Street by Street

WEST MIDLANDS

PLUS BROMSGROVE, CANNOCK, KIDDERMINSTER, LICHFIELD, NUNEATON, REDDITCH, ROYAL LEAMINGTON SPA, RUGBY, TAMWORTH, WARWICK

Enlarged Areas Birmingham, Coventry, Walsall, Wolverhampton

lst edition May 2001

© Automobile Association Developments Limited 2001

This product includes map data licensed from Ordnance Survey® with the permission of the Controller of Her Majesty's Stationery Office. © Crown copyright 2000. All rights reserved. Licence No: 399221.

Published by AA Publishing (a trading name of Automobile Association Developments Limited, whose registered office is Norfolk House, Priestley Road, Basingstoke, Hampshire, RG24 9NY. Registered number 1878835).

Mapping produced by the Cartographic Department of The Automobile Association.

A CIP Catalogue record for this book is available from the British Library.

Printed by G. Canale & C. s.p.a., Torino, Italy

The contents of this atlas are believed to be correct at the time of the latest revision. However, the publishers cannot be held responsible for loss occasioned to any person acting or refraining from action as a result of any material in this atlas, nor for any errors, omissions or changes in such material. The publishers would welcome information to correct any errors or omissions and to keep this atlas up to date. Please write to Publishing, The Automobile Association, Fanum House, Basing View, Basingstoke, Hampshire, RG21 4EA.

Ref: MX035

Key to map pages	ii-iii
Key to map symbols	iv-1
Enlarged scale pages	2-9
Street by Street	10-201
Index – towns & villages	202-203
Index – streets	204-261
Index – featured places	261-273

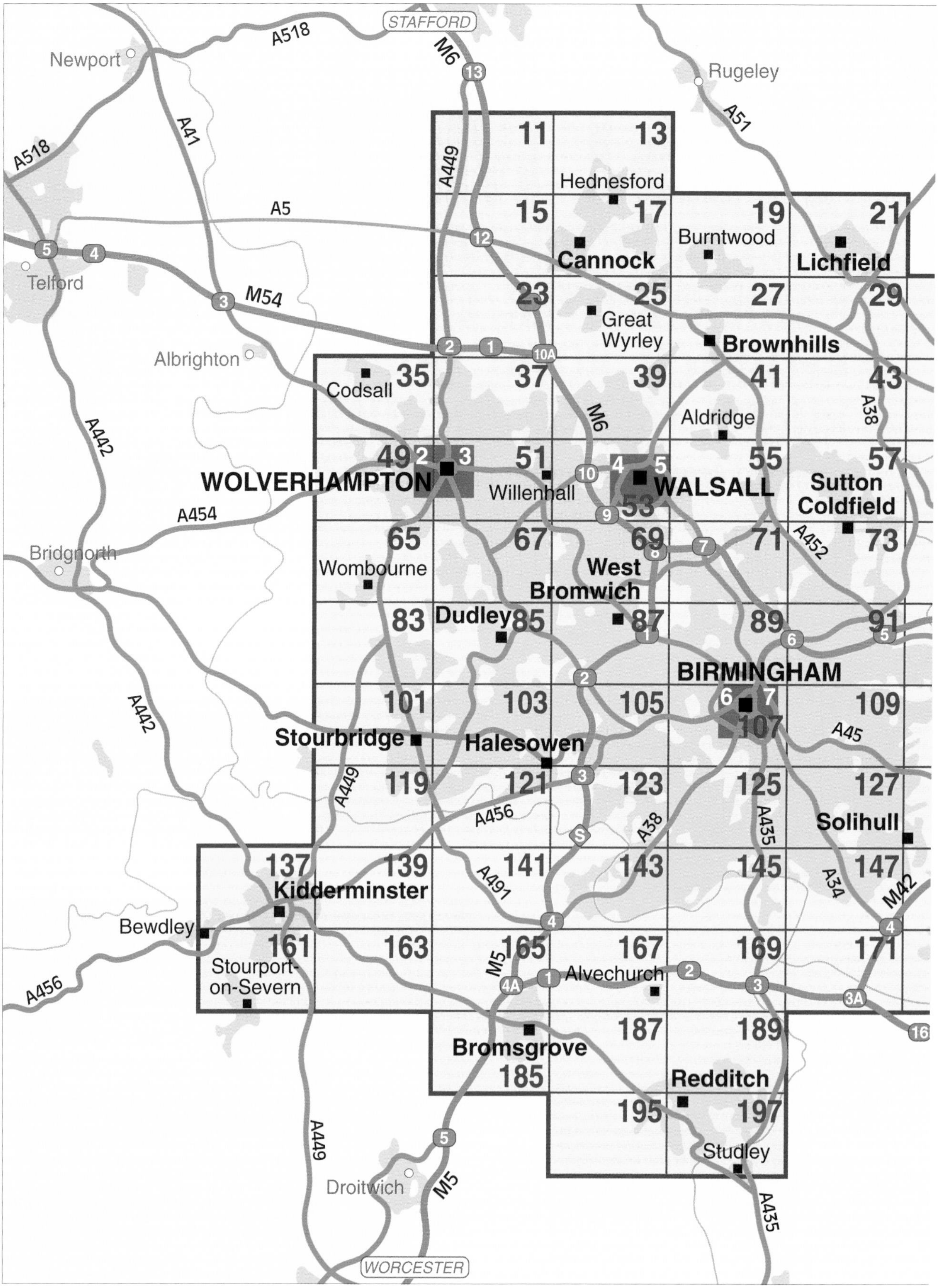

Newport

A518

A41

A518

A5

Telford 5 4

M54 3

Albrighton

A442

Bridgnorth

A454

A442

STAFFORD

M6 13

Rugeley

A449

A51

| 11 | 13 |
Hednesford

| 15 | 17 |
12 **Cannock** Burntwood **Lichfield**
| 19 | 21 |

| 23 | 25 | 27 | 29 |
2 1 10A Great Wyrley **Brownhills**

Codsall | 35 | 37 | 39 | 41 | 43 |
Aldridge A38

M6

WOLVERHAMPTON | 49 2 3 | 51 | 55 | 57 |
10 4 5 **Sutton Coldfield**
Willenhall 9 53 **WALSALL**
7 A452

Wombourne | 65 | 67 | 69 | 71 | 73 |
6

West Bromwich

Dudley | 83 85 | 87 | 89 | 91 |
1 5

2 **BIRMINGHAM**
6 7

Stourbridge | 101 | 103 | 105 | 107 | 109 |
Halesowen A45

| 119 | 121 | 123 | 125 | 127 |
3 **Solihull**
A456 S A38 A435 A34 M42

| 137 | 139 | 141 | 143 | 145 | 147 |
Kidderminster A491 4 M42

Bewdley | 161 | 163 | 165 | 167 | 169 | 171 |
4A 1 Alvechurch 2 3 3A
Stourport-on-Severn M5

A456 | 187 | 189 |
Bromsgrove 16

| 185 | **Redditch** |
195 197

A449 5

Droitwich M5 A435

Studley

M5

WORCESTER

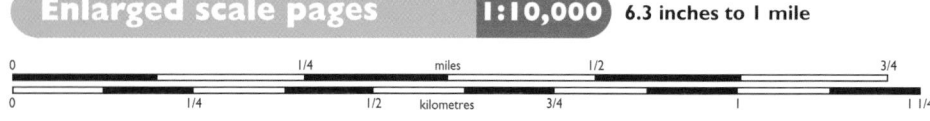

Enlarged scale pages **1:10,000** 6.3 inches to 1 mile

| 0 | 1/4 | miles | 1/2 | 3/4 |
| 0 | 1/4 | 1/2 kilometres | 3/4 | 1 | 1 1/4 |

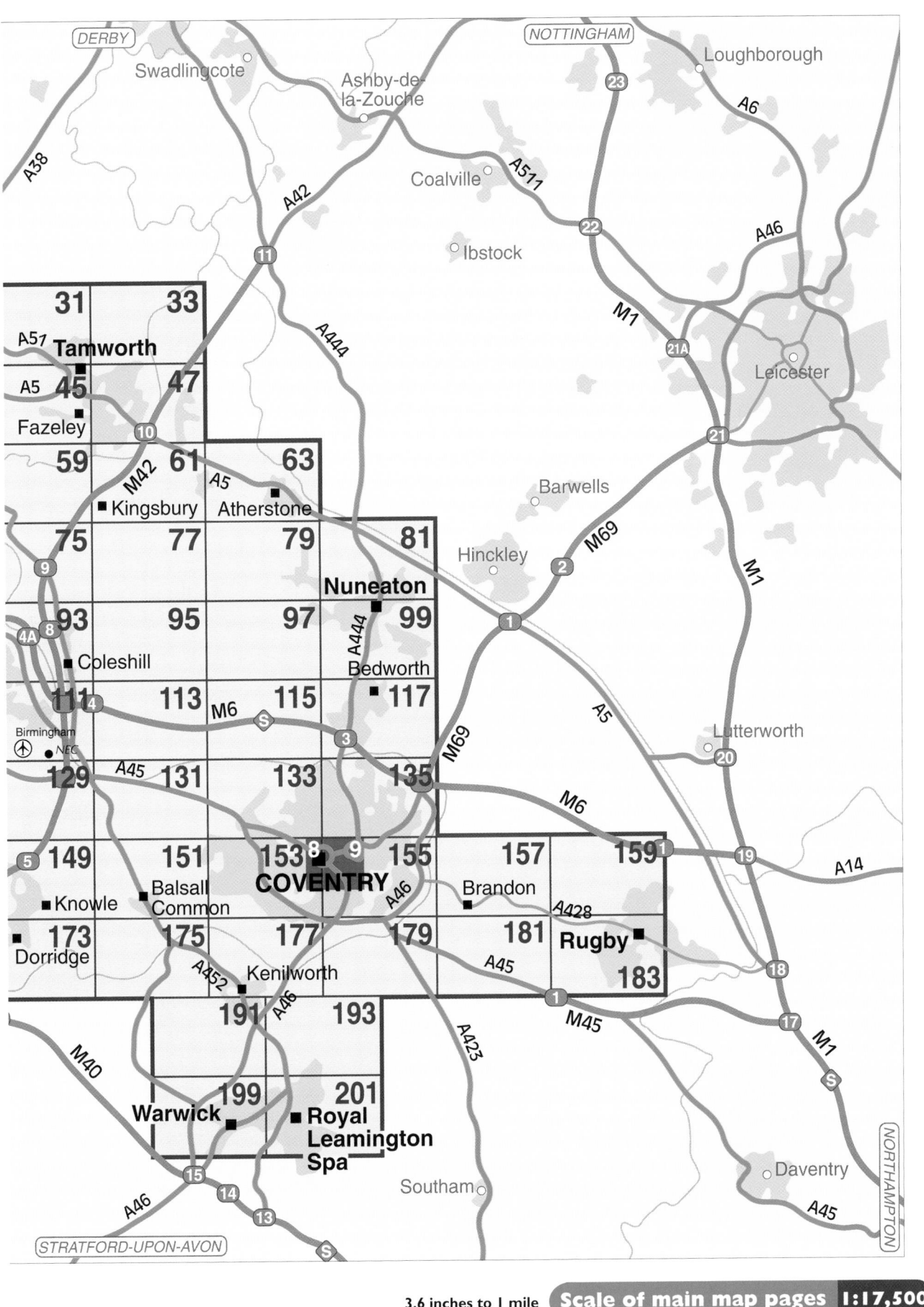

DERBY

NOTTINGHAM

Loughborough

Swadlingcote

Ashby-de-
la-Zouche

Coalville

A511

Ibstock

A46

M1

A6

A38

A57

A42

A444

A5

31 33

Tamworth

A5 45 47

Fazeley

11

10

M1

21A

Leicester

59 61 63

M42

A5

Kingsbury Atherstone

Barwells

21

75 77 79 81

9

Nuneaton

Hinckley

M69

M1

93 95 97 99

A444

4A 8

Coleshill Bedworth

2

Lutterworth

111 113 115 117

A5

Birmingham

NEC

4 M6 S

3

20

M69

M6

129 131 133 135

A45

5 149 151 153 8 9 155 157 159 1

19 A14

COVENTRY

Knowle Balsall A46 Brandon

Common A428

173 175 177 179 181 183

Dorridge Rugby

A452 Kenilworth A45 18

A46 1 17 M1

191 193 M45 S

M40 A423

Warwick 199 201

Royal Daventry

Leamington

Spa

15 Southam

14

13 A45

STRATFORD-UPON-AVON S

NORTHAMPTON

3.6 inches to 1 mile **Scale of main map pages** 1:17,500

0 1/2 miles 1

0 1/2 1 kilometres 1 1/2 2

Junction 9	Motorway & junction
Services	Motorway service area
	Primary road single/dual carriageway
Services	Primary road service area
	A road single/dual carriageway
	B road single/dual carriageway
	Other road single/dual carriageway
	Restricted road
	Private road
← ←	One way street
	Pedestrian street
	Track/ footpath
	Road under construction
[- - - - -]	Road tunnel
P	Parking

P+🚌	Park & Ride
🚌	Bus/coach station
	Railway & main railway station
	Railway & minor railway station
⊖	Underground station
⊖	Light railway & station
+++++++++	Preserved private railway
LC	Level crossing
•—•—•—•—•	Tramway
- - - - - -	Ferry route
....	Airport runway
- · - · - · -	Boundaries- borough/ district
▼▼▼▼▼▼▼	Mounds
93	Page continuation 1:17,500
7	Page continuation to enlarged scale 1:10,000

Symbol	Description	Symbol	Description
	River/canal lake, pier		Toilet with disabled facilities
	Aqueduct lock, weir		Petrol station
465 ▲ Winter Hill	Peak (with height in metres)	PH	Public house
	Beach	PO	Post Office
	Coniferous woodland		Public library
	Broadleaved woodland	i	Tourist Information Centre
	Mixed woodland		Castle
	Park		Historic house/ building
	Cemetery	Wakehurst Place NT	National Trust property
	Built-up area	M	Museum/ art gallery
	Featured building	†	Church/chapel
⌐⌐⌐⌐⌐⌐⌐⌐⌐	City wall		Country park
A&E	Accident & Emergency hospital		Theatre/ performing arts
	Toilet		Cinema

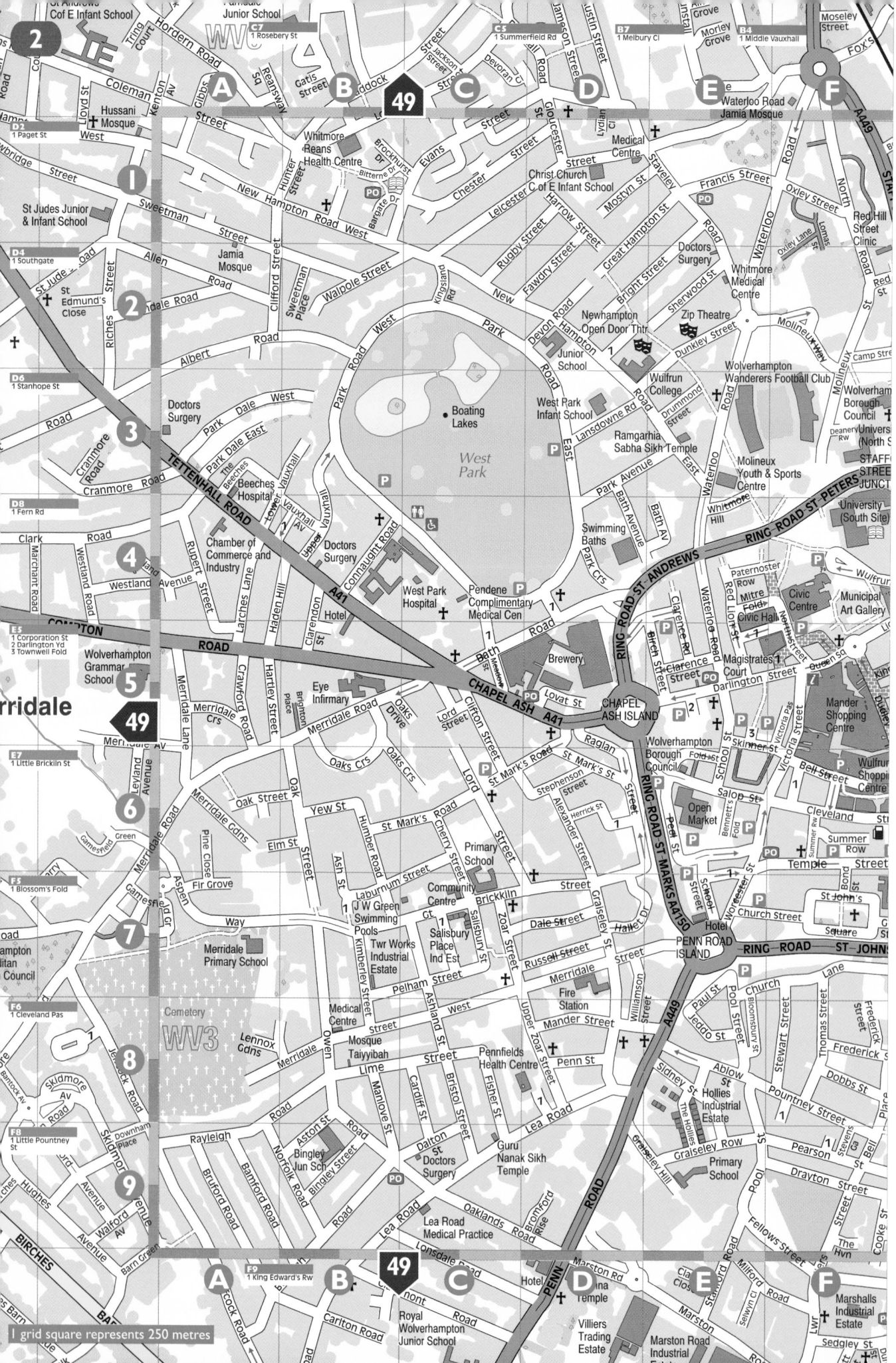

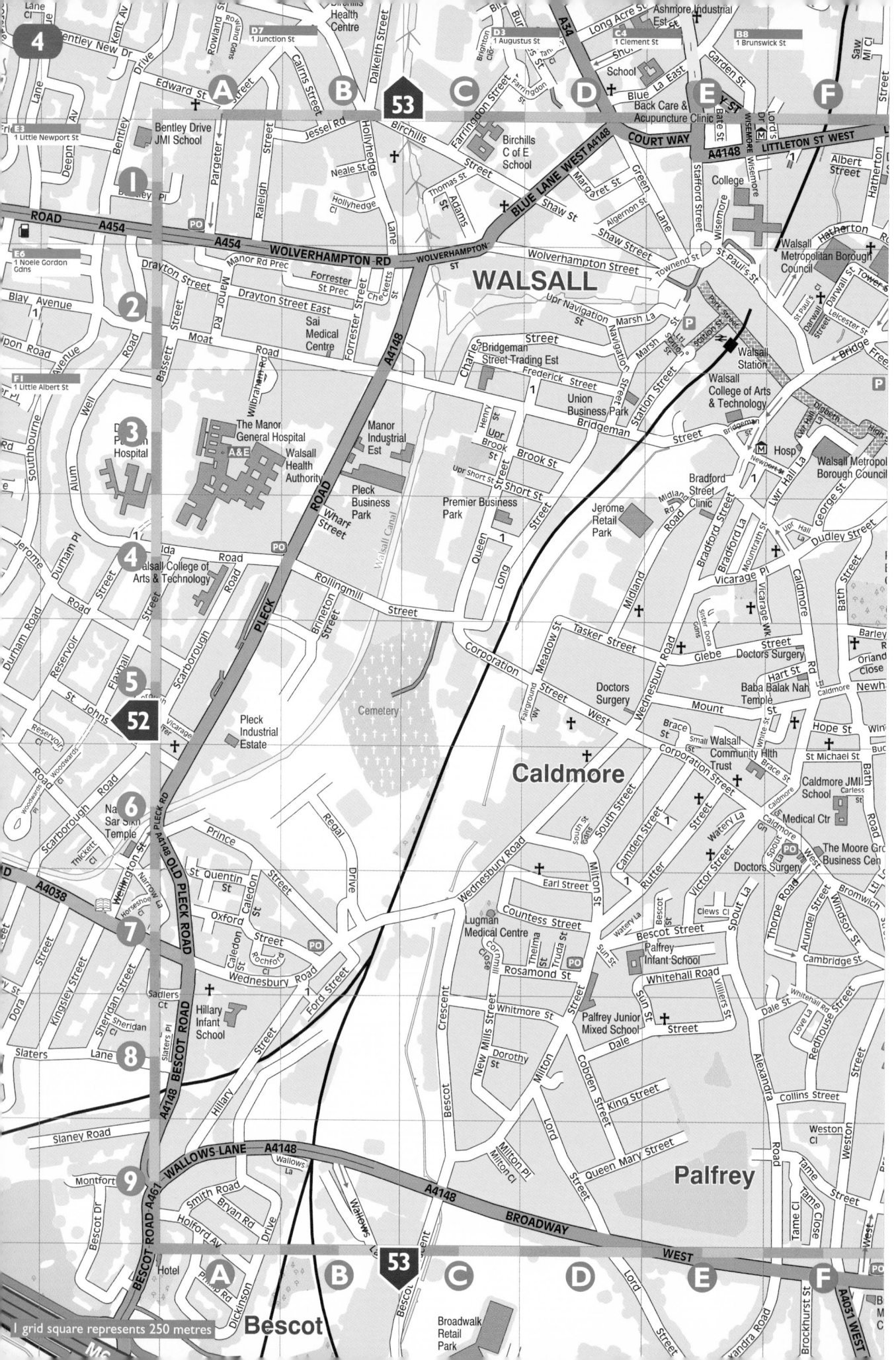

WALSALL

Caldmore

Palfrey

Bescot

1 grid square represents 250 metres

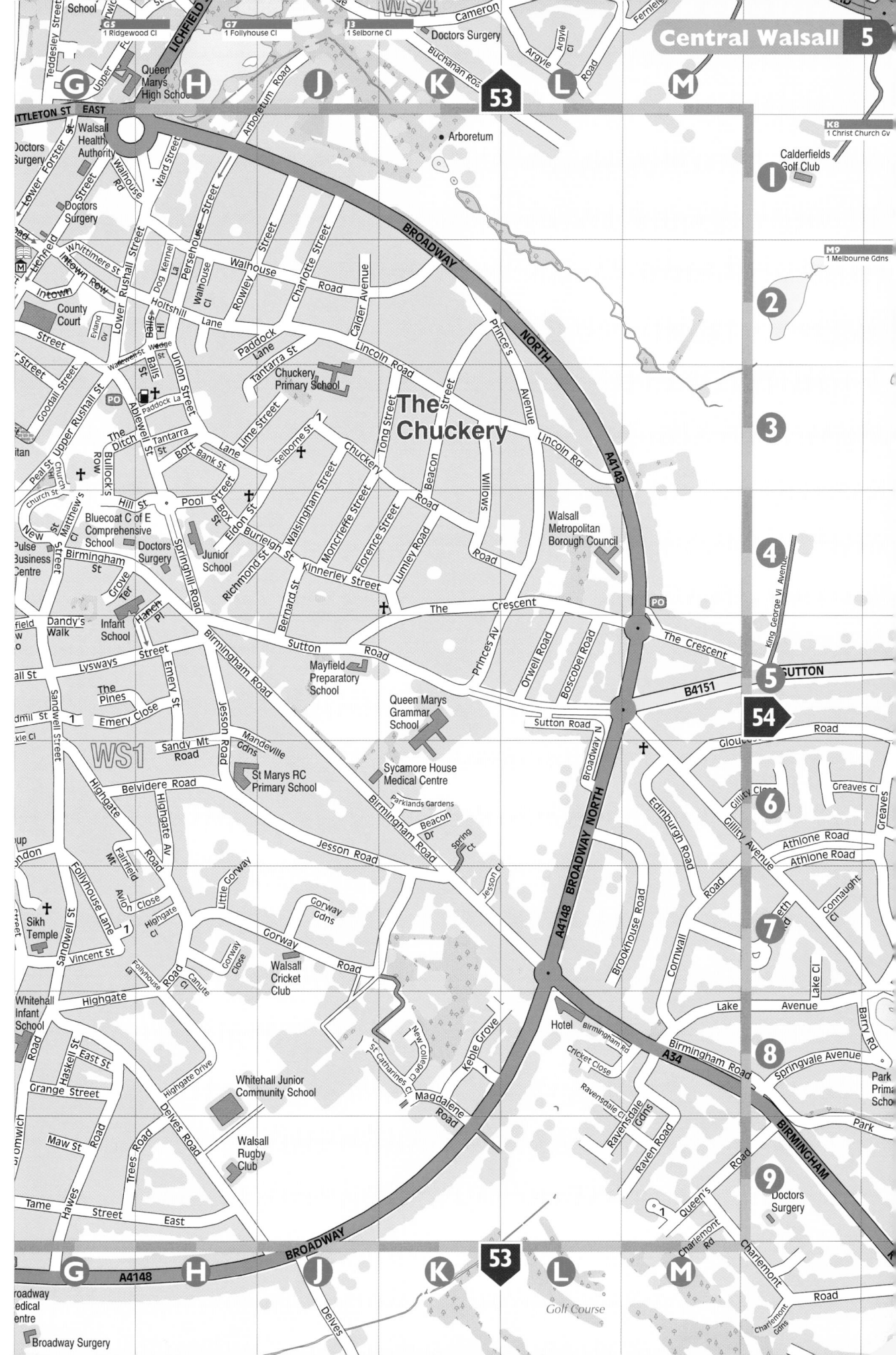

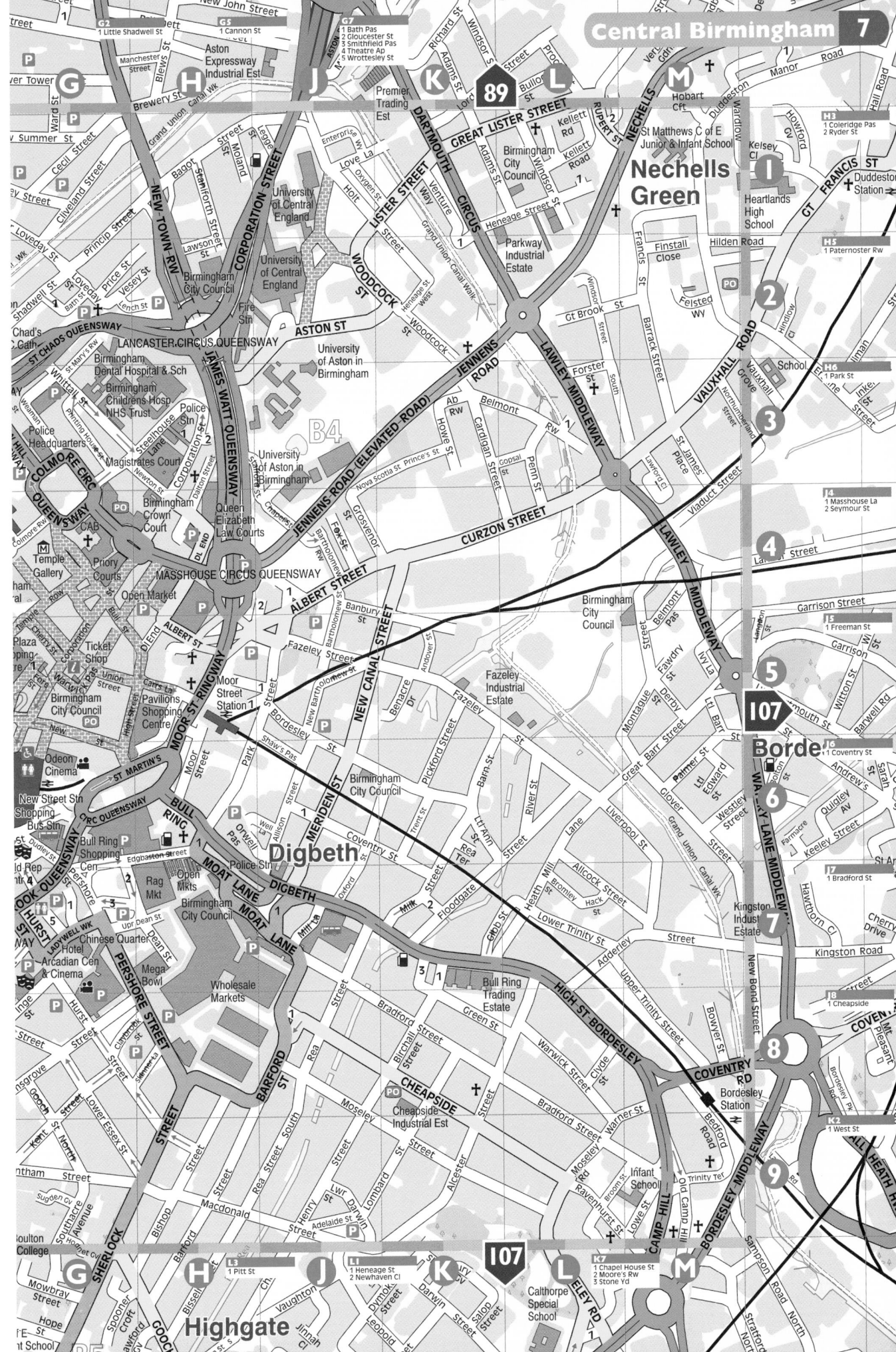

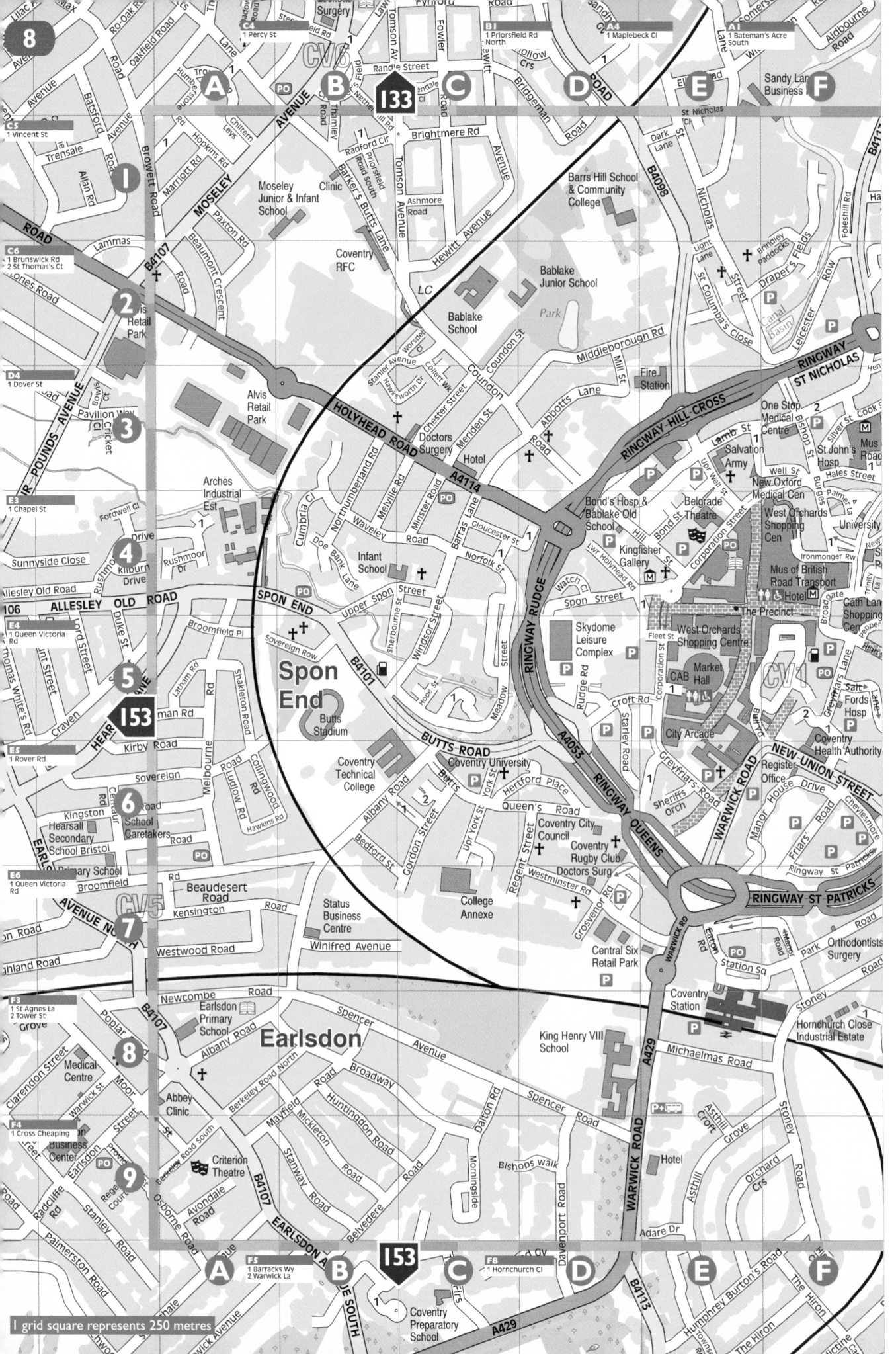

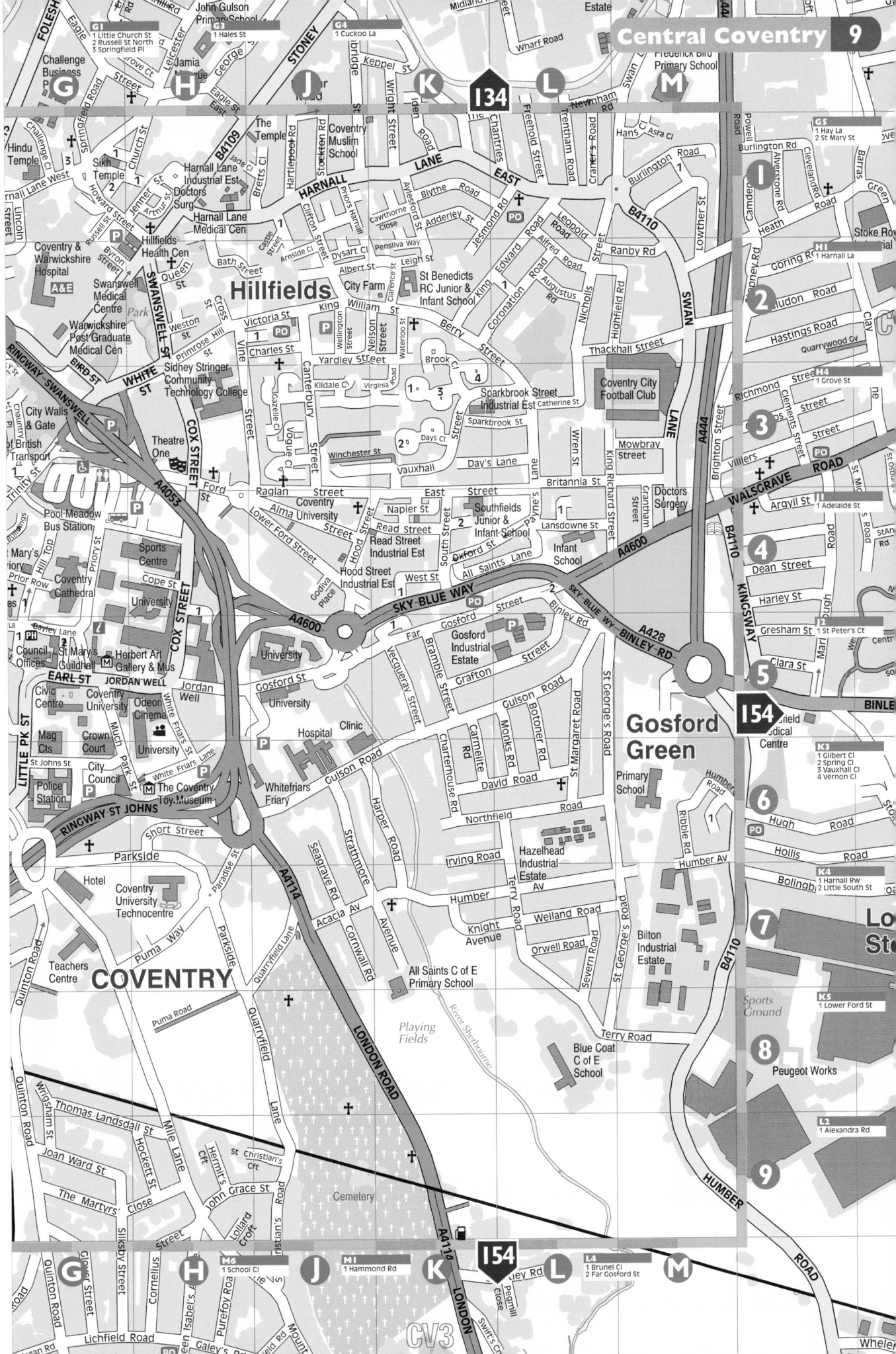

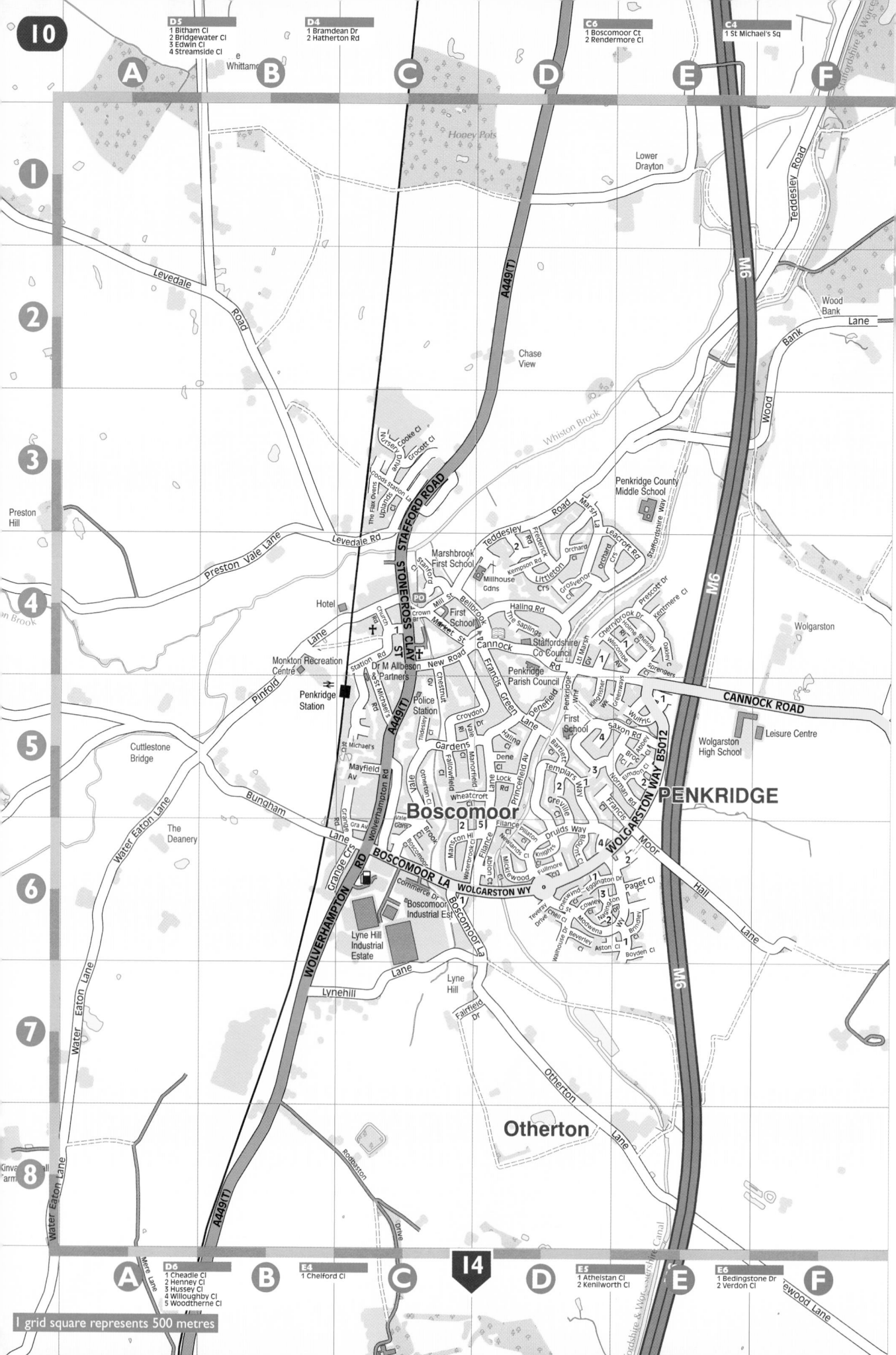

A   B   C   D   E   F

Honey Pots

Lower Drayton

1

Wood Bank

Levedale Road

Chase View

Whiston Brook

Wood Bank Lane

2

Preston Hill

Penkridge County Middle School

3

Preston Vale Lane

Levedale Rd

STAFFORD ROAD

Nursen Drive

Cooke Cl

Grocott Cl

The Flax Ovens

Goods Station La

Uplands

A449(T)

Marsh La

Leacroft Rd

Staffordshire Wy

Wolgarston

Marshbrook First School

Teddesley

Rd

Frederick

Littleton

Crs

Orchard

Grosvenor

Crs

Prescott Dr

Kentmere Cl

M6

4

an Brook

Hotel

Monkton Recreation Centre

Lane

Station Rd

Crown

Mill St

STONECROSS CLAY ST

Church

Market St

Millhouse Gdns

Kempson Rd

Haling Rd

Bellbrook

First School

The Saplings

Cannock

Staffordshire Co Council

Cherrybrook Dr

Shelney

Wicombe

Oakely

Sprengers

Wolgarston

Pinfold

Penkridge Station

Dr M Allbeson & Partners

New Road

Chestnut

Francis Green

Lane

Penkridge Parish Council

Denefield

Penkridge Wlf

First School

Wulfric

Greenways

CANNOCK ROAD

Leisure Centre

5

Cuttlestone Bridge

Water Eaton Lane

Bungham

Rd

Grange Crs

St Michael's

Police Station

Croydon

Dr

Gardens

Fallowfield

Vale

Haling

Dene

Saxon Rd

Bartlett

Francis

Wolgarston High School

A449(T)

B5012

6

The Deanery

Water Eaton Lane

WOLVERHAMPTON RD

Grange

Rd

Wolverhampton Rd

Mayfield Av

Wheatcroft

Manorfield

Lane

Lock Rd

Princefield Av

Templars Way

Greville

Druids Way

WOLGARSTON WY

Blount Cl

Boscomoor

BOSCOMOOR LA

Commerce Dr

Boscomoor Industrial Est

Manton Hl

Watercroft

Filance

Fullmore

Knights

Pilaston

Brock

Normas Rd

Elmdon

PENKRIDGE

Moor

Paget Cl

Hall

Lane

7

Lyne Hill Industrial Estate

WOLGARSTON WY

BOSCOMOOR La

Lynehill

Lane

Lyne Hill

Fairfield Dr

Cherwynd

Eggington Dr

Cowley

Modwena

Teresa Drive

Odell

Beverley

Walmoude Dr

Aston Cl

Boyden Cl

Brodey

Otherton

Lane

M6

8

Kinva

arm

Water Eaton Lane

Mere Lane

A449(T)

Rodbaston

Drive

Otherton

ndshire & Worcestershire Canal

A   B   C   D   E   F

1 grid square represents 500 metres

C8
1 Addison Cl
2 Lotus Dr
3 Pye Green Rd

C7
1 Margaret Dr
2 Windrush Rd

B6
1 Partridge Cl

A7
1 Oaklands Cl

A6
1 Ashdale Cl
2 Nightingale Cl
3 Raven Cl

A   B   C   D   E   F

1

2

3

4

11

5

6

7

8

White House

Heart of England

Marquis's Drive

Brindley Road

Cemetery

Badger Slade Wood

Cemetery

Penkridge Bank

Cannock Chase Forest

Broadhurst Green

Brindley Heath

A34(T)

Pottal Valley

Road

Green

Broadhurst

Chad's Ditch

Broadhurst Green

Brindley Road

Pye Green

Plantation Pine Rd
Spruce Rd
Tower Rd
Croft Av
Clarke Av
Cotton Gy
Cedar Gy
Cotswood Rd
Mendip Road
Heather Rd
Brail Rd

STAFFORD ROAD

Dogingtree Estate

Sycamore Wy
Maple Dr
Birch
Almond Rd
Lime Rd
Fir Cl
Ash Vw
Oak Tree
Cherry
Elm Cl
Hawthorne Rd
Beech

Huntington CP School

Fisher St
Tudor Road
Peel
Cowley
Bondway
Daisy
Stone Pine Cl
Corsican
Beech Pine
White Bark Cl
Turelian Cl
Rydal Cl
Corsican
Rosehill
Heather Ms
Bradbury
Rowley Cl
Greenwood
Woodland

Green Heath Rd
Green Lane

Cannock Chase Football Club

Pye Green Valley CP School

Green Heath

WS12

Kenmore
Unwood
Kinross
Chalcot
Coppermill
Thornhill Gdns
Braemar Gdns
Melrose Rd
Balmoral
Viewfield Av
Hedgerow Cl
Maycroft Cl
Hillside Cl
Abbey Rd
Ebenezer St
Lomax Rd
Wilcox Av
Florence St
Mount Street
Mary St

A34(T)

Littleton Business Park

Littleton Dr
Holly La
Robin Cl
Redwing Dr
Woodstock Dr
Swift Cl
Badger

Huntington

Foxfields

Squirrel Cl

PO
pillaton dr
Teddesley Wy

Fieldhouse
Broadway
J & C Brooke St
Foster Avenue
View Street
Blake County High School
William Baxter Special School
Millcent Av
Blewitt Street
Mavis Rd
Winsor Av
Mill Pool
McChie St

West Hill

Primary School

Doctors Surg

Limepit Lane
Sycamore Grn
Elizabeth Rd
Ann Crs
Westminster Rd
Holly St
Pye Pt St

Lichen Cl
Bracken Cl
Heather Dr
Ling Rd
Corse Gv
Fern Rd
Moss Cl

Herbert

Gravel Lane
Lowland

A34(T)

STAFFORD ROAD

Cavan's Wood

Rosemary Dr
Wardle Av
Cornhill
Clarion
Primary School
Glen Cl
Pl
Philip Gv
Way
Wells Rd
Snowdon
Speedy
Trent Rd
Bath Rd
Abbots Fld
West Chadsmoor Clnc
Lovatt St
Doctors Surgery
Chadsmoor Primary School
Moorland Rd
Princess Medical Practice Street
Grasmere Pl
Pye Grn Rd
Keats Av
Shelley Rd
Elliott
Redhill Primary School
James Terrace
Montrose Ct
Orion Wy
Stratford Wy
Saturn Rd
Marina
Belt Road
Wyvern
Apollo
Mercury Rd
Robin
Blake St
Platt Street
Haig Cl
Smalley Cl
Bradford St
Burgoyne St
Dovedale
Queen
Granary Cl
Western Rd

West Chadsmoor

High Town

Moorhill School

Redhill Road

Milton Road

Benton Rd

Centi Av

John Street

Hednesford Station

ROAD B5013

Stafford Lane

Anglesey St
Ewkett St
Cornwall

Moorhill School

16

Chadsmoor

D5
1 Buckthorn Cl

D6
1 Ardgay Dr
2 Mitcham Cl
3 Sheraton Cl

E5
1 Evergreen Hts
2 Mountain Pine Cl
3 Rowley Cl
4 Whitethorn Cl

E8
1 Richmond Cl

F6
1 Common Vw

F7
1 Bluebell Cl

A   B   C   D   E   F

1 grid square represents 500 metres

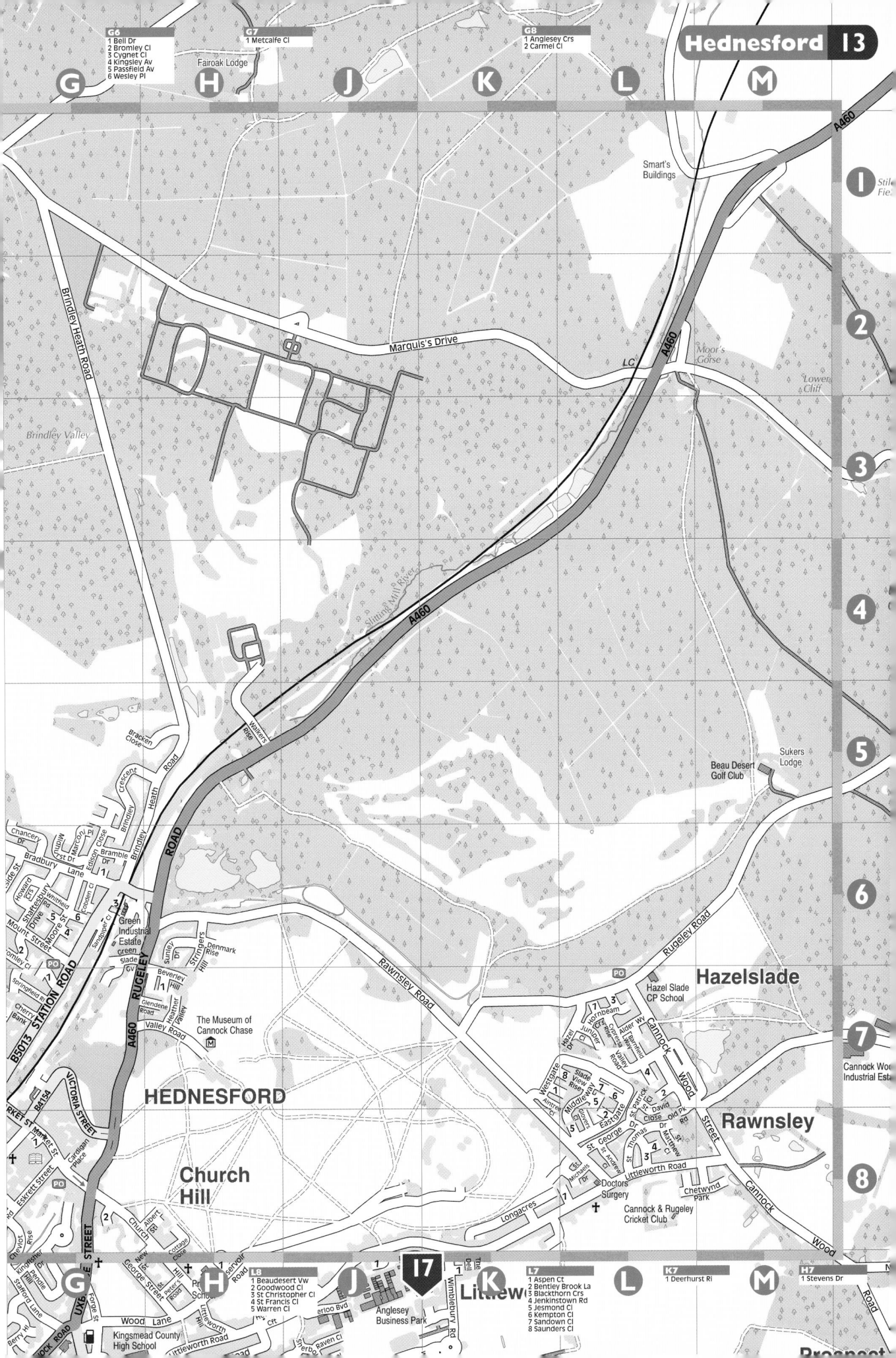

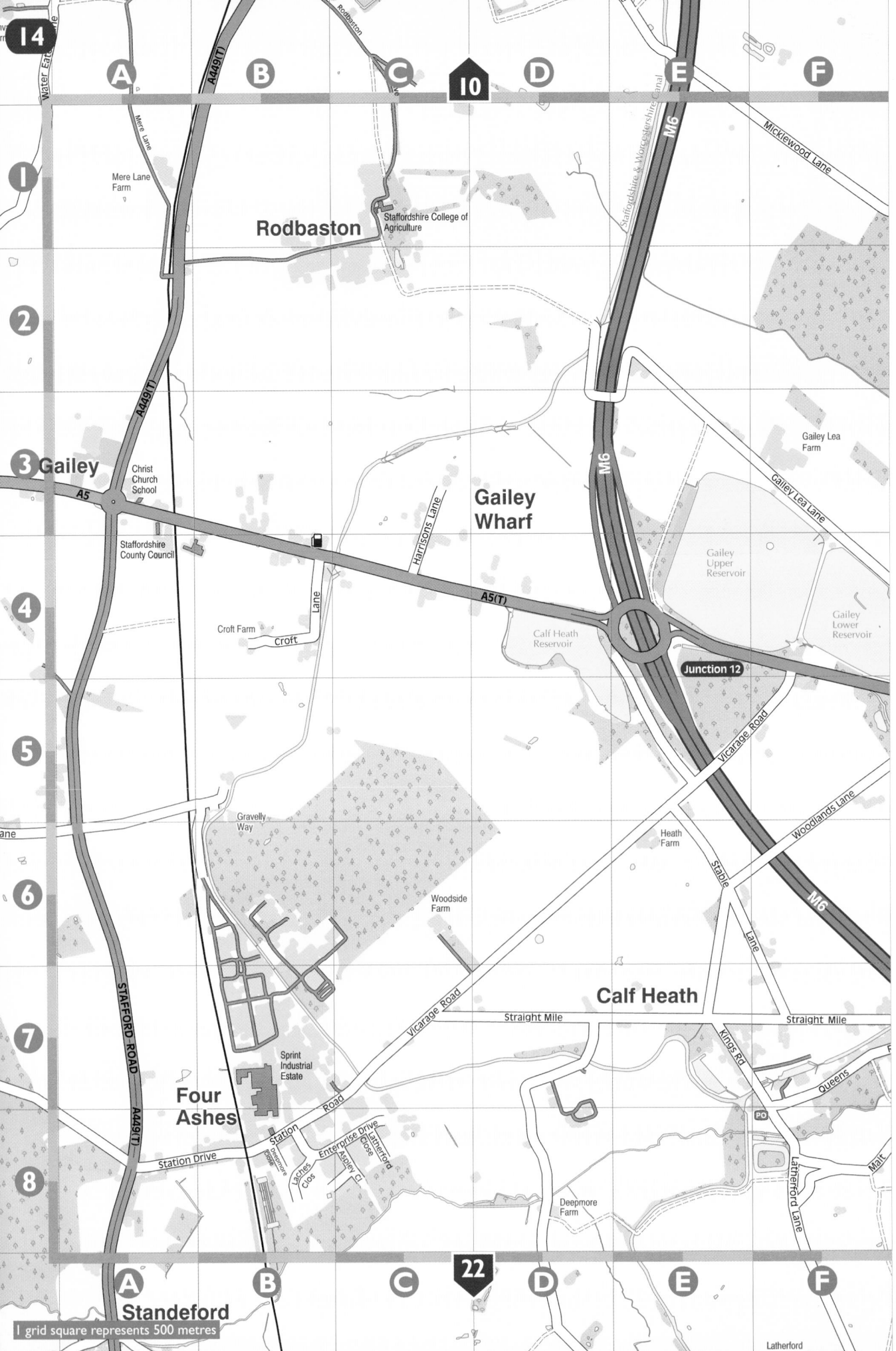

G H J K L M

M5
1 Burnham Gn

M6
1 Coppice Ct
2 Southgate End
3 Spinney Farm Rd
4 Wellfield Cl

11

I

2

C

3

NEW PENKRI

4

16

5

6

7

8

Horsemoor Wood

Micklewood

Micklewood Lane

Fullmoor Wood

Fullmoor Lodge

Mansty Wood

Cocksparrow Lane

Parkside Lane

B5012

Parkside Lane

Church Road

Hatherton

Sandy Lane

Hatton Rd

Sunfield Rd

Sunfield Rd

Alton Gv

Waverley

Gowland Dr

Gowland

Keeling Dr

Adamson Cl

Boyden Cl

Hatherton Cl

Sherbrook

Rowhott

Hatherton

Gorsey

Elms

Dr

Chaseley AV

Downesway

Rowan Rd

The

Chaseley Cr

Holder Drive

Dursley

Small Hi Cl

Pasture

Orchard

Galley Lea Lane

Oak Lane

A5(T)

Oak Farm

Church Lane

Four Crosses

Poplar Lane

Dorchester Rd

Exeter Road

Meriden Close

Bideford Way

ASCOT

Kendal

Grove

Littlemere

Ullesmere

Conway Rd

Carlisle Rd

Skipton Place

Langdales

Wolverham

Leamington

Riley Close

Whitby

Drive

Longfor

Banbur

Doctors Surgery

Bil

Berwick Dr

16

5

6

Prin Sch

WOLVERHAM

Hotel

Oak Lane

Four Crosses Lane

Catsbridge Lane

Wood Lane

Great Saredon

House Lane

Saredon Hall Farm

Wedge's Mills

PO

Hall Meadow

Woodhaven

Linkway Retail Park

Avo Bus Par

7

WOLVERHAMPTON ROAD

A460

Lodge La

8

G H J K L M

M6

23

South Staffs Business P

Middle Hill

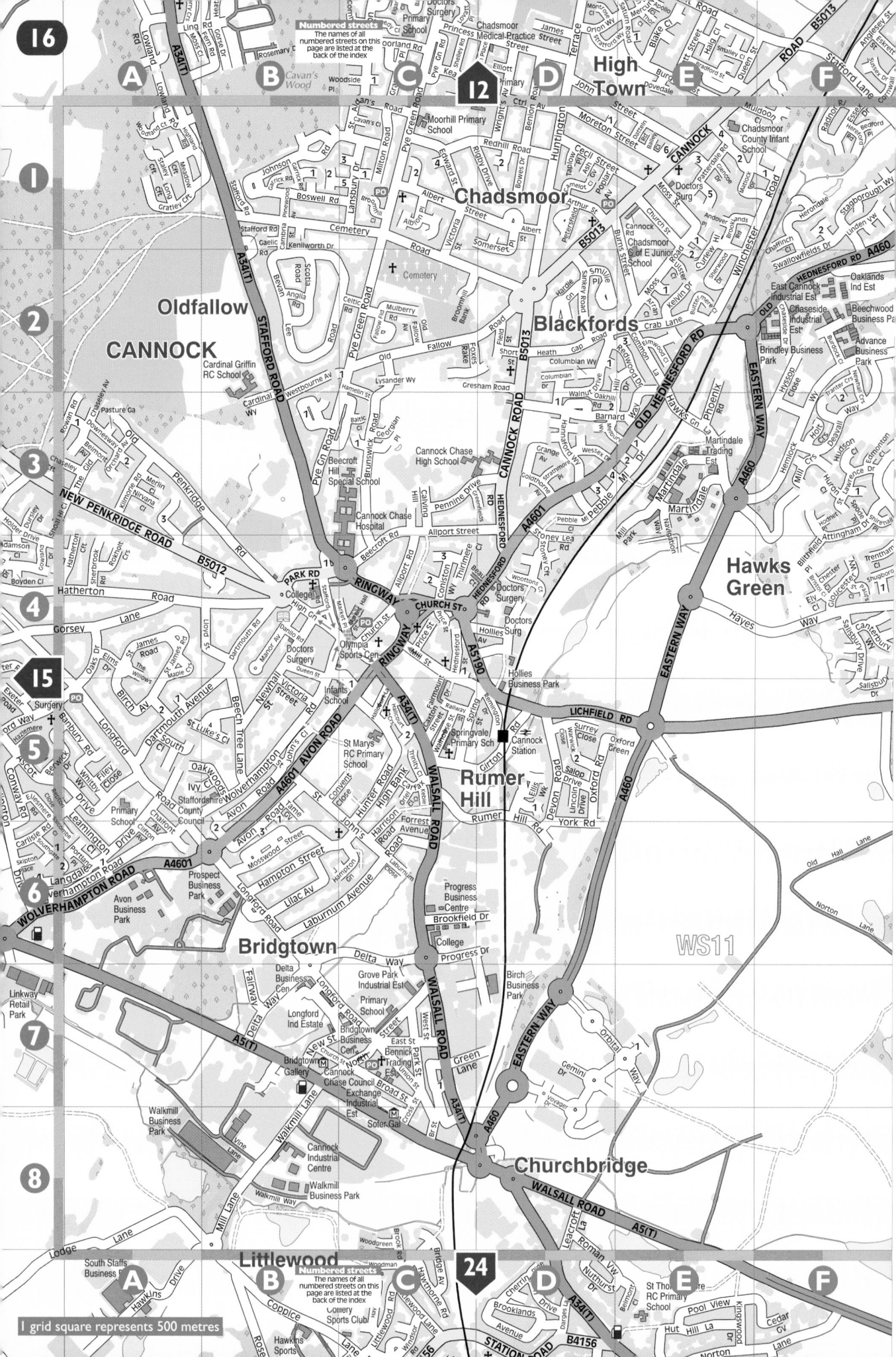

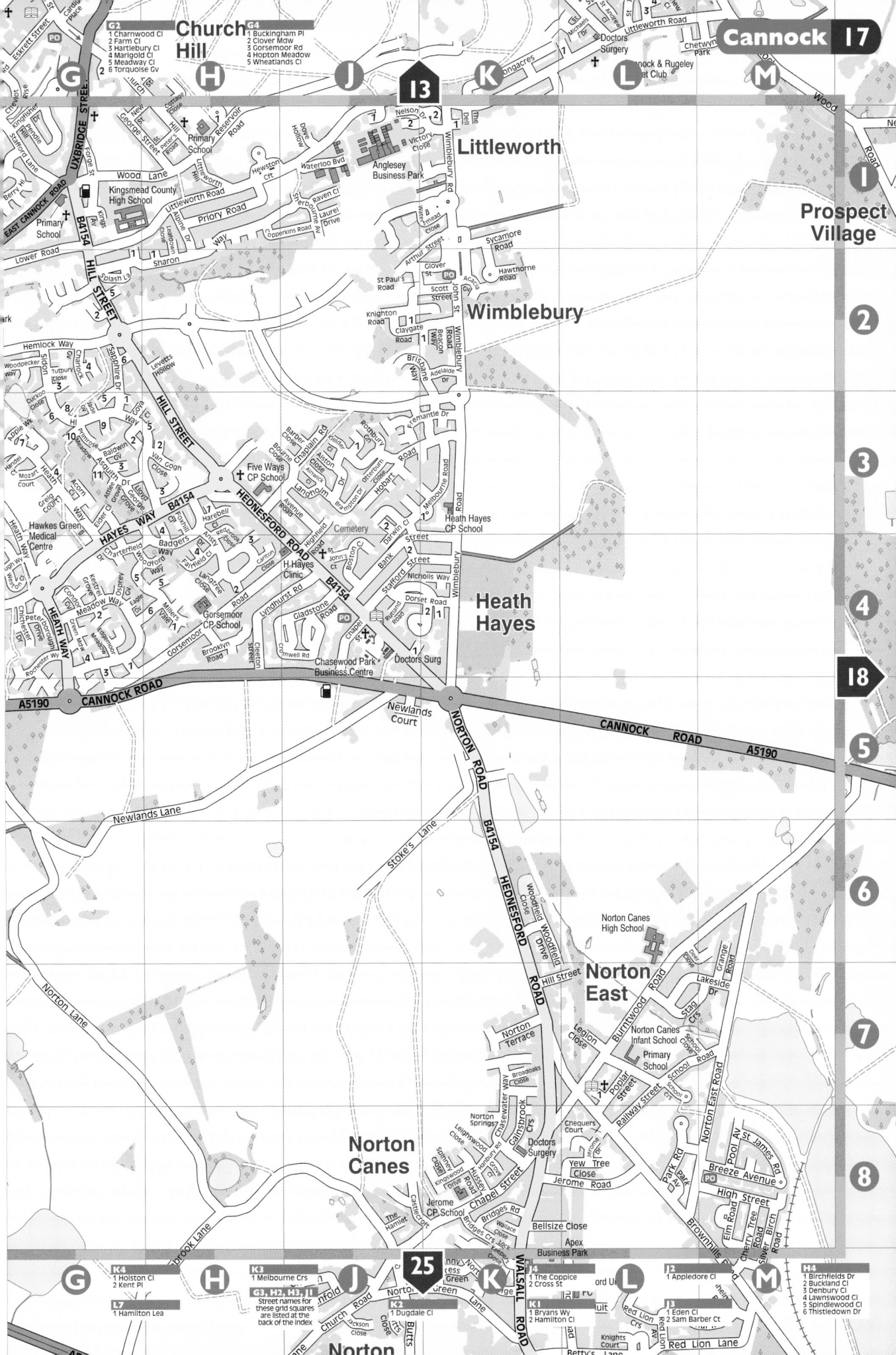

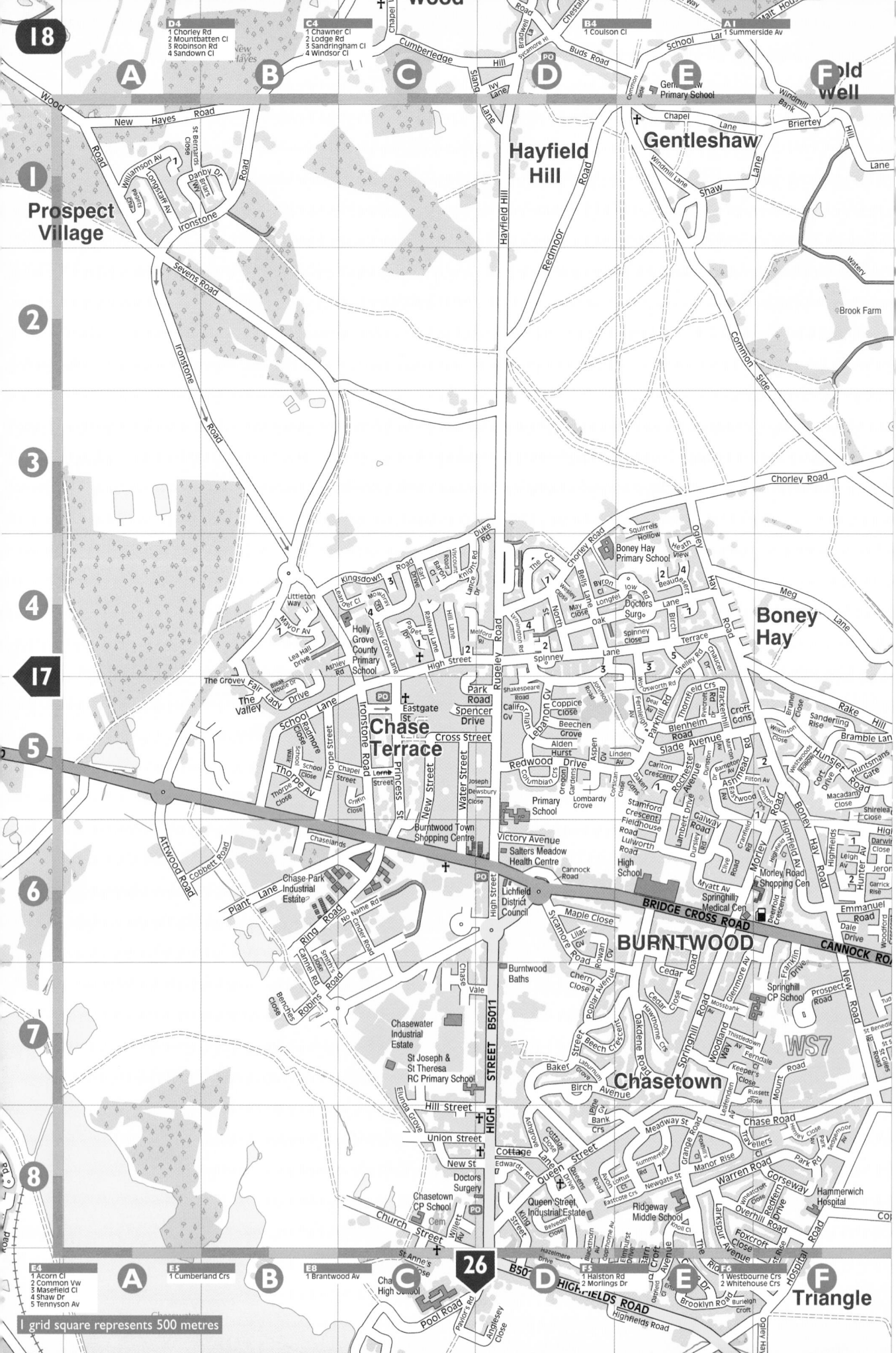

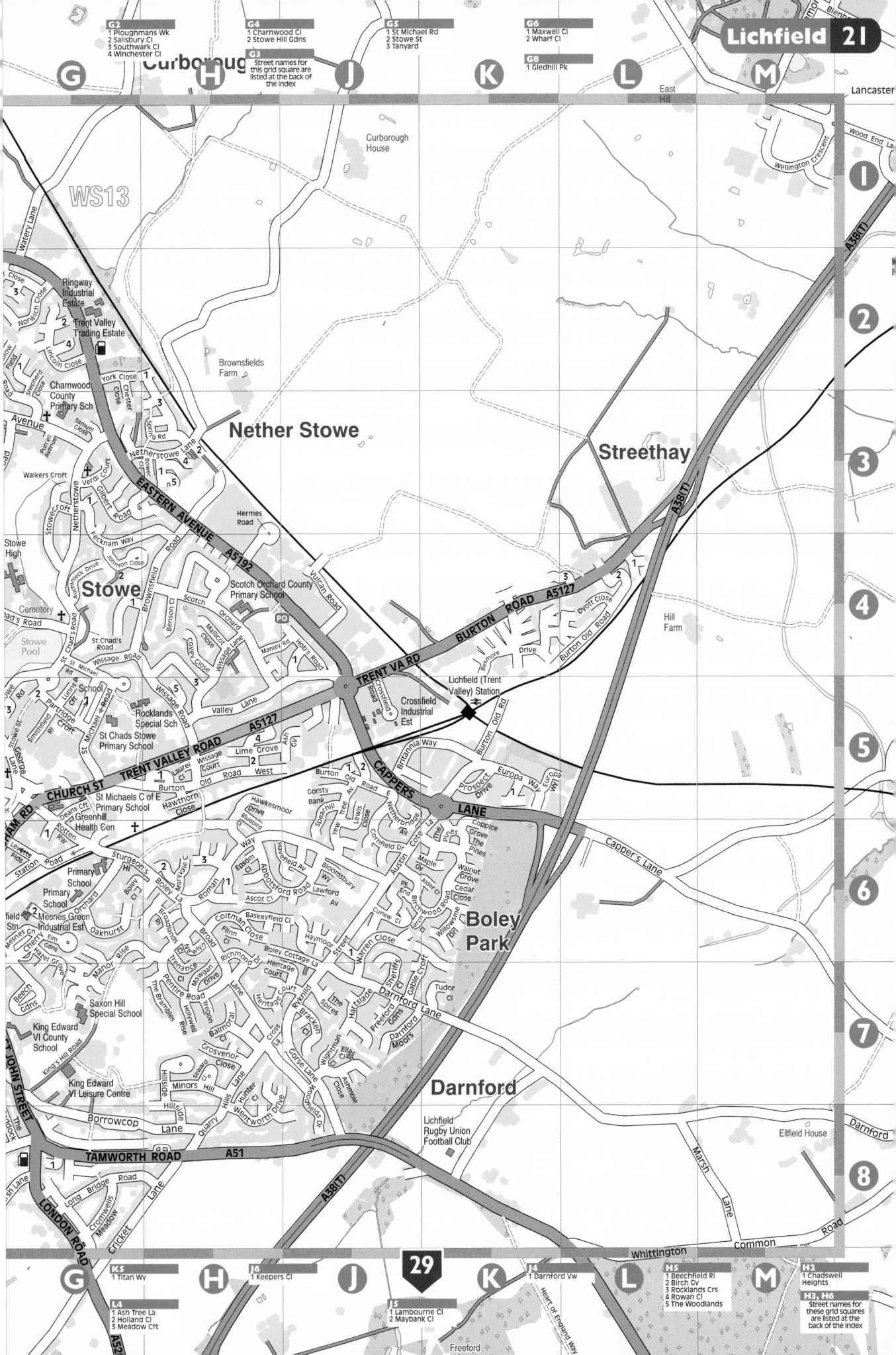

WS13

Curborough

Curborough House

Brownsfields Farm

Nether Stowe

Streethay

East Hill

Lancaster

Wood End La

Wellington Crescent

A38(T)

Ringway Industrial Estate

Trent Valley Trading Estate

Charnwood County Primary Sch

Walkers Croft

Stowe High

Stowe

Cemetery

Stowe Pool

Hermes Road

EASTERN AVENUE A5192

Scotch Orchard County Primary School

PO

BURTON ROAD A5127

Hill Farm

St Chad's Road

Rocklands Special Sch

St Chads Stowe Primary School

TRENT VA RD

Lichfield (Trent Valley) Station

Crossfield Industrial Est

TRENT VALLEY ROAD A5127

CHURCH ST

St Michaels C of E Primary School

Greenhill Health Cen

Lime Grove West

Burton Old Road

CAPPERS

LANE

Britannia Way

Prospect Drive

Europa Way

Capper's Lane

Primary School

Primary School

Mesnes Green Industrial Est

Oakhurst

Hawkesmoor Drive

Corsty Bank

Boley Park

Walnut Grove

Cedar Close

Coppice Grove The Pines

Saxon Hill Special School

Abbotsford Road

Bloomsbury Wy

Lawford Av

King Edward VI County School

King Edward VI Leisure Centre

Boley Cottage La

Heritage Court

Richmond La

Darnford Lane

Tudor

Darnford Moors

Darnford

Lichfield Rugby Union Football Club

Ellfield House

Darnford

TAMWORTH ROAD A51

Borrowcop Lane

London Road

A38(T)

Marsh Lane

Whittington Common

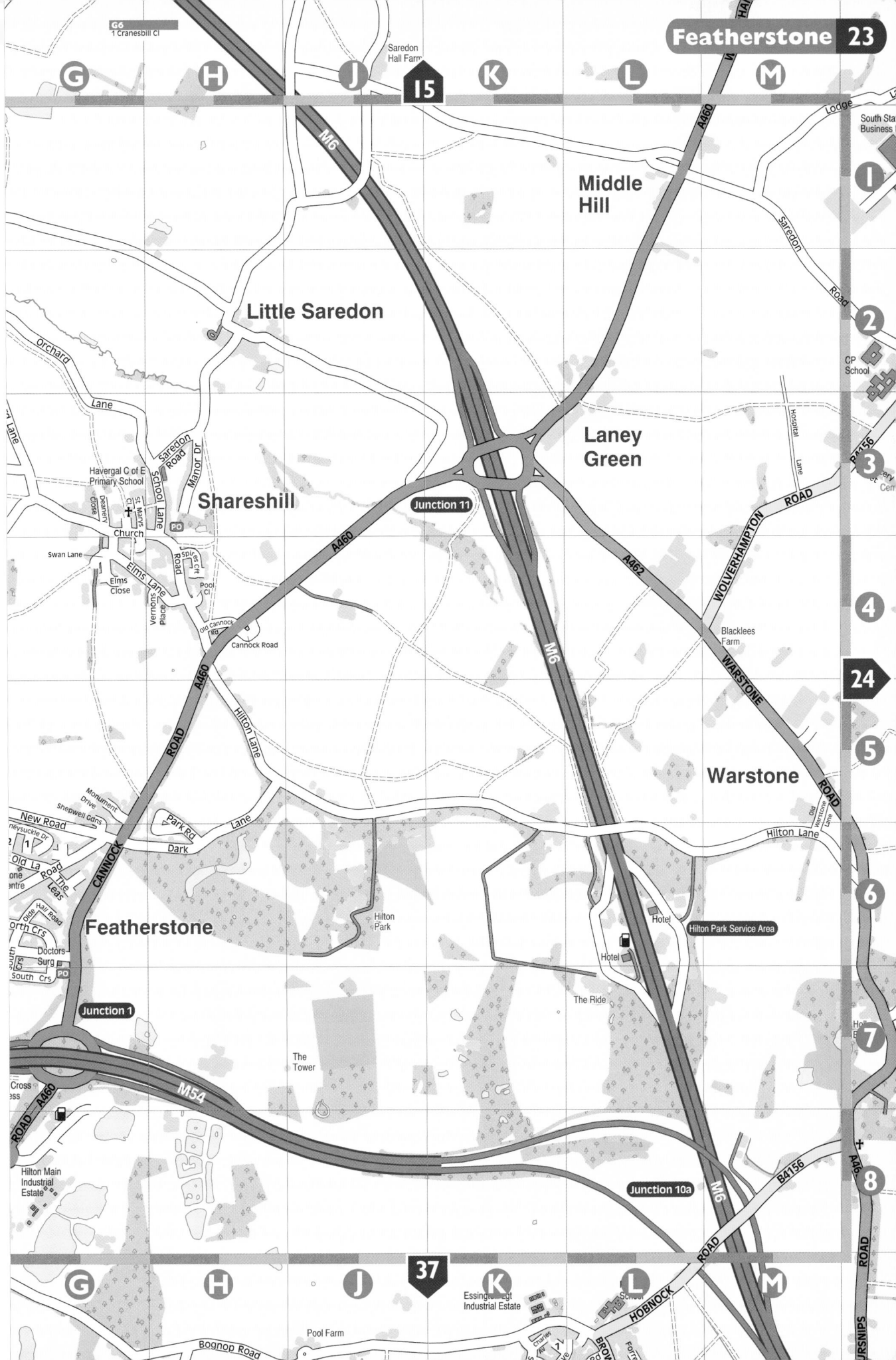

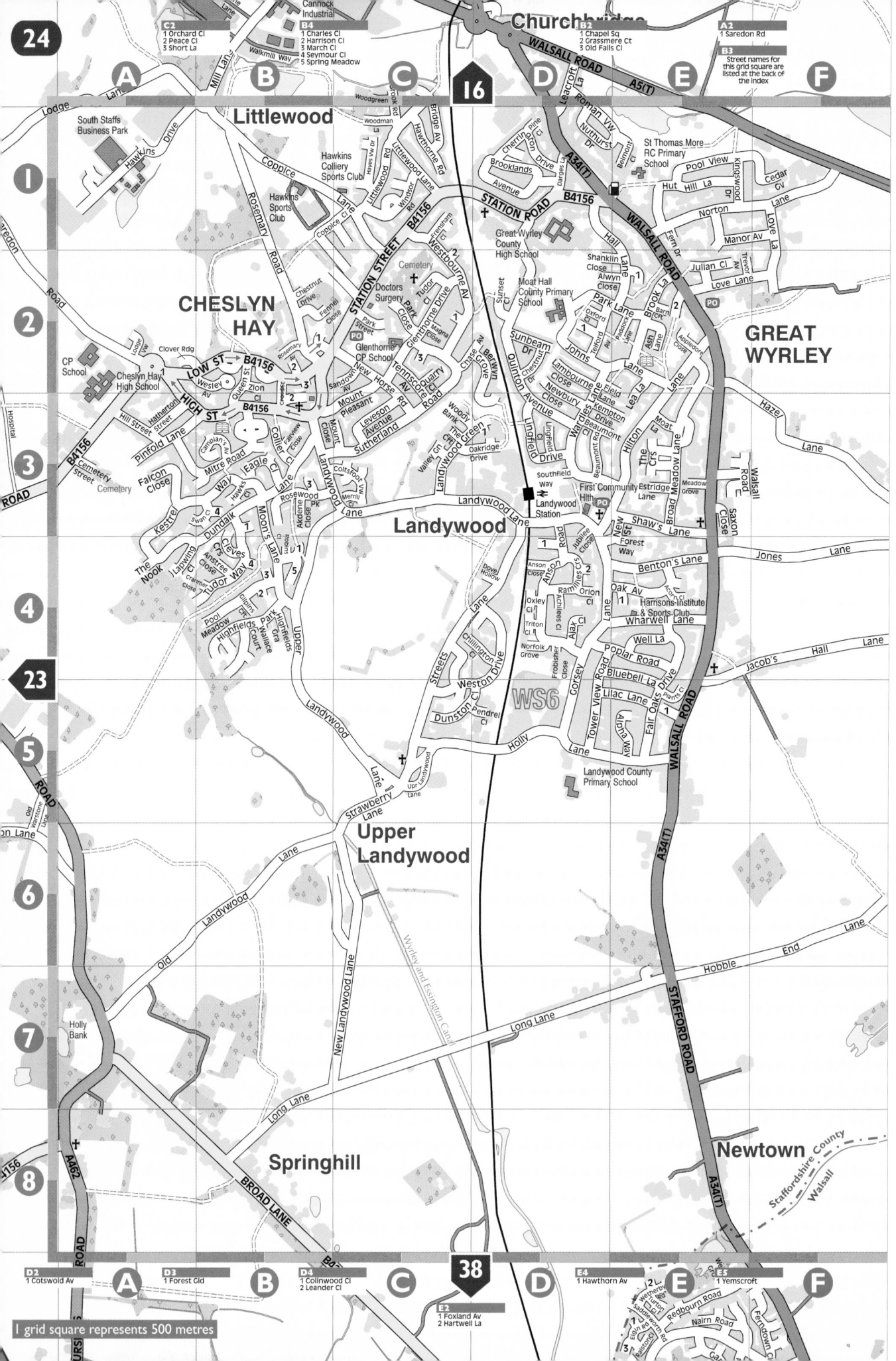

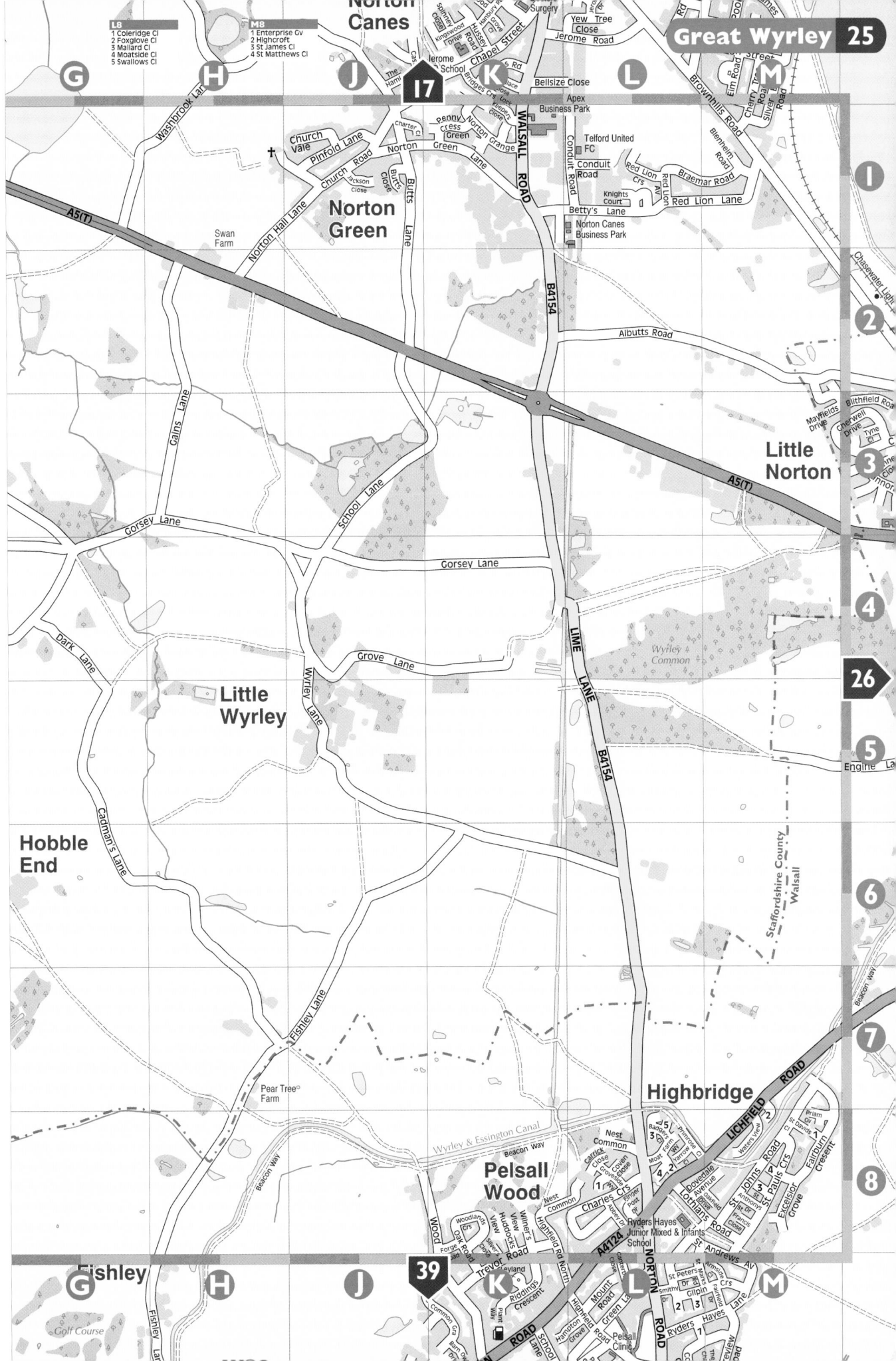

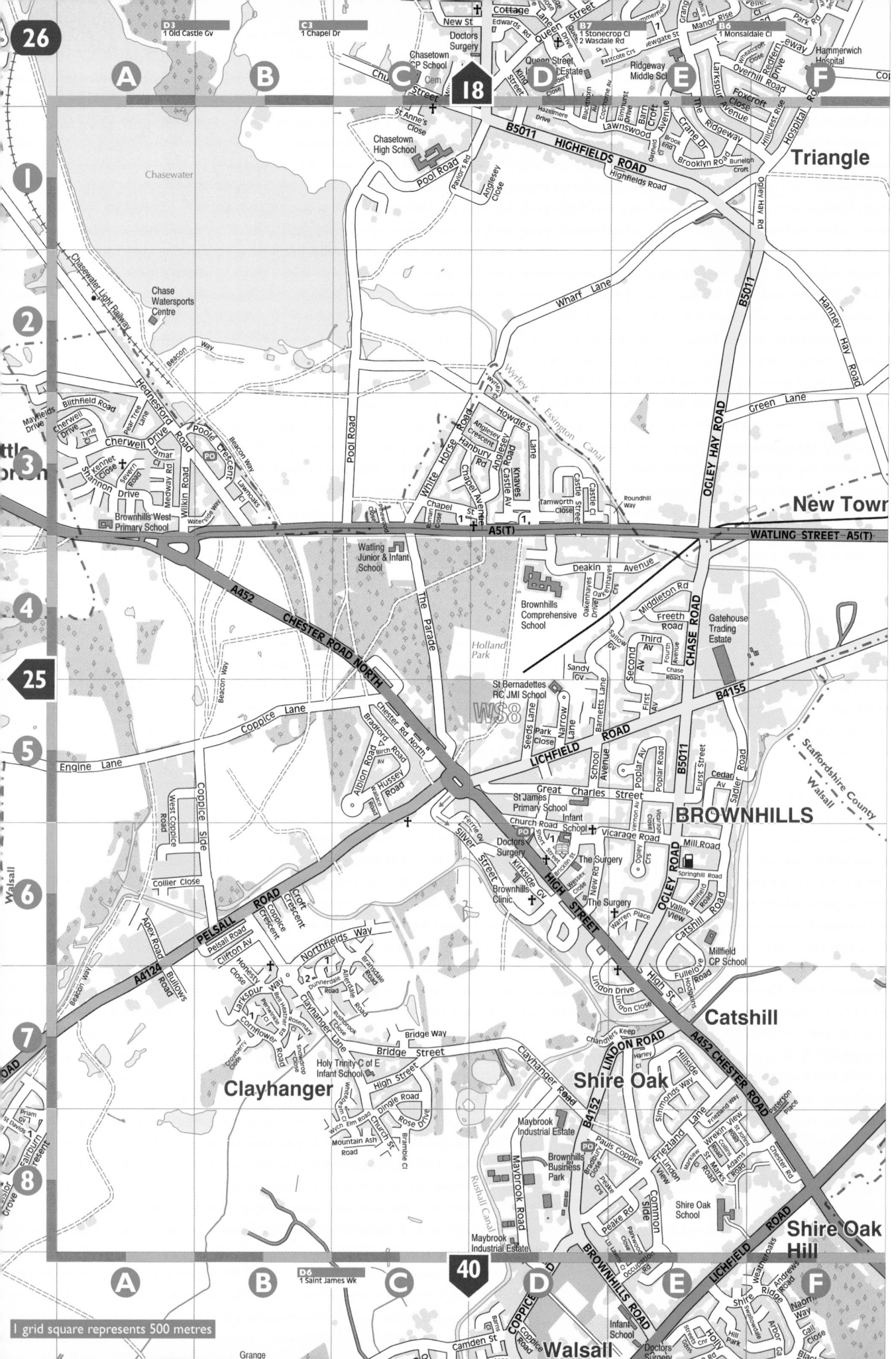

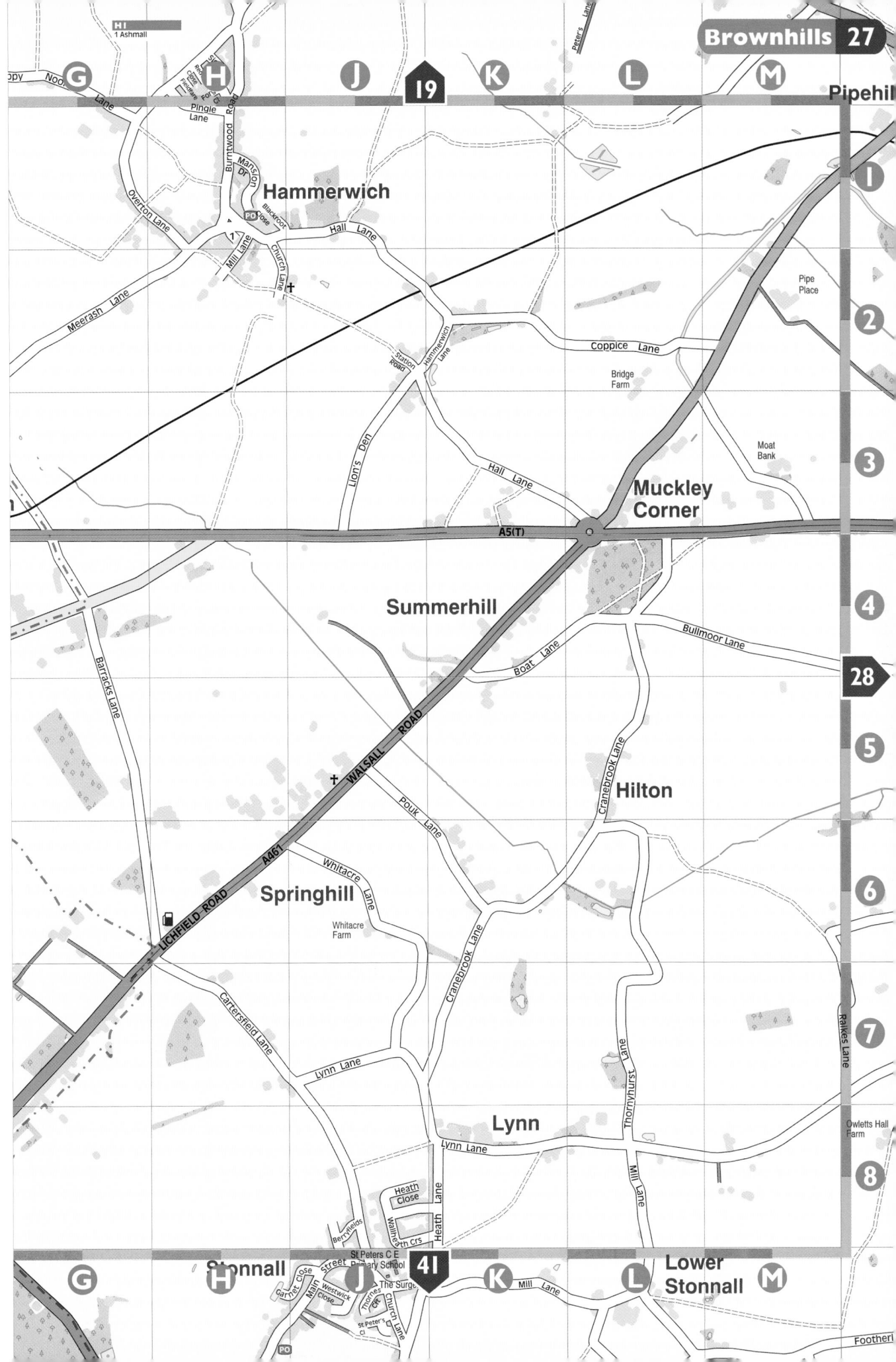

Pipehil

H1
1 Ashmall

G H J 19 K L M

I

Copy Nook
Lane

Pingle
Lane

Overton Lane

Burntwood Road

Manson Dr

Blackroot Close

Hammerwich

PO Close

For Croft
Fountains

Meerash Lane

Mill Lane

Church Lane

Hall Lane

Station
Road

Hammerwich Lane

2

Pipe
Place

Coppice Lane

Bridge
Farm

3

Moat
Bank

Lion's Den

Hall Lane

**Muckley
Corner**

A5(T)

Summerhill

Bullmoor Lane

4

28

Barracks Lane

Boat Lane

Cranebrook Lane

5

WALSALL ROAD

Pouk Lane

Hilton

A461

Whitacre Lane

Springhill

Whitacre
Farm

Cranebrook Lane

6

LICHFIELD ROAD

Cattersfield Lane

Lynn Lane

Thornyhurst Lane

Raikes Lane

7

Lynn

Lynn Lane

Mill Lane

Owletts Hall
Farm

8

Heath
Close

Berryfields

Wallheath Crs

Heath Lane

G H J 41 K L M

Garnet Close

Main Street

Westwick
Close

Thornes

St Peters C E
Primary School

The Surge

Stonnall

Church Lane

Mill Lane

**Lower
Stonnall**

St Peter's
Cl

PO

Footheri

Peter's Lane

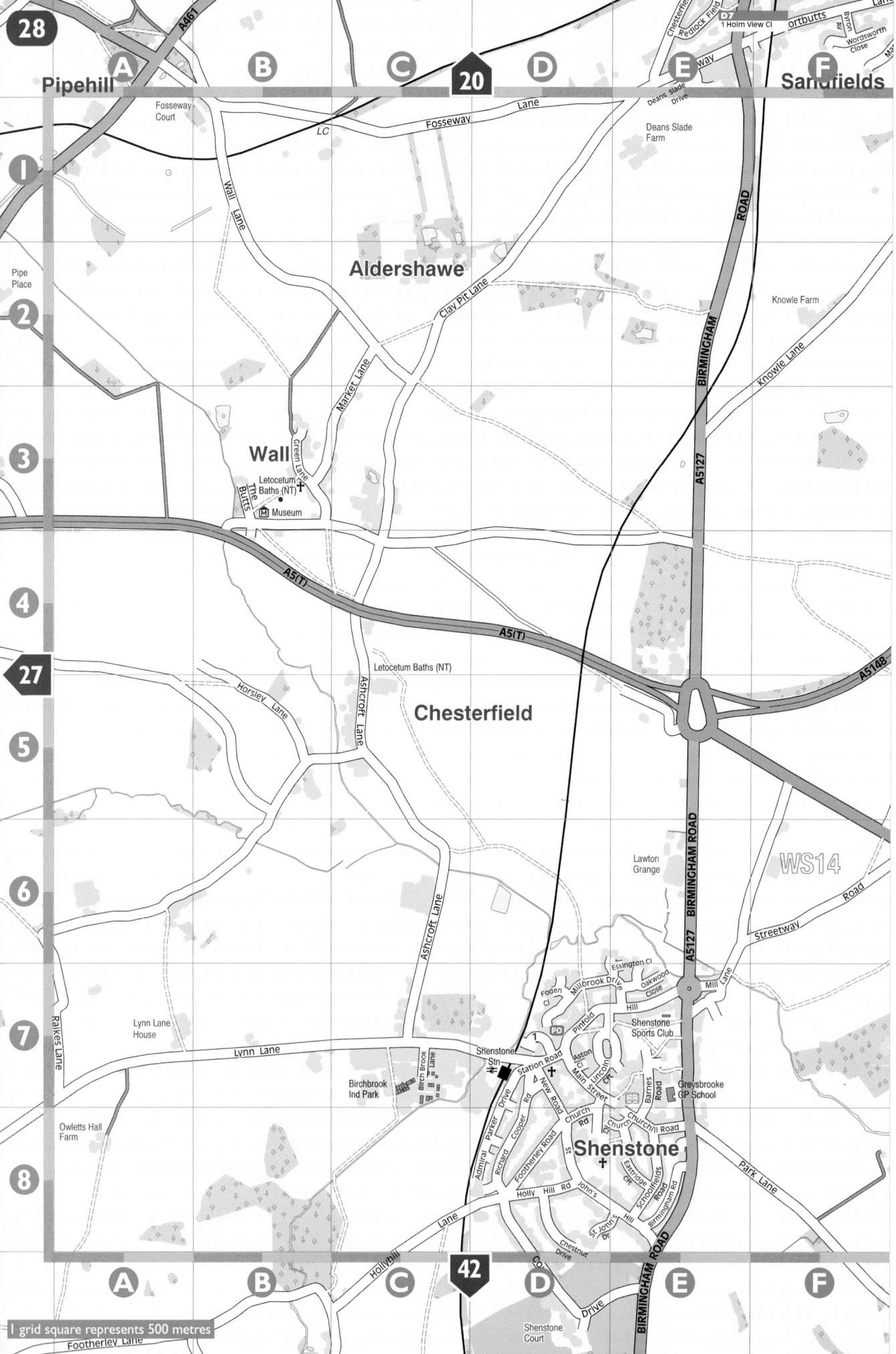

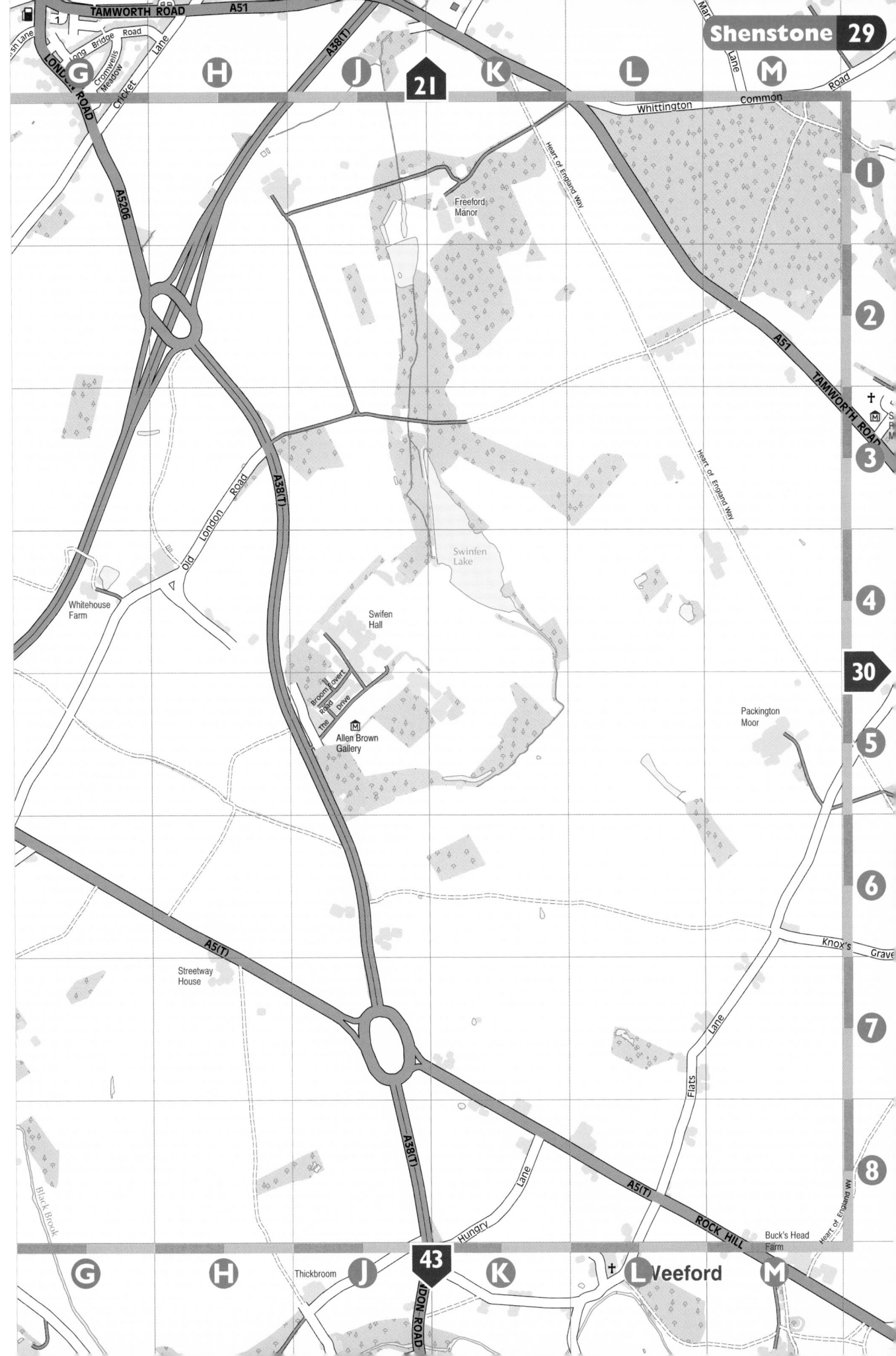

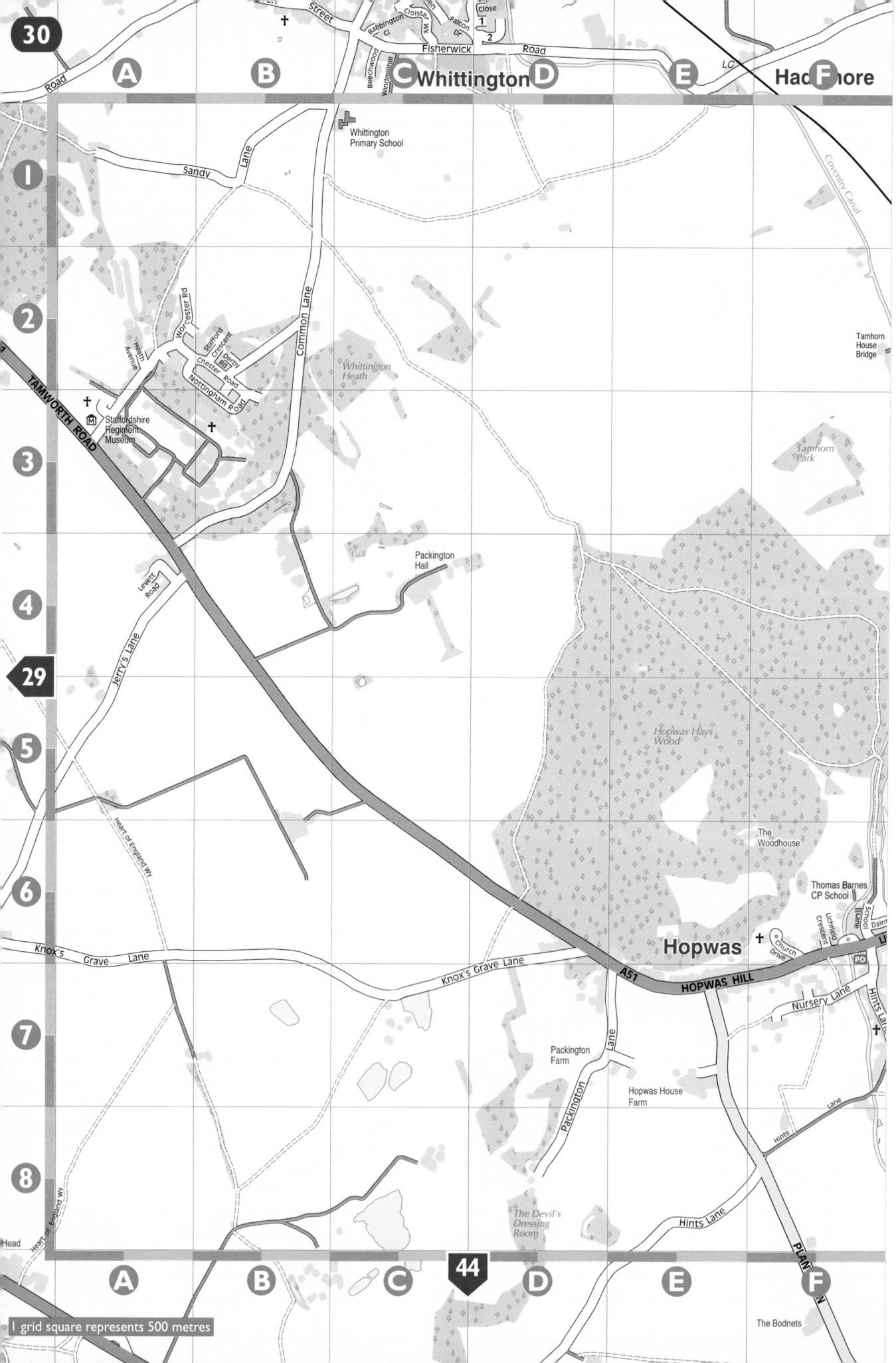

A   B   C **Whittington** D   E   **Had** F **more**

Fisherwick Road

I

Sandy Lane

Whittington Primary School

2

Worcester Rd
Heath Avenue
Stafford Crescent
Chester Derby Road
Nottingham Road
Common Lane
Whittington Heath

Tamhorn House Bridge

TAMWORTH ROAD

Staffordshire Regiment Museum

3

Tamhorn Park

Packington Hall

Levett Road

4

Jerry's Lane

Heart of England Wy

Hopwas Hays Wood

5

The Woodhouse

6

Thomas Barnes CP School

Knox's Grave Lane

Knox's Grave Lane

Church Drive
Lichfield Crescent
School Lane
Hopwas   A51
HOPWAS HILL
Hints Lane
Nursery Lane

PO

7

Packington Farm

Packington Lane

Hopwas House Farm

Hints Lane

8

Heart of England Wy

The Devil's Dressing Room

Hints Lane

PLAN

Head

A   B   C

D   E   F

The Bodnets

1 grid square represents 500 metres

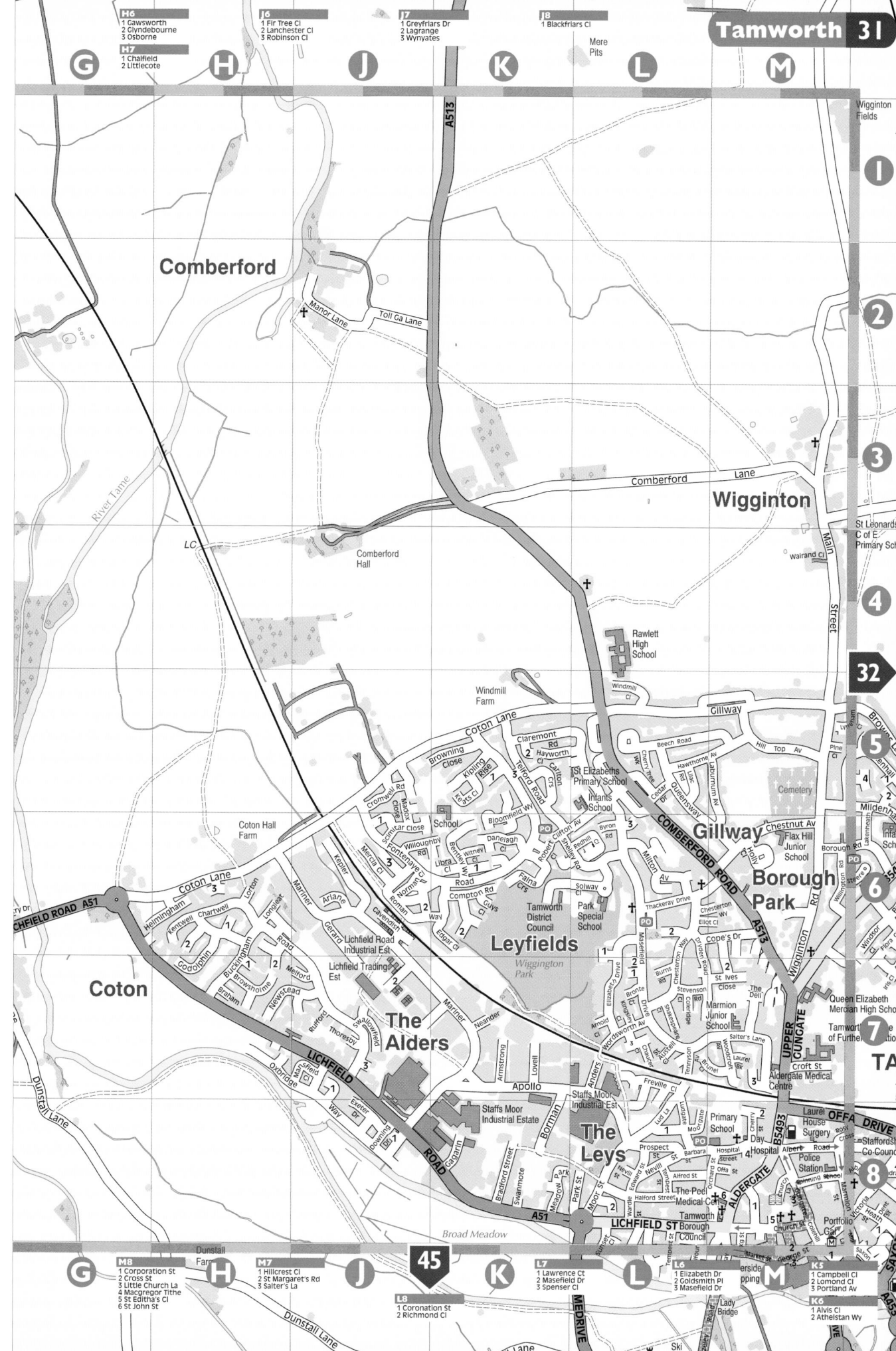

G H J K L M

Wiggington Fields

1

2

3

4

32

5

6

7

8

Comberford

River Tame

LC

Comberford Hall

Coton Hall Farm

Coton Lane

Coton

LICHFIELD ROAD A51

Kentwell

Godolphin

Buckingham

Braham

Browsholme

Newstead

Rufford

Thoresby

Melford

Swallowfield

The Alders

Oxbridge

LICHFIELD

Exeter Dr

A513

Manor Lane

Toll Ga Lane

Comberford Lane

Wigginton

St Leonards C of E. Primary Sch

Walrand Cl

Rawlett High School

Windmill Farm

Windmill

Gillway

Gillway

Hill Top Av

Cemetery

Flax Hill Junior School

Borough Park

Coton Lane

Claremont Rd

Browning Close

Kipling

Rise

Telford Road

Hayworth

Carlton Crs

St Elizabeths Primary School

Infants School

Beech Road

Hawthorne Rd

Lilac Rd

Lilac

Cherry Tree

Cedar

Laburnum Av

Pine Cl

Cromwell Rd

Maddox Close

Kett's Cl

School

Scimitar Close

Willoughby

Bentley Way

Witney

Bloomfield Wy

Danelagh

Libra Rd

Robert Clifton Av

Byron Cl

Redhill

Shelley Rd

Queensway

Milton

Holly

COMBERFORD ROAD

Chestnut Av

Borough Rd

Fontenaye Cl

Merca Cl

Norman

Road

Compton Rd

Faina Crs

Guys Cl

Solway

Park Special School

Av

Thackeray Drive

Chesterton Way

Eliot Cl

Marmion Rd

Borough Rd

Willington Rd

Helmingham

Chartwell

Lorton

Longleat

Kepler

Mariner

Arlane

Gerard

Cavendish

Roman

Edgar Cl

Way

Lichfield Road Industrial Est

Lichfield Trading Est

Tamworth District Council

Leyfields

Wiggington Park

St Ives Close

Cope's Dr

Burns Cr

Stevenson

The Dell

UPPER GUNGATE

Queen Elizabeth Mercian High Scho

Tamworth lege of Further ation

TA

Elizabeth's Drive

Bronte

Coleridge

Shakespeare

Marmion Junior School

Arnold

Wordsworth Av

Salter's Lane

Laurel

Croft St

Aldergate Medical Centre

Mariner

Neander

Mariner

Apollo

Borman

Lovell

Armstrong

Staffs Moor Industrial Est

Alders

Freville Cl

Ludgate

Moorgate

Primary School

Cherry St

Hospital Street

Laurel House Day Surgery

OFFA DRIVE

Staffordsh Co-Counc

The Leys

Prospect St

Offa St

Alfred St

Nevill St

Edward St

Halford Street

The Peel Medical Ce

Tamworth Borough Council

Police Station

Portfolio Ga

ALDERGATE

Church

Victoria

Heath

Bradford Street

Swanmote

Park St

Moor St

Meadow

Wartle

Sunset

Barbara

Tempest

LICHFIELD ST

Market St

George St

Saxon

A51

Broad Meadow

Dunstall Farm

Dunstall Lane

45

MEDRIVE

Lady Bridge

Ski

G H J K L M

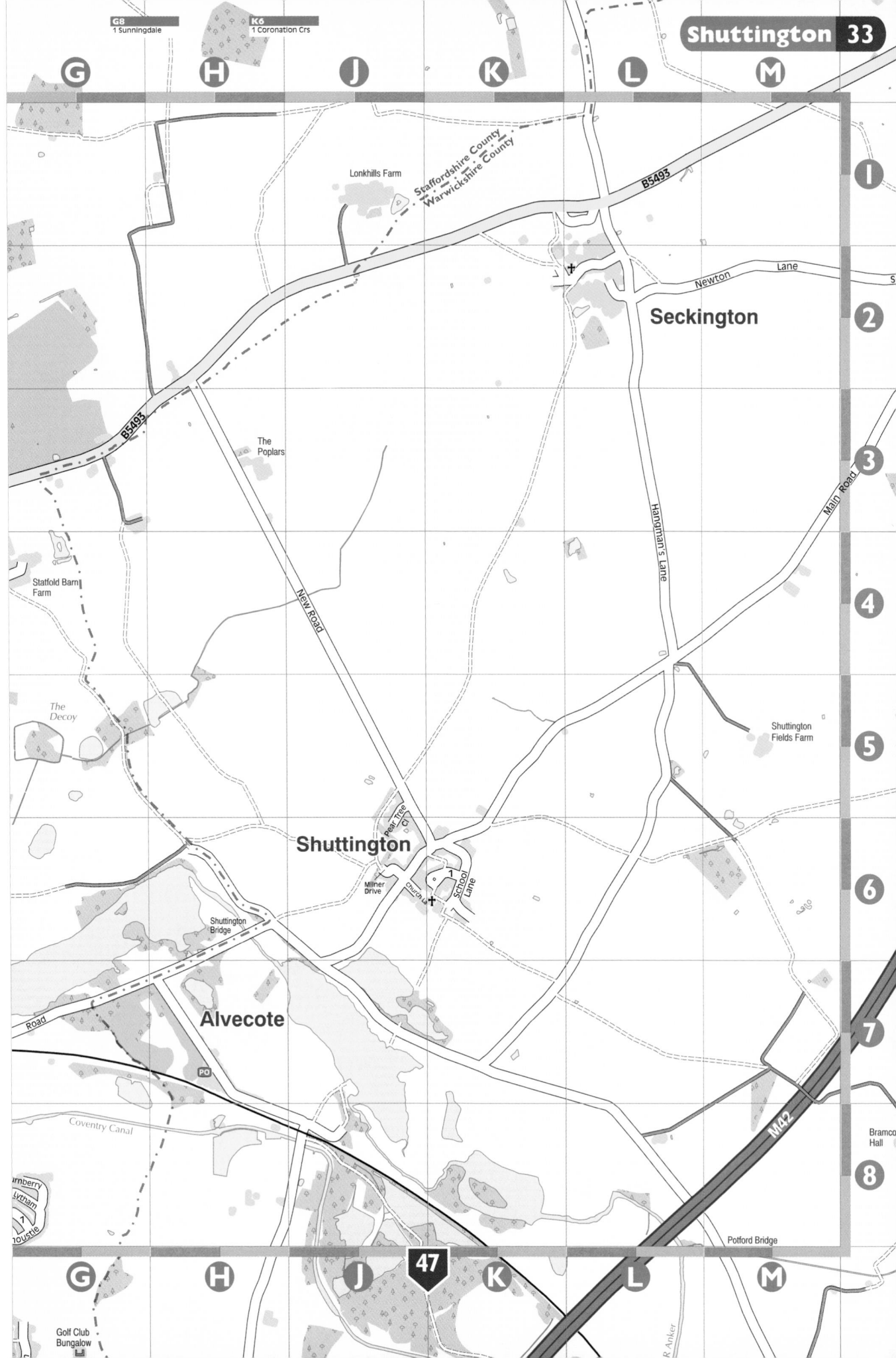

G8
1 Sunningdale

K6
1 Coronation Crs

G H J K L M

I

Lonkhills Farm

Staffordshire County
Warwickshire County

✝

B5493

Newton Lane

S

Seckington

2

B5493

The Poplars

3

Hangman's Lane

Main Road

New Road

4

Statfold Barn
Farm

Shuttington
Fields Farm

5

The Decoy

Pear Tree Cl

Shuttington

1

School Lane

6

Milner Drive

Church Ld

✝

Shuttington
Bridge

Road

Alvecote

7

PO

M42

Bramco
Hall

8

Coventry Canal

Potford Bridge

urnberry
ytham

1

oustie

Golf Club
Bungalow

R Anker

G H J **47** K L M

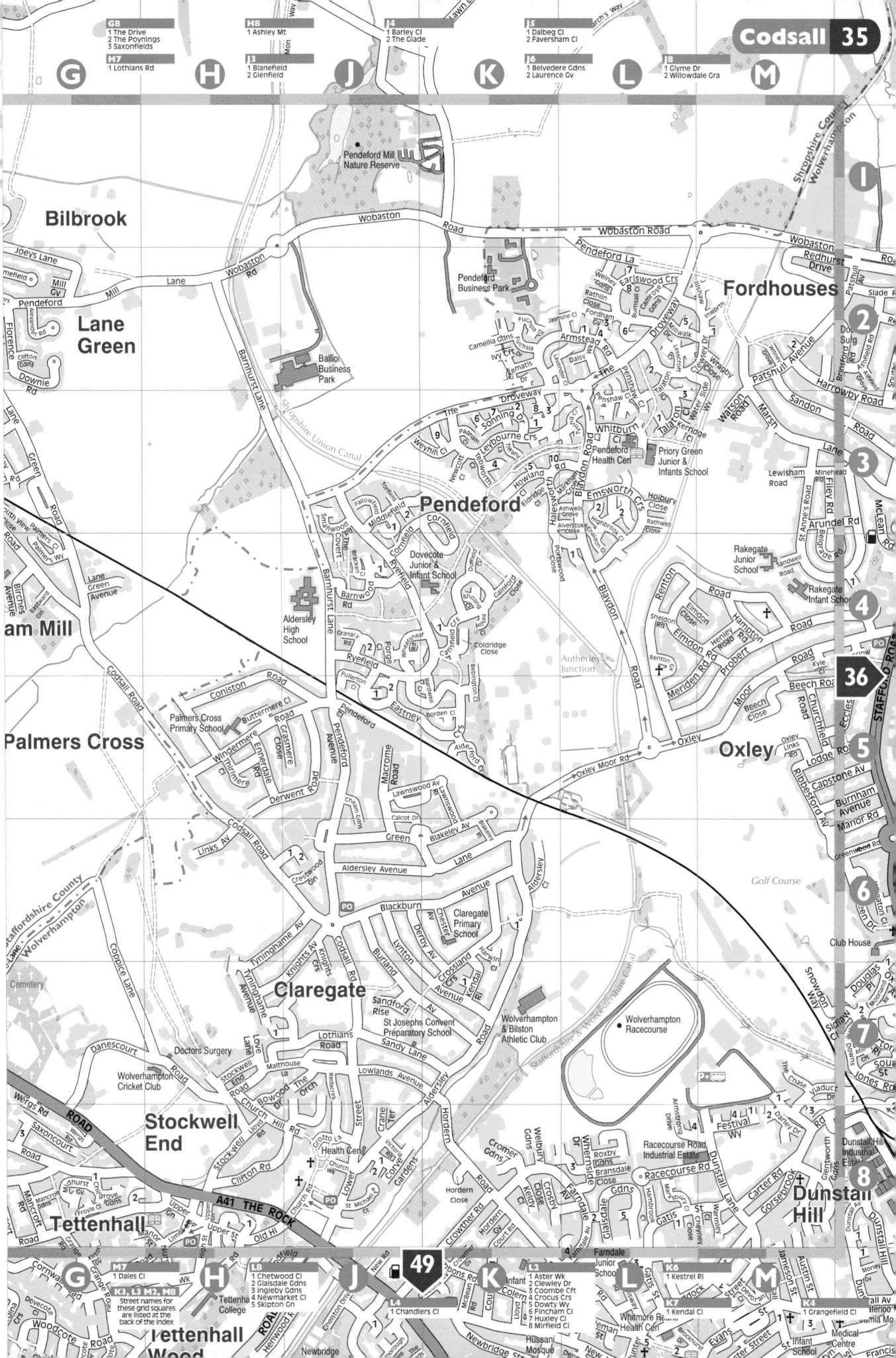

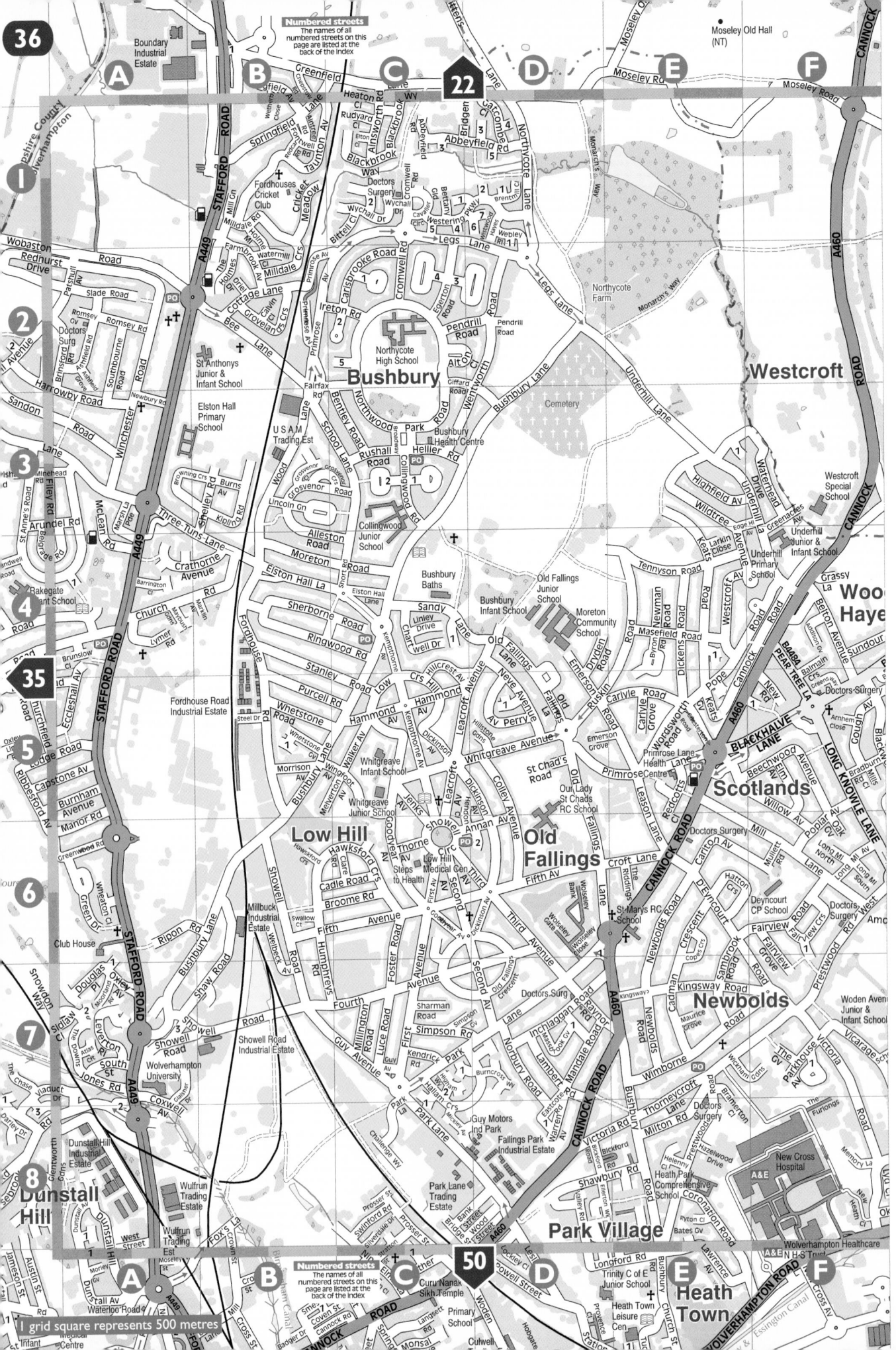

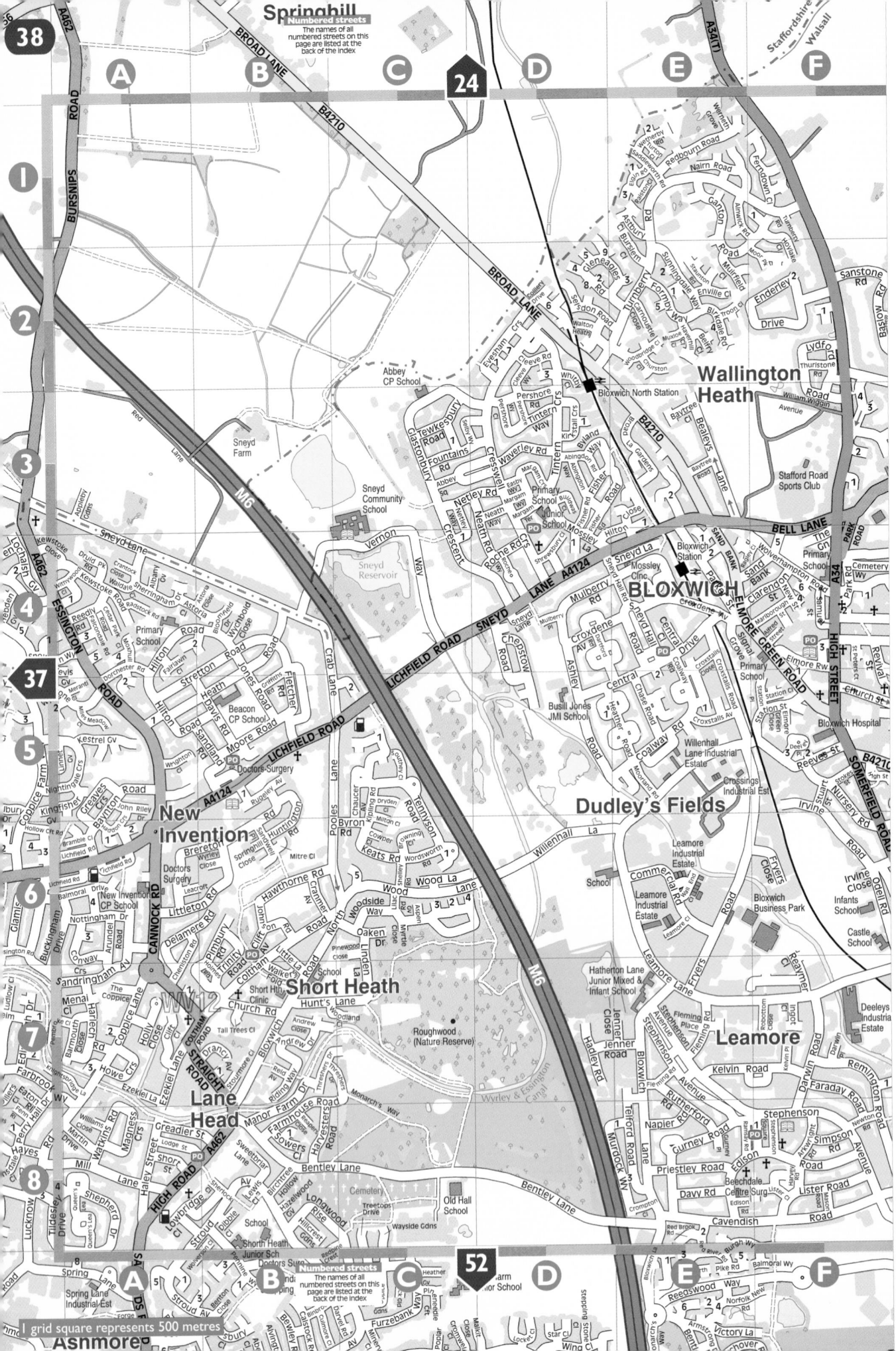

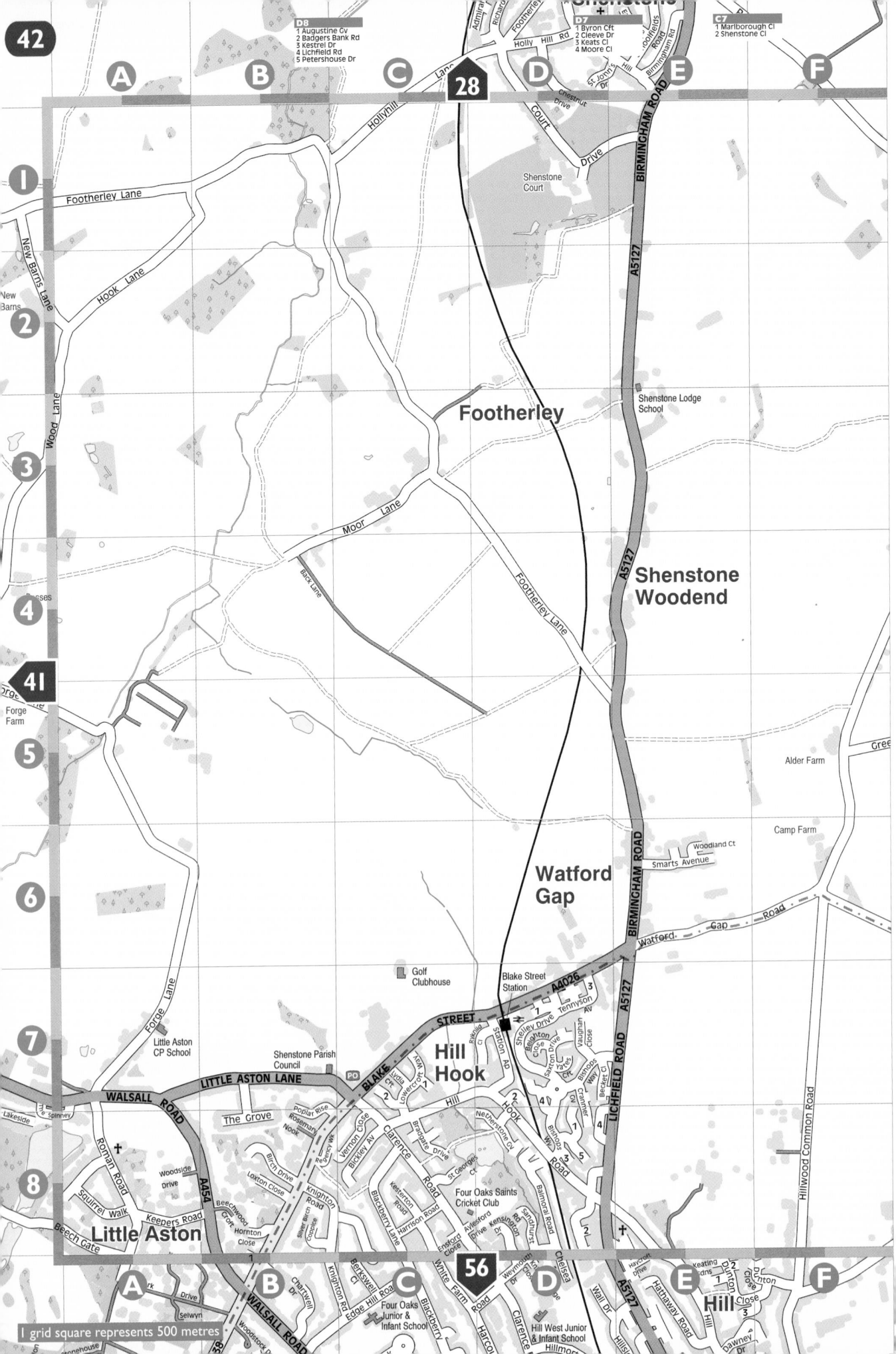

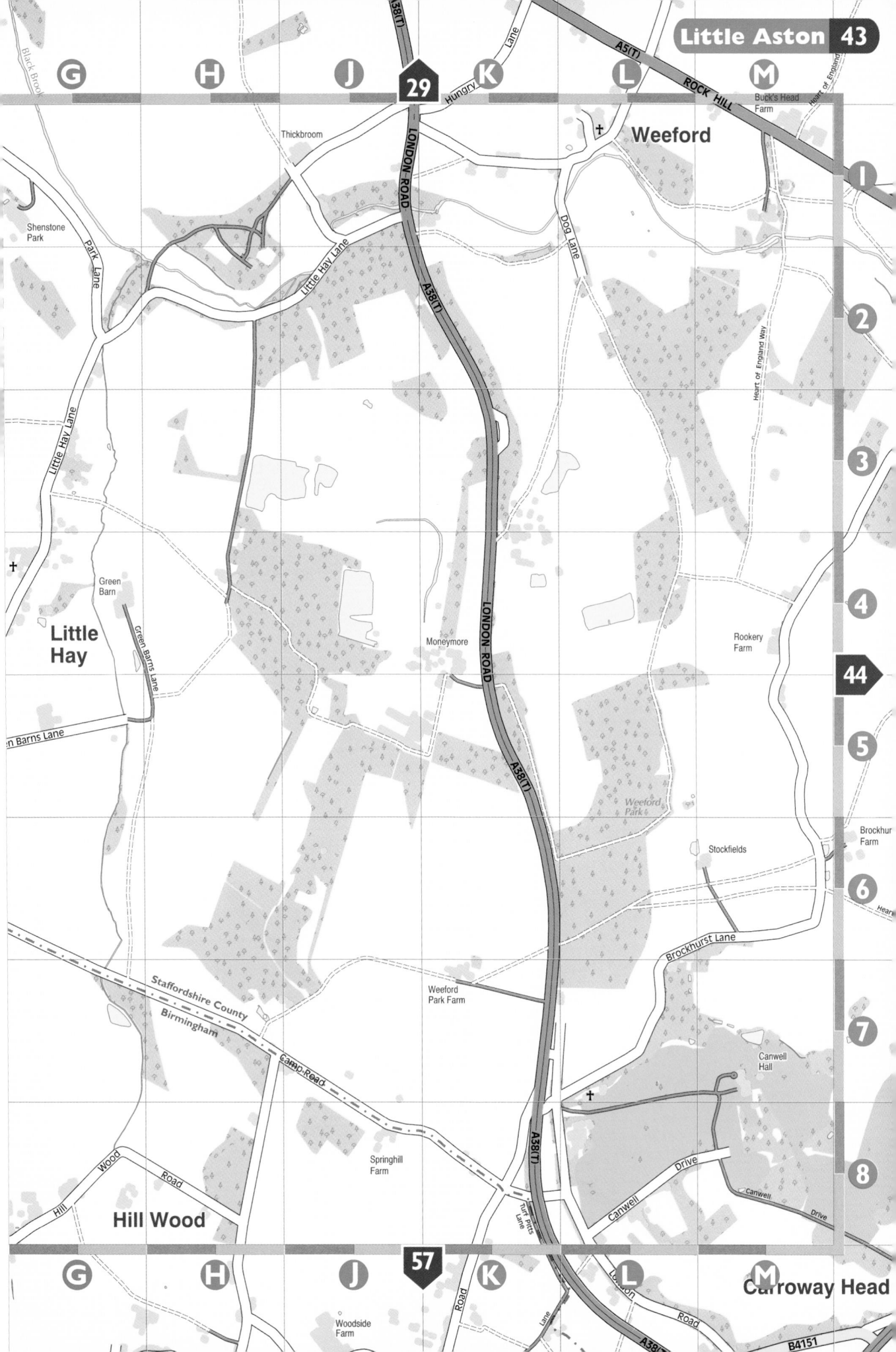

G H J **29** K L M I

Black Brook

Hungry Lane

A5(T) ROCK HILL

Buck's Head Farm

Thickbroom

Weeford

Shenstone Park

Park Lane

Little Hay Lane

A38(T)

LONDON ROAD

Dog Lane

Heart of England Way

2

Little Hay Lane

3

Little Hay

Green Barn

Green Barns Lane

Moneymore

LONDON ROAD

A38(T)

Rookery Farm

4

44

Weeford Park

Stockfields

Brockhur Farm

5

6

Hea

Green Barns Lane

Brockhurst Lane

Staffordshire County

Birmingham

Weeford Park Farm

7

Camp Road

Canwell Hall

8

Springhill Farm

A38(T)

Canwell Drive

Canwell Drive

Hill Wood Road

Hill Wood

Turf Pitts Lane

Canwell Drive

G H J **57** K L M

Carroway Head

Woodside Farm

Road

Road

Lane

London Road

A38

B4151

44

30

58

A B C D E F

1 2 3 4 **43** 5 6 7 8

's Head

Heart of England W

A5(T)

ROCK HILL

Hints Lane

The Drell's Room

The Bodnets

Hints Lane

Kendall's Wood

Rookery Lane

School Lane

Hints

Hints C

Bangley Farm

A5(T)

HINTS R

PLANTATION LA

Bourne Brook

SUTTO

Lower Bangley

Bangley Lane

Catston Close

Gainsborough Drive

Kirkland Way

Waggoner's Lane

Brockhurst Farm

Heart of England Way

Hints Farm

Hill Farm

Great Bangley Farm

Bangley Lane

SUTTON ROAD

A453

CRANEBROOK HILL

Drayton Lane

Oak Farm

roway Head

CARROWAY HEAD HILL

Shirrall Drive

well

Drive

Shirrall Hall Farm

B4151

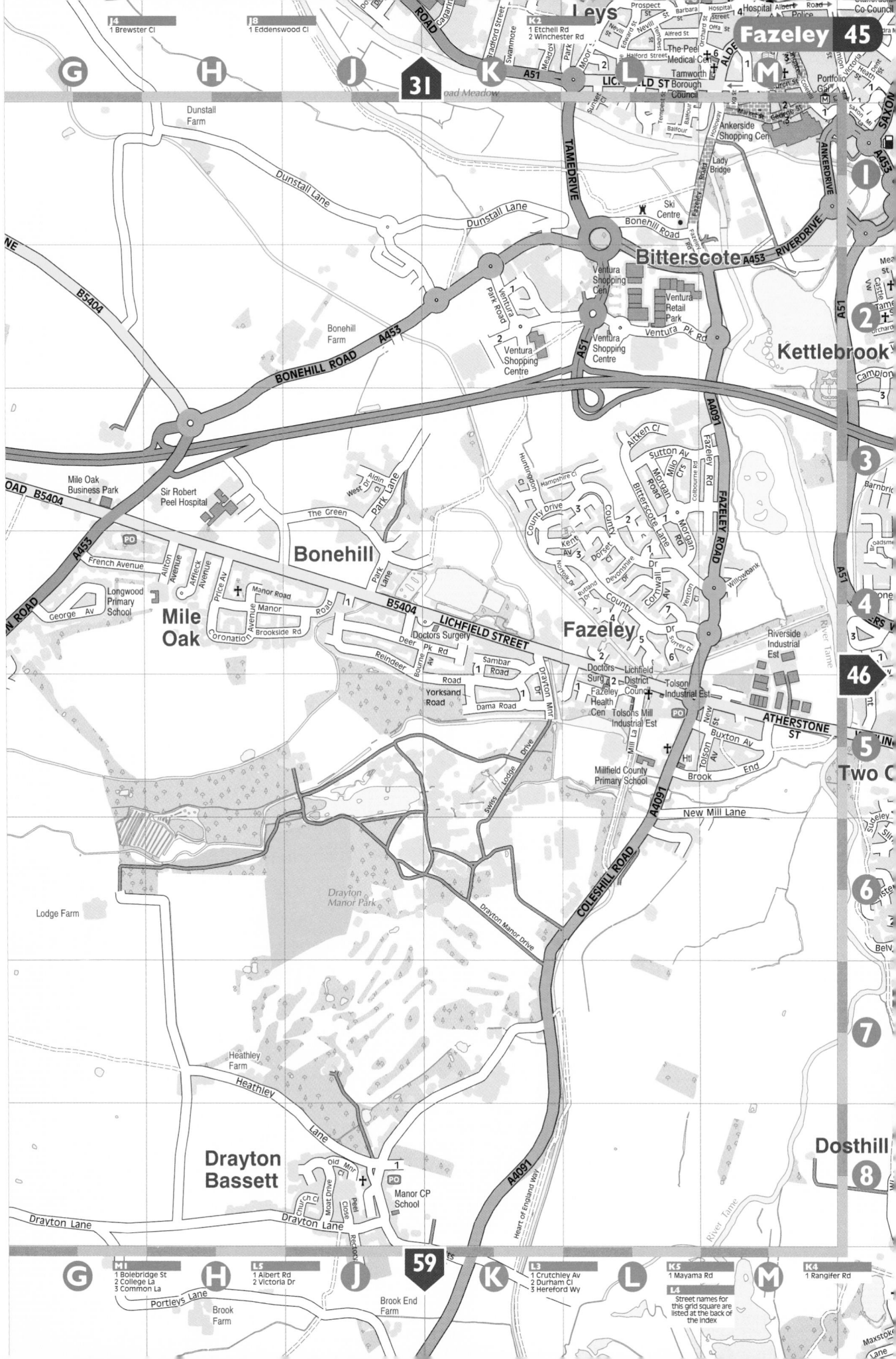

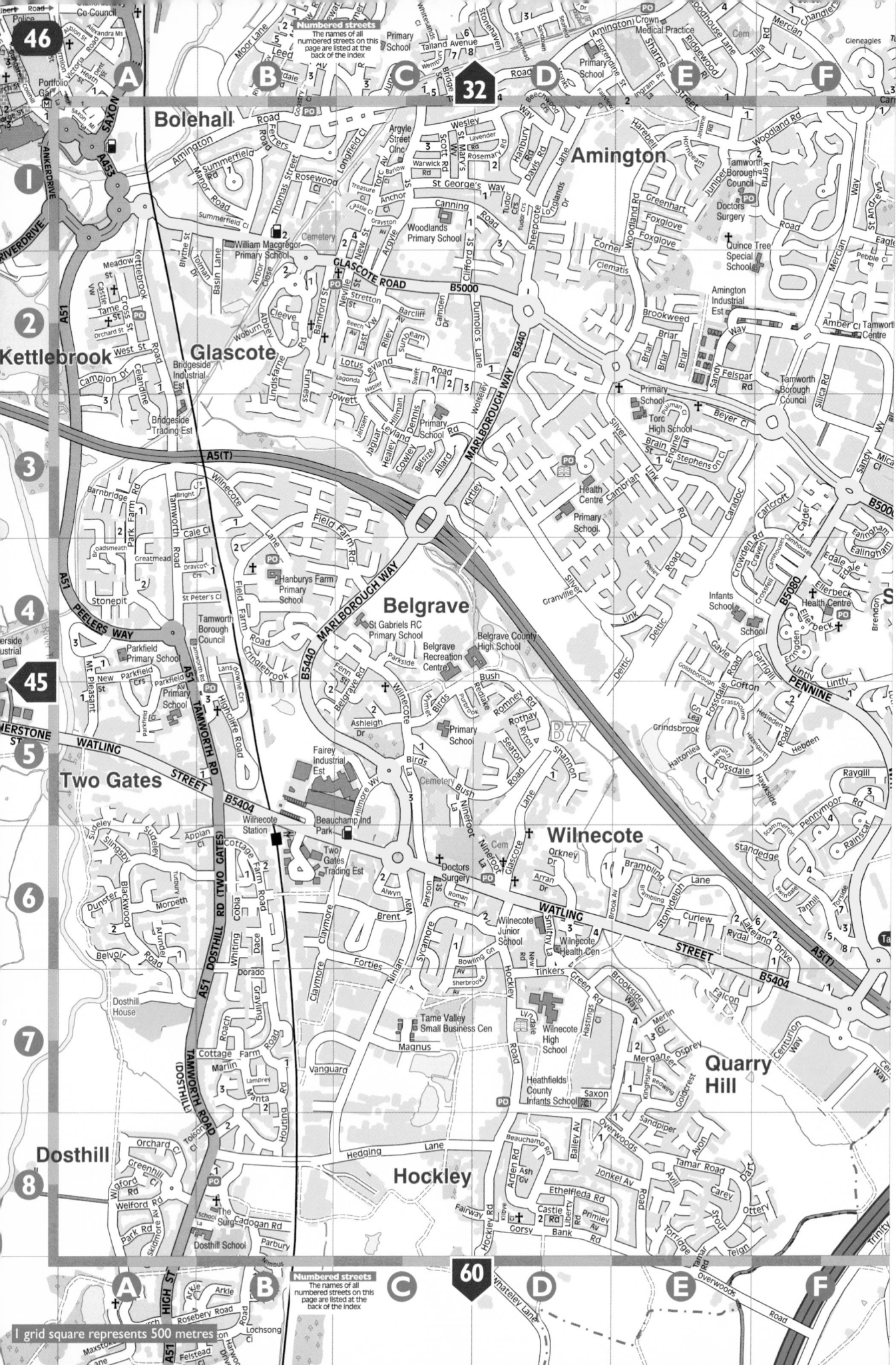

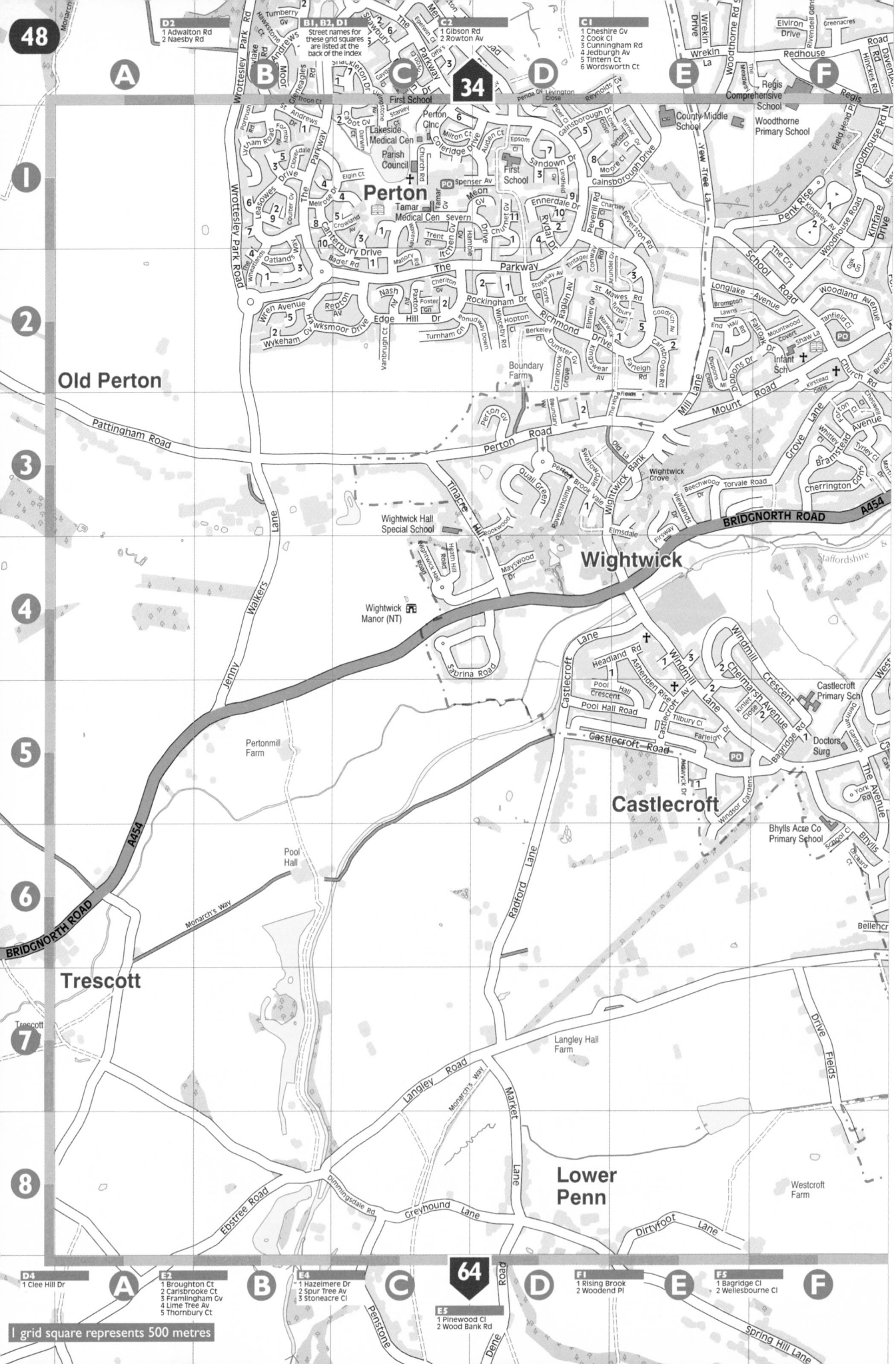

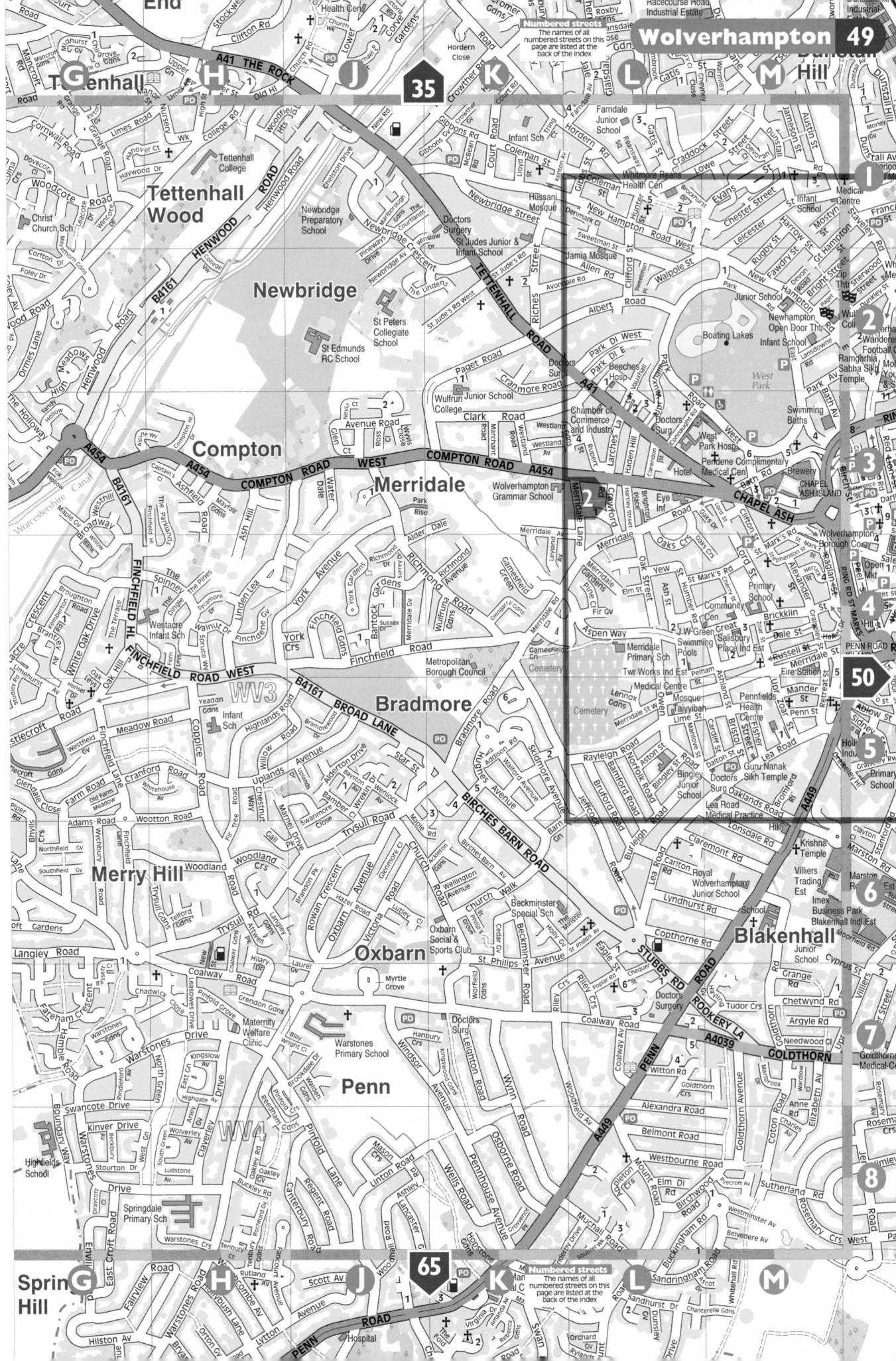

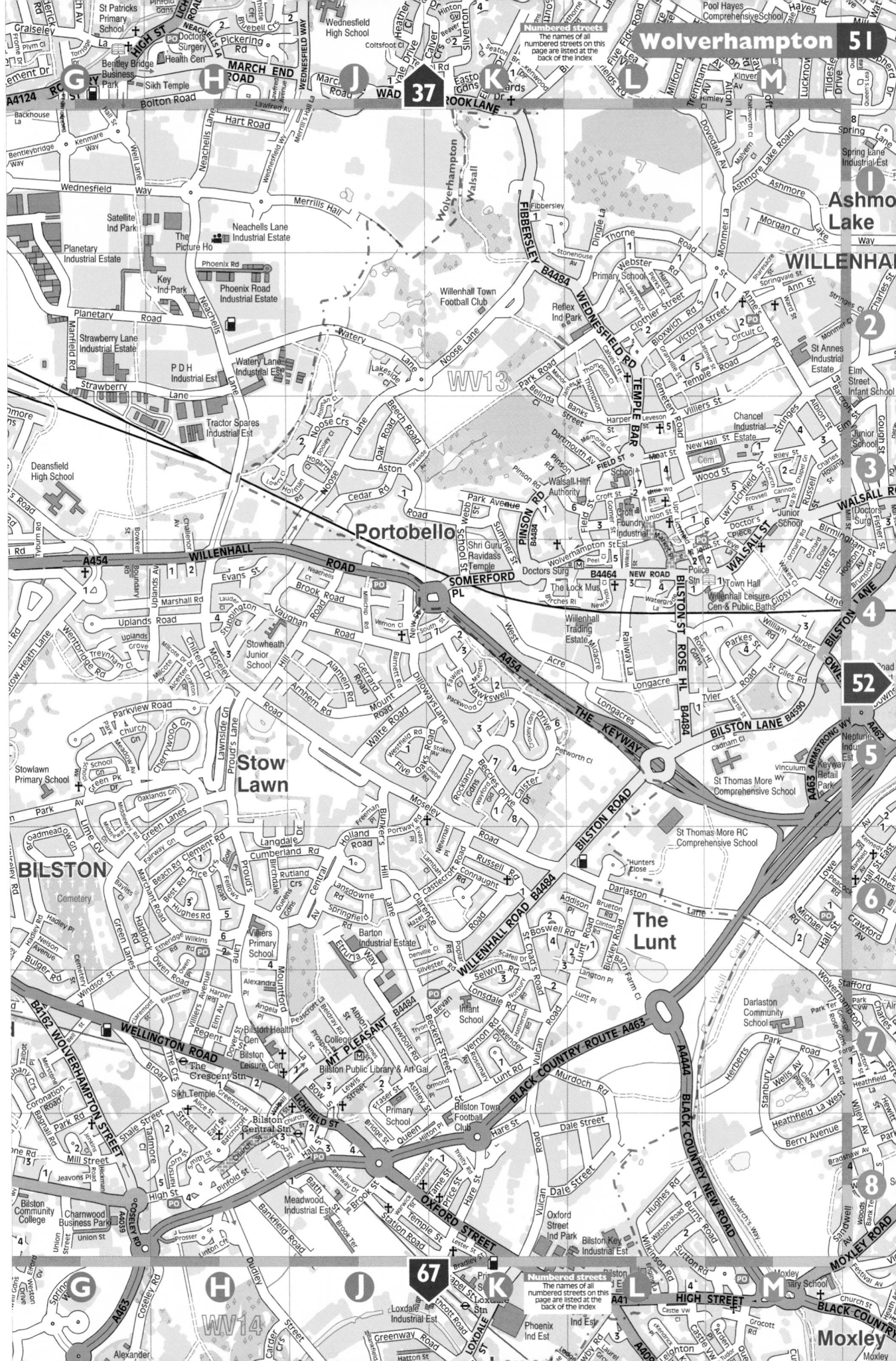

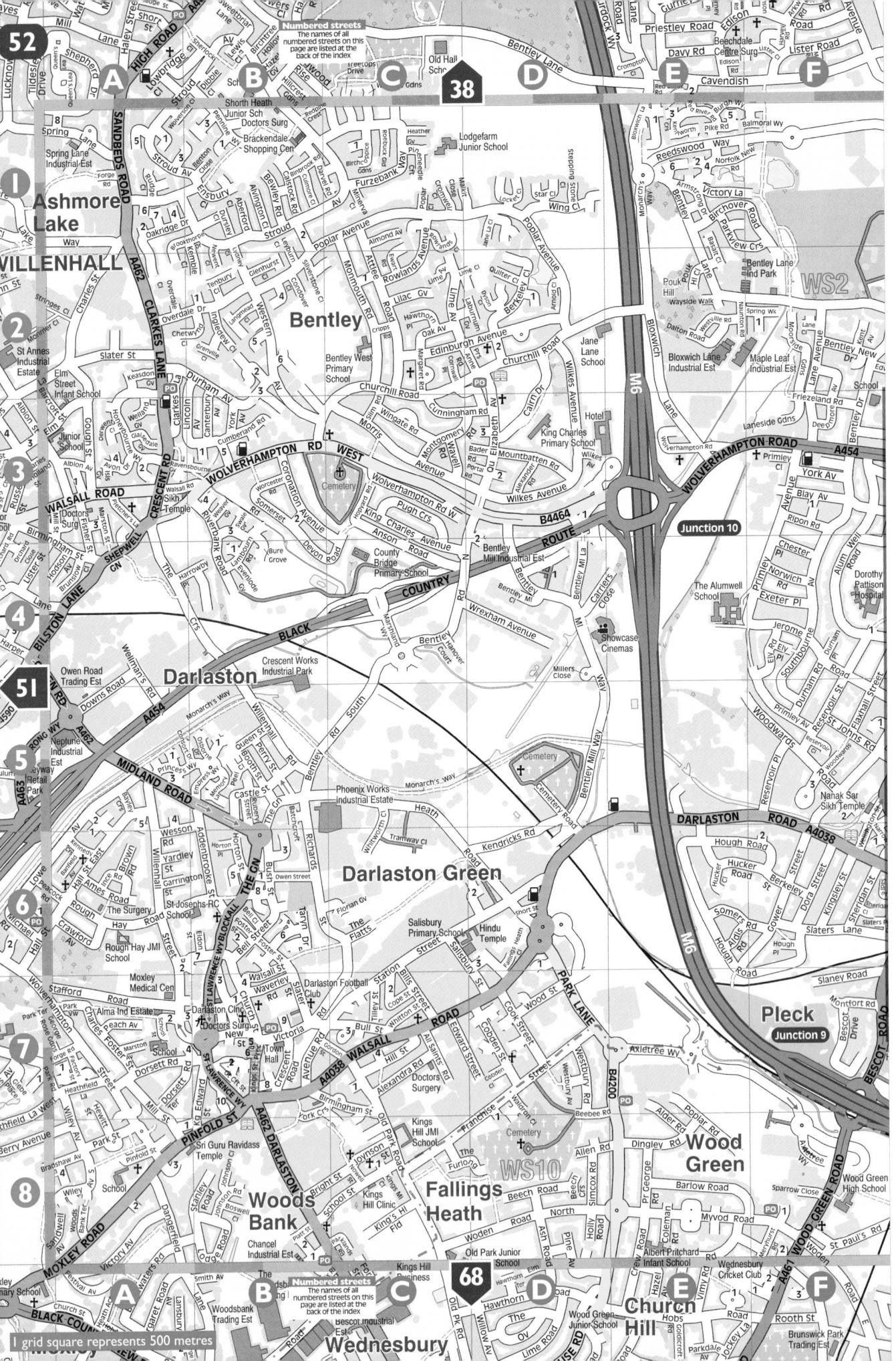

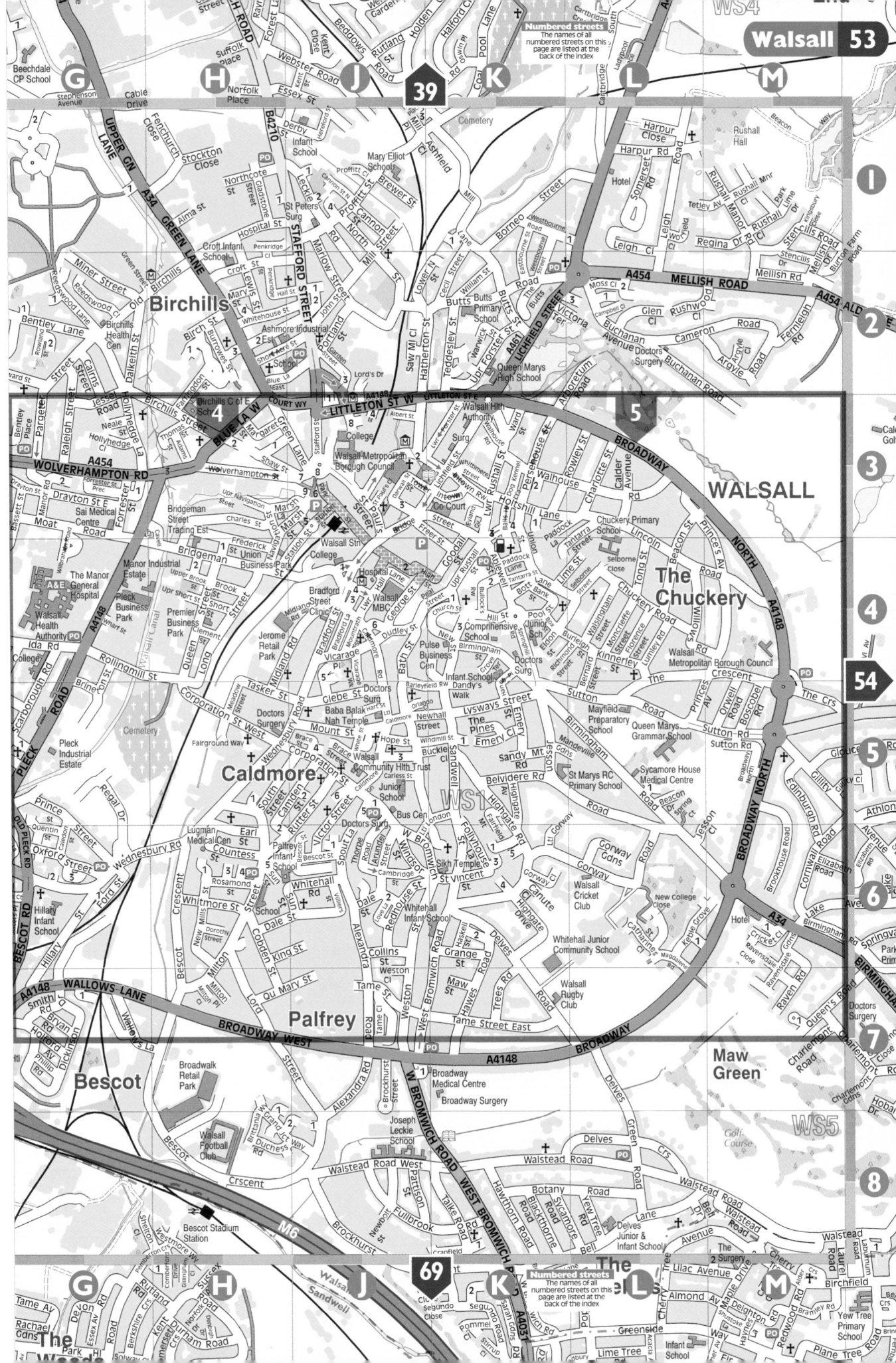

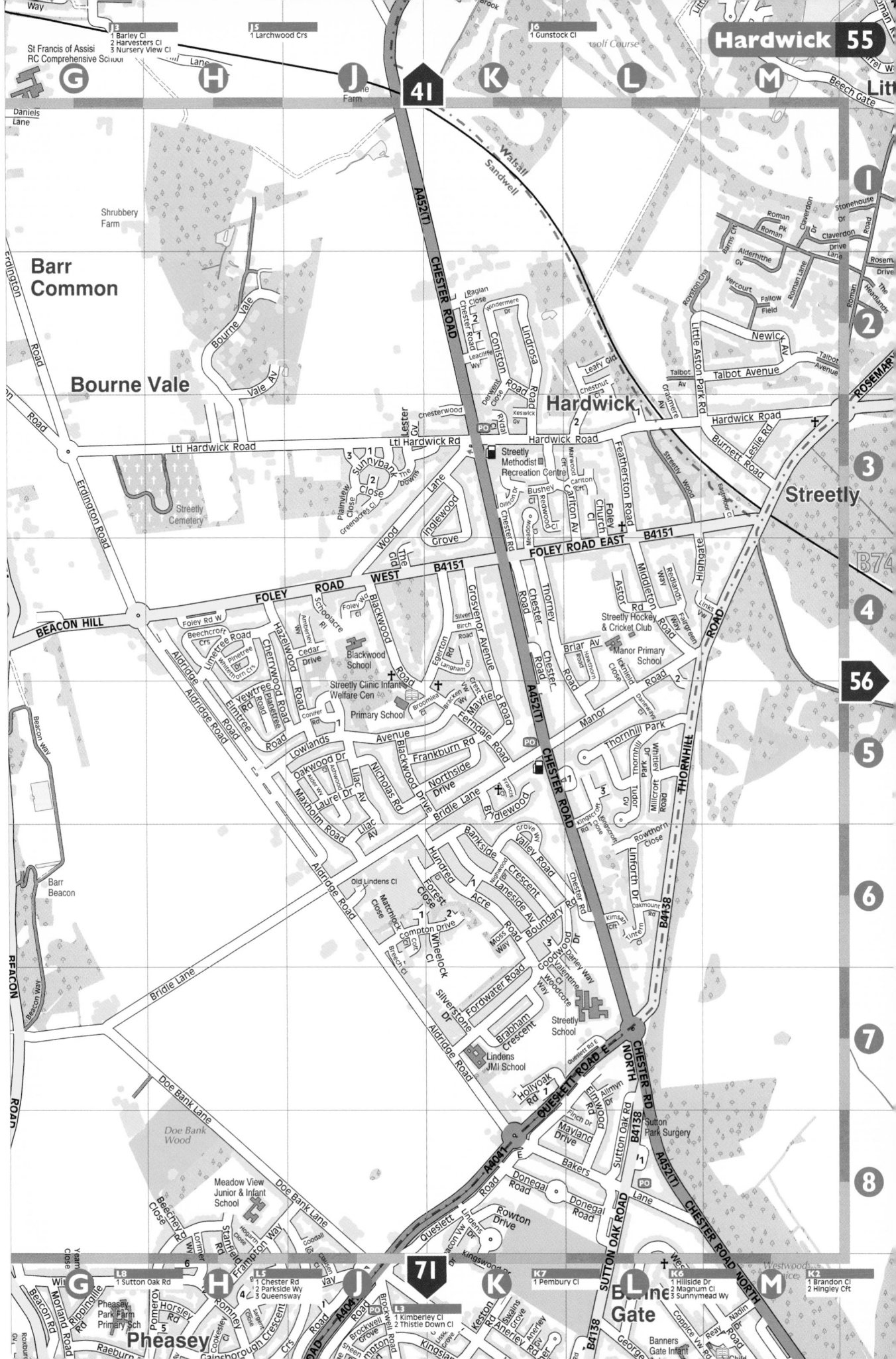

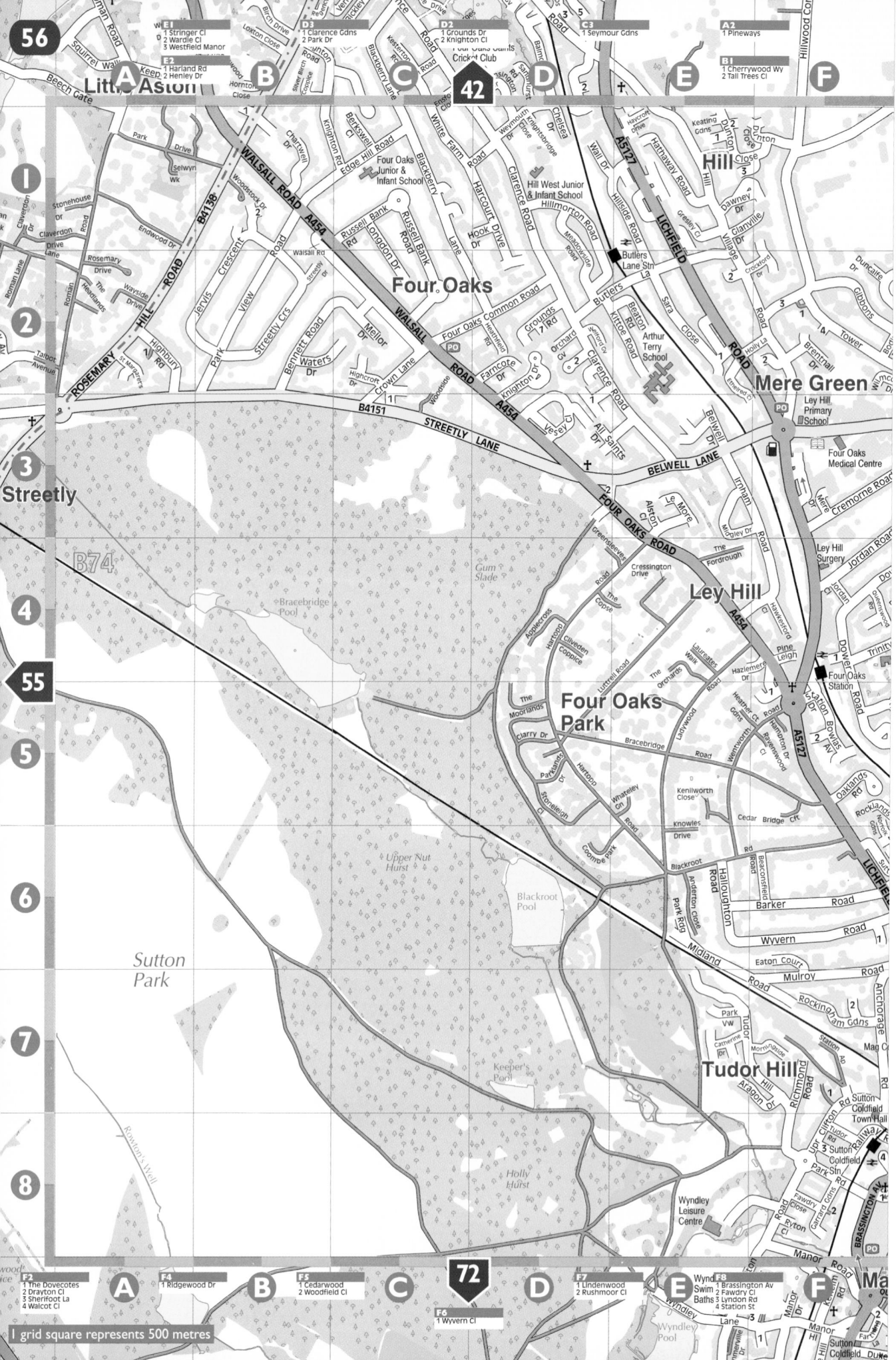

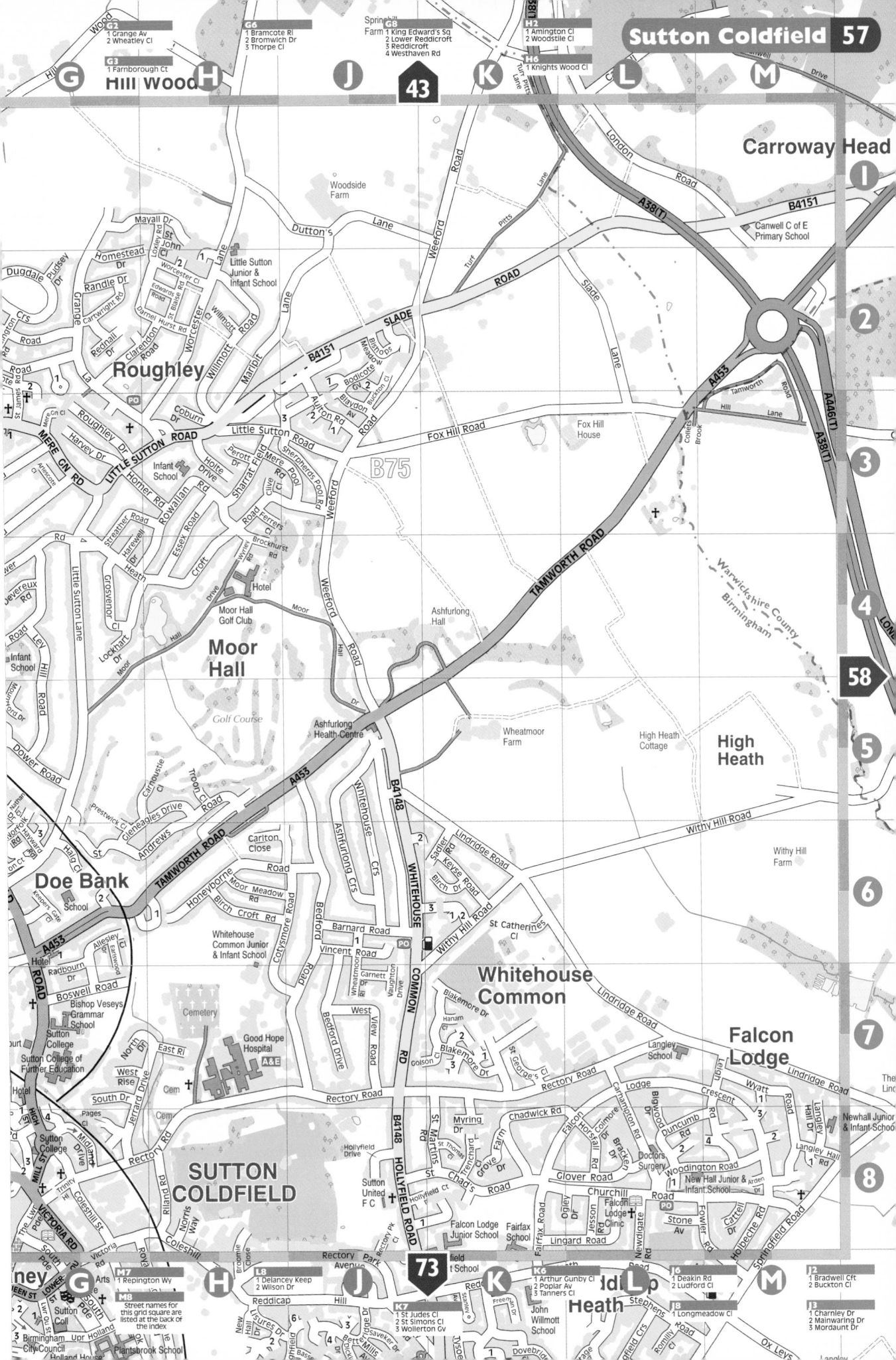

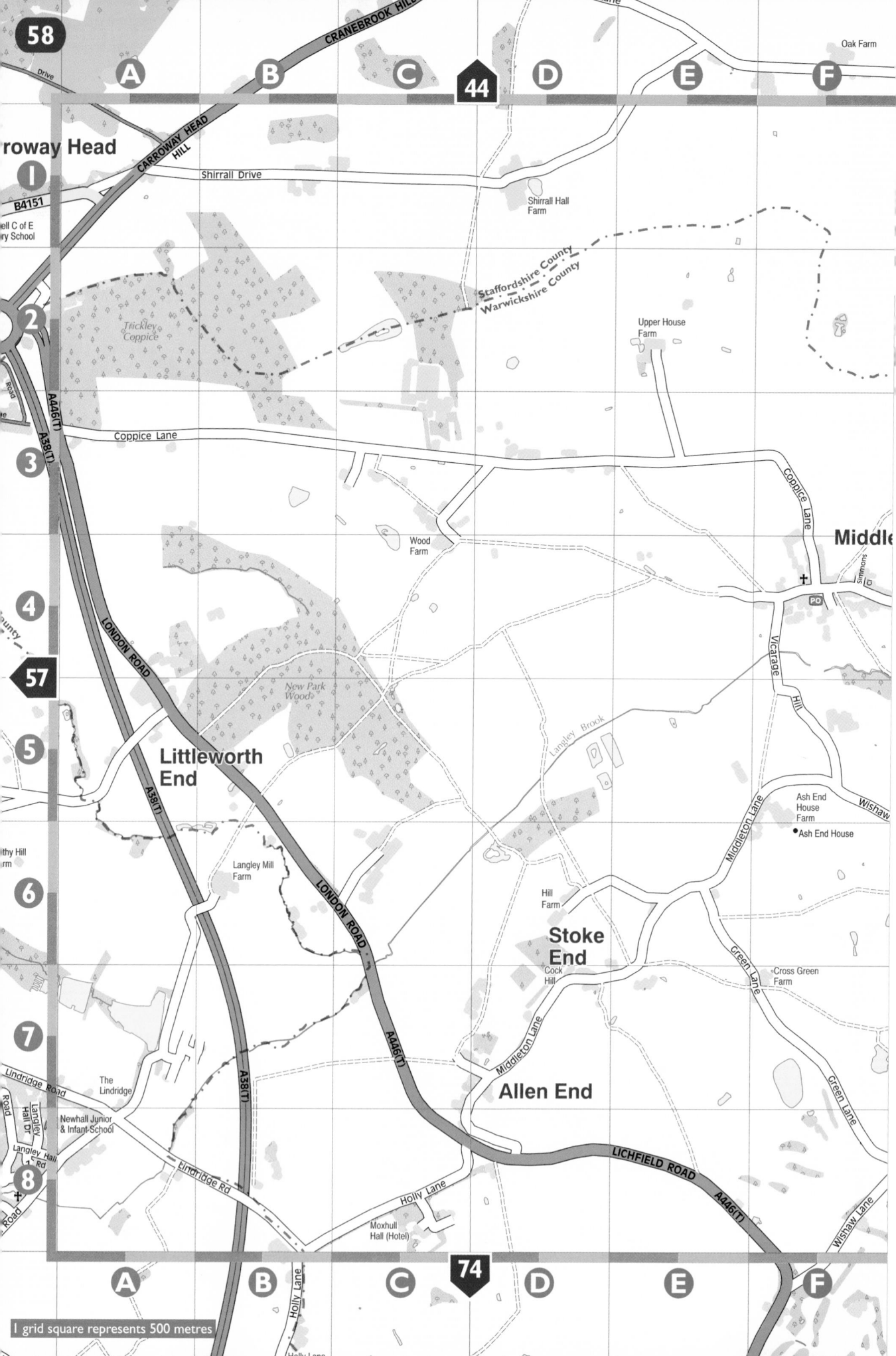

A   B   C   44   D   E   F

CRANEBROOK HILL

Oak Farm

roway Head

I

B4151

ell C of E
ry School

Shirrall Drive

Shirrall Hall
Farm

CARROWAY HEAD HILL

Staffordshire County
Warwickshire County

2

A446(T)

Trickley
Coppice

Upper House
Farm

Road

A38(T)

Coppice Lane

3

Coppice Lane

Wood
Farm

Middle

PO

LONDON ROAD

4

Vicarage Hill

57

5

New Park
Wood

Langley Brook

Littleworth
End

A38(T)

Ash End
House
Farm

Ash End House

Middleton Lane

thy Hill
rm

6

Langley Mill
Farm

Hill
Farm

Stoke
End

Green Lane

Cross Green
Farm

Cock
Hill

7

Lindridge Road

The
Lindridge

A446(T)

Middleton Lane

Allen End

Road

Langley Hall Dr

Newhall Junior
& Infant School

LICHFIELD ROAD

A446(T)

8

Langley
Hall
Rd

Lindridge Rd

Holly Lane

Moxhull
Hall (Hotel)

Green Lane

Wishaw Lane

Road

A   B   Holly Lane   C   74   D   E   F

1 grid square represents 500 metres

Dosthill

Drayton Bassett

L8
1 Bodymoor Heath La

G

H

Drayton La

Old Mnr Cl

Moat Drive

Church Cl

Drayton Lane

Rectory Cl

Manor CP School

PO

J

45

Salts La

K

Heart of England Way

L

River Tame

M

1
Maxstoke

Slade Lane

Portleys Lane

Brook Farm

Brook End Farm

A4091

Gallows Brook

2

...ton

Church Lane

Crowberry Lane

Middleton Pool

Middleton Hall

New House Farm

B78

Heart of England Way

Birmingham & Fazeley Canal

Heart of England Way

MWORTH

3

4

River Tame

Cliff H...

60

Cliff

5

Hunts Green

Lane

A4091

Wishaw Lane

Brick Kiln Lane

Aston Villa Football Club

Lower Farm

Bodymoor

Heath

Road

Broomey Croft Farm

Heart of England Way

M42

6

7

Bodymoor Heath

Kingsbury Water Park

Centenary Way

8

Middleton House Farm

North Wood

G

A4091

H

J

75

K

L

Bodymoor

M

G4
1 Islington Crs
2 St Michael's Cl
3 The Woodlands
4 Woodside Cl

G8
1 Charles St
2 Edinburgh Rd
3 Hawthorn Av

Hall End

STREET

A5(T)

Brown

New St

Long

Birch Coppice
Industrial E

Birch Coppice
I

47

Freasley

Penmire
Brook

Gypsy Lane

Lower House Lane

Lower House
Farm

A5(T)

I

The Cre

Manor Cl

Hill

Top

2

3

Overhouse
Farm

House

Lane

Watery Lane

Delves
Farm

Lower

**Edge
Hill**

Boulters

Delves Crs

Lane

Lane

**BADDESLEY
ENSOR**

Jean

4

PO

62

PO

St Church

Tamworth

Birchfield

**Wood
End**

Road

Speedwell

Cft

Bake

Park Roa

Speedwell

Lane

Roth

Hill

Walnut

Croft

5

Glenville
Av

Johnson
d School

Wood

Poplars
Farm

Waste
Farm

Common

Hurley

White's
Farm

Main Road

6

Heanley Lane

Heanley
Farm

Heanley Lane

Hipsley Lane

7

Cottage
Farm

8

Meadow
Rd

Cemetery

Hipsley Lane

Coronation Rd

Edmonds

Bee

Queens Way

Orchard Cl

Cherry

High View

Hurley

Hurley
Primary
School

Atherstone Lane

Hurley
Hall Farm

77

Atherstone Lane

Boultbee's
Farm

Knowle

Hill

Holly
Dr

herstone
Road
East House
Drive

G

H

J

K

L

M

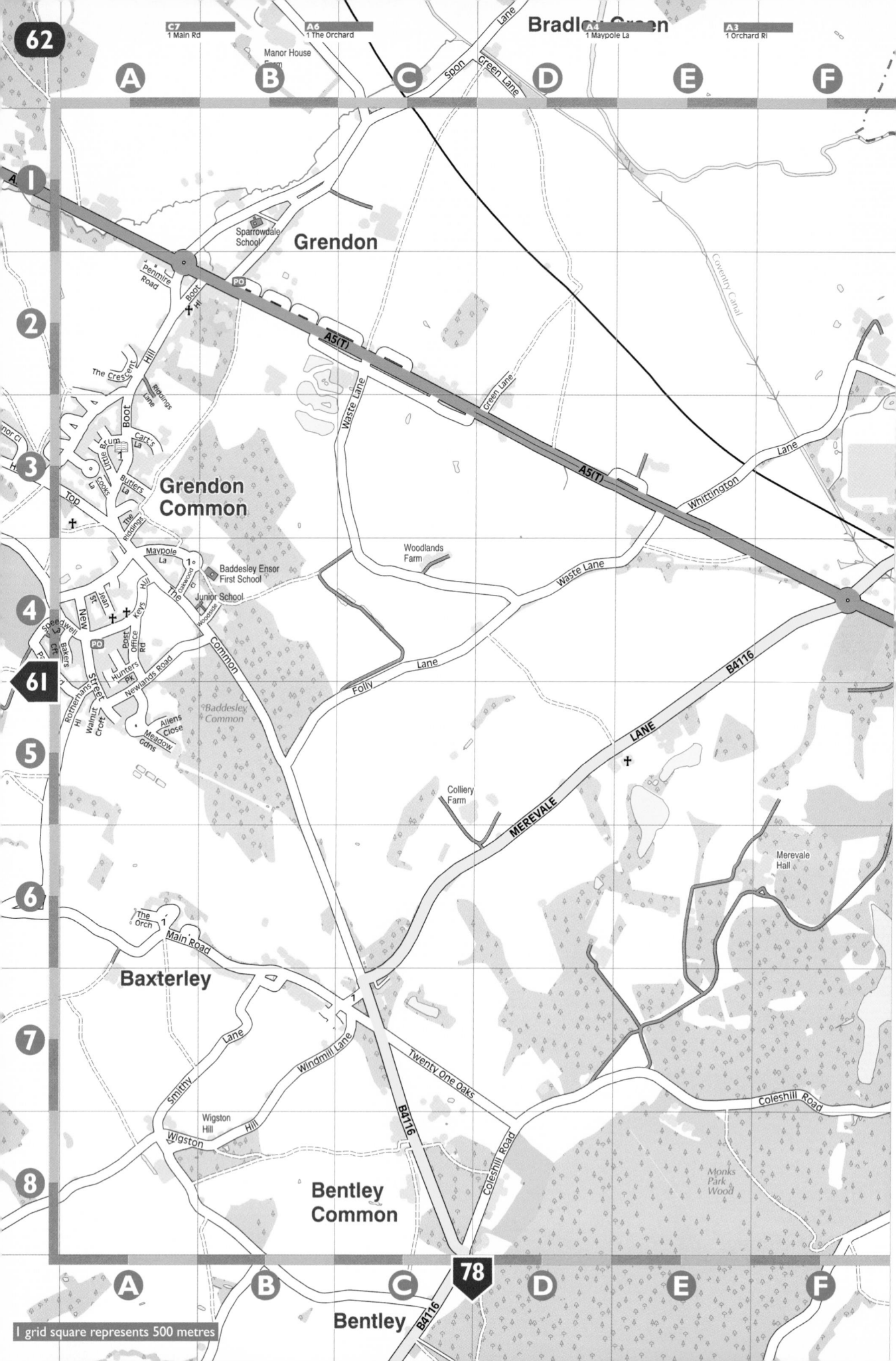

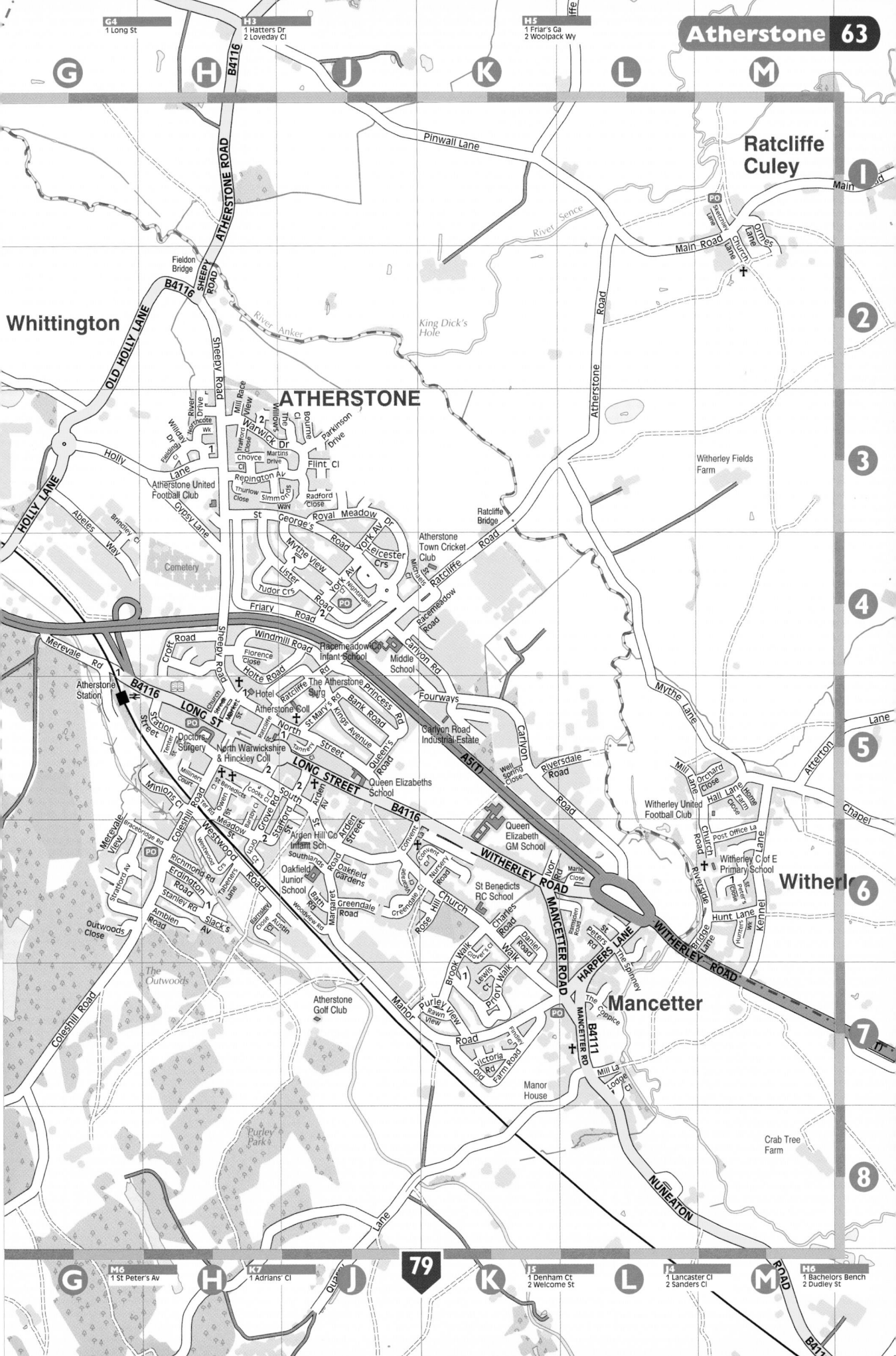

G   H   J   K   L   M

1

Ratcliffe
Culey

PO
Sketchley
Lane
Main Road

Ormes
Church Lane
Lane

2

Whittington

River Sence

Main Road

Atherstone
Road

Fieldon
Bridge

ATHERSTONE

River Anker

King Dick's
Hole

3

Witherley Fields
Farm

OLD HOLLY LANE

ATHERSTONE ROAD

SHEEPY ROAD

B4416

Sheepy Road

Mill Race View

The Willows

Warwick Dr

Bourne Cl

Parkinson
Drive

Holly
Lane

Willow Dr

River
Brook
Wk

Beechcote

Fielding
Cl

Trafford Close

Choyce
Cl

Martins
Drive

Flint Cl

Repington Av

Thurlow
Close

Simmonds
Way

Radford
Close

Atherstone United
Football Club

Gypsy Lane

Mythe View

Lister
Crs

York Rd

Nightingale

York Av

Leicester
Crs

St George's
Road

Royal Meadow
Dr

Ratcliffe
Bridge

Atherstone
Town Cricket
Club

4

HOLLY LANE

Merevale Rd

Cemetery

Abeles
Way

Brinkley Cl

Tudor Crs

Friary
Road

PO

Atherstone
Coll

Windmill Road

Florence
Close

Holte Road

Racemeadow Co
Infant School

Middle
School

Racemeadow
Road

Carlyon Rd

Michaels

Ratcliffe Road

Ratcliffe Road

5

Atherstone
Station

B4416

Croft Road

Sheepy Road

Church

Market
St

Hotel

The Atherstone
Surg

Ratcliffe

St Mary's Rd

Bank Road

Kings Avenue

Princess Rd

Fourways

Carlyon Road
Industrial Estate

Well
Spring
Close

Carlyon
Road

Riversdale
Road

Mill Lane

Orchard
Close

Hall Lane
Farm

Atterton
Lane

Chapel
Lane

LONG ST

Station
Street

PO

North
Street

Doctors
Surgery

Temple St

North Warwickshire
& Hinckley Coll

St Benedicts

Cocks Cl

Queen's
Road

A5(T)

Queen Road

Tanners

LONG STREET

Queen Elizabeths
School

B4416

A5(T)

Queen
Elizabeth
GM School

Witherley United
Football Club

Witherley C of E
Primary School

Witherle

6

Milliners
court

South

Stafford
Rd

Arden
Street

Meadow

Grove Rd

Convent

Nursery

Queen
Elizabeth
GM School

WITHERLEY ROAD

MANCETTER ROAD

Post Office La

Church
Road

Hunt Lane

Kennel

Lane

Hanbury

Minions Cl

Coleshill Road

Westwood

Westwood Road

Bracebridge Rd

Richmond Rd

Erdington
Road

Tabbers
Lane

Stanley Rd

Ambien
Road

Slack's
Av

Austin

Bansley
Close

Arden Hill Co
Infant Sch

Oakfield
Gardens

Oakfield
Junior
School

Southlands

Leith
Woodway Rd

Margaret
Road

Greendale
Road

Convent

St Benedicts
RC School

Charles
Road

Daniel
Road

Marie
Close

Convent
Road

St Peters
Rd

HARPERS LANE

The Spinney

Bridge
Lane

Riversdale

7

Stratford Av

PO

Merevale
View

Outwoods
Close

The
Outwoods

Atherstone
Golf Club

Manor
Road

Church
Hill

Rose Hill

Brook Walk

Purley View

Rawn
View

Lewis
Ct

Clover's Cl

Priory Walk

PO

Victoria
Rd

Old
Farm Road

Finchley Cl

NUNEATON

MANCETTER RD

B4111

Mill La

Lodge
Cl

Mancetter

The
Coppice

Crab Tree
Farm

WITHERLEY ROAD

8

Purley
Park

Manor
House

B4111

B4111

M6
1 St Peter's Av

K7
1 Adrians' Cl

J5
1 Denham Ct
2 Welcome St

J4
1 Lancaster Cl
2 Sanders Cl

H6
1 Bachelors Bench
2 Dudley St

64

D6
1 Bankside
2 Greenlands
3 Wedgwood Cl

Ebstree Road

C8
1 Crane Hollow
2 Millside
3 The Shales
4 Wodehouse Cl

B8
1 The Croft
2 Heathlands
3 Longford Cl

C7
Street names for this grid square are listed at the back of the index

B7
1 Bloomfield Cl
2 Brindley Cl
3 Wombrook Dl

Westcroft Farm

Greyhound Road

Penstone Lane

Dene Road

Lane

Spring Hill Lane

Trysull Holloway

Orton Lane

Showell Lane

Blackpit Lane

Orton

Flash Lane

Union Lane

Awbridge Bridge

Staffordshire & Worcestershire Canal

Monarch's Way

Orton Hill

Connaught Drive

Bearnett Lane

Manor House

Bell Road

Bell Road

Trysull

White PH

School Road

Strathmore Crs

Chequers Av

Orton Lane

Sutherland Dr

School Cl

All Saints C of E Primary School

Trysull Road

Bratch Hollow

Bratch Lane

Ladywell Cl

Victoria Gv

Billy Buns Lane

Bratch Park

Common Road

Station Road

Bullmeadow Lane

Meadow Lane

Bull Lane

Hazel Grove

The Bratch

Mount Road

St Benedict Biscop Primary School

School Road

Smallbrook Lane

Felashill Road

Woodford Lane

Bratch Common Road

Clap Gate Rd

Monarch's Way

Bumble Hole Meadows

Penleigh Gdns

Adpe Cl

Woden Cl

Hatch Heath Close

Churchward Grove

Mount Pleasant Avenue

Primary School

Bramblewood

Waverley Gdns

Police Stn

Felashill Cl

Lockside

Ounsdale Road

West...

Ounsdale Crs

The Grange

Wombourne Cricket Tennis & Bowling Club

Church Rd

Doctors Surg

Maypole Gallery

Smestow Gate

WOMBOURNE

Wombrook Ind Est

Smestow Bridge Industrial Est

Pool House Road

The Meadlands

Forge va Wy

Quiendale

Mariburn Wy

Giggetty

St Bernadettes RC Primary School

Spines Clinc

Lindale Drive

Planks Lane

Windsor

Bramber Dr

Kirkstone Crs

Sandringham Rd

Ounsdale

Cannon Rd

Rennison Drive

Walk Lane

Gravel Hill Surg

Civic Cen

Rookery Drive

Redcliffe

Copper Beech Dr

Greenhill Road

Maypole

High Street

Mosey's Hill Rd

Battlefield

Sunny Hl

Special Sch

Brook Road

Wool Road

Redhill Av

Glendale Close

Pinewood

Common Road

The Longlands

High Mdw

The Broadway

Beggars Bush La

Heathfields

Heath House Dr

Miller's Dale

Milfields

Stockley Brook

Lane Lane Gv

Swindol Way

Foley Gv

Furnace Rd

Honeway Drive

Waterfalls

Bricktbridge Rd

Van Diemans Rd

Jenks Road

Giggetty Lane

Lilac Dr

Elder Gv

Birch Hl Av

Lamb Crs

Elm Tree La

Blakeley

Whites Wood Lane

Woodlands

Sytch Lane

Greenhill Gdns

Greenfields Road

Cedars Av

Oaks Dr

School

Greenfields Road

Westleigh Rd

Calvin Cl

B4176

Ee View

Rd Dean Road

Chapel St

Chapel

W Coms Dr

Park Av

Griffiths Dr

Greenhill Farm

Nursery

Carder St

Gate Cl

Common Road

NORTH ROAD

Clap Gate Cl

Park

D7
1 Woodhill Cl

A

D8
1 Chartwell Dr
2 Cranwell Gn
3 Honeybourne Crs
4 The Willows

B

E4
1 Balmoral Dr
2 Ednam Gv

C 82 D

E7
1 Maypole Ct
2 Rushford Av
3 Saint Benedicts Rd

E

E8
1 Blakeley Heath Dr
2 Chestnut Dr
3 Hawkswell Av
4 Highfields Dr

F

E6
1 Sunridge Av
2 Windmill Bank

I grid square represents 500 metres

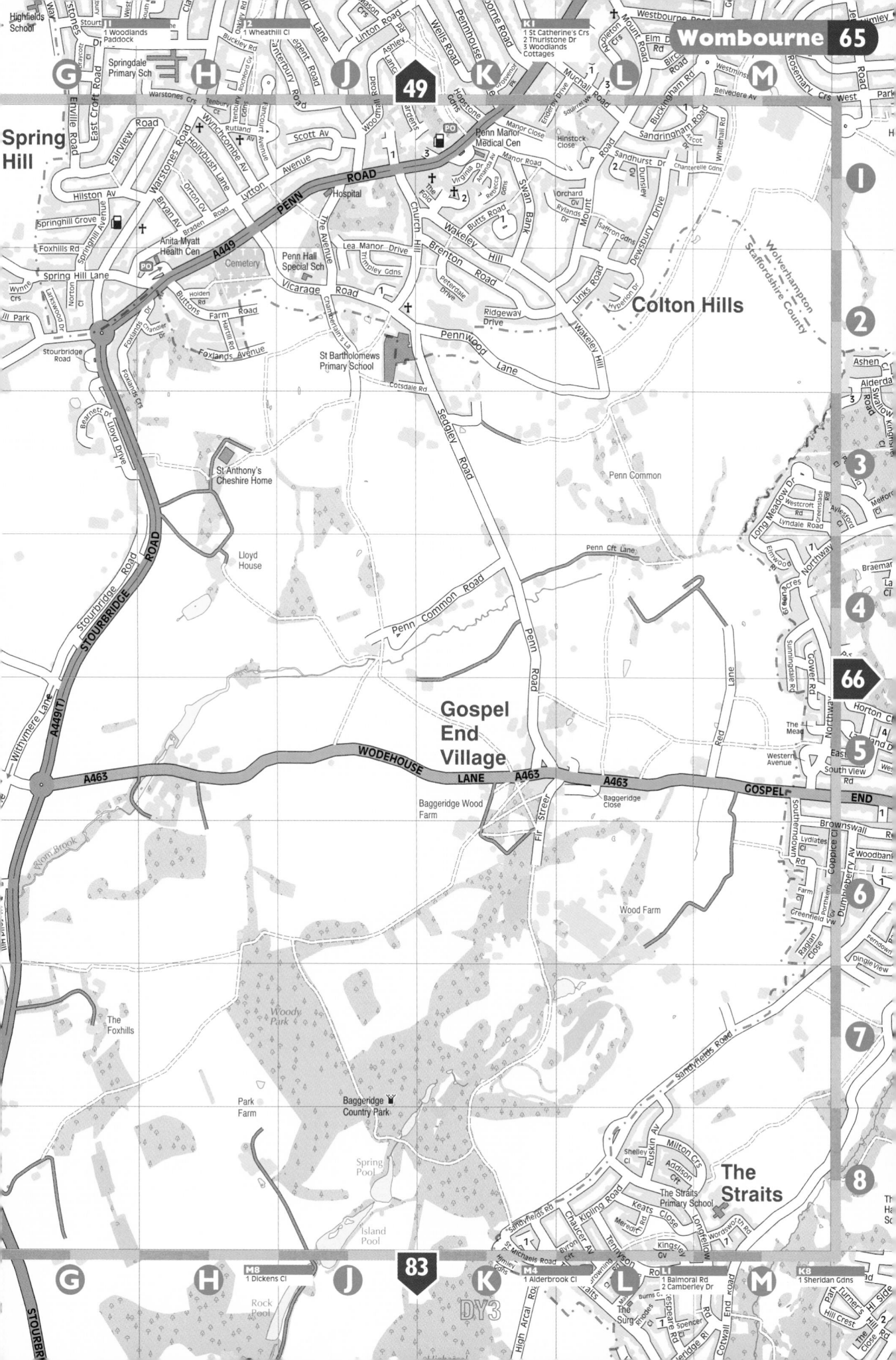

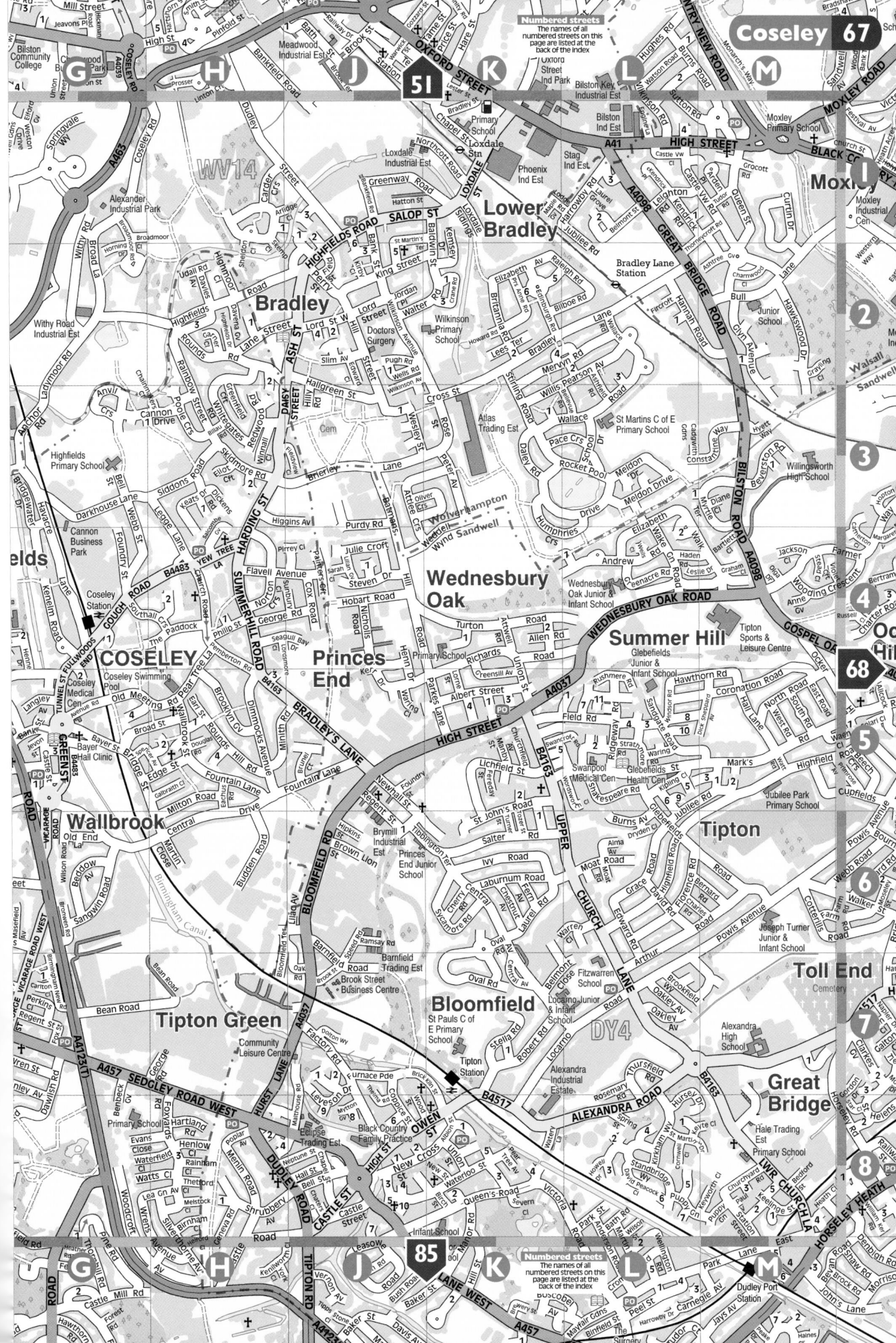

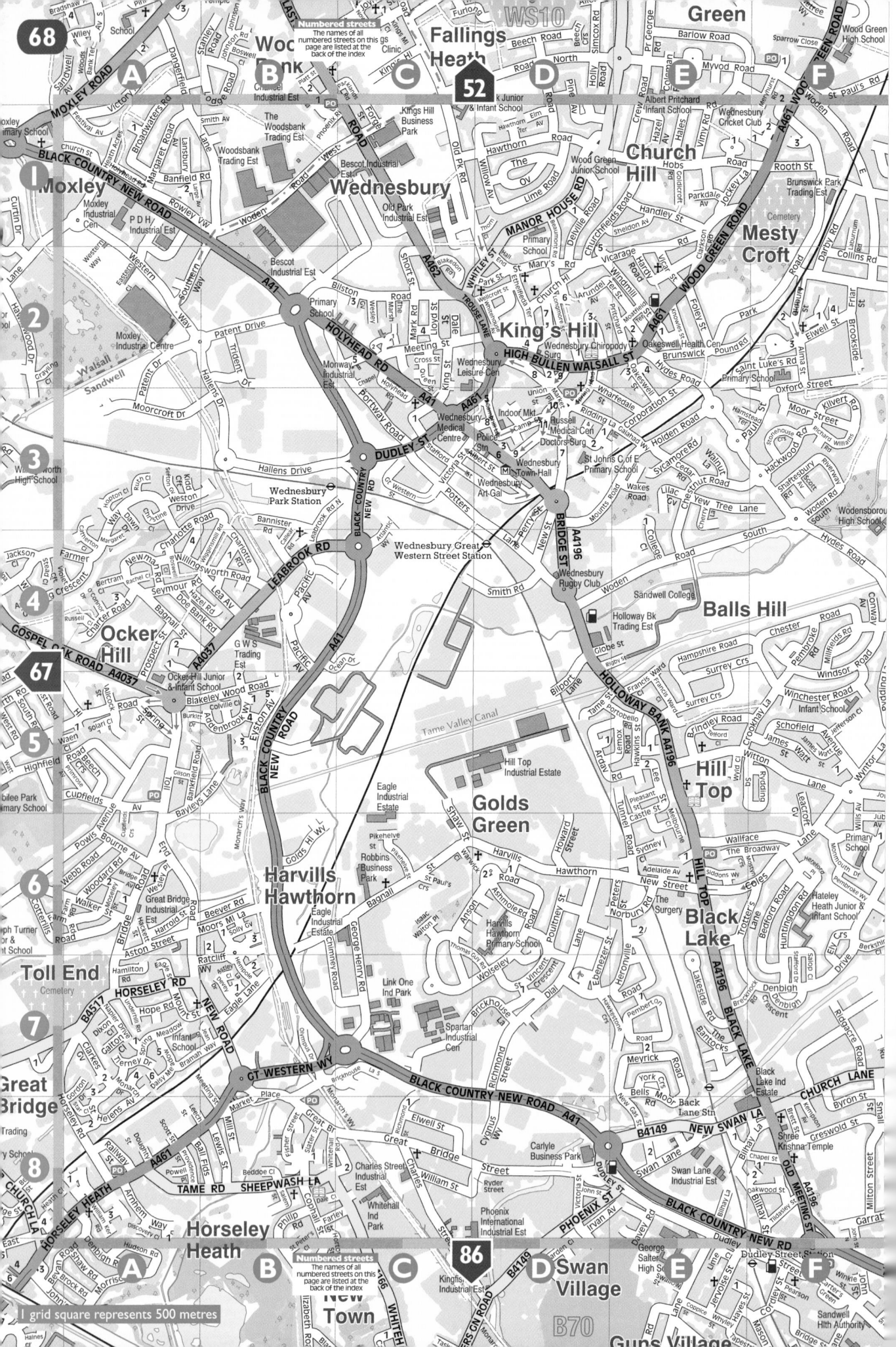

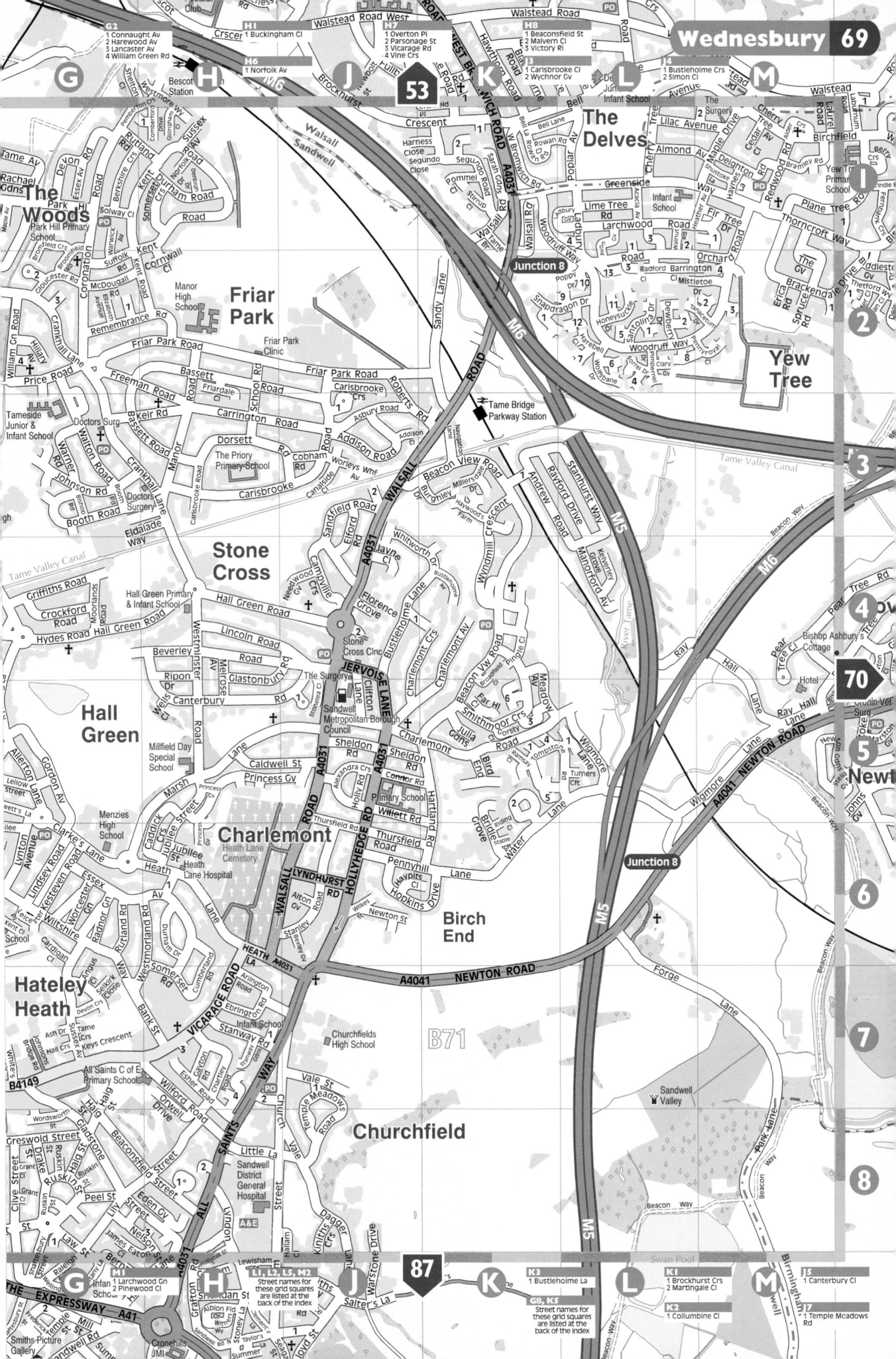

Grid reference lists

G2
1 Connaught Av
2 Harewood Av
3 Lancaster Av
4 William Green Rd

H1
1 Buckingham Cl

H6
1 Norfolk Av

J1
1 Overton Pl
2 Parsonage St
3 Vicarage Rd
4 Vine Crs

H8
1 Beaconsfield St
2 Malvern Cl
3 Victory Ri

J3
1 Carisbrooke Cl
2 Wychnor Gv

J4
1 Bustleholme Crs
2 Simon Cl

53

87

70

Areas and places:
The Woods, Friar Park, The Delves, Yew Tree, Stone Cross, Hall Green, Charlemont, Hateley Heath, Birch End, Churchfield

Roads: M6, M5, A4031, A4041 Newton Road, A41 The Expressway, B71, B4149

Junction 8

L1, L2, L5, M2
street names for these grid squares are listed at the back of the index

K3
1 Bustleholme La

K5
1 Brockhurst Crs
2 Martingale Cl

M5
1 Canterbury Cl

G8, K5
Street names for these grid squares are listed at the back of the index

K2
1 Collumbine Cl

M1
1 Temple Meadows Rd

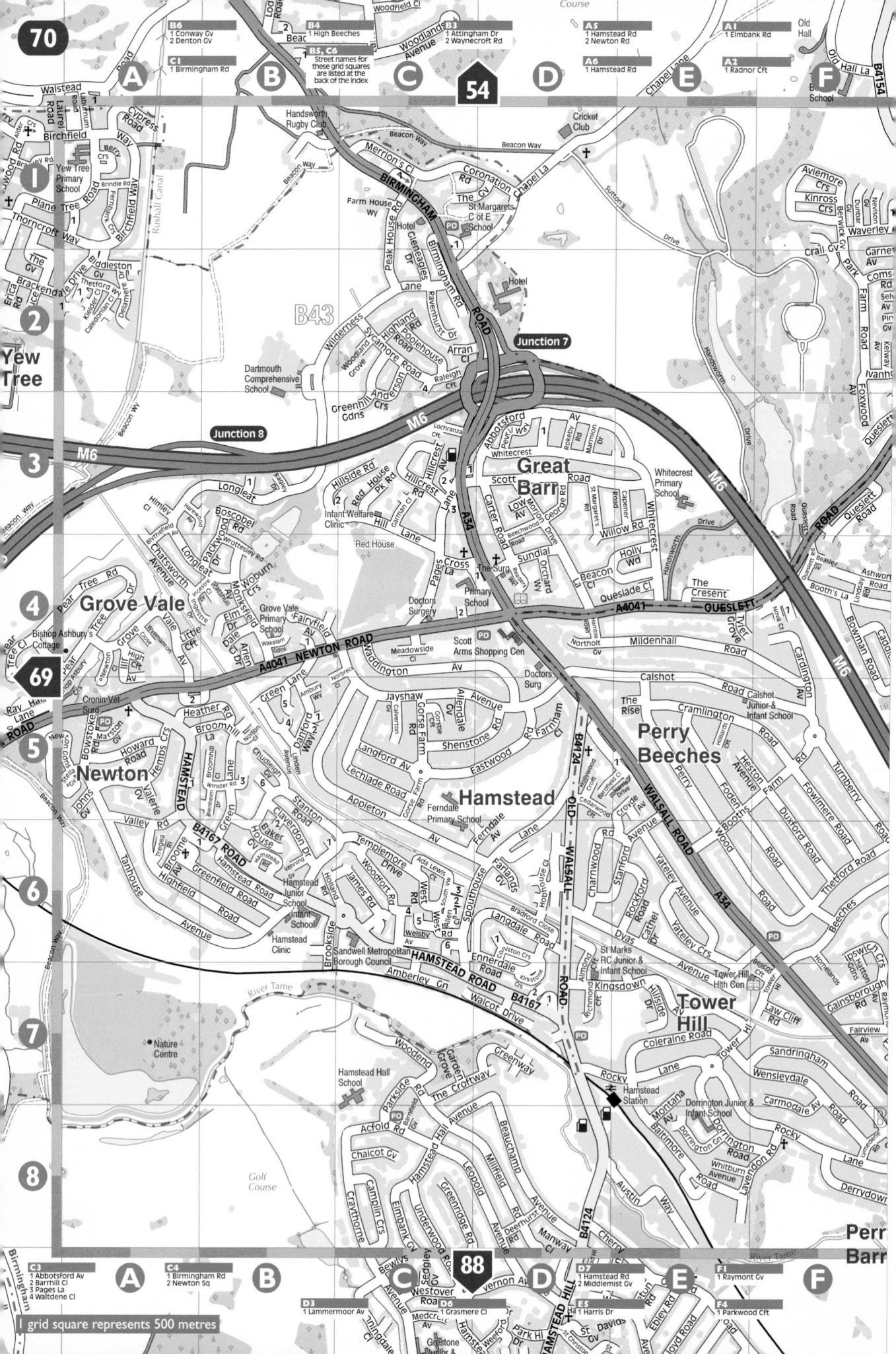

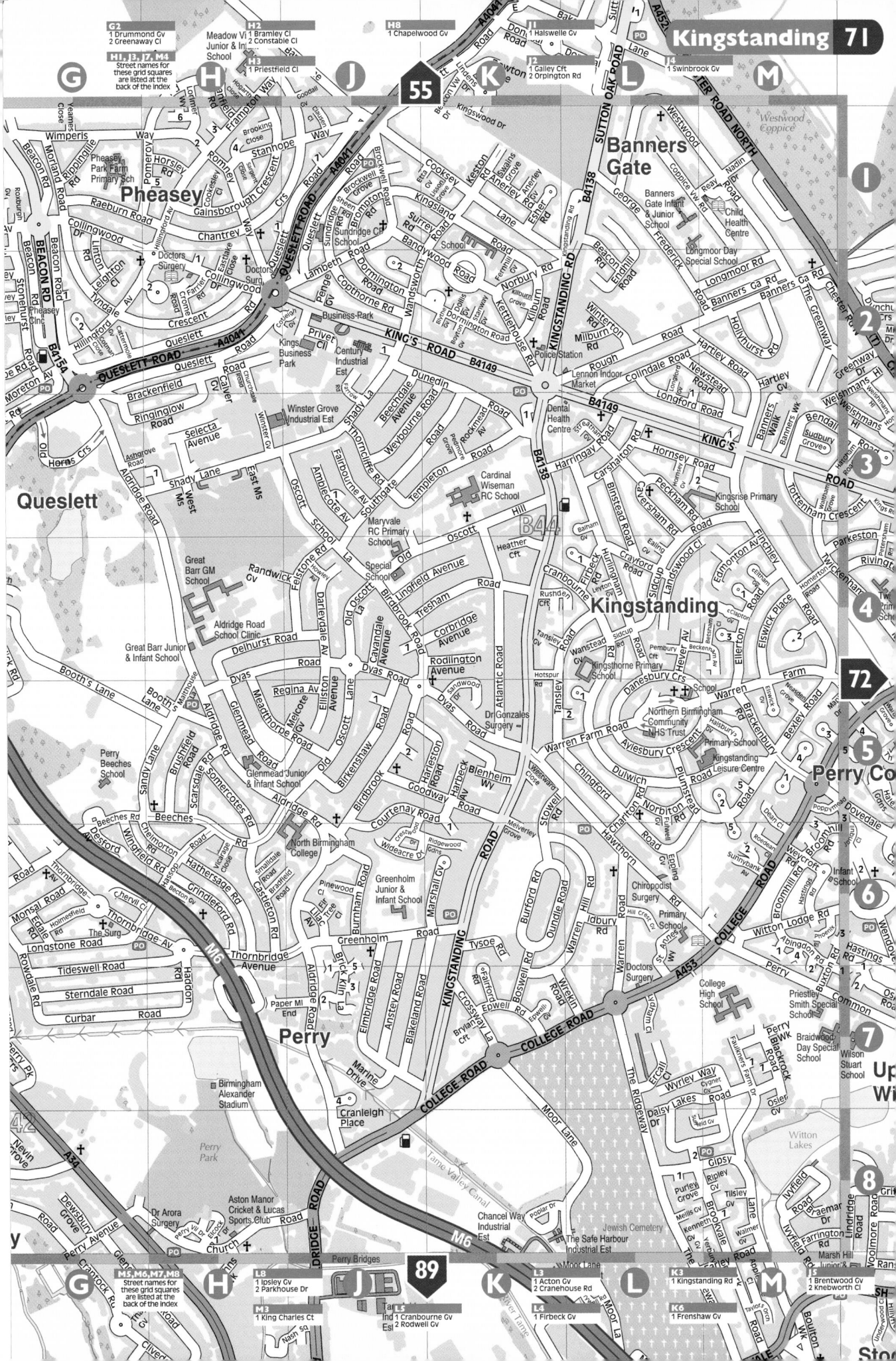

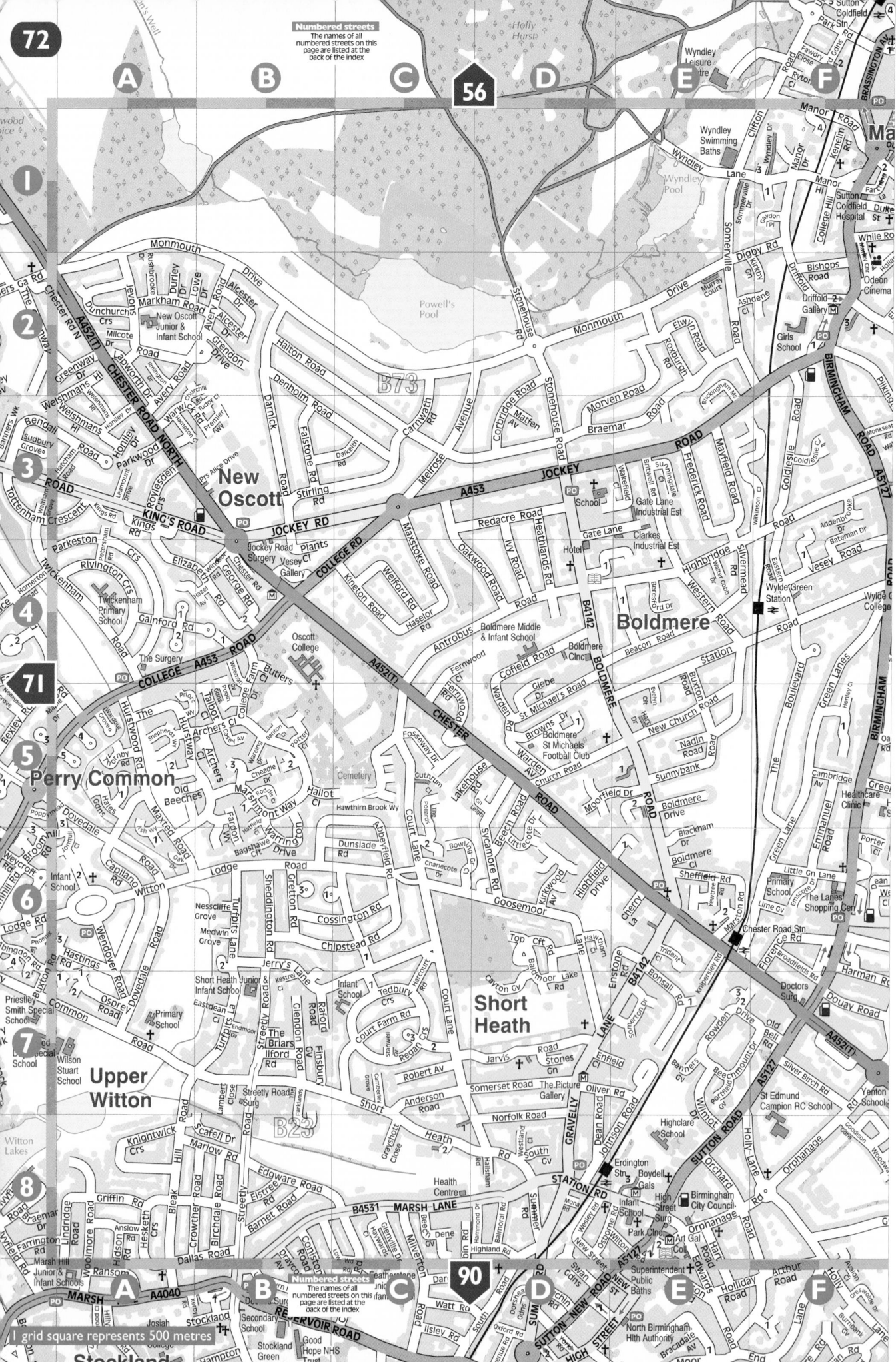

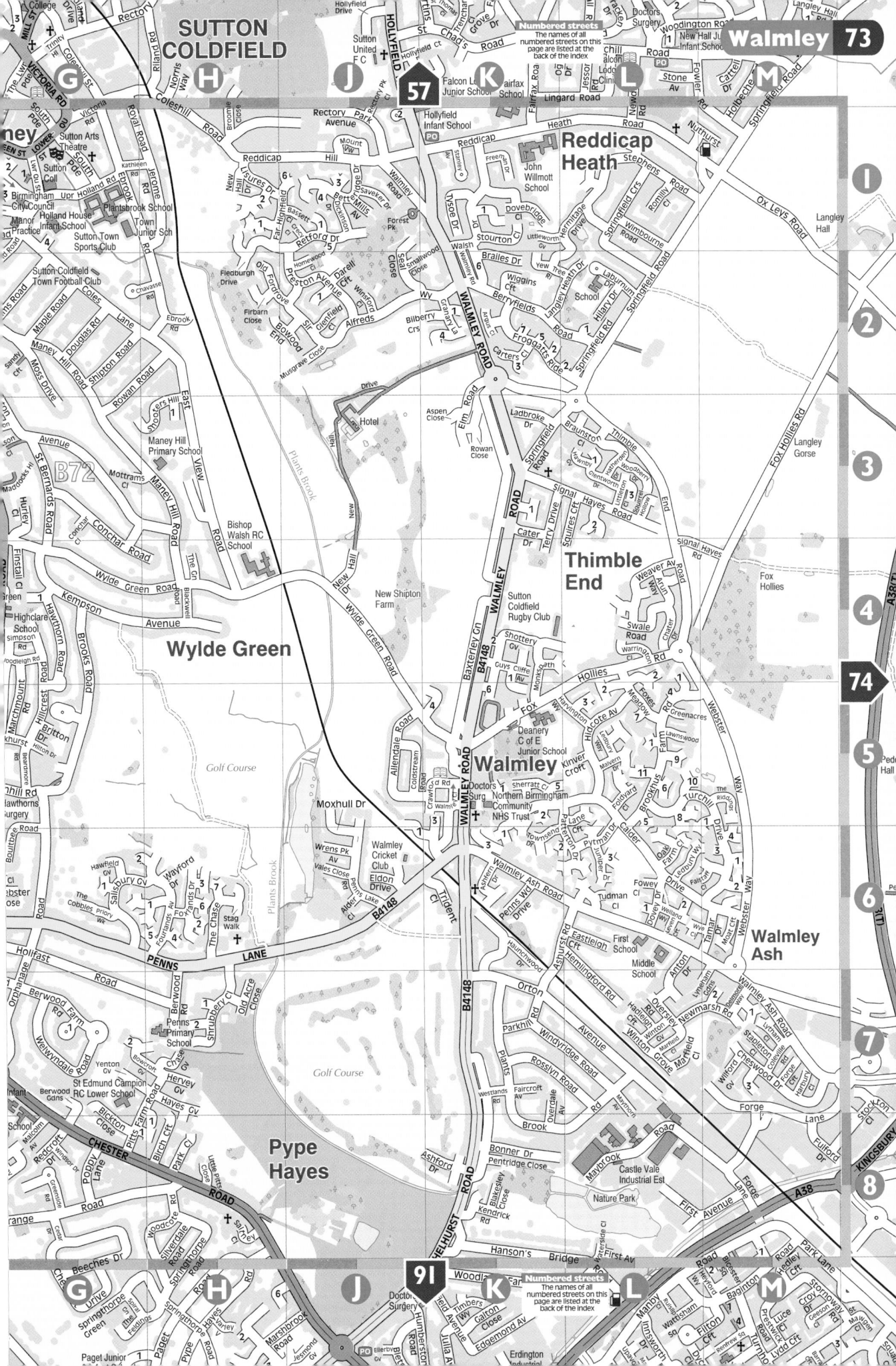

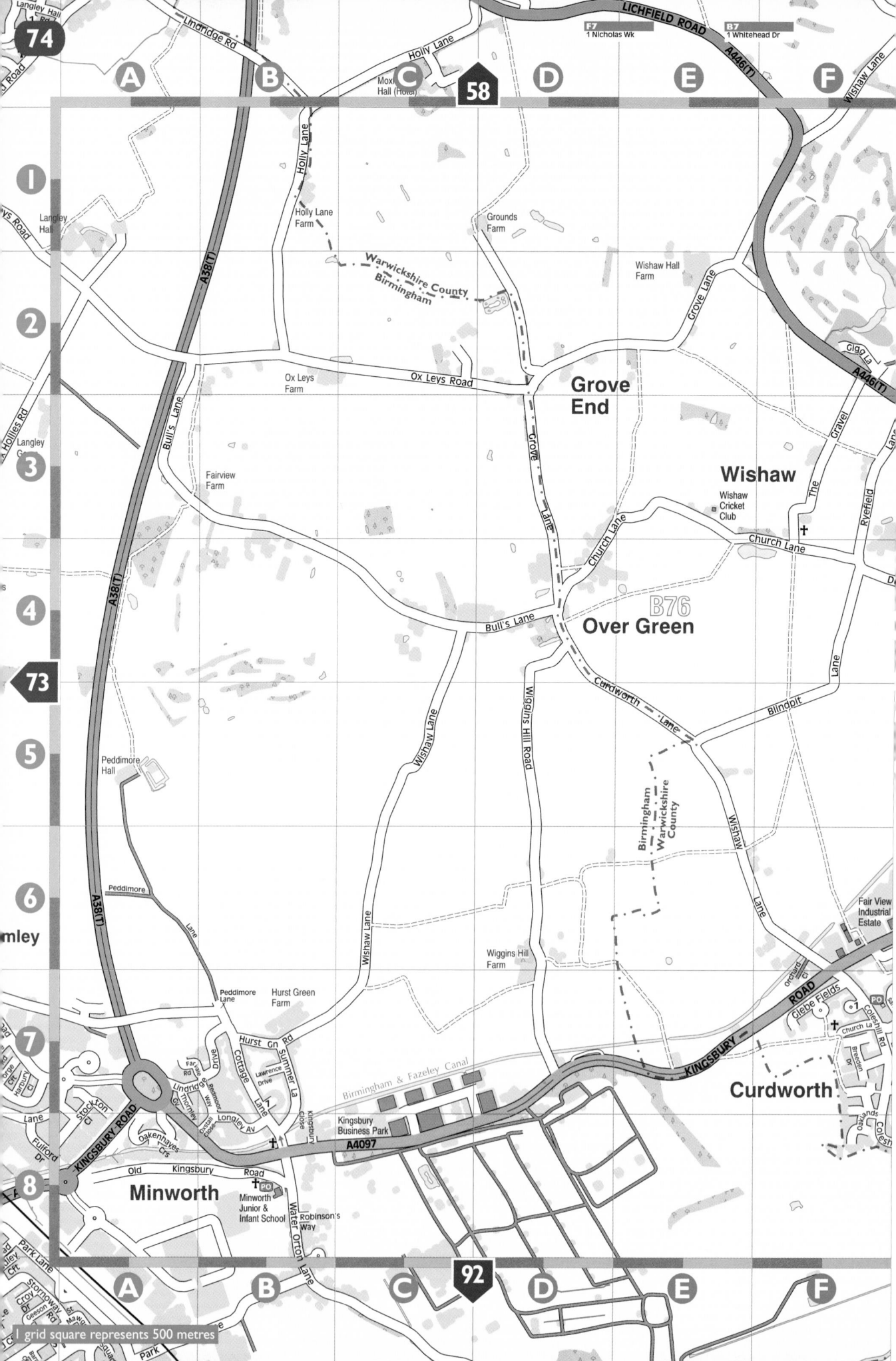

Langley Hall

Lindridge Rd

LICHFIELD ROAD

F7
1 Nicholas Wk

B7
1 Whitehead Dr

A446(T)

Wishaw Lane

A   B   Holly Lane   C   58   D   E   F

Moxhull Hall (Hotel)

1

Langley Hall

Holly Lane Farm

Grounds Farm

Wishaw Hall Farm

2

A38(T)

Bull's Lane

Ox Leys Farm

Ox Leys Road

Grove Lane

Grove End

Wishaw Hall Farm

Gigg La

A446(T)

3

Langley G

Fairview Farm

Wishaw

Wishaw Cricket Club

Church Lane

The Gravel

Ryefield

A Hollies Rd

Church Lane

4

Bull's Lane

B76

Over Green

Wiggins Hill Road

Lane

73

Peddimore Hall

Curdworth   Lane

Blindpit

Lane

5

Wishaw Lane

Birmingham Warwickshire County

Wishaw Lane

6

Peddimore

mley

Lane

Wiggins Hill Farm

Fair View Industrial Estate

Peddimore Lane

Hurst Green Farm

KINGSBURY

orchard

Glebe Fields

Colshill Rd

Church La

7

Hurst Gn Rd

Summer La

Lawrence Drive

Lindridge Rd

Longley Av

ROAD

PO

Bredon Dr

Oaksands

Coleshill

Curdworth

Birmingham & Fazeley Canal

Kingsbury Business Park

Stockton Cl

Longley Av

Kingsbury Close

A   B   C   92   D   E   F

8

Fulford Dr

Old   Kingsbury   Road

A4097

PO

Minworth

Minworth Junior & Infant School

Water Orton Lane

Robinson's Way

Park Lane

Stornoway Rd

1 grid square represents 500 metres

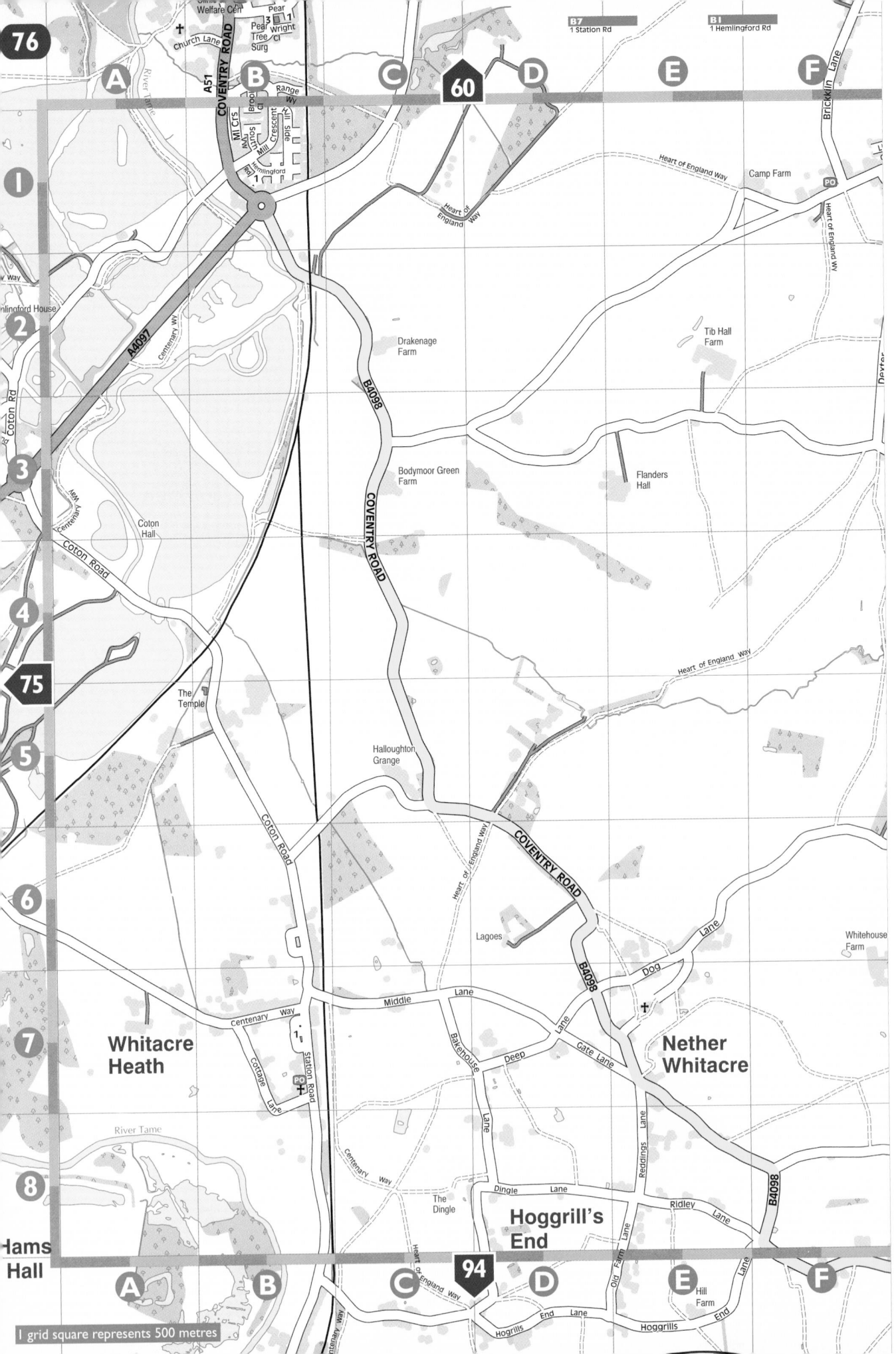

A B C 60 D E F

I

2

3

4

75

5

6

7

8

Drakenage Farm

Bodymoor Green Farm

The Temple

Halloughton Grange

Whitacre Heath

River Tame

Tib Hall Farm

Camp Farm

Flanders Hall

Heart of England Way

Heart of England Way

Heart of England Way

Lagoes

Whitehouse Farm

Nether Whitacre

Hoggrill's End

The Dingle

Hill Farm

A B 94 C D E F

Hams Hall

Coventry Road

Coton Road

Centenary Way

Middle Lane

Bakehouse Lane

Deep Lane

Gate Lane

Dingle Lane

Ridley Lane

Old Farm Lane

Reddings Lane

Dog Lane

Brickkiln Lane

B4098

A4097

A51

River Tame

Church Lane

Pear Tree Cl

Pear Wright

Range Wy

Mill Crs

Brook Cl

Mill South

Crescent

Hemlingford

Mill Side

Hemlingford House

Coton Rd

New Centenary Way

Coton Hall

Coton Road

Cottage Lane

Station Road

PO

Hoggrills End Lane

Hoggrills End Lane

1 grid square represents 500 metres

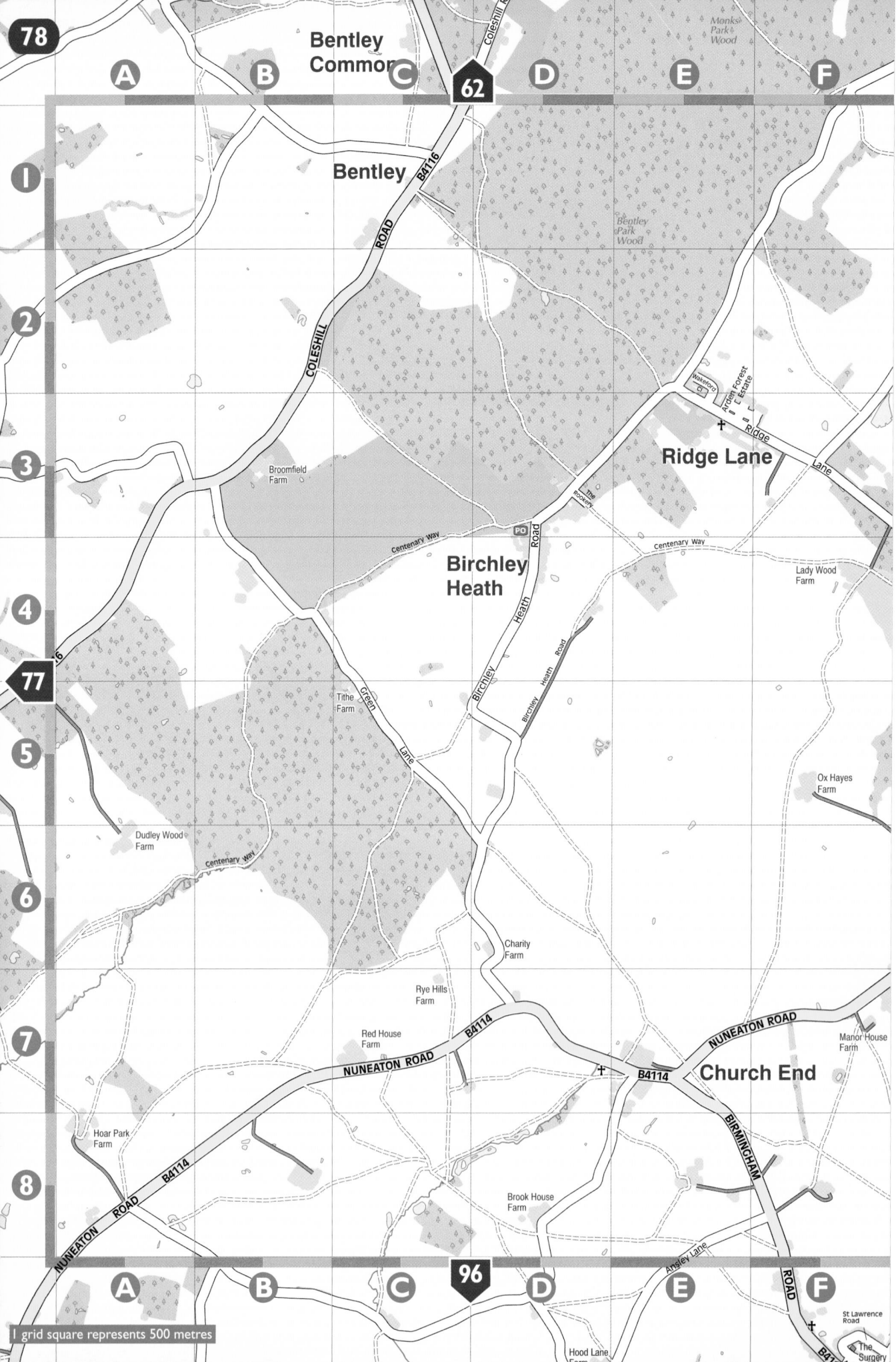

Bentley Common

Bentley

Bentley Park Wood

Monks Park Wood

Coleshill R

62

Coleshill Road

B4116

Broomfield Farm

Wakeford Cl

Arden Forest Estate

Ridge

Ridge Lane

Lane

The Rookery

PO

Centenary Way

Centenary Way

Birchley Heath

Lady Wood Farm

Birchley Heath Road

Birchley Heath Road

77

16

Green

Tithe Farm

Lane

Ox Hayes Farm

Dudley Wood Farm

Centenary Way

Charity Farm

Rye Hills Farm

Red House Farm

B4114

Nuneaton Road

NUNEATON ROAD

Manor House Farm

Church End

B4114

Hoar Park Farm

NUNEATON ROAD

B4114

BIRMINGHAM

Brook House Farm

Ansley Lane

ROAD

St Lawrence Road

B4?1

Hood Lane Farm

The Surgery

96

G H J **63** K L M

I

2

J5
1 Nursery Rd   L5
1 Beech Cl   L6
1 Silverbirch Cl

NUNEATON ROAD

B4171

LC

Woodford Lane

Apple Road

Pye Lane

Grange Road

3

Oldbury Farm

Purley Chase Lane

Oldbury Reservoir

Quarry Lane

Oldbury

White Hall Farm

Hartshill Green

White Hall Cl

Cherryfield

Charnwood Drive

Newbrook

Atherstone Road

Newdegate

Trentham Road

4

80

Oldbury Road

Oldbury Road

Pipers Lane

Centenary Way

Centenary Way

Hartshill Hayes Country Park

Nuneaton Road

Castle View

Oldbury View

Castle Road

Cemetery

Cemetery Lane

Hartshill

The Woodlands

Michael Drayton Middle School

Elm Wy

Hillside

Springhill

Drayton Close

Church Close

PO

Hartshill School

Chapel End

Nathaniel Newton First School

Victoria Road

5

Coleshill Road

B4114

Ansley Hall

ROAD

West View

St Johns Close

Thorncliffe Wy

Cornish Close

Limes Coppice

Moorwood Lane

Ash Dr

Moorwood Crs

Walnut Cl

Laurel Cl

Hazel Cl

Laurel Cl

Moor Meadow Rd

Hayes Road

Moor Rd

Moorwood Cl

School Hill

Orchard Close

Grange Close

CAM

6

Ansley Common

Bretts Hall Est

Moorbrooke

ANSLEY COMMON COLESHILL ROAD

Willow Cl

Alders Lane

Chancery Lane

PO

Salisbury Dr

Lincoln Avenue

B4114

Bucks Hill

CV10

Plough Hill

Westminster Drive

Orchard

Almond Av

7

Centenary Way

Plough Hill

Cemetery

Freesland Ri

Hitton Av

Merlin

Avenue

Zorfina Cl

Fraser Close

Fraser Dr

Trafford Dr

Melfort Cl

School Lane

The Rookery

Galley Common First School

Hill Farm

Marlowe Cl

Chesterton Dr

Blake Close

Browning Dr

Ruskin Cl

Swinburn Cl

Selby Wy

Wimbourne

Bertina Cl

Frensham Drive

Burnaby Cl

Carnette Crt

Mallerin Cl

Waltham Crescent

Bucks Hill

8

G H J **97** K L M

Tunnel Road

Haunchwood Road

Orford

Conrek Park Dr

St Peter's

Rock Cl

Dryden Cl

Carlyle Cl

Bronte Dr

Sheridan Dr

Kitchen Cl

Auden Cl

Orwell Cl

Addison Cl

Milton

Keats

Chesterton Dr

Fielding Wy

PO

Galley Road

Mayflair Dr

Galley Common Medical Centre

Doctors Surg

Chaucer Dr

Hardy Cl

Thackeray Close

M3
1 Stoneleigh Cl

Sherbourne Avenue

Waverley Avenue

M4
1 Kipling Cl

Barons Croft

Knowles

Porth

Drive

Spin

1 grid square represents 500 metres

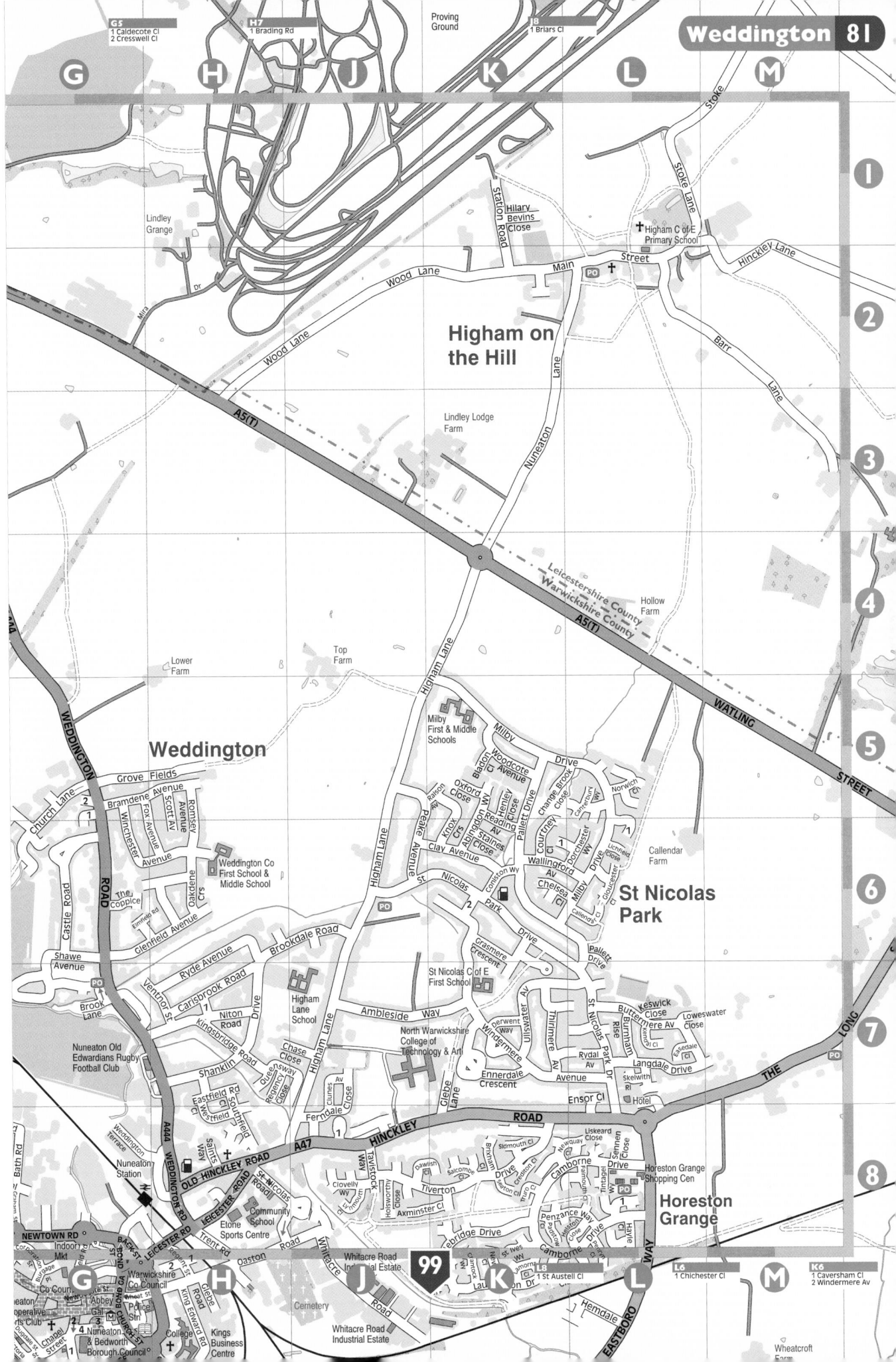

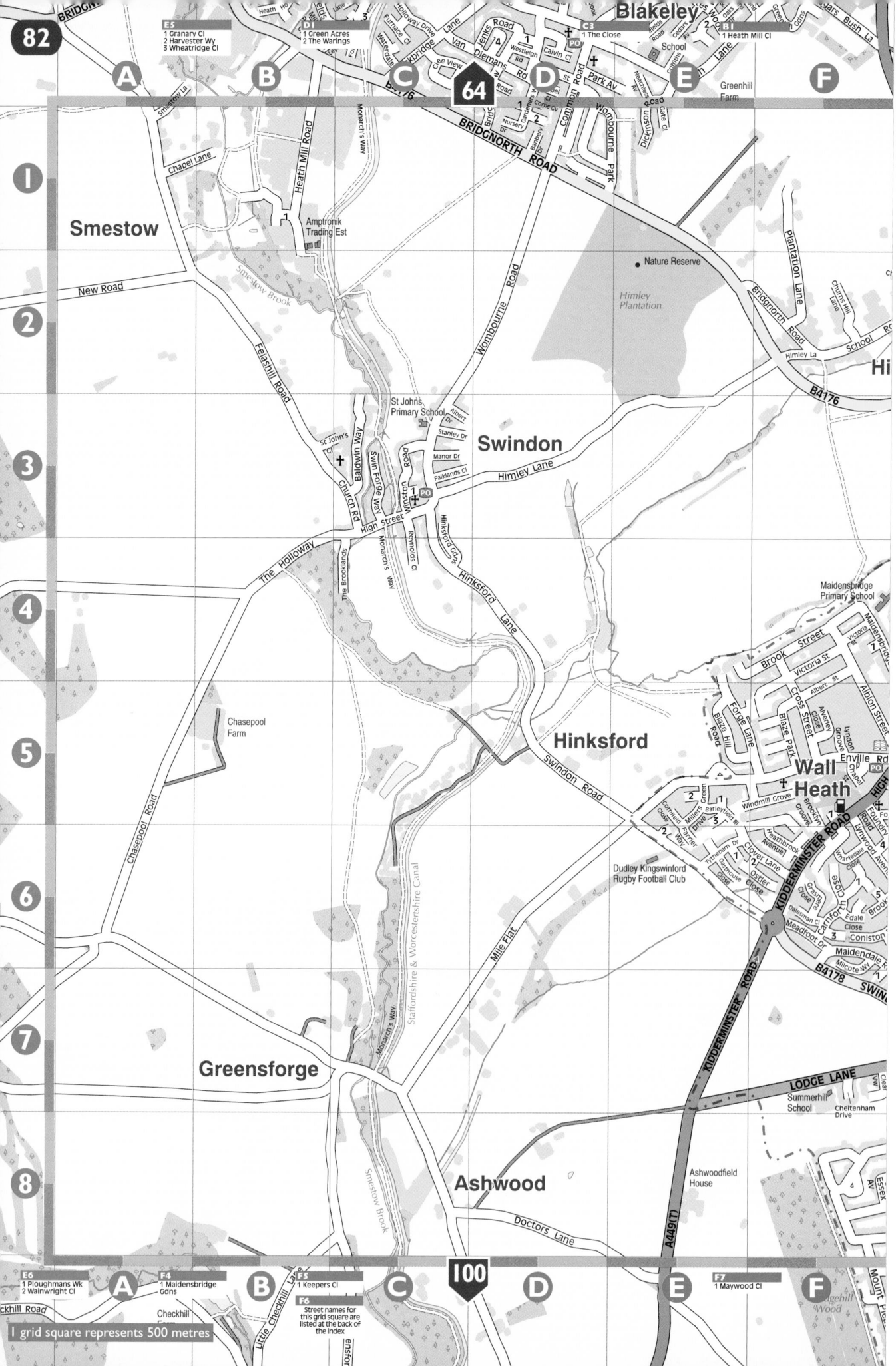

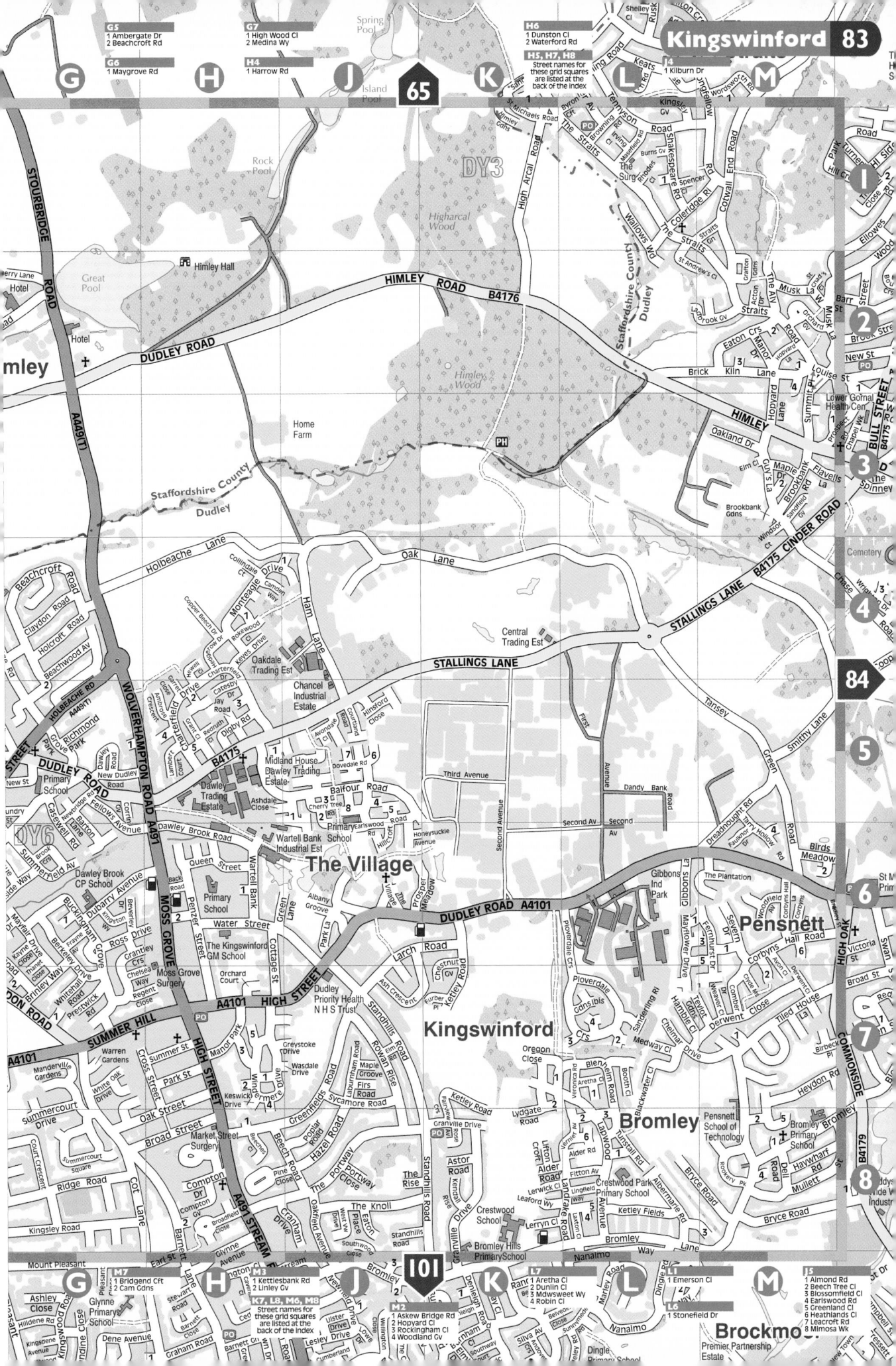

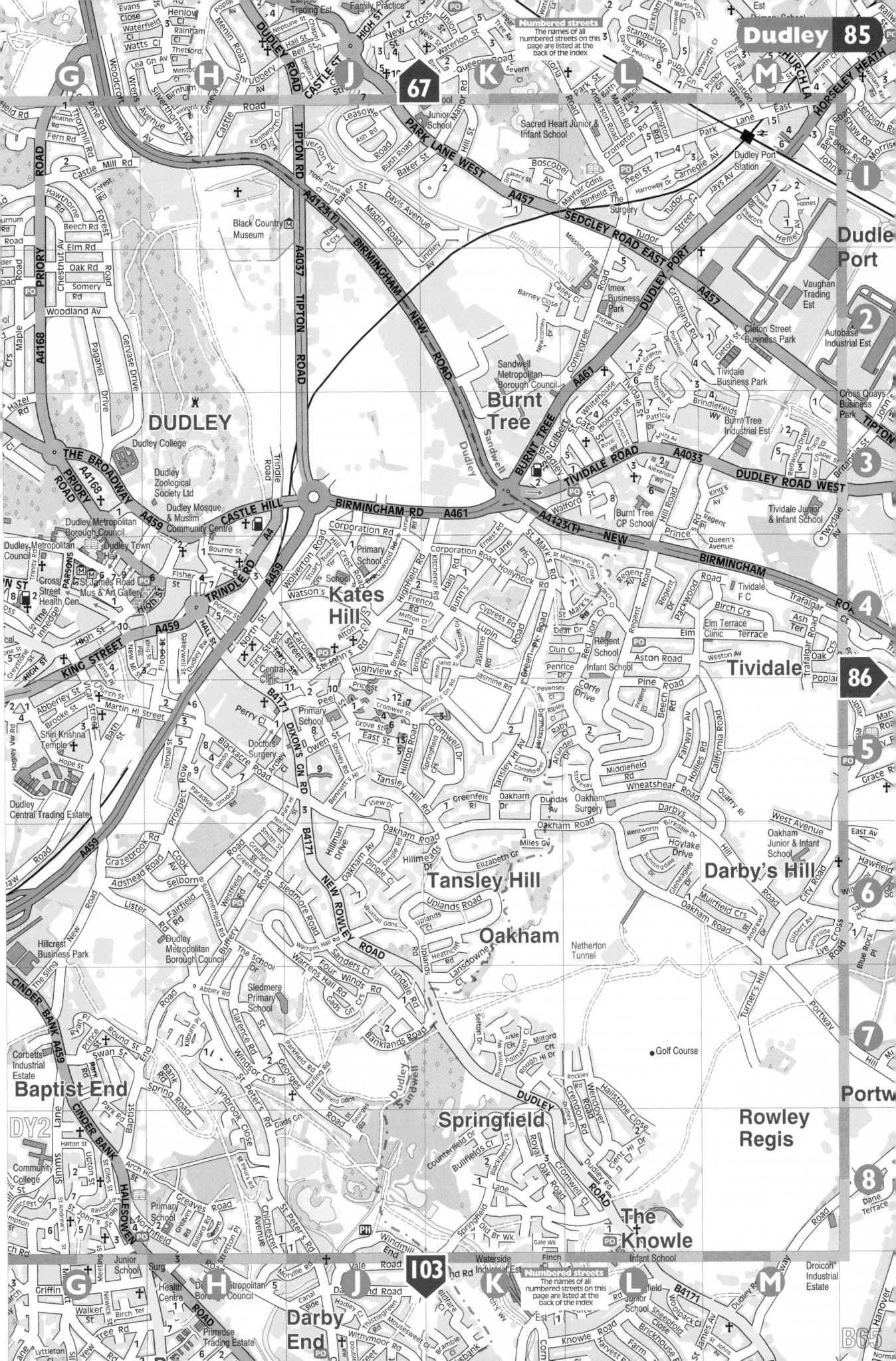

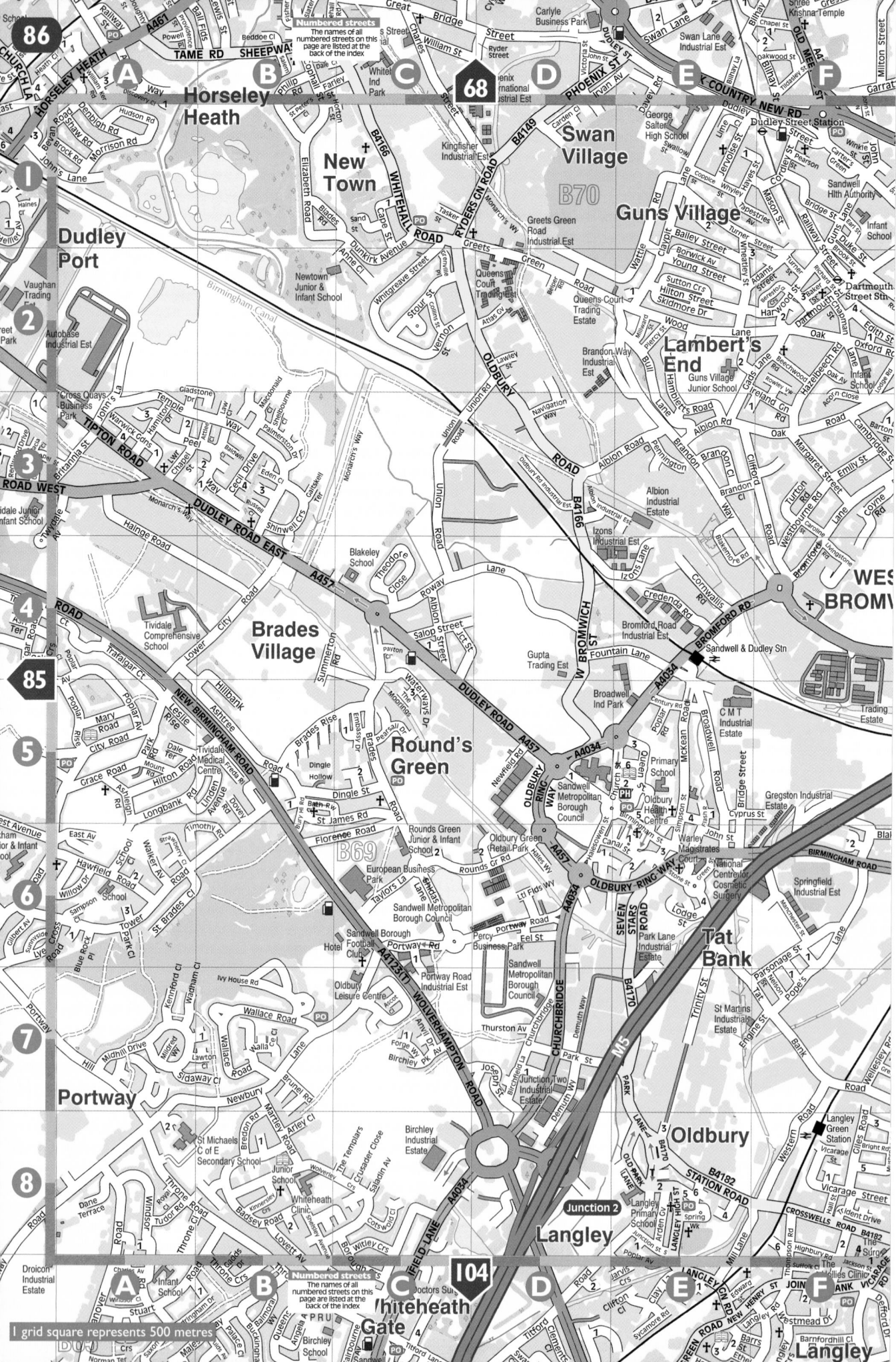

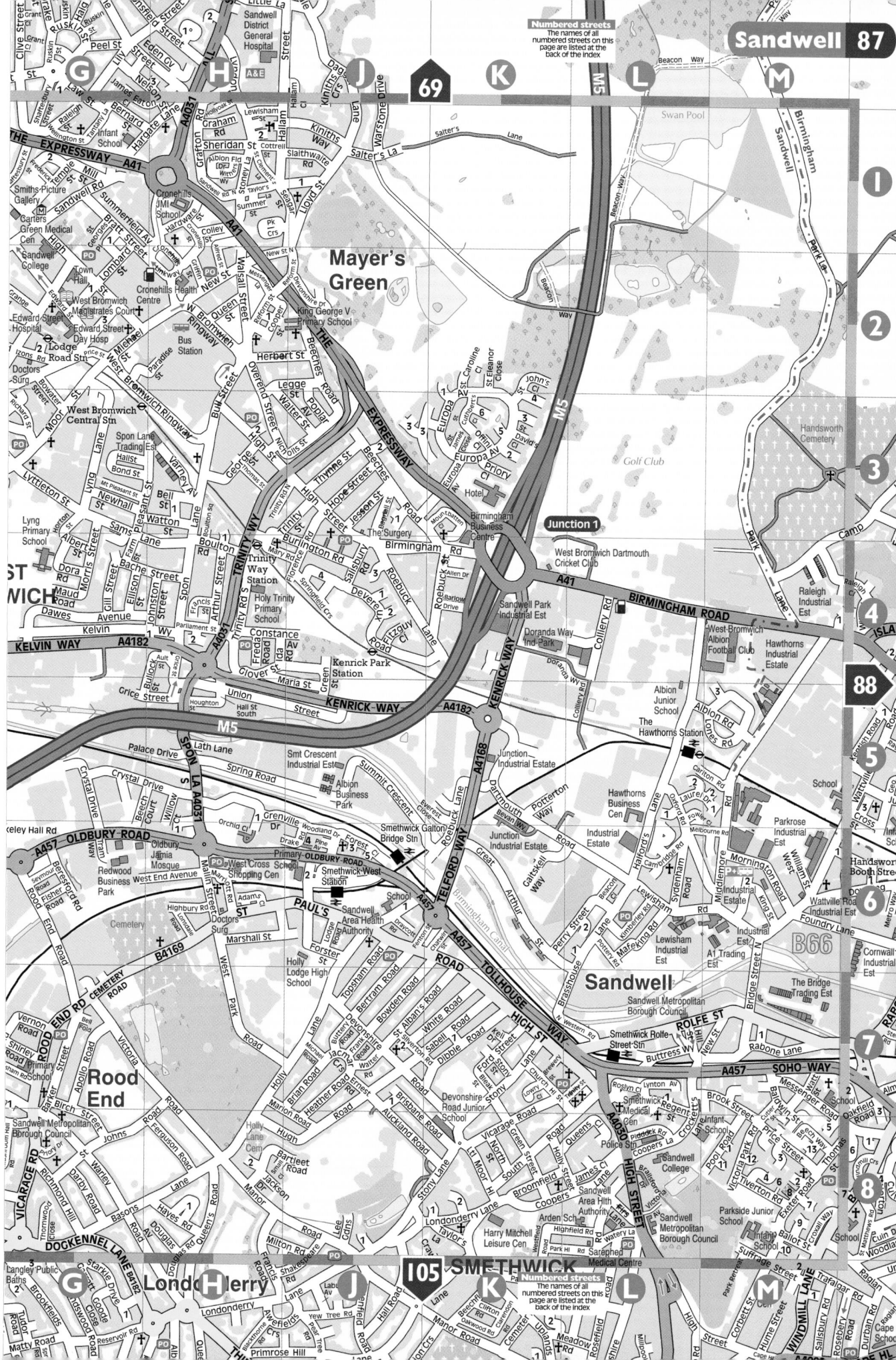

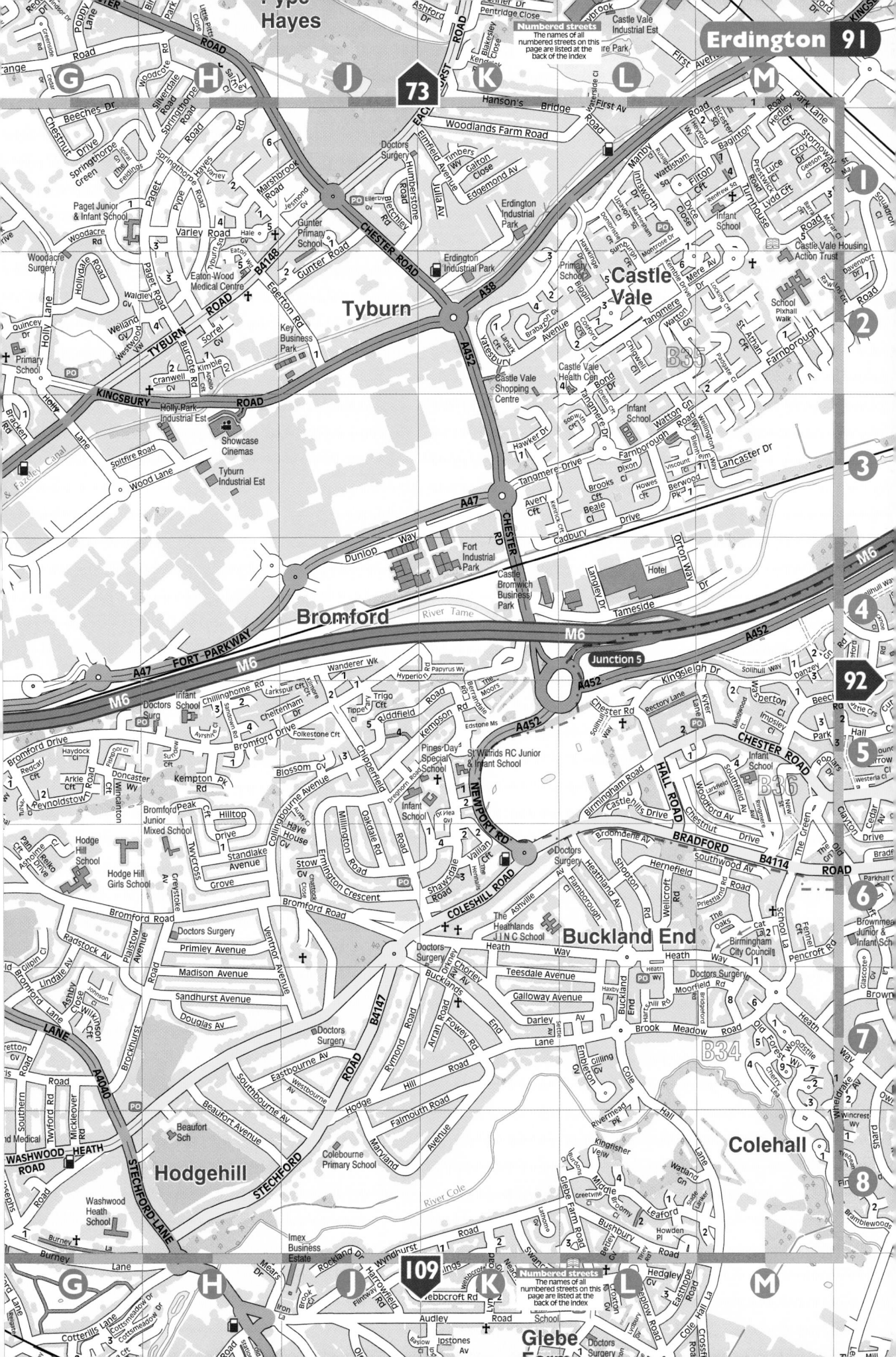

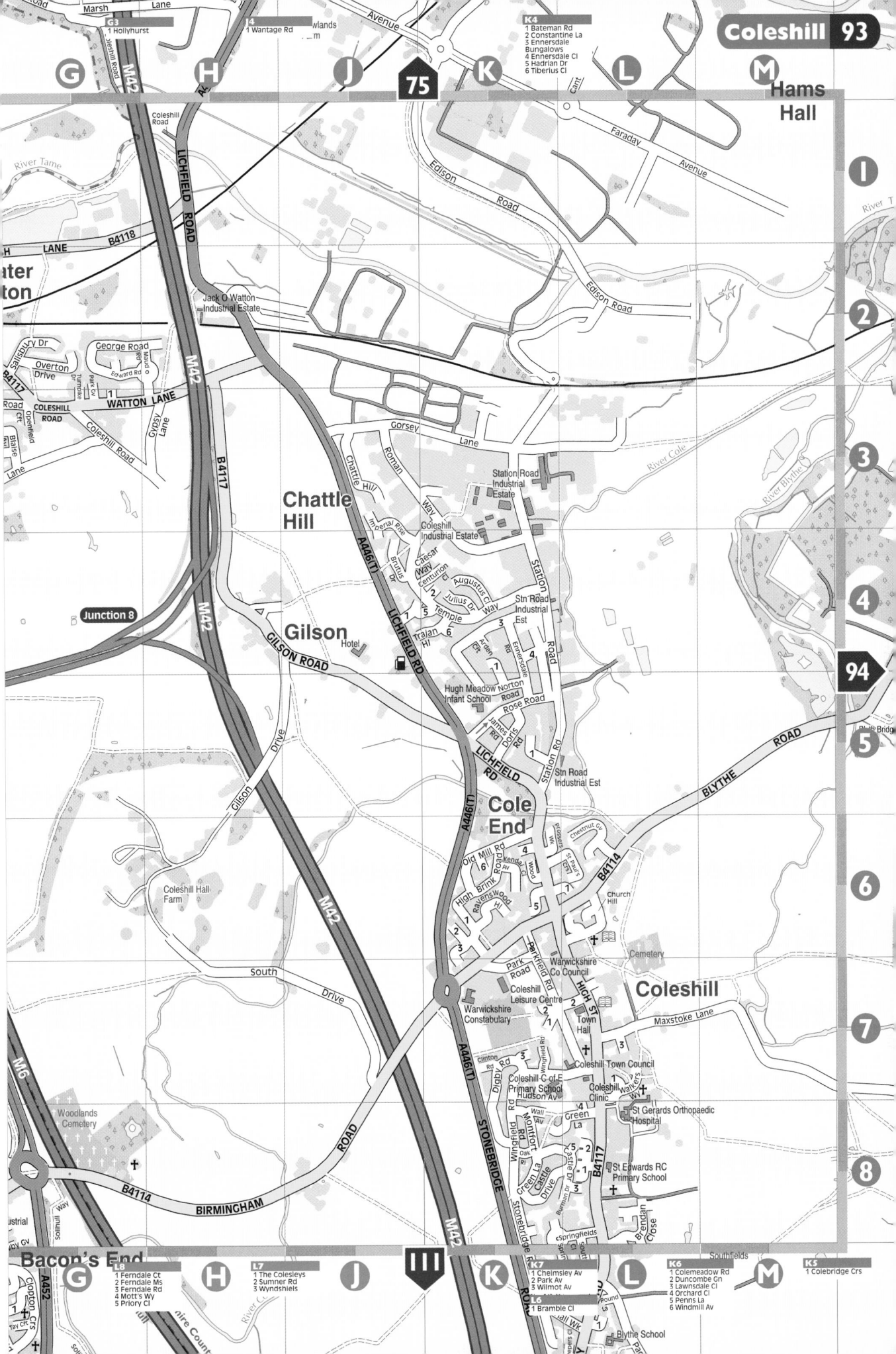

Hams
Hall

I
2
3
4
94
5
6
7
8

75

River Tame

Marsh Lane

G3
1 Hollyhurst

J4
1 Wantage Rd

lands

Avenue

K4
1 Bateman Rd
2 Constantine La
3 Ennersdale Bungalows
4 Ennersdale Cl
5 Hadrian Dr
6 Tiberius Cl

LANE

B4118

LICHFIELD ROAD

M42

B4117

George Road

Salisbury Dr

Overton Drive

Maud

Edward Rd

Park Ct

WATTON LANE

Gypsy Lane

Coleshill Road

COLESHILL Road

Blaise Lane

Openfield

Road

Edison Road

Faraday Avenue

River T

Edison Road

Jack O Watton Industrial Estate

Gorsey Lane

Station Road Industrial Estate

River Cole

River Blythe

Chattle Hill

Roman Way

Chattle Hill

Imperial Rise

A446(T)

Brutus Dr

Caesar Way

Centurion Cl

Augustus Way

Julius Dr

Temple

Trajan Hl

Coleshill Industrial Estate

Station Road

Stn Road Industrial Est

Arden Ryck

Ennersdale

Junction 8

GILSON ROAD

Gilson

Hotel

LICHFIELD RD

Hugh Meadow Norton Road

Rose Road

Station Rd

James Rd

Doris Rd

Infant School

M42

Gilson Drive

LICHFIELD RD

A446(T)

Stn Road Industrial Est

BLYTHE ROAD

Blyth Bridge

Cole End

Old Mill Rd

Kenc Av

Wood

Chestnut Cv

St Paul's Wk

B4114

High Brink Road

Ravenswood

Pleasant Wk

Coleshill Hall Farm

Church Hill

Cemetery

Park Road

arkfield Rd

Warwickshire Co Council

HIGH ST

Coleshill

South Drive

Coleshill Leisure Centre

Warwickshire Constabulary

Town Hall

Maxstoke Lane

M6

Woodlands Cemetery

A446(T)

Clinton Rd

Digbl Rd

Coleshill C of E Primary School

Hudson Av

Wall Av

Green La

Coleshill Town Council

Coleshill Clinic

Walker

St Gerards Orthopaedic Hospital

STONEBRIDGE

Monfort Rd

Winding

Oak Cl

Green La

Castle Drive

Castle Dr

B4117

St Edwards RC Primary School

Brendan Close

B4114

BIRMINGHAM

ROAD

Springfields

STONEBRIDGE

Southfields

A452

Clopton Crs

G
1 Ferndale Ct
2 Ferndale Ms
3 Ferndale Rd
4 Mott's Wy
5 Priory Cl

H

J

L7
1 The Colesleys
2 Sumner Rd
3 Wyndshiels

K

L6
1 Bramble Cl

L

K6
1 Chelmsley Av
2 Park Av
3 Wilmot Av

M

K5
1 Colebridge Crs

K6
1 Colemeadow Rd
2 Duncombe Gn
3 Lawnsdale Cl
4 Orchard Cl
5 Penns La
6 Windmill Av

Blythe School

G   H   J   K   L   M

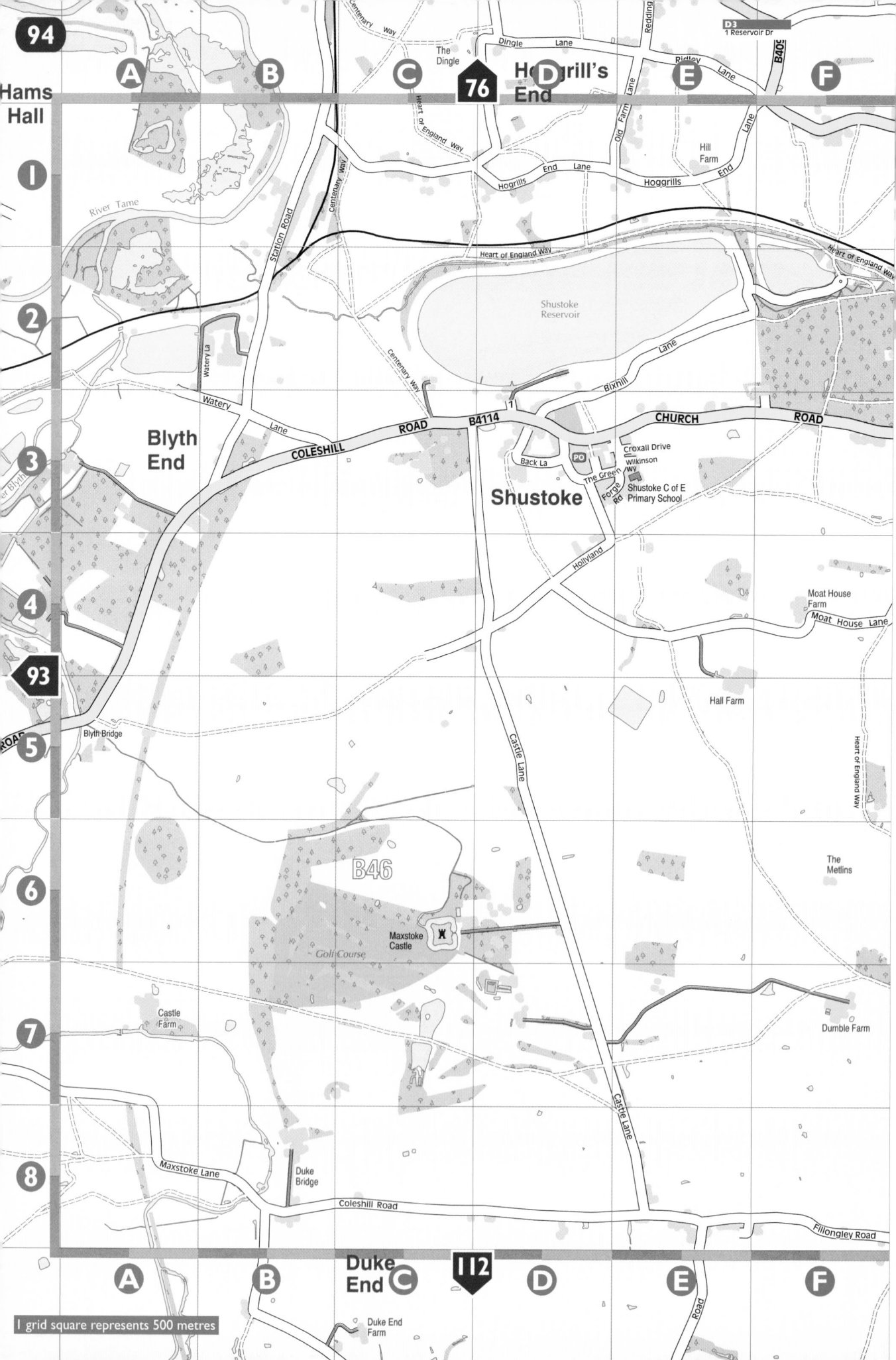

A   B   C   76   D   E   F

Hams
Hall

1

River Tame

2

Watery La

Watery

Blyth
End

COLESHILL   ROAD   B4114

3

Blyth

4

93

5

Blyth Bridge

6

7

Castle
Farm

8

Maxstoke Lane

Duke
Bridge

Coleshill Road

A   B   Duke   C   112   D   E   F
End

1 Reservoir Dr   B4098   D3

Centenary Way

Dingle   Lane
The
Dingle

Heart of England Way

Hogrill's
End

Hogrills   End   Lane

Old   Farm   Lane

Ridley   Lane

Hoggrills   End

Hill
Farm

Heart of England Way

Heart of England Way

Shustoke
Reservoir

Centenary Way

Bixhill   Lane

CHURCH   ROAD

Back La

PO

The Green

Forge Rd

Croxall Drive

Wilkinson
Wy

Shustoke C of E
Primary School

Shustoke

Hollyland

Castle Lane

B46

Maxstoke
Castle

Golf Course

Moat House
Farm

Moat House Lane

Hall Farm

The
Metlins

Heart of England Way

Dumble Farm

Castle Lane

Fillongley Road

1 grid square represents 500 metres

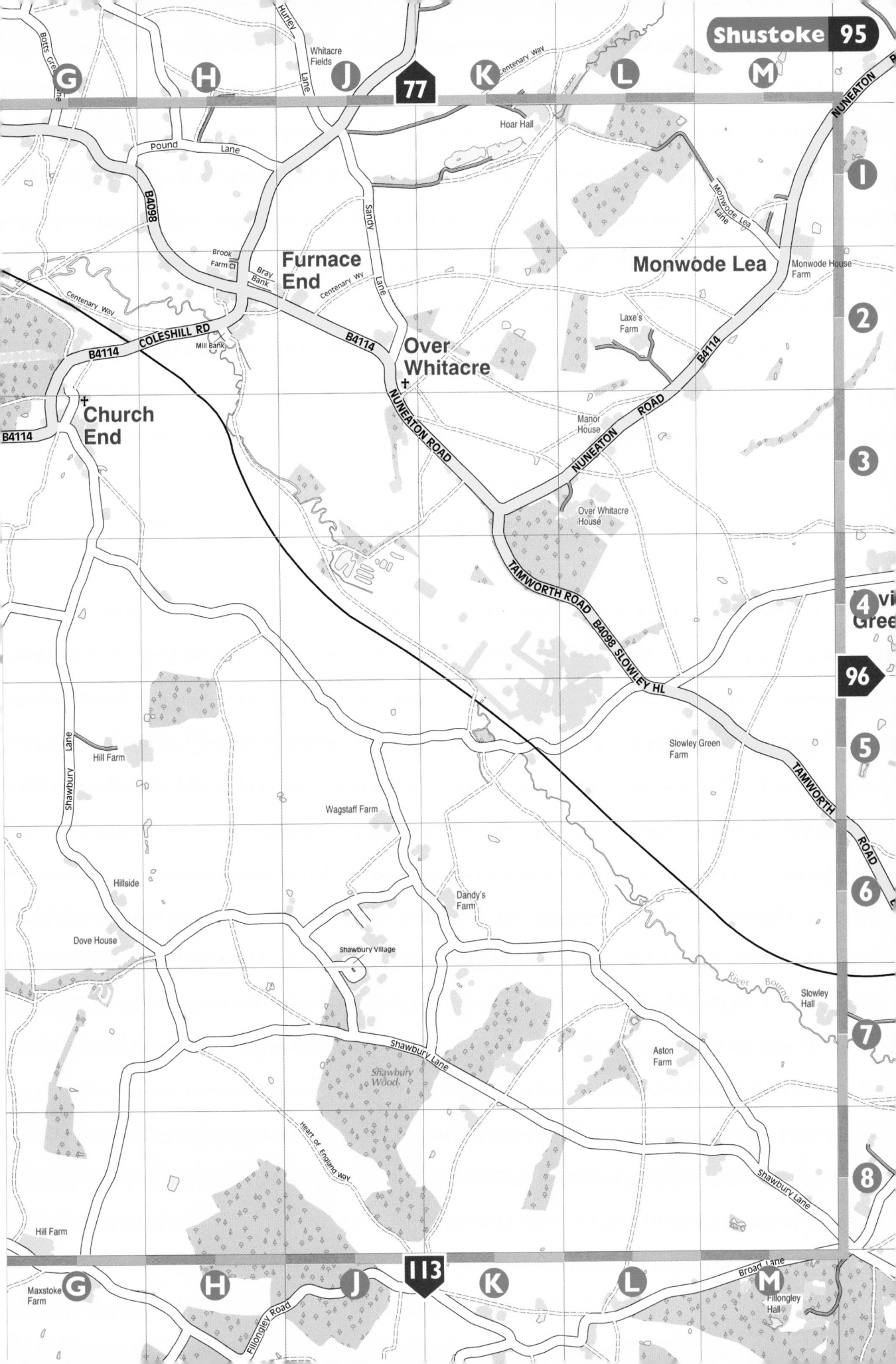

G H J 77 K L M

Botts Green Lane

Whitacre Fields

Hurley Lane

Centenary Way

Hoar Hall

Monwode Lea Lane

1

Pound Lane

Brook Farm Cl

Bray Bank

Furnace End

Sandy Lane

Centenary Wy

Monwode Lea

Monwode House Farm

B4098

Centenary Way

COLESHILL RD

Mill Bank

B4114

B4114

Over Whitacre

Laxe's Farm

B4114

2

B4114

B4114

Church End

NUNEATON ROAD

Manor House

NUNEATON ROAD

3

Over Whitacre House

TAMWORTH ROAD

4 vi Gree

B4098 SLOWLEY HL

96

Slowley Green Farm

5

Hill Farm

Shawbury Lane

TAMWORTH

Wagstaff Farm

ROAD

6

Hillside

Dandy's Farm

Dove House

Shawbury Village

River Bourne

Slowley Hall

7

Shawbury Lane

Aston Farm

Shawbury Wood

Heart of England Way

8

Shawbury Lane

Broad Lane

Hill Farm

G H J 113 K L M

Maxstoke Farm

Fillongley Road

Fillongley Hall

B4114

NUNEATON ROAD

F5
1 Hawthorne Av

F1
1 Ludford Cl
2 Malthouse Cl

E5
1 James St

JHA

Brook House
Farm

Ansley Lane

ROAD

B4112

St Lawrence
Road

The
Surgery

Ansley

A B C D E F

1

Monwode House
Farm

Hood Lane
Farm

**Ballard's
Green**

2

Bourne Brook

Ansley La

Arley
Wood

3

PO

Herbert Fowler
Middle School

Arley House
Farm

Arley Hall
Farm

Elm
Gv

Beech
Gv

Ash
Gv

Oak Av

Church

Church Lane

**Old
Arley**

Woodside

Arley Sports
Centre

Meadow
Cft

Rowling
Cft

Hill Top

**Devitts
Green**

4

Rectory
Road

Bournebrook
Vw

Station Road

Spinney

Arley Industrial
Estate

Firtree Lane

Hollick
Cfts

George Street

7

Charles Street

Sycamore
Crescent

1

5

TAMWORTH ROAD

Springs
Hill

Colliers Way

Frederick Road

Arley
Industrial
Estate

Spring Hill
Industrial
Estate

View
River Rw

Daffern
Avenue

Morgan
Close

Ransome Road

Gun Hill

PO

Arley & Gun
Hill School

**New
Arley**

B4098

Lichfield
Close

St Michael's
Close

6

Stonehouse Lane

Spring Hill

Fourfields
Way

**Gun
Hill**

Slowley
Hall

Tipper's Hill Lane

Spring Hill
Medical
Centre

Lamp Lane

7

Tamworth
Rd

Fillongley
Lodge

Tipper's Hill

The
Uplands

PARK LANE

8

Mill Lane

TAMWORTH ROAD

bury Lane

Hall Lane

B4098 ROAD

B4102

Wood End Lane

**Wood
End**

A B C D E F

ROAD

Castle Hills

Berryfields

ongley

79

G H J K L M

98

115

G H J K L M

Common

First School

Hill Farm

The Rookery Lane

Marlowe Cl

Chesterton

Sheridan Dr

Bronte

Browning Cl

Blake Close

Ruskin Cl

Swinburn Cl

Selby Wy

Wimbourne Cl

Waltham Crescent

PO

St Peter's

Valley Road

Doctors Surg

Hilcman

Rock Cl

Smyle

Auden

Wells Ln

Keats Cl

Addison

Chesterton

Hardy Cl

Dickens Cl

Chaucer Drive

Thackeray Close

Sherbourne Avenue

Hampton Drive

Beverley Avenue

Portland Drive

Knowles Spin

Bar Cr

I

Galley Common Medical Centre

Tunnel Road

Orford Rd

Court Court

Park Dr

Haunchwood Way

Centenary Way

Mayfair Dr

Park Lane

Doctors Surgery

Kingswood Road

Berwyn Way

Way

Hill Farm

Croft Mead

PO

Nuthurst Crs

Centenary Way

Centenary Way

Robinson's End

Robins Way

Park Lane Primary School

Wenlock Way

Client Dr

Quantock Dr

Presselly Cl

Mendip Drive

Wiclif

St Pauls C of E Fi School

2

Pennine Way

Snowdon

Tower View Crs

Ashe Rd

Cheviot Cl

Cotswold

Cromdale Close

Malvern Av

PO

Arley Lane

Nuthurst Lane

ANSLEY ROAD B4112

ANSLEY ROAD

Tower Farm

Stockingford

Nuthurst Heath Farm

Seeswood Pool

3

Centenary Way

ASTLEY LANE

4

Church Lane

Church Farm

Lodge Farm

98

Temple House

5

Astley

Astley Castle

Astley C of E Sch

Castle Dr

6

Red Lane

Astley Lane

7

LANE

Windmill Lane

PARK

B4102

8

Howe Green

Cowley Wood

Cottage Farm

Green Lane

New Road

Astley Lane

Sole End Farm

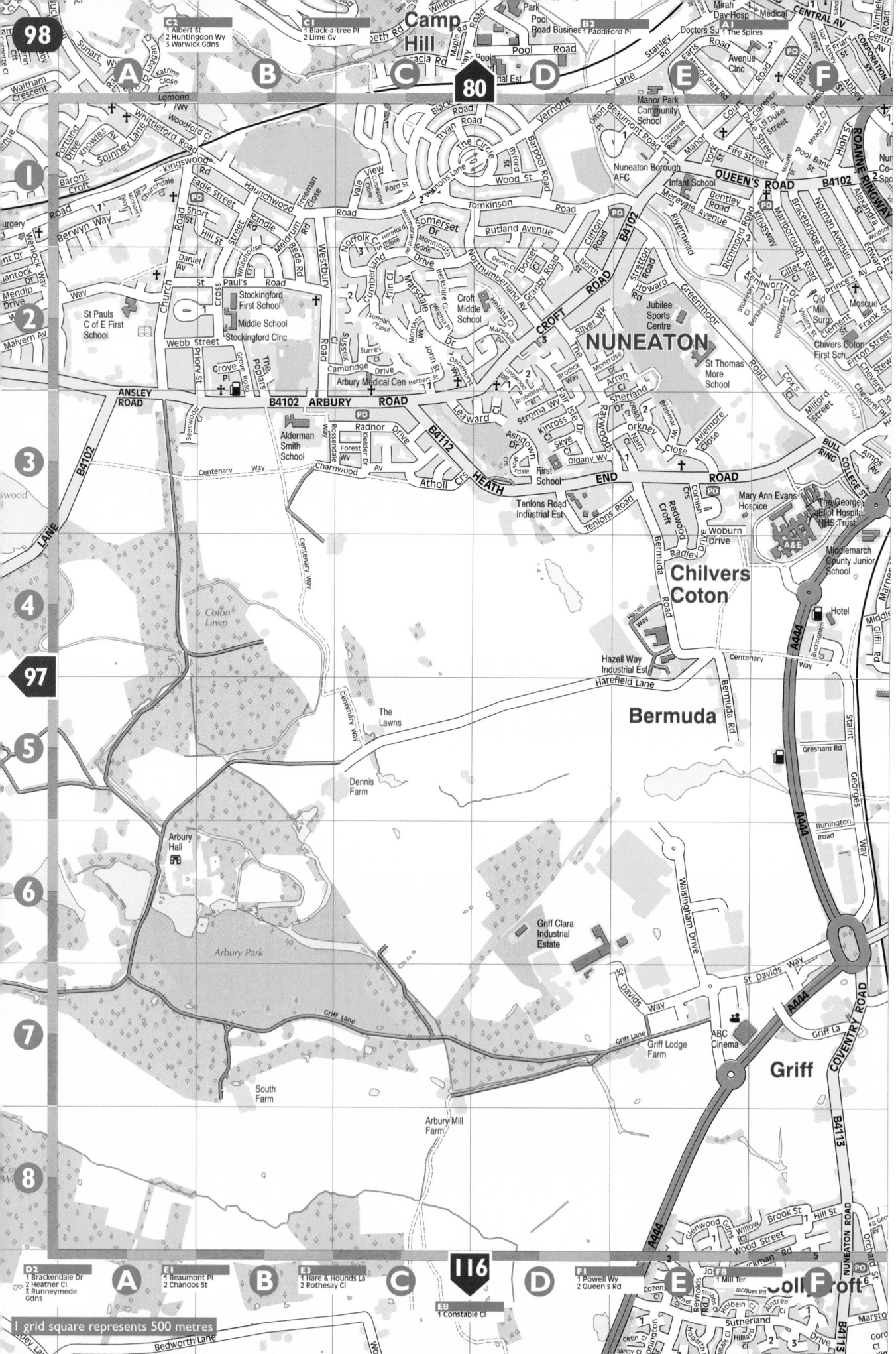

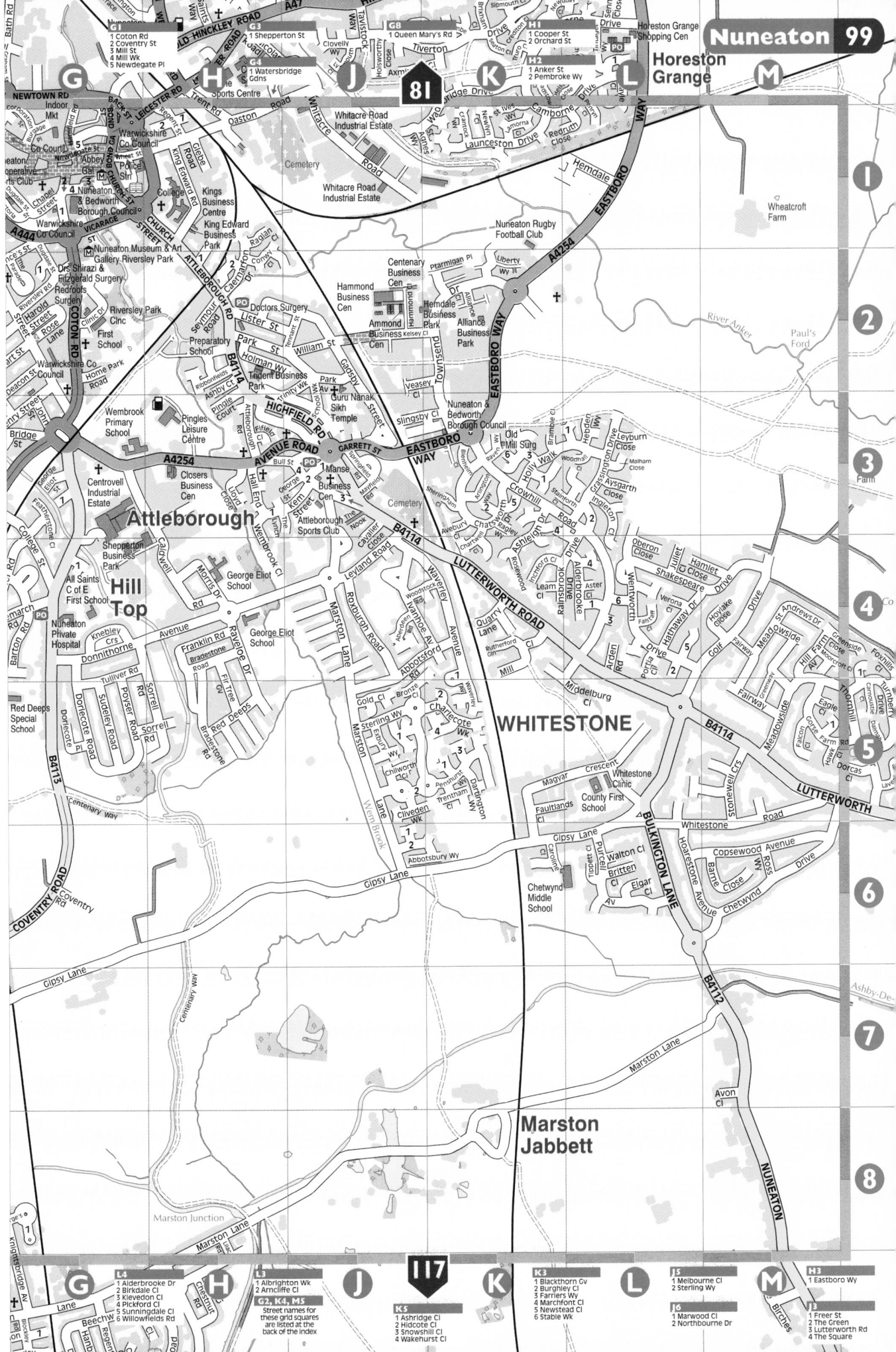

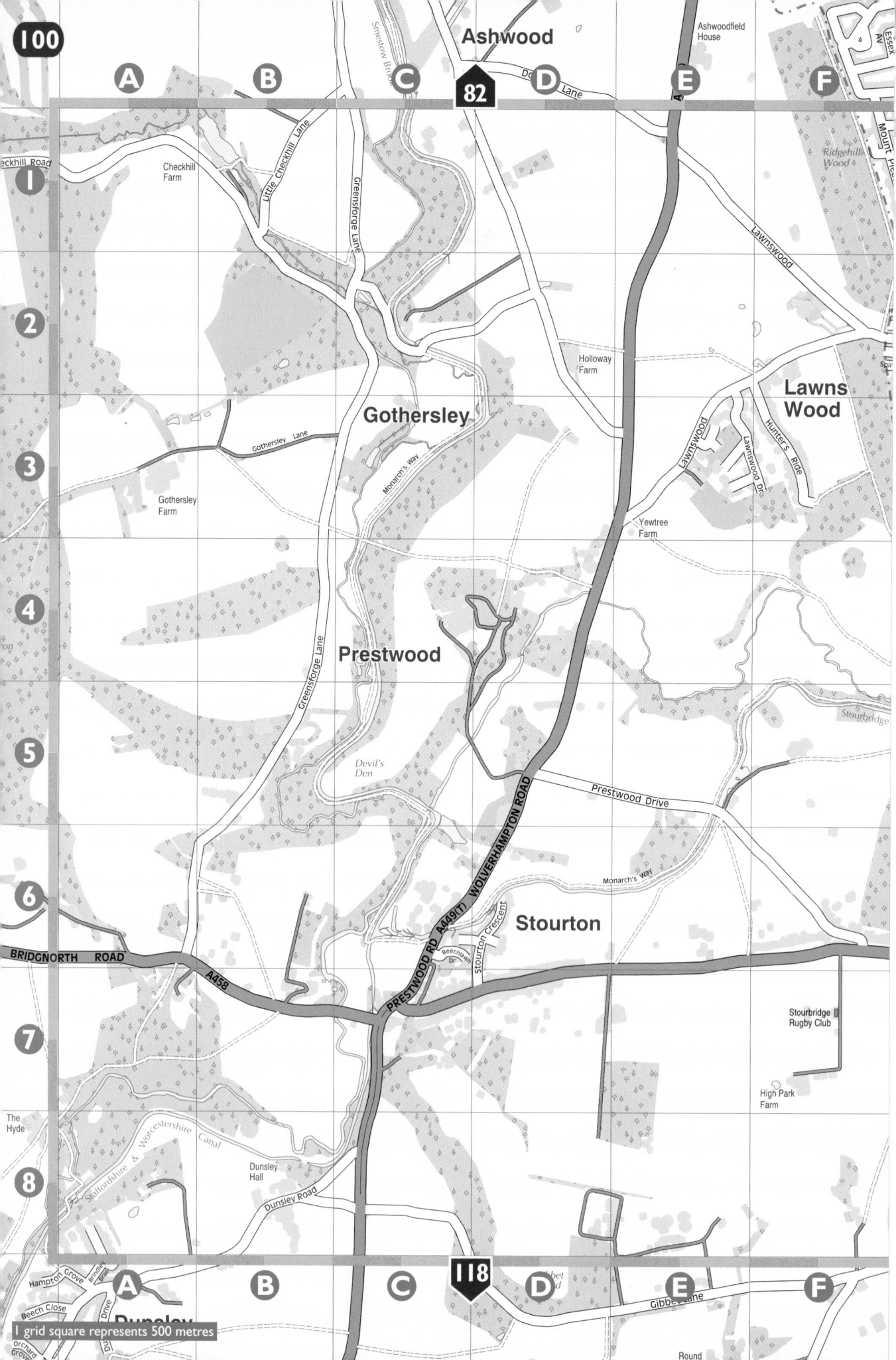

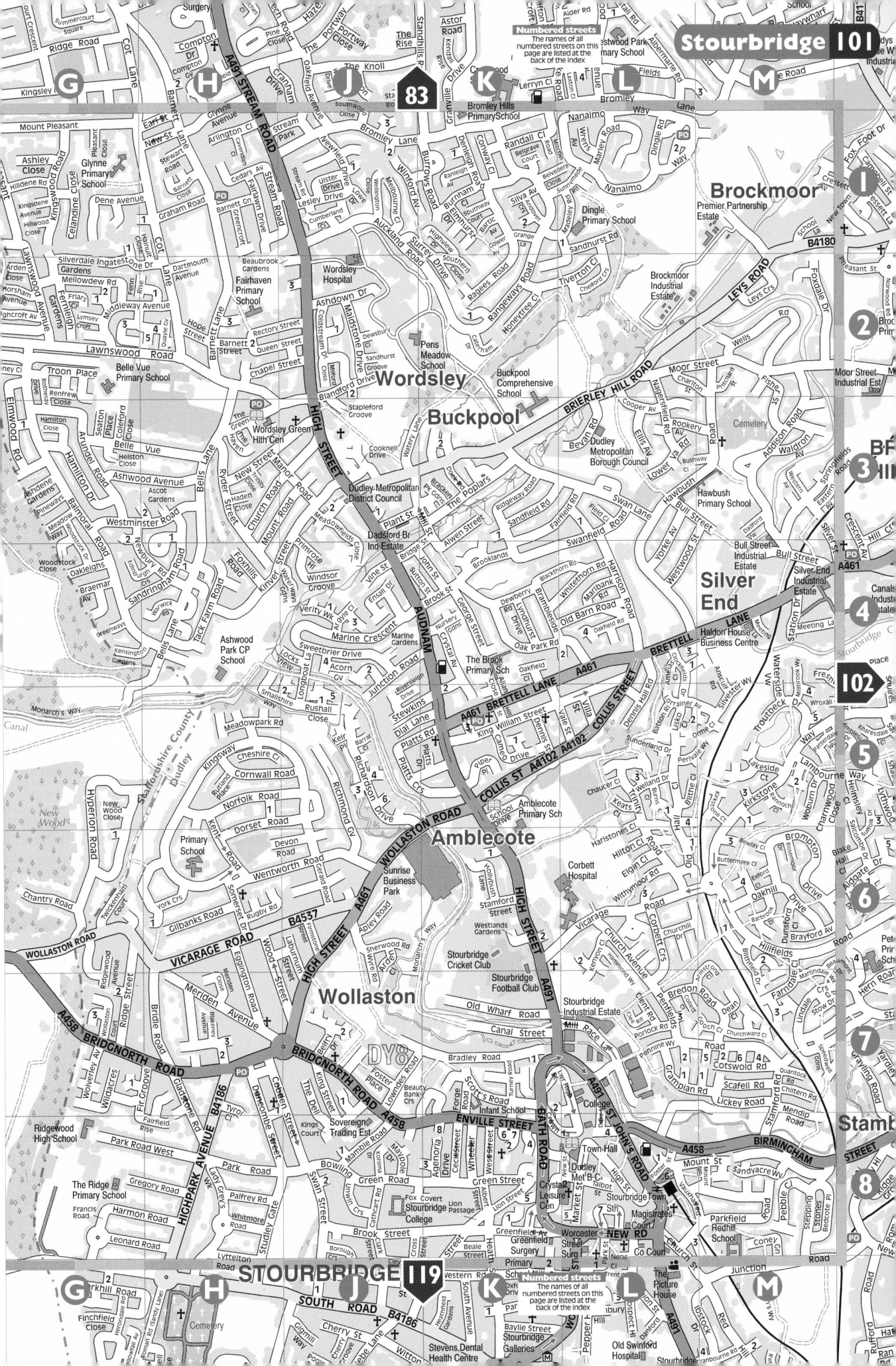

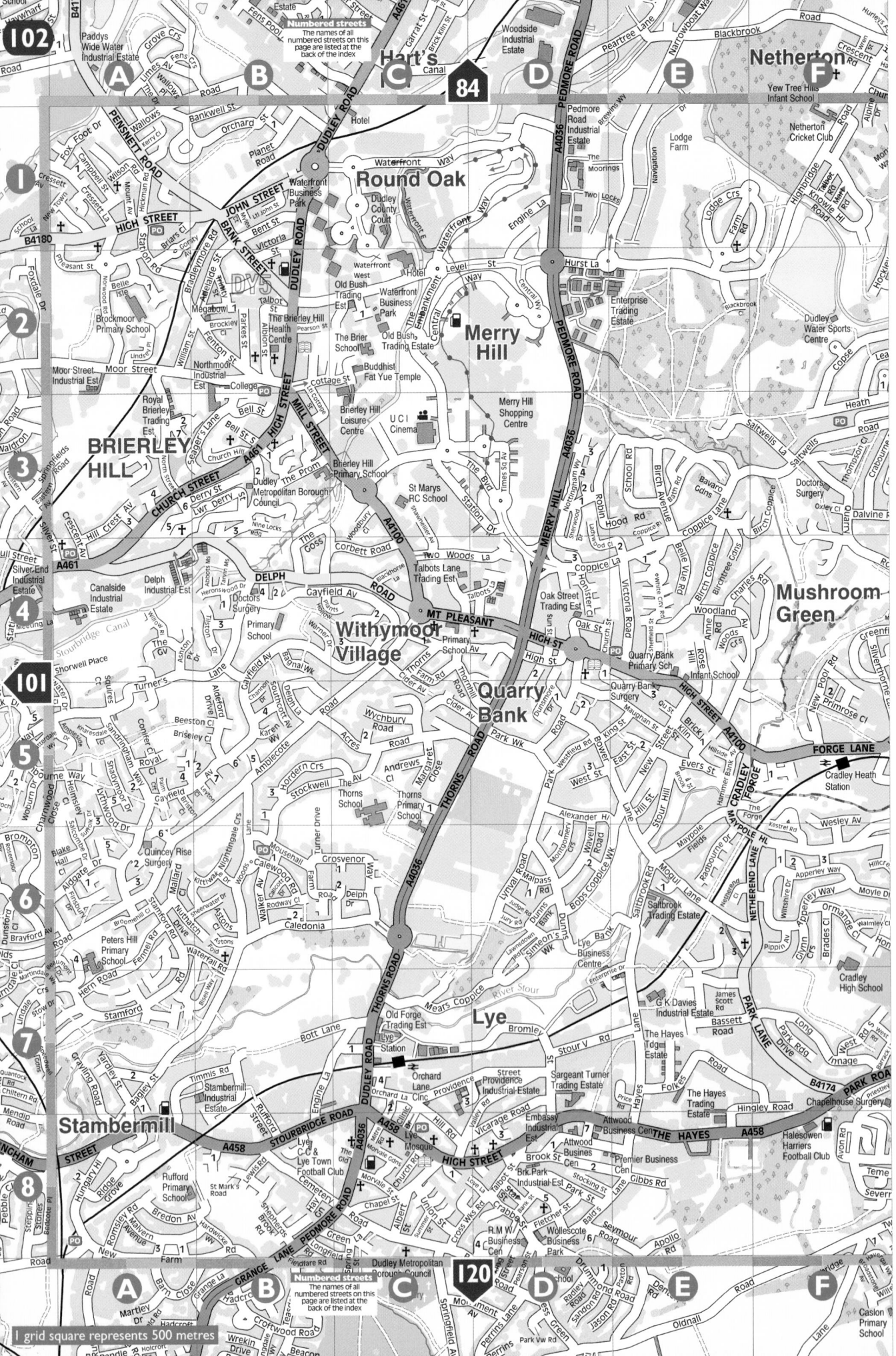

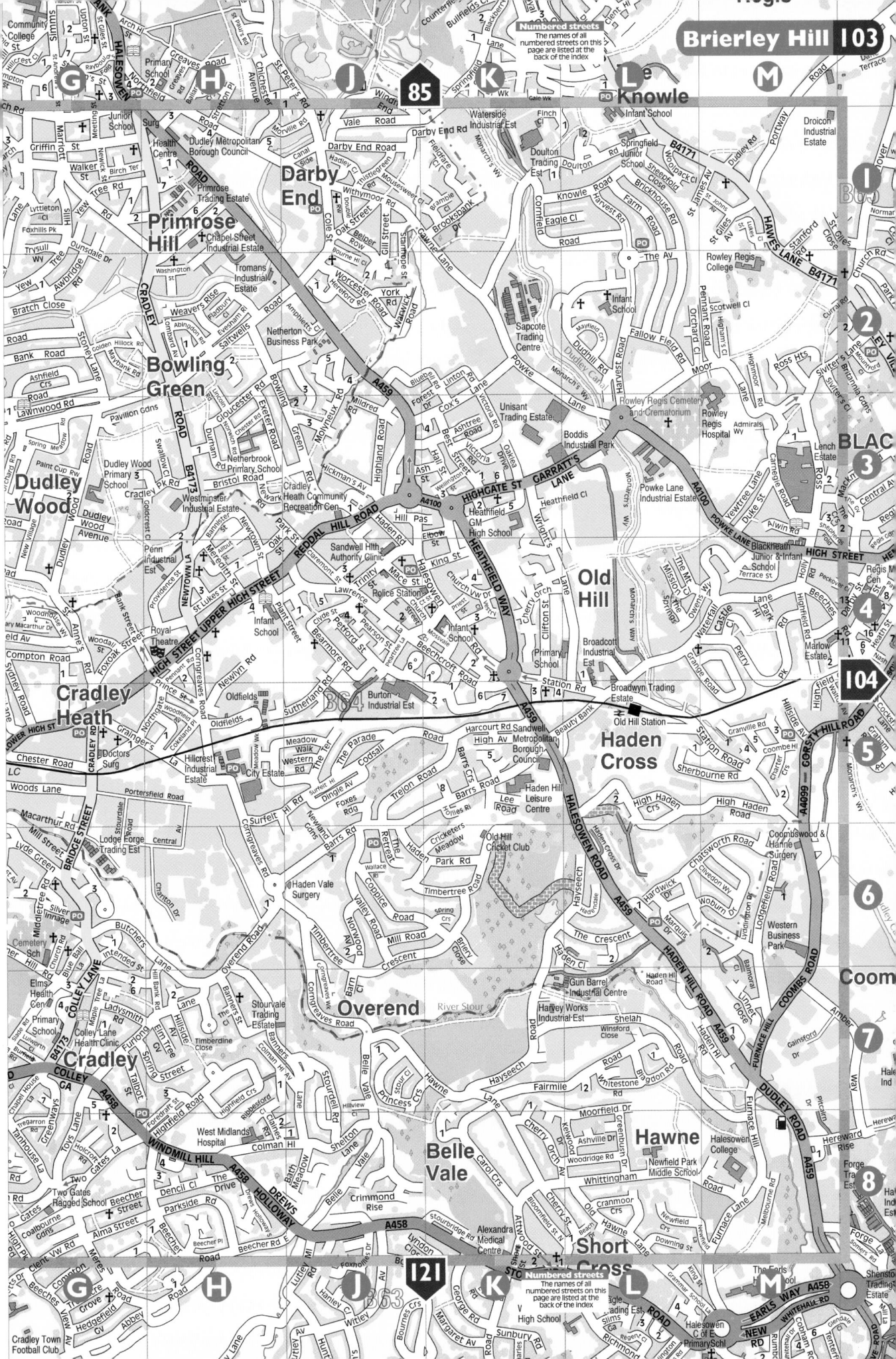

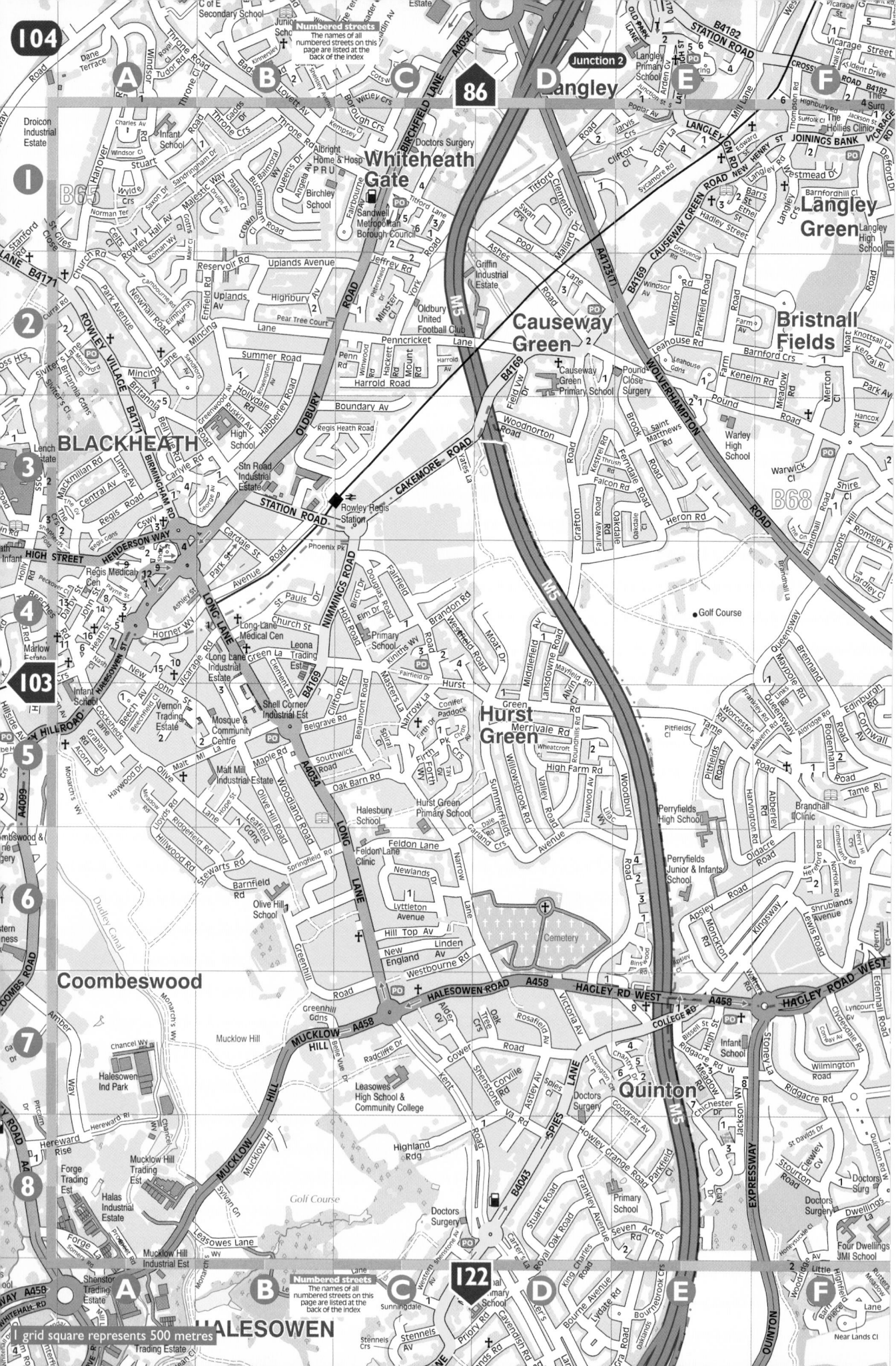

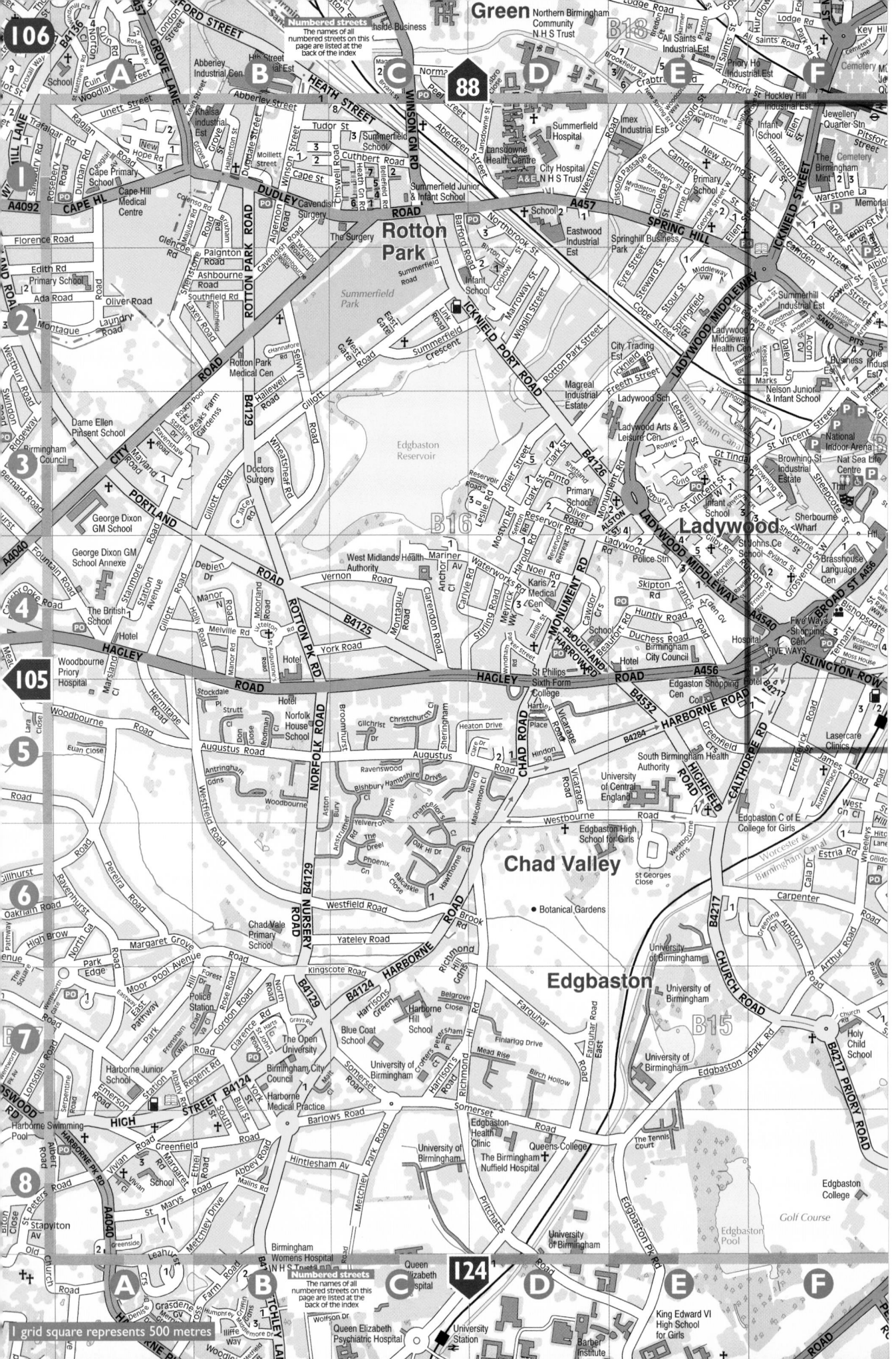

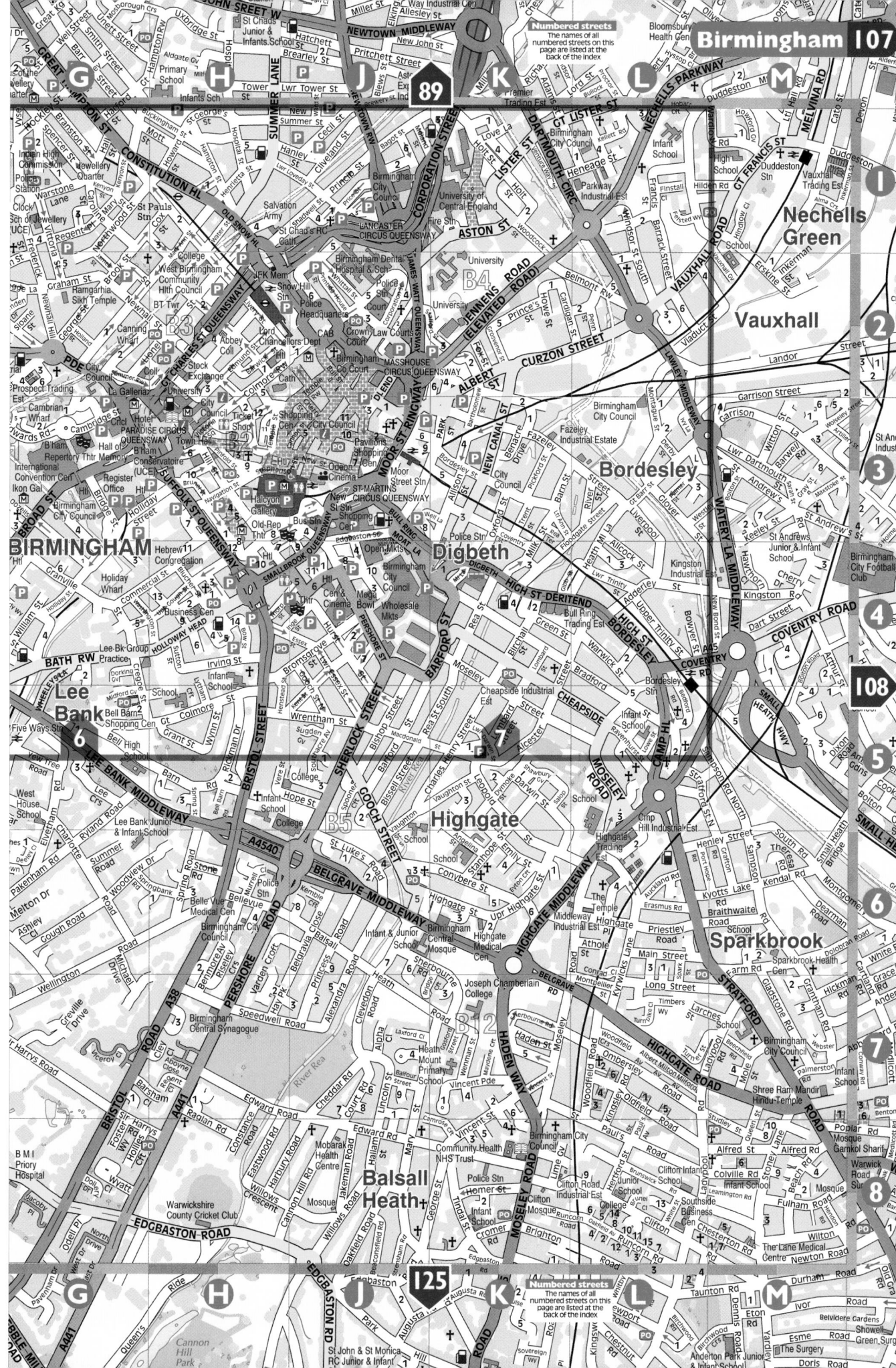

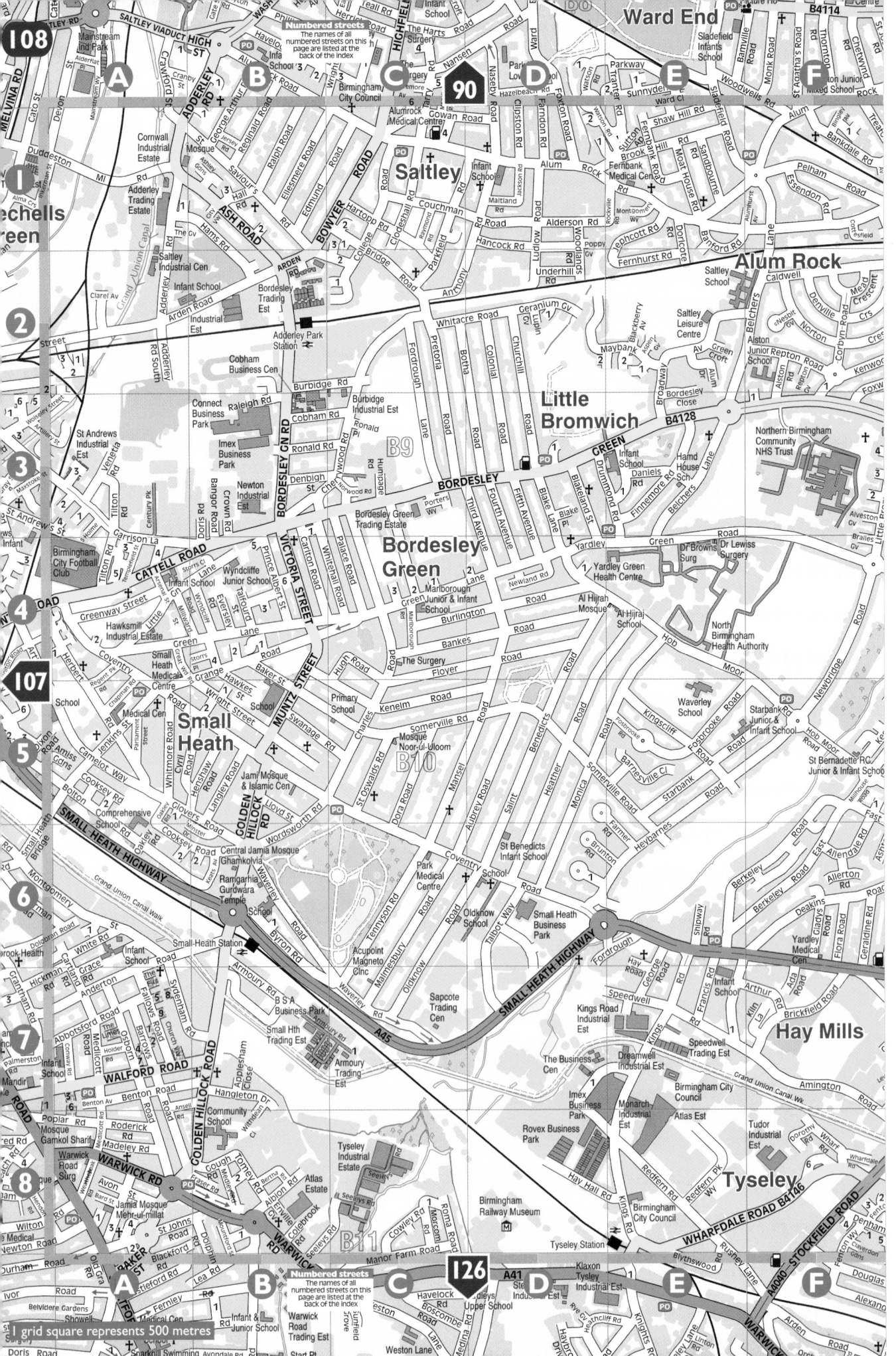

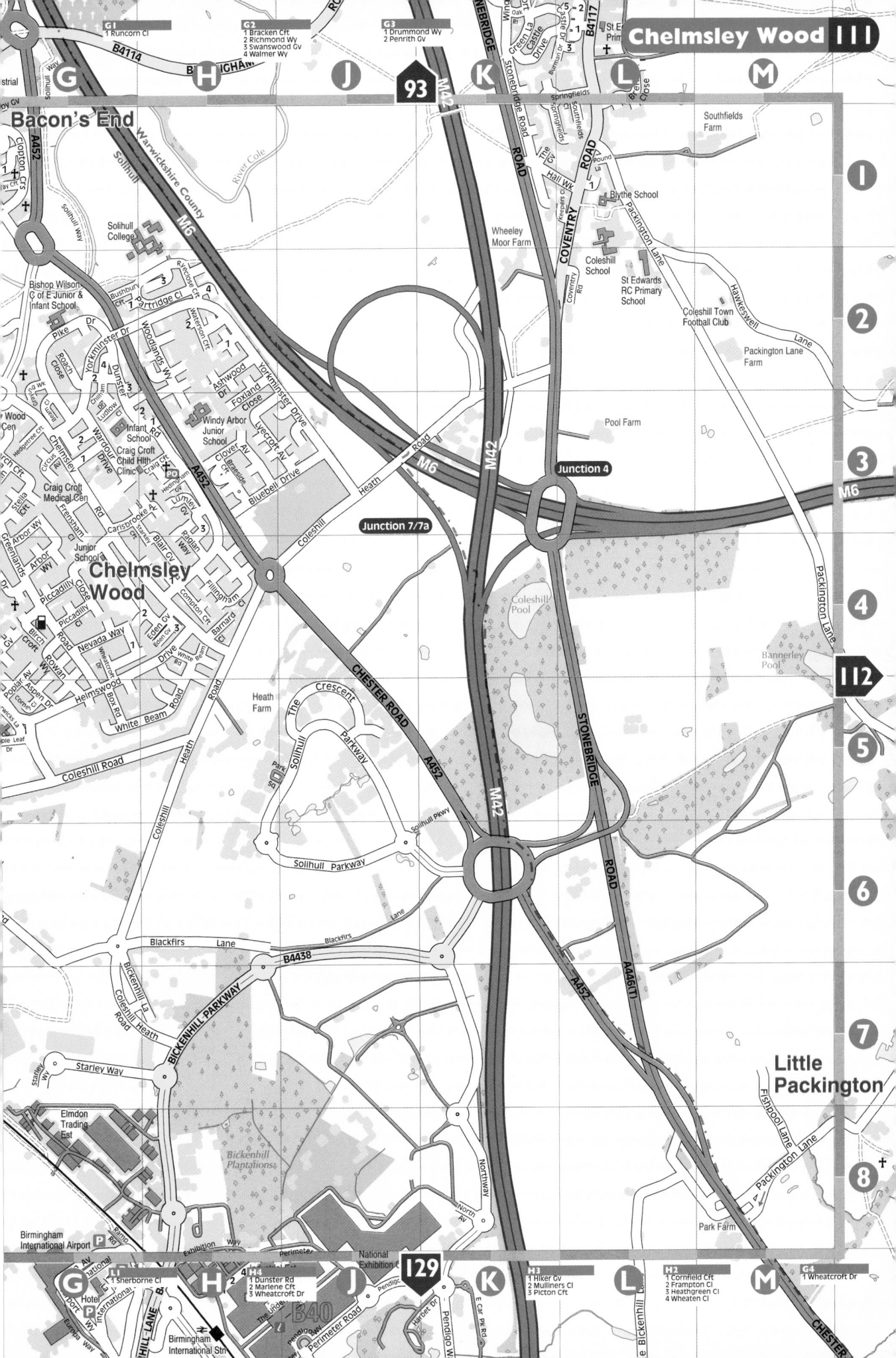

Bacon's End

G1
1 Runcorn Cl

G2
1 Bracken Cft
2 Richmond Wy
3 Swanswood Gv
4 Walmer Wy

G3
1 Drummond Wy
2 Penrith Gv

93

Solihull College

Bishop Wilson C of E Junior & Infant School

Windy Arbor Junior School

Infant School

Craig Croft Child Hlth Clinic

Craig Croft Medical Cen

Chelmsley Wood

Junior School

Junction 7/7a

Junction 4

Wheeley Moor Farm

Coleshill School

Blythe School

St Edwards RC Primary School

Coleshill Town Football Club

Packington Lane Farm

Southfields Farm

Pool Farm

Coleshill Pool

Bannerley Pool

112

Heath Farm

The Crescent

Solihull Parkway

Park Sq

Solihull Parkway

Solihull Pkwy

Blackfirs Lane

Blackfirs Lane

B4438

Bickenhill Parkway

Coleshill Heath

Coleshill Road

Starley Way

Starley Way

Elmdon Trading Est

Bickenhill Plantations

Birmingham International Airport

Little Packington

Park Farm

National Exhibition Centre

129

Birmingham International Stn

G
1 Sherborne Cl

H
1 Dunster Rd
2 Marlene Cft
3 Wheatcroft Dr

H3
1 Hiker Gv
2 Mulliners Cl
3 Picton Cft

H2
1 Cornfield Cft
2 Frampton Cl
3 Heathgreen Cl
4 Wheaten Cl

G4
1 Wheatcroft Dr

G   H   J   **95**   K   L   M

I

2

3

4

114

5

6

7

8

G   H   **131**   J   K   L   M

Hill Farm

Maxstoke Hall Farm

Fillongley Hall

Broad Lane

England way

Bentley's Farm

Bentley Lane

Fillongley Road

High House Farm

Heart of England Way

Broad Lane

Pump

Fillor Hou

Wood Corner Farm

Manor House Farm

Blabers Hall Farm

Green End

Newhall Green

White House Farm

Daniels Wood

M6

MERIDEN ROAD

Chape G er

Kinwalsey

Kinwalsey Lane

Lane

B4102

B4102

Birchley Hays Wood

oods

Outwoods Farm

Coventry Way

Close Wood

Meigs Wood

Heart of England Way

Butler's End

Becks Lane

Ivy House Farm

High Ash Farm

Lodge Green Lane North

Shaft L

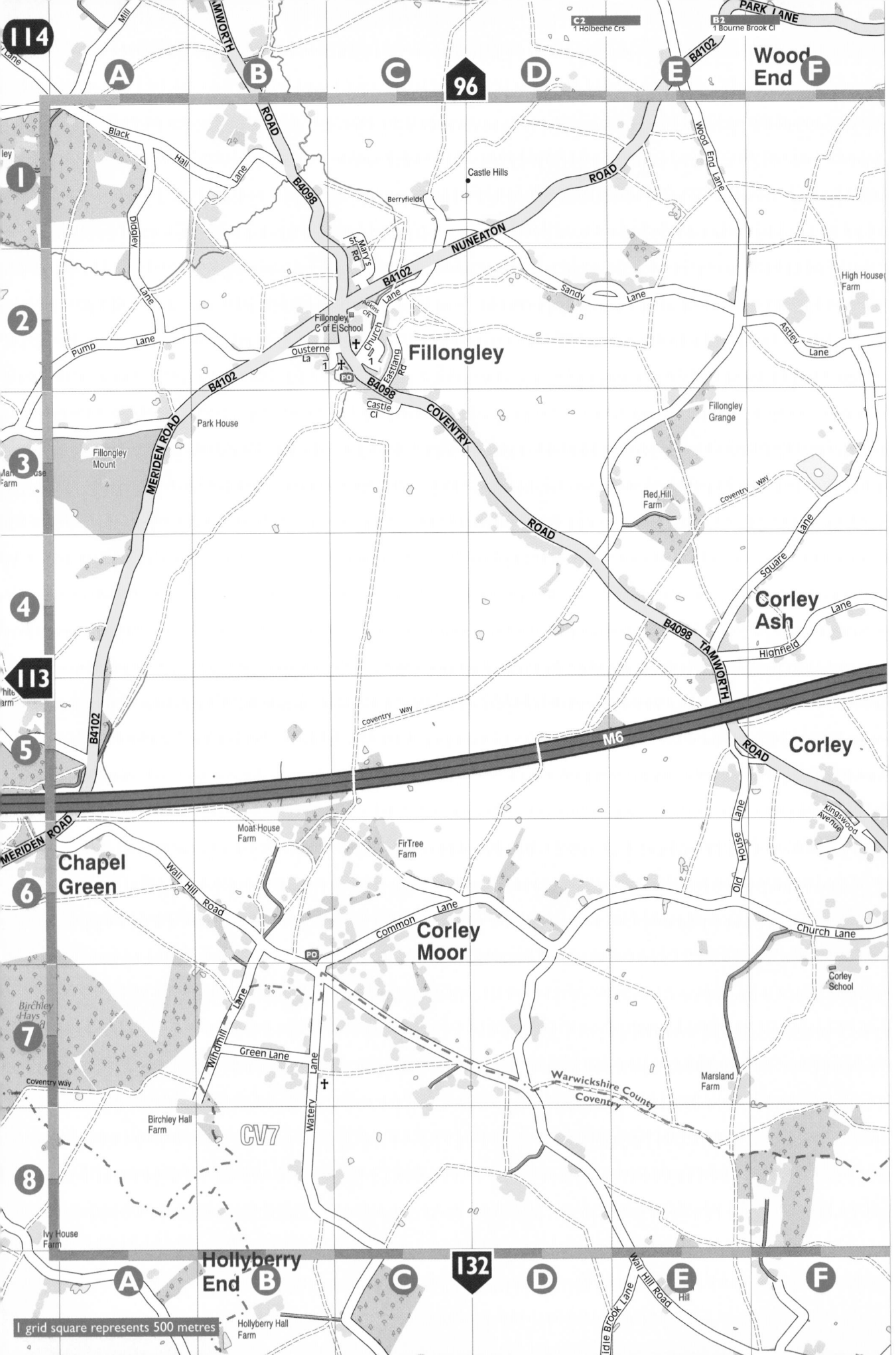

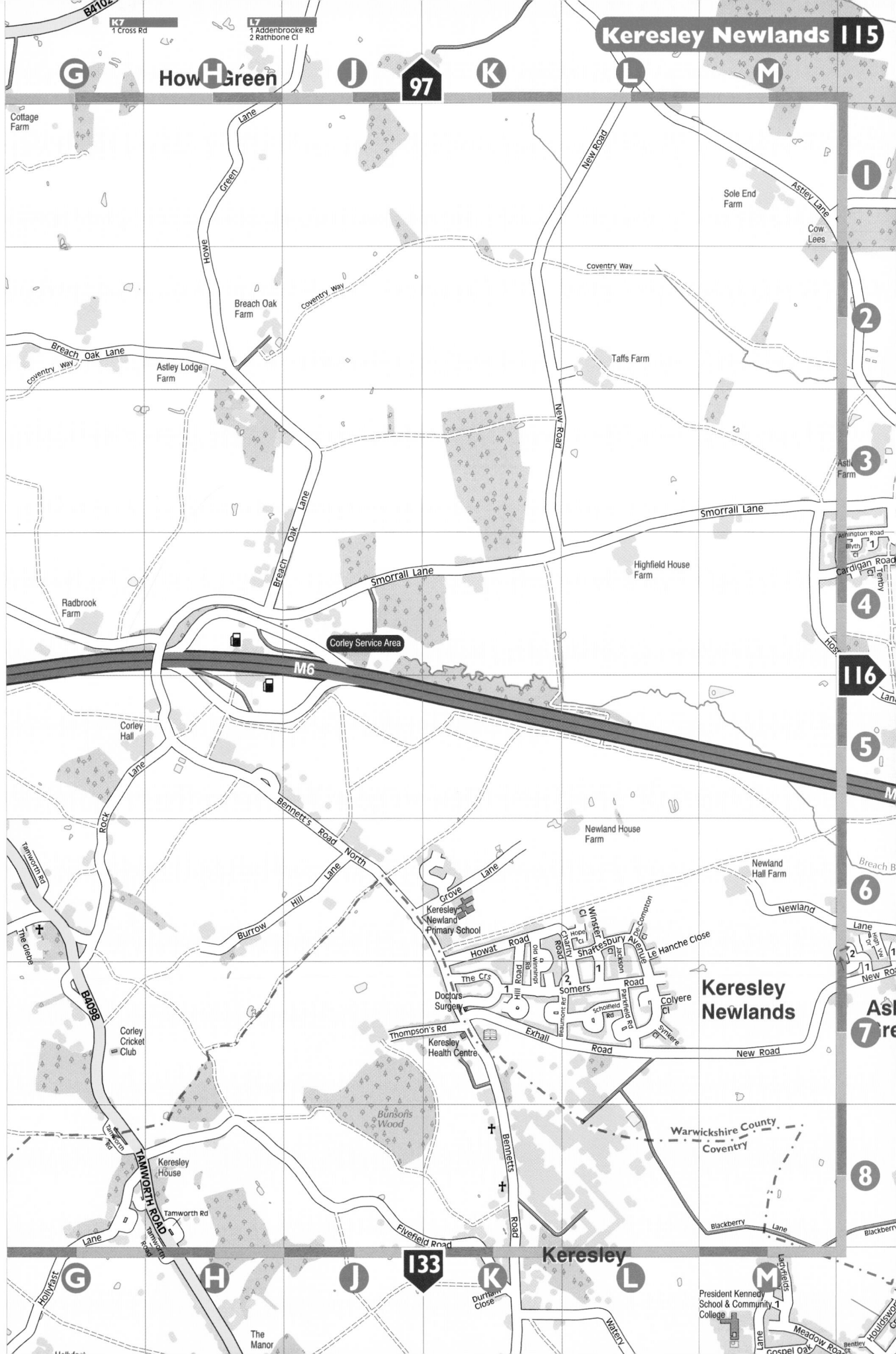

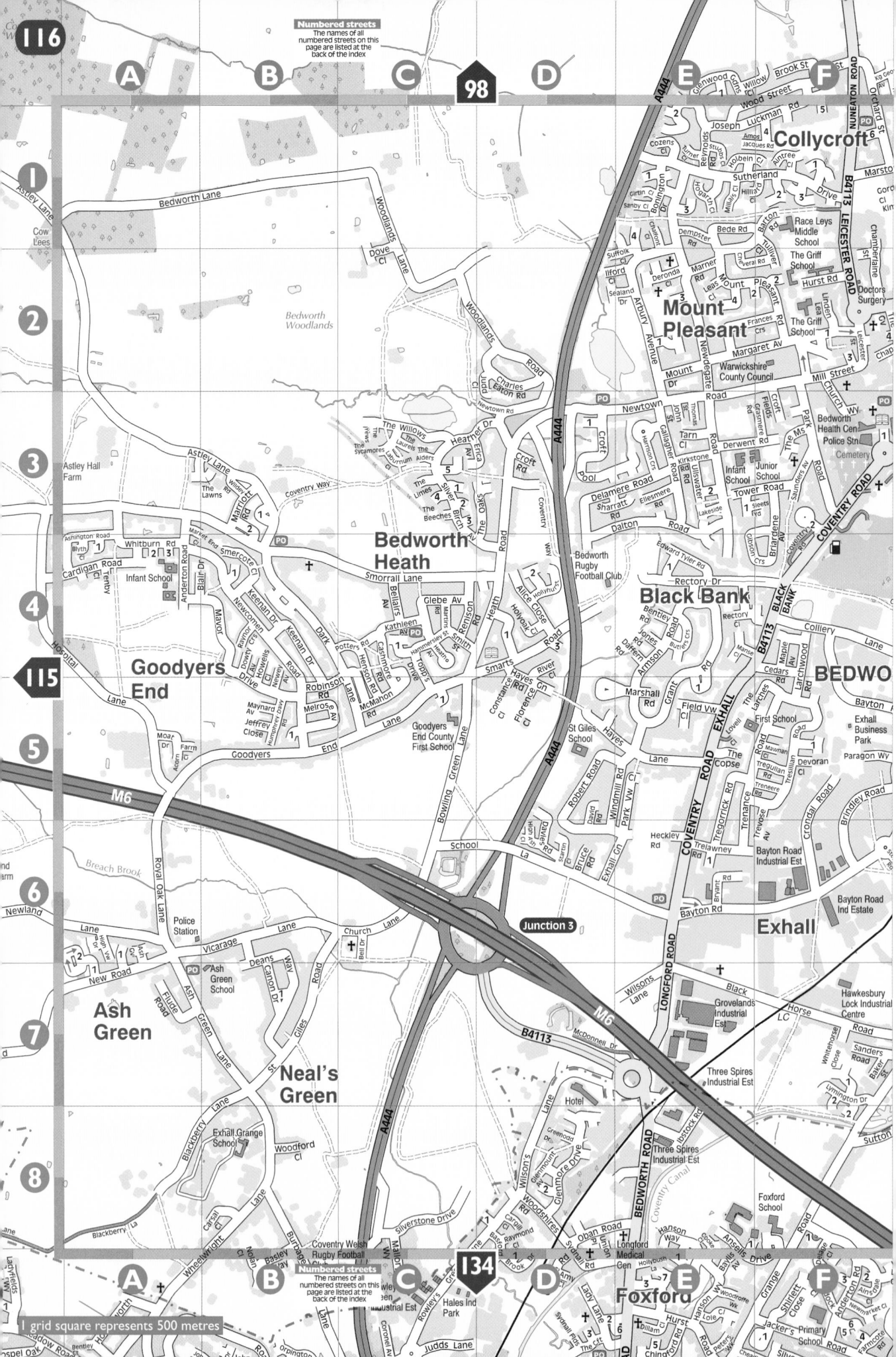

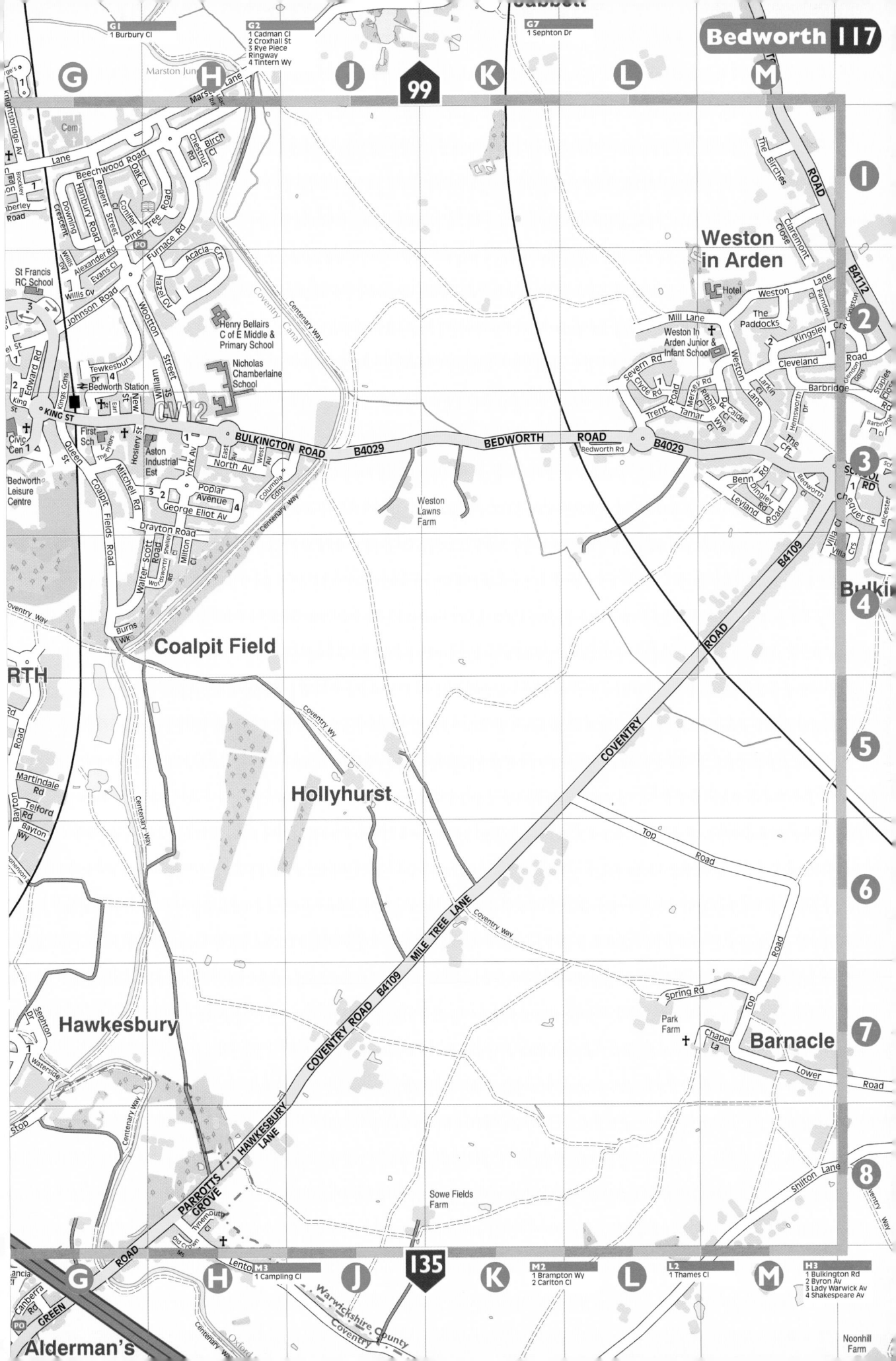

G1
1 Burbury Cl

G2
1 Cadman Cl
2 Croxhall St
3 Rye Piece Ringway
4 Tintern Wy

G7
1 Sephton Dr

G H J 99 K L M I

Marston Jun

Cem

Marston Lane

Weston in Arden

Knightsbridge Av
Blackley Cl
Chamberley Road

Beechwood Road
Hanbury Road
Downing Crescent
Regent Street
Conifer Street
Oak Cl
Chestnut Rd
Birch Rd

The Birches

ROAD
B4112

I

Pine Tree Rd
Acacia Crs
Hazel Gv
Furnace Rd
PO

Claremont Close
Compton Crs

2

St Francis RC School
Willis Rd
Willis Gv
Alexander Rd
Evans Cl
Johnson Road
Wooten Street
William Street

Henry Bellairs C of E Middle & Primary School

Nicholas Chamberlaine School

Hotel
Weston In Arden Junior & Infant School

Mill Lane
The Paddocks
Weston Lane
Kingsley
Cleveland
Larkin Rd

Weston Lane
Barbridge

Staples Rd
Barbridge Gdns

Edward Rd
King St
Tewkesbury Dr
Kings Cohs
Bedworth Station
KING ST
Earl Street
New Street
CV12

Severn Rd
Clyde Rd
Trent Road
Mersey Rd
Ribble Rd
Wye
Tamar
De Calder Rd
Larkin Rd
Hemsworth

3
SCHOOL RD
Chequer St
Leicester Rd

Queen Street
First Sch
The Drives
York Av
East Av
West Av
North Av
Aston Industrial Est
Mitchell Rd
George Eliot Av
Poplar Avenue
Columbia Gdns
BULKINGTON ROAD
B4029
BEDWORTH ROAD
Bedworth Rd
B4029
Benn Rd
Dingley Rd
Leyland Road
Bedworth Road
Villa Cl
Villa Crs
The Cft

Bulki
4

Bedworth Leisure Centre
Coalpit Fields Road
Drayton Road
Walter Scott Road
Shelley Rd
Osworth Rd
Milton
Wo

B4109

Coventry Canal
Centenary Way
Centenary way

Weston Lawns Farm

Burns WK
Centenary Way

Coventry Wy

Coalpit Field

RTH
Martindale Rd
Telford Rd
Bayton Wy
Bayton

Centenary Way

COVENTRY ROAD

5

Hollyhurst

Top Road

6

Spring Rd

Sephton Dr
Waterside
Stop

Hawkesbury

Park Farm
Chapel La
Barnacle
7

Shilton Lane
8

Centenary Way
HAWKESBURY LANE
PARROTTS GROVE
Tynemouth
Old Crown
Ms

MILE TREE LANE
COVENTRY ROAD
B4109
Coventry Way

Sowe Fields Farm

Lower Road
Top Road

Canberra Rd
PO
GREEN
ROAD
Lentor
Warwickshire County
Coventry
Oxford

G H 135 J K L M

M3
1 Campling Cl

M2
1 Brampton Wy
2 Carlton Cl

L2
1 Thames Cl

H3
1 Bulkington Rd
2 Byron Av
3 Lady Warwick Av
4 Shakespeare Av

Alderman's

Noonhill Farm

A B C **100** D E F

A2
1 The Grazings

Dunsley
Hall

Dunsley Road

Hampton Grove

Bindeley

Dunsley Road

Gibbet
Wood

Gibbet Lane

1

ch Close

Dunsley Drive

Dunsley

Orchard
Grove

Dunsley Road

Gibraltar

Round
Hill

Whittington Hall Lane

2

Mill

Pine
Larch

Blackley's Walk

Hawthorne Way

Willow
Road

Redwo
Elm
Lume
Gv

od Road

Cl

Cl

Whittington
Farm

Dark Lane

1

Horse Br Lane

A449(T)

Whittington
Common

3

Whittington

Whittington Hall Lane

Cookley Lane

Windsor Holloway

4

Highgrove
Farm

River Stour

Bunker's
Hill
Wood

5

North Worcestershire Path

6

New Road

Iverley House
Farm

Sugar Loaf Lane

Caunsall

North Worcestershire Path

Caunsall Road

Fairy
Glen

A451

7

Beech
Tree

Common Barn Lane

A449(T)

Beechtree Lane

STOURBRIDGE ROAD

Five Ways

Austcliffe
Farm

A451

8

Austcliffe
House Farm

A449(T)

White
Farm

138

ER
ROAD A449(T)

A B C D E F

borough

Ismere
House

A451

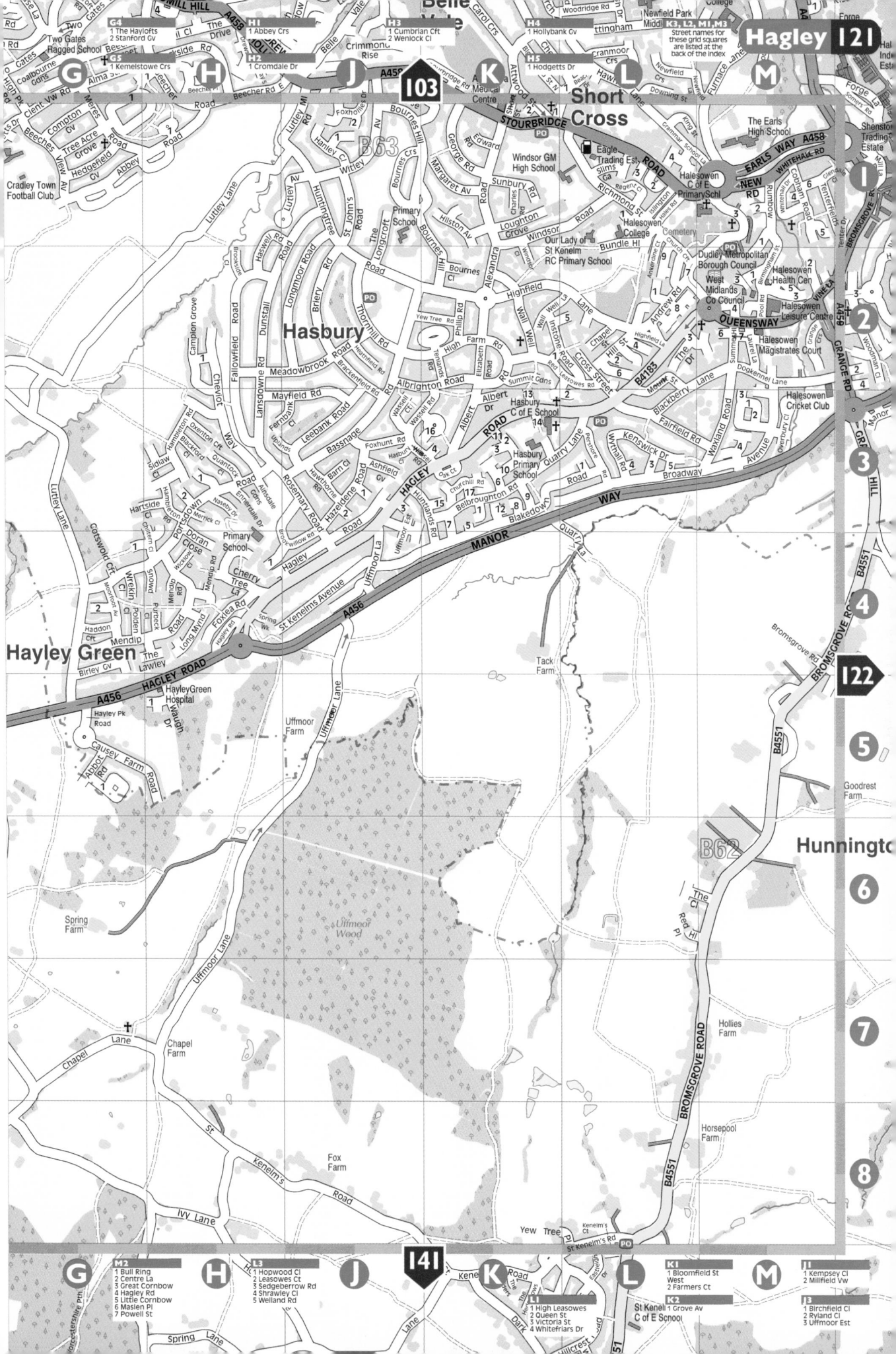

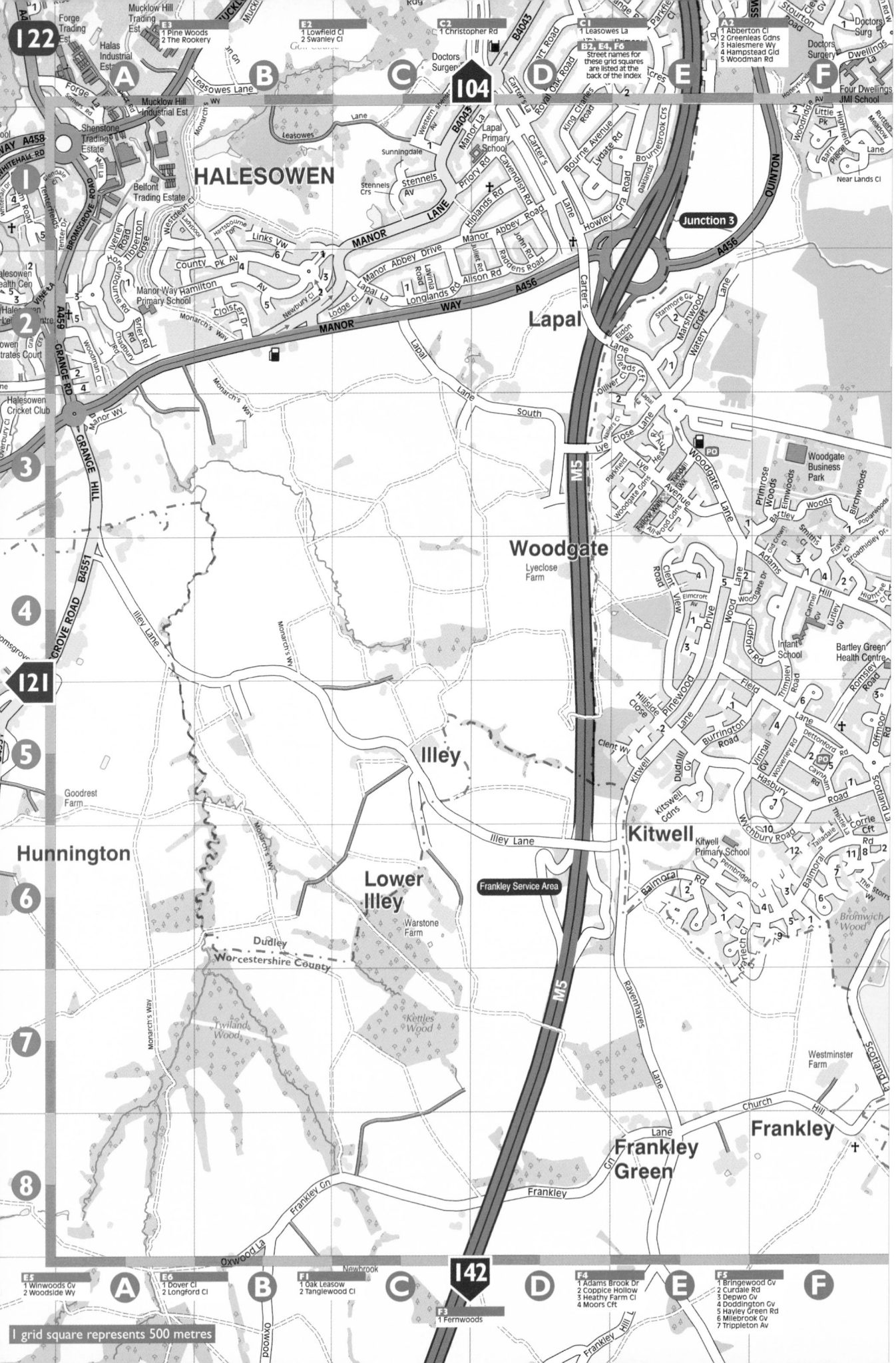

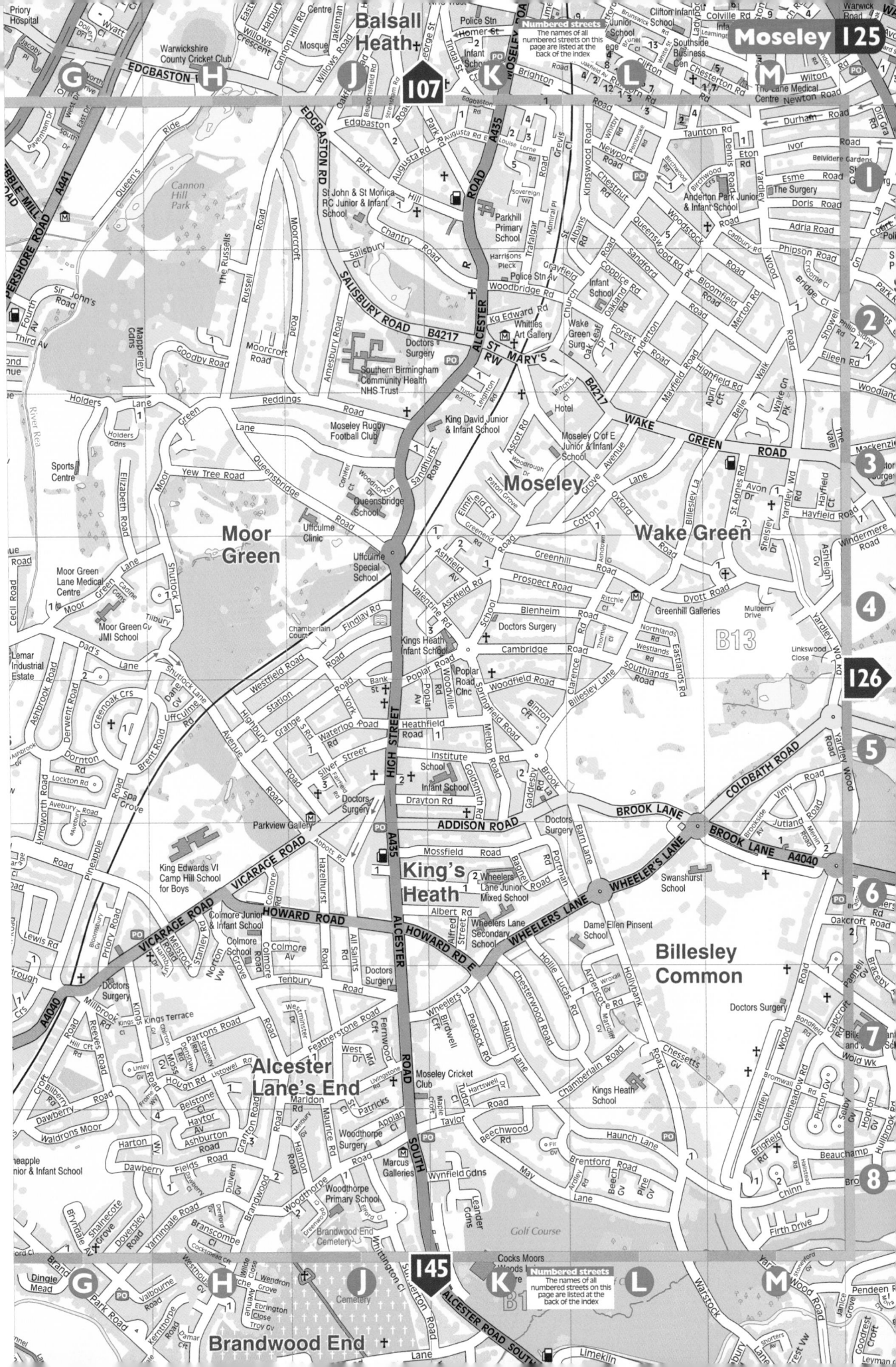

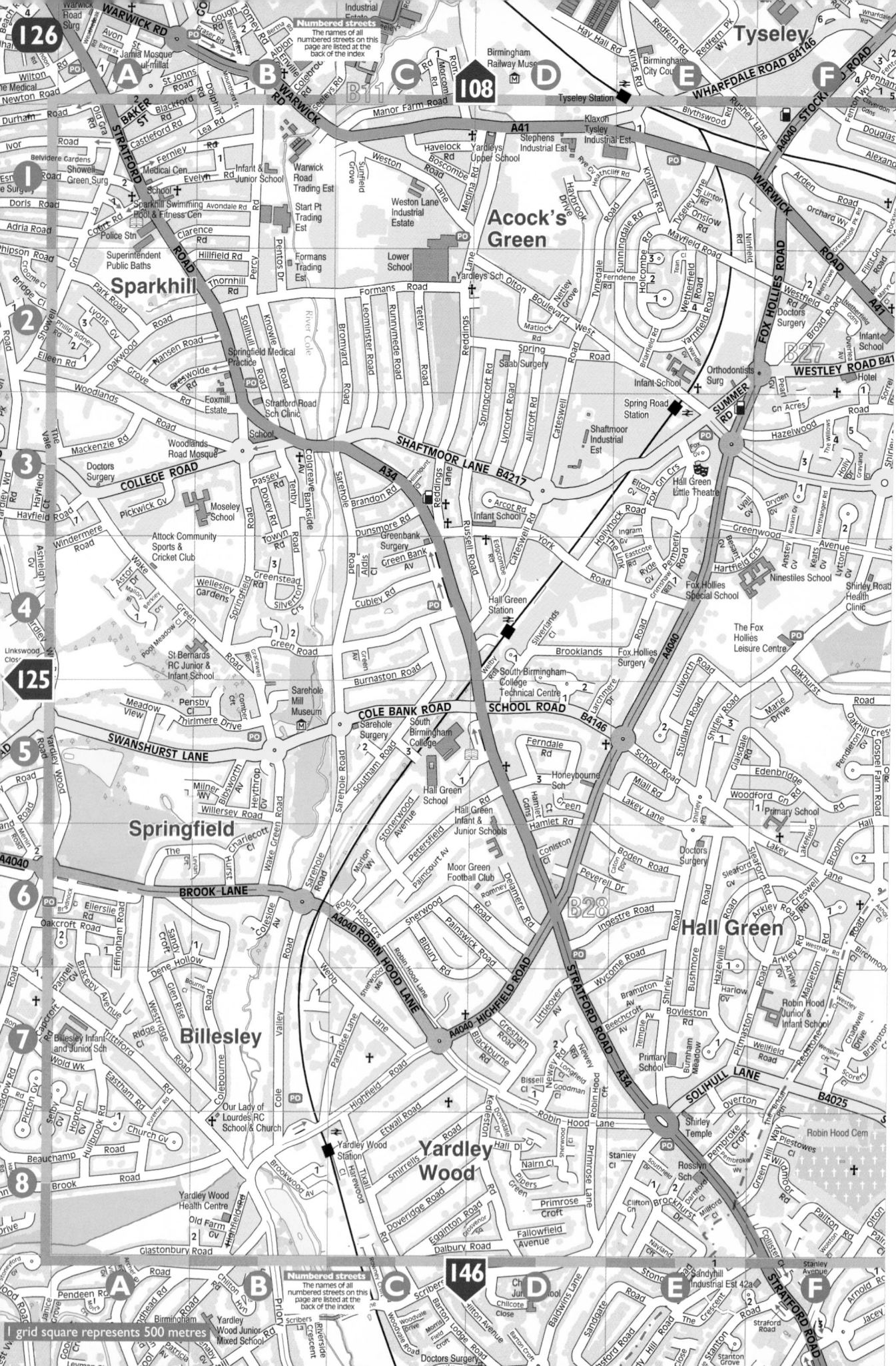

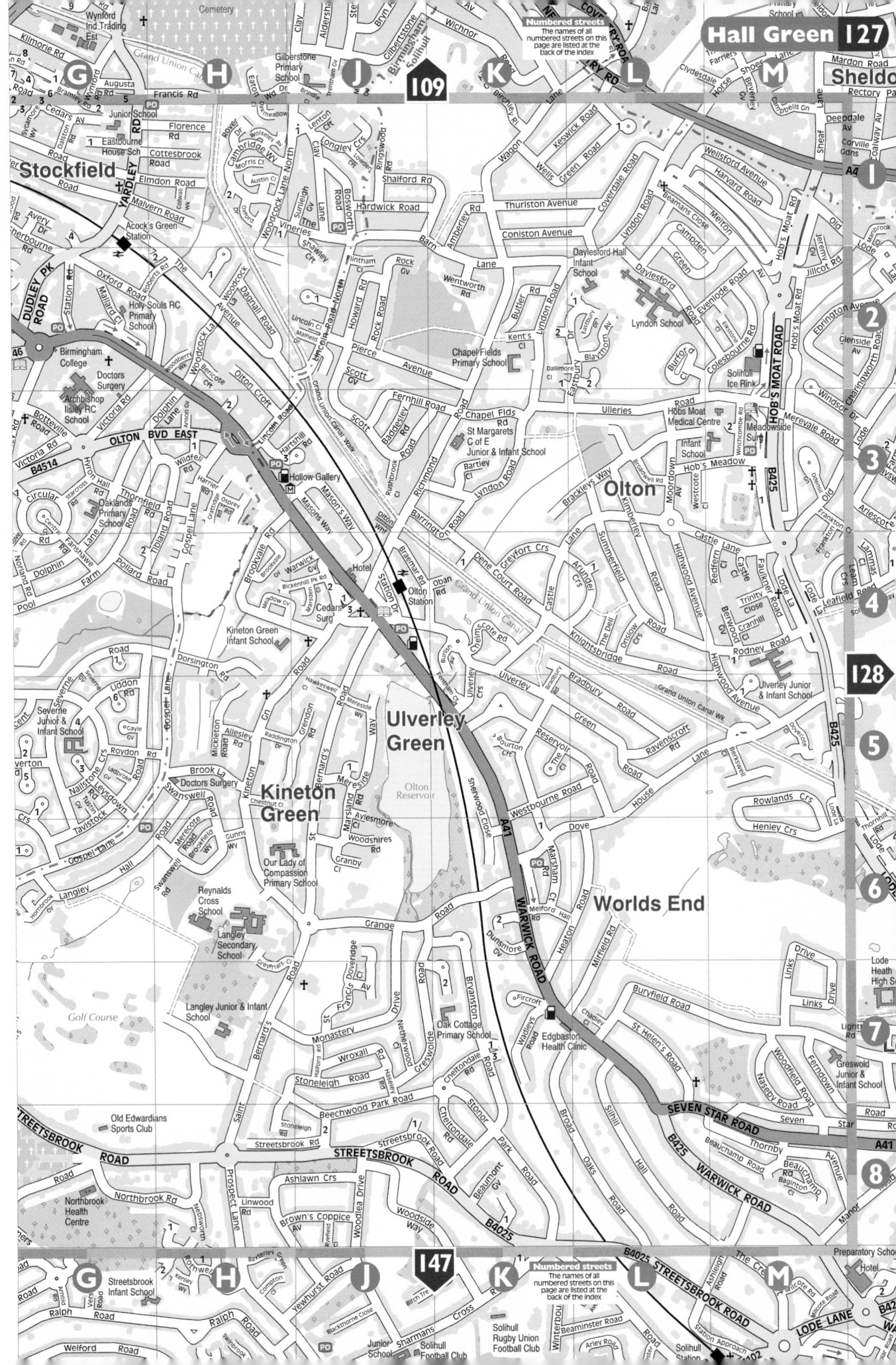

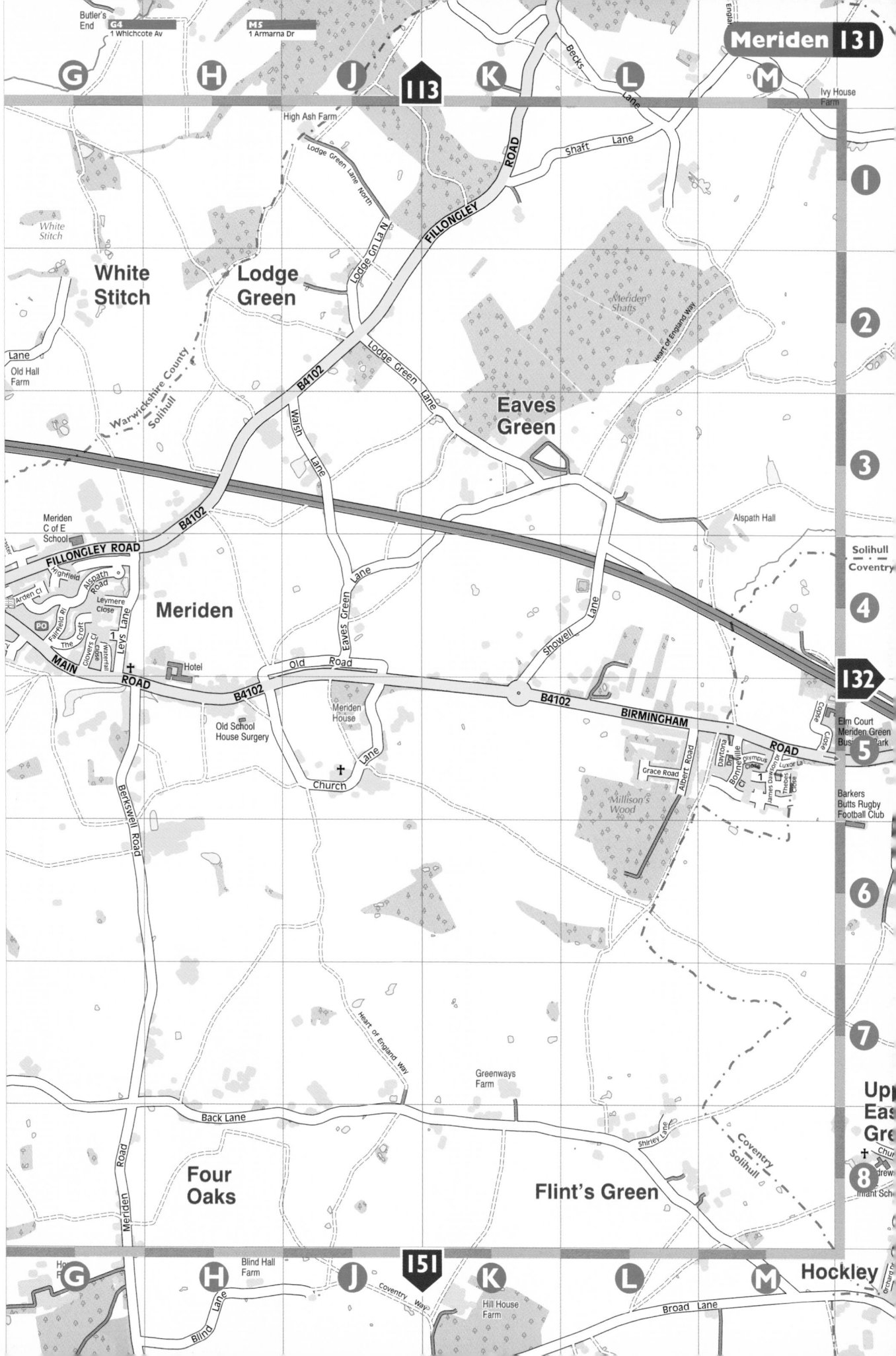

Butler's End G4
1 Whichcote Av

M5
1 Armarna Dr

G   H   J   113   K   L   M

I

Ivy House Farm

High Ash Farm

Lodge Green Lane North

FILLONGLEY ROAD

Shaft Lane

Becks Lane

White Stitch

Lane

Lodge Gn La N

Meriden Shafts

Heart of England Way

2

White Stitch

Lodge Green

B4102

Lodge Green Lane

Walsh Lane

Eaves Green

Warwickshire County
Solihull

Lane
Old Hall Farm

Alspath Hall

3

Solihull
Coventry

4

Meriden C of E School

FILLONGLEY ROAD

Highfield

Alspath Road

Arden Cl

Leymere Close

Fairfield Ri

Oliver's Cl

The Croft

Waterfall Close

Leys Lane

Meriden

Eaves Green Lane

Showell Lane

Lane

PO

Hotel

132

Elm Court
Meriden Green
Business Park

MAIN   ROAD   B4102   Old   Road

Church Lane

Meriden House

Old School House Surgery

B4102   BIRMINGHAM   ROAD

Copse Close

Daytona Dr

Bonneville Cl

Olympus Close

James Dawson Dr

Thebes Cl

Luxor La

Grace Road   1

Albert Road

5

Barkers Butts Rugby Football Club

Berkswell Road

Millison's Wood

6

Heart of England Way

7

Greenways Farm

Up
Eas
Gre

8

Back Lane

Four Oaks

Meriden   Road

Shirley Lane

Coventry
Solihull

Flint's Green

mant Sch

G   H   151   J   K   L   M   **Hockley**

Blind Hall Farm

Blind   Lane

Coventry Way

Hill House Farm

Broad   Lane

Orchard

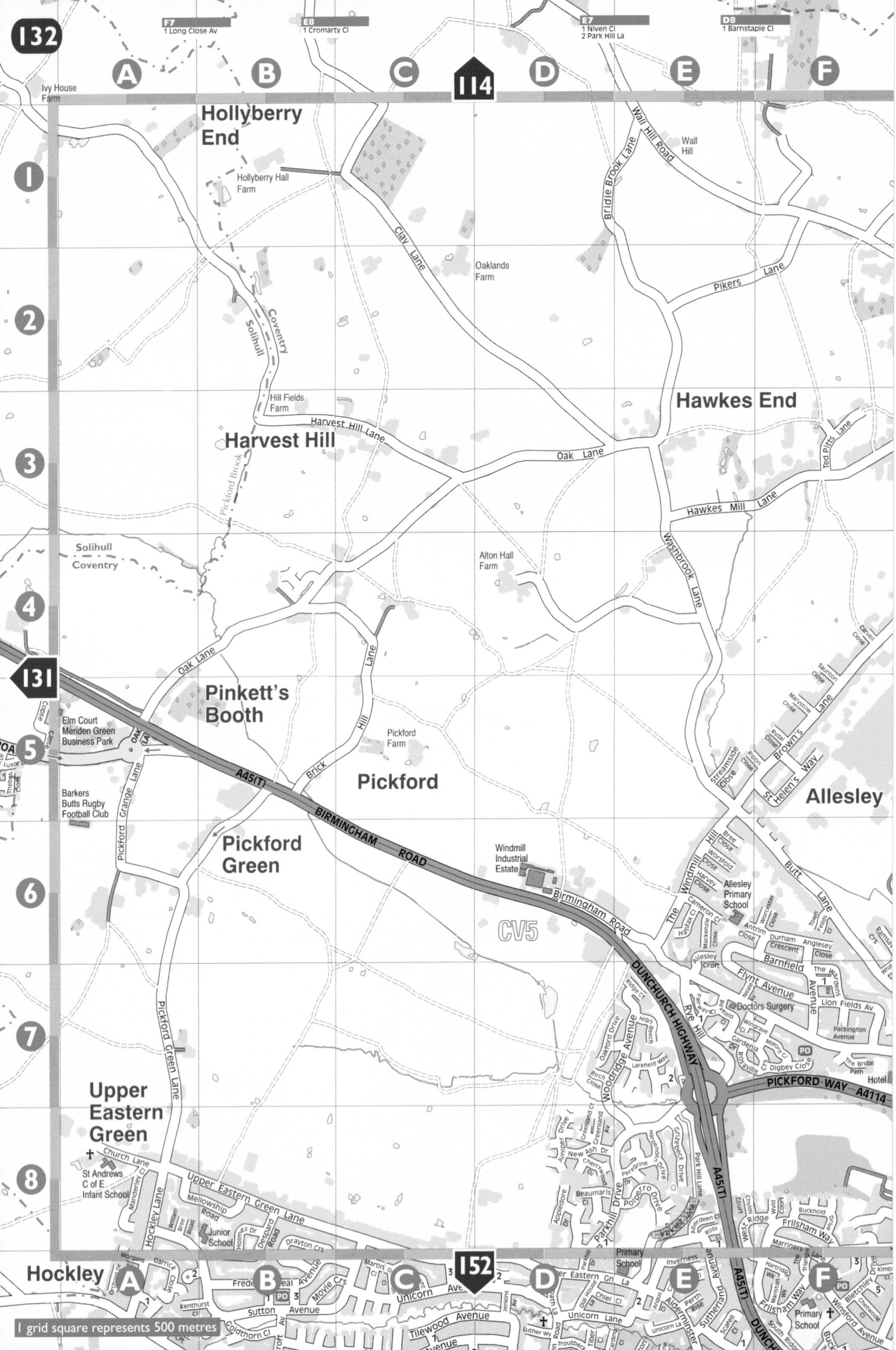

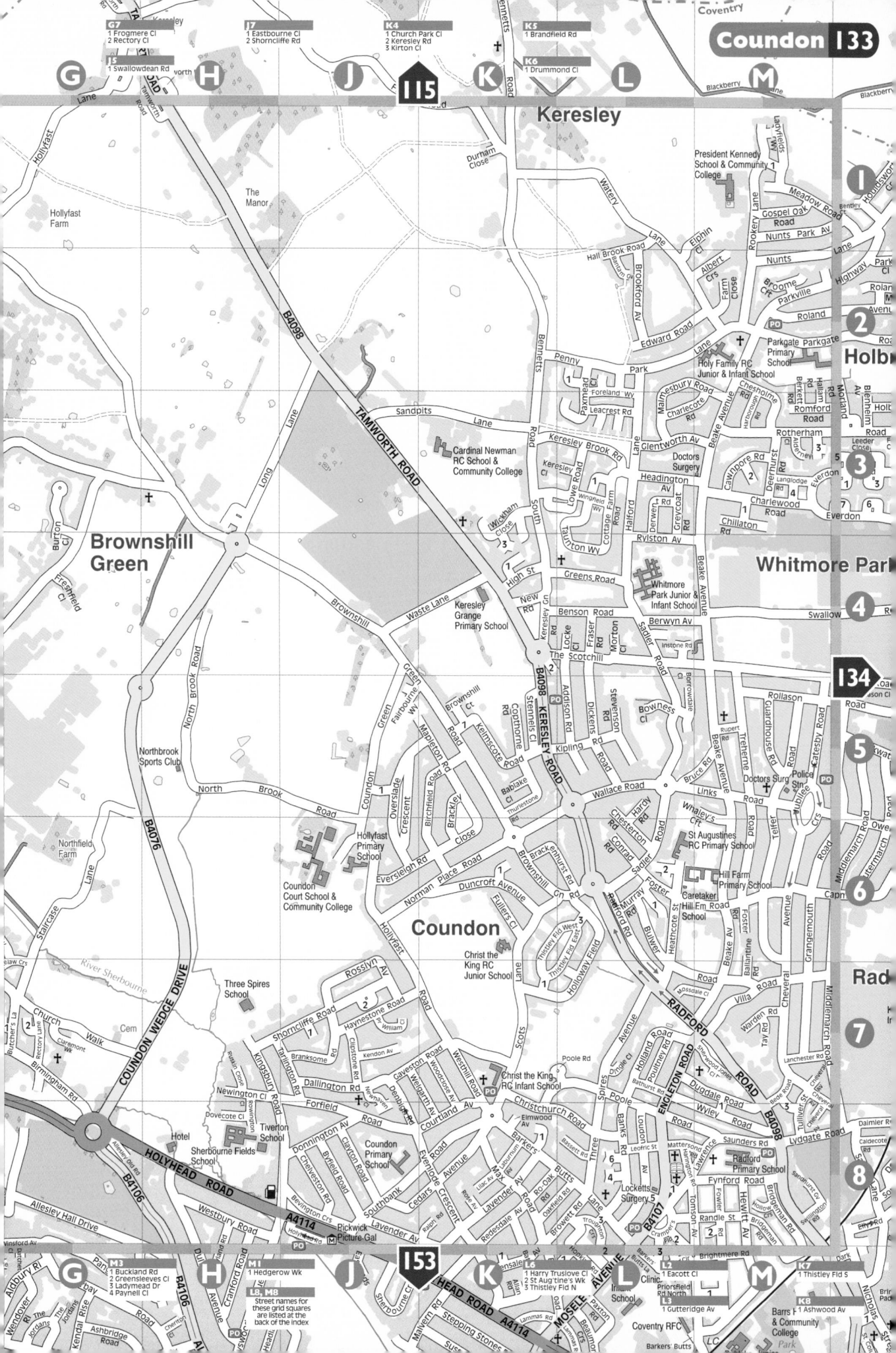

G   H   J   115   K   L   M

I1

Coventry

Keresley

President Kennedy
School & Community
College

Hollyfast
Farm

The Manor

Ladyfields

Meadow Road

Houldsworth

Bendley

Gospel Oak
Road

Nuts Park Av

Holb

Brownshill
Green

Cardinal Newman
RC School &
Community College

Keresley
Grange
Primary School

Whitmore
Park Junior &
Infant School

Whitmore Park

134

Northbrook
Sports Club

Hollyfast
Primary
School

Coundon
Court School &
Community College

Coundon

St Augustines
RC Primary School

Hill Farm
Primary School

Rad

River Sherbourne

Three Spires
School

Christ the
King RC
Junior School

RADFORD

Radford
Primary School

Hotel

Sherbourne Fields
School

Tiverton
School

Coundon
Primary
School

Christ the King
RC Infant School

Pickwick
Picture Gal.

HOLYHEAD ROAD

HEAD ROAD A4114

Coventry RFC

Barkers Butts

G   H   J   153   K   L   M

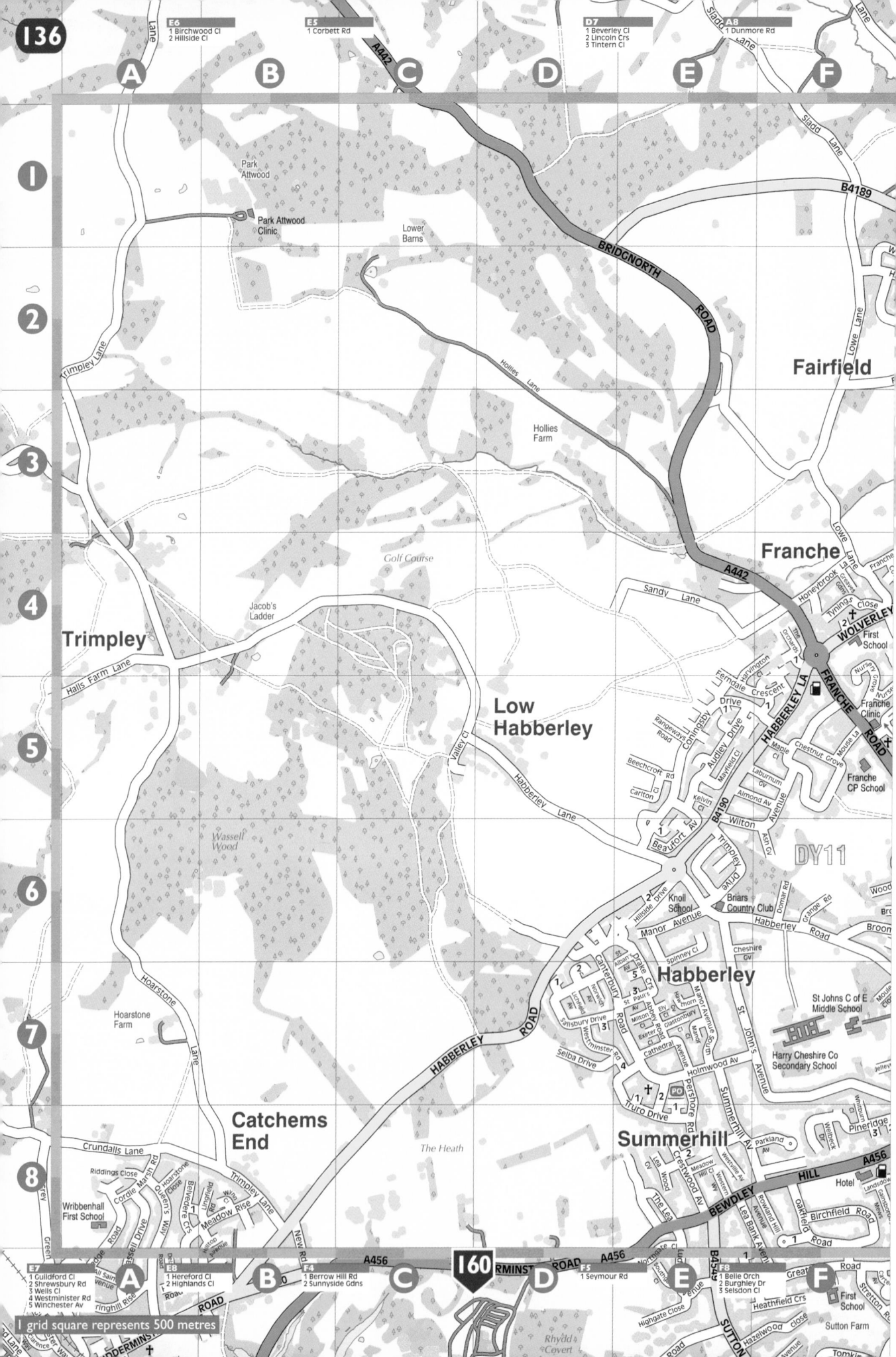

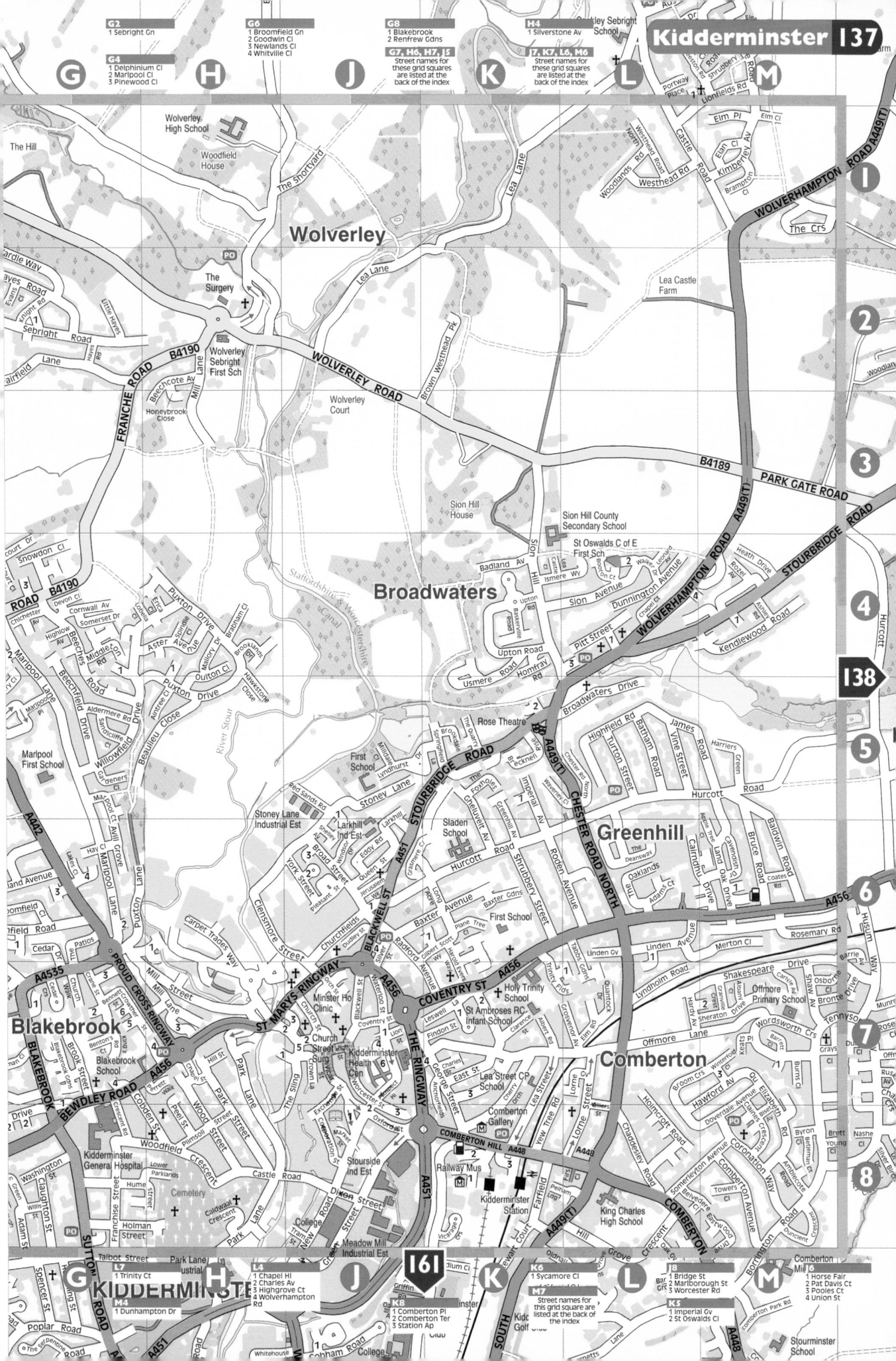

Austcliffe
House Farm

A   B   C   **118**   D   E   F

Five Ways

Whitehouse
Farm

Ismere
House

1

The Crs

OVERHILLTON ROAD A449(T)

Axborough Lane

STOURBRIDGE ROAD

A451

2

Roseberry
Gdns

Clifton Rd

New Rd

Grove

Woodland

Waggon Lane

Waggon Lane

Churchill Lane

Scuthorpe Rd

Wheatmill

Mill Lane

Station

Brookside Way

Elm Dr

3

RK GATE ROAD

A451

STOURBRIDGE ROAD

Woodhouse
Farm

Kennels

Wannerton Road

MILL CT

Forge Lane

PO

137

4

Hurcott Lane

Hurcott Wood

Wannerton
Farm

A456

Swan Cl

Hampshire Lane

Lynwood

The

5

Hurcott

Park
Hall

A456

New Wood Lane

6

BIRMINGHAM ROAD

A456

Deansford Lane

Bissell Wood

Rosemary Rd

Husum Way

Drive

Barrie

Shaw Av

Osborne Cl

Bronte Drive

Munro Cl

Tennyson

Rosetti Cl

Little Dunclent
Farm

7

School

Dunbar Way

Grays Cl

Offmore Farm
Close

Offmore
Farm

Ruskin Av

Chaucer Crs

Burns Cl

Byron Cl

Bedeme

Nashe Cl

Brett
Young
Cl

Prior Cl

Elmdale

Silver Birch

8

Ashdene
Close

Mount
Segg

Mearse
Farm

Road

Dunclent Crescent

A   B   C   **162**   D   E   F

Comberton
Middle Sch

1 grid square represents 500 metres

Stourminster
School

Dunclent

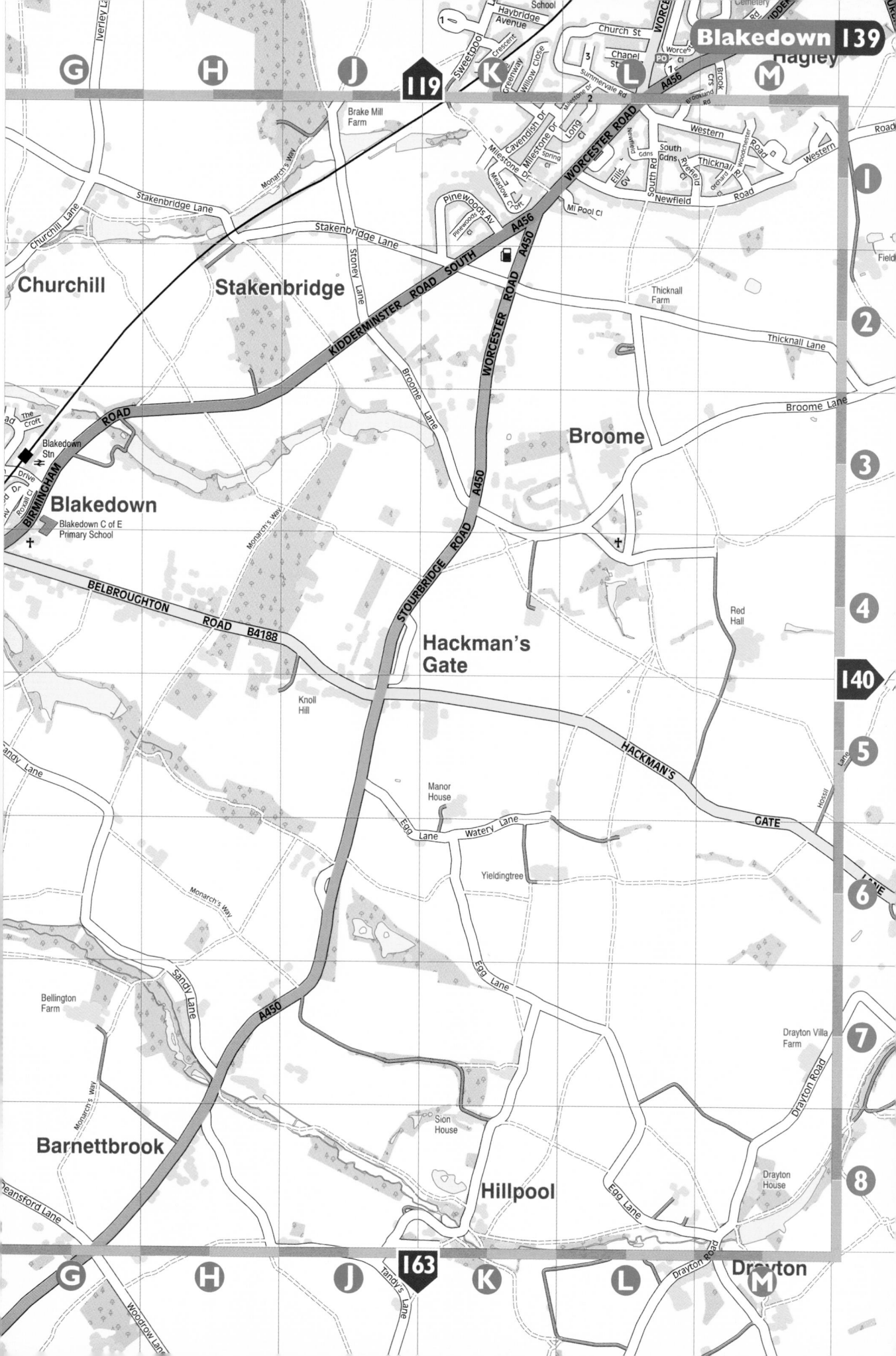

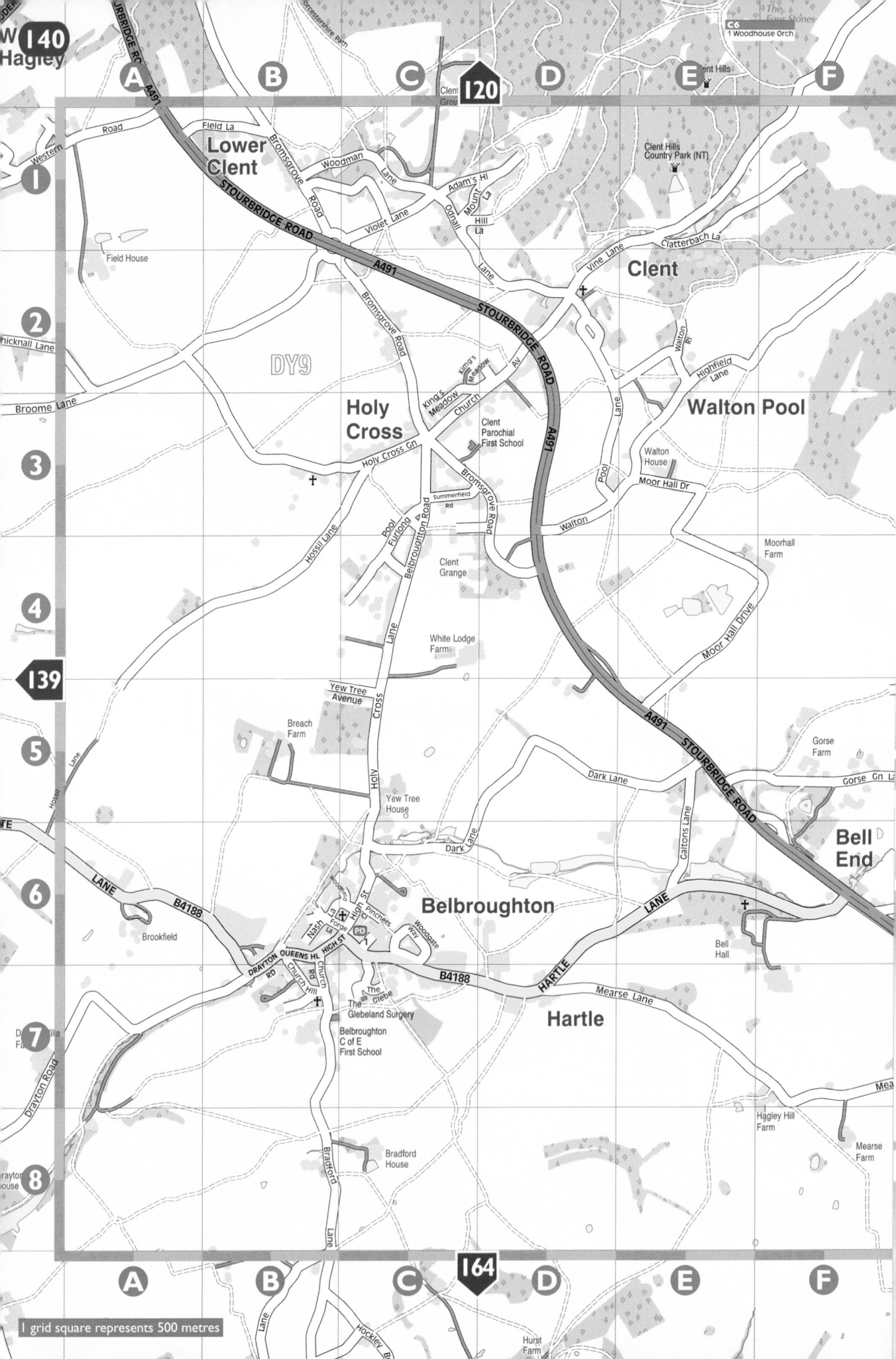

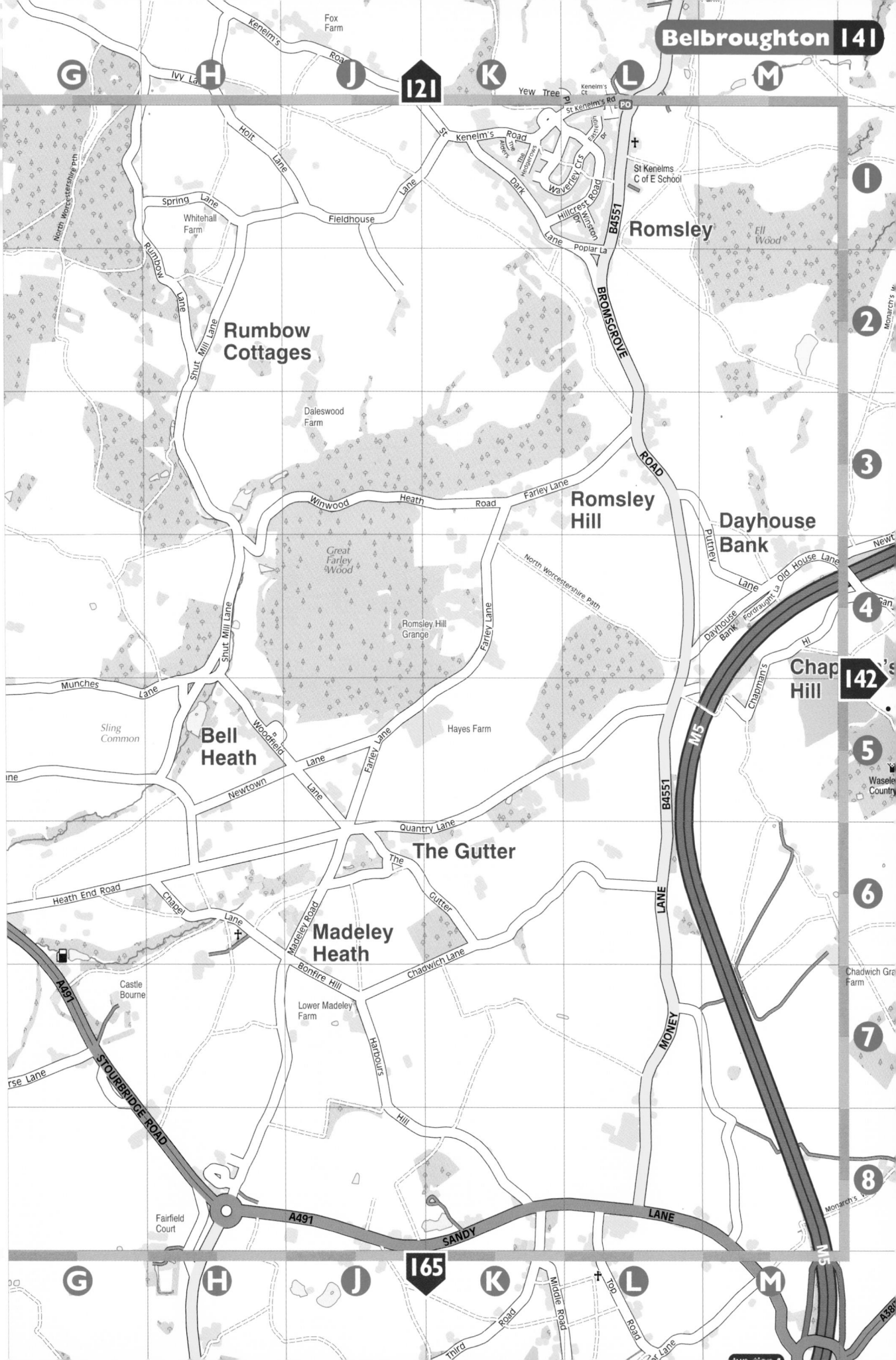

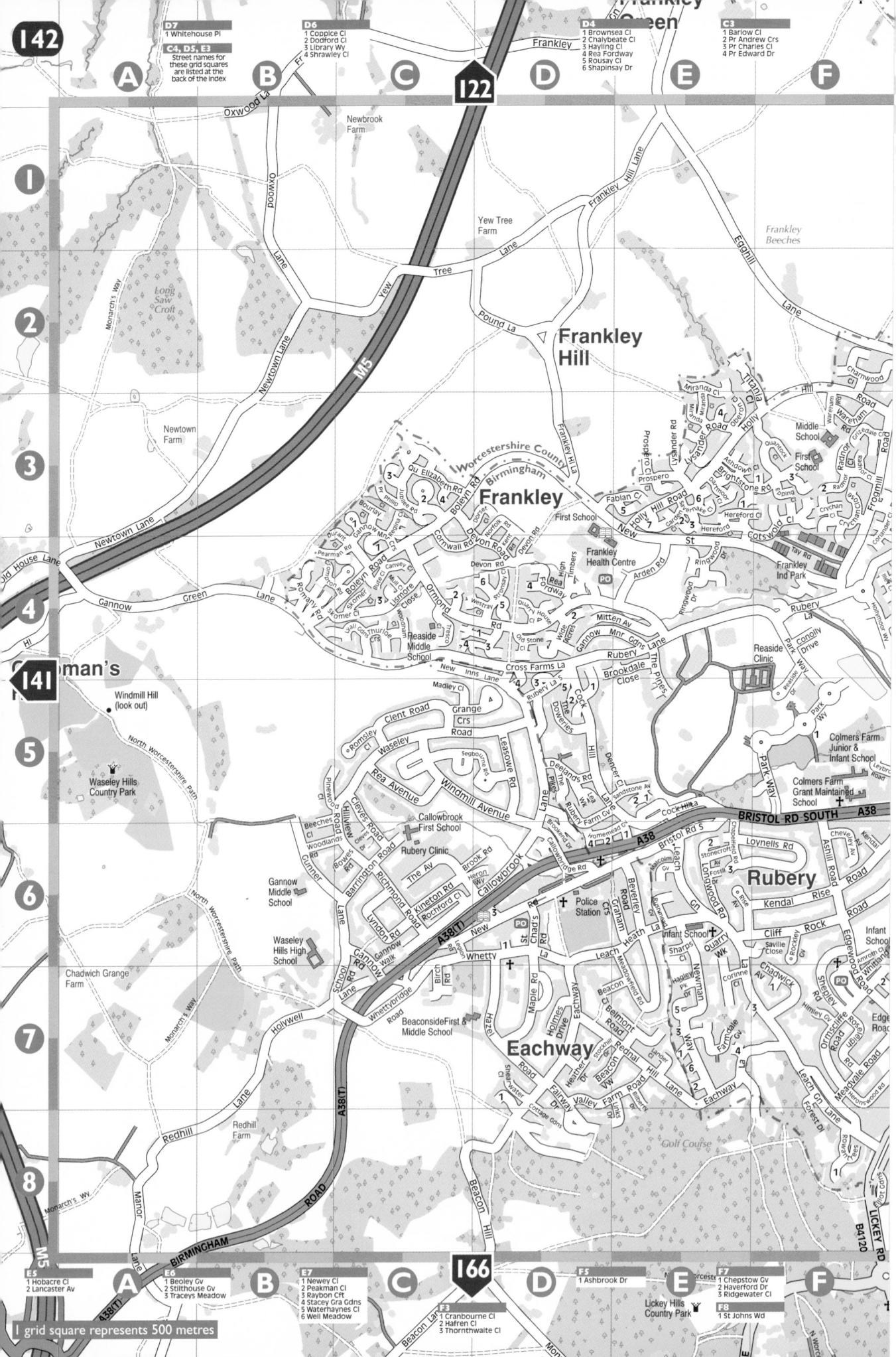

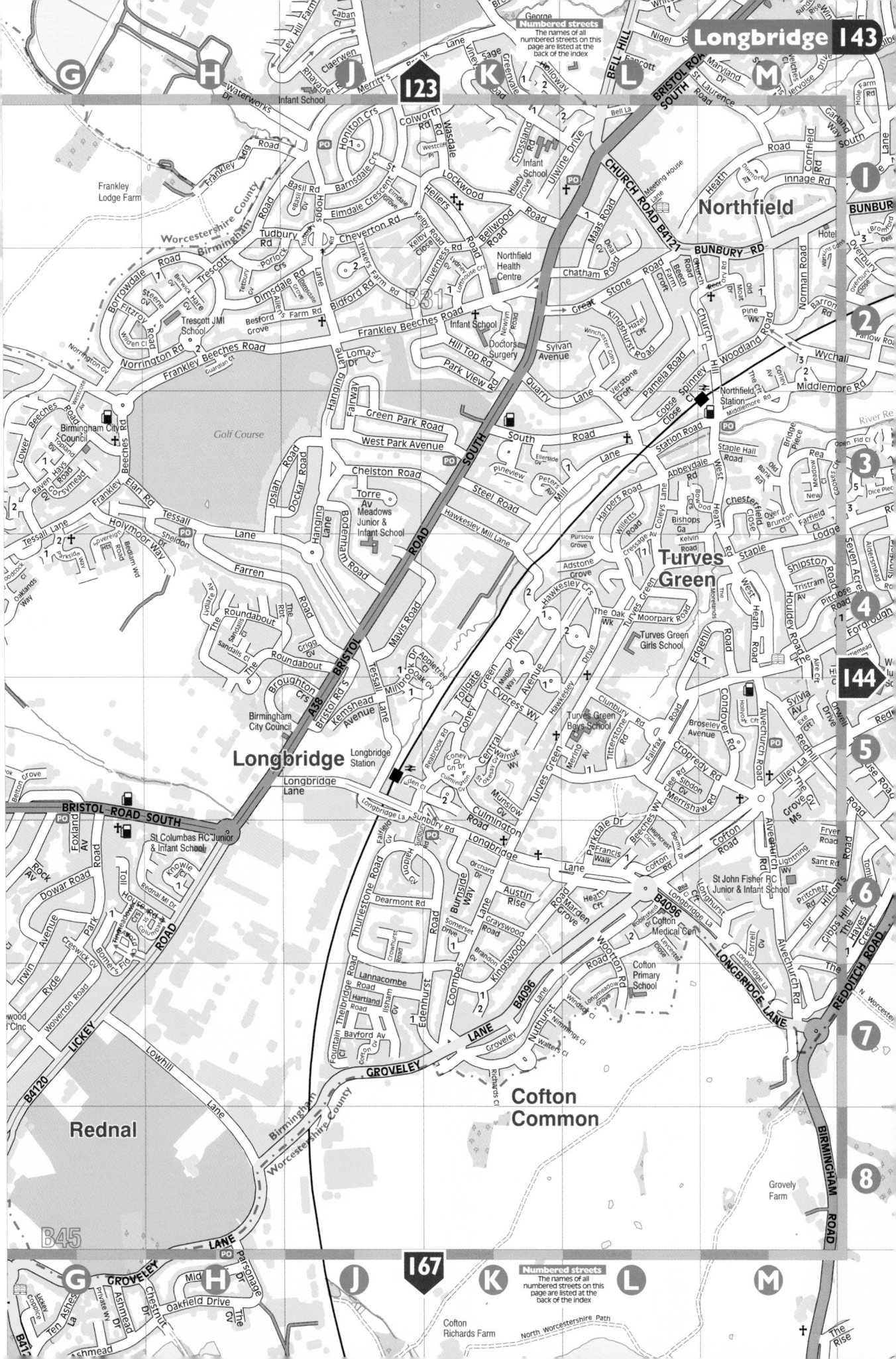

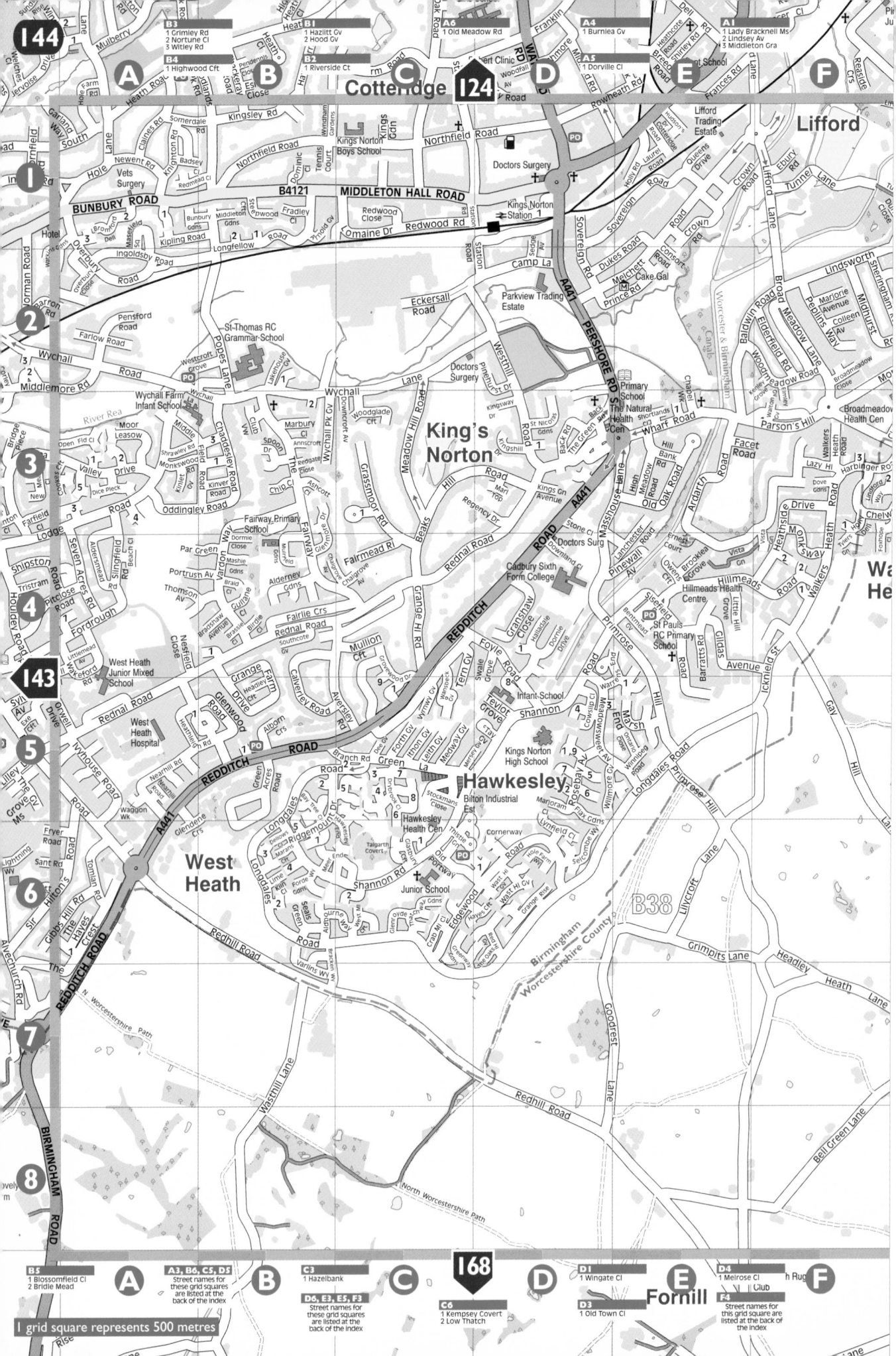

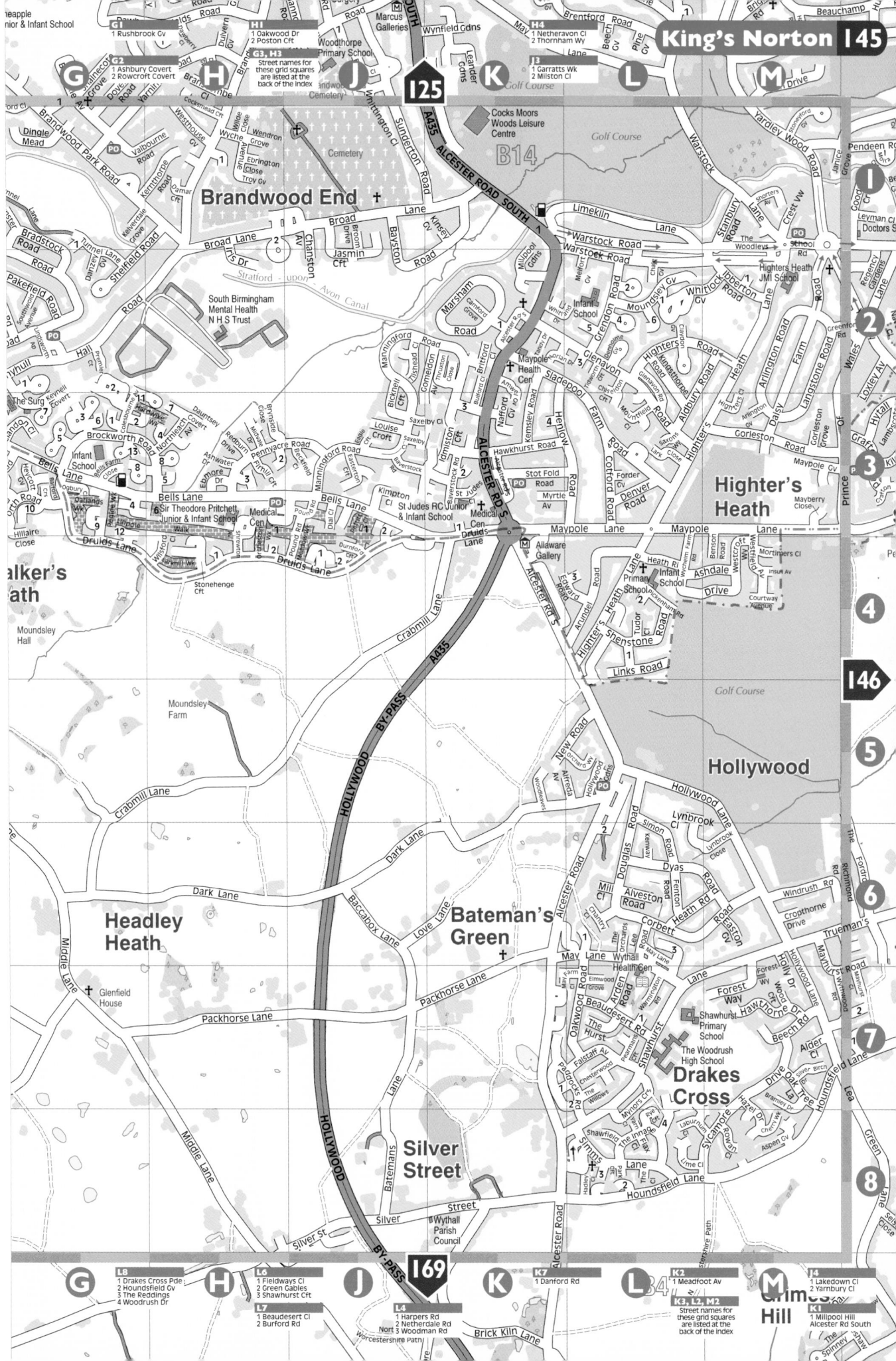

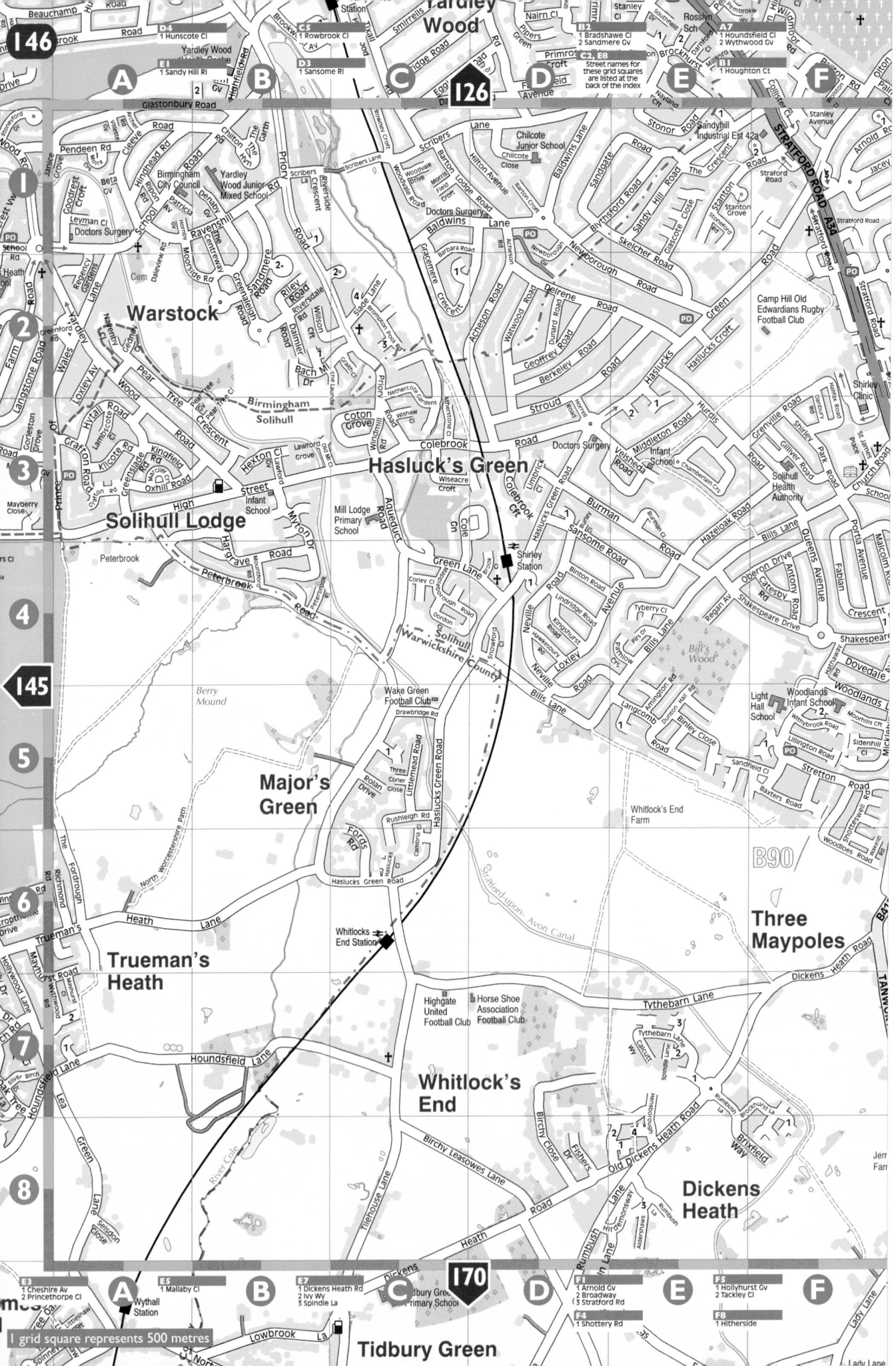

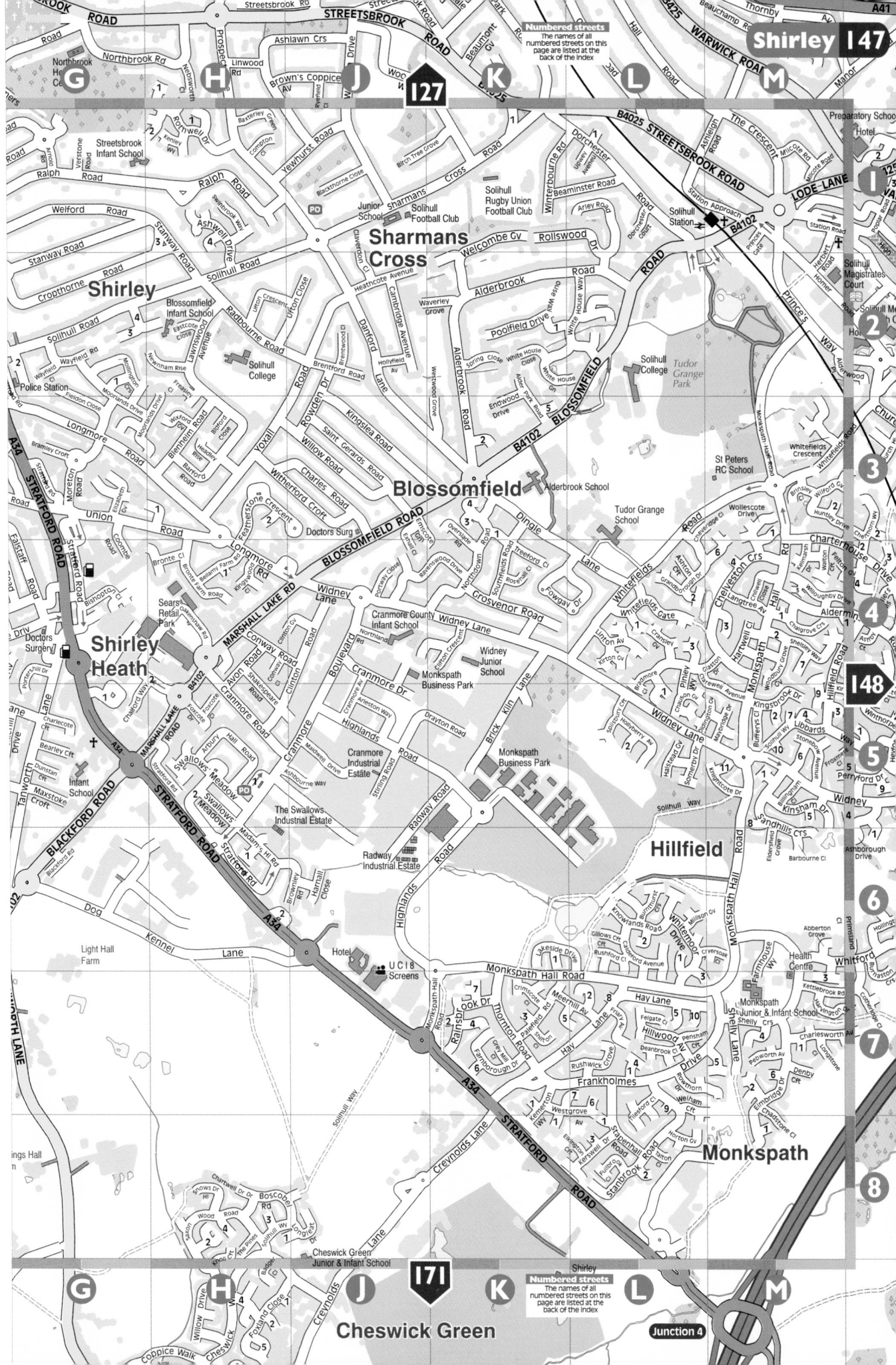

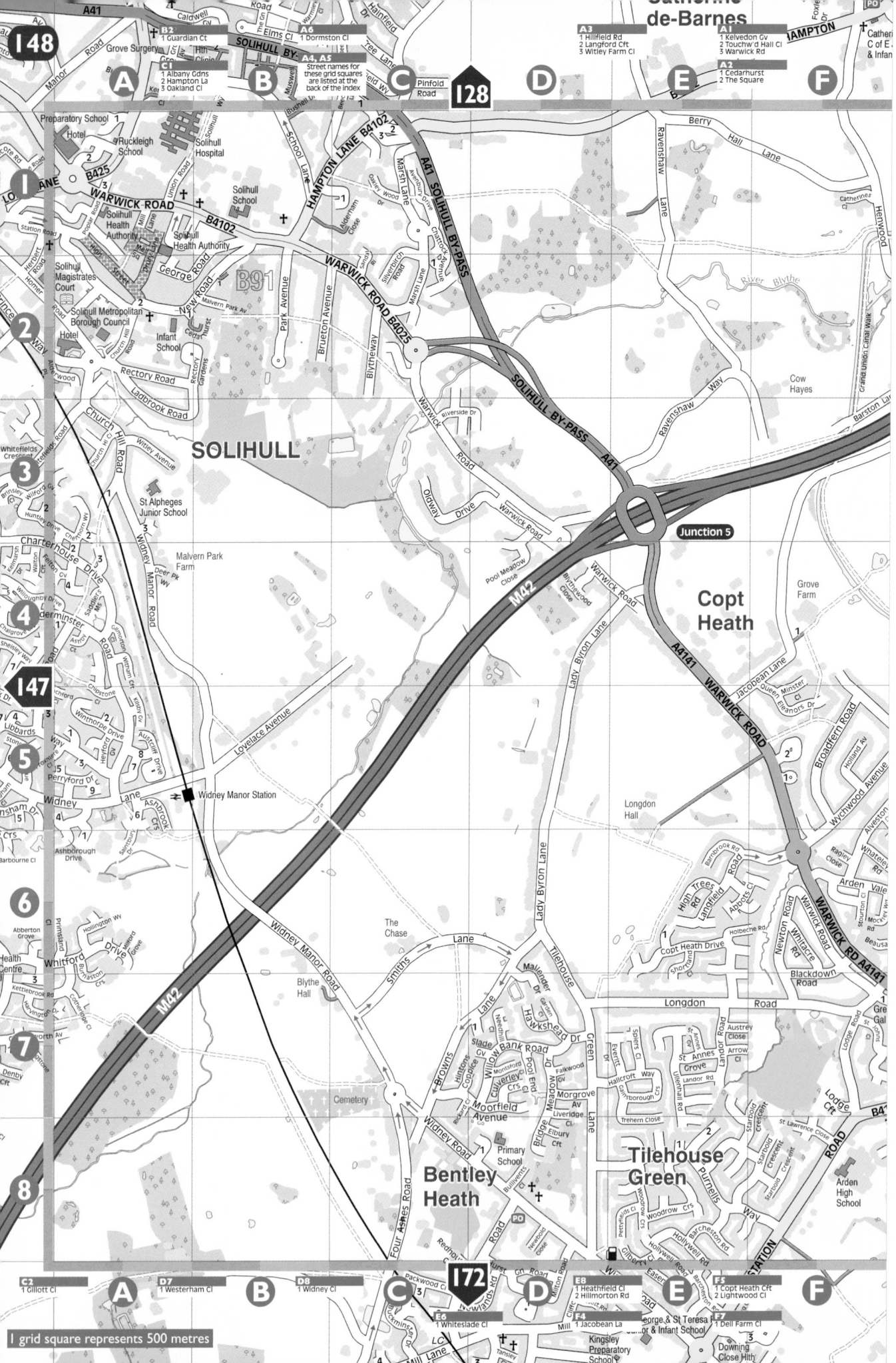

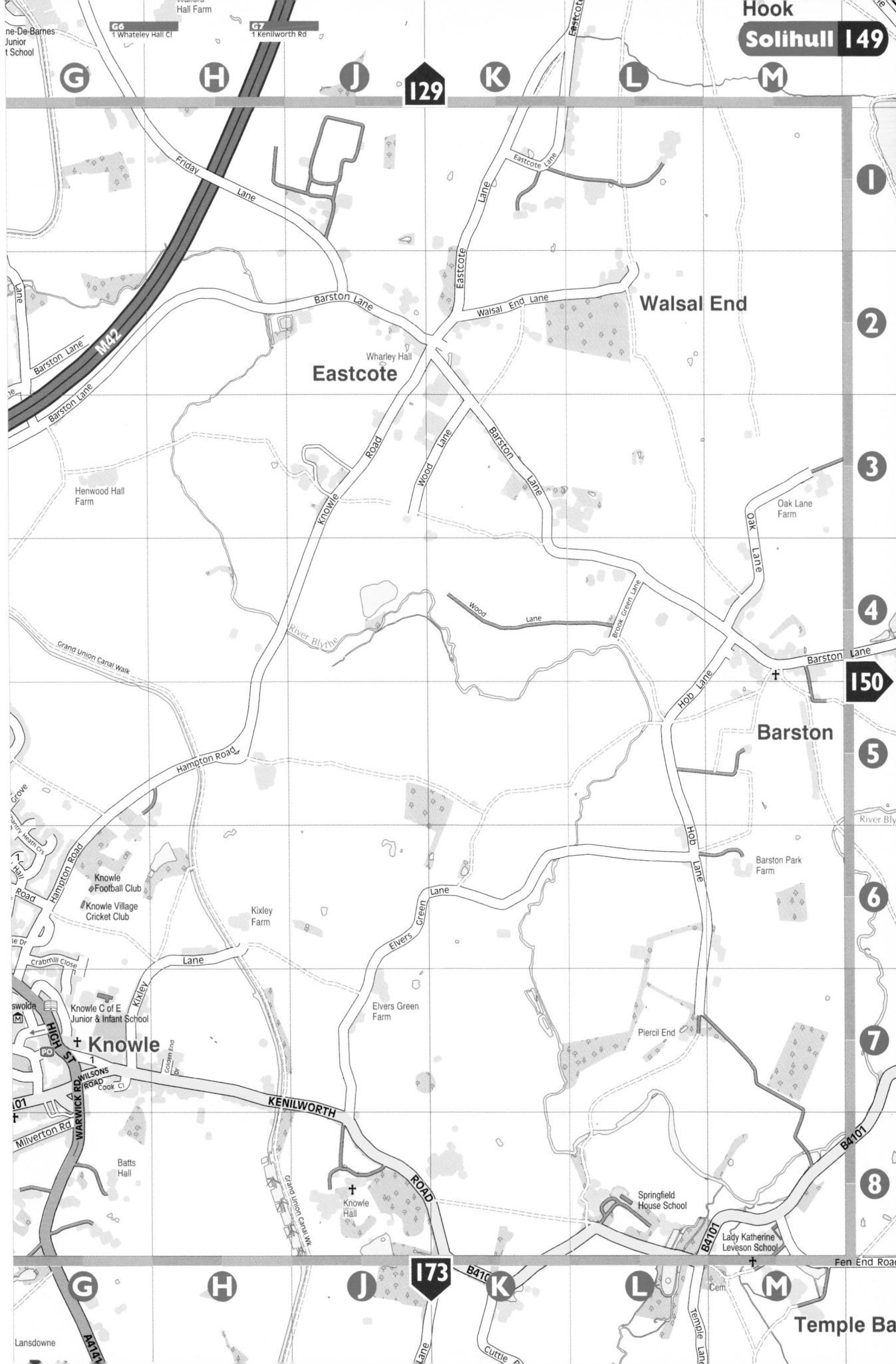

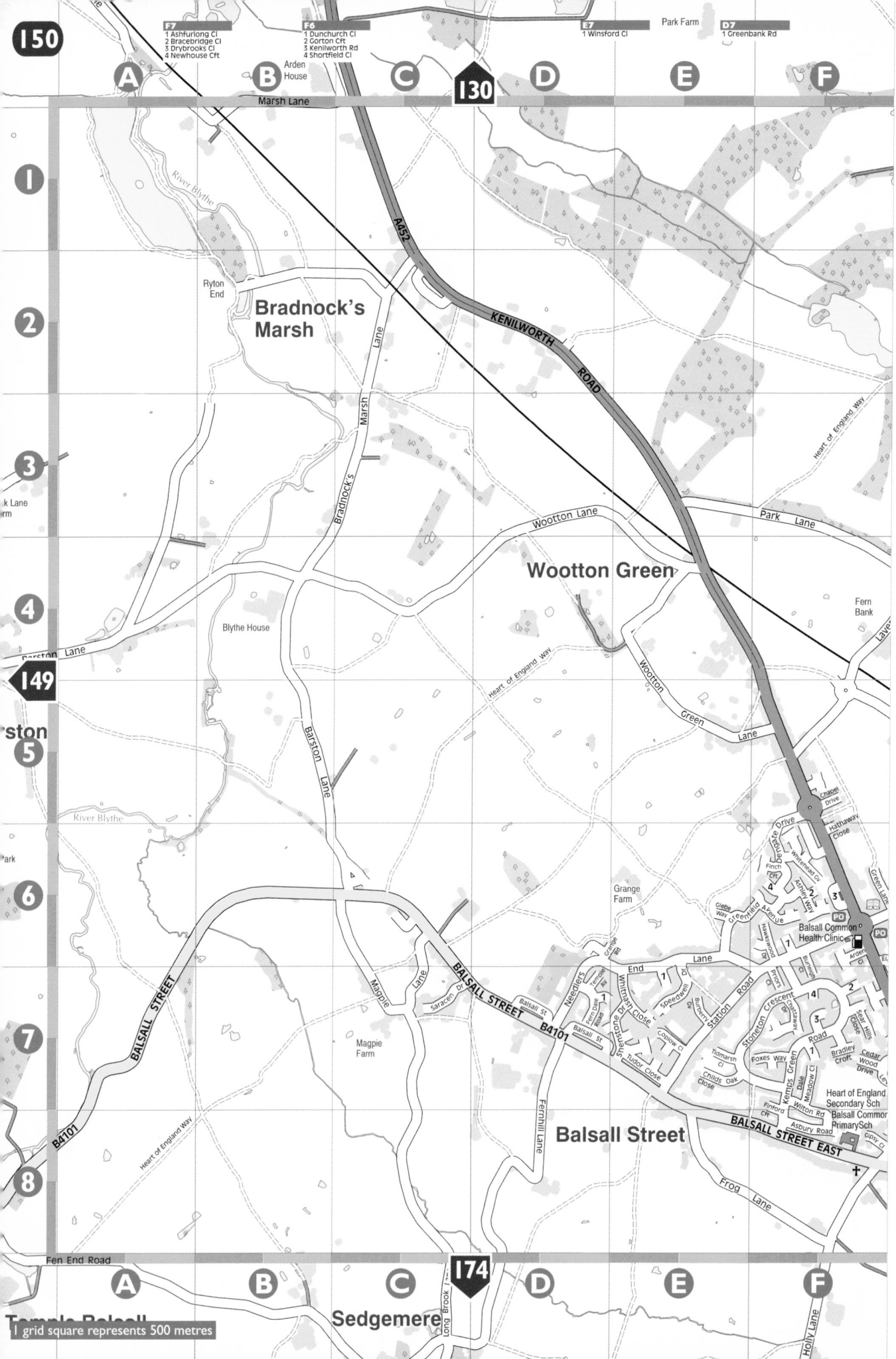

A B C D E F

F7
1 Ashfurlong Cl
2 Bracebridge Cl
3 Drybrooks Cl
4 Newhouse Cft

F6
1 Dunchurch Cl
2 Gorton Cft
3 Kenilworth Rd
4 Shortfield Cl

E7
1 Winsford Cl

Park Farm

D7
1 Greenbank Rd

Arden House

Marsh Lane

1

River Blythe

2

Ryton End

Bradnock's Marsh

3

k Lane rm

4

Blythe House

149

rston

5

River Blythe

6

Grange Farm

Magpie Farm

7

Magpie Lane

8

Fen End Road

A B C D E F

Sedgemere

174

Temple Balsall

Wootton Green

Fern Bank

KENILWORTH ROAD

A452

Wootton Lane

Park Lane

Heart of England Way

Wootton Green Lane

Bradnock's Marsh Lane

Barston Lane

Garston Lane

Heart of England Way

BALSALL STREET

B4101

Saracen Dr

Balsall St

Needlers End Lane

Whitnash Close

Fernhill Lane

Balsall Street

BALSALL STREET EAST

Frog Lane

Heart of England Way

B4101

Chapel Drive

Hathaway Close

Denbigh Drive

Balsall Common Health Clinic

Greenfield Avenue

Station Road

Stoneton Crescent

Heart of England Secondary Sch

Balsall Common Primary Sch

Holly Lane

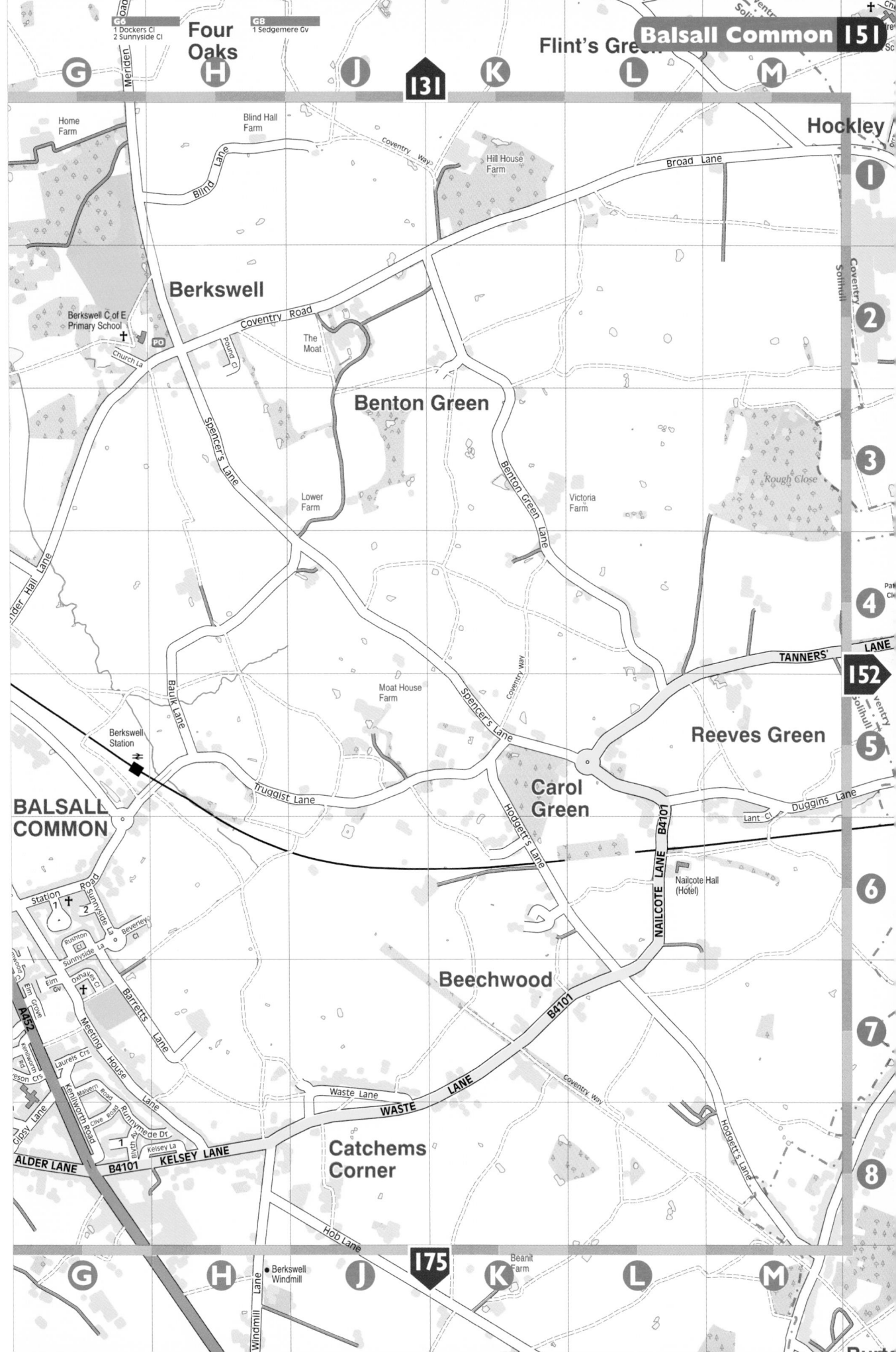

Four Oaks

G6
1 Dockers Cl
2 Sunnyside Cl

G8
1 Sedgemere Gv

G   H   J   **131**   K   L   M

Flint's Green

Hockley

Home Farm

Blind Hall Farm

Coventry Way

Hill House Farm

Broad Lane

1

Coventry

Solihull

Blind Lane

Berkswell

Berkswell C of E Primary School

PO

Church La

Coventry   Road

The Moat

Pound Cl

2

Benton Green

Spencer's Lane

Lower Farm

Benton Green Lane

Victoria Farm

Rough Close

3

Tender Hall Lane

4

Pa
Cle

TANNERS'   LANE

Baulk Lane

Berkswell Station

Moat House Farm

Spencer's Lane

Coventry Way

152

Coventry   Solihull

5

Reeves Green

BALSALL COMMON

Truggist Lane

Carol Green

Hodgett's Lane

B4101

Duggins Lane

Lant Cl

Station Road

Sunnyside La

1   2

Beverley Cl

Rughton Cl

Sunnyside La

Oxhayes

NAILCOTE   LANE

Nailcote Hall (Hotel)

6

Elm Gv

Barretts Lane

Beechwood

B4101

7

A452

Meeting House Lane

Laurels Crs

Kenilworth Road

Malvern Road

Clive Road

Runnymede Dr.

Kelsey La

Waste Lane

WASTE   LANE

Coventry   Way

Hodgett's Lane

Gipsy Lane

ALDER LANE   B4101   KELSEY LANE

Catchems Corner

8

Hob Lane

Beanit Farm

Berkswell Windmill

Windmill Lane

G   H   J   **175**   K   L   M

Burt

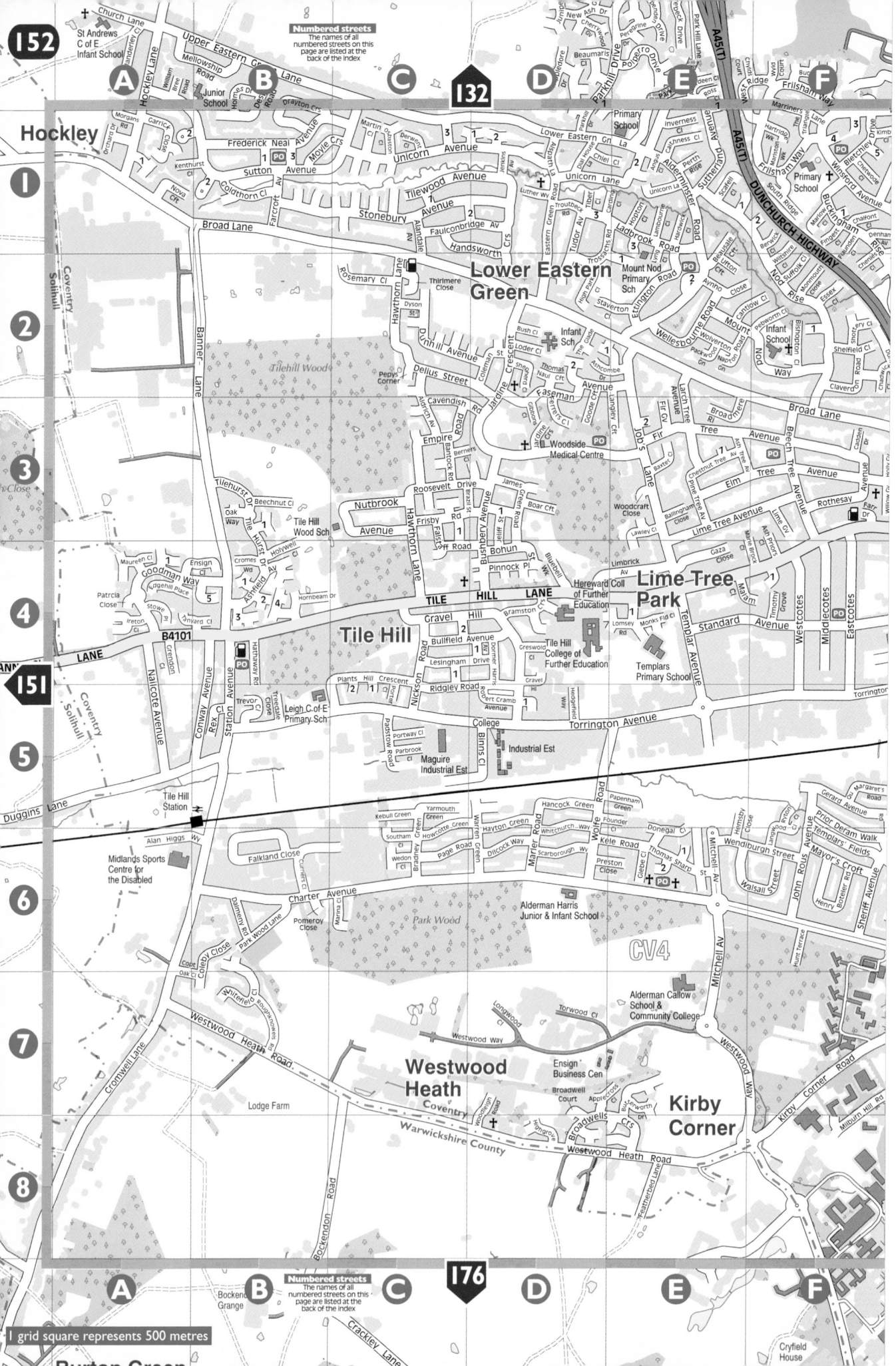

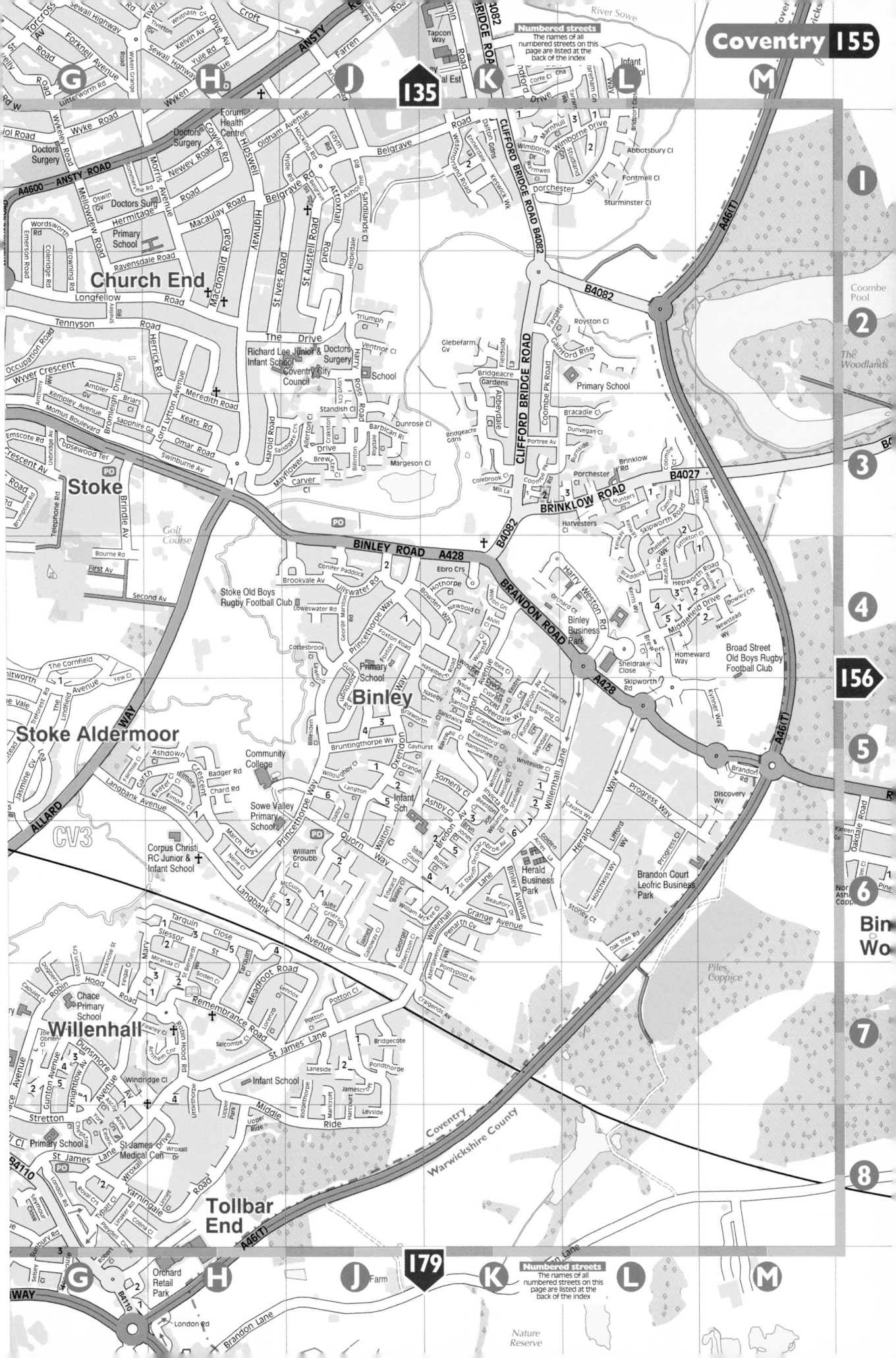

G H J K L M

1 Rooks Nest
The Grange
J2

B4029

I

2

3

4

158

5

6

7

8

B4027 COVENTRY ROAD

The Crescent

The Surgery

Hall Grove

Barr Lane

BROAD STREET

THE CRESCENT

Brinklow C of E First School

Ell Lane

Oxford Canal Walk

Town Thorns

Brinklow Road

Brinklow

Oxford Canal

Green Lane

Skidwith Cl

Great Balance

George

Birch Close

Colledge

1

Coventry Road

Yew Tree Hill

Posters

Potter

Heath Lane

PO

RUGBY RD

Butcher's Cl

Coventry Way

Coventry Way

Brays Cv

RUGBY ROAD

Rugby Road

Cathiron Lane

All Oaks Wood

Brinklow

Heath Lane

Coventry Way

Abbey Hall Farm

B4455

Hill Farm

QUEENS ROAD

Bretford

Kings Newnham Lane

Newnham Hall

Brandon Grange Farm

A428 BRANDON ROAD

Vicarage Farm

A428

River Avon

Avon Ho

Dalton Close

Fitzalan Close

Kings Newnham Road

School Street

Smithy Lane

PO

Holly Gv

Church Lawford

Green

B4455

COVENTRY ROAD

The Grange

Hall Lane

Coronation Road

Church Road

RUGBY ROAD

Marston

G H J K L M

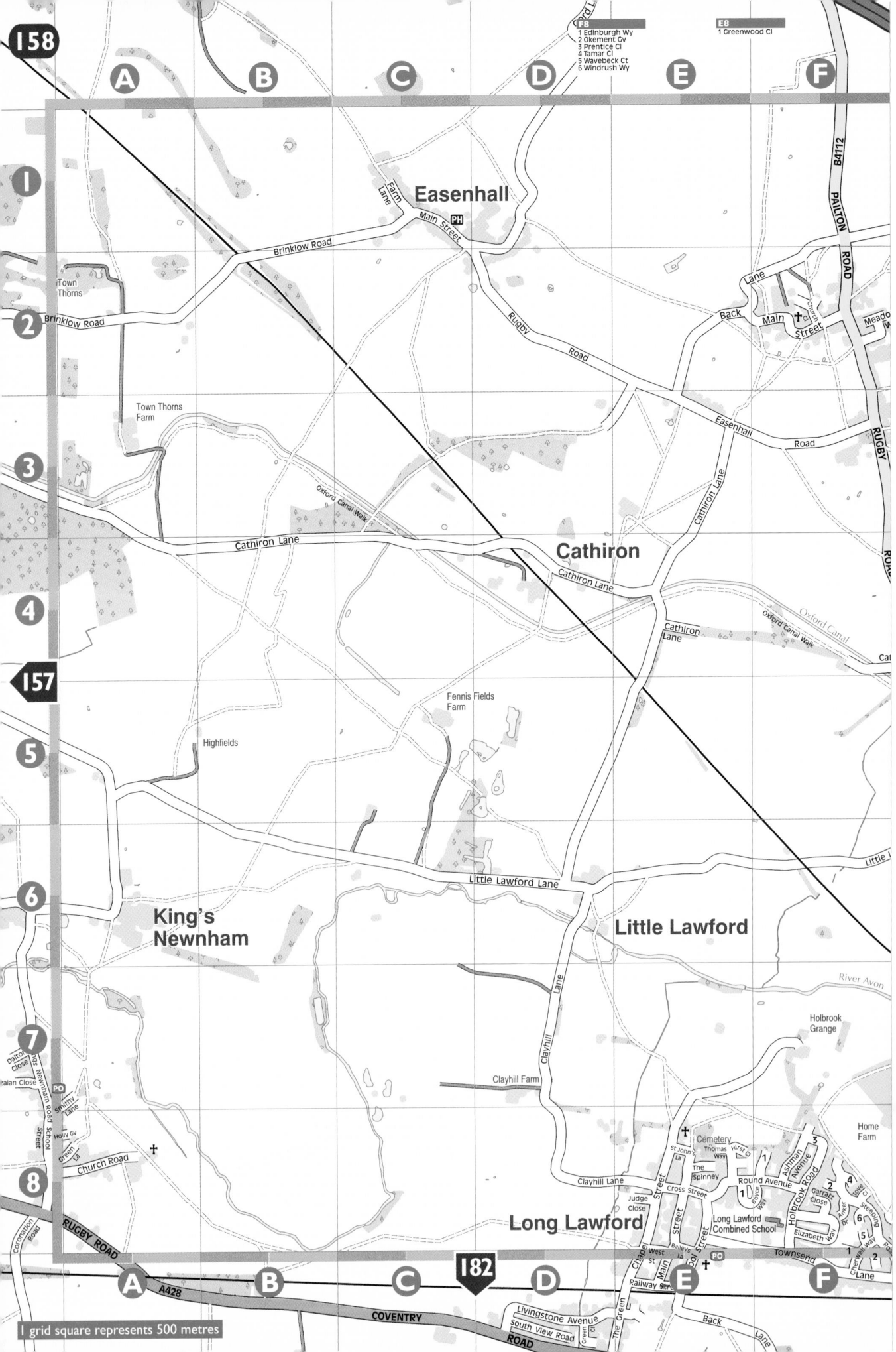

G · H · J · K · L · M

I

2

Junct

3

4

5

6

7

8

Harborough
Magna

Harborough
Parva

Cosford

River Swift

Valley
Drive

Lower
Lodge Farm

Leigh
Road

Haynes Way

Hotel

Brownsover

Oxford Canal Walk

Crawford Lane

B4112 HARBOROUGH ROAD

MAIN STREET

Penkine

Almond
GV

PO

Newbold Leisure
Centre

Newbold
FC

Parkfield Road

Newbold Road

Grange Road

Meadow Road

Lea Crescent

NEWBOLD ROAD

Brownsover

Pamcot

Avonmere

Egerton Cl

Norman

Allesley
Road

Cotterell Road

Morris Cl

Yates Avenue

Fosterd Road

Newbold Riverside
Primary

**Newbold
on Avon**

B4112

Haetams Way

Empetor Way

Glebe Farm Rd

Tiber
Way

Consul

Midland
Trading
Estate

Road

Pretorian
Way

Avenue

Benman

Chariot

Sparta Close

Consul Road

Forum

Drive

Old Leicester Road

Midland
Trading
Estate

Midland Trading Estate

Elliots Field
Retail Park

Hotel

Picnic
Area

Oxford Canal Path

Boughton
Road
Industrial
Estate

Thomson Cl

River Avon

LEICESTER ROAD

A426

Permian Close

Boughton Road

A426

Hunters Lane

Orchard
Business Park

Woodside

Park

NEWBOLD ROAD

Wood Street

Worcester
St

Essex St

Lancaster Road

Princes St

Hill St

K6
1 Quarry Cl
2 Robotham Rd

PO

Terrace
Industrial
Estate

Sandown

Eskdale

Grize

Copeland

Parker

Matlock Cl

Rose

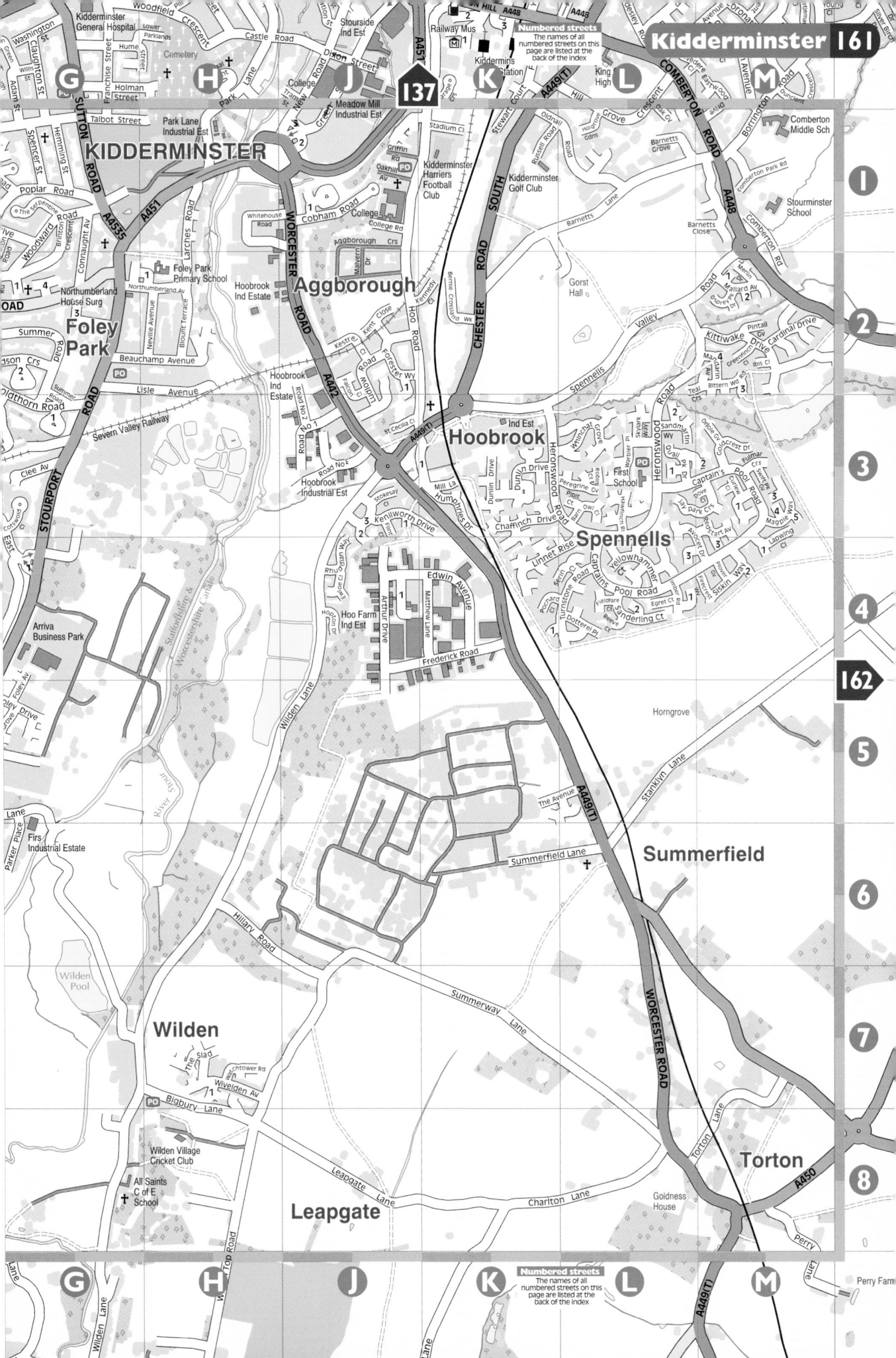

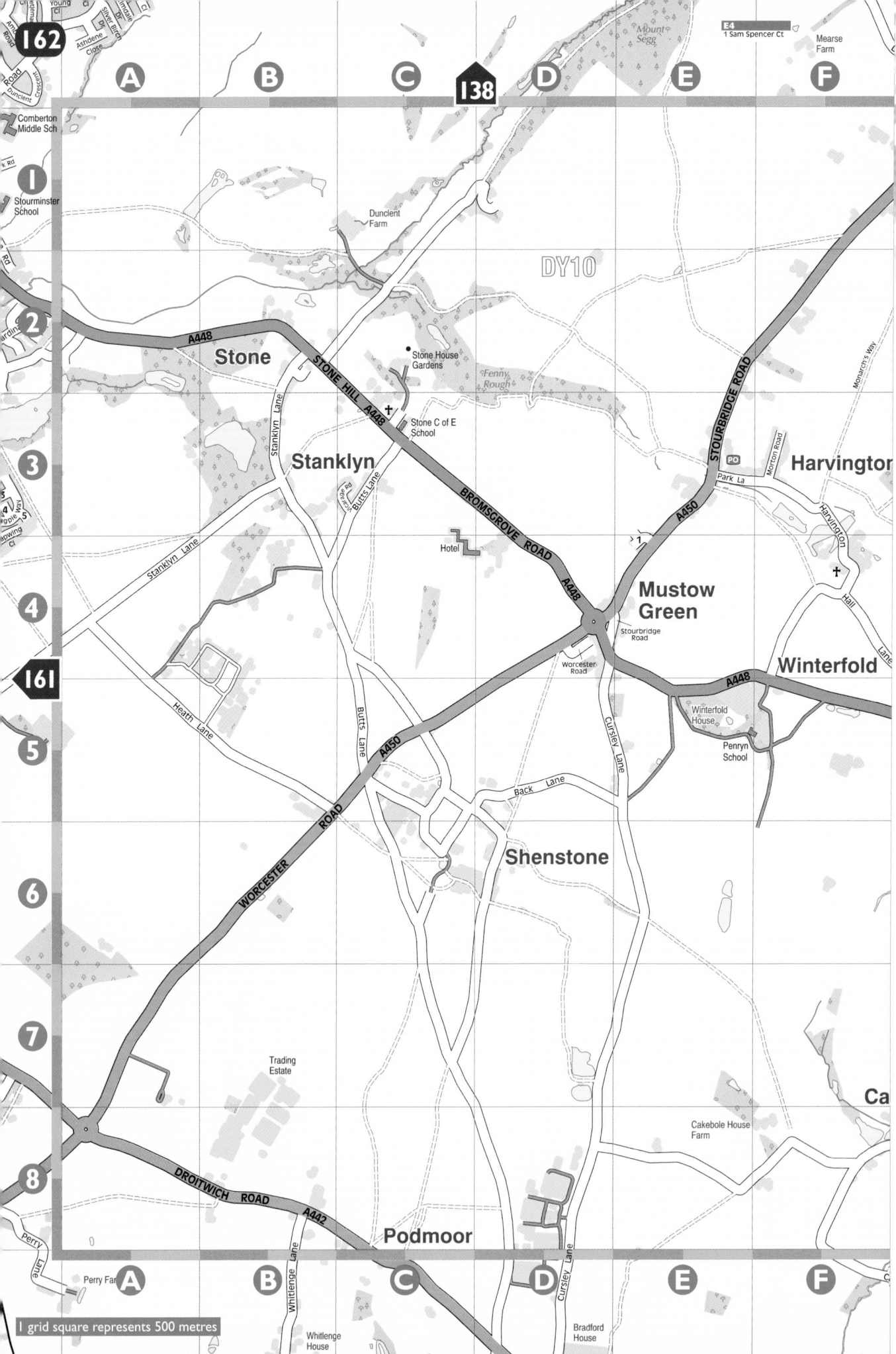

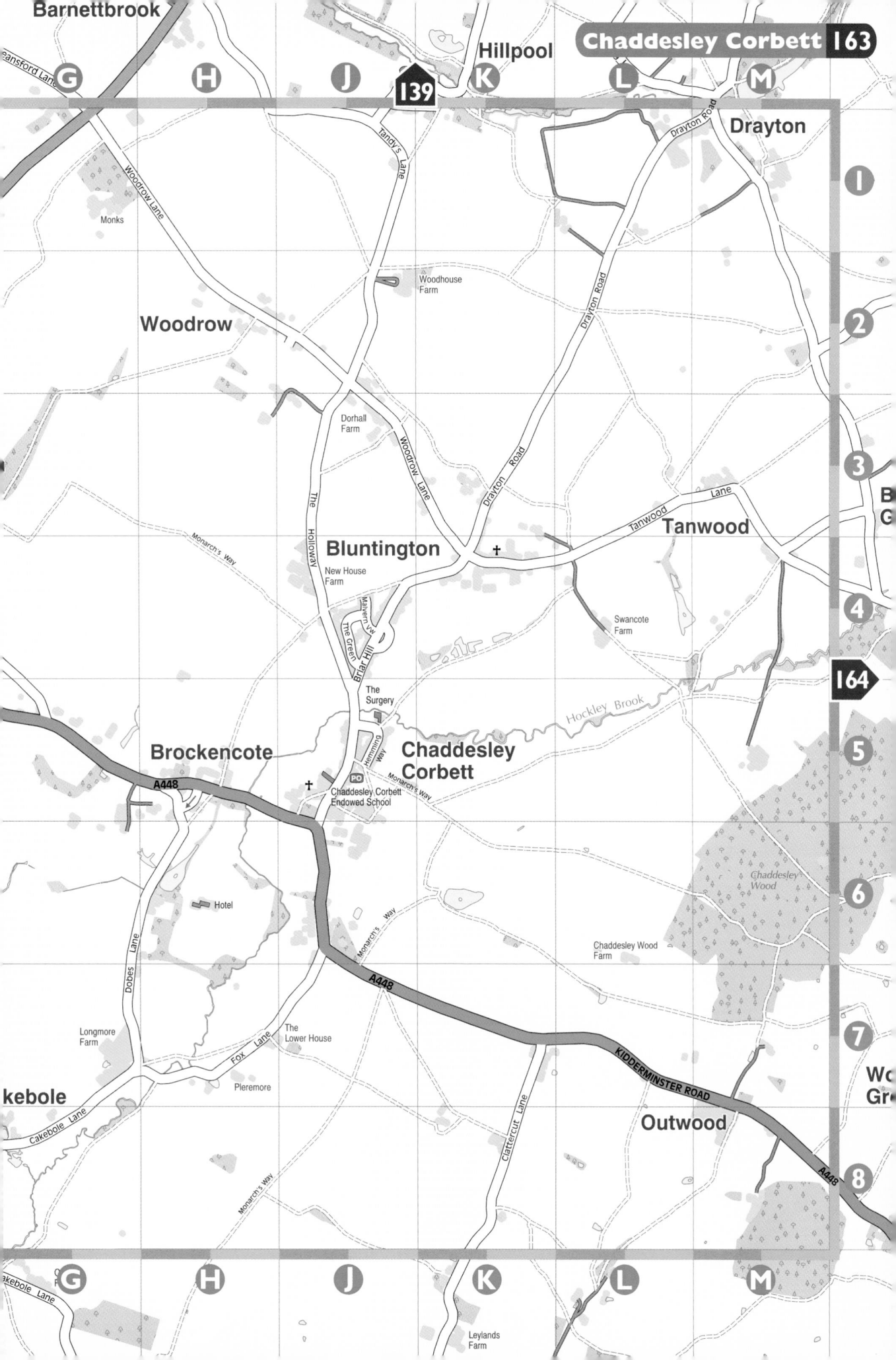

Barnettbrook

G H J **139** K L M

Hillpool

Drayton

1

Woodrow Lane

Monks

2

Woodhouse Farm

Woodrow

Drayton Road

Tandy's Lane

3

B G

Dorhall Farm

Woodrow Lane

Tanwood Lane

Tanwood

The Holloway

Bluntington

Drayton Road

✝

New House Farm

Swancote Farm

4

Malvern Vw

Monarch's Way

The Green

Brien Hill

164

The Surgery

Hockley Brook

5

Brockencote

Hemming Way

Chaddesley Corbett

PO

✝

Chaddesley Corbett Endowed School

Monarch's Way

Chaddesley Wood

A448

Hotel

Dobes Lane

Monarch's Way

6

Chaddesley Wood Farm

Longmore Farm

The Lower House

A448

7

Fox Lane

Pleremore

KIDDERMINSTER ROAD

Wo Gr

kebole

Cakebole Lane

Clattercut Lane

Outwood

A448

8

Monarch's Way

G H J K L M

Leylands Farm

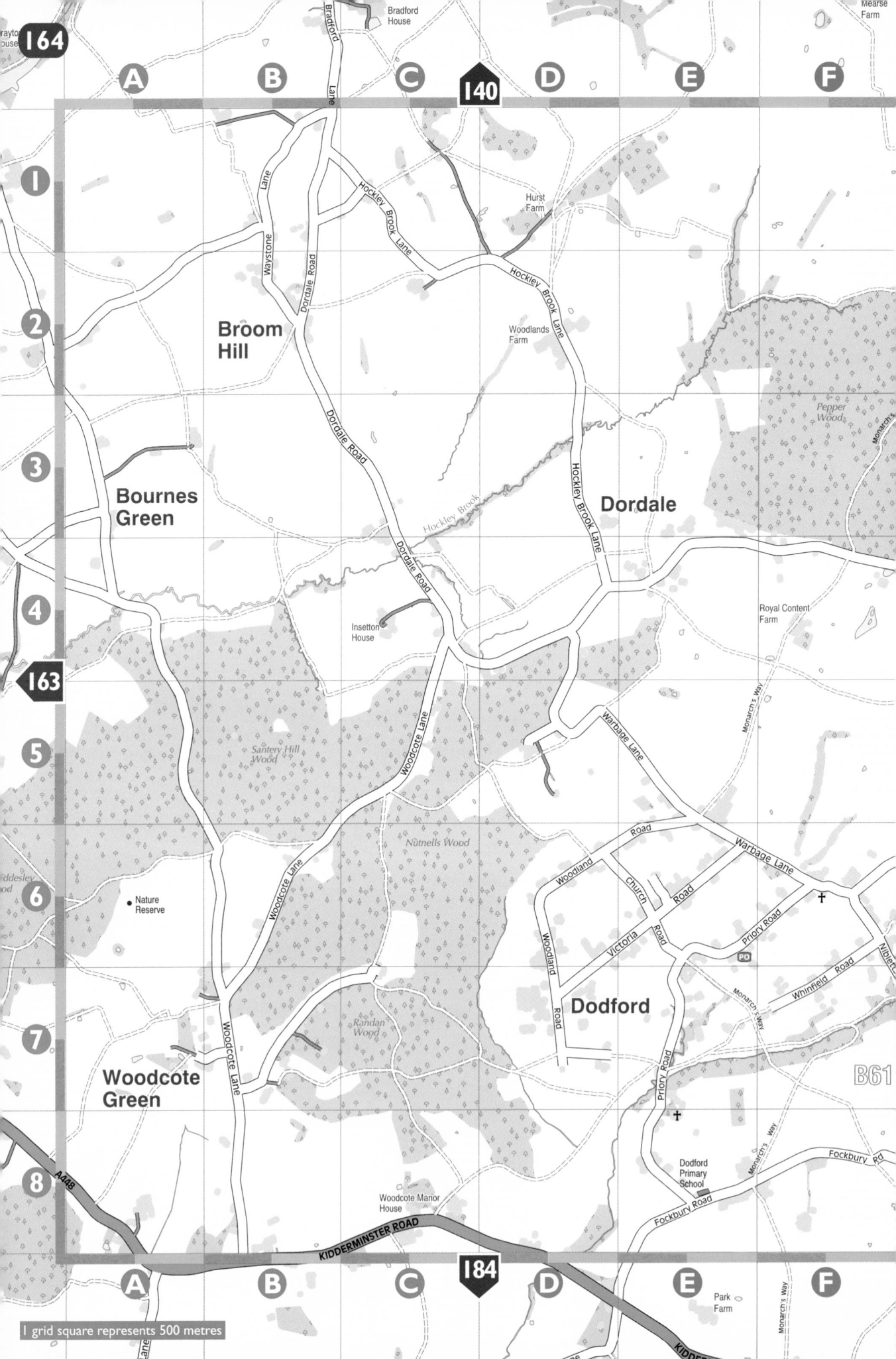

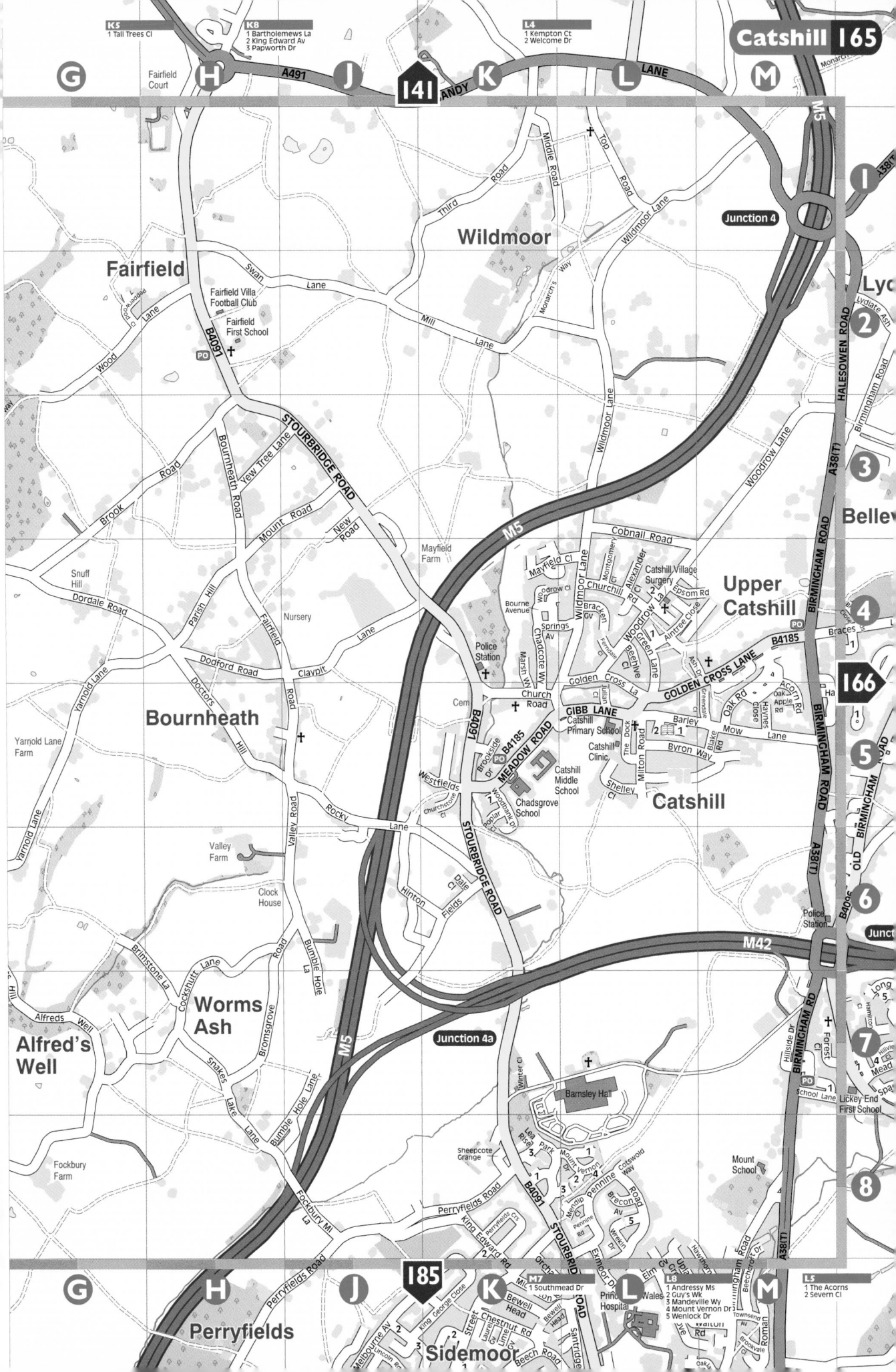

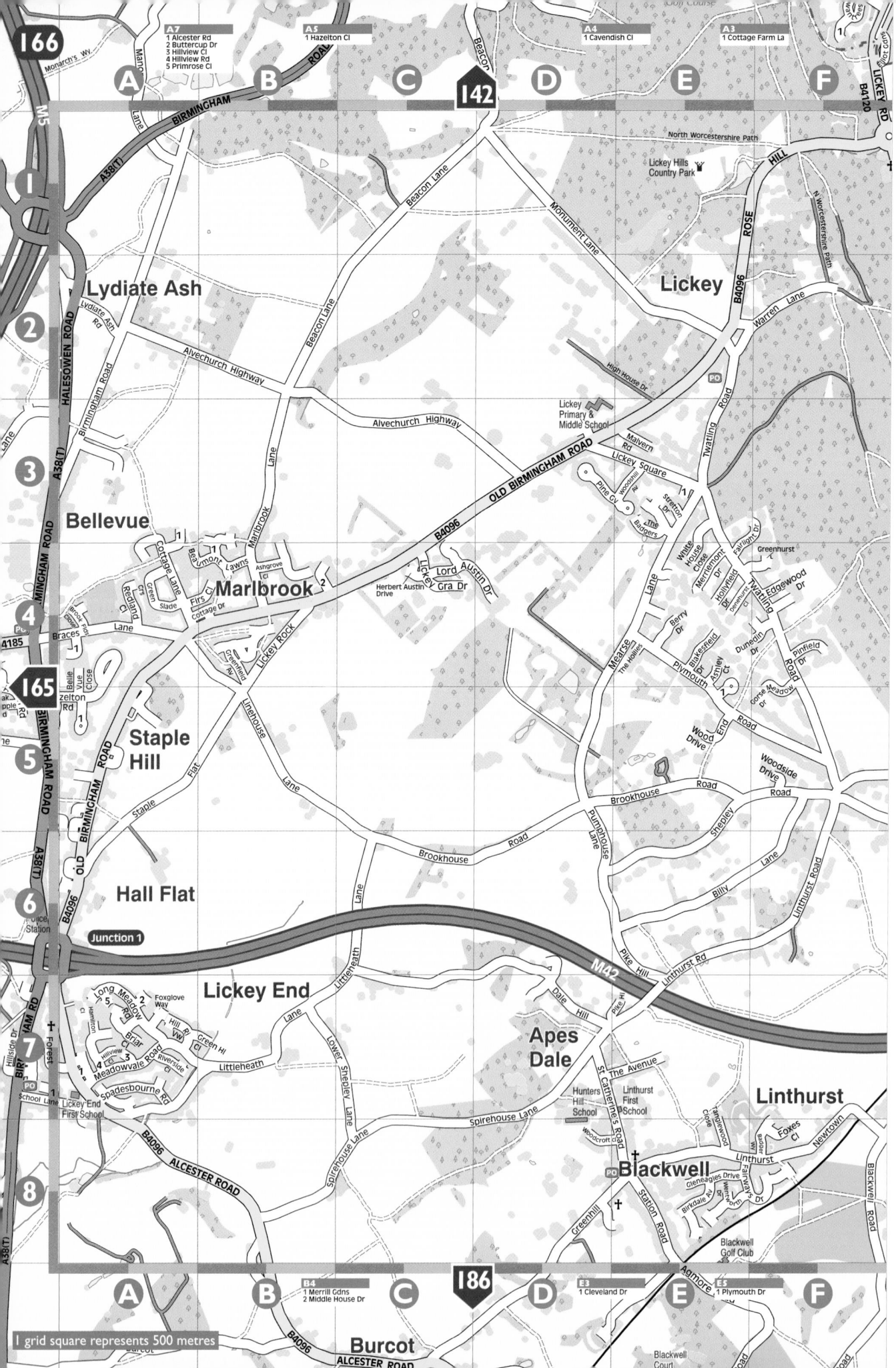

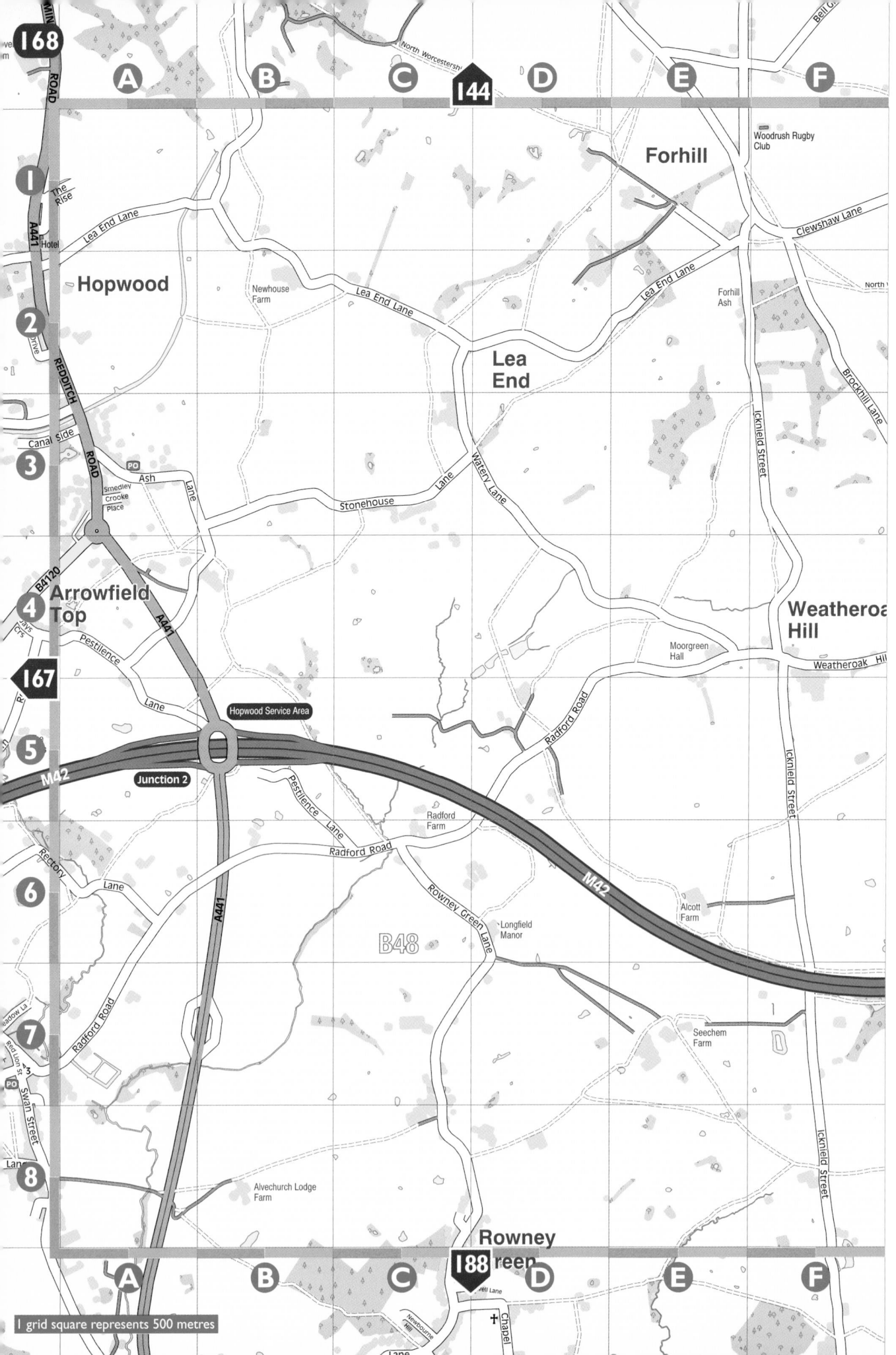

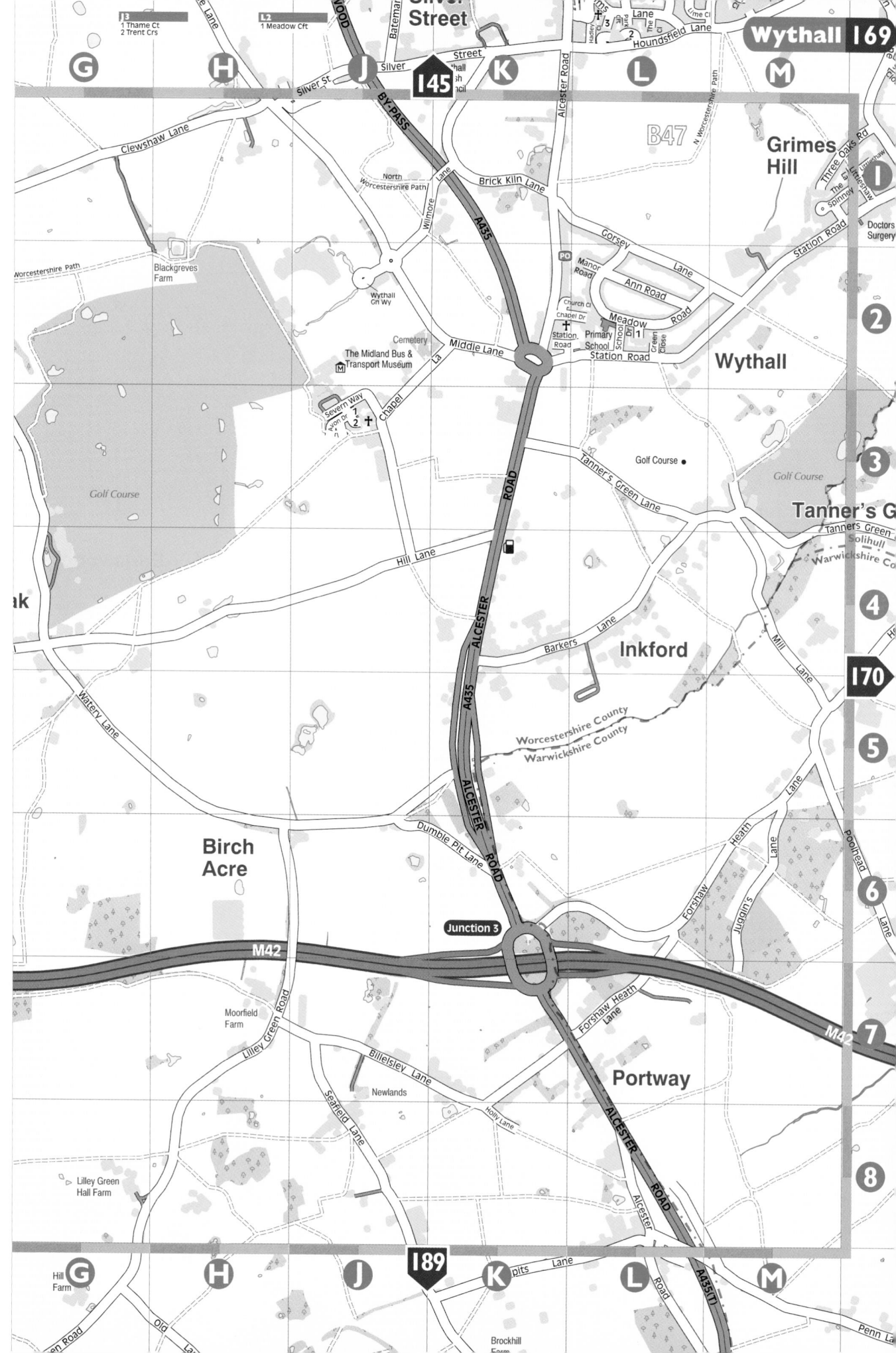

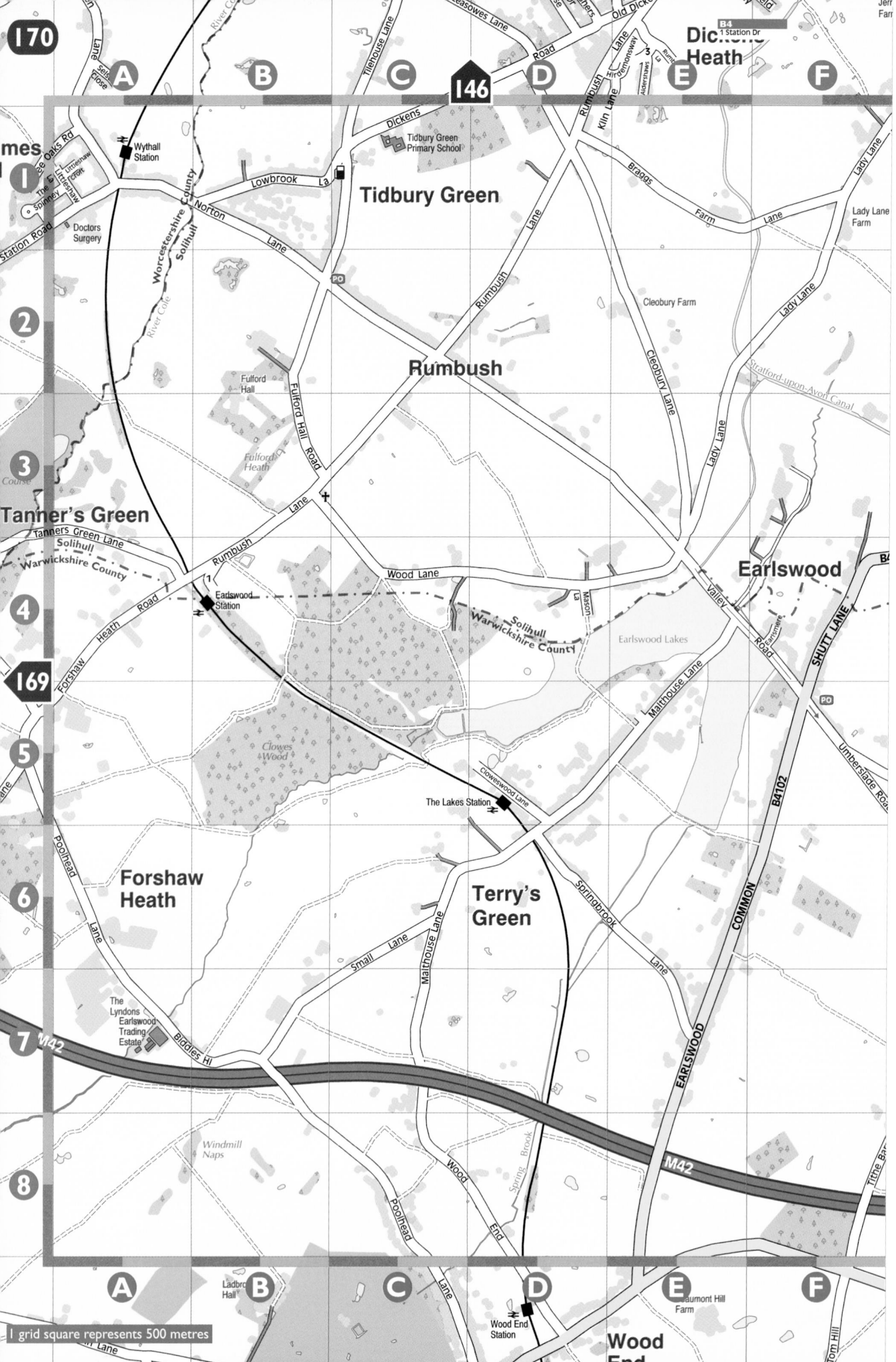

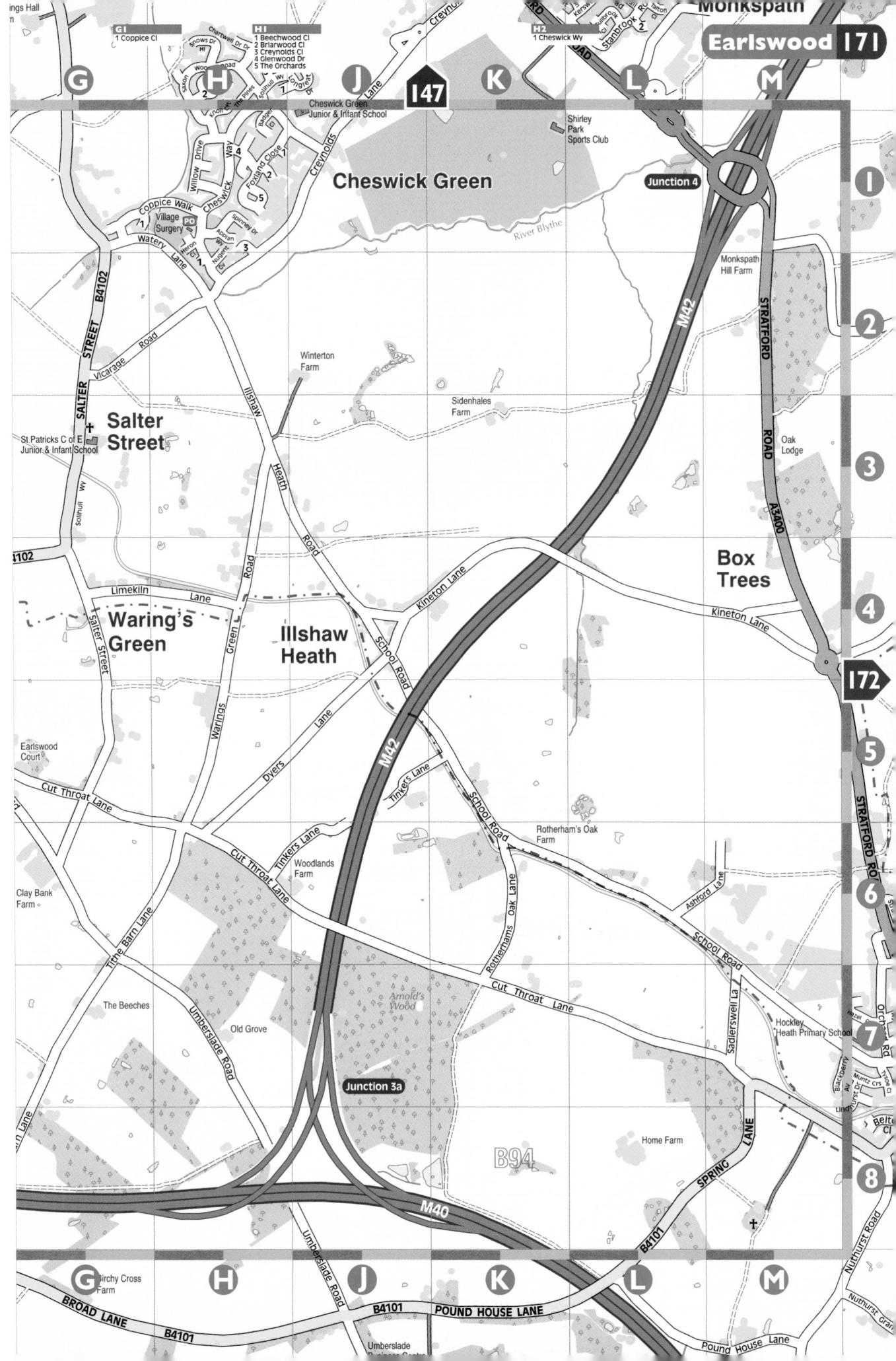

Bentley Heath

Tilehouse Green

Arden High School

148

St George & St Teresa RC Junior & Infant School

Kingsley Preparatory School

Downing Close Hlth Clinic

Knowle & Dorridge Cricket Club

Four Ashes

Dorridge Junior & Infant School

Knowle Grove

Dorridge Gallery

The Sheila Godfrey Clinic

Kitchen Gal

DORRIDGE

Bentley Manor

The Surg Dorridge Stn

Norton Green

Earlswood

Packwood Gullet

Parkfield

171

Solihull
Warwickshire County

Dorridge Cricket Club

Windmill Lane

Mill Pool Lane

Darley Green

Ivy House Farm

Aylesbury House (Hotel)

Packwood Towers

Packwood

AYLESBURY ROAD

Vicarage Road

Vicarage Road

STRATFORD ROAD

A3400

B4101

Park View

Meadow Close

Hockley Heath

Hockley Heath Pavilion (Sports Centre)

Belton Cl

B4459 OLD WARWICK ROAD

Glasshouse Lane

Grove Lane

Packwood Lane

Packwood House (NT)

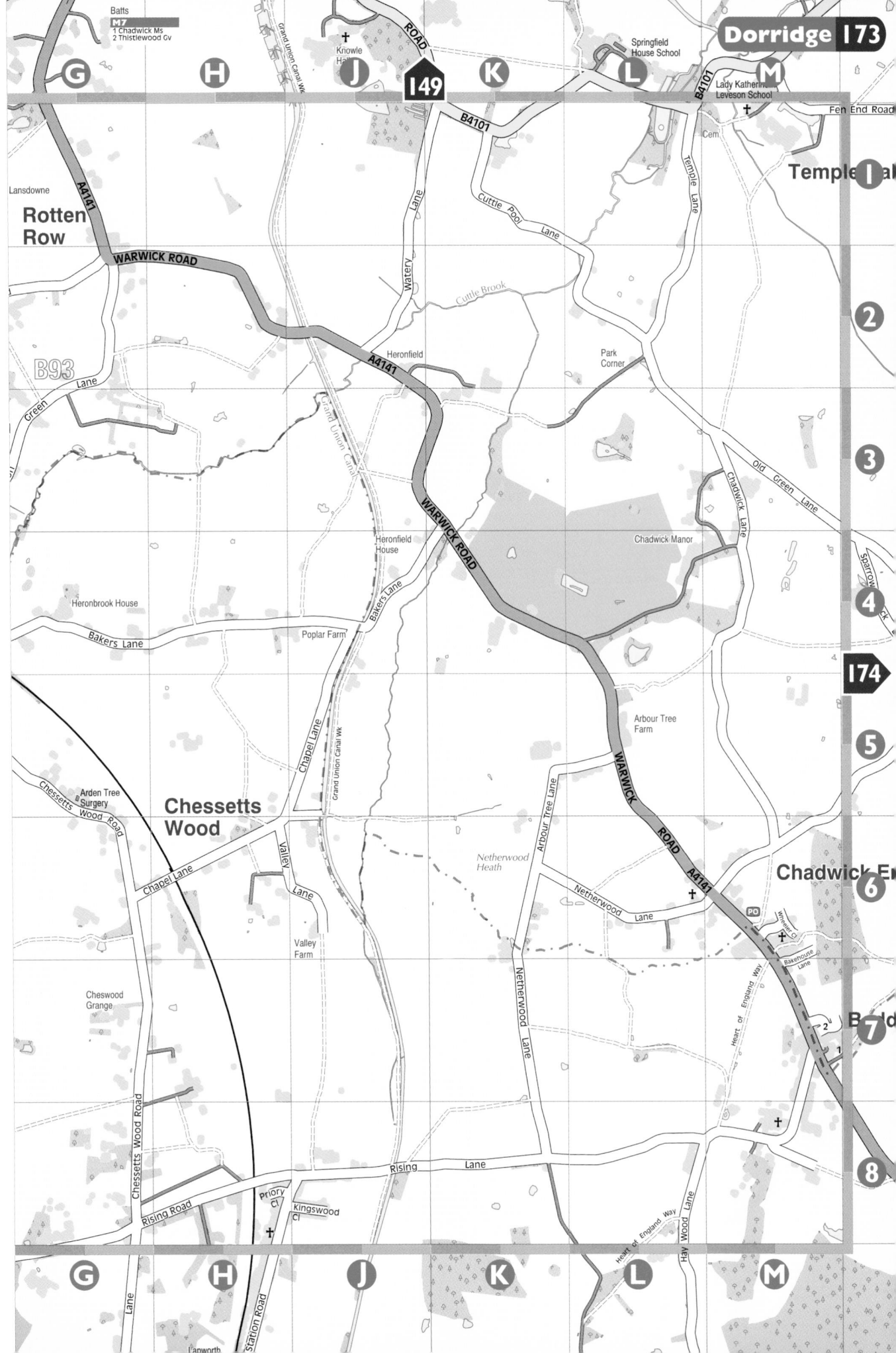

Batts
M7
1 Chadwick Ms
2 Thistlewood Gv

Knowle Hall

Springfield House School

Lady Katherine Leveson School

G **H** **J** **K** **L** **M**

149

B4101

ROAD

Temple

Cuttle Pool Lane

Watery Lane

Cuttle Brook

Park Corner

Fen End Road

Cem

Temple Lane

1

Lansdowne

Rotten Row

A4141

WARWICK ROAD

Heronfield

A4141

2

B93

Green Lane

Grand Union Canal

Old Green Lane

Chadwick Lane

Sparrow...

3

WARWICK ROAD

Heronfield House

Chadwick Manor

4

Heronbrook House

Bakers Lane

Poplar Farm

Bakers Lane

174

Arbour Tree Farm

5

Chapel Lane

Grand Union Canal Wk

WARWICK

Chessetts Wood

Arden Tree Surgery

Chessetts Wood Road

Chapel Lane

Valley Lane

Netherwood Heath

Arbour Tree Lane

Netherwood Lane

ROAD

A4141

Chadwick E

6

PO

Wheeler Cl

Valley Farm

Netherwood Lane

Bakehouse Lane

Cheswood Grange

Chessetts Wood Road

Heart of England Way

2

B **ld**

7

1

Rising Lane

8

Priory Cl

Rising Road

Kingswood Cl

Heart of England Way

Hay Wood Lane

Station Road

G **H** **J** **K** **L** **M**

Lanworth

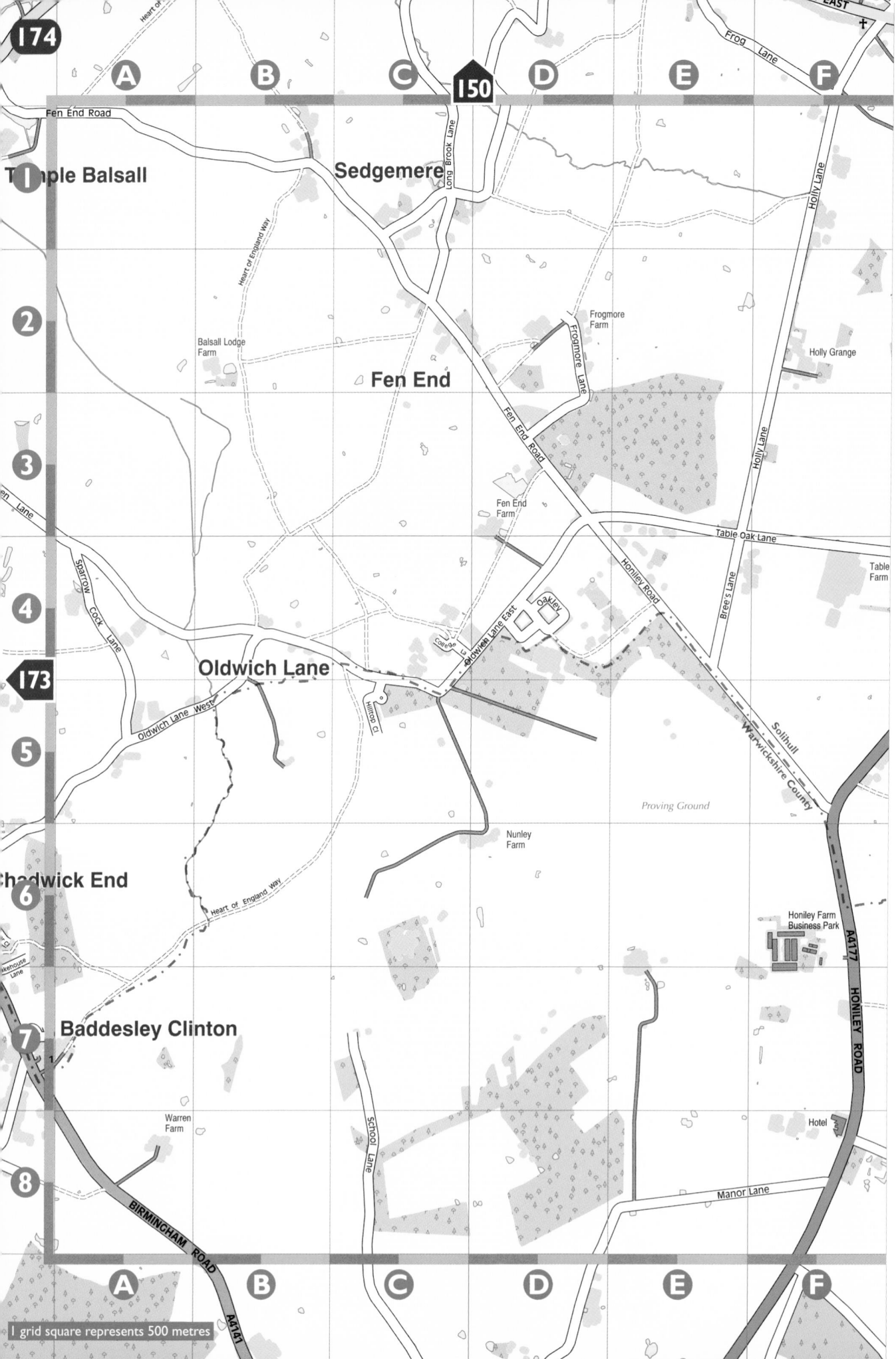

A **B** **C** **D** **E** **F**

Fen End Road

T|nple Balsall

Sedgemere

Heart of England Way

Frog Lane

Holly Lane

1

Frogmore Farm

2

Balsall Lodge Farm

Holly Grange

Fen End

Frogmore Lane

Fen End Road

3

Fen End Farm

Table Oak Lane

Lane

Sparrow Cock Lane

Honiley Road

Holly Lane

Bree's Lane

Table Farm

4

Oakley

Oldwich Lane

Cottage Ln

Oldwich Lane East

5

Oldwich Lane West

Hilltop Cl

Solihull

Warwickshire County

Proving Ground

Chadwick End

6

Nunley Farm

Heart of England Way

Honiley Farm Business Park

 kehouse Lane

A4177

HONILEY ROAD

Baddesley Clinton

7

Warren Farm

School Lane

Hotel

8

BIRMINGHAM ROAD

Manor Lane

A4141

A **B** **C** **D** **E** **F**

1 grid square represents 500 metres

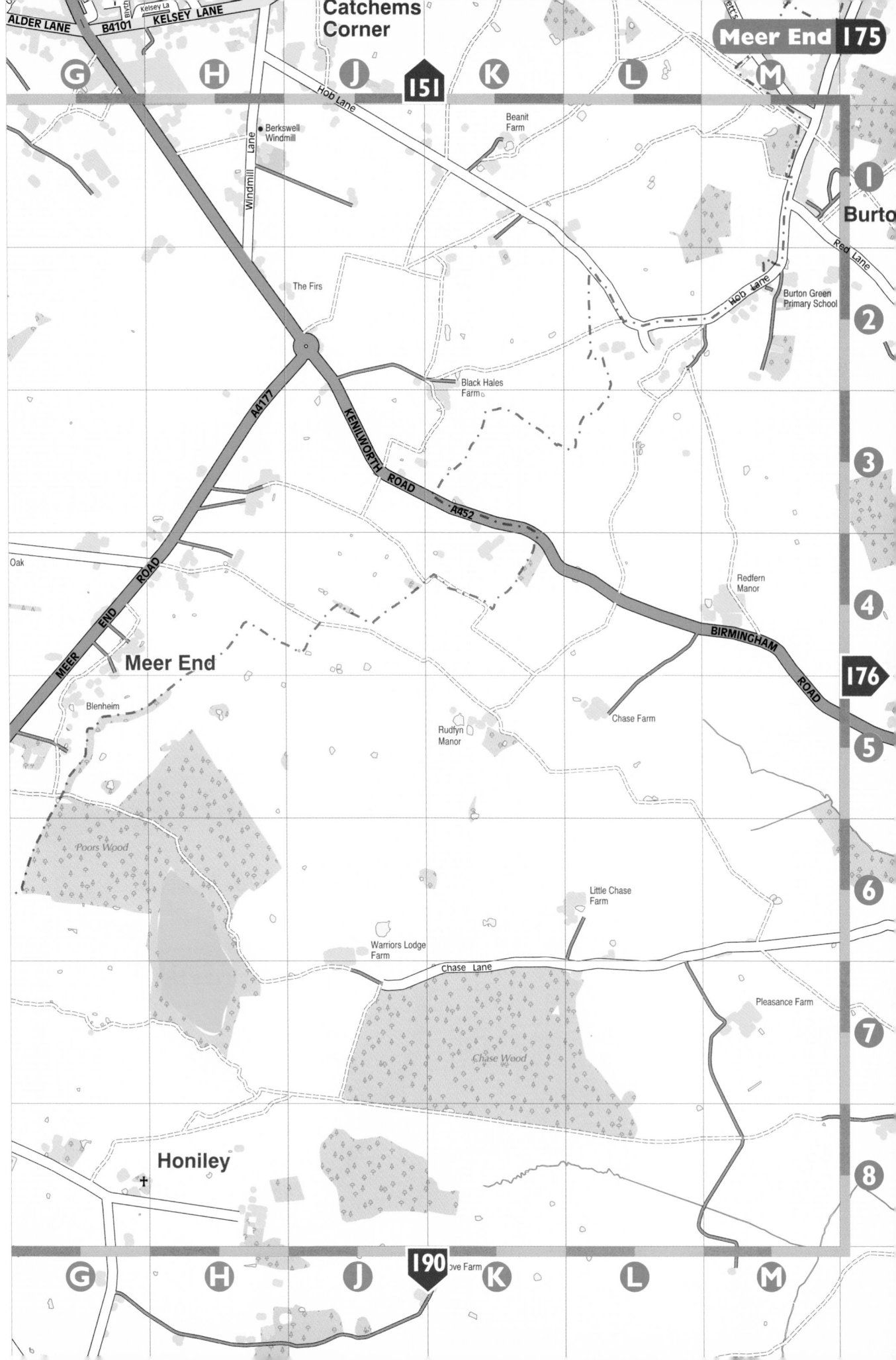

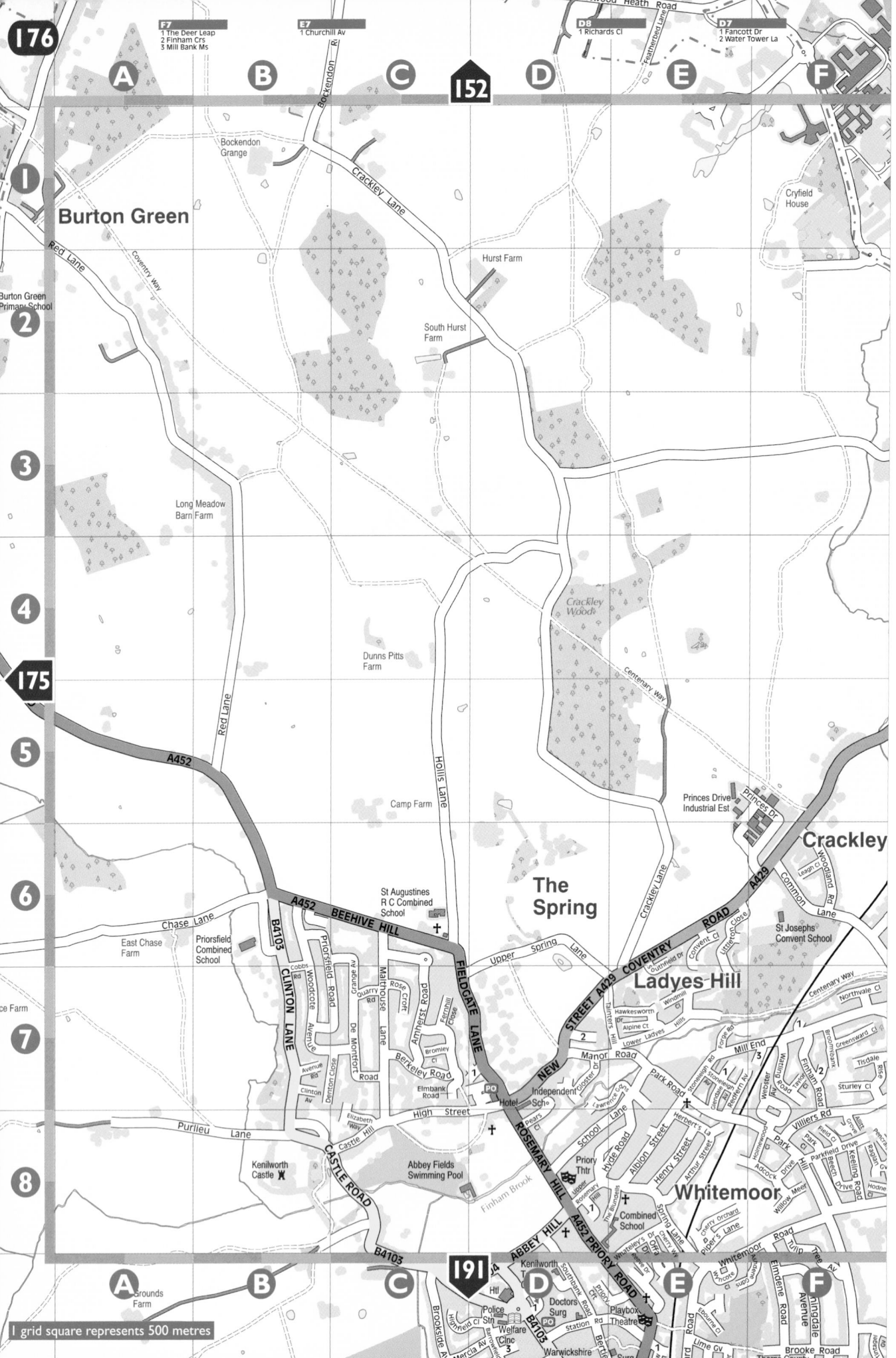

University of Warwick

G6
1 Butler Cl
2 Whitehead Dr

G7
1 Admiral Gdns
2 Angus Cl
3 Bodnant Wy
4 Cotton Dr
5 Framlingham Gv

G8
1 Chatsworth Gv
2 Denewood Wy
3 Harlech Cl
4 Kew Cl
5 Penryhn Cl
6 Powis Gv
7 Tappinger Gv

153

Bishop Ullathorne RC School

Coventry Warwickshire County

The Leasowes

Finham

Finham Primary School

King's Hill

Wainbody Wood School

Gibbet Hill

King's Hill Lane

Wainbody Wood Farm

Cryfield Grange

King's Hill Lane

178

Westley Bridge

Finham Brook

Manor Fields Farm

Millburn Grange

CV8

Highland Road

Inchbrook Road

Dalehouse Lane

Kingswood Farm

Dalehouse Lane Industrial Estate

Lulworth Park

Centenary Way

Finham Brook

Golf Course

Golf Club

Walkers Orchard

Vicarage Road

Crew Lane

Park Hill County Middle Sch

Park Hill

Crewe Farm

Kenilworth School

Kenilworth Rugby

Courthouse Cft

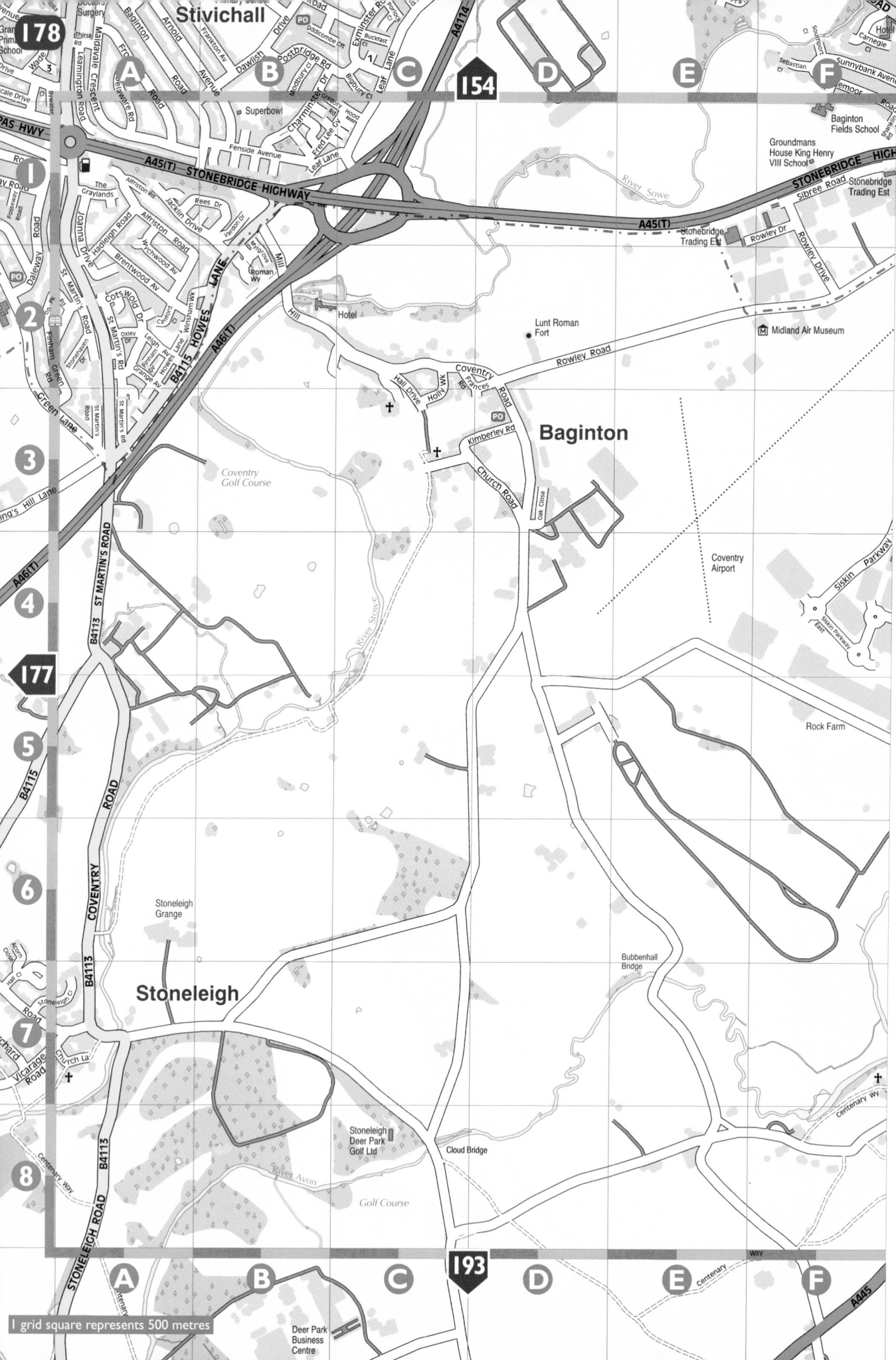

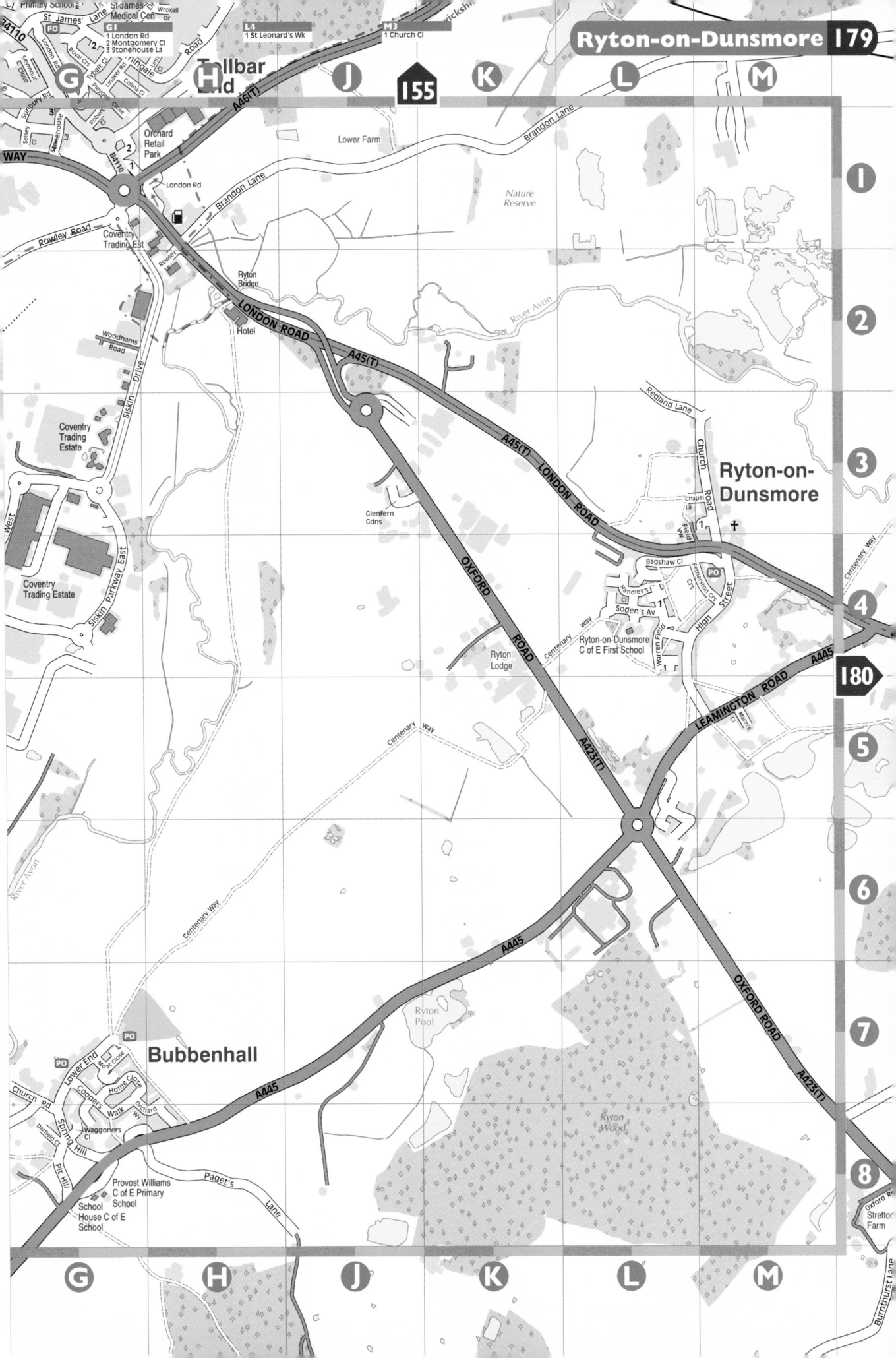

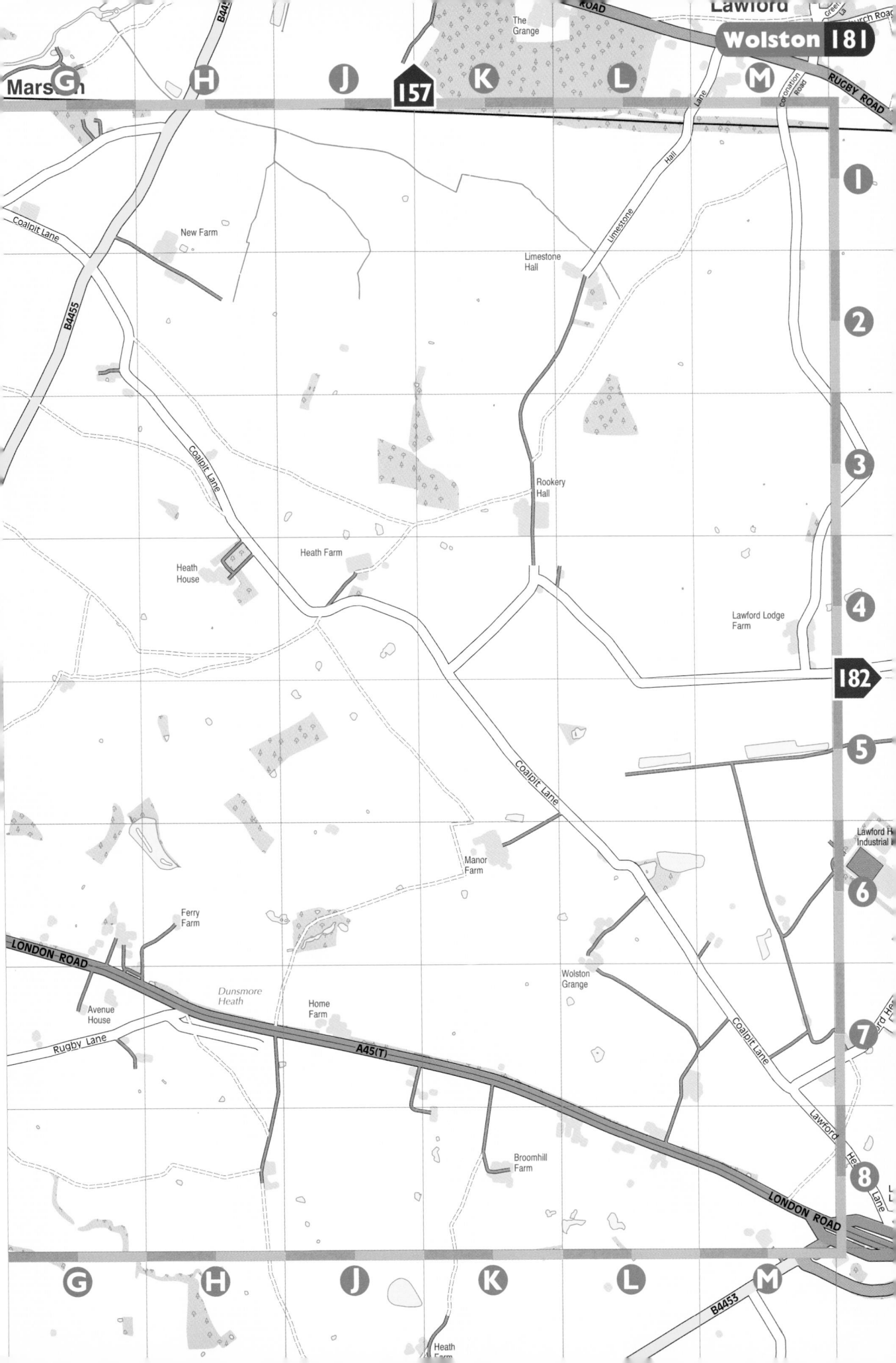

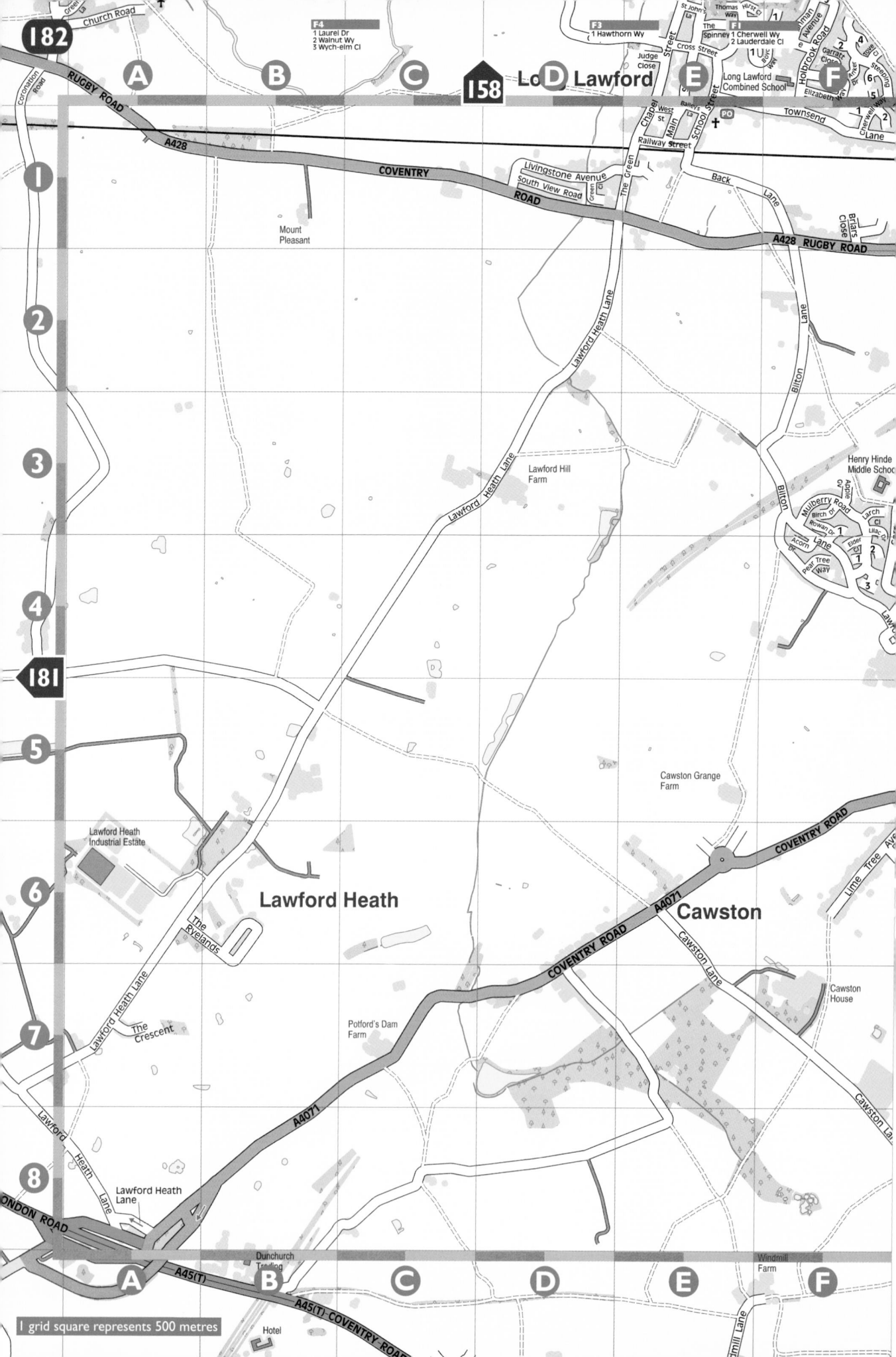

182

A428 RUGBY ROAD

Church Road

Coronation Road

Green

A B C D Lawford E F

158 Lo

F4
1 Laurel Dr
2 Walnut Wy
3 Wych-elm Cl

F3
1 Hawthorn Wy

F1
1 Cherwell Wy
2 Lauderdale Cl

St John's
The
Spinney

Thomas
Way

Street
Cross Street

Aman
Avenue

Holbrook Road

Steeping

Garratt
Close

Long Lawford
Combined School

Elizabeth Wy

Judge
Close

Chapel
St

West
St

Main
Street

School Street

PO

Bailey's
La

Townsend

Back
Lane

Cherwell Wy
Lane

Railway Street

Livingstone Avenue

South View Road

COVENTRY ROAD

Green

The Green

A428 RUGBY ROAD

Briars
Close

1

Mount
Pleasant

2

Bilton Lane

3

Lawford Heath Lane

Lawford Hill
Farm

Henry Hinde
Middle School

Mulberry Road

Birch Dr

Rowan Dr

Apple
Dr

Larch
Cl

Lilac Cl

Acorn
Dr

Elder
Dr

Pear Tree
Way

Bilton Lane

4

181

5

Cawston Grange
Farm

Lawford Heath
Industrial Estate

COVENTRY ROAD

Lime Tree Av

6

The
Ryelands

Lawford Heath

A4071

Cawston

Cawston Lane

Cawston
House

Lawford Heath Lane

The
Crescent

7

Potford's Dam
Farm

A4071

Cawston Lane

8

ONDON ROAD

Lawford Heath
Lane

Lawford Heath
Lane

Dunchurch
Trading

Windmill
Farm

A45(T)

A45(T) COVENTRY ROAD

A B C D E F

Mill Lane

Hotel

G7
1 Hewell Cl

M8
1 Aldborough La
2 Alderbrook Cl
3 Broad Heath Cl
4 Clarendon Cl
5 Cornhampton Cl
6 Daybrook Cl
7 Draycott Cl

G   H   J   167   K   L   M

Wheeley Road
Wheeley Farm
Scarfield Hill

Cobley Hill

I

Alvechurch Station

Worcester & Birmingham Canal

2
Grange Lane
Cattespool
Grange Farm

Stoney Lane
3
Stoney Lane Farm
River Arrow

4
Oxleasows Farm

Brockhill Lane
188
Shortwood Farm
Butler's Hill Wood
5

HM Prison
Lakeside
Brockhill Farm
6
Brockhill Lane

The Park
The Park
The Drive
The Lake
Hewell Grange
Hewell Kennels
Brockhill Lane
Brockhill Wood
7
Lower Farm

Holyoakes Lane
Gypsy Lane
Longmoor Close
Carthorse Lane
Butler's Hill
BROCKHILL
Kerswell Cl
DRIVE
Birchensale
8
B4184
Appletree Lane
Boot Piece
Lowen La
Salter's Lane

HEWELL LANE
Tack Farm
195

G   H   J   K   L   M

SALTER'S LANE   B4184   BROCKHILL DRIVE

Bridley Moor High School
Pitcheroak

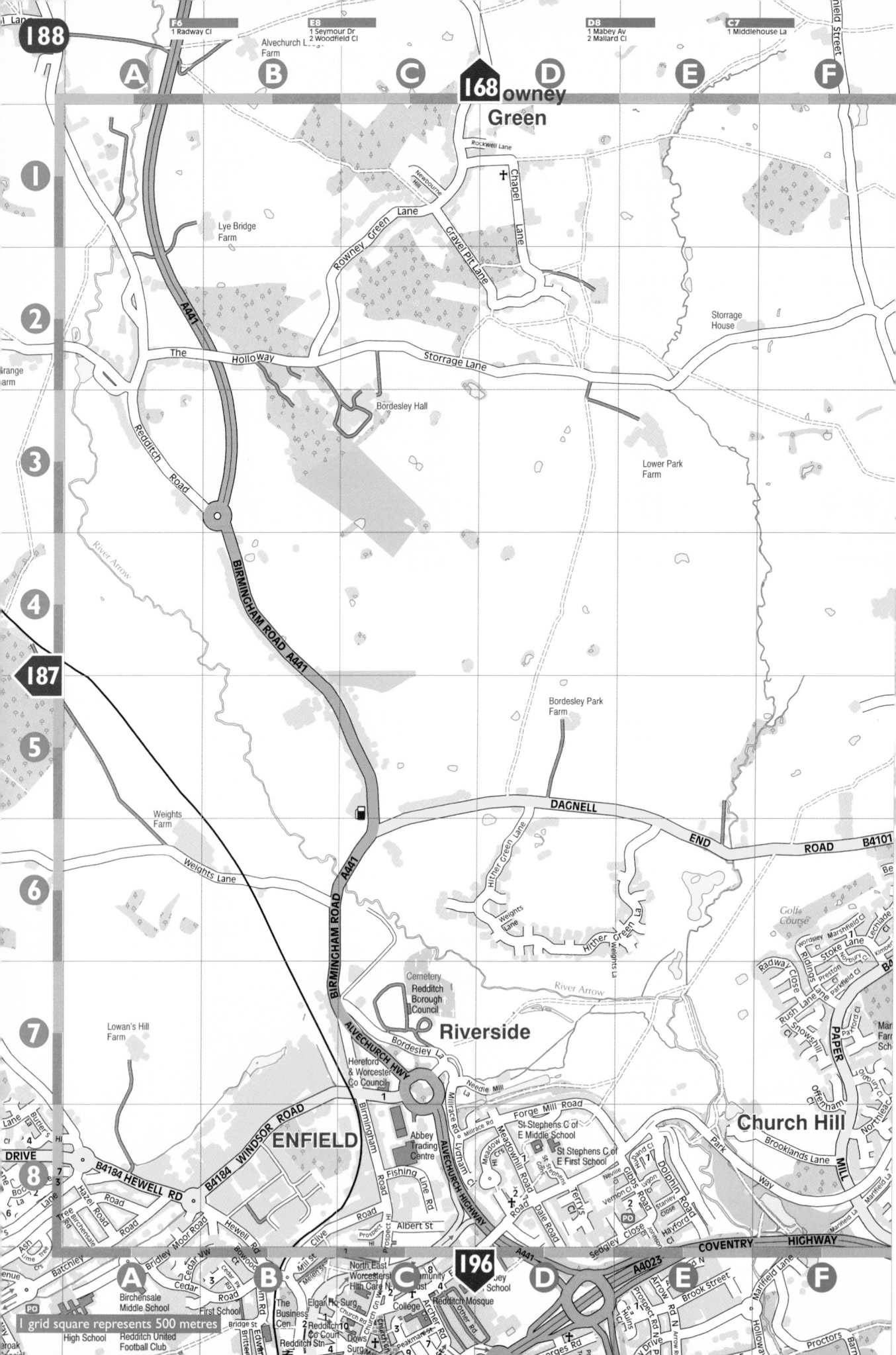

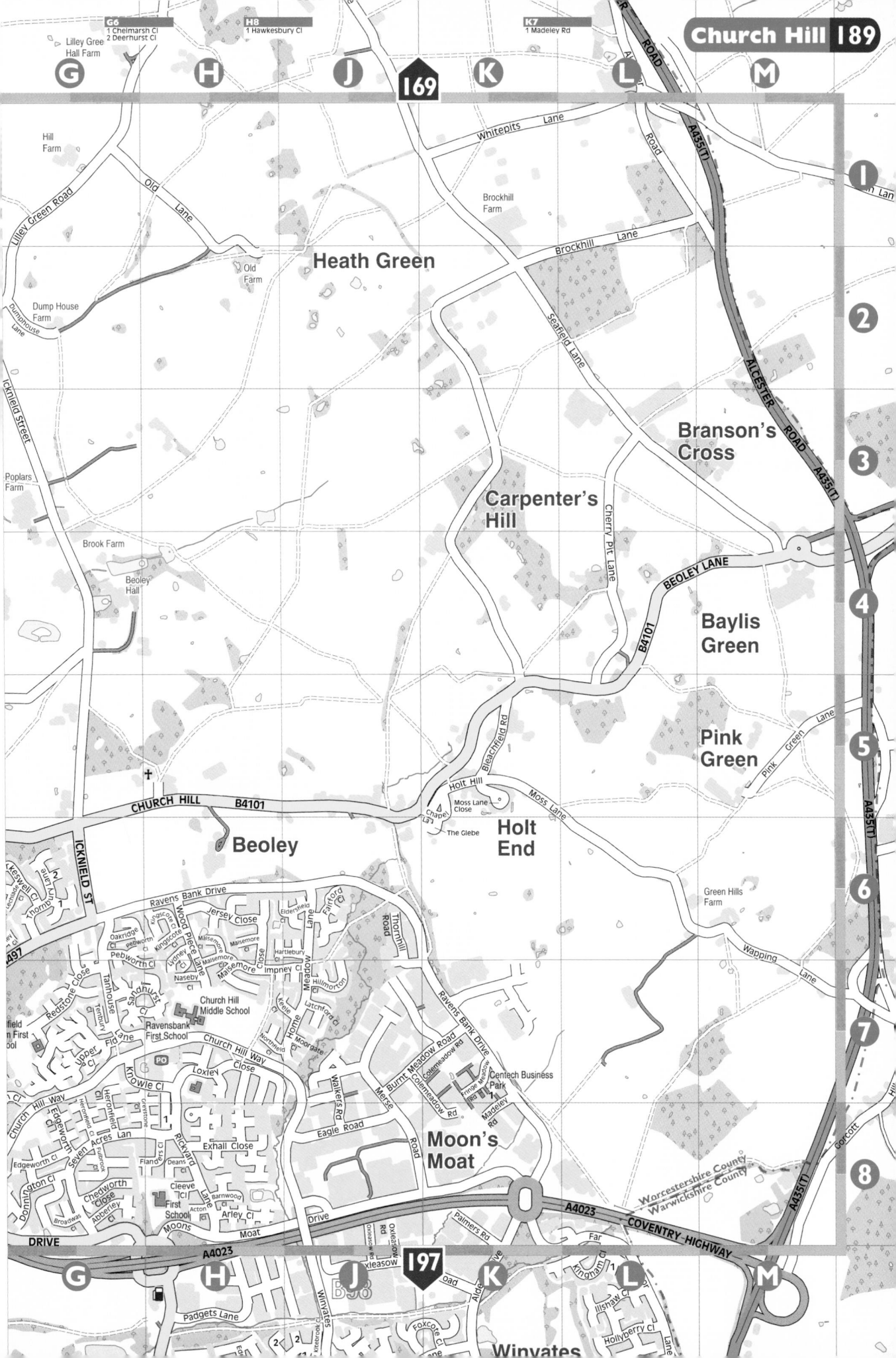

G6
1 Chelmarsh Cl
2 Deerhurst Cl

H8
1 Hawkesbury Cl

K7
1 Madeley Rd

G **H** **J** 169 **K** **L** **M**

I

2

3

4

5

6

7

8

Lilley Gree
Hall Farm

Hill
Farm

Old Lane

Lilley Green Road

Icknield Street

Dumphouse Lane

Dump House
Farm

Poplars
Farm

Brook Farm

Beoley
Hall

Old
Farm

Heath Green

Whitepits Lane

Brockhill
Farm

Brockhill Lane

Seafield Lane

ALCESTER ROAD

A435(T)

Branson's Cross

Carpenter's Hill

Cherry Pit Lane

BEOLEY LANE

Baylis Green

B4101

Pink Green

Pink Green Lane

A435(T)

CHURCH HILL B4101

Beoley

ICKNIELD ST

Bleachfield Rd

Holt Hill

Chapel La

The Glebe

Moss Lane Close

Moss Lane

Holt End

Green Hills
Farm

Wapping Lane

Keswell Dr

Thornhill

Ravens Bank Drive

Jersey Close

Eldersfield
Lane

Fairford

Thornhill Road

Oakridge
Pebworth

Kinscote

Wood Piece Lane

Lydney

Maisemore
Close

Hartlebury

Impney Rd

Keble

Pebworth Cl

Naseby

Maisemore

Maisemore

Hillmorton

Church Hill
Middle School

Redstone Close

Sandhurst

Tamhouse
Fld Lane
Tenbury

Ravensbank
First School

PO

Keele

Home
Meadow
Latchford Rd

Northfield

Moorgate

Ravens Bank Drive

Colemeadow Rd

Fringe Meadow

Centech Business
Park

Church Hill Way

Loxley
Close

Knowle Cl

Upper Cl

Exhall Close

Edgeworth
Cl

Donnington Cl

Seven Acres Lan

Rickyard
Close

Flanders

Deans

Cleeve
Close

Broadway

Abberley

Barnwood

Arley Cl

Acton

First
School

Moons Moat

Eagle Road

Walkers Rd

Merse Rd

Burnt Meadow Road

Colemeadow
Rd

Madeley

Ravens Bank Drive

Moon's Moat

Worcestershire County
Warwickshire County

A4023

COVENTRY HIGHWAY

DRIVE

A4023

Padgets Lane

G **H** **J** 197 **K** **L** **M**

Winyates

Oxleasow Rd

Palmers Rd

Gorcott

A435(T)

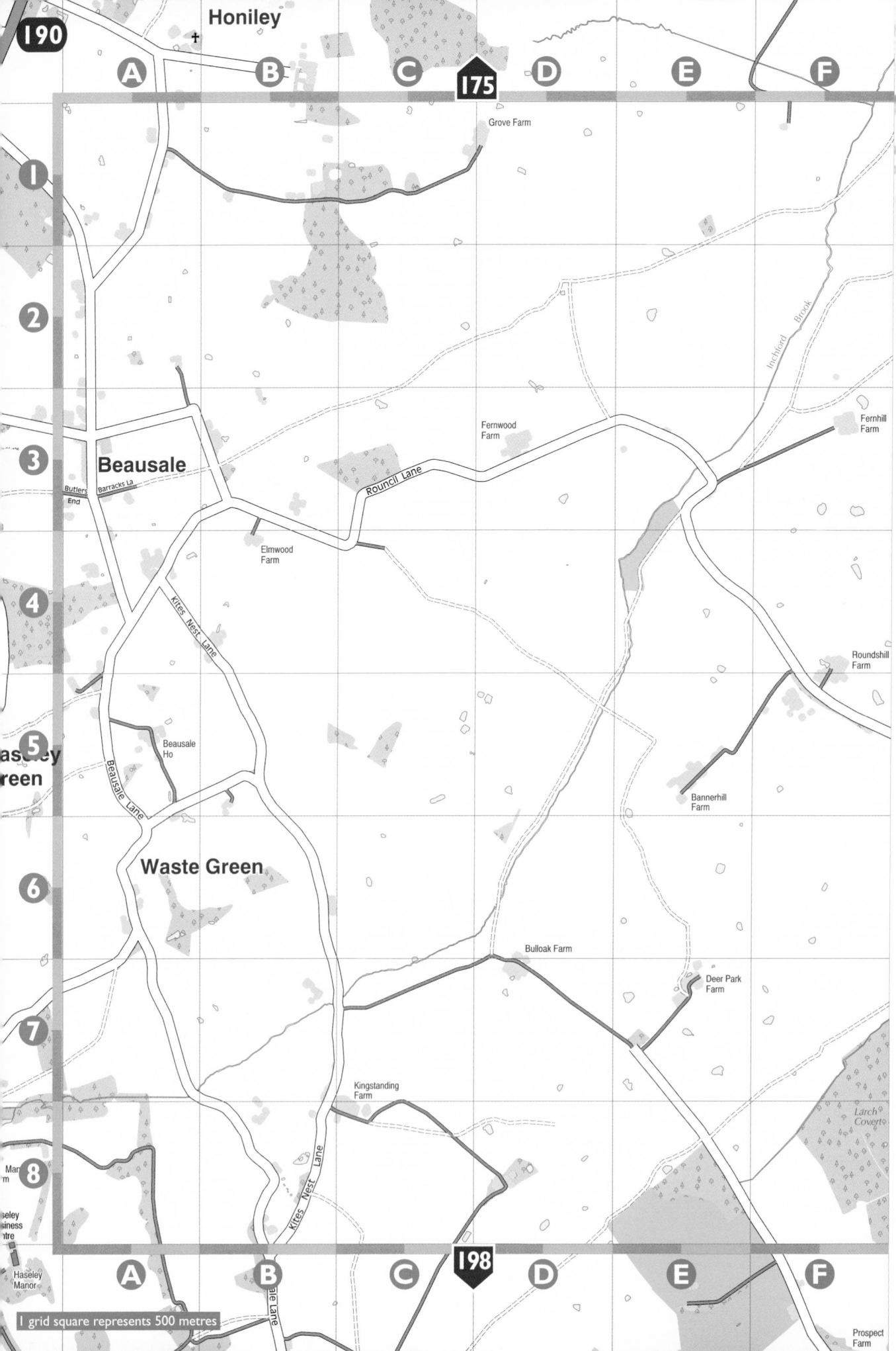

190

Honiley

A B **175** C D E F

1

Grove Farm

2

Inchford Brook

Fernhill Farm

3 Beausale

Butlers End Barracks La

Rouncil Lane

Fernwood Farm

Elmwood Farm

4

Kites Nest Lane

Roundshill Farm

aseley reen

5

Beausale Ho

Beausale Lane

Bannerhill Farm

Waste Green

6

Bulloak Farm

Deer Park Farm

7

Kingstanding Farm

Larch Covert

Man

8

Kites Nest Lane

eseley siness ntre

Haseley Manor

A B **198** C D E F

ale Lane

Prospect Farm

I grid square represents 500 metres

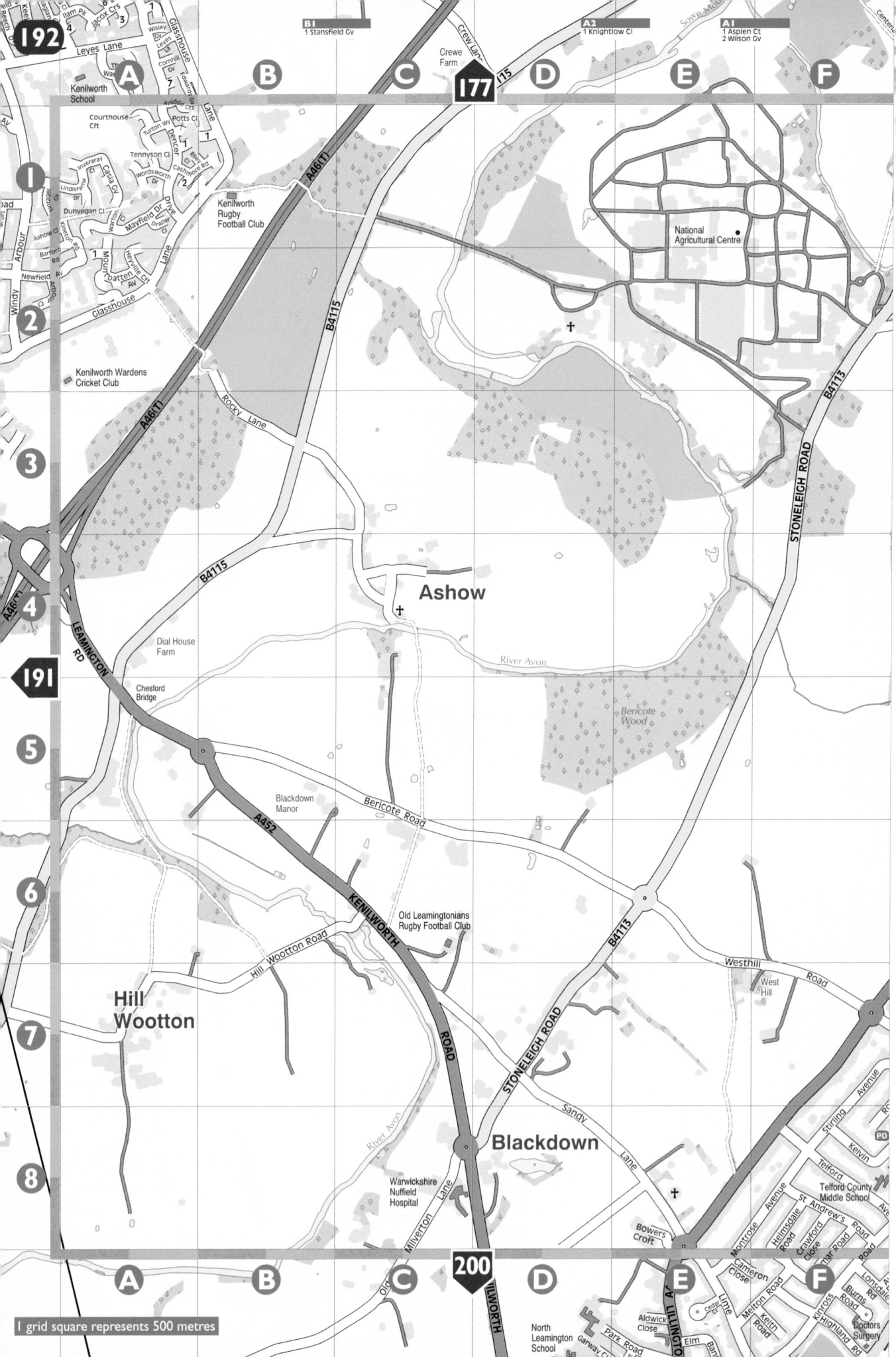

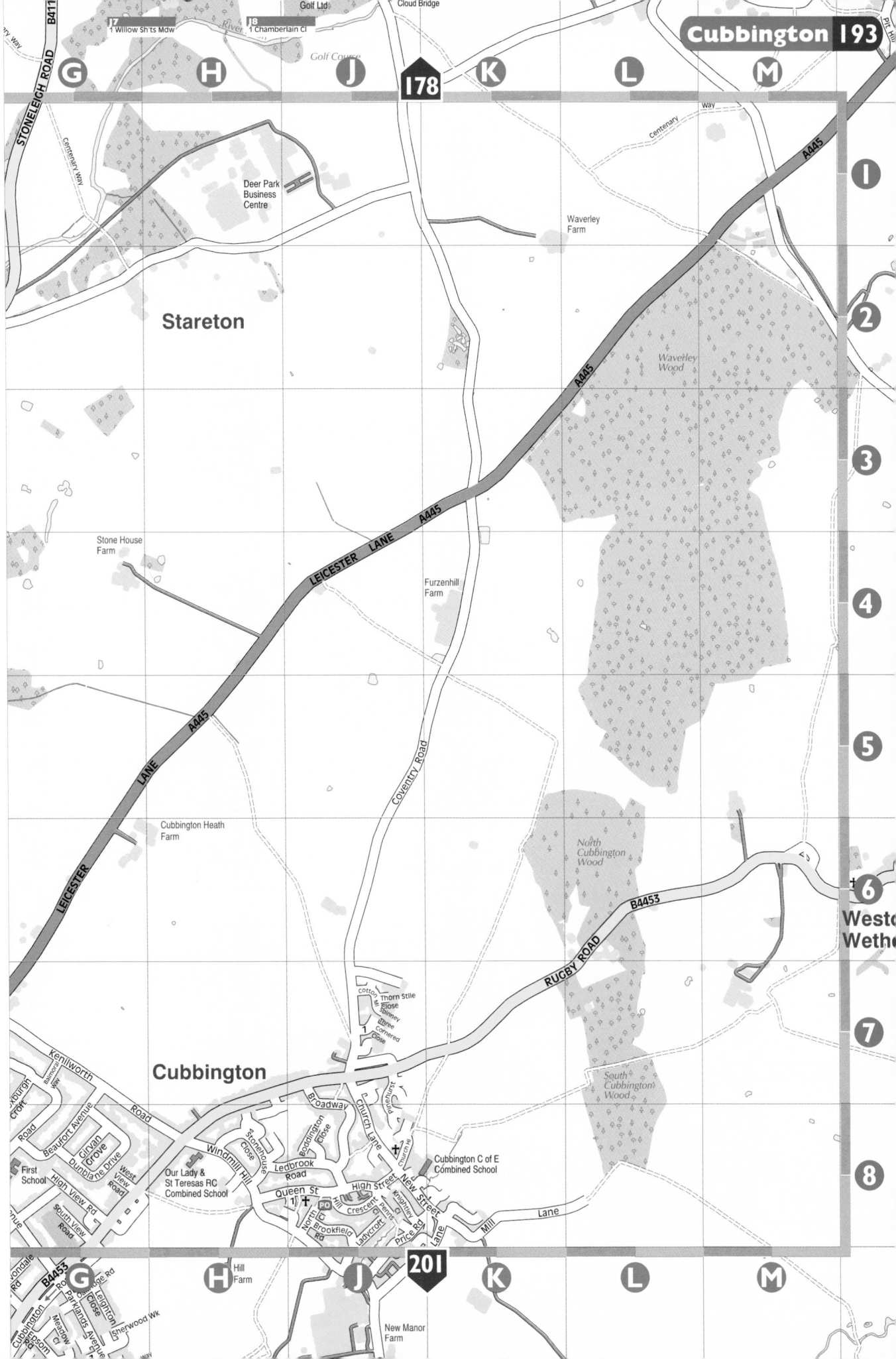

Stareton

Cubbington

Deer Park Business Centre

Waverley Farm

Waverley Wood

Stone House Farm

LEICESTER LANE A445

Furzenhill Farm

A445

Coventry Road

Cubbington Heath Farm

North Cubbington Wood

LEICESTER LANE

B4453

RUGBY ROAD

South Cubbington Wood

Cotton Mill Close
Thorn Stile Close
Three Spinney cornered Close

Kenilworth Road

Beaufort Avenue
Girvan Grove
Dunblane Drive

Windmill Hill

Broadway

Church Lane

Parkhurst

Boddington Close

West View Road

Ledbrook Road

Stonehouse Close

Our Lady & St Teresas RC Combined School

Cubbington C of E Combined School

Queen St

High Street

Crescent

New Street

Knightley

Price Rd

Mill Lane

Lane

First School

High View Rd

South View Road

Brookfield

Ladycroft

Kenilworth

B4453

Leighton Close

Parklands Avenue

Sherwood Wk

Hill Farm

New Manor Farm

Weste Wethe

G H J K L M

1 2 3 4 5 6 7 8

178

201

Golf Ltd

Cloud Bridge

Golf Course

River

1 Willow Sh'ts Mdw

1 Chamberlain Cl

STONELEIGH ROAD B411

Centenary Way

Centenary Way

Way

A445

Centenary Way

B4453

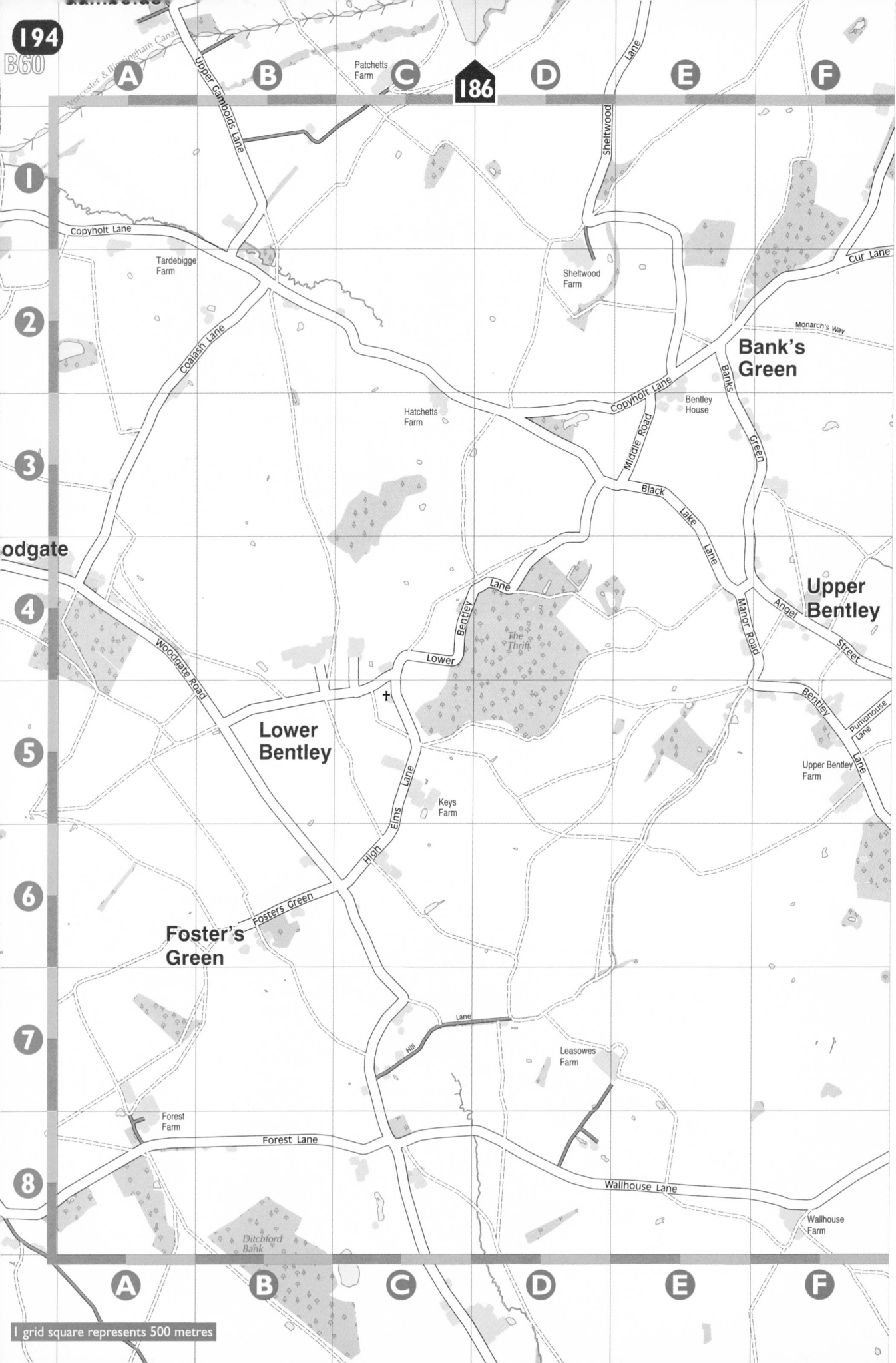

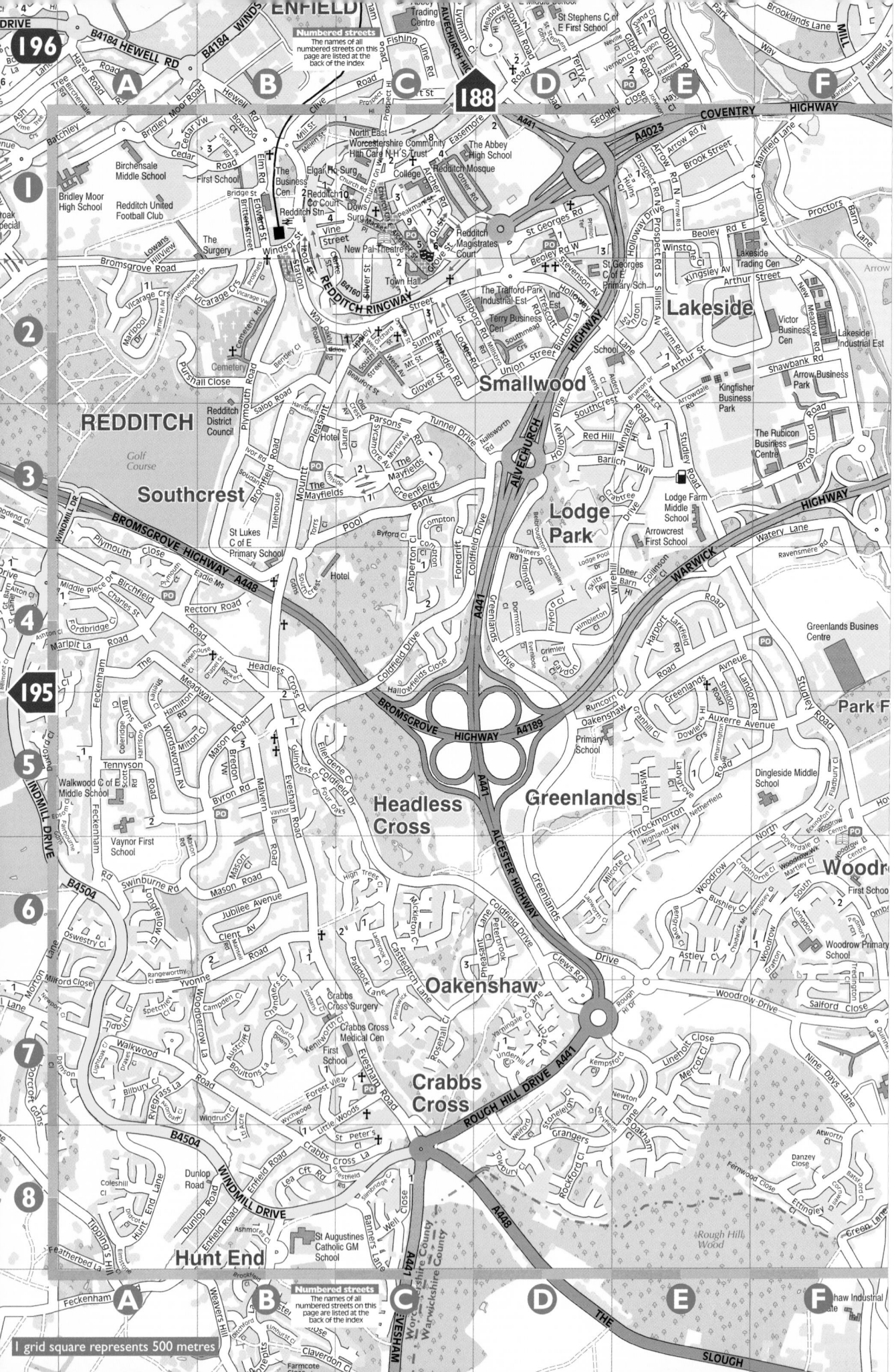

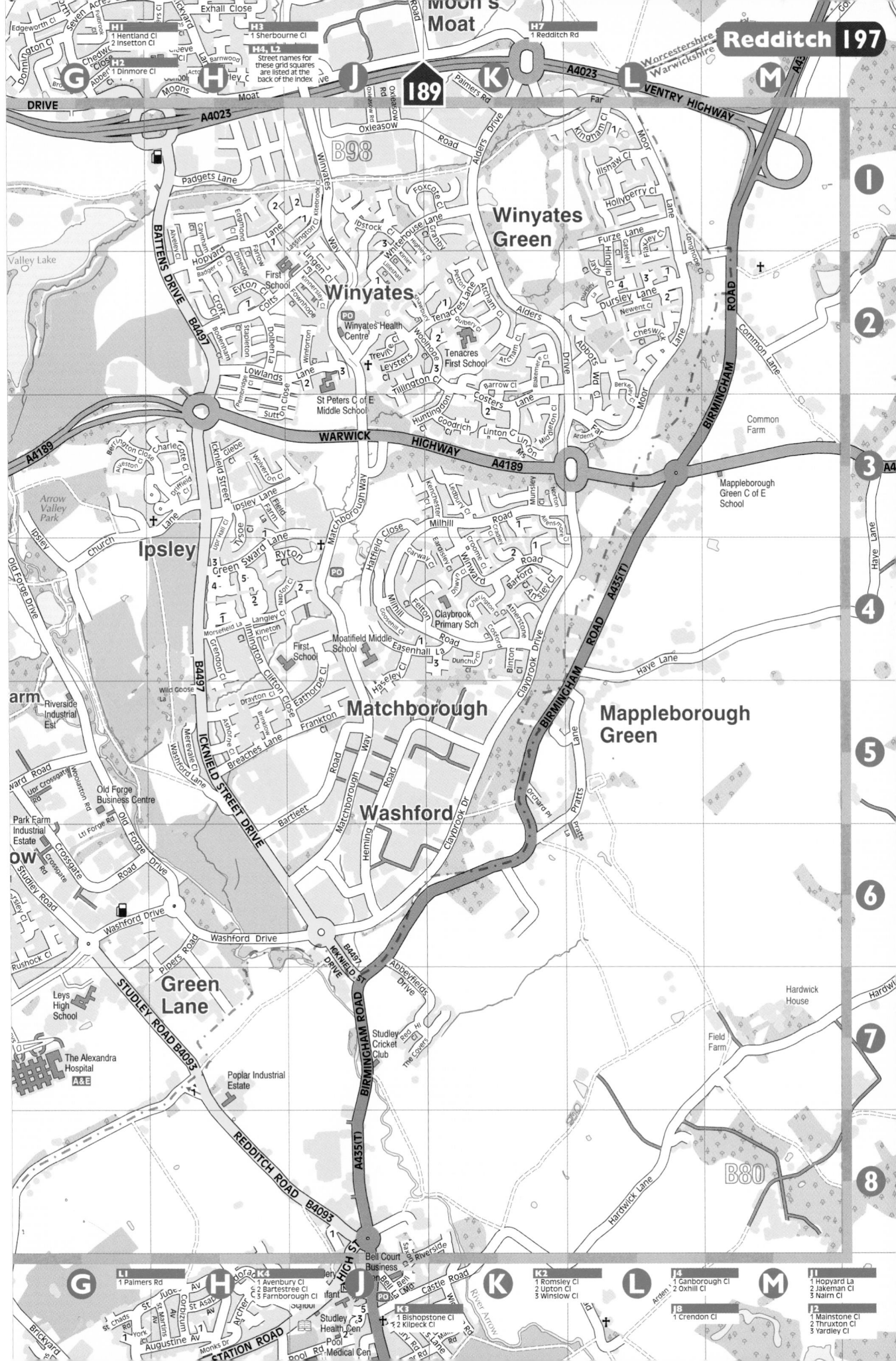

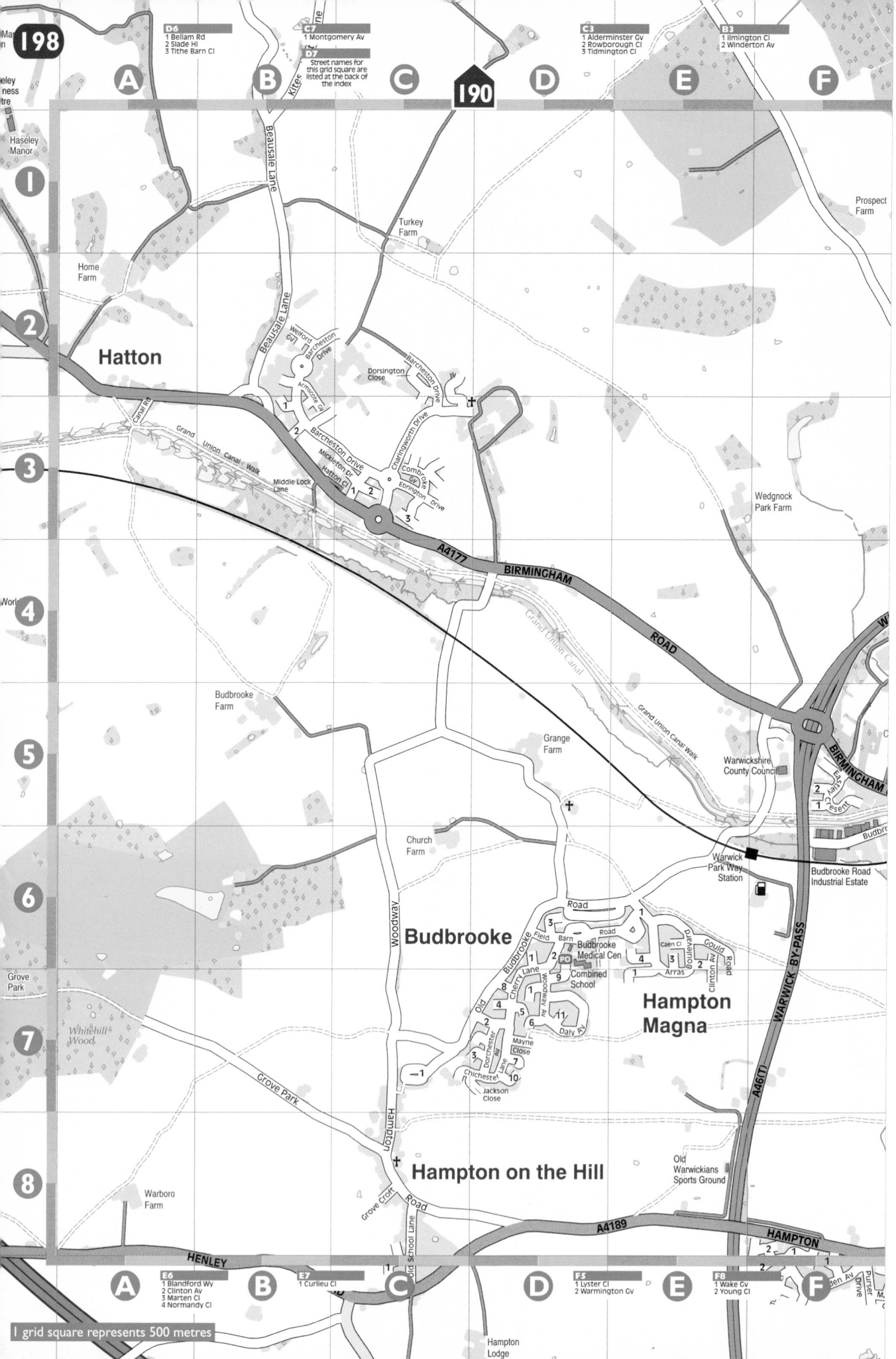

192

Blackdown

I

2

3

4

199

5

6

7

8

Milverton

Myton

CV32

ROYAL
LEAMINGTON
SPA

River Leam

Leamington Spa Station

Heathcote

1 grid square represents 500 metres

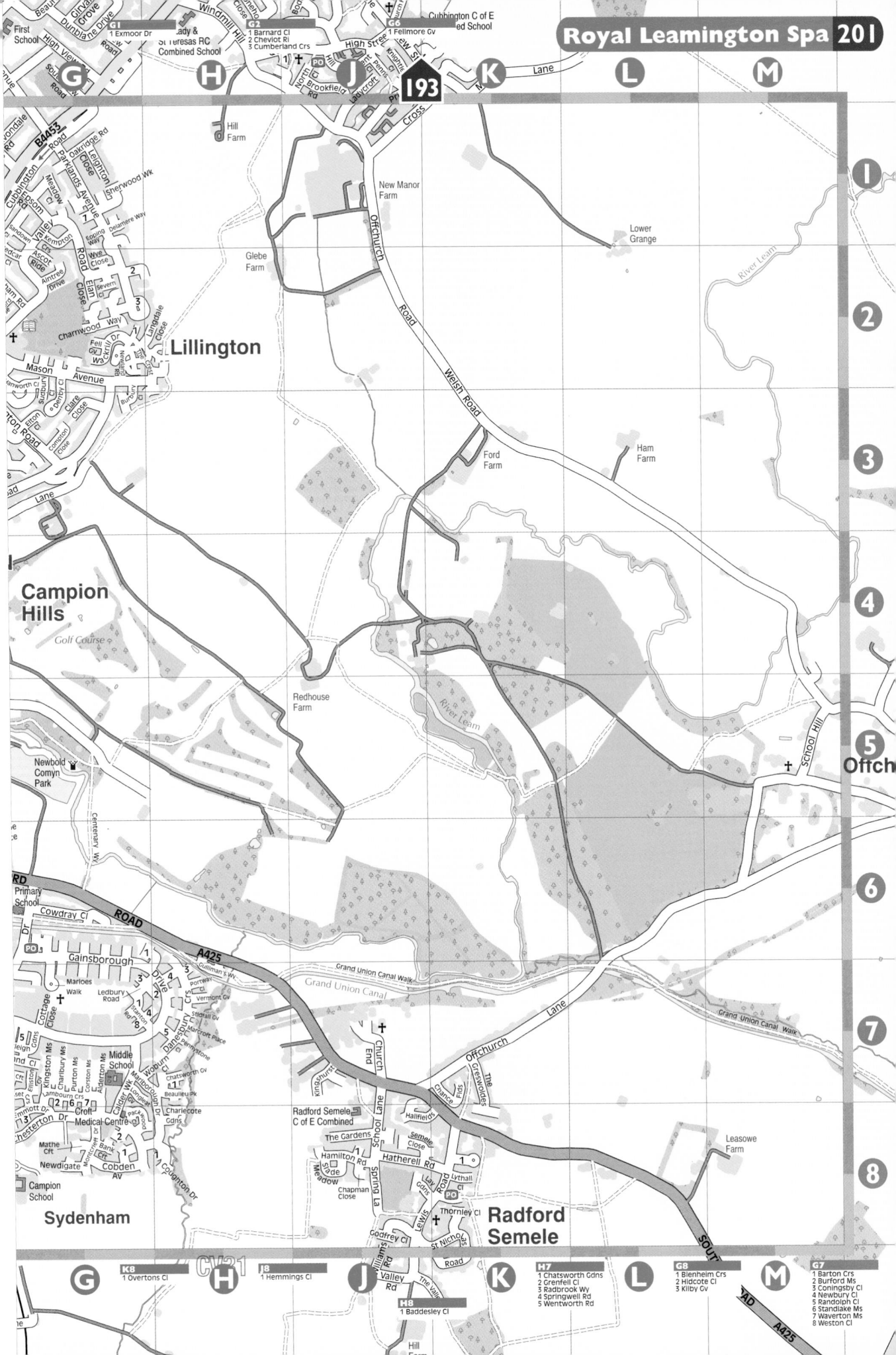

G H J K L M

193

I
2
3
4
5 Offch
6
7
8

Lillington

Campion
Hills

Golf Course

Newbold
Comyn
Park

New Manor
Farm

Hill
Farm

Glebe
Farm

Lower
Grange

River Leam

Ford
Farm

Ham
Farm

Redhouse
Farm

River Leam

School Hill

Offch

Welsh Road

Offchurch Road

Cross

Sydenham

Radford
Semele

Radford Semele
C of E Combined

Campion
School

Newbold Comyn
Park

A425

ROAD

Cowdray Cl

Gainsborough

Grand Union Canal Walk
Grand Union Canal

Grand Union Canal Walk

Offchurch Lane

The Greswoldes

Church End

Leasowe
Farm

SOUT
AD
A425

CV31

H8
1 Baddesley Cl

H7
1 Chatsworth Gdns
2 Grenfell Cl
3 Radbrook Wy
4 Springwell Rd
5 Wentworth Rd

G8
1 Blenheim Crs
2 Hidcote Cl
3 Kilby Gv

M
1 Barton Crs
2 Burford Ms
3 Coningsby Cl
4 Newbury Cl
5 Randolph Cl
6 Standlake Ms
7 Waverton Ms
8 Weston Cl

G1
1 Exmoor Dr

G2
1 Barnard Cl
2 Cheviot Ri
3 Cumberland Crs

G6
1 Fellmore Gv

Cubbington C of E
ed School

St Teresas RC
Combined School

Lady &
Combined School

B4453

Acock's Green 126 D1
Aggborough 161 J2
Alcester Lane's End 125 H7
Alderman's Green 135 G1
Aldershawe 28 C2
The Alders 31 J7
Aldridge 40 E7
Alfred's Well 165 G7
Allen End 58 D7
Allesley 132 F5
Alum Rock 108 E2
Alvechurch 167 J7
Alvecote 33 H7
Amblecote 101 K6
Amington 46 D1
Ansley 96 F1
Ansley Common 79 K6
Apes Dale 166 D7
Arrowfield Top 167 M4
Ash Green 116 A7
Ashmore Lake 51 M1
Ashmore Park 37 K4
Ashow 192 C4
Ashwood 82 C8
Astley 97 H6
Aston 89 L7
Aston Fields 185 L5
Atherstone 63 J3
Attleborough 99 G3
Bacon's End 111 G1
Baddesley Clinton 174 A7
Baddesley Ensor 62 B3
Baginton 178 D3
Ballard's Green 96 B2
Balls Hill 68 E4
Balsall Common 151 G5
Balsall Heath 107 J8
Balsall Street 150 D8
Bank's Green 194 E2
Banners Gate 71 L1
Baptist End 85 G7
Barnacle 117 M7
Barnettbrook 139 G8
Barnt Green 166 E6
Barnt Green 167 H5
Barr Common 55 G2
Barston 149 M5
Bartley Green 123 H5
Batchley 195 L2
Bateman's Green 145 K6
Baxterley 62 A7
Baylis Green 189 M4
Bearwood 105 L3
Beausale 190 A3
Bedworth 116 F5
Bedworth Heath 116 C4
Beech Lanes 105 J6
Beechwood 151 K7
Belbroughton 140 D6
Belgrave 46 C4
Bell End 140 F6
Belle Vale 103 K8
Bellevue 166 A3
Bell Green 134 F5
Bell Heath 141 H5
Bentley 52 B2
Bentley 78 B1
Bentley Common 62 B8
Bentley Heath 148 C8
Benton Green 151 J3
Beoley 189 H6
Berkswell 151 H2
Bermuda 98 E5
Bescot 53 G7
Bickenhill 129 H4
Bilbrook 35 G1
Billesley 126 A7
Billesley Common 125 L6
Bilston 51 G6
Bilton 183 G6
Binley 155 J5
Binley Woods 156 A6
Birch Acre 169 H6
Birchan Coppice 160 F4
Birch End 69 K6
Birches Green 90 E2
Birchfield 89 H4
Birchills 53 H2
Birchley Heath 78 C4
Birchmoor 47 J6
Birmingham 6 C7
Bitterscote 45 L2
Black Bank 116 E4
Blackdown 192 D8
Blackfords 16 D2
Blackheath 103 M3
Black Lake 68 E6
Blackstone 160 B4
Blackwell 166 E8
Blakebrook 137 G7
Blakedown 139 G3
Blakeley 64 E8
Blakenall Heath 39 G5
Blakenhall 49 M6
Bloomfield 67 K7
Blossomfield 147 J3
Bloxwich 38 E4
Bluntington 163 J4
Blyth End 94 A3
Bodymoor Heath 59 L8
Boldmere 72 E4
Bolehall 46 A1
Boley Park 21 K6
Bonehill 45 J4
Boney Hay 18 F4
Bordesley Green 108 C4
Borough Park 31 M6
Boscomoor 10 C5
Botts Green 77 H8
Bournbrook 124 E3
Bournes Green 164 A3
Bourne Vale 55 G2
Bournheath 165 H5
Bournville 124 D6
Bowling Green 103 H2
Box Trees 171 M4
Brades Village 86 B4
Bradley 67 H2

Bradmore 49 J5
Bradnock's Marsh 150 B2
Bramford 66 E6
Brandon 156 D8
Brandwood End 145 H1
Branson's Cross 189 L3
The Bratch 64 D5
Bretford 157 J6
Bridge End 199 L8
Bridgetown 16 B6
Brierley Hill 102 A3
Brinklow 157 J2
Brinsford 22 B6
Bristnall Fields 104 F2
Broad Green 186 E3
Broadwaters 137 J4
Brockencote 163 H5
Brockmoor 101 M1
Bromford 91 J4
Bromley 83 L8
Bromsgrove 185 M3
Broome 139 L3
Broom Hill 164 B2
Brownhills 26 E5
Brown's Green 88 D1
Brownshill Green 133 G4
Bubbenhall 179 H7
Buckland End 91 L6
Buckpool 101 K3
Budbrooke 198 C6
Burcot 186 C1
Burlish Park 160 D6
Burnt Tree 85 K3
Burntwood 18 C6
Burntwood Green 19 H7
Burton Green 176 A1
Bushbury 36 C2
Cakebole 162 F7
Caldecote 80 D3
Caldmore 4 C6
Calf Heath 14 D6
California 123 K3
Camp Hill 80 C8
Campion Hills 201 G4
Canley 153 G7
Cannock 16 A2
The Cape 199 H4
Carol Green 151 K5
Carpenter's Hill 189 K3
Carraway Head 57 M1
Castle Bromwich 92 A5
Castlecroft 48 E5
Castle Vale 91 C7
Catchems Corner 151 J8
Catchems End 136 B8
Catherine-de-Barnes 128 E8
Cathiron 158 D4
Catshill 26 E7
Catshill 165 L5
Caunsall 118 A6
Causeway Green 104 D2
Cawston 182 E6
Chaddesley Corbett 163 J5
Chadsmoor 16 C1
Chad Valley 106 D6
Chadwick End 173 M6
Chapel End 79 M5
Chapel Fields 153 J3
Chapel Green 114 A6
Chapman's Hill 141 M4
Charford 185 J5
Charlemont 69 H6
Chase Terrace 18 C5
Chasetown 18 D7
Chattle Hill 93 J5
Chelmsley Wood 111 G4
Cheslyn Hay 24 B2
Chessetts Wood 173 H5
Chesterfield 28 C5
Cheswick Green 171 J1
Cheylesmore 154 C6
Chilvers Coton 98 E4
Chorley 19 J3
The Chuckery 5 K3
Churchbridge 16 D8
Church End 78 E7
Church End 95 G3
Church End 155 G2
Churchfield 69 J8
Church Hill 13 H8
Church Hill 68 E1
Church Hill 188 E8
Churchill 139 G2
Church Lawford 157 M8
Cinder Hill 66 D4
Claregate 35 H7
Clayhanger 26 B7
Clent 140 E2
Cliff 59 M5
Coalpit Field 117 H4
Coal Pool 39 K8
Cobley Hill 187 J1
Codsall 34 D1
Cofton Common 143 K7
Cofton Hackett 167 H2
Cole End 93 K5
Colehall 91 M8
Coleshill 93 K6
Collycroft 116 F1
Colton Hills 65 L2
Comberford 31 H2
Comberton 137 L7
Compton 49 H3
Cooksey Corner 184 B7
Coombeswood 103 M7
Copt Heath 148 E4
Corley 114 F5
Corley Ash 114 E4
Corley Moor 114 C6
Coseley 67 G4
Cosford 159 K2
Coton 31 G7
Cotteridge 124 C8
Coundon 133 J6
Court House Green 134 E6
Coven Heath 22 A7
Crabbs Cross 196 C7
Crackley 176 F6

Cradley 103 G7
Cradley Heath 103 G5
Creswell Green 19 J3
Cross Green 22 B4
Cubbington 193 H7
Curdworth 74 E7
Dam Mill 34 F4
Darby End 103 H1
Darby's Hill 85 M6
Darlaston 52 A4
Darlaston Green 52 C6
Darley Green 172 E5
Darnford 21 K7
Daw End 39 M8
Dayhouse Bank 141 M3
Deepfields 66 F4
The Delves 69 L1
Devitts Green 96 A4
Dickens Heath 146 E8
Digbeth 7 J6
Dodford 164 D7
Doe Bank 57 G6
Dogingtree Estate 12 B5
Dordale 164 D3
Dordon 47 K8
Dorridge 172 E2
Dosthill 45 M8
Drakes Cross 145 L7
Drayton 163 M1
Drayton Bassett 45 H8
Druids Heath 41 G4
Dudley 85 H3
Dudley Port 86 A1
Dudley's Fields 38 D5
Dudley Wood 103 G3
Duke End 112 C1
Dunsley 118 A1
Dunstall Hill 35 M8
Eachway 142 D7
Earlsdon 8 A8
Earlswood 170 E4
Easenhall 158 C1
Eastcote 149 J2
Eaves Green 131 K3
Edgbaston 106 D7
Edge Hill 61 G3
Edgwick 134 C5
Edial 19 J7
Elcock's Brook 195 H7
Elmdon 128 E2
Elmdon Heath 128 C6
Emscote 199 L5
Enfield 188 B8
Erdington 90 E2
Essington 37 K2
Ettingshall 50 D8
Ettingshall Park 66 B2
Eve Hill 84 E3
Exhall 116 F6
Fairfield 136 F2
Fairfield 165 G2
Falcon Lodge 57 M7
Fallings Heath 52 C8
Farewell 19 L1
Fazeley 45 L4
Featherstone 23 G6
Fen End 174 C2
Fillongley 114 C2
Finham 177 M2
Finstall 186 C4
Fishley 39 G1
Five Ways 118 E8
Flint's Green 131 K8
Foleshill 134 D5
Foley Park 161 G2
Footherley 42 C3
Fordbridge 110 E2
Fordhouses 35 M2
Forhill 168 E1
Forshaw Heath 170 A6
Foster's Green 194 A6
Foul End 77 G3
Four Ashes 14 A7
Four Ashes 172 A2
Four Crosses 15 H6
Four Oaks 56 C2
Four Oaks 131 H8
Four Oaks Park 56 D5
Foxford 134 E1
Foxlydiate 195 J2
Franche 136 F4
Frankley 122 F8
Frankley 142 D3
Frankley Green 122 E8
Frankley Hill 142 D2
Freasley 61 G1
Friar Park 69 H2
Furnace End 95 J2
Gailey Wharf 14 D3
Galley Common 79 L8
Garrets Green 109 L4
Gentleshaw 18 E1
Gibbet Hill 177 J3
Gib Heath 88 E6
Giggetty 64 C8
Gilbertstone 109 K7
Gillway 31 L6
Gilson 93 J4
Glascote 46 A2
Glebe Farm 109 K1
Golds Green 68 C5
Goldthorn Park 66 B1
Goodyers End 116 A4
Gornalwood 84 A2
Gorsley Ley 19 G6
Goscote 39 K5
Gosford Green 9 L5
Gospel End Village 65 K5
Gothersley 100 C3
Gravelly Hill 90 D3
Great Barr 70 D3
Great Bridge 67 M7
Great Heath 134 C6
Great Saredon 15 H7
Great Wyrley 24 E2
Green End 113 J4
Green Heath 12 E6
Greenhill 137 L6

Greenlands 196 D5
Green Lane 153 L8
Green Lane 197 H7
Greensforge 82 B7
Grendon 62 B1
Grendon Common 62 A3
Griff 98 F7
Griffin's Hill 124 E5
Grimes Hill 169 M1
Grove End 74 D2
Grove Vale 70 A4
Gun Hill 96 D6
Guns Village 86 E1
The Gutter 141 J6
Guy's Cliffe 199 K3
Habberley 136 E7
Hackman's Gate 139 K4
Haden Cross 103 L5
Hagley 120 B7
Halesowen 122 A1
Hall End 47 K8
Hall Flat 166 A6
Hall Green 69 G3
Hall Green 126 E6
Hall Green 134 F2
Hammerwich 27 H1
Hampton in Arden 129 M7
Hampton Magna 198 E7
Hampton on the Hill 198 C8
Hamstead 70 C5
Handsworth 88 B3
Handsworth Wood 88 F2
Harborne 105 L7
Harborough Magna 159 G2
Harborough Parva 159 G3
Harden 39 K6
Hardwick 55 K3
Hartle 140 D7
Hartshill 79 M4
Hart's Hill 84 C8
Hartshill Green 79 L3
Harvest Hill 132 B3
Harvills Hawthorn 68 B6
Harvington 162 F3
Hasbury 121 J2
Hasluck's Green 146 C3
Hateley Heath 69 G7
Hatherton 15 K4
Hatton 198 A2
Hawkesbury 117 G7
Hawkes End 132 E3
Hawkesley 144 C5
Hawks Green 16 E4
Hawne 103 L8
Hayfield Hill 18 D1
Hayley Green 121 G4
Hay Mills 108 F7
Hazelslade 13 L7
Headless Cross 196 C5
Headley Heath 145 G6
Heath End 39 K4
Heath Green 189 J2
Heath Hayes 17 K4
Heath Town 50 E1
Hednesford 13 G7
Henley Green 135 H5
Higham on the Hill 81 K2
Highbridge 25 L7
Highgate 107 K5
High Heath 40 A3
High Heath 57 M5
Highter's Heath 145 M3
High Town 12 D8
Hill 56 E1
Hillfield 147 L6
Hillfields 9 H2
Hill Hook 42 C7
Hillpool 139 K8
Hill Top 68 E5
Hill Top 96 E4
Hill Top 99 G4
Hill Wood 43 G8
Hill Wootton 192 A7
Hilton 27 L5
Himley 82 F2
Hinksford 82 D5
Hints 44 B3
Hobble End 25 G6
Hockley 46 C8
Hockley 151 M1
Hockley Heath 172 B7
Hodgehill 91 H8
Hoggrill's End 76 D8
Holbrooks 134 A2
Holly Bank 40 F2
Hollyberry End 132 B1
Hollyhurst 117 J5
Hollywood 145 M5
Holt End 189 K6
Holy Cross 140 C3
Honiley 175 H8
Hoobrook 161 K3
Hook End 129 M8
Hopwas 30 E6
Hopwood 168 A2
Horeston Grange 81 L8
Horseley Heath 68 A8
Howe Green 97 H8
Hunnington 121 M6
Hunt End 196 A8
Huntington 12 B7
Hunts Green 59 G6
Hurcott 138 C5
Hurley 61 G8
Hurley Common 60 F6
Hurst Green 104 D5
Hurst Hill 66 D5
Illey 122 C5
Ilshaw Heath 171 H4
Inkford 169 L4
Ipsley 197 G4
Iverley 119 H5
Kates Hill 85 J4
Kendal End 167 H3
Kenilworth 191 J2
Keresley 133 K1
Keresley Newlands 115 M7
Kettlebrook 45 M2

Kidderminster 161 G1
Kineton Green 127 H5
Kingsbury 60 B7
King's Heath 125 J6
Kings Hill 177 M3
King's Hill 68 D2
Kingshurst 92 E6
King's Newnham 158 A6
King's Norton 144 C3
Kingstanding 71 L4
Kingswinford 83 K7
Kinwalsey 113 K6
Kirby Corner 152 E7
Kitt's Green 110 A1
Kitwell 122 E6
Knowle 149 G7
Knowle Grove 172 F2
The Knowle 85 L8
The Laches 22 D2
Ladyes Hill 176 E7
Ladywood 106 E3
Lakeside 196 E2
Lambert's End 86 E2
Landywood 24 C3
Lane Green 35 G2
Lane Head 38 A7
Lanesfield 66 E1
Laney Green 23 L3
Langley 86 D8
Langley Green 104 F1
Lapal 122 D2
Lawford Heath 182 B6
Lawns Wood 100 F2
Lea End 168 D2
Lea Hall 109 L3
Lea Marston 75 L6
Leamonsley 20 C6
Leamore 38 E7
Leapgate 161 J8
Lee Bank 6 C9
Leek Wootton 191 L7
Leighswood 40 E5
Ley Hill 56 E4
The Leys 31 L8
Lichfield 20 D4
Lickey 166 E2
Lickey End 166 B7
Lickhill 160 C8
Lifford 144 F1
Lillington 201 H2
Lime Tree Park 152 E4
Linthurst 166 F7
Little Aston 42 A8
Little Bloxwich 39 H2
Little Bromwich 108 D3
Little Hay 43 G4
Little Heath 134 D4
Little Lawford 158 E6
Little Norton 25 M3
Little Packington 111 M7
Little Saredon 23 H2
Littlewood 24 E2
Littleworth 17 K1
Littleworth End 58 A5
Little Wyrley 25 H5
Lode Heath 128 C3
Lodge Green 131 H2
Lodge Hill 123 M3
Lodge Park 196 D3
Londonderry 105 G3
London Fields 84 C3
Longbridge 143 H5
Longford 134 D1
Long Lawford 158 D8
Lower Bentley 194 B5
Lower Bradley 67 K1
Lower Clent 140 B1
Lower Eastern Green 152 C2
Lower Gornal 84 C1
Lower Illey 122 C6
Lower Penn 48 D8
Lower Stoke 154 E4
Lower Stonnall 41 L4
Low Habberley 136 D5
Low Hill 36 B6
Lozells 89 G6
The Lunt 51 L6
Lutley 120 F3
Lydiate Ash 166 A2
Lye 102 D7
Lyndon Green 109 K6
Lynn 27 K8
Madeley Heath 141 J6
Major's Green 146 B5
Mancetter 63 L7
Maney 72 F1
Manor House 135 G3
Mappleborough Green 197 L5
Marlbrook 166 B4
Marston 75 L3
Marston 157 G8
Marston Green 110 E5
Marston Jabbett 99 K8
Matchborough 197 J5
Maw Green 53 M7
Maxstoke 112 F3
Mayer's Green 87 J2
Meer End 175 G4
Mere Green 56 F2
Meriden 131 H4
Merridale 49 J3
Merry Hill 49 G6
Mesty Croft 68 E1
Middle Bickenhill 129 L2
Middle Hill 23 L1
Middle Stoke 154 E2
Middleton 58 F4
Mile Oak 45 H4
Mill Green 41 L6
Milverton 200 B2
Minworth 74 A8
Monkspath 147 L8
Monmore Green 50 E5
Monwode Lea 95 L2
Moon's Moat 189 K8
Moor Green 125 H4
Moor Hall 57 H4
Moseley 50 E4

Moseley 125 K3	Perry Common 71 M5	Shard End 92 B8	Swan Village 86 D1	Wednesfield 37 H7
Mount Pleasant 116 E2	Perry Crofts 32 A6	Shareshill 23 H3	Swindon 82 D3	Weeford 43 L1
Mount Pleasant 195 G8	Perryfields 185 H1	Sharmans Cross 147 J1	Sydenham 201 L3	Weoley Castle 123 K4
Moxley 67 M1	Perton 48 C1	Sheldon 109 M8	Tamworth 46 D2	Wergs 34 D7
Muckley Corner 27 L3	Pheasey 71 C1	Shelfield 40 A5	Tanner's Green 169 M3	West Chadsmoor 12 D7
Mushroom Green 102 F4	Piccadilly 60 D5	Shenley Fields 123 J6	Tansley Hill 85 K6	Westcroft 36 F2
Mustow Green 162 E4	Pickford 132 C5	Shenstone 28 D8	Tanwood 163 L3	West Hagley 119 M8
Myton 200 A6	Pickford Green 132 B6	Shenstone 162 D6	Tardebigge 186 E6	West Heath 144 A6
Neal's Green 116 B7	Pillaton 11 G6	Shenstone Woodend 42 E4	Tat Bank 86 E6	West Hill 12 E7
Nechells 90 B5	Pinkett's Booth 132 B5	Shire Oak 26 D7	Temple Balsall 173 M1	Weston in Arden 117 M1
Nechells Green 7 M1	Pink Green 189 M5	Shire Oak Hill 26 F8	Ten Acres 124 F5	Westwood Heath 152 C7
Nechells Green 107 M1	Pinley 154 E6	Shirley 147 C2	Terry's Green 170 D6	Whateley 60 C2
Nether Stowe 21 H3	Pipehill 19 M8	Shirley Heath 147 G4	Tettenhall 35 G8	Whitacre Heath 76 A7
Netherton 84 F8	Pleck 52 F7	Short Cross 103 L8	Tettenhall Wood 49 H1	Whiteheath Gate 104 C1
Nether Whitacre 76 E7	Plough Hill 79 L6	Short Heath 38 B7	Thimble End 73 K4	Whitehouse Common 57 K7
New Arley 96 F5	Podmoor 162 C8	Short Heath 72 D7	Thornes 41 J2	Whitemoor 176 E8
New Bilton 183 H3	Polesworth 47 L4	Shustoke 94 D3	Three Maypoles 146 F6	Whitestone 99 K5
Newbold on Avon 159 J8	Portobello 51 J3	Shuttington 33 J6	Tidbury Green 170 C1	Whitley 154 D7
Newbolds 36 E7	Portway 86 A7	Sidemoor 185 K1	Tile Cross 110 C3	Whitlock's End 146 C7
Newbridge 49 H2	Portway 169 L7	Silver End 101 M4	Tile Hill 152 C4	Whitmore Park 133 M4
Newhall Green 113 M4	Potter's Green 135 K4	Silver Street 145 J8	Tilehouse Green 148 E8	Whittington 63 G2
New Invention 38 A5	Prestwood 100 C4	Slade Heath 22 C3	Timberhonger 184 C4	Whittington 118 A3
New Oscott 72 B3	Priestfield 50 F7	Slideslow 186 A3	Tipper's Hill 96 C7	Whoberley 153 G3
Newton 70 A5	Primrose Hill 103 H1	Small Heath 108 A5	Tipton 67 L6	Wigginton 31 M3
Newtown 24 E8	Princes End 67 J4	Smallwood 196 D2	Tipton Green 67 H7	Wightwick 48 D4
New Town 26 F5	Prospect Village 17 M1	Smestow 82 A1	Tividale 85 M4	Wilden 161 H7
New Town 86 B1	Pye Green 12 D4	Smethwick 105 K1	Tollbar End 178 F1	Wildmoor 165 K1
Newtown 89 G8	Pype Hayes 73 H8	Soho 88 A7	Toll End 67 M7	Willenhall 51 M2
Northfield 143 M1	Quarry Bank 102 D5	Solihull 148 A3	Torton 161 M8	Willenhall 155 G7
Norton 119 J3	Quarry Heath 11 G5	Solihull Lodge 146 A3	Tower Hill 70 E7	Wilnecote 46 D6
Norton Canes 17 J8	Quarry Hill 46 E7	Southcrest 196 A3	Trescott 48 A7	Wimblebury 17 K2
Norton East 17 L7	Queslett 71 G3	South Yardley 109 H7	Triangle 26 F1	Windy Arbour 191 L2
Norton Green 25 J1	Quinton 104 E7	Sparkbrook 107 M6	Trueman's Heath 146 A6	Winson Green 88 D8
Norton Green 172 F3	Radford 134 A7	Sparkhill 126 A2	Trysull 64 A4	Winterfold 162 F4
Nuneaton 98 D2	Radford Semele 201 K8	Spennells 161 L4	Tudor Hill 56 E7	Winyates 197 J2
Oaken 34 A3	Ratcliffe Culey 63 M1	Spon End 8 B5	Turves Green 123 L4	Winyates Green 197 K1
Oakenshaw 196 C7	Rawnsley 13 M8	Springfield 3 K2	Tutnall 186 E4	Wishaw 74 E3
Oakham 85 K6	Reddicap Heath 73 L1	Springfield 85 K8	Two Gates 46 A5	Witherley 63 M6
Ocker Hill 68 A4	Redditch 196 A3	Springfield 126 A6	Tyburn 91 J2	Withybed Green 167 J2
Old Arley 96 D3	Rednal 143 G8	Springhill 24 B8	Tyseley 108 E8	Withymoor Village 102 C4
Oldbury 79 J3	Reeves Green 151 L5	Springhill 27 H6	Ulverley Green 127 J5	Witton 89 J2
Oldbury 86 E8	Ridgacre 105 G7	Spring Hill 65 C1	Upper Bentley 194 F4	Wollaston 101 J7
Old Fallings 36 D6	Ridge Lane 78 E3	The Spring 176 D6	Upper Catshill 165 M4	Wollescote 120 C1
Oldfallow 16 A2	Riverside 188 C7	Stakenbridge 139 H2	Upper Eastern Green 132 A7	Wolston 180 F2
Old Hill 103 L4	Robinson's End 97 J2	Stambermill 102 A8	Upper Gambolds 186 A8	Wolverhampton 3 J4
Old Milverton 199 L2	Rodbaston 14 B1	Standeford 22 A1	Upper Gornal 66 C7	Wolverley 137 J1
Old Perton 48 A2	Romsley 141 L1	Stanklyn 162 B3	Upper Landywood 24 C6	Wombourne 64 B7
Old Swinford 119 L2	Romsley Hill 141 L3	Staple Hill 166 A5	Upper Stoke 134 F8	Woodcock Hill 123 J5
Oldwich Lane 174 B4	Rood End 87 G7	Stareton 193 H2	Upper Witton 72 A7	Woodcote 191 J6
Olton 127 L3	Roseville 66 E5	Stechford 109 J2	Vauxhall 107 M2	Woodcote Green 164 A7
Orton 64 D2	Rotten Row 173 G1	Stirchley 124 E6	Vigo 40 D3	Wood End 37 G6
Orton Hill 64 E3	Rotton Park 106 C1	Stivichall 154 A8	The Village 83 J6	Wood End 61 H4
Otherton 10 D8	Roughley 57 G2	Stockfield 127 G1	Wake Green 125 L4	Wood End 96 F8
Ounsdale 64 D7	Round Oak 102 C1	Stockingford 97 M3	Walker's Heath 144 F4	Wood End 135 G3
Outwood 163 L8	Round's Green 86 C5	Stockland Green 90 A1	Walkwood 195 L7	Woodgate 122 D4
Outwoods 112 F7	Rowley Regis 85 M8	Stockwell End 35 C8	Wall 28 B3	Woodgate Valley 123 G2
Overend 103 J7	Rowley's Green 134 C1	Stoke 155 C3	Wallbrook 67 G6	Wood Green 52 E8
Over Green 74 D4	Rowney Green 168 D8	Stoke Aldermoor 155 G5	Wall Heath 82 F5	Wood Hayes 36 F4
Overslade 183 J4	Royal Leamington Spa 201 H3	Stoke End 58 D6	Wallington Heath 38 E2	Wood Hill 156 F1
Over Whitacre 95 J2	Rubery 142 E6	Stoke Heath 134 E7	Walmley 73 K5	Woodhouses 19 L6
Oxbarn 49 J6	Rugby 183 M4	Stoke Heath 185 H8	Walmley Ash 73 M6	Woodloes Park 199 H4
Oxley 35 M5	Ruiton 84 B1	Stone 162 B2	Walsal End 149 L2	Woodrow 163 H2
Packmores 199 J5	Rumbow Cottages 141 H2	Stonebridge 129 M3	Walsall 5 L1	Woodrow 196 F6
Packwood 172 E6	Rumbush 170 C2	Stone Cross 69 H4	Walsall Wood 40 D1	Woods Bank 52 B8
Packwood Gullet 172 D4	Rumer Hill 16 C5	Stoneleigh 185 L4	Walsgrave on Sowe 135 M6	Woodsetton 66 C6
Palfrey 4 E9	Rushall 40 A6	Stoneydelph 46 F4	Walton Pool 140 E3	Woodside 84 D7
Palmers Cross 34 F5	Russell's Hall 84 C5	Stoney Hill 185 L4	Ward End 90 E8	The Woods 69 G1
Park Farm 196 F5	Ryton-on-Dunsmore 179 M3	Stonnall 41 H1	Waring's Green 171 G4	Woodway Park 135 J5
Parkfield 50 D8	St Godwalds 186 A6	Stourbridge 100 D6	Warley Woods 105 J4	Wootton Green 150 D4
Park Gate 184 E2	St Helena 47 K4	Stourton 100 B1	Warstock 146 A2	Wordsley 101 J2
Park Hill 177 F8	St Johns 191 K3	Stowe 21 G4	Warstone 23 M5	Worlds End 127 L6
Park Village 36 D8	St Nicolas Park 81 L6	Stow Lawn 51 H5	Warwick 199 L7	Worms Ash 165 H7
Pedmore 120 B5	Salter Street 171 G3	The Straits 65 M8	Washford 197 J5	Wribbenhall 160 A1
Pelsall 39 M2	Saltley 108 C1	Streethay 21 L3	Washwood Heath 90 C7	Wyken 135 H8
Pelsall Wood 25 K8	Sandfields 20 F8	Streetly 55 M3	Waste Green 190 A6	Wylde Green 73 H4
Pendeford 35 J3	Sandwell 87 L7	Stretton-on-Dunsmore 180 E8	Water Orton 92 F2	Wythall 169 J3
Penkridge 10 E5	Scotlands 36 E5	Stubber's Green 40 C5	Watford Gap 42 D6	Yardley 109 H5
Penn 49 J7	Seckington 33 L2	Summerfield 161 L6	Weatheroak Hill 168 F4	Yardley Wood 126 C8
Pensnett 83 M6	Sedgemere 174 C1	Summerhill 27 J4	Webheath 195 J4	Yew Tree 69 M2
Perry 71 H7	Sedgley 66 C5	Summer Hill 67 L4	Weddington 81 G5	
Perry Barr 70 F8	Selly Oak 124 B4	Summerhill 136 E8	Wednesbury 68 B1	
Perry Beeches 70 E5	Selly Park 124 E4	Sutton Coldfield 57 L6	Wednesbury Oak 67 K4	

USING THE STREET INDEX

Street names are listed alphabetically. Each street name is followed by its postal town or area locality, the Postcode District, the page number, and the reference to the square in which the name is found.

Example: **Abberley** TAM/AM/WIL B77 .... 47 G3 🔳

Some entries are followed by a number in a blue box. This number indicates the location of the street within the referenced grid square. The full street name is listed at the side of the map page.

GENERAL ABBREVIATIONS

ACC .... ACCESS	COT .... COTTAGE	FLDS .... FIELDS	INF .... INFIRMARY	N .... NORTH
ALY .... ALLEY	COTS .... COTTAGES	FLS .... FALLS	INFO .... INFORMATION	NE .... NORTH EAST
AP .... APPROACH	CP .... CAPE	FLS .... FLATS	INT .... INTERCHANGE	NW .... NORTH WEST
AR .... ARCADE	CPS .... COPSE	FM .... FARM	IS .... ISLAND	O/P .... OVERPASS
ASS .... ASSOCIATION	CR .... CREEK	FT .... FORT	JCT .... JUNCTION	OFF .... OFFICE
AV .... AVENUE	CREM .... CREMATORIUM	FWY .... FREEWAY	JTY .... JETTY	ORCH .... ORCHARD
BCH .... BEACH	CRS .... CRESCENT	FY .... FERRY	KG .... KING	OV .... OVAL
BLDS .... BUILDINGS	CSWY .... CAUSEWAY	GA .... GATE	KNL .... KNOLL	PAL .... PALACE
BND .... BEND	CT .... COURT	GAL .... GALLERY	L .... LAKE	PAS .... PASSAGE
BNK .... BANK	CTRL .... CENTRAL	GDN .... GARDEN	LA .... LANE	PAV .... PAVILION
BR .... BRIDGE	CTS .... COURTS	GDNS .... GARDENS	LDG .... LODGE	PDE .... PARADE
BRK .... BROOK	CTYD .... COURTYARD	GLD .... GLADE	LGT .... LIGHT	PH .... PUBLIC HOUSE
BTM .... BOTTOM	CUTT .... CUTTINGS	GLN .... GLEN	LK .... LOCK	PK .... PARK
BUS .... BUSINESS	CV .... COVE	GN .... GREEN	LKS .... LAKES	PKWY .... PARKWAY
BVD .... BOULEVARD	CYN .... CANYON	GND .... GROUND	LNDG .... LANDING	PL .... PLACE
BY .... BYPASS	DEPT .... DEPARTMENT	GRA .... GRANGE	LTL .... LITTLE	PLN .... PLAIN
CATH .... CATHEDRAL	DL .... DALE	GRG .... GARAGE	LWR .... LOWER	PLNS .... PLAINS
CEM .... CEMETERY	DM .... DAM	GT .... GREAT	MAG .... MAGISTRATE	PLZ .... PLAZA
CEN .... CENTRE	DR .... DRIVE	GTWY .... GATEWAY	MAN .... MANSIONS	POL .... POLICE STATION
CFT .... CROFT	DRO .... DROVE	GV .... GROVE	MD .... MEAD	PR .... PRINCE
CH .... CHURCH	DRY .... DRIVEWAY	HGR .... HIGHER	MDW .... MEADOWS	PREC .... PRECINCT
CHA .... CHASE	DWGS .... DWELLINGS	HL .... HILL	MEM .... MEMORIAL	PREP .... PREPARATORY
CHYD .... CHURCHYARD	E .... EAST	HLS .... HILLS	MKT .... MARKET	PRIM .... PRIMARY
CIR .... CIRCLE	EMB .... EMBANKMENT	HO .... HOUSE	MKTS .... MARKETS	PROM .... PROMENADE
CIRC .... CIRCUS	EMBY .... EMBASSY	HOL .... HOLLOW	ML .... MALL	PRS .... PRINCESS
CL .... CLOSE	ESP .... ESPLANADE	HOSP .... HOSPITAL	ML .... MILL	PRT .... PORT
CLFS .... CLIFFS	EST .... ESTATE	HRB .... HARBOUR	MNR .... MANOR	PT .... POINT
CMP .... CAMP	EX .... EXCHANGE	HTH .... HEATH	MS .... MEWS	PTH .... PATH
CNR .... CORNER	EXPY .... EXPRESSWAY	HTS .... HEIGHTS	MSN .... MISSION	PZ .... PIAZZA
CO .... COUNTY	EXT .... EXTENSION	HVN .... HAVEN	MT .... MOUNT	QD .... QUADRANT
COLL .... COLLEGE	F/O .... FLYOVER	HWY .... HIGHWAY	MTN .... MOUNTAIN	QU .... QUEEN
COM .... COMMON	FC .... FOOTBALL CLUB	IMP .... IMPERIAL	MTS .... MOUNTAINS	QY .... QUAY
COMM .... COMMISSION	FK .... FORK	IN .... INLET	MUS .... MUSEUM	R .... RIVER
CON .... CONVENT	FLD .... FIELD	IND EST .... INDUSTRIAL ESTATE	MWY .... MOTORWAY	RBT .... ROUNDABOUT

RD ....ROAD	SER ....SERVICE AREA	STR ....STREAM	TWR ....TOWER	VW ....VIEW
RDG ....RIDGE	SH ....SHORE	STRD ....STRAND	U/P ....UNDERPASS	W ....WEST
REP ....REPUBLIC	SHOP ....SHOPPING	SW ....SOUTH WEST	UNI ....UNIVERSITY	WD ....WOOD
RES ....RESERVOIR	SKWY ....SKYWAY	TDG ....TRADING	UPR ....UPPER	WHF ....WHARF
RFC ....RUGBY FOOTBALL CLUB	SMT ....SUMMIT	TER ....TERRACE	V ....VALE	WK ....WALK
RI ....RISE	SOC ....SOCIETY	THWY ....THROUGHWAY	VA ....VALLEY	WKS ....WALKS
RP ....RAMP	SP ....SPUR	TNL ....TUNNEL	VIAD ....VIADUCT	WLS ....WELLS
RW ....ROW	SPR ....SPRING	TOLL ....TOLLWAY	VIL ....VILLA	WY ....WAY
S ....SOUTH	SQ ....SQUARE	TPK ....TURNPIKE	VIS ....VISTA	YD ....YARD
SCH ....SCHOOL	ST ....STREET	TR ....TRACK	VLG ....VILLAGE	YHA ....YOUTH HOSTEL
SE ....SOUTH EAST	STN ....STATION	TRL ....TRAIL	VLS ....VILLAS	

POSTCODE TOWNS AND AREA ABBREVIATIONS

ACGN ....Acock's Green
ALDR ....Aldridge
ALE/KHTH/YWD ....Alcester Lane'sEnd/King's Heath/Yardley Wood
ALVE ....Alvechurch
AST/WIT ....Aston/Witton
ATHST ....Atherstone
BDMR/CCFT ....Bradmore/Castlecroft
BDWTH ....Bedworth
BEWD ....Bewdley
BFLD/HDSWWD ....Birchfield/Handsworth Wood
BHAMNEC ....Birmingham N.E.C.
BHTH/HG ....Balsall Heath/Highgate
BILS/COS ....Bilston/Coseley
BKDE/SHDE ....Buckland End/Shard End
BKHL/PFLD ....Blakenhall/Priestfield
BLKHTH/ROWR ..Blackheath/Rowley Regis
BLOX/PEL ....Bloxwich/Pelsall
BNTWD ....Burntwood
BORD ....Bordesley
BRGRVE ....Bromsgrove east
BRGRVW ....Bromsgrove west
BRLYHL ....Brierley Hill
BRWNH ....Brownhills
BTACH/HAR ..Bishop's Tachbrook/Harbury
BVILLE ....Bournville
CBHAM ....Central Birmingham
CBHAMNE ..Central Birmingham northeast
CBHAMNW ....Central Birmingham north-west
CBHAMW ....Central Birmingham west

CBROM ....Castle Bromwich
CDSL ....Codsall
CDYHTH ....Cradley Heath
CHWD/FDBR/MGN ....Chelmsley Wood/Fordbridge/Marston Green
CNCK/NC ....Cannock/Norton Canes
COV ....Coventry
COVE ....Coventry east
COVEN ....Coven
COVN ....Coventry north
COVS ....Coventry south
COVW ....Coventry west
CRTAM ....Central & Rural Tamworth
CSCFLD/WYGN ....Central Sutton Coldfield/Wylde Green
CSHL/WTROR ....Coleshill/Water Orton
CVALE ....Castle Vale
DARL/WED ....Darlaston/Wednesbury
DIG/EDG ....Digbeth/Edgbaston
DOR/KN ....Dorridge/Knowle
DROIT ....Droitwich
DSYBK/YTR ....Daisy Bank/Yew Tree
DUDN ....Dudley north
DUDS ....Dudley south
DUNHL/THL/PER ....Dunstall Hill/Tettenhall/Perton
EDG ....Edgbaston
ERDE/BCHGN ....Erdington east/Birches Green
ERDW/GRVHL ....Erdington west/Gravelly Hill

ETTPK/GDPK/PENN ....Ettingshall Park/Goldthorn Park/Penn
FOAKS/STRLY ....Four Oaks/Streetly
GTB/HAM ....Great Barr/Hamstead
GTWY ....Great Wyrley
HAG/WOL ....Hagley/Wollescote
HALE ....Halesowen
HDSW ....Handsworth
HEDN ....Hednesford
HHTH/SAND ....Hateley Heath/Sandwell
HIA/OLT ....Hampton in Arden/Olton
HLGN/YWD ....Hall Green/Yardley Wood
HLYWD ....Hollywood
HOCK/TIA ....Hockley Heath/Tanworth-in-Arden
HRBN ....Harborne
HWK/WKHTH ....Hawkesley/Walker's Heath
KGSTG ....Kingstanding
KGSWFD ....Kingswinford
KIDD ....Kidderminster
KIDDW ....Kidderminster west
KINVER ....Kinver
KNWTH ....Kenilworth
LDYWD/EDGR ....Ladywood/Edgbaston Reservoir
LGLYGN/QTN ....Langley Green/Quinton
LGN/SDN/BHAMAIR ....Lyndon Green/Sheldon/Birmingham Airport
LICH ....Lichfield
LICHS ....Lichfield south
LOZ/NWT ....Lozells/Newtown
MGN/WHC ....Mere Green/Whitehouse

Common
MKTBOS/BARL/STKG ....Market Bosworth/Barlestone/Stoke Golding
MOS/BIL ....Moseley/Billesley
NFLD/LBR ....Northfield/Longbridge
NUN ....Nuneaton
NUNW/HART ....Nuneaton west/Hartshill
OLDBY ....Oldbury
PBAR/PBCH ....Perry Bar/Perry Beeches
PENK ....Penkridge
POL/KGSB/FAZ ....Polesworth/Kingsbury/Fazeley
RBRY ....Rubery
RCOVN/BALC/EX ....Rural Coventry north/Balsall Common/Exhall
REDE ....Redditch east
REDW ....Redditch west
RIDG/WDGT ....Ridgacre/Woodgate
RLSN ....Royal Leamington Spa north
RLSS ....Royal Leamington Spa south
RMSLY ....Romsley
RRUGBY ....Rural Rugby
RSTAF ....Rural Stafford
RUGBYN/HIL ....Rugby north/Hillmorton
RUGBYS/DCH ....Rugby south/Dunchurch
RUGE ....Rugeley
RUSH/SHEL ....Rushall/Shelfield
RWWCK/WEL ....Rural Warwick/Wellesbourne
SCFLD/BOLD ..Sutton Coldfield/Boldmere
SEDG ....Sedgley
SHHTH ....Short Heath

SHLY ....Shirley
SLYOAK ....Selly Oak
SMHTH ....Small Heath
SMTHWK ....Smethwick
SMTHWKW ....Smethwick west
SOLH ....Solihull
SPARK ....Sparkhill/Sparkbrook
STETCH ....Stetchford
STRBR ....Stourbridge
STRPT ....Stourport-on-Severn
STUD ....Studley
TAM/AM/WIL ....Tamworth/Amington/Wilnecote
TLHL/CAN ....Tile Hill/Canley
TPTN/OCK ....Tipton/Ocker Hill
VAUX/NECH ....Vauxhall/Nechells
WALM/CURD ....Walmley/Curdworth
WASH/WDE ...Washwood Heath/Ward End
WBROM ....West Bromwich
WLNHL ....Willenhall
WMBN ....Wombourne
WNSFLD ....Wednesfield
WOLV ....Wolverhampton
WOLVN ....Wolverhampton north
WSL ....Walsall
WSLW ....Walsall west
WSNGN ....Winson Green
WWCK ....Warwick
YDLY ....Yardley

Index - streets

Abb - Ald

A

Abberley TAM/AM/WIL B77 .... 47 G3
Abberley Cl HALE B63 .... 121 K3
REDE B98 .... 188 C8
Abberley Rd LGLYGN/QTN B68 .... 104 F5
SEDG DY3 .... 84 A1
Abberley St DUDS DY2 .... 85 G5
SMTHWK B66 .... 88 B8
Abberton Cl HALE B63 .... 122 A2
Abberton Gv SOLH B91 .... 147 M6
Abberton Wy TLHL/CAN CV4 .... 177 H2
Abbess Gv YDLY B25 .... 109 J4
Abbey Cl BRGRVE B60 .... 185 M3
PENK ST19 .... 10 E5
Abbey Crs HALE B63 .... 121 H1
LGLYGN/QTN B68 .... 105 H4
Abbey Cft POL/KGSB/FAZ B78 .... 47 L3
Abbeydale Cl COVS CV3 .... 155 K2
Abbeydale Rd NFLD/LBR B31 .... 143 L3
Abbey Dr BLOX/PEL WS3 .... 25 L8
Abbey End KNWTH CV8 .... 191 K1
Abbeyfield Rd
ERDW/GRVHL B23 .... 72 C5
WOLV WV10 .... 36 C1
Abbeyfields Dr STUD B80 .... 197 J6
Abbey Gn NUN CV11 .... 80 F8
Abbey Green Ct
POL/KGSB/FAZ B78 .... 47 L4
Abbey HI KNWTH CV8 .... 191 K1
Abbey Rd COVS CV3 .... 154 E7
DUDS DY2 .... 85 H7
ERDW/GRVHL B23 .... 90 B3
HALE B63 .... 121 G1
HRBN B17 .... 106 B8
KIDDW DY11 .... 136 E7
REDW B97 .... 196 C1
SEDG DY3 .... 84 A2
SMTHWK B67 .... 105 H4
TAM/AM/WIL B77 .... 46 B2
Abbey Sq BLOX/PEL WS3 .... 38 C3
Abbey St HEDN WS12 .... 12 F6
NUN CV11 .... 80 F8
SEDG DY3 .... 84 A2
Abbey St North WSNGN B18 .... 88 B8
Abbey Vw POL/KGSB/FAZ B78 .... 47 M5
Abbey Wy COVS CV3 .... 154 D7
Abbot Rd HALE B63 .... 121 G5
Abbotsbury Cl COVE CV2 .... 155 L1
Abbotsbury Wy NUN CV11 .... 99 J4
Abbots Cl DOR/KN B93 .... 148 E6
RUSH/SHEL WS4 .... 40 A7
Abbotsford Av SLYOAK B29 .... 123 M6
Abbotsford Dr DUDN DY1 .... 84 C6
Abbotsford Rd LICHS WS14 .... 21 H6
NUN CV11 .... 99 J4
SPARK B11 .... 108 A7
Abbots Ms BRLYHL DY5 .... 102 B4
Abbots Rd ALE/KHTH/YWD B14 .... 125 J6
Abbots Wy BDMR/CCFT WV3 .... 49 J4
WSNGN B18 .... 88 F7
Abbots Wood Cl REDE B98 .... 197 L2
Abbotts Cl STRPT DY13 .... 161 H7
Abbotts La COV CV1 .... 8 D3
Abbotts Pl BLOX/PEL WS3 .... 39 H4
Abbotts Rd ERDE/BCHGN B24 .... 90 D4
Abbotts St BLOX/PEL WS3 .... 39 H3
RLSS CV31 .... 200 D6
Abbotts Wk COVS CV3 .... 156 A6
Abdon Av SLYOAK B29 .... 123 M6
Abeles Wy ATHST CV9 .... 63 G3
Abercorn Rd COVW CV5 .... 153 K3
Aberdeen Cl COVW CV5 .... 132 E8

Aberdeen Rd NUN CV11 .... 99 J4
Aberdeen St WSNGN B18 .... 106 C1
Aberford Cl SHHTH WV12 .... 52 B1
Abergavenny Wk COVS CV3 .... 155 K7
Abigails Cl
LGN/SDN/BHAMAIR B26 .... 109 M6
Abingdon Cl WOLV WV1 .... 50 F3
Abingdon Rd BLOX/PEL WS3 .... 38 D3
DUDS DY2 .... 103 H2
ERDW/GRVHL B23 .... 71 M6
WOLV WV1 .... 50 F3
Abingdon Wy BLOX/PEL WS3 .... 38 D3
CVALE B35 .... 91 L2
NUN CV11 .... 81 K6
Ablewell St WSL WS1 .... 5 G3
Ablon Ct PENK ST19 .... 10 D6
Ablow St BKHL/PFLD WV2 .... 2 E8
Abnalls Cft LICH WS13 .... 20 D4
Abnalls La LICH WS13 .... 20 A5
LICH WS13 .... 20 D4
Abney Dr BILS/COS WV14 .... 66 D4
Ab Rw CBHAMNE B4 .... 7 K3
Acacia Av BEWD DY12 .... 160 A2
CHWD/FDBR/MGN B37 .... 92 D7
COV CV1 .... 9 J7
DSYBK/YTR WS5 .... 69 L1
Acacia Cl
CHWD/FDBR/MGN B37 .... 92 D7
DUDN DY1 .... 84 E2
OLDBY B69 .... 85 M3
Acacia Crs BDWTH CV12 .... 117 H2
CDSL WV8 .... 34 F2
Acacia Dr BILS/COS WV14 .... 66 E6
Acacia Gv HEDN WS12 .... 17 K2
RUGBYN/HIL CV21 .... 183 L6
Acacia Rd BVILLE B30 .... 124 C5
NUNW/HART CV10 .... 80 C8
RLSN CV32 .... 200 B4
Acfold Rd BFLD/HDSWWD B20 .... 70 C8
Achal Cl COVN CV6 .... 134 D3
Acheson Rd HLGN/YWD B28 .... 146 D1
Achilees Cl GTWY WS6 .... 24 E4
Achilles Rd COVN CV6 .... 134 E7
Ackleton Gdns BDMR/CCFT WV3 .... 49 K6
Ackleton Gv SLYOAK B29 .... 123 K5
Acorn Cl ACGN B27 .... 108 F8
BDWTH CV12 .... 116 A5
BNTWD WS7 .... 18 E4
BVILLE B30 .... 124 C5
CNCK/NC WS11 .... 17 G3
GTWY WS6 .... 24 E4
KNWTH CV8 .... 177 M6
WBROM B70 .... 86 F3
Acorn Dr RUGBYS/DCH CV22 .... 182 F4
Acorn Gdns SLYOAK B29 .... 124 E5
Acorn Gv CBHAMW B1 .... 6 A4
CDSL WV8 .... 34 C3
STRBR DY8 .... 101 J4
Acorn Rd BRGRVW B61 .... 165 M5
RMSLY B62 .... 104 A5
WNSFLD WV11 .... 37 L4
The Acorns BRGRVW B61 .... 165 L5
Acorn St COVS CV3 .... 154 F5
WLNHL WV13 .... 52 A3
Acre Ri SHHTH WV12 .... 37 M8
Acres Rd BRLYHL DY5 .... 102 C5
Acton Cl REDE B98 .... 189 H8
Acton Dr SEDG DY3 .... 83 M2
Acton Gv BILS/COS WV14 .... 66 F1
WOLV WV10 .... 71 L3
Ada Lewis Ct GTB/HAM B43 .... 70 C6
Adam Rd COVN CV6 .... 134 E6
Adams Brook Dr
RIDG/WDGT B32 .... 122 F4
Adams Cl SMTHWK B66 .... 87 H6

TPTN/OCK DY4 .... 67 K4
Adams Ct KIDD DY10 .... 137 L6
Adam's Hl HAG/WOL DY9 .... 140 C1
RIDG/WDGT B32 .... 122 F4
Adamson Cl CNCK/NC WS11 .... 15 M4
Adams Rd BDMR/CCFT WV3 .... 49 G6
BRWNH WS8 .... 26 E8
Adams St RUGBYN/HIL CV21 .... 183 J2
VAUX/NECH B7 .... 7 K1
WBROM B70 .... 86 E2
WSLW WS2 .... 4 C1
Adam St KIDD DY11 .... 137 G8
Adare Dr COVS CV3 .... 8 D9
Ada Rd SMTHWK B66 .... 105 M2
YDLY B25 .... 108 F7
Ada Wrighton Cl SHHTH WV12 .. 38 A6
Adcock Dr KNWTH CV8 .... 176 F8
Addenbrooke Crs KIDDW DY11 .. 160 E4
Addenbrooke Dr
SCFLD/BOLD B73 .... 72 F3
Addenbrooke Rd
RCOVN/BALC/EX CV7 .... 115 L7
SMTHWK B67 .... 105 K2
Addenbrooke St BLOX/PEL WS3 .. 39 G6
DARL/WED WS10 .... 52 B5
Addenbrook Wy
TPTN/OCK DY4 .... 68 B5
Adderley Cl WASH/WDE B8 .... 90 B8
WASH/WDE B8 .... 108 B1
Adderley Park Cl
WASH/WDE B8 .... 108 C1
Adderley Rd WASH/WDE B8 .... 108 A2
Adderley Rd South
WASH/WDE B8 .... 108 A2
Adderley St BORD B9 .... 7 L7
COV CV1 .... 9 K1
Addingham Cl WWCK CV34 .... 199 J4
Addison Cl CNCK/NC WS11 .... 12 C8
DARL/WED WS10 .... 69 J3
NUNW/HART CV10 .... 79 K8
Addison Cft SEDG DY3 .... 65 L8
Addison Gv WNSFLD WV11 .... 36 F4
Addison Pl BILS/COS WV14 .... 51 K6
CSHL/WTROR B46 .... 92 F2
Addison Rd
ALE/KHTH/YWD B14 .... 125 K6
BDMR/CCFT WV3 .... 49 K5
BRLYHL DY5 .... 101 M3
COVN CV6 .... 133 L5
DARL/WED WS10 .... 69 J3
RUGBYS/DCH CV22 .... 183 H3
VAUX/NECH B7 .... 90 A5
Addison St DARL/WED WS10 .... 68 D3
Addison Ter DARL/WED WS10 .. 68 D3
Adelaide Av WBROM B70 .... 68 E6
Adelaide Dr HEDN WS12 .... 17 K2
Adelaide Rd RLSN CV32 .... 200 C5
Adelaide St BHTH/HG B12 .... 7 J9
BRLYHL DY5 .... 102 B2
COV CV1 .... 9 J1
REDW B97 .... 196 B1
Adelaide Wk BKHL/PFLD WV2 .... 3 J8
Adey Rd WNSFLD WV11 .... 37 K5
Adkins Cft
RCOVN/BALC/EX CV7 .... 114 C2
Adkins La SMTHWK B67 .... 105 K4
Admington Rd STETCH B33 .... 110 A5
Admiral Gdns KNWTH CV8 .... 177 G7
Admiral Parker Dr LICHS WS14.... 28 D8
Admiral Pl MOS/BIL B13 .... 125 K1
Admirals Wy
BLKHTH/ROWR B65 .... 103 M3
Adonis Cl CRTAM B79 .... 32 A7
Adrian Cft MOS/BIL B13 .... 126 A4
Adrians' Cl ATHST CV9 .... 63 K7
Adria Rd SPARK B11 .... 125 M1

Adshead Rd DUDS DY2 .... 85 G6
Adstone Gv NFLD/LBR B31 .... 143 L4
Adwalton Rd
DUNHL/THL/PER WV6 .... 48 D2
Affleck Av POL/KGSB/FAZ B78 .... 45 H4
Agenoria Dr STRBR DY8 .... 101 K8
Aggborough Crs KIDD DY10 .... 161 J1
Agincourt Rd COVS CV3 .... 154 C7
Agmore La BRGRVE B60 .... 186 F2
Agmore Rd BRGRVE B60 .... 186 E1
Ainsbury Rd COVW CV5 .... 153 J5
Ainsdale Cl COVE CV2 .... 134 F1
STRBR DY8 .... 119 K3
Ainsdale Gdns HALE B63 .... 121 H3
Ainsworth Rd WOLV WV10 .... 36 C1
Aintree Cl BDWTH CV12 .... 116 F1
BRGRVW B61 .... 165 L4
COVN CV6 .... 134 C8
HEDN WS12 .... 13 K7
WOLV WV10 .... 137 H5
Aintree Dr RLSN CV32 .... 201 G2
Aintree Gv BKDE/SHDE B34 .... 92 B7
Aintree Rd WOLV WV10 .... 36 B1
Aintree Wy DUDN DY1 .... 84 C3
Aire Cft NFLD/LBR B31 .... 143 M4
Airfield Dr ALDR WS9 .... 54 C2
Airport Wy BHAMNEC B40 .... 129 H2
HIA/OLT B92 .... 129 H2
Aitken Cl POL/KGSB/FAZ B78 .... 45 L3
Ajax Cl GTWY WS6 .... 24 D4
Akdene Cl GTWY WS6 .... 24 B3
Akrill Cl WBROM B70 .... 68 F8
Alamein Rd WLNHL WV13 .... 51 J4
Alandale Av COVW CV5 .... 152 C1
Alan Higgs Wy TLHL/CAN CV4 .. 152 A6
Albany Cl KIDD DY10 .... 137 M7
Albany Crs BILS/COS WV14 .... 51 G7
Albany Gdns SOLH B91 .... 148 C1
Albany Gv KGSWFD DY6 .... 83 J6
SHHTH WV12 .... 38 A4
Albany Rd COVW CV5 .... 8 A8
HRBN B17 .... 106 A7
Albany Ter RLSN CV32 .... 200 C4
Albemarle Rd STRBR DY8 .... 119 K3
Albermarle Rd KGSWFD DY6 .... 83 L8
Albert Clarke Dr SHHTH WV12 .. 38 A6
Albert Cl CDSL WV8 .... 34 C1
Albert Crs COVN CV6 .... 133 M2
Albert Davie Dr HEDN WS12 .... 17 J1
Albert Dr HALE B63 .... 121 K3
SEDG DY3 .... 82 C3
Albert Rd ALE/KHTH/YWD B14 .. 125 K6
AST/WIT B6 .... 89 J6
BRGRVW B61 .... 185 J5
COVW CV5 .... 131 L5
CRTAM B79 .... 31 M8
ERDW/GRVHL B23 .... 90 B2
HALE B63 .... 121 K3
HDSW B21 .... 88 C4
HRBN B17 .... 105 M8
KIDD DY10 .... 137 K7
LGLYGN/QTN B68 .... 105 G5
POL/KGSB/FAZ B78 .... 45 L5
STETCH B33 .... 109 H2
WOLV WV1 .... 2 A2
Albert Sq RUGBYN/HIL CV21 .. 183 M2
Albert St BRLYHL DY5 .... 84 B6
CBHAMNE B4 .... 7 H5
CNCK/NC WS11 .... 16 C1
COV CV1 .... 9 J2
DARL/WED WS10 .... 68 C3
DIG/EDG B5 .... 7 J5
HAG/WOL DY9 .... 102 C8
HEDN WS12 .... 13 H8
KGSWFD DY6 .... 82 F5
NUNW/HART CV10 .... 98 C2

REDE B98 .... 188 C8
RLSN CV32 .... 200 A4
RUGBYN/HIL CV21 .... 183 L2
STRBR DY8 .... 101 K8
TPTN/OCK DY4 .... 67 K5
WBROM B70 .... 87 G4
WSL WS1 .... 4 F1
WWCK CV34 .... 199 H6
Albert St East OLDBY B69 .... 86 F6
Albion Av WLNHL WV13 .... 52 A3
Albion Field Dr HHTH/SAND B71 .. 87 H1
Albion Industrial Est
WBROM B70 .... 86 D3
Albion Pl CNCK/NC WS11 .... 16 C1
Albion Rd BRWNH WS8 .... 26 C5
HDSW B21 .... 88 B4
HHTH/SAND B71 .... 87 L5
SPARK B11 .... 108 B8
WBROM B70 .... 86 D3
Albion St BILS/COS WV14 .... 51 J7
BRLYHL DY5 .... 102 B2
CBHAMW B1 .... 6 B3
CRTAM B79 .... 32 A8
KGSWFD DY6 .... 82 F5
KNWTH CV8 .... 176 E8
OLDBY B69 .... 86 C4
TPTN/OCK DY4 .... 67 K8
WLNHL WV13 .... 51 M3
WOLV WV1 .... 3 H5
Alborn Crs HWK/WKHTH B38 .. 144 B5
Albrighton Rd HALE B63 .... 121 J2
Albrighton Wk NUN CV11 .... 99 L3
Albright Rd LGLYGN/QTN B68 .. 105 H1
Albutts Rd CNCK/NC WS11 .... 25 L2
Alcester Dr SCFLD/BOLD B73 .... 72 B2
WLNHL WV13 .... 51 H5
Alcester Hwy REDE B98 .... 196 D5
Alcester Rd ALVE B48 .... 169 L8
BRGRVE B60 .... 166 A7
BRGRVE B60 .... 186 E5
HLYWD B47 .... 169 K1
MOS/BIL B13 .... 125 K2
Alcester Rd South
ALE/KHTH/YWD B14 .... 145 K3
Alcester St BHTH/HG B12 .... 7 K9
REDW B97 .... 196 C1
Alcombe Gv STETCH B33 .... 109 J5
Alcott Cl DOR/KN B93 .... 172 D3
Alcott Gv STETCH B33 .... 110 B2
Alcott La
CHWD/FDBR/MGN B37 .... 110 D5
The Alcove BLOX/PEL WS3 .... 39 H3
Aldborough La REDW B97 .... 187 M8
Aldbourne Rd COV CV1 .... 134 A8
Aldbury Ri COVW CV5 .... 153 G1
Aldbury Rd
ALE/KHTH/YWD B14 .... 145 L3
Aldeburgh Cl BLOX/PEL WS3 .. 38 E2
Aldeford Dr BRLYHL DY5 .... 102 B5
Alden Hurst BNTWD WS7 .... 18 D5
Alderbrook Cl REDW B97 .... 187 M8
SEDG DY3 .... 65 M4
Alderbrooke Dr NUN CV11 .... 99 L4
Alderbrook Rd SOLH B91 .... 147 K2
Alder Cl HLYWD B47 .... 145 M7
LICHS WS14 .... 21 K6
WALM/CURD B76 .... 73 J6
Alder Coppice SEDG DY3 .... 66 A3
Alder Crs DSYBK/YTR WS5 .... 69 H1
Alder Dl BDMR/CCFT WV3 .... 49 J4
Alderdale Av SEDG DY3 .... 66 A2
Alderdale Crs HIA/OLT B92 .... 128 C6
Alder Dr CHWD/FDBR/MGN B37.. 110 F4
Alderflat Pl VAUX/NECH B7 .... 90 A4

Ald - Arl 205

Alderford Cl CDSL WV8 35 K5
Aldergate CRTAM B79 31 M8
Alder Gv RMSLY B62 104 C7
Alderham Cl SOLH B91 148 C1
Alderhithe Gv FOAKS/STRLY B74 55 M2
Alder La NFLD/LBR B31 124 A7
RCOVN/BALC/EX CV7 151 G8
Alderlea Cl STRBR DY8 119 L3
Alderley Rd BRGRVW B61 185 H5
Alderman's Green Rd
COVN CV6 134 F2
Alder Meadow Cl COVN CV6 134 B1
Aldermere Rd KIDDW DY11 137 G5
Alderminster Gv
RWWCK/WEL CV35 198 C3
Alderminster Rd COVW CV5 152 E1
SOLH B91 147 M4
Aldermoor La COVS CV3 154 E5
Alderney Cl COVN CV6 133 M3
Alderney Gdns
HWK/WKHTH B38 144 B4
Alder Park Rd SOLH B91 147 K2
Alderpits Rd BKDE/SHDE B34 92 B7
Alder Rd BHTH/HG B12 125 L1
COVN CV6 134 E3
DARL/WED WS10 52 E7
KGSWFD DY6 83 K8
Alders Cl REDE B98 196 D2
Alders Dr REDE B98 197 K1
Aldersea Dr AST/WIT B6 89 K6
Aldersgate
POL/KGSB/FAZ B78 60 B6
Aldershaw Rd
LGN/SDN/BHAMAIR B26 109 J8
Aldershaws SHLY B90 146 E8
Alders La NUNW/HART CV10 79 L6
Aldersley Av
DUNHL/THL/PER WV6 35 J6
Aldersley Cl
DUNHL/THL/PER WV6 35 K6
Aldersley Rd
DUNHL/THL/PER WV6 35 K8
Aldersmead Rd NFLD/LBR B31 144 A4
Alderson Rd WASH/WDE B8 108 D1
The Alders BDWTH CV12 116 C3
RMSLY B62 141 K1
Alderton Cl SOLH B91 147 M4
Alderton Dr BDMR/CCFT WV3 49 J5
Alderton Ms RLSS CV31 201 G7
Alder Wy BRGRVE B60 185 M3
FOAKS/STRLY B74 55 J5
HEDN WS12 13 L7
Alderwood Pl SOLH B91 147 M2
Alderwood Ri SEDG DY3 66 B8
Aldgate Dr BRLYHL DY5 102 A6
Aldgate Gv LOZ/NWT B19 89 H8
Aldin Cl POL/KGSB/FAZ B78 45 J3
Aldington Cl REDE B98 196 D4
Aldis Cl HLGN/YWD B28 126 C4
Aldis Rd WSLW WS2 52 E6
Aldrich Av TLHL/CAN CV4 152 C3
Aldridge Cl LGLYGN/QTN B68 105 G1
POL/KGSB/FAZ B78 47 K5
STRBR DY8 101 J5
Aldridge Rd FOAKS/STRLY B74 41 L8
FOAKS/STRLY B74 55 H4
LGLYGN/QTN B68 104 F5
PBAR/PBCH B42 89 J2
RUSH/SHEL WS4 53 M2
Aldridge St DARL/WED WS10 52 B6
Aldrin Wy TLHL/CAN CV4 153 H8
Aldwick Cl RLSN CV32 200 E1
Aldwych Cl ALDR WS9 40 F5
Aldwyck Dr BDMR/CCFT WV3 48 E5
Alexander Cl BRGRVW B61 165 L4
Alexander Hl BRLYHL DY5 102 D5
Alexander Rd ACGN B27 126 F1
BDWTH CV12 117 G2
CDSL WV8 35 G2
SMTHWKW B67 105 J3
WSLW WS2 52 D3
Alexander St BDMR/CCFT WV3 2 D6
Alexandra Av HDSW B21 88 B6
Alexandra Crs HHTH/SAND B71 69 J5
Alexandra Ms CRTAM B79 32 A8
Alexandra Pl BILS/COS WV14 51 H7
Alexandra Rd BVILLE B30 124 E6
COV CV1 9 L2
DARL/WED WS10 52 C7
DIG/EDG B5 107 J7
ETTPK/GDPK/PENN WV4 49 L8
HALE B63 121 K2
HDSW B21 88 B6
RLSS CV31 200 E7
RUGBYN/HIL CV21 183 M1
TPTN/OCK DY4 67 L8
WSL WS1 4 E8
Alexandra St DUDN DY1 84 F4
NUN CV11 98 F1
Alexandra Wy ALDR WS9 40 F8
TPTN/OCK DY4 85 L3
Alex Grierson Cl COVS CV3 155 J6
Alfall Rd COVE CV2 134 F8
Alford Cl RBRY B45 143 G6
Alfreda Av HLYWD B47 145 K5
Alfred Green Cl
RUGBYS/DCH CV22 183 L3
Alfred Rd COV CV1 9 L1
HDSW B21 88 C5
SPARK B11 107 M8
Alfred St ALE/KHTH/YWD B14 125 K6
AST/WIT B6 89 M5
BHTH/HG B12 107 M8
BLOX/PEL WS3 38 F4
CRTAM B79 31 L8
DARL/WED WS10 52 A8
RUGBYN/HIL CV21 183 K2
SMTHWK B66 87 M6
WBROM B70 87 H1
Alfreds Well BRGRVW B61 165 G7
Alfriston Rd COVS CV3 178 A1
Algernon Rd LDYWD/EDGR B16 106 B1
Algernon St WSLW WS2 4 D1
Alice Cl BDWTH CV12 116 D4
Alice St BILS/COS WV14 51 H7
Alison Cl TPTN/OCK DY4 67 L3
Alison Dr STRBR DY8 119 J3
Alison Rd RMSLY B62 122 C2
Alison Sq COVN CV6 134 F1
Allan Cl STRBR DY8 101 K4
Allan Rd COVN CV6 153 K1
Allard TAM/AM/WIL B77 46 C3
Allard Wy COVS CV3 155 G6
Allbut St CDYHTH B64 103 H4
Allcock St BORD B9 7 L7
TPTN/OCK DY4 68 A5
Allcroft Rd SPARK B11 126 D3
Allenby Cl KGSWFD DY6 83 L8
Allen Cl GTB/HAM B43 70 C6
Allendale Gv GTB/HAM B43 70 C5
Allendale Rd WALM/CURD B76 73 J5
YDLY B25 108 F6
Allen Dr DARL/WED WS10 52 A7
WBROM B70 87 K4
Allen Rd DARL/WED WS10 52 D8
TPTN/OCK DY4 67 K4
Allens Cl ATHST CV9 62 A5
SHHTH WV12 37 M8
Allens Croft Rd
ALE/KHTH/YWD B14 124 F8
Allens Farm Rd NFLD/LBR B31 143 H2
Allens La BLOX/PEL WS3 39 K3
Allensmead TAM/AM/WIL B77 46 A3
Allensmore Cl REDE B98 197 K3
Allens Rd WSNGN B18 88 D7
Allen St WBROM B70 86 F2
Allerdale Rd BRWNH WS8 26 C7
Allerton Cl COVE CV2 155 J3
Allerton La HHTH/SAND B71 69 G5
Allerton Rd YDLY B25 108 F6
Allesley Cl MGN/WHC B75 57 G6
Allesley Cft COVW CV5 132 E7
Allesley Hall Dr COVW CV5 133 G8
Allesley Old Rd COV CV1 8 B5
COVW CV5 133 G8
Allesley Rd HIA/OLT B92 127 H5
RUGBYN/HIL CV21 159 K7
Allesley St AST/WIT B6 89 J8
Alleston Rd WOLVN WV10 36 B4
Alleyne Gv ERDE/BCHGN B24 90 E3
Alleyne Rd ERDE/BCHGN B24 90 E4
The Alley SEDG DY3 83 M2
Alliance Wy COVE CV2 134 E8
Allied Cl COVN CV6 134 B3
Allingham Gv GTB/HAM B43 71 H1
Allington Cl DSYBK/YTR WS5 54 B5
Allison St DIG/EDG B5 7 J6
Allitt Gv KNWTH CV8 176 F8
Allman Rd ERDE/BCHGN B24 90 F1
Allmyn Dr FOAKS/STRLY B74 55 L7
Allport Rd CNCK/NC WS11 16 C4
Allport St CNCK/NC WS11 16 C4
All Saints Av BEWD DY12 160 A1
All Saints Dr FOAKS/STRLY B74 56 D3
All Saints La COV CV1 9 K4
All Saints Rd
ALE/KHTH/YWD B14 125 J6
BDWTH CV12 116 D4
BKHL/PFLD WV2 3 H8
BRGRVW B61 185 L2
DARL/WED WS10 52 C7
WSNGN B18 88 E8
WWCK CV34 199 L4
All Saints' St WSNGN B18 88 E8
All Saints Wy HHTH/SAND B71 69 H8
Allsops Cl
BLKHTH/ROWR B65 103 K1
Allwell Dr
ALE/KHTH/YWD B14 145 K3
Allwood Gdns RIDG/WDGT B32 122 E3
Alma Av TPTN/OCK DY4 67 L6
Alma Crs VAUX/NECH B7 107 M1
Alma Pl DUDS DY2 85 G4
Alma St COV CV1 9 J4
DARL/WED WS10 52 A7
DARL/WED WS10 68 F2
HALE B63 103 G8
LOZ/NWT B19 89 J7
SMTHWK B66 88 A7
WLNHL WV13 51 M3
WOLVN WV10 3 M3
WSLW WS2 53 H1
Alma Wy LOZ/NWT B19 89 H6
Almond Av DSYBK/YTR WS5 69 L1
KIDDW DY11 136 E5
NUNW/HART CV10 80 A7
RLSN CV32 200 D2
WSLW WS2 52 C1
Almond Cl BLOX/PEL WS3 39 K3
SLYOAK B29 123 L7
Almond Cft PBAR/PBCH B42 70 D7
Almond Gv
DUNHL/THL/PER WV6 50 A1
RUGBYN/HIL CV21 159 J6
WWCK CV34 199 L4
Almond Rd HEDN WS12 12 B5
KGSWFD DY6 83 J5
Almond Tree Av COVE CV2 135 G3
Alnwick Cl HEDN WS12 17 J3
Alnwick Rd BLOX/PEL WS3 38 E1
Alperton Dr HAG/WOL DY9 120 C3
Alpha Cl BHTH/HG B12 107 J7
Alpha Wy GTWY WS6 24 E5
Alpine Ct KNWTH CV8 176 E7
Alpine Dr DUDS DY2 102 F1
HEDN WS12 17 H1
Alpine Ri COVS CV3 153 L8
Alpine Wy DUNHL/THL/PER WV6 49 G3
Alport Cft BORD B9 107 M3
Alspath La COVW CV5 152 D1
Alspath Rd
RCOVN/BALC/EX CV7 131 G4
Alston Cl FOAKS/STRLY B74 56 E3
HEDN WS12 17 J3
SOLH B91 128 B7
Alston Gv BORD B9 108 F3
Alston Rd BORD B9 108 F2
OLDBY B69 86 C6
SOLH B91 128 B7
Alston St LDYWD/EDGR B16 106 D3
Althorpe Dr DOR/KN B93 172 B2
Althorpe St RLSS CV31 200 E6
Alton Av SHHTH WV12 37 L8
Alton Cl COVE CV2 135 H3
REDW B97 195 M4
WOLVN WV10 36 C2
Alton Gv CNCK/NC WS11 15 M4
DUDS DY2 85 H5
HHTH/SAND B71 69 J6
Alton Rd SLYOAK B29 124 D2
Alum Cl COVN CV6 134 B5
Alum Dr BORD B9 108 E2
Alumhurst Av WASH/WDE B8 108 F1
Alum Rock Rd WASH/WDE B8 90 B8
Alumwell Cl WSLW WS2 52 F4
Alum Well Rd WSLW WS2 52 F4
Alvaston Cl BLOX/PEL WS3 39 G2
Alvechurch Hwy BRGRVE B60 166 A2
REDE B98 188 C7
Alvechurch Rd HALE B63 121 K3
NFLD/LBR B31 143 M5
Alveley Cl REDE B98 197 H1
Alverley Cl KGSWFD DY6 82 F5
Alverstoke Cl COVEN WV9 35 K3
Alverstone Rd COVE CV2 154 E1
Alverton Cl TAM/AM/WIL B77 60 A1
Alveston Cl REDE B98 197 G3
Alveston Gv BORD B9 108 F3
DOR/KN B93 148 F6
Alveston Rd HLYWD B47 145 L6
Alvin Cl COVS CV3 155 K4
RMSLY B62 104 D5
Alvington Cl SHHTH WV12 52 B1
Alvis Cl CRTAM B79 31 K6
Alwen St STRBR DY8 101 K4
Alwin Rd BLKHTH/ROWR B65 103 M3
Alwold Rd SLYOAK B29 123 K3
Alwyn TAM/AM/WIL B77 46 C6
Alwyn Cl GTWY WS6 24 D2
Alwyn Rd RUGBYS/DCH CV22 183 G6
Amanda Av
ETTPK/GDPK/PENN WV4 65 K1
Amanda Dr
LGN/SDN/BHAMAIR B26 109 K4
Amber Cl TAM/AM/WIL B77 46 F2
Amber Dr OLDBY B69 86 E8
Ambergate Cl BLOX/PEL WS3 39 G2
Ambergate Dr KGSWFD DY6 83 G5
Amber Gv HEDN WS12 17 G3
Amberley Gn GTB/HAM B43 70 C7
Amberley Gv AST/WIT B6 89 L2
Amberley Rd HIA/OLT B92 127 K2
Amberley Wy FOAKS/STRLY B74 55 J4
Amber Wy RMSLY B62 103 M7
Amberwood Cl WSLW WS2 52 B2
Ambien Rd ATHST CV9 63 H6
Amblecote Av KGSTG B44 71 J3
Amblecote Rd BRLYHL DY5 102 B5
KIDD DY10 137 M8
Ambler Gv COVE CV2 155 G2
Ambleside COVE CV2 135 J3
RIDG/WDGT B32 123 G4
Ambleside Cl BILS/COS WV14 67 J1
Ambleside Dr BRLYHL DY5 102 A5
Ambleside Wy BRGRVE B60 185 M4
KGSWFD DY6 83 H7
NUN CV11 81 J7
Ambrose Cl WLNHL WV13 51 J3
Ambrose Crs KGSWFD DY6 83 H5
Ambury Wy GTB/HAM B43 70 B5
Amelas Cl STRBR DY8 101 L5
Amersham Cl COVW CV5 152 F1
RIDG/WDGT B32 105 J8
Amesbury Rd MOS/BIL B13 125 J2
Ames Rd DARL/WED WS10 52 A6
Amherst Av BFLD/HDSWWD B20 88 E2
Amherst Rd KNWTH CV8 176 C7
Amicombe TAM/AM/WIL B77 47 G4
Amington Cl MGN/WHC B75 57 H2
Amington Rd SHLY B90 146 E5
TAM/AM/WIL B77 46 A1
YDLY B25 108 F7
Amiss Gdns SMHTH B10 108 A5
Amity Cl SMTHWK B66 87 M8
Amos Av NUNW/HART CV10 98 F3
WNSFLD WV11 36 F6
Amos Jacques Rd BDWTH CV12 116 E1
Amos La WNSFLD WV11 37 G7
Amos Rd HAG/WOL DY9 120 D3
Amphlett Cft TPTN/OCK DY4 85 M1
Amphletts Cl DUDS DY2 103 J2
Ampton Rd EDG B15 106 F6
Amroth Cl RBRY B45 142 F6
Amwell Gv ALE/KHTH/YWD B14 145 K2
Amy Cl COVN CV6 134 D1
Anchorage Rd
ERDW/GRVHL B23 90 B2
FOAKS/STRLY B74 56 F7
Anchor Cl LDYWD/EDGR B16 106 C4
TAM/AM/WIL B77 46 C1
Anchorfields KIDD DY10 137 K7
Anchor La BILS/COS WV14 66 F3
Anchor Rd ALDR WS9 40 F7
BILS/COS WV14 67 G3
Anchorway Rd COVS CV3 177 M1
Anders CRTAM B79 31 L7
Andersleigh Dr
BILS/COS WV14 66 E5
Anderson Av
RUGBYS/DCH CV22 183 L5
Anderson Crs GTB/HAM B43 70 C3
Anderson Rd ERDW/GRVHL B23 72 C7
SMTHWK B66 105 L4
SMTHWKW B67 105 L3
TPTN/OCK DY4 67 L8
Anderton Cl FOAKS/STRLY B74 56 E6
Anderton Park Rd
MOS/BIL B13 125 L2
Anderton Rd BDWTH CV12 116 A4
COVE CV2 116 F8
SPARK B11 108 A7
Anderton St CBHAMW B1 6 A4
Andover Crs KGSWFD DY6 101 K1
Andover Pl CNCK/NC WS11 16 E1
Andover St DIG/EDG B5 7 K5
Andressy Ms BRGRVW B61 165 L8
Andrew Cl SHHTH WV12 38 B7
Andrew Dr SHHTH WV12 38 B7
Andrew Gdns HDSW B21 88 C4
Andrew Rd HALE B63 121 L2
HHTH/SAND B71 69 K5
TPTN/OCK DY4 67 L4
Andrews Cl BRLYHL DY5 102 C5
Andrews Rd ALDR WS9 40 F1
Anerley Gv KGSTG B44 71 K1
Anerley Rd KGSTG B44 71 K1
Angela Av BLKHTH/ROWR B65 104 B1
COVE CV2 135 J4
Angela Pl BILS/COS WV14 51 H7
Angelica Cl DSYBK/YTR WS5 69 L2
Angelina St BHTH/HG B12 107 K6
Angel Pas STRBR DY8 101 L8
Angel St DUDN DY1 84 F5
REDW B97 194 F4
Anglesey Av CBROM B36 92 F7
Anglesey Cl BNTWD WS7 26 D1
COVW CV5 132 F6
Anglesey Crs BRWNH WS8 26 D3
HEDN WS12 13 G8
Anglesey Rd BRWNH WS8 26 D3
LICH WS13 20 F3
Anglesey St HEDN WS12 12 F8
LOZ/NWT B19 89 G6
Angless Wy KNWTH CV8 191 K2
Anglian Rd ALDR WS9 40 B7
Anglia Rd CNCK/NC WS11 16 B2
Angorfa Cl LICH WS13 20 D6
Angus Cl COVW CV5 152 E1
HHTH/SAND B71 69 G7
KNWTH CV8 177 G7
Anita Av TPTN/OCK DY4 85 L3
Anita Cft ERDW/GRVHL B23 90 C3
Ankadine Rd STRBR DY8 101 M7
Anker Cl BNTWD WS7 19 H7
Ankerdine Ct HALE B63 121 L2
Ankerdrive CRTAM B79 45 M1
Anker Dr RRUGBY CV23 158 F8
Ankermoor Cl
BKDE/SHDE B34 91 M7
Ankerside POL/KGSB/FAZ B78 47 L2
Anker St NUN CV11 99 H2
Anker Vw POL/KGSB/FAZ B78 47 L5
Annan Av WOLVN WV10 36 C6
Ann Crs CNCK/NC WS11 12 C7
Ann Cft
LGN/SDN/BHAMAIR B26 128 B1
Anne Cl WBROM B70 86 C2
Anne Crs COVS CV3 155 G8
Anne Gv TPTN/OCK DY4 67 M4
Anne Rd BRLYHL DY5 102 E4
ETTPK/GDPK/PENN WV4 49 M8
SMTHWK B66 88 A6
Ann Rd HLYWD B47 169 L2
Annscroft HWK/WKHTH B38 144 B3
Ann St WLNHL WV13 51 M2
Ansbro Cl WSNGN B18 88 D8
Ansculf Rd STRBR DY8 101 M4
Ansell Rd ERDE/BCHGN B24 90 D4
SPARK B11 108 A7
WWCK CV34 199 H6
Ansells Dr COVN CV6 116 E8
Ansley Cl REDE B98 197 K4
Ansley Common
NUNW/HART CV10 79 L6
Ansley La RCOVN/BALC/EX CV7 96 D3
Ansley Rd NUNW/HART CV10 97 H2
NUNW/HART CV10 98 A3
Anslow Gdns WNSFLD WV11 37 K4
Anslow Rd ERDW/GRVHL B23 72 A8
Anson Av LICH WS13 20 E5
Anson Cl BNTWD WS7 19 G6
DUNHL/THL/PER WV6 34 C8
GTWY WS6 24 D4
RUGBYS/DCH CV22 183 G3
Anson Gv ACGN B27 127 H3
Anson Rd GTWY WS6 24 D4
WBROM B70 68 C6
WSLW WS2 52 C3
Anson Wy COVE CV2 135 K5
Anstey Cft
CHWD/FDBR/MGN B37 110 E1
Anstey Gv ACGN B27 126 F4
Anstey Rd KGSTG B44 71 J7
Anston Wy WNSFLD WV11 37 H6
Anstree Cl GTWY WS6 24 B4
Anstruther Rd EDG B15 106 C6
Ansty Dr HEDN WS12 17 H3
Ansty Rd COVE CV2 135 K7
Antelope Gdns WWCK CV34 199 G5
Anthony Rd WASH/WDE B8 108 C2
Anthony Wy COVE CV2 155 G3
Anton Dr WALM/CURD B76 73 L7
Antony Rd SHLY B90 146 F4
Antrim Cl COVW CV5 132 E6
Antringham Gdns EDG B15 106 B5
Antrobus Rd HDSW B21 88 C4
SCFLD/BOLD B73 72 C4
Anvil Crs BILS/COS WV14 67 G3
Anvil Dr OLDBY B69 86 C7
Apex Rd BRWNH WS8 26 A6
Apley Rd STRBR DY8 101 J6
Apollo CRTAM B79 31 K7
Apollo Cl CNCK/NC WS11 12 E8
Apollo Cft ERDE/BCHGN B24 91 H2
Apollo Rd HAG/WOL DY9 102 E8
LGLYGN/QTN B68 87 G7
Apollo Wy BFLD/HDSWWD B20 89 G4
WWCK CV34 200 B8
Apperley Wy HALE B63 102 F6
Appian Cl ALE/KHTH/YWD B14 125 J8
TAM/AM/WIL B77 46 A6
Appian Wy SHLY B90 171 H1
Appleby Cl
ALE/KHTH/YWD B14 125 H8
Appleby Gdns WNSFLD WV11 38 A3
Appleby Gv SHLY B90 147 M7
Applecross FOAKS/STRLY B74 56 D4
Applecross Cl TLHL/CAN CV4 152 D7
Appledore Cl GTWY WS6 24 E2
HEDN WS12 17 J2
Appledore Dr COVW CV5 132 D8
Appledore Rd DSYBK/YTR WS5 54 B5
Appledorne Gdns
BKDE/SHDE B34 91 M7
Apple Gv RUGBYS/DCH CV22 182 F3
Apple Pie La NUNW/HART CV10 79 M2
Applesham Cl SPARK B11 108 B7
Appleton Av GTB/HAM B43 70 C5
STRBR DY8 119 L3
Appleton Cl BVILLE B30 124 C5
Appleton Crs
ETTPK/GDPK/PENN WV4 49 L8
Apple Tree Cl ERDW/GRVHL B23 89 M1
KIDD DY10 137 M5
Appletree Cl NFLD/LBR B31 143 J4
Appletree Gv ALDR WS9 40 F8
DUNHL/THL/PER WV6 36 A8
Appletree La REDW B97 187 M8
Apple Wk CNCK/NC WS11 17 G3
Applewood Gv CDYHTH B64 103 K5
The Approach RLSS CV31 200 D7
April Cft MOS/BIL B13 125 M3
Apse Cl WMBN WV5 64 D6
Apsley Cl LGLYGN/QTN B68 104 E6
Apsley Gv DOR/KN B93 172 D3
ERDE/BCHGN B24 90 E3
Apsley Rd LGLYGN/QTN B68 104 E6
Aqueduct La ALVE B48 167 K6
Aqueduct Rd SHLY B90 146 C3
Aragon Dr RLSS CV31 200 B7
SCFLD/BOLD B73 56 E7
Arbor Cl TAM/AM/WIL B77 46 B2
Arboretum Rd WSL WS1 5 H1
The Arboretum TLHL/CAN CV4 177 H2
Arbor Ga ALDR WS9 40 F1
Arbor Wy
CHWD/FDBR/MGN B37 111 G4
Arbour Cl KNWTH CV8 191 M2
RUGBYS/DCH CV22 183 H6
Arbour Tree La DOR/KN B93 173 K6
Arbury Av BDWTH CV12 116 E2
COVN CV6 134 C3
Arbury Cl RLSN CV32 200 E2
Arbury Dr STRBR DY8 101 H2
Arbury Hall Rd SHLY B90 147 H5
Arbury Rd NUNW/HART CV10 98 B3
Arcal St SEDG DY3 66 C6
Archer Cl DARL/WED WS10 68 C2
LGLYGN/QTN B68 104 F1
Archer Ct HAG/WOL DY9 120 C3
Archer Rd ALE/KHTH/YWD B14 146 A1
BLOX/PEL WS3 39 J7
KNWTH CV8 191 J2
REDE B98 196 C1
Archers Cl ERDW/GRVHL B23 72 A5
Archery Flds WWCK CV34 199 K8
Archery Rd
RCOVN/BALC/EX CV7 130 F4
RLSS CV31 200 C5
Arch Hill St DUDS DY2 85 G8
Archibald Rd LOZ/NWT B19 89 G5
Arch Rd COVE CV2 135 J8
Arcot Rd HLGN/YWD B28 126 D3
Ardarth Rd HWK/WKHTH B38 144 E3
Ardav Rd WBROM B70 68 D5
Arden Av ATHST CV9 63 J5
Arden Cl RCOVN/BALC/EX CV7 131 G4
RCOVN/BALC/EX CV7 150 F6
RLSS CV31 200 F8
RUGBYS/DCH CV22 183 H8
STRBR DY8 101 J7
STRBR DY8 101 G2
TAM/AM/WIL B77 32 C8
WWCK CV34 199 L4
Ardencote Rd MOS/BIL B13 125 L7
Arden Cft CSHL/WTROR B46 93 K4
HIA/OLT B92 128 A1
Arden Dr DOR/KN B93 172 D3
LGN/SDN/BHAMAIR B26 109 K6
MGN/WHC B75 57 M8
SCFLD/BOLD B73 72 F5
Arden Forest Est
NUNW/HART CV10 78 E3
Arden Gv LDYWD/EDGR B16 106 E4
OLDBY B69 86 E8
Arden Meads HOCK/TIA B94 172 A7
Arden Oak Rd
LGN/SDN/BHAMAIR B26 110 B8
Arden Pl DARL/WED WS10 67 M1
Arden Rd ACGN B27 126 F1
AST/WIT B6 89 H5
DOR/KN B93 172 D4
HLYWD B47 145 L7
KNWTH CV8 191 M2
NUN CV11 99 L4
RBRY B45 142 E4
SMTHWKW B67 105 L1
TAM/AM/WIL B77 46 D8
WASH/WDE B8 108 A2
Ardens Cl REDE B98 197 L3
Arden St ATHST CV9 63 J6
COVW CV5 153 K4
Arden Vale Rd DOR/KN B93 148 F6
Arderne Dr
CHWD/FDBR/MGN B37 110 E4
Ardgay Dr HEDN WS12 12 D6
Ardingley Wk BRLYHL DY5 101 M6
Ardley Cl DUDS DY2 85 H5
Ardley Rd ALE/KHTH/YWD B14 125 L8
Aretha Cl KGSWFD DY6 83 L7
Argus Cl WALM/CURD B76 73 K2
Argyle Av TAM/AM/WIL B77 46 B1
Argyle Cl RUSH/SHEL WS4 53 M2
STRBR DY8 101 J4
Argyle Rd BKHL/PFLD WV2 49 M7
RUSH/SHEL WS4 53 M2
Argyle St TAM/AM/WIL B77 46 C2
VAUX/NECH B7 90 A5
Argyll St COVE CV2 154 E2
Ariane CRTAM B79 31 J6
Ariel Wy RUGBYS/DCH CV22 183 H7
Arion Cl TAM/AM/WIL B77 32 B8
Arkall Cl CRTAM B79 32 A6
Arkle TAM/AM/WIL B77 60 B1
Arkle Cft BLKHTH/ROWR B65 85 K7
CBROM B36 91 G5
Arkle Dr COVE CV2 135 K6
Arklet Cl NUNW/HART CV10 80 A8
Arkley Gv HLGN/YWD B28 126 F6
Arkley Rd HLGN/YWD B28 126 F6
Arkwright Rd RIDG/WDGT B32 105 G8
WSLW WS2 38 F8
Arlen Dr GTB/HAM B43 70 B4
Arlescote Cl MGN/WHC B75 57 G3
Arlescote Rd HIA/OLT B92 128 A4
Arleston Wy SHLY B90 147 J5
Arley Cl KIDDW DY11 160 E3
OLDBY B69 86 B8

REDE B98 189 H8
Arley Dr STRBR DY8 119 J2
Arley Gv
ETTPK/GDPK/PENN WV4 49 H8
Arley La NUNW/HART CV10 97 G3
Arley Ms RLSN CV32 200 B4
Arley Rd SLYOAK B29 124 D2
SOLH B91 147 L1
WASH/WDE B8 90 B7
Arlidge Cl BILS/COS WV14 67 H1
Arlidge Crs KNWTH CV8 177 G8
Arlington Av RLSN CV32 200 D3
Arlington Cl KGSWFD DY6 101 H1
Arlington Ct STRBR DY8 119 M1
Arlington Gv
ALE/KHTH/YWD B14 145 M3
Arlington Ms RLSN CV32 200 D3
Arlington Rd
ALE/KHTH/YWD B14 145 M2
HHTH/SAND B71 69 H7
Arlington Wy NUN CV11 99 K3
Arlon Av NUNW/HART CV10 80 B6
Armada Cl ERDW/GRVHL B23 90 B4 1
Armarna Dr COVW CV5 131 M5 1
Armfield St COVN CV6 134 E5
Armorial Rd COVS CV3 153 M7
Armoury Rd SPARK B11 108 B6
Armscote Gv
RWWCK/WEL CV35 198 B2
Armscott Rd COVE CV2 135 G7
Armside Cl BLOX/PEL WS3 39 L1
Armson Rd
RCOVN/BALC/EX CV7 116 E4
Armstead Rd COVEN WV9 35 L2
Armstrong CRTAM B79 31 K7
Armstrong Av COVS CV3 154 E4
Armstrong Cl
RUGBYS/DCH CV22 183 J4 1
STRBR DY8 101 M7
Armstrong Dr CBROM B36 92 D4
DUNHL/THL/PER WV6 35 L7
WSLW WS2 52 E1
Armstrong Wy WLNHL WV13 51 M5
Arncliffe Cl NUN CV11 99 L3 2
Arne Rd COVE CV2 135 L7
Arnhem Cl WNSFLD WV11 36 F5
Arnhem Cnr COVS CV3 155 H7
Arnhem Rd WLNHL WV13 51 J5
Arnhem Wy TPTN/OCK DY4 68 A8
Arnold Av COVS CV3 154 A8
Arnold Cl CRTAM B79 31 L7
WSLW WS2 52 D2
Arnold Gv BVILLE B30 144 B1
SHLY B90 146 F1 1
Arnold Rd SHLY B90 146 F1
Arnolds La CSHL/WTROR B46 112 D2
Arnold St RUGBYN/HIL CV21 183 M2
Arnotdale Dr HEDN WS12 12 D6
Arnside Cl COV CV1 9 J2
Arnwood Cl WSLW WS2 52 D3 1
Arosa Dr HRBN B17 123 M2
Arps Rd CDSL WV8 34 D2
Arran Cl CNCK/NC WS11 16 E2
GTB/HAM B43 70 C2
NUNW/HART CV10 98 D2
Arran Dr TAM/AM/WIL B77 46 D6
Arran Rd BKDE/SHDE B34 91 K7
Arran Wy CBROM B36 92 E6
Arras Bvd RWWCK/WEL CV35 198 E7
Arras Rd DUDS DY2 85 J3
Arrow Cl DOR/KN B93 148 E7
Arrowdale Rd REDE B98 196 E3
Arrowfield Gn
HWK/WKHTH B38 144 B6 1
Arrow Rd BLOX/PEL WS3 39 J7
Arrow Rd North REDE B98 196 E1
Arrow Rd South REDE B98 196 E1
Arsenal St BORD B9 108 A4
Arthingworth Cl COVS CV3 155 J4 1
Arthur Dr KIDDW DY11 161 J4
Arthur Gunby Cl
MGN/WHC B75 57 K6 1
Arthur Pl CBHAMW B1 6 B4
Arthur Rd EDG B15 106 F7
ERDE/BCHGN B24 90 F1
HDSW B21 88 D5
TPTN/OCK DY4 67 L7
YDLY B25 108 E7
Arthur St BILS/COS WV14 51 H7 1
BKHL/PFLD WV2 50 B7
CNCK/NC WS11 16 D1
COV CV1 9 H1
HEDN WS12 17 J2
KNWTH CV8 176 E8
REDE B98 196 E2
SMHTH B10 107 M4
WBROM B70 87 H4
Artillery St BORD B9 107 M3
Arton Cft ERDE/BCHGN B24 90 D3
Arundel TAM/AM/WIL B77 46 A6
Arundel Av DARL/WED WS10 68 D2
Arundel Cl WWCK CV34 199 K5
Arundel Crs HIA/OLT B92 127 L4
Arundel Dr OLDBY B69 85 K5
Arundel Gv
DUNHL/THL/PER WV6 48 E2
Arundel Pl SPARK B11 107 L6 1
Arundel Rd
ALE/KHTH/YWD B14 145 L4
BRGRVE B60 185 M4
COVS CV3 154 B7
SHHTH WV12 38 A6
STRBR DY8 101 G3
WOLVN WV10 35 M3
Arundel St WSL WS1 4 F7
Arun Wy WALM/CURD B76 73 L4
Asbury Rd DARL/WED WS10 69 J3
RCOVN/BALC/EX CV7 150 F8
Ascot Cl BDWTH CV12 116 F1 1
COVS CV3 155 G7
LDYWD/EDGR B16 106 D3 1
LICHS WS14 21 H6
OLDBY B69 86 C7
Ascot Dr CNCK/NC WS11 15 M5
DUDN DY1 84 D3
ETTPK/GDPK/PENN WV4 65 L1
Ascot Gdns STRBR DY8 101 H3
Ascot Ride RLSN CV32 201 G2
Ascot Rd MOS/BIL B13 125 K3
Ash Av BHTH/HG B12 107 L8 1
Ashborough Dr SOLH B91 148 A6
Ashbourne Cl CNCK/NC WS11 16 E1 1
Ashbourne Rd BLOX/PEL WS3 39 G2
ETTPK/GDPK/PENN WV4 66 C2
LDYWD/EDGR B16 106 B2
WOLV WV1 50 E2
Ashbourne Wy SHLY B90 147 H5
Ashbridge Rd COVW CV5 153 G1
Ashbrook Crs SOLH B91 148 A5
Ashbrook Dr RBRY B45 142 F5 1
Ashbrook Gv BVILLE B30 125 G5
Ashbrook Ri NUNW/HART CV10 79 M3
Ashbrook Rd BVILLE B30 125 G5
Ashburn Gv WLNHL WV13 52 A3 2
Ashburton Rd
ALE/KHTH/YWD B14 125 H8
COVE CV2 135 J6
Ashbury Covert BVILLE B30 145 G2 1
Ashby Cl CBROM B36 91 G7
COVS CV3 155 K5
Ashby Ct NUN CV11 99 H3
SOLH B91 148 A4
Ashby Rd CRTAM B79 31 M8
Ash Cl CDSL WV8 34 E2
Ashcombe Av
BFLD/HDSWWD B20 88 C2 1
Ashcombe Dr TLHL/CAN CV4 152 D2
Ashcombe Gdns
ERDE/BCHGN B24 91 H2 1
Ashcott Cl HWK/WKHTH B38 144 B3
Ash Ct RUGBYS/DCH CV22 183 J6
Ash Crs CHWD/FDBR/MGN B37 92 D7
KGSWFD DY6 83 J7
Ashcroft Cl COVE CV2 135 L5 1
Ashcroft Gv BFLD/HDSWWD B20 89 H3
Ashcroft La LICHS WS14 28 C5
Ashcroft Wy
RCOVN/BALC/EX CV7 135 M5
Ashdale Cl COVS CV3 156 C6
HEDN WS12 12 A6 1
KGSWFD DY6 83 H5
Ashdale Dr ALE/KHTH/YWD B14 145 L4
Ashdale Gv
LGN/SDN/BHAMAIR B26 109 L5
Ashdale Rd TAM/AM/WIL B77 32 B8
Ashdene Cl KIDD DY10 138 A8
SCFLD/BOLD B73 72 E2
Ashdene Gdns KNWTH CV8 191 M1
STRBR DY8 101 G3
Ashdown Cl COVS CV3 155 H5
MOS/BIL B13 125 L4
RBRY B45 142 E3
Ashdown Dr NUNW/HART CV10 98 D3
STRBR DY8 101 J2
Ash Dr BRGRVW B61 165 L4
HHTH/SAND B71 69 G7
KNWTH CV8 191 L1
NUNW/HART CV10 79 L5
Ashen Cl
ETTPK/GDPK/PENN WV4 66 A2
Ashenden Ri BDMR/CCFT WV3 48 E4
Ashenhurst Rd DUDN DY1 84 D5
Ashe Rd NUNW/HART CV10 97 M2
Ashes Rd OLDBY B69 104 D1
Ashfern Dr WALM/CURD B76 73 K6
Ashfield Av
ALE/KHTH/YWD B14 125 K4
TLHL/CAN CV4 152 B4
Ashfield Cl BLOX/PEL WS3 53 J1
Ashfield Crs DUDS DY2 103 G2
HAG/WOL DY9 120 D2
Ashfield Gv HALE B63 121 J3
WOLVN WV10 36 A2
Ashfield Rd
ALE/KHTH/YWD B14 125 K4
BDMR/CCFT WV3 49 H3
BILS/COS WV14 67 L2
KNWTH CV8 191 M2
WOLVN WV10 36 A2
Ashford Dr BDWTH CV12 116 E2 1
SEDG DY3 66 C6
WALM/CURD B76 73 J8
Ashford La HOCK/TIA B94 171 L6
Ashfurlong Cl
RCOVN/BALC/EX CV7 150 F7 1
Ashfurlong Crs MGN/WHC B75 57 J6
Ash Gn DUDN DY1 66 E8
Ash Green La
RCOVN/BALC/EX CV7 116 A7
Ashgrove BNTWD WS7 18 D8
Ash Gv BHTH/HG B12 107 M8 1
CNCK/NC WS11 16 D1
HAG/WOL DY9 120 B2
KIDDW DY11 136 F6
LICH WS13 21 J5
POL/KGSB/FAZ B78 60 B6
RCOVN/BALC/EX CV7 96 C3
RCOVN/BALC/EX CV7 116 A6
SEDG DY3 84 A3
TAM/AM/WIL B77 46 D8
Ashgrove Cl BRGRVE B60 166 B4
Ashgrove Rd KGSTG B44 71 G3
Ash Hl BDMR/CCFT WV3 49 H4
Ashill Rd RBRY B45 142 F6
Ashington Gv COVS CV3 154 E8
Ashington Rd BDWTH CV12 116 A4
Ashlands Cl CRTAM B79 32 A6
Ashland St BDMR/CCFT WV3 2 C7
Ash La ALVE B48 168 A3
GTWY WS6 24 E2
Ashlawn Crs SOLH B91 127 H8
Ashlawn Rd RUGBYS/DCH CV22 183 J8
Ashlea POL/KGSB/FAZ B78 47 K8 1
Ashleigh Dr
BFLD/HDSWWD B20 88 F3 1
NUN CV11 99 K4
TAM/AM/WIL B77 46 C5
Ashleigh Gv MOS/BIL B13 125 M4
Ashleigh Rd OLDBY B69 86 A5
SOLH B91 147 M1
Ashley Cl EDG B15 107 G6
KGSWFD DY6 101 G1
STRBR DY8 119 H3
Ashley Ct RBRY B45 166 E4
Ashley Crs WWCK CV34 199 M7
Ashley Gdns CDSL WV8 34 D1
WASH/WDE B8 108 B1
Ashley Mt
DUNHL/THL/PER WV6 35 H8 1
Ashley Rd BLOX/PEL WS3 38 D4
BNTWD WS7 18 B4
ERDW/GRVHL B23 90 C2
ETTPK/GDPK/PENN WV4 49 J8
KIDD DY10 137 M4
Ashley St BILS/COS WV14 51 J7
BLKHTH/ROWR B65 104 A4
Ashley Wy
RCOVN/BALC/EX CV7 150 F6
Ashmall BNTWD WS7 27 H1 1
Ashman Av RRUGBY CV23 158 F8
Ashmead Dr RBRY B45 167 G1
Ashmead Gv ERDE/BCHGN B24 90 E3
Ashmead Ri RBRY B45 167 G1
Ashmead Rd BNTWD WS7 18 E5
Ash Ms ACGN B27 109 G8 1
Ashmole Cl LICHS WS14 21 J7
Ashmole Rd WBROM B70 68 D6
Ashmore Av WNSFLD WV11 37 L4
Ashmore Lake Rd SHHTH WV12 51 M1
Ashmore Lake Wy SHHTH WV12 51 M1
Ashmore Rd BVILLE B30 124 D8
COVN CV6 8 C1
Ashmores Cl REDW B97 196 B8
Asholme Cl CBROM B36 91 G6
Ashorne Cl ACGN B27 126 F6
COVE CV2 135 G3 1
COVE CV2 135 H3 1
REDE B98 197 H5
Ashover Gv WSNGN B18 106 C1 1
Ashow Cl KNWTH CV8 191 M1
Ashperton Cl REDE B98 196 C4
Ash Priors Cl TLHL/CAN CV4 152 F3
Ashridge Cl NUN CV11 99 K5 1
Ash Rd DARL/WED WS10 52 D8
DUDN DY1 84 F2
TPTN/OCK DY4 85 J1
WASH/WDE B8 108 B1
Ashstead Cl WALM/CURD B76 73 M7 1
Ash St BDMR/CCFT WV3 2 B6
BILS/COS WV14 67 J2
BLOX/PEL WS3 39 H4
CDYHTH B64 103 J3
Ash Ter OLDBY B69 85 M4
Ashton Cl REDW B97 195 M4
Ashton Cft
LDYWD/EDGR B16 106 E3 1
SOLH B91 147 L4
Ashton Dr RUSH/SHEL WS4 40 A2
Ashton Park Dr BRLYHL DY5 102 A4
Ashton Rd YDLY B25 108 F6
Ash Tree Av TLHL/CAN CV4 152 E3
Ash Tree Dr
LGN/SDN/BHAMAIR B26 109 H6
Ashtree Gv BILS/COS WV14 67 M2
Ash Tree La LICH WS13 21 L4 1
Ashtree Rd BLOX/PEL WS3 39 L2
Ash Tree Rd BVILLE B30 124 E7
Ashtree Rd CDYHTH B64 103 K3
OLDBY B69 86 B5
Ash Tree Rd REDW B97 195 M1
Ashurst Cl COVN CV6 116 F8 2
Ashurst Rd WALM/CURD B76 73 K7
Ash Vw HEDN WS12 12 B5
Ashville Av BKDE/SHDE B34 91 K6
Ashville Dr HALE B63 103 L8
Ashwater Dr
ALE/KHTH/YWD B14 145 H3
Ash Wy ERDW/GRVHL B23 72 A5
SPARK B11 107 M8 2
Ashwell Dr SHLY B90 147 H1
Ashwells Gv COVEN WV9 35 K3
Ashwin Rd HDSW B21 88 D6
Ashwood Av COVN CV6 133 K8 1
STRBR DY8 101 G3
Ashwood Cl FOAKS/STRLY B74 55 J5
Ashwood Dr
CHWD/FDBR/MGN B37 111 H2
Ashwood Gv
ETTPK/GDPK/PENN WV4 49 L8 1
Ashwood Rd NUNW/HART CV10 80 C7
Ashworth Rd PBAR/PBCH B42 70 F4
Askew Bridge Rd SEDG DY3 83 M2 1
Askew Cl SEDG DY3 66 C8
Aspbury Cft CBROM B36 92 B4
Aspen Cl ACGN B27 126 F2 1
TLHL/CAN CV4 152 B4 1
WALM/CURD B76 73 K3
Aspen Ct HEDN WS12 13 L7 1
Aspen Dr
CHWD/FDBR/MGN B37 111 G5
Aspen Gdns BFLD/HDSWWD B20 88 F4
Aspen Gv BNTWD WS7 18 D5
BORD B9 108 E2
HLYWD B47 145 M8
SHHTH WV12 38 C6
The Aspens POL/KGSB/FAZ B78 60 A6
Aspen Wk STRPT DY13 160 C8
Aspen Wy BDMR/CCFT WV3 2 A7
Asplen Ct KNWTH CV8 192 A1 1
Aspley Cl WOLVN WV10 14 C8
Aspley La WOLVN WV10 22 B2
Asquith Dr CNCK/NC WS11 17 G3
OLDBY B69 86 B3 1
Asquith Rd WASH/WDE B8 90 F8
Asra Cl COVE CV2 9 M1
SMTHWK B66 87 L5 1
Assheton Cl
RUGBYS/DCH CV22 183 G5 1
Astbury Av SMTHWKW B67 105 K2
Astbury Cl BLOX/PEL WS3 38 E1
WOLV WV1 50 E4
Aster Av KIDDW DY11 137 H4
Aster Cl NUN CV11 99 L4
Aster Wk COVEN WV9 35 L2 1
Asthill Cft COVS CV3 8 E8
Asthill Gv COVS CV3 8 E9
Astley Av COVN CV6 134 C3
RMSLY B62 104 D7
Astley Cl REDE B98 196 E6
RLSN CV32 200 B3
TPTN/OCK DY4 68 B7
Astley La NUNW/HART CV10 97 K7
RCOVN/BALC/EX CV7 114 F2
Astley Rd HDSW B21 88 B4
Aston Brook St AST/WIT B6 89 J7
Aston Brook St East
AST/WIT B6 89 K8 1
Aston Bury EDG B15 106 B5
Aston Church Rd VAUX/NECH B7 90 A6
WASH/WDE B8 90 B7
Aston Cl BILS/COS WV14 67 L1 1
LICHS WS14 28 D7
PENK ST19 10 D6
Aston Hall Rd AST/WIT B6 89 L5
Aston La BFLD/HDSWWD B20 89 J3
Aston Rd BRGRVE B60 185 K7
COVW CV5 153 K4
DUDS DY2 84 F5
NUN CV11 80 F8
OLDBY B69 85 L4
WLNHL WV13 51 J3
Aston Rd North AST/WIT B6 89 K7
Astons Cl BRLYHL DY5 102 B6
Astons Fold BRLYHL DY5 102 B6
Aston St BDMR/CCFT WV3 2 B9
CBHAMNE B4 7 J2
TPTN/OCK DY4 68 A7
Astor Dr MOS/BIL B13 126 A4
Astoria Cl SHHTH WV12 38 B4
Astor Rd FOAKS/STRLY B74 55 L4
KGSWFD DY6 83 K8
Atcham Cl REDE B98 197 K2
Athelstan Cl PENK ST19 10 E5 1
Athelstan Gv
DUNHL/THL/PER WV6 34 C8
Athelstan Wy CRTAM B79 31 K6 2
Athena Dr RLSS CV31 200 B8
Atherstone Cl REDE B98 197 K4
SHLY B90 146 C3
Atherstone La ATHST CV9 77 J1
Atherstone Rd ATHST CV9 63 L3
ATHST CV9 77 H1
CSHL/WTROR B46 77 K8
NUNW/HART CV10 79 M3
WOLV WV1 50 F3 2
Atherstone St
POL/KGSB/FAZ B78 45 M5
Atherston Pl TLHL/CAN CV4 153 H7 1
Athlone Rd DSYBK/YTR WS5 54 A5
Athol Cl RIDG/WDGT B32 123 H5
Athole St BHTH/HG B12 107 L6
Atholl Crs NUNW/HART CV10 98 C3
Athol Rd COVE CV2 135 L7
Atlantic Rd KGSTG B44 71 K5
Atlantic Wy DARL/WED WS10 68 C4
Atlas Cft WOLVN WV10 36 A7
Atlas Gv WBROM B70 86 D2
Attenborough Cl LOZ/NWT B19 89 H8
Atterton La ATHST CV9 63 M5
Attingham Dr CNCK/NC WS11 16 F4
GTB/HAM B43 70 B3 1
Attleborough La
CSHL/WTROR B46 92 E4
Attleborough Rd NUN CV11 99 H3
Attlee Cl OLDBY B69 86 B3
Attlee Crs BILS/COS WV14 67 J3
Attlee Gv CNCK/NC WS11 17 G3
Attlee Rd WSLW WS2 52 C2
Attoxhall Rd COVE CV2 155 J1
Attwell Pk BDMR/CCFT WV3 49 H6
Attwell Rd TPTN/OCK DY4 67 K4
Attwood Cl WASH/WDE B8 90 C7 1
Attwood Crs COVE CV2 135 G7
Attwood Gdns
ETTPK/GDPK/PENN WV4 50 C8
Attwood Rd BNTWD WS7 18 A6
Attwood St HAG/WOL DY9 102 D8 1
HALE B63 103 K8
Atworth Cl REDE B98 196 F8
Aubrey Rd RIDG/WDGT B32 105 J6
SMHTH B10 108 D6
Auchinleck Dr LICH WS13 21 G4
Auckland Dr CBROM B36 92 D5
Auckland Rd KGSWFD DY6 101 J1
SMTHWKW B67 87 J8
SPARK B11 107 L6
Auden Cl NUNW/HART CV10 97 K1
Auden Ct DUNHL/THL/PER WV6 48 D1
Audley Dr KIDDW DY11 136 E5
Audley Rd STETCH B33 109 J1
Audnam STRBR DY8 101 J4
Augusta Pl RLSN CV32 200 D5
Augusta Rd ACGN B27 109 G8
MOS/BIL B13 125 J1
Augusta Rd East MOS/BIL B13 125 K1
Augusta St WSNGN B18 6 C1
Augustine Gv
FOAKS/STRLY B74 42 D8 1
WSNGN B18 88 D7 1
Augustus Cl CSHL/WTROR B46 93 K4
Augustus Ct EDG B15 106 D5 1
Augustus Rd COV CV1 9 L2
EDG B15 106 B5
Augustus St WSLW WS2 4 D3 1
Aulton Rd MGN/WHC B75 57 J3
Ault St WBROM B70 87 H4
Austcliff Cl REDW B97 196 B7
Austcliff Dr SOLH B91 148 A5
Austen Cl NUNW/HART CV10 79 K8
Austen Pl EDG B15 106 F5
Austin Cl ACGN B27 127 H1
ATHST CV9 63 H6
DUDN DY1 84 D3
Austin Cote La LICHS WS14 21 J6
Austin Cft CBROM B36 92 C4
Austin Dr COVN CV6 134 E6
Austin Edwards Dr
WWCK CV34 199 M5 1
Austin Ri NFLD/LBR B31 143 K6
Austin Rd BRGRVE B60 185 J5
HDSW B21 88 A4
Austin St DUNHL/THL/PER WV6 49 M1
Austin Wy PBAR/PBCH B42 70 E8
Austrey Cl DOR/KN B93 148 E7
Austrey Gv SLYOAK B29 123 L5 1
Austrey Rd KGSWFD DY6 83 L8 2
Austwick Cl WWCK CV34 199 J4
Austy Cl CBROM B36 91 J5
Autumn Berry Gv SEDG DY3 66 C7 1
Autumn Cl RUSH/SHEL WS4 40 A3
Autumn Dr LICH WS13 21 H3 1
RUSH/SHEL WS4 40 A3
SEDG DY3 84 B2
Autumn Gv LOZ/NWT B19 89 G7 1
Auxerre Av REDE B98 196 E5
Avalon Cl ERDE/BCHGN B24 90 F1
Avebury Cl NUN CV11 99 K3
Avebury Gv BVILLE B30 125 G6
Avebury Rd BVILLE B30 125 G5
Ave Maria Cl CDYHTH B64 103 J4 1
Avenbury Cl REDE B98 197 K4 1
Avenbury Dr SOLH B91 148 C1
Avenue Cl DOR/KN B93 172 E2
VAUX/NECH B7 89 L8
Avenue Perry WOLVN WV10 36 D5
Avenue Rd ALE/KHTH/YWD B14 125 H5
BILS/COS WV14 67 G5
BLKHTH/ROWR B65 104 B4
DARL/WED WS10 52 B7
DOR/KN B93 172 E2
DUDS DY2 84 C7
DUNHL/THL/PER WV6 49 J3
ERDW/GRVHL B23 90 D1
HDSW B21 88 B3
HEDN WS12 17 J3
KNWTH CV8 176 B7
NUN CV11 99 H3
RLSS CV31 200 D6
RUGBYN/HIL CV21 183 J1
VAUX/NECH B7 89 L7
The Avenue ACGN B27 127 H2
BDMR/CCFT WV3 48 F5
BLKHTH/ROWR B65 103 L2
BRGRVE B60 166 D7
COVS CV3 154 E7
ETTPK/GDPK/PENN WV4 65 J1
KIDD DY10 138 F4
KIDDW DY11 161 K5
RBRY B45 142 C6
Averill Rd
LGN/SDN/BHAMAIR B26 109 L5
Avern Cl TPTN/OCK DY4 67 M7 1
Aversley Rd HWK/WKHTH B38 144 B5
Avery Cft CVALE B35 91 K3
Avery Dr ACGN B27 127 G1
Avery Myers Cl
LGLYGN/QTN B68 86 F8 1
Avery Rd SCFLD/BOLD B73 72 B2
SMTHWK B66 88 B7
Aviemore Cl NUNW/HART CV10 98 E3
Aviemore Crs GTB/HAM B43 70 F1
Avill TAM/AM/WIL B77 46 E8
Avill Gv KIDDW DY11 137 G6
Avington Cl SEDG DY3 66 B6 1
Avion Cl WSL WS1 5 G7
Avocet Cl COVN CV6 134 F3
STETCH B33 109 J2 1
Avocet Dr KIDD DY10 161 L3
Avon TAM/AM/WIL B77 46 E8
Avonbank Cl REDW B97 196 A7
Avon Cl BDWTH CV12 99 M7
BRGRVE B60 185 K7
BRLYHL DY5 83 M6
DUNHL/THL/PER WV6 48 D1 1
Avon Crs BLOX/PEL WS3 39 L4
Avoncroft Rd BRGRVE B60 185 H8
Avondale Cl KGSWFD DY6 83 J5
Avondale Rd COVW CV5 8 A9
DUNHL/THL/PER WV6 49 K2
KNWTH CV8 156 D8
RLSN CV32 200 F1
SPARK B11 126 B1
Avon Dr CBROM B36 92 D6
HLYWD B47 169 J3
MOS/BIL B13 125 M3
WLNHL WV13 52 A3
Avon Gv DSYBK/YTR WS5 69 L2
Avonlea Ri RLSN CV32 200 A3
Avonmere RUGBYN/HIL CV21 159 J7
Avon Rd BLOX/PEL WS3 39 J4
BNTWD WS7 18 D8
CNCK/NC WS11 16 B5
HALE B63 102 F8
KIDDW DY11 160 F2
KNWTH CV8 191 J2
SHLY B90 147 H5
STRBR DY8 119 K2
Avon St COVE CV2 134 F8
RUGBYN/HIL CV21 183 L1 1
SPARK B11 108 A8
WWCK CV34 199 L6
Awbridge Br WMBN WV5 64 C3
Awbridge Rd DUDS DY2 103 G2
Awefields Crs SMTHWKW B67 105 H1
Awson St COVN CV6 134 D7
Axborough La KIDD DY10 138 A1
Axholme Rd COVE CV2 155 J1
Axletree Wy DARL/WED WS10 52 E7
Axminster Cl NUN CV11 81 J8
Ayala Cft CBROM B36 91 J5 1
Aylesbury Cl HOCK/TIA B94 172 A7 2
Aylesbury Crs KGSTG B44 71 L5
Aylesbury Rd HOCK/TIA B94 172 B6
Aylesford Cl SEDG DY3 65 M3
Aylesford Dr
CHWD/FDBR/MGN B37 110 E6 1
FOAKS/STRLY B74 42 C8
Aylesford Rd HDSW B21 88 B4
Aylesford St COV CV1 9 K1
RLSS CV31 200 E7
Aylesmore Cl HIA/OLT B92 127 J5
RIDG/WDGT B32 123 G4 2
Aynho Cl COVW CV5 152 E2
Ayre Rd ERDE/BCHGN B24 90 F1
Ayrshire Cl CBROM B36 91 H5
Ayrton Cl DUNHL/THL/PER WV6 48 E1
Aysgarth Cl NUN CV11 99 L3
Azalea Cl CDSL WV8 34 F2
Azalea Gv BORD B9 108 D3 1
Aziz Isaac Cl LGLYGN/QTN B68 87 G7 1

B

Babbacombe Rd COVS CV3 154 B8
Babington Rd HDSW B21 88 C6
Bablake Cl COVN CV6 133 K5
Bablake Cft HIA/OLT B92 127 L4 1
Babors Fld BILS/COS WV14 66 E2

Babworth Cl *COVEN* WV9 ...... 35 L3 ⬛
Baccabox La *HLYWD* B47 .... 145 J6
Bacchus Rd *WSNGN* B18 .... 88 D7
Bachelors Bench *ATHST* CV9 ...... 63 H6 ⬛
Bache St *WBROM* B70 .... 87 G4
Bach Mill Dr
  ALE/KHTH/YWD B14 .... 146 B2
Backcester La *LICH* WS13 .... 20 F5
Backcrofts *CNCK/NC* WS11 .... 16 C5
Backhouse La *WLNHL* WV13 .... 51 L1
  WNSFLD WV11 .... 51 C1
Back La *ALDR* WS9 .... 41 K6
  CSHL/WTROR B46 .... 94 D3
  KIDD DY10 .... 162 D5
  LICHS WS14 .... 42 B4
  RCOVN/BALC/EX CV7 .... 131 H8
  RRUGBY CV23 .... 158 E2
  RRUGBY CV23 .... 182 L1
  WWCK CV34 .... 199 J7 ⬛
Back Rd *HWK/WKHTH* B38 .... 144 D3
  HWK/WKHTH B38 .... 144 D3
  KGSWFD DY6 .... 83 H6
Back St *NUN* CV11 .... 81 G8
Badby Leys *RUGBYS/DCH* CV22 .. 183 K6
Baddesley Rd *RLSS* CV31 .... 201 H8 ⬛
Baddesley Rd *HIA/OLT* B92 ...... 127 J3
  WSLW WS2 .... 52 D3
Bader Rd *DUNHL/THL/PER* WV6 .. 48 B2
  WSLW WS2 .... 52 D3
Badger Cl *HEDN* WS12 .... 12 A7
  REDE B98 .... 197 H2
  SHLY B90 .... 171 H1
Badger Dr *WOLVN* WV10 .... 3 H1
Badger Rd *COVS* CV3 .... 155 H5
Badgers Bank Rd
  FOAKS/STRLY B74 .... 42 D8 ⬛
Badgers Cl *BLOX/PEL* WS3 .... 25 L8
Badgers Cft *RMSLY* B62 .... 103 M6 ⬛
The Badgers *RBRY* B45 .... 166 E3
Badger St *HAG/WOL* DY9 .... 102 C7 ⬛
  SEDG DY3 .... 66 C8
Badgers Wy *HEDN* WS12 .... 17 H4
Badger Wy *BRGRVE* B60 .... 166 F8
Badland Av *KIDD* DY10 .... 137 K4
Badminton Cl *DUDN* DY1 .... 84 D2 ⬛
Badsey Cl *NFLD/LBR* B31 .... 144 A1
Badsey Rd *OLDBY* B69 .... 86 B8
Baffin Cl *RUGBYS/DCH* CV22 ... 183 J4 ⬛
Baggeridge Cl *SEDG* DY3 .... 65 L5
Baggott St *BKHL/PFLD* WV2 .... 50 A6 ⬛
Baginton Cl *SOLH* B91 .... 127 M8
Baginton Rd *COVS* CV3 .... 153 M7
  CVALE B35 .... 91 M1 ⬛
Bagley St *HAG/WOL* DY9 .... 102 A7
Bagnall Cl
  LGN/SDN/BHAMAIR B26 .... 109 H7
Bagnall Rd *BILS/COS* WV14 .... 51 C7
Bagnall St *BLOX/PEL* WS3 .... 39 G6
  TPTN/OCK DY4 .... 68 C6
  TPTN/OCK DY4 .... 68 A4
  WBROM B70 .... 87 J3
Bagnall Wk *BRLYHL* DY5 .... 102 B4
Bagnell Rd *ALE/KHTH/YWD* B14 .. 125 K6
Bagot St *CBHAMNE* B4 .... 7 J2
Bagridge Cl *BDMR/CCFT* WV3 ..... 48 F5 ⬛
Bagridge Rd *BDMR/CCFT* WV3 ..... 48 F5
Bagshaw Cl *KNWTH* CV8 .... 179 L4
Bagshawe Cft
  ERDW/GRVHL B23 .... 72 B6
Bagshaw Rd *STETCH* B33 .... 109 J2
Bailey Av *TAM/AM/WIL* B77 .... 46 D8
Bailey Cl *CNCK/NC* WS11 .... 16 E1
Bailey Rd *BILS/COS* WV14 .... 50 F6
Bailey's La *RRUGBY* CV23 .... 158 E8
Bailey St *WBROM* B70 .... 86 E1
  WOLVN WV10 .... 3 J4
Bakehouse La *CSHL/WTROR* B46 .. 76 C7
  DOR/KN B93 .... 173 M7
  RUGBYN/HIL CV21 .... 183 K2
  RLSS CV31 .... 201 G2
Baker Av *BILS/COS* WV14 .... 66 D3
  RLSS CV31 .... 200 D6
Baker House Gv *GTB/HAM* B43 ..... 70 B6
Baker Rd *BILS/COS* WV14 .... 67 J2 ⬛
Bakers Cft *ATHST* CV9 .... 62 A4
Bakers Gdns *CDSL* WV8 .... 34 C1
Baker's La *ALDR* WS9 .... 40 F7
  COVW CV5 .... 153 J3
  DOR/KN B93 .... 173 G4
  FOAKS/STRLY B74 .... 55 K8
Baker St *BNTWD* WS7 .... 18 D7
  BORD B9 .... 108 B4
  COVN CV6 .... 116 F7
  HDSW B21 .... 88 D5
  SPARK B11 .... 126 A1
  TPTN/OCK DY4 .... 85 J1
  WBROM B70 .... 86 F2
Bakers Wy *CDSL* WV8 .... 34 C1
Bakewell Cl *BLOX/PEL* WS3 .... 39 G2
  COVS CV3 .... 155 K5
Balaclava Rd
  ALE/KHTH/YWD B14 .... 125 J5 ⬛
Bala Cl *STRPT* DY13 .... 160 D8
Balcaskie Cl *EDG* B15 .... 106 C6
Balden Rd *RIDG/WDGT* B32 .... 105 J6
Baldmoor Lake Rd
  ERDW/GRVHL B23 .... 72 C6
Bald's La *HAG/WOL* DY9 .... 102 D8
Baldwin Cl *OLDBY* B69 .... 86 B3
Baldwin Cft *COVN* CV6 .... 134 F4
Baldwin Gv *CNCK/NC* WS11 .... 17 C3
Baldwin Rd *BVILLE* B30 .... 144 E2
  KIDD DY10 .... 137 M5
Baldwins La *HLGN/YWD* B28 ..... 146 D1
Baldwin St *BILS/COS* WV14 .... 67 K1
  SMTHWK B66 .... 87 M7
Baldwin Wy *SEDG* DY3 .... 82 C3
Balfour *CRTAM* B79 .... 45 L1
Balfour Dr *OLDBY* B69 .... 86 B3 ⬛
Balfour Rd *KGSWFD* DY6 .... 83 J5
Balfour St *BHTH/HG* B12 .... 107 J7
Balham Gv *KGSTG* B44 .... 71 L3
Balking Cl *BILS/COS* WV14 .... 66 F2 ⬛
Ballantine Rd *COVN* CV6 .... 133 M7
Ballarat Wk *STRBR* DY8 .... 101 K8 ⬛
Ballard Crs *DUDS* DY2 .... 85 H8
Ballard Rd *DUDS* DY2 .... 85 H8
Ballard Wk
  CHWD/FDBR/MGN B37 .... 92 E7
Ball Flds *TPTN/OCK* DY4 .... 68 A8

Ballingham Cl *TLHL/CAN* CV4 ... 152 E3
Balliol Rd *COVE* CV2 .... 154 F1
Ball La *COVEN* WV9 .... 22 A7
Ballot St *SMTHWK* B66 .... 87 M8
Balls Hl *WSL* WS1 .... 5 H2
Balls St *WSL* WS1 .... 5 H2
Balmain Crs *WNSFLD* WV11 .... 36 F5
Balmoral Cl *COVE* CV2 .... 135 J7
  LICHS WS14 .... 21 H7
  RMSLY B62 .... 103 M6
  RUSH/SHEL WS4 .... 40 B6
Balmoral Dr *HEDN* WS12 .... 12 D6
  SHHTH WV12 .... 37 M6
  WMBN WV5 .... 64 E4 ⬛
Balmoral Rd *CBROM* B36 .... 92 E6
  ERDW/GRVHL B23 .... 72 D8
  ETTPK/GDPK/PENN WV4 .... 65 L1 ⬛
  FOAKS/STRLY B74 .... 42 D8
  RIDG/WDGT B32 .... 122 E6
  STRBR DY8 .... 101 C3
Balmoral Vw *DUDN* DY1 .... 84 C3
Balmoral Wy
  BLKHTH/ROWR B65 .... 104 B1
  RLSN CV32 .... 193 C7
  WSLW WS2 .... 52 E1
Balsall Heath Rd *DIG/EDG* B5 ... 107 J6
Balsall St *RCOVN/BALC/EX* CV7 . 150 D7
Balsall St East
  RCOVN/BALC/EX CV7 .... 150 E8
Baltic Cl *CNCK/NC* WS11 .... 16 C3
Baltimore Rd *PBAR/PBCH* B42 ..... 70 E8
Balvenie Wy *DUDN* DY1 .... 84 D2
Bamber Cl *BDMR/CCFT* WV3 .... 49 J5
Bamburgh *TAM/AM/WIL* B77 .... 46 A6 ⬛
Bamburgh Gv *RLSN* CV32 .... 200 C3
Bamford Cl *BLOX/PEL* WS3 .... 39 G2
Bamford Dr *BDMR/CCFT* WV3 .... 2 A9
  BLOX/PEL WS3 .... 39 G2
Bamford St *TAM/AM/WIL* B77 ..... 46 B2
Bampton Av *BNTWD* WS7 .... 18 E5
Bamville Rd *WASH/WDE* B8 .... 90 E8
Banbery Dr *WMBN* WV5 .... 82 D1
Banbrook Cl *HIA/OLT* B92 .... 128 B5
Banbury Cft
  CHWD/FDBR/MGN B37 .... 110 D3
Banbury Rd *CNCK/NC* WS11 ...... 15 M5
  WWCK CV34 .... 199 J3
Banbury St *DIG/EDG* B5 .... 7 J4
Bancroft Cl *DUDN* DY1 .... 66 F6 ⬛
Bandywood Rd *KGSTG* B44 .... 71 J1
Baneberry Dr *WOLVN* WV10 .... 22 F6
Banfield Av *DARL/WED* WS10 ...... 52 A6
Banfield Rd *DARL/WED* WS10 ...... 68 A1
Banford Rd *WASH/WDE* B8 .... 108 E1
Bangham Pit Rd *NFLD/LBR* B31 .. 123 J6
Bangley La *POL/KGSB/FAZ* B78 ... 44 E5
Bangor Rd *BORD* B9 .... 108 B3
Bank Crs *BNTWD* WS7 .... 18 D8
Bankdale Rd *WASH/WDE* B8 .... 108 F1
Bankes Rd *SMHTH* B10 .... 108 C4
Bank Farm *HAG/WOL* DY9 .... 120 A4
Bankfield Dr *RLSN* CV32 .... 200 A4
Bankfield Rd *BILS/COS* WV14 ..... 51 H8
  TPTN/OCK DY4 .... 68 A5
Banklands Rd *DUDS* DY2 .... 85 J7
Bank Rd *ATHST* CV9 .... 63 J5
  DUDS DY2 .... 85 H7
  SEDG DY3 .... 84 A2
Banks Gn *REDW* B97 .... 194 E2
Bankside *GTB/HAM* B43 .... 70 C6 ⬛
  MOS/BIL B13 .... 126 B3
  WMBN WV5 .... 64 D6 ⬛
Bankside Crs *FOAKS/STRLY* B74 .. 55 K6
Bankside Wy *ALDR* WS9 .... 40 F3
Banks Rd *COVN* CV6 .... 133 L8
Banks St *WLNHL* WV13 .... 51 L3
Bank St *ALE/KHTH/YWD* B14 ..... 125 J5
  BILS/COS WV14 .... 67 J1
  BRLYHL DY5 .... 102 B1
  CDYHTH B64 .... 103 G4
  HAG/WOL DY9 .... 102 D8
  HEDN WS12 .... 17 J4
  HHTH/SAND B71 .... 69 G7
  RUGBYN/HIL CV21 .... 183 L2 ⬛
  WOLVN WV10 .... 36 C3
  WSL WS1 .... 5 H3
Bankwell St *BRLYHL* DY5 .... 102 B1
Banner La *TLHL/CAN* CV4 .... 152 B2
Bannerlea Rd
  CHWD/FDBR/MGN B37 .... 92 D8
Bannerley Rd *STETCH* B33 ...... 110 A3
Banners Gate Rd
  SCFLD/BOLD B73 .... 71 M2
Banners Gv *ERDW/GRVHL* B23 ..... 72 E7
Banners La *HALE* B63 .... 103 H1
  REDW B97 .... 196 C8
Banners St *HALE* B63 .... 103 H1
Banners Wk *KGSTG* B44 .... 71 M3
Bannister St *CDYHTH* B64 .... 103 H3
Banstead Cl *BKHL/PFLD* WV2 ...... 50 C6
Bantam Gv *COVN* CV6 .... 133 L2
Bantams Cl *STETCH* B33 .... 110 A3
Bant Mill Rd *BRGRVE* B60 ...... 185 L4 ⬛
Banton Cl *ERDW/GRVHL* B23 ...... 72 B5
The Bantocks *WBROM* B70 .... 68 E7
Bantock Gdns *BDMR/CCFT* WV3 .... 49 J4
Bantock Rd *TLHL/CAN* CV4 ...... 152 C3
Banton Cl *ERDW/GRVHL* B23 ...... 72 B5
Bantry Cl
  LGN/SDN/BHAMAIR B26 .... 128 A1
Baptist End Rd *DUDS* DY2 .... 85 G8
Barbara Rd *HLGN/YWD* B28 ...... 126 E8
Barbara St *CRTAM* B79 .... 31 L8
Barber Cl *HEDN* WS12 .... 17 J3
Barbers La *HIA/OLT* B92 .... 129 C7 ⬛
Barbican Ri *COVE* CV2 .... 155 J3
Barbridge Rd *BDWTH* CV12 ...... 117 M3
Barbrook Dr *BRLYHL* DY5 .... 101 M6
Barby Rd *RUGBYS/DCH* CV22 ..... 183 L4
Barcheston Dr
  RWWCK/WEL CV35 .... 198 B3

Barcheston Rd *DOR/KN* B93 ..... 148 E8
  SLYOAK B29 .... 123 L4
Barclay Rd *SMTHWKW* B67 .... 105 J4
Barcliff Av *TAM/AM/WIL* B77 ..... 46 C2
Barcroft *WLNHL* WV13 .... 51 M2
Bardfield Cl *PBAR/PBCH* B42 ..... 70 D5
Bardon Dr *SHLY* B90 .... 147 H3 ⬛
Bard St *SPARK* B11 .... 108 A8
Bardwell Cl *CDSL* WV8 .... 35 K5
Barford Cl *COVS* CV3 .... 155 H5 ⬛
  DARL/WED WS10 .... 52 A5 ⬛
  REDE B98 .... 197 K4
  WALM/CURD B76 .... 73 K1 ⬛
Barford Crs
  ALE/KHTH/YWD B14 .... 145 G3
Barford Rd *KNWTH* CV8 .... 191 M2 ⬛
  SHLY B90 .... 147 H3
  WSNGN B18 .... 106 C1
Barford St *DIG/EDG* B5 .... 107 J5
Bargate Dr *DUNHL/THL/PER* WV6 .. 2 B1
Bargery Rd *WNSFLD* WV11 .... 37 L4
Barham Cl *SHLY* B90 .... 147 L8 ⬛
Barker Rd *FOAKS/STRLY* B74 ..... 56 F6
Barker's Butts La *COVN* CV6 ..... 8 C6
  COVN CV6 .... 133 K8
Barkers La *HLYWD* B47 .... 169 K4
Barker St *LGLYGN/QTN* B68 ...... 87 G8
  LOZ/NWT B19 .... 88 F6
Bark Piece *RIDG/WDGT* B32 ..... 123 G2
Barlands Cft *BKDE/SHDE* B34 .... 92 A7 ⬛
Barle Gv *CBROM* B36 .... 92 D6
Barley Cl *ALDR* WS9 .... 55 J3 ⬛
  CDSL WV8 .... 35 J4 ⬛
  SEDG DY3 .... 66 D6 ⬛
Barley Cft *BRGRVE* B60 .... 185 H6
  DUNHL/THL/PER WV6 .... 48 B2 ⬛
Barleyfield Ri *KGSWFD* DY6 ...... 82 E5
Barleyfield Rw *WSL* WS1 .... 4 F5
The Barley Lea *COVS* CV3 ...... 154 F5
Barley Mow La *BRGRVW* B61 ..... 165 L5
Barlich Wy *REDE* B98 .... 196 D3
Barlow Cl *LGLYGN/QTN* B68 ..... 104 C2 ⬛
  RBRY B45 .... 142 C3 ⬛
  TAM/AM/WIL B77 .... 46 C1
Barlow Ct *POL/KGSB/FAZ* B78 .... 60 B7 ⬛
Barlow Dr *WBROM* B70 .... 87 K4
  DARL/WED WS10 .... 52 E8
Barlow Rd *COVE* CV2 .... 135 M7 ⬛
  DARL/WED WS10 .... 52 C7
Barlows Rd *EDG* B15 .... 106 B8
Barmouth Cl *SHHTH* WV12 .... 38 A7
Barnabas Rd
  ERDW/GRVHL B23 .... 90 D1 ⬛
Barnaby Sq *WOLVN* WV10 .... 36 D1 ⬛
Barnack Av *COVS* CV3 .... 153 M8
Barnack Dr *WWCK* CV34 .... 199 J4 ⬛
Barnard Cl
  CHWD/FDBR/MGN B37 .... 111 H4
  RLSN CV32 .... 201 L8 ⬛
Barnard Pl *BKHL/PFLD* WV2 .... 50 C7
Barnard Rd *MGN/WHC* B75........ 57 J6
  WNSFLD WV11 .... 37 K4
Barnard Wy *CNCK/NC* WS11 .... 16 D3
Barn Av *SEDG* DY3 .... 66 A6
Barnbridge *TAM/AM/WIL* B77 ..... 46 A3
Barnbrook Rd *DOR/KN* B93 ...... 148 E6
Barn Cl *BRGRVE* B60 .... 185 J7 ⬛
  BVILLE B30 .... 124 F7
  CDYHTH B64 .... 103 J7
  HAG/WOL DY9 .... 120 A1
  HALE B63 .... 121 J3
  LICH WS13 .... 20 F2
  POL/KGSB/FAZ B78 .... 47 K7
Barn Cft *BNTWD* WS7 .... 26 E1
  GTWY WS6 .... 24 E2
  RIDG/WDGT B32 .... 123 J4
Barncroft Rd *OLDBY* B69 .... 85 L5 ⬛
Barncroft St *WBROM* B70 .... 68 E5 ⬛
Barne Cl *NUN* CV11 .... 99 M6
Barnes Cl *STETCH* B33 .... 110 C3
Barnes Hl *SLYOAK* B29 .... 123 K3
Barnes Rd *LICHS* WS14 .... 28 E7
Barnesville Cl *SMHTH* B10 ...... 108 E5
Barnet Rd *ERDW/GRVHL* B23 ...... 72 B8
Barnett Cl *BILS/COS* WV14 ...... 67 H1 ⬛
  KGSWFD DY6 .... 101 H1
Barnett Gn *KGSWFD* DY6 .... 101 H1
Barnett La *KGSWFD* DY6 .... 83 H8
Barnett Rd *WLNHL* WV13 .... 51 J4
Barnetts Cl *KIDD* DY10 .... 161 L1
Barnetts Gv *KIDD* DY10 .... 161 L1
Barnetts La *BRWNH* WS8 .... 26 D5
  KIDD DY10 .... 161 L1
Barnett St *STRBR* DY8 .... 101 H2
  TPTN/OCK DY4 .... 85 J1
  TPTN/OCK DY4 .... 85 J3 ⬛
Barney Cl *TPTN/OCK* DY4 .... 85 K2
Barn Farm Ct *BILS/COS* WV14 .... 51 L6
Barnfield Av *COVW* CV5........ 132 F6
Barnfield Cl *LICHS* WS14 .... 20 F7
Barnfield Dr *HIA/OLT* B92 ..... 128 D7
Barnfield Gv
  BFLD/HDSWWD B20 .... 70 C8
Barnfield Rd *BRGRVW* B61 ..... 185 J4 ⬛
  RMSLY B62 .... 104 B6
  TPTN/OCK DY4 .... 67 B6
  WOLV WV1 .... 50 E3
Barnfield Wy *HEDN* WS12 .... 13 L7
Barnford Cl *SMHTH* B10 .... 108 A4 ⬛
Barnford Crs *LGLYGN/QTN* B68 .. 104 E2
Barnfordhill Cl
  LGLYGN/QTN B68 .... 104 F1
Barn Gn *BDMR/CCFT* WV3 .... 49 K6
Barnhurst La *CDSL* WV8 .... 35 H7
Barn La *HDSW* B21 .... 88 C6
  HIA/OLT B92 .... 127 J1
  MOS/BIL B13 .... 125 L6
Barn Meadow *YDLY* B25 .... 109 H4
Barnmoor Ri *SOLH* B91 .... 128 A6 ⬛
Barn Owl Cl *KIDD* DY10 .... 161 L3 ⬛
Barn Owl Dr *BLOX/PEL* WS3 ...... 39 K1
Barnpark Covert *BVILLE* B30 ... 145 G3 ⬛
Barn Piece *RIDG/WDGT* B32 ..... 122 F1
Barnsbury Av
  CSCFLD/WYGN B72 .... 73 G7 ⬛
Barns Cl *ALDR* WS9 .... 40 D1
Barns Cft *FOAKS/STRLY* B74 ..... 55 M2

Barnsdale Crs *NFLD/LBR* B31 ... 143 J1
Barns La *RUSH/SHEL* WS4 .... 40 A5
Barnsley Cl *ATHST* CV9 .... 63 H6
  HRBN B17 .... 105 J4
Barnstaple Cl *COVW* CV5 .... 132 D8 ⬛
Barnstaple Rd *SMTHWK* B66 ...... 87 M8 ⬛
Barn St *DIG/EDG* B5 .... 7 K6
Barnswood Cl *CNCK/NC* WS11 ..... 15 M5
Barnt Green Rd *RBRY* B45 ...... 167 C2
Barnwood Cl *REDE* B98 .... 189 H8
Barnwood Rd *CDSL* WV8 .... 35 H4
  RIDG/WDGT B32 .... 123 K1
Baron Cl *BNTWD* WS7 .... 18 C4
Barons Cl *HRBN* B17 .... 105 M7 ⬛
Baron's Cft *COVS* CV3 .... 154 C6
  NUNW/HART CV10 .... 98 A1
Baron's Field Rd *COVS* CV3 .... 154 B6
Barpool Rd *NUNW/HART* CV10 ..... 98 D1
Barrack La *HALE* B63 .... 102 F7
Barrack Rd *BLOX/PEL* WS3 .... 39 H5
  BRWNH WS8 .... 27 C4
  RWWCK/WEL CV35 .... 190 A3
Barrack St *VAUX/NECH* B7 .... 7 M2
  WBROM B70 .... 68 E5 ⬛
  WWCK CV34 .... 199 J6 ⬛
Barracks Wy *COV* CV1 .... 8 F5 ⬛
Barra Cft *CVALE* B35 .... 91 M1 ⬛
Barrar Cl *STRBR* DY8 .... 101 J5
Barras Gn *COV* CV2 .... 154 E1
Barras La *COV* CV1 .... 8 C4
Barratts Cft *BRLYHL* DY5 .... 84 A4 ⬛
Barratts Rd *HWK/WKHTH* B38 ... 144 E5 ⬛
Barr Common Cl *ALDR* WS9 .... 54 F2
Barr Common Rd *ALDR* WS9 .... 54 E1
Barrett Cl *KIDD* DY10 .... 137 M7
Barretts La
  RCOVN/BALC/EX CV7 .... 151 C7
Barrhill Cl *GTB/HAM* B43 .... 70 C3 ⬛
Barrie Av *KIDD* DY10 .... 138 A6
Barrington Cl *DSYBK/YTR* WS5 ... 69 L2
  WOLVN WV10 .... 36 A4
Barrington Rd *HIA/OLT* B92 .... 127 J4
  RBRY B45 .... 142 C6
  RUGBYS/DCH CV22 .... 183 C3
Barr Lakes La *DSYBK/YTR* WS5 ... 54 C6
Barr La
  MKTBOS/BARL/STKG CV13 ..... 81 M2
  RRUGBY CV23 .... 157 J1
Barron Rd *NFLD/LBR* B31 .... 143 J2
Barrow Cl *COVE* CV2 .... 135 M7
  REDE B98 .... 197 K2
Barrowfield La *KNWTH* CV8 ..... 191 K1
Barrow Hill Rd *BRLYHL* DY5 ..... 84 A4
Barrow Rd *KNWTH* CV8 .... 191 K1
Barrows La
  LGN/SDN/BHAMAIR B26 .... 109 L7
Barrows Rd *SPARK* B11 .... 108 A7
Barrow Wk *DIG/EDG* B5 .... 107 J6 ⬛
Barrs Crs *CDYHTH* B64 .... 103 K5
Barrs Rd *CDYHTH* B64 .... 103 J5
Barrs St *LGLYGN/QTN* B68 ...... 104 E1
Barr St *LOZ/NWT* B19 .... 89 C8
  SEDG DY3 .... 84 A2
Barry Rd *DSYBK/YTR* WS5 .... 54 A6
Barsby Cl *ATHST* CV9 .... 63 H6
Barsham Cl *DIG/EDG* B5 .... 107 C7
Barsham Dr *BRLYHL* DY5 .... 102 A5 ⬛
Barston Cl *COVN* CV6 .... 134 C2
Barston La *HIA/OLT* B92 .... 149 M4
  RCOVN/BALC/EX CV7 .... 150 B5
  SOLH B91 .... 148 F3
Bartestree Cl *REDE* B98 .... 197 K4 ⬛
Bartholemews La
  BRGRVW B61 .... 165 K8 ⬛
Bartholomew Rw *CBHAMNE* B4 ..... 7 J4
Bartholomew St *DIG/EDG* B5 ...... 7 J5
Bartic Av *KGSWFD* DY6 .... 101 K4
Bartleet Rd *REDE* B98 .... 197 H6
  SMTHWK B67 .... 87 H8
Bartlett Cl *COVN* CV6 .... 134 C3
  PENK ST19 .... 10 D5
  TPTN/OCK DY4 .... 67 M4
Bartley Cl *HIA/OLT* B92 .... 127 K3
Bartley Dr *NFLD/LBR* B31 ...... 123 J5
Bartley Woods
  RIDG/WDGT B32 .... 122 F3
Barton Crs *RLSS* CV31 .... 201 C7 ⬛
Barton Cft *HLGN/YWD* B28 ..... 146 D1
Barton Dr *DOR/KN* B93 .... 172 F1
Barton La *KGSWFD* DY6 .... 83 G5
Barton Lodge Rd
  HLGN/YWD B28 .... 146 C1
Barton Rd *BDWTH* CV12 .... 116 F1
  COVN CV6 .... 134 D3 ⬛
  ETTPK/GDPK/PENN WV4 .... 66 D1 ⬛
  NUNW/HART CV10 .... 99 C4
  RUGBYS/DCH CV22 .... 183 H5
Bartons Bank *LOZ/NWT* B19 ...... 89 J6
Barton's Meadow *COVE* CV2 .... 134 F8
Barton St *WBROM* B70 .... 86 F3
Barwell Cl *DOR/KN* B93 .... 172 C1 ⬛
  RLSN CV32 .... 200 D3
Barwell Rd *BORD* B9 .... 107 M3
Barwick St *COV* CV1 .... 8 D4 ⬛
Basalt Cl *WSLW* WS2 .... 52 E1
Basant Cl *WWCK* CV34 .... 199 L6 ⬛
Bascote Brook Dr *COVN* CV6 ... 116 D8
Basford Dr *NFLD/LBR* B31 ...... 143 J1
Basil Gv *NFLD/LBR* B31 .... 143 J1
Basil Rd *NFLD/LBR* B31 .... 143 J1
Basin La *TAM/AM/WIL* B77 .... 46 B2
Baskerville Rd *KIDD* DY10 ..... 137 K4
Baskeyfield Cl *LICHS* WS14 ..... 21 H4
Basley Wy *COVN* CV6 .... 134 B1
Baslow Cl *BLOX/PEL* WS3 .... 38 F2
  STETCH B33 .... 109 J1
Baslow Rd *BLOX/PEL* WS3 .... 38 F2
Basons La *LGLYGN/QTN* B68 ...... 87 C8
Bassano Rd
  BLKHTH/ROWR B65 .... 104 A4 ⬛
Bassenthwaite Ct
  KGSWFD DY6 .... 83 H7 ⬛
Bassett Cl
  ETTPK/GDPK/PENN WV4 .... 49 C7
  SHHTH WV12 .... 52 B1 ⬛
  WALM/CURD B76 .... 73 J1 ⬛

Bassett Cft *SMHTH* B10 .... 107 M5 ⬛
Bassett Rd *COVN* CV6 .... 133 L8
  DARL/WED WS10 .... 69 G3
  HALE B63 .... 102 E7
Bassetts Gv
  CHWD/FDBR/MGN B37 .... 92 C8
Bassett St *WSLW* WS2 .... 4 A3
Bassnage Rd *HALE* B63 .... 121 J3
Batchcroft *BILS/COS* WV14 ...... 51 H8
  DARL/WED WS10 .... 52 B5
Batchelor Cl *STRBR* DY8 .... 101 K5 ⬛
Batchley Rd *REDW* B97 .... 195 M1
Bateman Dr *SCFLD/BOLD* B73 ..... 72 F4
Bateman Rd
  CSHL/WTROR B46 .... 93 K4 ⬛
Bateman's Acre South
  COVN CV6 .... 8 A1 ⬛
Batemans La *HLYWD* B47 .... 145 J8
Bates Cl *WALM/CURD* B76 .... 73 M5 ⬛
Bates Gv *WNSFLD* WV11 .... 36 E8
Bates Hl *REDW* B97 .... 196 B1 ⬛
Bates Rd *COVW* CV5 .... 153 J6
Bate St *ETTPK/GDPK/PENN* WV4 .. 66 C2 ⬛
Bath Av *WOLV* WV1 .... 2 D3
Batheaston Cl
  HWK/WKHTH B38 .... 144 B6 ⬛
Bath Meadow *HALE* B63 .... 103 J8
Bath Pas *DIG/EDG* B5 .... 7 G7 ⬛
Bath Pl *RLSS* CV31 .... 200 D6
Bath Rd *ATHST* CV9 .... 63 J6
  BRLYHL DY5 .... 102 E3
  CNCK/NC WS11 .... 16 C2
  NUN CV11 .... 81 G8
  STRBR DY8 .... 101 K7
  TPTN/OCK DY4 .... 67 L8
  WOLV WV1 .... 2 C5
  WSL WS1 .... 4 F5
Bath Rw *EDG* B15 .... 6 C8
  OLDBY B69 .... 86 B5
Bath St *BILS/COS* WV14 .... 51 J8
  CBHAMNE B4 .... 7 G2
  COV CV1 .... 9 H2
  DUDS DY2 .... 85 G5
  RLSS CV31 .... 200 D6
  RUGBYN/HIL CV21 .... 183 M2 ⬛
  SEDG DY3 .... 66 C4
  WLNHL WV13 .... 51 M4 ⬛
  WOLV WV1 .... 3 J6 ⬛
  WSL WS1 .... 4 F4
Bathurst Cl
  RUGBYS/DCH CV22 .... 183 J5 ⬛
Bathurst Rd *COVN* CV6 .... 133 L7
Bathway Rd *COVS* CV3 .... 177 L1 ⬛
Batmans Hill Rd *BILS/COS* WV14 . 67 J3
Batsford Cl *REDE* B98 .... 196 D1 ⬛
Batsford Rd *COVN* CV6 .... 153 K1
Batson Ri *STRBR* DY8 .... 101 L5
Battenhall Rd *HRBN* B17 .... 105 J4
Battens Cl *REDE* B98 .... 196 D2
Battens Dr *REDE* B98 .... 197 H1
Battenfield Hl *WMBN* WV5 .... 64 F6
Battlefield La *WMBN* WV5 .... 64 F6
Baulk La *RCOVN/BALC/EX* CV7 .. 151 H5
Bavaro Gdns *BRLYHL* DY5 .... 102 E3
Baverstock Rd
  ALE/KHTH/YWD B14 .... 145 J3
Bawnmore Ct
  RUGBYS/DCH CV22 .... 183 H5 ⬛
Bawnmore Pk
  RUGBYS/DCH CV22 .... 183 H5
Bawnmore Rd
  RUGBYS/DCH CV22 .... 183 H5
Baxter Av *KIDD* DY10 .... 137 K6
Baxter Cl *TLHL/CAN* CV4 .... 152 S5
Baxter Ct *RLSS* CV31 .... 200 E6 ⬛
Baxter Gdns *KIDD* DY10 .... 137 K6
Baxterley Gn *SOLH* B91 .... 147 H1
  WALM/CURD B76 .... 73 K4
Baxters Rd *SHLY* B90 .... 146 F5
Bayer St *BILS/COS* WV14 .... 67 G5
Bayford Av
  LGN/SDN/BHAMAIR B26 .... 128 A1
  NFLD/LBR B31 .... 143 J7
Bayley Crs *DARL/WED* WS10 ...... 52 A5
Bayley La *COV* CV1 .... 9 G5
Bayleys La *TPTN/OCK* DY4 .... 68 A6
Baylie St *STRBR* DY8 .... 119 K1
Baylis Av *COVN* CV6 .... 134 E1
Bayliss Av *BILS/COS* WV14 ...... 66 E3
  WNSFLD WV11 .... 37 K5
Bayliss Cl *BILS/COS* WV14 ...... 51 C6
  NFLD/LBR B31 .... 123 M8
Baynton Rd *SHHTH* WV12 .... 38 A6
Bayston Rd
  ALE/KHTH/YWD B14 .... 145 J7
Bayswater Rd
  BFLD/HDSWWD B20 .... 89 H4
  SEDG DY3 .... 84 D3
Bayton Rd
  RCOVN/BALC/EX CV7 .... 116 F7
Bayton Wy
  RCOVN/BALC/EX CV7 .... 117 G6
Baytree Cl *BLOX/PEL* WS3 .... 38 E3
Bay Tree Cl *COVE* CV2 .... 135 H4
  HWK/WKHTH B38 .... 144 B5
Baytree Rd *BLOX/PEL* WS3 .... 38 E3
Baywell Cl *SHLY* B90 .... 147 L6 ⬛
Beach Av *BHTH/HG* B12 .... 107 M8 ⬛
  BILS/COS WV14 .... 52 A4
Beach Brook Cl *SPARK* B11 .... 107 M8 ⬛
Beachburn Wy
  BFLD/HDSWWD B20 .... 88 C2
Beach Cl *NFLD/LBR* B31 .... 144 A4
Beachcroft Rd *KGSWFD* DY6 ..... 83 C5 ⬛
Beach Dr *HALE* B63 .... 103 L8
Beach Rd *BILS/COS* WV14 .... 51 H6
  SPARK B11 .... 107 M8 ⬛
Beach St *HALE* B63 .... 103 L8 ⬛
Beachwood Av *KGSWFD* DY6 ...... 83 C4
Beacon Cl *GTB/HAM* B43 .... 70 D4
  RBRY B45 .... 142 D7
  SMTHWK B66 .... 87 L6
Beacon Dr *WSL* WS1 .... 5 K6
Beaconfields *LICH* WS13 .... 20 E5 ⬛
Beacon Gdns *LICH* WS13 .... 20 E4

Beacon HI ALDR WS9 ... 55 G4
AST/WIT B6 ... 89 J5
RBRY B45 ... 142 C8
Beacon La BRGRVE B60 ... 166 B2
SEDG DY3 ... 66 C4
Beacon Ri ALDR WS9 ... 54 F2
HAG/WOL DY9 ... 120 B1
SEDG DY3 ... 66 C4
Beacon Rd ALDR WS9 ... 54 F6
COVN CV6 ... 134 B2
DSYBK/YTR WS5 ... 54 B8
GTB/HAM B43 ... 71 G2
KGSTG B44 ... 71 L1
SCFLD/BOLD B73 ... 72 E4
SHHTH WV12 ... 38 A5 □
Beaconsfield Av
ETTPK/GDPK/PENN WV4 ... 50 B8 □
RUGBYS/DCH CV22 ... 183 L4
Beaconsfield Dr
ETTPK/GDPK/PENN WV4 ... 50 B8 □
Beaconsfield Rd BHTH/HG B12 ... 125 J1
COVE CV2 ... 154 F3
FOAKS/STRLY B74 ... 56 F6
Beaconsfield St
HHTH/SAND B71 ... 69 G8
RLSS CV31 ... 200 F1
Beacon St BILS/COS WV14 ... 66 D4
LICH WS13 ... 20 E5
WSL WS1 ... 5 K4
Beacon Vw RBRY B45 ... 142 D7
Beacon View Dr KGSTG B44 ... 71 K1
Beacon View Rd
HHTH/SAND B71 ... 69 K3
HEDN WS12 ... 17 K2
RUSH/SHEL WS4 ... 40 A8
Beacon Wy ALDR WS9 ... 40 E2
Beadborough Wk ALDR WS9 ... 40 F4 □
Beake Av COVN CV6 ... 133 M7
Beakes Rd SMTHWKW B67 ... 105 K2
Beaks Farm Gdns
LDYWD/EDGR B16 ... 106 B3
Beaks Hill Rd HWK/WKHTH B38 ... 144 C4
Beak St CBHAMW B1 ... 6 F6
Beale CI CVALE B35 ... 91 L3
Beale St STRBR DY8 ... 101 K8
Bealeys Av WNSFLD WV11 ... 37 G5
Bealeys La BLOX/PEL WS3 ... 38 E3
Beamans CI COVN CV6 ... 133 M7
Beaminster Rd SOLH B91 ... 147 K1
Beamish CI COVE CV2 ... 135 L7 □
Bean Cft RIDG/WDGT B32 ... 123 G3
Beanfield Av COVS CV3 ... 177 K1
Bean Rd DUDS DY2 ... 85 H5
TPTN/OCK DY4 ... 67 G7
Beardmore Rd
CSCFLD/WYGN B72 ... 73 G5
Bear HI ALVE B48 ... 167 M8
Bearhill Dr ALVE B48 ... 167 M7
Bear Lane CI
POL/KGSB/FAZ B78 ... 47 L3 □
Bearmore Rd CDYHTH B64 ... 103 J4
Bearley Cft SHLY B90 ... 147 G5
Bearnett Dr
ETTPK/GDPK/PENN WV4 ... 65 G3
Bearnett La WMBN WV5 ... 64 F4
Bearwood Rd SMTHWKW B66 ... 105 L3
Beasley Gv PBAR/PBCH B42 ... 70 F4
Beaton CI WLNHL WV13 ... 51 J3
Beaton Rd FOAKS/STRLY B74 ... 56 E2
Beatrice St BLOX/PEL WS3 ... 39 C7
Beatrice Wk TPTN/OCK DY4 ... 85 L3 □
Beatty Dr RUGBYS/DCH CV22 ... 183 H3
Beaubrook Gdns STRBR DY8 ... 101 H2
Beauchamp Av
BFLD/HDSWWD B20 ... 70 D8
KIDDW DY11 ... 161 G2
RLSN CV32 ... 200 D4
Beauchamp CI
CHWD/FDBR/MGN B37 ... 110 F3 □
WALM/CURD B76 ... 73 M6 □
Beauchamp Gdns WWCK CV34 ... 199 M6
Beauchamp HI RLSN CV32 ... 200 C4
Beauchamp Rd KNWTH CV8 ... 191 J3
MOS/BIL B13 ... 125 M8
RLSN CV32 ... 200 D4 □
SOLH B91 ... 127 L8
TAM/AM/WIL B77 ... 46 D8
WWCK CV34 ... 199 M5
Beau Ct CNCK/NC WS11 ... 16 C4
Beaudesert BNTWD WS7 ... 18 E4
Beaudesert CI HLYWD B47 ... 145 L7 □
Beaudesert Rd
BFLD/HDSWWD B20 ... 88 F5
COVW CV5 ... 8 A7
HLYWD B47 ... 145 L7
Beaudesert Vw HEDN WS12 ... 13 L8 □
Beaufell CI WWCK CV34 ... 199 J4 □
Beaufort Av CBROM B36 ... 91 H7
KIDDW DY11 ... 136 E6
RLSN CV32 ... 193 G8
Beaufort Dr COVS CV3 ... 155 K6
Beaufort Rd LDYWD/EDGR B16 ... 106 D4
Beaufort St REDW B97 ... 196 C2
Beaufort Wy ALDR WS9 ... 54 F1
Beaulieu Av KGSWFD DY6 ... 101 K1 □
Beaulieu CI KIDDW DY11 ... 137 C5
Beaulieu Pk RLSS CV31 ... 201 H7
Beaumaris CI COVW CV5 ... 132 D8
DUDN DY1 ... 84 D2
Beaumont Av GTWY WS6 ... 24 D3
TPTN/OCK DY4 ... 67 J7 □
Beaumont Crs COVN CV6 ... 8 A1
Beaumont Dr BRLYHL DY5 ... 101 M6
HRBN B17 ... 123 M1
Beaumont Gdns WSNGN B18 ... 88 D7 □
Beaumont Gv SOLH B91 ... 127 K8
Beaumont Lawns BRGRVE B60 ... 166 A4
Beaumont PI NUN CV11 ... 98 E1 □
Beaumont Rd BVILLE B30 ... 124 C7
DARL/WED WS10 ... 68 D1
GTWY WS6 ... 24 D3
NUN CV11 ... 98 D1
RCOVN/BALC/EX CV7 ... 115 L7
RMSLY B62 ... 104 C5
Beausale Cft COVW CV5 ... 152 E2
Beausale Dr DOR/KN B93 ... 148 F6
Beausale La RWWCK/WEL CV35 ... 190 A5

Beauty Bank CDYHTH B64 ... 103 K5
Beauty Bank Crs STRBR DY8 ... 101 J7
Beaver CI WNSFLD WV11 ... 37 K8
Bebington CI COVEN WV9 ... 35 K4
Beccles Dr WLNHL WV13 ... 51 K5
RCOVN/BALC/EX CV7 ... 96 C3
WWCK CV34 ... 199 M4 □
Beech Hurst
HWK/WKHTH B38 ... 144 C5 □
Beechlawn Dr KINVER DY7 ... 100 C6
Beechmore Rd
LGN/SDN/BHAMAIR B26 ... 109 K8
Beechmount Dr
ERDW/GRVHL B23 ... 72 E7
Beechnut CI SOLH B91 ... 128 B8 □
TLHL/CAN CV4 ... 152 B3
Beechnut La SOLH B91 ... 128 C8
Beech Park Dr RBRY B45 ... 167 C5 □
Beech Pine CI HEDN WS12 ... 12 E5
Beech Rd BRGRVW B61 ... 185 K1
BVILLE B30 ... 124 C6
COVN CV6 ... 133 M8 □
CRTAM B79 ... 31 L5
DARL/WED WS10 ... 52 D8
DUDN DY1 ... 85 G1
ERDW/GRVHL B23 ... 72 D6
HLYWD B47 ... 145 M7
KGSWFD DY6 ... 83 H8
OLDBY B69 ... 85 L5
STRBR DY8 ... 119 J2
WLNHL WV13 ... 51 J3
WOLVN WV10 ... 35 M5
Beech Tree Av TLHL/CAN CV4 ... 152 F3
WNSFLD WV11 ... 37 G5 □
Beech Tree CI KGSWFD DY6 ... 83 J5 □
REDW B97 ... 195 L1
Beech Tree La CNCK/NC WS11 ... 16 B5
Beechtree La KIDD DY10 ... 118 D7
Beechtree Rd ALDR WS9 ... 40 C3
Beech Wk HWK/WKHTH B38 ... 144 D5 □
Beech Wy SMTHWK B66 ... 87 M8
Beechwood Av COVW CV5 ... 153 J4
WNSFLD WV11 ... 36 F5
Beechwood CI BLOX/PEL WS3 ... 38 F2 □
SHLY B90 ... 171 H1 □
Beechwood Crs
TAM/AM/WIL B77 ... 32 D8
Beechwood Cft
FOAKS/STRLY B74 ... 42 B8
KNWTH CV8 ... 191 K3
Beechwood Dr
DUNHL/THL/PER WV6 ... 48 E3
Beechwood Park Rd SOLH B91 ... 127 J8
Beechwood Rd
ALE/KHTH/YWD B14 ... 125 K8
BDWTH CV12 ... 117 G1
DUDS DY2 ... 85 J4
GTB/HAM B43 ... 70 D4
NUNW/HART CV10 ... 80 B7
SMTHWKW B67 ... 105 J5
WBROM B70 ... 86 F2
Beecroft Av LICH WS13 ... 20 F4
Beecroft Rd CNCK/NC WS11 ... 16 C4
Beehive CI BRGRVW B61 ... 165 L4
Beehive HI KNWTH CV8 ... 176 B6
Beehive La WALM/CURD B76 ... 75 G7
Bee La WOLVN WV10 ... 36 B2
Beeston CI AST/WIT B6 ... 89 L6 □
BRLYHL DY5 ... 102 A5
COVS CV3 ... 155 K5
Beeton Rd WSNGN B18 ... 88 C7
Beet St BLKHTH/ROWR B65 ... 104 A4 □
Beever Rd TPTN/OCK DY4 ... 68 B6
Beggars Bush La WMBN WV5 ... 64 F8
Beighton CI FOAKS/STRLY B74 ... 42 D7
Beilby Rd BVILLE B30 ... 124 F7
Belbroughton CI REDE B98 ... 196 D5
Belbroughton Rd
HAG/WOL DY9 ... 140 C4
HALE B63 ... 121 K3
KIDD DY10 ... 139 C4
STRBR DY8 ... 119 J2
Belchers La BORD B9 ... 108 E3
Beldray Rd BILS/COS WV14 ... 51 J7
Belfry CI BLOX/PEL WS3 ... 38 E2
Belfry Dr STRBR DY8 ... 101 J7
The Belfry
DUNHL/THL/PER WV6 ... 48 B1 □
Belgrade Rd WOLVN WV10 ... 35 M3
Belgrave Ct KGSWFD DY6 ... 101 K1 □
Belgrave Middleway
DIG/EDG B5 ... 107 J6
Belgrave Rd BHTH/HG B12 ... 107 K7
COVE CV2 ... 155 H1
RMSLY B62 ... 104 B5
TAM/AM/WIL B77 ... 46 C5
Belgrave Sq COVE CV2 ... 155 J1
Belgrave Ter HDSW B21 ... 88 E6 □
Belgrave Wk WSLW WS2 ... 52 F2 □
Belgravia CI DIG/EDG B5 ... 107 J6
Belgrove CI EDG B15 ... 106 C7
Belinda CI WLNHL WV13 ... 51 K2
Bellairs Av BDWTH CV12 ... 116 C4
Bellam Rd
RWWCK/WEL CV35 ... 198 D6 □
Bellamy CI SHLY B90 ... 147 H4 □
Bellamy Farm Rd SHLY B90 ... 147 H4
Bellamy La WNSFLD WV11 ... 37 G6
Bell Barn Rd EDG B15 ... 6 D9
Bellbrook PENK ST19 ... 10 C4
Bellbrooke CI COVE CV2 ... 134 F4
Bell CI CBROM B36 ... 92 F7
DARL/WED WS10 ... 68 C7
LICH WS13 ... 20 D4 □
Bellcroft LDYWD/EDGR B16 ... 6 A6
Bell Dr DSYBK/YTR WS5 ... 53 L8
RCOVN/BALC/EX CV7 ... 116 C6
Bellefield Av WSNGN B18 ... 106 C1 □
Bellefield Rd WSNGN B18 ... 106 C1
Belle Isle BRLYHL DY5 ... 102 A2
Bellemere Rd HIA/OLT B92 ... 129 M8
Bellencroft Gdns
BDMR/CCFT WV3 ... 48 D5 □
Belle Orch KIDDW DY11 ... 136 F8 □
Belle Vue DIG/EDG B5 ... 107 H6
Bellevue DIG/EDG B5 ... 107 H6
Belle Vue CI BRGRVE B60 ... 166 A5
Belle Vue Dr RMSLY B62 ... 104 B7
Belle Vue Gdns
BLKHTH/ROWR B65 ... 104 A2 □
Bellevue Rd BILS/COS WV14 ... 67 K3

Belle Vue Rd BRLYHL DY5 ... 102 E4
Bellevue Rd
LGN/SDN/BHAMAIR B26 ... 109 L6
Bellevue St BILS/COS WV14 ... 66 D3
Belle Vue Ter HIA/OLT B92 ... 129 L7
Belle Wk MOS/BIL B13 ... 125 M3
Bellfield CI KINVER DY7 ... 100 C6
Bell Fold LGLYGN/QTN B68 ... 87 C7
Bell Green La HWK/WKHTH B38 ... 144 F8
Bell Green Rd COVN CV6 ... 134 F5
Bell Heather Rd BRWNH WS8 ... 26 B7
Bell HI NFLD/LBR B31 ... 123 J8
Bell Holloway NFLD/LBR B31 ... 123 K8
Bellington Cft SHLY B90 ... 147 L7 □
Bellis St LDYWD/EDGR B16 ... 106 D4
Bell La BLOX/PEL WS3 ... 38 F4
DSYBK/YTR WS5 ... 69 K1
NFLD/LBR B31 ... 143 L1
STETCH B33 ... 110 C4
Bellman CI DARL/WED WS10 ... 52 B6 □
Bell Meadow HAG/WOL DY9 ... 119 M5
Bell Meadow Wy
ALE/KHTH/YWD B14 ... 145 H3 □
Bell PI BKHL/PFLD WV2 ... 2 F9
Bell Rd DSYBK/YTR WS5 ... 54 B7
DUDS DY2 ... 85 C8 □
WMBN WV5 ... 64 A4
Bells Farm CI
ALE/KHTH/YWD B14 ... 145 G3
Bells La BNTWD WS7 ... 18 D4
HWK/WKHTH B38 ... 145 G3
STRBR DY8 ... 101 H4
Bells Moor Rd WBROM B70 ... 68 E7
Bell St BILS/COS WV14 ... 51 G7
BILS/COS WV14 ... 67 G3
BRLYHL DY5 ... 84 B6
BRLYHL DY5 ... 102 B3
DARL/WED WS10 ... 52 B6
TPTN/OCK DY4 ... 67 J8
WBROM B70 ... 87 H3
WOLV WV1 ... 2 F6
Bell St South BRLYHL DY5 ... 102 B3
Bell Tower Ms RLSN CV32 ... 200 D2
Bell Vue Rd BLKHTH/ROWR B65 ... 104 A3
Bellwood Rd NFLD/LBR B31 ... 143 K1
Belmont Av CNCK/NC WS11 ... 16 A3
Belmont CI ALDR WS9 ... 40 E6
GTWY WS6 ... 24 E1
REDW B97 ... 195 M4
TPTN/OCK DY4 ... 67 K7
Belmont Covert
NFLD/LBR B31 ... 123 M7 □
Belmont Dr RLSN CV32 ... 200 E3
Belmont Gdns BILS/COS WV14 ... 67 L1 □
Belmont Pas BCHAMNE B4 ... 7 M5
Belmont Rd BRLYHL DY5 ... 84 D7
COVN CV6 ... 134 E6 □
ETTPK/GDPK/PENN WV4 ... 49 L8
HAG/WOL DY9 ... 120 C1
HDSW B21 ... 88 A5
RBRY B45 ... 142 D7
RUGBYS/DCH CV22 ... 183 L5
SMTHWK B66 ... 105 L3
TAM/AM/WIL B77 ... 46 C6 □
Belmont Rd East HDSW B21 ... 88 A5 □
Belmont Rw DRBHAMNE B4 ... 7 K3
Belmont St BILS/COS WV14 ... 67 L1
Belper DUDN DY1 ... 84 F4
Belper Rd BLOX/PEL WS3 ... 39 C2
WBROM B70 ... 86 D2
Belper Rw DUDS DY2 ... 103 J1
Belsize TAM/AM/WIL B77 ... 46 C3
Belstone CI
ALE/KHTH/YWD B14 ... 125 H8
Belton Av WNSFLD WV11 ... 36 F1
Belton CI HOCK/TIA B94 ... 172 A8
Belton Gv RBRY B45 ... 143 G5
Belt Rd HEDN WS12 ... 12 E8
Belvedere Av
ETTPK/GDPK/PENN WV4 ... 49 M8
Belvedere CI BNTWD WS7 ... 18 D8
CRTAM B79 ... 32 A6
KGSWFD DY6 ... 101 K1
KIDD DY10 ... 137 L2
Belvedere Crs BEWD DY12 ... 136 A8
Belvedere Dr BRGRVW B61 ... 185 L1 □
Belvedere Gdns
DUNHL/THL/PER WV6 ... 35 J6 □
Belvedere Rd COVW CV5 ... 153 L5
ERDE/BCHGN B24 ... 90 E3
Belvide Gdns CDSL WV8 ... 34 D1
Belvide Gv SLYOAK B29 ... 123 M5
Belvidere Gdns SPARK B11 ... 125 M1
Belvidere Rd WSL WS1 ... 5 G6
Belvoir TAM/AM/WIL B77 ... 46 A6
Belvoir CI DUDN DY1 ... 84 C3
Belwell Dr FOAKS/STRLY B74 ... 56 E3
Belwell La FOAKS/STRLY B74 ... 56 E3
Bembridge CI WNSFLD WV11 ... 37 M5 □
Bembridge Rd STETCH B33 ... 109 L2
Benacre Dr DIG/EDG B5 ... 7 K5
Benbeck Gv TPTN/OCK DY4 ... 67 G6
Benches BNTWD WS7 ... 18 B7
Bendall Rd KGSTG B44 ... 71 M3
Benedictine Rd COVS CV3 ... 154 A6
Benedon Rd
LGN/SDN/BHAMAIR B26 ... 109 L6
Bengrove CI REDE B98 ... 196 E6
Benion Rd CNCK/NC WS11 ... 16 D1
Benmore Av DIG/EDG B5 ... 107 H7
Bennett Av DUDN DY1 ... 66 F7
Bennett Dr WWCK CV34 ... 199 M6
Bennett Rd FOAKS/STRLY B74 ... 56 B2
Bennett's Fold BKHL/PFLD WV2 ... 2 E6
Bennett's HI CBHAMNW B3 ... 6 F5
DUDS DY2 ... 85 J5
Bennetts Rd
RCOVN/BALC/EX CV7 ... 115 K8
WASH/WDE B8 ... 90 B7
Bennett's Rd North
RCOVN/BALC/EX CV7 ... 115 H5
Bennetts Rd South
RCOVN/BALC/EX CV7 ... 133 K2
Bennett St KIDDW DY11 ... 137 G7
LOZ/NWT B19 ... 89 H5

RUGBYN/HIL CV21 ... 183 K2 □
Ben Nevis Wy STRBR DY8 ... 101 L7 □
Bennfield Rd
RUGBYN/HIL CV21 ... 183 L2
Benn Rd BDWTH CV12 ... 117 M3
Benson Av
ETTPK/GDPK/PENN WV4 ... 50 A7
LICH WS13 ... 21 H4
Benson CI DUNHL/THL/PER WV6 ... 34 C7
COVN CV6 ... 133 L4
WSNGN B18 ... 88 D7
Benson Vw CRTAM B79 ... 32 A5
Bent Av WRDG/WDGT B32 ... 105 H7
Benthall Rd COVN CV6 ... 134 D3
Bentham Ct NFLD/LBR B31 ... 123 K8 □
Bentleybridge Wy WLNHL WV13 ... 51 G1
Bentley Brook La HEDN WS12 ... 13 L7 □
Bentley CI REDW B97 ... 196 B2
RLSN CV32 ... 200 F2
Bentley Ct COVN CV6 ... 134 A1
Bentley Dr CDSL WV8 ... 34 D1 □
WSLW WS2 ... 52 F3
Bentley Farm CI
DOR/KN B93 ... 172 C1 □
Bentley Gv SLYOAK B29 ... 123 K5 □
Bentley La
RCOVN/BALC/EX CV7 ... 113 G3
REDW B97 ... 194 F5
SHHTH WV12 ... 38 B8
WSLW WS2 ... 52 E1
Bentley Mill CI WSLW WS2 ... 52 D4
Bentley Mill La WSLW WS2 ... 52 D4
Bentley Mill Wy WSLW WS2 ... 52 D4
Bentley New Dr WSLW WS2 ... 52 E2
Bentley Rd CBROM B36 ... 92 B6
NUN CV11 ... 98 E1
RCOVN/BALC/EX CV7 ... 116 E4
WOLVN WV10 ... 36 C3
Bentley Rd North WSLW WS2 ... 52 C4
Bentley Rd South
DARL/WED WS10 ... 52 B5
Bentley Wy CRTAM B79 ... 31 K6
Bentmead Gv
HWK/WKHTH B38 ... 144 E4
Benton Av SPARK B11 ... 108 A7
Benton CI SHHTH WV12 ... 52 B1
Benton Crs BLOX/PEL WS3 ... 39 H3
Benton Green La
RCOVN/BALC/EX CV7 ... 151 K3
Benton Rd SPARK B11 ... 108 A7
Benton's Ct KIDDW DY11 ... 137 G7
Benton's La GTWY WS6 ... 24 E4
Bentons Mill Cft
VAUX/NECH B7 ... 90 A5 □
The Bentree COVS CV3 ... 154 F5
Bent St BRLYHL DY5 ... 102 B1
Ben Willetts Wk
BLKHTH/ROWR B65 ... 104 A4 □
Beoley CI CSCFLD/WYGN B72 ... 73 G4 □
Beoley Gv RBRY B45 ... 142 E6 □
Beoley La REDE B98 ... 189 L4
Beoley Rd East REDE B98 ... 196 E5
Beoley Rd West REDE B98 ... 196 D2
Berberry CI BVILLE B30 ... 124 B7
Berenska Dr RLSN CV32 ... 200 E3
Beresford Av COVN CV6 ... 134 C4
Beresford Crs WBROM B70 ... 86 F2
Beresford Dr SCFLD/BOLD B73 ... 72 E4
Beresford Rd BLOX/PEL WS3 ... 39 J5
OLDBY B69 ... 87 G6
Bericote Cft ACGN B27 ... 127 H2
Bericote Rd RLSN CV32 ... 192 C5
Berkeley CI
DUNHL/THL/PER WV6 ... 48 D2
NUNW/HART CV10 ... 98 D2
REDE B98 ... 197 L2
WSLW WS2 ... 52 D2
Berkeley Dr KGSWFD DY6 ... 83 G6
Berkeley Rd KNWTH CV8 ... 176 C7
SHLY B90 ... 146 D2
YDLY B25 ... 108 E6
Berkeley Rd East YDLY B25 ... 108 F6
Berkeley Rd North COVW CV5 ... 8 A8
Berkeswell CI REDE B98 ... 188 F6
Berkett Rd COVN CV6 ... 133 M2
Berkley Cts MOS/BIL B13 ... 126 A4
Berkley CI BRGRVE B60 ... 185 M5
Berkley St CBHAMW B1 ... 6 C6
Berkshire CI HHTH/SAND B71 ... 68 F6
NUNW/HART CV10 ... 98 C2
Berkshire Crs DARL/WED WS10 ... 69 G1
The Berkshire BLOX/PEL WS3 ... 38 E2 □
Berkswell CI DUDN DY1 ... 84 C2
FOAKS/STRLY B74 ... 56 C1
HIA/OLT B92 ... 127 M5
Berkswell Rd COVN CV6 ... 134 E3
ERDE/BCHGN B24 ... 90 F1
RCOVN/BALC/EX CV7 ... 131 C5
Bermuda CI DUDN DY1 ... 66 F7
Bermuda Rd NUNW/HART CV10 ... 98 E5
Bernard PI HRBN B17 ... 105 M3
LGLYGN/QTN B68 ... 105 G3
TPTN/OCK DY4 ... 67 L6
Bernard St HHTH/SAND B71 ... 87 G1
WSL WS1 ... 5 J5
Berners CI TLHL/CAN CV4 ... 152 C3
Berners St LOZ/NWT B19 ... 89 G6
Bernhard Dr HDSW B21 ... 88 C5 □
Bernie Crossland Wk
KIDD DY10 ... 161 K2
Bernwall CI STRBR DY8 ... 119 K1 □
Berrandale Rd CBROM B36 ... 91 K5
Berrington CI REDE B98 ... 197 G3
Berrington Dr BILS/COS WV14 ... 66 F5
Berrington Rd
NUNW/HART CV10 ... 80 B6
RLSS CV31 ... 200 F7
Berrington Wk DIG/EDG B5 ... 107 J6 □
Berrow Dr EDG B15 ... 106 D6
Berrow Hill Rd KIDDW DY11 ... 136 F4 □
Berrowside Rd
BKDE/SHDE B34 ... 92 C7 □
Berrow Vw BRGRVE B60 ... 185 H6 □
Berry Av DARL/WED WS10 ... 51 M8
Berrybush Gdns SEDG DY3 ... 66 C6 □
Berry CI LOZ/NWT B19 ... 89 H7
Berry Crs DSYBK/YTR WS5 ... 55 H2

Berry Dr *ALDR* WS9 ... 40 C8
RBRY B45 ... 166 E4
Berryfield Rd
LGN/SDN/BHAMAIR B26 ... 110 B8
Berryfields *ALDR* WS9 ... 27 J8
ALDR WS9 ... 40 C8
RCOVN/BALC/EX CV7 ... 114 C1
Berryfields Rd *WALM/CURD* B76 .. 73 K2
Berry Hall La *SOLH* B91 ... 148 E1
Berry Hl *HEDN* WS12 ... 17 G1
Berry La *BRGRVW* B61 ... 184 B6
Berry Rd *DUDN* DY1 ... 85 G1 1
WASH/WDE B8 ... 90 C8
Berry St *COV* CV1 ... 9 K2
WOLV WV1 ... 3 G5
WSNGN B18 ... 88 D7
Bertha Rd *SPARK* B11 ... 108 B8
Bertie Rd *KNWTH* CV8 ... 191 K1
Bertram Cl *TPTN/OCK* DY4 ... 68 A4
Bertram Rd *BORD* B9 ... 108 B4 1
SMTHWKW B67 ... 87 J7
Berwick Cl *COVW* CV5 ... 152 F1
WWCK CV34 ... 199 J3 1
Berwick Dr *CNCK/NC* WS11 ... 15 M5
Berwick Gv *GTB/HAM* B43 ... 70 F1
NFLD/LBR B31 ... 143 H2
Berwicks La
CHWD/FDBR/MGN B37 ... 110 F5
Berwood Farm Rd
CSCFLD/WYGN B72 ... 73 G7
Berwood Gdns
ERDE/BCHGN B24 ... 73 G7
Berwood Gv *HIA/OLT* B92 ... 127 M4
Berwood La *ERDE/BCHGN* B24 .. 91 J2 1
Berwood Rd *CSCFLD/WYGN* B72 .. 73 H7
Berwyn Av *COVN* CV6 ... 133 L4
Berwyn Gv *GTWY* WS6 ... 24 D2
Berwyn Wy *NUNW/HART* CV10 ... 98 A1
Besant Gv *ACGN* B27 ... 126 E3
Besbury Cl *DOR/KN* B93 ... 172 C3
Bescot Crs *DARL/WED* WS10 ... 53 H8
WSL WS1 ... 4 C8
Bescot Cft *PBAR/PBCH* B42 ... 70 F6
Bescot Dr *WSLW* WS2 ... 52 F7
Bescot Rd *WSLW* WS2 ... 4 A8
Bescot St *WSL* WS1 ... 4 D7
Besford Gv *NFLD/LBR* B31 ... 143 H2
SHLY B90 ... 147 M7 2
Bessborough Rd *YDLY* B25 ... 109 H5
Best Av *KNWTH* CV8 ... 177 G6
Best Rd *BILS/COS* WV14 ... 51 H6
Best St *CDYHTH* B64 ... 103 K3
Beswick Gdns
RUGBYS/DCH CV22 ... 183 H6
Beswick Gv *STETCH* B33 ... 109 L1 1
Beta Gv *ALE/KHTH/YWD* B14 ... 146 A1
Betjeman Ct *KIDD* DY10 ... 137 M8
Betjeman Pl *WOLVN* WV10 ... 36 E4 1
Betley Gv *STETCH* B33 ... 109 L1
Betony Cl *DSYBK/YTR* WS5 ... 69 L2 2
Betsham Cl *KGSTG* B44 ... 71 M4
Bettany Gld *WOLVN* WV10 ... 36 C1
Betteridge Dr *WALM/CURD* B76 ... 73 J1
Bettina Cl *NUNW/HART* CV10 ... 79 M8
Bettman Cl *COVS* CV3 ... 154 C7
Bett Rd *BFLD/HDSWWD* B20 ... 88 C2
Betty's La *CNCK/NC* WS11 ... 25 L1
Bevan Av
ETTPK/GDPK/PENN WV4 ... 66 C1
Bevan Cl *BILS/COS* WV14 ... 51 K7
RUSH/SHEL WS4 ... 40 A4
Bevan Lee Rd *CNCK/NC* WS11 ... 16 B2
Bevan Rd *BRLYHL* DY5 ... 101 L3
TPTN/OCK DY4 ... 85 M1
Bevan Wy *SMTHWK* B66 ... 87 K5
Beverley Av *NUNW/HART* CV10 ... 97 M1
Beverley Cl
CSCFLD/WYGN B72 ... 73 H6 1
KIDDW DY11 ... 136 D7 1
PENK ST19 ... 10 D6
RCOVN/BALC/EX CV7 ... 151 G6
Beverley Court Rd
RIDG/WDGT B32 ... 104 F7
Beverley Crs
ETTPK/GDPK/PENN WV4 ... 66 D1
Beverley Cft *ERDW/GRVHL* B23 ... 90 B4
Beverley Dr *KGSWFD* DY6 ... 83 G6
Beverley Gv
LGN/SDN/BHAMAIR B26 ... 109 M8
Beverley Hl *HEDN* WS12 ... 13 H7
Beverley Rd *HHTH/SAND* B71 ... 69 H4
RBRY B45 ... 142 E6
RLSN CV32 ... 200 B4
Beverly Dr *TLHL/CAN* CV4 ... 177 H3
Beverston Rd
DUNHL/THL/PER WV6 ... 48 E1
TPTN/OCK DY4 ... 67 M3
Bevington Crs *COVN* CV6 ... 133 J8
Bevington Rd *AST/WIT* B6 ... 89 K5
Bevin Rd *WSLW* WS2 ... 52 C2 1
Bewdley Dr *WOLV* WV1 ... 50 F3
Bewdley Hl *KIDDW* DY11 ... 136 E8
Bewdley Rd *BVILLE* B30 ... 124 F5
KIDDW DY11 ... 137 G8
STRPT DY13 ... 160 D8
Bewdley Rd North *STRPT* DY13 .. 160 B6
Bewell Head *BRGRVW* B61 ... 185 K1
Bewlay Cl *BRLYHL* DY5 ... 101 M6
Bewley Rd *SHHTH* WV12 ... 52 B1
Bewlys Av *BFLD/HDSWWD* B20 ... 88 C1
Bexfield Cl *COVW* CV5 ... 132 E7
Bexhill Gv *EDG* B15 ... 6 D8
Bexley Gv *HHTH/SAND* B71 ... 69 J6
Bexley Rd *KGSTG* B44 ... 71 M5
Bexmore Dr *LICH* WS13 ... 21 K4
Beyer Cl *TAM/AM/WIL* B77 ... 46 E3
Bhylls Crs *BDMR/CCFT* WV3 ... 49 G6
Bhylls La *BDMR/CCFT* WV3 ... 48 F6
Bibbey's Gn *WOLVN* WV10 ... 36 D1 2
Bibsworth Av *MOS/BIL* B13 ... 126 B5
Bibury Rd *HLGN/YWD* B28 ... 126 C6
Bicester Sq *CVALE* B35 ... 91 M1 2
Bickenhill La *BHAMNEC* B40 ... 129 G1
CHWD/FDBR/MGN B37 ... 111 G6
Bickenhill Park Rd *HIA/OLT* B92 .. 127 H4
Bickenhill Pkwy
CHWD/FDBR/MGN B37 ... 111 H7
Bickenhill Rd
CHWD/FDBR/MGN B37 ... 110 F6
Bickford Rd *AST/WIT* B6 ... 89 L4
WOLVN WV10 ... 36 D8
Bickington Rd *RIDG/WDGT* B32 .. 123 H4
Bickley Av *FOAKS/STRLY* B74 ... 42 C8
SPARK B11 ... 108 A7 1
Bickley Gv
LGN/SDN/BHAMAIR B26 ... 109 M8
Bickley Rd *BILS/COS* WV14 ... 51 L7
RUSH/SHEL WS4 ... 40 A6
Bicknell Cft
ALE/KHTH/YWD B14 ... 145 J3
Bickton Cl *ERDE/BCHGN* B24 ... 73 G7
Biddings La *BILS/COS* WV14 ... 66 F3
Biddles Hl *HOCK/TIA* B94 ... 170 A7
Biddlestone Pl
DARL/WED WS10 ... 51 M6 1
Biddleston Gv *DSYBK/YTR* WS5 ... 70 A2
Bideford Dr *SLYOAK* B29 ... 124 A4
Bideford Rd *COVE* CV2 ... 135 G6
SMTHWK B66 ... 87 M8 3
Bideford Wy *CNCK/NC* WS11 ... 15 M5
Bidford Cl *SHLY* B90 ... 147 H3
Bidford Rd *NFLD/LBR* B31 ... 143 J2
Bierton Rd *YDLY* B25 ... 109 G5
Bigbury Cl *COVS* CV3 ... 154 C8
Bigbury La *STRPT* DY13 ... 161 H7
Biggin Cl *CVALE* B35 ... 91 L2
DUNHL/THL/PER WV6 ... 34 C8 2
Biggin Hall Crs *COVS* CV3 ... 154 F3
Bigwood Dr *MGN/WHC* B75 ... 57 L7
RIDG/WDGT B32 ... 123 G4
Bilberry Cl *STRPT* DY13 ... 160 C8
Bilberry Crs *HEDN* WS12 ... 12 A8
WALM/CURD B76 ... 73 J2
Bilberry Dr *RBRY* B45 ... 142 E7
Bilberry Rd
ALE/KHTH/YWD B14 ... 125 G7
COVE CV2 ... 135 H3 2
Bilboe Rd *BILS/COS* WV14 ... 67 K2
Bilbrook Ct *CDSL* WV8 ... 34 F2 1
Bilbrook Gv *CDSL* WV8 ... 34 F2 2
SLYOAK B29 ... 123 K3 1
Bilbrook Rd *CDSL* WV8 ... 34 E1
Bilbury Cl *REDW* B97 ... 196 A7
Bilhay La *WBROM* B70 ... 68 E8
Bilhay St *WBROM* B70 ... 68 F8 2
Billau Rd *BILS/COS* WV14 ... 67 H3
Billelsley La *ALVE* B48 ... 169 J7
Billesden Cl *COVS* CV3 ... 155 J5
Billesley La *MOS/BIL* B13 ... 125 L5
Billingham Cl *SOLH* B91 ... 147 M5
Billing Rd *COVW* CV5 ... 153 H2
Billingsley Rd
LGN/SDN/BHAMAIR B26 ... 109 L5
Billinton Cl *COVE* CV2 ... 155 J3
Bills La *SHLY* B90 ... 146 D5
Billsmore Gn *HIA/OLT* B92 ... 128 A6
Bills St *DARL/WED* WS10 ... 52 C7
Billy Buns La *WMBN* WV5 ... 64 E5
Billy La *BRGRVE* B60 ... 166 E6
Billy Wright Cl
ETTPK/GDPK/PENN WV4 ... 49 H7
Bilport La *DARL/WED* WS10 ... 68 D5
Bilston La *WLNHL* WV13 ... 51 M5
Bilston Rd *BKHL/PFLD* WV2 ... 3 L8
DARL/WED WS10 ... 68 B2
TPTN/OCK DY4 ... 67 M3
WLNHL WV13 ... 51 L6
WOLV WV1 ... 3 H6
Bilston St *DARL/WED* WS10 ... 52 B7 1
DARL/WED WS10 ... 52 A7 3
SEDG DY3 ... 66 B5
WLNHL WV13 ... 51 L4
Bilton Grange Rd
LGN/SDN/BHAMAIR B26 ... 109 K6
Bilton La *RRUGBY* CV23 ... 182 F3
Bilton Rd *RUGBYS/DCH* CV22 ... 183 L3 1
Bilton Street Island *WOLV* WV1 ... 3 H6
Binbrook Rd *SHHTH* WV12 ... 52 B1
Bincomb Av
LGN/SDN/BHAMAIR B26 ... 109 M7
Binfield St *TPTN/OCK* DY4 ... 85 L1
Bingley Av *WASH/WDE* B8 ... 108 F1
Bingley St *BDMR/CCFT* WV3 ... 2 B9
Binley Av *COVS* CV3 ... 155 K6
Binley Cl
LGN/SDN/BHAMAIR B26 ... 109 H7
SHLY B90 ... 146 E5
Binley Gv *COVS* CV3 ... 155 K6 1
Binley Rd *COV* CV1 ... 9 L4
COVE CV2 ... 9 M5
COVS CV3 ... 154 E3
Binns Cl *TLHL/CAN* CV4 ... 152 D5
Binstead Rd *KGSTG* B44 ... 71 L3
Binswood Av *RLSN* CV32 ... 200 D3
Binswood Cl *COVE* CV2 ... 135 H3
Binswood Rd *RMSLY* B62 ... 104 E6
Binswood St *RLSN* CV32 ... 200 C3
Binton Cl *REDE* B98 ... 197 K4
Binton Cft *MOS/BIL* B13 ... 125 K5
Binton Rd *COVE* CV2 ... 135 H3
SHLY B90 ... 146 D4
Birbeck Pl *BRLYHL* DY5 ... 83 M7
Birchall St *BHTH/HG* B12 ... 7 K8
Birch Av *BNTWD* WS7 ... 18 D7
BRLYHL DY5 ... 102 E3
BRWNH WS8 ... 26 C5
CNCK/NC WS11 ... 16 A5
Birch Brook La *LICHS* WS14 ... 28 C7
Birch Cl *BDWTH* CV12 ... 117 H1
BVILLE B30 ... 124 B7
COVW CV5 ... 132 D7
POL/KGSB/FAZ B78 ... 60 B6
Birch Coppice *BRLYHL* DY5 ... 102 E4
DUDS DY2 ... 102 F3
WMBN WV5 ... 64 C7 1
Birchcoppice Gdns *SHHTH* WV12 .. 52 C1
Birch Crs *OLDBY* B69 ... 85 M4
Birch Cft *ALDR* WS9 ... 41 G5
CHWD/FDBR/MGN B37 ... 111 G4
Birchcroft *COVEN* WV9 ... 22 A3
Birch Cft *ERDE/BCHGN* B24 ... 73 H8
Birch Croft Rd *MGN/WHC* B75 ... 57 H6
Birchdale *BILS/COS* WV14 ... 51 J8
Birchdale Av *ERDW/GRVHL* B23 ... 90 C2
Birchdale Rd *ERDW/GRVHL* B23 ... 72 B8
Birch Dr *FOAKS/STRLY* B74 ... 42 B8
MGN/WHC B75 ... 57 K6
RMSLY B62 ... 104 C4
RUGBYS/DCH CV22 ... 182 F3
Birchensale Rd *REDW* B97 ... 188 A8
Birches Av *CDSL* WV8 ... 35 G4
Birches Barn Av
BDMR/CCFT WV3 ... 49 K6
Birches Barn Rd
BDMR/CCFT WV3 ... 49 K5
Birches Cl *MOS/BIL* B13 ... 125 K4 1
Birches Green Rd
ERDE/BCHGN B24 ... 90 F3
Birches La *ALVE* B48 ... 167 K7
KNWTH CV8 ... 191 L2
Birches Park Rd *CDSL* WV8 ... 34 E3
Birches Ri *WLNHL* WV13 ... 51 K4
Birches Rd *CDSL* WV8 ... 34 F3
The Birches *BDWTH* CV12 ... 117 M1
Birchfield Av
DUNHL/THL/PER WV6 ... 34 F7
Birchfield Cl *ATHST* CV9 ... 61 G4
HALE B63 ... 121 J3 1
Birchfield Crs *HAG/WOL* DY9 ... 120 D2 1
Birchfield Dr *STRPT* DY13 ... 160 C8
Birchfield La *OLDBY* B69 ... 104 C1
Birchfield Rd
BFLD/HDSWWD B20 ... 89 H4
COVN CV6 ... 133 K6
HAG/WOL DY9 ... 120 D2
KIDDW DY11 ... 136 F8
LOZ/NWT B19 ... 89 H5
PBAR/PBCH B42 ... 89 H2
REDW B97 ... 195 K2
Birchfields Dr *HEDN* WS12 ... 17 H4 1
Birchfields Rd *SHHTH* WV12 ... 37 L8
Birchfield Wy *DSYBK/YTR* WS5 ... 69 M1
Birchgate *HAG/WOL* DY9 ... 120 D1
Birchglade *BDMR/CCFT* WV3 ... 49 H4 1
Birchgrave Cl *COVN* CV6 ... 134 E6 3
Birch Gv *LGLYGN/QTN* B68 ... 105 H6 1
LICH WS13 ... 21 H5 2
POL/KGSB/FAZ B78 ... 47 H6
Birch Hill Av *WMBN* WV5 ... 64 D8
Birch Hollow *EDG* B15 ... 106 D7
Birchills St *WSLW* WS2 ... 4 B1
Birch La *ALDR* WS9 ... 41 H4
LGLYGN/QTN B68 ... 105 H6
RUSH/SHEL WS4 ... 40 A4
Birchley Heath Rd
NUNW/HART CV10 ... 78 D5
Birchley Park Av *OLDBY* B69 ... 86 C7
Birchley Ri *HIA/OLT* B92 ... 109 K8
Birchmoor Cl *HLGN/YWD* B28 ... 126 F6
Birchmoor Rd
POL/KGSB/FAZ B78 ... 47 J5
Birchover Rd *WSLW* WS2 ... 52 E1
Birch Rd *AST/WIT* B6 ... 89 L3
LGLYGN/QTN B68 ... 105 H6
RBRY B45 ... 142 C7
SEDG DY3 ... 66 D4
WNSFLD WV11 ... 37 K4
Birch Rd East *AST/WIT* B6 ... 89 L2
Birch St *LGLYGN/QTN* B68 ... 87 G7
TPTN/OCK DY4 ... 67 K8
WOLV WV1 ... 2 E5
WSLW WS2 ... 53 H2
Birch Ter *BNTWD* WS7 ... 18 E4
DUDS DY2 ... 103 G1
Birchtree Gdns *BRLYHL* DY5 ... 102 E4
Birch Tree Gv *SOLH* B91 ... 147 J1
Birchtree Hollow *SHHTH* WV12 ... 38 B8
Birchtree Rd *NUNW/HART* CV10 ... 80 A7
Birchtrees *ERDE/BCHGN* B24 ... 91 H1 1
Birchtrees Dr *STETCH* B33 ... 110 B3 1
Birch Wk *LGLYGN/QTN* B68 ... 105 H6
Birchway Cl *RLSN* CV32 ... 200 A4 1
Birchwood Av
POL/KGSB/FAZ B78 ... 47 K6
Birchwood Cl *KIDDW* DY11 ... 136 E6 1
WNSFLD WV11 ... 37 L2 1
Birchwood Crs *BHTH/HG* B12 ... 125 L1
Birchwood Rd *BHTH/HG* B12 ... 125 L1
COVS CV3 ... 156 A6
ETTPK/GDPK/PENN WV4 ... 49 L8
LICHS WS14 ... 21 J6
Birchwoods *RIDG/WDGT* B32 ... 122 F3
Birchy Cl *SHLY* B90 ... 146 D7
Birchy Leasowes La *SHLY* B90 ... 146 C8
Birdbrook Rd *KGSTG* B44 ... 71 J5
Bird End *HHTH/SAND* B71 ... 69 K5
Bird Grove Ct *COV* CV1 ... 134 B8
Birdhope *TAM/AM/WIL* B77 ... 47 G4 2
Birdie Cl *HWK/WKHTH* B38 ... 144 B4
Birdlip Gv *RIDG/WDGT* B32 ... 105 G7
Birds Bush Rd *TAM/AM/WIL* B77 ... 46 C5
Birds Meadow *BRLYHL* DY5 ... 83 M6
Bird St *COV* CV1 ... 9 G2
LICH WS13 ... 20 E5
SEDG DY3 ... 84 A2
Birdwell Cft *MOS/BIL* B13 ... 125 K7
Birkdale Av *BRGRVE* B60 ... 166 E8
SLYOAK B29 ... 124 D4 1
Birkdale Cl *NUN* CV11 ... 99 L4 2
STRBR DY8 ... 119 K4
WOLV WV1 ... 50 E3 1
Birkdale Dr *OLDBY* B69 ... 85 L6
Birkdale Gv *SLYOAK* B29 ... 124 E5
Birkdale Rd *BLOX/PEL* WS3 ... 38 E2
Birkenshaw Rd *KGSTG* B44 ... 71 J5
Birley Gv *HALE* B63 ... 121 G5
Birmingham New Rd
BILS/COS WV14 ... 66 F4
DUDN DY1 ... 67 G7
ETTPK/GDPK/PENN WV4 ... 66 C1
Birmingham Rd *ALDR* WS9 ... 40 E8
ALDR WS9 ... 54 E1
ALVE B48 ... 167 M1
BKHL/PFLD WV2 ... 3 G9
BLKHTH/ROWR B65 ... 104 A3 1
BLKHTH/ROWR B65 ... 104 A4 1
BRGRVE B60 ... 165 M7
BRGRVW B61 ... 166 A1
BRGRVW B61 ... 185 L2 1
CBROM B36 ... 91 L5
COVW CV5 ... 132 D6
CSCFLD/WYGN B72 ... 72 F5
CSHL/WTROR B46 ... 92 D3
DSYBK/YTR WS5 ... 5 M8
DUDN DY1 ... 85 J3
GTB/HAM B43 ... 70 C1 1
GTB/HAM B43 ... 70 C4 1
HAG/WOL DY9 ... 120 B7
HALE B63 ... 121 M1 1
HHTH/SAND B71 ... 87 L4
HWK/WKHTH B38 ... 143 M8
KIDD DY10 ... 138 A6
KNWTH CV8 ... 175 M4
LICH WS13 ... 20 F6
LICHS WS14 ... 28 E8
MGN/WHC B75 ... 42 E6
NUNW/HART CV10 ... 78 E8
OLDBY B69 ... 86 F6
RCOVN/BALC/EX CV7 ... 130 E3
REDE B98 ... 188 C7
REDW B97 ... 188 B4
RWWCK/WEL CV35 ... 174 A8
STUD B80 ... 197 M3
WALM/CURD B76 ... 75 L6
WBROM B70 ... 87 J4
WSL WS1 ... 5 H5
WWCK CV34 ... 198 F5
Birmingham St *DARL/WED* WS10 .. 52 B7
DUDS DY2 ... 85 H4 1
HALE B63 ... 121 M2
OLDBY B69 ... 86 E5
STRBR DY8 ... 101 L8
WLNHL WV13 ... 51 M3
WSL WS1 ... 5 G4
Birnham Cl *TPTN/OCK* DY4 ... 67 H8
Bisell Wy *BRLYHL* DY5 ... 102 B7
Biset Av *KIDD* DY10 ... 137 M8
Bishbury Cl *EDG* B15 ... 106 C5
Bishop Asbury Crs
GTB/HAM B43 ... 69 M5
Bishop Cl *RBRY* B45 ... 142 C4 1
Bishop Hall Crs *BRGRVE* B60 ... 185 J6
Bishop Rd *DARL/WED* WS10 ... 69 C3
Bishops Cl *DUDS* DY2 ... 85 J5 1
SMTHWK B66 ... 106 A1 1
Bishops Ga *NFLD/LBR* B31 ... 143 L3
Bishopsgate St *EDG* B15 ... 6 B7
Bishops Meadow
MGN/WHC B75 ... 57 J2
Bishops Rd *SCFLD/BOLD* B73 ... 72 F2
Bishopstone Cl *REDE* B98 ... 197 K3 1
Bishop St *COV* CV1 ... 8 F3
DIG/EDG B5 ... 7 H9
STRPT DY13 ... 160 E8
Bishops Wk *COVW* CV5 ... 8 C9
Bishops Wy *FOAKS/STRLY* B74 ... 42 D7
Bishopton Cl *COVW* CV5 ... 152 F2
SHLY B90 ... 147 G4
Bishopton Rd *SMTHWKW* B67 ... 105 K4
Bishton Gv *DUDS* DY2 ... 103 H1 1
Bissel Dr *DARL/WED* WS10 ... 68 F2 1
Bissell Cl *HLGN/YWD* B28 ... 126 D7
Bissell St *DIG/EDG* B5 ... 107 J5
RIDG/WDGT B32 ... 104 E7
Bissel St *BILS/COS* WV14 ... 51 K8 1
Bisset Crs *RLSS* CV31 ... 200 F7
Bitham Cl *PENK* ST19 ... 10 D5 1
Biton Cl *HRBN* B17 ... 105 M8
Bittell Cl *WOLVN* WV10 ... 36 C1
Bittell Farm Rd *RBRY* B45 ... 167 L4
Bittell La *RBRY* B45 ... 167 J5
Bittell Rd *RBRY* B45 ... 167 H5
Bitterne Dr *DUNHL/THL/PER* WV6 .. 2 B1
Bittern Wood Rd *KIDD* DY10 ... 161 M2
Bitterscote La
POL/KGSB/FAZ B78 ... 45 L3
Bixhill La *CSHL/WTROR* B46 ... 94 D3
Blackacre Rd *DUDS* DY2 ... 85 H5
Black-a-tree Pl
NUNW/HART CV10 ... 98 C1 1
Black-a-tree Rd
NUNW/HART CV10 ... 98 C1
Black Bank
RCOVN/BALC/EX CV7 ... 116 F4
Blackberry Av *BORD* B9 ... 108 E2
HOCK/TIA B94 ... 171 M7
Blackberry Cl *DUDN* DY1 ... 84 C5
Blackberry La *ALDR* WS9 ... 40 F1
BLKHTH/ROWR B65 ... 85 K8
COVN CV6 ... 134 F7
FOAKS/STRLY B74 ... 42 C8
HALE B63 ... 121 L3
RCOVN/BALC/EX CV7 ... 115 M8
Blackbird Cft *CBROM* B36 ... 92 E6
Blackbrook Cl *DUDS* DY2 ... 102 E2
Blackbrook Rd *DUDS* DY2 ... 84 E8
Blackbrook Wy *WOLVN* WV10 ... 36 C1
Blackburn Av
DUNHL/THL/PER WV6 ... 35 J6
Blackburne Rd *HLGN/YWD* B28 .. 126 D7
Blackburn Rd *COVN* CV6 ... 134 D2
Blackbushe Cl *HRBN* B17 ... 105 K6 1
Blackcat Cl
CHWD/FDBR/MGN B37 ... 110 E2 1
Black Country New Rd
BILS/COS WV14 ... 51 L7
Black Country Route
BILS/COS WV14 ... 51 K7
Blackdown *TAM/AM/WIL* B77 ... 47 G4
Blackdown Cl *RBRY* B45 ... 142 E3 1
Blackdown Rd *DOR/KN* B93 ... 148 F7
Blackfirs La
CHWD/FDBR/MGN B37 ... 111 H6
Blackford Cl *HALE* B63 ... 121 H3
KIDDW DY11 ... 160 E4
Blackford Rd *SHLY* B90 ... 147 G6
SPARK B11 ... 126 A1
Blackford St *WSNGN* B18 ... 88 C8 1
Blackfriars Cl *CRTAM* B79 ... 31 J8 1
Blackgreaves La
WALM/CURD B76 ... 75 K4
Black Hall La
RCOVN/BALC/EX CV7 ... 114 A1
Blackhalve La *WNSFLD* WV11 ... 36 E5
Blackham Dr *SCFLD/BOLD* B73 ... 72 E6
Blackham Rd *WNSFLD* WV11 ... 37 K5
Black Haynes Rd *SLYOAK* B29 ... 123 L6
Blackhorse La *BRLYHL* DY5 ... 102 C4
Black Horse La *KIDD* DY10 ... 137 H7 1
Black Horse Rd
RCOVN/BALC/EX CV7 ... 116 E7
Black Lake *HHTH/SAND* B71 ... 68 E7
Black Lake La *BRGRVE* B60 ... 194 E3
Black La *RLSN* CV32 ... 200 F3
Blacklow Rd *WWCK* CV34 ... 199 L4
Blackman Wy
RUGBYN/HIL CV21 ... 183 K1
Blackmoor Cft *STETCH* B33 ... 110 B3 2
Blackmore La *BRGRVE* B60 ... 185 L2
Blackpit La *WMBN* WV5 ... 64 C2
Black Prince Av *COVS* CV3 ... 154 C7
Blackrock Rd *ERDW/GRVHL* B23 .. 71 M7
Blackroot Cl *BNTWD* WS7 ... 27 H1
Blackroot Rd *FOAKS/STRLY* B74 ... 56 E6
Blackshaw Dr *COVE* CV2 ... 135 K7 2
Blacksmiths La
HOCK/TIA B94 ... 172 A7 3
Blackstich La *REDW* B97 ... 195 L4
Blackthorn Av *BNTWD* WS7 ... 26 D1
Blackthorn Cl *BVILLE* B30 ... 124 A8
TLHL/CAN CV4 ... 153 H8
Blackthorn Crs *HEDN* WS12 ... 13 L7 3
Blackthorne Cl *SOLH* B91 ... 147 J1
Blackthorne Rd *DSYBK/YTR* WS5 .. 53 K8
DUDN DY1 ... 84 D1
KNWTH CV8 ... 191 L2
SMTHWKW B67 ... 105 H1
Blackthorn Gv *NUN* CV11 ... 99 K3 1
Blackthorn Rd *BVILLE* B30 ... 124 A7
CBROM B36 ... 92 A5
STRBR DY8 ... 101 K4
Blackwatch Rd *COVN* CV6 ... 134 A5
Blackwater Cl *BRLYHL* DY5 ... 83 L8
Blackwell Rd *BRGRVE* B60 ... 186 D1
COVN CV6 ... 134 C5 1
CSCFLD/WYGN B72 ... 73 H4
RBRY B45 ... 167 G7
Blackwell St *KIDD* DY10 ... 137 J7
Blackwood Av
RUGBYS/DCH CV22 ... 183 H3
WNSFLD WV11 ... 36 F5
Blackwood Dr *FOAKS/STRLY* B74 .. 55 J5
Blackwood Rd *BRGRVE* B60 ... 185 M3
FOAKS/STRLY B74 ... 55 J4
TAM/AM/WIL B77 ... 46 A6
Blades Rd *WBROM* B70 ... 86 B1
Bladon Cl *NUN* CV11 ... 81 K5
Blaenwern Dr *HALE* B63 ... 102 F6 1
Blagdon Rd *HALE* B63 ... 103 L7
Blair Dr *BDWTH* CV12 ... 116 B4
Blair Gv *CHWD/FDBR/MGN* B37 ... 111 H4
Blakebrook *KIDDW* DY11 ... 137 G8 1
Blakebrook Cl *KIDDW* DY11 ... 137 G7 1
Blakebrook Gdns *KIDDW* DY11 ... 137 G7
Blake Cl *CNCK/NC* WS11 ... 12 E8
NUNW/HART CV10 ... 79 L8
RUGBYS/DCH CV22 ... 183 G3
Blakedon Rd *DARL/WED* WS10 ... 68 C2
Blakedown Rd *HALE* B63 ... 121 K3
Blake Hall Cl *BRLYHL* DY5 ... 101 M6
Blakeland Rd *KGSTG* B44 ... 71 L4
Blakelands Av *RLSS* CV31 ... 200 F7 1
Blakeland St *BORD* B9 ... 108 D3
Blake La *BORD* B9 ... 108 D3
Blakeley Av
DUNHL/THL/PER WV6 ... 35 K6
Blakeley Hall Gdns *OLDBY* B69 .. 86 F6 2
Blakeley Hall Rd *OLDBY* B69 ... 86 F6
Blakeley Heath Dr
WMBN WV5 ... 64 E8 1
Blakeley Ri
DUNHL/THL/PER WV6 ... 35 K6
Blakeley Wood Rd
TPTN/OCK DY4 ... 68 A5
Blakemere Av *YDLY* B25 ... 109 J5
Blakemere Cl *REDE* B98 ... 197 K2
Blakemore Cl
RIDG/WDGT B32 ... 123 K2 1
Blakemore Dr *MGN/WHC* B75 ... 57 K7
Blakemore Rd *ALDR* WS9 ... 40 F2
WBROM B70 ... 86 E3
Blakenall Cl *BLOX/PEL* WS3 ... 39 H4
Blakenall Heath *BLOX/PEL* WS3 ... 39 H5
Blakenall La *BLOX/PEL* WS3 ... 39 H5
Blakenall Rw *BLOX/PEL* WS3 ... 39 H5
Blakeney Av *HRBN* B17 ... 105 L6
STRBR DY8 ... 101 H7
Blakeney Cl *SEDG* DY3 ... 66 A5 1
Blakenhale Rd *STETCH* B33 ... 109 M4
Blake Pl *BORD* B9 ... 108 D3
Blake Rd *BRGRVW* B61 ... 165 M5
Blakesfield Dr *RBRY* B45 ... 166 E4
Blakesley Cl *WALM/CURD* B76 ... 73 K8
Blakesley Ms *YDLY* B25 ... 109 H5
Blakesley Rd *YDLY* B25 ... 109 H4
Blake St *FOAKS/STRLY* B74 ... 42 C7
Blakewood Cl
BKDE/SHDE B34 ... 92 A8 1
Blandford Av *CBROM* B36 ... 92 C4
Blandford Dr *COVE* CV2 ... 135 K8
STRBR DY8 ... 101 J3
Blandford Gdns *BNTWD* WS7 ... 19 G7
Blandford Rd *RIDG/WDGT* B32 ... 105 J8
RLSN CV32 ... 200 A4 2
Blandford Wy
RWWCK/WEL CV35 ... 198 E6 1
Blanefield *CDSL* WV8 ... 35 J3 1
Blay Av *WSLW* WS2 ... 52 F3
Blaydon Av *MGN/WHC* B75 ... 57 J3
Blaydon Rd *COVEN* WV9 ... 35 L4
Blaythorn Av *HIA/OLT* B92 ... 127 L2
Blaze Hill Rd *KGSWFD* DY6 ... 82 E5
Blaze Pk *KGSWFD* DY6 ... 82 F5
Bleachfield Rd *REDE* B98 ... 189 K5
Bleak Hill Rd *ERDW/GRVHL* B23 ... 72 A8
Bleak House Dr *BNTWD* WS7 ... 18 B5
Bleakhouse Rd
LGLYGN/QTN B68 ... 105 G4
Bleak St *SMTHWKW* B67 ... 87 K7
Blenheim Av *COVN* CV6 ... 134 A2
Blenheim Cl *NUN* CV11 ... 99 K3
RUSH/SHEL WS4 ... 40 B6 1
Blenheim Crs *BRGRVE* B60 ... 185 L5
RLSS CV31 ... 201 G8 1
Blenheim Dr *GTB/HAM* B43 ... 70 B5
Blenheim Rd *BNTWD* WS7 ... 18 E5
CNCK/NC WS11 ... 25 M1
KGSWFD DY6 ... 83 K7 1
MOS/BIL B13 ... 125 K4

SHHTH WV12 .... 37 M7
SHLY B90 .... 147 H3
Blenheim Wy CVALE B35 .... 91 L3
DUDN DY1 .... 84 C3
KGSTG B44 .... 71 K5
Bletchley Dr COVW CV5 .... 152 F1
Bletchley Rd ERDE/BCHGN B24 .. 91 J1
Blewitt Cl CBROM B36 .... 92 B5
Blewitt St BRLYHL DY5 .... 84 A7
HEDN WS12 .... 12 F7
Blews St AST/WIT B6 .... 89 J8
Blind La RCOVN/BALC/EX CV7 ... 151 H1
Blindpit La WALM/CURD B76 .... 74 F5
Blithe Cl STRBR DY8 .... 101 L5
Blithfield Dr BRLYHL DY5 ..... 101 M6
Blithfield Gv
ERDE/BCHGN B24 .... 73 G8
Blithfield Pl CNCK/NC WS11 ... 16 F4
Blithfield Rd BRWNH WS8 ...... 26 A3
Blockall DARL/WED WS10 .... 52 B6
Blockley Rd BDWTH CV12 .... 117 C1
Blondvil St COVS CV3 .... 154 A6
Bloomfield Cl WMBN WV5 .... 64 B7
Bloomfield Crs LICHS WS13 .... 20 E5
Bloomfield Dr SHHTH WV12 ..... 38 B4
Bloomfield Rd MOS/BIL B13 .... 125 L2
TPTN/OCK DY4 .... 67 J6
Bloomfield St North HALE B63 . 103 K8
Bloomfield St West
HALE B63 .... 121 K1
Bloomfield Ter TPTN/OCK DY4 .. 67 H7
Bloomfield Wy CRTAM B79 ...... 31 K6
Bloomsbury Gv
ALE/KHTH/YWD B14 .... 125 C6
Bloomsbury St BKHL/PFLD WV2 .. 2 E7
VAUX/NECH B7 .... 89 M8
Bloomsbury Wy LICHS WS14 ..... 21 J6
Blossomfield Cl
HWK/WKHTH B38 .... 144 B5
KGSWFD DY6 .... 83 J5
Blossomfield Rd SOLH B91 ..... 147 K3
Blossom Gv CBROM B36 .... 91 H5
Blossom Hl ERDE/BCHGN B24 .... 90 E1
Blossom's Fold WOLV WV1 ...... 2 E3
Blossomville Wy ACGN B27 ..... 109 G8
Blount Cl PENK ST19 .... 10 D6
Blount Ter KIDDW DY11 .... 161 H2
Blowers Green Crs DUDS DY2 ... 84 F6
Blower's Green Rd DUDS DY2 ... 84 F6
Bloxam Gdns
RUGBYS/DCH CV22 .... 183 K3
Bloxam Pl RUGBYN/HIL CV21 .... 183 L2
Bloxcidge St LGLYGN/QTN B68 .. 86 F8
Bloxwich La WSLW WS2 .... 38 E7
WSLW WS2 .... 39 H6
Bloxwich Rd North
SHHTH WV12 .... 38 B7
Bloxwich Rd South
WLNHL WV13 .... 51 L2
Blucher St CBHAMW B1 .... 6 E7
Blue Ball La HALE B63 .... 103 C7
Bluebell Cl HEDN WS12 .... 12 F7
STRBR DY8 .... 101 G3
Bluebell Crs WNSFLD WV11 ..... 37 H8
Bluebell Dr
CHWD/FDBR/MGN B37 .... 111 H3
Bluebell La GTWY WS6 .... 24 D4
Bluebell Rd ALDR WS9 .... 40 F2
CDYHTH B64 .... 103 J2
DUDN DY1 .... 84 F2
Bluebell Wk TLHL/CAN CV4 ..... 152 D4
Bluebellwood Cl
WALM/CURD B76 .... 73 L2
Bluebird Cl LICHS WS14 .... 21 H5
Blue Cedars STRBR DY8 .... 101 G7
Blue Lake Rd DOR/KN B93 ...... 172 F3
Blue La East WSLW WS2 .... 53 H2
Blue La West WSLW WS2 .... 4 C1
Blue Rock Pl OLDBY B69 .... 86 A7
Blundell Rd SPARK B11 .... 108 B8
The Blundells KNWTH CV8 ...... 176 D8
Blyth Av RCOVN/BALC/EX CV7 ... 151 C3
Blyth Br CSHL/WTROR B46 ...... 94 A5
Blyth Cl BDWTH CV12 .... 116 A4
Blythe Cl BNTWD WS7 .... 19 H7
REDW B97 .... 196 B6
Blythefield Av GTB/HAM B43 ... 70 A4
Blythe Gdns CDSL WV8 .... 34 D1
Blythe Gv KGSTG B44 .... 71 K2
Blythe Rd COV CV1 .... 9 K1
CSHL/WTROR B46 .... 93 M5
Blythe St TAM/AM/WIL B77 ..... 46 A2
Blythesway ALVE B48 .... 167 L7
Blytheway SOLH B91 .... 148 C2
Blythewood Cl DOR/KN B93 ..... 148 D4
Blythsford Rd HLGN/YWD B28 ... 146 D1
Blythswood Rd SPARK B11 ...... 126 E1
Blyton Cl LDYWD/EDGR B16 ..... 106 D1
Boar Cft TLHL/CAN CV4 .... 152 D3
Board School Gdns SEDG DY3 ... 66 C7
Boar Hound Cl WSNGN B18 ...... 106 C1
Boat La LICHS WS14 .... 27 K4
Boatman's La ALDR WS9 .... 40 C3
Bobbington Wy DUDS DY2 .... 85 H8
Bobs Coppice Wk BRLYHL DY5 ... 102 D6
Bockendon Rd TLHL/CAN CV4 .... 176 B1
Boddington Cl RLSN CV32 ...... 193 J8
Bodenham Rd REDE B98 .... 197 H2
Bodenham Rd
LGLYGN/QTN B68 .... 104 F5
NFLD/LBR B31 .... 143 J3
Boden Rd HLGN/YWD B28 .... 126 E6
Bodens La ALDR WS9 .... 54 E6
Bodicote Gv MGN/WHC B75 ...... 57 J2
Bodington Rd MGN/WHC B75 ..... 56 F2
Bodmin Cl DSYBK/YTR WS5 ...... 54 B6
Bodmin Gv VAUX/NECH B7 .... 89 M8
Bodmin Ri DSYBK/YTR WS5 ...... 54 B6
Bodmin Rd COVE CV2 .... 135 K8
DUDS DY2 .... 103 H3
Bodnant Wy KNWTH CV8 .... 177 G7
Bodymoor Heath La
WALM/CURD B76 .... 59 L8
Bodymoor Heath Rd
POL/KGSB/FAZ B78 .... 59 J7
WALM/CURD B76 .... 75 L1
Bognop Rd WNSFLD WV11 .... 37 H1

Bohun St TLHL/CAN CV4 .... 152 D4
Boldmere Cl SCFLD/BOLD B73 ... 72 E6
Boldmere Dr SCFLD/BOLD B73 ... 72 E5
Boldmere Gdns
SCFLD/BOLD B73 .... 72 E5
Boldmere Rd SCFLD/BOLD B73 ... 72 D4
Bolebridge St CRTAM B79 ...... 45 M1
Boley Cl LICHS WS14 .... 21 H6
Boley Cottage La LICHS WS14 .. 21 H6
Boley La LICHS WS14 .... 21 H6
Boleyn Cl GTWY WS6 .... 24 B3
Boleyn Rd RBRY B45 .... 142 C4
Bolingbroke Rd COVS CV3 ...... 154 E4
Bolney Rd RIDG/WDGT B32 ...... 105 J8
Bolton Cl COVS CV3 .... 154 C8
Bolton Rd SMHTH B10 .... 107 M5
WNSFLD WV11 .... 37 G8
Bolton St BORD B9 .... 107 M3
Bolton Wy BLOX/PEL WS3 .... 38 D2
Bomers Fld RBRY B45 .... 143 G6
Bond Cl CVALE B35 .... 91 L2
Bondfield Rd MOS/BIL B13 ..... 125 M7
Bond Ga NUN CV11 .... 99 G1
Bond Sq WSNGN B18 .... 106 E1
Bond St BILS/COS WV14 .... 66 E5
BKHL/PFLD WV2 .... 2 F7
BLKHTH/ROWR B65 .... 104 C2
BVILLE B30 .... 124 E6
COV CV1 .... 8 E4
LOZ/NWT B19 .... 6 C2
NUN CV11 .... 81 G8
RUGBYN/HIL CV21 .... 183 K2
WBROM B70 .... 87 G3
Bondway HEDN WS12 .... 12 D5
Bonehill Rd POL/KGSB/FAZ B78 . 45 H1
Bone Mill La WOLV WV1 .... 2 F1
Boney Hay Rd BNTWD WS7 .... 18 F5
Bonfire Hl HAG/WOL DY9 .... 141 J7
Bonham Gv YDLY B25 .... 109 H4
Boningale Wy DOR/KN B93 ...... 172 B2
Bonington Dr BDWTH CV12 ...... 116 E1
Bonner Dr WALM/CURD B76 ...... 73 K8
Bonner Gv ALDR WS9 .... 40 D8
Bonneville Cl COVW CV5 .... 131 M5
Bonniksen Cl RLSS CV31 .... 200 D8
Bonnington Wy
GTB/HAM B43 .... 71 H1
Bonsall Rd ERDW/GRVHL B23 .... 72 E7
Bonville Gdns WOLVN WV10 ..... 36 C1
Booth Cl BLOX/PEL WS3 .... 39 H5
KGSWFD DY6 .... 83 J7
LICH WS13 .... 20 E3
Boot Hl ATHST CV9 .... 62 A3
Booth Rd DARL/WED WS10 .... 69 G3
Booths Farm Rd
PBAR/PBCH B42 .... 70 E6
Booth's La PBAR/PBCH B42 ..... 71 H5
Booth St BLOX/PEL WS3 .... 39 C5
DARL/WED WS10 .... 52 B5
HDSW B21 .... 88 A6
HEDN WS12 .... 12 F7
Booton Ct KIDD DY10 .... 137 L4
Boot Piece La REDW B97 .... 187 M8
Bordeaux Cl DUDN DY1 .... 84 C2
Borden Cl CDSL WV8 .... 35 K5
Bordesley Cl BORD B9 .... 108 E3
Bordesley Ct RLSN CV32 .... 200 E2
Bordesley Gn BORD B9 .... 108 C3
Bordesley Gn East STETCH B33 . 109 J3
Bordesley Green Rd BORD B9 ... 108 B3
Bordesley Park Rd
SMHTH B10 .... 107 M4
Bordesley St DIG/EDC B5 ...... 7 J5
Bore St LICH WS13 .... 20 F6
Borman CRTAM B79 .... 31 K8
Borneo St RUSH/SHEL WS4 ...... 53 K1
Borough Crs OLDBY B69 .... 86 C8
STRBR DY8 .... 101 J8
Borough Rd CRTAM B79 .... 31 M6
Borrington Rd KIDD DY10 ...... 161 M1
Borrowcop La LICH WS13 .... 21 G8
Borrowdale Cft BRLYHL DY5 .... 101 N1
COVN CV6 .... 133 L4
Borrowdale Dr RLSN CV32 ...... 200 A3
Borrowdale Gv
NFLD/LBR B31 .... 143 H2
Borrowdale Rd NFLD/LBR B31 ... 143 G2
Borrow St WLNHL WV13 .... 51 L2
Borwick Av WBROM B70 .... 86 E2
Boscobel Av TPTN/OCK DY4 ..... 85 K1
Boscobel Cl DUDN DY1 .... 84 D2
Boscobel Rd GTB/HAM B43 ...... 70 B3
SHLY B90 .... 147 H8
WSL WS1 .... 5 L5
Boscombe Av SPARK B11 .... 108 A7
Boscombe Rd SPARK B11 .... 126 C1
Boscomoor Cl PENK ST19 .... 10 C6
Boscomoor La PENK ST19 .... 10 C6
Boston Cl HEDN WS12 .... 13 K6
Boston Gv KGSTG B44 .... 71 M5
Boston Pl COVN CV6 .... 134 B5
Bosty La ALDR WS9 .... 40 B8
Boswell Cl DARL/WED WS10 ..... 52 B8
DARL/WED WS10 .... 68 A4
Boswell Dr COVE CV2 .... 135 L7
COVE CV2 .... 135 L6
Boswell Rd BILS/COS WV14 ..... 51 K6
CNCK/NC WS11 .... 16 B1
FOAKS/STRLY B74 .... 57 G7
KGSTG B44 .... 71 K7
RUGBYS/DCH CV22 .... 183 J6
Bosworth Cl SEDG DY3 .... 66 D7
Bosworth Dr
CHWD/FDBR/MGN B37 .... 110 D3
Bosworth Rd
LGN/SDN/BHAMAIR B26 .... 127 J1
Botany Dr SEDG DY3 .... 66 B8
Botany Rd DSYBK/YTR WS5 ...... 53 K8
Botha Rd BORD B9 .... 108 C2
Botoner Rd COV CV1 .... 9 L5
Botteley Rd WBROM B70 .... 68 E7
Bottetourt Rd HRBN B17 .... 123 J2
Bott La HAG/WOL DY9 .... 102 B7
WSL WS1 .... 5 H3

Bottrill St NUN CV11 .... 80 F8
Bott Rd COVW CV5 .... 153 H5
Botts Green La
CSHL/WTROR B46 .... 77 G8
Boughton Rd YDLY B25 .... 109 G6
The Boulevard BRLYHL DY5 ..... 102 C3
SCFLD/BOLD B73 .... 72 F5
Boultbee Rd CSCFLD/WYGN B72 .. 73 C6
Boulters La ATHST CV9 .... 61 H4
Boulton Dr BNTWD WS7 .... 18 E5
Boulton Rd SMHTH B21 .... 88 C6
SMTHWK B66 .... 88 B7
SOLH B91 .... 128 A6
WBROM B70 .... 87 H4
Boultons La REDW B97 .... 196 B5
Boulton Sq WBROM B70 .... 87 H4
Boulton Wk ERDW/GRVHL B23 .... 89 M1
Boundary Av
BLKHTH/ROWR B65 .... 104 C3
Boundary Crs SEDG DY3 .... 84 A2
Boundary Hl SEDG DY3 .... 84 A1
Boundary Pl HDSW B21 .... 87 M4
Boundary Rd ALDR WS9 .... 40 D2
FOAKS/STRLY B74 .... 55 K6
WLNHL WV13 .... 51 C4
Boundary Wy
DUNHL/THL/PER WV6 .... 48 D3
ETTPK/GDPK/PENN WV4 .... 49 G7
Bourlay Cl RBRY B45 .... 142 C3
Bournbrook Rd SLYOAK B29 ..... 124 D2
Bourne Av BRGRVW B61 .... 165 K4
POL/KGSB/FAZ B78 .... 45 J5
RMSLY B62 .... 122 D1
TPTN/OCK DY4 .... 68 A6
Bournbrook Cl DUDS DY2 .... 85 G8
Bourne Brook Cl
RCOVN/BALC/EX CV7 .... 114 B2
Bournbrook Crs RMSLY B62 ..... 122 E1
Bournbrook Vw
RCOVN/BALC/EX CV7 .... 96 C4
Bourne Cl ATHST CV9 .... 63 J3
HEDN WS12 .... 17 H3
MOS/BIL B13 .... 126 A7
SOLH B91 .... 128 C7
Bourne Gn RIDG/WDGT B32 ...... 105 J7
Bourne Hill Cl DUDS DY2 ...... 103 J1
Bourne Rd AST/WIT B6 .... 89 M6
COVS CV3 .... 155 C4
Bournes Cl HALE B63 .... 121 K2
Bournes Crs HALE B63 .... 121 J1
Bournes Hl HALE B63 .... 121 J1
Bourne St BILS/COS WV14 ...... 66 E6
DUDS DY2 .... 85 H4
Bourne V ALDR WS9 .... 55 H2
Bourne Way Gdns
SLYOAK B29 .... 124 E5
Bournheath Rd BRGRVW B61 ..... 165 H3
Bournville La BVILLE B30 ..... 124 B6
Bourton Cl DSYBK/YTR WS5 ..... 69 L2
Bourton Cft HIA/OLT B92 ...... 127 K5
Bourton Dr RLSS CV31 .... 200 F8
Bourton Rd HIA/OLT B92 .... 127 K6
Bovey Cft WALM/CURD B76 ...... 73 L6
Bovingdon Rd CVALE B35 .... 91 L3
Bowater Av STETCH B33 .... 109 H4
Bowater St WBROM B70 .... 87 C2
Bowbrook Av SHLY B90 .... 147 L8
Bowcroft Gv ERDE/BCHGN B24 ... 73 C7
Bowden Cl STETCH B33 .... 109 J3
Bowden Wy COVS CV3 .... 155 J4
Bowdler Rd BKHL/PFLD WV2 ..... 3 H9
Bowen Av
ETTPK/GDPK/PENN WV4 .... 66 E2
Bowen-cooke Av CDSL WV8 ...... 34 C7
Bowen St
ETTPK/GDPK/PENN WV4 .... 50 C8
Bower Cl LICH WS13 .... 21 H3
Bowercourt Cl SOLH B91 .... 147 M3
Bower La BRLYHL DY5 .... 102 D5
Bowers Cft RLSN CV32 .... 192 E8
Bowes Dr CNCK/NC WS11 .... 16 D1
Bowes Rd RBRY B45 .... 142 C6
Bowfell Cl COVW CV5 .... 152 F1
Bowling Green Av
TAM/AM/WIL B77 .... 46 C6
Bowling Green Cl
DARL/WED WS10 .... 52 B6
ERDW/GRVHL B23 .... 72 C6
Bowling Green La
BFLD/HDSWWD B20 .... 88 E5
RCOVN/BALC/EX CV7 .... 116 C6
Bowling Green Rd BORD B9 ..... 108 A4
DUDS DY2 .... 103 H2
STRBR DY8 .... 101 J2
Bowling Green St
WWCK CV34 .... 199 H7
Bowls Ct COVW CV5 .... 153 K2
Bowman Rd PBAR/PBCH B42 ...... 70 F4
Bowman's Ri WOLV WV1 .... 50 E2
Bowmore Rd BRGRVE B60 .... 185 M4
Bowness Cl COVN CV6 .... 133 L5
Bowood Ct REDW B97 .... 196 B1
Bowood Crs NFLD/LBR B31 ...... 143 L3
Bowood Dr
DUNHL/THL/PER WV6 .... 35 H8
Bowood End WALM/CURD B76 ..... 73 H2
Bowshot Cl CBROM B36 .... 92 B4
Bowstoke Rd GTB/HAM B43 ...... 70 A5
Bow St BILS/COS WV14 .... 51 J7
CBHAMW B1 .... 6 F8
WLNHL WV13 .... 51 L4
Bowyer Rd WASH/WDE B8 .... 108 B2
Bowyer St BORD B9 .... 7 M8
Boxhill Cl AST/WIT B6 .... 89 K7
The Boxhill COVS CV3 .... 154 F4
Boxnott Cl REDW B97 .... 195 L3
Box Rd CHWD/FDBR/MGN B37 ..... 111 C5
Box St WSL WS1 .... 5 H4
Box Trees Rd HOCK/TIA B94 .... 172 A4
Boyce Wy RRUGBY CV23 .... 158 F8
Boyd Cl COVE CV2 .... 135 K5
Boyden Cl CNCK/NC WS11 .... 15 M4
PENK ST19 .... 10 C6
Boyd Gv ACGN B27 .... 126 F3
Boydon Cl BKHL/PFLD WV2 ...... 50 E7
Boylston Rd HLGN/YWD B28 ..... 126 E7

Boyne Rd
LGN/SDN/BHAMAIR B26 .... 109 M6
Boyton Gv KGSTG B44 .... 71 K2
Brabazon Gv CVALE B35 .... 91 K2
Brabham Cl KIDDW DY11 .... 137 H4
Brabham Crs FOAKS/STRLY B74 .. 55 K7
Bracadale Av ERDE/BCHGN B24 .. 90 D4
Bracadale Cl COVS CV3 .... 155 L3
Bracebridge Rd ATHST CV9 ..... 63 G6
ERDE/BCHGN B24 .... 90 D4
FOAKS/STRLY B74 .... 56 E5
POL/KGSB/FAZ B78 .... 60 A7
Bracebridge St AST/WIT B6 .... 89 J7
NUN CV11 .... 98 F1
Braceby Av MOS/BIL B13 .... 126 A6
Braces La BRGRVE B60 .... 165 M4
Brace St WSL WS1 .... 4 E6
Brackenbury Rd KGSTG B44 ..... 71 M5
Bracken Cl BNTWD WS7 .... 19 C6
CDSL WV8 .... 35 J4
HEDN WS12 .... 13 C5
LICHS WS14 .... 21 J7
RUGBYS/DCH CV22 .... 183 J4
Bracken Cft
CHWD/FDBR/MGN B37 .... 111 G2
Brackendale Dr DSYBK/YTR WS5 . 69 M2
NUNW/HART CV10 .... 98 D2
Brackendale Wy HAG/WOL DY9 ... 120 B1
Bracken Dr MGN/WHC B75 .... 57 L8
RUGBYS/DCH CV22 .... 183 J4
Brackenfield Rd HALE B63 ..... 121 J2
KGSTG B44 .... 71 C3
Bracken Gv BRGRVW B61 .... 165 L4
Brackenhill Rd BNTWD WS7 ..... 18 E5
Brackenhurst Rd COVN CV6 ..... 133 K6
Bracken Park Gdns STRBR DY8 .. 101 K3
Bracken Rd ERDE/BCHGN B24 .... 91 C3
HEDN WS12 .... 12 A8
HWK/WKHTH B38 .... 144 B6
Bracken Wy FOAKS/STRLY B74 ... 55 K5
Bracken Wd DSYBK/YTR WS5 ..... 54 B8
Brackenwood Dr WNSFLD WV11 ... 37 K8
Bracklesham Wy
TAM/AM/WIL B77 .... 32 E7
Brackley Av
BFLD/HDSWWD B20 .... 89 G4
Brackley Cl COVN CV6 .... 133 K6
Brackleys Wy HIA/OLT B92 ..... 127 K3
Bradburne Wy VAUX/NECH B7 .... 89 L8
Bradbury Cl BRWNH WS8 .... 26 D8
Bradbury Dr HIA/OLT B92 ...... 127 K5
Bradbury La HEDN WS12 .... 12 E5
Braddock Cl COVS CV3 .... 155 L4
Brade Dr COVE CV2 .... 135 M7
Braden Rd
ETTPK/GDPK/PENN WV4 .... 65 H1
Brades Cl HALE B63 .... 102 F6
Brades Ri OLDBY B69 .... 86 B5
Brades Rd OLDBY B69 .... 86 C5
Bradestone Rd NUN CV11 .... 99 H5
Bradewell Rd CBROM B36 .... 92 B4
Bradfield Rd PBAR/PBCH B42 ... 71 H6
Bradford Cl GTB/HAM B43 ...... 70 D6
WSL WS1 .... 4 E4
Bradford La HAG/WOL DY9 ...... 140 B8
Bradford Rd BRWNH WS8 .... 26 C5
CBROM B36 .... 91 L6
DUDS DY2 .... 84 D7
Bradford St CNCK/NC WS11 ..... 12 E8
CRTAM B79 .... 31 K8
DIG/EDC B5 .... 7 J7
WSL WS1 .... 4 E4
Bradgate Cl SHHTH WV12 .... 38 A7
Bradgate Dr FOAKS/STRLY B74 .. 42 C8
Brading Rd
NUNW/HART CV10 .... 81 H7
Bradley Cft
RCOVN/BALC/EX CV7 .... 150 F7
Bradley La BILS/COS WV14 ..... 67 K2
Bradleymore Rd BRLYHL DY5 .... 102 A2
Bradley Rd BKDE/SHDE B34 ..... 92 B7
BKHL/PFLD WV2 .... 50 C6
STRBR DY8 .... 101 K7
Bradleys Cl CDYHTH B64 .... 103 J6
Bradley's La BILS/COS WV14 ... 67 J3
Bradley St BILS/COS WV14 ..... 67 K1
BRLYHL DY5 .... 83 M6
TPTN/OCK DY4 .... 85 K3
Bradley Thursfield Ct
KIDDW DY11 .... 137 H6
Bradmore Cl SOLH B91 .... 147 L5
Bradmore Gv SLYOAK B29 .... 123 L5
Bradmore Rd BDMR/CCFT WV3 .... 49 K5
Bradney Gn TLHL/CAN CV4 ...... 152 C6
Bradnick Pl TLHL/CAN CV4 ..... 152 C8
Bradnock Cl MOS/BIL B13 ...... 126 A6
Bradnock's Marsh La
HIA/OLT B92 .... 150 C3
Bradshaw Av DARL/WED WS10 .... 51 M8
HWK/WKHTH B38 .... 144 B4
Bradshaw Cl TPTN/OCK DY4 ..... 85 L2
Bradshawe Cl
ALE/KHTH/YWD B14 .... 146 B2
Bradshaw St WOLV WV1 .... 3 H5
Bradstock Rd BVILLE B30 ...... 145 C1
Bradwall Rd MGN/WHC B75 ...... 57 J2
Braemar Av NUNW/HART CV10 .... 81 C5
Braemar Cl COVE CV2 .... 135 J7
SEDG DY3 .... 66 A4
SHHTH WV12 .... 38 A6
Braemar Dr ERDW/GRVHL B23 .... 71 M8
Braemar Gdns HEDN WS12 .... 13 J2
Braemar Rd CNCK/NC WS11 ...... 25 L1
HIA/OLT B92 .... 127 H4
RLSN CV32 .... 200 F1
SCFLD/BOLD B73 .... 72 D3
Braemar Wy NUNW/HART CV10 .... 98 E3
Braeside Cft
CHWD/FDBR/MGN B37 .... 111 H3
Braeside Wy BLOX/PEL WS3 ..... 39 K2
Brafield Leys
RUGBYS/DCH CV22 .... 183 L7
Bragg Rd BFLD/HDSWWD B20 ..... 89 H3
Braggs Farm La SHLY B90 ...... 170 E1

Braham CRTAM B79 .... 31 H7
Braid Cl HWK/WKHTH B38 .... 144 B4
Brailes Cl HIA/OLT B92 .... 128 C6
Brailes Dr WALM/CURD B76 ..... 73 K2
Brailsford Cl WNSFLD WV11 .... 37 J5
Brailsford Dr SMTHWK B66 ..... 87 L8
Brain St TAM/AM/WIL B77 ...... 46 E3
Braithwaite Cl KGSWFD DY6 .... 83 H7
Braithwaite Rd SPARK B11 ..... 107 L6
Brake La STRBR DY8 .... 119 J7
Brakesmead RLSS CV31 .... 200 D8
Bramah Wy TPTN/OCK DY4 .... 68 A7
Bramber Dr WMBN WV5 .... 64 D7
Bramber Wy STRBR DY8 .... 119 K3
Bramble Cl AST/WIT B6 .... 89 J6
BRWNH WS8 .... 26 C8
CDYHTH B64 .... 103 K1
CSHL/WTROR B46 .... 93 L6
NFLD/LBR B31 .... 123 K8
NUN CV11 .... 99 K3
SHHTH WV12 .... 38 A6
Bramble Dell BORD B9 .... 108 E2
Bramble Dr HEDN WS12 .... 13 C6
Bramble Gn DUDN DY1 .... 66 D8
Bramble La BNTWD WS7 .... 18 F5
Brambleside STRBR DY8 .... 101 K4
The Brambles HAG/WOL DY9 ..... 120 B2
LICHS WS14 .... 21 H7
WALM/CURD B76 .... 73 L5
Bramble St COV CV1 .... 9 K5
Bramblewood WMBN WV5 .... 64 C6
Bramblewood Dr
BDMR/CCFT WV3 .... 49 J5
Bramblewoods BKDE/SHDE B34 ... 92 A8
Brambling TAM/AM/WIL B77 ..... 46 E6
Brambling Ri KIDD DY10 .... 161 M4
Bramcote Ri HIA/OLT B92 ...... 128 A6
Bramcote Ri
FOAKS/STRLY B74 .... 57 G6
Bramcote Rd RIDG/WDGT B32 .... 105 G8
Bramdean Dr PENK ST19 .... 10 C4
Bramdene Av NUNW/HART CV10 ... 81 C5
Bramerton Cl WNSFLD WV11 ..... 36 E7
Bramford Dr DUDN DY1 .... 66 F7
Bramley Cl DSYBK/YTR WS5 ..... 54 B5
GTB/HAM B43 .... 71 H2
Bramley Cft SHLY B90 .... 147 C2
Bramley Dr BFLD/HDSWWD B20 ... 88 F2
HLYWD B47 .... 145 M7
Bramley Mews Ct ACGN B27 ..... 127 G1
Bramley Rd ACGN B27 .... 109 G8
DSYBK/YTR WS5 .... 69 M1
Brampton Av HLGN/YWD B28 ..... 126 E7
Brampton Cl KIDD DY10 .... 137 M1
Brampton Crs HIA/OLT B92 ..... 126 F7
Brampton Dr HEDN WS12 .... 17 J3
Brampton Wy BDWTH CV12 .... 117 M2
Bramshall Dr DOR/KN B93 ...... 172 C2
Bramshaw Cl
ALE/KHTH/YWD B14 .... 145 K3
Bramstead Av
DUNHL/THL/PER WV6 .... 48 F3
Bramston Crs TLHL/CAN CV4 .... 152 D4
Bramwell Gdns COVN CV6 .... 116 D8
Brancaster Rd TAM/AM/WIL B77 . 32 E7
Branchal Rd ALDR WS9 .... 41 G4
Branch Rd HWK/WKHTH B38 ...... 144 B5
Branden Rd ALVE B48 .... 167 L7
Brandfield Rd COVN CV6 .... 133 K5
Brandhall La LGLYGN/QTN B68 .. 104 F4
Brandhall Rd LGLYGN/QTN B68 .. 104 F4
Brandon Cl FOAKS/STRLY B74 ... 55 K2
SEDG DY3 .... 66 C6
WBROM B70 .... 86 E3
Brandon Gv NFLD/LBR B31 ...... 143 K6
Brandon La KNWTH CV8 .... 156 D7
Brandon Pde RLSN CV32 .... 200 E5
Brandon Pk BDMR/CCFT WV3 ..... 49 J6
Brandon Pl BKDE/SHDE B34 ..... 92 B6
Brandon Rd COVS CV3 .... 155 L5
HLGN/YWD B28 .... 126 C3
KNWTH CV8 .... 157 G7
RMSLY B62 .... 104 C5
SOLH B91 .... 128 A6
Brandon Wy BRLYHL DY5 .... 102 C3
WBROM B70 .... 86 E3
Brandwood Gv
ALE/KHTH/YWD B14 .... 125 H8
Brandwood Park Rd
ALE/KHTH/YWD B14 .... 145 G1
Brandwood Rd
ALE/KHTH/YWD B14 .... 125 H8
Branfield Cl BILS/COS WV14 ... 66 E4
Branksome Av HDSW B21 .... 88 D5
Branksome Rd COVN CV6 .... 133 J7
Branscombe Cl
ALE/KHTH/YWD B14 .... 125 H8
Bransdale Av COVN CV6 .... 134 B2
Bransdale Cl
DUNHL/THL/PER WV6 .... 35 L8
Bransdale Rd BRWNH WS8 .... 26 C6
Bransford Av TLHL/CAN CV4 .... 153 H8
Bransford Ri SOLH B91 .... 128 F3
Branstree Dr COVN CV6 .... 134 B3
Brantford Rd YDLY B25 .... 109 G5
Branthill Cft SOLH B91 .... 147 M4
Brantley Av BDMR/CCFT WV3 .... 49 G4
Brantley Rd AST/WIT B6 .... 89 L3
Branton Hill La ALDR WS9 ..... 41 G8
Brantwood Av BNTWD WS7 .... 18 E3
Brasshouse La SMTHWK B66 ..... 87 K7
Brassie Cl HWK/WKHTH B38 ..... 144 B4
Brassington Av
SCFLD/BOLD B73 .... 56 F8
Bratch Cl DUDS DY2 .... 103 C2
Bratch Common Rd WMBN WV5 .... 64 C5
Bratch Hollow WMBN WV5 .... 64 C5
Bratch La WMBN WV5 .... 64 C5
Bratch Pk WMBN WV5 .... 64 C5
Brathay Cl COVS CV3 .... 154 B7
Bratt St WBROM B70 .... 87 C1
Braunston Cl WALM/CURD B76 ... 73 L3
Bray Bank CSHL/WTROR B46 ..... 95 H3
Brayford Av BRLYHL DY5 .... 101 M6
COVS CV3 .... 154 A7
Braymoor Rd STETCH B33 .... 110 C4
Brays Cl RRUGBY CV23 .... 157 J2

Bray's La COVE CV2 ...... 154 E2
Brays Rd
  LGN/SDN/BHAMAIR B26 ...... 109 L8
Bray St WLNHL WV13 ...... 51 M3
Braytoft Cl COVN CV6 ...... 134 A3
Brazil St TLHL/CAN CV4 ...... 152 C3
Breaches La REDE B98 ...... 197 H5
Breach Oak La
  RCOVN/BALC/EX CV7 ...... 115 H4
Breakback Rd BRGRVW B61 ...... 185 H5
Bream TAM/AM/WIL B77 ...... 46 B6
Bream Cl
  CHWD/FDBR/MGN B37 ...... 111 G3
Breamore Crs DUDN DY1 ...... 84 D2
Brean Av
  LGN/SDN/BHAMAIR B26 ...... 109 K8
Brearley St HDSW B21 ...... 88 B5
  LOZ/NWT B19 ...... 89 H8
Brecknell Ri KDDN DY10 ...... 137 K5
Brecknock Rd HHTH/SAND B71 ...... 68 E7
Brecon Av COVW CV5 ...... 132 E6
Brecon Dr BFLD/HDSWWD B20 ...... 88 F5
Brecon Dr STRBR DY8 ...... 101 M7
Bredon Av COVS CV3 ...... 155 K6
  HAG/WOL DY9 ...... 102 A8
  KIDDW DY11 ...... 160 E4
Bredon Ct HALE B63 ...... 121 L2
Bredon Cft WSNGN B18 ...... 88 E8
Bredon Rd BRGRVE B60 ...... 185 H6
  OLDBY B69 ...... 86 B8
  STRBR DY8 ...... 101 L7
Bredon Vw REDW B97 ...... 196 B5
Breech Cl FOAKS/STRLY B74 ...... 55 J6
Bree Cl COVW CV5 ...... 132 E6
Breeden Dr WALM/CURD B76 ...... 74 F7
Breedon Rd BVILLE B30 ...... 124 E8
Breedon Wy RUSH/SHEL WS4 ...... 40 A4
Breen Rydding Dr
  BILS/COS WV14 ...... 66 F4
Bree's La KNWTH CV8 ...... 174 E4
Breeze Av CNCK/NC WS11 ...... 17 M8
Brelades Cl DUDN DY1 ...... 84 C2
Brendan Cl CSHL/WTROR B46 ...... 93 L8
Brendon TAM/AM/WIL B77 ...... 46 F4
Brendon Wy NUNW/HART CV10 ...... 97 L2
Brennand Rd LGLYGN/QTN B68 ...... 104 F4
Brent TAM/AM/WIL B77 ...... 46 C6
Brentford Rd
  ALE/KHTH/YWD B14 ...... 125 K8
  SOLH B91 ...... 147 J2
Brentmill Cl NUNW/HART CV10 ...... 36 D1
Brentnall Dr MGN/WHC B75 ...... 56 F2
Brenton Rd
  ETTPK/GDPK/PENN WV4 ...... 65 K1
Brent Rd BVILLE B30 ...... 125 G5
Brentwood Av COVS CV3 ...... 178 A2
Brentwood Cl SOLH B91 ...... 147 J2
Brentwood Gv KGSTG B44 ...... 71 J5
Brenwood Cl KGSWFD DY6 ...... 82 F6
Brereton Cl DUDS DY2 ...... 85 J5
Brereton Rd SHHTH WV12 ...... 38 A6
Brese Av WWCK CV34 ...... 199 K4
Bretby Gv ERDW/GRVHL B23 ...... 72 E7
Bretford Rd COVE CV2 ...... 135 G4
Bretshall Cl SHLY B90 ...... 147 H3
Brett Dr RIDG/WDGT B32 ...... 123 G5
Brettell La BRLYHL DY5 ...... 102 A4
  STRBR DY8 ...... 101 K5
Brettell St DUDS DY2 ...... 84 F6
Bretton Rd ACGN B27 ...... 127 H3
Bretts Cl COV CV1 ...... 9 J1
Bretts Hall Est
  NUNW/HART CV10 ...... 79 K6
Brett St HHTH/SAND B71 ...... 68 F8
Brett Young Cl KIDD DY10 ...... 137 M8
Brevitt Rd BKHL/PFLD WV2 ...... 50 F7
Brewers Cl COVS CV3 ...... 155 L4
Brewers Dr BLOX/PEL WS3 ...... 39 L4
Brewer St WS2 ...... 53 J1
Brewery St AST/WIT B6 ...... 89 J8
  DUDS DY2 ...... 85 J4
  HDSW B21 ...... 88 B5
  SMTHWKW B67 ...... 87 K7
  TPTN/OCK DY4 ...... 85 K1
Brewood Rd WOLVN WV10 ...... 22 A4
Brewster Cl COVE CV2 ...... 155 J3
  POL/KGSB/FAZ B78 ...... 45 J4
Breydon Gv WLNHL WV13 ...... 51 K5
Brian Rd SMTHWKW B67 ...... 87 J7
Briansway COVN CV6 ...... 134 C2
Briar TAM/AM/WIL B77 ...... 46 E2
Briar Av FOAKS/STRLY B74 ...... 55 L4
Briarbeck RUSH/SHEL WS4 ...... 40 A5
Briar Cl BRGRVE B60 ...... 166 A7
  ERDE/BCHGN B24 ...... 90 E1
  HEDN WS12 ...... 12 E5
  RLSN CV32 ...... 200 F3
Briardene Av BDWTH CV12 ...... 116 F4
Briarfield Rd SPARK B11 ...... 126 E2
Briar Hl KIDD DY10 ...... 163 J5
Briars Cl BRLYHL DY5 ...... 102 A1
  COVE CV2 ...... 155 G3
  NUN CV11 ...... 81 J8
  RRUGBY CV23 ...... 182 F1
The Briars ERDW/GRVHL B23 ...... 72 B7
Briars Wy HEDN WS12 ...... 18 A1
Briar Wood Cl
  BKHL/PFLD WV2 ...... 50 E6
Briarwood Cl SHLY B90 ...... 171 H1
Brickbridge La WMBN WV5 ...... 64 C8
Brickfield Rd YDLY B25 ...... 108 F7
Brickheath Rd WOLV WV1 ...... 50 C2
Brickhill Dr
  CHWD/FDBR/MGN B37 ...... 110 C3
Brick Hill La COVW CV5 ...... 132 B5
Brickhouse La South
  TPTN/OCK DY4 ...... 68 B7
Brickhouse Rd
  BLKHTH/ROWR B65 ...... 103 L1
Brickkiln St BRWNH WS8 ...... 26 C5
Brickkiln La ATHST CV9 ...... 76 F1
Brick Kiln La HLYWD B47 ...... 169 K1
  KGSTG B44 ...... 71 J6
  POL/KGSB/FAZ B78 ...... 59 C7
  SEDG DY3 ...... 83 L2
  SOLH B91 ...... 147 K5
Brick Kiln St BRLYHL DY5 ...... 84 C8

BRLYHL DY5 ...... 102 E5
  TPTN/OCK DY4 ...... 67 J7
Brickkiln St WLNHL WV13 ...... 51 K4
Brick St SEDG DY3 ...... 66 B5
Brickyard Rd ALDR WS9 ...... 40 D4
Bridal Pth COVW CV5 ...... 132 F7
The
  HLGN/YWD B28 ...... 126 F8
Briddsland Rd STECH B33 ...... 110 C3
Brideake Cl COVS CV3 ...... 155 K2
Bridge Av GTWY WS6 ...... 16 C8
  TPTN/OCK DY4 ...... 68 A6
Bridgeburn Rd NFLD/LBR B31 ...... 123 J5
Bridge Cl SPARK B11 ...... 125 M2
Bridgecote COVS CV3 ...... 155 L3
Bridge Cft BHTH/HG B12 ...... 107 J7
Bridge Cross Rd BNTWD WS7 ...... 18 E6
Bridge End WWCK CV34 ...... 199 K8
Bridgeford Rd BKDE/SHDE B34 ...... 91 M7
Bridgelands Wy
  BFLD/HDSWWD B20 ...... 89 H4
Bridge La ATHST CV9 ...... 63 L6
Bridgeman Cft CBROM B36 ...... 92 A5
Bridgeman Rd COV CV6 ...... 133 M8
Bridgeman St WSLW WS2 ...... 4 D3
Bridgemary Cl WOLVN WV10 ...... 36 D1
Bridge Meadow Dr
  DOR/KN B93 ...... 148 D8
Bridgend Cft BRLYHL DY5 ...... 83 M7
Bridge Piece NFLD/LBR B31 ...... 143 M3
Bridge Rd RUSH/SHEL WS4 ...... 39 M4
  TPTN/OCK DY4 ...... 68 A6
  WASH/WDE B8 ...... 108 C2
Bridges Crs CNCK/NC WS11 ...... 17 K8
Bridges Rd CNCK/NC WS11 ...... 17 K8
Bridge St ATHST CV9 ...... 77 G1
  BILS/COS WV14 ...... 51 J8
  BILS/COS WV14 ...... 67 G5
  BRWNH WS8 ...... 26 C7
  CBHAMW B1 ...... 6 D7
  CNCK/NC WS11 ...... 16 C8
  COVN CV6 ...... 134 E6
  DARL/WED WS10 ...... 68 D3
  HALE B63 ...... 103 G6
  KIDD DY10 ...... 137 J8
  NUN CV11 ...... 99 G3
  OLDBY B69 ...... 86 E5
  POL/KGSB/FAZ B78 ...... 47 L4
  REDW B97 ...... 196 B1
  STRBR DY8 ...... 101 J4
  TAM/AM/WIL B77 ...... 32 C8
  WBROM B70 ...... 86 F1
  WLNHL WV13 ...... 51 K4
  WOLVN WV10 ...... 36 C2
  WSL WS1 ...... 4 F2
  WWCK CV34 ...... 200 A5
Bridge St North SMTHWK B66 ...... 87 M7
Bridge St West LOZ/NWT B19 ...... 89 H7
Bridget St RUGBYN/HIL CV21 ...... 183 K2
Bridgewater Av OLDBY B69 ...... 104 E1
Bridgewater Cl PENK ST19 ...... 10 D5
Bridgewater Crs DUDS DY2 ...... 85 J4
Bridgewater Dr BILS/COS WV14 ...... 67 G3
Bridgewater St
  TAM/AM/WIL B77 ...... 32 C8
Bridge Wy BRWNH WS8 ...... 26 C7
Bridgnorth Av WMBN WV5 ...... 82 D1
Bridgnorth Gv SHHTH WV12 ...... 37 M7
Bridgnorth Rd
  DUNHL/THL/PER WV6 ...... 49 G3
  KIDDW DY11 ...... 136 D2
  KINVER DY7 ...... 101 G7
  SEDG DY3 ...... 64 A8
  STRBR DY8 ...... 101 J7
Bridgwater Cl ALDR WS9 ...... 40 D1
Bridle Brook La
  RCOVN/BALC/EX CV7 ...... 132 E1
Bridle Gv HHTH/SAND B71 ...... 69 K5
Bridle La FOAKS/STRLY B74 ...... 55 H7
Bridle Md HWK/WKHTH B38 ...... 144 B5
Bridle Rd RUGBYN/HIL CV21 ...... 183 J1
  STRBR DY8 ...... 101 J7
Bridlewood FOAKS/STRLY B74 ...... 55 K5
Bridley Moor Rd REDW B97 ...... 196 A1
Bridport Cl COVE CV2 ...... 155 L1
Brierfield Wy HIA/OLT B92 ...... 127 H6
Brierley Hill Rd BRLYHL DY5 ...... 101 L3
Brierley La BILS/COS WV14 ...... 67 J3
Brierley Rd COVE CV2 ...... 135 C5
Brier Road Rd HALE B63 ...... 122 A2
Briertey Hill La RUGE WS15 ...... 18 F1
Briery Cl DYHTH B64 ...... 103 K6
Briery Rd HALE B63 ...... 121 J2
Brigfield Crs MOS/BIL B13 ...... 125 M8
Brigfield Rd MOS/BIL B13 ...... 125 M8
Bright Crs TAM/AM/WIL B77 ...... 46 A3
Brightmere Rd COVN CV6 ...... 8 C1
Brighton Cl WSLW WS2 ...... 53 H2
Brighton Pl BDMR/CCFT WV3 ...... 2 B5
Brighton Rd BHTH/HG B12 ...... 107 K8
Brighton St COVE CV2 ...... 9 M3
Bright Rd LGLYGN/QTN B68 ...... 86 F8
Brightstone Cl WOLVN WV10 ...... 36 D1
Brightstone Rd RBRY B45 ...... 142 E3
Bright St COVN CV6 ...... 134 C7
  DARL/WED WS10 ...... 52 B8
  STRBR DY8 ...... 101 H7
  WOLV WV1 ...... 2 D2
Brightwalton Rd COVS CV3 ...... 154 B6
Brightwell Crs DOR/KN B93 ...... 172 C2
Brill Cl TLHL/CAN CV4 ...... 153 G8
Brimstone La BRGRVW B61 ...... 165 G6
Brindle Av COVS CV3 ...... 155 G3
Brindle Cl
  LGN/SDN/BHAMAIR B26 ...... 109 J8
Brindlefields Wy TPTN/OCK DY4 ...... 85 J3
Brindle Rd DSYBK/YTR WS5 ...... 70 A1
Brindley Av WNSFLD WV11 ...... 37 L4
Brindley Brae KINVER DY7 ...... 118 A1
Brindley Cl ATHST CV9 ...... 63 G3
  PENK ST19 ...... 10 E6
  STRBR DY8 ...... 101 J4
  WMBN WV5 ...... 64 B7
  WSLW WS2 ...... 38 E8
Brindley Ct TPTN/OCK DY4 ...... 67 J8
Brindley Crs HEDN WS12 ...... 13 C6
Brindley Dr CBHAMW B1 ...... 6 C5
Brindley Heath Rd HEDN WS12 ...... 13 G6
Brindley Paddocks COV CV1 ...... 8 E2
Brindley Rd HEDN WS12 ...... 12 D1

HHTH/SAND B71 ...... 68 E5
  RCOVN/BALC/EX CV7 ...... 116 F6
Brindley St STRPT DY13 ...... 160 D8
Brineton Gv SLYOAK B29 ...... 123 L4
Brineton St WSLW WS2 ...... 4 A5
Bringewood Gv
  RIDG/WDGT B32 ...... 122 F5
Brinklow Cl REDE B98 ...... 197 H5
Brinklow Cft BKDE/SHDE B34 ...... 92 B6
Brinklow Rd COVS CV3 ...... 155 L3
  RRUGBY CV23 ...... 157 L2
  SLYOAK B29 ...... 123 K3
Brinley Wy KGSWFD DY6 ...... 83 G7
Brinsford La WOLVN WV10 ...... 22 B6
Brinsford Rd WOLVN WV10 ...... 36 A2
Brinsley Cl SOLH B91 ...... 147 M3
Brinsley Rd
  LGN/SDN/BHAMAIR B26 ...... 109 M5
Brinton Cl KIDDW DY11 ...... 161 G2
Brinton Crs KIDDW DY11 ...... 161 G1
Brisbane Cl COVS CV3 ...... 154 C7
Brisbane Rd SMTHWKW B67 ...... 87 J7
Brisbane Wy HEDN WS12 ...... 17 J2
Briscoe Rd COVN CV6 ...... 134 A1
Briseley Cl BRLYHL DY5 ...... 102 A5
Bristam Ct OLDBY B69 ...... 86 C7
Bristnall Hall La
  LGLYGN/QTN B68 ...... 105 G2
Bristnall Hall Rd
  LGLYGN/QTN B68 ...... 105 G2
Bristol Cl CNCK/NC WS11 ...... 16 F4
Bristol Rd COVW CV5 ...... 153 K3
  DIG/EDG B5 ...... 107 G8
  DUDS DY2 ...... 103 H3
  ERDW/GRVHL B23 ...... 90 C2
  SLYOAK B29 ...... 124 B5
Bristol Rd South NFLD/LBR B31 ...... 143 J4
  NFLD/LBR B31 ...... 143 J4
  RBRY B45 ...... 142 E6
Bristol St BDMR/CCFT WV3 ...... 2 C8
  BILS/COS WV14 ...... 51 J8
  DIG/EDG B5 ...... 107 H5
Briston Cl BRLYHL DY5 ...... 102 A5
Britannia Gdns
  BLKHTH/ROWR B65 ...... 104 A2
Britannia Rd BILS/COS WV14 ...... 67 K2
  BLKHTH/ROWR B65 ...... 104 A2
Britannia St COVE CV2 ...... 9 L3
  OLDBY B69 ...... 86 A3
Britannia Wy LICHS WS14 ...... 21 J5
Britford Cl ALE/KHTH/YWD B14 ...... 145 K2
Briton Rd COVE CV2 ...... 154 E1
Brittan Cl BKDE/SHDE B34 ...... 92 C7
Brittania Wy WSL WS1 ...... 53 H8
Britten Cl NUN CV11 ...... 99 L6
Britten St REDW B97 ...... 196 B1
Britton Dr CSCFLD/WYGN B72 ...... 73 G5
Britwell Rd SCFLD/BOLD B73 ...... 72 E3
Brixfield Wy SHLY B90 ...... 146 E8
Brixham Cl NUN CV11 ...... 81 K8
Brixham Dr COVE CV2 ...... 135 C2
Brixham Rd LDYWD/EDGR B16 ...... 106 B1
Brixworth Cl COVS CV3 ...... 155 J5
Broad Acres NFLD/LBR B31 ...... 123 J7
Broad Cft TPTN/OCK DY4 ...... 68 A7
Broadfern Rd DOR/KN B93 ...... 148 F5
Broadfield Cl HHTH/SAND B71 ...... 69 K5
  KGSWFD DY6 ...... 83 H8
Broadfields HAG/WOL DY9 ...... 119 L7
Broadfields Rd
  ERDW/GRVHL B23 ...... 72 C8
Broadgate COV CV1 ...... 8 F5
Broad Ground Rd REDE B98 ...... 196 F3
Broad Heath Cl REDW B97 ...... 187 M8
Broadheath Dr RUSH/SHEL WS4 ...... 40 B5
Broadhidley Dr
  RIDG/WDGT B32 ...... 122 F4
Broadhurst Gn HEDN WS12 ...... 12 C2
Broadhurst Green Rd
  HEDN WS12 ...... 12 B3
Broadlands Cl TLHL/CAN CV4 ...... 153 G3
Broadlands Dr BRLYHL DY5 ...... 84 C8
Broadlands Ri LICHS WS14 ...... 21 H6
Broad La ALE/KHTH/YWD B14 ...... 145 H2
  BDMR/CCFT WV3 ...... 49 J5
  BLOX/PEL WS3 ...... 38 F5
  LICHS WS14 ...... 21 H6
  RCOVN/BALC/EX CV7 ...... 113 J2
  RCOVN/BALC/EX CV7 ...... 151 L1
  RUSH/SHEL WS4 ...... 40 A4
  TLHL/CAN CV4 ...... 153 G3
  WNSFLD WV11 ...... 37 H3
Broad Lane Gdns BLOX/PEL WS3 ...... 38 E3
Broad La North SHHTH WV12 ...... 37 M7
Broad La South SHHTH WV12 ...... 37 L7
Broadlee TAM/AM/WIL B77 ...... 47 G4
Broad Meadow ALDR WS9 ...... 40 F4
Broadmeadow Cl BVILLE B30 ...... 144 F2
Broadmeadow Gn
  BILS/COS WV14 ...... 51 G6
Broad Meadow La BVILLE B30 ...... 144 F2
  GTWY WS6 ...... 24 C3
Broadmeadows Rd
  SHHTH WV12 ...... 38 C5
Broadmere Ri TLHL/CAN CV4 ...... 152 E3
Broadmoor Av
  LGLYGN/QTN B68 ...... 105 H3
Broadmoor Cl BILS/COS WV14 ...... 67 G1
Broadmoor Rd BILS/COS WV14 ...... 67 G1
Broad Oaks WALM/CURD B76 ...... 73 L5
Broadoaks Cl CNCK/NC WS11 ...... 17 K7
Broad Oaks Rd SOLH B91 ...... 127 K8
Broad Park Rd COVE CV2 ...... 135 H6
Broad Rd ACGN B27 ...... 126 F2
Broadsmeath
  TAM/AM/WIL B77 ...... 46 A3
Broadstone Av BLOX/PEL WS3 ...... 39 H6
  HALE B63 ...... 120 F1
Broadstone Cl
  ETTPK/GDPK/PENN WV4 ...... 50 B3
Broadstone Rd
  LGN/SDN/BHAMAIR B26 ...... 109 K3
Broad St BILS/COS WV14 ...... 51 G7
  BILS/COS WV14 ...... 67 C5
  BRGRVW B61 ...... 185 K1
  BRLYHL DY5 ...... 84 A7
  CBHAMW B1 ...... 6 B7

CNCK/NC WS11 ...... 16 C7
  COVN CV6 ...... 134 C6
  EDG B15 ...... 6 A8
  KGSWFD DY6 ...... 83 H8
  KIDD DY10 ...... 137 J6
  OLDBY B69 ...... 86 E8
  RRUGBY CV23 ...... 157 K2
  WOLV WV1 ...... 3 G4
  WWCK CV34 ...... 199 K6
Broad Street Jetty
  COVN CV6 ...... 134 C6
Broad Street Jct WOLV WV1 ...... 3 H4
Broadwas Cl REDE B98 ...... 189 C8
Broadwater COVW CV5 ...... 153 L5
Broadwaters Av
  DARL/WED WS10 ...... 68 A1
Broadwaters Dr KIDD DY10 ...... 137 L5
Broad Wy RUSH/SHEL WS4 ...... 40 A3
Broadway BDMR/CCFT WV3 ...... 49 C4
  CDSL WV8 ...... 34 C2
  COVW CV5 ...... 8 B8
  HEDN WS12 ...... 12 D7
  LGLYGN/QTN B68 ...... 105 C4
  RLSN CV32 ...... 193 J7
  SHLY B90 ...... 146 F1
Broadway Av BORD B9 ...... 108 E3
  HALE B63 ...... 121 J3
Broadway Cft
  LGLYGN/QTN B68 ...... 105 C4
  LGN/SDN/BHAMAIR B26 ...... 109 L7
Broadway North WSL WS1 ...... 5 L6
The Broadway
  BFLD/HDSWWD B20 ...... 89 H3
  DUDN DY1 ...... 84 E2
  HHTH/SAND B71 ...... 68 E6
  STRBR DY8 ...... 119 H7
  WMBN WV5 ...... 64 B8
Broadway West WSL WS1 ...... 4 C9
Broadwell Ct TLHL/CAN CV4 ...... 152 D7
Broadwell Rd HIA/OLT B92 ...... 127 L3
  OLDBY B69 ...... 86 E5
Broadwells Crs TLHL/CAN CV4 ...... 152 D8
Broadyates Gv YDLY B25 ...... 109 C7
Broadyates Rd YDLY B25 ...... 109 C7
Brobury Cft SHLY B90 ...... 147 H1
Broc Cl PENK ST19 ...... 10 C2
Brockenhurst Rd COVN CV6 ...... 116 F7
Brockeridge Cl SHHTH WV12 ...... 38 A1
Brocket Cl STRPT DY15 ...... 160 C7
Brockhall Gv
  CHWD/FDBR/MGN B37 ...... 92 D8
Brockhill Dr REDW B97 ...... 187 M8
Brockhill La ALVE B48 ...... 168 F2
  BRGRVE B60 ...... 187 C4
  REDE B98 ...... 189 K2
  REDW B97 ...... 187 L7
Brockhurst Crs
  DSYBK/YTR WS5 ...... 69 K1
Brockhurst Dr
  DUNHL/THL/PER WV6 ...... 2 B1
  HLGN/YWD B28 ...... 126 E8
  TLHL/CAN CV4 ...... 152 B3
Brockhurst La MGN/WHC B75 ...... 43 L7
  SHLY B90 ...... 146 E8
Brockhurst Pl
  DSYBK/YTR WS5 ...... 53 K8
Brockhurst Rd CBROM B36 ...... 91 C7
  MGN/WHC B75 ...... 57 H4
Brockhurst St DSYBK/YTR WS5 ...... 53 J7
Brockley Cl BRLYHL DY5 ...... 102 B2
Brockley Gv MOS/BIL B13 ...... 125 C4
Brockley Pl VAUX/NECH B7 ...... 90 A6
Brockmoor Cl HAG/WOL DY9 ...... 120 A3
Brock Rd TPTN/OCK DY4 ...... 85 M1
Brockwell Gv KGSTG B44 ...... 71 J1
Brockwell Rd KGSTG B44 ...... 71 J1
Brockworth Rd BVILLE B30 ...... 145 C3
Brocton Cl
  ETTPK/GDPK/PENN WV4 ...... 66 E2
Brodick Wy NUNW/HART CV10 ...... 98 D2
Brogden Cl HHTH/SAND B71 ...... 69 G5
Bromage Av POL/KGSB/FAZ B78 ...... 60 A7
Bromfield Cl AST/WIT B6 ...... 89 J6
Bromfield Crs DARL/WED WS10 ...... 69 G2
Bromfield Rd REDW B97 ...... 196 B3
Bromford Cl
  ERDW/GRVHL B23 ...... 72 C8
Bromford Crs ERDE/BCHGN B24 ...... 90 E3
  OLDBY B69 ...... 86 E5
  WASH/WDE B8 ...... 90 F4
  WBROM B70 ...... 86 F4
Bromford Dell NFLD/LBR B31 ...... 144 A1
Bromford Dr CBROM B36 ...... 91 G5
Bromford Hl
  BFLD/HDSWWD B20 ...... 89 G2
Bromford La ERDE/BCHGN B24 ...... 90 E3
  OLDBY B69 ...... 86 E5
  WASH/WDE B8 ...... 90 F4
  WBROM B70 ...... 86 F4
Bromford Ri BDMR/CCFT WV3 ...... 2 D9
Bromford Rd CBROM B36 ...... 90 F6
  DUDS DY2 ...... 84 E7
  WBROM B70 ...... 86 E4
Bromleigh Dr COVE CV2 ...... 155 C3
Bromley BRLYHL DY5 ...... 83 M8
Bromley Cl HEDN WS12 ...... 13 C6
  KNWTH CV8 ...... 179 G6
Bromley Gdns CDSL WV8 ...... 34 E1
Bromley La KGSWFD DY6 ...... 101 J1
Bromley Pl
  ETTPK/GDPK/PENN WV4 ...... 49 L8
Bromley St BKHL/PFLD WV2 ...... 50 A6
  BORD B9 ...... 7 L7
  HAG/WOL DY9 ...... 102 D7
Brompton Dr BRLYHL DY5 ...... 101 M6
Brompton Lawns
  DUNHL/THL/PER WV6 ...... 48 E2
Brompton Pool Rd
  HLGN/YWD B28 ...... 145 C2
Brompton Rd KGSTG B44 ...... 71 J1
Bromsgrove Eastern By-pass
  BRGRVE B60 ...... 185 J7
Bromsgrove Hwy BRGRVE B60 ...... 186 E5
  REDE B98 ...... 196 C5
  REDW B97 ...... 195 L2
Bromsgrove Rd BRGRVW B61 ...... 165 H7
  HAG/WOL DY9 ...... 140 B1

HALE B63 ...... 122 A6
  KIDD DY10 ...... 162 C3
  REDW B97 ...... 195 L2
  RMSLY B62 ...... 121 M5
Bromsgrove St DIG/EDG B5 ...... 6 F8
  KIDD DY10 ...... 137 J7
Bromwich Cl COVS CV3 ...... 155 K6
Bromwich Dr MGN/WHC B75 ...... 57 C6
Bromwich La HAG/WOL DY9 ...... 119 M6
Bromwynd Cl
  BKHL/PFLD WV2 ...... 49 M7
Bromyard Av
  WALM/CURD B76 ...... 73 L5
Bromyard Rd SPARK B11 ...... 126 C2
Bronte Cl NUNW/HART CV10 ...... 79 K8
  SHLY B90 ...... 147 H4
Bronte Ct CRTAM B79 ...... 31 C7
Bronte Dr CNCK/NC WS11 ...... 17 C3
  KIDD DY10 ...... 137 M7
Bronte Farm Rd SHLY B90 ...... 147 H4
Bronte Rd BKHL/PFLD WV2 ...... 50 D7
Bronwen Rd BILS/COS WV14 ...... 67 C6
Bronze Cl NUN CV11 ...... 99 J5
Brook Av TAM/AM/WIL B77 ...... 46 D6
Brookbank Av BKDE/SHDE B34 ...... 92 E7
Brookbank Gdns SEDG DY3 ...... 83 M3
Brookbank Rd SEDG DY3 ...... 83 M3
Brook Cl ALDR WS9 ...... 40 E2
  COV CV1 ...... 9 K2
  LGN/SDN/BHAMAIR B26 ...... 109 H8
  LICH WS13 ...... 20 E4
  PENK ST19 ...... 10 C6
  POL/KGSB/FAZ B78 ...... 76 B7
  SHLY B90 ...... 146 D4
  STETCH B33 ...... 109 J1
Brook Crs HAG/WOL DY9 ...... 119 M8
  HAG/WOL DY9 ...... 120 D2
  KGSWFD DY6 ...... 83 C6
Brook Cft
  CHWD/FDBR/MGN B37 ...... 110 F6
  LGN/SDN/BHAMAIR B26 ...... 109 M1
Brookdale KIDD DY10 ...... 137 K5
  SEDG DY3 ...... 84 A2
Brookdale Cl RBRY B45 ...... 142 E3
Brookdale Dr
  ETTPK/GDPK/PENN WV4 ...... 49 H7
Brookdale Rd NUNW/HART CV10 ...... 81 H1
Brook Dr RIDG/WDGT B32 ...... 123 H4
Brooke Cl WWCK CV34 ...... 199 K8
Brook End BNTWD WS7 ...... 26 E1
  POL/KGSB/FAZ B78 ...... 45 L5
Brookend Dr RBRY B45 ...... 142 D6
Brooke Rd HEDN WS12 ...... 12 D7
  KNWTH CV8 ...... 191 M1
Brooke St DUDS DY2 ...... 85 H5
Brook Farm Cl CSHL/WTROR B46 ...... 95 H2
Brookfield Cl ALDR WS9 ...... 40 E4
Brookfield Dr CNCK/NC WS11 ...... 16 C6
Brookfield Rd ALDR WS9 ...... 40 E4
  CDSL WV8 ...... 34 F2
  RLSN CV32 ...... 193 J3
  WSNGN B18 ...... 88 D8
Brook Fields Cl BRGRVE B60 ...... 166 A4
Brookfields Rd
  LGLYGN/QTN B68 ...... 105 G1
Brookfield Wy HIA/OLT B92 ...... 127 H6
  TPTN/OCK DY4 ...... 67 L7
Brookford Av COVN CV6 ...... 133 L2
Brook Green La HIA/OLT B92 ...... 149 L4
Brook Gv CDSL WV8 ...... 34 F2
Brookhill Cl SHHTH WV12 ...... 38 A4
Brook Hill Rd WASH/WDE B8 ...... 108 L1
Brook Holloway HAG/WOL DY9 ...... 120 C2
Brook House Cl WOLVN WV10 ...... 22 F7
Brook House La WOLVN WV10 ...... 22 F7
Brookhouse La WOLVN WV10 ...... 22 D7
Brookhouse Rd BRGRVE B60 ...... 166 C6
  DSYBK/YTR WS5 ...... 5 L7
Brookhus Farm Rd
  WALM/CURD B76 ...... 73 L5
Brooking Cl GTB/HAM B43 ...... 71 H1
Brookland Rd ALDR WS9 ...... 40 D2
  HAG/WOL DY9 ...... 119 L8
Brooklands STRBR DY8 ...... 101 K4
Brooklands Av GTWY WS6 ...... 24 D1
Brooklands Cl
  HLGN/YWD B28 ...... 126 D4
Brooklands Dr
  ALE/KHTH/YWD B14 ...... 125 J8
  KIDDW DY11 ...... 137 H4
Brooklands Gv ALDR WS9 ...... 40 D3
Brooklands La REDE B98 ...... 188 F8
Brooklands Pde WOLV WV1 ...... 50 F3
Brooklands Rd CNCK/NC WS11 ...... 16 E1
  HLGN/YWD B28 ...... 126 D4
The Brooklands SEDG DY3 ...... 82 C4
Brook La ALDR WS9 ...... 40 D2
  ALE/KHTH/YWD B14 ...... 125 J5
  GTWY WS6 ...... 24 E2
  HIA/OLT B92 ...... 127 H5
  MOS/BIL B13 ...... 125 L5
  NUNW/HART CV10 ...... 81 G7
Brooklea BDWTH CV12 ...... 116 D3
Brooklea Gv HWK/WKHTH B38 ...... 144 E4
Brooklyn Av AST/WIT B6 ...... 89 K6
Brooklyn Gv BILS/COS WV14 ...... 67 H5
  KGSWFD DY6 ...... 82 F5
Brooklyn Rd BNTWD WS7 ...... 26 E1
  COV CV1 ...... 134 B7
  HEDN WS12 ...... 17 H4
Brookmans Av RIDG/WDGT B32 ...... 123 H1
Brookmeadow Ct
  HLGN/YWD B28 ...... 126 C7
Brook Meadow Rd
  BKDE/SHDE B34 ...... 91 L7
  RUSH/SHEL WS4 ...... 40 A5
Brook Rd BRGRVW B61 ...... 165 G3
  BRGRVW B61 ...... 185 J4
  EDG B15 ...... 106 C6
  GTWY WS6 ...... 16 C8
  LGLYGN/QTN B68 ...... 104 E3
  RBRY B45 ...... 142 C6
  STRBR DY8 ...... 119 M2
  WLNHL WV13 ...... 51 J4
  WMBN WV5 ...... 64 D7
Brooksbank Dr CDYHTH B64 ...... 103 K1

Brooksby Gv *DOR/KN* B93 ...... **172** E3 🔟
Brooks Cft *CVALE* B35 .... **91** L3
Brookshaw Wy *COVE* CV2 ...... **135** K5
Brookside *DARL/WED* WS10 ...... **68** F2
GTB/HAM B43 .... **70** B7
NFLD/LBR B31 .... **123** K8
RRUGBY CV23 .... **180** D7
SEDG DY3 .... **84** B3
Brookside Av *COWV* CV5 .... **153** G2
KNWTH CV8 .... **191** J1
MOS/BIL B13 .... **125** M6
Brookside CI *ALVE* B48 .... **167** M7 🔟
ERDW/GRVHL B23 .... **72** A6 🔟
HALE B63 .... **121** H2
RUGBYS/DCH CV22 .... **183** L4
WMBN WV5 .... **64** C7 🔟
Brookside Dr *BRGRVW* B61 ...... **165** K5
Brookside Rd
POL/KGSB/FAZ B78 .... **45** H4
Brookside Wy *KGSWFD* DY6 ...... **82** F6
KIDD DY10 .... **138** F3
TAM/AM/WIL B77 .... **46** D7
Brooks Rd *CSCFLD/WYGN* B72 ... **73** G4
Brook St *BDWTH* CV12 .... **98** F8
BILS/COS WV14 .... **51** J8
BRLYHL DY5 .... **102** E5
CBHAMNW B3 .... **6** D3
HAG/WOL DY9 .... **102** D8 🔟
KGSWFD DY6 .... **82** F4
KIDDW DY11 .... **137** G7
KNWTH CV8 .... **180** E2 🔟
REDE B98 .... **196** E1 🔟
SEDG DY3 .... **66** E6
SEDG DY3 .... **84** A2
SMTHWK B66 .... **87** M7
STRBR DY8 .... **101** K4
STRBR DY8 .... **101** J8
TPTN/OCK DY4 .... **67** J7
WBROM B70 .... **86** F1
WSLW WS2 .... **4** C3
WWCK CV34 .... **199** J7 🔟
Brook Ter *BILS/COS* WV14 ...... **51** J8
Brookthorpe Dr *SHHTH* WV12 ... **52** A1
Brook V *BEWD* DY12 .... **160** A2
Brookvale Av *COVS* CV3 .... **155** J4
Brookvale CI *BRGRVW* B60 ...... **185** M1
HIA/OLT B92 .... **127** H4
Brookvale Park Rd
ERDW/GRVHL B23 .... **71** M8
Brookvale Rd *AST/WIT* B6 .... **89** L2
HIA/OLT B92 .... **127** H4
Brook Wk *ATHST* CV9 .... **63** K7
RIDG/WDGT B32 .... **123** H3
Brookweed *TAM/AM/WIL* B77 ... **46** E2
Brookwillow Rd *HALE* B63 ...... **121** H3
Brookwood Av *HLGN/YWD* B28 ... **126** B8
Broom CI *BRGRVE* B60 .... **185** M3 🔟
RUGBYS/DCH CV22 .... **183** J4 🔟
Broom Covert Rd *LICHS* WS14 ... **29** J5
Broom Cft *KIDD* DY10 .... **137** L7
Broomcroft Rd
CHWD/FDBR/MGN B37 .... **92** D8
Broomdene Av *BKDE/SHDE* B34 ... **91** L6
Broom Dr *ALE/KHTH/YWD* B14 ... **145** J1
Broome Av *GTB/HAM* B43 .... **70** A6
Broome Cft *COVN* CV6 .... **133** M2
Broomehill CI *BRLYHL* DY5 ...... **102** E5
Broome La *HAG/WOL* DY9 .... **139** J2
HAG/WOL DY9 .... **139** M3
Broome Rd *WOLVN* WV10 .... **36** B6
Broomfield *SMTHWK* B67 .... **87** M7
Broomfield CI *KIDDW* DY11 ...... **136** F6
Broomfield Gn *KIDDW* DY11 ...... **137** L1 🔟
Broomfield PI *COWV* CV5 .... **8** A5 🔟
Broomfield Ri
NUNW/HART CV10 .... **98** D3
Broomfield Rd *COWV* CV5 .... **153** K4
DARL/WED WS10 .... **69** G2
ERDW/GRVHL B23 .... **90** B3
KIDDW DY11 .... **136** F6
Broomfields CI *SOLH* B91 .... **128** B8 🔟
Broomhall Av *WNSFLD* WV11 ... **37** H7 🔟
Broom Hall Crs *ACGN* B27 .... **127** C5 🔟
Broom Hall Gv *ACGN* B27 .... **127** G5 🔟
Broomhill Bank *CNCK/NC* WS11 ... **16** C2
Broomhill CI *CNCK/NC* WS11 .... **16** L1
GTB/HAM B43 .... **70** B5
Broomhill La *GTB/HAM* B43 .... **70** A5
Broomhill Rd *ERDW/GRVHL* B23 ... **71** M6
Broomhurst *EDG* B15 .... **106** C5
Broomie CI *MGN/WHC* B75 ...... **73** H1
Broomlea CI *FOAKS/STRLY* B74 ... **55** J5
Broom Rd *DSYBK/YTR* WS5 ...... **69** M2 🔟
DUDN DY1 .... **84** E1
Broom St *BHTH/HG* B12 .... **7** L9
Broomybank *KNWTH* CV8 .... **176** F7
Broomy CI *STETCH* B33 .... **91** L8
STRPT DY13 .... **160** B8
Broseley Av *NFLD/LBR* B31 ...... **143** L5
Broseley Brook CI *BORD* B9 ...... **108** A4 🔟
Brosil Av *BFLD/HDSWWD* B20 ... **88** C2
Brotherton Av *REDW* B97 .... **195** K3
Brougham St *LOZ/NWT* B19 ...... **88** F6 🔟
Brough CI *BILS/COS* WV14 ...... **66** C2
VAUX/NECH B7 .... **89** M7 🔟
Broughton Ct
DUNHL/THL/PER WV6 .... **48** E2 🔟
Broughton Crs *NFLD/LBR* B31 ... **143** H5
Broughton Rd *BDMR/CCFT* WV3 ... **49** G4
BFLD/HDSWWD B20 .... **88** E5
HAG/WOL DY9 .... **120** B2
Browett Rd *COVN* CV6 .... **133** K8
Brownfield Rd *BKDE/SHDE* B34 ... **92** A7
Brownhills Rd *BRWNH* WS8 ..... **26** D8
CNCK/NC WS11 .... **17** L8
Browning Av *WWCK* CV34 .... **200** E3 🔟
Browning Cl *CRTAM* B79 .... **31** K5
KIDD DY10 .... **137** M7 🔟
NUNW/HART CV10 .... **79** G3
SHHTH WV12 .... **38** C6
Browning Crs *WOLVN* WV10 .... **36** A3
Browning Rd *BNTWD* WS7 .... **19** G6
COVE CV2 .... **155** G1 🔟
SEDG DY3 .... **83** L1
Brownley Rd *SHLY* B90 .... **147** J6
Brown Lion St *TPTN/OCK* DY4 ... **67** J6
Brownlow St *RLSN* CV32 .... **200** E3

Brown Rd *DARL/WED* WS10 ...... **52** A6
Brown's Coppice Av *SOLH* B91 ... **127** H8
Browns Dr *SCFLD/BOLD* B73 ..... **72** D5
Brownsea Cl *RBRY* B45 .... **142** D4 🔟
Brownsea Dr *CBHAMNW* B1 ..... **6** E7 🔟
Brownsfield Rd *LICH* WS13 ...... **21** H3 🔟
Browns Gn
BFLD/HDSWWD B20 .... **88** D2 🔟
Brownshill Ct *COVN* CV6 .... **133** K5
Brownshill Green Rd *COVN* CV6 ... **133** K6
COVW CV5 .... **133** J4
Brownshore La *WNSFLD* WV11 ... **37** L2
Brown's La *COWV* CV5 .... **132** F5
CRTAM B79 .... **32** A5
DOR/KN B93 .... **148** C7
POL/KGSB/FAZ B78 .... **47** K8
Brownsover CI *CBROM* B36 ...... **91** M4 🔟
Brownsover La
RUGBYS/HIL CV21 .... **159** M6
Brownsover Rd
RUGBYS/HIL CV21 .... **159** J6
Brown St *BKHL/PFLD* WV2 .... **50** B6
Brownswall Rd *SEDG* DY3 .... **65** M6
Brown Westhead Pk
KIDD DY10 .... **137** K3
Browsholme *CRTAM* B79 .... **31** H7
Bruce CI *COVN* CV6 .... **133** L5
KIDD DY10 .... **137** M6
RCOVN/BALC/EX CV7 .... **116** D6
Bruce Williams Wy
RUGBYS/DCH CV22 .... **183** M3
SOLH B91 .... **148** B2
Brueton Av *BRGRVE* B60 .... **185** L5
SOLH B91 .... **148** B2
Brueton Dr *ERDE/BCHGN* B24 ... **90** E2
REDE B98 .... **196** E2
Brueton Rd *BILS/COS* WV14 .... **51** L6
Bruford Rd *BDMR/CCFT* WV3 ... **2** A9
Brunel CI *BHTH/HG* B12 .... **107** L8
BNTWD WS7 .... **18** F5
COVE CV2 .... **9** L4 🔟
CRTAM B79 .... **31** L7
STRPT DY13 .... **160** E8
Brunel CI *BILS/COS* WV14 .... **67** J5
Brunel Ga *CDSL* WV8 .... **34** C7 🔟
Brunel Rd *OLDBY* B69 .... **86** B7
Brunel St *CBHAM* B2 .... **6** E6
Brunel Wk *POL/KGSB/FAZ* B78 ... **47** L2
Brunel Wy *BKHL/PFLD* WV2 ..... **50** E6
Brunslow CI *WLNHL* WV13 .... **52** A4
WOLVN WV10 .... **36** A4
Brunswick Ga *STRBR* DY8 .... **119** L4
Brunswick Park Rd
DARL/WED WS10 .... **68** E2
Brunswick Rd *BHTH/HG* B12 ... **107** L8
CNCK/NC WS11 .... **16** C3
COV CV1 .... **8** D6 🔟
HDSW B21 .... **88** D4
Brunswick St *CBHAMW* B1 ...... **6** B8 🔟
RLSS CV31 .... **200** E7
WSLW WS2 .... **4** B8 🔟
Brunswick Ter
DARL/WED WS10 .... **68** D2 🔟
Bruntingthorpe Wy *COVS* CV3 ... **155** J5
Brunton CI *COVS* CV3 .... **155** M4 🔟
Brunton Rd *SMHTH* B10 .... **108** D6
Brushfield Rd *PBAR/PBCH* B42 ... **71** H5
Brutus Dr *CSHL/WTROR* B46 .... **93** J4
Bryan Av
ETTPK/GDPK/PENN WV4 ...... **65** H1
Bryan Rd *WSLW* WS2 .... **4** A9
Bryanston CI *COVE* CV2 .... **155** L1 🔟
Bryanston Rd *SOLH* B91 .... **127** K7
Bryans Wy *HEDN* WS12 .... **17** K1 🔟
Bryant Rd *RCOVN/BALC/EX* CV7 ... **116** E6
Bryant St *WSNGN* B18 .... **88** C3
Bryce Rd *BRLYHL* DY5 .... **83** L8
Brylan Cft *KGSTG* B44 .... **71** K7
Brympton Rd *COVS* CV3 .... **155** G3
Bryn Arden Rd
LGN/SDN/BHAMAIR B26 .... **109** J8
Bryndale Av
ALE/KHTH/YWD B14 .... **125** G8
Bryn Jones CI *COVS* CV3 .... **155** K6
Brynmawr Rd *BILS/COS* WV14 ... **66** D2
Bryn Rd *COVN* CV6 .... **134** D6
Brynside CI *BVILLE* B30 .... **145** K3
Bryony Gdns
DARL/WED WS10 .... **52** B6 🔟
Bryony Rd *SLYOAK* B29 .... **123** M6
Buchanan Av *RUSH/SHEL* WS4 ... **53** L2 🔟
Buchanan CI *RUSH/SHEL* WS4 ... **53** L2 🔟
Buchanan Rd
RUGBYS/DCH CV22 .... **183** J4
RUSH/SHEL WS4 .... **53** L2
Buchan CI *NUNW/HART* CV10 ... **97** K1
Buckbury CI *HAG/WOL* DY9 ..... **120** B3 🔟
Buckbury Cft *SHLY* B90 .... **147** M7 🔟
Buckden *TAM/AM/WIL* B77 ..... **47** G4 🔟
Buckfast CI *BRGRVW* B61 .... **185** H4
COVS CV3 .... **154** C8
Buckhold Dr *COWV* CV5 .... **132** F8
Buckingham CI
DARL/WED WS10 .... **69** H1 🔟
NUNW/HART CV10 .... **98** F4
Buckingham Dr *SHHTH* WV12 ... **37** M6
Buckingham Gv *KGSWFD* DY6 ... **83** C6
Buckingham Ms
SCFLD/BOLD B73 .... **72** E3
Buckingham PI *HEDN* WS12 ..... **17** G4 🔟
Buckingham Ri *COWV* CV5 .... **152** F1
DUDN DY1 .... **84** D2 🔟
Buckingham Rd
BLKHTH/ROWR B65 .... **104** D1
CBROM B36 .... **92** D6
CRTAM B79 .... **31** H7
ETTPK/GDPK/PENN WV4 ...... **65** L1
Buckingham St *LOZ/NWT* B19 ... **6** D1
Buckland CI *HEDN* WS12 .... **17** H4 🔟
Buckland End *BKDE/SHDE* B34 ... **91** L7
Buckland Rd *COVN* CV6 .... **133** M5 🔟
Bucklands End La
BKDE/SHDE B34 .... **91** K7
Buckle CI *WSL* WS1 .... **4** F6 🔟
Buckley Rd
ETTPK/GDPK/PENN WV4 ...... **49** H8

RLSN CV32 .... **200** F3
The Buckleys *ALVE* B48 .... **167** L7
Buckminster Dr *DOR/KN* B93 ... **172** C1
Bucknall Rd *WNSFLD* WV11 ..... **37** L4
Bucknell CI *SOLH* B91 .... **128** A8
Buckridge CI
HWK/WKHTH B38 .... **144** B6 🔟
Bucks HI *NUNW/HART* CV10 .... **79** M6
Buckthorn CI *HEDN* WS12 .... **12** D5 🔟
Buckton CI *MGN/WHC* B75 ...... **57** J2 🔟
Budbrook CI *COVE* CV2 .... **135** H3
Budbrooke Rd *WWCK* CV34 ..... **198** F6
Budbrook Gv *BKDE/SHDE* B34 ... **92** C7
Budden Rd *TPTN/OCK* DY4 ...... **67** H6
Bude Rd *DSYBK/YTR* WS5 .... **54** B6
Buffery Rd *DUDS* DY2 .... **85** J5 🔟
Bufferys CI *SOLH* B91 .... **147** M5 🔟
Buildwas CI *NFLD/LBR* WS5 ..... **38** C3
Bulford CI *ALE/KHTH/YWD* B14 ... **145** K3
Bulger Rd *BILS/COS* WV14 .... **51** G6
Bulkington La *NUN* CV11 .... **99** L5
Bulkington Rd *BDWTH* CV12 ... **117** H3 🔟
Bullace Cft *EDG* B15 .... **124** B2
Bulldog La *LICH* WS13 .... **20** F4 🔟
Buller St
ETTPK/GDPK/PENN WV4 ...... **50** C8
Bullfield Av *TLHL/CAN* CV4 ...... **152** C4
Bullfields CI *BLKHTH/ROWR* B65 ... **85** K8
Bullfinch CI *DUDN* DY1 .... **84** C5
Bullimore Gv *KNWTH* CV8 .... **191** J1 🔟
Bullivents CI *DOR/KN* B93 .... **148** D8
Bull La *BILS/COS* WV14 .... **67** M2
WBROM B70 .... **86** E2
WMBN WV5 .... **64** F6
Bullmeadow La *WMBN* WV5 .... **64** E6
Bullmoor La *LICHS* WS14 .... **27** L4
Bullock's Rw *WSL* WS1 .... **5** G3
Bullock St *VAUX/NECH* B7 ...... **89** L8
WBROM B70 .... **87** H5
Bullows Rd *BRWNH* WS8 .... **26** A7
Bull Ring *DIG/EDG* B5 .... **7** H6
HALE B63 .... **121** M2 🔟
KIDD DY10 .... **137** J7 🔟
NUNW/HART CV10 .... **98** F3
Bull's Head La *COVS* CV3 .... **154** E4
Bull's La *WALM/CURD* B76 ...... **74** A3
Bull St *BRLYHL* DY5 .... **101** L3
CBHAM B2 .... **7** G4
DARL/WED WS10 .... **51** L8
RLSN CV32 .... **200** F1
Burns Av *COVE* CV2 .... **154** F2
CRTAM B79 .... **31** L7
DARL/WED WS10 .... **51** L8
RLSN CV32 .... **200** F1
Bullus Rd *STRPT* DY13 .... **160** E8
Bull Yd *COV* CV1 .... **8** E5 🔟
Bulwell CI *AST/WIT* B6 .... **89** L6 🔟
Bulwer Rd *COVN* CV6 .... **133** L6
Bulwick CI *COVS* CV3 .... **155** M4 🔟
Bumble Hole La *BRGRVW* B61 ... **165** H8
Bumblehole Mdw *WMBN* WV5 ... **64** D6
Bunbury Gdns *NFLD/LBR* B31 ... **144** A1
Bunbury Rd *NFLD/LBR* B31 ...... **144** A1
Bundle HI *HALE* B63 .... **121** L2
Bungay Lake La *BRGRVW* B61 ... **184** D3
Bungham La *PENK* ST19 .... **10** B5
Bunker's Hill La *BILS/COS* WV14 ... **52** A2
Bunn's La *DUDS* DY2 .... **85** K4
Buntsford HI *BRGRVE* B60 ...... **185** J7
Buntsford Park Rd
BRGRVE B60 .... **185** K7
Bunyan PI *CNCK/NC* WS11 ...... **16** C1 🔟
Burbage CI *WOLVN* WV10 .... **36** C7 🔟
Burbages La *COVN* CV6 .... **116** B8
Burberry Gv
RCOVN/BALC/EX CV7 .... **150** F2
Burbidge Rd *BORD* B9 .... **108** B2
Burbury CI *BDWTH* CV12 .... **117** G1 🔟
RLSN CV32 .... **201** G3
Burbury Ct *WWCK* CV34 .... **199** M5 🔟
Burbury St *LOZ/NWT* B19 .... **89** G7
Burcot Av *BRGRVE* B60 .... **185** M1
WOLV WV1 .... **50** E3
Burcote Rd *ERDE/BCHGN* B24 ... **91** H2
Burcot La *BRGRVE* B60 .... **185** M2
Burdock CI *DSYBK/YTR* WS5 .... **69** L2 🔟
HEDN WS12 .... **16** F2
Burdock Rd *SLYOAK* B29 .... **123** L7
Burdons CI *STETCH* B33 .... **91** L8
Bure Gv *WLNHL* WV13 .... **52** B4
Burfield Rd *HALE* B63 .... **103** G7
Burford CI *DSYBK/YTR* WS5 ..... **69** L1 🔟
HIA/OLT B92 .... **127** L2
Burford Ms *RLSS* CV31 .... **201** G7 🔟
Burford Rd *HLYWD* B47 .... **145** J7 🔟
KGSTG B44 .... **71** K6
Burgage PI *NUN* CV11 .... **99** G1
Burges *COV* CV1 .... **8** F3
Burges Gv *WWCK* CV34 .... **199** K4 🔟
Burgess Cft *HIA/OLT* B92 .... **128** D6 🔟
Burghley CI *NUN* CV11 .... **99** K3 🔟
Burghley Dr *HHTH/SAND* B71 ... **69** K3
KIDDW DY11 .... **136** F8 🔟
Burghley Wk *BRLYHL* DY5 .... **101** M5 🔟
Burgh Wy *WSLW* WS2 .... **52** E1
Burgoyne St *CNCK/NC* WS11 ... **12** E8
Burhill Wy
CHWD/FDBR/MGN B37 .... **110** F1
Burke Av *MOS/BIL* B13 .... **126** B4 🔟
Burkitt Dr *TPTN/OCK* DY4 .... **68** A5
Burland Av
DUNHL/THL/PER WV6 .... **35** J6
Burleigh CI *HEDN* WS12 .... **12** E5
RCOVN/BALC/EX CV7 .... **150** C1 🔟
SHHTH WV12 .... **37** M7 🔟
Burleigh Cft *BNTWD* WS7 .... **26** E1
Burleigh Rd *BDMR/CCFT* WV3 ... **49** G6
Burleigh St *WSL* WS1 .... **5** H4
Burleton Rd *STETCH* B33 .... **110** C3
Burley CI *SHLY* B90 .... **146** D3
Burlington Av *WBROM* B70 ..... **87** H4
Burlington Rd *AST/WIT* B6 ...... **89** J7 🔟
Burlish Av *HIA/OLT* B92 .... **127** K4
Burlish CI *STRPT* DY13 .... **160** C7
Burlish Crossing *STRPT* DY13 ... **160** C7
Burman CI *SHLY* B90 .... **146** E3

Burman Dr *CSHL/WTROR* B46 ... **93** K8
Burman Rd *SHLY* B90 .... **146** D3
Burmese Wy *BLKHTH/ROWR* B65 ... **85** K7
Burnaby CI *NUNW/HART* CV10 ... **79** M8
Burnaby Rd *COVN* CV6 .... **134** A5
Burnaston Crs *SHLY* B90 .... **148** A6
Burnaston Rd *HLGN/YWD* B28 ... **126** C3
Burnbank Gv *ERDE/BCHGN* B24 ... **90** F1
Burn CI *SMTHWK* B67 .... **105** L1
Burnel Gdns *BDMR/CCFT* WV3 ... **49** J5 🔟
Burnel Rd *SLYOAK* B29 .... **123** L3
Burnet Gv *WOLVN* WV10 .... **22** F5
Burnett Rd *FOAKS/STRLY* B74 ... **55** M3
Burney La *WASH/WDE* B8 .... **91** C8 🔟
Burnfields CI *ALDR* WS9 .... **40** E6
Burnham Av *WOLVN* WV10 ..... **36** A5
YDLY B25 .... **109** G7
Burnham CI *KGSWFD* DY6 ...... **101** K1
Burnham Gn *CNCK/NC* WS11 ... **15** M5 🔟
Burnham Meadow
HLGN/YWD B28 .... **126** E7
Burnham Ri *NUN* CV11 .... **81** E7
Burnham Rd *COVS* CV3 .... **154** E7
KGSTG B44 .... **71** J6
Burnhill Gv *SLYOAK* B29 .... **123** L5
Burnlea Gv *NFLD/LBR* B31 ...... **144** A4 🔟
Burnsall CI
CHWD/FDBR/MGN B37 .... **110** D3
COVEN WV9 .... **35** L2
Burnsall Gv *COVW* CV5 .... **153** H5
Burnsall Rd *COVW* CV5 .... **153** H5
Burns Av *TPTN/OCK* DY4 .... **67** L6
WOLVN WV10 .... **36** B3
WWCK CV34 .... **199** G8
Burns CI *KIDD* DY10 .... **137** M7
LICHS WS14 .... **20** F7
REDW B97 .... **196** A5
STRBR DY8 .... **101** L5
Burns Dr *BNTWD* WS7 .... **19** G6
Burns Gv *SEDG* DY3 .... **83** L1
Burnside *COVS* CV3 .... **155** L3
RUGBYS/DCH CV22 .... **183** J3
Burnside Gdns *DSYBK/YTR* WS5 ... **54** B7
Burnside Wy *NFLD/LBR* B31 .... **143** K6
Burns PI *DARL/WED* WS10 ...... **51** L8 🔟
Burns Rd *COVE* CV2 .... **154** F2
CRTAM B79 .... **31** L7
DARL/WED WS10 .... **51** L8
RLSN CV32 .... **200** F1
Burns St *CNCK/NC* WS11 .... **16** D1
Burns Wk *BDWTH* CV12 .... **117** G4
Burnthurst Crs *SOLH* B91 .... **147** L6
Burnt Meadow Rd *REDE* B98 ... **189** J7
Burnt Oak Dr *STRBR* DY8 .... **101** L8 🔟
Burnt Tree *TPTN/OCK* DY4 ...... **85** K3
Burntwood Rd *BNTWD* WS7 .... **27** H1
CNCK/NC WS11 .... **17** L2
Burrington Rd *RIDG/WDGT* B32 ... **122** E5
Burrowes St *WSLW* WS2 .... **53** H2
Burrow Hill CI *CBROM* B36 ..... **92** A5
Burrow Hill La
RCOVN/BALC/EX CV7 .... **115** H6
Burrows Rd *KGSWFD* DY6 ...... **101** K1
Burslem CI *BLOX/PEL* WS3 ...... **38** E1
Bursnips Rd *WNSFLD* WV11 ..... **38** A1
Burton Av *RUSH/SHEL* WS4 ..... **39** M6
Burton CI *COWV* CV5 .... **133** C4
CRTAM B79 .... **32** A6
Burton Crs *WOLVN* WV10 .... **3** J5
Burton Farm Rd
RUSH/SHEL WS4 .... **53** M2
Burton La *REDE* B98 .... **196** D2
Burton Old Rd *LICH* WS13 .... **21** K4
LICHS WS14 .... **21** K5
Burton Old Rd East *LICHS* WS14... **21** J5
Burton Old Rd West *LICH* WS13 ... **21** H5
Burton Rd *DUDN* DY1 .... **84** E2
LICH WS13 .... **21** K4
WOLVN WV10 .... **3** K2
Burton Wood Dr
BFLD/HDSWWD B20 .... **89** H3
Buryfield Rd *SOLH* B91 .... **127** L7
Bury Hill Rd *OLDBY* B69 .... **86** B6
Bury Rd *RLSS* CV31 .... **200** C6
Busby CI *COVS* CV3 .... **155** K6
Bush Av *SMTHWK* B66 .... **88** A8 🔟
Bushbery Av *TLHL/CAN* CV4 .... **152** D4
Bushbury Cft
CHWD/FDBR/MGN B37 .... **111** G2
Bushbury La *WOLVN* WV10 ..... **36** B7
Bushbury Rd *STETCH* B33 .... **91** L8
WOLVN WV10 .... **36** E7
Bush CI *TLHL/CAN* CV4 .... **152** D2
Bushell Dr *SOLH* B91 .... **148** B1
Bushey Fields Rd *DUDN* DY1 ... **84** C6 🔟
Bush Gv *BLOX/PEL* WS3 .... **39** L3
HDSW B21 .... **88** A4
Bushley CI *REDE* B98 .... **196** E6
Bushley Cft *SOLH* B91 .... **147** M5 🔟
Bushman Wy *BKDE/SHDE* B34 ... **92** C8
Bushmore Rd *HLGN/YWD* B28 ... **126** E7
Bush Rd *DUDS* DY2 .... **103** G3 🔟
TPTN/OCK DY4 .... **85** J1
Bush St *DARL/WED* WS10 .... **52** B6
Bushway CI *BRLYHL* DY5 .... **101** L3
Bushwood Dr *DOR/KN* B93 ..... **172** E2 🔟
Bushwood Rd *SLYOAK* B29 ..... **123** M4
Bustleholme Av
HHTH/SAND B71 .... **69** K4
Bustleholme Crs
HHTH/SAND B71 .... **69** J4 🔟
Bustleholme La
HHTH/SAND B71 .... **69** K3 🔟
Butcher's La *RRUGBY* CV23 ..... **157** K2
Butcher's La *COWV* CV5 .... **133** G7
HALE B63 .... **103** G6
Butchers Rd *HIA/OLT* B92 .... **129** L7 🔟
Butcroft Gdns
DARL/WED WS10 .... **52** C7 🔟
Bute CI *NFLD/LBR* B31 .... **123** J8
SHHTH WV12 .... **37** M7
Butler CI *KNWTH* CV8 .... **177** G6 🔟
Butler Rd *HIA/OLT* B92 .... **127** K4
Butlers CI *BFLD/HDSWWD* B20 ... **88** E2
ERDW/GRVHL B23 .... **72** B4

Butlers Crs
RCOVN/BALC/EX CV7 .... **116** E4
Butlers End *RWWCK/WEL* CV35 ... **190** A3
Butler's Hill La *REDW* B97 .... **187** M8
Butler St *WBROM* B70 .... **86** E1 🔟
Butlin Rd *COVN* CV6 .... **134** A1
Butlin St *VAUX/NECH* B7 .... **89** L6
Buttercup CI *DSYBK/YTR* WS5 ... **69** L2 🔟
Buttercup Dr *BRGRVE* B60 ...... **166** A7 🔟
Butterfield CI
DUNHL/THL/PER WV6 .... **48** B2 🔟
Butterfield Rd *BRLYHL* DY5 ..... **83** M6 🔟
Buttermere *TAM/AM/WIL* B77 ... **46** F6 🔟
Buttermere CI *NUN* CV11 .... **81** L7
Buttermere CI *BRLYHL* DY5 ..... **101** M6
CNCK/NC WS11 .... **155** K6 🔟
COVS CV3 .... **155** K6 🔟
DUNHL/THL/PER WV6 .... **35** H5
Buttermere Ct
DUNHL/THL/PER WV6 .... **48** D1 🔟
Buttermere Dr
RIDG/WDGT B32 .... **123** K2 🔟
WNSFLD WV11 .... **37** L3
Buttermere Gv *WNSFLD* WV11 ... **37** L3
Buttermere Rd *STRPT* DY13 .... **160** D7
Butterworth CI *BILS/COS* WV14 ... **66** E4
Butterworth Dr *TLHL/CAN* CV4 ... **152** E7
Buttery Rd *SMTHWK* B67 .... **87** J7
Butt La *COWV* CV5 .... **132** F6
Buttons Farm Rd
ETTPK/GDPK/PENN WV4 ...... **65** H2
Buttress Wy *SMTHWK* B66 ..... **87** L7
Butts *COV* CV1 .... **8** C6
Butts CI *CNCK/NC* WS11 .... **25** J1
Butts La *CNCK/NC* WS11 .... **25** J1
KIDD DY10 .... **162** C5
Butts Rd *COV* CV1 .... **8** C6
ETTPK/GDPK/PENN WV4 ...... **65** K1
RUSH/SHEL WS4 .... **53** K2
Butts St *RUSH/SHEL* WS4 .... **53** K2
The Butts *LICHS* WS14 .... **28** B3
RUSH/SHEL WS4 .... **53** K2
Buxton Av *POL/KGSB/FAZ* B78 ... **45** M5
Buxton CI *BLOX/PEL* WS3 .... **39** G2
Buxton Rd *BLOX/PEL* WS3 ...... **39** G2
DUDS DY2 .... **85** G7
ERDW/GRVHL B23 .... **71** M7
SCFLD/BOLD B73 .... **72** E4
Byfield CI *STETCH* B33 .... **110** C4
Byfield Rd *COVN* CV6 .... **133** J8
Byfleet CI
ETTPK/GDPK/PENN WV4 ...... **66** E2
Byford CI *REDE* B98 .... **196** C3
Byford St *NUNW/HART* CV10 ... **98** D1
Byland *TAM/AM/WIL* B77 .... **46** B2 🔟
Bylands CI *BRGRVW* B61 .... **185** J4
Byland Wy *BLOX/PEL* WS3 ...... **38** D3
By Pass Rd *TAM/AM/WIL* B77 ... **32** E8
Byrchen Moor Gdns
BRLYHL DY5 .... **83** M6 🔟
Byrne Rd *BKHL/PFLD* WV2 ...... **50** B6
Byron Av *AST/WIT* B6 .... **89** M2
BDWTH CV12 .... **117** H3 🔟
LICHS WS14 .... **20** F8
Byron CI *BNTWD* WS7 .... **18** D4
KIDD DY10 .... **137** M8
SMHTH B10 .... **108** B6 🔟
Byron Crs *DUDN* DY1 .... **66** F8
Byron Gdns *HHTH/SAND* B71 ... **68** F8
Byron PI *CNCK/NC* WS11 .... **12** D8
Byron Rd *CRTAM* B79 .... **31** L6
REDW B97 .... **196** B5
SHHTH WV12 .... **38** C6
SMHTH B10 .... **108** B6
WOLVN WV10 .... **36** E4
Byron St *BRLYHL* DY5 .... **84** B6
COV CV1 .... **9** G2
HHTH/SAND B71 .... **68** F8
Byron Wy *BRGRVW* B61 .... **165** L5
Bywater CI *COVS* CV3 .... **153** M8
Byways *BLOX/PEL* WS3 .... **39** G2

C

Caban CI *NFLD/LBR* B31 .... **123** J8
Cable Dr *WSLW* WS2 .... **39** G8
Cable St *BKHL/PFLD* WV2 .... **3** K9
Cabot Gv *DUNHL/THL/PER* WV6 ... **48** F1
Cadbury Dr *CVALE* B35 .... **91** K4
Cadbury Rd *MOS/BIL* B13 .... **125** M1
Cadbury Wy *HRBN* B17 .... **105** M8
Cadden Dr *TLHL/CAN* CV4 ...... **152** F3
Caddick Crs *HHTH/SAND* B71 ... **69** H6
Caddick Rd *PBAR/PBCH* B42 ... **70** F4
Caddick St *BILS/COS* WV14 ..... **67** L3
Cadgwith Gdns *BILS/COS* WV14 ... **67** L3
Cadine Gdns *MOS/BIL* B13 ..... **125** G4
Cadle Rd *WOLVN* WV10 .... **36** B6
Cadman CI *BDWTH* CV12 .... **117** G2 🔟
Cadman Crs *WOLVN* WV10 ..... **36** E7
Cadman's La *GTWY* WS6 .... **25** G5
Cadnam CI *HRBN* B17 .... **124** A2
WLNHL WV13 .... **51** M5
Cadogan Rd *TAM/AM/WIL* B77 ... **46** B8
Caen CI *RWWCK/WEL* CV35 ..... **198** E6
Caernarfon Dr *NUN* CV11 .... **99** H2
Caernarvon CI *SHHTH* WV12 ... **38** A6 🔟
Caernarvon Wy *DUDN* DY1 ...... **84** C3
Caesar Rd *KNWTH* CV8 .... **191** J2
Cairndhu Dr *KIDD* DY10 .... **137** L6
Cairn Dr *WSLW* WS2 .... **52** D3
Cairns St *WSLW* WS2 .... **53** G2
Caister *TAM/AM/WIL* B77 .... **32** E7
Caister Dr *WLNHL* WV13 .... **51** M5
Caistor CI *POL/KGSB/FAZ* B78 ... **44** F5
Caithness CI *COWV* CV5 .... **152** C1
Cakemore Rd *RMSLY* B62 .... **104** C3
Cala Dr *EDG* B15 .... **106** F6
Calcot Dr *DUNHL/THL/PER* WV6 ... **35** J6
Calcutt Wy *SHLY* B90 .... **146** E7

Caldecote Cl
  NUNW/HART CV10 .... 81 G5 🔲
Caldecote Gv *BORD* B9 .... 109 G4
Caldecote Rd *COVN* CV6 .... 134 A8
Caldeford Av *SHLY* B90 .... 147 L6
Calder *TAM/AM/WIL* B77 .... 46 F3
Calder Av *WSL* WS1 .... 5 J2
Calder Cl *BDWTH* CV12 .... 117 M3
  COVS CV3 .... 154 C6
Calder Dr *WALM/CURD* B76 .... 73 L5
Calderfields Cl
  RUSH/SHEL WS4 .... 53 L2 🔲
Calder Gv *BFLD/HDSWWD* B20 .... 88 D3
Calder Ri *DUDN* DY1 .... 66 D7
Calder Rd *STRPT* DY13 .... 160 C6
Calder Wk *RLSS* CV31 .... 201 G8
Caldmore Av *WSL* WS1 .... 4 E6
Caldmore Rd *WSL* WS1 .... 4 F4
Caldwall Crs *KIDDW* DY11 .... 137 H8
Caldwell Gv *SOLH* B91 .... 128 A8
Caldwell Rd *BORD* B9 .... 108 F2
  NUN CV11 .... 99 H4
Caldwell St *HHTH/SAND* B71 .... 69 H5
Caldy Wk *STRPT* DY13 .... 160 C7 🔲
Cale Cl *TAM/AM/WIL* B77 .... 46 A3
Caledonia *BRLYHL* DY5 .... 102 B6
Caledonian Cl *GTB/HAM* B43 .... 70 A2
Caledonia Rd *BKHL/PFLD* WV2 .... 3 J9
Caledonia St *BILS/COS* WV14 .... 51 J7 🔲
Caledon St *WSLW* WS2 .... 4 A7
Calewood Rd *BRLYHL* DY5 .... 102 B6
Californian Gv *BNTWD* WS7 .... 18 D5
California Rd *OLDBY* B69 .... 85 M5
California Wy *RIDG/WDGT* B32 .... 123 K2
Callaghan Gv *CNCK/NC* WS11 .... 17 G3 🔲
Callcott Dr *BRLYHL* DY5 .... 102 A6
Callear Rd *DARL/WED* WS10 .... 68 B4
Callendar Cl *NUN* CV11 .... 81 L6
Calley Cl *TPTN/OCK* DY4 .... 85 K2
Callowbridge Rd *RBRY* B45 .... 142 C6
Callowbrook La *RBRY* B45 .... 142 D6
Callow Hill La *REDW* B97 .... 195 K7
Callow Hill Rd *ALVE* B48 .... 167 K6
Callows La *KIDD* DY10 .... 137 J7 🔲
Calmere Cl *COVE* CV2 .... 135 K5
Calshot Rd *PBAR/PBCH* B42 .... 70 E5
Calstock Rd *SHHTH* WV12 .... 52 B1
Calthorpe Cl *DSYBK/YTR* WS5 .... 54 C7
Calthorpe Rd
  BFLD/HDSWWD B20 .... 89 G3
  DSYBK/YTR WS5 .... 54 B7
  EDG B15 .... 106 E5
Caludon Park Av *COVE* CV2 .... 135 L2
Caludon Rd *COVE* CV2 .... 154 E1
Calver Crs *WNSFLD* WV11 .... 37 K3
Calver Gv *KGSTG* B44 .... 71 H2
Calverley Rd *HWK/WKHTH* B38 .... 144 B4
Calverton Gv *GTB/HAM* B43 .... 70 C5
Calves Cft *WLNHL* WV13 .... 51 L2
Calvin Cl *WMBN* WV5 .... 64 D8
  WOLVN WV10 .... 36 B2
Calving Hl *CNCK/NC* WS11 .... 16 C3
Camberley Crs
  ETTPK/GDPK/PENN WV4 .... 66 C3
  SEDG DY3 .... 66 C3
Camberley Dr
  ETTPK/GDPK/PENN WV4 .... 65 L1 🔲
Camberley Rd *KGSWFD* DY6 .... 101 L1 🔲
Camberwell Ter *RLSS* CV31 .... 200 E6
Camborne Dr *NUN* CV11 .... 81 K8
Camborne Rd *DSYBK/YTR* WS5 .... 54 B8
Cambourne Rd
  BLKHTH/ROWR B65 .... 104 A2
Cambrai Dr *HLGN/YWD* B28 .... 126 C5 🔲
Cambria Cl *SHLY* B90 .... 146 C6
Cambrian *TAM/AM/WIL* B77 .... 46 D3
Cambria St *CNCK/NC* WS11 .... 16 A4
Cambridge Av *SCFLD/BOLD* B73 .... 72 F5
  SOLH B91 .... 147 J2
Cambridge Cl *ALDR* WS9 .... 40 E7
Cambridge Crs *EDG* B15 .... 107 H6 🔲
Cambridge Dr
  CHWD/FDBR/MGN B37 .... 110 D4
  NUNW/HART CV10 .... 98 B2
Cambridge Rd *DUDS* DY2 .... 84 E6
  MOS/BIL B13 .... 125 K4
  SMTHWK B66 .... 87 L6
Cambridge St *CBHAMW* B1 .... 6 D5
  COV CV1 .... 134 C8
  WBROM B70 .... 86 F3
  WOLVN WV10 .... 3 H1
  WSL WS1 .... 4 F1
Cambridge Wy *ACGN* B27 .... 127 L1
Camden Cl *CBROM* B36 .... 91 L5 🔲
  DSYBK/YTR WS5 .... 69 L1 🔲
Camden Dr *CBHAMW* B1 .... 6 B3
  TAM/AM/WIL B77 .... 46 C2
Camden St *ALDR* WS9 .... 40 C1
  CBHAMW B1 .... 6 C4
  COVE CV2 .... 154 E1
  WSL WS1 .... 4 D6
  WSNGN B18 .... 106 E1
Camden Wy *KGSWFD* DY6 .... 83 H4
Camellia Gdns *COVEN* WV9 .... 35 K2
Camelot Cl *CNCK/NC* WS11 .... 16 D1
Camelot Wy *SMTHH* B10 .... 108 A5
Cameo Dr *STRBR* DY8 .... 101 K5
  RLSN CV32 .... 200 E1
Cameron Cl *COVW* CV5 .... 132 E6
  RLSN CV32 .... 200 E1
Cameron Rd *RUSH/SHEL* WS4 .... 53 L2
Camford Gv
  ALE/KHTH/YWD B14 .... 145 K2
Cam Gdns *BRLYHL* DY5 .... 83 M7 🔲
Camhouses *TAM/AM/WIL* B77 .... 46 F4
Camino Rd *RIDG/WDGT* B32 .... 123 L2 🔲
Camomile Cl *DSYBK/YTR* WS5 .... 69 L2 🔲
  RUSH/SHEL WS4 .... 53 L2
Campbell Cl *CRTAM* B79 .... 31 K5 🔲
  RUSH/SHEL WS4 .... 53 L2
Campbell Pl *DARL/WED* WS10 .... 52 B7 🔲
Campbells Gn
  LGN/SDN/BHAMAIR B26 .... 109 M8
Campbell St *BRLYHL* DY5 .... 83 M7 🔲
  DUDS DY2 .... 85 H5 🔲
  RUGBYN/HIL CV21 .... 183 J2
Campden Rd *REDW* B97 .... 196 B7

Campden Gn *HIA/OLT* B92 .... 127 L2
Camp HI *BHTH/HG* B12 .... 107 L5
Camp Hill Dr *NUNW/HART* CV10 .... 80 B7
Camphill La *DARL/WED* WS10 .... 68 D3 🔲
Camp Hill Rd *NUNW/HART* CV10 .... 80 A6
Campian's Av *GTWY* WS6 .... 24 B3
Campion Cl *COVS* CV3 .... 154 B7
  DSYBK/YTR WS5 .... 69 L2 🔲
  WMBN WV5 .... 64 C7 🔲
Campion Dr *TAM/AM/WIL* B77 .... 46 A2
  WOLVN WV10 .... 22 E6
Campion Gn *RLSN* CV32 .... 200 E3 🔲
Campion Gv *HALE* B63 .... 121 H2
Campion Rd *RLSN* CV32 .... 200 E3
Campion Ter *RLSN* CV32 .... 200 E4
Camp La *HDSW* B21 .... 87 M3
  HWK/WKHTH B38 .... 144 D2
Camplea Cft
  CHWD/FDBR/MGN B37 .... 110 C3
Camplin Crs *BFLD/HDSWWD* B20 .... 70 C8
Camp Rd *MGN/WHC* B75 .... 43 H7
Campville Crs *HHTH/SAND* B71 .... 69 J4
Campville Gv
  CHWD/FDBR/MGN B37 .... 92 D8 🔲
Camp Wood Cl *SLYOAK* B29 .... 124 C5
Camrose Cft *BHTH/HG* B12 .... 107 J7
  BKDE/SHDE B34 .... 91 M7 🔲
Camrose Gdns *COVEN* WV9 .... 35 L2
Camsey La *BNTWD* WS7 .... 19 J5
Camville *COVS* CV3 .... 155 L3
Canal La *ERDE/BCHGN* B24 .... 90 E4
Canal Rd *COVN* CV6 .... 134 C5
  RWWCK/WEL CV35 .... 198 A3
Canal Side *ALVE* B48 .... 167 M3 🔲
  DUDS DY2 .... 103 J1
Canalside Cl *BLOX/PEL* WS3 .... 39 H3 🔲
  HHTH/SAND B71 .... 69 J3
Canal St *BRLYHL* DY5 .... 84 C8
  OLDBY B69 .... 86 D6
  STRBR DY8 .... 101 K7
Canary Cl *LOZ/NWT* B19 .... 89 G5 🔲
Canberra Rd *COVE* CV2 .... 135 L5
  DSYBK/YTR WS5 .... 54 A8
Canford Cl *BHTH/HG* B12 .... 107 K6 🔲
  COVS CV3 .... 178 A2
Canford Crs *CDSL* WV8 .... 34 C2
Canley Ford *COVW* CV5 .... 153 J6
Canley Rd *COVW* CV5 .... 153 J4
Cannel Rd *BNTWD* WS7 .... 18 D6
Canning Cl *DSYBK/YTR* WS5 .... 54 B7
Canning Gdns *WSNGN* B18 .... 106 C1 🔲
Canning Rd *DSYBK/YTR* WS5 .... 54 B7
  TAM/AM/WIL B77 .... 46 C1
Cannock Rd *BNTWD* WS7 .... 18 D6
  CNCK/NC WS11 .... 16 E1
  HEDN WS12 .... 17 L5
  PENK ST19 .... 10 D4
  SHHTH WV12 .... 38 A6
  WOLVN WV10 .... 3 H1
  WOLVN WV10 .... 36 D1
Cannocks La *TLHL/CAN* CV4 .... 153 H7
Cannock Wood Rd *HEDN* WS12 .... 13 M8
Cannock Wood St *HEDN* WS12 .... 13 L7
Cannon Cl *TLHL/CAN* CV4 .... 153 J7
Cannon Dr *BILS/COS* WV14 .... 67 G3
Cannon Hill Rd *BHTH/HG* B12 .... 107 H8
  TLHL/CAN CV4 .... 153 H7
Cannon Park Rd *TLHL/CAN* CV4 .... 153 J8
Cannon Rd *WMBN* WV5 .... 64 E7
Cannon St *CBHAM* B2 .... 7 G5 🔲
  WLNHL WV13 .... 51 M3
  WSLW WS2 .... 53 J1
Cannon St North *WSLW* WS2 .... 53 J1 🔲
Canon Dr *RCOVN/BALC/EX* CV7 .... 116 B7
Canon Hudson Cl *COVS* CV3 .... 155 G7 🔲
Canterbury Cl
  BLKHTH/ROWR B65 .... 104 C1 🔲
  BLOX/PEL WS3 .... 25 L8
  HHTH/SAND B71 .... 69 J5 🔲
Canterbury Dr *BNTWD* WS7 .... 19 H6
  CHWD/FDBR/MGN B37 .... 110 E6
  DUNHL/THL/PER WV6 .... 48 B1
Canterbury Rd
  BFLD/HDSWWD B20 .... 89 H4
  ETTPK/GDPK/PENN WV4 .... 49 H8
  HHTH/SAND B71 .... 69 H5
  KIDDW DY11 .... 136 D6
Canterbury St *COV* CV1 .... 9 J2
Canterbury Wy *CNCK/NC* WS11 .... 16 F4
  NUN CV11 .... 81 L5
Cantlow Cl *COVW* CV5 .... 152 E2
Cantlow Rd *MOS/BIL* B13 .... 125 L7 🔲
Canton La *WALM/CURD* B76 .... 75 L8
Canute Cl *WSL* WS1 .... 5 H7
Canvey Cl *RBRY* B45 .... 142 C4
Canwell Av
  CHWD/FDBR/MGN B37 .... 92 D8
Canwell Dr *MGN/WHC* B75 .... 43 L8
Canwell Gdns *BILS/COS* WV14 .... 66 F1
Capcroft Rd *MOS/BIL* B13 .... 125 M7
Cape HI *SMTHWK* B66 .... 105 M1
Capener Rd *GTB/HAM* B43 .... 70 E3
Capern Gv *RIDG/WDGT* B32 .... 105 K8
Cape Rd *WWCK* CV34 .... 199 H5
Cape St *WBROM* B70 .... 86 C1
  WSNGN B18 .... 106 B1
Capethorn Rd *SMTHWK* B66 .... 105 L2
Capilano Rd *ERDW/GRVHL* B23 .... 72 A6
Capmartin Rd *COVN* CV6 .... 133 M6
Capper's La *LICHS* WS14 .... 21 J5
Capponfield Cl *BILS/COS* WV14 .... 66 F2
Capstone Av *WOLVN* WV10 .... 35 M5
  WSNGN B18 .... 106 C1
Captain's Cl *BDMR/CCFT* WV3 .... 47 M5
Captains Pool Rd *KIDD* DY10 .... 161 L4
  KIDD DY10 .... 161 L3
Capulet Cl *COVS* CV3 .... 155 G7
  RUGBYS/DCH CV22 .... 183 J7
Caradoc *TAM/AM/WIL* B77 .... 46 E3
Caradoc Cl *COVE* CV2 .... 135 H6
Carcroft Rd *YDLY* B25 .... 109 G5

Cardale Cft *COVS* CV3 .... 155 K5
Cardale St *BLKHTH/ROWR* B65 .... 104 B3
Carden Cl *WBROM* B70 .... 86 D1
Carder Crs *BILS/COS* WV14 .... 67 H1
Carder Dr *BRLYHL* DY5 .... 102 A3
Cardiff Cl *BDMR/CCFT* WV3 .... 2 C8
Cardigan Dr *RUSH/SAND* B71 .... 69 G6
Cardigan Dr *SHHTH* WV12 .... 37 M7 🔲
Cardigan Pl *HEDN* WS12 .... 13 G8
Cardigan Rd *BDWTH* CV12 .... 116 A4
Cardigan St *CBHAMNE* B4 .... 7 K3
Cardinal Crs *BRGRVW* B61 .... 185 H4
Cardinal Dr *KIDD* DY10 .... 161 M2
Cardinal Wy *CNCK/NC* WS11 .... 16 B3
Carding Cl *COVW* CV5 .... 152 D1
Cardington Av *PBAR/PBCH* B42 .... 70 F4
Cardoness Pl *DUDN* DY1 .... 84 D3 🔲
Cardy Cl *REDW* B97 .... 195 L1
Careless Gn *HAG/WOL* DY9 .... 120 D1
Carey *TAM/AM/WIL* B77 .... 46 E8
Carey St *COVN* CV6 .... 134 F4
Carfax *CNCK/NC* WS11 .... 16 C5
Cargill Cl *COVN* CV6 .... 116 D8
Carhampton Rd *MGN/WHC* B75 .... 57 L7
Carisbroke *TAM/AM/WIL* B77 .... 46 E3
Carisbrooke Av
  CHWD/FDBR/MGN B37 .... 111 G3
Carisbrooke Cl
  DARL/WED WS10 .... 69 J3 🔲
Carisbrooke Ct
  DUNHL/THL/PER WV6 .... 48 E2 🔲
Carisbrooke Crs
  DARL/WED WS10 .... 69 J2
Carisbrooke Dr *RMSLY* B62 .... 122 B2 🔲
Carisbrooke Gdns
  WOLVN WV10 .... 36 C2 🔲
Carisbrooke Rd
  DARL/WED WS10 .... 69 H3
  DUNHL/THL/PER WV6 .... 48 E2
  HRBN B17 .... 105 M4
  WOLVN WV10 .... 36 C2
Carisbrook Rd
  NUNW/HART CV10 .... 81 H7
Carlcroft *TAM/AM/WIL* B77 .... 46 F3
Carless Av *HRBN* B17 .... 105 M6
Carless St *WSL* WS1 .... 4 F6
Carlisle Cl *CNCK/NC* WS11 .... 15 M6
Carlisle St *WSNGN* B18 .... 88 C8
Carl St *WSLW* WS2 .... 39 H8
Carlton Av *BILS/COS* WV14 .... 51 K6 🔲
  FOAKS/STRLY B74 .... 55 J3
  HAG/WOL DY9 .... 120 C2
  HDSW B21 .... 88 B4 🔲
  WNSFLD WV11 .... 36 E6
Carlton Cl *BDWTH* CV12 .... 117 M2 🔲
  DUDN DY1 .... 67 G7
  HEDN WS12 .... 17 H4
  KIDDW DY11 .... 136 E5
  MGN/WHC B75 .... 57 H6
  REDW B97 .... 195 M4
Carlton Crs *BNTWD* WS7 .... 18 E5
  CRTAM B79 .... 31 K5
Carlton Cft *FOAKS/STRLY* B74 .... 55 L3
Carlton Ms *CBROM* B36 .... 92 B5 🔲
Carlton Rd *BDMR/CCFT* WV3 .... 49 L6
  BORD B9 .... 108 B4
  COVN CV6 .... 134 D4
  RUGBYS/DCH CV22 .... 183 H4
  SMTHWK B66 .... 87 L5
Carlyle Av *KIDD* DY10 .... 137 M7
Carlyle Gv *WOLVN* WV10 .... 36 E5
Carlyle Rd *BLKHTH/ROWR* B65 .... 104 A3
  BRGRVW B60 .... 185 M5
  LDYWD/EDGR B16 .... 106 C4
  LOZ/NWT B19 .... 89 G5
  WOLVN WV10 .... 36 D5
Carlyon Rd *ATHST* CV9 .... 63 K5
Carmel Cl *HEDN* WS12 .... 13 C8 🔲
Carmel Gv *RIDG/WDGT* B32 .... 122 F4
Carmelite Rd *COV* CV1 .... 9 K5
Carmichael Cl *LICHS* WS14 .... 21 H6 🔲
Carmodale Av *PBAR/PBCH* B42 .... 70 F7
Carnbroe Av *COVS* CV3 .... 155 K6
Carnegie Av *TPTN/OCK* DY4 .... 85 L1
Carnegie Cl *COVS* CV3 .... 154 F8
Carnegie Dr *DARL/WED* WS10 .... 68 E2 🔲
Carnegie Rd
  BLKHTH/ROWR B65 .... 103 M3
Carnford Rd
  LGN/SDN/BHAMAIR B26 .... 109 M7
Carnforth Cl *KGSWFD* DY6 .... 82 F6
Carnforth Rd *BRGRVW* B60 .... 185 M4
Carnoustie *TAM/AM/WIL* B77 .... 32 F8
Carnoustie Cl *BLOX/PEL* WS3 .... 38 E2 🔲
  BRGRVW B61 .... 185 H5 🔲
  MGN/WHC B75 .... 57 H5
Carnwath Rd *SCFLD/BOLD* B73 .... 72 C3
Carol Av *BRGRVW* B61 .... 185 H2
Carol Crs *HALE* B63 .... 103 K8
  WNSFLD WV11 .... 37 J7
Caroline Cl *NUN* CV11 .... 99 K6
Caroline Rd *MOS/BIL* B13 .... 125 K1 🔲
Caroline St *CBHAMW* B1 .... 6 D2
  DUDS DY2 .... 85 J4
  WBROM B70 .... 86 F3
Carpenter Rd *EDG* B15 .... 106 F6
Carpenter's Rd *LOZ/NWT* B19 .... 89 G6
Carpet Trades Wy *KIDDW* DY11 .... 137 H6
Carrick Cl *BLOX/PEL* WS3 .... 25 L8
Carriers Cl *WSLW* WS2 .... 52 D4
Carrington Rd *DARL/WED* WS10 .... 69 H3
Carroway Head HI
  MGN/WHC B75 .... 58 A1
Carrs La *CBHAMNE* B4 .... 7 H5
Carsal Cl *RCOVN/BALC/EX* CV7 .... 116 B8
Carshalton Rd *KGSTG* B44 .... 71 L3
Cartbridge Crs *BLOX/PEL* WS3 .... 39 K7
Cartbridge La *RUSH/SHEL* WS4 .... 39 L8
Cartbridge La South
  RUSH/SHEL WS4 .... 39 L8
Carter Av *CDSL* WV8 .... 34 F2
  KIDDW DY11 .... 160 F1
Carter Rd *COVS* CV3 .... 154 E5
  DUNHL/THL/PER WV6 .... 35 M8
  GTB/HAM B43 .... 70 D3
Carters Cl *BRGRVW* B60 .... 185 H6
  WALM/CURD B76 .... 73 K2

Cartersfield La *ALDR* WS9 .... 27 H7
Carter's Gn *WBROM* B70 .... 86 F1
Carters Hurst *STETCH* B33 .... 109 M4 🔲
Carter's La *RMSLY* B62 .... 104 D8
Carthorse La *REDW* B97 .... 187 M8
Carthusian Rd *COVS* CV3 .... 154 A5
Cartland Rd *BVILLE* B30 .... 124 F6
  SPARK B11 .... 108 A2
Cartmel Cl *COVW* CV5 .... 152 E1 🔲
Cart's La *ATHST* CV9 .... 62 A3
The Cartway
  DUNHL/THL/PER WV6 .... 48 B1 🔲
Cartwright Gdns *OLDBY* B69 .... 86 A3 🔲
Cartwright Rd *MGN/WHC* B75 .... 57 G2
Cartwright St *BKHL/PFLD* WV2 .... 3 G9
Carvell Cl *COVW* CV5 .... 132 F4
Carver Cl *COVE* CV2 .... 155 J3
Carver Gdns *STRBR* DY8 .... 119 J3
Carver St *WSNGN* B18 .... 6 A2
Cascade Cl *COVS* CV3 .... 154 C7
Casewell Rd *KGSWFD* DY6 .... 83 C5
Casey Av *ERDW/GRVHL* B23 .... 72 B5
Cash Joynson Av
  DARL/WED WS10 .... 52 A5 🔲
Cashmore Av *RLSS* CV31 .... 200 D8
Cashmore Rd *BDWTH* CV12 .... 116 C4
  KNWTH CV8 .... 192 A1
Cash's La *COV* CV1 .... 134 B7
Casia Gv *KNWTH* CV8 .... 192 A1
Caslon Crs *STRBR* DY8 .... 119 H1
Caslon Rd *HALE* B63 .... 103 G7 🔲
Caspian Wy *COVE* CV2 .... 135 L5 🔲
Cassandra Cl *BRLYHL* DY5 .... 84 A3 🔲
  TLHL/CAN CV4 .... 177 H2 🔲
Cassowary Rd
  BFLD/HDSWWD B20 .... 88 D2 🔲
Castello Dr *CBROM* B36 .... 92 B4
Castlebridge Rd *WNSFLD* WV11 .... 37 L6 🔲
Castle Cl *BRWNH* WS8 .... 26 D3
  CDYHTH B64 .... 103 M4
  COVS CV3 .... 154 D1
  HIA/OLT B92 .... 127 M4
  RCOVN/BALC/EX CV7 .... 114 C3
  TAM/AM/WIL B77 .... 46 A1
  WWCK CV34 .... 199 J7 🔲
Castle Crs *CBROM* B36 .... 92 A5
Castlecroft *CNCK/NC* WS11 .... 17 J8
Castle Cft *LGLYGN/QTN* B68 .... 105 H5 🔲
Castlecroft Av *BDMR/CCFT* WV3 .... 48 C5
Castlecroft Gdns
  BDMR/CCFT WV3 .... 48 E5 🔲
Castlecroft La *BDMR/CCFT* WV3 .... 48 D5
  BILS/COS WV14 .... 51 J6
Castleditch La *REDE* B98 .... 196 C6 🔲
Castle Dr *CSHL/WTROR* B46 .... 93 K8
  NUNW/HART CV10 .... 97 J6
  SHHTH WV12 .... 37 M8 🔲
Castle Dyke *LICH* WS13 .... 20 F6 🔲
Castleford Rd *SPARK* B11 .... 126 A1
Castleford Rd *ALDR* WS9 .... 40 E2
Castle Gv *STRBR* DY8 .... 119 M2 🔲
Castle Hts *CDYHTH* B64 .... 103 M5 🔲
Castle HI *DUDN* DY1 .... 85 H3
  KNWTH CV8 .... 176 C8
Castlehill Rd *ALDR* WS9 .... 41 G2
Castlehills Dr *CBROM* B36 .... 91 L5
Castle La *BEWD* DY12 .... 160 A2
  CSHL/WTROR B46 .... 94 D5
  HIA/OLT B92 .... 127 K4
  WWCK CV34 .... 199 J7 🔲
Castle Ms *RUGBYN/HIL* CV21 .... 183 M2 🔲
Castle Mill Rd *DUDN* DY1 .... 85 G1
Castle Rd *ALDR* WS9 .... 40 E3
  KIDD DY10 .... 137 L1
  KIDDW DY11 .... 137 H8
  KNWTH CV8 .... 191 J1
  NUNW/HART CV10 .... 79 M4
  NUNW/HART CV10 .... 81 G6
  SLYOAK B29 .... 123 L3
  TAM/AM/WIL B77 .... 46 B1
  TPTN/OCK DY4 .... 85 H1
Castle Rd East
  LGLYGN/QTN B68 .... 105 H5
Castle Rd West
  LGLYGN/QTN B68 .... 105 G5
Castle St *BILS/COS* WV14 .... 67 J3
  BRWNH WS8 .... 26 D3
  COV CV1 .... 9 J2
  DARL/WED WS10 .... 52 B5
  DUDN DY1 .... 85 H4
  RUGBYN/HIL CV21 .... 183 L2
  SEDG DY3 .... 66 B5
  TPTN/OCK DY4 .... 67 J8
  WBROM B70 .... 68 E6
  WOLV WV1 .... 3 G5
Castleton Cl *BLOX/PEL* WS3 .... 39 C2
  PBAR/PBCH B42 .... 71 H6
Castleton St *DUDS* DY2 .... 85 G8 🔲
Castle Vw *DUDN* DY1 .... 84 F3
  NUNW/HART CV10 .... 79 M4
  TAM/AM/WIL B77 .... 46 A2
Castle View Cl *DARL/WED* WS10 .... 67 L1
Castle View Rd *DARL/WED* WS10 .... 67 L1
Caswell Rd *RLSS* CV31 .... 200 F1
  SEDG DY3 .... 66 A5
Cat And Kittens La *WOLVN* WV10 .... 22 C7
Cater Dr *WALM/CURD* B76 .... 73 K3
Caterham Dr *STRBR* DY8 .... 101 K2
Catesby Dr *KGSWFD* DY6 .... 83 H5
Catesby Rd *COVN* CV6 .... 133 M5
  SHLY B90 .... 146 F4
Cateswell Rd *HLGN/YWD* B28 .... 126 D4
Cathcart Rd *STRBR* DY8 .... 101 J8
Cathedral Av *KIDDW* DY11 .... 136 F7
Cathedral Cl *LICH* WS13 .... 20 F7
Cathedral Ri *LICH* WS13 .... 20 E5 🔲
Cathel Dr *PBAR/PBCH* B42 .... 70 E6
Catherine De Barnes La
  HIA/OLT B92 .... 129 G7
Catherine Dr *SCFLD/BOLD* B73 .... 56 F7
Catherine Rd *BILS/COS* WV14 .... 66 E4
Catherines Cl *SOLH* B91 .... 148 F1 🔲
Catherine St *AST/WIT* B6 .... 89 L6 🔲
  COV CV1 .... 9 L3
Catherton Cl *TPTN/OCK* DY4 .... 68 A3
Cathiron La *RRUGBY* CV23 .... 157 K2

  RRUGBY CV23 .... 158 F4
Catholic La *SEDG* DY3 .... 66 A6
Catisfield Cl *CDSL* WV8 .... 35 K4
Cat La *BKDE/SHDE* B34 .... 91 M6
Cato St *BDMR/CCFT* WV3 .... 126 E6
Cato St North *VAUX/NECH* B7 .... 107 M1
Cato St North *VAUX/NECH* B7 .... 90 A7
Catsbridge La *CNCK/NC* WS11 .... 15 L4
Catshill Rd *BRWNH* WS8 .... 26 E6
Cattell Dr *MGN/WHC* B75 .... 57 M8
Cattell Rd *BORD* B9 .... 108 A4
  WWCK CV34 .... 199 J6
Cattells Gv *VAUX/NECH* B7 .... 90 A7
Cattermole Gv *GTB/HAM* B43 .... 71 G2
Cattock Hurst Dr
  CSCFLD/WYGN B72 .... 73 H6 🔲
Causeway *BLKHTH/ROWR* B65 .... 104 A3
Causeway Green Rd
  LGLYGN/QTN B68 .... 104 E2
Causeway Rd *BILS/COS* WV14 .... 67 H5 🔲
The Causeway *YDLY* B25 .... 109 H8
Causey Farm Rd *HALE* B63 .... 121 G5
Cavalier Circ *WOLVN* WV10 .... 36 C1
Cavalier Cl *NUN* CV11 .... 99 J4
Cavandale Av *KGSTG* B44 .... 71 J4
Cavan's Cl *CNCK/NC* WS11 .... 16 C1
Cavans Wy *COVS* CV3 .... 155 L5
Cavell Rd *DUDS* DY2 .... 85 K4 🔲
Cavendish Cl *BRGRVE* B60 .... 166 A4 🔲
  HWK/WKHTH B38 .... 144 F4 🔲
  KGSWFD DY6 .... 101 H1
Cavendish Dr *HAG/WOL* DY9 .... 139 K1
  KIDD DY10 .... 137 M6
Cavendish Gdns *WSLW* WS2 .... 52 E1 🔲
Cavendish Rd
  LDYWD/EDGR B16 .... 106 B2
  RMSLY B62 .... 122 D1
  TLHL/CAN CV4 .... 152 C3
  WOLV WV1 .... 50 F4
  WSLW WS2 .... 38 E8
Cavendish Wy *ALDR* WS9 .... 40 F8
Caversham Cl *NUN* CV11 .... 81 K6 🔲
Caversham Rd *KGSTG* B44 .... 71 L3
Cawdon Gv *DOR/KN* B93 .... 172 C3
Cawdor Crs *LDYWD/EDGR* B16 .... 106 D4
Cawnpore Rd *COVN* CV6 .... 133 M3
Cawston La *RUGBYS/DCH* CV22 .... 182 E6
Cawston Wy
  RUGBYS/DCH CV22 .... 183 G5 🔲
Cawthorne Cl *COV* CV1 .... 9 K1
Caxton Gv *KGSTG* B44 .... 72 A4 🔲
Caxton St *CNCK/NC* WS11 .... 16 C5
Caynham Cl *REDE* B98 .... 197 H1
Caynham Rd *RIDG/WDGT* B32 .... 122 F5
Cayton Gv *ERDW/GRVHL* B23 .... 72 D7
Cecil Dr *OLDBY* B69 .... 86 B3
Cecil Rd *ERDE/BCHGN* B24 .... 90 D2
  SLYOAK B29 .... 125 G4
Cecil St *CBHAMNE* B4 .... 7 G1
  CNCK/NC WS11 .... 16 D1
  RUSH/SHEL WS4 .... 53 K2
  STRBR DY8 .... 101 K8
Cecily Rd *COVS* CV3 .... 154 B6
Cedar Av *BILS/COS* WV14 .... 66 E6
  BRWNH WS8 .... 26 E5
  CBROM B36 .... 92 A4
Cedar Bridge Cft
  FOAKS/STRLY B74 .... 56 E5
Cedar Cl *BNTWD* WS7 .... 18 E7
  BVILLE B30 .... 124 B7
  DSYBK/YTR WS5 .... 69 M1
  HEDN WS12 .... 12 E4
  LGLYGN/QTN B68 .... 105 C5 🔲
  LICHS WS14 .... 21 K6
  POL/KGSB/FAZ B78 .... 60 B7 🔲
  RLSN CV32 .... 200 E1
  STRBR DY8 .... 119 H3 🔲
Cedar Crs *KIDDW* DY11 .... 137 G7
Cedar Dr *BRGRVE* B60 .... 185 L4
  CRTAM B79 .... 31 L5
  ERDE/BCHGN B24 .... 73 C8
  FOAKS/STRLY B74 .... 55 J4
  KIDDW DY11 .... 137 G6
Cedar Gv *BDMR/CCFT* WV3 .... 49 K6
  CDSL WV8 .... 34 F2 🔲
  GTWY WS6 .... 24 F1
  HAG/WOL DY9 .... 119 L7 🔲
  WWCK CV34 .... 199 J4
Cedarhill Dr *CNCK/NC* WS11 .... 16 D3 🔲
Cedarhurst *RIDG/WDGT* B32 .... 105 L8
  SOLH B91 .... 148 A2 🔲
Cedar Park Rd *REDW* B97 .... 196 B1
  SHHTH WV12 .... 38 A4
Cedar Rd *BNTWD* WS7 .... 18 E7
  BVILLE B30 .... 124 C7
  DARL/WED WS10 .... 52 A1
  DUDN DY1 .... 84 F2 🔲
  NUNW/HART CV10 .... 80 B7
  REDW B97 .... 196 A1
  TPTN/OCK DY4 .... 67 H8 🔲
  WLNHL WV13 .... 51 J3
Cedars Av *ACGN* B27 .... 127 G1
  COVN CV6 .... 133 J8
  KGSWFD DY6 .... 101 H1
  WMBN WV5 .... 64 A5
Cedars Rd *RCOVN/BALC/EX* CV7 .... 116 F4
The Cedars *YDLY* B25 .... 109 J4
Cedar Ter *BRGRVE* B60 .... 185 L4 🔲
Cedar Vw *REDW* B97 .... 196 A1
Cedar Wy *NFLD/LBR* B31 .... 143 K4 🔲
  WNSFLD WV11 .... 37 C6
Cedarwood *FOAKS/STRLY* B74 .... 56 F5 🔲
Cedarwood Cft *PBAR/PBCH* B42 .... 70 D5
Cedar Wood Dr
  RCOVN/BALC/EX CV7 .... 150 F7
Cedar Wood Rd *SEDG* DY3 .... 84 A1
Cedric Cl *COVS* CV3 .... 155 G8
Celandine *CNCK/NC* WS11 .... 16 C2
Celandine Cl *STRBR* DY8 .... 101 G1
Celandine Rd *COVE* CV2 .... 135 H3 🔲
  DUDN DY1 .... 84 E1 🔲
The Celandines *WMBN* WV5 .... 64 C4
Celbury Wy *GTB/HAM* B43 .... 70 B5 🔲
Celtic Rd *CNCK/NC* WS11 .... 16 C2
Celts Cl *BLKHTH/ROWR* B65 .... 104 A1
Cemetery La *NUNW/HART* CV10 .... 79 M4
  WSNGN B18 .... 88 E5

Cemetery Rd CNCK/NC WS11 ..... 16 B1
 HAG/WOL DY9 ..... 102 B8
 LGLYGN/QTN B68 ..... 87 C7
 REDW B97 ..... 196 B2
 SMTHWKW B67 ..... 105 K1
 WLNHL WV13 ..... 51 L2
 WSLW WS2 ..... 52 D5
Cemetery St BILS/COS WV14 ..... 51 C6
 GTWY WS6 ..... 24 A3
Cemetery Wy BLOX/PEL WS3 ..... 38 F4
Centaur Rd COVW CV5 ..... 153 K3
Centenary Cl NFLD/LBR B31 ..... 143 L4
Centenary Dr HDSW B21 ..... 88 C4
Centenary Rd TLHL/CAN CV4 ..... 153 H6
Centenary Wy CSHL/WTROR B46 ..... 77 K8
 KNWTH CV8 ..... 176 E4
 NUNW/HART CV10 ..... 98 E4
 RLSS CV31 ..... 200 B6
 WALM/CURD B76 ..... 75 M1
 WWCK CV34 ..... 199 J6
Centenrary Wy COVS CV3 ..... 156 C3
Central Av BILS/COS WV14 ..... 51 J8
 BLKHTH/ROWR B65 ..... 104 A3
 CNCK/NC WS11 ..... 12 D8
 COVE CV2 ..... 155 H1
 HAG/WOL DY9 ..... 120 C2
 NFLD/LBR B31 ..... 143 K5
 NUN CV11 ..... 80 F8
 RLSS CV31 ..... 200 D1
 TPTN/OCK DY4 ..... 67 K6
Central Cl BLOX/PEL WS3 ..... 38 E4
Central Dr BILS/COS WV14 ..... 67 H6
 BLOX/PEL WS3 ..... 38 D5
 SEDG DY3 ..... 84 A3
Central Gv ACGN B27 ..... 127 G3
Central Rd BRGRVW B60 ..... 185 L4
Central Wy BRLYHL DY5 ..... 102 C2
Centre La HALE B63 ..... 121 M2
The Centreway
 ALE/KHTH/YWD B14 ..... 146 B1
Centurion Cl CSHL/WTROR B46 ..... 93 J4
Centurion Wy TAM/AM/WIL B77 ..... 46 F1
Century Pk BORD B9 ..... 108 A3
Century Rd OLDBY B69 ..... 86 E5
Ceolmund Crs
 CHWD/FDBR/MGN B37 ..... 110 F2
Chace Av COVS CV3 ..... 154 F8
Chaceley Cl COVE CV2 ..... 135 L5
Chaceley Gv
 ERDW/GRVHL B23 ..... 72 B6
Chadbury Cft SOLH B91 ..... 147 M5
Chadbury Rd HALE B63 ..... 122 K2
Chadcote Wy BRGRVW B61 ..... 165 K4
Chaddersley Cl RBRY B45 ..... 142 D5
Chaddesley Cl OLDBY B69 ..... 86 B8
 REDE B98 ..... 196 D4
Chaddesley Dr
 HAG/WOL DY9 ..... 119 M4
Chaddesley Rd HALE B63 ..... 121 K3
 HWK/WKHTH B38 ..... 144 B3
 KIDD DY10 ..... 137 L8
Chadley Cl SOLH B91 ..... 127 L7
Chad Rd DUDN DY1 ..... 66 F6
 EDG B15 ..... 106 D5
Chad's Ditch HEDN WS12 ..... 12 C3
Chadshunt Cl CBROM B36 ..... 92 B3
Chadsmoor Ter VAUX/NECH B7 ..... 89 M7
Chadstone Cl SHLY B90 ..... 147 M4
Chadswell Hts LICH WS13 ..... 21 H2
 LICH WS13 ..... 21 H3
Chad Valley Cl HRBN B17 ..... 106 B7
Chadwell Dr HIA/OLT B92 ..... 126 F7
Chadwell Gdns CDSL WV8 ..... 34 D1
Chadwich La HAG/WOL DY9 ..... 141 J7
Chadwick Av RBRY B45 ..... 142 F7
Chadwick Cl COVW CV5 ..... 152 F2
 ETTPK/GDPK/PENN WV4 ..... 49 C7
Chadwick La DOR/KN B93 ..... 173 M3
Chadwick Ms DOR/KN B93 ..... 173 M7
Chadwick Rd MGN/WHC B75 ..... 57 K8
Chadwick Ms REDE B98 ..... 196 E6
Chaffcombe Rd
 LGN/SDN/BHAMAIR B26 ..... 110 A7
Chaffinch Cl HEDN WS12 ..... 16 F2
 SEDG DY3 ..... 66 A3
Chaffinch Dr CBROM B36 ..... 92 F6
 KIDD DY10 ..... 161 K3
Chaffinch Rd HAG/WOL DY9 ..... 120 B2
Chainmakers Ct BILS/COS WV14 ..... 67 C2
Chain Wk LOZ/NWT B19 ..... 89 H5
Chalcot Dr HEDN WS12 ..... 12 D6
Chalcot Gv BFLD/HDSWWD B20 ..... 70 C8
Chaldon Cl COVEN WV9 ..... 35 L5
Chale Gv ALE/KHTH/YWD B14 ..... 145 L2
Chalfield CRTAM B79 ..... 31 H7
Chalfont Av CNCK/NC WS11 ..... 16 A5
Chalfont Cl BDWTH CV12 ..... 116 E1
 COVW CV5 ..... 152 F1
Chalfont Pl HAG/WOL DY9 ..... 120 C3
Chalford Rd
 ERDW/GRVHL B23 ..... 72 A5
Chalford Wy SHLY B90 ..... 147 H4
Chalgrove Av HWK/WKHTH B38 ..... 144 C4
Chalgrove Crs SOLH B91 ..... 147 M4
Challenge Cl COV CV1 ..... 9 G1
Challenge Wy WOLVN WV10 ..... 36 C8
Challenor Av WLNHL WV13 ..... 51 H3
Chalybeate Cl RBRY B45 ..... 142 D4
Chamberlain Cl OLDBY B69 ..... 86 B3
 RLSN CV32 ..... 193 J8
Chamberlain Ct MOS/BIL B13 ..... 125 J4
Chamberlain Crs SHLY B90 ..... 146 E3
Chamberlaine St BDWTH CV12 ..... 116 F1
Chamberlain Rd MOS/BIL B13 ..... 125 K7
Chamberlain's La
 ETTPK/GDPK/PENN WV4 ..... 65 J2
Chance Cft LGLYGN/QTN B68 ..... 104 F5
Chance Flds RLSS CV31 ..... 201 K7
Chancellor's Cl EDG B15 ..... 106 C5
 TLHL/CAN CV4 ..... 177 H1
Chancel Wy RMSLY B62 ..... 104 A8
Chancery Dr HEDN WS12 ..... 13 G6
Chancery La NUNW/HART CV10 ..... 79 M6
Chancery Wy BRLYHL DY5 ..... 102 D3
Chanders Rd WWCK CV34 ..... 199 H4
Chandler Dr
 ETTPK/GDPK/PENN WV4 ..... 65 H2

Chandlers Cl COVEN WV9 ..... 35 L4
 REDW B97 ..... 196 B7
Chandlers Dr TAM/AM/WIL B77 ..... 32 F8
Chandlers Keep BRWNH 26 D7
Chandos St COVE CV2 ..... 154 E2
 NUN CV11 ..... 98 E1
 RLSN CV32 ..... 200 D4
Change Brook Cl NUN CV11 ..... 81 K5
Channon Dr BRLYHL DY5 ..... 102 B5
Chanston Av
 ALE/KHTH/YWD B14 ..... 145 J1
Chanterelle Gdns
 ETTPK/GDPK/PENN WV4 ..... 65 L1
Chantrey Crs BILS/COS WV14 ..... 51 K6
 GTB/HAM B43 ..... 71 H1
The Chantries COV CV1 ..... 9 K1
Chantry Av BLOX/PEL WS3 ..... 39 H5
Chantry Cl HLYWD B47 ..... 145 L6
Chantry Dr RMSLY B62 ..... 104 E7
Chantry Heath Crs
 DOR/KN B93 ..... 148 F5
Chantry Rd HDSW B21 ..... 88 D5
 KINVER DY7 ..... 101 C6
 MOS/BIL B13 ..... 125 J1
The Chantry WWCK CV34 ..... 199 L4
Chapel Ash WOLV WV1 ..... 2 C5
Chapel Ash Island WOLV WV1 ..... 2 D5
Chapel Av BRWNH WS8 ..... 26 C3
Chapel Cl CDYHTH B64 ..... 103 M5
 WMBN WV5 ..... 64 D8
Chapel Ct KIDD DY10 ..... 137 L4
Chapel Dr BRWNH WS8 ..... 26 C3
 HLYWD B47 ..... 169 K2
 RCOVN/BALC/EX CV7 ..... 150 F7
Chapel Farm Cl COVS CV3 ..... 155 G7
Chapelfield Rd RBRY B45 ..... 142 E5
Chapel Fields Rd HIA/OLT B92 ..... 127 K3
Chapel Gn WLNHL WV13 ..... 51 M3
Chapel Hl KIDD DY10 ..... 137 L4
Chapel House La HALE B63 ..... 103 C8
Chapelhouse Rd
 CHWD/FDBR/MGN B37 ..... 110 D3
Chapel House St BHTH/HG B12 ..... 7 K7
Chapel La ALVE B48 ..... 188 D1
 CDSL WV8 ..... 34 C2
 GTB/HAM B43 ..... 70 D1
 HAG/WOL DY9 ..... 141 H6
 HLYWD B47 ..... 169 J3
 HOCK/TIA B94 ..... 173 G6
 KNWTH CV8 ..... 179 L3
 LICHS WS14 ..... 20 F7
 RCOVN/BALC/EX CV7 ..... 117 M7
 REDE B98 ..... 189 K5
 RMSLY B62 ..... 121 G7
 RUGE WS15 ..... 18 E1
 SEDG DY3 ..... 82 A1
 SLYOAK B29 ..... 123 H3
Chapel Rw WWCK CV34 ..... 199 J6
Chapel Sq GTWY WS6 ..... 24 B2
Chapel St BDWTH CV12 ..... 116 F2
 BILS/COS WV14 ..... 67 K1
 BKHL/PFLD WV2 ..... 50 B6
 BLOX/PEL WS3 ..... 39 K2
 BLOX/PEL WS3 ..... 39 H5
 BNTWD WS7 ..... 18 B5
 BRGRVE B60 ..... 185 L3
 BRLYHL DY5 ..... 84 A6
 BRLYHL DY5 ..... 102 B3
 BRLYHL DY5 ..... 102 D4
 BRWNH WS8 ..... 26 C3
 CBHAMNE B4 ..... 7 J4
 CNCK/NC WS11 ..... 17 K8
 COV CV1 ..... 8 E3
 DARL/WED WS10 ..... 68 C2
 DUDS DY2 ..... 103 H1
 HAG/WOL DY9 ..... 102 C8
 HAG/WOL DY9 ..... 119 L8
 HALE B63 ..... 121 L2
 HDSW B21 ..... 88 B6
 HEDN WS12 ..... 17 J4
 KGSWFD DY6 ..... 82 F5
 KIDDW DY11 ..... 137 H7
 NUN CV11 ..... 99 G8
 OLDBY B69 ..... 86 C6
 REDW B97 ..... 196 B4
 RLSS CV31 ..... 200 E6
 RRUGBY CV23 ..... 182 E1
 RUGBYN/HIL CV21 ..... 183 L2
 STRBR DY8 ..... 119 L1
 STRBR DY8 ..... 119 L1
 TPTN/OCK DY4 ..... 67 J8
 WBROM B70 ..... 68 F8
 WMBN WV5 ..... 64 D8
 WWCK CV34 ..... 199 J6
Chapel Wk SMTHWKW B67 ..... 105 K1
Chapel Wk BRGRVE B60 ..... 185 L3
 BVILLE B30 ..... 144 E2
 SEDG DY3 ..... 84 A3
Chapelwood Gv
 PBAR/PBCH B42 ..... 71 H8
Chaplain Rd HEDN WS12 ..... 17 J3
Chapman Cl RLSS CV31 ..... 201 J8
Chapman Rd SMTH B10 ..... 108 A5
Chapman's Hi BRGRVW B61 ..... 141 M5
Chapmans Pas CBHAMW B1 ..... 6 E7
Chapman St WBROM B70 ..... 86 F2
Chard Rd COVS CV3 ..... 155 H5
Charfield Cl BVILLE B30 ..... 124 B6
Charford Rd BRGRVE B60 ..... 185 K5
Charingworth Dr
 RWWCK/WEL CV35 ..... 198 D1
Charingworth Rd HIA/OLT B92 ..... 128 A3
Charity Rd
 RCOVN/BALC/EX CV7 ..... 115 K6
Charlbury Av
 CHWD/FDBR/MGN B37 ..... 110 D3
Charlbury Crs
 LGN/SDN/BHAMAIR B26 ..... 109 K5
Charlbury Ms RLSS CV31 ..... 201 G7
Charlecote Cft SHLY B90 ..... 147 G5
Charlecote Dr DUDN DY1 ..... 84 C2
 ERDW/GRVHL B23 ..... 72 C6
Charlecote Gdns RLSS CV31 ..... 201 H8
 SCFLD/BOLD B73 ..... 72 E5
Charlecote Ri WLNHL WV13 ..... 51 K5
Charlecote Rd COVN CV6 ..... 133 L3
Charlecote Wk NUN CV11 ..... 99 K5

Charlecott Cl MOS/BIL B13 ..... 126 B6
Charlemont Av HHTH/SAND B71 ..... 69 K5
Charlemont Cl DSYBK/YTR WS5 ..... 54 A7
Charlemont Crs
 HHTH/SAND B71 ..... 69 J5
Charlemonte Cl HEDN WS12 ..... 17 H2
Charlemont Gdns
 DSYBK/YTR WS5 ..... 53 M7
Charlemont Rd HHTH/SAND B71 ..... 69 J5
Charles Av BLKHTH/ROWR B65 ..... 104 A1
 ETTPK/GDPK/PENN WV4 ..... 49 M8
 KIDD DY10 ..... 137 L4
 WNSFLD WV11 ..... 37 K1
Charles Cl GTWY WS6 ..... 24 B4
 WASH/WDE B8 ..... 108 B1
Charles Crs BLOX/PEL WS3 ..... 25 L8
Charles Dr VAUX/NECH B7 ..... 89 M7
Charles Eaton Rd BDWTH CV12 ..... 116 D2
Charles Edward Rd
 LGN/SDN/BHAMAIR B26 ..... 109 H7
Charlesfield Rd
 RUGBYS/DCH CV22 ..... 183 L5
Charles Foster St
 DARL/WED WS10 ..... 52 A7
Charles Gardner Rd
 RLSS CV31 ..... 200 E7
Charles Henry St DIG/EDG B5 ..... 107 J5
Charles Holland St WLNHL WV13 ..... 51 M3
Charles Rd AST/WIT B6 ..... 89 L4
 ATHST CV9 ..... 63 K6
 BFLD/HDSWWD B20 ..... 89 C4
 BRLYHL DY5 ..... 102 E4
 HALE B63 ..... 121 K1
 SMHTH B10 ..... 108 C5
 SOLH B91 ..... 147 J3
 STRBR DY8 ..... 119 J1
 TPTN/OCK DY4 ..... 67 L6
Charles St ATHST CV9 ..... 61 G8
 COV CV1 ..... 9 L2
 KIDD DY10 ..... 137 K7
 NUN CV11 ..... 80 E8
 RCOVN/BALC/EX CV7 ..... 96 E5
 REDW B97 ..... 196 A4
 RUGBYS/DCH CV22 ..... 183 K3
 WBROM B66 ..... 88 A6
 WBROM B70 ..... 68 C8
 WLNHL WV13 ..... 52 A2
 WSLW WS2 ..... 4 C3
 WWCK CV34 ..... 199 L5
Charles Wk
 BLKHTH/ROWR B65 ..... 86 A8
Charles Warren Cl
 RUGBYN/HIL CV21 ..... 183 M2
Charleswoth Av SHLY B90 ..... 147 M7
Charleville Rd LOZ/NWT B19 ..... 88 F6
Charlewood Rd COVN CV6 ..... 133 M3
Charlock Gv HEDN WS12 ..... 17 C2
Charlotte Cl TPTN/OCK DY4 ..... 85 L3
Charlotte Rd BVILLE B30 ..... 124 E7
 DARL/WED WS10 ..... 68 A4
 EDG B15 ..... 107 C5
Charlotte St CBHAMNW B3 ..... 6 D4
 DUDN DY1 ..... 84 F5
 RLSS CV31 ..... 200 D7
 RUGBYN/HIL CV21 ..... 183 M2
 WSL WS1 ..... 5 J2
Charlton Rd KGSTG B44 ..... 71 L6
Charlton St BRLYHL DY5 ..... 101 L2
 DUDN DY1 ..... 84 F4
Charminster Av YDLY B25 ..... 109 H5
Charminster Dr COVS CV3 ..... 178 B1
Charnley Dr MGN/WHC B75 ..... 57 J3
Charnwood Av
 NUNW/HART CV10 ..... 98 B3
 SEDG DY3 ..... 66 A3
Charnwood Cl BILS/COS WV14 ..... 67 M2
 BRLYHL DY5 ..... 101 M6
 HEDN WS12 ..... 17 G2
 LICH WS13 ..... 21 C4
 RBRY B45 ..... 142 F2
Charnwood Ct
 HAG/WOL DY9 ..... 120 C3
Charnwood Dr
 NUNW/HART CV10 ..... 79 L3
Charnwood Rd
 DSYBK/YTR WS5 ..... 69 L1
 PBAR/PBCH B42 ..... 70 D6
Charnwood Wy RLSN CV32 ..... 201 G2
Charter Appoach
 WWCK CV34 ..... 199 H7
 WWCK CV34 ..... 199 H8
Charter Av TLHL/CAN CV4 ..... 152 B6
Charter Cl CNCK/NC WS11 ..... 25 J1
Charter Crs CDYHTH B64 ..... 103 M5
Charterfield Dr HEDN WS12 ..... 17 C4
 KGSWFD DY6 ..... 83 G1
Charterhouse Dr SOLH B91 ..... 147 M4
Charterhouse Rd COV CV1 ..... 9 K5
Charter Rd TPTN/OCK DY4 ..... 68 A4
Charters Av CDSL WV8 ..... 34 F4
The Charters LICH WS13 ..... 20 F4
Charter St BRLYHL DY5 ..... 84 C8
Chartist Rd WASH/WDE B8 ..... 90 B7
Chartley Cl DOR/KN B93 ..... 172 C2
 DUNHL/THL/PER WV6 ..... 48 D1
Chartley Rd ERDW/GRVHL B23 ..... 90 A4
 HHTH/SAND B71 ..... 69 H7
The Chartway BLOX/PEL WS3 ..... 39 M1
Chartwell CRTAM B79 ..... 31 H6
Chartwell Cl DUDN DY1 ..... 66 F7
 NUN CV11 ..... 99 K4
Chartwell Dr FOAKS/STRLY B74 ..... 56 B1
 SHLY B90 ..... 147 H8
 WMBN WV5 ..... 64 D8
 WOLVN WV10 ..... 36 C4
Chase Av GTWY WS6 ..... 24 C2
Chase Gv ERDE/BCHGN B24 ..... 73 H7
Chaselands BNTWD WS7 ..... 18 B6
Chase La KNWTH CV8 ..... 175 K7
Chaseley Av CNCK/NC WS11 ..... 16 A3
Chaseley Cft CNCK/NC WS11 ..... 15 M3
Chaseley Gdns BNTWD WS7 ..... 19 C6
Chasepool Rd SEDG DY3 ..... 82 A6
Chase Rd BLOX/PEL WS3 ..... 38 G5
 BNTWD WS7 ..... 18 E8
 BRWNH WS8 ..... 26 E4

 SEDG DY3 ..... 83 M4
Chaseside Dr HEDN WS12 ..... 16 F2
The Chase DUNHL/THL/PER WV6 ..... 35 M7
 WALM/CURD B76 ..... 73 H6
Chase V BNTWD WS7 ..... 18 C7
Chase Vw
 ETTPK/GDPK/PENN WV4 ..... 66 C3
Chasewater Wy CNCK/NC WS11 ..... 17 K8
Chater Dr WALM/CURD B76 ..... 73 L4
Chaters Cl TPTN/OCK DY4 ..... 68 A4
Chatham Cl COVS CV3 ..... 155 G5
Chatham Rd NFLD/LBR B31 ..... 143 L2
Chatsworth Av GTB/HAM B43 ..... 70 A4
Chatsworth Cl
 CSCFLD/WYGN B72 ..... 73 H6
 SHHTH WV12 ..... 37 M8
 SHLY B90 ..... 147 H8
Chatsworth Dr NUN CV11 ..... 99 K3
Chatsworth Gdns RLSS CV31 ..... 201 H7
 RLSS CV31 ..... 201 H7
Chatsworth Ri COVS CV3 ..... 154 C8
Chatsworth Rd CDYHTH B64 ..... 103 L6
Chattaway Dr
 RCOVN/BALC/EX CV7 ..... 150 F7
Chattaway St VAUX/NECH B7 ..... 90 A6
Chattle Hl CSHL/WTROR B46 ..... 93 J3
Chattock Av SOLH B91 ..... 148 C1
Chattock Cl CBROM B36 ..... 91 J6
Chatwell Gv SLYOAK B29 ..... 123 M3
Chatwin Pl BILS/COS WV14 ..... 67 J2
Chatwin St SMTHWK B66 ..... 87 K6
Chatwins Whf TPTN/OCK DY4 ..... 67 K8
Chaucer Av SEDG DY3 ..... 65 L8
 SHHTH WV12 ..... 38 C5
 TPTN/OCK DY4 ..... 67 M5
Chaucer Cl BILS/COS WV14 ..... 67 J2
 CRTAM B79 ..... 31 L7
 ERDW/GRVHL B23 ..... 89 M2
 LICHS WS14 ..... 20 F7
 STRBR DY8 ..... 101 L5
Chaucer Crs KIDD DY10 ..... 138 A7
Chaucer Dr BNTWD WS7 ..... 18 E4
 NUNW/HART CV10 ..... 97 L1
Chaucer Gv ACGN B27 ..... 126 F3
 BRGRVE B60 ..... 185 M5
 RUGBYS/DCH CV22 ..... 183 K7
Chauntry Pl COV CV1 ..... 9 G3
Chauson Gv SOLH B91 ..... 147 L5
Chavasse Rd CSCFLD/WYGN B72 ..... 73 G2
Chawner Cl BNTWD WS7 ..... 18 C4
Chawn Hl HAG/WOL DY9 ..... 120 A2
Chawnhill Cl HAG/WOL DY9 ..... 120 A2
Chawn Park Dr HAG/WOL DY9 ..... 120 A2
Chaynes Gv STETCH B33 ..... 110 B3
Chaytor Rd POL/KGSB/FAZ B78 ..... 47 L5
Cheadle Cl COVN CV6 ..... 134 E1
 PENK ST19 ..... 10 D6
Cheadle Dr ERDW/GRVHL B23 ..... 72 B5
Cheam Cl COVN CV6 ..... 134 E4
Cheam Gdns
 DUNHL/THL/PER WV6 ..... 35 J2
Cheapside BHTH/HG B12 ..... 7 J8
 DIG/EDG B5 ..... 7 J8
 WLNHL WV13 ..... 51 L4
Cheatham St VAUX/NECH B7 ..... 90 A7
Checketts St WSLW WS2 ..... 4 B2
Checkley Cft
 WALM/CURD B76 ..... 73 K5
Cheddar Rd BHTH/HG B12 ..... 107 J7
Chedworth Cl REDE B98 ..... 189 C7
Chedworth Cl REDE B98 ..... 189 G8
 SLYOAK B29 ..... 123 M7
Cheedon Cl DOR/KN B93 ..... 172 C3
Chelford Cl PENK ST19 ..... 10 E4
Chelford Crs KGSWFD DY6 ..... 101 L2
Chell Cl PENK ST19 ..... 10 D6
Chells Gv MOS/BIL B13 ..... 125 M8
Chelmar Cl CBROM B36 ..... 92 D5
Chelmar Dr BRLYHL DY5 ..... 83 L7
Chelmarsh Av BDMR/CCFT WV3 ..... 48 E4
Chelmarsh Cl REDE B98 ..... 189 G6
Chelmorton Rd PBAR/PBCH B42 ..... 71 G5
Chelmscote Rd HIA/OLT B92 ..... 127 K4
Chelmsley Av
 CSHL/WTROR B46 ..... 93 K7
Chelmsley Cir
 CHWD/FDBR/MGN B37 ..... 110 D5
Chelmsley Gv STETCH B33 ..... 110 C2
Chelmsley La
 CHWD/FDBR/MGN B37 ..... 110 D5
Chelmsley Rd
 CHWD/FDBR/MGN B37 ..... 110 E2
Chelney Wk COVS CV3 ..... 155 L4
Chelsea Cl NUN CV11 ..... 81 K6
 RIDG/WDGT B32 ..... 123 K1
Chelsea Dr FOAKS/STRLY B74 ..... 56 G7
Chelsea Wy KGSWFD DY6 ..... 83 G7
Chelston Dr
 DUNHL/THL/PER WV6 ..... 35 K6
Chelston Rd NFLD/LBR B31 ..... 143 J1
Cheltenham Cft COVE CV2 ..... 135 K6
Cheltenham Dr CBROM B36 ..... 91 H5
 KGSWFD DY6 ..... 82 F7
Chelthorn Wy SOLH B91 ..... 148 A3
Cheltondale Rd SOLH B91 ..... 127 K7
Chelveston Crs SOLH B91 ..... 147 M4
Chelveston Rd COVN CV6 ..... 133 J3
Chelwood Dr
 ETTPK/GDPK/PENN WV4 ..... 50 F8
Chelwood Gv COVE CV2 ..... 135 K4
Chelworth Rd
 HWK/WKHTH B38 ..... 144 F3
Chem Rd BILS/COS WV14 ..... 50 F8
Chenies Cl COVW CV5 ..... 152 C2
Cheniston Rd SHHTH WV12 ..... 37 M2
Chepstow Cl COVS CV3 ..... 155 G8
 DUNHL/THL/PER WV6 ..... 48 D1
Chepstow Gv RBRY B45 ..... 142 F7
Chepstow Rd BLOX/PEL WS3 ..... 38 D8
 WOLVN WV10 ..... 22 B8
Chequerfield Dr
 BDMR/CCFT WV3 ..... 49 L7
Chequers Av WMBN WV5 ..... 64 E4
Chequers Ct CNCK/NC WS11 ..... 17 L8

Chequer St BDMR/CCFT WV3 ..... 49 L7
Cherhill Covert BVILLE B30 ..... 145 G3
Cherington Cl REDE B98 ..... 197 K4
Cherington Rd SLYOAK B29 ..... 124 C5
Cheriton Cl COVW CV5 ..... 153 H1
Cheriton Gv
 DUNHL/THL/PER WV6 ..... 48 C2
Cherrington Cl DR GTWY WV6 ..... 24 D1
Cherrington Gdns
 DUNHL/THL/PER WV6 ..... 48 F3
 HAG/WOL DY9 ..... 120 A5
Cherrington Wy SOLH B91 ..... 147 M4
Cherry Bank HEDN WS12 ..... 13 G7
Cherrybrook Dr REDE ST19 ..... 10 D4
Cherrybrook Wy COVE CV2 ..... 135 G4
Cherry Cl ATHST CV9 ..... 77 G1
 BNTWD WS7 ..... 18 D7
 COVN CV6 ..... 134 B3
Cherry Crs BRGRVW B61 ..... 185 J3
 ERDE/BCHGN B24 ..... 90 D2
Cherry Dr BORD B9 ..... 107 M4
Cherry Gn DUDN DY1 ..... 84 D1
Cherry Gv RUGBYS/DCH CV22 ..... 183 J5
 SMTHWK B66 ..... 88 B3
 STRBR DY8 ..... 119 J1
Cherry Hill Av RBRY B45 ..... 167 G5
Cherry Hill Dr RBRY B45 ..... 167 G5
Cherry Hill Rd RBRY B45 ..... 167 G5
Cherry La DARL/WED WS10 ..... 68 E3
 RWWCK/WEL CV35 ..... 198 D7
 SCFLD/BOLD B73 ..... 72 E6
 SEDG DY3 ..... 82 F2
Cherry Lea BKDE/SHDE B34 ..... 91 M7
Cherry Orch CDYHTH B64 ..... 103 K4
 KIDD DY10 ..... 137 K7
 KNWTH CV8 ..... 176 E8
 LICHS WS14 ..... 21 G6
Cherry Orchard Av HALE B63 ..... 103 K8
Cherry Orchard Crs
 HALE B63 ..... 103 K7
Cherry Orchard Dr
 BRGRVW B61 ..... 185 J2
Cherry Orchard Rd
 BFLD/HDSWWD B20 ..... 70 D8
Cherry Pit La REDE B98 ..... 189 L3
Cherry Rd TPTN/OCK DY4 ..... 67 K6
Cherry St BDMR/CCFT WV3 ..... 2 G5
 CBHAM B2 ..... 7 G5
 CRTAM B79 ..... 31 M8
 HALE B63 ..... 103 K8
 STRBR DY8 ..... 119 J1
 WWCK CV34 ..... 199 L5
Cherry Tree Av DSYBK/YTR WS5 ..... 69 L3
 NUNW/HART CV10 ..... 80 C7
Cherrytree Ct HAG/WOL DY9 ..... 120 C4
Cherry Tree Gdns CDSL WV8 ..... 34 F2
Cherry Tree La CDSL WV8 ..... 34 F2
 HALE B63 ..... 121 H4
Cherry Tree Rd CNCK/NC WS11 ..... 25 M1
 HEDN WS12 ..... 12 B5
 KGSWFD DY6 ..... 83 J5
Cherry Tree Wk CRTAM B79 ..... 31 L5
 REDW B97 ..... 195 M1
Cherry Wk HLYWD B47 ..... 145 M8
Cherry Wy KNWTH CV8 ..... 176 E8
Cherrywood Crs SOLH B91 ..... 148 A5
Cherrywood Gn BILS/COS WV14 ..... 51 K1
Cherrywood Gv COVW CV5 ..... 132 B3
Cherrywood Rd BORD B9 ..... 108 B3
 FOAKS/STRLY B74 ..... 55 L4
Cherrywood Wy
 FOAKS/STRLY B74 ..... 56 B1
Chervil Cl PBAR/PBCH B42 ..... 71 G6
Chervil Ri WOLVN WV10 ..... 3 L2
Cherwell Dr BRWNH WS8 ..... 25 M3
 CBROM B36 ..... 92 D5
Cherwell Wy RRUGBY CV23 ..... 182 F1
Chesford Br KNWTH CV8 ..... 192 K5
Chesford Crs COVN CV6 ..... 134 F3
 WWCK CV34 ..... 199 M5
Chesham St RLSS CV31 ..... 200 F6
Cheshire Av SHLY B90 ..... 146 E3
Cheshire Cl
 RUGBYS/DCH CV22 ..... 183 G5
 STRBR DY8 ..... 101 H5
Cheshire Gv
 DUNHL/THL/PER WV6 ..... 48 C1
 KIDDW DY11 ..... 136 E6
Cheshire Rd AST/WIT B6 ..... 89 L3
 SMTHWKW B67 ..... 105 L1
 WSLW WS2 ..... 52 D3
Chesholme Rd COVN CV6 ..... 133 M2
The Chesils COVS CV3 ..... 154 A7
Cheslyn Dr GTWY WS6 ..... 24 B3
Chessetts Gv MOS/BIL B13 ..... 125 L7
Chessetts Wood Rd
 HOCK/TIA B94 ..... 173 G5
Chester Av DUNHL/THL/PER WV6 ..... 35 K6
Chester Cl
 CHWD/FDBR/MGN B37 ..... 110 E3
 CNCK/NC WS11 ..... 16 F4
 LICH WS13 ..... 21 G2
 WLNHL WV13 ..... 52 B3
Chesterfield Cl NFLD/LBR B31 ..... 143 M3
Chesterfield Rd LICHS WS14 ..... 20 E5
Chestergate ERDE/BCHGN B24 ..... 91 H1
Chester Pl WSLW WS2 ..... 52 F4
Chester Ri LGLYGN/QTN B68 ..... 105 G5
Chester Rd ALDR WS9 ..... 41 J4
 BRWNH WS8 ..... 26 E1
 CBROM B36 ..... 91 L5
 CBROM B36 ..... 92 D6
 CDYHTH B64 ..... 103 G5
 CHWD/FDBR/MGN B37 ..... 110 F1
 CSHL/WTROR B46 ..... 111 J4
 CVALE B35 ..... 91 K2
 DUDS DY2 ..... 103 H3
 ERDE/BCHGN B24 ..... 91 J1
 ERDW/GRVHL B23 ..... 55 L5
 FOAKS/STRLY B74 ..... 55 L5
 HHTH/SAND B71 ..... 68 C2
 LICHS WS14 ..... 30 B2
 RCOVN/BALC/EX CV7 ..... 129 M1
 SCFLD/BOLD B73 ..... 72 B4
Chester Rd North BRWNH WS8 ..... 26 B4
 FOAKS/STRLY B74 ..... 55 L7

KIDD DY10......137 L5
SCFLD/BOLD B73......55 L8
Chester Rd South KIDD DY10......161 K2
Chester St AST/WIT B6......89 K8
COV CV1......8 C3
DUNHL/THL/PER WV6......2 C1
Chesterton Av
BHTH/HG B12......107 M8 ②
Chesterton Cl SOLH B91......127 J8 ②
Chesterton Dr
NUNW/HART CV10......97 K1
RLSS CV31......200 F8
Chesterton Rd BHTH/HG B12......107 L8
COVN CV6......133 L5
WOLVN WV10......36 E5
Chesterton Wy CRTAM B79......31 L6
HLYWD B47......145 L7
Chesterwood Gdns
BFLD/HDSWWD B20......89 H3 ②
Chesterwood Rd MOS/BIL B13......125 K7
Chestnut Av CRTAM B79......31 M6
DUDN DY1......85 G2
KNWTH CV8......191 K2
TPTN/OCK DY4......67 K6
Chestnut Cl CDSL WV8......34 D3 ②
CNCK/NC WS11......17 G3 ②
FOAKS/STRLY B74......55 L3
HIA/OLT B92......127 H5
POL/KGSB/FAZ B78......60 B7 ②
STRBR DY8......119 G2 ②
Chestnut Ct CBROM B36......92 C6
Chestnut Crs NUNW/HART CV10......80 C8
Chestnut Dr CBROM B36......91 L5
ERDE/BCHGN B24......91 G1
GTWY WS6......24 B2
LICHS WS14......28 D8
RBRY B45......167 C1
RUSH/SHEL WS4......39 M5
WMBN WV5......64 E8 ②
Chestnut Fld
RUGBYN/HIL CV21......183 L2
Chestnut Gv CSHL/WTROR B46......93 L6
KGSWFD DY6......83 K7
KIDDW DY11......136 F5
KNWTH CV8......180 E2 ②
PENK ST19......10 C4
TLHL/CAN CV4......152 E3 ②
Chestnut Pl BLOX/PEL WS3......39 H7
Chestnut Rd BDWTH CV12......117 H1
BLOX/PEL WS3......39 J7
BRGRVW B61......185 K1
DARL/WED WS10......68 C3
LGLYGN/QTN B68......105 C6
MOS/BIL B13......125 L1
Chestnuts Av
LGN/SDN/BHAMAIR B26......109 M6
The Chestnuts BDWTH CV12......116 C3 ②
Chestnut Tree Av
TLHL/CAN CV4......152 E3 ②
Chestnut Wy BDMR/CCFT WV3......49 H5
Chestom Rd BILS/COS WV14......50 F6
Cheston Rd VAUX/NECH B7......89 L7
Cheswell Cl
DUNHL/THL/PER WV6......48 F3
Cheswick Cl COVN CV6......134 E6 ②
REDE B98......197 L2
WLNHL WV13......51 K5 ②
Cheswick Wy SHLY B90......171 H2 ②
Cheswood Dr WALM/CURD B76......73 M7
Chesworth Rd BRGRVE B60......185 M4
Chetland Cft HIA/OLT B92......128 D6 ②
Chettle Rd BILS/COS WV14......67 K2 ②
Chetwode Cl COVW CV5......152 F1
Chetwood Cl
DUNHL/THL/PER WV6......35 L8 ②
WSLW WS2......52 A2
Chetwynd Dr NUN CV11......99 M6
Chetwynd Pk HEDN WS12......13 L8
Chetwynd Rd BKHL/PFLD WV2......49 M7
POL/KGSB/FAZ B78......47 L5
WASH/WDE B8......90 F4
Cheveley Av RBRY B45......142 F6
Chevening Cl SEDG DY3......66 C6 ②
Cheveral Av COVN CV6......133 M7
Cheveral Rd BDWTH CV12......116 E2
Cheverel Pl NUN CV11......98 F2
Cheverel St NUN CV11......98 F2
Cheveridge Cl SOLH B91......147 L4
Cheverton Rd NFLD/LBR B31......143 J2 ②
Cheviot TAM/AM/WIL B77......47 C4
Cheviot Cl NUNW/HART CV10......97 M2
Cheviot Ri HEDN WS12......17 C1
RLSN CV32......201 G2 ②
Cheviot Rd BKHL/PFLD WV2......50 D6
STRBR DY8......101 L7 ②
Cheviot Wy HALE B63......121 H2
Cheylesmore COV CV1......8 F6
Cheylesmore Cl
SCFLD/BOLD B73......72 F1 ②
Cheyne Gdns
HLGN/YWD B28......146 C2 ②
Cheyne Wk BRLYHL DY5......102 A6 ②
Cheyney Cl
DUNHL/THL/PER WV6......35 L8
Chichester Av DUDS DY2......85 H8
KIDDW DY11......137 C4
Chichester Cl NUN CV11......81 L6 ②
Chichester Dr CNCK/NC WS11......17 C4
RIDG/WDGT B32......104 E8
Chichester Gv
CHWD/FDBR/MGN B37......110 F4
Chichester La
RWWCK/WEL CV35......198 C7
Chideock Hl COVS CV3......153 L7
Chiel Cl COVW CV5......152 D1
Chigwell Cl CVALE B35......91 L2
Chilcote Cl HLGN/YWD B28......146 D1
Childs Av BILS/COS WV14......66 E3
Childs Oak Cl
RCOVN/BALC/EX CV7......150 C1
Chilgrove Gdns
DUNHL/THL/PER WV6......35 C8
Chilham Dr
CHWD/FDBR/MGN B37......111 C3
Chillaton Rd COVN CV6......133 M3
Chillingham TAM/AM/WIL B77......46 A6 ②

Chillinghome Rd CBROM B36......91 J5 ②
Chillington Cl GTWY WS6......24 C4
Chillington Dr CDSL WV8......34 D1
DUDN DY1......84 D2
Chillington Flds WOLV WV1......50 L4
Chillington Pl BILS/COS WV14......51 C8 ②
Chillington Rd TPTN/OCK DY4......68 A4 ②
Chillington St WOLV WV1......3 L8
Chiltern Cl HALE B63......121 C3
SEDG DY3......84 B2 ②
Chiltern Dr WLNHL WV13......51 H4
Chiltern Leys COVN CV6......8 A1
Chiltern Rd STRBR DY8......101 M7
TAM/AM/WIL B77......47 C4
The Chilterns COVW CV5......152 F1 ②
Chilton Rd ALE/KHTH/YWD B14......146 B1
Chilwell Cl SOLH B91......147 M4
Chilwell Cft LOZ/NWT B19......89 J7
Chilworth Av WNSFLD WV11......37 K6
Chilworth Cl AST/WIT B6......89 K7 ②
NUN CV11......99 J5
Chimes Cl STETCH B33......110 C4
Chingford Cl STRBR DY8......101 L1 ②
Chingford Rd COVN CV6......134 E1
KGSTG B44......71 L5
Chinley Gv KGSTG B44......72 A4
Chinn Brook Rd MOS/BIL B13......125 M8
Chip Cl HWK/WKHTH B38......144 B3
Chipperfield Rd CBROM B36......91 J5
Chipstead Rd ERDW/GRVHL B23......72 B6
Chipstone Cl SOLH B91......148 A5
Chirbury Gv NFLD/LBR B31......143 M4 ②
Chirk Cl KIDDW DY11......161 J5 ②
Chirton Gv ALE/KHTH/YWD B14......125 H7
Chiseldon Cft
ALE/KHTH/YWD B14......145 L2 ②
Chisholm Gv ACGN B27......127 C5 ②
Chiswell Rd WSNGN B18......106 C1
Chivington Cl SHLY B90......147 M7 ②
Chorley Av BKDE/SHDE B34......91 K6
Chorley Gdns BILS/COS WV14......50 F8 ②
Chorley Rd BNTWD WS7......18 D4 ②
Choyce Cl ATHST CV9......63 H3
Christchurch Cl EDG B15......106 C5
Christ Church Gdns LICH WS13......20 D6
Christ Church Gv WSL WS1......5 K8 ②
Christchurch La LICH WS13......20 D6
Christchurch Rd COVN CV6......133 K7
Christine Cl DARL/WED WS10......68 A3
Christopher Rd BKHL/PFLD WV2......3 J9
RMSLY B62......122 C2 ②
SLYOAK B29......124 A3 ②
Chub TAM/AM/WIL B77......46 B6 ②
Chubb St WOLV WV1......3 H4 ②
Chuckery Rd WSL WS1......5 J3
Chudleigh Gv GTB/HAM B43......70 B5
Chudleigh Rd ERDW/GRVHL B23......90 C1
Church Av HAG/WOL DY9......140 C3
STRBR DY8......101 L6
Churchbridge OLDBY B69......86 D7
Church Cl ATHST CV9......61 G4
CHWD/FDBR/MGN B37......92 E7
HLYWD B47......169 K2
KNWTH CV8......179 M3 ②
LICHS WS14......28 D8
NUNW/HART CV10......79 M5
POL/KGSB/FAZ B78......45 J8
RCOVN/BALC/EX CV7......96 C3
RRUGBY CV23......158 F2
Church Cft HALE B63......121 L1
HRBN B17......105 L7
Church Cross Vw BRLYHL DY5......84 B5
Churchdale Cl
NUNW/HART CV10......98 A1
Churchdale Rd KGSTG B44......71 H2
Church Down Cl REDW B97......196 B7
Church Dr BVILLE B30......124 F6
POL/KGSB/FAZ B78......30 F6
Church End RLSS CV31......201 J7
Churchfield Av TPTN/OCK DY4......67 K5
Churchfield Cl COVEN WV9......22 A3
VAUX/NECH B7......90 A7 ②
Churchfield Rd WOLVN WV10......35 M5
Churchfields BRGRVW B61......185 K3
KIDD DY10......137 J6
Churchfields Gdns
BRGRVW B61......185 K2 ②
Churchfields Rd BRGRVW B61......185 K2
DARL/WED WS10......68 D2
Church St DUDS DY2......85 C5 ②
Church Gdns WOLVN WV10......50 E1 ②
BILS/COS WV14......51 C5
Church Gn BFLD/HDSWWD B20......88 D3
BILS/COS WV14......51 C5
Church Gn East REDW B97......196 C1
Church Gn West REDW B97......196 C1
Church Gv MOS/BIL B13......126 A8
Church Hl BRLYHL DY5......102 B3
CSHL/WTROR B46......93 L6
DARL/WED WS10......68 D2 ②
ETTPK/GDPK/PENN WV4......65 J1
HAG/WOL DY9......140 B7
HEDN WS12......13 C8
NFLD/LBR B31......143 L2
REDE B98......189 G5
RIDG/WDGT B32......122 E8
RLSN CV32......193 J8
RLSN CV32......200 C5
RRUGBY CV23......180 D8
WSL WS1......5 G3
Church Hill Cl SOLH B91......148 A3
Church Hill Rd
BFLD/HDSWWD B20......88 F4
DUNHL/THL/PER WV6......35 H7
SOLH B91......148 A3
Church Hill St SMTHWKW B67......87 K7
Church Hill Wy REDE B98......189 G8
Churchill Av COVN CV6......134 C4
KNWTH CV8......176 E7 ②
Churchill Cl OLDBY B69......86 A3 ②
Churchill Dr
BLKHTH/ROWR B65......103 M3 ②
STRBR DY8......101 L6
Churchill Gdns SEDG DY3......66 A6 ②
Churchill La KIDD DY10......138 F3
Churchill Pl STETCH B33......109 M4
Churchill Rd BORD B9......108 D2

BRGRVW B61......165 L4
HALE B63......121 K3
LICHS WS14......28 E8
MGN/WHC B75......57 L8
RUGBYS/DCH CV22......183 L4
SCFLD/BOLD B73......72 A3
WSLW WS2......52 C1
Church La ALDR WS9......41 J1
AST/WIT B6......89 L5
ATHST CV9......63 M1
BFLD/HDSWWD B20......88 D3
BKHL/PFLD WV2......2 E7
BNTWD WS7......27 H1
BRGRVW B61......185 K3
CDSL WV8......34 D1
CNCK/NC WS11......15 K5
COVE CV2......154 F2
COVEN WV9......22 A3
COVW CV5......132 A8
CRTAM B79......31 M8
CRTAM B79......33 J6
CSHL/WTROR B46......112 E3
HALE B63......121 M1 ②
HHTH/SAND B71......69 G7
HIA/OLT B92......129 H4
KNWTH CV8......177 M7
NUNW/HART CV10......81 C6
NUNW/HART CV10......97 H4
POL/KGSB/FAZ B78......59 C4
POL/KGSB/FAZ B78......60 B7
RCOVN/BALC/EX CV7......96 D3
RCOVN/BALC/EX CV7......114 C2
RCOVN/BALC/EX CV7......114 F6
RCOVN/BALC/EX CV7......116 C6
RCOVN/BALC/EX CV7......131 J5
RCOVN/BALC/EX CV7......151 C2
RLSN CV32......193 J7
RLSN CV32......200 E2
STETCH B33......109 K2
WALM/CURD B76......74 C4
WALM/CURD B76......74 F7
WALM/CURD B76......75 L7
Church Moat Wy
BLOX/PEL WS3......38 F5 ②
Churchover Cl
WALM/CURD B76......73 H7 ②
Church Park Cl COVN CV6......133 K4 ②
Church Pth
RWWCK/WEL CV35......198 D7 ②
Church Pl BLOX/PEL WS3......39 H5
Church Rd ALDR WS9......41 J2
AST/WIT B6......89 L4
ATHST CV9......63 M6
BDMR/CCFT WV3......49 J6
BILS/COS WV14......67 H4
BLKHTH/ROWR B65......104 A2
BLOX/PEL WS3......39 H5
BNTWD WS7......19 H6
BRGRVW B61......164 E6
BRGRVW B61......165 K5
BRGRVW B61......185 K2
BRWNH WS8......26 D6
CDSL WV8......34 C1
CNCK/NC WS11......15 L4
CNCK/NC WS11......25 J1
CSCFLD/WYGN B72......72 F2 ②
CSHL/WTROR B46......94 E3
DUDS DY2......84 F8
DUNHL/THL/PER WV6......35 J8
DUNHL/THL/PER WV6......48 C1
DUNHL/THL/PER WV6......48 F2
EDG B15......106 F7
ERDE/BCHGN B24......90 E1
HAG/WOL DY9......102 C8
HAG/WOL DY9......140 B6
HALE B63......103 C7 ②
KNWTH CV8......178 D3
KNWTH CV8......179 C5
KNWTH CV8......179 M3
LGN/SDN/BHAMAIR B26......109 J5
LGN/SDN/BHAMAIR B26......110 A8
LICHS WS14......28 D8
MOS/BIL B13......125 L5
NFLD/LBR B31......143 L1
NUNW/HART CV10......79 M5
NUNW/HART CV10......98 A2
PBAR/PBCH B42......71 H8
PENK ST19......10 C4
POL/KGSB/FAZ B78......47 L8
REDW B97......195 K3
REDW B97......196 C1
RRUGBY CV23......158 A8
SEDG DY3......82 C3
SHHTH WV12......38 B7
SHLY B90......146 F3
SMTHWKW B67......105 K1
STETCH B33......109 K3
STRBR DY8......101 H3
STRBR DY8......119 M2
TAM/AM/WIL B77......60 A1
WMBN WV5......64 F6
WOLVN WV10......23 G3
WOLVN WV10......36 A4
YDLY B25......109 J5
Church Sq OLDBY B69......86 E6 ②
Churchstone Cl BRGRVW B61......165 K5
Church St ATHST CV9......63 H5
BILS/COS WV14......51 H8
BKHL/PFLD WV2......2 E7
BLOX/PEL WS3......38 F5
BNTWD WS7......18 C8
BRGRVW B61......185 K3
BRLYHL DY5......84 B6
BRLYHL DY5......102 A3
BRLYHL DY5......102 A4
BRWNH WS8......26 C8
CBHAMNW B3......6 F4
CDYHTH B64......103 J4
CNCK/NC WS11......16 B7
CNCK/NC WS11......16 E1
CNCK/NC WS11......16 C4
COV CV1......9 H1
CRTAM B79......31 M8
DARL/WED WS10......52 B7
DARL/WED WS10......67 M1
DUDS DY2......85 C5
HAG/WOL DY9......119 L8

SMTHWKW B67......105 K1
Clarendon Sq RLSN CV32......200 D4
Clarendon St BDMR/CCFT WV3......2 B3
BLOX/PEL WS3......38 F4
COV CV5......153 K4
RLSN CV32......200 E3
Clare Rd BLOX/PEL WS3......39 K7
WOLVN WV10......36 C5
Clare's Ct KIDDW DY11......137 C7 ②
Clarewell Av SOLH B91......147 L4
Clarion Wy CNCK/NC WS11......12 C8
Clarke's Av HEDN WS12......12 E4
KNWTH CV8......191 L2
Clarkes Gv TPTN/OCK DY4......68 A7
Clarke's La HHTH/SAND B71......69 G6
WLNHL WV13......52 A2
Clarke St REDW B97......196 B1
Clark Rd BDMR/CCFT WV3......49 K3
Clarkson Rd DARL/WED WS10......68 C2
Clark St COVN CV6......134 E4
LDYWD/EDGR B16......106 D3
STRBR DY8......101 J8
Clarry Dr FOAKS/STRLY B74......56 D5
Clary Gv DSYBK/YTR WS5......69 L2
Clatterbach La HAG/WOL DY9......140 E1
Clattercut La DROIT WR9......163 K8
Claughton Rd DUDS DY2......85 H4 ②
Claughton St KIDDW DY11......137 C8
Clausen Cl GTB/HAM B43......71 J1
Clavedon Cl NFLD/LBR B31......123 J6 ②
Claverdon Cl SOLH B91......147 L5
Claverdon Dr FOAKS/STRLY B74......55 M1
GTB/HAM B43......70 B5
Claverdon Gdns ACGN B27......108 F8
Claverdon Rd COVW CV5......152 F2
Claverley Dr
ETTPK/GDPK/PENN WV4......49 H8
Clay Av NUN CV11......81 K3
Claybrook Dr STUD B80......197 K6
Claybrook St DIG/EDG B5......7 C8
Claycroft Ter DUDN DY1......66 F7 ②
Claydon Gv
ALE/KHTH/YWD B14......145 L2 ②
Claydon Rd KGSWFD DY6......83 C4
Clay Dr RIDG/WDGT B32......104 E8
Claygate Rd HEDN WS12......17 J2
Clayhanger La BRWNH WS8......26 E7
Clayhanger Rd BRWNH WS8......26 D7
Clayhill La RRUGBY CV23......158 D8
Clay La COVE CV2......154 E1
COVW CV5......132 C1
LGN/SDN/BHAMAIR B26......127 J1
OLDBY B69......104 E1
Claymore TAM/AM/WIL B77......46 B7
Claypit Cl WBROM B70......86 E2 ②
Claypit La BRGRVW B61......165 J4
TAM/AM/WIL B77......18 C2
Claypit La WBROM B70......86 E2
Clay St PENK ST19......10 C4
Clayton Cl BKHL/PFLD WV2......50 A6
Clayton Dr BRGRVE B60......185 M6
CBROM B36......92 A5
Clayton Rd BILS/COS WV14......66 F6
COVN CV6......133 J8
WASH/WDE B8......90 B8
Clear Vw KGSWFD DY6......82 F7
Clearwell Gdns DUDN DY1......84 C2 ②
Cleasby TAM/AM/WIL B77......47 C4
Clee Av KIDDW DY11......161 C3
Clee Hill Dr BDMR/CCFT WV3......48 D1 ②
Clee Hill Rd SEDG DY3......84 A1
Clee Rd DUDS DY2......84 E6
LGLYGN/QTN B68......105 G1
NFLD/LBR B31......143 L5
STRBR DY8......101 L7
Cleeton St HEDN WS12......17 H4
Cleeve TAM/AM/WIL B77......46 B2
Cleeve Cl REDE B98......189 H8
Cleeve Dr FOAKS/STRLY B74......42 D7 ②
Cleeve Rd ALE/KHTH/YWD B14......146 A1
BLOX/PEL WS3......38 D2
Cleeves Av RLSS CV31......200 B7 ②
Cleeve Wy BLOX/PEL WS3......38 D3
Clee View Meadow SEDG DY3......66 B3
Clee View Rd WMBN WV5......64 C8
Clematis TAM/AM/WIL B77......46 D2
Clematis Dr COVEN WV9......35 K2
Clemens St RLSS CV31......200 E6
Clement Pl BILS/COS WV14......51 H6 ②
Clement Rd BILS/COS WV14......51 H6
RMSLY B62......104 B4
Clements Rd OLDBY B69......104 D1
Clements Rd YDLY B25......109 H5
Clements St COVE CV2......154 E2
Clement St CBHAMW B1......6 B4
NUN CV11......98 F2
WSLW WS2......4 C4 ②
Clemson St WLNHL WV13......51 L3 ②
Clennon Ri COVE CV2......135 H5
Clensmore St KIDD DY10......137 H6
Clent Av KIDDW DY11......160 F4
REDW B97......196 B6
Clent Dr HAG/WOL DY9......120 A7
NUNW/HART CV10......97 M2
Clent Hill Dr BLKHTH/ROWR B65......85 L8
Clent Rd HDSW B21......88 B4
LGLYGN/QTN B68......105 G5
RBRY B45......142 C5
STRBR DY8......101 L7
Clent View Rd HALE B63......121 G1
RIDG/WDGT B32......122 E4
STRBR DY8......119 J3 ②
Clent Wy RIDG/WDGT B32......122 D5
Cleobury La HOCK/TIA B94......170 E2
Cleton St TPTN/OCK DY4......85 M2 ②
Clevedon Av CBROM B36......92 C5 ②
Clevedon Rd BHTH/HG B12......107 J7
Cleveland Cl WLNHL WV13......51 H4 ②
WNSFLD WV11......37 K4 ②
Cleveland Dr CNCK/NC WS11......16 F1 ②
Cleveland Pas WOLV WV1......2 F6 ②
BKHL/PFLD WV2......3 H7
COVE CV2......154 E1
Cleveland St BKHL/PFLD WV2......2 F6
DUDN DY1......84 F4 ②
STRBR DY8......119 J1

Cleveley Dr *NUNW/HART* CV10 ...... 80 B6
Cleves Crs *GTWY* WS6 .... 24 A3
Cleves Dr *RBRY* B45 .... 142 C6
Cleves Rd *RBRY* B45 .... 142 C5
Clewley Dr *COVEN* WV9 .... 35 L2 🖪
Clewley Gv *RIDG/WDGT* B32 .... 104 F8
Clews Cl *WSL* WS1 .... 4 E7
Clewshaw La *HWK/WKHTH* B38 ... 168 F1
Clews Rd *REDE* B98 .... 196 D6
Cley Cl *DIG/EDG* B5 .... 107 H7
Clifden Dr *KNWTH* CV8 .... 177 C7
Cliffe Dr *STETCH* B33 .... 109 M2
Cliffe Rd *RLSN* CV32 .... 200 B4
Cliffe Wy *WWCK* CV34 .... 199 L5
Cliff Hall La *POL/KGSB/FAZ* B78 ... 59 M5
Clifford Bridge Rd *COVE* CV2 ...... 135 K7
  COVS CV3 .... 155 K3
Clifford St *DOR/KN* B93 .... 172 D1
  SMTHWKW B67 .... 105 K4
  WBROM B70 .... 86 E3
Clifford St *DUDN* DY1 .... 84 F5 🖪
  DUNHL/THL/PER WV6 .... 2 A2
  LOZ/NWT B19 .... 89 H6
  TAM/AM/WIL B77 .... 46 C2
Clifford Wk *LOZ/NWT* B19 .... 89 H6
Cliff Rock Rd *RBRY* B45 .... 142 F6
Clift Av *SHHTH* WV12 .... 38 B6
Clift Cl *SHHTH* WV12 .... 38 A7
Clifton Av *ALDR* WS9 .... 41 C5
  BRWNH WS8 .... 26 B7
  CNCK/NC WS11 .... 16 A6
  CRTAM B79 .... 31 K6
Clifton Cl *AST/WIT* B6 .... 89 K6
  OLDBY B69 .... 104 D1
  REDE B98 .... 197 H4
Clifton Crs *SHLY* B90 .... 147 K4
Clifton Gdns *CDSL* WV8 .... 35 C2
Clifton Gn *HLGN/YWD* B28 .... 126 E8
Clifton La *CRTAM* B79 .... 32 F2
  HHTH/SAND B71 .... 69 J3
Clifton Gdns *CRTAM* B79 .... 31 K5
  BHTH/HG B12 .... 107 L8
  CBROM B36 .... 92 C5
  DUNHL/THL/PER WV6 .... 35 H8
  KIDDW DY11 .... 160 E4
  NUNW/HART CV10 .... 98 D1
  RMSLY B62 .... 104 B5
  RUGBYN/HIL CV21 .... 183 M2
  SCFLD/BOLD B73 .... 72 E1
  SMTHWKW B67 .... 105 K1
Clifton St *BDMR/CCFT* WV3 ....
  BILS/COS WV14 .... 66 D4
  CDYHTH B64 .... 103 K4
  COV CV1 .... 9 J1
  STRBR DY8 .... 119 K1
Clinic Dr *HAG/WOL* DY9 .... 102 C8
  NUN CV11 .... 99 C2
Clinton Av *KNWTH* CV8 .... 176 B7
  RWWCK/WEL CV35 .... 198 E6 🖪
Clinton Crs *BNTWD* WS7 .... 18 F5
Clinton Cv *SHLY* B90 .... 147 H4
Clinton La *KNWTH* CV8 .... 176 B7
Clinton Rd *BILS/COS* WV14 .... 51 L6
  COVN CV6 .... 134 D3
  CSHL/WTROR B46 .... 93 K7
  SHLY B90 .... 147 J5
Clinton St *RLSS* CV31 .... 200 E6 🖪
  WSNGN B18 .... 88 C8 🖪
Clipper Vw
  LDYWD/EDGR B16 .... 106 C4
Clipstone Rd *COVN* CV6 .... 133 J7
Clipston Rd *WASH/WDE* B8 .... 90 D8
Clissold Cl *DIG/EDG* B5 .... 107 J6 🖪
Clissold Pas *WSNGN* B18 .... 106 E1
Clissold St *WSNGN* B18 .... 106 E1
Clive Cl *MGN/WHC* B75 .... 57 H3
Cliveden Av *ALDR* WS9 .... 40 F4
  PBAR/PBCH B42 .... 89 C1
Cliveden Coppice
  FOAKS/STRLY B74 .... 56 D4
Cliveden Wk *NUN* CV11 .... 99 J5
Clivedon Wy *CDYHTH* B64 .... 103 L6
Cleveland St *CBHAMNE* B4 .... 7 C1
Clive Rd *BNTWD* WS7 .... 18 E6
  BRGRVE B60 .... 185 M5
  RCOVN/BALC/EX CV7 .... 151 C4
  REDW B97 .... 188 B3
  RIDG/WDGT B32 .... 105 H6
Clive St *HHTH/SAND* B71 .... 69 C8
Clockfields Dr *STRBR* DY8 .... 101 L4
Clock La *HIA/OLT* B92 .... 129 H3
Clockmill Av *BLOX/PEL* WS3 .... 39 J2
Clockmill Pl *BLOX/PEL* WS3 .... 39 K2
Clockmill Rd *BLOX/PEL* WS3 .... 39 J2
Clodeshall Rd *WASH/WDE* B8 ...... 108 C1
Cloister Cft *COVE* CV2 .... 135 K2
Cloister Crofts *RLSN* CV32 .... 200 D2
Cloister Dr *RMSLY* B62 .... 122 B2
Cloister Wy *RLSN* CV32 .... 200 D2
Clonmel Rd *BVILLE* B30 .... 124 E7
Clopton Crs
  CHWD/FDBR/MGN B37 .... 110 C1
Clopton Rd *STETCH* B33 .... 110 A5
The Close *DARL/WED* WS10 .... 68 C2 🖪
  HALE B63 .... 103 H7
  HIA/OLT B92 .... 127 K5
  HLYWD B47 .... 145 L8
  HRBN B17 .... 105 K6
  KNWTH CV8 .... 156 D8
  RLSS CV31 .... 200 E7
  RMSLY B62 .... 121 L6
  SEDG DY3 .... 82 C3 🖪
  SEDG DY3 .... 66 B6
Clothier Gdns *WLNHL* WV13 .... 51 L2 🖪
Clothier St *WLNHL* WV13 .... 51 L2
Cloudbridge Dr *HIA/OLT* B92 ..... 128 D6 🖪
Cloud Gn *HIA/OLT* CV4 .... 153 H8
Cloudsley Gv *HIA/OLT* B92 .... 127 K2 🖪
Clovelly Gdns *COVE* CV2 .... 135 C8 🖪
Clovelly Rd *COVE* CV2 .... 134 F8
Clovelly Wy *NUN* CV11 .... 81 J8
Clover Av
  CHWD/FDBR/MGN B37 .... 111 H3
Cloverdale
  DUNHL/THL/PER WV6 .... 48 B1
Clover Dr *RIDG/WDGT* B32 .... 123 C3
Clover Hl *DSYBK/YTR* WS5 .... 54 C5
Clover La *KGSWFD* DY6 .... 82 E6

Clover Lea Sq *WASH/WDE* B8 ...... 90 E7 🖪
Clover Ley *WOLVN* WV10 .... 3 L3
Clover Mdw *HEDN* WS12 .... 17 C4 🖪
Clover Piece *TPTN/OCK* DY4 ...... 68 A7 🖪
Clover Rdg *GTWY* WS6 .... 24 A2
Clover Rd *SLYOAK* B29 .... 123 L6
Club La *WOLVN* WV10 .... 22 A7
Club Rw *SEDG* DY3 .... 66 C8
Club Vw *HWK/WKHTH* B38 .... 144 B3
Clunbury Cft *BKDE/SHDE* B34 .... 91 M8 🖪
Clunbury Rd *NFLD/LBR* B31 .... 143 L5
Clun Cl *DUDS* DY2 .... 85 K4
Clunes Av *NUN* CV11 .... 81 J7
Clun Rd *NFLD/LBR* B31 .... 123 K7
Clyde Av *RMSLY* B62 .... 104 C5
Clyde Ms *BRLYHL* DY5 .... 83 M7
Clyde Rd *BDWTH* CV12 .... 117 L2
  DOR/KN B93 .... 172 E3
Clydesdale
  LGN/SDN/BHAMAIR B26 .... 109 L8
Clydesdale Rd *RIDG/WDGT* B32 ... 104 F7
Clyde St *BHTH/HG* B12 .... 7 L8
  CDYHTH B64 .... 103 J4
Coach House Ri
  TAM/AM/WIL B77 .... 46 D6 🖪
Coalash La *BRGRVE* B60 .... 194 A2
Coalbourne Gdns *HALE* B63 ...... 103 C8
Coalbourn La *STRBR* DY8 .... 101 K6 🖪
Coalheath La *RUSH/SHEL* WS4 ... 40 A5
Coalpit Fields Rd *BDWTH* CV12 .. 117 C3
Coalpit La *KNWTH* CV8 .... 181 C1
Coal Pool La *BLOX/PEL* WS3 ..... 39 K6 🖪
Coalport Rd *WOLV* WV1 .... 50 E4
Coalway Av
  ETTPK/GDPK/PENN WV4 .... 49 L7
  LGN/SDN/BHAMAIR B26 .... 128 A1
Coalway Gdns *BDMR/CCFT* WV3 ... 49 H7
Coalway Rd *BLOX/PEL* WS3 .... 38 C4
  ETTPK/GDPK/PENN WV4 .... 49 H7
Coates Rd *KIDD* DY10 .... 137 M6
Coat of Arms Bridge Rd
  COVS CV3 .... 153 L7
Cobbett Rd *BNTWD* WS7 .... 18 A6
The Cobbles *CSCFLD/WYGN* B72 .. 73 C6
Cobbs Rd *KNWTH* CV8 .... 176 B7
Cobden Av *RLSS* CV31 .... 201 C8
Cobden Cl *DARL/WED* WS10 .... 52 D7
  HEDN WS12 .... 13 C6
  TPTN/OCK DY4 .... 67 K5 🖪
Cobden Gdns *BHTH/HG* B12 .... 107 J7 🖪
Cobden St *COVN* CV6 .... 134 C8
  DARL/WED WS10 .... 52 D7
  KIDDW DY11 .... 137 C2
  STRBR DY8 .... 101 H7
  WSL WS1 .... 4 D8
Cobham Cl *BRGRVE* B60 .... 185 K6
  CVALE B35 .... 91 K2 🖪
Cobham Court Ms
  HAG/WOL DY9 .... 120 B7 🖪
Cobham Rd *BORD* B9 .... 108 B3
  DARL/WED WS10 .... 69 J3
  HALE B63 .... 121 M1
  KIDDW DY11 .... 161 J1
  STRBR DY8 .... 119 L3
Cobia *TAM/AM/WIL* B77 .... 46 B6
Cob La *NFLD/LBR* B31 .... 124 A6
Cobley Hl *ALVE* B48 .... 187 J1
Cobnall Rd *BRGRVW* B61 .... 165 L3
Cobs Fld *BVILLE* B30 .... 124 A2
Coburg Cft *TPTN/OCK* DY4 .... 68 A7 🖪
Coburn Dr *MGN/WHC* B75 .... 57 H3
Cochrane Cl *HAG/WOL* DY9 .... 120 A5
  TPTN/OCK DY4 .... 68 A7 🖪
Cochrane Rd *BRLYHL* DY5 .... 84 D8
  DUDS DY2 .... 84 D7 🖪
Cockermouth Cl *RLSN* CV32 ..... 200 B3 🖪
Cock Hill La *RBRY* B45 .... 142 D5 🖪
Cocksheds La *RMSLY* B62 .... 104 A5
Cockshut Hl
  LGN/SDN/BHAMAIR B26 .... 109 L5
Cockshutt La *BRGRVW* B61 .... 165 H7
Cockshutts La *BKHL/PFLD* WV2 ... 50 B6
Cocksmead Cft
  ALE/KHTH/YWD B14 .... 125 H6
Cocksparrow La *CNCK/NC* WS11 .. 15 L1
Cocksparrow St *WWCK* CV34 ...... 199 H4 🖪
Cockspur St *POL/KGSB/FAZ* B78 .. 47 J6
Cockthorpe Cl *HRBN* B17 .... 105 K6
Cocton Cl *DUNHL/THL/PER* WV6 ... 34 C8
Codsall Gdns *CDSL* WV8 .... 34 C1
Codsall Rd *CDSL* WV8 .... 35 C4
  CDYHTH B64 .... 103 J5
  DUNHL/THL/PER WV6 .... 35 H3
Cofield Rd *SCFLD/BOLD* B73 ..... 72 D4
Cofton Church La *RBRY* B45 ..... 167 H3
Cofton Ct *RBRY* B45 .... 143 H6 🖪
Cofton Gv *NFLD/LBR* B31 .... 143 J7
Cofton Lake Rd *RBRY* B45 .... 167 C2
Cofton Rd *NFLD/LBR* B31 .... 143 L6
Cokeland Pl *CDYHTH* B64 .... 103 H5
Colaton Cl *WOLVN* WV10 .... 50 C1
Colbek Ct *NUNW/HART* CV10 ..... 97 J7 🖪
Colbourne Grove Dr
  RLSN CV32 .... 200 B3 🖪
Colbourne Rd
  POL/KGSB/FAZ B78 .... 45 L3
  TPTN/OCK DY4 .... 85 L1 🖪
Colbrand Gv *EDG* B15 .... 107 H5 🖪
Coldbath Rd *MOS/BIL* B13 .... 125 M5
Coldfield Dr *REDE* B98 .... 196 D4
Coldridge Cl *COVEN* WV9 .... 35 K4
Coldstream Dr *STRBR* DY8 .... 101 J2
Coldstream Rd *WALM/CURD* B76... 73 J5
Cole Bank Rd *HLGN/YWD* B28 .... 126 C5
Colebourne Rd *MOS/BIL* B13 .... 126 B7
Colebridge Crs
  CSHL/WTROR B46 .... 93 K5 🖪
Colebrook Cl *COVS* CV3 .... 155 K3
Colebrook Cft *SHLY* B90 .... 146 D3
Colebrook Rd *SHLY* B90 .... 146 C3
  SPARK B11 .... 108 B8
Coleby Cl *TLHL/CAN* CV4 .... 152 B7
Cole Ct
  CHWD/FDBR/MGN B37 .... 110 F3 🖪
Coleford Cl *REDW* B97 .... 195 H1
  STRBR DY8 .... 101 G3

Coleford Dr
  CHWD/FDBR/MGN B37 .... 110 E3
Cole Gn *SHLY* B90 .... 146 C3
Cole Hall La *BKDE/SHDE* B34 .... 91 M8 🖪
  STETCH B33 .... 109 L1
Colehill *CRTAM* B79 .... 31 M8
Colehurst Cft *SHLY* B90 .... 147 K7 🖪
Coleman Rd *DARL/WED* WS10 ..... 53 L8
Coleman St
  DUNHL/THL/PER WV6 .... 49 K1
  TLHL/CAN CV4 .... 152 D2
Colemeadow Rd
  CSHL/WTROR B46 .... 93 K6 🖪
  MOS/BIL B13 .... 125 M8
  REDE B98 .... 189 J7
Colenso Rd *SMTHWK* B66 .... 106 A1
Coleraine Rd *PBAR/PBCH* B42 .... 70 E7
Coleridge Cl *BLOX/PEL* WS3 ..... 25 L8 🖪
  CRTAM B79 .... 31 L7
  REDW B97 .... 196 A5
  SHHTH WV12 .... 38 C6 🖪
Coleridge Dr
  DUNHL/THL/PER WV6 .... 48 C1
Coleridge Pas *CBHAMNE* B4 ...... 7 H3 🖪
Coleridge Ri *SEDG* DY3 .... 83 L1
Coleridge Rd *COVE* CV2 .... 155 C1
  GTB/HAM B43 .... 70 C6 🖪
Colesbourne Av *BVILLE* B30 ..... 145 C3
Colesbourne Rd *HIA/OLT* B92 .... 127 M2
Coleshill Cl *REDW* B97 .... 196 A3
Coleshill Heath Rd
  CHWD/FDBR/MGN B37 .... 111 C7
  CHWD/FDBR/MGN B37 .... 111 J4
Coleshill Rd *ATHST* CV9 .... 62 D8
  BKDE/SHDE B34 .... 91 K6
  CHWD/FDBR/MGN B37 .... 111 C5
  CSHL/WTROR B46 .... 92 F3
  MGN/WHC B75 .... 57 H8
  NUNW/HART CV10 .... 79 H5
  POL/KGSB/FAZ B78 .... 45 L6
  WALM/CURD B76 .... 74 F8
Coleshill St *CSCFLD/WYGN* B72 .. 57 C8
Coleside Av *MOS/BIL* B13 .... 126 B6
Coles La *CSCFLD/WYGN* B72 ...... 73 C2
  HHTH/SAND B71 .... 68 E6
The Colesleys
  CSHL/WTROR B46 .... 93 L7 🖪
Cole St *DUDS* DY2 .... 103 J1
Cole Valley Rd *HLGN/YWD* B28 ... 126 B7
Coleview Crs *STETCH* B33 .... 110 C2
Coleville Rd *WALM/CURD* B76 .... 73 M7
Coleys La *NFLD/LBR* B31 .... 143 L3
Colgreave Av *MOS/BIL* B13 ...... 126 B3
Colina Cl *COVS* CV3 .... 155 C8
Colindale Rd *KGSTG* B44 .... 71 L2
Colinwood Cl *GTWY* WS6 .... 24 D4 🖪
Colledge Cl *RRUGBY* CV23 .... 157 H2
Colledge Rd *COVN* CV6 .... 134 B4
Colleen Av *BVILLE* B30 .... 144 F2
College Cl *DARL/WED* WS10 ...... 68 E3
College Dr *BFLD/HDSWWD* B20 ... 88 D3
  RLSN CV32 .... 200 D3
College Farm Dr
  ERDW/GRVHL B23 .... 72 B5
College Hl *SCFLD/BOLD* B73 ..... 72 F7
College La *CRTAM* B79 .... 45 M1 🖪
  KNWTH CV8 .... 174 C4
College Rd *BFLD/HDSWWD* B20 ... 88 C3
  BRGRVE B60 .... 185 L3
  DUNHL/THL/PER WV6 .... 49 H1
  KGSTG B44 .... 71 J8
  KIDD DY10 .... 161 J1
  MOS/BIL B13 .... 126 A3
  RMSLY B62 .... 104 E7
  SCFLD/BOLD B73 .... 72 C4
  STRBR DY8 .... 119 L1 🖪
  WASH/WDE B8 .... 108 C2
College St *NUNW/HART* CV10 ..... 98 F3
  WSNGN B18 .... 106 E1
College Vw
  DUNHL/THL/PER WV6 .... 49 H2
College Wk *BRGRVE* B60 .... 185 L3
Collet Rd *CDSL* WV8 .... 34 C8
Collets Brook *MGN/WHC* B75 .... 57 L3
Collets Gv
  CHWD/FDBR/MGN B37 .... 110 D1 🖪
Collett Wk *COV* CV1 .... 8 C2
Colley Av *WOLVN* WV10 .... 36 D5
Colley Ga *HALE* B63 .... 103 G7
Colley La *HALE* B63 .... 103 C7 🖪
Colley Orch *HALE* B63 .... 103 C7 🖪
Colley St *WBROM* B70 .... 87 H1
Collier Cl *BRWNH* WS8 .... 26 A6
  GTWY WS6 .... 24 B3
Colliers Cl *SHHTH* WV12 .... 37 M7
Colliers Dr *RCOVN/BALC/EX* CV7 . 96 C5
Colliery Dr *BLOX/PEL* WS3 ...... 38 C2
Colliery La
  RCOVN/BALC/EX CV7 .... 116 F4
Colliery Rd *HHTH/SAND* B71 ..... 87 L5
  WOLV WV1 .... 3 M5
Collindale Ct *KGSWFD* DY6 ...... 83 H4
Collingbourne Av *CBROM* B36 ... 91 H6
Collingdon Av
  LGN/SDN/BHAMAIR B26 .... 110 A7 🖪
Colling Wk
  CHWD/FDBR/MGN B37 .... 92 E8 🖪
Collingwood Av
  RUGBYS/DCH CV22 .... 183 G4
Collingwood Dr *GTB/HAM* B43 ... 71 C1
Collingwood Rd *COVW* CV5 .... 8 A6
  WOLVN WV10 .... 36 C3
Collins Cl *RIDG/WDGT* B32 ...... 104 E8 🖪
Collins Cl *TLHL/CAN* CV4 .... 153 H8
Collins Hl *LICH* WS13 .... 20 C5
Collinson Cl *REDE* B98 .... 196 E4
Collins Rd *BRWNH* WS8 .... 26 E8
  DARL/WED WS10 .... 68 F2
  WWCK CV34 .... 200 B8
Collis Cl *BRGRVE* B60 .... 185 J6
Collis St *STRBR* DY8 .... 101 K5
Collister Cl *SHLY* B90 .... 126 F8
Collumbine Cl
  DSYBK/YTR WS5 .... 69 K2 🖪

  RMSLY B62 .... 104 C5
Coningsby Cl *RLSS* CV31 .... 201 C3 🖪
Coningsby Dr *KIDDW* DY11 .... 136 E5
Conington Gv *HRBN* B17 .... 105 L8
Coniston *TAM/AM/WIL* B77 .... 46 F6 🖪
Coniston Av *HIA/OLT* B92 .... 127 K1
Coniston Cl *BRGRVE* B60 .... 185 M4
  HLGN/YWD B28 .... 126 D6
Coniston Crs *GTB/HAM* B43 ...... 70 D6
  STRPT DY13 .... 160 D7
Coniston Dr *COVW* CV5 .... 152 B1 🖪
  KGSWFD DY6 .... 82 F6
Coniston Rd *COVW* CV5 .... 153 K4
  DUNHL/THL/PER WV6 .... 35 H5
  ERDW/GRVHL B23 .... 72 B8
  FOAKS/STRLY B74 .... 55 K2
  RLSN CV32 .... 200 B4
Coniston Wy *CNCK/NC* WS11 ...... 16 C4
  NUN CV11 .... 81 K6
Connaught Av
  DARL/WED WS10 .... 69 C2 🖪
  KIDDW DY11 .... 161 C2
Connaught Cl *DSYBK/YTR* WS5 ... 54 A6
Connaught Dr *WMBN* WV5 .... 64 E4
Connaught Gv *BILS/COS* WV14 .... 51 K6
  WOLV WV1 .... 2 B4
Connops Wy *HAG/WOL* DY9 .... 102 C8 🖪
Connor Rd *HHTH/SAND* B71 ...... 69 J5
Conolly Dr *RBRY* B45 .... 142 F5
Conrad Cl *BHTH/HG* B12 .... 107 L6
  RUGBYS/DCH CV22 .... 183 K7
Conrad Rd *COVN* CV6 .... 133 L6
Consort Crs *BRLYHL* DY5 .... 84 A7 🖪
Consort Dr *DARL/WED* WS10 ...... 52 A5
Consort Rd *BVILLE* B30 .... 144 E2
Constable Cl *BDWTH* CV12 .... 98 E8 🖪
  GTB/HAM B43 .... 71 H2 🖪
The Constables
  LGLYGN/QTN B68 .... 104 F3 🖪
Constance Av *WBROM* B70 .... 87 H4
Constance Cl
  RCOVN/BALC/EX CV7 .... 116 D5
Constance Rd *DIG/EDG* B5 .... 107 H8
Constantine La
  CSHL/WTROR B46 .... 93 K4 🖪
Constantine Wy *BILS/COS* WV14 .. 67 L3
Constitution Hl *DUDS* DY2 ...... 85 H5 🖪
  LOZ/NWT B19 .... 6 E1
Consul Rd *RUGBYN/HIL* CV21 ..... 159 L7
Convent Rd *ATHST* CV9 .... 63 K6
  CNCK/NC WS11 .... 16 B5
  KNWTH CV8 .... 176 E6
Convent La *ATHST* CV9 .... 63 J6
Conway Av *HHTH/SAND* B71 ...... 68 F4
  LGLYGN/QTN B68 .... 104 F3 🖪
  RIDG/WDGT B32 .... 104 F7
  TLHL/CAN CV4 .... 152 B5
Conway Cl *DUDN* DY1 .... 67 C7 🖪
  KGSWFD DY6 .... 101 K1
  SHLY B90 .... 147 H4
Conway Crs *SHHTH* WV12 .... 38 A6
Conway Gv *GTB/HAM* B43 .... 70 B6 🖪
Conway Rd *BRGRVE* B60 .... 185 K4
  CHWD/FDBR/MGN B37 .... 110 C2
  CNCK/NC WS11 .... 15 M5
  DUNHL/THL/PER WV6 .... 48 D2
  RLSN CV32 .... 200 B5
  SHLY B90 .... 147 H4
  SPARK B11 .... 108 A7
Conwy Cl *NUN* CV11 .... 99 J4
  WSLW WS2 .... 52 E1 🖪
Conybere St *BHTH/HG* B12 .... 107 K6
Conyworth Cl *ACGN* B27 .... 127 H1 🖪
Cook Av *DUDS* DY2 .... 85 H6
Cook Cl *DOR/KN* B93 .... 149 C7
  DUNHL/THL/PER WV6 .... 48 C7
Cooke Cl *COVN* CV6 .... 116 E8
  PENK ST19 .... 10 C3
  WWCK CV34 .... 199 K3 🖪
Cookes Cft *NFLD/LBR* B31 .... 144 A3
Cookesley Cl *GTB/HAM* B43 ...... 71 H1
Cooke St *BKHL/PFLD* WV2 .... 50 A6
Cooknell Dr *STRBR* DY8 .... 101 J3
Cook Rd *BLOX/PEL* WS3 .... 39 H3
Cooks Cl *ATHST* CV9 .... 63 H5
Cooksey La *KGSTG* B44 .... 71 K1
Cooksey Rd *SMHTH* B10 .... 107 M5 🖪
Cooks La *ATHST* CV9 .... 62 A3
  CHWD/FDBR/MGN B37 .... 110 C1
  STETCH B33 .... 110 C2
Cook St *COV* CV1 .... 8 F3
  DARL/WED WS10 .... 52 C7
  VAUX/NECH B7 .... 90 A6
Coombe Ct *COVS* CV3 .... 155 L3
Coombe Cft *COVEN* WV9 .... 35 J2
Coombe Dr *COVS* CV3 .... 156 C6 🖪
Coombe Hl *CDYHTH* B64 .... 103 M5
Coombe Pk *FOAKS/STRLY* B74 .... 56 D6
Coombe Park Rd *COVS* CV3 .... 155 K3
Coombe Rd *BFLD/HDSWWD* B20 .. 89 J4
  SHLY B90 .... 147 C3
Coombes La *NFLD/LBR* B31 .... 143 K7
Coombe St *COVS* CV3 .... 154 F3
Coombs Rd *RMSLY* B62 .... 103 M7
Co-operative St *COVN* CV6 ...... 134 F2
Cooper Av *BRLYHL* DY5 .... 101 L3
Cooper Cl *BRGRVE* B60 .... 185 J6
  WBROM B70 .... 87 J3 🖪
Coopers Hl *ALVE* B48 .... 167 J4
Coopers La *SMTHWK* B66 .... 87 L8
  SMTHWKW B67 .... 87 K8
Coopers Rd *BFLD/HDSWWD* B20 .. 88 E2
Cooper St *NUN* CV11 .... 99 H1 🖪
  WBROM B70 .... 87 H2
  WOLV WV1 .... 3 M9
Coopers Wk *KNWTH* CV8 .... 179 C7
Cope Arnolds Cl *COVN* CV6 ...... 134 D1 🖪
Copeley Hl *AST/WIT* B6 .... 90 A4
Copes Crs *WOLVN* WV10 .... 36 E7
Cope's Dr *CRTAM* B79 .... 31 L6
Cope St *BLOX/PEL* WS3 .... 39 C7
  COV CV1 .... 9 H4
  DARL/WED WS10 .... 52 C7
  WSNGN B18 .... 106 C2

Cophall St *TPTN/OCK* DY4 .... 68 B8
Cophams CI *HIA/OLT* B92 .... 128 A3 🔲
Copland PI *TLHL/CAN* CV4 .... 152 C4 🔲
Coplow CI *RCOVN/BALC/EX* CV7 .... 150 E7
Coplow St *LDYWD/EDGR* B16 .... 106 D2
Coplow Ter
  LDYWD/EDGR B16 .... 106 D2 🔲
Copnor Gv
  LGN/SDN/BHAMAIR B26 .... 109 J7
Coppenhall Gv *STECH* B33 .... 109 L2 🔲
Copperas St *COVE* CV2 .... 134 F3 🔲
Copper Beech CI *COVN* CV6 .... 134 C4
Copperbeech CI
  RIDG/WDGT B32 .... 105 K8
Copper Beech Dr *KGSWFD* DY6 .... 83 H4
  WMBN WV5 .... 64 F7
Copperfield Rd *COVE* CV2 .... 154 F2
Copperfields *LICHS* WS14 .... 21 H6 🔲
Copperkins Rd *HEDN* WS12 .... 17 H1
Coppermill CI *WALM/CURD* B76 .... 12 D6
Coppice Av *HAG/WOL* DY9 .... 120 D2
Coppice CI *BNTWD* WS7 .... 18 D5
  GTWY WS6 .... 24 B1
  RBRY B45 .... 142 D6 🔲
  REDW B97 .... 196 A2 🔲
  SEDG DY3 .... 66 A6
  SHLY B90 .... 171 C1 🔲
  WNSFLD WV11 .... 37 L4 🔲
Coppice Ct *CNCK/NC* WS11 .... 15 M6 🔲
Coppice Crs *BRWNH* WS8 .... 26 B6
Coppice Dr *ACGN* B27 .... 126 F3 🔲
  POL/KGSB/FAZ B78 .... 47 K6
Coppice Farm Wy *SHHTH* WV12 .... 37 M4
Coppice Gv *LICHS* WS14 .... 21 K6
Coppice Hts *KIDDW* DY11 .... 160 F4
Coppice Hollow
  RIDG/WDGT B32 .... 122 F4 🔲
Coppice La *ALDR* WS9 .... 40 D4
  BNTWD WS7 .... 18 D5
  BRLYHL DY5 .... 102 E4 🔲
  BRWNH WS8 .... 26 B5
  CNCK/NC WS11 .... 24 B1
  DUNHL/THL/PER WV6 .... 34 F7
  POL/KGSB/FAZ B78 .... 58 A3
  SHHTH WV12 .... 38 A7
Coppice Ri *BRLYHL* DY5 .... 102 E3
Coppice Rd *ALDR* WS9 .... 40 D1
  BDMR/CCFT WV3 .... 49 H5
  BILS/COS WV14 .... 66 E5
  CDYHTH B64 .... 103 J6
  HIA/OLT B92 .... 128 C6
  MOS/BIL B13 .... 125 L2
Coppice Side *BRWNH* WS8 .... 26 B5
Coppice St *TPTN/OCK* DY4 .... 67 J7
  WBROM B70 .... 86 E1
The Coppice *ATHST* CV9 .... 63 L7
  BFLD/HDSWWD B20 .... 88 E3 🔲
  COVS CV3 .... 154 F5
  HEDN WS12 .... 17 J4 🔲
  NUNW/HART CV10 .... 81 C6
  SHHTH WV12 .... 38 A7
  TPTN/OCK DY4 .... 68 A4 🔲
Coppice View Rd
  SCFLD/BOLD B73 .... 71 L1
Coppice Wk *SHLY* B90 .... 171 C1 🔲
Copplestone CI
  BKDE/SHDE B34 .... 91 M7 🔲
Copps Rd *RLSN* CV32 .... 200 B5
Coppy Hall Av *ALDR* WS9 .... 40 F4
Coppy Nook La *BNTWD* WS7 .... 18 F8
Copse CI *COVW* CV5 .... 131 M5
  NFLD/LBR B31 .... 143 L3
Copse Crs *BLOX/PEL* WS3 .... 39 L1
Copse Rd *DUDS* DY2 .... 102 F2
The Copse *FOAKS/STRLY* B74 .... 56 D4
  RCOVN/BALC/EX CV7 .... 116 C5
Copsewood Av *NUN* CV11 .... 99 M6
Copsewood Ter *COVS* CV3 .... 155 G3
Copstone Dr *SLYOAK* B29 .... 123 M5
Copston Gv *SLYOAK* B29 .... 123 M5
Copthall Rd *HDSW* B21 .... 88 A3
Copt Heath Cft *DOR/KN* B93 .... 148 F5 🔲
Copt Heath Dr *DOR/KN* B93 .... 148 E6
Copthorne Av *BNTWD* WS7 .... 26 D1
Copthorne Rd *BDMR/CCFT* WV3 .. 49 L6
  COVN CV6 .... 133 K5
  KGSTG B44 .... 71 J2
Copt Oak CI *TLHL/CAN* CV4 .... 152 A6
Copyholt La *BRGRVE* B60 .... 194 A1
  BRGRVE B60 .... 194 D3
Coral CI *COVW* CV5 .... 153 G3
Coralin CI
  CHWD/FDBR/MGN B37 .... 110 F3
Corbett CI *BRGRVE* B60 .... 185 M5
Corbett Crs *STRBR* DY8 .... 101 L6
Corbett Rd *BRLYHL* DY5 .... 102 C4
  HLYWD B47 .... 145 L6
  KIDDW DY11 .... 136 E5 🔲
Corbetts CI *HIA/OLT* B92 .... 129 M6
Corbett St *SMTHWK* B66 .... 105 M1
Corbin Rd *POL/KGSB/FAZ* B78 .... 47 K7
Corbison CI *WWCK* CV34 .... 199 H4
Corbridge Av *KGSTG* B44 .... 71 K4
Corbridge Rd *SCFLD/BOLD* B73 .... 72 D3
Corbyn Rd *BORD* B9 .... 108 F2
  DUDN DY1 .... 84 D5
Corbyns CI *BRLYHL* DY5 .... 83 M6
Corbyns Hall La *BRLYHL* DY5 .... 83 M6
Corbyns Hall Rd *BRLYHL* DY5 .... 83 M6
Cordelia Wy *RUGBYS/DCH* CV22 .. 183 J7
Cordle Marsh Rd *BEWD* DY12..... 136 A8
Cordley St *WBROM* B70 .... 86 F1
Corfe CI *COVE* CV2 .... 135 K4
  DUNHL/THL/PER WV6 .... 48 D2
  RIDG/WDGT B32 .... 105 K8
Corfe Dr *OLDBY* B69 .... 85 L5
Corfe Rd *BILS/COS* WV14 .... 66 E5
Corfton Dr
  DUNHL/THL/PER WV6 .... 49 G2
Coriander CI *NFLD/LBR* B31 .... 142 F4
Corinne CI *RBRY* B45 .... 142 E7
Corinne Cft
  CHWD/FDBR/MGN B37 .... 110 E1
Corisande Rd *SLYOAK* B29........ 124 A3
Corley Av *NFLD/LBR* B31 .... 143 M2
Corley CI *SHLY* B90 .... 146 C4
Corley Vw
  RCOVN/BALC/EX CV7 .... 116 A6 🔲

Cornbrook Rd *SLYOAK* B29 .... 123 K7
Cornbury Gv *SHLY* B90 .... 147 H1 🔲
Corncrake CI
  CSCFLD/WYGN B72 .... 73 H3 🔲
Corncrake Dr *CBROM* B36......... 92 E5
Corncrake Rd *SEDG* DY3 .... 84 B2
Corndon CI *KIDDW* DY11 .... 160 F3
Cornel *TAM/AM/WIL* B77 .... 46 D1
Cornel CI
  CHWD/FDBR/MGN B37 .... 111 G5
Cornelius St *COVS* CV3........ 154 B5
Cornerway *HWK/WKHTH* B38...... 144 D6
Cornets End La
  RCOVN/BALC/EX CV7 .... 130 C6
Cornfield *CDSL* WV8 .... 35 J4
Cornfield Av *BRGRVE* B60 .... 185 H7
Cornfield CI *KGSWFD* DY6 .... 82 E5
Cornfield Cft
  CHWD/FDBR/MGN B37 .... 111 H2 🔲
  WALM/CURD B76 .... 73 K2 🔲
Cornfield Dr *LICHS* WS14 .... 21 J6
Cornfield Rd
  BLKHTH/ROWR B65 .... 103 K1
  NFLD/LBR B31 .... 143 M1
The Cornfield *COVS* CV3 .... 155 G4
Cornflower CI *WOLVN* WV10 ...... 22 E2 🔲
Cornflower Crs *DUDS* DY2 .... 85 K5
Cornflower Rd *BRWNH* WS8........ 26 B7
Corngreaves Rd *CDYHTH* B64 .... 103 H4
The Corngreaves
  BKDE/SHDE B34 .... 92 A7 🔲
Corngreaves Wk *CDYHTH* B64 .... 103 J6
Cornhampton CI *REDW* B97 ...... 187 M8 🔲
Cornhill *CNCK/NC* WS11 .... 12 C8
Corn HI *DSYBK/YTR* WS5 .... 54 C5
  WOLV WV1 .... 3 H5
Cornhill Gv *BVILLE* B30 .... 125 C6 🔲
  KNWTH CV8 .... 177 C8
Cornish CI *NUNW/HART* CV10 .... 79 K5
Cornish Crs *NUNW/HART* CV10.... 98 E3
Corn Mill HI *RIDG/WDGT* B32 .... 123 J4
Cornmill CI *WSL* WS13 .... 4 C7
Cornmill Gv
  DUNHL/THL/PER WV6 .... 48 B2 🔲
Cornovian CI
  DUNHL/THL/PER WV6 .... 34 C8 🔲
Corns Gv *WMBN* WV5........ 64 D8
Cornwall CI *KIDDW* DY11 .... 137 G4
  LGLYGN/QTN B68 .... 104 F5
  POL/KGSB/FAZ B78 .... 45 L4
Cornwall CI *ALDR* WS9 .... 40 E4
  DARL/WED WS10 .... 69 H2
  KGSWFD DY6 .... 83 H5 🔲
  WWCK CV34 .... 199 K4 🔲
Cornwall Ga *SHHTH* WV12........ 37 M8 🔲
Cornwallis Rd
  RUGBYS/DCH CV22 .... 182 F4
  WBROM B70 .... 86 E4
Cornwall PI *RLSN* CV32 .... 200 B4
  WSLW WS2 .... 52 C2
Cornwall Rd
  BFLD/HDSWWD B20 .... 88 D3
  COV CV1 .... 9 J7
  DSYBK/YTR WS5........ 5 M7
  DUNHL/THL/PER WV6 .... 49 G1
  HEDN WS12 .... 12 F8
  RBRY B45 .... 142 C3
  STRBR DY8 .... 101 H5
Cornwall St *CBHAMNW* B3 .... 6 E4
Cornwell CI *REDE* B98 .... 196 F8 🔲
  TPTN/OCK DY4 .... 67 L8
Cornyx La *SOLH* B91 .... 128 B7
Coronation Av
  POL/KGSB/FAZ B78 .... 45 H4
  POL/KGSB/FAZ B78 .... 47 M3
  WLNHL WV13 .... 52 B3
Coronation Crs *CRTAM* B79 ...... 33 K6 🔲
Coronation Rd *ALDR* WS9 .... 40 D2
  ATHST CV9 .... 77 G1
  BILS/COS WV14 .... 51 G7
  COV CV1 .... 9 L2
  DARL/WED WS10 .... 69 G2
  GTB/HAM B43 .... 70 C1
  RRUGBY CV23 .... 157 M8
  RUSH/SHEL WS4 .... 39 M3
  SLYOAK B29 .... 124 D3
  TPTN/OCK DY4 .... 67 M5
  WASH/WDE B8 .... 90 D7 🔲
  WNSFLD WV11 .... 36 E8
Coronation St *CRTAM* B79 .... 31 L8 🔲
Coronation Ter *BRGRVE* B60...... 185 M6
Coronation Wy *KIDD* DY10 ...... 137 M8
Coronel Av *COVN* CV6 .... 134 C1
Corporation Rd *DUDS* DY2 .... 85 K4
Corporation St *CBHAM* B2 .... 7 G5
  CBHAMNE B4 .... 7 H3
  COV CV1 .... 8 E4
  CRTAM B79 .... 31 M8 🔲
  DARL/WED WS10 .... 68 E3 🔲
  KIDD DY10 .... 137 J8
  NUN CV11 .... 80 F8
  RUGBYN/HIL CV21 .... 183 L2
  WOLV WV1 .... 2 E5
  WSL WS1 .... 4 E6
Corporation St West *WSLW* WS2 .. 4 C5
Correen *TAM/AM/WIL* B77 ...... 47 C3 🔲
Corrie Cft
  LGN/SDN/BHAMAIR B26 ...... 109 M6
  RIDG/WDGT B32 .... 122 F6
Corrin Gv *KGSWFD* DY6 .... 83 G5
Corser St *DUDN* DY1 .... 84 D3
  STRBR DY8 .... 119 L2
  WOLV WV1 .... 3 L6
Corsican CI *BNTWD* WS7 .... 18 D5
  SHHTH WV12 .... 38 C6 🔲
Corsican Dr *HEDN* WS12 .... 12 E5
Corston Ms *RLSS* CV31 .... 201 C7 🔲
Cort Dr *BNTWD* WS7 .... 18 E5
Corvedale Rd *SLYOAK* B29........ 123 L7
Corve Gdns
  DUNHL/THL/PER WV6 .... 35 J8
Corve Vw *SEDG* DY3 .... 66 A4 🔲
Corville Gdns
  LGN/SDN/BHAMAIR B26 ...... 127 M1
Corville Rd *RMSLY* B62........ 104 D7
Corwen Cft *NFLD/LBR* B31 .... 123 J7
Cory Cft *TPTN/OCK* DY4 .... 67 L8 🔲
Coseley Rd *BILS/COS* WV14....... 51 G8

Cosford CI *REDE* B98 .... 197 K4
  RLSN CV32 .... 200 F2
Cosford Crs *CVALE* B35 .... 91 L2
Cosford Dr *DUDS* DY2 .... 85 J8 🔲
Cosford La *RRUGBY* CV23 .... 159 L3
Cossington Rd
  ERDW/GRVHL B23 .... 72 B6
Costers La *REDE* B98 .... 197 K4
Coten End *WWCK* CV34 .... 199 K6
Cotford Rd
  ALE/KHTH/YWD B14 .... 145 L3
Cotheridge CI *SHLY* B90 .... 148 A7
Cot La *STRBR* DY8 .... 101 H1
Cotleigh Gv *KGSTG* B44 .... 71 H2
Cotman CI *BDWTH* CV12 .... 116 E1 🔲
  GTB/HAM B43 .... 71 G2
Coton La *CRTAM* B79 .... 31 H6
  ERDW/GRVHL B23 .... 90 D1 🔲
Coton Rd
  ETTPK/GDPK/PENN WV4 ...... 49 M8
  NUN CV11 .... 99 C1 🔲
  WALM/CURD B76 .... 75 M3
Cotsdale Rd
  ETTPK/GDPK/PENN WV4 ...... 65 J2
Cotswold Av *GTWY* WS6 .... 24 D2 🔲
Cotswold CI *ALDR* WS9 .... 41 C4
  KIDDW DY11 .... 161 C3
  OLDBY B69 .... 86 C8
  RBRY B45 .... 142 E4
Cotswold Crs *NUNW/HART* CV10 .. 97 M2
Cotswold Cft *HALE* B63 .... 121 C3
Cotswold Dr *COVS* CV3 .... 178 A2
Cotswold Gv *SHHTH* WV12 ...... 37 M4 🔲
Cotswold Rd *BKHL/PFLD* WV2 .... 50 D6
  HEDN WS12 .... 12 E5
  STRBR DY8 .... 101 M7
Cotswold Wy *BRGRVW* B61....... 165 L8
  HEDN WS12 .... 17 H1
  RLSS CV31 .... 201 C7 🔲
  WNSFLD WV11 .... 37 C7
Cottage Dr *BRGRVE* B60 .... 166 A4
Cottage Farm La
  BRGRVE B60 .... 166 A3 🔲
Cottage Farm Rd *COVN* CV6...... 133 L4
  TAM/AM/WIL B77 .... 46 B6
Cottage Gdns *RBRY* B45 .... 142 D7
Cottage La *BNTWD* WS7 .... 18 D8
  BRGRVE B60 .... 166 A3
  CSHL/WTROR B46 .... 76 B7
  WALM/CURD B76 .... 74 B7
  WOLVN WV10 .... 36 B2
Cottage St *BRLYHL* DY5 .... 102 B2
  KGSWFD DY6 .... 83 H6
Cottage Vw *CDSL* WV8 .... 34 F1 🔲
Cotterell Rd *RUGBYN/HIL* CV21 .. 159 K7
Cotteridge Rd *BVILLE* B30........ 144 E1
Cotterills Av *WASH/WDE* B8 ...... 109 C1 🔲
Cotterills La *WASH/WDE* B8 ...... 109 C1
Cotterills Rd *TPTN/OCK* DY4 .... 67 M6
Cottesbrook CI *COVS* CV3 .... 155 J4
Cottesbrook Rd *ACGN* B27 ...... 127 H1
Cottesfield CI *WASH/WDE* B8 .... 108 F1
Cottesmore CI
  HHTH/SAND B71 .... 69 K5 🔲
Cottle CI *WSLW* WS2 .... 52 D2 🔲
Cotton Dr *KNWTH* CV8 .... 177 C7 🔲
Cotton Gv *HEDN* WS12 .... 12 E4
Cotton La *MOS/BIL* B13 .... 125 L3
Cotton Mill Spinney *RLSN* CV32 .. 193 J7
Cotton Pool Rd *BRGRVW* B61 .... 185 J3 🔲
Cottrell St *HHTH/SAND* B71 ...... 87 H1
Cottsmeadow Dr
  WASH/WDE B8 .... 109 C1
Cotwall End Rd *SEDG* DY3........ 83 M1
Cotysmore Rd *MGN/WHC* B75 .... 57 H6
Couchman Rd *WASH/WDE* B8 .... 108 C1
Coughton Dr *RLSS* CV31 .... 201 H8
Coulson CI *BNTWD* WS7 .... 18 B4 🔲
Coulter Gv
  DUNHL/THL/PER WV6........ 48 B1
Coulter La *BNTWD* WS7 .... 19 J5
Coundon Gn *COVN* CV6 .... 133 J5
Coundon Rd *COV* CV1 .... 8 C3
Coundon St *COV* CV1 .... 8 C3
Coundon Wedge Dr *COVW* CV5 .. 133 C7
Counterfield Dr
  BLKHTH/ROWR B65 .... 85 K8
Countess Dr *RUSH/SHEL* WS4 .... 40 B6
Countess Rd *NUN* CV11 .... 98 E1
The Countess's Cft
  COVS CV3 .... 154 B6 🔲
Countess St *WSL* WS1 .... 4 C7
Countinghouse Wy
  BRGRVE B60 .... 185 J7 🔲
County CI *BVILLE* B30 .... 125 G7 🔲
  RIDG/WDGT B32........ 123 G2
County Dr *POL/KGSB/FAZ* B78 .... 45 K4
County La *KINVER* DY7 .... 119 H5
County Park Av *RMSLY* B62 ...... 122 B2 🔲
Courtaulds Wy *COVN* CV6........ 134 B7
Court CI *KIDDW* DY11 .... 136 F4
Court Crs *KGSWFD* DY6 .... 83 G8
Court Dr *LICHS* WS14 .... 42 D1
Courtenay Rd *KGSTG* B44 .... 71 J6
Court Farm Rd
  ERDW/GRVHL B23........ 72 C7
Courthouse Cft *KNWTH* CV8...... 192 A1
Courtland Av *COVN* CV6 .... 133 K8
Courtland Rd *KGSWFD* DY6 ...... 83 J5
Courtlands CI *DIG/EDG* B5 ...... 107 G7 🔲
The Courtlands
  DUNHL/THL/PER WV6........ 49 J1
Court La *ERDW/GRVHL* B23....... 72 C5
Court Leet *COVS* CV3 .... 156 B6
Court Leet Rd *COVS* CV3 .... 154 C6
Courtney CI *NUN* CV11 .... 81 K6
Court Oak Gv *RIDG/WDGT* B32 .. 105 K7
Court Oak Rd *HRBN* B17 .... 105 J7
  RIDG/WDGT B32........ 105 J7
Court Pas *DUDN* DY1 .... 85 G4 🔲
Court Rd *BTHTY/HG* B12 .... 107 J7
  DUNHL/THL/PER WV6 .... 49 K1
  ETTPK/GDPK/PENN WV4 ...... 66 C1
  SPARK B11 .... 126 A1
Court St *CDYHTH* B64 .... 103 J4

RLSS CV31 .... 200 E6
Court Wy *WSLW* WS2 .... 4 D1
Courtway Av
  ALE/KHTH/YWD B14 .... 145 M4
Cousins St *BKHL/PFLD* WV2 ...... 50 B6
Coveley Gv *WSNGN* B18........ 88 E8
Coven CI *BLOX/PEL* WS3 .... 25 L8
Coven Gv *SLYOAK* B29 .... 123 M3
Coven St *WOLVN* WV10 .... 3 H1
Coventry Hwy *REDE* B98 .... 189 L8
Coventry Rd *BDWTH* CV12 ...... 116 F4
  BTACH/HAR CV33 .... 193 J5
  COVS CV3 .... 156 C3
  CSHL/WTROR B46 .... 111 J2
  HIA/OLT B92 .... 129 M2
  KNWTH CV8 .... 176 E7
  LGN/SDN/BHAMAIR B26 ...... 109 J7
  LGN/SDN/BHAMAIR B26 ...... 128 D1 🔲
  NUNW/HART CV10 .... 99 C6
  POL/KGSB/FAZ B78 .... 76 C3
  RCOVN/BALC/EX CV7 .... 114 C3
  RCOVN/BALC/EX CV7 .... 117 J7
  RCOVN/BALC/EX CV7 .... 151 K7
  RRUGBY CV23 .... 157 J2
  RUGBYS/DCH CV22 .... 182 D7
  SMHTH B10 .... 7 M8
  WWCK CV34 .... 199 L3
Coventry Road Exhall
  RCOVN/BALC/EX CV7 .... 116 E6
Coventry St *COVE* CV2 .... 154 E1
  DIG/EDG B5 .... 7 J6 🔲
  KIDD DY10 .... 137 J7
  NUN CV11 .... 99 C1 🔲
  STRBR DY8 .... 101 L8 🔲
  WOLV WV1 .... 50 E3
Coventry Wy *BDWTH* CV12........ 116 B3
  KNWTH CV8 .... 180 D2
  RCOVN/BALC/EX CV7 .... 113 M7
  RCOVN/BALC/EX CV7 .... 151 J1
Cove PI *COVE* CV2 .... 135 C6
Coverdale Rd *HIA/OLT* B92 ...... 127 L1
Coverley PI *RUGBYS/DCH* CV22 .. 183 J2
The Covers *STUD* B80 .... 197 J7
Covert La *STRBR* DY8 .... 119 H4
The Covert *CDSL* WV8 .... 35 J4
Covey CI *LICH* WS13 .... 21 H4
Cowan CI *RUGBYS/DCH* CV22 .... 182 F4
Cowdray CI *RLSS* CV31 .... 201 C6
Cow La *POL/KGSB/FAZ* B78........ 60 D2
Cowles CT *YDLY* B25 .... 109 J4
Cowley *TAM/AM/WIL* B77 .... 46 C3
Cowley CI *CBROM* B36 .... 92 D4
  PENK ST19 .... 10 D6
Cowley Dr *ACGN* B27 .... 127 H1 🔲
  DUDN DY1 .... 84 D3
Cowley Gn *HEDN* WS12 .... 12 D5
Cowley Rd *COVE* CV2 .... 155 H1
  SPARK B11 .... 108 C8
Cowper CI *SHHTH* WV12 .... 38 C6
  WWCK CV34 .... 199 K4 🔲
Cowslip CI *HWK/WKHTH* B38 .... 144 D5
  SLYOAK B29 .... 123 L6
Coxcroft Av *BRLYHL* DY5 .... 102 D4 🔲
Coxmoor CI *BLOX/PEL* WS3 ...... 38 D2 🔲
Cox Rd *BILS/COS* WV14 .... 67 J4
Cox's CI *NUNW/HART* CV10 ...... 98 F2
Cox's La *CDYHTH* B64 .... 103 K3
Cox St *CBHAMNW* B3 .... 6 E2
  COV CV1 .... 9 H3
Coxwell Av *WOLVN* WV10 .... 36 A7
Coxwell Gdns
  LDYWD/EDGR B16 .... 106 D3 🔲
Coyne CI *TPTN/OCK* DY4 .... 67 H8 🔲
Coyne Rd *WBROM* B70 .... 86 F3
Cozens CI *BDWTH* CV12 .... 116 E1
Crabbe St *HAG/WOL* DY9 .... 102 D8
Crabbs Cross La *REDW* B97 ...... 196 B8
Crab La *CNCK/NC* WS11 .... 16 E2
  SHHTH WV12 .... 38 B4
Crabmill CI *DOR/KN* B93 .... 149 C6
Crab Mill CI *HWK/WKHTH* B38 .. 144 C6
Crabmill La *COVN* CV6 .... 134 D6
  HWK/WKHTH B38 .... 145 C5
Crabourne Rd *DUDS* DY2........ 85 J8 🔲
Crabtree CI *HHTH/SAND* B71 .... 69 K5 🔲
  NFLD/LBR B31 .... 144 A3 🔲
  REDE B98 .... 196 D3
Crabtree Dr *BRGRVW* B61........ 185 K2
Crabtree La *BRGRVW* B61 .... 185 J2
Crabtree Rd *WSNGN* B18 .... 88 E8
Crackley La *KNWTH* CV8 .... 176 C1
Craddock Dr *NUNW/HART* CV10.. 80 A6
Craddock Rd *SMTHWKW* B67 .... 87 J7 🔲
Craddock St
  DUNHL/THL/PER WV6........ 49 J1
Cradley CI *REDE* B98 .... 197 K3
Cradley Cft *HDSW* B21........ 88 B2
Cradley Flds *HALE* B63 .... 103 H8 🔲
Cradley Forge *HALE* B63 .... 102 E5
Cradley Park Rd *DUDS* DY2...... 103 C3
Cradley Rd *CDYHTH* B64 .... 103 C5
  DUDS DY2 .... 103 C3
Cradock Rd *WASH/WDE* B8 ...... 90 C8 🔲
Craig CI *RLSS* CV31 .... 200 F8 🔲
Craig Cft
  CHWD/FDBR/MGN B37 .... 111 H3
Craigends Av *COVS* CV3 .... 155 J7
Crail Gv *GTB/HAM* B43 .... 70 F2
Crakston CI *COVE* CV2 .... 155 J3
Cramlington Rd
  PBAR/PBCH B42 .... 70 E5
Cramnore CI *TPTN/OCK* DY4 .... 67 L5 🔲
Cramper's Fld *COVN* CV6........ 133 L8
Cramp HI *DARL/WED* WS10 ...... 52 B7 🔲
Cranbourne Cha *COVE* CV2 ...... 135 K8
Cranbourne Gv
  DUNHL/THL/PER WV6........ 48 D2
Cranbourne PI
  HHTH/SAND B71 .... 87 H1 🔲
Cranbourne Rd *KGSTG* B44 ...... 71 K4
  STRBR DY8 .... 119 L1

Craneberry Rd *STECH* B33 .... 110 C2
Cranebrook HI
  LICH/FAZ B78 .... 44 B8
Cranebrook La *LICHS* WS14...... 27 K7
Crane CI *WWCK* CV34 .... 199 H4
Crane Dr *BNTWD* WS7 .... 26 E1
Crane Fld *LICH* WS13 .... 20 E4
Crane Hollow *WMBN* WV5 .... 64 C3 🔲
Cranehouse Rd *KGSTG* B44 ...... 71 L3
Cranemoor CI *VAUX/NECH* B7 .... 90 A7 🔲
Craner's Rd *COV* CV1 .... 9 L1
Cranesbill CI *WOLVN* WV10 ...... 23 C6 🔲
Cranesbill Rd *SLYOAK* B29 ...... 123 L7
Cranes Park Rd
  LGN/SDN/BHAMAIR B26 ...... 110 A8
Crane St *KIDDW* DY11 .... 137 G7
Crane Ter *DUNHL/THL/PER* WV6 .. 35 J8
Cranfield Gv
  LGN/SDN/BHAMAIR B26 ...... 109 K5
Cranfield PI *DSYBK/YTR* WS5 .... 69 K1
Cranfield Rd *BNTWD* WS7 .... 18 E6
Cranford Gv *SOLH* B91........ 148 A4 🔲
Cranford Rd *BDMR/CCFT* WV3 .. 49 C5
  COVW CV5........ 153 H1
Cranford St *SMTHWK* B66 .... 88 A8
Cranford Wy *SMTHWK* B66 ...... 88 A8
Cranham CI *REDW* B97 .... 195 M5
Cranham Dr *KGSWFD* DY6........ 83 H8
Cranhill CI *HIA/OLT* B92 .... 127 M4
Crankhall La *DARL/WED* WS10 .. 69 C2
Cranleigh CI *ALDR* WS9 .... 40 F8
  SHHTH WV12 .... 38 A3 🔲
Cranleigh PI *KGSTG* B44 .... 71 J8
Cranley Dr *CDSL* WV8 .... 34 D1
Cranmer Av *SHHTH* WV12 .... 38 B6
Cranmer CI *GTWY* WS6 .... 24 B1
Cranmere Av
  DUNHL/THL/PER WV6........ 34 E7
Cranmer Gv *FOAKS/STRLY* B74 .. 42 D7
Cranmoor Crs *HALE* B63 .... 103 L8
Cranmore Av *HDSW* B21........ 88 B6
  SHLY B90 .... 147 J5
Cranmore Bvd *SHLY* B90 .... 147 H5 🔲
Cranmore Dr *SHLY* B90 .... 147 J4
Cranmore Rd *BDMR/CCFT* WV3 .. 49 K2
  CBROM B36 .... 92 C4
  SHLY B90 .... 147 H5
Cransley Gv *SOLH* B91 .... 147 L4
Crantock CI *SHHTH* WV12 .... 38 A4
Crantock Rd *PBAR/PBCH* B42 .... 89 C1
Crantock Wy *NUN* CV11 .... 99 K1
Cranwell Gn *WMBN* WV5 .... 64 D8 🔲
Cranwell Gv *ERDE/BCHGN* B24 .. 91 L2
Cranwell Wy *CVALE* B35 .... 91 L2 🔲
Crathie CI *COVE* CV2........ 135 K7
Crathorne Av *WOLVN* WV10 ...... 36 A4
Craufurd Ct *STRBR* DY8 .... 119 L2 🔲
Craufurd St *STRBR* DY8 .... 119 L2 🔲
Craven *TAM/AM/WIL* B77 .... 46 F4
Craven Av *COVS* CV3 .... 156 A6
Craven Rd *RUGBYN/HIL* CV21 .... 183 M1
Craven St *BKHL/PFLD* WV2 ...... 50 C6
  COVW CV5........ 153 K3
Crawford Av *DARL/WED* WS10 .. 52 A6
  ETTPK/GDPK/PENN WV4 ...... 66 D2
  SMTHWKW B67 .... 87 J8
Crawford CI *RLSN* CV32 .... 200 F1
Crawford Rd *BDMR/CCFT* WV3 .. 2 A5
  WALM/CURD B76 .... 75 K5
Crawford St *WASH/WDE* B8 ...... 90 A8
Crawshaws Rd *CBROM* B36 ...... 92 A4
Crayford Rd *KGSTG* B44 .... 71 L4
Craythorne Av
  BFLD/HDSWWD B20 .... 70 C8
Crecy CI *WALM/CURD* B76 .... 73 J1
Crecy Rd *COVS* CV3 .... 154 C6
Credenda Rd *WBROM* B70 .... 86 E4
Crediton CI *NUN* CV11 .... 81 K8
Cregoe St *EDG* B15........ 6 D8
Cremore Av *WASH/WDE* B8 ...... 90 C8
Cremorne Rd *MGN/WHC* B75 .... 56 F5
Crendon CI *STUD* B80 .... 197 J7
Crendon Rd *BLKHTH/ROWR* B65 .. 85 L7
Crescent Av *BRLYHL* DY5 .... 102 A3
  COVS CV3 .... 154 F3
The Crescent Grange Rd
  HAG/WOL DY9 .... 120 A1 🔲
Crescent Rd *DARL/WED* WS10 .. 52 B7
  DUDS DY2 .... 84 D3
  KIDDW DY11 .... 137 G7
  WLNHL WV13 .... 52 A3
Crescent Stennels *RMSLY* B62 .. 122 C1
The Crescent *ATHST* CV9 .... 62 A2
  BILS/COS WV14 .... 51 H7
  BLKHTH/ROWR B65 .... 103 M3
  BNTWD WS7 .... 18 D4
  BRGRVE B60 .... 185 A4
  CDYHTH B64 .... 103 L6
  CSHL/WTROR B46 .... 111 J5
  DARL/WED WS10 .... 68 E1 🔲
  DUDN DY1 .... 85 J1
  DUNHL/THL/PER WV6........ 48 F2
  GTB/HAM B43 .... 70 E4
  GTWY WS6 .... 24 E3
  HAG/WOL DY9 .... 119 K8
  HIA/OLT B92 .... 129 M6
  KIDD DY10 .... 137 M1
  RCOVN/BALC/EX CV7 .... 115 K7
  RRUGBY CV23 .... 157 K1
  RRUGBY CV23 .... 182 A7
  SHLY B90 .... 146 E1
  SOLH B91 .... 147 M1
  WLNHL WV13 .... 52 A4
  WSL WS1 .... 5 K4
  WSL WS1 .... 5 K4
  WSNGN B18 .... 88 F7
Cressage Av *NFLD/LBR* B31 ...... 143 L4
Cressage Rd *COVE* CV2 .... 135 L7
Cressett Av *BRLYHL* DY5 .... 101 M1
Cressett La *BRLYHL* DY5 .... 102 A1
Cressington Dr
  FOAKS/STRLY B74........ 56 E4
Cresswell CI
  NUNW/HART CV10 .... 81 C5 🔲
Cresswell Crs *BLOX/PEL* WS3 .... 38 D3

Cresswell Gv
ERDE/BCHGN B24 91 H1 3
The Crest *NFLD/LBR* B31 143 M7
RLSN CV32 201 G2
Crest Vw *ALE/KHTH/YWD* B14 145 M1
FOAKS/STRLY B74 55 K4
Crestwood *TAM/AM/WIL* B77 32 E8 1
Crestwood Av *KIDDW* DY11 136 E8
Crestwood Dr *KGSTG* B44 71 J6
Crestwood Gln
DUNHL/THL/PER WV6 35 J6
Creswell Rd *HLGN/YWD* B28 126 F6
Creswick Gv *RBRY* B45 143 G6
Crew La *KNWTH* CV8 177 J8
Crew Rd *DARL/WED* WS10 68 E1
Creynolds Cl *SHLY* B90 171 H1 3
Creynolds La *SHLY* B90 147 K8
Cricket Cl *COVW* CV5 153 K2
DSYBK/YTR WS5 5 L8
Cricketers Meadow
CDYHTH B64 103 K6
Cricket La *LICHS* WS14 29 G1
Cricket Meadow *SEDG* DY3 66 C8
WOLVN WV10 36 B1
Crick La *BFLD/HDSWWD* B20 88 E5
Cricklewood Dr *RMSLY* B62 122 B2 3
Crigdon *POL/KGSB/FAZ* B78 47 G3 3
Crimmond Ri *HALE* B63 103 J8
Crimscote Cl *SHLY* B90 147 K7
Cringlebrook *TAM/AM/WIL* B77 46 B4
Cripps Rd *WSLW* WS2 52 C2
Crockett's La *SMTHWK* B66 87 L8
Crocketts Rd *HDSW* B21 88 B6
Crockett St *DUDN* DY1 84 E3
Crockford Dr *MGN/WHC* B75 56 E2
Crockford Rd *HHTH/SAND* B71 69 G4
Crocus Crs *COVEN* WV9 35 L2 2
Croft Av *HEDN* WS12 12 E4
Croft Cl *REDE* B98 197 H2
RRUGBY CV23 180 D7 1
WWCK CV34 200 A6
YDLY B25 109 J5
Croft Crs *BRWNH* WS8 26 B6
Croft Down Rd *HIA/OLT* B92 128 B1
Croftdown Rd *HRBN* B17 105 K7
Crofters Cl *STRBR* DY8 119 M1 1
Crofters Ct *EDG* B15 106 C7
Croft Flds *BDWTH* CV12 116 F3
Croft Gdns *BNTWD* WS7 18 E5
Croft La *WOLVN* WV10 14 B4
WOLVN WV10 36 D6
Croft Md *NUNW/HART* CV10 97 G2
Croft Pool *BDWTH* CV12 116 D3
Croft Rd *ATHST* CV9 63 H4
BDWTH CV12 116 D3
COV CV1 8 D5
LGN/SDN/BHAMAIR B26 109 J5
NUNW/HART CV10 98 D2
RWWCK/WEL CV35 191 L6
The Crofts *WALM/CURD* B76 73 L5 3
Croft St *CRTAM* B79 31 M7
WLNHL WV13 51 L3
WSLW WS2 53 H2
The Croft *BDWTH* CV12 117 M3
COVN CV6 134 D1
DSYBK/YTR WS5 54 B5
DUDS DY2 84 D7 2
GTWY WS6 24 C3
KIDD DY10 139 G3
KIDDW DY11 160 E2
NFLD/LBR B31 143 M2
RCOVN/BALC/EX CV7 131 G4
SEDG DY3 66 C4 1
WLNHL WV13 51 L3 1
WMBN WV5 64 B8 1
The Croftway
BFLD/HDSWWD B20 70 C7
Croftwood Rd *HAG/WOL* DY9 120 B1
Cromarty Cl *COVW* CV5 132 E8 1
Cromdale *TAM/AM/WIL* B77 47 G4 1
Cromdale Cl *NUNW/HART* CV10 97 L2
Cromdale Dr *HALE* B63 121 H2 1
Cromer Gdns
DUNHL/THL/PER WV6 35 K8
Crome Rd *GTB/HAM* B43 71 H2
Cromer Rd *BHTH/HG* B12 107 K8
RLSN CV32 200 F3
Cromes Wd *TLHL/CAN* CV4 152 B4
Crompton Cl *WSLW* WS2 38 E8
Crompton Rd
BFLD/HDSWWD B20 89 G5
RBRY B45 142 B4
TPTN/OCK DY4 85 L1
VAUX/NECH B7 90 A5
Crompton St *WWCK* CV34 199 H7
Cromwell Cl *BLKHTH/ROWR* B65 85 K8
WSLW WS2 52 C1
Cromwell Dr *DUDS* DY2 85 K5
Cromwell La *RIDG/WDGT* B32 123 H5
TLHL/CAN CV4 152 A7
Cromwell Rd *CRTAM* B79 31 J5
HEDN WS12 17 H4
WOLVN WV10 36 C1
Cromwells Meadow *LICHS* WS14 21 G8
Cromwell St *COVN* CV6 134 D7
DUDS DY2 85 J5 1
VAUX/NECH B7 89 M8
Crondal Pl *EDG* B15 106 F6 1
Crondal Rd
RCOVN/BALC/EX CV7 116 F6
Cronehills Linkway *WBROM* B70 87 H2
Cronehills St *WBROM* B70 87 H1
Crookham Cl *HRBN* B17 105 K6
Crookhay La *HHTH/SAND* B71 68 E5
Crook La *ALDR* WS9 54 E7
Croome Cl *COVN* CV6 153 K1 1
REDE B98 197 K3
SPARK B11 125 M2
Cropredy Rd *NFLD/LBR* B31 143 L5
Cropthorne Cl *REDE* B98 196 E6
Cropthorne Dr *HLYWD* B47 145 M6
Cropthorne Rd *SHLY* B90 147 H1 3
Crosbie Rd *COVW* CV5 153 J2
HRBN B17 105 M7
Crosby Cl *CBHAMW* B1 6 A4
DUNHL/THL/PER WV6 35 K8
Cross Cheaping *COV* CV1 8 F4 1
Cross Cl *CDYHTH* B64 103 K3 1
Cross Farm Rd *HRBN* B17 124 B1
Cross Farms La *RBRY* B45 142 D4
Crossfell *TAM/AM/WIL* B77 46 F4
Crossfield Rd *LICH* WS13 21 J5
STETCH B33 109 L2
Cross Fields Rd *WWCK* CV34 199 K5 1
Crossgate Rd *DUDS* DY2 84 D7
REDE B98 197 G6
Cross In Hand La *LICH* WS13 20 D4 2
Crosskey Cl *STETCH* B33 110 C3 1
Cross Keys *LICH* WS13 20 F5
Crossland Crs
DUNHL/THL/PER WV6 35 K7
Crossland Rd *NFLD/LBR* B31 143 K1
Cross La *GTB/HAM* B43 70 C4
LICHS WS14 21 H7
RLSN CV32 201 J1
SEDG DY3 66 B5
Crossley St *DUDS* DY2 103 H1 1
Cross Pl *SEDG* DY3 66 C4 2
Cross Rd *COVN* CV6 134 D5
RCOVN/BALC/EX CV7 115 K7 1
RLSN CV32 200 B4 1
Cross St *BILS/COS* WV14 67 K3
BLKHTH/ROWR B65 104 A4 2
BLOX/PEL WS3 39 L4
BNTWD WS7 18 C5
CNCK/NC WS11 16 C8
COV CV1 9 H2
CRTAM B79 31 M8 2
DARL/WED WS10 68 C2
DUDN DY1 84 F4
GTWY WS6 24 B3
HALE B63 121 L2
HDSW B21 88 A5
HEDN WS12 17 J4 2
KGSWFD DY6 82 F5
LGLYGN/QTN B68 104 E1 2
NUNW/HART CV10 98 B2
RLSN CV32 200 E4
RRUGBY CV23 158 E8
STRBR DY8 101 H2 2
TAM/AM/WIL B77 46 A2
WLNHL WV13 51 L4
WOLV WV1 3 M6
WWCK CV34 199 K6 1
Cross St South *BKHL/PFLD* WV2 50 A6
Cross Wk *POL/KGSB/FAZ* B78 47 L7
Cross Walks Rd *HAG/WOL* DY9 102 C8
Crossway La *KGSTG* B44 71 K7
Crossway Rd *COVS* CV3 177 M1
Crosswells Rd *LGLYGN/QTN* B68 86 F8
Crowberry Cl *BRWNH* WS8 26 B7
Crowberry La
POL/KGSB/FAZ B78 59 G4
Crowden Rd *TAM/AM/WIL* B77 46 E4
Crowesbridge Ms
BILS/COS WV14 66 F5 1
Crowhill Rd *NUN* CV11 99 K3
Crowhurst Rd *NFLD/LBR* B31 143 J6
Crowland Av
DUNHL/THL/PER WV6 48 C1
Crowle Dr *HAG/WOL* DY9 102 A8 1
Crowmere Rd *COVE* CV2 135 K6
Crown Br *PENK* ST19 10 C4
Crown Cl *BLKHTH/ROWR* B65 104 B1
BRGRVW B61 185 K3
SEDG DY3 66 B4
Crown Ct *DARL/WED* WS10 52 A5 3
Crown Gn *COVN* CV6 134 C3
Crown La *FOAKS/STRLY* B74 56 C3
KIDD DY10 137 J7
STRBR DY8 101 K7
Crown Meadow *ALVE* B48 167 L7
Crownmeadow Dr
TPTN/OCK DY4 68 B6 1
Crown Rd *BORD* B9 108 B3
BVILLE B30 144 E1
Crown St *WOLV* WV1 36 B8
Crown Ter *RLSS* CV31 200 D6 3
Crown Wk *TPTN/OCK* DY4 85 L3 3
Crown Wy *RLSN* CV32 200 F2
Crows Nest Cl
WALM/CURD B76 73 K2 2
Crowther Gdns *HALE* B63 103 G6 1
Crowther Gv
DUNHL/THL/PER WV6 49 K1
Crowther Rd
DUNHL/THL/PER WV6 35 K8
ERDW/GRVHL B23 72 B8
Crowther St *KIDDW* DY11 137 G7
WOLVN WV10 50 C1
Croxall Dr *CSHL/WTROR* B46 94 E3
Croxall Wy *SMTHWK* B66 87 M8
Croxdene Av *BLOX/PEL* WS3 38 D4
Croxhall St *BDWTH* CV12 117 G2 2
Croxley Gdns *WLNHL* WV13 51 K5
Croxstalls Av *BLOX/PEL* WS3 38 E5
Croxstalls Cl *BLOX/PEL* WS3 38 E4
Croxstalls Pl *BLOX/PEL* WS3 38 E5 1
Croxstalls Rd *BLOX/PEL* WS3 38 E4
Croxton Gv *STETCH* B33 109 L1
Croyde Av *PBAR/PBCH* B42 70 E5
Croydon Cl *COVS* CV3 154 C7
Croydon Dr *PENK* ST19 10 C5
Croydon Rd *ERDE/BCHGN* B24 90 E4
SLYOAK B29 124 D2
Croy Dr *CVALE* B35 91 M1
Cruisehill La *REDW* B97 195 H8
Crummock Cl *COVN* CV6 134 B2 1
Crumpfields La *REDW* B97 195 J5
Crusader Cl *OLDBY* B69 86 C8
Crutch La *DROIT* WR9 184 A8
Crutchley Av
POL/KGSB/FAZ B78 45 L3 1
Crychan Cl *RBRY* B45 142 F3
Cryersoak Cl *SHLY* B90 147 L6
Cryfield Grange Rd
TLHL/CAN CV4 177 G3
Cryfield Hts *TLHL/CAN* CV4 177 H3
Crystal Av *STRBR* DY8 101 K4
Crystal Dr *SMTHWK* B66 87 G5
Cubbington Rd *COVN* CV6 134 E2
RLSN CV32 200 E2
Cubley Rd *HLGN/YWD* B28 126 C4
Cuckoo Cl *HEDN* WS12 17 G3
Cuckoo La *COV* CV1 9 G4 1
Cuckoo Rd *VAUX/NECH* B7 90 A5
Cuin Dr *SMTHWK* B66 88 A8
Cuin Rd *SMTHWK* B66 88 A8
Culey Gv *STETCH* B33 110 B3
Culford Dr *RIDG/WDGT* B32 123 G5
Culham Cl *ACGN* B27 127 H3 2
Cullwick St *WOLV* WV1 50 E6
Culmington Gv *NFLD/LBR* B31 143 K5
Culmington Rd *NFLD/LBR* B31 143 K5
Culmore Cl *SHHTH* WV12 52 B1
Culmore Rd *RMSLY* B62 104 C4 1
Culpepper Cl *NUNW/HART* CV10 98 C1
Culverhouse Dr *STRBR* DY8 101 L4 1
Culverley Crs *DOR/KN* B93 148 D7
Culwell St *WOLVN* WV10 3 H3
Culworth Cl *RLSS* CV31 200 D8
Culworth Rw *COVN* CV6 134 C5
Cumberford Av *STETCH* B33 110 C4 1
Cumberland Av *DIG/EDG* B5 107 J6 1
Cumberland Cl *KGSWFD* DY6 101 J1
Cumberland Crs *BNTWD* WS7 18 E5 1
RLSN CV32 201 G2 3
Cumberland Dr
NUNW/HART CV10 98 C2
POL/KGSB/FAZ B78 45 L4 1
Cumberland Rd *BILS/COS* WV14 51 H6
CNCK/NC WS11 16 E1 2
HHTH/SAND B71 69 H7
LGLYGN/QTN B68 104 F5
WLNHL WV13 52 B3
Cumberland St *CBHAMW* B1 6 B6
Cumbria Cl *COV* CV1 8 B4
Cumbrian Cft *HALE* B63 121 H3 1
Cumming St *RLSS* CV31 200 E6 3
Cundall Cl *RLSS* CV31 200 F7 3
Cunningham Rd
DUNHL/THL/PER WV6 48 C1 3
WSLW WS2 52 C3
Cunningham Wy North
RUGBYS/DCH CV22 183 G3 1
RUGBYS/DCH CV22 183 G4 1
Cupfields Av *TPTN/OCK* DY4 68 A5
Cupfields Crs *TPTN/OCK* DY4 68 A6
Curbar Rd *PBAR/PBCH* B42 71 G7
Curborough Rd *LICH* WS13 20 F2
Curdale Rd *RIDG/WDGT* B32 122 F5 2
Curdworth La *WALM/CURD* B76 74 D4
Cur La *REDW* B97 194 F2
Curlew *TAM/AM/WIL* B77 46 E6
Curlew Cl *KIDD* DY10 161 M3
LICHS WS14 21 J6
Curlew Hl *CNCK/NC* WS11 16 E2
Curlews Cl *ERDW/GRVHL* B23 72 A5 2
Curlieu Cl *RWWCK/WEL* CV35 198 E7 1
Curral Rd *BLKHTH/ROWR* B65 103 M2
Curriers Cl *TLHL/CAN* CV4 152 B6
Curtin Dr *DARL/WED* WS10 67 M1
Curtis Cl *SMTHWK* B66 106 A1 2
Curtis Rd *COVE* CV2 135 H7
Curzon Av *COVN* CV6 134 C5
Curzon St *BKHL/PFLD* WV2 50 B6
CBHAMNE B4 7 K4
Cuthbert Rd *WSNGN* B18 106 C1
Cutlers Rough Cl
NFLD/LBR B31 123 K8 2
Cutler St *SMTHWK* B66 87 M8
Cutsdean Cl *NFLD/LBR* B31 123 K7
Cutshill Cl *CBROM* B36 92 A5
Cut Throat La *HOCK/TIA* B94 171 G5
The Cutting *RUSH/SHEL* WS4 53 K1 1
Cuttle Mill La *WALM/CURD* B76 75 H2
Cuttle Pool La *DOR/KN* B93 173 K1
Cutworth Cl *WALM/CURD* B76 73 L2 2
Cygnet Cl *ALVE* B48 167 L6 1
HEDN WS12 13 G6 3
Cygnet Gv *ERDW/GRVHL* B23 71 L7
Cygnet La *BRLYHL* DY5 84 A6
Cygnet Rd *WBROM* B70 68 E8 1
Cygnus Wy *WBROM* B70 68 D8
Cymbeline Wy
RUGBYS/DCH CV22 183 H7
Cypress Av *SEDG* DY3 66 B8
Cypress Cft *COVS* CV3 155 K5
Cypress Gdns *KGSWFD* DY6 101 H1 1
Cypress Gv *NFLD/LBR* B31 143 J4 1
Cypress Ri *HEDN* WS12 13 L7
Cypress Rd *DSYBK/YTR* WS5 70 A1
DUDS DY2 85 K4
Cypress Sq *ACGN* B27 109 G8 3
Cypress Wy *NFLD/LBR* B31 143 K5
Cyprus Cl *SLYOAK* B29 123 L6
Cyprus St *BKHL/PFLD* WV2 49 M6
OLDBY B69 86 E5 1
Cyril Rd *SMHTH* B10 108 A5

D

Dace *TAM/AM/WIL* B77 46 B6
Dacer Cl *BVILLE* B30 124 F8
Dadford Vw *BRLYHL* DY5 101 M3
Dad's La *MOS/BIL* B13 125 G4
Daffern Av *RCOVN/BALC/EX* CV7 96 E5
Daffern Rd
RCOVN/BALC/EX CV7 116 E4
Daffodil Cl *SEDG* DY3 66 C6
Daffodil Pl *DSYBK/YTR* WS5 54 B5
Daffodil Rd *DSYBK/YTR* WS5 54 B5
Daffodil Wy *NFLD/LBR* B31 143 J5 1
Dagger La *HHTH/SAND* B71 69 J8
Dagnall Rd *ACGN* B27 127 H2
Dagnell End Rd *REDE* B98 188 D5
Daimler Cl *CBROM* B36 92 D4
Daimler Rd
ALE/KHTH/YWD B14 146 B2
COVN CV6 134 A8
Dainton Gv *RIDG/WDGT* B32 123 G4
Daintree Cft *COVS* CV3 154 A6
Daintry Dr *POL/KGSB/FAZ* B78 30 F6
Dairy Cl *TPTN/OCK* DY4 67 M8 1
Dairy Ct *LGLYGN/QTN* B68 105 H6
Daisy Bank *HEDN* WS12 12 D5
Daisy Bank Cl *BLOX/PEL* WS3 39 M3
Daisy Bank Crs *DSYBK/YTR* WS5 54 B5
Daisy Dr *ERDW/GRVHL* B23 71 L8
Daisy Farm Rd
ALE/KHTH/YWD B14 145 M3
Daisy Meadow *TPTN/OCK* DY4 68 A7
Daisy Rd *LDYWD/EDGR* B16 106 D3 3
Daisy St *BILS/COS* WV14 67 J3
DUNHL/THL/PER WV6 49 L1 3
Daisy Wk *COVEN* WV9 35 L2
Dalbeg Cl *CDSL* WV8 35 J5 1
Dalbury Rd *HLGN/YWD* B28 126 C8
Dalby Cl *COVS* CV3 155 J6
Dalby Rd *BLOX/PEL* WS3 39 K7
Dale Cl *BRGRVW* B61 165 K6
GTB/HAM B43 70 B4
SMTHWKW B67 105 L2
TPTN/OCK DY4 68 B8
WWCK CV34 199 L5 1
Dalecote Av *HIA/OLT* B92 128 C5
Dale Dr *BNTWD* WS7 18 F6
Dale End *CBHAMNE* B4 7 H5
DARL/WED WS10 52 B7 2
NUNW/HART CV10 80 C8
Dale Hl *BRGRVE* B60 166 D7
Dalehouse La *KNWTH* CV8 177 G7
Dale Meadow Cl
RCOVN/BALC/EX CV7 150 F7
Dale Rd *REDE* B98 188 D8
RMSLY B62 104 D5
SLYOAK B29 124 C2
STRBR DY8 119 K3
Dales Cl
DUNHL/THL/PER WV6 35 M7 1
Dalesman Cl *KGSWFD* DY6 82 F6
Dale St *BDMR/CCFT* WV3 2 D7
BILS/COS WV14 51 K8
DARL/WED WS10 68 C2
RLSS CV31 200 C5
RUGBYN/HIL CV21 183 L1
SMTHWK B66 105 L2
WSL WS1 4 D8
Dale Ter *OLDBY* B69 86 A5
Daleview Rd
ALE/KHTH/YWD B14 146 A2
Daleway Rd *COVS* CV3 177 M2
Dalewood Cft
LGN/SDN/BHAMAIR B26 109 K7
Dalewood Rd
CHWD/FDBR/MGN B37 92 D8 3
Daley Cl *CBHAMW* B1 6 A4
Daley Rd *BILS/COS* WV14 67 K3
Dalkeith Av *RUGBYS/DCH* CV22 183 H6
Dalkeith Rd *SCFLD/BOLD* B73 72 C3
Dalkeith St *WSLW* WS2 53 G2
Dallas Rd *ERDW/GRVHL* B23 90 A1
Dallimore Cl *HIA/OLT* B92 127 K2
Dallington Rd *COVN* CV6 133 J7
Dalloway Cl *DIG/EDG* B5 107 H7 1
Dalmeny Rd *TLHL/CAN* CV4 152 B6
Dalston Cl *DUDS* DY2 85 H7 1
Dalston Rd *ACGN* B27 127 G1
Dalton Cl *RRUGBY* CV23 157 M7
Dalton Gdns *COVE* CV2 155 K1
Dalton Rd *BDWTH* CV12 116 D3
COVW CV5 8 C9
WSLW WS2 52 E2
Dalton St *BDMR/CCFT* WV3 2 C9
CBHAMNE B4 7 H4
Dalvine Rd *DUDS* DY2 102 F3
Dalwood Cl *BILS/COS* WV14 66 F6
Daly Av *RWWCK/WEL* CV35 198 D7
Damar Cft *ALE/KHTH/YWD* B14 145 H1
Dama Rd *POL/KGSB/FAZ* B78 45 K5
Dame Agnes Gv *COVN* CV6 134 F5
Damien Cl *SMTHWKW* B67 87 K8 1
Damson Cl *REDW* B97 195 M7
WNSFLD WV11 37 L7 2
Damson La *SOLH* B91 128 C8
Damson Pkwy *HIA/OLT* B92 128 D2
Damson Rd
RWWCK/WEL CV35 198 D7 2
Dam St *LICH* WS13 20 F5
Danbury Cl *WALM/CURD* B76 73 L3 1
Danbury Rd *SHLY* B90 146 F2
Danby Dr *HEDN* WS12 18 A1
Danby Gv *ERDE/BCHGN* B24 90 F3
Dando Rd *DUDS* DY2 85 H5
Dandy Bank Rd *KGSWFD* DY6 83 L5
Dandy's Wk *WSL* WS1 5 G5
Dane Gv *MOS/BIL* B13 125 H5
Danelagh Cl *CRTAM* B79 31 K6
Dane Rd *COVE* CV2 154 F1
Danesbury Crs *KGSTG* B44 71 L5
RLSS CV31 201 H7
Danes Cl *WNSFLD* WV11 37 K1
Danescourt Rd
DUNHL/THL/PER WV6 35 G7
Daneswood Dr *ALDR* WS9 40 D2 1
Daneswood Rd *COVS* CV3 156 C6 2
Dane Ter *BLKHTH/ROWR* B65 86 A8
Daneways Cl *FOAKS/STRLY* B74 55 L5
Danford Cl *STRBR* DY8 119 L1
Danford Gdns *SMHTH* B10 108 A5 1
Danford La *SOLH* B91 147 J2
Danford Rd *HLYWD* B47 145 K7 1
Danford Wy *GTB/HAM* B43 70 B5
Dangerfield La *DARL/WED* WS10 52 A8
Daniel Av *NUNW/HART* CV10 98 A2
Daniel Rd *ATHST* CV9 63 K6
Daniels La *ALDR* WS9 55 G1
Daniels Rd *BORD* B9 108 E3
Danilo Rd *CNCK/NC* WS11 16 B4
Danks St *TPTN/OCK* DY4 85 L3 3
Danzey Cl *REDE* B98 196 F8
Danzey Green Rd *CBROM* B36 91 M4
Danzey Gv *BVILLE* B30 145 G2
Daphne Cl *COVE* CV2 135 G2 1
Darby Cl *BILS/COS* WV14 66 E3
Darby End Rd
BLKHTH/ROWR B65 103 J1
DUDS DY2 103 J1
Darby Rd *DARL/WED* WS10 68 F2
LGLYGN/QTN B68 87 G8
Darbys Hill Rd *OLDBY* B69 85 L5
Darby St *BLKHTH/ROWR* B65 104 A4
Darell Cft *WALM/CURD* B76 73 J2
Daren Cl *CBROM* B36 92 D5
Dare Rd *ERDW/GRVHL* B23 90 C1
Darfield Ct *KNWTH* CV8 179 G8
Darges La *GTWY* WS6 24 D1
Darkhouse La *BILS/COS* WV14 67 G3
Dark La *BDWTH* CV12 116 B4
BRGRVE B60 185 H7
COV CV1 8 E1
GTWY WS6 25 G4
HAG/WOL DY9 140 C6
HWK/WKHTH B38 145 H6
KINVER DY7 118 A2
LICH WS13 19 L4
POL/KGSB/FAZ B78 47 J5
RMSLY B62 141 K1
WNSFLD WV11 23 H6
WOLVN WV10 22 B5
Darlaston La *BILS/COS* WV14 51 L6
Darlaston Rd *DARL/WED* WS10 52 B8
WSLW WS2 52 E5
Darley Av *BKDE/SHDE* B34 91 K7
Darleydale Av *KGSTG* B44 71 J4
Darley Dr *DUNHL/THL/PER* WV6 35 M8
Darley Green Rd *DOR/KN* B93 172 F4
Darley Wy *FOAKS/STRLY* B74 55 K6
Darlington St
DARL/WED WS10 52 B8 1
WOLV WV1 2 E5
Darlington Yd *WOLV* WV1 2 E5 2
Darnbrook *TAM/AM/WIL* B77 47 G4 3
Darnel Cft *SMHTH* B10 107 M4 2
Darnel Hurst Rd *MGN/WHC* B75 57 G2
Darnford Cl *COVE* CV2 135 K6 2
CSCFLD/WYGN B72 73 H6 2
HLGN/YWD B28 126 E8
Darnford La *LICHS* WS14 21 J7
Darnford Moors *LICHS* WS14 21 J7
Darnford Vw *LICH* WS13 21 J4 1
Darnick Rd *SCFLD/BOLD* B73 72 B2
Darnley Rd
LDYWD/EDGR B16 106 E3 2
Darrach Cl *COVE* CV2 135 J3
Darris Rd *SLYOAK* B29 124 E5 2
Dart *TAM/AM/WIL* B77 46 E8
Dartford Rd *BLOX/PEL* WS3 38 D4
Dartington Wy *NUN* CV11 99 K5
Dartmoor Cl *RBRY* B45 142 E3
Dartmouth Av *BLOX/PEL* WS3 39 J8
CNCK/NC WS11 16 A5
STRBR DY8 101 H2
WLNHL WV13 51 K3
Dartmouth Cl *BLOX/PEL* WS3 39 J8
CNCK/NC WS11 16 A5 1
Dartmouth Crs
BILS/COS WV14 51 L6 1
Dartmouth Dr *ALDR* WS9 40 D8
Dartmouth Pl *BLOX/PEL* WS3 39 J7
Dartmouth Rd *CNCK/NC* WS11 16 B4
COVE CV2 135 G8
SLYOAK B29 124 D3
SMTHWK B66 87 K5
Dartmouth St *BKHL/PFLD* WV2 3 H8 1
WBROM B70 87 G1
Dart St *BORD* B9 107 M4
Darvel Rd *SHHTH* WV12 52 B1
Darwall St *WSL* WS1 4 F2
Darwin Cl *BNTWD* WS7 18 F6
COVE CV2 135 L7 3
HEDN WS12 17 J4
Darwin Ct *DUNHL/THL/PER* WV6 48 C1
Darwin Pl *WSLW* WS2 38 F7
Darwin Rd *WSLW* WS2 38 F7
Darwin St *BHTH/HG* B12 107 K5
Dassett Gv *BORD* B9 109 G3
Dassett Rd *DOR/KN* B93 172 D1
Datchet Cl *COVW* CV5 153 G1
Datteln Rd *CNCK/NC* WS11 16 E1
D'aubeny Rd *TLHL/CAN* CV4 152 F5
Dauntsey Covert *BVILLE* B30 145 H3
Davena Dr *SLYOAK* B29 123 J3 1
Davena Gv *BILS/COS* WV14 67 H2
Davenport Dr *BRGRVE* B60 185 M4 2
CVALE B35 92 A2
Davenport Rd
DUNHL/THL/PER WV6 34 F8
WNSFLD WV11 37 J7
Daventry Gv *RIDG/WDGT* B32 105 G7
Daventry Rd *COVS* CV3 154 B6
Davey Rd *BFLD/HDSWWD* B20 89 J4
WBROM B70 86 E1
David Peacock Cl *TPTN/OCK* DY4 67 L8
David Rd *BFLD/HDSWWD* B20 88 F3
COV CV1 9 K6
RCOVN/BALC/EX CV7 116 D6
RUGBYS/DCH CV22 183 H5
TPTN/OCK DY4 67 L6
Davidson Av *RLSS* CV31 200 E6
Davidson Rd *LICHS* WS14 20 F6 2
The Davids *NFLD/LBR* B31 124 A7
Davies Av *BILS/COS* WV14 67 H2
Davies Rd *RCOVN/BALC/EX* CV7 116 D6
Davis Av *TPTN/OCK* DY4 85 J1
Davis Cl *RLSN* CV32 200 B3
Davis Gv
LGN/SDN/BHAMAIR B26 109 H7
Davison Rd *SMTHWKW* B67 105 K2
Davis Rd *SHHTH* WV12 38 B5
TAM/AM/WIL B77 46 D1
Davy Rd *WSLW* WS2 38 E8
Dawberry Cl
ALE/KHTH/YWD B14 125 H8
Dawberry Fields Rd
ALE/KHTH/YWD B14 125 G8
Dawberry Rd
ALE/KHTH/YWD B14 125 G8
Daw End *RUSH/SHEL* WS4 40 A7
Daw End La *RUSH/SHEL* WS4 39 M7
Dawes Av *WBROM* B70 87 G4
Dawes Cl *COVE* CV2 154 E1
Dawley Brook Rd *KGSWFD* DY6 83 H6
Dawley Crs
CHWD/FDBR/MGN B37 110 F4
Dawley Rd *KGSWFD* DY6 83 G5
Dawlish Cl *NUN* CV11 81 J8
Dawlish Dr *COVS* CV3 154 B8
Dawlish Rd *DUDN* DY1 66 F8
SLYOAK B29 124 D3
SMTHWK B66 87 M8 2
Dawn Dr *DARL/WED* WS10 68 A3
Dawney Dr *MGN/WHC* B75 56 E1
Dawn Rd *NFLD/LBR* B31 123 J7
Dawson Av *BILS/COS* WV14 66 D3
Dawson Rd *BRGRVW* B61 185 J3
COVS CV3 154 E4
HDSW B21 88 C5

Dawson Sq *BILS/COS* WV14 ...... 51 G8 ⬛
Dawson St *BLOX/PEL* WS3 ...... 39 H5
　SMTHWK B66 ...... 105 L2
Day Av *WNSFLD* WV11 ...... 37 J6
Daybrook Cl *REDW* B97 ...... 187 M8 ⬛
Dayhouse Bank *RMSLY* B62 ...... 141 M4
Daylesford Rd *HIA/OLT* B92 ...... 127 L2
Days Cl *COV* CV1 ...... 9 K3
Day's La *COV* CV1 ...... 9 K3
Daytona Dr *COVW* CV5 ...... 131 M5
Deacon St *NUN* CV11 ...... 99 G2
Deakin Av *BRWNH* WS8 ...... 26 D4
Deakin Rd *ERDE/BCHGN* B24 ...... 90 D2
　MGN/WHC B75 ...... 57 J6 ⬛
Deakins Rd *YDLY* B25 ...... 108 F6
Deal Av *BNTWD* WS7 ...... 18 E5
Deal Dr *DUDS* DY2 ...... 85 K4
Deal Gv *NFLD/LBR* B31 ...... 143 L1
Deanbrook Cl *SHLY* B90 ...... 147 L7
Dean Cl *CSCFLD/WYGN* B72 ...... 72 F6
　KGSTG B44 ...... 71 M5
　STRBR DY8 ...... 101 M7
Dean Ct *CDSL* WV8 ...... 34 C8
Deanery Cl *WOLVN* WV10 ...... 23 G3
Deanery Rw *WOLV* WV1 ...... 2 F5
Dean Rd *ERDW/GRVHL* B23 ...... 72 D8
　RUSH/SHEL WS4 ...... 40 A6
　WMBN WV5 ...... 64 D8
Deans Cl *REDE* B98 ...... 189 H8
Deans Cft *LICH* WS13 ...... 21 G6
Deansfield Rd *WOLV* WV1 ...... 50 E3
Deansford La *KIDD* DY10 ...... 138 D5
Deans Pl *BLOX/PEL* WS3 ...... 39 K7
Dean's Rd *WOLV* WV1 ...... 50 E2
Deans Slade Dr *LICHS* WS14 ...... 28 E1
Deanston Cft *COVE* CV2 ...... 135 K4
Dean St *COVE* CV2 ...... 154 C2
　DIG/EDG B5 ...... 7 H7
　SEDG DY3 ...... 66 B5 ⬛
Deansway *BRGRVW* B61 ...... 185 H4
Deans Wy *RCOVN/BALC/EX* CV7 ...... 116 B7
Deansway *WWCK* CV34 ...... 199 H4
The Deansway *KIDD* DY10 ...... 137 L8
Dearman Rd *SPARK* B11 ...... 107 M6
Dearmont Rd *NFLD/LBR* B31 ...... 143 J6
Dearne Ct *SEDG* DY3 ...... 66 E7
Deavall Wy *CNCK/NC* WS11 ...... 16 F3
Debden Cl *DOR/KN* B93 ...... 172 C3
Debenham Crs *YDLY* B25 ...... 109 H4
Debenham Rd *YDLY* B25 ...... 109 H4
Deblen Dr *LDYWD/EDGR* B16 ...... 106 B4
Deborah Cl
　ETTPK/GDPK/PENN WV4 ...... 50 A7 ⬛
De-compton Cl
　RCOVN/BALC/EX CV7 ...... 115 L6
Deedmore Cl *COVE* CV2 ...... 135 G5
Deegan Cl *COVE* CV2 ...... 134 E7
Dee Gv *CNCK/NC* WS11 ...... 16 B6 ⬛
　HWK/WKHTH B38 ...... 144 C5
Deelands Rd *RBRY* B45 ...... 142 D5
Deeley *TAM/AM/WIL* B77 ...... 46 B6
Deeley Cl *CDYHTH* B64 ...... 103 J6 ⬛
　EDG B15 ...... 107 G6
Deeley Dr *TPTN/OCK* DY4 ...... 68 A7 ⬛
Deeley Pl *BLOX/PEL* WS3 ...... 38 F5
Deeley St *BLOX/PEL* WS3 ...... 38 F5 ⬛
　BRLYHL DY5 ...... 102 C4
Deepdale *POL/KGSB/FAZ* B78 ...... 47 H4 ⬛
Deepdale Av
　LGN/SDN/BHAMAIR B26 ...... 127 M1
Deepdale La *DUDN* DY1 ...... 84 C2
Deepdales *WMBN* WV5 ...... 64 C7
Deep La *CSHL/WTROR* B46 ...... 76 D7
Deeplow Cl
　CSCFLD/WYGN B72 ...... 73 G1 ⬛
Deepmoor Rd *STETCH* B33 ...... 109 K2
Deepmore Av *WSLW* WS2 ...... 52 F3
Deepmore Cl *WOLVN* WV10 ...... 14 B8
Deepmore Rd
　RUGBYS/DCH CV22 ...... 183 H5
Deepwood Cl *RUSH/SHEL* WS4 ...... 39 M5
Deer Barn Hl *REDE* B98 ...... 196 K4
Deer Cl *BLOX/PEL* WS3 ...... 39 G4
　CNCK/NC WS11 ...... 17 L6
Deerdale Wy *COVS* CV3 ...... 155 K5
Deerfold Crs *BNTWD* WS7 ...... 18 F6
Deerhill *TAM/AM/WIL* B77 ...... 47 G4
Deerhurst Ri *HEDN* WS12 ...... 13 K7 ⬛
Deerhurst Rd
　BFLD/HDSWWD B20 ...... 70 D8
　COVN CV6 ...... 133 M3
The Deer Leap *KNWTH* CV8 ...... 176 F7 ⬛
Dee Rd *BLOX/PEL* WS3 ...... 39 J4
Deerpark Dr *WWCK* CV34 ...... 199 H5
Deer Park Rd
　POL/KGSB/FAZ B78 ...... 45 J4
Deer Park Wy *SOLH* B91 ...... 148 A4
Defford Av *RUSH/SHEL* WS4 ...... 40 A4
Defford Dr *LGLYGN/QTN* B68 ...... 104 F1
Deighton Rd *DSYBK/YTR* WS5 ...... 69 M1
Delage Cl *COV* CV2 ...... 134 F1
Delamere Av *CBROM* B36 ...... 92 B4
Delamere Dr *GTB/HAM* B43 ...... 70 A2
Delamere Rd *BDWTH* CV12 ...... 116 D3
　BEWD DY12 ...... 160 A1
　HLGN/YWD B28 ...... 126 D6
　SHHTH WV12 ...... 38 A6
Delamere Wy *RLSN* CV32 ...... 201 G1
Delancey Keep
　MGN/WHC B75 ...... 57 L8 ⬛
Delaware Rd *COVS* CV3 ...... 154 A8
Delhi Av *COVN* CV6 ...... 134 B4
Delhurst Av
　ETTPK/GDPK/PENN WV4 ...... 66 C2
Delhurst Rd *KGSTG* B44 ...... 71 H4
Delius St *TLHL/CAN* CV4 ...... 152 C2
Della Dr *RIDG/WDGT* B32 ...... 123 H5
Dell Cl *COVS* CV3 ...... 148 F7 ⬛
Dell Farm Cl *DOR/KN* B93 ...... 148 F7 ⬛
Dellow Gv *ALVE* B48 ...... 167 L8 ⬛
Dellows Cl *HWK/WKHTH* B38 ...... 144 B6
Dell Rd *BRLYHL* DY5 ...... 83 M8
　BVILLE B30 ...... 124 E8
The Dell *CRTAM* B79 ...... 31 M7
　HEDN WS12 ...... 17 K1
　HIA/OLT B92 ...... 127 L4
　LICH WS13 ...... 20 D6

NFLD/LBR B31 ...... 123 H7
　STRBR DY8 ...... 101 J7
Delmore Wy *WALM/CURD* B76 ...... 73 M7
Delph Dr *BRLYHL* DY5 ...... 102 C6
Delphinium Cl *BORD* B9 ...... 108 D2 ⬛
　KIDDW DY11 ...... 137 G4 ⬛
Delph La *BRLYHL* DY5 ...... 102 B5
Delph Rd *BRLYHL* DY5 ...... 102 B4
Delrene Rd *HLGN/YWD* B28 ...... 146 D2
Delta Wy *CNCK/NC* WS11 ...... 16 B7
Deltic *TAM/AM/WIL* B77 ...... 46 E4
Delves Crs *ATHST* CV9 ...... 61 H4
　DSYBK/YTR WS5 ...... 53 L8
Delves Green Rd
　DSYBK/YTR WS5 ...... 53 L7
Delves Rd *WSL* WS1 ...... 5 H8
Delville Rd *DARL/WED* WS10 ...... 68 D2
De Marnham Cl *WBROM* B70 ...... 87 J4 ⬛
De Montfort Rd *KNWTH* CV8 ...... 176 C7
De Montfort Wy *TLHL/CAN* CV4 ...... 153 G7
De Moram Gv *HIA/OLT* B92 ...... 128 D6
Dempster Rd *BDWTH* CV12 ...... 116 E1
Demuth Wy *OLDBY* B69 ...... 86 D7
Denaby Gv *ALE/KHTH/YWD* B14 ...... 146 B1
Denbigh Cl *DUDN* DY1 ...... 84 D3
Denbigh Crs *HHTH/SAND* B71 ...... 68 F7
Denbigh Dr *DARL/WED* WS10 ...... 69 H1
　HHTH/SAND B71 ...... 68 F7
Denbigh Rd *COVN* CV6 ...... 133 J7
　TPTN/OCK DY4 ...... 86 A1
Denbigh St *BORD* B9 ...... 108 B3
Denbury Cl *HEDN* WS12 ...... 17 H4 ⬛
Denby Cl *RLSN* CV32 ...... 201 G3
　VAUX/NECH B7 ...... 89 M8
Denby Cft *SHLY* B90 ...... 147 M7
Dencer Cl *RBRY* B45 ...... 142 D5
Dencer Dr *KNWTH* CV8 ...... 192 A1
Dencil Cl *HALE* B63 ...... 103 H8
Dene Av *KGSWFD* DY6 ...... 101 G1
Dene Cl *PENK* ST19 ...... 10 D5
Dene Court Rd *HIA/OLT* B92 ...... 127 K4
Denefield *PENK* ST19 ...... 10 D5
Denegate Cl
　WALM/CURD B76 ...... 73 M7 ⬛
Dene Hollow *MOS/BIL* B13 ...... 126 A7
Denehurst Cl *RBRY* B45 ...... 166 E4
Denehurst Wy
　NUNW/HART CV10 ...... 98 C2
Dene Rd
　ETTPK/GDPK/PENN WV4 ...... 64 D1
　STRBR DY8 ...... 119 K2
Denewood Av
　BFLD/HDSWWD B20 ...... 88 E3
Denewood Wy *KNWTH* CV8 ...... 177 G8 ⬛
Denford Gv
　ALE/KHTH/YWD B14 ...... 125 H8
Dengate Dr
　RCOVN/BALC/EX CV7 ...... 150 F6
Denham Av *COVW* CV5 ...... 152 F1
Denham Ct *ATHST* CV9 ...... 63 J5 ⬛
Denham Gdns *BDMR/CCFT* WV3 ...... 48 F5
Denham Rd *ACGN* B27 ...... 108 F8
Denholme Gv
　ALE/KHTH/YWD B14 ...... 145 L2
Denholm Rd *SCFLD/BOLD* B73 ...... 72 B2
Denise Dr *BILS/COS* WV14 ...... 66 F5
　CHWD/FDBR/MGN B37 ...... 110 D1
　HRBN B17 ...... 124 A1
Denleigh Rd *KGSWFD* DY6 ...... 101 K1
Denmark Ri *HEDN* WS12 ...... 13 H6
Denmead Dr *WNSFLD* WV11 ...... 37 K5 ⬛
Denmore Gdns *WOLV* WV1 ...... 50 F3
Dennett Cl *WWCK* CV34 ...... 199 K3 ⬛
Dennis *TAM/AM/WIL* B77 ...... 46 C3
Dennis Hall Rd *STRBR* DY8 ...... 101 L5
Dennis Rd *BHTH/HG* B12 ...... 125 M1
　COVE CV2 ...... 134 F8
Dennis St *STRBR* DY8 ...... 101 K5
Denshaw Cft *COVE* CV2 ...... 135 L5
Denshaw Rd
　ALE/KHTH/YWD B14 ...... 125 H7
Denton Cl *KNWTH* CV8 ...... 176 B7
Denton Cft *DOR/KN* B93 ...... 172 B2
Denton Gv *GTB/HAM* B43 ...... 70 B6 ⬛
　STETCH B33 ...... 109 H3 ⬛
Denton Rd *HAG/WOL* DY9 ...... 120 E1
Dent St *CRTAM* B79 ...... 32 A8
Denver Rd *ALE/KHTH/YWD* B14 ...... 145 L3
Denville Cl *BILS/COS* WV14 ...... 51 J6
Denville Crs *BORD* B9 ...... 108 F2
Denville Rd *RLSN* CV32 ...... 200 E2
Depwo Gv *RIDG/WDGT* B32 ...... 122 F5 ⬛
Derby Av *DUNHL/THL/PER* WV6 ...... 35 J6
Derby Dr
　CHWD/FDBR/MGN B37 ...... 110 F3
Derby Rd *LICHS* WS14 ...... 30 B2
Derby St *DIG/EDG* B5 ...... 7 M5
　WSLW WS2 ...... 53 H1
Dereham Cl *WASH/WDE* B8 ...... 108 A1 ⬛
Dereham Ct *RLSN* CV32 ...... 200 E2
Dereham Wk *BILS/COS* WV14 ...... 67 J3 ⬛
Derek Av *POL/KGSB/FAZ* B78 ...... 47 J1
Dereton Cl *DUDN* DY1 ...... 84 C5 ⬛
Dering Cl *COVE* CV2 ...... 135 H5
Deronda Cl *BDWTH* CV12 ...... 116 E2
Derron Av
　LGN/SDN/BHAMAIR B26 ...... 109 J8
Derry Cl *HRBN* B17 ...... 123 L2
　KNWTH CV8 ...... 180 E2 ⬛
Derrydown Cl
　ERDW/GRVHL B23 ...... 90 C2 ⬛
Derrydown Rd *PBAR/PBCH* B42 ...... 70 F8
Derry St *BKHL/PFLD* WV2 ...... 3 G9
　BRLYHL DY5 ...... 102 A3
Dersingham Dr *COVN* CV6 ...... 134 F3
Derwent Av *STRPT* DY13 ...... 160 D8
Derwent Cl *BRLYHL* DY5 ...... 83 M7 ⬛
　COVW CV5 ...... 152 C1
　FOAKS/STRLY B74 ...... 55 K3
　RLSN CV32 ...... 200 B4 ⬛
　WLNHL WV13 ...... 52 A3
Derwent Gv *BNTWD* WS7 ...... 19 H7
　BVILLE B30 ...... 125 G4 ⬛
　CNCK/NC WS11 ...... 16 B6 ⬛
Derwent Rd *BDWTH* CV12 ...... 116 E3
　BVILLE B30 ...... 125 G5
　COVN CV6 ...... 133 L3
　DUNHL/THL/PER WV6 ...... 35 H5

Derwent Wy *BRGRVE* B60 ...... 185 M4 ⬛
　NUN CV11 ...... 81 K7
Desford Av *PBAR/PBCH* B42 ...... 71 G6
Despard Rd *COWW* CV5 ...... 132 B8
Dettonford Rd
　RIDG/WDGT B32 ...... 122 F6
Devereux Cl *CBROM* B36 ...... 92 A5 ⬛
　TLHL/CAN CV4 ...... 152 A4 ⬛
Devereux Rd *MGN/WHC* B75 ...... 57 G4
　WBROM B70 ...... 87 J4
Devey Dr *TPTN/OCK* DY4 ...... 68 B7
Devine Cft *TPTN/OCK* DY4 ...... 67 L8 ⬛
Devitts Cl *SHLY* B90 ...... 147 K6 ⬛
Devon Cl *KIDDW* DY11 ...... 137 G4
　NUNW/HART CV10 ...... 98 D2
Devon Crs *ALDR* WS9 ...... 40 C4
　DUDS DY2 ...... 84 D6
　HHTH/SAND B71 ...... 68 C2
Devon Gv *COVE* CV2 ...... 134 F8
Devon Rd *CNCK/NC* WS11 ...... 16 D5
　DARL/WED WS10 ...... 69 G1
　RBRY B45 ...... 142 C3
　SMTHWKW B67 ...... 105 J6
　STRBR DY8 ...... 101 H6
　WLNHL WV13 ...... 52 B4
　WOLV WV1 ...... 2 D2
Devonshire Av *WSNGN* B18 ...... 88 D7
Devonshire Dr *HHTH/SAND* B71 ...... 87 J2
　POL/KGSB/FAZ B78 ...... 45 L4
Devonshire Rd
　BFLD/HDSWWD B20 ...... 88 D3
　SMTHWKW B67 ...... 87 J7
Devonshire St *WSNGN* B18 ...... 88 D7
Devon St *VAUX/NECH* B7 ...... 108 A1
Devoran Cl
　DUNHL/THL/PER WV6 ...... 49 M1
　RCOVN/BALC/EX CV7 ...... 116 F5
Dewberry Dr *DSYBK/YTR* WS5 ...... 69 L2
Dewberry Rd *STRBR* DY8 ...... 101 K4
Dewhurst Cft *STETCH* B33 ...... 109 M2 ⬛
Dewsbury Av *COVS* CV3 ...... 153 M8
Dewsbury Cl *STRBR* DY8 ...... 101 J2
Dewsbury Dr *BNTWD* WS7 ...... 19 G7
　ETTPK/GDPK/PENN WV4 ...... 65 L2
Dewsbury Gv *PBAR/PBCH* B42 ...... 71 G8
Dexter La *ATHST* CV9 ...... 77 G2
Dexter Wy *POL/KGSB/FAZ* B78 ...... 47 K5
Deykin Av *AST/WIT* B6 ...... 89 L3
D'eyncourt Rd *WNSFLD* WV11 ...... 36 E5
Dial Cl *ALE/KHTH/YWD* B14 ...... 145 J3
Dial House La *COVW* CV5 ...... 152 D1
Dial La *STRBR* DY8 ...... 101 J5
　WBROM B70 ...... 68 D7
Diamond Gv *HEDN* WS12 ...... 17 G3 ⬛
Diamond Park Dr *STRBR* DY8 ...... 101 J4 ⬛
Diana Cl *ALDR* WS9 ...... 40 F2
Diana Dr *COVE* CV2 ...... 135 J4
Diane Cl *TPTN/OCK* DY4 ...... 67 M3
Dibble Cl *WNHL* WV12 ...... 38 B8
Dibble Rd *SMTHWKW* B67 ...... 87 K7
Dibdale Rd *DUDN* DY1 ...... 84 D2
Dibdale St *DUDN* DY1 ...... 84 D3
Dice Pleck *NFLD/LBR* B31 ...... 144 A3
Dickens Cl *NUNW/HART* CV10 ...... 97 L1
　SEDG DY3 ...... 65 M8 ⬛
Dickens Gv
　ALE/KHTH/YWD B14 ...... 145 L2 ⬛
Dickens Heath Rd *SHLY* B90 ...... 146 E7 ⬛
　SHLY B90 ...... 146 E8 ⬛
Dickens Rd *BILS/COS* WV14 ...... 67 H3
　COVN CV6 ...... 133 L5
　RUGBYS/DCH CV22 ...... 183 K7
　WOLVN WV10 ...... 36 E5
　WWCK CV34 ...... 199 M5
Dickinson Av *WOLVN* WV10 ...... 36 C5
Dickinson Ct
　RUGBYS/DCH CV22 ...... 183 L4
Dickinson Dr *WALM/CURD* B76 ...... 73 J1
　WSLW WS2 ...... 53 G7
Dickinson Rd *WMBN* WV5 ...... 82 E1
Dick Sheppard Av
　TPTN/OCK DY4 ...... 67 M5
Didcot Cl *REDW* B97 ...... 196 A8
Diddington Av
　HLGN/YWD B28 ...... 126 E8 ⬛
Diddington La *HIA/OLT* B92 ...... 130 A5 ⬛
Didgley Gv
　CHWD/FDBR/MGN B37 ...... 92 E8 ⬛
Didgley La
　RCOVN/BALC/EX CV7 ...... 114 A1
Didsbury Rd
　RCOVN/BALC/EX CV7 ...... 116 E4 ⬛
Digbeth *DIG/EDG* B5 ...... 7 J7
　WSL WS1 ...... 4 F5
Digbey Cl *COVW* CV5 ...... 132 F7
Digby Crs *CSHL/WTROR* B46 ...... 92 F2 ⬛
Digby Dr
　CHWD/FDBR/MGN B37 ...... 110 F7
Digby Rd *CSHL/WTROR* B46 ...... 93 K7
　KGSWFD DY6 ...... 83 H5
　SCFLD/BOLD B73 ...... 72 C2
Dilcock Wy *TLHL/CAN* CV4 ...... 152 D6
Dilke Rd *ALDR* WS9 ...... 40 D8
Dillam Cl *COVN* CV6 ...... 134 C1
Dillotford Av *COVS* CV3 ...... 154 C7 ⬛
Dilloways La *WLNHL* WV13 ...... 51 J4
Dilwyn Cl *REDE* B98 ...... 197 K4
Dimbles Hl *LICH* WS13 ...... 20 F4
Dimbles La *LICH* WS13 ...... 20 E5
Dimmingsdale Bank
　RIDG/WDGT B32 ...... 123 G1
Dimmingsdale Rd
　ETTPK/GDPK/PENN WV4 ...... 48 B8
Dimminsdale *WLNHL* WV13 ...... 51 L4 ⬛
Dimmocks Av *BILS/COS* WV14 ...... 67 H5
Dimmock St
　ETTPK/GDPK/PENN WV4 ...... 50 C8
Dimsdale Gv *NFLD/LBR* B31 ...... 143 J2
Dimsdale Rd *NFLD/LBR* B31 ...... 143 H2
Dinedor *REDE* B98 ...... 197 H2 ⬛
Dingle Av *CDYHTH* B64 ...... 103 J5
Dingle Cl *BVILLE* B30 ...... 124 B6
　COVN CV6 ...... 133 L7
Dingle Hollow *OLDBY* B69 ...... 86 B5
Dingle La *CSHL/WTROR* B46 ...... 76 D4
　SOLH B91 ...... 147 K3
　WLNHL WV13 ...... 51 L1

Dingle Md *ALE/KHTH/YWD* B14 ...... 145 G1
Dingle Rd *BRWNH* WS8 ...... 26 C8
　DUDS DY2 ...... 85 J6
　HAG/WOL DY9 ...... 119 M3
　KGSWFD DY6 ...... 101 L1
　WMBN WV5 ...... 64 D8
Dingle St *OLDBY* B69 ...... 86 B5
The Dingle *BDMR/CCFT* WV3 ...... 49 H4
　NUNW/HART CV10 ...... 80 C7
　OLDBY B69 ...... 86 B5 ⬛
　SHLY B90 ...... 147 H8 ⬛
　SLYOAK B29 ...... 124 C3
Dingle Vw *SEDG* DY3 ...... 66 A6
Dingley Rd *BDWTH* CV12 ...... 117 M3
　DARL/WED WS10 ...... 52 E8
Dinham Gdns *DUDN* DY1 ...... 84 C2 ⬛
Dinmore Av *NFLD/LBR* B31 ...... 143 M1
Dinmore Cl *REDE* B98 ...... 197 H2 ⬛
Dippons Dr
　DUNHL/THL/PER WV6 ...... 48 E2
Dippons Mill Cl
　DUNHL/THL/PER WV6 ...... 48 E2
Dirtyfoot La
　ETTPK/GDPK/PENN WV4 ...... 48 E8
Discovery Cl *TPTN/OCK* DY4 ...... 68 A8
Discovery Wy *COVS* CV3 ...... 155 M5
The Ditch *WSL* WS1 ...... 5 G3
Ditton Cl *RUGBYS/DCH* CV22 ...... 183 C4
Ditton Gv *NFLD/LBR* B31 ...... 143 K7 ⬛
Dixon Cl *CVALE* B35 ...... 91 L3
　TPTN/OCK DY4 ...... 68 A7
Dixon Rd *SMHTH* B10 ...... 107 M5
Dixon's Green Rd *DUDS* DY2 ...... 85 J5
Dixon St *BKHL/PFLD* WV2 ...... 50 C7
　KIDD DY10 ...... 137 J8
Dobbins Oak Rd *HAG/WOL* DY9 ...... 120 B4
Dobbs Mill Cl *SLYOAK* B29 ...... 124 F3 ⬛
Dobbs St *BKHL/PFLD* WV2 ...... 2 F8
Dobes La *KIDD* DY10 ...... 163 G7
Dockar Rd *NFLD/LBR* B31 ...... 143 J3
Dockers Cl
　RCOVN/BALC/EX CV7 ...... 151 G6 ⬛
Dock La *DUDN* DY1 ...... 84 F4
Dock Meadow Dr
　ETTPK/GDPK/PENN WV4 ...... 66 C1
Dock Rd *STRBR* DY8 ...... 101 K3
The Dock *BRGRVW* B61 ...... 165 L5
　HAG/WOL DY9 ...... 102 D8 ⬛
Doctors Hl *BRGRVW* B61 ...... 165 H4
　HAG/WOL DY9 ...... 120 A2
Doctors La *KGSWFD* DY6 ...... 82 D8
Doctor's Piece *WLNHL* WV13 ...... 51 M3
Dodd Av *WWCK* CV34 ...... 200 A6
Doddington Gv
　RIDG/WDGT B32 ...... 122 F5 ⬛
Dodds La *LICH* WS13 ...... 19 G2
Dodford Cl *RBRY* B45 ...... 142 D6 ⬛
Dodford Rd *BRGRVW* B61 ...... 165 H4
Dodgson Cl *COVN* CV6 ...... 134 E1 ⬛
Doe Bank La *ALDR* WS9 ...... 55 H7
　COV CV1 ...... 8 B4
Doe Bank Rd *TPTN/OCK* DY4 ...... 68 A4
Dogberry Cl *COVS* CV3 ...... 155 C7
Dogge Lane Cft *ACGN* B27 ...... 126 F3 ⬛
Dogkennel La *HALE* B63 ...... 121 M2
　LGLYGN/QTN B68 ...... 87 G8
Dog Kennel La *SHLY* B90 ...... 147 G6
　WSL WS1 ...... 5 H2
Dog La *BRGRVW* B61 ...... 184 A7
　CSHL/WTROR B46 ...... 76 E7
　LICHS WS14 ...... 43 L1
　TAM/AM/WIL B77 ...... 32 F7
Dogpool La *BVILLE* B30 ...... 124 F4
Doidge Rd *ERDW/GRVHL* B23 ...... 90 B2
Dolben La *REDE* B98 ...... 197 H2
Dollery Dr *DIG/EDG* B5 ...... 107 G8
Dollis Gv *KGSTG* B44 ...... 71 K2
Dollman St *VAUX/NECH* B7 ...... 107 M2 ⬛
Dolman Rd *AST/WIT* B6 ...... 89 J3
Dolobran Rd *SPARK* B11 ...... 107 M6
Dolomite Av *COVW* CV5 ...... 153 H4
Dolphin Cl *BLOX/PEL* WS3 ...... 39 K4
Dolphin La *ACGN* B27 ...... 127 G4
Dolphin Rd *REDE* B98 ...... 188 D3
　SPARK B11 ...... 108 B8
Dolton Wy *TPTN/OCK* DY4 ...... 67 J7
Domar Rd *KIDDW* DY11 ...... 136 F6
Dominic Cl *BVILLE* B30 ...... 144 B1
Doncaster Cl *COVE* CV2 ...... 135 H6
Doncaster Wy *CBROM* B36 ...... 91 C5
Don Cl *EDG* B15 ...... 106 B5
Donegal Cl *TLHL/CAN* CV4 ...... 152 E6
Donegal Rd *FOAKS/STRLY* B74 ...... 55 K8
Dongan Rd *WWCK* CV34 ...... 199 M2 ⬛
Donibristle Cft *CVALE* B35 ...... 91 L1
Donnington Av *COVN* CV6 ...... 133 J8
Donnington Cl *REDE* B98 ...... 189 G8
Donnithorne Av
　NUNW/HART CV10 ...... 99 G4
Dooley Cl *WLNHL* WV13 ...... 51 J3
Doone Cl *COVE* CV2 ...... 135 J7
Dorado *TAM/AM/WIL* B77 ...... 46 B7
Doran Cl *HALE* B63 ...... 121 H4
Doranda Wy *HHTH/SAND* B71 ...... 87 K4
Dora Rd *HDSW* B21 ...... 88 C6
　SMHTH B10 ...... 108 C6
　WBROM B70 ...... 87 G4
Dora St *WSLW* WS2 ...... 52 F6
Dorcas Cl *NUN* CV11 ...... 99 M5
Dorchester Av
　RWWCK/WEL CV35 ...... 198 D7
Dorchester Ct *SHHTH* WV12 ...... 38 A5 ⬛
Dorchester Dr *HRBN* B17 ...... 123 M1
Dorchester Rd *CNCK/NC* WS11 ...... 15 M4
　HAG/WOL DY9 ...... 120 B3
　SHHTH WV12 ...... 38 A5
　SOLH B91 ...... 147 L1
Dorchester Wy *COVE* CV2 ...... 135 K4
Dordale Rd *HAG/WOL* DY9 ...... 164 B2
Dordon Cl *SHLY* B90 ...... 146 E6
Dordon Rd *POL/KGSB/FAZ* B78 ...... 47 K5
Doreen Gv *ERDE/BCHGN* B24 ...... 90 F3
Doris Rd *BORD* B9 ...... 108 B4
　CSHL/WTROR B46 ...... 93 K5
　SPARK B11 ...... 125 M1

Dorking Gv *EDG* B15 ...... 6 D7
Dorlcote Rd *WASH/WDE* B8 ...... 108 E1
Dorlecote Pl *NUNW/HART* CV10 ...... 99 G5
Dorlecote Rd *NUNW/HART* CV10 ...... 99 G5
Dormer Av *TAM/AM/WIL* B77 ...... 32 C8
Dormer Harris Av
　TLHL/CAN CV4 ...... 152 D4
Dormer Pl *RLSN* CV32 ...... 200 D5
Dormie Cl *HWK/WKHTH* B38 ...... 144 B4
Dormington Rd *KGSTG* B44 ...... 71 J2
Dormston Cl *REDE* B98 ...... 196 D4
　SOLH B91 ...... 148 A6 ⬛
Dormston Dr *SEDG* DY3 ...... 66 B5
　SLYOAK B29 ...... 123 K3
Dormy Dr *NFLD/LBR* B31 ...... 143 L6
Dorncliffe Av *STETCH* B33 ...... 110 B6
Dorney Cl *COVW* CV5 ...... 153 J5
Dornie Dr *HWK/WKHTH* B38 ...... 144 B4
Dornton Rd *BVILLE* B30 ...... 125 G5
Dorothy Powell Wy
　COVE CV2 ...... 135 K4 ⬛
Dorothy Rd *SMTHWKW* B67 ...... 105 L2
　SPARK B11 ...... 108 F8
Dorridge Cl *REDW* B97 ...... 195 M4
Dorridge Cft *DOR/KN* B93 ...... 172 D3
Dorridge Rd *DOR/KN* B93 ...... 172 E3
Dorrington Gn *PBAR/PBCH* B42 ...... 70 E8
Dorrington Rd *PBAR/PBCH* B42 ...... 70 E8
Dorset Cl *NUNW/HART* CV10 ...... 98 D2
　POL/KGSB/FAZ B78 ...... 45 L4
　RBRY B45 ...... 142 D3
Dorset Dr *ALDR* WS9 ...... 40 C4
Dorset Pl *BLOX/PEL* WS3 ...... 39 G6 ⬛
Dorset Rd *COV* CV1 ...... 134 A8
　HEDN WS12 ...... 17 J4
　HRBN B17 ...... 105 M2
　STRBR DY8 ...... 101 H6
　WASH/WDE B8 ...... 90 A8
Dorsett Rd *DARL/WED* WS10 ...... 52 A7
　DARL/WED WS10 ...... 69 H3
　STRPT DY13 ...... 160 D8
Dorsett Road Ter
　DARL/WED WS10 ...... 52 A7
Dorsheath Gdns
　ERDW/GRVHL B23 ...... 90 D1
Dorsington Cl
　RWWCK/WEL CV35 ...... 198 C2
Dorsington Rd *ACGN* B27 ...... 127 H4
Dorstone Covert *BVILLE* B30 ...... 145 G3
Dorville Cl *HWK/WKHTH* B38 ...... 144 A5 ⬛
Dosthill Road (Two Gates)
　TAM/AM/WIL B77 ...... 46 B7
Dotterel Pl *KIDD* DY10 ...... 161 L4
Douay Rd *ERDE/BCHGN* B24 ...... 72 F2
Double Rw *DUDS* DY2 ...... 103 J1
Doughty St *TPTN/OCK* DY4 ...... 68 A8
Douglas Av *CBROM* B36 ...... 91 H7
　LGLYGN/QTN B68 ...... 87 H8
Douglas Davies Cl
　SHHTH WV12 ...... 52 A1 ⬛
Douglas Pl *WOLVN* WV10 ...... 36 A7
Douglas Rd *ACGN* B27 ...... 126 F1
　BILS/COS WV14 ...... 67 H5
　CSCFLD/WYGN B72 ...... 73 G2
　HDSW B21 ...... 88 C5
　HLYWD B47 ...... 145 L6
　LGLYGN/QTN B68 ...... 105 H1
　RMSLY B62 ...... 104 C4
Douglass Rd *DUDS* DY2 ...... 85 H5
Doulton Cl *COVE* CV2 ...... 135 J4 ⬛
　RIDG/WDGT B32 ...... 123 K2
Doulton Rd *BLKHTH/ROWR* B65... 103 J2
Dovebridge Cl *WALM/CURD* B76 ... 73 K1
Dove Cl *BDWTH* CV12 ...... 116 C2
　BNTWD WS7 ...... 19 H7
　DARL/WED WS10 ...... 68 F1 ⬛
　KIDD DY10 ...... 161 L3
　YDLY B25 ...... 109 J5
Dovecote Cl *COVN* CV6 ...... 133 H8
　DUNHL/THL/PER WV6 ...... 49 G1
　SOLH B91 ...... 127 M5
　TPTN/OCK DY4 ...... 68 A8 ⬛
Dovecote Rd *BRGRVW* B61 ...... 185 J4
The Dovecotes
　MGN/WHC B75 ...... 56 F2 ⬛
Dovedale *CNCK/NC* WS11 ...... 12 E8
Dovedale Av *BLOX/PEL* WS3 ...... 25 L8
　COVN CV6 ...... 134 D3
　SHHTH WV12 ...... 51 L1
　SHLY B90 ...... 147 K4
Dovedale Ct
　ETTPK/GDPK/PENN WV4 ...... 66 D3 ⬛
Dovedale Dr *HLGN/YWD* B28 ...... 126 D7
Dovedale Rd *ERDW/GRVHL* B23 ... 72 A7
　ETTPK/GDPK/PENN WV4 ...... 66 C2
　KGSWFD DY6 ...... 83 J5
Dove Dr *STRBR* DY8 ...... 101 L5 ⬛
Dove Gdns *HWK/WKHTH* B38 ...... 144 F3
Dove Hollow *GTWY* WS6 ...... 24 D4
　HEDN WS12 ...... 17 J1
Dovehouse Flds *LICHS* WS14 ...... 20 F7
Dove House La *HIA/OLT* B92 ...... 127 K6
Dovehouse Pool Rd
　AST/WIT B6 ...... 89 J5 ⬛
Dover Cl *RIDG/WDGT* B32 ...... 122 E6 ⬛
Dovercourt Rd
　LGN/SDN/BHAMAIR B26 ...... 110 A8
Doverdale Av *KIDD* DY10 ...... 137 M8
Doverdale Cl *HALE* B63 ...... 103 J8 ⬛
　REDE B98 ...... 196 F6
Dover Farm Cl
　TAM/AM/WIL B77 ...... 46 F5 ⬛
Dove Rdg *STRBR* DY8 ...... 101 L6 ⬛
Doveridge Cl *SOLH* B91 ...... 127 J7
Doveridge Rd *HLGN/YWD* B28 ...... 126 C8
Doversley Rd
　ALE/KHTH/YWD B14 ...... 125 G8
Dove St *BILS/COS* WV14 ...... 51 H7
　COV CV1 ...... 8 D4 ⬛
　WSNGN B18 ...... 97 H2
Dovestone
　POL/KGSB/FAZ B78 ...... 47 H4 ⬛
Dove Wy *CBROM* B36 ...... 92 D5
Dovey Dr *WALM/CURD* B76 ...... 73 L6
Dovey Rd *MOS/BIL* B13 ...... 126 B3
　OLDBY B69 ...... 86 B5
Dowar Rd *RBRY* B45 ...... 143 G5

Dowells Gdns *STRBR* DY8 .... 101 H2
The Doweries *RBRY* B45 .... 142 D5
Dower Rd *MGN/WHC* B75 .... 56 F4
Dowler's Hill Crs *REDE* B98 .... 196 E5
Dowles Cl *SLYOAK* B29 .... 123 M7
Dowles Rd *KIDDW* DY11 .... 160 F3
Dowley Cft *COVS* CV3 .... 155 M4
Downcroft Av
HWK/WKHTH B38 .... 144 C3
Downderry Wy *COVN* CV6 .... 134 E7
Downend Cl *WOLVN* WV10 .... 36 D1
Downes Ct *TPTN/OCK* DY4 .... 67 J8
Downesway *CNCK/NC* WS11 ..... 16 A3
Downey Cl *SPARK* B11 .... 107 M6
Downfield Cl *BLOX/PEL* WS3 ..... 38 E1
Downfield Dr *SEDG* DY3 .... 66 C7
Downham Cl *DSYBK/YTR* WS5 .. 54 C5
Downham Pl
BDMR/CCFT WV3 .... 49 K5
Downie Rd *CDSL* WV8 .... 35 G2
Downing Cl
BLKHTH/ROWR B65 .... 104 A4
DOR/KN B93 .... 172 E1
WNSFLD WV11 .... 37 L6
Downing Crs *BDWTH* CV12 .... 117 G1
Downing Dr *CRTAM* B79 .... 31 J8
Downing St *HALE* B63 .... 103 L8
SMTHWK B66 .... 88 A6
Downland Cl *HWK/WKHTH* B38 .. 144 D4
Downsell Rd *REDW* B97 .... 195 L3
Downsfield Rd
LGN/SDN/BHAMAIR B26 .... 109 M6
Downside Rd *ERDE/BCHGN* B24 .. 90 C4
Downs Rd *WLNHL* WV13 .... 52 A5
The Downs *FOAKS/STRLY* B74 .... 55 J3
WOLVN WV10 .... 36 A7
Downton Cl *COVE* CV2 .... 135 L5
Downton Crs *STETCH* B33 .... 110 C2
Dowty Av *BDWTH* CV12 .... 116 B4
Dowty Wy *COVEN* WV9 .... 35 L2
Doyle Dr *COVN* CV6 .... 134 D2
Dragoon Flds *BRGRVE* B60 .... 185 M5
Drake Cl *BLOX/PEL* WS3 .... 38 F4
Drake Crs *KIDDW* DY11 .... 136 E6
Drake Rd *BLOX/PEL* WS3 .... 39 G4
ERDW/GRVHL B23 .... 90 A2
SMTHWK B66 .... 87 H6
Drakes Cl *REDW* B97 .... 196 A7
Drakes Cross Pde
HLYWD B47 .... 145 L8
Drakes Hill Cl *KINVER* DY7 .... 119 G1
Drake St *COVN* CV6 .... 134 B6
HHTH/SAND B71 .... 69 G8
Drancy Av *SHHTH* WV12 .... 38 B7
Draper Cl *KNWTH* CV8 .... 192 A1
Draper's Flds *COV* CV1 .... 8 F2
Drawbridge Rd *SHLY* B90 .... 146 C5
Draycote Cl *HIA/OLT* B92 .... 128 B6
Draycott Av *ERDW/GRVHL* B23 .... 72 B8
Draycott Cl
ETTPK/GDPK/PENN WV4 .... 49 G8
REDW B97 .... 187 M8
Draycott Crs
TAM/AM/WIL B77 .... 46 B4
Draycott Dr *NFLD/LBR* B31 .... 123 J6
Draycott Rd *COVE* CV2 .... 134 F6
SMTHWK B66 .... 87 J6
Drayton Cl *MGN/WHC* B75 .... 56 F2
NUNW/HART CV10 .... 79 L5
REDE B98 .... 197 H5
Drayton Ct *BRGRVE* B60 .... 185 M5
WWCK CV34 .... 199 J3
Drayton Crs *COVW* CV5 .... 132 B8
Drayton La *POL/KGSB/FAZ* B78 ...... 44 D8
Drayton Leys
RUGBYS/DCH CV22 .... 183 L6
Drayton Manor Dr
POL/KGSB/FAZ B78 .... 45 K4
Drayton Rd
ALE/KHTH/YWD B14 .... 125 J5
BDWTH CV12 .... 117 G3
HAG/WOL DY9 .... 140 B7
KIDD DY10 .... 163 K3
SHLY B90 .... 147 J5
SMTHWK B66 .... 105 L4
Drayton St *BKHL/PFLD* WV2 .... 2 F9
Drayton St East *WSLW* WS2 .... 4 A2
Drayton Wy *NUNW/HART* CV10 .... 80 A6
Dreadnought Rd *BRLYHL* DY5 .... 83 M6
The Dreel *EDG* B15 .... 106 C6
Dreghorn Rd *CBROM* B36 .... 91 J5
Drem Cft *CVALE* B35 .... 91 L2
Dresden Cl
ETTPK/GDPK/PENN WV4 .... 66 E1
Drew Crs *HAG/WOL* DY9 .... 120 B2
KNWTH CV8 .... 191 L1
Drew Rd *HAG/WOL* DY9 .... 120 B2
Drews Holloway *HALE* B63 .... 103 H8
Drews Holloway South
HALE B63 .... 103 H8
Drews La *WASH/WDE* B8 .... 90 E7
Drews Meadow Cl
ALE/KHTH/YWD B14 .... 145 G3
Dreyer Cl *RUGBYS/DCH* CV22 ...... 183 G3
Driffield Cl *REDE* B98 .... 197 H3
Driffold *SCFLD/BOLD* B73 .... 72 F2
Driftwood Cl
HWK/WKHTH B38 .... 144 B6
Drive Flds
ETTPK/GDPK/PENN WV4 .... 48 F7
The Drive *ALVE* B48 .... 167 M2
BFLD/HDSWWD B20 .... 88 E3
BLOX/PEL WS3 .... 39 J3
BRLYHL DY5 .... 84 A8
CDSL WV8 .... 34 D2
COVE CV2 .... 155 H2
DUNHL/THL/PER WV6 .... 35 G8
ERDW/GRVHL B23 .... 90 C3
HALE B63 .... 103 H8
HALE B63 .... 121 L2
LICHS WS14 .... 29 J5
REDW B97 .... 187 G7
RUSH/SHEL WS4 .... 40 A4
Droitwich Rd *KIDD* DY10 .... 162 A8
Dronfield Rd *COVE* CV2 .... 154 F2
Drovers Wy *BRGRVE* B60 .... 185 J7
The Droveway *COVEN* WV9 .... 35 K3
Droylsdon Park Rd *COVS* CV3 .... 177 M2

Druid Park Rd *SHHTH* WV12 .... 38 A4
Druid Rd *COVE* CV2 .... 154 F2
Druids Av *ALDR* WS9 .... 41 G5
BLKHTH/ROWR B65 .... 104 B1
Druids La *ALE/KHTH/YWD* B14 .... 145 K4
HWK/WKHTH B38 .... 145 G4
Druids Wk *ALDR* WS9 .... 40 E2
Druids Wy *PENK* ST19 .... 10 D6
Drummond Cl *COVN* CV6 .... 133 K6
WNSFLD WV11 .... 37 L3
Drummond Gv *GTB/HAM* B43 ... 71 G2
Drummond Rd *BORD* B9 .... 108 D3
BRGRVE B60 .... 185 M5
HAG/WOL DY9 .... 120 D1
Drummond St *WOLV* WV1 .... 2 E3
Drummond Wy
CHWD/FDBR/MGN B37 .... 111 G3
Drury La *CDSL* WV8 .... 34 D1
RUGBYN/HIL CV21 .... 183 L2
SOLH B91 .... 148 A2
STRBR DY8 .... 101 L8
Drybrook Cl *HWK/WKHTH* B38 .... 144 C5
Drybrooks Cl
RCOVN/BALC/EX CV7 .... 150 F7
Dryden Cl *KNWTH* CV8 .... 191 K2
NUNW/HART CV10 .... 79 K8
SHHTH WV12 .... 38 C5
TPTN/OCK DY4 .... 67 L6
Dryden Gv *ACGN* B27 .... 126 F3
Dryden Pl *BLOX/PEL* WS3 .... 39 J6
RUGBYS/DCH CV22 .... 183 J2
Dryden Rd *BLOX/PEL* WS3 .... 39 J6
CRTAM B79 .... 31 L6
WOLVN WV10 .... 36 D4
Dryden Wk
RUGBYS/DCH CV22 .... 183 J2
Drylea Gv *CBROM* B36 .... 91 K5
Dual Wy *HEDN* WS12 .... 12 A5
Dubarry Av *KGSWFD* DY6 .... 83 G6
Duchess Rd *LDYWD/EDGR* B16 ..... 106 E4
WSL WS1 .... 53 H8
Duckhouse Rd *WNSFLD* WV11 .... 37 H6
Duck La *CDSL* WV8 .... 34 F3
Duddeston Manor Rd
VAUX/NECH B7 .... 7 M1
Duddeston Mill Rd
VAUX/NECH B7 .... 107 M1
Dudding Rd
ETTPK/GDPK/PENN WV4 .... 50 B8
Dudhill Rd *CDYHTH* B64 .... 103 L2
Dudley Cl *BLKHTH/ROWR* B65 .... 85 K7
Dudley Crs *WNSFLD* WV11 .... 37 J7
Dudley Gn *RLSN* CV32 .... 200 F3
Dudley Park Rd *ACGN* B27 .... 127 G2
Dudley Port *TPTN/OCK* DY4 .... 85 L2
Dudley Rd *BKHL/PFLD* WV2 .... 3 G8
BLKHTH/ROWR B65 .... 85 K7
BRLYHL DY5 .... 102 B1
HAG/WOL DY9 .... 102 C7
HALE B63 .... 103 M7
KGSWFD DY6 .... 83 G5
KNWTH CV8 .... 191 K3
OLDBY B69 .... 86 C5
RMSLY B62 .... 103 M8
SEDG DY3 .... 66 B6
TPTN/OCK DY4 .... 67 H8
WSNGN B18 .... 106 B1
Dudley Rd East *OLDBY* B69 .... 86 A3
Dudley Rd West *OLDBY* B69 .... 85 M3
Dudley Rw *DUDS* DY2 .... 85 H4
Dudley St *ATHST* CV9 .... 63 H6
BILS/COS WV14 .... 67 H1
COVN CV6 .... 134 E4
DARL/WED WS10 .... 68 C3
DIG/EDG B5 .... 7 G6
KIDD DY10 .... 137 J6
SEDG DY3 .... 66 B5
WBROM B70 .... 68 E8
WOLV WV1 .... 2 F5
WSL WS1 .... 4 F4
Dudley Wk
ETTPK/GDPK/PENN WV4 .... 50 A8
Dudley Wood Av *DUDS* DY2 .... 103 G3
Dudley Wood Rd *DUDS* DY2 .... 103 G4
Dudmaston Wy *DUDN* DY1 .... 84 C2
Dudnill Gv *RIDG/WDGT* B32 .... 122 E5
Duffield Cl *CDSL* WV8 .... 35 K4
Dufton Rd *RIDG/WDGT* B32 .... 105 J8
Dugdale Cl *HEDN* WS12 .... 17 K2
Dugdale Crs *MGN/WHC* B75 .... 57 G2
Dugdale Rd *COVN* CV6 .... 133 L7
Dugdale St *NUN* CV11 .... 99 G1
WSNGN B18 .... 106 B1
Duggins La
RCOVN/BALC/EX CV7 .... 151 M5
Duke Barn Fld *COVE* CV2 .... 134 E8
Duke Rd *BNTWD* WS7 .... 18 C4
Dukes Rd *BVILLE* B30 .... 144 D2
Duke St *BDMR/CCFT* WV3 .... 49 L6
BLKHTH/ROWR B65 .... 103 M3
COVW CV5 .... 153 K3
CSCFLD/WYGN B72 .... 72 F1
NUN CV11 .... 98 E1
RLSN CV32 .... 200 E4
RUGBYN/HIL CV21 .... 183 L1
SEDG DY3 .... 66 B8
STRBR DY8 .... 101 L8
WBROM B70 .... 86 F1
WNSFLD WV11 .... 37 H8
WOLV WV1 .... 3 J6
Dukes Wy *POL/KGSB/FAZ* B78 .... 47 L7
Dulvern Gv
ALE/KHTH/YWD B14 .... 125 H8
Dulverton Av *COVW* CV5 .... 153 H1
Dulverton Rd *AST/WIT* B6 .... 89 L4
Dulwich Gv *KGSTG* B44 .... 71 M5
Dulwich Rd *KGSTG* B44 .... 71 L5
Dumbleberry Av *SEDG* DY3 .... 66 A6
Dumblederry La *ALDR* WS9 .... 40 C5
Dumble Pit La *HLYWD* B47 .... 169 J6
Dumolo's La *TAM/AM/WIL* B77 .... 46 C2
Dumphouse La *ALVE* B48 .... 189 G2
Dunard Rd *SHLY* B90 .... 146 D2
Dunbar Cl *KIDD* DY10 .... 138 A7
Dunbar Gv *GTB/HAM* B43 .... 70 F1
Dunblane Dr *RLSN* CV32 .... 193 G8
Duncalfe Dr *MGN/WHC* B75 .... 56 F2
Duncan Dr *RUGBYS/DCH* CV22 .... 183 H7

Duncan Edwards Cl
DUDN DY1 .... 84 E5
Duncan St *BKHL/PFLD* WV2 .... 50 A6
Dunchurch Cl
RCOVN/BALC/EX CV7 .... 150 F6
REDE B98 .... 197 K4
Dunchurch Crs *SCFLD/BOLD* B73 .. 72 A2
Dunchurch Dr *NFLD/LBR* B31 .. 123 J6
Dunchurch Hwy *COVW* CV5 .... 132 E7
TLHL/CAN CV4 .... 153 G3
Dunchurch Rd
RUGBYS/DCH CV22 .... 183 K7
Dunclent Crs *KIDD* DY10 .... 137 M8
Duncombe Gn
CSHL/WTROR B46 .... 93 K6
Duncombe Gv *HRBN* B17 .... 105 K6
Duncombe St *STRBR* DY8 .... 101 H7
Duncroft Av *COVN* CV6 .... 133 K6
Duncroft Rd
LGN/SDN/BHAMAIR B26 .... 109 K5
Duncumb Rd *MGN/WHC* B75 .... 57 L8
Dundalk La *GTWY* WS6 .... 24 B4
Dundas Av *OLDBY* B69 .... 85 K5
Dunedin Dr *RBRY* B45 .... 166 E4
Dunedin Rd *KGSTG* B44 .... 71 J2
Dunhampton Dr *KIDD* DY10 ... 137 M4
Dunhill Av *TLHL/CAN* CV4 .... 152 C2
Dunkirk Av *WBROM* B70 .... 86 C1
Dunkley St *WOLV* WV1 .... 2 E2
Dunley Cft *SHLY* B90 .... 147 K7
Dunlin Cl *ERDW/GRVHL* B23 .... 90 A3
KGSWFD DY6 .... 83 L7
WOLVN WV10 .... 22 E6
Dunlin Dr *KIDD* DY10 .... 161 K3
Dunlop Rd *REDW* B97 .... 196 A8
Dunlop Wy *ERDE/BCHGN* B24 .... 91 J4
Dunmore Rd *BEWD* DY12 .... 136 A8
Dunnerdale Rd *BRWNH* WS8 .... 26 B7
Dunnigan Rd *RIDG/WDGT* B32 .... 123 K2
Dunnington Av *KIDD* DY10 .... 137 L4
Dunnose Cl *COVN* CV6 .... 134 C5
Dunns Bank *BRLYHL* DY5 .... 102 D6
Dunn's La *POL/KGSB/FAZ* B78 .... 47 M7
Dunrose Cl *COVE* CV2 .... 155 J3
Dunsfold Cl
ETTPK/GDPK/PENN WV4 .... 66 E2
Dunsfold Cft *AST/WIT* B6 .... 89 K7
Dunsford Cl *BRLYHL* DY5 .... 101 M6
Dunsford Rd *SMTHWK* B66 .... 105 L3
Dunsink Rd *BFLD/HDSWWD* B20 .. 89 K4
Dunslade Crs *BRLYHL* DY5 .... 102 D5
Dunslade Rd *ERDW/GRVHL* B23 ..... 72 C6
Dunsley Dr *KINVER* DY7 .... 118 A1
STRBR DY8 .... 101 J2
Dunsley Gv
ETTPK/GDPK/PENN WV4 .... 65 L1
Dunsley Rd *KINVER* DY7 .... 100 B8
Dunsmore Av *COVS* CV3 .... 155 G8
Dunsmore Dr *BRLYHL* DY5 .... 102 D5
Dunsmore Gv *SOLH* B91 .... 127 K6
Dunsmore Rd *HLGN/YWD* B28 ...... 126 C4
Dunstall Av
DUNHL/THL/PER WV6 .... 36 A8
Dunstall Cl *REDW* B97 .... 195 M3
Dunstall Gv *SLYOAK* B29 .... 123 K5
Dunstall Hl
DUNHL/THL/PER WV6 .... 36 A8
Dunstall La
DUNHL/THL/PER WV6 .... 35 M8
POL/KGSB/FAZ B78 .... 31 G7
Dunstall Rd
DUNHL/THL/PER WV6 .... 49 M1
HALE B63 .... 121 H2
Dunstan Cft *SHLY* B90 .... 147 G5
Dunster *TAM/AM/WIL* B77 .... 46 A6
Dunster Cl *BVILLE* B30 .... 144 F1
Dunster Gv
DUNHL/THL/PER WV6 .... 48 D2
Dunster Pl *COVN* CV6 .... 134 B2
Dunster Rd
CHWD/FDBR/MGN B37 .... 111 H4
Dunston Cl *GTWY* WS6 .... 24 C5
KGSWFD DY6 .... 83 H6
Dunston Dr *BNTWD* WS7 .... 18 E5
Dunsville Dr *COVE* CV2 .... 135 K5
Dunton Cl *MGN/WHC* B75 .... 56 E1
Dunton Coppice
WALM/CURD B76 .... 75 J5
Dunton Hall Rd *SHLY* B90 .... 146 E5
Dunton La *WALM/CURD* B76 .... 74 F4
Dunton Rd
CHWD/FDBR/MGN B37 .... 110 D1
Dunvegan Cl *COVS* CV3 .... 155 L3
KNWTH CV8 .... 192 A1
Dunvegan Rd
ERDE/BCHGN B24 .... 90 E1
Durant Cl *RBRY* B45 .... 142 B4
Durban Rd *SMTHWK* B66 .... 106 A1
Durbar Av *COVN* CV6 .... 134 B5
D'urberville Rd *BKHL/PFLD* WV2 .. 50 D6
Durham Av *WLNHL* WV13 .... 52 A2
Durham Cl *BRGRVW* B61 .... 185 J1
POL/KGSB/FAZ B78 .... 45 L3
RCOVN/BALC/EX CV7 .... 133 K1
Durham Crs *COVW* CV5 .... 132 F6
Durham Cft
CHWD/FDBR/MGN B37 .... 110 E3
Durham Dr *HHTH/SAND* B71 .... 69 H6
Durham Pl *WSLW* WS2 .... 52 F4
Durham Rd
BLKHTH/ROWR B65 .... 104 C1
DARL/WED WS10 .... 69 H1
DUDS DY2 .... 103 H3
SPARK B11 .... 125 M1
STRBR DY8 .... 101 H5
WSLW WS2 .... 52 F5
Durley Dean Rd *SLYOAK* B29 .... 124 A3
Durley Dr *SCFLD/BOLD* B73 .... 72 A2
Durley Rd *YDLY* B25 .... 109 G8
Durlston Cl *TAM/AM/WIL* B77 .... 32 D8
Durlston Gv *HLGN/YWD* B28 ...... 126 E5
Durnford Cft
ALE/KHTH/YWD B14 .... 145 J4
Dursley Cl *HIA/OLT* B92 .... 127 M5
SHHTH WV12 .... 52 B1
Dursley Dr *CNCK/NC* WS11 .... 15 M3
Dursley La *REDE* B98 .... 197 L2
Dursley Rd *BNTWD* WS7 .... 18 E6

Dusthouse La *BRGRVE* B60 .... 186 B6
Dutton Rd *COVE* CV2 .... 135 H2
Dutton's La *MGN/WHC* B75 .... 57 J1
Duxford Cl *REDW* B97 .... 195 M5
Duxford Rd *PBAR/PBCH* B42 .... 70 F5
Dwellings La *RIDG/WDGT* B32 .... 104 F8
Dyas Av *PBAR/PBCH* B42 .... 70 E6
Dyas Rd *HLYWD* B47 .... 145 L6
KGSTG B44 .... 71 H5
Dyce Cl *CVALE* B35 .... 91 L1
Dyers La *HOCK/TIA* B94 .... 171 H5
KNWTH CV8 .... 180 E2
Dymoke St *BHTH/HG* B12 .... 107 K5
Dymond Rd *COVN* CV6 .... 134 A2
Dyott Cl *LICH* WS13 .... 21 L4
Dyott Rd *MOS/BIL* B13 .... 125 L4
Dysart Cl *COV* CV1 .... 9 J2
Dyson Cl *WSLW* WS2 .... 52 D2
Dysons Gdns *WASH/WDE* B8 ...... 90 C8
Dyson St *TLHL/CAN* CV4 .... 152 C2

E

Eachelhurst Rd
ERDE/BCHGN B24 .... 91 J1
Eachus Rd *BILS/COS* WV14 .... 67 H5
Eachway *RBRY* B45 .... 142 D7
Eachway La *RBRY* B45 .... 142 E7
Eacott Cl *COVN* CV6 .... 133 L2
Eadie Ms *REDW* B97 .... 196 A4
Eadie St *NUNW/HART* CV10 .... 98 A1
Eagle Cl *BLKHTH/ROWR* B65 .... 103 K1
DUDN DY1 .... 84 D4
GTWY WS6 .... 24 B3
NUN CV11 .... 99 M5
Eagle Cft *ALE/KHTH/YWD* B14 ...... 145 J3
Eagle Dr *TAM/AM/WIL* B77 .... 46 F1
Eagle Gdns *ERDE/BCHGN* B24 .... 90 E3
Eagle Gv *CBROM* B36 .... 92 E5
HEDN WS12 .... 17 G4
Eagle La *TPTN/OCK* DY4 .... 68 B7
Eagle Rd *REDE* B98 .... 189 J8
Eagle St *BDMR/CCFT* WV3 .... 49 L6
BKHL/PFLD WV2 .... 3 K8
COV CV1 .... 134 B8
RLSS CV31 .... 200 E7
TPTN/OCK DY4 .... 68 A7
Eagle St East *COV* CV1 .... 134 B8
Ealing Gv *KGSTG* B44 .... 71 L4
Ealingham *TAM/AM/WIL* B77 .... 46 F3
Eardisley Cl *REDE* B98 .... 197 K4
Earl Dr *BNTWD* WS7 .... 18 C4
Earlsbury Gdns
BFLD/HDSWWD B20 .... 89 H4
Earls Court Rd *HRBN* B17 .... 105 L7
The Earl's Cft *COVS* CV3 .... 154 B6
Earlsdon Av North *COVW* CV5 .... 153 K4
Earlsdon Av South *COVW* CV5 .... 8 A9
Earlsdon St *COVW* CV5 .... 153 K5
Earls Ferry Gdns
RIDG/WDGT B32 .... 122 F6
Earlsmead Rd *HDSW* B21 .... 88 A5
Earlsmere *HOCK/TIA* B94 .... 170 F4
Earls Rd *NUN* CV11 .... 80 E8
RUSH/SHEL WS4 .... 40 A6
Earlston Wy *GTB/HAM* B43 .... 70 B5
Earl St *BDWTH* CV12 .... 117 G3
BILS/COS WV14 .... 51 H8
BILS/COS WV14 .... 67 H5
COV CV1 .... 9 G5
KGSWFD DY6 .... 101 H1
RLSN CV32 .... 200 E4
RUGBYN/HIL CV21 .... 183 M2
WBROM B70 .... 86 F1
WSL WS1 .... 4 D7
Earls Wy *HALE* B63 .... 121 M1
Earlswood Common
HOCK/TIA B94 .... 170 E7
Earlswood Ct
BFLD/HDSWWD B20 .... 88 E3
Earlswood Crs *COVEN* WV9 .... 35 L2
Earlswood Dr *MGN/WHC* B75 .... 57 G6
Earlswood Rd *DOR/KN* B93 .... 172 B3
KGSWFD DY6 .... 83 J5
Easby Wy *BLOX/PEL* WS3 .... 38 D3
WASH/WDE B8 .... 90 C8
Easedale Cl *COVS* CV3 .... 153 M7
NUN CV11 .... 81 L7
Easemore Rd *REDE* B98 .... 196 C1
Easenhall Cl *DOR/KN* B93 .... 172 E1
Easenhall La *REDE* B98 .... 197 J4
Easenhall Rd *RRUGBY* CV23 .... 158 E3
Easmore Cl
ALE/KHTH/YWD B14 .... 145 H3
East Av *BDWTH* CV12 .... 117 H3
COVE CV2 .... 154 E2
OLDBY B69 .... 86 A6
WNSFLD WV11 .... 37 G7
Eastboro Wy *NUN* CV11 .... 99 H3
Eastbourne Av *BKDE/SHDE* B34 .. 91 H7
Eastbourne Cl *COVN* CV6 .... 133 J7
Eastbourne St *RUSH/SHEL* WS4 .... 53 K2
Eastbrook Cl
WALM/CURD B76 .... 73 H1
Eastbury Dr *HIA/OLT* B92 .... 127 L3
East Cannock Rd *HEDN* WS12 .... 17 G1
East Car Park Rd
BHAMNEC B40 .... 129 K1
Eastcote Cl *SHLY* B90 .... 147 H2
Eastcote Crs *BNTWD* WS7 .... 18 D8
Eastcote La *HIA/OLT* B92 .... 129 L8
Eastcote Rd *ACGN* B27 .... 126 E4
WOLVN WV10 .... 36 D8
Eastcotes *TLHL/CAN* CV4 .... 152 F4
East Croft Rd
ETTPK/GDPK/PENN WV4 .... 65 G1
Eastdean Cl *ERDW/GRVHL* B23 .... 72 A7
East Dene *RLSN* CV32 .... 200 F3
East Dr *DIG/EDG* B5 .... 125 G1
Eastern Av *BRLYHL* DY5 .... 101 M3
LICH WS13 .... 20 E2
Eastern Cl *DARL/WED* WS10 .... 68 A2
Eastern Green Rd *COVW* CV5 .... 152 D2
Eastern Rd *SCFLD/BOLD* B73 .... 72 F4
SLYOAK B29 .... 124 F2
Eastern Wy *CNCK/NC* WS11 .... 16 D8

HEDN WS12 .... 16 F2
Easterton Cft
ALE/KHTH/YWD B14 .... 145 J3
East Farm Cft *SMTHH* B10 .... 108 B5
Eastfield Dr *HIA/OLT* B92 .... 128 C5
Eastfield Gv *WOLV* WV1 .... 3 M5
Eastfield Pl
RUGBYN/HIL CV21 .... 183 L2
Eastfield Retreat *WOLV* WV1 .... 3 M5
Eastfield Rd *BORD* B9 .... 109 G3
NUNW/HART CV10 .... 81 H7
RLSN CV32 .... 200 E5
TPTN/OCK DY4 .... 67 L5
WOLV WV1 .... 3 M5
Eastgate *HEDN* WS12 .... 13 L8
East Ga *LDYWD/EDGR* B16 .... 106 C2
Eastgate St *BNTWD* WS7 .... 18 C5
East Gn *ETTPK/GDPK/PENN* WV4 .. 49 H7
East Gv *RLSS* CV31 .... 200 E7
Eastham Rd *MOS/BIL* B13 .... 126 A7
East Holme *BORD* B9 .... 108 A3
Easthope Rd *STETCH* B33 .... 109 L1
East House Dr *ATHST* CV9 .... 77 H1
Eastlake Cl *GTB/HAM* B43 .... 71 H2
Eastlands Gv *COVW* CV5 .... 153 J1
Eastlands Rd *MOS/BIL* B13 .... 125 L4
Eastlang Rd
RCOVN/BALC/EX CV7 .... 114 C2
Eastleigh *SEDG* DY3 .... 65 M5
Eastleigh Av *COVW* CV5 .... 153 K6
Eastleigh Cft *WALM/CURD* B76 .... 73 L6
Eastleigh Dr *RMSLY* B62 .... 141 L1
Eastleigh Gv *YDLY* B25 .... 109 H5
Eastley Crs *WWCK* CV34 .... 198 F5
East Meadway *STETCH* B33 .... 110 B2
East Ms *KGSTG* B44 .... 71 H3
Eastmoor Cl *FOAKS/STRLY* B74 .... 55 M3
Eastney Crs *CDSL* WV8 .... 35 J5
Eastnor Cl *KIDDW* DY11 .... 161 J3
REDE B98 .... 196 C4
Eastnor Gv *RLSS* CV31 .... 200 F6
Easton Gdns *WNSFLD* WV11 .... 37 K8
Easton Gv *ACGN* B27 .... 127 G4
HLYWD B47 .... 145 M6
East Park Wy *WOLV* WV1 .... 50 E4
East Pathway *HRBN* B17 .... 106 A7
Eastridge Cft *LICHS* WS14 .... 28 E8
East Ri *MGN/WHC* B75 .... 57 H7
East Rd *BRGRVE* B60 .... 185 L4
STRPT DY13 .... 160 E8
TPTN/OCK DY4 .... 67 M5
WOLVN WV10 .... 22 E6
East St *BRLYHL* DY5 .... 102 E5
CNCK/NC WS11 .... 16 C7
COV CV1 .... 9 K4
DUDS DY2 .... 85 J5
KIDD DY10 .... 137 K7
SEDG DY3 .... 84 A2
TAM/AM/WIL B77 .... 46 B8
WOLV WV1 .... 3 J6
WSL WS1 .... 5 G8
East Union St
RUGBYS/DCH CV22 .... 183 L3
East Vw *TAM/AM/WIL* B77 .... 46 C2
East View Rd *WALM/CURD* B76 .... 73 H2
Eastville *NFLD/LBR* B31 .... 143 M2
Eastward Gln *CDSL* WV8 .... 35 G4
East Wy *BHAMNEC* B40 .... 129 K2
HIA/OLT B92 .... 129 L2
Eastway *HRBN* B17 .... 106 A7
Eastwood Av *BNTWD* WS7 .... 18 E5
Eastwood Dr *KIDD* DY10 .... 137 M8
Eastwood Rd *BHTH/HG* B12 .... 107 H8
GTB/HAM B43 .... 70 C5
Easy La *RUGBYN/HIL* CV21 .... 183 K2
Eatesbrook Rd *STETCH* B33 .... 110 A2
Eathorpe Cl *BKDE/SHDE* B34 .... 92 B7
COVE CV2 .... 135 G4
REDE B98 .... 197 J5
Eaton Av *WBROM* B70 .... 86 E1
Eaton Cl *RLSN* CV32 .... 200 B3
Eaton Ct *FOAKS/STRLY* B74 .... 56 F6
Eaton Crs *SEDG* DY3 .... 83 M2
Eaton Pl *KGSWFD* DY6 .... 83 J8
Eaton Ri *SHHTH* WV12 .... 37 M7
Eaton Rd *COV* CV1 .... 8 E7
Eaton Wd *ERDE/BCHGN* B24 .... 91 H2
Eaton Wood Dr
LGN/SDN/BHAMAIR B26 .... 109 H8
Eaves Court Dr *SEDG* DY3 .... 66 A3
Eaves Green Gdns *ACGN* B27 ... 108 F8
Eaves Green La
RCOVN/BALC/EX CV7 .... 131 J4
Ebbw Vale Ter *COVS* CV3 .... 154 B6
Ebenezer St *BILS/COS* WV14 .... 66 F5
HEDN WS12 .... 12 E6
WBROM B70 .... 68 D7
Ebley Rd *BFLD/HDSWWD* B20 .... 88 E1
Ebmore Dr *ALE/KHTH/YWD* B14 .. 145 H3
Eborall Cl *WWCK* CV34 .... 199 J3
Ebourne Cl *KNWTH* CV8 .... 191 L1
Ebrington Av *HIA/OLT* B92 .... 127 M2
Ebrington Cl
ALE/KHTH/YWD B14 .... 145 H1
Ebrington Dr
RWWCK/WEL CV35 .... 198 C3
Ebrington Rd *HHTH/SAND* B71 ...... 69 H7
Ebro Crs *COVS* CV3 .... 155 K4
Ebrook Rd *CSCFLD/WYGN* B72 .... 73 G1
Ebstree Rd
ETTPK/GDPK/PENN WV4 .... 48 B8
Eburne Rd *COVE* CV2 .... 135 G2
Ebury Rd *BVILLE* B30 .... 144 F1
Eccles Cl *COVE* CV2 .... 135 G5
Eccleshall Av *WOLVN* WV10 .... 36 A5
Ecclestone Rd *WNSFLD* WV11 .... 37 L5
Echells Cl *BRGRVW* B61 .... 185 H3
Echo Wy
ETTPK/GDPK/PENN WV4 .... 66 E1
Eckersall Rd *HWK/WKHTH* B38 .... 144 C2
Eckington Cl *REDE* B98 .... 196 F5
Ecton Leys *RUGBYS/DCH* CV22 .... 183 L6
Edale *TAM/AM/WIL* B77 .... 46 F4
Edale Cl
ETTPK/GDPK/PENN WV4 .... 66 C2
KGSWFD DY6 .... 82 F6
Edale Rd *PBAR/PBCH* B42 .... 71 G6
Edale Wy *COVN* CV6 .... 134 E6

Eddenswood Cl
POL/KGSB/FAZ B78 .... 45 J8
Eddish Rd STECH B33 .... 109 M1
Eddy Rd KIDD DY10 .... 137 J6
Edenbridge Rd HLGN/YWD B28 .. 126 F5
Eden Cl HEDN WS12 .... 17 J3
NFLD/LBR B31 .... 143 J5
OLDBY B69 .... 86 B3
Eden Ct KNWTH CV8 .... 191 M1
Edendale Rd
LGN/SDN/BHAMAIR B26 .... 109 M7
Eden Gv CHWD/FDBR/MGN B37.. 111 H4
HHTH/SAND B71 .... 69 G8
Edenhall Rd RIDG/WDGT B32 .. 104 F7
Edenhurst Rd NFLD/LBR B31 .. 143 K7
Eden Rd HIA/OLT B92 .... 128 B2
RCOVN/BALC/EX CV7 .... 135 L4
Edensor Cl WOLVN WV10.......... 3 K1
Edgar Cl CRTAM B79 .... 31 K6
Edgbaston Park Rd EDG B15 .. 106 C7
Edgbaston Rd BHTH/HG B12 .. 125 J1
DIG/EDG B5 .... 107 G8
SMTHWK B66 .... 105 M2
Edgbaston St DIG/EDG B5 .... 7 G6
Edgcombe Rd HLGN/YWD B28.. 126 D4
Edgefield Rd COVE CV2 .... 135 L5
Edge HI POL/KGSB/FAZ B78 .... 60 F3
Edge Hill Av WOLVN WV10.......... 36 E4
Edge Hill Dr
DUNHL/THL/PER WV6 .... 48 C2
SEDG DY3 .... 66 A3
Edgehill Pl TLHL/CAN CV4 .... 152 A4
Edgehill Rd FOAKS/STRLY B74.. 56 C1
NFLD/LBR B31 .... 143 L4
Edgemond Av ERDE/BCHGN B24.. 91 K1
Edgemoor Meadow HEDN WS12.. 17 G4
Edge St BILS/COS WV14.......... 67 G5
Edgewood Cl RDBRY B45 .... 103 K5
Edgewood Dr RBRY B45 .... 166 F4
Edgewood Rd
HWK/WKHTH B38 .... 144 C6
RBRY B45 .... 142 F6
Edgeworth Cl REDE B98 .... 189 G8
SHHTH WV12 .... 52 A1
Edgmond Av REDE B98 .... 197 H1
Edgware Rd ERDW/GRVHL B23 .. 72 B8
Edgwick Rd COVN CV6 .... 134 D6
Edinburgh Av WSLW WS2 .... 52 C2
Edinburgh Cl KIDD DY10 .... 137 J5
Edinburgh Ct
ERDE/BCHGN B24 .... 91 H1
Edinburgh Crs RLSS CV31 .... 200 D7
STRBR DY8 .... 101 G4
Edinburgh Dr RUSH/SHEL WS4 .. 40 B6
SHHTH WV12 .... 37 M7
Edinburgh La WSLW WS2 .... 52 E1
Edinburgh Rd ATHST CV9 .... 61 G8
BILS/COS WV14 .... 67 K2
DSYBK/YTR WS5 .... 5 M6
DUDS DY2 .... 85 H7
LGLYGN/QTN B68 .... 104 F5
NUNW/HART CV10 .... 80 B7
Edinburgh Wy RRUGBY CV23 .. 158 F8
Edingale Rd COVE CV2 .... 135 K5
Edison Cl HEDN WS12 .... 13 G6
Edison Gv RIDG/WDGT B32 .. 105 H8
WSLW WS2 .... 38 E8
Edison Rd WALM/CURD B76.......... 93 K1
Edith Rd SMTHWK B66 .... 105 M2
Edith St WBROM B70 .... 86 F2
Edmondes Cl WWCK CV34 .. 199 K4
Edmonds Cl STETCH B33 .... 109 M3
Edmondscote Rd RLSN CV32 .. 200 B5
Edmonds Rd CDYHTH B64 .... 103 G3
Edmonton Av KGSTC B44 .... 71 M4
Edmoor Cl SHHTH WV12 .... 38 A7
Edmund Cl COV CV1 .... 134 B8
SEDG DY3 .... 66 C7
WASH/WDE B8 .... 108 B1
Edmund St CBHAMNW B3.......... 6 F4
Ednall La BRGRVE B60 .... 185 L3
Ednam Cl HHTH/SAND B71 .... 69 K5
Ednam Gv WMBN WV5 .... 64 E4
Ednam Rd DUDN DY1 .... 85 G3
ETTPK/GDPK/PENN WV4 .... 50 A7
Edsome Wy CBROM B36 .... 91 K5
Edstone Cl DOR/KN B93 .... 172 D1
Edstone Ms CBROM B36 .... 91 K5
Edward Av ALDR WS9 .... 40 E6
Edward Bailey Cl COVS CV3 .. 155 J6
Edward Cl BILS/COS WV14 .... 67 J2
Edward Ct TAM/AM/WIL B77 .. 46 D1
Edward Fisher Dr
TPTN/OCK DY4 .... 67 L8
Edward Rd
ALE/KHTH/YWD B14 .... 145 K4
BDWTH CV12 .... 117 G3
BHTH/HG B12 .... 107 J8
COVN CV6 .... 133 L2
CSHL/WTROR B46 .... 93 G3
DIG/EDG B5 .... 107 H7
DUNHL/THL/PER WV6 .... 34 C8
HALE B63 .... 121 K1
LGLYGN/QTN B68 .... 105 C5
SMTHWKW B67 .... 105 K1
TPTN/OCK DY4 .... 67 L6
Edwards Gv KNWTH CV8 .... 177 G8
Edwards Rd BNTWD WS7 .... 18 D8
DUDS DY2 .... 103 G1
ERDE/BCHGN B24 .... 72 E8
MGN/WHC B75.......... 57 H2
Edward St CBHAMNW B1.......... 6 B5
CNCK/NC WS11 .... 16 C1
COVN CV6 .... 134 C8
CRTAM B79 .... 31 L8
DARL/WED WS10 .... 52 C7
DUDN DY1 .... 84 F4
ETTPK/GDPK/PENN WV4 .... 50 D7
LGLYGN/QTN B68 .... 104 E1
NUN CV11 .... 98 F1
REDW B97 .... 196 B1
RLSN CV32 .... 200 A4
RUGBYN/HIL CV21 .... 183 K1
WBROM B70 .... 87 G2
WSLW WS2 .... 52 F4
WWCK CV34 .... 199 H6

Edward Tyler Rd BDWTH CV12.. 116 E4
Edwin Av KIDDW DY11 .... 161 K4
Edwin Cl PENK ST19 .... 10 D5
Edwin Ct BRGRVE B60 .... 185 J6
Edwin Crs BRGRVE B60 .... 185 K5
Edyth Rd COVE CV2 .... 155 L1
Edyvean Cl RUGBYS/DCH CV22 .. 183 J1
Eel St OLDBY B69 .... 86 D6
Effingham Rd MOS/BIL B13 .. 126 A7
Egbert Cl AST/WIT B6.......... 89 M5
Egelwin Cl
DUNHL/THL/PER WV6.......... 34 C8
Egerton Cl RUGBYN/HIL CV21 .. 159 K7
Egerton Rd ERDE/BCHGN B24 .. 91 H2
FOAKS/STRLY B74 .... 55 K4
WOLVN WV10 .... 36 C2
Egghill La RIDG/WDGT B32 .. 142 E1
Eggington Dr PENK ST19 .... 10 D6
Eggington Rd STRBR DY8 .... 101 H6
Egginton Rd HLGN/YWD B28 .. 126 C8
Egg La HAG/WOL DY9 .... 139 J6
Egmont Gdns WNSFLD WV11 .. 37 K8
Egret Cl KIDD DY10 .... 161 L4
Eider Cl KIDD DY10 .... 161 M4
Eileen Gdns
CHWD/FDBR/MGN B37 .... 110 C1
Eileen Rd SPARK B11 .... 125 M2
Elan Av STRPT DY13 .... 160 C6
Elan Cl KIDD DY10 .... 137 M1
RLSN CV32 .... 201 G2
SEDG DY3 .... 84 B2
Elan Rd NFLD/LBR B31 .... 143 C3
SEDG DY3 .... 66 A3
Elborow St
RUGBYN/HIL CV21 .... 183 L2
Elbow St CDYHTH B64 .... 103 K4
Elbury Cft DOR/KN B93 .... 148 D8
Elcock Dr PBAR/PBCH B42 .... 71 H8
Eldalade Wy DARL/WED WS10 .. 69 G4
Elderberry Wy COVE CV2 .... 134 F7
Elder Cl CNCK/NC WS11 .... 17 G3
POL/KGSB/FAZ B78 .... 60 B6
RUGBYS/DCH CV22 .... 182 F4
Elderfield Rd BVILLE B30 .... 144 F2
Elder Gv WMBN WV5 .... 64 D7
Elder La BNTWD WS7 .... 19 C6
Eldersfield Cl REDE B98 .... 189 H6
Eldersfield Gv SOLH B91 .... 147 M6
Eldon Dr WERDW/GRVHL B23 .. 90 C3
Eldon Rd DLYWD/EDGR B16 .. 106 D4
RIDG/WDGT B32 .... 122 E2
Eldon St DARL/WED WS10 .... 52 B6
WSL WS1 .... 5 H4
Eld Rd COVN CV6 .... 134 C6
Eleanor Rd BILS/COS WV14 .... 51 H7
Electric Av AST/WIT B6 .... 89 M5
Elford Cl ALE/KHTH/YWD B14 .. 125 J8
Elford Gv BILS/COS WV14 .... 67 G1
CHWD/FDBR/MGN B37 .... 110 F4
Elford Rd HHTH/SAND B71 .... 69 J4
HRBN B17 .... 123 M2
SLYOAK B29 .... 123 M2
Elgar Cl CNCK/NC WS11 .... 12 C8
LICH WS13 .... 20 F3
NUN CV11 .... 99 L6
Elgar Crs BRLYHL DY5 .... 84 B6
Elgar Rd COVN CV6 .... 134 F5
Elgin Cl SEDG DY3 .... 66 C4
STRBR DY8 .... 101 L6
Elgin Gv YDLY B25 .... 109 C6
Elgin Rd BLOX/PEL WS3 .... 38 E1
Elias Cl LICHS WS14 .... 21 J7
Eliot Cl CRTAM B79 .... 31 L6
WWCK CV34 .... 199 J3
Eliot Ct RUGBYS/DCH CV22 .. 183 J2
Eliot Cft BILS/COS WV14 .... 67 H3
Eliot St VAUX/NECH B7.......... 90 A5
Elizabeth Av BILS/COS WV14 .. 67 K2
DARL/WED WS10 .... 69 G2
ETTPK/GDPK/PENN WV4 .... 49 M8
POL/KGSB/FAZ B78 .... 47 L3
Elizabeth Crt WWCK CV34 .. 199 M7
Elizabeth Crs LGLYGN/QTN B68 .. 105 H3
Elizabeth Dr CRTAM B79 .... 31 L6
Elizabeth Gv DUDS DY2 .... 85 K6
SHLY B90 .... 147 G3
Elizabeth Ms OLDBY B69 .... 85 L3
Elizabeth Rd CNCK/NC WS11 .. 12 C7
DSYBK/YTR WS5 .... 54 A6
HALE B63 .... 121 K2
MOS/BIL B13 .... 125 C3
RLSS CV31 .... 200 C7
SCFLD/BOLD B73 .... 72 A4
STETCH B33 .... 109 H2
TPTN/OCK DY4 .... 86 B1
Elizabeth Wk TPTN/OCK DY4 .. 67 L4
Elizabeth Wy KNWTH CV8 .. 176 C6
RRUGBY CV23 .... 158 F8
Elkington Cft SHLY B90 .... 147 K8
Elkington St AST/WIT B6 .... 89 J3
COVN CV6 .... 134 D5
Elkstone Cl HIA/OLT B92 .... 127 M2
Elkstone Covert
ALE/KHTH/YWD B14 .... 145 G3
Ellacombe Rd COVE CV2 .... 135 H5
Ellards Dr WNSFLD WV11 .... 37 K8
Ellen St WSNGN B18 .... 6 A1
Ellenvale Cl BILS/COS WV14 .. 66 E5
Ellerbeck TAM/AM/WIL B77 .. 46 F4
Ellerby Gv ERDE/BCHGN B24 .. 91 J1
Ellerdene Cl REDE B98 .... 196 B5
Ellerside Gv NFLD/LBR B31 .. 143 K3
Ellerslie Cl BRLYHL DY5 .... 102 B5
Ellerslie Rd KGSTC B44 .... 71 M4
Ellerton Rd KGSTC B44 .... 71 M4
Ellerton Wk WOLVN WV10.......... 36 D8
Ellesmere Rd BDWTH CV12.. 116 E3
CNCK/NC WS11.......... 15 M5
WASH/WDE B8 .... 108 A4
Ellice Dr CBROM B36 .... 92 F6
Elliot Gdns RBRY B45 .... 142 F8

Elliott Cl CNCK/NC WS11 .... 12 D8
Elliott Rd SLYOAK B29 .... 124 C3
Elliotts La CDSL WV8 .... 34 E2
Elliott's Rd TPTN/OCK DY4 .... 67 J8
Ellis Av BRLYHL DY5 .... 101 L3
Ellison St WBROM B70 .... 87 G4
Ellis St CBHAMW B1.......... 6 E7
Elliston Av KGSTC B44 .... 71 J5
Elliston Gv RLSS CV31 .... 201 C7
Ellis Wk CNCK/NC WS11 .... 16 D5
Ell La RRUGBY CV23 .... 157 K1
Ellowes Rd SEDG DY3 .... 84 A1
Ellys Rd COV CV1 .... 134 A8
Elm Av BHTH/HG B12 .... 107 L8
BILS/COS WV14 .... 51 H7
DARL/WED WS10 .... 68 D1
WNSFLD WV11 .... 36 F5
Elmay Rd
LGN/SDN/BHAMAIR B26 .... 109 L6
Elm Bank MOS/BIL B13 .... 125 L2
Elm Bank Cl RLSN CV32 .... 200 E1
Elmbank Gv BFLD/HDSWWD .. 70 C8
Elmbank Rd DSYBK/YTR WS5 .. 70 A1
KNWTH CV8 .... 176 C7
Elmbridge Cl HALE B63 .... 103 H8
Elmbridge Dr SHLY B90 .... 147 M7
Elmbridge Rd KGSTG B44 .... 71 J7
Elmbridge Wy SEDG DY3 .... 66 C7
Elm Cl COVS CV3 .... 156 A6
KIDD DY10 .... 137 M1
SEDG DY3 .... 83 M3
STRBR DY8 .... 119 G3
Elm Cft LGLYGN/QTN B68 .... 105 C6
Elmcroft Av RIDG/WDGT B32 .. 122 C4
Elmcroft Gdns WOLVN WV10 .. 36 C2
Elmcroft Rd
LGN/SDN/BHAMAIR B26 .... 109 M7
Elmdale RMSLY B62 .... 104 E6
Elmdale Crs NFLD/LBR B31 .. 143 J1
Elmdale Dr ALDR WS9 .... 41 G5
KIDD DY10 .... 138 A8
Elmdale Gv NFLD/LBR B31 .. 143 J1
Elmdale Rd BILS/COS WV14 .. 66 E6
Elm Dale Rd
ETTPK/GDPK/PENN WV4 .... 49 L8
Elmdene Cl KNWTH CV8 .... 180 E1
Elmdene Rd KNWTH CV8 .... 191 M1
Elmdon Cl HIA/OLT B92 .... 128 B3
PENK ST19 .... 10 E5
WOLVN WV10 .... 35 L4
Elmdon Coppice
HIA/OLT B92 .... 128 D6
Elmdon La
CHWD/FDBR/MGN B37 .... 110 D6
LGN/SDN/BHAMAIR B26 .... 128 E2
Elmdon Park Rd HIA/OLT B92.. 128 B3
Elmdon Rd ACGN B27 .... 127 C1
CHWD/FDBR/MGN B37 .... 110 E6
SLYOAK B29 .... 124 C3
WOLVN WV10 .... 35 L4
Elm Dr GTB/HAM B43 .... 70 B4
KIDD DY10 .... 138 F3
RMSLY B62 .... 104 C4
Elm Farm Av
CHWD/FDBR/MGN B37 .... 110 D6
Elm Farm Rd BKHL/PFLD WV2 .. 50 B6
Elmfield Av ERDE/BCHGN B24 .. 91 J1
Elmfield Crs MOS/BIL B13 .... 125 K3
Elmfield Rd CBROM B36 .... 92 C6
NUNW/HART CV10 .... 81 C6
Elm Gdns LICHS WS14 .... 21 G6
Elm Gn DUDN DY1 .... 66 E8
Elm Gv ATHST CV9 .... 77 C1
BRGRVW B61 .... 185 L1
CDSL WV8 .... 34 E2
CHWD/FDBR/MGN B37 .... 92 D7
HEDN WS12 .... 12 B5
KINVER DY7 .... 118 A2
RCOVN/BALC/EX CV7 .... 96 C3
RCOVN/BALC/EX CV7 .... 151 C7
Elmhurst Av
BLKHTH/ROWR B65 .... 104 A2
Elmhurst Dr BNTWD WS7 .... 26 E1
KGSWFD DY6 .... 101 K1
Elmhurst Rd COVN CV6 .... 134 E1
HDSW B21 .... 88 C4
Elmley Cl DUDN DY1 .... 66 F6
KIDDW DY11 .... 160 F2
Elmley Gv BVILLE B30 .... 144 F2
DUNHL/THL/PER WV6 .... 48 D2
Elmore Cl
CHWD/FDBR/MGN B37 .... 110 E1
COVS CV3 .... 155 H5
Elmore Green Cl BLOX/PEL WS3.. 38 F5
Elmore Green Rd BLOX/PEL WS3.. 38 E4
Elmore Rd RUGBYS/DCH CV22.. 183 K4
STETCH B33 .... 109 L2
Elmore Rw BLOX/PEL WS3 .... 38 F4
Elm Pl KIDD DY10 .... 137 M1
Elm Rd BLOX/PEL WS3 .... 39 H7
BVILLE B30 .... 124 D5
CNCK/NC WS11 .... 17 M8
DUDN DY1 .... 85 G2
KGSWFD DY6 .... 83 J7
KIDD DY10 .... 137 L7
REDW B97 .... 196 B1
RLSN CV32 .... 200 F2
WALM/CURD B76 .... 73 K3
Elms Cl SOLH B91 .... 128 B8
WOLVN WV10 .... 23 G4
Elmsdale DUNHL/THL/PER WV6.. 48 D3
Elmsdale Ct WSL WS1 .... 5 L6
Elms Dr CNCK/NC WS11 .... 16 A4
Elms La WOLVN WV10 .... 23 G4
Elms Rd CSCFLD/WYGN B72 .. 72 F2
Elmstead Av STETCH B33 .... 110 B6
Elmstead Cl DSYBK/YTR WS5 .. 54 C4
Elmstead Wd DSYBK/YTR WS5 .. 54 C5
The Elms BDWTH CV12 .... 116 C3
RWWCK/WEL CV35 .... 191 C7
Elmstone Cl REDW B97 .... 196 A6
Elm St BDMR/CCFT WV3 .... 2 A6
WLNHL WV13 .... 51 M3
Elm Ter OLDBY B69 .... 85 L4
Elm Tree Av TLHL/CAN CV4 .. 152 L3
Elm Tree Cl POL/KGSB/FAZ B78 .. 46 D7
WMBN WV5 .... 64 D8

Elm Tree Gv HALE B63 .... 103 H7
Elm Tree Ri HIA/OLT B92 .... 129 L7
Elm Tree Rd BVILLE B30 .... 124 E7
HRBN B17 .... 105 L7
Elmtree Rd FOAKS/STRLY B74 .. 55 H5
Elm Tree Wy CDYHTH B64 .. 103 K4
Elm Wy NUNW/HART CV10 .. 79 L5
Elmwood Av COVN CV6 .... 133 K8
WNSFLD WV11 .... 37 G6
Elmwood Cl CNCK/NC WS11 .. 16 E2
RCOVN/BALC/EX CV7 .... 150 F6
Elmwood Gdns
BFLD/HDSWWD B20 .... 88 F3
Elmwood Gv HLYWD B47 .... 145 L7
Elmwood Ri SEDG DY3 .... 65 M4
Elmwood Rd
ERDE/BCHGN B24 .... 91 C3
FOAKS/STRLY B74 .... 55 L7
STRBR DY8 .... 101 G2
Elmwoods RIDG/WDGT B32 .. 122 F3
Elphin Cl COVN CV6 .... 133 L1
Elphinstone End
CSCFLD/WYGN B72 .... 73 G7
Elsee Rd RUGBYN/HIL CV21 .. 183 L2
Elsma Rd LGLYGN/QTN B68 .. 105 C5
Elston Hall La WOLVN WV10 .. 36 B4
Elstree Rd ERDW/GRVHL B23 .. 72 B8
Elswick Rd KGSTB B44 .... 71 M5
Elswick Pl KGSTG B44 .... 71 M4
Elsworth Gv YDLY B25 .... 109 C7
Eltham Gv KGSTG B44 .... 71 M4
Eltham Rd COVS CV3 .... 154 C6
Elton Cl RLSN CV32 .... 201 C3
WOLVN WV10 .... 36 C1
Elton Cft DOR/KN B93 .... 172 D1
Elton Gv ACGN B27 .... 126 E3
Eltonia Cft
LGN/SDN/BHAMAIR B26 .... 109 M7
Elunda Gv BNTWD WS7 .... 18 C7
Elva Cft CBROM B36 .... 92 D4
Elvers Green La DOR/KN B93 .. 149 J6
Elvetham Rd EDG B15 .... 6 C9
Elviron Dr DUNHL/THL/PER WV6.. 34 F8
Elwells Cl
ETTPK/GDPK/PENN WV4 .... 66 E2
Elwell St DARL/WED WS10 .... 68 F2
WBROM B70 .... 68 C8
Elwy Cir
RCOVN/BALC/EX CV7 .... 116 A6
Elwyn Rd SCFLD/BOLD B73 .... 72 A2
Ely Cl BLKHTH/ROWR B65 .... 104 C1
CHWD/FDBR/MGN B37 .... 110 F3
CNCK/NC WS11 .... 16 F4
COVE CV2 .... 135 L7
KIDDW DY11 .... 136 E7
Ely Crs HHTH/SAND B71 .... 68 F7
Ely Gv RIDG/WDGT B32 .... 123 K1
Ely Pl WSLW WS2 .... 52 F4
Ely Rd WSLW WS2 .... 52 F4
Emay Cl WBROM B70 .... 68 D5
The Embankment BRLYHL DY5 .. 102 C2
Embassy Dr EDG B15 .... 6 A9
OLDBY B69 .... 86 C5
Embassy Wk COVE CV2 .... 135 H5
Emberton Wy TAM/AM/WIL B77 .. 32 D8
Embleton Gv BKDE/SHDE B34 .. 91 L7
Emerald Wy RLSS CV31 .... 200 B8
Emerson Cl SEDG DY3 .... 83 L1
Emerson Gv WOLVN WV10 .... 36 D5
Emerson Rd COVE CV2 .... 155 C1
HRBN B17 .... 106 A7
WOLVN WV10 .... 36 D4
Emery Cl COVE CV2 .... 135 J6
ERDW/GRVHL B23 .... 90 B4
WSL WS1 .... 5 C5
Emery St WSL WS1 .... 5 H5
Emily Gdns
LDYWD/EDGR B16 .... 106 D2
Emily Rd
LGN/SDN/BHAMAIR B26 .... 109 H7
Emily St BHTH/HG B12 .... 107 K6
WBROM B70 .... 86 F3
Emmanuel Rd BNTWD WS7 .. 18 F6
SCFLD/BOLD B73 .... 72 F6
Emmeline St BORD B9 .... 107 M4
Emott Dr RLSS CV31 .... 200 B5
Emperor Wy RUGBYN/HIL CV21.. 159 K6
Empire Cl ALDR WS9 .... 40 C5
Empire Rd TLHL/CAN CV4 .... 152 C3
Empress Wy DARL/WED WS10 .. 52 B5
Emscote Dr SCFLD/BOLD B73.. 72 F6
Emscote Gn SOLH B91 .... 147 J3
Emscote Rd AST/WIT B6 .... 89 K4
COVS CV3 .... 155 C3
WWCK CV34 .... 199 L6
Emscote Arts Rd COVEN WV9 .. 35 L3
End Hall Rd
DUNHL/THL/PER WV6.......... 48 E2
Endhill Rd KGSTG B44 .... 71 L2
Endicott Rd AST/WIT B6 .... 89 K4
Endmoor Gv ERDW/GRVHL B23 .. 72 B7
Endsleigh Gdns RLSS CV31 .. 200 F7
Endsleigh Gv HLGN/YWD B28.. 126 E5
Endwood Court Rd
BFLD/HDSWWD B20 .... 88 D2
Endwood Dr FOAKS/STRLY B74 .. 56 A1
SOLH B91 .... 147 K3
Enfield Cl ERDW/GRVHL B23 .. 72 D7
Enfield Rd BLKHTH/ROWR B65... 104 D2
COVE CV2 .... 154 F2
EDG B15 .... 6 D9
REDW B97 .... 196 B8
Enford Cl BKDE/SHDE B34 .... 92 B7
Engine La BRLYHL DY5.......... 102 D1
BRWNH WS8 .... 26 A5

DARL/WED WS10 .... 67 L1
HAG/WOL DY9 .... 102 B8
TAM/AM/WIL B77 .... 46 E3
Engine St OLDBY B69 .... 86 E7
SMTHWK B66 .... 87 M7
England Crs RLSS CV31 .... 200 C6
Englestede Cl
BFLD/HDSWWD B20 .... 88 D2
Engleton Rd COVN CV6 .... 133 L8
Englewood Dr
HLGN/YWD B28 .... 126 E5
Ennerdale Cl RLSN CV32 .... 200 B3
Ennerdale Crs NUN CV11 .... 81 K7
Ennerdale Dr
DUNHL/THL/PER WV6.......... 48 D1
HALE B63 .... 121 H3
Ennerdale La COVE CV2.......... 155 L1
Ennerdale Rd
DUNHL/THL/PER WV6.......... 35 H5
GTB/HAM B43 .... 70 C6
STRPT DY13 .... 160 D7
Ennerdale Bungalows
CSHL/WTROR B46 .... 93 K4
Ennersdale Cl
CSHL/WTROR B46 .... 93 K4
Ennersdale Rd
CSHL/WTROR B46 .... 93 K4
Enright Cl RLSN CV32 .... 200 B5
Ensall Dr STRBR DY8 .... 101 J4
Ensbury Cl SHHTH WV12 .... 52 B1
Ensdale Rw WLNHL WV13 .... 51 L2
Ensdon Gv KGSTC B44 .... 71 M4
Ensford Cl FOAKS/STRLY B74 .. 56 C1
Ensign Cl TLHL/CAN CV4 .... 152 A4
Ensor Cl NUN CV11 .... 81 K7
Enstone Rd DUDN DY1 .... 84 D5
ERDW/GRVHL B23 .... 72 E7
Enterprise Dr HAG/WOL DY9 .. 102 D7
WOLVN WV10 .... 14 B8
Enterprise Gv BLOX/PEL WS3 .. 25 M8
Enterprise Wy CBHAMNE B4.......... 7 J1
Enville Cl BLOX/PEL WS3 .... 38 E2
Enville Gv SPARK B11 .... 108 B8
Enville Pl STRBR DY8 .... 101 K8
Enville Rd
ETTPK/GDPK/PENN WV4 .... 49 G8
KGSWFD DY6 .... 83 B1
SEDG DY3 .... 84 B1
Enville St STRBR DY8 .... 101 K8
Epping Cl BLOX/PEL WS3 .... 39 K7
RBRY B45 .... 71 L6
Epping Gv KGSTG B44 .... 71 J6
Epping Wy RLSN CV32 .... 201 G1
Epsom Cl BDWTH CV12 .... 116 F1
DUNHL/THL/PER WV6 .... 48 D1
LICHS WS14 .... 21 H6
REDW B97 .... 195 M5
Epsom Dr COVS CV3 .... 155 C7
Epsom Gv KGSTG B44 .... 71 M5
Epsom Rd BRGRVW B61 .... 165 L4
RLSN CV32 .... 201 G1
RUGBYS/DCH CV22 .... 183 H4
Epwell Cl KGSTG B44 .... 71 K7
Epwell Rd KGSTG B44 .... 71 K7
Erasmus Rd SPARK B11 .... 107 L6
Ercall Cl ERDW/GRVHL B23 .. 71 L7
Erdington Hall Rd
ERDE/BCHGN B24 .... 90 D3
Erdington Rd ALDR WS9 .... 54 F2
ATHST CV9 .... 63 H6
Erica Av BDWTH CV12 .... 116 C3
Erica Cl KIDDW DY11 .... 137 H4
SLYOAK B29 .... 123 L5
Erica Rd DSYBK/YTR WS5 .... 69 M2
Eric Grey Cl COVE CV2 .... 134 E8
Eringden TAM/AM/WIL B77 .. 46 F4
Erithway Rd COVS CV3 .... 177 M1
Ermington Crs CBROM B36 .. 91 J6
Ermington Rd
ETTPK/GDPK/PENN WV4 .... 50 B8
Ernest Clarke Cl SHHTH WV12 .. 52 A1
Ernest Ct HWK/WKHTH B38 .. 144 E4
Ernest Richards Rd
BDWTH CV12 .... 116 F1
Ernest Rd BHTH/HG B12 .... 125 M1
DUDS DY2 .... 85 J7
SMTHKW B67 .... 87 J7
Ernest St CBHAMW B1.......... 6 C8
Ernsford Av COVS CV3 .... 154 E4
Ernsford Cl DOR/KN B93 .... 172 D3
Erskine St VAUX/NECH B7 .... 107 M2
Erwood Cl REDW B97 .... 195 M3
Esher Dr COVS CV3 .... 154 C6
Esher Rd HHTH/SAND B71.......... 71 K1
KGSTC B44 .... 71 K1
Eskdale Cl WOLV WV1 .... 50 E3
Eskdale Wk BRLYHL DY5 .... 101 M5
Eskrett St HEDN WS12 .... 12 E8
Esme Rd SPARK B11 .... 125 M1
Esmond Cl BVILLE B30 .... 124 B8
Essendon Rd WASH/WDE B8 .. 108 F1
Essex Av DARL/WED WS10 .... 69 G1
HHTH/SAND B71 .... 69 G8
KGSWFD DY6 .... 82 F8
Essex Cl COVW CV5.......... 152 F2
KNWTH CV8 .... 191 J5
Essex Dr HEDN WS12 .... 16 F1
Essex Gdns STRBR DY8 .... 101 H6
Essex Rd DUDS DY2 .... 84 D7
MGN/WHC B75.......... 57 H4
Essex St DIG/EDG B5 .... 6 F8
RUGBYN/HIL CV21 .... 183 K1
WSLW WS2 .... 53 H8
Essington Cl LICHS WS14 .... 20 E8
LICHS WS14.......... 21 C7
STRBR DY8 .... 101 J5
Essington Rd SHHTH WV12.......... 37 M4
Essington St LDYWD/EDGR B16.. 6 D7
Essington Wy WOLV WV1 .... 50 F4
Este Rd
LGN/SDN/BHAMAIR B26 .... 109 L5
Esterton Cl COVN CV6 .... 134 A3
Estria Rd EDG B15 .... 106 F6
Estridge La GTWY WS6.......... 24 E3
Etchell Rd POL/KGSB/FAZ B78 .. 45 K2
Ethelfield Rd COVE CV2 .... 154 F2
Ethelred Rd TAM/AM/WIL B77 .. 46 E3
Ethelfleda Rd TAM/AM/WIL B77 .. 46 D3

Ethelfleda Ter *DARL/WED* WS10.... **68** D2
Ethelred Cl *FOAKS/STRLY* B74.... **56** E2
Ethel Rd *HRBN* B17 .... **106** D8
Ethel St *CBHAMW* B1 .... **6** F5
  LGLYGN/QTN B68 .... **104** C1
  SMTHWKW B67 .... **105** K3
Etheridge Rd *BILS/COS* WV14 .... **51** H6
Eton Cl *SEDG* DY3 .... **66** D6
Eton Dr *STRBR* DY8 .... **119** L2
Eton Rd *BHTH/HG* B12.......... **125** M1
Etruria Wy *BILS/COS* WV14 ...... **51** J6
Etta Gv *KGSTG* B44 .... **71** J1
Ettingley Cl *REDE* B98 .... **196** F8
Ettingshall Park Farm La
  ETTPK/GDPK/PENN WV4 ...... **66** B1
Ettingshall Rd *BILS/COS* WV14 .... **66** E4
  BKHL/PFLD WV2 .... **50** E6
Ettington Cl *DOR/KN* B93 ...... **172** B3
Ettington Rd *AST/WIT* B6 ...... **89** J5
  COVW CV5.......... **152** C2
Ettymore Cl *SEDG* DY3 .... **66** B5
Ettymore Rd *SEDG* DY3 .... **66** B5
Ettymore Rd West *SEDG* DY3.... **66** A5
Etwall Rd *HLGN/YWD* B28 ...... **126** C8
Euan Cl *HRBN* B17 .... **106** E1
Eunal Ct *REDE* B97 .... **196** C8
Europa Av *WBROM* B70.......... **87** K3
Europa Wy
  LGN/SDN/BHAMAIR B26 ...... **129** G1
  LICHS **21** K5
Euston Crs *COVS* CV3 .... **155** G7
Euston Pl *RLSN* CV32 .... **200** D5
Evans Cl *BDWTH* CV12 .... **117** G2
  KIDDW DY11 .... **137** G2
  TPTN/OCK DY4 .... **67** G8
Evans Cft *POL/KGSB/FAZ* B78 .... **45** L4
Evans Pl *BILS/COS* WV14 ...... **51** J6
Evans Rd *RUGBYS/DCH* CV22 .... **183** G3
Evans St *BILS/COS* WV14 ...... **66** D4
  DUNHL/THL/PER WV6.......... **2** C1
  WLNHL WV13 .... **51** H4
Eva Rd *LGLYGN/QTN* B68 ...... **105** G3
  WSNGN B18 .... **88** C7
Eve La *DUDN* DY1 .... **66** D8
Evelyn Av *COVN* CV6 .... **134** C3
Evelyn Cft *SCFLD/BOLD* B73.... **72** E5
Evelyn Rd *SPARK* B11.......... **126** A1
Evenlode Cl *REDE* B98 .... **196** F6
Evenlode Crs *COVN* CV6 ...... **133** K8
Evenlode Gv *WLNHL* WV13 .... **52** B4
Evenlode Rd *HIA/OLT* B92...... **127** L2
Everdon Rd *COVN* CV6 .... **133** M3
Everest Cl *SMTHWK* B66 ...... **87** J5
Everest Rd *BFLD/HDSWWD* B20.... **88** E2
  RUGBYS/DCH CV22 .... **183** J5
  WSLW WS2 .... **52** D2 🔢
Everglade Rd
  POL/KGSB/FAZ B78 .... **60** F3
Evergreen Cl *BILS/COS* WV14.... **66** F5
Evergreen Hts *HEDN* WS12 .... **12** E5 🔢
Everitt Dr *DOR/KN* B93 .... **148** E7
Eversleigh Rd *COVN* CV6 ...... **133** J6
Eversley Dl *ERDE/BCHGN* B24 .... **90** E3
Eversley Gv *SEDG* DY3 .... **66** A3
  WNSFLD WV11 .... **37** G7
Eversley Rd *BORD* B9 .... **108** B4 🔢
Evers St *BRLYHL* DY5 .... **102** E5
Everton Rd *WASH/WDE* B8 ...... **109** G1 🔢
Eves Cft *RIDG/WDGT* B32 ...... **123** G4
Evesham Crs *BLOX/PEL* WS3 .... **38** D2
Evesham Ri *DUDS* DY2.......... **103** H2
Evesham Rd *REDW* B97.......... **196** D6
Evesham St *REDW* B97 .... **196** C2 🔢
Eveson Rd *STRBR* DY8 .... **119** H3
Evreux Wy
  RUGBYN/HIL CV21 .... **183** L2 🔢
Ewart Rd *WSLW* WS2 .... **52** C2
Ewell Rd *ERDE/BCHGN* B24...... **90** F1
Ewhurst Av *SLYOAK* B29 ...... **124** D4 🔢
Ewhurst Cl *WLNHL* WV13 .... **51** K5 🔢
Ewloe Cl *KIDDW* DY11 .... **161** J4
Exbury Cl *COVEN* WV9 .... **35** K3 🔢
Exbury Wy *NUN* CV11 .... **99** J5
Excelsior Gv *BLOX/PEL* WS3 .... **38** F4 🔢
Exchange St *BRLYHL* DY5 ...... **102** B1 🔢
  KIDD DY10.......... **137** J2
The Exchange *BLOX/PEL* WS3 .... **38** F4 🔢
Exe Cft *NFLD/LBR* B31 .... **143** M5
Exeter Cl *COVS* CV3 .... **155** H5
  KIDDW DY11.......... **136** E7
Exeter Dr
  CHWD/FDBR/MGN B37.......... **110** D5
  CRTAM B79 .... **31** J8
Exeter Pas *CBHAMW* B1 .... **6** F8 🔢
Exeter Pl *WSLW* WS2 .... **52** F4
Exeter Rd *CNCK/NC* WS11 .... **15** M5
  DUDS DY2 .... **103** H3
  SLYOAK B29 .... **124** D3
  SMTHWK B66 .... **87** M8
Exeter St *CBHAMW* B1 .... **6** F8 🔢
Exford Cl *BRLYHL* DY5 .... **101** M6
Exhall Cl *REDE* B98 .... **189** H8
  SOLH B91 .... **147** J3
Exhall Gn *RCOVN/BALC/EX* CV7 .. **116** D6
Exhall Rd *RCOVN/BALC/EX* CV7 .. **115** K7
Exham Cl *WWCK* CV34 .... **199** J4 🔢
Exhibition Wy *BHAMNEC* B40.... **129** H1
Exminster Rd *COVS* CV3 ...... **154** C3 🔢
Exmoor Dr *BRGRVW* B61 ...... **165** L8
  RLSN CV32 .... **201** G1 🔢
Exmoor Gn *WNSFLD* WV11 .... **37** G6
Exmouth Cl *COVE* CV2 .... **135** G6
The Expressway *WBROM* B70 .... **87** G1
Exton Cl *RCOVN/BALC/EX* CV7 .. **116** A7 🔢
Exton Wy *WASH/WDE* B8 ...... **90** B8
Eyffler Cl *WWCK* CV34 .... **199** H6 🔢
Eyland Gv *WSL* WS1 .... **5** G2
Eymore Cl *SLYOAK* B29 .... **123** M7
Eyre St *WSNGN* B18 .... **106** C1
Eyston Av *TPTN/OCK* DY4 ...... **68** B5
Eyton Cl *REDE* B98.......... **197** H2
Eyton Cft *BHTH/HG* B12 ...... **107** K6
Ezekiel La *SHHTH* WV12.......... **38** A1

F

Fabian Cl *COVS* CV3 .... **155** H6 🔢
  RBRY B45 .... **142** D3
Fabian Crs *SHLY* B90 .... **146** F4
Facet Rd *HWK/WKHTH* B38...... **144** E3
Factory La *BRGRVW* B61 ...... **185** J4
Factory Rd *TPTN/OCK* DY4 ...... **67** J7
  WSNGN B18 .... **88** D7
Factory St *DARL/WED* WS10...... **52** A7
Fairbanks Cl *COVE* CV2 .... **135** L6 🔢
Fairbourne Av
  BLKHTH/ROWR B65 .... **104** C1
  KGSTG B44 .... **71** J3
Fairbourne Gdns *REDW* B97...... **196** A5
Fairbourne Wy *COVN* CV6...... **133** J5
Fairburn Cresent *BLOX/PEL* WS3.. **25** M8
Faircroft *KNWTH* CV8.......... **191** K2
Faircroft Av *WALM/CURD* B76.... **73** K7
Faircroft Rd *CBROM* B36.......... **92** B4
Fairfax Rd *NUN/WHC* B75 ...... **73** K1
  NFLD/LBR B31 .... **143** L5
  WOLV WV10 .... **36** B2
Fairfield Cl *HEDN* WS12 ...... **17** H4
Fairfield Ct *COVS* CV3 .... **154** E6 🔢
Fairfield Dr *BLOX/PEL* WS3 .... **39** M1
  CDSL WV8 .... **34** C2
  PENK SV19 .... **10** C7
  RMSLY B62 .... **104** C4
Fairfield Gv *RMSLY* B62 ...... **104** C4 🔢
Fairfield La *KIDDW* DY11 ...... **136** F2
Fairfield Mt *WSL* WS1 .... **5** G6
Fairfield Rd
  RCOVN/BALC/EX CV7.......... **131** G4
  STRBR DY8 .... **101** G8
Fairfield Rd
  ALE/KHTH/YWD B14.......... **125** J5
  BRGRVW B61 .... **165** H4
  DUDS **85** H6
  HALE B63 .... **121** L3
  RMSLY B62 .... **104** C4
  STRBR DY8 .... **100** C4 🔢
Fairfields Hl *POL/KGSB/FAZ* B78.. **47** K5
Fairford Cl *REDE* B98.......... **189** J6
Fairford Gdns *BNTWD* WS7 .... **19** G7
  STRBR DY8 .... **101** J2 🔢
Fairford Rd *KGSTG* B44 .... **71** K7
Fairgreen Gdns *BRLYHL* DY5 .... **84** A8 🔢
Fairgreen Wy *FOAKS/STRLY* B74 .. **55** L4
  SLYOAK B29 .... **124** D4 🔢
Fairground Wy *WSL* WS1 ...... **4** D5
Fairhaven Cft *RMSLY* B62 ...... **104** C4 🔢
Fairhills *SEDG* DY3 .... **66** B5 🔢
Fairholme Rd *CBROM* B36...... **90** F6
Fairhurst Dr *RLSN* CV32 .... **200** C2
Fair Isle Dr *NUNW/HART* CV10 .. **98** D2
Fair Lady Dr *BNTWD* WS7 ...... **18** E5
Fairlands Pk *TLHL/CAN* CV4 .... **153** J8
Fairlawn Cl *WNWD* WV12 ...... **38** A4
Fairlawn Dr *KGSWFD* DY6 ...... **101** H1
Fairlawns
  LGN/SDN/BHAMAIR B26 ...... **109** K4
  WALM/CURD B76 .... **73** L5 🔢
Fairlie Crs *HWK/WKHTH* B38...... **144** B4
Fairlight Dr *RBRY* B45 .... **166** E4
Fairmead Ri *HWK/WKHTH* B38.... **144** C4
Fairmile Cl *COVS* CV3 .... **155** G5
Fairmile Rd *HALE* B63 .... **103** K7
Fairmont Rd *BRGRVE* B60...... **185** M5
Fairmount Dr *CNCK/NC* WS11 .... **16** C5
Fairoak Dr *BRGRVE* B60.......... **185** K7
  DUNHL/THL/PER WV6.......... **48** E2
Fair Oaks Dr *GTWY* WS6.......... **24** E5
Fairview Av *PBAR/PBCH* B42 .... **70** F7
Fairview Cl *GTWY* WS6.......... **24** B3
  TAM/AM/WIL B77 .... **32** D8
  WNSFLD WV11 .... **36** F6 🔢
Fairview Crs *KGSWFD* DY6 ...... **83** K7
  WNSFLD WV11 .... **36** F6
Fairview Gv *WNSFLD* WV11...... **36** F6
Fairview Rd *DUDN* DY1 .... **84** E3
  ETTPK/GDPK/PENN WV4 ...... **65** G1
  WNSFLD WV11 .... **36** F6
Fairway *CNCK/NC* WS11 ...... **16** B7
  NFLD/LBR B31 .... **143** J5
  NUN CV11 .... **99** M5
  RUSH/SHEL WS4 .... **40** B4
  TAM/AM/WIL B77 .... **46** C8
Fairway Av *OLDBY* B69 .... **85** L5
Fairway Gn *OLDBY* B69 .... **85** L5
Fairway Ri *KNWTH* CV8.......... **177** G7
Fairway Rd *LGLYGN/QTN* B68 .... **104** D4
Fairways Av *STRBR* DY8 .... **119** J3
Fairways Cl *COVW* CV5.......... **132** E7
  STRBR DY8 .... **119** J3
Fairways Dr *BRGRVE* B60...... **166** E8
The Fairways *RLSN* CV32 ...... **200** B3
The Fairway *HWK/WKHTH* B38 .. **144** B3
Fairyfield Av *GTB/HAM* B43 ...... **70** D6
Fakenham Cft *HRBN* B17 ...... **105** K6 🔢
Falcon *TAM/AM/WIL* B77.......... **46** B8
Falcon Av *COVS* CV3 .... **155** K5
Falcon Cl *CNCK/NC* WS11 ...... **16** A3 🔢
  GTWY WS6 .... **24** A3
  KIDD DY10.......... **161** J2
  NUN CV11 .... **99** M5
Falcon Crs *BILS/COS* WV14...... **66** D3
Falcondale Av *SHHTH* WV12...... **38** A4
Falconhurst Rd *SLYOAK* B29 .... **124** A3
Falcon Lodge Crs
  MGN/WHC B75.......... **57** L8
Falcon Pl *OLDBY* B69 .... **86** A6 🔢
Falcon Ri *STRBR* DY8 .... **101** C7 🔢
Falcon Rd *LGLYGN/QTN* B68 .... **104** D3
Falcon Wy *DUDN* DY1 .... **84** D4
Falfield Cl *OLDBY* B69 .... **86** B7 🔢
Falfield Gv *NFLD/LBR* B31.......... **143** H6
Falkland Cl *TLHL/CAN* CV4.......... **152** B6
Falkland Cft *BVILLE* B30.......... **124** F7
Falklands Cl *SEDG* DY3.......... **82** C3
Falkland Wy *CBROM* B36...... **92** F8
Falkwood Gv *DOR/KN* B93 ...... **148** D7
Fallindale Rd
  LGN/SDN/BHAMAIR B26 ...... **109** M7

Fallings Heath Cl
  DARL/WED WS10 .... **52** D6
Fallowfield *WBROM* B70 .... **35** J3
Fallow Fld *CNCK/NC* WS11 ...... **16** C2
Fallowfield
  DUNHL/THL/PER WV6 ...... **48** B1 🔢
Fallow Fld *FOAKS/STRLY* B74 .... **55** M2
Fallowfield Av *HLGN/YWD* B28 .. **126** D8
Fallowfield Cl *PENK* SV19 ...... **10** C5
Fallow Field Rd
  BLKHTH/ROWR B65.......... **103** L2
Fallowfield Rd *DSYBK/YTR* WS5.... **54** C5
  HALE B63 .... **121** H2
  HIA/OLT B92 .... **128** A3
Fallowfields Cl *BRGRVW* B61 .... **185** J2 🔢
Fallows Rd *SPARK* B11.......... **108** A7
Fallow Wk *RIDG/WDGT* B32 .... **122** C3
Falmouth Cl *NUN* CV11 ...... **81** L8
Falmouth Dr *TAM/AM/WIL* B77 .. **32** D8
Falmouth Rd *BKDE/SHDE* B34 .. **91** J8
  DSYBK/YTR WS5.......... **54** B6
Falna Crs *CRTAM* B79.......... **31** K6
Falstaff Av *HLYWD* B47 .... **145** J4
Falstaff Cl *NUN* CV11 .... **99** L4
  WALM/CURD B76.......... **73** L6
Falstaff Ct *RUGBYS/DCH* CV22 .. **183** H7
Falstaff Rd *SHLY* B90 .... **147** G3
  TLHL/CAN CV4 .... **152** C3
Falstone Rd *SCFLD/BOLD* B73 .. **72** B3
Fancott Dr *KNWTH* CV8 .... **176** D7 🔢
Fancott Rd *NFLD/LBR* B31 ...... **123** L8
Fancourt Av
  ETTPK/GDPK/PENN WV4 ...... **49** H8
Fane Rd *WNSFLD* WV11 .... **37** L4
Fanshawe Rd *ACGN* B27 ...... **127** C4
Faraday Av *RIDG/WDGT* B32 .... **105** H8
  WALM/CURD B76 .... **75** J8
Faraday Rd *WSLW* WS2 .... **38** F7
Farber Rd *COVE* CV2 .... **135** L7
Farbrook Wy *SHHTH* WV12...... **37** M7
Farcroft Av *COVW* CV5.......... **152** B1
  HDSW B21 .... **88** B3
Farcroft Gv *HDSW* B21 .... **88** B4
Farcroft Rd *HDSW* B21 .... **88** B4
Fardon Wy *ERDW/GRVHL* B23 .. **72** B5
Fareham Crs
  ETTPK/GDPK/PENN WV4 ...... **49** G7
Farewell La *BNTWD* WS7 ...... **19** J7
Farfield *KIDD* DY10.......... **137** K8
Farfield Cl *NFLD/LBR* B31 ...... **143** M3
Far Gosford St *COV* CV1 ...... **9** K5
  COVE CV2 .... **9** L4 🔢
Far Highfield *WALM/CURD* B76 .. **73** H1
Far Hill Cl *HHTH/SAND* B71 .... **69** K5
Farlands Dr *STRBR* DY8 ...... **119** L2 🔢
Farlands Gv *GTB/HAM* B43 ...... **70** D6
Farlands Rd *STRBR* DY8 ...... **119** L2
Farleigh Dr *BDMR/CCFT* WV3 .. **48** E5
Farleigh Rd
  DUNHL/THL/PER WV6 ...... **48** E2
Farley La *HAG/WOL* DY9 ...... **141** J5
Farley Rd *ERDW/GRVHL* B23.... **89** M1
Farley St *RLSS* CV31 .... **200** E6
  TPTN/OCK DY4 .... **68** B8
Farlow Cl *COVN* CV6 .... **134** E7 🔢
  REDE B98 .... **197** H1
Farlow Cft
  CHWD/FDBR/MGN B37.......... **110** D6 🔢
Farlow Rd *NFLD/LBR* B31 ...... **144** A2
Farmacre *BORD* B9 .... **107** M3 🔢
Farman Rd *COVW* CV5.......... **153** K3
Farmbridge Cl *WSLW* WS2 ...... **52** B2 🔢
Farmbridge Rd *WSLW* WS2 .... **52** B2 🔢
Farmbrook Av *WOLVN* WV10 .. **36** B2
Farm Cl *CDSL* WV8 .... **34** F3
  COVN CV6 .... **133** M2
  CRTAM B79 .... **32** A6
  HEDN WS12 .... **17** G2 🔢
  HIA/OLT B92 .... **128** A3
  KIDDW DY11 .... **160** F3
  SEDG DY3 .... **65** M6 🔢
  STECH B33 .... **109** K2
Farmcote Rd *COVE* CV2 .... **134** F1
  STECH B33 .... **109** L1 🔢
Farm Cft *LOZ/NWT* B19 .... **89** G7
Farmcroft Rd *HAG/WOL* DY9 .. **120** C3
Farmdale Gv *RBRY* B45.......... **142** E7
Farmer Rd *SMHTH* B10.......... **108** E6
Farmers Cl *WALM/CURD* B76 .. **73** H1
Farmers Ct *HALE* B63 .... **121** K1 🔢
Farmers Rd *BRGRVE* B60...... **185** J7
Farmer Ward Rd *KNWTH* CV8.... **191** G7
Farmer Wy *TPTN/OCK* DY4 ...... **67** M4
Farmhouse Rd *SHHTH* WV12...... **38** B4
Farm House Wy *GTB/HAM* B43 .. **70** C1
Farmhouse Wy *SHLY* B90 ...... **147** M7
Farm La *RUGBY* CV23 .... **158** C1
Farmoor Gv *BKDE/SHDE* B34 .. **92** C7
Far Moor La *REDE* B98.......... **189** L8
Farmoor Wy *WOLVN* WV10 .... **36** C1 🔢
Farm Rd *BDMR/CCFT* WV3 .... **49** G5
  BLKHTH/ROWR B65.......... **103** L1
  BRLYHL DY5 .... **102** C4
  DUDS DY2 .... **102** E1
  KNWTH CV8 .... **191** J5
  LGLYGN/QTN B68 .... **104** E2
  REDE B98 .... **196** E2
  RLSN CV32 .... **200** F2
  SMTHWKW B67 .... **105** J2
  SPARK B11 .... **107** M7
  TPTN/OCK DY4 .... **67** M6
Farmside Gn *COVEN* WV9 ...... **35** K3 🔢
Farmstead Cl *WSL* WS1 ...... **53** J8 🔢
Farmstead Rd *HIA/OLT* B92.... **128** A3
The Farmstead *COVS* CV3...... **154** F5
Farm St *LOZ/NWT* B19 .... **89** G7
  WBROM B70.......... **87** G3
  WSLW WS2 .... **53** J1 🔢
Farnborough Cl *REDE* B98 .... **197** K4 🔢
Farnborough Ct
  MGN/WHC B75.......... **57** G3 🔢
Farnborough Dr *SHLY* B90 .... **147** K7
Farnborough Rd *CVALE* B35.... **91** L3
Farnbury Cft
  HWK/WKHTH B38 .... **144** F3 🔢
Farncote Dr *FOAKS/STRLY* B74.... **56** D2

Farndale Av *COVN* CV6 .... **134** B2
  DUNHL/THL/PER WV6 ...... **35** L8
Farndale Cl *BRLYHL* DY5 ...... **101** M7
Farndon Av
  CHWD/FDBR/MGN B37.......... **110** F6
Farndon Cl *BDWTH* CV12...... **117** M2
Farndon Rd *WASH/WDE* B8 ...... **90** D8
Farnham Cl *GTB/HAM* B43 ...... **70** D5
Farnham Rd *HDSW* B21.......... **88** B3
Farnhurst Rd *CBROM* B36...... **90** F6
Farnol Rd
  LGN/SDN/BHAMAIR B26 ...... **109** K5
Farnworth Gv *CBROM* B36...... **92** C4
Farquhar Rd *EDG* B15.......... **106** D7
  MOS/BIL B13 .... **125** K2 🔢
Farquhar Rd East *EDG* B15...... **106** D7
Farr Dr *TLHL/CAN* CV4 .... **152** F3
Farren Rd *COVE* CV2 .... **135** J8
  NFLD/LBR B31 .... **143** H4
Farrier Cl *BRGRVE* B60.......... **185** J6
  WALM/CURD B76 .... **73** K5 🔢
Farrier Rd *GTB/HAM* B43 ...... **71** H2
Farriers Mi *BLOX/PEL* WS3 ...... **39** J1
The Farriers
  LGN/SDN/BHAMAIR B26 ...... **109** M8
Farriers Wy *NUN* CV11 .... **99** K3 🔢
Farrier Wy *KGSWFD* DY6 ...... **82** E6
Farringdon St *WSLW* WS2 ...... **4** C1
Farrington Rd
  ERDW/GRVHL B23 .... **71** M8
  ETTPK/GDPK/PENN WV4 ...... **66** C3
Farrow Rd *KGSTG* B44 .... **71** J2
Farthing La *CSCFLD/WYGN* B72 .. **72** F1
  WALM/CURD B76 .... **75** G7
Farthing Pools Cl
  CSCFLD/WYGN B72 .... **73** G1 🔢
Farvale Rd *WALM/CURD* B76 .... **74** A7
Farway Gdns *CDSL* WV8 .... **34** D3
Far Wood Rd *NFLD/LBR* B31 .... **123** H5
Faseman Av *TLHL/CAN* CV4 .... **152** D3
Fashoda Rd *SLYOAK* B29 ...... **124** F4
Fastlea Rd *RIDG/WDGT* B32 .... **123** H4
Fastmoor Ov *STECH* B33 ...... **110** C4
Fast Pits Rd *YDLY* B25 .... **108** F5
Fatherless Barn Crs
  HALE B63 .... **103** G8 🔢
Faulconbridge Av *COVW* CV5.... **152** C1
Faulkland Crs *WOLV* WV1 ...... **3** G3 🔢
Faulkner Cl *STRBR* DY8 ...... **119** K1 🔢
Faulkner Rd *HIA/OLT* B92...... **127** M4
Faulkners Farm Dr
  ERDW/GRVHL B23 .... **71** M7
Faultlands Cl *NUN* CV11 ...... **99** K5
Faversham Cl *CDSL* WV8 ...... **35** J5 🔢
  WSLW WS2 .... **52** B2 🔢
Fawdry Cl *SCFLD/BOLD* B73 .... **56** F8 🔢
Fawdry St *DIG/EDG* B5 .... **7** M5
  SMTHWK B66 .... **88** A3 🔢
  WOLV WV1 .... **2** D2
Fawley Cl *COVS* CV3 .... **155** G7
  WLNHL WV13 .... **51** K5
Fawley Gv *ALE/KHTH/YWD* B14 .. **124** F8
Fawsley Leys
  RUGBYS/DCH CV22 .... **183** L6
Faygate Cl *COVS* CV3 .... **155** K2
Fazeley Rd *POL/KGSB/FAZ* B78 .. **45** L1
Fazeley St *DIG/EDG* B5 .... **7** J5
Featherbed La *LICH* WS13...... **20** C2
  REDW B97 .... **195** M6
  TLHL/CAN CV4 .... **152** E8
Featherstone Cl
  NUNW/HART CV10 .... **99** G3
  SHLY B90 .... **147** H3 🔢
Featherstone Crs *SHLY* B90 .... **147** H4
Featherstone La *WOLVN* WV10 .. **22** F5
Featherstone Rd
  ALE/KHTH/YWD B14.......... **125** J7
  FOAKS/STRLY B74.......... **55** L3
Feckenham Rd *REDW* B97...... **196** L3
Fecknam Wy *LICH* WS13 ...... **21** G3
Feiashill Rd *SEDG* DY3.......... **82** B2
Felbrigg Cl *BRLYHL* DY5 ...... **102** B5 🔢
The Feldings *ERDE/BCHGN* B24 .. **91** G1
Feldon La *RMSLY* B62 .... **104** C6
Felgate Cl *SHLY* B90 .... **147** L7
Fellbrook Cl *STECH* B33 ...... **109** K1
Fell Gv *HDSW* B21.......... **88** A4
  RLSN CV32 .... **201** G2
Fellmeadow Rd *STECH* B33 .... **109** L3
Fellmeadow Wy *SEDG* DY3 ...... **66** C6 🔢
Fellmore Gv *RLSS* CV31 ...... **201** G6 🔢
Fellows La *HRBN* B17 .... **105** L7
Fellows Rd *BILS/COS* WV14...... **51** H6
Fellows St *BKHL/PFLD* WV2 .... **2** E9
Felspar Rd *TAM/AM/WIL* B77 .... **46** B2
Felstead Cl *TAM/AM/WIL* B77 .. **60** A1
Felsted Wy *VAUX/NECH* B7 .... **7** M2
Felstone Rd *KGSTG* B44 .... **71** J4
Feltham Cl *STECH* B33 .... **110** C4
Felton Cl *COVE* CV2 .... **135** J4
  REDE B98 .... **197** J3
Felton Cft *STECH* B33 .... **109** L2 🔢
Felton Gv *SOLH* B91 .... **147** M4
Fenbourne Cl *RUSH/SHEL* WS4 .. **40** C4
Fenchurch Cl *WSLW* WS2...... **53** L1
Fencote Av
  CHWD/FDBR/MGN B37.......... **110** E1
Fen End Rd
  RCOVN/BALC/EX CV7 .... **173** M1
Fenmere Cl
  ETTPK/GDPK/PENN WV4 ...... **50** B8
Fennel Cl *GTWY* WS6 .... **24** B2
Fennel Cft *BKDE/SHDE* B34 .... **91** M6
Fennel Rd *BRLYHL* DY5 .... **102** A6
Fennis Cl *DOR/KN* B93 .... **172** D2
Fenn Ri *SHHTH* WV12.......... **37** M7
  STRBR DY8 .... **101** G2
Fenn St *TAM/AM/WIL* B77 ...... **46** B4
Fens Crs *BRLYHL* DY5 .... **84** B3
Fenside Av *COVS* CV3.......... **178** B1
Fens Pool Av *BRLYHL* DY5 ...... **84** B3
The Fensway *BKDE/SHDE* B34 .. **91** L8 🔢
Fenter Cl *MOS/BIL* B13 .... **107** K8 🔢

Fentham Cl *HIA/OLT* B92......... **129** M7
Fentham Ct *HIA/OLT* B92......... **127** K4
Fentham Gn *HIA/OLT* B92 ...... **129** L6 🔢
Fentham Rd *AST/WIT* B6 ...... **89** M7
  ERDW/GRVHL B23 .... **90** B2
  HIA/OLT B92 .... **129** L6
Fenton Rd *ACGN* B27 .... **108** F8
  HLYWD B47 .... **145** L6
Fenton St *BRLYHL* DY5.......... **102** B2
  SMTHWK B66 .... **87** J6
Fenton Wy *ACGN* B27 .... **126** F1
Fenwick Cl *REDW* B97.......... **195** M4
Fereday Rd *ALDR* WS9 .... **40** F2
Fereday's Cft *SEDG* DY3 ...... **66** B6
Fereday St *TPTN/OCK* DY4 ...... **67** K5
Ferguson Dr *KIDDW* DY11 ...... **160** E4
Ferguson Rd *LGLYGN/QTN* B68 .. **87** H8
Ferguson St *WNSFLD* WV11 .... **37** L4
Fern Av *TPTN/OCK* DY4 .... **67** K6
Fernbank Cl *HALE* B63.......... **121** H3
Fernbank Crs *DSYBK/YTR* WS5.... **70** A1
Fernbank Rd *WASH/WDE* B8 .... **108** E1
Fern Cl *BILS/COS* WV14.......... **66** F5
  COVE CV2 .... **135** G3 🔢
  RUSH/SHEL WS4 .... **40** A4
Fern Cft *LICH* WS13 .... **20** C4 🔢
Ferndale Av *GTB/HAM* B43 ...... **70** D6
Ferndale Cl *BNTWD* WS7 ...... **18** E7
  BRGRVW B61 .... **165** L4
  HAG/WOL DY9 .... **119** L8 🔢
  NUN CV11 .... **81** J8
Ferndale Crs *CSHL/WTROR* B46 .. **93** L8 🔢
Ferndale Dr *KNWTH* CV8 ...... **191** L3
Ferndale Ms
  CSHL/WTROR B46 .... **93** L8 🔢
Ferndale Pk *HAG/WOL* DY9 .... **120** K5
Ferndale Rd *COVS* CV3 .... **156** B6
  CSHL/WTROR B46 .... **93** L8 🔢
  FOAKS/STRLY B74 .... **55** K5
  HLGN/YWD B28 .... **126** D5
  LGLYGN/QTN B68 .... **104** E3
  LICH WS13 .... **20** C3
Fern Dale Rd
  RCOVN/BALC/EX CV7 .... **150** D7
Ferndale Rd *WNSFLD* WV11 .... **37** M2
Fern Dell Cl *CNCK/NC* WS11 .... **16** A3 🔢
Ferndene Rd *SPARK* B11 ...... **126** D2
Ferndown Av *SEDG* DY3 ...... **66** A6
Ferndown Cl *BLOX/PEL* WS3 .... **38** F1
  LGN/SDN/BHAMAIR B26 ...... **109** L7
  TLHL/CAN CV4 .... **152** D2 🔢
Ferndown Ct
  RUGBYS/DCH CV22 .... **183** J4 🔢
Ferndown Gdns *WNSFLD* WV11 .. **37** K8
Ferndown Rd
  RUGBYS/DCH CV22 .... **183** J4
  SOLH B91 .... **127** M7
Ferndown Ter
  RUGBYS/DCH CV22 .... **183** J4 🔢
Fern Dr *GTWY* WS6 .... **24** C1
Ferney Hill Av *REDW* B97...... **196** A2
Fernhill Cl *KNWTH* CV8.......... **176** C7
Fernhill Dr *RLSN* CV32 .... **200** F4
Fernhill Gv *KGSTG* B44 .... **71** K2
Fernhill La
  RCOVN/BALC/EX CV7 .... **150** D7
Fernhill Rd *HIA/OLT* B92......... **127** J3
Fernhurst Dr *BRLYHL* DY5...... **83** M6
Fernhurst Rd *WASH/WDE* B8 .... **108** E2
Fernleigh Av *BNTWD* WS7 ...... **18** E5
Fernleigh Gdns *STRBR* DY8 .... **101** G2
Fernleigh Rd *RUSH/SHEL* WS4 .. **53** M2
Fernley Rd *SPARK* B11 .... **126** A1
Fern Leys *BDMR/CCFT* WV3 .... **49** H4
Fernside Rd *BDMR/CCFT* WV3 .. **2** D8 🔢
  DUDN DY1 .... **85** G1
  ERDE/BCHGN B24 .... **90** E1
  HEDN WS12 .... **12** B8
Fernside Gdns *SPARK* B11 .... **125** M2 🔢
Fernwood Cl *REDE* B98.......... **196** E8
  SCFLD/BOLD B73 .... **72** C4
Fernwood Cft
  ALE/KHTH/YWD B14.......... **125** J7
  TPTN/OCK DY4 .... **85** K1 🔢
Fernwood Rd *SCFLD/BOLD* B73 .. **72** C5
Fernwoods *RIDG/WDGT* B32 .. **122** F3 🔢
Ferrers Cl *MGN/WHC* B75 ...... **57** H3
  TLHL/CAN CV4 .... **152** D3
Ferrers Rd *TAM/AM/WIL* B77 .. **46** B3
Ferrie Gv *BRWNH* WS8.......... **26** C5
Ferris Gv *ACGN* B27 .... **126** F1
Festival Av *DARL/WED* WS10 .... **68** B1
Festival Ms *HEDN* WS12.......... **12** D7
Festival Wy
  DUNHL/THL/PER WV6.......... **35** M8
Fetherston Crs *KNWTH* CV8 .... **179** L4
Ffernfail Ct *ERDW/GRVHL* B23 .. **72** C8 🔢
Fibbersley *WLNHL* WV13 ...... **51** K1
  WNSFLD WV11 .... **51** K1
Fibbersley Bank *WLNHL* WV13 .. **51** K1 🔢
Fiddlers Gn *HIA/OLT* B92......... **129** L6 🔢
Field Barn Rd
  RWWCK/WEL CV35 .... **198** D6
Field Cl *BLOX/PEL* WS3 .... **39** M3
  BLOX/PEL WS3 .... **39** G5
  KNWTH CV8 .... **176** F8
  LGN/SDN/BHAMAIR B26 ...... **109** L7
  STRBR DY8 .... **101** L3
  WWCK CV34 .... **199** M6 🔢
Field Cottage Dr *STRBR* DY8 .. **119** M2 🔢
Fieldfare *BNTWD* WS7 .... **19** H8
Fieldfare Cl *BLKHTH/ROWR* B65.. **103** K1
Fieldfare Cft *KIDD* DY10 ...... **161** L4
Fieldfare Rd *HAG/WOL* DY9 .... **119** M8
Fieldgate La *KNWTH* CV8 ...... **176** C6
Field Head La *WWCK* CV34 .... **199** M7
Fieldhead Pl
  DUNHL/THL/PER WV6.......... **35** M8
Fieldhead Rd *SPARK* B11 ...... **126** E2 🔢
Fieldhouse La *RMSLY* B62...... **141** J1
Fieldhouse Rd *BNTWD* WS7 .... **18** E6
  ETTPK/GDPK/PENN WV4 ...... **66** C1
  HEDN WS12 .... **12** D6

YDLY B25 .... 109 C5
Fielding Cl ATHST CV9 .... 63 H3
Field La GTWY WS6 .... 24 D2
  HAG/WOL DY9 .... 140 A1
  RIDG/WDGT B32 .... 122 C5
  RUSH/SHEL WS4 .... 39 M3
  SOLH B91 .... 128 E8
  STRBR DY8 .... 119 L2
Field Ms DUDS DY2 .... 103 J3
Fieldon Br ATHST CV9 .... 63 H2
Fieldon Cl SHLY B90 .... 147 C2
Field Rd BLOX/PEL WS3 .... 39 G4
  DUDS DY2 .... 85 J4
  LICH WS13 .... 20 F2
  TPTN/OCK DY4 .... 67 K5
Fieldside La COVS CV3 .... 155 K2
Field St BILS/COS WV14 .... 67 J2
  CNCK/NC WS11 .... 16 D2
  WLNHL WV13 .... 51 L3
  WOLVN WV10 .... 3 J2
Field Vw KNWTH CV8 .... 179 L3
Fieldview Cl BILS/COS WV14 .... 67 H3
Field View Cl
  RCOVN/BALC/EX CV7 .... 116 E5
Field View Dr
  BLKHTH/ROWR B65 .... 104 D3
Field Wk ALDR WS9 .... 40 F6
Field Wy HOCK/TIA B94 .... 172 A7
Fieldways Cl HLYWD B47 .... 145 L6
Fife Rd COVW CV5 .... 153 K3
Fife St NUN CV11 .... 98 E1
Fifield Cl NUN CV11 .... 99 H3
Fifield Gv STECH B33 .... 109 K2
Fifth Av BORD B9 .... 108 D3
  WOLVN WV10 .... 36 B6
Filance Cl PENK ST19 .... 10 D6
Filance La PENK ST19 .... 10 D6
Filey TAM/AM/WIL B77 .... 32 D8
Filey Cl CNCK/NC WS11 .... 16 A5
Filey Rd WOLVN WV10 .... 35 M3
Fillingham Cl
  CHWD/FDBR/MGN B37 .... 111 H4
Fillongley Rd CSHL/WTROR B46 .... 94 F8
  RCOVN/BALC/EX CV7 .... 131 C4
  RCOVN/BALC/EX CV7 .... 131 K1
Filton Av BNTWD WS7 .... 18 E5
Filton Cft CVALE B35 .... 111 M1
Fimbrell Cl STRBR DY8 .... 101 L5
Finbury Cl HIA/OLT B92 .... 127 K4
Finchall Cft HIA/OLT B92 .... 128 C6
Fincham Cl COVEN WV9 .... 35 L2
Finch Cl BLKHTH/ROWR B65 .... 103 K1
Finch Cft RCOVN/BALC/EX CV7 .... 150 F6
Finchdene Gv BDMR/CCFT WV3 .... 49 H4
Finch Dr FOAKS/STRLY B74 .... 55 L8
Finches End BKDE/SHDE B34 .... 92 A8
Finchfield Cl STRBR DY8 .... 119 C1
Finchfield Gdns
  BDMR/CCFT WV3 .... 49 J4
Finchfield HI BDMR/CCFT WV3 .... 49 J5
Finchfield La BDMR/CCFT WV3 .... 49 C5
Finchfield Rd BDMR/CCFT WV3 .... 49 J5
Finchfield Rd West
  BDMR/CCFT WV3 .... 49 G4
Finchley Cl SEDG DY3 .... 84 B5
Finchley Rd KGSTG B44 .... 71 M3
Finchmead Gv STECH B33 .... 110 C3
Finchpath Rd WBROM B70 .... 68 E7
Finch Rd LOZ/NWT B19 .... 89 C5
Findlay Rd ALE/KHTH/YWD B14 .... 125 J4
Findley Cl ATHST CV9 .... 63 K7
Findon Rd WASH/WDE B8 .... 90 F7
Findon St KIDD DY10 .... 137 K7
Fineacre La RUGBY CV23 .... 180 A8
Finford Cft
  RCOVN/BALC/EX CV7 .... 150 F7
Fingal Cl COVS CV3 .... 155 C7
Finger Post Dr BLOX/PEL WS3 .... 25 L8
Fingest Cl COVW CV5 .... 155 L5
Finham Crs KNWTH CV8 .... 176 F7
Finham Green Rd COVS CV3 .... 177 M2
Finham Gv COVS CV3 .... 178 A2
Finham Rd KNWTH CV8 .... 176 F7
Finlarigg Dr EDG B15 .... 106 D7
Finmere Cl COVS CV3 .... 153 M8
Finmere Rd BORD B9 .... 108 E3
Finney Well Cl BILS/COS WV14 .... 66 F2
Finsbury Dr BRLYHL DY5 .... 102 A6
Finsbury Gv ERDW/GRVHL B23 .... 72 B7
Finstall Cl CSCFLD/WYGN B72 .... 73 C4
  VAUX/NECH B7 .... 7 M2
Finstall Rd BRGRVE B60 .... 186 A5
Finwood Cl HIA/OLT B92 .... 128 C2
Fir Av BHTH/HG B12 .... 107 L8
Firbank Cl BVILLE B30 .... 124 C6
Firbank Wy BLOX/PEL WS3 .... 39 K3
Firbarn Cl WALM/CURD B76 .... 73 H2
Firbeck Gv KGSTG B44 .... 71 L4
Firbeck Rd KGSTG B44 .... 71 L4
Fir Cl HEDN WS12 .... 12 B5
Fircroft BILS/COS WV14 .... 67 L2
Fir Cft BRLYHL DY5 .... 102 A5
Fircroft NFLD/LBR B31 .... 123 K5
  POL/KGSB/FAZ B78 .... 60 A6
  SOLH B91 .... 127 K7
Fircroft Cl BRGRVE B60 .... 185 H7
  CNCK/NC WS11 .... 16 E2
Firecrest
  ERDW/GRVHL B23 .... 71 M6
  HEDN WS12 .... 17 G3
Firecrest Wy KIDD DY10 .... 161 M4
Fir Gv ALE/KHTH/YWD B14 .... 125 K8
  BDMR/CCFT WV3 .... 2 A7
  STRBR DY8 .... 101 C7
  TLHL/CAN CV4 .... 152 E3
Firhill Cft ALE/KHTH/YWD B14 .... 145 H3
Firmstone St STRBR DY8 .... 101 J6
Firsbrook Cl
  DUNHL/THL/PER WV6 .... 49 L1
Firs Cl BRGRVE B60 .... 166 A4
  KIDD DY10 .... 137 L8
Firs Dr RUGBYS/DCH CV22 .... 183 K3
  SHLY B90 .... 146 E4
Firs Farm Dr CBROM B36 .... 91 K6
Firsholm Cl SCFLD/BOLD B73 .... 72 E6
Firs La SMTHWKW B67 .... 87 L8

Firs Rd KGSWFD DY6 .... 83 J7
Firs St DUDS DY2 .... 85 H4
First Av BORD B9 .... 108 C4
  BRWNH WS8 .... 26 E5
  COVS CV3 .... 155 G4
  KGSWFD DY6 .... 83 L5
  SLYOAK B29 .... 124 F2
  WALM/CURD B76 .... 73 L8
  WOLVN WV10 .... 36 C6
First Exhibition Av
  BHAMNEC B40 .... 129 H1
The Firs BDWTH CV12 .... 116 C3
  COVW CV5 .... 153 M5
  POL/KGSB/FAZ B78 .... 60 B6
  SPARK B11 .... 108 A7
First Meadow Piece
  RIDG/WDGT B32 .... 123 J1
Fir St SEDG DY3 .... 65 K6
Firsvale Rd WNSFLD WV11 .... 37 K8
Firsway DUNHL/THL/PER WV6 .... 48 E4
Firswood Rd STETCH B33 .... 110 A4
Firth Dr ALE/KHTH/YWD B14 .... 125 H8
  RMSLY B62 .... 104 C5
Firth Park Crs RMSLY B62 .... 104 C5
Fir Tree Av TLHL/CAN CV4 .... 152 E3
Fir Tree Cl CRTAM B79 .... 31 J6
  KGSTG B44 .... 71 J6
  REDW B97 .... 196 B1
Fir Tree Dr DSYBK/YTR WS5 .... 69 M1
  SEDG DY3 .... 66 C6
Fir Tree Gv NUN CV11 .... 99 H4
  SCFLD/BOLD B73 .... 72 D4
Firtree La RCOVN/BALC/EX CV7 .... 96 E5
Fir Tree Rd BDMR/CCFT WV3 .... 49 H6
Firtree Rd ERDE/BCHGN B24 .... 90 F3
Fisher Rd BLOX/PEL WS3 .... 38 D3
  COVN CV6 .... 134 C5
  OLDBY B69 .... 87 G6
Fishers Dr SHLY B90 .... 146 D8
Fisher St BDMR/CCFT WV3 .... 2 C8
  BRLYHL DY5 .... 101 M2
  DUDS DY2 .... 85 H4
  HEDN WS12 .... 12 D5
  TPTN/OCK DY4 .... 68 B8
  TPTN/OCK DY4 .... 85 L2
  WLNHL WV13 .... 52 A3
Fish HI REDW B97 .... 196 C1
Fishing Line Rd REDE B98 .... 188 C8
Fishley Cl BLOX/PEL WS3 .... 39 G1
Fishley La BLOX/PEL WS3 .... 25 J7
Fishponds Rd KNWTH CV8 .... 191 J2
Fishpool Cl CBROM B36 .... 91 C5
Fishpool La
  RCOVN/BALC/EX CV7 .... 111 M7
Fitters Mill Cl DIG/EDG B5 .... 107 J7
Fitton Av KGSWFD DY6 .... 83 L8
Fitton St NUN CV11 .... 98 F2
Fitzalan Cl RRUGBY CV23 .... 157 M7
Fitzgerald Pl BRLYHL DY5 .... 101 M7
Fitzguy Cl WBROM B70 .... 87 J4
Fitzmaurice Rd WNSFLD WV11 .... 37 K6
Fitz Roy Av HRBN B17 .... 105 K6
Fitzroy Cl COVE CV2 .... 135 M7
Fitzroy Rd NFLD/LBR B31 .... 143 G2
Fivefield Rd
  RCOVN/BALC/EX CV7 .... 115 J8
Five Fields Rd SHHTH WV12 .... 37 L8
Five Oaks Rd WLNHL WV13 .... 51 J5
Flackwell Rd
  ERDW/GRVHL B23 .... 72 C6
Fladbury Cl DUDS DY2 .... 103 H2
  REDE B98 .... 196 F5
Fladbury Crs SLYOAK B29 .... 124 B3
Fladbury Gdns LOZ/NWT B19 .... 89 L1
Flamborough Cl
  BKDE/SHDE B34 .... 91 L6
Flamborough Wy DUDS DY1 .... 66 F6
Flanders Cl REDE B98 .... 189 C8
Flanders Dr KGSWFD DY6 .... 83 H5
Flash La WMBN WV5 .... 64 C3
Flash Rd OLDBY B69 .... 86 E6
Flats La LICHS WS14 .... 29 L7
The Flats BRGRVW B61 .... 185 K2
The Flatts DARL/WED WS10 .... 52 D3
Flaunden Cl COVW CV5 .... 152 F2
Flavel Crs RLSS CV31 .... 200 D6
Flavell Av BILS/COS WV14 .... 67 H4
Flavell Cl RIDG/WDGT B32 .... 122 F4
Flavells La SEDG DY3 .... 83 M3
  YDLY B25 .... 109 G5
Flavell St DUDN DY1 .... 66 F7
Flavel Rd BRGRVE B60 .... 185 J6
Flax Cl HLYWD B47 .... 145 L8
Flax Gdns HWK/WKHTH B38 .... 144 D5
Flaxhall St WSLW WS2 .... 52 F5
Flaxley Rd REDE B98 .... 197 L2
Flaxley Rd STETCH B33 .... 109 K2
The Flax Ovens PENK ST19 .... 10 C3
Flaxton Gv STETCH B33 .... 109 L1
Flecknoe Cl CBROM B36 .... 92 A4
Flecknose St COVS CV3 .... 155 G7
Fledburgh Dr WALM/CURD B76 .... 73 H2
Fleet St CBHAMNW B3 .... 6 D4
  COV CV1 .... 8 E5
Fleetwood Gv
  LGN/SDN/BHAMAIR B26 .... 109 L4
Fleming Pl WSLW WS2 .... 38 E7
Fleming Rd RIDG/WDGT B32 .... 105 H8
  WSLW WS2 .... 38 E7
Flemmynge Cl CDSL WV8 .... 34 C1
Fletchamstead Hwy
  COVW CV5 .... 153 G4
  TLHL/CAN CV4 .... 153 G4
Fletcher Gv DOR/KN B93 .... 172 F1
Fletcher Rd SHHTH WV12 .... 38 B4
Fletcher's La WLNHL WV13 .... 52 A3
Fletcher St HAG/WOL DY9 .... 102 D8
Fletchworth Ga COVW CV5 .... 153 H5
Fletton Gv
  ALE/KHTH/YWD B14 .... 145 L2
Flinkford Cl DSYBK/YTR WS5 .... 54 A7
Flinn Cl LICHS WS14 .... 21 H6
Flint Cl ATHST CV9 .... 63 J3
  KIDDW DY11 .... 161 J3
Flint Green Rd ACGN B27 .... 126 E2
Flintham Cl ACGN B27 .... 127 J2
The Flintway STETCH B33 .... 109 J1
Floodgate St DIG/EDG B5 .... 7 K7

Flood St DUDS DY2 .... 85 H4
Flora Cl CRTAM B79 .... 32 A6
Flora Rd YDLY B25 .... 108 F6
Florence Av
  ETTPK/GDPK/PENN WV4 .... 66 D1
  SPARK B11 .... 107 M7
Florence Cl ATHST CV9 .... 63 H4
  RCOVN/BALC/EX CV7 .... 116 D5
Florence Gv HHTH/SAND B71 .... 69 J4
Florence Rd ACGN B27 .... 127 H1
  ALE/KHTH/YWD B14 .... 125 K5
  CDSL WV8 .... 35 G2
  ERDW/GRVHL B23 .... 72 F6
  HDSW B21 .... 88 B5
  OLDBY B69 .... 86 B6
  SMTHWK B66 .... 105 M1
  TPTN/OCK DY4 .... 67 L6
  WBROM B70 .... 87 J4
Florence St CBHAMW B1 .... 6 E8
  HEDN WS12 .... 12 E6
  WSL WS1 .... 5 J4
Florendine St TAM/AM/WIL B77 .... 32 D8
Florian Gv DARL/WED WS10 .... 52 C6
Florida Wy KGSWFD DY6 .... 83 L8
Flowerdale Cl BILS/COS WV14 .... 66 F5
Flowerdale Dr COVE CV2 .... 134 F7
Floyds La RUSH/SHEL WS4 .... 40 A7
Floyer Rd SMHTH B10 .... 108 C4
Flude Rd RCOVN/BALC/EX CV7 .... 116 A7
Flyford Cl REDE B98 .... 196 D4
Flyford Cft SLYOAK B29 .... 123 K3
Flynt Av COVW CV5 .... 132 E7
Fockbury Mill La BRGRVW B61 .... 165 J8
Fockbury Rd BRGRVW B61 .... 164 E8
Foden Cl LICHS WS14 .... 28 D7
Foden Rd PBAR/PBCH B42 .... 70 E5
Foinavon Cl BLKHTH/ROWR B65 .... 85 K7
Fold St WOLV WV1 .... 2 E6
The Fold DARL/WED WS10 .... 52 B7
  ETTPK/GDPK/PENN WV4 .... 65 K1
Foldyard Cl WALM/CURD B76 .... 73 L5
Foleshill Rd COV CV1 .... 8 F1
  COVN CV6 .... 134 B7
Foley Dr DUNHL/THL/PER WV6 .... 48 F2
  KIDDW DY11 .... 161 C5
Foley Church Cl
  FOAKS/STRLY B74 .... 55 L3
Foley Dr DUNHL/THL/PER WV6 .... 49 C2
  KIDDW DY11 .... 160 F5
Foley Gv KIDDW DY11 .... 160 F5
  WMBN WV5 .... 64 C8
Foley Rd HAG/WOL DY9 .... 119 M3
  WASH/WDE B8 .... 90 F7
Foley Rd East FOAKS/STRLY B74 .... 55 L4
Foley Rd West FOAKS/STRLY B74 .... 55 H4
Foley St DARL/WED WS10 .... 68 C2
Foley Wood Cl FOAKS/STRLY B74 .... 55 J4
Foliot Flds YDLY B25 .... 109 H5
Folkes Rd HAG/WOL DY9 .... 102 E7
Folkestone Cft CBROM B36 .... 91 J5
Folliott Rd STETCH B33 .... 109 L2
Follyhouse Cl WSL WS1 .... 5 G7
Follyhouse La WSL WS1 .... 5 G7
Folly La ATHST CV9 .... 62 C5
Fontenaye Rd CRTAM B79 .... 31 J6
Fontley Cl
  LGN/SDN/BHAMAIR B26 .... 109 L4
Fontmell Cl COVS CV3 .... 155 L1
Fontwell Rd WOLVN WV10 .... 36 B1
Footherley Cl LICHS WS14 .... 42 A1
  LICHS WS14 .... 42 D4
Footherley Rd LICHS WS14 .... 28 D8
Fordbridge Cl REDW B97 .... 196 A4
Fordbridge Rd
  CHWD/FDBR/MGN B37 .... 110 D1
Ford Brook La BLOX/PEL WS3 .... 39 M4
Forder Gv ALE/KHTH/YWD B14 .... 145 L3
Forde Way Gdns
  HWK/WKHTH B38 .... 144 B6
Fordfield Rd STETCH B33 .... 110 A1
Fordham Gv COVEN WV9 .... 35 L2
Fordhouse La BVILLE B30 .... 124 F7
Fordhouse Rd BRGRVE B60 .... 185 L4
  WOLVN WV10 .... 36 B4
Ford La LICH WS13 .... 19 L3
Fordraught La RMSLY B62 .... 141 M4
The Fordrift
  CHWD/FDBR/MGN B37 .... 110 E8
Ford Rd BRGRVW B61 .... 185 J4
Fordrough YDLY B25 .... 108 D6
Fordrough La WASH/WDE B8 .... 108 C2
The Fordrough
  FOAKS/STRLY B74 .... 56 E4
  NFLD/LBR B31 .... 143 M4
  SHLY B90 .... 146 A6
Fords Rd SHLY B90 .... 146 C6
Ford St COV CV1 .... 9 H3
  NUNW/HART CV10 .... 98 C1
  SMTHWKW B67 .... 87 K7
  WSLW WS2 .... 4 B8
  WSNGN B18 .... 88 F8
Fordwater Rd FOAKS/STRLY B74 .... 55 K7
Fordwell Cl COVW CV5 .... 153 K2
Foredraft Cl RIDG/WDGT B32 .... 123 C3
Foredraft St HALE B63 .... 103 H8
Foredrift Cl REDE B98 .... 196 C4
Foredrove La HIA/OLT B92 .... 128 C2
Forelands Gv BRGRVW B61 .... 185 H5
Foreland Wy COVN CV6 .... 133 C3
Forest Av BLOX/PEL WS3 .... 39 H6
Forest Cl BRGRVE B60 .... 165 M7
  FOAKS/STRLY B74 .... 55 J6
  SMTHWK B66 .... 87 J6
Forest Dl RBRY B45 .... 142 F7
Forest Dr CDYHTH B64 .... 103 J3
  HRBN B17 .... 106 B7
Forester's Wy KIDD DY10 .... 161 J2
Forest Ga SHHTH WV12 .... 38 B5
Forest Gld GTWY WS6 .... 24 D3
Forest Hill Rd
  LGN/SDN/BHAMAIR B26 .... 110 A8
Forest La WASH/WDE B8 .... 90 C5
  BRGRVE B60 .... 194 B8
Forest Pk WALM/CURD B76 .... 73 J1
Forest Pl BLOX/PEL WS3 .... 39 J7
Fore St CBHAM B4 .... 7 G5
Forest Rd DOR/KN B93 .... 172 E2

DUDN DY1 .... 85 G1
LGLGYGN/QTN B68 .... 105 G6
MOS/BIL B13 .... 125 L2
YDLY B25 .... 109 G7
Forest Vw REDW B97 .... 196 B7
Forest Wy GTWY WS6 .... 24 C4
  HLYWD B47 .... 145 M7
  NUNW/HART CV10 .... 98 C3
Forfield Pl RLSS CV31 .... 200 E6
Forfield Rd COVN CV6 .... 133 J8
Forge Cl BNTWD WS7 .... 19 H8
  CDSL WV8 .... 35 J4
Forge Dr BRGRVW B61 .... 185 K2
Forge La ALDR WS9 .... 41 K7
  BNTWD WS7 .... 19 K7
  CDYHTH B64 .... 102 F5
  FOAKS/STRLY B74 .... 42 A7
  HAG/WOL DY9 .... 140 B6
  HHTH/SAND B71 .... 69 L7
  KGSWFD DY6 .... 82 E5
  KIDD DY10 .... 138 F4
  LICH WS13 .... 20 E4
  LICHS WS14 .... 41 M5
  RMSLY B62 .... 104 A8
  WALM/CURD B76 .... 73 M8
Forge Leys WMBN WV5 .... 64 C7
Forge Mill Rd REDE B98 .... 188 D8
Forge Rd BLOX/PEL WS3 .... 25 K8
  CSHL/WTROR B46 .... 94 D3
  DARL/WED WS10 .... 51 M7
  KNWTH CV8 .... 176 E7
  SHHTH WV12 .... 52 A1
  STRBR DY8 .... 101 K7
Forge St DARL/WED WS10 .... 68 C1
  HEDN WS12 .... 17 C1
The Forge HALE B63 .... 102 E5
Forge Valley Wy WMBN WV5 .... 64 C7
Forge Wy COVN CV6 .... 134 A2
  OLDBY B69 .... 86 C7
Forknell Av COVE CV2 .... 135 G2
Formans Rd SPARK B11 .... 126 C2
Formby Av
  DUNHL/THL/PER WV6 .... 48 B1
Formby Wy BLOX/PEL WS3 .... 38 E2
Forrell Gv NFLD/LBR B31 .... 143 M6
Forrest Av CNCK/NC WS11 .... 16 C6
  WNSFLD WV11 .... 37 L1
Forrester St WSLW WS2 .... 4 B2
Forrester Street Prec WSLW WS2 .... 4 B2
Forrest Rd KNWTH CV8 .... 191 J1
Forshaw Heath La
  HOCK/TIA B94 .... 169 L6
Forshaw Heath Rd
  HOCK/TIA B94 .... 170 A5
Forster St SMTHWKW B67 .... 87 J6
  VAUX/NECH B7 .... 7 L3
Forsythia Cl NFLD/LBR B31 .... 123 K5
Forsythia Gv CDSL WV8 .... 34 E2
Fort Crs ALDR WS9 .... 40 E2
Forth Dr
  CHWD/FDBR/MGN B37 .... 110 F1
Forth Gv HWK/WKHTH B38 .... 144 C5
Forth Wy RMSLY B62 .... 104 C5
Forties TAM/AM/WIL B77 .... 46 C6
Fortnum Cl STETCH B33 .... 110 A3
Forton Cl DUNHL/THL/PER WV6 .... 48 F3
Fort Pkwy ERDE/BCHGN B24 .... 90 F5
Forum Dr RUGBYN/HIL CV21 .... 159 K8
Fosberry Cl WWCK CV34 .... 199 M5
Fosbrooke Rd SMHTH B10 .... 108 C5
Fossdale Rd TAM/AM/WIL B77 .... 46 E5
Fosse Cl LICHS WS14 .... 20 E8
Fosseway LICHS WS14 .... 28 C1
Fosseway Dr ERDE/BCHGN B23 .... 72 C5
Fosseway La LICHS WS14 .... 28 C1
Fosseway Rd COVS CV3 .... 177 M1
Fossil Dr RBRY B45 .... 142 E6
Foster Av BILS/COS WV14 .... 66 F4
  HEDN WS12 .... 12 B8
Fosterd Rd RUGBYN/HIL CV21 .... 159 K8
Foster Gdns DUNHL/THL/PER WV6 .... 48 C2
Foster Pl STRBR DY8 .... 101 J7
Foster Rd COVN CV6 .... 133 L6
  WOLVN WV10 .... 36 C7
Fosters Gn BRGRVE B60 .... 194 B6
Foster St BLOX/PEL WS3 .... 39 H5
  DARL/WED WS10 .... 52 B6
Foster St East STRBR DY8 .... 101 L8
Foster Wy DIG/EDG B5 .... 107 G8
Fotherley Brook Rd ALDR WS9 .... 41 K8
Founder Cl TLHL/CAN CV4 .... 152 D5
Foundry La BLOX/PEL WS3 .... 39 J2
  SMTHWK B66 .... 88 B6
Foundry Rd KGSWFD DY6 .... 82 F5
  WSNGN B18 .... 88 B8
Foundry St BILS/COS WV14 .... 67 G4
  KGSWFD DY6 .... 82 F5
  TPTN/OCK DY4 .... 67 J5
Fountain Cl NFLD/LBR B31 .... 143 J7
Fountain La BILS/COS WV14 .... 67 H5
  OLDBY B69 .... 86 D4
Fountain Rd HRBN B17 .... 105 M4
Fountains Rd BLOX/PEL WS3 .... 38 C3
Fountains Wy BLOX/PEL WS3 .... 38 C3
Four Acres RIDG/WDGT B32 .... 123 G1
Four Ashes Rd DOR/KN B93 .... 172 B2
Four Crosses La WOLVN WV10 .... 15 H7
Four Crosses Rd
  RUSH/SHEL WS4 .... 40 A4
Fourfields Wy
  RCOVN/BALC/EX CV7 .... 96 D6
Fourlands Av CSCFLD/WYGN B72 .... 73 H6
Fourlands Rd NFLD/LBR B31 .... 123 J7
Four Oaks Cl REDE B98 .... 196 B5
Four Oaks Common Rd
  FOAKS/STRLY B74 .... 56 C2
Four Oaks Rd FOAKS/STRLY B74 .... 56 D3
Four Pounds Av COVW CV5 .... 153 K2
Four Stones Cl SOLH B91 .... 147 L4
Four Stones Gv DIG/EDG B5 .... 107 J7
Fourth Av BORD B9 .... 108 D3
  BRWNH WS8 .... 26 E4
  SLYOAK B29 .... 125 G2
  WOLVN WV10 .... 36 B7
Fourways ATHST CV9 .... 63 J5
Four Winds Rd DUDS DY2 .... 85 J6

Fowey Cl WALM/CURD B76 .... 73 L6
Fowey Rd BKDE/SHDE B34 .... 91 K7
Fowgay Dr SOLH B91 .... 147 K4
Fowler Cl CDSL WV8 .... 34 C7
  SMTHWK B66 .... 87 L5
Fowler Pl STRPT DY13 .... 160 E8
Fowler Rd COVN CV6 .... 133 M8
  MGN/WHC B75 .... 57 H7
Fowler St BKHL/PFLD WV2 .... 50 A7
  VAUX/NECH B7 .... 89 M8
Fowlmere Rd PBAR/PBCH B42 .... 70 F5
Fownhope Cl REDE B98 .... 197 J2
Fox Av NUNW/HART CV10 .... 81 C5
Foxbury Dr DOR/KN B93 .... 172 E2
Foxcote Av HDSW B21 .... 88 C6
Foxcote Cl REDE B98 .... 197 J1
  SHLY B90 .... 147 H5
Foxcote Dr SHLY B90 .... 147 H5
Foxcote La HAG/WOL DY9 .... 120 F2
Fox Covert STRBR DY8 .... 101 J8
Foxcroft Cl BNTWD WS7 .... 18 E8
Foxdale Dr BRLYHL DY5 .... 101 M2
Foxdale Gv STETCH B33 .... 110 A2
Foxes Meadow
  WALM/CURD B76 .... 73 L5
Foxes Rake CNCK/NC WS11 .... 16 C2
Foxes Rdg CDYHTH B64 .... 103 J5
Foxes Wy RCOVN/BALC/EX CV7 .... 119 L2
Foxfield Dr STRBR DY8 .... 119 L2
Foxfields Wy HEDN WS12 .... 12 A6
Fox Foot Dr BRLYHL DY5 .... 102 A1
Foxford Cl CBROM B36 .... 92 B4
  CSCFLD/WYGN B72 .... 73 H6
Foxford Crs COVN CV6 .... 134 F1
Foxglove TAM/AM/WIL B77 .... 46 E1
Foxglove Cl BLOX/PEL WS3 .... 25 L8
  COVN CV6 .... 134 A3
  WNSFLD WV11 .... 37 J8
  WOLVN WV10 .... 22 F6
Foxglove Crs
  CHWD/FDBR/MGN B37 .... 110 C2
Foxglove Rd DUDN DY1 .... 84 D1
  HDSW B21 .... 88 B6
Fox Green Crs ACGN B27 .... 126 E3
Fox Gv ACGN B27 .... 126 E3
Fox HI SLYOAK B29 .... 124 A5
Foxhill Cl HEDN WS12 .... 17 H3
Fox Hill Cl SLYOAK B29 .... 124 A5
Foxhill La ALVE B48 .... 167 H8
Fox Hill Rd MGN/WHC B75 .... 57 K3
Foxhill's Cl BNTWD WS7 .... 18 E8
Foxhills Pk DUDS DY2 .... 103 G1
Foxhills Rd
  ETTPK/GDPK/PENN WV4 .... 65 G2
  STRBR DY8 .... 101 H4
The Foxholes KIDD DY10 .... 137 K5
Foxhollies Dr HALE B63 .... 121 J1
Fox Hollies Rd ACGN B27 .... 126 F2
  WALM/CURD B76 .... 73 K5
Fox Hollow
  DUNHL/THL/PER WV6 .... 49 G3
Foxhope Cl HWK/WKHTH B38 .... 144 F4
Foxhunt Rd HALE B63 .... 121 J3
Foxland Av GTWY WS6 .... 24 E2
  RBRY B45 .... 143 G6
Foxland Cl
  CHWD/FDBR/MGN B37 .... 111 H3
  SHLY B90 .... 171 H1
Foxlands Av
  ETTPK/GDPK/PENN WV4 .... 65 H2
Foxlands Crs
  ETTPK/GDPK/PENN WV4 .... 65 G2
Foxlands Dr CSCFLD/WYGN B72 .... 73 H6
  ETTPK/GDPK/PENN WV4 .... 65 G2
  SEDG DY3 .... 66 B8
Fox La BRGRVW B61 .... 185 H5
  KIDD DY10 .... 163 H7
  LICH WS13 .... 20 E1
Foxlea Rd HALE B63 .... 121 H4
Foxley Dr SOLH B91 .... 128 E8
Foxlydiate Crs REDW B97 .... 195 L1
Foxlydiate La REDW B97 .... 195 J3
Foxmeadow Cl SEDG DY3 .... 66 C6
Foxoak St CDYHTH B64 .... 103 G4
Fox's La WOLV WV1 .... 36 B8
Fox St CBHAMNE B4 .... 7 J4
  DUDN DY1 .... 67 G7
Foxton Rd COVS CV3 .... 155 J4
  WASH/WDE B8 .... 90 D8
Fox Wk ALDR WS9 .... 40 F2
Foxwalks Av BRGRVW B61 .... 185 H5
Foxwell Gv BORD B9 .... 109 G3
Foxwell Rd BORD B9 .... 108 F3
Foxwood Av GTB/HAM B43 .... 70 F2
Foxwood Gv
  CHWD/FDBR/MGN B37 .... 92 D8
Foxwood Rd
  CHWD/FDBR/MGN B37 .... 92 D8
  POL/KGSB/FAZ B78 .... 47 K5
Foxyards Cl TPTN/OCK DY4 .... 67 H8
Foxyards Rd TPTN/OCK DY4 .... 67 H8
Foyle Rd HWK/WKHTH B38 .... 144 D4
Fozdar Crs BILS/COS WV14 .... 66 E4
Fradley Cl BVILLE B30 .... 144 B1
Framefield Dr SOLH B91 .... 128 C7
Framlingham Gv
  DUNHL/THL/PER WV6 .... 48 E2
  KNWTH CV8 .... 177 G7
Frampton Cl BVILLE B30 .... 124 B6
  CHWD/FDBR/MGN B37 .... 111 H2
Frampton Wk COVE CV2 .... 155 K1
Frampton Wy GTB/HAM B43 .... 71 H1
Frances Av WWCK CV34 .... 199 L6
Frances Crs BDWTH CV12 .... 116 E2
Frances Dr BLOX/PEL WS3 .... 38 F3
Frances Havergal Cl
  RLSS CV31 .... 200 D7
Frances Rd BVILLE B30 .... 124 E8
  ERDW/GRVHL B23 .... 90 B2
  KNWTH CV8 .... 178 C2
  LOZ/NWT B19 .... 89 C7
Franchecourt Dr KIDD DY10 .... 136 F4
Franche Cl KIDDW DY11 .... 136 F6
Franchise Gdns
  DARL/WED WS10 .... 52 D8

Franchise St DARL/WED WS10 52 C8
KIDDW DY11 137 G8
PBAR/PBCH B42 89 J3 1
Franciscan Rd COVS CV3 154 A5
Francis Cl FOAKS/STRLY B74 55 K5
KGSWFD DY6 83 H5 3
PENK ST19 10 D5
POL/KGSB/FAZ B78 47 L3
Francis Green La PENK ST19 10 D4
Francis Rd ACGN B27 109 H8
BRGRVE B60 185 K6
LDYWD/EDGR B16 106 E4
LICH WS13 20 E3
SMTHWKW B67 87 H8
STETCH B33 109 H2
STRBR DY8 101 G8
STRPT DY13 160 C7
YDLY B25 108 E7
Francis St COVN CV6 134 C7
VAUX/NECH B7 7 M1
WBROM B70 87 H4
WOLV WV1 2 E1
Francis Wk NFLD/LBR B31 143 L6
Francis Ward Cl HHTH/SAND B71 68 E5
Frankburn Rd FOAKS/STRLY B74 55 J5
Frankfort St LOZ/NWT B19 89 H7
Frankholmes Dr SHLY B90 147 L7
Frankland Rd COVN CV6 134 E4
Frankley Av RMSLY B62 104 E8 2
Frankley Beeches Rd
NFLD/LBR B31 143 H2
Frankley Gn RMSLY B62 122 B8
Frankley Green La
RIDG/WDGT B32 122 D8
Frankley Hill La RBRY B45 142 D3
RIDG/WDGT B32 142 D1
Frankley La NFLD/LBR B31 123 G7
Frankley Lodge Rd
NFLD/LBR B31 143 H1
Frankley Rd LGLYGN/QTN B68 104 E5
Franklin Dr BNTWD WS7 18 F7
Franklin Gv TLHL/CAN CV4 152 C4 2
Franklin Rd BVILLE B30 124 D8
NUN CV11 99 H4
Franklin St WSNGN B18 88 C8
Franklin Wy BVILLE B30 124 D6
Franklyn Cl
DUNHL/THL/PER WV6 34 C8
Frankpledge Rd COVS CV3 154 C5
Frank Rd SMTHWKW B67 87 J7
Frank St BHTH/HG B12 107 K6 2
NUN CV11 98 F2
Franks Wy STETCH B33 109 J3 1
Frank Tommey Cl
BLKHTH/ROWR B65 104 A4 7
Frankton Av COVS CV3 154 B8
Frankton Cl HIA/OLT B92 127 M4
REDE B98 197 J5
Frankton Gv BORD B9 108 F3 3
Frankton La RRUGBY CV23 180 E8
Frankwell Dr COVE CV2 135 J4
Fraser Cl NUNW/HART CV10 79 M7
Fraser Rd COVN CV6 133 L4
SPARK B11 108 A8
Fraser St BILS/COS WV14 51 J7
Frayne Av KGSWFD DY6 83 G6
Freasley Cl SHLY B90 147 H2
Freasley Rd BKDE/SHDE B34 92 B8 1
Freda Ri OLDBY B69 86 B5
Freda Rd WBROM B70 87 H4
Fredas Gv HRBN B17 123 L1
Frederick Neal Av COVW CV5 152 B1
Frederick Rd AST/WIT B6 89 L5 1
EDG B15 106 F5
ERDW/GRVHL B23 90 B3
KIDDW DY11 161 K4
LGLYGN/QTN B68 105 H6
PENK ST19 10 D3
RCOVN/BALC/EX CV7 96 D5
SCFLD/BOLD B73 72 E3
SLYOAK B29 124 B3
SPARK B11 126 A1 1
STETCH B33 109 H2 2
WNSFLD WV11 37 G8
Fredericks Cl STRBR DY8 119 J1
Frederick St BKHL/PFLD WV2 2 F8
CBHAMW B1 6 C2
RUGBYS/DCH CV22 183 K2
WBROM B70 87 G1
WSLW WS2 4 C3
Frederick William St
WLNHL WV13 51 M3 3
Fred Lee Gv COVS CV3 178 B1
Freeboard La KNWTH CV8 180 C6
Freeburn Cswy TLHL/CAN CV4 153 G6
Freeford Gdns LICHS WS14 21 J7
Freeland Gv KGSWFD DY6 101 K1 2
Freeman Cl NUNW/HART CV10 98 B1
Freeman Dr WALM/CURD B76 73 L5 1
Freeman Pl BILS/COS WV14 51 J5
Freeman Rd DARL/WED WS10 69 G2
VAUX/NECH B7 89 M7 3
Freemans Cl RLSN CV32 200 C4
Freeman St COVN CV6 134 D7
DIG/EDG B5 7 J5 1
WOLVN WV10 3 L4
Freemantle Rd
RUGBYS/DCH CV22 183 C3 2
Freer Rd AST/WIT B6 89 H5
Freer St NUN CV11 99 J3 1
WSL WS1 4 F2
Freesland Ri NUNW/HART CV10 79 M7
Freeth Rd BRWNH WS8 26 E4
Freeth St LDYWD/EDGR B16 106 E3
OLDBY B69 86 D5 1
Freezeland St BILS/COS WV14 50 F7 1
Fremantle Dr HEDN WS12 17 J3
Fremont Dr DUDN DY1 84 C2
French Av POL/KGSB/FAZ B78 45 G4
French Rd DUDS DY2 85 J4
Frensham Cl
CHWD/FDBR/MGN B37 111 G3
GTWY WS6 24 C1
Frensham Dr NUNW/HART CV10 79 M8
Frensham Wy HRBN B17 106 A7
Frenshaw Gv KGSTG B44 71 K6 1
Freshfield Cl COVW CV5 133 G4
Freshwater Dr BRLYHL DY5 101 M4
Fretton Cl COVN CV6 134 D6
Freville Cl CRTAM B79 31 L7
Frevill Rd COVN CV6 134 F5
Friardale Cl DARL/WED WS10 69 H2
Friar Park Rd DARL/WED WS10 69 G2
Friars Cl COVS CV3 156 C6
STRBR DY8 101 G2
Friar's Ga ATHST CV9 63 H5 1
Friars Gorse KINVER DY7 101 G6 1
Friars' Rd COV CV1 8 F6
Friars St WWCK CV34 199 H7
Friar St DARL/WED WS10 68 F2
Friary Av LICH WS13 20 E6
SHLY B90 147 L7
Friary Cl RWWCK/WEL CV35 198 D7 3
Friary Crs RUSH/SHEL WS4 40 A7
Friary Gdns HDSW B21 88 B3
Friary Rd ATHST CV9 63 H4
HDSW B21 88 C3
Friary St NUN CV11 80 F8
The Friary LICH WS13 20 E7
Friday Acre LICH WS13 20 E4
Friday La HIA/OLT B92 149 H1
Friesland Dr WOLV WV1 50 F2
Friezeland Rd WSLW WS2 52 F3
Friezland La BRWNH WS8 26 E8
Friezland Wy BRWNH WS8 26 E8
Frilsham Wy COVW CV5 132 F8
Fringe Green Cl BRGRVE B60 185 L6
Fringe Meadow Rd REDE B98 189 K7
Frinton Gv HDSW B21 88 A6
Frisby Rd RIDG/WDGT B32 105 J8
TLHL/CAN CV4 152 C3
Friston Av LDYWD/EDGR B16 6 A7
Friswell Dr COVN CV6 134 D5 1
Frobisher Cl GTWY WS6 24 D4
Frobisher Rd COVS CV3 154 A8
RUGBYS/DCH CV22 183 G4
Frodesley Rd
LGN/SDN/BHAMAIR B26 109 M5
Froggatt Rd BILS/COS WV14 51 H6 2
Froggatts Ride
WALM/CURD B76 73 K2
Frog La LICH WS13 20 F6
RCOVN/BALC/EX CV7 150 E8
Frogmere Cl COVW CV5 133 G7 1
Frogmill Rd NFLD/LBR B31 142 F3
Frogmore La KNWTH CV8 174 D2
Frome Dr WNSFLD WV11 37 G8
Frome Wy ALE/KHTH/YWD B14 125 G7
Frost St BKHL/PFLD WV2 50 E7
Froxmere Cl SOLH B91 147 M5
Froyle Cl DUNHL/THL/PER WV6 35 G8
Froysell St WLNHL WV13 51 M3
Fryer Av RLSN CV32 200 C3
Fryer Rd NFLD/LBR B31 143 M6
Fryers Cl BLOX/PEL WS3 38 F6
Fryers Rd WSLW WS2 38 E7
Fryer St WOLV WV1 3 G4
Frythe Cl KNWTH CV8 177 G7
Fuchsia Dr COVEN WV9 35 K2
Fugelmere Cl HRBN B17 105 K6
Fulbrook Cl REDE B98 189 G8
Fulbrook Gv SLYOAK B29 123 K5 1
Fulbrook Rd COVE CV2 135 G4
DUDN DY1 84 E4 1
Fulford Dr WALM/CURD B76 73 M8
Fulford Gv
LGN/SDN/BHAMAIR B26 110 A7
Fulford Hall Rd HOCK/TIA B94 170 B2
Fulham Rd SPARK B11 107 M8
Fullbrook Cl SHLY B90 147 L8
Fullbrook Rd DSYBK/YTR WS5 53 J8
Fullelove Rd BRWNH WS8 26 E7
Fullers Cl COVN CV6 133 K6
Fullerton Cl CDSL WV8 35 J4
Fullmore Cl PENK ST19 10 D6
Fullwood Cl COVE CV2 135 J3
Fullwood Crs DUDS DY2 84 C7
Fullwoods End BILS/COS WV14 67 G5
Fulmar Crs KIDD DY10 161 M3
Fulton Cl BRGRVE B60 185 M4
Fulwell Gv KGSTG B44 71 L5
Fulwood Av RMSLY B62 104 D5
Furber Pl KGSWFD DY6 83 K7
Furlong La HALE B63 103 G7
Furlong Meadow
NFLD/LBR B31 144 A3 2
Furlongs Rd SEDG DY3 66 B7
The Furlongs STRBR DY8 119 M2 2
WOLVN WV10 36 F8
The Furlong DARL/WED WS10 52 C8
Furlong Wk SEDG DY3 84 B1
Furnace Cl WMBN WV5 64 C8
Furnace Hl HALE B63 103 M7
RMSLY B62 103 M7
Furnace La HALE B63 103 M8
Furnace Pde TPTN/OCK DY4 67 J7
Furnace Rd BDWTH CV12 117 H2
DUDS DY2 85 G5 2
Furness TAM/AM/WIL B77 46 B2
Furness Cl BLOX/PEL WS3 38 D2 3
The Furrows BRGRVE B60 185 H7
Furst St BRWNH WS8 26 E5
Furzebank Wy SHHTH WV12 52 C1
Furze La REDE B98 197 L1
Furze Wy DSYBK/YTR WS5 54 B5
Fynford Rd COVN CV6 133 M8

G

Gable Cft LICHS WS14 21 J7
Gables Cl RUGBYS/DCH CV22 183 H5
The Gables POL/KGSB/FAZ B78 47 L3 2
Gaddesby Rd
ALE/KHTH/YWD B14 125 K5
Gadds Dr BLKHTH/ROWR B65 104 B1
Gadsby Av WNSFLD WV11 37 L6
Gadsby St NUN CV11 99 J2
Gads Gn DUDS DY2 85 H8
Gads Green Crs DUDS DY2 85 J7
Gads La DUDN DY1 85 G4 2
WBROM B70 86 E2
Gadwall Cft ERDW/GRVHL B23 89 M2
Gaelic Rd CNCK/NC WS11 16 B1
Gagarin CRTAM B79 31 K8
Gaiafields Rd LICH WS13 20 F4
Gaialands Crs LICH WS13 20 F4 2
Gaia La LICH WS13 20 E5
Gail Cl ALDR WS9 40 F1
Gailey Cft KGSTG B44 71 J2 1
Gailey Lea La PENK ST19 14 F3
Gail Pk BDMR/CCFT WV3 49 H6
Gainford Cl COVEN WV9 35 K4
Gainford Ri COVS CV3 155 K2
Gainford Rd KGSTG B44 71 J2 1
Gainsborough Crs DOR/KN B93 148 E7
GTB/HAM B43 71 H1
Gainsborough Dr
BDWTH CV12 116 E1 2
DUNHL/THL/PER WV6 48 D1
POL/KGSB/FAZ B78 44 F5
RLSS CV31 201 G6
Gainsborough Hl STRBR DY8 119 L2
Gainsborough Ms KIDDW DY11 136 F8
Gainsborough Pl DUDN DY1 84 C3
Gainsborough Rd
PBAR/PBCH B42 70 F7
Gainsbrook Crs CNCK/NC WS11 17 K8
Gains La BLOX/PEL WS3 25 H3
Gairloch Rd WNSFLD WV11 37 M4 2
Gaitskell Ter OLDBY B69 86 B3
Gaitskell Wy SMTHWK B66 87 K6
Galahad Wy DARL/WED WS10 68 E3
Galbraith Cl BILS/COS WV14 67 H5
Galena Wy AST/WIT B6 89 J7
Gale Wk BLKHTH/ROWR B65 85 K8
Galey's Rd COVS CV3 154 B5
Gallagher Rd BDWTH CV12 116 E3
The Galliards TLHL/CAN CV4 177 H1
Galliers Cl TAM/AM/WIL B77 46 D8 1
Galloway Av BKDE/SHDE B34 91 K7
Gallows Hl WWCK CV34 199 M8
Galmington Dr COVS CV3 153 M7 1
Galton Cl ERDE/BCHGN B24 91 K1
TPTN/OCK DY4 68 A7
Galton Rd SMTHWKW B67 105 K4
Galtons La HAG/WOL DY9 140 E6
Galway Rd BNTWD WS7 18 E5
Gamesfield Gn BDMR/CCFT WV3 49 K4
Gammage St DUDS DY2 84 F5
Gamson Cl KIDD DY10 161 J1 1
Ganborough Cl REDE B98 197 J4 1
Gandy Rd SHHTH WV12 37 L7
Gannahs Farm Cl
WALM/CURD B76 73 K2 3
Gannow Green La RBRY B45 142 A4
Gannow Manor Crs RBRY B45 142 C4
Gannow Manor Gdns
RBRY B45 142 D4
Gannow Rd RBRY B45 142 C6
Gannow Wk RBRY B45 142 C6
Ganton Rd BLOX/PEL WS3 38 E1
Garage Cl TAM/AM/WIL B77 32 B8 2
Garden Cl DOR/KN B93 148 D7
RBRY B45 142 E3
WASH/WDE B8 90 E8 1
Garden Ct WWCK CV34 199 J6
Garden Crs BLOX/PEL WS3 39 K2
Garden Cft ALDR WS9 40 F6
Gardeners Cl KIDDW DY11 137 G5
Gardeners Wy WMBN WV5 82 D1
Garden Gv BFLD/HDSWWD B20 70 C7
Gardenia Dr COVW CV5 132 E7
The Gardens ERDW/GRVHL B23 90 C2
KNWTH CV8 191 L2
RLSS CV31 201 J8
Garden St WSLW WS2 53 J2
Garden Wk BILS/COS WV14 51 K7
SEDG DY3 84 A3
Garden Wy KNWTH CV8 191 L3 1
Garfield Rd
LGN/SDN/BHAMAIR B26 109 M5
Garganey Ct KIDD DY10 161 K4 1
Garibaldi Ter BRGRVE B60 185 L4
Garland Crs RMSLY B62 104 C5
Garland St BORD B9 108 A2 1
Garland Wy NFLD/LBR B31 143 M1
Garlick Dr KNWTH CV8 177 G7
Garman Cl GTB/HAM B43 70 C3
Garner Cl BILS/COS WV14 67 H2
Garnet Av GTB/HAM B43 70 F2
Garnet Cl ALDR WS9 41 H1
Garnett Dr MGN/WHC B75 57 J7
Garnette Cl NUNW/HART CV10 79 M8
Garrard Gdns SCFLD/BOLD B73 56 F8
Garrat St BRLYHL DY5 84 C8
Garratt Cl LGLYGN/QTN B68 105 G1
RRUGBY CV23 158 F8
Garratt's La CDYHTH B64 103 K3
Garratt St HHTH/SAND B71 69 G8
Garratts Wk
ALE/KHTH/YWD B14 145 J3 1
Garret Cl KGSWFD DY6 83 H4
Garretts Green La
LGN/SDN/BHAMAIR B26 109 L6
STETCH B33 109 M5
Garrett St NUN CV11 99 J3
Garrick Cl COVW CV5 152 A1
Garrick Ri BNTWD WS7 18 E6
Garrick Rd CNCK/NC WS11 16 B1
LICH WS13 20 D3
Garrick St WOLV WV1 3 G6
Garrigill TAM/AM/WIL B77 46 E4
Garrington St DARL/WED WS10 52 A6
Garrison La BORD B9 107 M3
Garrison St BORD B9 108 A2 1
Garth Crs COVS CV3 155 G5
The Garth ALE/KHTH/YWD B14 146 B1
LICH WS13 20 F3
Garway Cl REDE B98 197 J4
RLSN CV32 200 D1
Garway Gv YDLY B25 108 F7
Garwood Rd
LGN/SDN/BHAMAIR B26 109 K3
Garyth Williams Cl
RUGBYS/DCH CV22 183 J5
Gas Sq BRGRVW B61 185 J4
Gas St CBHAMW B1 6 C6
RLSS CV31 200 D6
RUGBYN/HIL CV21 183 M2
Gatacre St SEDG DY3 84 B2 2
Gatcombe Cl WOLVN WV10 36 D1
Gatcombe Rd DUDN DY1 84 C3 3
Gate Cl WMBN WV5 64 E8
Gatehouse Fold DUDS DY2 85 H4 4
Gatehouse La BDWTH CV12 116 E3 1
Gate La CSHL/WTROR B46 76 D7
HOCK/TIA B94 172 A2
SCFLD/BOLD B73 72 D3
Gateley Cl REDE B98 197 L1
Gateley Rd LGLYGN/QTN B68 105 H6
Gateside Rd COVN CV6 134 C3
Gate St SEDG DY3 66 C6 3
TPTN/OCK DY4 85 L3
WASH/WDE B8 90 B8
Gatis St DUNHL/THL/PER WV6 35 L8
Gatwick Rd CVALE B35 91 M1 3
Gauden Rd HAG/WOL DY9 120 B4
Gaulby Wk COVS CV3 155 L4 1
The Gaunts ALVE B48 167 M7
Gaveston Rd COVN CV6 133 J7
RLSN CV32 200 C4
Gawne La DUDS DY2 103 J1
Gawsworth CRTAM B79 31 H6 1
Gaydon Cl COVN CV6 134 E5
DUNHL/THL/PER WV6 34 C8
REDE B98 196 D4
Gaydon Gv SLYOAK B29 123 L3
Gaydon Pl SCFLD/BOLD B73 72 F1
Gaydon Rd ALDR WS9 54 E1
HIA/OLT B92 128 B2
Gayer St COVN CV6 134 D4
Gayfield Av BRLYHL DY5 102 A5
Gay Hill La HWK/WKHTH B38 144 F5
Gayhurst Cl COVS CV3 155 J5
Gayhurst Dr YDLY B25 109 J5
Gayle TAM/AM/WIL B77 46 E4
Gayle Gv ACGN B27 127 G5
Gayton Rd HHTH/SAND B71 69 H7
Gaywood Cft EDG B15 6 D9 1
Gaza Cl TLHL/CAN CV4 152 E4
Gazelle Cl COV CV1 9 J3
Geach St LOZ/NWT B19 89 H7
Gedney Cl ALE/KHTH/YWD B14 146 A2 1
Geeson Cl CVALE B35 91 M1
Gee St LOZ/NWT B19 89 H7
Gemini Dr CNCK/NC WS11 16 D7
Geneva Rd TPTN/OCK DY4 85 H1
Genge Av
ETTPK/GDPK/PENN WV4 66 C1 1
Genners La RIDG/WDGT B32 123 G5
Genthorn Cl
ETTPK/GDPK/PENN WV4 66 D1 2
Gentian Cl NFLD/LBR B31 123 K7
Geoffery Cl COVE CV2 134 F8
Geoffrey Cl WALM/CURD B76 73 M6 2
Geoffrey Rd SHLY B90 146 D2
SPARK B11 126 A2 1
George Arthur Rd
WASH/WDE B8 108 B1
George Av BLKHTH/ROWR B65 104 B3
POL/KGSB/FAZ B78 45 G4
George Birch Cl RRUGBY CV23 157 J2
George Bird Cl SMTHWK B66 87 L7 1
George Cl DUDS DY2 85 J5 3
George Eliot Av BDWTH CV12 117 H3
George Eliot Rd COV CV1 134 B8
George Eliot St
NUNW/HART CV10 99 G3
George Frederick Rd
SCFLD/BOLD B73 71 L1
George Henry Rd TPTN/OCK DY4 68 C6
George Hodgkinson Cl
TLHL/CAN CV4 152 D2 2
George La LICH WS13 21 G5
George Marston Rd COVS CV3 155 J4
George Park Cl COVE CV2 135 G4
George Rd ALVE B48 167 L7
BILS/COS WV14 67 H4
CSHL/WTROR B46 93 G2
ERDW/GRVHL B23 90 A2
GTB/HAM B43 70 D3
HALE B63 121 K1
LGLYGN/QTN B68 105 G3
SCFLD/BOLD B73 72 B4
SLYOAK B29 124 C3
SOLH B91 148 A2
TPTN/OCK DY4 67 H7
WWCK CV34 199 L5
YDLY B25 108 E7
George Robertson Cl COVS CV3 155 J6
George Rose Gdns
DARL/WED WS10 51 M7
George's Pde BKHL/PFLD WV2 3 G6
George St BHTH/HG B12 107 K8
BKHL/PFLD WV2 2 F7
BRGRVW B61 185 K3 1
CBHAMNW B3 6 C4
COV CV1 134 C8
CRTAM B79 45 M1
DUDN DY1 66 F7
HDSW B21 88 A5
HEDN WS12 17 G1
KIDD DY10 137 K7
LOZ/NWT B19 88 F6
NUN CV11 99 H3
RCOVN/BALC/EX CV7 96 E5
RLSS CV31 200 E6
RUGBYN/HIL CV21 183 K2
STRBR DY8 101 K4
WBROM B70 87 H3
WLNHL WV13 51 L1 1
WSL WS1 4 F4
George Street Ringway
BDWTH CV12 116 F2 1
George St West WSNGN B18 106 E1
Georgian Pl CNCK/NC WS11 16 C3
Georgina Av BILS/COS WV14 67 H2 1
Geraldine Rd YDLY B25 108 F6
Gerald Rd STRBR DY8 101 J6
Geranium Gv BORD B9 108 D2
Geranium Rd DUDS DY2 85 K5 1
Gerard CRTAM B79 31 J6
Gerard Av TLHL/CAN CV4 152 F5
Gerardsfield Rd STETCH B33 110 B2
Germander Dr
DSYBK/YTR WS5 69 L2 3
Gerrard Cl LOZ/NWT B19 89 H6
Gerrard Rd WLNHL WV13 51 J4
Gerrard St LOZ/NWT B19 89 G7
WWCK CV34 199 K7 1
Gervase Dr DUDN DY1 85 G2
Geston Rd DUDN DY1 84 D5
Gheluvelt Av KIDD DY10 137 K5
Gibbet Hill Rd TLHL/CAN CV4 177 G2
Gibbet La KINVER DY7 118 E1
Gibbins Rd SLYOAK B29 124 A4
Gibb La BRGRVW B61 165 L5
Gibbons Cl TLHL/CAN CV4 152 D3
Gibbons Gv
DUNHL/THL/PER WV6 49 J1
Gibbons Hill Rd SEDG DY3 66 B3
Gibbons La BRLYHL DY5 83 L6
Gibbons Rd
DUNHL/THL/PER WV6 49 K1
MGN/WHC B75 56 F2
Gibbs Cl COVE CV2 135 M7
Gibbs Hill Rd NFLD/LBR B31 143 M6
Gibbs Rd HAG/WOL DY9 102 E8
REDE B98 188 E8
Gibb St BORD B9 7 K7
Gibson Crs BDWTH CV12 116 E3
Gibson Dr BFLD/HDSWWD B20 88 F5
Gibson Rd BFLD/HDSWWD B20 88 F5
DUNHL/THL/PER WV6 48 C2 1
Gideon Cl
LGN/SDN/BHAMAIR B26 109 H7 1
Gideons Cl SEDG DY3 66 B8
Gielgud Wy
RCOVN/BALC/EX CV7 135 M5
Giffard Rd WOLV WV1 50 F6
WOLVN WV10 36 C2
Giffard Wy WWCK CV34 199 J4 3
Giffords Cft LICH WS13 20 E4
Diggetty La WMBN WV5 64 C7
Gigg La WALM/CURD B76 74 F2
Gigmill Wy STRBR DY8 119 J1
Gilbanks Rd STRBR DY8 101 H6
Gilberry Cl DOR/KN B93 148 E8
Gilbert Av OLDBY B69 85 M6
RUGBYS/DCH CV22 183 H3
Gilbert Cl COV CV1 9 K3 1
WNSFLD WV11 37 L6
Gilbert La WMBN WV5 64 F6
Gilbert Rd BRGRVE B60 185 J6
LICH WS13 21 G3
SMTHWK B66 105 M1
Gilbert Scott Wy KIDD DY10 137 J6
Gilbertstone Av
LGN/SDN/BHAMAIR B26 109 J8
Gilbertstone Cl REDE B98 196 C4 2
Gilbert St TPTN/OCK DY4 85 K3
Gilbeys Cl STRBR DY8 101 J4 3
Gilby Rd LDYWD/EDGR B16 106 E4
Gilchrist Dr EDG B15 106 C5
Gildas Av HWK/WKHTH B38 144 E4
Giles Cl COVN CV6 134 A3 3
HIA/OLT B92 128 D6
STETCH B33 109 J2
Giles Rd LGLYGN/QTN B68 86 F8
LICH WS13 20 E2
Gilfil Rd NUNW/HART CV10 98 F4
Gilldown Pl EDG B15 106 F6
Gillespie Cft AST/WIT B6 89 K6
Gillet Cl NUN CV11 98 F2
Gillhurst Rd HRBN B17 105 M6
Gillians Wk COVE CV2 135 L5
Gilling Gv BKDE/SHDE B34 91 L7
Gillingham Cl DARL/WED WS10 69 H1
Gillity Av DSYBK/YTR WS5 5 M6
Gillity Cl DSYBK/YTR WS5 5 M6
Gilliver Rd SHLY B90 146 F3
Gillman Cl
LGN/SDN/BHAMAIR B26 128 B1 2
Gillott Cl SOLH B91 148 C2 1
Gillott Rd LDYWD/EDGR B16 106 A4
Gillows Cft SHLY B90 147 L6
Gillscroft Rd STETCH B33 109 L2
Gill St DUDS DY2 103 J2
WBROM B70 87 G4
Gillway CRTAM B79 31 M5
Gilmorton Cl HRBN B17 105 M6
SOLH B91 148 A4
Gilpin Cl CBROM B36 91 G7
Gilpin Crs BLOX/PEL WS3 39 L1
Gilpins Cft GTWY WS6 24 B4
Gilson Dr CSHL/WTROR B46 93 H5
Gilson Rd CSHL/WTROR B46 93 H4
Gilson St TPTN/OCK DY4 68 A5
Gilson Wy
CHWD/FDBR/MGN B37 92 E7 1
Gilwell Rd BKDE/SHDE B34 92 C7
Gipsy Cl RCOVN/BALC/EX CV7 150 F8
Gipsy La ERDW/GRVHL B23 71 M8
NUNW/HART CV10 99 G7
RCOVN/BALC/EX CV7 151 G8
WLNHL WV13 51 M4
Girdlers Cl COVS CV3 153 M8
Girtin Cl BDWTH CV12 116 E1
Girton Rd CNCK/NC WS11 16 D5
Girvan Gv RLSN CV32 193 G8
Gisborn Cl SMTHH B10 107 M5 4
Gisburn Cl WWCK CV34 199 K4
Gladeside Cl RUSH/SHEL WS4 40 A5
The Glades ALDR WS9 40 F6
The Glade CDSL WV8 35 J4 2
CNCK/NC WS11 16 A3
FOAKS/STRLY B74 55 J4
HAG/WOL DY9 102 C8
LGN/SDN/BHAMAIR B26 128 B1
TLHL/CAN CV4 152 D2
Gladiator Wy
RUGBYN/HIL CV21 159 K6 1
Gladstone Dr OLDBY B69 86 A2
Gladstone Gv KGSWFD DY6 83 H5 4
Gladstone Rd DOR/KN B93 172 E3
ERDW/GRVHL B23 90 B2
HEDN WS12 17 J4
LGN/SDN/BHAMAIR B26 109 H7 2
SPARK B11 107 M7
STRBR DY8 101 H7
Gladstone St AST/WIT B6 89 L5
DARL/WED WS10 52 C7 2
HHTH/SAND B71 69 G8
RUGBYN/HIL CV21 183 J1
WSLW WS2 53 H1
Gladys Rd SMTHWKW B67 105 K3
YDLY B25 108 F6

Glaisdale Av COVN CV6 134 C2
Glaisdale Gdns
DUNHL/THL/PER WV6 35 L8 2
Glaisdale Rd HLGN/YWD B28 126 E5
Glaisedale Gv WLNHL WV13 52 A3
Glaisher Dr WOLVN WV10 36 A7
Glamis Rd SHHTH WV12 37 M6
Glanville Dr MGN/WHC B75 56 E1
Glasbury Cft HWK/WKHTH B38 144 C6
Glascote Cl SHLY B90 146 E2
Glascote Gv BKDE/SHDE B34 92 A7
Glascote La TAM/AM/WIL B77 46 D6
Glascote Rd TAM/AM/WIL B77 46 B2
Glasscroft Cottages
BNTWD WS7 19 K6
Glasshouse Hl STRBR DY8 119 M2
Glasshouse La HOCK/TIA B94 172 C8
KNWTH CV8 177 G8
Glastonbury Cl KIDDW DY11 136 E7
Glastonbury Crs BLOX/PEL WS3 38 C3
Glastonbury Rd
ALE/KHTH/YWD B14 126 A8
HHTH/SAND B71 69 H5
Glastonbury Wy
BLOX/PEL WS3 38 C4 1
Glaston Dr SOLH B91 147 L5 1
Gleads Cft RIDG/WDGT B32 122 E2
Gleave Rd SLYOAK B29 124 C4
Glebe Av BDWTH CV12 116 C4
Glebe Cl REDE B98 197 H3
TLHL/CAN CV4 152 E6
Glebe Crs KNWTH CV8 191 L2
RUGBYN/HIL CV21 183 J2
Glebe Dr SCFLD/BOLD B73 72 D5
Glebefarm Gv COVS CV3 155 K2
Glebe Farm Rd
RUGBYN/HIL CV21 159 K6
STETCH B33 91 L8
Glebe Flds WALM/CURD B76 74 F7
Glebefields Rd TPTN/OCK DY4 67 L5
Glebeland Cl LDYWD/EDGR B16 6 A7 1
Glebe La NUN CV11 81 K8
STRBR DY8 119 J1
Glebe Pl DARL/WED WS10 51 M1
RLSS CV31 200 F6
Glebe Rd ALVE B48 167 L6
NUN CV11 99 H1
SOLH B91 128 B8
WLNHL WV13 51 K5
Glebe St WSL WS1 4 E5
The Glebe HAG/WOL DY9 140 C7
RCOVN/BALC/EX CV7 115 G6
REDE B98 189 K6
Glebe Wy RCOVN/BALC/EX CV7 150 E6
Gledhill Pk LICHS WS14 21 G8 1
Gleeson Dr WWCK CV34 199 J4 1
Glenavon Rd
ALE/KHTH/YWD B14 145 L2
Glen Cl HEDN WS12 12 B8
RUSH/SHEL WS4 53 L2
Glencoe Dr CNCK/NC WS11 16 E1
Glencoe Rd COVS CV3 154 F4
SMTHWK B66 106 A1
Glen Ct DUNHL/THL/PER WV6 49 J4 1
Glencroft Rd HIA/OLT B92 128 B2
Glendale Av KNWTH CV8 176 E8
Glendale Cl BDMR/CCFT WV3 49 G5
HALE B63 121 M1
Glendale Ct TAM/AM/WIL B77 46 F7 1
Glendale Dr STETCH B33 109 K2 1
WMBN WV5 64 E7
Glendawn Cl CNCK/NC WS11 16 E2 2
Glendene Crs HWK/WKHTH B38 144 A6
Glendene Rd HEDN WS12 13 G7
Glen Devon Cl RBRY B45 142 E3 3
Glendon Rd ERDW/GRVHL B23 72 B7
Glendon Wy DOR/KN B93 172 B2
Glendower Av COVW CV5 153 H3
Glendower Rd ALDR WS9 40 F4
PBAR/PBCH B42 71 G8
Gleneagles TAM/AM/WIL B77 32 F8
Gleneagles Dr BRGRVE B60 166 E8
GTB/HAM B43 70 C1
MGN/WHC B75 57 G6
OLDBY B69 85 L6
Gleneagles Rd BLOX/PEL WS3 38 D2
COVE CV2 135 J7
DUNHL/THL/PER WV6 34 B8
LGN/SDN/BHAMAIR B26 109 L5
Glenelg Dr STRBR DY8 119 M3
Glenelg Ms DSYBK/YTR WS5 54 B8 2
Glenfern Gdns KNWTH CV8 179 J3
Glenfern Rd BILS/COS WV14 66 E5
Glenfield CDSL WV8 35 J3 2
Glenfield Av NUNW/HART CV10 81 G6
Glenfield Cl REDW B97 196 B7 1
SOLH B91 148 A5 2
WALM/CURD B76 73 J2
Glenfield Gv SLYOAK B29 124 E4
Glengarry Cl RIDG/WDGT B32 122 F6 2
Glengarry Gdns
BDMR/CCFT WV3 49 K4
Glenhurst Cl WSLW WS2 52 B2
Glenmead Rd KGSTG B44 71 H5
Glenmore Av BNTWD WS7 18 E7
Glenmore Cl BDMR/CCFT WV3 49 J6
Glenmore Dr COVN CV6 116 D8
HWK/WKHTH B38 144 B4
Glenmount Av COVN CV6 116 D8
Glenn St COVN CV6 134 B2
Glen Park Rd SEDG DY3 84 B3
Glenpark Rd WASH/WDE B8 90 C8
Glenridding Cl COVN CV6 116 D8 2
Glen Ri MOS/BIL B13 126 A7
Glen Rd SEDG DY3 66 C7
STRBR DY8 119 K2
Glenroy Cl COVE CV2 135 J7
Glenroyde HWK/WKHTH B38 144 C6
Glen Side RIDG/WDGT B32 123 H3
Glenside Av HIA/OLT B92 127 M2
Glenthorne Dr GTWY WS6 24 C2
Glenthorne Rd
ERDE/BCHGN B24 90 E3
Glenthorne Wy
ERDE/BCHGN B24 90 E3 2
Glentworth Av COVN CV6 133 L3
Glentworth Dr WALM/CURD B76 73 L3
Glentworth Gdns
DUNHL/THL/PER WV6 35 M8
Glenville Av ATHST CV9 61 G5
Glenville Dr ERDW/GRVHL B23 72 B5 2
Glenwood Cl BRLYHL DY5 102 B5 3
Glenwood Dr SHLY B90 171 H1 4
Glenwood Gdns BDWTH CV12 116 F3
Glenwood Ri ALDR WS9 41 H2
Glenwood Rd
HWK/WKHTH B38 144 B5
Globe St DARL/WED WS10 68 D4
Gloster Dr KNWTH CV8 176 D7
Gloucester Cl LICH WS13 20 F2 1
NUN CV11 81 L6
Gloucester Pl WLNHL WV13 52 B3 2
Gloucester Rd DARL/WED WS10 69 G2
DSYBK/YTR WS5 5 M6
DUDS DY2 103 H3
Gloucester St COV CV1 8 C4
DIG/EDG B5 7 G7 2
RLSS CV31 200 E6 6
Gloucester Wy
CHWD/FDBR/MGN B37 110 E4
CNCK/NC WS11 16 F4
Glover Cl HLGN/YWD B28 126 D7 1
Glover Rd MGN/WHC B75 57 K8
Glover's Cl ATHST CV9 63 K6
HEDN WS12 13 L8
RCOVN/BALC/EX CV7 131 G4
Glovers Cft
CHWD/FDBR/MGN B37 110 D2
Glovers Field Dr
VAUX/NECH B7 90 A6 1
Glovers Rd SMHTH B10 108 A5
Glover St BORD B9 7 M6
COVS CV3 154 B5
HEDN WS12 17 K2
REDE B98 196 C2
WBROM B70 87 H4
Glyme Dr
DUNHL/THL/PER WV6 35 J8 1
Glyn Av BILS/COS WV14 67 M2
Glyndebourne CRTAM B79 31 H6 2
Glyn Dr BILS/COS WV14 67 M2 1
Glyn Farm Rd RIDG/WDGT B32 105 G8
Glynn Crs HALE B63 102 F6
Glynne Av KGSWFD DY6 101 H1
Glyn Rd RIDG/WDGT B32 105 H7
Glynside Av RIDG/WDGT B32 105 G8
Godfrey Cl RLSS CV31 201 J8
Godiva Pl COV CV1 9 J4
Godolphin CRTAM B79 31 H7
Godson Crs KIDDW DY11 160 F2
Godson Pl KIDDW DY11 161 G2 2
Goffs Cl RIDG/WDGT B32 123 K2
Gofton TAM/AM/WIL B77 46 E5
Gold Cl NUN CV11 99 J5
Goldcrest TAM/AM/WIL B77 46 E7
Goldcrest Cl DUDS DY2 103 H3
Goldcrest Cft CBROM B36 92 E5
Goldcrest Dr KIDD DY10 161 M3
Golden Acres La COVS CV3 155 K6
Goldencrest Dr OLDBY B69 86 C5 2
Golden Cft
BFLD/HDSWWD B20 88 D4 1
WNSFLD WV11 37 L5
Golden Cross La BRGRVW B61 165 L5
Golden End Dr DOR/KN B93 149 H7
Golden Hillock Rd DUDS DY2 103 G2
SMHTH B10 108 B6
SPARK B11 108 B8
Goldfinch Cl SLYOAK B29 124 B5
Goldfinch Rd HAG/WOL DY9 120 A2 1
Goldicroft Rd DARL/WED WS10 68 E1
Goldieslie Cl SCFLD/BOLD B73 72 F3
Goldieslie Rd SCFLD/BOLD B73 72 F3
Goldsborough TAM/AM/WIL B77 46 E4
Golds Hill Gdns HDSW B21 88 D6
Golds Hill Rd HDSW B21 88 D5
Golds Hill Wy TPTN/OCK DY4 68 B6
Goldsmith Av
RUGBYS/DCH CV22 183 K6 1
WWCK CV34 199 G8
Goldsmith Pl CRTAM B79 31 L6 2
Goldsmith Rd
ALE/KHTH/YWD B14 125 K5
BLOX/PEL WS3 39 J5
Goldstar Wy STETCH B33 110 A3
Goldthorn Av
ETTPK/GDPK/PENN WV4 49 M8
Goldthorn Cl COVW CV5 152 B1
Goldthorn Crs
ETTPK/GDPK/PENN WV4 49 L7
Goldthorne Av CNCK/NC WS11 16 D3
LGN/SDN/BHAMAIR B26 128 A1
Goldthorne Cl REDW B97 196 A4 1
Goldthorne Wk BRLYHL DY5 102 B5 4
Goldthorn Hl
ETTPK/GDPK/PENN WV4 49 M7
Goldthorn Pl KIDDW DY11 161 G3 1
Goldthorn Rd
ETTPK/GDPK/PENN WV4 49 M7
KIDDW DY11 160 F2
Golf Dr NUN CV11 99 M4
Golf La BILS/COS WV14 51 H6
Golson Cl MGN/WHC B75 57 J7
Gomeldon Av
ALE/KHTH/YWD B14 145 K2
Gomer St WLNHL WV13 51 L3
Gomer St West WLNHL WV13 51 L3 3
Gooch Cl STRBR DY8 101 L7
Gooch St DIG/EDG B5 107 J5
Gooch St North DIG/EDG B5 7 G8
Goodall Gv GTB/HAM B43 55 J8
Goodall St WSL WS1 5 G3
Goodby Rd MOS/BIL B13 125 H2
Goode Av WSNGN B18 88 E8
Goode Cl LGLYGN/QTN B68 105 G1
Goode Cft TLHL/CAN CV4 152 D3
Goodere Av
POL/KGSB/FAZ B78 47 L5 2
Goodere Dr POL/KGSB/FAZ B78 47 L3
Goodeve Wk MGN/WHC B75 57 M8 2
Goodison Gdns
ERDE/BCHGN B24 72 F8
Goodman Cl HLGN/YWD B28 126 D7
Goodman St CBHAMW B1 6 A4
Goodman Wy TLHL/CAN CV4 152 A4
Goodrest Av RMSLY B62 104 E7
Goodrest Cft
ALE/KHTH/YWD B14 146 A1
Goodrest La HWK/WKHTH B38 144 D7
Goodrich Av
DUNHL/THL/PER WV6 48 E2
Goodrich Cl REDE B98 197 K3
Goodrich Covert BVILLE B30 145 G3 3
Goods Station La PENK ST19 10 C3
Goodway Rd HIA/OLT B92 128 C2
KGSTG B44 71 J5
Goodwin Cl KIDDW DY11 137 G6 2
Goodwood Cl CBROM B36 91 H5 1
COVS CV3 155 G7 4
HEDN WS12 13 L8 2
Goodwood Dr FOAKS/STRLY B74 55 K7
Goodwyn Av LGLYGN/QTN B68 105 H6
Goodyear Av WOLVN WV10 36 C5
Goodyear Rd SMTHWKW B67 105 H3
Goodyers End La
RCOVN/BALC/EX CV7 116 B5
Goosehill Cl REDE B98 197 J4
Goosemoor La
ERDW/GRVHL B23 72 D6
Goostry Cl TAM/AM/WIL B77 46 B1
Goostry Rd TAM/AM/WIL B77 32 B8 3
Gopsal St CBHAMNE B4 7 L3
Gordon Av
ETTPK/GDPK/PENN WV4 66 D2
HHTH/SAND B71 69 G5
LOZ/NWT B19 89 H6
Gordon Cl BDWTH CV12 116 F1
OLDBY B69 86 B3 4
Gordon Crs BRLYHL DY5 84 C8
Gordon Dr TPTN/OCK DY4 68 A8
Gordon Pl BILS/COS WV14 51 G8 3
Gordon Rd HRBN B17 106 B7
LOZ/NWT B19 89 G5
Gordon St BKHL/PFLD WV2 3 H8
COV CV1 8 C7
DARL/WED WS10 52 B7
RLSS CV31 200 E6
Gorey Cl WNSFLD WV11 37 M5
Gorge Rd SEDG DY3 66 C5
Goring Rd COVE CV2 154 E1
Gorleston Gv
ALE/KHTH/YWD B14 145 M3
Gorleston Rd
ALE/KHTH/YWD B14 145 M3
Gorsebrook Rd
DUNHL/THL/PER WV6 36 A8 2
Gorse Cl CHWD/FDBR/MGN B37 111 G3 1
RUGBYS/DCH CV22 183 J4
SLYOAK B29 123 L5
Gorse Dr HEDN WS12 12 B8
Gorse Farm Rd GTB/HAM B43 70 C5
NUN CV11 99 M5
Gorsefield Rd BKDE/SHDE B34 92 A8
Gorse Green La HAG/WOL DY9 140 F5
Gorse La LICHS WS14 21 J7
Gorse Meadow Dr RBRY B45 166 F5
Gorsemoor Rd HEDN WS12 17 G4 3
Gorsemoor Wy
WNSFLD WV11 37 M2 1
Gorse Rd DUDN DY1 84 E1
WNSFLD WV11 37 L5
Gorseway BNTWD WS7 18 F8
COVW CV5 153 G2
Gorsey La CNCK/NC WS11 15 M4
CNCK/NC WS11 25 G3
CSHL/WTROR B46 93 J3
GTWY WS6 24 D5
HLYWD B47 169 L1
Gorsey Wy ALDR WS9 40 C8
Gorsly Piece RIDG/WDGT B32 123 G1
Gorstey Lea BNTWD WS7 19 G6
Gorstie Cft GTB/HAM B43 70 C5
Gorsty Av BRLYHL DY5 102 A1
Gorsty Bank LICHS WS14 21 J5
Gorsty Cl HHTH/SAND B71 69 K5
Gorsty Hayes CDSL WV8 34 D2
Gorsty Hill Rd RMSLY B62 103 M5
Gorsy Bank Rd
TAM/AM/WIL B77 46 D8
Gorsymead Gv NFLD/LBR B31 143 G3
Gorsy Rd RIDG/WDGT B32 123 H1
Gorsy Wy NUNW/HART CV10 80 B8
Gorton Cft
RCOVN/BALC/EX CV7 150 F6 2
Gorway Cl WSL WS1 5 H7
Gorway Gdns WSL WS1 5 J7
Gorway Rd WSL WS1 5 J7
Goscote Cl BLOX/PEL WS3 39 K6
Goscote La BLOX/PEL WS3 39 J4
Goscote Lodge Crs
BLOX/PEL WS3 39 L6
Goscote Pl BLOX/PEL WS3 39 L6
Goscote Rd BLOX/PEL WS3 39 K4
Gosford St BHTH/HG B12 107 K7
COV CV1 9 J5
Gospel End Rd SEDG DY3 65 L5
Gospel End St SEDG DY3 66 B6
Gospel Farm Rd ACGN B27 126 F5
Gospel La ACGN B27 127 G6
Gospel Oak Rd COVN CV6 133 M1
TPTN/OCK DY4 67 M4
Gosport Cl WOLV WV1 50 F6
Gosport Rd COVN CV6 134 C5 3
Goss Cft SLYOAK B29 124 B4
Gossett La KNWTH CV8 156 D6
Gossey La STETCH B33 110 A3
The Goss BRLYHL DY5 102 B4
Gotham Rd
LGN/SDN/BHAMAIR B26 109 J7
Gothersley La KINVER DY7 100 B3
Goths Cl BLKHTH/ROWR B65 104 A1
Gough Av WNSFLD WV11 36 F5
Gough Rd BILS/COS WV14 67 G4 1
EDG B15 107 G6
SPARK B11 108 B8
Gough St CBHAMW B1 6 E7
WLNHL WV13 52 A3
WOLV WV1 3 J5
Gould Av East KIDDW DY11 160 E3
Gould Av West KIDDW DY11 160 E4
Gould Firm La ALDR WS9 41 J7
Gould Rd RWWCK/WEL CV35 198 E6
Gowan Rd WASH/WDE B8 108 C1
Gower Av KGSWFD DY6 101 K1
Gower Rd RMSLY B62 104 C7
SEDG DY3 65 M4
Gower St BKHL/PFLD WV2 3 J8
LOZ/NWT B19 89 H6
WLNHL WV13 51 L3 4
WSLW WS2 52 F6
Gowland Dr CNCK/NC WS11 15 M4
Goya Cl HEDN WS12 17 G3
Gozzard St BILS/COS WV14 51 J8
Gracemere Crs HLGN/YWD B28 146 C1
Grace Rd COVW CV5 131 L5
OLDBY B69 86 A5
SPARK B11 108 A7
TPTN/OCK DY4 67 L6
Gracewell Rd MOS/BIL B13 126 B4
Grafton Cl REDE B98 196 F6
Grafton Crs BRGRVE B60 185 J6
Grafton Dr WLNHL WV13 51 H4
Grafton Gdns SEDG DY3 83 M2
Grafton La BRGRVW B61 185 G6
Grafton Pl BILS/COS WV14 51 J6 1
Grafton Rd HDSW B21 88 B4
HHTH/SAND B71 87 H1
LGLYGN/QTN B68 104 D3
SHLY B90 146 A3
SPARK B11 107 M6
Grafton St COV CV1 9 K5
Graham Cl COVN CV6 134 F5
TPTN/OCK DY4 67 M4
Graham Crs RBRY B45 142 D6
Graham Rd HHTH/SAND B71 87 H1
RMSLY B62 104 A5
STRBR DY8 101 H1
YDLY B25 109 G7
Graham St CBHAMW B1 6 C3
LOZ/NWT B19 89 G6
NUN CV11 80 F8
Grainger Cl TPTN/OCK DY4 68 B7 1
Grainger's La CDYHTH B64 103 G5
Grainger St DUDS DY2 85 H6
Graiseley Hl BKHL/PFLD WV2 2 D9
Graiseley La WNSFLD WV11 37 G8
Graiseley Rw BKHL/PFLD WV2 2 E9
Graiseley St BDMR/CCFT WV3 2 D7
Graith Cl ALE/KHTH/YWD B14 146 C2
Grammar School La HALE B63 121 L1
Grampian Rd STRBR DY8 101 L7
Granary Cl HEDN WS12 12 F8
KGSWFD DY6 82 E5 1
Granary La WALM/CURD B76 73 K2
Granary Rd BRGRVE B60 185 J7
CDSL WV8 35 J4
The Granary ALDR WS9 40 F7
Granborough Cl COVS CV3 155 K5
Granbourne Rd WSLW WS2 52 B1 2
Granby Av STETCH B33 110 A4
Granby Cl HIA/OLT B92 127 J6
REDE B98 197 K1
Granby Rd NUNW/HART CV10 98 D2
Grandborough Dr SOLH B91 147 L4
Grand Cl SMTHWK B66 105 M2 1
Grand Junction Wy WSL WS1 53 H8
Grand Union Canal
WWCK CV34 199 L5
Grand Union Canal Wk
CBHAMNE B4 6 F2
DOR/KN B93 149 H8
RLSS CV31 201 J7
RWWCK/WEL CV35 198 E5
SOLH B91 148 F2
SPARK B11 108 A6
WWCK CV34 200 A6
YDLY B25 108 E7
Grandys Cft
CHWD/FDBR/MGN B37 110 D3 1
Grange Av ALDR WS9 40 E4
CNCK/NC WS11 16 D3
COVS CV3 155 K6
COVS CV3 178 A2
KNWTH CV8 176 C7
MGN/WHC B75 57 G2 1
PENK ST19 10 C6
Grange Cl NUNW/HART CV10 80 A6
TAM/AM/WIL B77 46 A5 1
WWCK CV34 200 A5
Grange Crs HALE B63 121 M2
PENK ST19 10 B6
RBRY B45 142 C5
RUSH/SHEL WS4 39 M5
Grange Farm Dr
HWK/WKHTH B38 144 B5
Grangefield Cl CDSL WV8 35 K4 1
Grange Hl RMSLY B62 122 A3
Grange Hill Rd
HWK/WKHTH B38 144 C4
Grange La BRGRVE B60 187 L2
HAG/WOL DY9 120 B1
KGSWFD DY6 101 K1
LICH WS13 20 A7
MGN/WHC B75 57 G2
Grangemouth Rd COVN CV6 133 M7
Grange Ri HWK/WKHTH B38 144 D6
Grange Rd ALE/KHTH/YWD B14 125 H5
AST/WIT B6 89 J5
BILS/COS WV14 66 F6
BKHL/PFLD WV2 49 M7
BNTWD WS7 18 E8
BORD B9 108 B5
CDYHTH B64 103 M5
CNCK/NC WS11 17 M7
COVN CV6 134 F1
DOR/KN B93 172 C4
DUDN DY1 84 F4
DUNHL/THL/PER WV6 35 G8
ERDE/BCHGN B24 72 F8
HAG/WOL DY9 120 A1
HALE B63 121 M2
HIA/OLT B92 127 J6
KIDDW DY11 136 F6
NUNW/HART CV10 79 M3
PENK ST19 10 C5
RCOVN/BALC/EX CV7 150 D6
REDE B98 196 D1 1
RLSN CV32 200 E2
RUGBYN/HIL CV21 159 J7
SLYOAK B29 124 D2
SMTHWK B66 105 L2
WBROM B70 86 F2
Grangers La REDE B98 196 D8
Grange St DUDN DY1 84 F4
WSL WS1 5 G8
The Grange WMBN WV5 64 E6
WWCK CV34 199 M6 2
Granhill Cl REDE B98 196 E5
Granoe Cl COVS CV3 155 J5
Granshaw Cl HWK/WKHTH B38 144 D4
Grant Cl HHTH/SAND B71 69 G8
KGSWFD DY6 83 H5
Grantham Cl BRLYHL DY5 101 M6 2
Grantham Rd SMTHWK B66 105 M2
SPARK B11 107 M7
Grantham St COVE CV2 9 M3
Grantley Crs KGSWFD DY6 83 G6
Grantley Dr
CHWD/FDBR/MGN B37 110 E2
Granton Cl
ALE/KHTH/YWD B14 125 H8 3
Granton Rd
ALE/KHTH/YWD B14 125 H8
Grantown Gv GTWY WS6 38 E1 2
Grant Rd COVS CV3 154 F3
RCOVN/BALC/EX CV7 116 E5
Grant St BLOX/PEL WS3 38 F5 3
EDG B15 6 E9
Granville TAM/AM/WIL B77 46 D4
Granville Cl BKHL/PFLD WV2 3 H8 2
BRGRVE B60 185 M4 1
Granville Crest KIDD DY10 137 M7
Granville Dr KGSWFD DY6 83 K8
Granville Rd CDYHTH B64 103 M5 3
DOR/KN B93 172 E3
Granville St BKHL/PFLD WV2 3 H8
CBHAMW B1 6 D7
RLSN CV32 200 E3
WLNHL WV13 51 L2
Grasdene Gv HRBN B17 124 A1
Grasmere Av COVS CV3 153 K7
DUNHL/THL/PER WV6 48 D1 5
FOAKS/STRLY B74 55 L2
Grasmere Cl
DUNHL/THL/PER WV6 35 H5
GTB/HAM B43 70 D6 1
KGSWFD DY6 82 F6
KIDD DY10 137 J6
WNSFLD WV11 37 G6
Grasmere Crs NUN CV11 81 K6
Grasmere Gv STRPT DY13 160 D7
Grasmere Pl CNCK/NC WS11 12 C8
Grasmere Rd BDWTH CV12 116 E3
HDSW B21 88 D6
Grasscroft Dr COVS CV3 154 C7 5
Grassholme TAM/AM/WIL B77 46 E5
Grassington Av WWCK CV34 199 K4
Grassington Dr
CHWD/FDBR/MGN B37 110 D4 1
NUN CV11 99 L3
Grassmere Ct GTWY WS6 24 B2 2
Grassmere Dr STRBR DY8 119 K2 1
Grassmoor Rd
HWK/WKHTH B38 144 C3
Grassy La WOLVN WV10 36 F4
Graston Cl LDYWD/EDGR B16 106 E3 3
Gratley Cft HEDN WS12 16 A1
Grattidge Rd HIA/OLT B92 127 H3
Gratton Ct COVS CV3 153 K7
Gravel Bank RIDG/WDGT B32 123 H3
Gravel Hl TLHL/CAN CV4 152 D4
WMBN WV5 64 F7
Gravel La HEDN WS12 11 M7
Gravelly Hl ERDE/BCHGN B24 90 C3
Gravelly Hl North
ERDE/BCHGN B24 90 C2
Gravelly La ALDR WS9 41 J3
ERDW/GRVHL B23 72 D8
Gravel Pit La ALVE B48 188 C1
The Gravel WALM/CURD B76 74 F3
Grayfield Av MOS/BIL B13 125 K2
Grayland Cl ACGN B27 126 F3
The Graylands COVS CV3 178 A1
Grayling TAM/AM/WIL B77 46 B7
Grayling Cl DARL/WED WS10 67 M2
Grayling Rd BRLYHL DY5 102 A7
Grayling Wk
CHWD/FDBR/MGN B37 111 G3
Gray Rd HEDN WS12 12 D7
Grays Cl KIDD DY10 137 M7
Grayshott Cl BRGRVW B61 185 H2
ERDW/GRVHL B23 72 C8
Grays Rd HRBN B17 106 B7
Grayston Av TAM/AM/WIL B77 46 C1
Gray St BORD B9 107 M3
Grayswood Av COVW CV5 153 H1
Grayswood Park Rd
RIDG/WDGT B32 105 G7
Grayswood Rd NFLD/LBR B31 143 K6
Grazebrook Cft
RIDG/WDGT B32 123 H5 1
Grazebrook Rd DUDS DY2 85 G6
Grazewood Cl SHHTH WV12 37 M6 1
Grazing La REDW B97 195 J3
The Grazings KINVER DY7 118 A2 1
Greadier St SHHTH WV12 38 A8
Great Arthur St SMTHWK B66 87 K6
Great Balance RRUGBY CV23 157 H2
Great Barn La REDW B97 195 M4
Great Barr St BORD B9 7 M6
Great Brickkiln St
BDMR/CCFT WV3 2 C7
Great Br TPTN/OCK DY4 68 B8
Great Bridge Rd
BILS/COS WV14 67 L1 3
Great Bridge St WBROM B70 68 C8
Great Brook St VAUX/NECH B7 7 L2
Great Charles St BRWNH WS8 26 D5
Great Charles Street Queensway
CBHAMNW B3 6 E4
Great Colmore St EDG B15 6 E9
Great Cornbow HALE B63 121 M2 3
Great Croft St DARL/WED WS10 52 B7
Greatfield Rd KIDDW DY11 160 F1
Great Francis St
VAUX/NECH B7 107 M1
Great Hampton Rw
LOZ/NWT B19 6 D1
Great Hampton St WOLV WV1 2 D2
WSNGN B18 89 G8

Greatheed Rd RLSN CV32 200 C4
Great King St LOZ/NWT B19 89 G7
Great Lister St VAUX/NECH B7 7 K1
Greatmead TAM/AM/WIL B77 46 A4
Great Stone Rd NFLD/LBR B31 143 L2
Great Tindal St
LDYWD/EDGR B16 106 E3 1
Great Western Cl WSNGN B18 88 C7 2
Great Western Dr
CDYHTH B64 103 L4 1
Great Western St
DARL/WED WS10 68 C3
WOLV WV1 3 G3
Great Western Wy STRPT DY13 160 E8
TPTN/OCK DY4 68 B7
Great Wood Rd BORD B9 108 A4
Greaves Av DSYBK/YTR WS5 54 A5
Greaves Cl DSYBK/YTR WS5 54 A5
WWCK CV34 200 A7
Greaves Crs SHHTH WV12 38 A5
Greaves Gdns KIDDW DY11 136 F4
Greaves Rd DUDS DY2 85 H8
Greaves Sq HWK/WKHTH B38 144 F4 2
Grebe Cl ERDW/GRVHL B23 89 M2
Greenacre Cl TAM/AM/WIL B77 32 F8 1
Greenacre Dr CDSL WV8 34 F3
Greenacre Rd TPTN/OCK DY4 67 L4
Green Acres ACGN B27 126 F3
WMBN WV5 82 D1 1
Greenacres
DUNHL/THL/PER WV6 34 F8
SEDG DY3 65 M4
WALM/CURD B76 73 L5
Greenacres Av WOLVN WV10 36 F4
Greenacres Cl FOAKS/STRLY B74 55 J3
Greenacres Rd BRGRVW B61 185 J2 2
Green Acres Rd
HWK/WKHTH B38 144 B5
Greenaleigh Rd
ALE/KHTH/YWD B14 146 B2
Green Av HLGN/YWD B28 126 C4
Greenaway Cl GTB/HAM B43 71 G2 2
Greenbank RBRY B45 167 H5
Green Bank Av HLGN/YWD B28 126 C4
Greenbank Gdns STRBR DY8 101 J3 1
Greenbank Rd
RCOVN/BALC/EX CV7 150 D7 1
Green Barns La LICHS WS14 42 F5
Greenbush Dr HALE B63 103 L8
Green Cl HLYWD B47 169 L2
RRUGBY CV23 182 D1
Green Ct HLGN/YWD B28 126 D5
Green Cft BORD B9 108 E2
Greencroft BILS/COS WV14 51 H7
KGSWFD DY6 101 H1
LICH WS13 20 E3
Greendale Cl ATHST CV9 63 J6
BRGRVW B61 165 M5
Greendale Rd ATHST CV9 63 J6
COVW CV5 153 H2
Green Dr RIDG/WDGT B32 123 G4
WOLVN WV10 36 A6
Greenend Rd MOS/BIL B13 125 K3
Greenfels Ri DUDS DY2 85 K5
Greenfield Av BRGRVE B60 166 B4
CDYHTH B64 102 F4
RCOVN/BALC/EX CV7 150 E6
STRBR DY8 101 K8
Greenfield Crs EDG B15 106 E5
Greenfield Cft BILS/COS WV14 67 H2
Greenfield La WOLVN WV10 22 B8 1
Greenfield Rd GTB/HAM B43 70 A6
HRBN B17 106 A8
SMTHWKW B67 105 J1
Greenfields ALDR WS9 40 E6 1
CNCK/NC WS11 16 C3
REDE B98 196 C3
Greenfields Rd KGSWFD DY6 83 J8
RUSH/SHEL WS4 40 B3
WMBN WV5 64 E8
The Green Fld COVS CV3 154 F5
Greenfield Vw SEDG DY3 65 M6
Greenfinch Cl KIDD DY10 161 M2
Greenfinch Rd CBROM B36 92 E5
HAG/WOL DY9 120 B2
Greenford Rd
ALE/KHTH/YWD B14 145 M2
Green Gables HLYWD B47 145 L6 2
Greenhart TAM/AM/WIL B77 46 E1
Green Heath Rd HEDN WS12 12 E5
Greenhill BRGRVE B60 166 D8
WMBN WV5 64 F7
Greenhill Av KIDD DY10 137 K5
Green Hill Cl BRGRVE B60 166 A7
Greenhill Cl SHHTH WV12 37 M8
TAM/AM/WIL B77 46 A8
Greenhill Dr SLYOAK B29 124 A4
Greenhill Gdns GTB/HAM B43 70 B3
RMSLY B62 104 B7
WMBN WV5 64 F8
Greenhill Rd CSCFLD/WYGN B72 72 F5
HDSW B21 88 B3
MOS/BIL B13 125 K4
RMSLY B62 104 B6 1
RUGBYS/DCH CV22 183 K4
SEDG DY3 66 D8 1
Greenhill Wy ALDR WS9 40 F4 2
Green Hill Wy SHLY B90 126 F8
Greenholm Rd KGSTG B44 71 J6
Greenhough Rd LICH WS13 20 E5
Greenhurst RBRY B45 166 F4
Greening Dr EDG B15 106 F6
Greenland Av COVW CV5 132 D8
Greenland Cl KGSWFD DY6 83 J5 2
Greenland Ct COVW CV5 132 D8
Greenland Ri HIA/OLT B92 128 B6
Greenland Rd SLYOAK B29 124 F4
Greenlands WMBN WV5 64 D6 2
Greenlands Av REDE B98 196 E5
Greenlands Dr REDE B98 196 D6
Greenlands Rd
CHWD/FDBR/MGN B37 111 G3
Green La ALDR WS9 41 J8
ATHST CV9 62 D3
BLOX/PEL WS3 39 G6
BNTWD WS7 19 H4
BNTWD WS7 26 F3
BORD B9 108 A4
BRGRVW B61 165 L4
CBROM B36 92 C5
CNCK/NC WS11 16 C7
COVS CV3 153 L7
CSHL/WTROR B46 93 K8
DUDN DY1 66 D8
DUNHL/THL/PER WV6 35 J6
GTB/HAM B43 70 B6
HAG/WOL DY9 102 B8
HDSW B21 88 A5
HWK/WKHTH B38 144 C5
KGSWFD DY6 83 H6
LICH WS13 19 G2
LICHS WS14 28 B3
NUNW/HART CV10 78 C5
NUNW/HART CV10 80 A6
POL/KGSB/FAZ B78 47 H6
POL/KGSB/FAZ B78 58 E6
RCOVN/BALC/EX CV7 114 B7
RCOVN/BALC/EX CV7 150 F6
REDW B97 195 K4
RIDG/WDGT B32 105 G7
RMSLY B62 104 B4
RRUGBY CV23 157 M8
RRUGBY CV23 157 H2
RUSH/SHEL WS4 40 B2
SHLY B90 146 C4
STUD B80 196 F8
WSLW WS2 4 D1
WSLW WS2 39 G7
WWCK CV34 199 J5
BILS/COS WV14 51 G6
SCFLD/BOLD B73 72 F6
Green Lea TAM/AM/WIL B77 46 E5
Greenleaf Cl COVW CV5 152 E2 1
Greenleas Gdns HALE B63 122 A2 2
Green Leigh ERDW/GRVHL B23 72 D5
Greenleighs SEDG DY3 66 B2
Greenly Rd
ETTPK/GDPK/PENN WV4 50 B8
Green Meadow HAG/WOL DY9 119 M5
WNSFLD WV11 37 J8 2
Green Meadow Cl WMBN WV5 64 C7
Green Meadow Rd
SHHTH WV12 37 M6 2
SLYOAK B29 123 K6
Green Mdw HEDN WS12 17 G4
Greenmoor Rd
NUNW/HART CV10 98 E2
Greenoak Crs BVILLE B30 125 G5
SEDG DY3 66 E6
Green Oak Rd CDSL WV8 34 F3
Greenodd Dr COVN CV6 116 D8
Green Park Av BILS/COS WV14 50 F5
Green Park Dr BILS/COS WV14 51 G5
Green Park Rd BRGRVE B60 185 M4
DUDS DY2 85 K4
NFLD/LBR B31 143 J3
Greenridge Rd
BFLD/HDSWWD B20 70 C8
Green Rd DUDS DY2 85 H6
MOS/BIL B13 126 B4
Green Rock La BLOX/PEL WS3 39 H4
Greenroyde HAG/WOL DY9 119 M4 2
Greensforge La KINVER DY7 100 B5
Greenside HRBN B17 106 A8
Greenside Cl NUN CV11 99 M4
Greenside Rd ERDE/BCHGN B24 73 G8
Greenside Wy DSYBK/YTR WS5 69 L1
Greensill Av TPTN/OCK DY4 67 K5
Green Slade Crs BRGRVE B60 166 A4
Greenslade Crs
NFLD/LBR B31 143 L3 1
Green Slade Gv HEDN WS12 13 G6
Greenslade Rd DSYBK/YTR WS5 54 A6
SEDG DY3 65 M3
SHLY B90 146 A3
Greensleeves FOAKS/STRLY B74 56 D3
Greensleeves Cl COVN CV6 133 M3 2
Greens Rd COVN CV6 133 L4
Greenstead Rd MOS/BIL B13 126 B4
Green St BTHH/HG B12 7 K8
BILS/COS WV14 67 G5
KIDD DY10 161 J1
OLDBY B69 86 E6
SMTHWKW B67 87 K8
STRBR DY8 101 K8
WBROM B70 87 J5
WSLW WS2 53 G2
Greensward Cl KNWTH CV8 176 F7
Green Sward La REDE B98 197 K1
The Greensward COVS CV3 155 L3 1
Greensway WNSFLD WV11 36 F5
The Green ALDR WS9 41 G7
BLOX/PEL WS3 38 F4
CBROM B36 91 M6
CSCFLD/WYGN B72 73 H4
CSHL/WTROR B46 94 D3
DARL/WED WS10 52 B6
HWK/WKHTH B38 144 D3
KIDD DY10 163 J4
LGLYGN/QTN B68 104 F3
NUN CV11 99 J3 2
POL/KGSB/FAZ B78 45 J5
POL/KGSB/FAZ B78 60 F1
POL/KGSB/FAZ B78 60 A7
RIDG/WDGT B32 104 E7 3
RRUGBY CV23 182 E1
RUGBYS/DCH CV22 183 G5
SOLH B91 128 B8
STRBR DY8 101 H3
TAM/AM/WIL B77 32 F7 1
Greenvale NFLD/LBR B31 123 K8
Greenvale Av
LGN/SDN/BHAMAIR B26 110 B7
Greenway ALDR WS9 40 F3
BFLD/HDSWWD B20 70 D7
NUN CV11 99 M5
POL/KGSB/FAZ B78 47 L2 1
SEDG DY3 66 C4
WWCK CV34 199 J4
Greenway Av STRBR DY8 101 J4 1
Greenway Dr SCFLD/BOLD B73 72 A2
Greenway Gdns
HWK/WKHTH B38 144 C6
SEDG DY3 66 C4
Greenway Rd BILS/COS WV14 67 J1
Greenways HALE B63 103 G8
NFLD/LBR B31 123 K5 3
PENK ST19 10 E5
STRBR DY8 101 G4
The Greenways RLSN CV32 200 F2 1
Greenway St BORD B9 108 A4
The Greenway
CHWD/FDBR/MGN B37 110 E7
HAG/WOL DY9 119 K8
SCFLD/BOLD B73 71 M2
Greenwood YDLY B25 109 H5
Greenwood Av ACGN B27 126 E3
BLKHTH/ROWR B65 104 B2 1
LGLYGN/QTN B68 86 F8 3
Greenwood Cl
ALE/KHTH/YWD B14 125 J8
RRUGBY CV23 158 E8 1
Greenwood Pk ALDR WS9 41 G4
HEDN WS12 12 F5
Greenwood Pl KGSTG B44 71 M4 2
Greenwood Rd ALDR WS9 40 F3
HHTH/SAND B71 68 F5 1
WOLVN WV10 36 A6
The Greenwoods STRBR DY8 101 J8 1
Greethurst Dr MOS/BIL B13 126 A3 1
Greets Green Rd WBROM B70 86 C1
Greetville Cl STETCH B33 91 L8
Gregory Av COVS CV3 153 L7
SLYOAK B29 123 L5
Gregory Cl DARL/WED WS10 68 D3 4
Gregory Dr DUDN DY1 84 E3
Gregory Hood Rd COVS CV3 154 B8
Gregory Rd STRBR DY8 101 G8
Greig Ct CNCK/NC WS11 17 G3
Grendon Cl REDE B98 197 H4
TLHL/CAN CV4 152 A4
Grendon Dr SCFLD/BOLD B73 72 B2
Grendon Gdns
ETTPK/GDPK/PENN WV4 49 H7
Grendon Rd
ALE/KHTH/YWD B14 145 L2
HIA/OLT B92 127 J5
POL/KGSB/FAZ B78 47 L4
Grenfell Cl RLSS CV31 201 H7 2
Grenfell Dr EDG B15 106 D5 2
Grenfell Rd BLOX/PEL WS3 39 H2
Grenville Av COVE CV2 154 F2
Grenville Cl
RUGBYS/DCH CV22 183 G4 2
WSLW WS2 52 B2
Grenville Dr ERDW/GRVHL B23 89 M2
SMTHWK B66 87 H5
Grenville Pl WBROM B70 86 C2
Grenville Rd DUDN DY1 84 C4
SHLY B90 146 F3
Gresham Av RLSN CV32 200 F3
Gresham Pl RLSN CV32 200 F3
Gresham Rd CNCK/NC WS11 16 C2
HLGN/YWD B28 126 D7
LGLYGN/QTN B68 86 F7
Gresham St COVE CV2 154 E3
Gresley Cl MGN/WHC B75 56 E1
Gresley Rd COVE CV2 135 H6
Gressel La STETCH B33 110 A2
Grestone Av
BFLD/HDSWWD B20 88 C2
Greswold Cl TLHL/CAN CV4 152 D4
Greswolde Dr ERDE/BCHGN B24 90 F1
Greswolde Park Rd ACGN B27 126 F2
Greswolde Rd SOLH B91 127 J7
SPARK B11 126 A2
The Greswoldes RLSS CV31 201 K7
Greswold Gdns STETCH B33 91 L8 2
Greswold St HHTH/SAND B71 68 F8
Gretna Rd COVS CV3 177 K1
Gretton Crs ALDR WS9 40 D8
Gretton Rd ALDR WS9 40 D8
ERDW/GRVHL B23 72 B6
Greville Cl PENK ST19 10 D5
Greville Dr EDG B15 107 G7
Greville Rd KNWTH CV8 191 J1
WWCK CV34 199 M4
Grevis Cl MOS/BIL B13 125 K1
Grevis Rd YDLY B25 109 J4 2
Greycoat Rd COVN CV6 133 L3
Greyfort Crs HIA/OLT B92 127 K4
Greyfriars Cl DUDN DY1 84 C2
HIA/OLT B92 127 H6
Greyfriars Dr CRTAM B79 31 J7 1
Greyfriars La COV CV1 8 F5
Greyfriars Rd COV CV1 8 E6
Greyhound La
ETTPK/GDPK/PENN WV4 48 C8
STRBR DY8 119 H3
Greyhurst Cft SOLH B91 147 M5 3
Grey Mill Cl SHLY B90 147 K7
Greystoke Av CBROM B36 91 H6
Greystoke Dr KGSWFD DY6 83 H7
Greystone Cl REDE B98 189 G7
Greystone Pas DUDN DY1 84 F4
Greystone St DUDS DY2 85 G4
Grey Tree Crs DOR/KN B93 172 C2
Grice St WBROM B70 87 G5
Griffin Cl BNTWD WS7 18 C5
Griffin Gdns HRBN B17 124 B1
Griffin Rd ERDW/GRVHL B23 72 A8
KIDD DY10 161 J1
RLSS CV31 200 A6
Griffins Brook Cl BVILLE B30 124 B6 1
Griffins Brook La BVILLE B30 124 A7
NFLD/LBR B31 124 A7
Griffin St DUDS DY2 103 G1
WBROM B70 87 H2
WOLV WV1 3 M6
Griffiths Dr WMBN WV5 64 E8
WNSFLD WV11 37 K4
Griffiths Rd DUDN DY1 66 E7 1
HHTH/SAND B71 69 G4
SHHTH WV12 38 B5
Griff La NUNW/HART CV10 98 B7
NUNW/HART CV10 98 F7
Grigg Gv NFLD/LBR B31 143 J4
Grimley Cl REDE B98 196 D4
Grimley La BRGRVE B60 186 C8
Grimley Rd NFLD/LBR B31 144 B3 1
Grimley Wy CNCK/NC WS11 16 D1 1
Grimpits La HWK/WKHTH B38 144 E6
Grimshaw Rd HLGN/YWD B28 126 E4
Grimston Cl COVS CV3 155 L3 2
Grimstone St WOLVN WV10 3 H3
Grindleford Rd PBAR/PBCH B42 71 H6
Grindle Rd COVN CV6 134 D1
Grindsbrook TAM/AM/WIL B77 46 E5
Gristhorpe Rd SLYOAK B29 124 E5
Grizebeck Dr COVW CV5 132 E8
Grizedale Cl RBRY B45 142 F3
Grocott Cl PENK ST19 10 C3
Grocott Rd DARL/WED WS10 67 M1
Grosmont Av BTHH/HG B12 107 L7 1
Grosvenor Av
BFLD/HDSWWD B20 89 G3
FOAKS/STRLY B74 55 K4
KIDD DY10 137 K7
Grosvenor Cl LICHS WS14 21 H7
MGN/WHC B75 57 G4
PENK ST19 10 D4
WOLVN WV10 36 B3
Grosvenor Crs WOLVN WV10 36 B3
Grosvenor Pk
ETTPK/GDPK/PENN WV4 49 K8
Grosvenor Rd AST/WIT B6 89 M5
BFLD/HDSWWD B20 89 G3
COV CV1 8 D7
ETTPK/GDPK/PENN WV4 66 C2
HRBN B17 105 L7
LGLYGN/QTN B68 104 E1
RLSS CV31 200 E8
SEDG DY3 84 B3
SOLH B91 147 K4
WOLVN WV10 36 B3
Grosvenor Sq HLGN/YWD B28 126 C8
Grosvenor St CBHAMNE B4 7 J4
WOLVN WV10 3 L3
Grosvenor St West
LDYWD/EDGR B16 6 A7
Grosvenor Wy BRLYHL DY5 102 B6
Grotto La DUNHL/THL/PER WV6 35 J8
Groucutt St BILS/COS WV14 67 G5 1
Grounds Dr FOAKS/STRLY B74 56 D2 1
Grounds Rd FOAKS/STRLY B74 56 D2
Grout St WBROM B70 86 C1 1
Grove Av HALE B63 121 K2 1
MOS/BIL B13 125 L3
SOLH B91 128 A8
Grove Cl CNCK/NC WS11 17 K8
Grove Cottage Rd BORD B9 108 B3 1
Grove Crs BLOX/PEL WS3 39 K2
BRLYHL DY5 84 A8
Grove Cft RWWCK/WEL CV35 198 C8
Grove Farm Dr MGN/WHC B75 57 K8
Grove Flds NUNW/HART CV10 81 G5
Grove Gdns HDSW B21 88 D3
Grove Hl DSYBK/YTR WS5 54 A5
Grove Hill Rd HDSW B21 88 D4
Groveland Rd TPTN/OCK DY4 85 L2
Grovelands Crs WOLVN WV10 36 B2
Grove La BFLD/HDSWWD B20 88 D3
BLOX/PEL WS3 25 J4
DUNHL/THL/PER WV6 48 F3
HDSW B21 88 D5
HOCK/TIA B94 172 E8
HRBN B17 124 A1
RCOVN/BALC/EX CV7 115 K6
SMTHWK B66 88 A8
WALM/CURD B76 74 D3
WSNGN B18 106 B1
Groveley La NFLD/LBR B31 143 K7
RBRY B45 167 G1
Grove Ms NFLD/LBR B31 143 M5
Grove Pk KGSWFD DY6 83 G5
RWWCK/WEL CV35 198 B7
Grove Pl NUNW/HART CV10 98 B2
RLSS CV31 200 E7
Grove Rd ALE/KHTH/YWD B14 125 H6
ATHST CV9 63 H6
DOR/KN B93 172 E1
LGLYGN/QTN B68 105 H4
NUNW/HART CV10 98 B2
SOLH B91 128 A8
SPARK B11 126 A2
Groveside Wy BLOX/PEL WS3 25 L8
Grove St COV CV1 9 H4 1
DUDS DY2 85 J5 5
REDE B98 196 C2
RLSN CV32 200 C4
WOLVN WV10 3 M2
WSNGN B18 106 B1
Grove Ter WSL WS1 5 G4
The Grove BDWTH CV12 116 F2
BLKHTH/ROWR B65 104 A3
BNTWD WS7 18 B5
BRLYHL DY5 102 A4
CSHL/WTROR B46 111 K1
DSYBK/YTR WS5 69 M2
ETTPK/GDPK/PENN WV4 50 C8
FOAKS/STRLY B74 42 B8
GTB/HAM B43 70 C1
HIA/OLT B92 129 L5
NFLD/LBR B31 143 M5
RBRY B45 167 H1
WASH/WDE B8 108 A1
WNSFLD WV11 36 F7
Grove Vale Av GTB/HAM B43 70 A4
Grove Wy FOAKS/STRLY B74 55 K6
Grovewood Dr
HWK/WKHTH B38 144 C4
Guardhouse Rd COVN CV6 133 M5
Guardian Ct NFLD/LBR B31 143 H2
SOLH B91 148 B2 1
Guardians Wy NFLD/LBR B31 123 J5 1
Guernsey Dr CBROM B36 92 F7
Guest Av WNSFLD WV11 37 G5
Guest Gv LOZ/NWT B19 89 G7
Guild Av BLOX/PEL WS3 39 H6
Guild Cl LDYWD/EDGR B16 106 E3
Guild Cft LOZ/NWT B19 89 H7
Guildford Cl KIDDW DY11 136 E7 1
Guildford Cft
CHWD/FDBR/MGN B37 110 D5
Guildford Dr LOZ/NWT B19 89 H7
Guildford St LOZ/NWT B19 89 H6 1
Guild Rd BRGRVE B60 185 K4
COVN CV6 134 B6
Guilsborough Rd COVS CV3 155 J4
Guinness Cl REDW B97 196 B5
Guiting Cl REDW B97 195 M4 1
Guiting Rd SLYOAK B29 123 L6
Gulistan Rd RLSN CV32 200 C4
Gullane Cl HWK/WKHTH B38 144 B4
The Gullet POL/KGSB/FAZ B78 47 K4
Gulliman's Wy RLSS CV31 201 H7
Gullswood Cl
ALE/KHTH/YWD B14 145 H3 3
Gulson Rd COV CV1 9 J6
Gumbleberrys Cl
WASH/WDE B8 109 G1 3
Gundry Cl RLSS CV31 200 E6 7
Gungate CRTAM B79 31 M8
Gun Hl RCOVN/BALC/EX CV7 96 E5
Gun La COVE CV2 134 E8
Gunmakers Wk LOZ/NWT B19 89 H6
Gunner La RBRY B45 142 B6
Gunns Wy HIA/OLT B92 127 H6
Guns La WBROM B70 86 F1
Gunstock Cl FOAKS/STRLY B74 55 J6 1
Gunter Rd ERDE/BCHGN B24 91 J2
Gunton Av COVS CV3 155 G8
Guphill Av COVW CV5 153 H3
Guphill La COVW CV5 153 H2
Gurnard TAM/AM/WIL B77 46 B7 1
Gurnard Cl WNSFLD WV11 37 M4
Gurney Pl WSLW WS2 38 E8
Gurney Rd WSLW WS2 38 E8
Guthrie Cl LOZ/NWT B19 89 H7
Guthrum Cl
DUNHL/THL/PER WV6 34 D8 1
ERDW/GRVHL B23 72 C5
Gutteridge Av COVN CV6 133 L3 1
The Gutter HAG/WOL DY9 141 J6
Guy Av WOLVN WV10 36 B7
Guy Pl East RLSN CV32 200 D4 3
Guy Pl West RLSN CV32 200 D4 4
Guy Rd KNWTH CV8 191 K3
Guy's Cliffe Av RLSN CV32 200 A3
WALM/CURD B76 73 K4
Guy's Cliffe Rd RLSN CV32 200 C5 1
Guy's Cliffe Ter WWCK CV34 199 K6 2
Guys Cl CRTAM B79 31 K6
WWCK CV34 199 L5 2
Guy's Cross Park Rd
WWCK CV34 199 K5
Guy's La SEDG DY3 83 M3
Guy St RLSN CV32 200 D4
WWCK CV34 199 K6
Guy's Wk BRGRVW B61 165 L8 2
Gwendoline Wy ALDR WS9 40 F1
Gypsy La ATHST CV9 63 H3
CSHL/WTROR B46 93 H3
KNWTH CV8 191 K4
POL/KGSB/FAZ B78 61 L1
REDW B97 187 G8

H

Habberley La KIDDW DY11 136 D5
Habberley Rd BEWD DY12 136 C7
BLKHTH/ROWR B65 104 B3
KIDDW DY11 136 F6
Habberley St KIDDW DY11 137 G7 3
Habberly Cft SOLH B91 147 M4 3
Hackett Cl BILS/COS WV14 66 D4
Hackett Dr SMTHWK B66 87 H6 1
Hackett Rd BLKHTH/ROWR B65 104 C2
Hackett St TPTN/OCK DY4 68 A6
Hackford Rd
ETTPK/GDPK/PENN WV4 66 D1
Hackmans Gate La
HAG/WOL DY9 139 L5
Hack St BORD B9 7 L7
Hackwood Rd DARL/WED WS10 68 F3
Hadcroft Gra HAG/WOL DY9 120 B1
Hadcroft Rd HAG/WOL DY9 120 A1
Haddock Rd BILS/COS WV14 51 G6
Haddon Crs SHHTH WV12 38 A6
Haddon Cft HALE B63 121 G4
Haddon End COVS CV3 154 C7
Haddon Rd PBAR/PBCH B42 71 H6
RLSN CV32 200 F3
Haddon St COVN CV6 134 E5
Haden Cl CDYHTH B64 103 K6
STRBR DY8 101 H3
Haden Crs WNSFLD WV11 37 K7
Haden Cross Dr CDYHTH B64 103 L6
Hadendale CDYHTH B64 103 L6
Haden Hl BDMR/CCFT WV3 2 A5
Haden Hill Rd CDYHTH B64 103 L6
HALE B63 103 L7
RMSLY B62 103 M7 1
Haden Park Rd CDYHTH B64 103 J6
Haden Rd CDYHTH B64 103 J3
TPTN/OCK DY4 67 L4
Haden St BTHH/HG B12 107 K7
Haden Wy BTHH/HG B12 107 K7
Hadfield Cl ERDE/BCHGN B24 91 J2 2
Hadfield Cft LOZ/NWT B19 89 G8 1
Hadfield Wy
CHWD/FDBR/MGN B37 110 E1 3
Hadland Rd STETCH B33 109 M4
Hadleigh Cft WALM/CURD B76 73 L7
Hadleigh Rd COVS CV3 178 A2
Hadley Cl DUDS DY2 103 J1
HLYWD B47 145 L8
Hadley Cft SMTHWK B66 87 L6 1
Hadley Pl BILS/COS WV14 51 G6
Hadley Rd BILS/COS WV14 51 G6
WSLW WS2 38 D7
Hadleys Cft
POL/KGSB/FAZ B78 60 B8 1
Hadley St LGLYGN/QTN B68 104 E1
Hadlow Cft STETCH B33 110 B6
Hadrian Cl RLSN CV32 200 F1
Hadrian Dr CSHL/WTROR B46 93 K4 1
Hadrians Cl TAM/AM/WIL B77 46 B5 1
Hadrians Wy RUGBYN/HIL CV21 159 K6
Hadyn Gv
LGN/SDN/BHAMAIR B26 109 M7
Hadzor Rd LGLYGN/QTN B68 105 H5
Hafren Cl RBRY B45 142 F3 2
Hafton Gv BORD B9 108 B4 3
Haggar St BKHL/PFLD WV2 50 A7
Hagley Cswy HAG/WOL DY9 120 D6
Hagley Cl HAG/WOL DY9 120 A7
Hagley Park Dr RBRY B45 142 E7

Hagley Rd HAG/WOL DY9 .... 120 A4
HALE B63 .... 121 M2
HRBN B17 .... 106 A4
LDYWD/EDGR B16 .... 106 D5
STRBR DY8 .... 119 M2
Hagley Rd West HRBN B17 .... 105 L4
LGLYGN/QTN B68 .... 105 L6
RIDG/WDGT B32 .... 104 E7
RMSLY B62 .... 104 D7
Hagley View Rd DUDS DY2 .... 85 G5
Hagley Wood La HAG/WOL DY9 .... 120 F7
Haig Cl CNCK/NC WS11 .... 12 E8
MGN/WHC B75 .... 57 G6
Haig Rd DUDS DY2 .... 85 K4
Haig St HHTH/SAND B71 .... 69 G7
Hailes Park Cl BKHL/PFLD WV2 .... 50 B7
Hailstone Cl BLKHTH/ROWR B65 .... 85 L7
Haines Cl TPTN/OCK DY4 .... 85 M1
Haines St WBROM B70 .... 87 H5
Hainfield Dr SOLH B91 .... 128 C8
Hainge Rd OLDBY B69 .... 86 A3
Hainult Cl STRBR DY8 .... 101 H1
Halberton St WSNGN B18 .... 106 B1
Haldon Gv NFLD/LBR B31 .... 143 J6
Hale Gv ERDE/BCHGN B24 .... 91 H1
Halecroft Av WNSFLD WV11 .... 37 H8
Hales Crs SMTHWKW B67 .... 105 J1
Halescroft Sq NFLD/LBR B31 .... 123 J7
Hales Gdns ERDW/GRVHL B23 .... 72 A5
Hales La SMTHWKW B67 .... 105 J1
Halesmere Wy HALE B63 .... 122 A2
Halesowen Rd BRGRVW B61 .... 166 A3
CDYHTH B64 .... 103 K5
DUDS DY2 .... 85 G8
RMSLY B62 .... 104 C7
Halesowen St OLDBY B69 .... 86 D6
RMSLY B62 .... 104 A5
Hales Rd DARL/WED WS10 .... 68 L1
HALE B63 .... 121 L1
Hales St COV CV1 .... 9 G3
Hales Wy OLDBY B69 .... 86 D6
Halesworth Rd COVEN WV9 .... 35 K3
Halewood Gv
HLGN/YWD B28 .... 126 E6
Haley St SHHTH WV12 .... 38 A3
Halfcot Av HAG/WOL DY9 .... 120 A2
Halford Crs BLOX/PEL WS3 .... 39 K8
Halford Gv ERDE/BCHGN B24 .... 91 J1
Halford La COVN CV6 .... 133 L3
Halford Rd SOLH B91 .... 127 J7
Halford's La SMTHWK B66 .... 87 L6
Halford St CRTAM B79 .... 31 L8
Halfshire La KIDD DY10 .... 138 F4
Halfway Cl KGSTG B44 .... 71 J7
Halifax Cl COVW CV5 .... 132 E6
Halifax Gv WSNGN B18 .... 106 C1
Halifax Rd SHLY B90 .... 146 F2
Haling Cl PENK ST19 .... 10 D5
Haling Rd PENK ST19 .... 10 D4
Halladale HWK/WKHTH B38 .... 144 D4
Hallam Cl HHTH/SAND B71 .... 87 J1
Hallam Crs WOLVN WV10 .... 36 C7
Hallam Crs COVN CV6 .... 133 M2
Hallams Cl KNWTH CV8 .... 156 D8
Hallam St BHTH/HG B12 .... 107 J8
HHTH/SAND B71 .... 87 H1
Hallbridge Cl BLOX/PEL WS3 .... 39 K3
Hallbridge Wy OLDBY B69 .... 85 M3
Hall Brook Rd
RCOVN/BALC/EX CV7 .... 133 L2
Hallchurch Rd DUDS DY2 .... 84 D6
Hall Cl KNWTH CV8 .... 177 M7
Hallcourt Cl CNCK/NC WS11 .... 16 C5
Hallcourt Crs CNCK/NC WS11 .... 16 C5
Hallcourt La CNCK/NC WS11 .... 16 C5
Hall Crs HHTH/SAND B71 .... 69 G7
Hallcroft Cl
CSCFLD/WYGN B72 .... 73 G6
Hallcroft Wy ALDR WS9 .... 41 G8
DOR/KN B93 .... 148 E7
Hall Dale Cl HLGN/YWD B28 .... 126 D8
Hall Dr CHWD/FDBR/MGN B37 .... 110 E6
HAG/WOL DY9 .... 120 B7
KNWTH CV8 .... 178 C2
Hall End DARL/WED WS10 .... 68 D2
NUN CV11 .... 99 H3
Hallens Dr DARL/WED WS10 .... 68 B3
Hallet Dr BDMR/CCFT WV3 .... 2 D7
Hallewell Rd LDYWD/EDGR B16 .... 106 B3
Hallfields RLSS CV31 .... 201 J8
Hall Green Rd COVE B34 .... 134 F3
HHTH/SAND B71 .... 69 H4
Hallgreen St BILS/COS WV14 .... 67 J2
Hall Gv BILS/COS WV14 .... 67 G5
RRUGBY CV23 .... 157 J1
Hall Hays Rd BKDE/SHDE B34 .... 92 C6
Hall La ALDR WS9 .... 40 C3
ATHST CV9 .... 63 M5
BILS/COS WV14 .... 66 D4
BLOX/PEL WS3 .... 39 K2
BNTWD WS7 .... 27 J1
COVE CV2 .... 135 K7
GTWY WS6 .... 24 D1
HAG/WOL DY9 .... 120 B7
TPTN/OCK DY4 .... 67 M5
Hall Meadow CNCK/NC WS11 .... 15 M7
HAG/WOL DY9 .... 120 B6
Hallmoor Rd STECH B33 .... 109 M2
Hallot Cl ERDW/GRVHL B23 .... 72 B5
Halloughton Rd
FOAKS/STRLY B74 .... 56 E6
Hallowfields Cl REDE B98 .... 196 C4
Hall Park St BILS/COS WV14 .... 50 F7
Hall Rd BFLD/HDSWWD B20 .... 88 E6
CBROM B36 .... 91 L5
RLSN CV32 .... 200 D4
SMTHWKW B67 .... 105 J1
WASH/WDE B8 .... 108 B1
Halls Farm La BEWD DY12 .... 136 A5
Hallstead Rd MOS/BIL B13 .... 125 M8
Hall St BILS/COS WV14 .... 51 J8
CDYHTH B64 .... 103 K3
DARL/WED WS10 .... 51 M6
DUDS DY2 .... 85 H4
LGLYGN/QTN B68 .... 86 F8
SEDG DY3 .... 66 B5
STRBR DY8 .... 119 L2
TPTN/OCK DY4 .... 67 J8
WBROM B70 .... 87 G3
WLNHL WV13 .... 51 M4
WNSFLD WV11 .... 37 G8
WSLW WS2 .... 53 H2
WSNGN B18 .... 6 D1
Hall St East DARL/WED WS10 .... 52 A6
Hall St South WBROM B70 .... 87 H5
Hall Wk CSHL/WTROR B46 .... 111 K1
Halsbury Gv KGSTG B44 .... 71 M5
Halston Rd BNTWD WS7 .... 18 F5
Halswelle Gv GTB/HAM B43 .... 71 J1
Haltonlea TAM/AM/WIL B77 .... 46 E5
Halton Rd SCFLD/BOLD B73 .... 72 B2
Halton St DUDS DY2 .... 85 G8
Hamar Wy
CHWD/FDBR/MGN B37 .... 110 F4
Hamberley Ct WSNGN B18 .... 88 B8
Hamble Cl BRLYHL DY5 .... 83 L7
Hambledon Cl COVEN WV9 .... 35 L3
Hamble Gv
DUNHL/THL/PER WV6 .... 48 C1
Hamble Rd
ETTPK/GDPK/PENN WV4 .... 49 G7
PBAR/PBCH B42 .... 70 D4
Hambleton Rd HALE B63 .... 121 H3
Hambletts Rd WBROM B70 .... 86 E2
Hambrook Cl
DUNHL/THL/PER WV6 .... 35 L8
Hambury Dr
ALE/KHTH/YWD B14 .... 125 H6
Hamelin St CNCK/NC WS11 .... 16 C2
Hamgreen La REDW B97 .... 195 H6
Hamilton Av HRBN B17 .... 105 L5
RMSLY B62 .... 122 A2
STRBR DY8 .... 101 G8
Hamilton Cl BDWTH CV12 .... 116 A4
BRGRVE B60 .... 185 H8
HEDN WS12 .... 17 K1
SEDG DY3 .... 66 A5
STRBR DY8 .... 101 G8
Hamilton Dr OLDBY B69 .... 86 A3
STRBR DY8 .... 101 G8
Hamilton Gdns WOLVN WV10 .... 36 C2
Hamilton Lea CNCK/NC WS11 .... 17 L1
Hamilton Rd COVE CV2 .... 154 E2
HDSW B21 .... 88 B5
KIDDW DY11 .... 160 F2
REDW B97 .... 196 A5
RLSS CV31 .... 201 J8
SMTHWKW B67 .... 105 J3
TPTN/OCK DY4 .... 68 A7
Hamilton St BLOX/PEL WS3 .... 39 G4
Hamilton Ter RLSN CV32 .... 200 D5
Ham La HAG/WOL DY9 .... 120 A3
KGSWFD DY6 .... 83 J4
Hamlet Cl NUN CV11 .... 99 L4
RUGBYS/DCH CV22 .... 183 H7
Hamlet Gdns HLGN/YWD B28 .... 126 D5
Hamlet Rd HLGN/YWD B28 .... 126 D6
The Hamlet CNCK/NC WS11 .... 17 J8
RWWCK/WEL CV35 .... 191 L6
Hammer Bank HALE B63 .... 102 E5
Hammersley Cl HALE B63 .... 103 G6
Hammersley St BDWTH CV12 .... 116 C4
Hammerwich La BNTWD WS7 .... 27 J3
Hammerwich Rd BNTWD WS7 .... 19 H7
Hammond Av WOLVN WV10 .... 36 C5
Hammond Dr ERDW/GRVHL B23 .... 72 D8
Hammond Wy STRBR DY8 .... 101 L6
Hampden Cl BRLYHL DY5 .... 102 E5
Hampden Retreat
BHTH/HG B12 .... 107 J7
Hampden Wy
RUGBYS/DCH CV22 .... 183 G6
Hamps Cl BNTWD WS7 .... 19 H6
Hampshire Cl COVS CV3 .... 155 K5
POL/KGSB/FAZ B78 .... 45 K3
Hampshire Dr EDG B15 .... 106 C5
Hampshire Rd HHTH/SAND B71 .... 68 E4
Hampson Cl SPARK B11 .... 107 M7
Hampstead Cl WNSFLD WV11 .... 37 G7
Hampstead Gld HALE B63 .... 122 A2
Hampton Av BRGRVE B60 .... 185 L5
NUNW/HART CV10 .... 97 M1
Hampton Cl CRTAM B79 .... 32 A6
REDE B98 .... 196 F6
SCFLD/BOLD B73 .... 72 A3
Hampton Court Rd HRBN B17 .... 105 K7
Hampton Dr FOAKS/STRLY B74 .... 56 F5
Hampton Gn CNCK/NC WS11 .... 16 B6
Hampton Gv BLOX/PEL WS3 .... 39 K1
Hampton La
RCOVN/BALC/EX CV7 .... 130 D5
SOLH B91 .... 148 C1
Hampton St AST/WIT B6 .... 89 H5
COVN CV6 .... 134 D7
DOR/KN B93 .... 149 G6
ERDW/GRVHL B23 .... 90 B1
RWWCK/WEL CV35 .... 198 C7
WOLVN WV10 .... 35 M4
WWCK CV34 .... 198 F8
Hampton St BILS/COS WV14 .... 66 F5
CNCK/NC WS11 .... 16 B6
DUDS DY2 .... 84 F8
LOZ/NWT B19 .... 6 E1
WWCK CV34 .... 199 H2
Hams La WALM/CURD B76 .... 75 K8
Hams Rd WASH/WDE B8 .... 108 B1
Hamstead Hall Av
BFLD/HDSWWD B20 .... 70 C8
Hamstead Hall Rd
BFLD/HDSWWD B20 .... 88 C1
Hamstead Hl
BFLD/HDSWWD B20 .... 88 D1
Hamstead Rd
BFLD/HDSWWD B20 .... 88 F4
GTB/HAM B43 .... 70 A5
GTB/HAM B43 .... 70 A6
GTB/HAM B43 .... 70 D7
Hamstead Ter DARL/WED WS10 .... 68 C5
Hanam Cl MGN/WHC B75 .... 57 K7
Hanbury Cl BRGRVE B60 .... 185 L5
HALE B63 .... 121 K3
Hanbury Crs
ETTPK/GDPK/PENN WV4 .... 49 J7
Hanbury Cft ACGN B27 .... 127 J2
Hanbury Hl STRBR DY8 .... 119 L1
Hanbury Rd BDWTH CV12 .... 117 G1
BRGRVE B60 .... 185 H8
BRWNH WS8 .... 26 C3
CNCK/NC WS11 .... 17 K8
DOR/KN B93 .... 172 D2
TAM/AM/WIL B77 .... 46 D1
WBROM B70 .... 86 E2
Hanch Pl WSL WS1 .... 5 H5
Hancock Gn TLHL/CAN CV4 .... 152 D5
Hancock Rd WASH/WDE B8 .... 108 D1
Hancox St LGLYGN/QTN B68 .... 104 F3
Handcross Gv COVS CV3 .... 153 L8
Handel Ct CNCK/NC WS11 .... 17 G3
Handley Gv NFLD/LBR B31 .... 143 G5
Handley's Cl KNWTH CV8 .... 179 L4
Handley St DARL/WED WS10 .... 68 E1
Handsworth Cl HDSW B21 .... 88 B6
Handsworth Crs COVW CV5 .... 152 C1
Handsworth Dr GTB/HAM B43 .... 70 E4
Handsworth New Rd
WSNGN B18 .... 88 C8
Handsworth Wood Rd
BFLD/HDSWWD B20 .... 88 D2
Hanford Cl COVN CV6 .... 134 C7
Hanging La NFLD/LBR B31 .... 143 J3
Hangleton Dr SPARK B11 .... 108 B7
Hangman's La CRTAM B79 .... 33 L3
Hanley Cl HALE B63 .... 121 J1
Hanley St LOZ/NWT B19 .... 6 F1
Hanlith TAM/AM/WIL B77 .... 46 E5
Hannaford Wy CNCK/NC WS11 .... 16 D3
Hannafore Rd
LDYWD/EDGR B16 .... 106 B2
Hannah Rd BILS/COS WV14 .... 67 L2
Hanney Hay Rd BNTWD WS7 .... 26 F2
Hannon Rd
ALE/KHTH/YWD B14 .... 125 J8
Hanover Cl AST/WIT B6 .... 89 J6
Hanover Ct
DUNHL/THL/PER WV6 .... 49 G1
WSLW WS2 .... 52 C4
Hanover Dr VAUX/NECH B7 .... 90 D5
Hanover Gdns
RUGBYN/HIL CV21 .... 183 M1
Hanover Pl CNCK/NC WS11 .... 16 C3
Hanover Rd
BLKHTH/ROWR B65 .... 104 A1
Hanover St BRGRVW B61 .... 185 K4
Hans Cl COV CV1 .... 9 M1
Hansell Dr DOR/KN B93 .... 172 C3
Hansom Rd RIDG/WDGT B32 .... 105 G8
Hanson Gv HIA/OLT B92 .... 109 K8
Hanson's Bridge Rd
ERDE/BCHGN B24 .... 73 K8
Hanson Wy COVN CV6 .... 116 E8
Hanwell Cl WALM/CURD B76 .... 73 M6
Hanwood Cl BHTH/HG B12 .... 107 K5
COVW CV5 .... 152 B1
Hanworth Cl RLSN CV32 .... 200 F2
Hanworth Rd WWCK CV34 .... 199 G5
Harald Cl DUNHL/THL/PER WV6 .... 34 C8
Harbeck Av KGSTG B44 .... 71 K5
Harberrow Cl HAG/WOL DY9 .... 119 L7
Harbet Dr BHAMNEC B40 .... 129 J1
Harbinger Rd HWK/WKHTH B38 .... 144 F1
Harborne La HRBN B17 .... 124 B1
SLYOAK B29 .... 124 B1
Harborne Park Rd HRBN B17 .... 106 A8
Harborne Rd EDG B15 .... 106 C6
SMTHWKW B67 .... 105 H4
Harborough Dr ALDR WS9 .... 40 E8
CBROM B36 .... 92 B4
Harborough Rd COVN CV6 .... 133 M3
RUGBYN/HIL CV21 .... 159 G5
Harborough Wk
HAG/WOL DY9 .... 119 M3
Harbours Cl BRGRVE B60 .... 185 H6
Harbours Hl HAG/WOL DY9 .... 141 J7
Harbury Cl REDE B98 .... 197 H4
WALM/CURD B76 .... 73 M7
Harbury Rd BHTH/HG B12 .... 107 H8
Harcourt COVS CV3 .... 155 J8
Harcourt Dr DUDN DY1 .... 84 B3
FOAKS/STRLY B74 .... 56 C1
Harcourt Gdns NUN CV11 .... 99 G2
Harcourt Rd CDYHTH B64 .... 103 K5
DARL/WED WS10 .... 68 D1
ERDW/GRVHL B23 .... 72 C7
Harden Cl BLOX/PEL WS3 .... 39 J6
Harden Gv BLOX/PEL WS3 .... 39 J6
Harden Rd BLOX/PEL WS3 .... 39 H6
Hardie Gn CNCK/NC WS11 .... 16 D2
Harding St BILS/COS WV14 .... 67 H4
Hardon Rd
ETTPK/GDPK/PENN WV4 .... 50 D8
Hardware St WBROM B70 .... 87 H1
Hardwick Cl COVW CV5 .... 152 E1
Hardwick Dr CDYHTH B64 .... 103 L6
Hardwicke Wy HAG/WOL DY9 .... 102 B8
Hardwick La STUD B80 .... 197 L8
Hardwike Wk BVILLE B30 .... 145 G3
Hardwyn Cl COVS CV3 .... 155 L4
Hardy Av KIDD DY10 .... 137 L2
Hardy Cl NUNW/HART CV10 .... 97 L1
RUGBYS/DCH CV22 .... 183 G3
Hardy Rd BLOX/PEL WS3 .... 39 J5
COVN CV6 .... 133 L5
DARL/WED WS10 .... 68 C2
Hardy Sq BKHL/PFLD WV2 .... 50 D7
Hare and Hounds La
NUNW/HART CV10 .... 98 E3
Harebell TAM/AM/WIL B77 .... 46 E1
Harebell Cl DSYBK/YTR WS5 .... 69 L2
HEDN WS12 .... 17 H3
WOLVN WV10 .... 22 E6
Harebell Crs DUDN DY1 .... 84 E1
Harebell Gdns
HWK/WKHTH B38 .... 144 D5
Harefield La NUNW/HART CV10 .... 98 D5
Harefield Rd COVE CV2 .... 154 F2
NUN CV11 .... 99 G1
Hare Gv NFLD/LBR B31 .... 143 H2
Haresfield Cl REDW B97 .... 196 B3
Hare St BILS/COS WV14 .... 51 K8
Harewood Dr MGN/WHC B75 .... 57 G4
Harewood Av
DARL/WED WS10 .... 69 G2
GTB/HAM B43 .... 70 A3
Harewood Cl HLGN/YWD B28 .... 126 C8
Harewood Rd COVW CV5 .... 153 G2
Harford St LOZ/NWT B19 .... 6 D1
Hargate La WBROM B70 .... 87 G1
Harger Ct KNWTH CV8 .... 191 K1
Hargrave Cl COVS CV3 .... 155 L4
CSHL/WTROR B46 .... 92 F2
Hargrave Rd SHLY B90 .... 146 B3
Hargreave Cl
WALM/CURD B76 .... 73 K6
Hargreaves St BKHL/PFLD WV2 .... 50 E6
Harington Rd COVN CV6 .... 133 L8
Harland Rd FOAKS/STRLY B74 .... 56 E2
Harlech Cl KNWTH CV8 .... 177 G8
OLDBY B69 .... 85 L4
RIDG/WDGT B32 .... 122 E7
Harlech Rd SHHTH WV12 .... 38 A7
Harlech Wy DUDN DY1 .... 84 D3
KIDDW DY11 .... 161 J3
Harleston Rd KGSTG B44 .... 71 K5
Harley Cl BRWNH WS8 .... 26 E7
Harley Dr BILS/COS WV14 .... 66 F1
Harley St COVE CV2 .... 154 E2
Harlow Gv HLGN/YWD B28 .... 126 E7
Harlstones Cl STRBR DY8 .... 101 L6
Harman Rd CSCFLD/WYGN B72 .... 72 F6
Harmar Cl WWCK CV34 .... 199 H4
Harmer Cl COVE CV2 .... 135 L6
Harmer St WSNGN B18 .... 88 E8
Harmon Rd STRBR DY8 .... 101 G8
Harnall Cl SHLY B90 .... 147 J6
Harnall La COV CV1 .... 9 H1
Harnall La East COV CV1 .... 9 J1
Harnall La West COV CV1 .... 8 F1
Harnall Rw COV CV1 .... 9 K4
Harness Cl DSYBK/YTR WS5 .... 69 J1
Harold Evers Wy KIDD DY10 .... 137 K6
Harold Rd COVE CV2 .... 155 H3
LDYWD/EDGR B16 .... 106 D4
SMTHWKW B67 .... 105 J2
Harold St NUN CV11 .... 99 G2
Harpenden Dr COVW CV5 .... 132 E8
Harper Av WNSFLD WV11 .... 37 G6
Harper Rd BILS/COS WV14 .... 51 H7
COV CV1 .... 9 J6
Harpers Cl ATHST CV9 .... 63 L7
Harpers Rd HLYWD B47 .... 145 L4
NFLD/LBR B31 .... 143 L3
Harper St WLNHL WV13 .... 51 L3
Harport Rd REDE B98 .... 196 E4
Harpur Cl RUSH/SHEL WS4 .... 53 L1
Harpur Rd RUSH/SHEL WS4 .... 53 L1
Harrier Rd ACGN B27 .... 127 H3
Harriers Gn KIDD DY10 .... 137 M5
Harriet Cl BRLYHL DY5 .... 83 M8
Harringay Dr STRBR DY8 .... 119 J2
Harringay Rd KGSTG B44 .... 71 K3
Harris Dr PBAR/PBCH B42 .... 70 E5
RUGBYS/DCH CV22 .... 183 K5
SMTHWK B66 .... 105 M2
Harrison Cl BLOX/PEL WS3 .... 39 G4
GTWY WS6 .... 24 B4
Harrison Crs BDWTH CV12 .... 116 E3
Harrison Rd CNCK/NC WS11 .... 16 C6
ERDE/BCHGN B24 .... 90 D1
FOAKS/STRLY B74 .... 42 C8
REDW B97 .... 196 A5
RUSH/SHEL WS4 .... 40 A3
STRBR DY8 .... 101 L4
Harrison's Fold DUDS DY2 .... 85 G8
Harrisons Gn EDG B15 .... 106 C7
Harrisons La ATHST CV9 .... 14 C4
Harrisons Pleck MOS/BIL B13 .... 125 K2
Harrison's Rd EDG B15 .... 106 C7
Harrison St BLOX/PEL WS3 .... 39 G4
Harris Rd COVS CV3 .... 154 F3
WWCK CV34 .... 199 G5
Harrold Av BLKHTH/ROWR B65 .... 104 C2
Harrold Rd BLKHTH/ROWR B65 .... 104 C2
Harrold St TPTN/OCK DY4 .... 68 A6
Harrold Ter LOZ/NWT B19 .... 89 G5
Harrop Wy STRBR DY8 .... 101 J5
Harrowby Dr TPTN/OCK DY4 .... 85 L1
Harrowby Pl WLNHL WV13 .... 52 A4
Harrowby Rd BILS/COS WV14 .... 67 L1
WOLVN WV10 .... 35 M2
Harrow Cl BRGRVE B60 .... 185 J7
COVN CV6 .... 116 E8
HAG/WOL DY9 .... 119 L7
Harrowfield Rd STECH B33 .... 109 J1
Harrow Rd KGSWFD DY6 .... 83 H4
SLYOAK B29 .... 124 D2
Harrow St WOLV WV1 .... 2 D1
Harry Perks St WLNHL WV13 .... 51 L2
Harry Rose Rd COVE CV2 .... 155 J3
Harry Weston Rd COVS CV3 .... 155 L4
Hart Dr SCFLD/BOLD B73 .... 72 E5
Hartfield Crs ACGN B27 .... 126 E4
Hartford Cl HRBN B17 .... 105 L6
Hartford Rd BRGRVE B60 .... 185 M4
Hartill Rd
ETTPK/GDPK/PENN WV4 .... 65 H2
Hartill St WLNHL WV13 .... 51 M5
Hartington Cl DOR/KN B93 .... 172 C2
Hartington Crs COVW CV5 .... 153 J4
Hartington Rd LOZ/NWT B19 .... 89 H5
Hartland Av BILS/COS WV14 .... 66 E5
COVE CV2 .... 134 F7
Hartland Rd HHTH/SAND B71 .... 69 K5
NFLD/LBR B31 .... 143 J7
TPTN/OCK DY4 .... 67 M8
Hartland St BRLYHL DY5 .... 84 B6
Hartlebury Cl DOR/KN B93 .... 172 G2
HEDN WS12 .... 17 G2
REDE B98 .... 189 H6
Hartlebury Rd HALE B63 .... 121 K3
Hartledon Rd HRBN B17 .... 105 M8
Hartle La HAG/WOL DY9 .... 140 D7
Hartlepool Rd COV CV1 .... 9 J1
Hartleyburn
TAM/AM/WIL B77 .... 46 E5
Hartley Dr ALDR WS9 .... 54 F1
Hartley Gv KGSTG B44 .... 71 M2
Hartley Pl EDG B15 .... 106 D5
Hartley Rd KGSTG B44 .... 71 L2
Hartley St BDMR/CCFT WV3 .... 2 B5
Harton Wy ALE/KHTH/YWD B14 .... 125 G3
Hartopp Rd FOAKS/STRLY B74 .... 56 D4
WASH/WDE B8 .... 108 C1
Hartridge Wk COVW CV5 .... 152 F1
Hart Rd ERDE/BCHGN B24 .... 72 E8
WNSFLD WV11 .... 51 H1
Hartsbourne Dr RMSLY B62 .... 122 B3
Harts Cl HRBN B17 .... 106 B7
Harts Green Rd HRBN B17 .... 105 L8
Hartshill Rd BKDE/SHDE B34 .... 91 L7
HIA/OLT B92 .... 127 H3
Hartshorn St BILS/COS WV14 .... 51 H8
Hartside Cl HALE B63 .... 121 G3
Hartslade LICHS WS14 .... 21 J7
Harts Rd WASH/WDE B8 .... 90 C8
Hart St WSL WS1 .... 4 F5
Hartswell Dr MOS/BIL B13 .... 125 K7
Hartwell Cl SOLH B91 .... 147 M4
Hartwell La GTWY WS6 .... 24 C2
Hartwell Rd ERDE/BCHGN B24 .... 90 F3
Harvard Cl DUDN DY1 .... 84 D1
Harvard Rd HIA/OLT B92 .... 127 M1
Harvest Cl BRGRVE B60 .... 185 H7
BVILLE B30 .... 124 F8
SEDG DY3 .... 66 C8
Harvesters Cl COVS CV3 .... 155 L3
FOAKS/STRLY B74 .... 55 J3
Harvesters Rd SHHTH WV12 .... 38 B8
Harvester Wy KGSWFD DY6 .... 82 E5
Harvest Gdns
LGLYGN/QTN B68 .... 104 E1
Harvest Hill La COVW CV5 .... 132 B3
Harvest Rd BLKHTH/ROWR B65 .... 103 L2
SMTHWKW B67 .... 105 H2
Harvey Cl COVW CV5 .... 132 E6
Harvey Dr MGN/WHC B75 .... 57 G3
Harvey Rd
LGN/SDN/BHAMAIR B26 .... 109 H6
WSLW WS2 .... 38 F3
Harvills Hawthorn WBROM B70 .... 68 D6
Harvine Wk STRBR DY8 .... 119 J2
Harvington Cl KIDDW DY11 .... 136 E5
Harvington Dr SHLY B90 .... 147 M7
Harvington Hall La KIDD DY10 .... 162 F3
Harvington Rd BILS/COS WV14 .... 66 F5
BRGRVE B60 .... 185 L5
HALE B63 .... 121 K3
LGLYGN/QTN B68 .... 104 E5
SLYOAK B29 .... 123 L5
Harvington Wy
WALM/CURD B76 .... 73 K5
Harwell Cl CRTAM B79 .... 32 A6
Harwin Cl DUNHL/THL/PER WV6 .... 35 K6
Harwood Drive
TAM/AM/WIL B77 .... 60 B1
Harwood Gv SHLY B90 .... 147 G5
Harwood Rd LICH WS13 .... 20 F2
Harwood St WBROM B70 .... 86 F2
Hasbury Cl HALE B63 .... 121 J3
Hasbury Rd RIDG/WDGT B32 .... 122 F5
Haselbech Rd COVS CV3 .... 155 K4
Haseley Cl REDE B98 .... 197 J5
RLSS CV31 .... 200 F3
Haseley Rd COVE CV2 .... 135 G4
HDSW B21 .... 88 C6
SOLH B91 .... 127 J7
Haselor Rd SCFLD/BOLD B73 .... 72 C4
Haselour Rd
CHWD/FDBR/MGN B37 .... 92 D8
Hasilwood Sq COVS CV3 .... 154 F3
Haskell St WSL WS1 .... 5 G8
Haslucks Cft SHLY B90 .... 146 E2
Haslucks Cft SHLY B90 .... 146 E2
Haslucks Green Rd SHLY B90 .... 146 E2
Hassop Rd PBAR/PBCH B42 .... 71 H6
Hastings Cl TAM/AM/WIL B77 .... 46 D7
Hastings Ct DUDN DY1 .... 84 C3
Hastings Rd BRGRVE B60 .... 185 J6
COVE CV2 .... 154 E1
ERDW/GRVHL B23 .... 71 M6
Haswell Rd HALE B63 .... 121 H2
Hatcham Rd KGSTG B44 .... 72 A3
Hatchett St LOZ/NWT B19 .... 89 J8
Hatchford Av HIA/OLT B92 .... 128 A2
Hatchford Brook Rd
HIA/OLT B92 .... 128 A2
Hatch Heath Cl WMBN WV5 .... 64 D6
Hateley Dr
ETTPK/GDPK/PENN WV4 .... 66 C1
Hatfield Cl ERDW/GRVHL B23 .... 72 B6
REDE B98 .... 197 J4
Hatfield Rd HAG/WOL DY9 .... 120 A1
LOZ/NWT B19 .... 89 H5
Hathaway Cl
RCOVN/BALC/EX CV7 .... 150 F3
WLNHL WV13 .... 51 K5
Hathaway Dr NUN CV11 .... 99 H4
WWCK CV34 .... 199 J3
Hathaway Gv MGN/WHC B75 .... 56 E1
SHLY B90 .... 146 F4
TLHL/CAN CV4 .... 152 B4
Hatherden Dr WALM/CURD B76 .... 73 L3
Hatherell Rd RLSS CV31 .... 201 J8
Hathersage Rd PBAR/PBCH B42 .... 71 H6
Hatherton Cft CNCK/NC WS11 .... 16 A4
Hatherton Gdns WOLVN WV10 .... 36 C3
Hatherton Rd BILS/COS WV14 .... 51 K7
CNCK/NC WS11 .... 15 M4
PENK ST19 .... 10 D4
WSL WS1 .... 4 F1
Hatherton St GTWY WS6 .... 24 A3
RUSH/SHEL WS4 .... 53 J2
WSL WS1 .... 4 F1
Hatters Dr ATHST CV9 .... 63 H3
Hattersley Gv SPARK B11 .... 126 E2
Hatton Cl RWWCK/WEL CV35 .... 198 B3
Hatton Crs WNSFLD WV11 .... 36 E6
Hatton Gdns PBAR/PBCH B42 .... 49 K2
CNCK/NC WS11 .... 15 L4
Hattons Gv CDSL WV8 .... 34 F3
Hatton St BILS/COS WV14 .... 67 J1

Haughton Rd
 BFLD/HDSWWD B20 .... 89 G4
Haunch La MOS/BIL B13 .... 125 K7
 WALM/CURD B76 .... 75 L5
Haunchwood Dr
 WALM/CURD B76 .... 73 K6
Haunchwood Park Dr
 NUNW/HART CV10 .... 97 J1
Haunchwood Rd
 NUNW/HART CV10 .... 98 B1
Havacre La BILS/COS WV14 .... 67 C3
Havefield Av LICHS WS14 .... 21 H6
Havelock Cl BDMR/CCFT WV3 .. 49 K5 🖸
Havelock Rd
 BFLD/HDSWWD B20 .... 89 G3
 SPARK B11 .... 126 C1
 WASH/WDE B8 .... 90 C8 🖸
Haven Cft GTB/HAM B43 ...... 70 B5 🖸
Haven Dr ACGN B27 .... 126 F2 🖸
The Haven ALE/KHTH/YWD B14 .. 146 B1
 BKHL/PFLD WV2 .... 2 F9
 STRBR DY8 .... 101 H3
Haverford Dr RBRY B45 .... 142 F7 🖸
Havergal Wk HALE B63 .... 120 F1
Haverhill Cl BLOX/PEL WS3 .... 38 E2
Hawbridge Cl SHLY B90 .... 147 M7 🖸
Hawbush Rd BLOX/PEL WS3 .... 39 J7
 BRLYHL DY5 .... 101 L3
Hawcroft Gv BKDE/SHDE B34 .. 92 A7
Hawes La BLKHTH/ROWR B65 .. 103 M1
Hawes Rd WSL WS1 .... 5 C9
Haweswater Dr KGSWFD DY6 .. 83 H7 🖸
Hawfield Cl OLDBY B69 .... 86 A6 🖸
Hawfield Gv CSCFLD/WYGN B72 .. 73 C6
Hawfield Rd OLDBY B69 .... 86 A6
Hawfinch TAM/AM/WIL B77 .... 46 E8 🖸
Hawfinch Ri KIDD DY10 .... 161 L3
Hawford Av KIDD DY10 .... 137 L8
Hawk Cl NUN CV11 .... 99 M5
Hawker Dr CVALE B35 .... 91 K3
Hawkesbury Cl REDE B98 ...... 189 H8 🖸
Hawkesbury La
 RCOVN/BALC/EX CV7 .... 117 H8
Hawkesbury Rd SHLY B90 ...... 146 D4
Hawkes Cl SLYOAK B29 .... 124 E5
Hawkesford Cl CBROM B36 .... 91 L5 🖸
 FOAKS/STRLY B74 .... 56 F4
Hawkesford Rd STETCH B33 .... 110 B2 🖸
Hawkes La HHTH/SAND B71 .... 68 E6 🖸
Hawkesley Crs NFLD/LBR B31 .. 143 K5
Hawkesley Dr NFLD/LBR B31 .. 143 K5
Hawkesley End
 HWK/WKHTH B38 .... 144 B5
Hawkesley Mill La
 NFLD/LBR B31 .... 143 K3
Hawkes Mill La COVW CV5 .... 132 E3
Hawkesmoor Dr LICHS WS14 .. 21 H5
Hawkes St BORD B9 .... 108 B4
Hawkestone Crs WBROM B70 .. 68 D7
Hawkestone Rd SLYOAK B29 .. 123 L6
Hawkeswell Cl HIA/OLT B92 .... 127 J5
Hawkeswell La
 CSHL/WTROR B46 .... 111 M2
Hawkesworth Dr KNWTH CV8 .. 176 E7
Hawkeyard Rd
 ERDE/BCHGN B24 .... 90 C4
Hawkhurst Rd
 ALE/KHTH/YWD B14 .... 145 K3
Hawkinge Dr CVALE B35 .... 91 L1
Hawkins Cl DIG/EDG B5 .... 107 J7 🖸
 LICH WS13 .... 20 F3 🖸
 RUGBYS/DCH CV22 .... 183 J4 🖸
Hawkins Cft TPTN/OCK DY4 .... 85 L2 🖸
Hawkins Dr CNCK/NC WS11 .... 24 A1
Hawkins Rd COVW CV5 .... 8 A6
Hawkins St WBROM B70 .... 68 E5
Hawkley Cl WOLV WV1 .... 50 F3 🖸
Hawkley Rd WOLV WV1 .... 50 F3
Hawkmoor Gdns
 HWK/WKHTH B38 .... 144 E5 🖸
Hawks Cl GTWY WS6 .... 24 B3
Hawksford Crs BNTWD WS7 .... 10 M6
Hawks Green La CNCK/NC WS11 .. 16 E3
Hawkshead Dr DOR/KN B93 .... 148 D7
Hawkside TAM/AM/WIL B77 .... 46 F5
Hawksmoor Dr
 DUNHL/THL/PER WV6 .... 48 B2
Hawkstone Cl KIDDW DY11 .... 137 H4
Hawkstone Cl CDSL WV8 .... 34 B8
Hawkswell Av WMBN WV5 ...... 64 E3 🖸
Hawkswell Dr WLNHL WV13 .... 51 K5
Hawkswood Dr
 DARL/WED WS10 .... 67 M2
 RCOVN/BALC/EX CV7 .... 150 F6
Hawkswood Gv
 ALE/KHTH/YWD B14 .... 145 M2 🖸
Hawksworth Dr COV CV1 .... 8 B3
Hawkyard Ct CNCK/NC WS11 .. 16 E1 🖸
Hawnby Gv WALM/CURD B76 .. 73 L3
Hawne Cl HALE B63 .... 103 J7 🖸
The Hawnelands HALE B63 .... 103 K8 🖸
Hawne La HALE B63 .... 103 J7 🖸
Hawskford Crs WOLVN WV10 .. 36 B6
Hawthorn Av ATHST CV9 .... 61 C8 🖸
 GTWY WS6 .... 24 E4 🖸
Hawthorn Brook Wy
 ERDW/GRVHL B23 .... 72 C5
Hawthorn Cl BORD B9 .... 107 M4
 ERDW/GRVHL B23 .... 72 C6
 LICH WS13 .... 21 H5
Hawthorn Coppice
 HAG/WOL DY9 .... 119 L2
Hawthorn Cft LGLYGN/QTN B68.. 105 H6
Hawthorne Av CRTAM B79 ...... 31 L5
 RCOVN/BALC/EX CV7 .... 96 F5 🖸
Hawthorne Cl KNWTH CV8 .... 180 E1
Hawthorne Crs BNTWD WS7 .... 18 E7
Hawthorne Dr HLYWD B47 ...... 145 M7
Hawthorne Gv SEDG DY3 .... 84 B3 🖸
Hawthorne La CDSL WV8 .... 34 C4
Hawthorne Rd
 BKHL/PFLD WV2 .... 50 B7 🖸
 BVILLE B30 .... 124 D4
 CBROM B36 .... 92 C6
 DUDN DY1 .... 85 G1
 EDG B15 .... 106 C6

 GTWY WS6 .... 24 C1
 HALE B63 .... 121 J3
 HEDN WS12 .... 12 B5
 HEDN WS12 .... 17 K2
 SHHTH WV12 .... 38 B6
 WNSFLD WV11 .... 37 L2 🖸
Hawthorne Ter
 NUNW/HART CV10 .... 80 D8
Hawthorne Wy KINVER DY7 .... 118 A2
Hawthorn Gv KIDDW DY11 .... 136 E7
Hawthorn La TLHL/CAN CV4 .. 152 C2
Hawthorn Pk
 BFLD/HDSWWD B20 .... 88 C2
Hawthorn Pl WSLW WS2 .... 52 C2
Hawthorn Rd BRGRVW B61 .... 165 L8
 BRLYHL DY5 .... 102 C5 🖸
 CSCFLD/WYGN B72 .... 73 G4
 DARL/WED WS10 .... 68 D1
 DSYBK/YTR WS5 .... 53 K8
 FOAKS/STRLY B74 .... 55 L4
 KGSTG B44 .... 71 L6
 REDW B97 .... 195 L1
 RLSS CV31 .... 200 D7
 RUSH/SHEL WS4 .... 39 M5
 TPTN/OCK DY4 .... 67 L5
 WOLV WV1 .... 50 F5 🖸

Hazel Cft
 CHWD/FDBR/MGN B37 ...... 110 F4
 NFLD/LBR B31 .... 143 L2
Hazelcroft POL/KGSB/FAZ B78 .. 60 A6 🖸
Hazeldene Rd HALE B63 .... 121 J3
 STECH B33 .... 110 C6 🖸
Hazel Dr HEDN WS12 .... 13 L7
 HLYWD B47 .... 145 M7
Hazeley Cl HRBN B17 .... 105 K6
Hazel Gdns ACGN B27 .... 127 C3 🖸
 CDSL WV8 .... 34 E1 🖸
Hazelgarth TAM/AM/WIL B77 .. 46 E5
Hazel Gv BDWTH CV12 .... 117 H2
 BILS/COS WV14 .... 51 J6
 HOCK/TIA B94 .... 172 A7
 LICHS WS14 .... 21 G6
 STRBR DY8 .... 119 G2
 WBROM B70 .... 87 G4 🖸
 WMBN WV5 .... 64 C6
Hazelhurst Rd
 ALE/KHTH/YWD B14 .... 125 J5
 CBROM B36 .... 148 E8 🖸
Hazel La GTWY WS6 .... 24 F3
Hazell Wy NUNW/HART CV10 .. 98 E4
Hazelmere Dr
 BDMR/CCFT WV3 .... 48 E4 🖸
 BNTWD WS7 .... 26 D1
Hazelmere Rd
 HLGN/YWD B28 .... 126 D5 🖸
Hazeloak Rd SHLY B90 .... 146 E4
Hazel Rd BDMR/CCFT WV3 .... 49 J6
 COVN CV6 .... 154 C4
 DUDN DY1 .... 85 G3
 KGSWFD DY6 .... 83 J8
 NUNW/HART CV10 .... 80 B8
 RBRY B45 .... 142 D7
 REDW B97 .... 188 A8
 TPTN/OCK DY4 .... 68 A4
Hazelton Cl BRGRVE B60 ...... 166 A5 🖸
 SOLH B91 .... 147 M4 🖸
Hazelton Rd BRGRVE B60 ...... 165 M5
Hazeltree Cft ACGN B27 .... 126 F3 🖸
Hazeltree Gv DOR/KN B93 .... 172 C2
Hazelville Gv HLGN/YWD B28 .. 126 E7
Hazelville Rd HLGN/YWD B28 .. 126 E7
Hazelwell Crs BVILLE B30 ...... 124 F7
Hazelwell Fordrough
 BVILLE B30 .... 124 F6
Hazelwell La BVILLE B30 .... 124 E6
Hazelwell Rd BVILLE B30 ...... 124 E7
Hazelwood Cl GTWY WS6 ...... 24 B3 🖸
 KIDDW DY11 .... 160 E1
Hazelwood Dr WNSFLD WV11 .. 36 E8
Hazelwood Gv SHHTH WV12 .. 38 B8
Hazelwood Rd ACGN B27 ...... 126 F3
 DUDN DY1 .... 66 D8
 FOAKS/STRLY B74 .... 55 H4
Hazlemere Cl COVW CV5 ...... 152 F1 🖸
Hazlemere Dr FOAKS/STRLY B74 .. 56 L4
Hazlemere Gv CNCK/NC WS11 .. 15 M5
Hazlitt Gv BVILLE B30 .... 144 B1 🖸
Headborough Rd COVE CV2 .... 134 E8
Headingley Rd HDSW B21 ...... 88 C3
Headington Av COVN CV6 ...... 133 J3
Headland Dr WASH/WDE B8 .... 90 B8 🖸
Headland Rd BDMR/CCFT WV3 .. 48 C4
The Headlands COVW CV5 .... 153 H1
 FOAKS/STRLY B74 .... 56 A2
Headless Cross Dr REDW B97 .. 196 B4
Headley Cft HWK/WKHTH B38 .. 144 B5
Headley Heath La
 HWK/WKHTH B38 .... 144 F6
Headley Ri SHLY B90 .... 147 H3
Heale Cl HALE B63 .... 102 E6 🖸
Healey TAM/AM/WIL B77 .... 46 C3
Health Centre Rd
 TLHL/CAN CV4 .... 177 G1
Heanley La ATHST CV9 .... 61 H6
 ATHST CV9 .... 77 H1
Heanor Cft AST/WIT B6 .... 89 M5 🖸
Hearsall Common COVW CV5 .. 153 J3
Hearsall La COVW CV5 .... 153 K3
Heartland Ms
 BLKHTH/ROWR B65 .... 103 M3 🖸
Heartlands Pkwy
 VAUX/NECH B7 .... 90 A8
Heartlands Pl WASH/WDE B8 .. 108 C1 🖸
Heart of England Wy
 CSHL/WTROR B46 .... 76 C8
 CSHL/WTROR B46 .... 94 F5
 DOR/KN B93 .... 173 M7
 KNWTH CV8 .... 174 B2
 LICH WS13 .... 19 M4
 POL/KGSB/FAZ B78 .... 45 K8
 POL/KGSB/FAZ B78 .... 60 B8 🖸
 RCOVN/BALC/EX CV7 .... 131 C2
 WALM/CURD B76 .... 59 L7
Heath Acres DARL/WED WS10 .. 68 A1
Heath Av BDWTH CV12 .... 116 C4
 LICHS WS14 .... 30 A2
Heathbank Dr HEDN WS12 .... 13 L7
Heath Bridge Cl BLOX/PEL WS3 .. 39 L5
Heathbrook Av KGSWFD DY6 .. 82 F6
Heathcliff Rd DUDS DY2 .... 85 K6
 SPARK B11 .... 126 D1
Heath Cl ALDR WS9 .... 27 J8
 BRGRVE B60 .... 185 J7
 BVILLE B30 .... 124 B8
 TPTN/OCK DY4 .... 67 M8
Heathcote Cl SOLH B91 .... 147 J2
Heathcote La WWCK CV34 .... 199 L8
Heathcote Rd BVILLE B30 ...... 124 E8
Heathcote St COVN CV6 .... 133 L6
Heath Crs COVN CV6 .... 134 D8 🖸
Heath Cft NFLD/LBR B31 ...... 143 L6
Heath Croft Rd MGN/WHC B75 .. 57 G4
Heath Dr KIDD DY10 .... 137 M4
Heath End Rd HAG/WOL DY9 .. 141 C6
 NUNW/HART CV10 .... 98 D2
Heather Av DSYBK/YTR WS5 .. 69 M1
Heather Cl CBROM B36 .... 92 D2 🖸
 NUNW/HART CV10 .... 98 D2 🖸
 RUGBYS/DCH CV22 .... 183 J4 🖸
 WNSFLD WV11 .... 37 J8
Heather Court Gdns
 FOAKS/STRLY B74 .... 56 E5
Heather Cft KGSTG B44 .... 71 K4
Heather Dl MOS/BIL B13 ...... 125 G3 🖸

Heather Dr BDWTH CV12 ...... 116 C3
 HEDN WS12 .... 12 B8
 RBRY B45 .... 142 D7
Heather Gv SHHTH WV12 ...... 52 C1
 SOLH B91 .... 148 C1
Heatherleigh Rd CBROM B36 .. 92 D5 🖸
Heather Ms HEDN WS12 .... 12 E5
Heather Rd BLOX/PEL WS3 .... 38 D5
 COVE CV2 .... 134 F3
 COVS CV3 .... 156 A6
 DUDN DY1 .... 85 G1
 GTB/HAM B43 .... 70 A5
 HEDN WS12 .... 12 E4
 SMHTH B10 .... 108 D5
 SMTHWKW B67 .... 87 J8
Heather Va HEDN WS12 .... 13 H7
Heath Farm Rd CDSL WV8 .... 34 F3 🖸
 STRBR DY8 .... 119 J2
Heathfield Av
 BFLD/HDSWWD B20 .... 88 F5 🖸
Heathfield Cl CDYHTH B64 .... 103 K3
 DOR/KN B93 .... 148 E8 🖸
Heathfield Crs KIDDW DY11 .. 160 F1
Heathfield Dr BLOX/PEL WS3 .. 38 F3 🖸
Heathfield Gdns STRBR DY8 .. 119 K1
Heathfield La DARL/WED WS10 .. 52 A7
Heathfield La West
 DARL/WED WS10 .... 51 M8
Heathfield Rd
 ALE/KHTH/YWD B14 .... 125 J5
 BEWD DY12 .... 160 A1
 BFLD/HDSWWD B20 .... 89 G4
 COVW CV5 .... 153 C3
 FOAKS/STRLY B74 .... 56 D2
 HALE B63 .... 121 J2
 LOZ/NWT B19 .... 88 F6
 REDW B97 .... 195 L4
Heathfield Wy CDYHTH B64 .... 103 K4
Heath Gap Rd CNCK/NC WS11 .. 16 D7
Heath Gdns SOLH B91 .... 128 B7 🖸
Heath Gn DUDN DY1 .... 66 D8
Heathgreen Cl
 CHWD/FDBR/MGN B37 ...... 111 H2 🖸
Heath Green Gv WSNGN B18 .. 106 C1 🖸
Heath Green Rd WSNGN B18 .. 106 C1
Heath Gv CDSL WV8 .... 34 F2 🖸
Heath Hill Rd
 DUNHL/THL/PER WV6 .... 48 C4
Heath House Dr WMBN WV5 .. 64 B8
Heath House La CDSL WV8 .... 33 J8
Heathland Av BKDE/SHDE B34.. 91 L6
Heathland Cl HEDN WS12 ...... 17 H3 🖸
Heathlands WMBN WV5 .... 64 B8 🖸
Heathlands Cl KGSWFD DY6 .. 83 J5 🖸
Heathlands Rd SCFLD/BOLD B73 .. 72 D3
The Heathlands
 BLKHTH/ROWR B65 .... 104 A4 🖸
 STRBR DY8 .... 119 M1 🖸
 WMBN WV5 .... 64 B8
Heath La HHTH/SAND B71 .... 69 H6
 KIDD DY10 .... 162 A5
 RRUGBY CV23 .... 157 H3
 STRBR DY8 .... 119 L2 🖸
Heathleigh Rd
 HWK/WKHTH B38 .... 144 A5
Heathley La POL/KGSB/FAZ B78.. 45 H7
Heathmere Av YDLY B25 .... 109 H5
Heathmere Dr
 CHWD/FDBR/MGN B37 ...... 110 D3
Heath Mill Cl SEDG DY3 .... 82 B1 🖸
Heath Mill La BORD B9 .... 7 L7
Heath Mill Rd SEDG DY3 .... 82 B1
Heath Rd ALE/KHTH/YWD B14.. 145 L4
 BVILLE B30 .... 124 B8
 DARL/WED WS10 .... 52 C5
 DUDS DY2 .... 102 F2 🖸
 HLYWD B47 .... 145 L6
 SHHTH WV12 .... 38 B5
 SOLH B91 .... 148 A1
Heath Rd South NFLD/LBR B31 .. 143 M1
Heathside Dr BLOX/PEL WS3 .. 39 L1 🖸
 HWK/WKHTH B38 .... 144 F4
Heath St BLKHTH/ROWR B65 .. 104 A4
 CRTAM B79 .... 32 A8
 HEDN WS12 .... 12 C6
 STRBR DY8 .... 101 K8
 WSNGN B18 .... 88 B8
Heath St South WSNGN B18 .. 106 D1 🖸
Heath Ter RLSN CV32 .... 200 B4
Heath Vw BNTWD WS7 .... 18 E4
Heath Wy BKDE/SHDE B34 .... 91 K6
 CNCK/NC WS11 .... 17 C3
Heathy Farm Cl
 RIDG/WDGT B32 .... 122 F4 🖸
Heathy Ri RIDG/WDGT B32 .... 122 E3
Heaton Cl WOLVN WV10 ...... 22 C8
Heaton Dr EDG B15 .... 106 C5
Heaton Rd SOLH B91 .... 127 K6
Heaton St WSNGN B18 .... 88 F8
Hebden TAM/AM/WIL B77 .... 46 F5
Hebden Av WWCK CV34 .... 199 J4
Hebden Gv HLGN/YWD B28 .. 146 C2 🖸
 WNSFLD WV11 .... 37 M4
Hebden Wy NUN CV11 .... 99 L3
Heckley Rd
 RCOVN/BALC/EX CV7 .... 116 E6
Hedera Cl DSYBK/YTR WS5 .... 69 M2 🖸
Hedgefield Gv HALE B63 ...... 121 G1
Hedgefield Wy TLHL/CAN CV4 .. 152 D5
Hedgerow Cl HEDN WS12 ...... 12 D6
Hedgerow Dr KGSWFD DY6 .... 83 H4
The Hedgerows
 NUNW/HART CV10 .... 80 D7
 RMSLY B62 .... 141 K1
 TAM/AM/WIL B77 .... 46 D5 🖸
Hedgerow Wk COVN CV6 ...... 133 M1 🖸
The Hedges WMBN WV5 .... 64 C7 🖸
Hedges Wy BRGRVE B60 ...... 185 M4 🖸
Hedgetree Cft
 CHWD/FDBR/MGN B37 ...... 111 C3
Hedingham Gv
 CHWD/FDBR/MGN B37 ...... 111 H3
Hedley Cft CVALE B35 .... 91 M1
Hedley Gv STETCH B33 .... 109 L1

CNCK/NC WS11 .... 16 D3
 HEDN WS12 .... 17 H3
Hednesford St CNCK/NC WS11 .. 16 C4
Heeley Rd SLYOAK B29 .... 124 D3
Heemstede La RLSN CV32 ...... 200 E8
Heenan Gv LICH WS13 .... 20 D3 🖸
Heera Cl COVN CV6 .... 134 B6 🖸
Helena Cl NUNW/HART CV10 .. 98 D2
Helena St CBHAMW B1 .... 6 C4 🖸
Helenny Cl WOLVN WV10 ...... 36 C8
Helen St COVN CV6 .... 134 D7
Hele Rd COVS CV3 .... 154 B7
Helford Cl TPTN/OCK DY4 .... 85 H1
Hellaby Cl CSCFLD/WYGN B72 .. 73 C1 🖸
Hellidon Cl RLSN CV32 .... 200 E3 🖸
Hellier Av TPTN/OCK DY4 .... 85 M1
Hellier Rd WOLVN WV10 .... 36 C3
Hellier St DUDS DY2 .... 85 C5 🖸
Helming Dr WOLV WV1 .... 50 F2
Helmingham CRTAM B79 ...... 31 G6
Helmsdale Rd RLSN CV32 ...... 192 F8 🖸
Helmsdale Wy SEDG DY3 ...... 66 C6
Helmsley Cl BRLYHL DY5 ...... 102 A5 🖸
Helmsley Rd WNSFLD WV11 .. 37 L5 🖸
Helmswood Dr
 CHWD/FDBR/MGN B37 ...... 111 G5
Helston Cl CRTAM B79 .... 32 A5 🖸
 DSYBK/YTR WS5 .... 54 B6
 NUN CV11 .... 81 K8
 STRBR DY8 .... 101 C3
Helstone Gv SPARK B11 .... 126 E2 🖸
Helston Rd DSYBK/YTR WS5 .. 54 A7
Hembs Crs GTB/HAM B43 ...... 70 A5
Hemdale NUN CV11 .... 99 L1
Hemingford Rd COVE CV2 .... 135 K5
Heming Rd REDE B98 .... 197 J6
Hemlingford Cft
 CHWD/FDBR/MGN B37 ...... 110 E6 🖸
Hemlingford Rd
 CHWD/FDBR/MGN B37 ...... 92 C7
 POL/KGSB/FAZ B78 .... 76 B1 🖸
 WALM/CURD B76 .... 73 K6
Hemlock Wy CNCK/NC WS11 .. 16 F3
 HEDN WS12 .... 17 C2
Hemmings Cl RLSS CV31 ...... 201 J3 🖸
 STRBR DY8 .... 101 K8 🖸
 WOLVN WV10 .... 3 K2
Hemmings St
 DARL/WED WS10 .... 52 A5 🖸
Hemming Cl KIDDW DY11 .... 161 C1
Hemming Wy KIDD DY10 ...... 163 J5
Hemplands Rd STRBR DY8 .... 101 K8 🖸
Hempole La TPTN/OCK DY4 .. 68 B7
Hemsby Cl TLHL/CAN CV4 .... 152 E6
Hemsworth Dr BDWTH CV12 .. 117 M3
Hemyock Rd SLYOAK B29 ...... 123 M5
Henbury Rd ACGN B27 .... 127 H2 🖸
Henderson Cl LICHS WS14 .... 21 H6 🖸
Henderson Wk
 TPTN/OCK DY4 .... 67 M5 🖸
Hendon Wy
 BLKHTH/ROWR B65 .... 104 A4
 WOLVN WV10 .... 36 C5
Hendon Cl SEDG DY3 .... 84 B3 🖸
 WOLVN WV10 .... 36 C5
Hendon Rd SPARK B11 .... 107 M8
Hendre Cl TLHL/CAN CV4 ...... 153 H3
Heneage St VAUX/NECH B7 .... 7 L1 🖸
Heneage St West VAUX/NECH B7 .. 7 K2
Henfield Cl WNSFLD WV11 .... 37 H7 🖸
Hengham Rd
 LGN/SDN/BHAMAIR B26 ...... 109 L4
Hen La COVN CV6 .... 134 B2
Henley Cl BLOX/PEL WS3 ...... 39 J4
 BNTWD WS7 .... 18 F8
 CRTAM B79 .... 32 A7
 NUN CV11 .... 81 K5
 SCFLD/BOLD B73 .... 72 C5
 TPTN/OCK DY4 .... 68 B8 🖸
Henley Crs SOLH B91 .... 127 M6 🖸
Henley Dr MGN/WHC B75 .... 56 E2 🖸
Henley Mill La COVE CV2 ...... 135 C6
Henley Rd COVE CV2 .... 135 C5
 RLSS CV31 .... 200 F8 🖸
 WOLVN WV10 .... 35 M4
Henley St SPARK B11 .... 107 L6
Henlow Cl TPTN/OCK DY4 .... 67 H8
Henlow Rd
 ALE/KHTH/YWD B14 .... 145 K3
The Hennalls CBROM B36 ...... 91 K6
Hennals Av REDW B97 .... 195 K2
Henn Dr TPTN/OCK DY4 .... 67 J4
Henne Dr BILS/COS WV14 ...... 67 C4
Henney Cl PENK ST19 .... 14 D7 🖸
Henn St TPTN/OCK DY4 .... 67 L5 🖸
Henrietta St CBHAMNW B3 ...... 6 F2
 COVN CV6 .... 134 C3
 LOZ/NWT B19 .... 6 F2
Henry Boteler Rd
 TLHL/CAN CV4 .... 152 F6
Henry Rd YDLY B25 .... 109 G7
Henry St COV CV1 .... 8 F3
 KNWTH CV8 .... 176 E8
 NUN CV11 .... 10 E6
 RUGBYN/HIL CV21 .... 183 L2 🖸
 WSLW WS2 .... 4 C3
Hensborough SHLY B90 .... 146 E7
Hensel Dr BDMR/CCFT WV3 .. 49 C5 🖸
Henshaw Gv YDLY B25 .... 109 C6 🖸
Henshaw Rd SMTH B10 .... 108 B5 🖸
Henson Rd BDWTH CV12 ...... 116 C4
Henstead St DIG/EDG B5 .... 6 F9
Hentland Cl REDE B98 .... 197 H1 🖸
Henwood Cl
 DUNHL/THL/PER WV6 .... 49 J2 🖸
Henwood La SOLH B91 .... 148 F1 🖸
Henwood Rd
 DUNHL/THL/PER WV6 .... 49 C2
Hepburn Cl ALDR WS9 .... 54 L1 🖸
Hepburn Edge
 ERDE/BCHGN B24 .... 90 F1 🖸
Hepworth Cl
 DUNHL/THL/PER WV6 .... 48 D1 🖸
Hepworth Rd COVS CV3 .... 155 L4 🖸
Herald Av COVW CV5 .... 153 G4
Herald Wy COVS CV3 .... 155 L6 🖸
Herbert Austin Dr BRGRVE B60 .. 166 C4
Herbert Rd ALDR WS9 .... 40 E4
 HDSW B21 .... 88 D4

SMTH B10 .... 108 A4
SMTHKW B67 .... 105 L4
SOLH B91 .... 147 M2
Herbert's La KNWTH CV8 .... 176 E8

Herbert Park Rd
DARL/WED WS10 .... 51 M7
Herbert St BILS/COS WV14 .. 50 F7
NUNW/HART CV10 .... 98 C2
REDW B97 .... 196 C1
WBROM B70 .... 87 H2
WOLV WV1 .... 3 C3
Herbhill Cl
ETTPK/GDPK/PENN WV4 ... 66 B1
Hereford Av BHTH/HG B12 .. 107 L7
Hereford Cl ALDR WS9 ..... 40 E5
KIDDW DY11 .... 136 E8
NUNW/HART CV10 .... 98 C1
RBRY B45 .... 142 E3
Hereford Pl HHTH/SAND B71 .. 68 F6
Hereford Rd DUDS DY2 .... 103 J2
HEDN WS12 .... 16 F1
LGLYGN/QTN B68 .... 104 F6
Hereford Sq WASH/WDE B8 . 90 A8
Hereford St WSLW WS2 .... 53 J1
Hereford Wy
POL/KGSB/FAZ B78 .... 45 L3
Hereward Rd RMSLY B62 ... 103 M8
Heritage Cl LGLYGN/QTN B68 105 G1
Heritage Ct LICHS WS14 .... 21 H7
TLHL/CAN CV4 .... 177 H2
Heritage Wy STETCH B33 .. 110 B2
Hermes Cl RLSS CV31 ..... 200 C8
Hermes Crs COVE CV2 .... 135 H6
Hermes Cl LICH WS13 ..... 21 H3
Hermitage La
POL/KGSB/FAZ B78 .... 47 J4
Hermitage Rd COVE CV2 ... 155 C1
EDG B15 .... 106 A5
ERDW/GRVHL B23 .... 90 B2
SOLH B91 .... 128 A8
The Hermitage SOLH B91 .. 128 A7
Hermitage Wy KNWTH CV8 .. 191 L1
Hermit's Cft COVS CV3 .... 9 H9
Hermit St SEDG DY3 ...... 84 B1
Hernall Cft
LGN/SDN/BHAMAIR B26 ... 109 L6
Herne Cl WSNGN B18 ..... 106 E1
Hernefield Rd BKDE/SHDE B34 91 H4
Hernehurst Rd WDGT B32 .. 105 G8
Hern Rd BRLYHL DY5 ..... 102 A7
Heron Cl ALVE B48 .... 167 L6
SHLY B90 .... 171 H2
Herondale HEDN WS12 .... 16 F1
Herondale Rd
LGN/SDN/BHAMAIR B26 ... 109 K7
STRBR DY8 .... 119 C1
Heronfield Cl REDE B98 ... 189 C7
Heronfield Dr NFLD/LBR B31 143 K7
Heronfield Wy SOLH B91 .. 128 C8
Heron Ml BLOX/PEL WS3 ... 39 J2
Heron Rd LGLYGN/QTN B68 . 104 E3
The Heronry
DUNHL/THL/PER WV6 ..... 48 D3
Herons Wy SLYOAK B29 ... 124 A2
Heronswood Dr BRLYHL DY5 102 B4
Heronswood Rd KIDD DY10 . 161 K3
RBRY B45 .... 142 F7
Heronville Dr WBROM B70 . 68 E6
Heronville Rd WBROM B70 . 68 C7
Heron Wy RBRY B45 ...... 142 C6
Herrick Rd COVE CV2 ..... 155 H2
WASH/WDE B8 .... 90 C4
Herrick St BDMR/CCFT WV3 . 2 D6
Herringshaw Cft
WALM/CURD B76 .... 73 J2
Hertford Pl COV CV1 ..... 8 C5
Hertford St BHTH/HG B12 .. 107 L8
Hertford Wy DOR/KN B93 .. 172 F1
Hervey Gv ERDE/BCHGN B24 73 H7
Hesket Av LGLYGN/QTN B68 105 C4
Hesketh Crs ERDW/GRVHL B23 72 A8
Hesleden TAM/AM/WIL B77 . 46 F5
Heslop Cl COVS CV3 ...... 155 K5
Hessian Cl BILS/COS WV14 . 66 F3
Heston Av PBAR/PBCH B42 . 70 E5
Hever Av KGSTG B44 ..... 71 L4
Hever Cl DUDN DY1 ...... 84 C2
Hewell Av BRGRVE B60 ... 185 K6
Hewell Cl KGSWFD DY6 ... 83 H4
NFLD/LBR B31 .... 143 K6
REDW B97 .... 187 C7
Hewell La BRGRVE B60 ... 186 E3
RBRY B45 .... 167 C5
REDW B97 .... 187 J8
Hewell Rd RBRY B45 ..... 167 H5
REDW B97 .... 188 B8
Hewitt Av COVN CV6 ..... 133 M8
Hewitt Cl LICH WS13 ..... 20 E3
Hewitt St DARL/WED WS10 . 52 A7
Hewston Cft HEDN WS12 .. 17 H1
Hexby Cl COVE CV2 ...... 135 L7
Hexham Wy DUDN DY1 ... 84 D3
Hexton Cl SHLY B90 ..... 146 B3
Hexworthy Av COVS CV3 .. 153 M8
Heybarnes Rd SMHTH B10 . 108 C6
Heybrook Cl COVE CV2 ... 135 C6
Heycott Gv HWK/WKHTH B38 145 C3
Heycroft TLHL/CAN CV4 ... 177 H1
Heydon Rd BRGRVE B60 .. 186 D4
BRLYHL DY5 .... 83 M8
Heyford Gv SOLH B91 .... 148 A5
Heyford Leys
RUGBYS/DCH CV22 .... 183 K7
Heyford Wy CVALE B35 ... 73 M8
Heygate Wy ALDR WS9 ... 41 C5
Heynesfield Rd STECH B33 . 110 A2
Heythrop Gv MOS/BIL B13 . 126 B5
Heyville Cft KNWTH CV8 .. 192 H1
Heywood Cl COVN CV6 ... 134 E6
Hibbert Cl RUGBYS/DCH CV22 183 K4
Hickman Av WOLV WV1 ... 50 D4
Hickman Gdns
LDYWD/EDGR B16 .... 106 C4
Hickman Rd BILS/COS WV14 51 C8
BRLYHL DY5 .... 102 A1
NUNW/HART CV10 .... 97 K1

SPARK B11 .... 107 M7
TPTN/OCK DY4 .... 67 K5
Hickman's Cl BDWTH CV12 . 103 J3
Hickmans Cl RMSLY B62 .. 104 E7
Hickman St HAG/WOL DY9 . 102 A7
Hickmerelands La SEDG DY3 66 B5
Hickory Ct CNCK/NC WS11 . 17 C3
Hickory Dr HRBN B17 ..... 105 M3
Hicks Cl WWCK CV34 ..... 199 J3
Hidcote Av WALM/CURD B76 73 L5
Hidcote Cl NUN CV11 ..... 99 K5
RLSS CV31 .... 201 C8
Hidcote Gv
CHWD/FDBR/MGN B37 .... 110 E6
STETCH B33 .... 110 A5
Hidcote Rd KNWTH CV8 ... 177 G7
Hidson Rd ERDW/GRVHL B23 90 A1
Higgins Av BILS/COS WV14 . 67 H3
Higgins La RIDG/WDGT B32 . 105 C8
Higgs Field Crs
BLKHTH/ROWR B65 .... 103 M4
Higgs Rd WNSFLD WV11 .. 37 L4
Higham La NUN CV11 ..... 81 J7
Higham's Cl
BLKHTH/ROWR B65 .... 103 M2
Higham Wy WOLVN WV10 . 36 C7
High Arcal Dr SEDG DY3 .. 66 D6
High Arcal Rd SEDG DY3 .. 83 K1
High Ash Cl
RCOVN/BALC/EX CV7 ..... 116 D6
High Av CDYHTH B64 ..... 103 K5
High Bank CNCK/NC WS11 . 16 C5
High Beech COVW CV5 ... 132 E7
High Beeches GTB/HAM B43 70 B4
Highbridge Rd DUDS DY2 . 102 F1
SCFLD/BOLD B73 .... 72 E4
High Brink Rd CSHL/WTROR B46 93 K6
Highbrook Cl COVEN WV9 . 35 L3
High Brow HRBN B17 ..... 105 M6
High Bullen DARL/WED WS10 68 D3
Highbury Av
BLKHTH/ROWR B65 .... 104 B2
Highbury Cl
BLKHTH/ROWR B65 .... 104 B2
Highbury Gn
NUNW/HART CV10 .... 80 A6
Highbury Rd
ALE/KHTH/YWD B14 ..... 125 H5
FOAKS/STRLY B74 .... 56 A2
LGLYGN/QTN B68 .... 86 F8
SMTHWK B66 .... 87 H6
High Clere CDYHTH B64 ... 103 L6
Highcliffe Rd TAM/AM/WIL B77 46 B5
Highcrest Cl NFLD/LBR B31 . 143 L6
High Cft ALDR WS9 .... 41 C8
Highcroft BLOX/PEL WS3 .. 25 M8
High Cft GTB/HAM B43 ... 70 A4
Highcroft Av STRBR DY8 .. 100 F2
Highcroft Cl HIA/OLT B92 . 128 A3
Highcroft Crs RLSN CV32 .. 200 A4
Highcroft Dr FOAKS/STRLY B74 56 C2
Highcroft Rd ERDW/GRVHL B23 90 C2
Highdown Crs SHLY B90 .. 147 L7
Highdown Rd RLSS CV31 .. 200 F7
High Elms La BRGRVE B60 . 194 C6
High Ercal Av BRLYHL DY5 . 102 A3
High Farm Rd HALE B63 .. 121 K2
RMSLY B62 .... 104 D5
Highfield RCOVN/BALC/EX CV7 131 G4
Highfield Av BILS/COS WV14 67 J1
BNTWD WS7 .... 18 F6
REDE B98 .... 196 B5
RUSH/SHEL WS4 .... 40 A5
TAM/AM/WIL B77 .... 32 E8
WOLVN WV10 .... 36 E3
Highfield Cl BNTWD WS7 .. 18 F6
HLGN/YWD B28 .... 126 B8
KNWTH CV8 .... 191 J1
Highfield Crs
BLKHTH/ROWR B65 .... 103 M5
HALE B63 .... 103 H7
WOLVN WV10 .... 36 F7
Highfield Dr ERDW/GRVHL B23 72 D6
Highfield La HAG/WOL DY9 140 E2
HALE B63 .... 121 L2
RCOVN/BALC/EX CV7 ..... 114 F4
RIDG/WDGT B32 .... 123 G1
Highfield Rd
ALE/KHTH/YWD B14 ..... 126 B8
BLKHTH/ROWR B65 .... 103 M4
BLOX/PEL WS3 .... 39 L1
BNTWD WS7 .... 18 F6
BRGRVW B61 .... 185 J5
COVE CV2 .... 9 M2
DUDS DY2 .... 85 J4
EDG B15 .... 106 E5
GTB/HAM B43 .... 70 A6
HALE B63 .... 103 H8
HEDN WS12 .... 17 J4
HLGN/YWD B28 .... 126 C7
KIDD DY10 .... 137 L5
MOS/BIL B13 .... 125 L2
NUN CV11 .... 99 H3
REDW B97 .... 196 B5
SEDG DY3 .... 66 B4
SMTHWK B67 .... 87 K8
STRBR DY8 .... 101 L3
TPTN/OCK DY4 .... 67 L6
WASH/WDE B8 .... 90 C8
Highfield Rd North
BLOX/PEL WS3 .... 25 K8
Highfields BNTWD WS7 ... 18 F6
BRGRVW B61 .... 185 J4
Highfields Dr BILS/COS WV14 67 H2
WMBN WV5 .... 64 E8
Highfields Gra GTWY WS6 . 24 B4
Highfields Pk GTWY WS6 .. 24 B4
Highfields Rd BILS/COS WV14 67 H2
SEDG DY3 .... 26 D1
The Highfields
DUNHL/THL/PER WV6 ... 48 E3
Highfield Ter RLSN CV32 .. 200 B4
Highfield Wy ALDR WS9 .. 41 G3
Highgate FOAKS/STRLY B74 55 M4
SEDG DY3 .... 66 C8
Highgate Av
ETTPK/GDPK/PENN WV4 . 49 H7
WSL WS1 .... 5 H6

Highgate Cl BHTH/HG B12 . 107 K6
KIDDW DY11 .... 160 E1
WSL WS1 .... 5 H7
Highgate Dr WSL WS1 ... 5 H8
Highgate Middleway
BHTH/HG B12 .... 107 K6
Highgate Pl BHTH/HG B12 . 107 L6
Highgate Rd BHTH/HG B12 . 107 L7
DUDS DY2 .... 84 D7
WSL WS1 .... 5 G8
Highgate St BHTH/HG B12 . 107 J6
CDYHTH B64 .... 103 J3
High Gra LICH WS13 .... 20 D4
High Gn CNCK/NC WS11 . 16 B4
Highgrove
DUNHL/THL/PER WV6 ... 49 G2
RUGBYS/DCH CV22 ..... 183 H6
TLHL/CAN CV4 .... 152 D8
Highgrove Ct KIDD DY10 . 137 L4
Highgrove Pl DUDN DY1 . 84 D3
High Haden Crs CDYHTH B64 103 L5
High Haden Rd CDYHTH B64 103 M5
High Heath Cl BVILLE B30 . 124 B8
High Hl WNSFLD WV11 ... 37 L3
High Holborn SEDG DY3 .. 66 B6
High House Dr RBRY B45 . 166 D2
High House La BRGRVE B60 186 E7
Highland Ms BILS/COS WV14 67 H4
Highland Rd CDYHTH B64 . 103 J3
COVW CV5 .... 153 K4
DUDN DY1 .... 84 E2
ERDW/GRVHL B23 .... 72 D8
GTB/HAM B43 .... 70 C2
HEDN WS12 .... 16 A1
KNWTH CV8 .... 177 G6
RLSN CV32 .... 200 A1
Highlands Cl KIDDW DY11 . 136 E8
WWCK CV34 .... 199 L5
SHLY B90 .... 147 J5
Highland Wy REDE B98 .. 196 E6
High Leasowes HALE B63 . 121 L1
Highley Cl KIDDW DY11 .. 160 F3
REDE B98 .... 197 J1
Highlow Av KIDDW DY11 . 137 C4
High Meadow Rd
HWK/WKHTH B38 .... 144 E3
High Mdw BRGRVE B60 .. 185 H6
DUNHL/THL/PER WV6 ... 49 G3
WMBN WV5 .... 64 E7
Highmoor Cl BILS/COS WV14 67 H2
SHHTH WV12 .... 37 M6
Highmoor Rd
BLKHTH/ROWR B65 ..... 103 M2
Highmore Dr RIDG/WDGT B32 123 C5
High Mount St HEDN WS12 . 12 F7
High Oak BRLYHL DY5 ... 84 A7
Highpark Av STRBR DY8 .. 101 H8
High Park Cl COVW CV5 .. 152 D2
SEDG DY3 .... 66 B4
SMTHWK B66 .... 87 M8
High Park Crs SEDG DY3 .. 66 B4
High Park Rd HALE B63 .. 102 F8
High Rdg ALDR WS9 ..... 40 D8
High Ridge Cl ALDR WS9 . 40 C8
DARL/WED WS10 .... 67 L1
High St ALDR WS9 .... 40 D2
ALDR WS9 .... 40 F7
ALE/KHTH/YWD B14 .... 125 J5
ATHST CV9 .... 61 G8
BDWTH CV12 .... 116 F3
BILS/COS WV14 .... 51 G8
BLKHTH/ROWR B65 ..... 103 M4
BLKHTH/ROWR B65 ..... 104 A4
BLOX/PEL WS3 .... 38 F5
BNTWD WS7 .... 18 D8
BRGRVE B60 .... 185 K3
BRGRVW B61 .... 185 K3
BRLYHL DY5 .... 84 A6
BRLYHL DY5 .... 102 A1
BRLYHL DY5 .... 102 D4
BRWNH WS8 .... 26 D6
CBHAM B2 .... 7 G5
CNCK/NC WS11 .... 17 M8
COV CV1 .... 8 F5
COVN CV6 .... 133 K4
CSHL/WTROR B46 ...... 93 K6
DARL/WED WS10 ...... 52 A7
DARL/WED WS10 ...... 67 L1
DOR/KN B93 .... 149 C2
DUDS DY2 .... 85 G4
DUNHL/THL/PER WV6 ... 49 H1
ERDE/BCHGN B24 ...... 90 D1
ERDW/GRVHL B23 ...... 72 E8
GTWY WS6 .... 24 A3
HAG/WOL DY9 .... 102 C8
HAG/WOL DY9 .... 140 C6
HALE B63 .... 121 M1
HIA/OLT B92 .... 129 C1
HRBN B17 .... 106 A8
KSGWFD DY6 .... 82 F5
KSGWFD DY6 .... 83 H7
KIDD DY10 .... 137 J7
KNWTH CV8 .... 176 C8
KNWTH CV8 .... 179 M4
LOZ/NWT B19 .... 89 J6
NUN CV11 .... 98 F1
POL/KGSB/FAZ B78 .... 47 M3
RIDG/WDGT B32 ...... 104 E7
RLSN CV32 .... 193 J8
RLSS CV31 .... 200 D6
SCFLD/BOLD B73 ...... 57 G7
SEDG DY3 .... 66 C3
SEDG DY3 .... 82 C3
SHLY B90 .... 146 A3
SMTHWK B66 .... 87 L8
SMTHWK B67 .... 87 A7
SOLH B91 .... 148 A1
STRBR DY8 .... 101 J3
TAM/AM/WIL B77 ...... 60 A1
TPTN/OCK DY4 .... 67 J3
WASH/WDE B8 .... 90 B8
WBROM B70 .... 87 G1
WMBN WV5 .... 64 F7

WNSFLD WV11 .... 37 C8
WSL WS1 .... 4 F3
WWCK CV34 .... 199 J7
High Street Bordesley BORD B9 7 L7
High Street Prec
DARL/WED WS10 .... 52 B7
Highters Cl
ALE/KHTH/YWD B14 .... 145 M3
Highter's Heath La
ALE/KHTH/YWD B14 .... 145 L4
Highters Rd
ALE/KHTH/YWD B14 .... 145 L2
High Timbers RBRY B45 .. 142 D4
Hightree Cl RIDG/WDGT B32 122 F4
High Trees BFLD/HDSWWD B20 88 D2
High Trees Cl REDE B98 .. 196 C6
High Trees Rd DOR/KN B93 148 E6
High Vw ATHST CV9 ...... 77 C1
BILS/COS WV14 .... 66 D4
Highview Dr KGSWFD DY6 . 101 K1
High View Dr
RCOVN/BALC/EX CV7 .... 116 A6
High View Rd RLSN CV32 . 193 C6
Highview St DUDS DY2 ... 85 J4
Highwaymans Cft
TLHL/CAN CV4 .... 153 H8
Highwood Av HIA/OLT B92 127 L4
High Wood Cl KGSWFD DY6 83 G7
Highwood Cft
HWK/WKHTH B38 .... 144 B4
Hiker Gv
CHWD/FDBR/MGN B37 .. 111 H3
Hilary Bevins Cl
MKTBOS/BARL/STKG CV13 81 K1
Hilary Crs DUDN DY1 ..... 66 F7
Hilary Dr ALDR WS9 ...... 40 E8
BDMR/CCFT WV3 .... 49 H6
WALM/CURD B76 .... 73 L2
Hilary Gv NFLD/LBR B31 .. 143 K1
Hilary Rd NUNW/HART CV10 80 C8
TLHL/CAN CV4 .... 153 H7
Hilden Rd VAUX/NECH B7 . 7 M2
Hilderic Crs DUDN DY1 ... 84 D6
Hilderstone Rd YDLY B25 . 109 C7
Hildicks Crs BLOX/PEL WS3 39 K6
Hildicks Pl BLOX/PEL WS3 . 39 K6
Hillaire Cl HWK/WKHTH B38 145 C4
Hillaries Rd ERDW/GRVHL B23 90 B3
Hillary Av DARL/WED WS10 69 G2
Hillary Crest SEDG DY3 ... 66 C8
Hillary Rd RUGBYS/DCH CV22 183 J5
STRPT DY13 .... 161 H6
Hillary St WSLW WS2 .... 4 A8
Hill Av ETTPK/GDPK/PENN WV4 66 D2
Hill Bank HAG/WOL DY9 .. 102 C8
Hillbank OLDBY B69 ..... 86 B5
Hill Bank Rd HALE B63 .. 103 H6
HWK/WKHTH B38 .... 144 B3
Hill Cl NFLD/LBR B31 ... 143 M4
RLSN CV32 .... 200 E2
SEDG DY3 .... 83 M1
Hill Crs RRUGBY CV23 .. 180 C7
Hill Crest RLSN CV32 .... 193 J8
SEDG DY3 .... 83 M1
Hillcrest Av BRLYHL DY5 . 102 A4
HALE B63 .... 102 F6
WOLVN WV10 .... 36 C5
Hillcrest Cl CRTAM B79 . 31 M7
DUDS DY2 .... 85 C8
Hill Crest Dr LICH WS13 . 20 E4
Hillcrest Gdns SHHTH WV12 38 B8
Hillcrest Gv KGSTG B44 .. 71 L6
Hillcrest Ri BNTWD WS7 . 26 F1
Hill Crest Rd DUDS DY2 .. 85 J4
MOS/BIL B13 .... 125 J3
Hillcrest Rd CSCFLD/WYGN B72 73 C5
GTB/HAM B43 .... 70 C3
NUNW/HART CV10 ..... 80 B8
POL/KGSB/FAZ B78 .... 47 K6
RMSLY B62 .... 141 K1
Hill Croft Rd
ALE/KHTH/YWD B14 .... 125 J5
Hillcroft Rd KGSWFD DY6 . 83 J6
Hillcross Wk CBROM B36 . 91 K6
CBROM B36 .... 91 K6
Hilldene Rd KGSWFD DY6 . 101 C1
Hill Dr CNCK/NC WS11 ... 16 C1
Hilldrop Gv HRBN B17 ... 124 B2
Hilleys Cft
CHWD/FDBR/MGN B37 .. 110 D2
Hill Farm Av NUN CV11 .. 99 M4
Hillfield Ms SOLH B91 ... 147 M5
Hillfield Rd RUGBYS/DCH CV22 183 J4
SOLH B91 .... 148 A3
SPARK B11 .... 126 B2
Hillfields SMTHKW B67 .. 105 H2
Hillfields Rd BRLYHL DY5 . 101 M6
Hill Fray Dr COVS CV3 ... 154 E8
Hill Grove Crs KIDD DY10 . 137 L8
Hillgrove Gdns KIDD DY10 . 161 L9
Hill Hook Rd FOAKS/STRLY B74 42 C7
Hill House La STETCH B33 . 109 K2
Hillhurst Gv CBROM B36 . 92 B4
Hilliard Cl BDWTH CV12 .. 116 E1
Hilliards Cft PBAR/PBCH B42 70 E5
Hillingford Av GTB/HAM B43 71 H1
Hill La BNTWD WS7 ..... 18 C4
BRGRVE B60 .... 185 K4
BRGRVE B60 .... 194 C7
GTB/HAM B43 .... 70 C3
HAG/WOL DY9 .... 140 C1
HLYWD B47 .... 169 J4
MGN/WHC B75 .... 57 M3
Hillman DR TAM/AM/WIL B77 46 C3
Hillman Dr DUDS DY2 ... 85 J6
Hillman Gv CBROM B36 .. 92 C4
Hillmeads Dr DUDS DY2 .. 85 J6
Hillmeads Rd HWK/WKHTH B38 144 E4
Hillmorton Cl REDE B98 .. 189 J7
Hillmorton Rd COVE CV2 . 135 C3
DOR/KN B93 .... 148 E8
FOAKS/STRLY B74 ..... 56 D1

Hill Pk ALDR WS9 .... 40 E1
Hill Pas CDYHTH B64 .... 103 J3
Hill Pl WNSFLD WV11 .... 37 L4
Hill Rise Vw BRGRVE B60 . 166 A2
Hill Rd HAG/WOL DY9 ... 102 C8
OLDBY B69 .... 85 L3
RCOVN/BALC/EX CV7 ... 115 K7
WLNHL WV13 .... 51 H4
Hillside BRWNH WS8 ..... 26 F7
Hill Side COVE CV2 ..... 134 E7
Hillside LICHS WS14 ..... 21 H8
NUNW/HART CV10 ..... 79 L5
Hill Side POL/KGSB/FAZ B78 76 B1
Hillside REDE B98 .... 196 B3
Hill Side SEDG DY3 ..... 84 A1
Hillside Av BLKHTH/ROWR B65 103 M5
BRLYHL DY5 .... 102 E5
HALE B63 .... 103 H7
Hillside Cl HEDN WS12 .. 12 E6
KIDDW DY11 .... 136 E6
RIDG/WDGT B32 ...... 122 E5
Hillside Crs BLOX/PEL WS3 39 K3
Hillside Cft HIA/OLT B92 . 128 C4
Hillside Dr BRGRVE B60 . 165 M7
CHWD/FDBR/MGN B37 . 110 D1
FOAKS/STRLY B74 ..... 55 K6
KIDDW DY11 .... 136 E6
NUNW/HART CV10 ..... 80 A6
PBAR/PBCH B42 ...... 70 E7
Hillside Gdns
CHWD/FDBR/MGN B37 . 110 D1
WOLV WV1 .... 50 E2
Hillside Rd DUDN DY1 ... 84 E1
ERDW/GRVHL B23 ..... 90 B3
FOAKS/STRLY B74 ..... 56 D1
GTB/HAM B43 .... 70 B3
Hillstone Gdns WOLVN WV10 36 D5
Hillstone Rd BKDE/SHDE B34 92 B8
Hill St BDWTH CV12 ..... 98 F8
BILS/COS WV14 .... 67 J2
BNTWD WS7 .... 18 C8
BRLYHL DY5 .... 102 E5
BRLYHL DY5 .... 102 B3
CBHAM B2 .... 6 F6
CNCK/NC WS11 .... 17 K7
COV CV1 .... 8 D4
DARL/WED WS10 ...... 52 C7
DUDS DY2 .... 84 F8
GTWY WS6 .... 24 A3
HAG/WOL DY9 .... 102 D8
HALE B63 .... 121 L2
HEDN WS12 .... 17 G2
KIDDW DY11 .... 137 H7
NUNW/HART CV10 ..... 98 B1
RLSN CV32 .... 200 E4
RUGBYN/HIL CV21 .... 183 L1
SEDG DY3 .... 66 C8
SMTHWK B66 .... 87 L7
STRBR DY8 .... 101 K5
TPTN/OCK DY4 .... 85 K1
WNSFLD WV11 .... 37 K2
WSL WS1 .... 5 G4
WWCK CV34 .... 199 H5
The Hill RIDG/WDGT B32 . 123 H3
Hill Top ATHST CV9 ..... 61 M3
COV CV1 .... 9 G4
HHTH/SAND B71 ...... 68 E6
REDW B97 .... 195 K4
Hilltop HAG/WOL DY9 ... 120 C2
Hilltop Av BEWD DY12 .. 160 B1
Hill Top Av CRTAM B79 . 31 M5
RMSLY B62 .... 104 C6
Hill Top Cl KGSTG B44 .. 71 J7
Hilltop Cl KNWTH CV8 .. 174 C5
Hilltop Dr CBROM B36 ... 91 H6
Hilltop Rd DUDS DY2 ... 85 J5
Hill Top Rd LGLYGN/QTN B68 105 G3
NFLD/LBR B31 .... 143 K2
Hill Vw ALDR WS9 ...... 40 F3
Hillview Cl BRGRVE B60 . 166 A7
HALE B63 .... 103 J7
Hillview Rd BRGRVE B60 . 166 A7
RBRY B45 .... 142 C5
Hill Village Rd MGN/WHC B75 56 F1
Hillville Gdns STRBR DY8 . 119 M2
Hill Wd BLOX/PEL WS3 .. 39 K3
Hillwood Av SHLY B90 .. 147 L7
Hillwood Cl STRBR DY8 .. 101 C1
Hillwood Common Rd
MGN/WHC B75 .... 42 F8
Hill Wood Rd MGN/WHC B75 43 C8
Hillwood Rd NFLD/LBR B31 123 J6
RMSLY B62 .... 104 A6
Hill Wootton Rd
RWWCK/WEL CV35 ..... 191 L7
Hill Farm Av NUN CV11 .. 99 M4
Hillyfields Rd ERDW/GRVHL B23 90 A1
Hilly Rd BILS/COS WV14 . 67 J3
Hilmore Wy TAM/AM/WIL B77 46 C5
Hilsea Cl COVEN WV9 ... 35 M4
Hilston Av
ETTPK/GDPK/PENN WV4 . 65 G1
HALE B63 .... 121 K1
Hilton Av HLGN/YWD B28 146 C1
NUNW/HART CV10 ..... 79 M7
Hilton Cl BLOX/PEL WS3 . 38 C4
STRBR DY8 .... 101 L6
Hilton Cross WOLVN WV10 22 F8
Hilton Dr CSCFLD/WYGN B72 73 C5
Hilton La GTWY WS6 .... 24 E3
SHHTH WV12 .... 23 H5
Hilton Pl BILS/COS WV14 . 51 J8
Hilton Rd
ETTPK/GDPK/PENN WV4 . 66 D1
OLDBY B69 .... 86 A5
SHHTH WV12 .... 38 A5
WNSFLD WV11 .... 22 F6
Hilton St WBROM B70 ... 86 E2
WOLVN WV10 .... 3 J2
Himbleton Cl REDE B98 .. 196 D4
Himbleton Cft SHLY B90 . 147 L7
Himley Av DUDN DY1 ... 84 D3
Himley Cl GTB/HAM B43 . 70 A3
SHHTH WV12 .... 37 L8
Himley Crs
ETTPK/GDPK/PENN WV4 . 50 A8
Himley Gdns SEDG DY3 .. 83 K1
Himley Gv RBRY B45 .... 142 F7
Himley La SEDG DY3 .... 82 D3

Himley Rd BDWTH CV12 .... 116 B3 ▯
  DUDN DY1 .... 84 C4
  SEDG DY3 .... 83 J2
Himley St DUDN DY1 .... 84 E4
Hinbrook Rd DUDN DY1 .... 84 C4
Hinchliffe Av BILS/COS WV14 .... 66 F3
Hinckes La
  DUNHL/THL/PER WV6 .... 34 F8
Hinckley La
  MKTBOS/BARL/STKG CV13 .... 81 M2
  RCOVN/BALC/EX CV7 .... 135 M5
Hinckley St DIG/EDG B5 .... 6 F7 ▯
Hincks St BKHL/PFLD WV2 .... 50 E6
Hind Cl WWCK CV34 .... 199 K3
Hindhead Rd
  ALE/KHTH/YWD B14 .... 146 A1
Hindlip Cl HALE B63 .... 121 K3 ▯
  REDE B98 .... 197 L1
Hindlow Cl VAUX/NECH B7 .... 107 M1
Hindon Gv ACGN B27 .... 127 C6 ▯
Hindon Sq EDG B15 .... 106 D5
Hingeston St WSNGN B18 .... 6 A1
Hingley Cft FOAKS/STRLY B74 .... 55 K2 ▯
Hingley Rd HALE B63 .... 102 E7
Hingley St CDYHTH B64 .... 103 H4 ▯
Hinksford Gdns SEDG DY3 .... 82 C3
Hinksford La SEDG DY3 .... 82 C4
Hinsford Cl KGSWFD DY6 .... 83 J5
Hinstock Cl
  ETTPK/GDPK/PENN WV4 .... 65 L1
Hinstock Rd BFLD/HDSWWD B20... 88 D4
Hintlesham Av EDG B15 .... 106 B8
Hinton Av ALVE B48 .... 167 L7
Hinton Flds BRGRVW B61 .... 165 J6
Hinton Gv WNSFLD WV11 .... 37 K8
Hintons Coppice DOR/KN B93 ... 148 C7
Hints Ct POL/KGSB/FAZ B78 .... 44 B3
Hints La POL/KGSB/FAZ B78 .... 30 F7
  POL/KGSB/FAZ B78 .... 44 C2
Hints Rd POL/KGSB/FAZ B78 .... 44 F3
Hipkins St TPTN/OCK DY4 .... 67 J6
Hiplands Rd RMSLY B62 .... 122 C1
Hipsley Cl CBROM B36 .... 92 A4 ▯
Hipsley La ATHST CV9 .... 61 J8
Hipsmoor Cl
  CHWD/FDBR/MGN B37 .... 110 D2 ▯
Hipswell Hwy COVE CV2 .... 155 H3 ▯
Hirdemonsway SHLY B90 .... 146 E8
Hirdemonsway SHLY B90 .... 146 E8
Hiron Cft COVS CV3 .... 154 A5
The Hiron COVS CV3 .... 154 A5
Hirst Cl RRUGBY CV23 .... 158 E8
Histons Dr CDSL WV8 .... 34 D3
Histons Hl CDSL WV8 .... 34 D3
Hitchcock Cl SMTHWKW B67 .... 87 H8 ▯
Hitches La EDG B15 .... 106 F6
Hitchman Ms RLSS CV31 .... 200 E8 ▯
Hitchman Rd RLSS CV31 .... 200 E7
Hither Green La REDE B98 .... 188 D6
Hitherside SHLY B90 .... 146 F8 ▯
Hoarestone Av NUN CV11 .... 99 L6
Hoarstone STRBR DY8 .... 119 K8 ▯
Hoarstone La BEWD DY12 .... 136 A8
Hoarstone La BEWD DY12 .... 136 A7
Hobacre Cl RBRY B45 .... 142 E5 ▯
Hobart Cft VAUX/NECH B7 .... 89 L8
Hobart Dr DSYBK/YTR WS5 .... 54 A7
Hobart Rd HEDN WS12 .... 17 J3
  TPTN/OCK DY4 .... 67 J4
Hobble End La GTWY WS6 .... 24 E7
Hobgate Rd WOLVN WV10 .... 3 L1
Hob Green Rd HAG/WOL DY9 ... 120 C3
Hobhouse Cl GTB/HAM B43 .... 70 D6
  RCOVN/BALC/EX CV7 .... 151 J8
Hobley St WLNHL WV13 .... 52 A3 ▯
Hobmoor Cft YDLY B25 .... 109 H6
Hob Moor Rd
  LGN/SDN/BHAMAIR B26 .... 109 J6 ▯
  SMTHH B10 .... 108 L4
  YDLY B25 .... 109 C5
Hobnock Rd WNSFLD WV11 .... 37 L1
Hobs Hole La ALDR WS9 .... 41 H6
Hob's Meadow HIA/OLT B92 .... 127 L3
Hob's Moat Rd HIA/OLT B92 .... 127 M3 ▯
Hobson Cl WSNGN B18 .... 88 E3 ▯
Hobson Rd SLYOAK B29 .... 124 F4
Hobs Rd DARL/WED WS10 .... 68 E1
  LICH WS13 .... 21 J4
Hobstone Hill La BNTWD WS7 .... 19 J4
Hockett St COVS CV3 .... 9 H9
Hocking Rd COVE CV2 .... 155 J1
Hockley Brook Cl WSNGN B18 ... 88 E3 ▯
Hockley Brook La
  HAG/WOL DY9 .... 164 C1
Hockley Cl LOZ/NWT B19 .... 89 H7
Hockley Hl WSNGN B18 .... 88 F7
Hockley La COVW CV5 .... 132 A8
  DUDS DY2 .... 85 G5
Hockley Pool Cl WSNGN B18 ... 88 F8 ▯
Hockley Rd BILS/COS WV14 .... 66 E6
  ERDW/GRVHL B23 .... 90 B1 ▯
  TAM/AM/WIL B77 .... 46 D8
Hockley St LOZ/NWT B19 .... 89 C8
  WSNGN B18 .... 6 C1
Hodge Hill Av HAG/WOL DY9 .... 120 D2 ▯
Hodge Hill Rd BKDE/SHDE B34... 91 J8
Hodge La TAM/AM/WIL B77 .... 32 F7
Hodgetts Cl SMTHWKW B67 .... 105 H2
Hodgetts Dr HALE B63 .... 121 H5 ▯
Hodgett's La
  RCOVN/BALC/EX CV7 .... 151 K5 ▯
Hodgkins Cl BRWNH WS8 .... 26 F7
Hodnell Cl CBROM B36 .... 92 A4
Hodnet Cl BILS/COS WV14 .... 50 FB ▯
  KNWTH CV8 .... 176 FB
Hodnet Gv DIG/EDG B5 .... 7 G9
  DIG/EDG B5 .... 107 J5 ▯
Hodnet Pl CNCK/NC WS11 .... 16 F3
Hodson Av WLNHL WV13 .... 52 A4
Hodson Cl WNSFLD WV11 .... 37 K5 ▯
Hoff Beck Court Ct
  BORD B9 .... 107 M3 ▯
Hogarth Cl BDWTH CV12 .... 116 E1
  GTB/HAM B43 .... 55 H8

  WLNHL WV13 .... 51 J3
Hoggrills End La
  CSHL/WTROR B46 .... 94 E1
Hoggs La NFLD/LBR B31 .... 143 J1
Hogrills End La
  CSHL/WTROR B46 .... 94 D1
Holbeache La KGSWFD DY6 .... 83 H4
Holbeache Rd KGSWFD DY6 .... 83 G5
  KINVER DY7 .... 100 E1
Holbeach Rd STETCH B33 .... 109 M3
Holbeche Crs
  RCOVN/BALC/EX CV7 .... 114 C2 ▯
Holbeche Rd DOR/KN B93 .... 148 E6
  MGN/WHC B75 .... 73 M1
Holbein Cl BDWTH CV12 .... 116 E1
Holberg Gv WNSFLD WV11 .... 37 K7
Holborn Av COVN CV6 .... 134 A3
Holborn Hl VAUX/NECH B7 .... 89 M5
Holbrook Av RUGBY/HIL CV21... 183 L1 ▯
Holbrook La COVN CV6 .... 134 B4 ▯
Holbrook Rd RRUGBY CV23 .... 158 F8
Holbrook Wy COVN CV6 .... 134 B4
Holbury Cl COVEN WV9 .... 35 L3
Holcombe Rd SPARK B11 .... 126 E2
Holcot Leys RUGBYS/DCH CV22... 183 L6
Holcroft Rd HAG/WOL DY9 .... 120 A1
  HALE B63 .... 103 C8
  KGSWFD DY6 .... 83 C4
Holcroft St BKHL/PFLD WV2 .... 50 E6 ▯
  TPTN/OCK DY4 .... 85 L3
Holden Cl ERDW/GRVHL B23 .... 90 C3
Holden Crs BLOX/PEL WS3 .... 39 J8
Holden Cft TPTN/OCK DY4 .... 85 L2 ▯
Holden Pl BLOX/PEL WS3 .... 53 J1
Holden Rd DARL/WED WS10 .... 68 E3
  ETTPK/GDPK/PENN WV4 .... 65 L2
Holder Dr CNCK/NC WS11 .... 15 M3
Holder Rd SPARK B11 .... 108 A7
  YDLY B25 .... 109 C6
Holders Gdns MOS/BIL B13 .... 125 C3
Holders La MOS/BIL B13 .... 125 C3
Holdford Rd AST/WIT B6 .... 89 K3
Holdgate Rd SLYOAK B29 .... 123 M6
Hole Farm Rd NFLD/LBR B31 ... 124 A8
Hole Farm Wy
  HWK/WKHTH B38 .... 144 D6
Hole La NFLD/LBR B31 .... 124 A7
Holford Av WSLW WS2 .... 4 A9
Holford Dr PBAR/PBCH B42 .... 89 J1
Holford Wy AST/WIT B6 .... 89 L2
  PBAR/PBCH B42 .... 89 K2
Holifast Rd CSCFLD/WYGN B72 ... 73 G6
Holioak Dr WWCK CV34 .... 199 L7
Holland Av DOR/KN B93 .... 148 F5
  LGLYGN/QTN B68 .... 105 L1
Holland Cl LICHS WS14 .... 21 L4 ▯
Holland Cft WALM/CURD B76... 75 M3
Holland Rd BILS/COS WV14 .... 51 J6
  COVN CV6 .... 133 L7
  CSCFLD/WYGN B72 .... 72 F2
  GTB/HAM B43 .... 70 B6
Holland Rd West AST/WIT B6 ... 89 K7
Hollands Pl BLOX/PEL WS3 .... 39 H4
Hollands Rd BLOX/PEL WS3 .... 39 H4
Holland St BHAMNW B3 .... 6 C4
  CSCFLD/WYGN B72 .... 72 F1 ▯
  DUDN DY1 .... 84 A1
  TPTN/OCK DY4 .... 68 A6 ▯
Hollemeadow Av BLOX/PEL WS3... 39 H4
Holliars Gv
  CHWD/FDBR/MGN B37 .... 92 D8
Hollick Crs RCOVN/BALC/EX CV7 .. 96 E5
Hollicombe Ter COVE CV2 .... 135 H5
Holliday Rd ERDE/BCHGN B24 ... 90 E1
  HDSW B21 .... 88 D6
Holliday St CBHAMW B1 .... 6 D6
  EDG B15 .... 6 C7
Hollie Lucas Rd MOS/BIL B13 ... 125 K6
Hollies Av CNCK/NC WS11 .... 16 C4
Hollies Cft DIG/EDG B5 .... 107 G8
Hollies Dr DARL/WED WS10 .... 68 C3 ▯
Hollies La KIDDW DY11 .... 136 D2
Hollies Ri CDYHTH B64 .... 103 K5
Hollies Rd OLDBY B69 .... 85 L5
  POL/KGSB/FAZ B78 .... 47 M5
Hollies St BRLYHL DY5 .... 84 B6
The Hollies AST/WIT B6 .... 89 M5 ▯
  BKHL/PFLD WV2 .... 2 E8
  RBRY B45 .... 166 E4
  STRPT DY13 .... 160 C7
Hollin Brow Cl DOR/KN B93 ... 172 F2 ▯
Hollingberry La
  WALM/CURD B76 .... 73 K2 ▯
Hollings Gv SOLH B91 .... 147 M5 ▯
Hollington Rd WOLV WV1 .... 50 F5
Hollington Wy SOLH B91 .... 148 A6
Hollinwell Cl BLOX/PEL WS3 .... 38 E2 ▯
Hollis La KNWTH CV8 .... 176 C5
Hollis Rd COVS CV3 .... 154 E3
Hollister Dr RIDG/WDGT B32 ... 123 K2
Holloway CRTAM B79 .... 45 M1
  NFLD/LBR B31 .... 123 J7
Holloway Bank
  DARL/WED WS10 .... 68 D5
Holloway Circus Queensway
  CBHAMW B1 .... 6 E7
Holloway Dr REDE B98 .... 196 F1
  REDE B98 .... 196 D3
  WMBN WV5 .... 64 C8
Holloway Fld COVW CV6 .... 133 L7
Holloway Head EDG B15 .... 6 E8
Holloway La REDE B98 .... 196 E2 ▯
Holloway Pk REDE B98 .... 196 E2 ▯
Holloway St SEDG DY3 .... 84 B1
  WOLV WV1 .... 50 E6
Holloway St West SEDG DY3 .... 66 B8
The Holloway ALVE B48 .... 188 A2
  DUNHL/THL/PER WV6 .... 48 F3
  KIDD DY10 .... 163 J3
  SEDG DY3 .... 82 B4
  STRBR DY8 .... 101 G6 ▯
  WWCK CV34 .... 199 H7 ▯
Hollow Crs COVN CV6 .... 133 M8
Hollow Cft NFLD/LBR B31 .... 143 M2 ▯
Hollow Croft Rd SHHTH WV12... 36 B2
Hollowtree La BRGRVE B60 .... 186 E2 ▯
Holly Av BHTH/HG B12 .... 107 L8 ▯
  SLYOAK B29 .... 124 F4

Hollybank Av WNSFLD WV11 .... 37 L2
Hollybank Cl BLOX/PEL WS3 .... 38 E3 ▯
Hollybank Gv HALE B63 .... 121 H4 ▯
Hollybank Rd MOS/BIL B13 .... 125 L7
Hollyberry Av SOLH B91 .... 147 L5
Hollyberry Cl REDE B98 .... 197 L1
Hollyberry Cft
  BKDE/SHDE B34 .... 92 A7 ▯
Holly Bush Gv RIDG/WDGT B32 .. 105 H6
Hollybush La CDSL WV8 .... 34 B3
  COVN CV6 .... 134 E1
  ETTPK/GDPK/PENN WV4 .... 65 H1
  STRBR DY8 .... 101 K6
Holly Cl CRTAM B79 .... 31 M6
  SHHTH WV12 .... 38 A7
Hollycot Gdns BHTH/HG B12 ... 107 K7 ▯
Hollycroft Rd HDSW B21 .... 88 B4
Hollydale Rd
  BLKHTH/ROWR B65 .... 104 B2
  ERDE/BCHGN B24 .... 91 G2
Holly Dell HWK/WKHTH B38 ... 144 F3
Holly Dr ACGN B27 .... 126 F3
  ATHST CV9 .... 77 H1
  HLYWD B47 .... 145 M6
Hollyfaste Rd STETCH B33 .... 109 M4 ▯
Hollyfast La
  RCOVN/BALC/EX CV7 .... 133 G1
Hollyfast Rd COVN CV6 .... 133 J6
Hollyfield Av SOLH B91 .... 147 J2
Hollyfield Ct MGN/WHC B75 .... 57 J8
Hollyfield Crs MGN/WHC B75 ... 73 J1 ▯
Hollyfield Dr MGN/WHC B75 .... 57 J8
  RBRY B45 .... 166 E4
Hollyfield Rd MGN/WHC B75 ... 57 J8
Holly Gv BDMR/CCFT WV3 .... 49 K6
  BRGRVW B61 .... 185 K2
  BVILLE B30 .... 124 D5
  LOZ/NWT B19 .... 88 F5
  RRUGBY CV23 .... 157 M8
  STRBR DY8 .... 101 K4 ▯
  TLHL/CAN CV4 .... 153 C3
Holly Grove La BNTWD WS7 ... 18 C4
Holly Hall Rd DUDS DY2 .... 84 E7
Hollyhedge Cl NFLD/LBR B31 .. 123 H7 ▯
  WSLW WS2 .... 4 B1
Hollyhedge La WSLW WS2 .... 52 C1
Hollyhedge Rd HHTH/SAND B71... 69 J6
Hollyhill La LICHS WS14 .... 42 C1
Holly Hill Rd LICHS WS14 .... 28 D8
  RBRY B45 .... 142 E3
Hollyhock Rd ACGN B27 .... 126 D4
  DUDS DY2 .... 85 K4
Hollyhurst BDWTH CV12 .... 116 D4
  CSHL/WTROR B46 .... 94 D4
Hollyhurst Dr STRBR DY8 .... 101 J2 ▯
Hollyhurst Gv
  LGN/SDN/BHAMAIR B26 .... 109 J7
  SHLY B90 .... 146 F5 ▯
Hollyhurst Rd SCFLD/BOLD B73... 71 M2
Hollyland CSHL/WTROR B46 .... 94 D4
Holly La ALDR WS9 .... 40 E1
  ALDR WS9 .... 41 K5
  ALVE B48 .... 169 K8
  ATHST CV9 .... 63 C3
  CHWD/FDBR/MGN B37 .... 110 D5
  ERDE/BCHGN B24 .... 72 E8
  ERDE/BCHGN B24 .... 90 F1
  GTWY WS6 .... 24 D5
  HEDN WS12 .... 12 A6
  KNWTH CV8 .... 174 F3
  MGN/WHC B75 .... 56 E2
  SMTHWK B66 .... 87 H6 ▯
  SMTHWK B66 .... 87 H7
  WALM/CURD B76 .... 74 B1
Hollymoor Wy NFLD/LBR B31 .. 142 F4
Hollymount RMSLY B62 .... 104 E6 ▯
Hollyoak Cft NFLD/LBR B31 .... 143 M5
Hollyoake Cl LGLYGN/QTN B68 ... 104 E3 ▯
Hollyoake Ct
  LGLYGN/QTN B68 .... 104 E3 ▯
Hollyoak Gv SOLH B91 .... 147 L4 ▯
Hollyoak Rd FOAKS/STRLY B74... 55 K7
Hollyoak St HHTH/SAND B71 ... 87 H1
Holly Park Dr ERDE/BCHGN B24 ... 90 F2
Holly Rd BLKHTH/ROWR B65 ... 103 M4
  BRGRVW B61 .... 185 K1
  BVILLE B30 .... 144 E1
  DARL/WED WS10 .... 52 D8
  DUDN DY1 .... 84 E2
  HDSW B21 .... 88 D5
  HHTH/SAND B71 .... 69 J5
  LDYWD/EDGR B16 .... 106 A4
  LGLYGN/QTN B68 .... 105 G5
Holly Stitches Rd
  NUNW/HART CV10 .... 80 C7
Holly St CNCK/NC WS11 .... 12 D7
  DUDN DY1 .... 84 C6
  RLSN CV32 .... 200 E4
  SMTHWKW B67 .... 87 K8
Holly Wk KNWTH CV8 .... 178 C3
  NUN CV11 .... 99 K3
  RLSN CV32 .... 200 E5
Hollywell Rd DOR/KN B93 .... 148 E8
  LGN/SDN/BHAMAIR B26 .... 109 M7
Hollywell St BILS/COS WV14 .... 66 E4
Holly Wd GTB/HAM B43 .... 70 E4
Hollywood By-pass
  HLYWD B47 .... 145 K4
Hollywood Cft PBAR/PBCH B42... 70 D5
Hollywood Gdns HLYWD B47 .... 145 L5
Hollywood La HLYWD B47 .... 145 L5
Holman Cl WLNHL WV13 .... 51 J3
Holman Rd WLNHL WV13 .... 51 H3
Holman St KIDDW DY11 .... 137 G8
Holman Wy NUN CV11 .... 99 H2
Holmcroft COVE CV2 .... 135 K5
Holmcroft Gdns COVEN WV9 ... 22 A3 ▯
Holmcroft Rd KIDD DY10 .... 137 L7
Holme Ml WOLVN WV10 .... 36 B1
Holme Ri PENK ST19 .... 10 E4
Holmes Dr COVW CV5 .... 132 B8
  RBRY B45 .... 142 D7
Holmesfield Rd PBAR/PBCH B42... 71 C6
Holmes Rd SHHTH WV12 .... 38 B6
The Holmes WOLVN WV10 .... 36 B2
Holme Wy RUSH/SHEL WS4 .... 39 M4
Holmewood Cl KNWTH CV8 .... 176 F4
Holmfield Rd COVE CV2 .... 154 F3

Holmsdale Rd COVN CV6 .... 134 C6
Holm View Cl LICHS WS14 .... 28 D7 ▯
Holmwood Av KIDDW DY11 .... 136 E7
Holmwood Dr REDW B97 .... 196 A6
Holmwood Rd BORD B9 .... 108 A4 ▯
Holston Cl HEDN WS12 .... 17 K4 ▯
Holsworth Cl
  TAM/AM/WIL B77 .... 46 B4 ▯
Holsworthy Cl NUN CV11 .... 81 J8
Holt Crs CNCK/NC WS11 .... 16 F3
Holte Dr MGN/WHC B75 .... 57 H3
Holte Rd AST/WIT B6 .... 89 L5 ▯
  ATHST CV9 .... 63 H4
  SPARK B11 .... 108 B8 ▯
Holt Hl REDE B98 .... 189 K5 ▯
Holt La RMSLY B62 .... 141 H1
Holt Rd RMSLY B62 .... 104 C4
Holtshill La WSL WS1 .... 5 H2
Holt St VAUX/NECH B7 .... 7 J1
The Holt RLSN CV32 .... 200 F1
Holwick TAM/AM/WIL B77 .... 46 F5 ▯
Holy Cross Gn HAG/WOL DY9 ... 140 C3
Holy Cross La HAG/WOL DY9 ... 140 C5
Holyhead Rd COVN CV6 .... 133 J8
  COVW CV5 .... 133 H8
  COVW CV5 .... 153 J1
Holyhead Wy HDSW B21 .... 88 A5
Holyoak Cl AST/WIT B6 .... 89 K4 ▯
  BDWTH CV12 .... 116 D4
  RUGBYS/DCH CV22 .... 183 G5 ▯
Holyoakes La REDW B97 .... 187 G7
Holy Well Cl
  LDYWD/EDGR B16 .... 106 E4 ▯
Holywell Cl TLHL/CAN CV4 .... 152 B4
Holywell La RBRY B45 .... 142 B7
Holywell Ri LICHS WS14 .... 21 H7
Home Cl KNWTH CV8 .... 179 C7
Homecroft Rd YDLY B25 .... 109 J5
Homedene Rd NFLD/LBR B31 ... 123 H6
Home Farm RWWCK/WEL CV35... 191 K7
Home Farm Cl ATHST CV9 .... 63 M5
Homefield Rd CDSL WV8 .... 34 F2
Homelands PBAR/PBCH B42 ... 70 F6
Homelea Rd YDLY B25 .... 109 H5
Homemead Gv RBRY B45 .... 142 D6
Home Meadow La REDE B98 ... 189 J7
Home Park Rd NUN CV11 .... 99 G2
Homer Hill Rd HALE B63 .... 102 F6
Homer Rd MGN/WHC B75 .... 57 G3
  SOLH B91 .... 147 M2
Homers Fold BILS/COS WV14 ... 51 H8 ▯
Homer St BHTH/HG B12 .... 107 K8
Homerton Rd KGSTG B44 .... 71 H4
Homestead Cl SEDG DY3 .... 66 C8 ▯
Homestead Dr MGN/WHC B75... 57 G2
Homestead Rd STETCH B33 ... 109 H4
Homeward Wy COVS CV3 .... 155 L4
Homewood Cl WALM/CURD B76 .. 73 J2
Homfray Cl KIDD DY10 .... 137 K5
Honesty Cl BRWNH WS8 .... 26 B6
Honeswode Cl
  BFLD/HDSWWD B20 .... 88 C6
Honeyborne Cl MGN/WHC B75... 57 H6
Honeybourne Cl COVW CV5 ... 152 F2 ▯
  HALE B63 .... 121 L2 ▯
Honeybourne Crs
  WMBN WV5 .... 64 D8 ▯
Honeybourne Rd HALE B63 ... 122 A2
  STETCH B33 .... 110 A5
Honeybourne Wy WLNHL WV13... 52 A3
Honeybrook Cl KIDDW DY11 ... 137 H3
Honeybrook La KIDDW DY11 ... 136 F4
Honeyfield Rd COV CV1 .... 134 B8
Honeysuckle Av KGSWFD DY6 ... 83 J6
Honeysuckle Cl
  RIDG/WDGT B32 .... 104 F8
Honeysuckle Dr COVE CV2 ... 134 F3
  DSYBK/YTR WS5 .... 69 L2
  WOLVN WV10 .... 22 F6
Honeysuckle Gv ACGN B27 ... 109 G8 ▯
Honeytree Cl KGSWFD DY6 ... 101 K2
Honiley Dr SCFLD/BOLD B73 ... 72 A3
Honiley Rd KNWTH CV8 .... 174 E4
  STETCH B33 .... 109 L3
Honiley Wy COVE CV2 .... 135 H4 ▯
Honister Cl BRLYHL DY5 .... 102 D4
Honiton Cl NFLD/LBR B31 .... 143 J1 ▯
Honiton Crs NFLD/LBR B31 ... 143 J1
Honiton Rd COVE CV2 .... 134 F8
Honiton Wk SMTHWK B66 ... 87 M8 ▯
Honiton Wy ALDR WS9 .... 40 D9
Honnington Ct SLYOAK B29 ... 123 K4 ▯
Honor Av
  ETTPK/GDPK/PENN WV4 .... 50 A8
Hood Gv BVILLE B30 .... 144 B1 ▯
Hood St COV CV1 .... 9 J4
Hood's Wy RUGBYS/DCH CV22... 183 H4
Hook Dr FOAKS/STRLY B74 ... 56 C1
Hook La LICHS WS14 .... 42 C1
Hooper St WSNGN B18 .... 106 D1 ▯
Hoo Rd KIDD DY10 .... 161 J2
Hoosen Cl RMSLY B62 .... 104 E7 ▯
Hope Cl RCOVN/BALC/EX CV7 ... 115 L6
Hopedale Cl COVE CV2 .... 155 J2
Hopedale Rd
  RIDG/WDGT B32 .... 105 G8 ▯
Hope Rd TPTN/OCK DY4 .... 68 A7
Hope St COV CV1 .... 8 C7
  DIG/EDG B5 .... 107 H5
  DUDS DY2 .... 85 G5
  RMSLY B62 .... 104 B5
  STRBR DY8 .... 101 H2
  WBROM B70 .... 87 J3
  WSL WS1 .... 4 F5
Hopgardens Av BRGRVE B60 ... 185 M3
Hopkins Dr HHTH/SAND B71 ... 69 J6
Hopkins Rd COVN CV6 .... 8 A1
Hopkins St BILS/COS WV14 .... 85 K3 ▯
Hopleys Cl TAM/AM/WIL B77 ... 46 C1 ▯
Hopstone Gdns
  ETTPK/GDPK/PENN WV4 .... 49 K8
Hopstone Rd SLYOAK B29 ... 123 L4
Hopton Cl COVW CV5 .... 152 E1

  DUNHL/THL/PER WV6 .... 48 D2
  TPTN/OCK DY4 .... 68 A3
Hopton Crs WNSFLD WV11 .... 37 J7
Hopton Crofts RLSN CV32 .... 200 A3 ▯
Hopton Dr KIDDW DY11 .... 161 J4
Hopton Gdns DUDN DY1 .... 84 E2 ▯
Hopton Gv MOS/BIL B13 .... 126 A8
Hopton Meadow HEDN WS12 ... 17 G4 ▯
Hopwas Gv
  CHWD/FDBR/MGN B37 .... 92 D8 ▯
Hopwas Hl POL/KGSB/FAZ B78... 30 E7
Hopwood Cl HALE B63 .... 121 L3 ▯
Hopwood Gv NFLD/LBR B31 ... 143 J7 ▯
Hopyard Cl SEDG DY3 .... 83 M2 ▯
Hopyard Gdns BILS/COS WV14 ... 66 F2 ▯
Hopyard La REDE B98 .... 197 J1 ▯
  SEDG DY3 .... 83 M2 ▯
Hopyard Rd WSLW WS2 .... 52 C3
Horace Partridge Rd
  DARL/WED WS10 .... 51 L8 ▯
Horace St BILS/COS WV14 .... 66 E5
Horatio Dr MOS/BIL B13 .... 125 K1 ▯
Hordern Cl
  DUNHL/THL/PER WV6 .... 35 K8
Hordern Crs BRLYHL DY5 .... 102 B5
Hordern Gv
  DUNHL/THL/PER WV6 .... 35 K8
Hordern Rd
  DUNHL/THL/PER WV6 .... 35 K8
Hornbeam TAM/AM/WIL B77 ... 46 E1
Hornbeam Cl SLYOAK B29 .... 123 M6 ▯
Hornbeam Crs HEDN WS12 .... 13 L7
Hornbeam Dr TLHL/CAN CV4 ... 152 B4
Hornbrook Gv HIA/OLT B92 ... 127 G6
Hornby Gv ALE/KHTH/YWD B14... 146 A1
Hornby Rd
  ETTPK/GDPK/PENN WV4 .... 66 A1
Hornchurch Cl COV CV1 .... 8 F8 ▯
Horndean Cl COVN CV6 .... 134 C5 ▯
Horner Wy BLKHTH/ROWR B65... 104 A4
Horne Wy BKDE/SHDE B34 .... 92 C8
Horning Dr BILS/COS WV14 .... 67 G2
Horninghold Cl COVS CV3 .... 155 J5 ▯
Hornsey Cl COVE CV2 .... 135 J6
Hornsey Gv KGSTG B44 .... 71 L3
Hornsey Rd KGSTG B44 .... 71 L3
Hornton Cl FOAKS/STRLY B74 ... 42 B8
Horrell Rd
  LGN/SDN/BHAMAIR B26 .... 109 L6 ▯
  SHLY B90 .... 146 D3
Horse Bridge La KINVER DY7 ... 118 A3
Horsecroft Dr
  HHTH/SAND B71 .... 69 L5 ▯
Horse Fair KIDD DY10 .... 137 J6 ▯
Horsehills Dr BDMR/CCFT WV3... 49 J3 ▯
Horselea Cft WASH/WDE B8 ... 109 G1
Horseley Flds WOLV WV1 .... 3 H5
Horseley Heath
  TPTN/OCK DY4 .... 85 M1 ▯
Horseley Rd TPTN/OCK DY4 ... 67 M7
Horseshoe Cl WSLW WS2 .... 52 F6 ▯
Horse Shoe Rd COVN CV6 .... 134 E1 ▯
Horse Shoes La
  LGN/SDN/BHAMAIR B26 .... 109 M8
The Horseshoe
  LGLYGN/QTN B68 .... 105 G3 ▯
Horsfall Rd MGN/WHC B75 .... 57 L8
Horsford Rd COVS CV3 .... 154 C7 ▯
Horsham Av STRBR DY8 .... 101 G2
Horsley La LICHS WS14 .... 28 B5
Horsley Rd GTB/HAM B43 .... 71 H1
Horton Cl DARL/WED WS10 ... 52 B3 ▯
  SEDG DY3 .... 66 A5
Horton Crs RUGBYS/DCH CV22... 183 J5 ▯
Horton Gv SHLY B90 .... 147 L8
Horton Pl DARL/WED WS10 ... 52 B6
Horton Sq BHTH/HG B12 .... 107 J6 ▯
Horton St DARL/WED WS10 ... 52 B6
  TPTN/OCK DY4 .... 68 B8
  WBROM B70 .... 87 C4
Hosiery St BDWTH CV12 .... 117 G3
Hospital La BDWTH CV12 .... 115 M4
  BILS/COS WV14 .... 66 F6
Hospital Rd BNTWD WS7 .... 26 F1
Hospital St CRTAM B79 .... 31 M6
  LOZ/NWT B19 .... 6 F1
  WOLV WV1 .... 3 H7
  WSLW WS2 .... 53 H1
Hossil La HAG/WOL DY9 .... 139 M5
Hotchkiss Wy COVS CV3 .... 155 L6
Hothersall Dr
  SCFLD/BOLD B73 .... 72 D5 ▯
Hothorpe Cl COVS CV3 .... 155 K4
Hotspur Rd KGSTG B44 .... 71 K4
Hough Pl WSLW WS2 .... 52 F6
Hough Rd ALE/KHTH/YWD B14... 125 H7
  WSLW WS2 .... 52 F6
Houghton Ct
  HLGN/YWD B28 .... 146 B1 ▯
Houghton St OLDBY B69 .... 86 D7 ▯
  WBROM B70 .... 87 H5
Houldey Rd NFLD/LBR B31 .... 143 M4
Houldsworth Crs COVN CV6 ... 134 A1
Houliston Cl DARL/WED WS10 ... 52 F8 ▯
Houndsfield Cl HLYWD B47 ... 146 A7 ▯
Houndsfield Gv HLYWD B47 ... 145 L8 ▯
Houndsfield La HLYWD B47 ... 145 L8
Housman Cl BRGRVE B60 .... 185 J5
Houting TAM/AM/WIL B77 .... 46 B8
The Houx STRBR DY8 .... 101 J5 ▯
Hove Av COVW CV5 .... 152 C1 ▯
Hovelands Cl COVE CV2 .... 135 C5 ▯
Hove Rd ACGN B27 .... 126 F4
Howard Av BRGRVW B61 .... 185 J2
Howard Cl COVW CV5 .... 152 D1 ▯
Howard Crs HEDN WS12 .... 13 G6
Howard Rd
  ALE/KHTH/YWD B14 .... 125 H6
  BFLD/HDSWWD B20 .... 88 C6
  BILS/COS WV14 .... 67 K2
  GTB/HAM B43 .... 70 A5
  HIA/OLT B92 .... 127 J2
  NUNW/HART CV10 .... 196 F5
  REDE B98 .... 196 F5
  WNSFLD WV11 .... 37 K5
  YDLY B25 .... 109 J5
Howard Rd East
  ALE/KHTH/YWD B14 .... 125 J6

Howard St *BKHL/PFLD* WV2 .... 3 G8
  COV CV1 .... 9 G1
  LOZ/NWT B19 .... 6 E1
  TPTN/OCK DY4 .... 67 M8 ⓫
  WBROM B70 .... 68 D6
Howarth Wy *AST/WIT* B6 .... 89 L6 ⓫
Howat Rd *RCOVN/BALC/EX* CV7 .. 115 K6
Howcotte Gn *TLHL/CAN* CV4 ...... 152 C6
Howden Pl *STECH* B33 .... 91 L8
Howdle's La *BRWNH* WS8 .... 26 D3
Howe Crs *SHHTH* WV12 .... 38 A7
Howe Green La
  NUNW/HART CV10 .... 115 H2
Howell Dr *TPTN/OCK* DY4 .... 67 L8
Howell Rd *BKHL/PFLD* WV2 .... 50 C6
Howells Cl *BDWTH* CV12 .... 116 B5
Howes Cft *CVALE* B35 .... 91 L3
Howes La *COVS* CV3 .... 178 A2
Howe St *CBHAMNE* B4 .... 7 K3
Howford Gv *VAUX/NECH* B7 ...... 107 M1
Howland Cl *COVEN* WV9 .... 35 K3
Howlette Rd *TLHL/CAN* CV4 ...... 152 C5 ⓫
Howley Av *KGSTG* B44 .... 71 J4
Howley Grange Rd *RMSLY* B62 .. 104 D8
Hoylake *TAM/AM/WIL* B77 .... 46 F1 ⓫
Hoylake Cl *BLOX/PEL* WS3 .... 38 F2
  NUN CV11 .... 99 M4
Hoylake Dr *OLDBY* B69 .... 85 L6
Hoylake Rd
  DUNHL/THL/PER WV6 .... 34 B8
Hoyland Wy *BVILLE* B30 .... 124 C5
Hubert Cft *SLYOAK* B29 .... 124 C3
Hubert Rd *SLYOAK* B29 .... 124 D3
Hubert St *AST/WIT* B6 .... 89 K8
Hucker Cl *WSLW* WS2 .... 52 E6
Hucker Rd *WSLW* WS2 .... 52 E6
Huddisdon Cl *WWCK* CV34 ...... 199 K4 ⓫
Huddlestone Cl *WOLVN* WV10 .... 22 E7
Huddocks Vw *BLOX/PEL* WS3 ...... 25 K8
Hudson Av *CSHL/WTROR* B46 .... 93 K7
Hudson Cl *CNCK/NC* WS11 .... 16 F5
Hudson Dr *BNTWD* WS7 .... 19 C7
Hudson Gv
  DUNHL/THL/PER WV6 .... 34 C8 ⓫
Hudson Rd *BFLD/HDSWWD* B20 .... 88 E1
  RUGBYS/DCH CV22 .... 183 J4
  TPTN/OCK DY4 .... 86 A1
Hudson's Dr *BVILLE* B30 .... 144 E1
Hudswell Dr *BRLYHL* DY5 .... 102 B5 ⓫
Hughes Av *BDMR/CCFT* WV3 .... 49 K5
Hughes Cl *WWCK* CV34 .... 199 H3
Hughes Pl *BILS/COS* WV14 .... 51 H6 ⓫
Hughes Rd *BILS/COS* WV14 .... 51 H6
  DARL/WED WS10 .... 51 L8
Hugh Rd *COVS* CV3 .... 154 E3
  SMHTH B10 .... 108 C4
  SMTHWKW B67 .... 87 H8
Huins Cl *REDE* B98 .... 196 E1
Hulland Pl *BRLYHL* DY5 .... 102 A2 ⓫
Hullbrook Rd *MOS/BIL* B13 .... 126 A8
Hulme Cl *COVS* CV3 .... 155 M4
Humber Av *COV* CV1 .... 9 K7
  COVS CV3 .... 9 M7
  WALM/CURD B76 .... 73 L6 ⓫
Humber Gv *CBROM* B36 .... 92 D4
Humber Rd *BDMR/CCFT* WV3 ...... 2 B6
  COVS CV3 .... 9 M6
Humberstone Rd
  ERDE/BCHGN B24 .... 91 J1
  SMTHWK B66 .... 105 M1
Humpage Rd *BORD* B9 .... 108 C3
Humphrey Av *BRGRVE* B60 ...... 185 J6
Humphrey Burton's Rd
  COVS CV3 .... 154 A5
Humphrey Middlemore Dr
  HRBN B17 .... 124 B1
Humphreys Rd *WOLVN* WV10 ..... 36 B6
Humphrey St *SEDG* DY3 .... 84 B2
Humphries Crs *BILS/COS* WV14 ... 67 K3
Humphries Dr *KIDD* DY10 .... 161 K3
Humphris St *WWCK* CV34 .... 199 M5
Hundred Acre Rd
  FOAKS/STRLY B74 .... 55 K6
Hungary Cl *HAG/WOL* DY9 .... 102 A8 ⓫
Hungary Hl *HAG/WOL* DY9 .... 102 A8
Hungerfield Rd *CBROM* B36 .... 92 A4
Hungerford Rd *STRBR* DY8 .... 119 J3
Hungry La *LICHS* WS14 .... 43 K1
Hunningham Gv *SOLH* B91 ...... 147 M5 ⓫
Hunscote Cl
  RIDG/WDGT B32 .... 122 E4 ⓫
Hunningham Crs *HALE* B63 ...... 121 M3 ⓫
Hunscote Cl *SHLY* B90 .... 146 D4 ⓫
Hunslet Rd *BNTWD* WS7 .... 18 F5
  RIDG/WDGT B32 .... 123 K1
Hunstanton Av *HRBN* B17 .... 105 K5
Hunstanton Cl *BRLYHL* DY5 ..... 102 A5 ⓫
Hunt Cl *RWWCK/WEL* CV35 ..... 198 D7 ⓫
Hunt End La *REDW* B97 .... 196 A8
Hunter Av *BNTWD* WS7 .... 18 F6
Hunter Cl *LICHS* WS14 .... 21 H7
Hunter Crs *BLOX/PEL* WS3 .... 39 K7
Hunter Rd *CNCK/NC* WS11 .... 16 C5
Hunters Cl *BILS/COS* WV14 .... 51 L6
  COVS CV3 .... 155 L3
Hunters La *RUGBYN/HIL* CV21 .. 159 L8
Hunter's Ride *KINVER* DY7 .... 100 F3
Hunters Pk *ATHST* CV9 .... 62 A5
Hunter's Wk *LOZ/NWT* B19 .... 88 F7
Hunter St *DUNHL/THL/PER* WV6 .. 2 B1
Hunters V *LOZ/NWT* B19 .... 89 G7
Hunters Wk *ATHST* CV9 .... 63 H6
Hunter Ter *COVW* CV5 .... 153 G5 ⓫
Huntingdon Cl
  POL/KGSB/FAZ B78 .... 45 K3
  REDE B98 .... 197 J3
Huntingdon Gdns *HALE* B63 ..... 103 G6 ⓫
Huntingdon Rd *COVW* CV5 .... 8 B3
  HHTH/SAND B71 .... 68 F6
Huntington Wy
  NUNW/HART CV10 .... 98 C2 ⓫
Huntington Rd *SHHTH* WV12 ...... 38 B6
Huntington Terrace Rd
  CNCK/NC WS11 .... 16 D1

Huntingtree Rd *HALE* B63 .... 121 J1
Huntlands Rd *HALE* B63 .... 121 J3
Hunt La *ATHST* CV9 .... 63 H6
Huntley Dr *SOLH* B91 .... 147 M3
Huntly Rd *LDYWD/EDGR* B16 .... 106 E4
Hunton Hl *ERDW/GRVHL* B23 .... 90 B2
Hunton Rd *ERDW/GRVHL* B23 .... 90 C2
Hunt Paddocks *KNWTH* CV8 ... 191 J4
Hunt's La *SHHTH* WV12 .... 38 B7
Huntsman Ga *BNTWD* WS7 .... 18 F5
Huntsmans Ri *HEDN* WS12 .... 12 A5
Hunts Mill Dr *BRLYHL* DY5 .... 84 A4
Hunts Rd *BVILLE* B30 .... 124 E6
Hunt Ter *TLHL/CAN* CV4 .... 152 F6
Hurcott La *KIDD* DY10 .... 138 A3
Hurcott Rd *KIDD* DY10 .... 137 L5
Hurdis Rd *SHLY* B90 .... 146 E3
Hurdlow Av *WSNGN* B18 .... 88 F8
Hurley Cl *CSCFLD/WYGN* B72 .... 73 G3
  DSYBK/YTR WS5 .... 54 B7
  RLSN CV32 .... 200 E3
Hurley Gv
  CHWD/FDBR/MGN B37 .... 92 D8
Hurley La *CSHL/WTROR* B46 .... 77 J8
Hurleys Fold *DUDS* DY2 .... 84 F8
Hurlingham Rd *KGSTG* B44 .... 71 L4
Hurn Wy *COVE* CV2 .... 134 F1 ⓫
Huron Cl *CNCK/NC* WS11 .... 16 F3
Hursey Dr *TPTN/OCK* DY4 .... 67 L8
Hurstbourne Crs *WOLV* WV1 ...... 50 F4
Hurst Cl *CBROM* B36 .... 92 C6
Hurstcroft Rd *STECH* B33 ...... 109 M2
Hurst Green Rd *DOR/KN* B93 ... 172 D1
  RMSLY B62 .... 104 C5
  WALM/CURD B76 .... 74 B7
Hurst La *BKDE/SHDE* B34 .... 92 B7
  BRLYHL DY5 .... 102 D2
  TPTN/OCK DY4 .... 67 H8
Hurst La North *BKDE/SHDE* B34 .. 92 C6
  CBROM B36 .... 92 C6
Hurst Rd *BDWTH* CV12 .... 116 F2 ⓫
  BILS/COS WV14 .... 66 E4
  COVN CV6 .... 134 E1
  SMTHWKW B67 .... 105 H3
Hurst St *DIG/EDG* B5 .... 7 G8
The Hurst *HLYWD* B47 .... 145 L7
  MOS/BIL B13 .... 126 A6
The Hurstway
  ERDW/GRVHL B23 .... 72 A5
Hurstwood Rd *KGSTG* B44 .... 72 A5
Hussey Cl *PENK* ST19 .... 10 D6 ⓫
Hussey Rd *BRWNH* WS8 .... 26 C5
  CNCK/NC WS11 .... 17 K8
Husum Wy *KIDD* DY10 .... 138 A6
Hut Hill La *GTWY* WS6 .... 24 E1
Hutton Av *WASH/WDE* B8 .... 90 D8
Hutton Rd *BFLD/HDSWWD* B20 .. 88 F4
  WASH/WDE B8 .... 90 B8 ⓫
Huxbey Dr *HIA/OLT* B92 .... 128 C5
Huxley Cl *COVEN* WV9 .... 35 L2 ⓫
Hyatt Sq *BRLYHL* DY5 .... 102 A6 ⓫
Hyde Cl *BRGRVE* B60 .... 185 M3
Hyde Pl *RLSN* CV32 .... 200 C5
Hyde Rd *COVE* CV2 .... 155 J1
  KNWTH CV8 .... 176 D8
  WNSFLD WV11 .... 37 H7
Hydes Rd *DARL/WED* WS10 .... 68 F4
  HHTH/SAND B71 .... 69 G4
The Hyde *HAG/WOL* DY9 .... 120 B3
Hyett Wy *TPTN/OCK* DY4 .... 67 M3
Hylda Rd *BFLD/HDSWWD* B20 .... 88 F4
Hylstone Crs *WNSFLD* WV11 ...... 37 H7
Hylton St *WSNGN* B18 .... 89 G8 ⓫
Hyperion Dr
  ETTPK/GDPK/PENN WV4 .... 65 L2
Hyperion Rd *CBROM* B36 .... 91 J4
  KINVER DY7 .... 101 G5
Hyron Hall Rd *ACGN* B27 .... 127 G3
Hyssop Cl *CNCK/NC* WS11 .... 16 F3
  VAUX/NECH B7 .... 89 L8
Hytall Rd *SHLY* B90 .... 146 A3
Hythe Gv *YDLY* B25 .... 109 H5 ⓫

I

Ibberton Rd
  ALE/KHTH/YWD B14 .... 145 M1
Ibex Cl *COVS* CV3 .... 155 K4
Ibis Cl *KIDD* DY10 .... 161 M2
Ibis Gdns *KGSWFD* DY6 .... 83 L7
Ibstock Cl *REDE* B98 .... 197 J1
Ibstock Dr *STRBR* DY8 .... 119 L1
Ibstock Rd *COVN* CV6 .... 116 E8
Icknield Cl *FOAKS/STRLY* B74 ..... 55 L4
Icknield Port Rd
  LDYWD/EDGR B16 .... 106 C2
Icknield Sq *LDYWD/EDGR* B16 .. 106 E2
Icknield St *ALVE* B48 .... 168 F3
  ALVE B48 .... 188 F2
  HWK/WKHTH B38 .... 144 F5
  REDE B98 .... 189 G6
  REDE B98 .... 197 H3
  WSNGN B18 .... 6 A2
  WSNGN B18 .... 88 F8 ⓫
Icknield Street Dr *REDE* B98 ..... 197 H5
  STUD B80 .... 197 H6
Ida Rd *WBROM* B70 .... 87 H4
Idbury Rd *KGSTG* B44 .... 71 L6
Iden Rd *COV* CV1 .... 134 C8
Idmiston Cft
  ALE/KHTH/YWD B14 .... 145 K3
Idonia Rd *DUNHL/THL/PER* WV6 .. 34 C8
Ilam Pk *KNWTH* CV8 .... 177 G8
Ilex Cl *WASH* CV34 .... 199 M6
Ilford Cl *BDWTH* CV12 .... 116 D2
Ilford Dr *COVS* CV3 .... 153 M8
Ilford Rd *ERDW/GRVHL* B23 .... 72 B7
Ilfracombe Gv *COVS* CV3 .... 153 L8
Iliffe Wy *HRBN* B17 .... 124 B1
Ilkley Gv
  CHWD/FDBR/MGN B37 .... 110 D3
Illey Cl *NFLD/LBR* B31 .... 142 F4
Illey La *RMSLY* B62 .... 122 A4
Illshaw *COVEN* WV9 .... 35 L2
Illshaw Cl *REDE* B98 .... 197 L1

Illshaw Heath Rd
  HOCK/TIA B94 .... 171 H2
Ilmington Cl *COVS* CV3 .... 153 M8 ⓫
  REDE B98 .... 197 H4
  RWWCK/WEL CV35 .... 198 B3 ⓫
Ilmington Dr *SCFLD/BOLD* B73 ... 72 A2
Ilmington Rd *SLYOAK* B29 .... 123 K4
Ilsham Gv *NFLD/LBR* B31 .... 143 J7
Ilsley Rd *ERDW/GRVHL* B23 ...... 90 C1
Imber Rd *KIDD* DY10 .... 161 L4
Imperial Av *KIDD* DY10 .... 137 K5
Imperial Gv *KIDD* DY10 .... 137 K5
Imperial Ri *CSHL/WTROR* B46 .... 93 J3
Imperial Rd *BORD* B9 .... 108 C4 ⓫
Impney Cl *REDE* B98 .... 189 H7
Impsley Cl *CBROM* B36 .... 91 M5
Inca Cl *COVS* CV3 .... 155 K5
Ince Rd *DARL/WED* WS10 .... 52 A6
Incestre Rd *GTB/HAM* B43 .... 70 A4
Inchbrook Rd *KNWTH* CV8 .... 177 G6
Inchcape Av
  BFLD/HDSWWD B20 .... 88 C2
Inchford Av *WWCK* CV34 .... 199 J3
Inchford Cl *NUN* CV11 .... 99 K4
Inchford Rd *HIA/OLT* B92 .... 128 C6
Inchlaggan Rd *WOLVN* WV10 ..... 36 D7
Ingatestone Dr *STRBR* DY8 ...... 101 G2
Ingestre Cl *BLOX/PEL* WS3 .... 38 D2 ⓫
  CNCK/NC WS11 .... 16 F4 ⓫
Ingestre Dr *GTB/HAM* B43 .... 70 A4
Inge St *DIG/EDG* B5 .... 7 G8
Ingestre Rd *HLGN/YWD* B28 .... 126 D6
  WOLVN WV10 .... 36 A4 ⓫
Ingham Wy *HRBN* B17 .... 105 K6
Ingleby Gdns
  DUNHL/THL/PER WV6 .... 35 L8 ⓫
Ingledew Cl *WSLW* WS2 .... 52 B2
Inglefield Rd *STECH* B33 .... 109 K2
Inglemere Gv *SLYOAK* B29 ...... 123 K6
Inglenook Dr
  BFLD/HDSWWD B20 .... 88 F3
Ingleton Cl *NUN* CV11 .... 99 L3
Ingleton Rd *WASH/WDE* B8 .... 90 E6
Inglewood Av
  BDMR/CCFT WV3 .... 49 K5 ⓫
Inglewood Cl *KGSWFD* DY6 .... 83 H8 ⓫
  RLSN CV32 .... 200 C2
Inglewood Gv *FOAKS/STRLY* B74 .. 55 K4
Inglewood Rd *SPARK* B11 .... 108 A8 ⓫
Ingoldsby Rd *NFLD/LBR* B31 ..... 144 A2
Ingot Cl *WSLW* WS2 .... 38 F7
Ingram Gv *ACGN* B27 .... 126 E3
Ingram Pit La *TAM/AM/WIL* B77 .. 32 E8
Ingram Pl *BLOX/PEL* WS3 .... 39 H4
Ingram Rd *BLOX/PEL* WS3 .... 39 H4
  COVW CV5 .... 153 H5
Inhedge St *SEDG* DY3 .... 66 C8
The Inhedge *DUDN* DY1 .... 85 G4
Inkberrow Rd *HALE* B63 .... 121 K3 ⓫
Inkerman Gv *WOLVN* WV10 .... 3 L4
Inkerman St *VAUX/NECH* B7 ... 107 M1
  WOLVN WV10 .... 3 L2
Inland Rd *ERDE/BCHGN* B24 ...... 90 F3
Innage Cl *RLSS* CV31 .... 200 E5
Innage Rd *NFLD/LBR* B31 .... 143 M1
The Innage *HLYWD* B47 .... 145 L7
Innis Rd *COVW* CV5 .... 153 J6
Innsworth Dr *CVALE* B35 .... 91 L1
Insetton Cl *REDE* B98 .... 197 H1 ⓫
Inshaw Cl *STECH* B33 .... 109 J2
Institute Rd
  ALE/KHTH/YWD B14 .... 125 K5
Instone Rd *COVN* CV6 .... 133 L4
  HALE B63 .... 121 L2 ⓫
Instow Cl *WNSFLD* WV11 .... 37 M5
Insull Av *ALE/KHTH/YWD* B14 ... 145 M4
Intended St *HALE* B63 .... 103 G6
International Dr
  LGN/SDN/BHAMAIR B26 .... 129 G1
Intown *WSL* WS1 .... 5 G2
Intown Rw *WSL* WS1 .... 5 G2
Inveraray Cl *KNWTH* CV8 .... 192 A1
Inverclyde Dr
  BFLD/HDSWWD B20 .... 88 C2
Inverness Cl *COVW* CV5 .... 152 E1
Inverness Rd *NFLD/LBR* B31 .... 143 K2
Invicta Rd *COVS* CV3 .... 155 K5
Inworth *COVEN* WV9 .... 35 M2
Ipsley Church La *REDE* B98 ..... 197 G3
Ipsley Gv *ERDW/GRVHL* B23 ...... 71 L8 ⓫
Ipsley La *REDE* B98 .... 197 H3
Ipsley St *REDE* B97 .... 196 C2
Ipstones Av *STECH* B33 .... 109 K1
Ipswich Crs *PBAR/PBCH* B42 ..... 70 F6
Ireland Green Rd *WBROM* B70 .... 86 E2
Ireton Cl *TLHL/CAN* CV4 .... 152 A4
Ireton Rd *BFLD/HDSWWD* B20 ... 88 E1
  WOLVN WV10 .... 36 B2
Iris Cl *CRTAM* B79 .... 32 A7
  DUDS DY2 .... 85 K4
  SLYOAK B29 .... 123 M5
Iris Dr *ALE/KHTH/YWD* B14 ..... 145 H1
Irnham Rd *FOAKS/STRLY* B74 ..... 56 E3
Iron Bridge Wk *HAG/WOL* DY9 .. 119 M5
Iron La *STECH* B33 .... 109 H1
Ironmonger Rw *COV* CV1 .... 8 F4
Ironstone Rd *BNTWD* WS7 .... 18 C5
Irvan Av *WBROM* B70 .... 68 D8
Irvine Cl *BLOX/PEL* WS3 .... 38 F6
Irvine Rd *BLOX/PEL* WS3 .... 38 F5
Irving Cl *LICH* WS13 .... 20 C3
  SEDG DY3 .... 83 L1
Irving Rd *COV* CV1 .... 9 K7
  HIA/OLT B92 .... 128 C1
  TPTN/OCK DY4 .... 67 L4 ⓫
Irving St *EDG* B15 .... 6 E8
Irwin Av *RBRY* B45 .... 143 G7
Isaac Walton Pl *WBROM* B70 ..... 68 C4
Isbourne Wy *BORD* B9 .... 107 M2 ⓫
Isis Gv *CBROM* B36 .... 92 A5
  WLNHL WV13 .... 52 A3
Island Dr *KIDD* DY10 .... 161 J1 ⓫
Island Rd *HDSW* B21 .... 88 A4
Islington *HALE* B63 .... 121 L1
Islington Crs *ATHST* CV9 .... 61 G4 ⓫
Islington Rw *EDG* B15 .... 6 A8
Ismere Rd *ERDE/BCHGN* B24 .... 90 F3

Ismere Wy *KIDD* DY10 .... 137 K4
Itchen Gv *DUNHL/THL/PER* WV6 .. 48 C2
Ithon Gv *HWK/WKHTH* B38 ...... 144 C5
Ivanhoe Av *NUN* CV11 .... 99 J4
Ivanhoe Rd *BKHL/PFLD* WV2 ..... 50 E7 ⓫
  GTB/HAM B43 .... 70 F2
  LICHS WS14 .... 20 F7
Ivanhoe St *DUDS* DY2 .... 84 E6
Ivatt Cl *RUSH/SHEL* WS4 .... 39 M6
Iverley Cl *KIDD* DY10 .... 119 C8
Iverley Rd *HALE* B63 .... 122 A2
Iverley Wk *HAG/WOL* DY9 .... 119 M3
Ivor Rd *ATHST* CV9 .... 63 K6
  COVN CV6 .... 133 K7
  REDW B97 .... 196 B3
  SPARK B11 .... 125 M1
Ivybridge Gv *PBAR/PBCH* B42 .... 89 C2
Ivybridge Rd *COVS* CV3 .... 154 B8
Ivy Cl *CNCK/NC* WS11 .... 16 A5
Ivy Cft *COVEN* WV9 .... 35 K2
Ivydale Av
  LGN/SDN/BHAMAIR B26 .... 110 A8
Ivy Farm La *TLHL/CAN* CV4 ..... 153 H7
Ivyfield Rd *ERDW/GRVHL* B23 .... 71 M8
Ivy Gv *NUNW/HART* CV10 .... 80 B7
  WSNGN B18 .... 106 C1 ⓫
Ivyhouse La *BILS/COS* WV14 ...... 66 F5
Ivyhouse Rd *HWK/WKHTH* B38 .. 144 A5
Ivy House Rd *OLDBY* B69 .... 86 B7
Ivy La *CBHAMNE* B4 .... 7 M5
  RMSLY B62 .... 121 H8
Ivy Lodge Cl
  CHWD/FDBR/MGN B37 .... 110 E5
Ivy Rd *BVILLE* B30 .... 124 E7
  DUDN DY1 .... 84 E1
  HDSW B21 .... 88 E6
  SCFLD/BOLD B73 .... 72 D4
  TPTN/OCK DY4 .... 67 K6
Ivy Wy *SHLY* B90 .... 146 E7 ⓫
Izod St *REDW* B97 .... 196 B1
Izons La *WBROM* B70 .... 86 E4
Izons Rd *WBROM* B70 .... 87 C2

J

Jacey Rd *LDYWD/EDGR* B16 ..... 106 B3
  SHLY B90 .... 146 F1
Jackdaw Cl *SEDG* DY3 .... 66 A3
Jackdaw Dr *CBROM* B36 .... 92 E5
Jacker's Rd *COVE* CV2 .... 134 F1
Jack Holden Av *BILS/COS* WV14 .. 66 E3
Jacklin Dr *COVS* CV3 .... 178 A1
Jackson Cl *CNCK/NC* WS11 .... 25 J1
  LGLYGN/QTN B68 .... 86 E8 ⓫
  RCOVN/BALC/EX CV7 .... 115 L6
  RWWCK/WEL CV35 .... 198 D7 ⓫
  SPARK B11 .... 107 M6 ⓫
  TPTN/OCK DY4 .... 67 M4
  WOLVN WV10 .... 22 E7 ⓫
Jackson Dr *SMTHWKW* B67 .... 87 H8
Jackson Rd *COVN* CV6 .... 134 B4
  LICH WS13 .... 20 F2 ⓫
  WASH/WDE B8 .... 108 D1
Jackson St
  DUNHL/THL/PER WV6 .... 49 M1 ⓫
  HAG/WOL DY9 .... 102 C2 ⓫
  LGLYGN/QTN B68 .... 104 F1
Jackson Wy *RIDG/WDGT* B32 ... 104 E8
Jacmar Crs *SMTHWKW* B67 .... 87 J7
Jacobean La *DOR/KN* B93 .... 148 F4 ⓫
Jacob's Hall La *GTWY* WS6 .... 24 E4
Jacoby Pl *EDG* B15 .... 107 C8
Jacox Crs *KNWTH* CV8 .... 177 C8
Jade Cl *COV* CV1 .... 9 H1
Jade Gv *HEDN* WS12 .... 17 C3
Jaffray Crs *ERDE/BCHGN* B24 .... 90 D2 ⓫
Jaffray Rd *ERDE/BCHGN* B24 ..... 90 D2
Jaguar *TAM/AM/WIL* B77 .... 46 C3
Jakeman Cl *REDE* B98 .... 197 J1 ⓫
Jakeman Rd *BHTH/HG* B12 .... 107 J8
James Bridge Cl *BLSLW* WS2 .... 52 F6 ⓫
James Cl *DARL/WED* WS10 .... 52 D6 ⓫
  SMTHWKW B67 .... 87 L8
James Dawson Dr *COVW* CV5 .. 131 M5
James Dee Cl *BRLYHL* DY5 ...... 102 E4 ⓫
James Eaton Cl *HHTH/SAND* B71 .. 69 C8
James Galloway Cl *COVS* CV3 ... 155 L8
James Green Rd *TLHL/CAN* CV4 .. 152 D3
Jameson Rd *AST/WIT* B6 .... 90 A3
Jameson St
  DUNHL/THL/PER WV6 .... 49 M1
James Rd *CSHL/WTROR* B46 ..... 93 K5
  GTB/HAM B43 .... 70 C6
  KIDD DY10 .... 137 L5
  SPARK B11 .... 108 D7 ⓫
James Scott Rd *HALE* B63 .... 102 E7
James St *BILS/COS* WV14 .... 51 J7
  CBHAMW B1 .... 6 D3
  CNCK/NC WS11 .... 12 D8
  NUN CV11 .... 80 E8
  RCOVN/BALC/EX CV7 .... 96 E5 ⓫
  RUGBYN/HIL CV21 .... 183 M2
  WLNHL WV13 .... 51 L3
James Turner St *WSNGN* B18 .... 88 C7
James Watt Dr
  BFLD/HDSWWD B20 .... 88 F5
James Watt Queensway
  CBHAMNE B4 .... 7 H2
James Watt St *HHTH/SAND* B71 .. 68 C8
  VAUX/NECH B7 .... 7 M1 ⓫
Jane Lane Cl *WSLW* WS2 .... 52 D1
Janice Gv *ALE/KHTH/YWD* B14 .. 145 M1
Janine Av *WNSFLD* WV11 .... 37 J6
Jaques Cl *CSHL/WTROR* B46 ...... 92 F3
Jardine Crs *TLHL/CAN* CV4 ..... 152 D3
Jardine Rd *AST/WIT* B6 .... 89 K4
Jarvis Crs *OLDBY* B69 .... 104 E1
Jarvis Rd *ERDW/GRVHL* B23 ...... 72 D7
Jarvis Wy *ERDE/BCHGN* B24 ...... 90 C5
  VAUX/NECH B7 .... 90 C5
Jasmin Cft *ALE/KHTH/YWD* B14 .. 145 J2
Jasmine Cl *COVEN* WV9 .... 35 K2
Jasmine Gv *BRGRVW* B61 .... 185 K1 ⓫
  CDSL WV8 .... 34 F2 ⓫

  COVS CV3 .... 155 G5
  RLSN CV32 .... 200 E3
Jasmine Rd *DUDS* DY2 .... 85 K4
  TAM/AM/WIL B77 .... 46 E1
Jasmine Wy *DARL/WED* WS10 .... 52 B6 ⓫
Jason Cl *TAM/AM/WIL* B77 .... 32 E8
Jason Rd *HAG/WOL* DY9 .... 120 D1
Jayne Cl *HHTH/SAND* B71 .... 69 J4
  WNSFLD WV11 .... 37 H6
Jay Park Crs *KIDD* DY10 .... 161 L3
Jay Rd *KGSWFD* DY6 .... 83 H5
Jays Av *TPTN/OCK* DY4 .... 85 M1
Jays Cl *REDE* B98 .... 197 L2
Jays Crs *ALVE* B48 .... 167 M4
Jayshaw Av *GTB/HAM* B43 .... 70 C5
Jean Dr *TPTN/OCK* DY4 .... 68 B7
Jean St *ATHST* CV9 .... 62 A4
Jeavons Pl *BILS/COS* WV14 .... 51 G8
Jedburgh Av
  DUNHL/THL/PER WV6 .... 48 C1 ⓫
Jedburgh Gv *COVS* CV3 .... 177 L1
Jeddo St *BKHL/PFLD* WV2 .... 2 E8
Jefferson Cl *HHTH/SAND* B71 .... 68 F5
Jeffrey Av
  ETTPK/GDPK/PENN WV4 .... 50 D7
Jeffrey Cl *BDWTH* CV12 .... 116 B5
Jeffrey Rd *BLKHTH/ROWR* B65 .. 104 C2
Jeffs Av *BKHL/PFLD* WV2 .... 3 H9
Jeliff St *TLHL/CAN* CV4 .... 152 D4
Jelleyman Cl *KIDDW* DY11 ...... 136 F7
Jenkins Av *COVW* CV5 .... 152 D1
Jenkins Cl *BILS/COS* WV14 .... 51 G8
Jenkinson Rd
  DARL/WED WS10 .... 68 B4 ⓫
Jenkins St *SMHTH* B10 .... 108 A5
Jenkinstown Rd *HEDN* WS12 ..... 13 L7 ⓫
Jenks Av *WOLVN* WV10 .... 36 C5
Jenks Rd *WMBN* WV5 .... 64 D8
Jennens Rd *CBHAMNE* B4 .... 7 K3
Jennens Rd (Elevated Rd)
  CBHAMNE B4 .... 7 J4
Jenner Cl *WSLW* WS2 .... 38 D7
Jenner Rd *WSLW* WS2 .... 38 D7
Jenner St *BKHL/PFLD* WV2 .... 3 J7
  COV CV1 .... 9 H1
Jennings St *CDYHTH* B64 .... 103 K3 ⓫
Jenny Cl *BILS/COS* WV14 .... 67 J4 ⓫
Jenny Walkers La
  DUNHL/THL/PER WV6 .... 48 B3
Jensen *TAM/AM/WIL* B77 .... 46 C3
Jenton Rd *RLSS* CV31 .... 200 F7
Jephcott Rd *WASH/WDE* B8 ..... 108 E2
Jephson Dr
  LGN/SDN/BHAMAIR B26 .... 109 K6
Jeremy Gv *HIA/OLT* B92 .... 127 M1
Jeremy Rd
  ETTPK/GDPK/PENN WV4 .... 50 A8
Jerome Dr *CNCK/NC* WS11 .... 17 L8
Jerome Rd *CNCK/NC* WS11 .... 17 K8
  CSCFLD/WYGN B72 .... 73 H1
  WSLW WS2 .... 52 F4
Jerome Wy *BNTWD* WS7 .... 18 F6
Jerrard Dr *MGN/WHC* B75 .... 57 G8
Jerry's La *ERDW/GRVHL* B23 ...... 72 B6
  LICHS WS14 .... 30 A5
Jersey Cl *REDE* B98 .... 189 H6
Jersey Cft *CBROM* B36 .... 92 F7
Jersey Rd *WASH/WDE* B8 .... 108 B1
Jerusalem Wk *KIDD* DY10 .... 137 J6
Jervis Cl *BRLYHL* DY5 .... 84 A6
Jervis Crs *FOAKS/STRLY* B74 ..... 56 B2
Jervis Rd *TAM/AM/WIL* B77 .... 46 B5
Jervoise Dr *NFLD/LBR* B31 ...... 124 A8 ⓫
Jervoise La *HHTH/SAND* B71 ...... 69 J4
Jervoise Rd *SLYOAK* B29 .... 123 K4
Jervoise St *WBROM* B70 .... 86 F3
Jesmond Cl *HEDN* WS12 .... 13 L7 ⓫
Jesmond Gv *ERDE/BCHGN* B24 .. 91 J1
Jesmond Rd *COV* CV1 .... 9 K2
Jessel Rd *WSLW* WS2 .... 4 B1
Jessie Rd *ALDR* WS9 .... 40 E4
Jesson Cl *WSL* WS1 .... 5 K7
Jesson Rd *BLKHTH/ROWR* B65 ... 57 L8
  SEDG DY3 .... 66 E7
  WSL WS1 .... 5 H5
Jesson St *WBROM* B70 .... 87 J3
Jevons Rd *SCFLD/BOLD* B73 ...... 72 A2
Jevon St *BILS/COS* WV14 .... 66 F5 ⓫
Jew's La *DUDN* DY1 .... 84 C1
Jiggins La *RIDG/WDGT* B32 ...... 123 G5
Jill Av *GTB/HAM* B43 .... 70 A4
Jillcot Rd *HIA/OLT* B92 .... 127 M2
Jim Forrest Cl *COVS* CV3 .... 155 K5 ⓫
Jinnah Cl *BHTH/HG* B12 .... 107 K5 ⓫
Joanna Dr *COVS* CV3 .... 178 A1
Joan St *BKHL/PFLD* WV2 .... 50 C7
Joan Ward St *COVS* CV3 .... 9 G9
Job's La *TLHL/CAN* CV4 .... 152 E3
Jockey Fld *SEDG* DY3 .... 66 C7
Jockey La *DARL/WED* WS10 .... 68 L1
Jockey Rd *SCFLD/BOLD* B73 ...... 72 B3
Jodrell St *NUN* CV11 .... 80 F8
Joe Obrien Cl *COVS* CV3 .... 155 G7
Joe Williams Cl *COVS* CV3 ...... 155 K6
Joeys La *CDSL* WV8 .... 35 G2
John Bosco Cl
  HHTH/SAND B71 .... 68 F6 ⓫
John Bright Cl *TPTN/OCK* DY4 ... 67 K5 ⓫
John Bright St *CBHAM* B2 .... 6 F6 ⓫
  CBHAMW B1 .... 6 F7 ⓫
Johndory *TAM/AM/WIL* B77 .... 46 B7 ⓫
John Fletcher Cl
  DARL/WED WS10 .... 52 F8 ⓫
John Grace St *COVS* CV3 .... 9 H9
John Harper St *WLNHL* WV13 .... 51 M3 ⓫
John Kempe Wy
  BHTH/HG B12 .... 107 L6 ⓫
John Knight Rd
  BDWTH CV12 .... 116 F1 ⓫
John Mcguire Crs *COVS* CV3 .... 155 J6 ⓫
John Nash Sq *KNWTH* CV8 ...... 191 K2
John O'gaunt Rd *KNWTH* CV8 ... 191 J2
John Riley Dr *SHHTH* WV12 .... 38 A5
John Rd *RMSLY* B62 .... 122 D1
John Rous Av *TLHL/CAN* CV4 ... 152 F6
Johns Gv *GTB/HAM* B43 .... 70 A5
John Shelton Dr *COVN* CV6 ..... 134 A1
John Simpson Cl *KNWTH* CV8 .. 180 C2

Johns La GTWY WS6 24 D2
OLDBY B69 86 A3
TPTN/OCK DY4 85 M1
Johnson Av RUGBYS/DCH CV22 183 H3
WNSFLD WV11 37 K6
Johnson Cl CBROM B36 91 G7
DARL/WED WS10 52 B8
LICH WS13 21 G4
REDE B98 188 E8
SPARK B11 108 A8 2
Johnson Dr CVALE B35 91 K2 2
Johnson Pl BILS/COS WV14 51 K6 3
Johnson Rd BDWTH CV12 117 G2
BNTWD WS7 18 D5
CNCK/NC WS11 16 B1
COVN CV6 134 E5
DARL/WED WS10 52 B8
DARL/WED WS10 69 G3
ERDW/GRVHL B23 72 D8
SHHTH WV12 38 B6
Johnsons Bridge Rd
HHTH/SAND B71 69 G7
Johnsons Gv LGLYGN/QTN B68 105 G5
Johnson St ATHST CV9 61 G4
BILS/COS WV14 66 D4
BKHL/PFLD WV2 3 G9
VAUX/NECH B7 90 A7 4
Johnstone St LOZ/NWT B19 89 H5
Johnston St WBROM B70 87 H4
John St BDWTH CV12 116 E3
BKHL/PFLD WV2 50 E7
BLKHTH/ROWR B65 104 A4
BRLYHL DY5 102 B1
CNCK/NC WS11 12 D8
HEDN WS12 17 K2
LOZ/NWT B19 88 F6
NUN CV11 99 G3
NUNW/HART CV10 98 C2
OLDBY B69 86 E6
RLSN CV32 200 D5 2
STRBR DY8 101 K4
TAM/AM/WIL B77 46 C1 2
WBROM B70 68 D8
WLNHL WV13 51 L4
WSLW WS2 53 J2
John St North HHTH/SAND B71 68 F8
John Thwaites Cl
RUGBYS/DCH CV22 183 L3 2
Joiners Cft HIA/OLT B92 128 C5 1
Joinings Bank
LGLYGN/QTN B68 104 F1
Jonathan Rd COVE CV2 135 K5
Jones Field Crs WOLV WV1 50 F3
Jones' La BNTWD WS7 19 K6
GTWY WS6 24 F4
Jones Rd RCOVN/BALC/EX CV7 116 E4
SHHTH WV12 38 B4
WOLVN WV10 36 A7
Jones Wood Cl
WALM/CURD B76 73 K6 2
Jonkel Av TAM/AM/WIL B77 46 D8
Jonquil Cl ERDW/GRVHL B23 72 A6
Jordan Cl KNWTH CV8 191 M3
MGN/WHC B75 56 F4
SMTHWK B66 87 M8 7
Jordan Leys TPTN/OCK DY4 67 M8 3
Jordan Pl BILS/COS WV14 67 J2
Jordan Rd MGN/WHC B75 56 F4
Jordans Cl REDW B97 196 B7
The Jordans COVW CV5 153 G1
Jordan Wy ALDR WS9 40 F4
Jordan Well COV CV1 9 G5
Jorden's Wk BEWD DY12 160 A1 1
Joseph Creighton Cl
COVS CV3 155 J6 2
Joseph Dewsbury Cl
BNTWD WS7 18 C5
Joseph Luckman Rd
BDWTH CV12 116 E1
Joseph St OLDBY B69 86 D7
Josiah Rd NFLD/LBR B31 143 H3
Jowett TAM/AM/WIL B77 46 B3
Jowett's La HHTH/SAND B71 68 F5
Joyberry Dr STRBR DY8 119 K2
Joyce Pool WWCK CV34 199 J6 5
Joynson St DARL/WED WS10 52 C8
Jubilee Av HHTH/SAND B71 68 F6
REDW B97 196 B6
Jubilee Cl BLOX/PEL WS3 39 J7
GTWY WS6 24 D4
Jubilee Crs COVN CV6 133 M6
Jubilee Dr North KIDDW DY11 160 F3
Jubilee Dr South KIDDW DY11 160 F3
Jubilee Rd BILS/COS WV14 67 L1
RBRY B45 142 C3
TPTN/OCK DY4 67 L6
Jubilee St HHTH/SAND B71 69 H6
RUGBYN/HIL CV21 183 J2
Judd Cl BDWTH CV12 116 D2
Judds La COVN CV6 134 C1
Judge Cl OLDBY B69 86 E6 2
RRUGBY CV23 158 E8
Judge Rd BRLYHL DY5 102 D6
Juggin's La HOCK/TIA B94 169 M6
Julia Av ERDE/BCHGN B24 91 K1
Julia Gdns HHTH/SAND B71 69 K5
Julian Cl BRGRVW B61 165 L5
COVE CV2 135 K5
GTWY WS6 24 E2
WOLV WV1 50 F3
Julian Rd WOLV WV1 50 F3
Julie Cft BILS/COS WV14 67 J4
Juliet Cl NUN CV11 99 L4
Juliet Dr RUGBYS/DCH CV22 183 H7
Juliet Rd RMSLY B62 122 C1
Julius Dr CSHL/WTROR B46 93 K4
Junction Rd BKHL/PFLD WV2 50 F6
BRGRVW B61 185 J2
HDSW B21 88 A5
STRBR DY8 101 J5
STRBR DY8 119 M1
Junction St DUDS DY2 84 F5 2
OLDBY B69 86 C4
WSL WS1 4 D7 1
Junction St South OLDBY B69 86 E8
The Junction STRBR DY8 101 J5 5
June Crs TAM/AM/WIL B77 32 C8
June Cft
LGN/SDN/BHAMAIR B26 110 B8
Juniper TAM/AM/WIL B77 46 E1
Juniper Cl ACGN B27 108 F8 4
HEDN WS12 13 L7
Juniper Dr COVW CV5 132 D8
WALM/CURD B76 73 L6
Juniper Ri HALE B63 103 G8 2
Jury Rd BRLYHL DY5 102 D6
Jury St WWCK CV34 199 J7
Jutland Rd MOS/BIL B13 125 M6

K

Kanzan Rd COVE CV2 135 G1
Kareen Gv COVS CV3 156 A6
Karen Cl NUNW/HART CV10 80 C6
Karen Wy BRLYHL DY5 102 B5
Karlingford Cl COVW CV5 153 H5 1
Katherine Rd SMTHWKW B67 105 K3
Kathleen Av BDWTH CV12 116 C4
Kathleen Rd CSCFLD/WYGN B72 73 G1
YDLY B25 109 G6
Katie Rd SLYOAK B29 124 C4
Katrine Cl NUNW/HART CV10 80 A8
Katrine Rd STRPT DY13 160 C7
Kayne Cl KGSWFD DY6 83 G6
Kaysbrook Dr RRUGBY CV23 180 E7
Kean Cl LICH WS13 20 C3
Keanscott Dr
LGLYGN/QTN B68 105 G1 3
Keasdon Gv WLNHL WV13 52 A2
Keating Gdns MGN/WHC B75 56 E1
Keats Av CNCK/NC WS11 12 C8
SMHTH B10 108 B6
Keats Cl CRTAM B79 31 K5
FOAKS/STRLY B74 42 D7 3
NUNW/HART CV10 79 L8
SEDG DY3 65 L8
STRBR DY8 101 L5
Keats Dr BILS/COS WV14 67 H3
Keats Gv ACGN B27 126 F4
WOLVN WV10 36 E5
Keats Pl KIDD DY10 137 M7
Keats Rd BLOX/PEL WS3 39 J6
COVE CV2 155 H3
SHHTH WV12 38 C6
WOLVN WV10 36 E4
Keble Cl BNTWD WS7 19 G6
CNCK/NC WS11 16 C5
Keble Gv
LGN/SDN/BHAMAIR B26 109 M7
WSL WS1 5 K8
Kebull Gn TLHL/CAN CV4 152 C5
Kedleston Cl BLOX/PEL WS3 38 E2 4
Kedleston Rd HLGN/YWD B28 126 D7
Keel Dr MOS/BIL B13 126 B4 2
Keele Cl REDE B98 189 H7
Keeley St BORD B9 107 M3
Keeling Dr CNCK/NC WS11 15 M4
Keelinge St TPTN/OCK DY4 67 M8
Keeling Rd KNWTH CV8 176 F8
Keenan Dr BDWTH CV12 116 B4
Keen St SMTHWK B66 106 A1
Keepers Cl ALDR WS9 40 D2
BNTWD WS7 18 E7
CSHL/WTROR B46 111 L1
KGSWFD DY6 82 F5 1
LICHS WS14 21 J6 1
Keepers Gate Cl MGN/WHC B75 57 G6
Keepers La CDSL WV8 34 E5
Keepers Rd FOAKS/STRLY B74 42 A8
Kegworth Cl COVN CV6 134 E1 4
Kegworth Rd ERDW/GRVHL B23 90 A4
Keir Cl RLSN CV32 200 E3
Keir Pl STRBR DY8 101 J5
Keir Rd DARL/WED WS10 69 G3
Keith Rd RLSN CV32 200 F1
Kelby Cl NFLD/LBR B31 143 J2
Kelby Rd NFLD/LBR B31 143 J1
Keldy Cl DUNHL/THL/PER WV6 35 K8
Kele Rd TLHL/CAN CV4 152 D6
Kelfield Av HRBN B17 123 M1
Kelia Dr SMTHWKW B67 87 K7
Kellett Rd VAUX/NECH B7 7 L1
Kelling Cl BRLYHL DY5 102 A5 4
Kellington Cl WASH/WDE B8 108 D1 1
Kelmarsh Dr SOLH B91 147 M4
Kelmscote Rd COVN CV6 133 K5
Kelmscott Rd HRBN B17 105 M6
Kelsall Cl WOLV WV1 50 F3
Kelsall Cft CBHAMW B1 6 A4
Kelsey Cl NUN CV11 99 J2
VAUX/NECH B7 107 M1 1
Kelsey La RCOVN/BALC/EX CV7 151 G8
Kelsey's Cl KNWTH CV8 180 D2
Kelso Gdns
DUNHL/THL/PER WV6 48 B1 4
Kelsull Cft
CHWD/FDBR/MGN B37 110 E3
Kelton Ct EDG B15 106 E6 1
Kelvedon Gv SOLH B91 148 A1 1
Kelverdale Gv
ALE/KHTH/YWD B14 145 G1
Kelverley Gv HHTH/SAND B71 69 L4
Kelvin Av COVE CV2 135 H8
Kelvin Cl KIDDW DY11 136 E5
Kelvin Dr CNCK/NC WS11 16 E2
Kelvin Pl WSLW WS2 38 F7
Kelvin Rd NFLD/LBR B31 143 L4
RLSN CV32 192 F8
WSLW WS2 38 E7
Kelvin Wy WBROM B70 87 G4
Kelway COVS CV3 155 L3
Kelway Av GTB/HAM B43 70 F2
Kelwood Dr HALE B63 103 K8
Kelynmead Rd STETCH B33 109 L3
Kemberton Cl
BDMR/CCFT WV3 49 G4 1
Kemberton Rd BDMR/CCFT WV3 49 G4
SLYOAK B29 123 L3
Kemble Cl SHHTH WV12 52 B1
Kemble Cft DIG/EDG B5 107 J6
Kemble Dr CVALE B35 91 L2
Kemelstowe Crs HALE B63 121 G5 1
Kemerton Wy SHLY B90 147 K8
Kemp Cl WWCK CV34 199 L6 3
Kempe Rd STETCH B33 109 L1
Kempley Av COVE CV2 155 G3
Kempsey Cl HALE B63 121 J1 1
HIA/OLT B92 127 L2 1
OLDBY B69 104 B1
REDE B98 196 F6
Kempsey Covert
HWK/WKHTH B38 144 C6 1
Kempsford Cl REDE B98 196 D7
Kemps Green Rd
RCOVN/BALC/EX CV7 150 F7
Kempson Av CSCFLD/WYGN B72 73 G4
HHTH/SAND B71 68 F8
Kempson Rd CBROM B36 91 K5
PENK ST19 10 D4
Kempsons Gv BILS/COS WV14 66 F2 3
Kempthorne Av WOLVN WV10 36 C5
Kempthorne Gdns
BLOX/PEL WS3 38 E3 2
Kempthorne Rd
BILS/COS WV14 51 K7 2
Kempton Cl HEDN WS12 13 L7 6
Kempton Ct BRGRVW B61 165 L4 1
Kempton Crs RLSN CV32 201 G1
Kempton Dr GTWY WS6 24 D3
Kempton Park Rd CBROM B36 91 H5
Kempton Wy STRBR DY8 119 J2
Kemsey Dr BILS/COS WV14 67 K1
Kemshead Av NFLD/LBR B31 143 J5
Kemsley Rd
ALE/KHTH/YWD B14 145 K3
Kem St NUN CV11 99 J3
Kenchester Cl REDE B98 197 K3
Kendal Av CSHL/WTROR B46 93 K6
RBRY B45 142 F6
RLSN CV32 200 A3
Kendal Cl BRGRVE B60 185 M4
DUNHL/THL/PER WV6 35 K7 1
NUN CV11 81 L7
REDE B98 197 L2 1
Kendal Ct CNCK/NC WS11 15 M5
Kendal Dr RBRY B45 167 H4
Kendal End Rd RBRY B45 167 G3
Kendal Gv HIA/OLT B92 128 D5
Kendall Ri KGSWFD DY6 83 K8
Kendal Ri COVW CV5 153 G1
DUNHL/THL/PER WV6 35 K7
LGLYGN/QTN B68 104 F2
Kendal Rise Rd RBRY B45 142 F6
Kendal Rd SPARK B11 107 M6
Kendlewood Rd KIDD DY10 137 M4
Kendon Av COVN CV6 133 J7
Kendrick Av BKDE/SHDE B34 110 B1
Kendrick Cl COVN CV6 134 E1 5
HIA/OLT B92 128 D7
Kendrick Pl BILS/COS WV14 67 L1
Kendrick Rd BILS/COS WV14 67 L1
ERDE/BCHGN B24 73 K8
WOLVN WV10 36 C7
Kendricks Rd DARL/WED WS10 52 D6
Kendrick St DARL/WED WS10 68 E2 2
Kenelm Rd BILS/COS WV14 67 G4
LGLYGN/QTN B68 104 E2
SCFLD/BOLD B73 72 F1
SMHTH B10 108 C5
Kenelm's Ct RMSLY B62 141 L1
Kenilworth Cl FOAKS/STRLY B74 56 E5
PENK ST19 10 E5 2
REDW B97 196 B7
STRBR DY8 101 H3 1
TPTN/OCK DY4 85 H1
Kenilworth Ct DUDN DY1 84 D5 2
Kenilworth Crs
ETTPK/GDPK/PENN WV4 66 C1
WSLW WS2 52 E1
Kenilworth Dr CNCK/NC WS11 16 B1
KIDDW DY11 161 J3
NUN CV11 98 E2
Kenilworth Rd
BFLD/HDSWWD B20 89 J4
COVS CV3 153 L6
DOR/KN B93 149 G7 1
DUNHL/THL/PER WV6 48 D1 6
HIA/OLT B92 150 D2
KNWTH CV8 175 J3
LGLYGN/QTN B68 105 H5
LICHS WS14 20 F7 3
RCOVN/BALC/EX CV7 130 A3
RCOVN/BALC/EX CV7 150 F6 3
RLSN CV32 192 C6
TAM/AM/WIL B77 46 C1 3
TLHL/CAN CV4 177 G4
Kenilworth St RLSN CV32 200 D5 3
Kenley Gv BVILLE B30 144 E3
Kenley Wy SHLY B90 147 H1
Kenmare Wy WNSFLD WV11 51 G1
Kenmore Av HEDN WS12 12 D6
Kenmure Rd STETCH B33 110 A6
Kennan Av RLSS CV31 200 D7
Kennedy Cl KIDD DY10 161 J2
TAM/AM/WIL B77 46 A4 1
Kennedy Crs DARL/WED WS10 52 A6
SEDG DY3 84 B1
Kennedy Cft
LGN/SDN/BHAMAIR B26 109 L6
Kennedy Dr RUGBYS/DCH CV22 183 G3
Kennedy Gv BVILLE B30 124 F7 1
Kennedy Rd WOLVN WV10 3 H3
Kennel La ATHST CV9 63 M6
Kennerley Rd
LGN/SDN/BHAMAIR B26 109 H7
Kennet Cl BRWNH WS8 26 A3
COVE CV2 135 G5
Kennet Gv CBROM B36 92 D5
Kenneth Gv ERDW/GRVHL B23 71 L8
Kennford Cl OLDBY B69 86 A7
Kennington Rd WOLVN WV10 36 D8 1
Kenpas Hwy COVS CV3 153 L8
Kenrick Cft CVALE B35 91 K3
Kenrick Wy SMTHWK B66 87 K5
WBROM B70 87 J5
Kensington Av BHTH/HG B12 125 L1 2
Kensington Cl
NUNW/HART CV10 80 A7
Kensington Ct
NUNW/HART CV10 80 A7 1
Kensington Dr
FOAKS/STRLY B74 42 D8
Kensington Gdns STRBR DY8 101 G4
Kensington Rd COVW CV5 8 A7
SHHTH WV12 37 M6
SLYOAK B29 124 E4
Kenswick Dr HALE B63 121 L3
Kent Av POL/KGSB/FAZ B78 45 L4
WSLW WS2 52 F2
Kent Cl ALDR WS9 40 F4
BLOX/PEL WS3 39 J8
COVS CV3 154 C7
HHTH/SAND B71 68 F6
KIDD DY10 161 J2
Kenthurst Cl COVW CV5 152 A1
Kentish Rd HDSW B21 88 A5
Kentmere Cl COVE CV2 135 J3
PENK ST19 10 E4
Kenton Av
DUNHL/THL/PER WV6 49 K1
Kent Pl DUDS DY2 84 E7
HEDN WS12 17 K4 2
Kent Rd BKHL/PFLD WV2 50 C6
DARL/WED WS10 69 H1
RBRY B45 142 D4
RMSLY B62 104 C7
STRBR DY8 101 H5
Kent's Cl HIA/OLT B92 127 K2
Kent St DIG/EDG B5 7 G9
SEDG DY3 66 C8
WSLW WS2 39 J8
Kent St North WSNGN B18 88 D8
Kentwell CRTAM B79 31 H6
Kenward Cft HRBN B17 105 K6
Kenway HLYWD B47 145 L6
Kenwick Rd HRBN B17 123 M1 2
Kenwood Rd BORD B9 108 F2 1
Kenyon Cl BRGRVE B60 185 K4
STRBR DY8 101 L7
Kenyon St CBHAMNW B3 6 D2
Kepler CRTAM B79 31 J6
Keppel Cl RUGBYS/DCH CV22 183 G4
Keppel St COV CV1 134 C8
Kerby Rd ERDW/GRVHL B23 90 A1
Keresley Brook Rd COVN CV6 133 K3
Keresley Cl COVN CV6 133 K3
SOLH B91 128 A8
Keresley Green Rd COVN CV6 133 K4
Keresley Gv SLYOAK B29 123 K3 3
Keresley Rd COVN CV6 133 K4 2
Kernthorpe Rd
ALE/KHTH/YWD B14 145 G1
Kerr Dr TPTN/OCK DY4 67 J5
Kerria Rd TAM/AM/WIL B77 46 F1
Kerridge Cl COVEN WV9 35 L3
Kerris Wy COVS CV3 155 L4
Kerry Cl BRLYHL DY5 102 A1
NFLD/LBR B31 123 K7
Kerry Hl BRGRVE B60 185 J7
Kersley Gdns WNSFLD WV11 37 K7
Kerswell Cl REDW B97 187 M8
Kerswell Dr SHLY B90 147 L8
Kesterton Rd FOAKS/STRLY B74 42 C8
Kesteven Cl EDG B15 106 F7 1
Kesteven Rd HHTH/SAND B71 69 G6
Keston Rd KGSTG B44 71 K1
Kestrel TAM/AM/WIL B77 46 E7 1
Kestrel Av YDLY B25 108 F5
Kestrel Cl ERDW/GRVHL B23 72 B7
KIDD DY10 161 J2
Kestrel Cft COVS CV3 155 K5
Kestrel Dr FOAKS/STRLY B74 42 D8 3
Kestrel Gv HEDN WS12 17 G4
SHHTH WV12 38 A5
SLYOAK B29 124 B5 1
Kestrel Ri
DUNHL/THL/PER WV6 35 K6 1
Kestrel Rd DUDN DY1 84 E5
HALE B63 102 F6
LGLYGN/QTN B68 104 D3
Kestrel Wy GTWY WS6 24 A3
Keswick Cl NUN CV11 81 L7
Keswick Dr KGSWFD DY6 83 H7
Keswick Gn RLSN CV32 200 B4
Keswick Gv FOAKS/STRLY B74 55 K3
Keswick Rd HIA/OLT B92 127 K1
Keswick Wk COVE CV2 155 K1
Ketley Cft BHTH/HG B12 107 K6 4
Ketley Flds KGSWFD DY6 83 L8
Ketley Hill Rd DUDN DY1 84 D5
Ketley Rd KGSWFD DY6 83 K7
Kettlebrook Rd SHLY B90 147 M7
TAM/AM/WIL B77 46 A1
Kettlehouse Rd KGSTG B44 71 K2
Kettlesbank Rd SEDG DY3 83 M3 1
Kettlewell Cl WWCK CV34 199 J4
Kettlewell Wy
CHWD/FDBR/MGN B37 110 D3
Ketton Gv STETCH B33 110 B6
Keviliok St COVS CV3 154 B7
Kew Cl CHWD/FDBR/MGN B37 110 D2
KNWTH CV8 177 G8 4
Kew Dr DUDN DY1 84 E3
Kew Gdns STETCH B33 109 H4
Kew Rd RUGBYN/HIL CV21 183 L1
Kewstoke Cl WNSFLD WV11 37 M4
Kewstoke Cft NFLD/LBR B31 123 J7 1
Kewstoke Rd SHHTH WV12 38 A4
Keyes Dr KGSWFD DY6 83 H4
Key Hl WSNGN B18 88 F8
Key Hill Dr WSNGN B18 89 G8
Keynell Covert BVILLE B30 145 G3
Keynes Dr BILS/COS WV14 51 J7 2
Keys Crs HHTH/SAND B71 69 G7
Keys Dr RUGBYS/DCH CV22 183 G2
Keyse Rd MGN/WHC B75 57 K6
Keys Hl ATHST CV9 62 A4
Keyte Cl TPTN/OCK DY4 67 L8
The Keyway WLNHL WV13 51 L5
Keyworth Cl TPTN/OCK DY4 67 M8
Khyber Cl DARL/WED WS10 52 A5 5
Kidd Cft DARL/WED WS10 68 A3
Kidderminster Rd BEWD DY12 160 A1
BRGRVW B61 185 J3 2
HAG/WOL DY9 119 M8
KGSWFD DY6 82 E7
KIDD DY10 119 G6
KIDD DY10 163 L7
Kidderminster Rd South
KIDD DY10 139 J2
Kielder Cl DSYBK/YTR WS5 70 A2
HEDN WS12 17 J3
Kielder Dr NUNW/HART CV10 98 C3
Kielder Gdns HAG/WOL DY9 119 M4 3
Kier's Bridge Cl TPTN/OCK DY4 85 L2 4
Kilburn Dr COVW CV5 153 K2
KGSWFD DY6 83 J4 1
Kilburn Gv KGSTG B44 71 K2
Kilburn Pl DUDS DY2 85 H7
Kilburn Rd KGSTG B44 71 K2
Kilby Av LDYWD/EDGR B16 106 E3
Kilbye Cl TAM/AM/WIL B77 46 D8
Kilby Gv RLSS CV31 201 G8 3
Kilbys Gv BFLD/HDSWWD B20 88 D3
Kilcote Rd SHLY B90 146 A3
Kildale Cl COV CV1 9 J3
Kildwick Wy WWCK CV34 199 J4 7
Kilmore Cft CBROM B36 91 J4
Kilmorie Rd ACGN B27 109 G8
CNCK/NC WS11 16 A3
Kiln Cl NUNW/HART CV10 98 C2
RLSN CV32 200 E3
Kiln La SHLY B90 170 D1
YDLY B25 108 F7
Kilnsey Gv WWCK CV34 199 J4
Kiln Wy POL/KGSB/FAZ B78 47 K4
Kilpeck Cl REDE B98 197 K3 2
Kilsby Gv SOLH B91 148 A5
Kilvert Rd DARL/WED WS10 68 F3
Kimberley TAM/AM/WIL B77 46 D6 3
Kimberley Av KIDD DY10 137 M1
WASH/WDE B8 90 C8 4
Kimberley Cl COVW CV5 152 D1 2
FOAKS/STRLY B74 55 L3 1
REDE B98 188 F6
Kimberley Pl DUDN DY1 66 F6 3
Kimberley Rd BDWTH CV12 116 F1
HIA/OLT B92 127 L3
KNWTH CV8 178 C3
RUGBYN/HIL CV21 183 M1
SMTHWK B66 87 L6
Kimberley St BDMR/CCFT WV3 2 B7
Kimble Cl COVW CV5 152 F1
Kimble Gv ERDE/BCHGN B24 91 H2
Kimg's Meadow HAG/WOL DY9 140 C2
Kimpton Cl
ALE/KHTH/YWD B14 145 J3
Kimsan Cft FOAKS/STRLY B74 55 L6
Kinchford Cl SOLH B91 147 M5
Kineton Cl REDE B98 197 H4
Kineton Cft RIDG/WDGT B32 123 H5
Kineton Green Rd HIA/OLT B92 127 H5
Kineton La HOCK/TIA B94 171 J4
Kineton Ri SEDG DY3 66 A3
Kineton Rd COVE CV2 135 G7
KNWTH CV8 191 M1
RBRY B45 142 C6
SCFLD/BOLD B73 72 C4
Kinfare Dr DUNHL/THL/PER WV6 48 F1
Kinfare Ri SEDG DY3 84 C1
King Charles Av WSLW WS2 52 C3
King Charles Cl KIDDW DY11 137 G7 4
King Charles Ct KGSTG B44 71 M3 1
King Charles Rd RMSLY B62 122 D1
King Edmund St DUDN DY1 84 F3
King Edward Av BRGRVW B61 165 K8 2
King Edward Rd BRGRVW B61 165 K8
COV CV1 9 K2
MOS/BIL B13 125 K2
NUN CV11 99 H1
RUGBYN/HIL CV21 183 M1
King Edwards Cl
BFLD/HDSWWD B20 88 F5 2
King Edwards Gdns
BFLD/HDSWWD B20 88 F6 2
King Edwards Rd CBHAMW B1 6 B4
King Edward's Rw
BKHL/PFLD WV2 2 F9 1
King Edward's Sq
SCFLD/BOLD B73 57 G8 1
King Edward St
DARL/WED WS10 52 B8
Kingfield Rd COVN CV6 134 B7
SHLY B90 146 A3
Kingfisher TAM/AM/WIL B77 46 E7
Kingfisher Av NUNW/HART CV10 80 A8
Kingfisher Cl SEDG DY3 66 A3
Kingfisher Ct ALVE B48 167 L6 2
Kingfisher Dr CBROM B36 92 E5
HEDN WS12 17 G1
STRBR DY8 119 G1 1
Kingfisher Gv KIDD DY10 161 M2 1
SHHTH WV12 37 M5
Kingfisher Veiw STETCH B33 91 L8
Kingfisher Wk PENK ST19 10 D5
Kingfisher Wy SLYOAK B29 124 B5
King George Av BRGRVW B61 185 J1 2
King George Cl BRGRVW B61 185 J1
King George Crs
RUSH/SHEL WS4 39 M7
King George Pl RUSH/SHEL WS4 39 M7
King George's Av BDWTH CV12 98 F8
COVN CV6 134 C3
King George Vi Av
DSYBK/YTR WS5 54 A5
Kingham Cl REDE B98 197 L1
SEDG DY3 84 A3
Kingham Covert BVILLE B30 145 H3 4
Kingland Dr RLSN CV32 200 A4
King Richard St COVE CV2 9 L3
Kings Av ATHST CV9 63 J5
HEDN WS12 17 G1
OLDBY B69 85 M3
Kingsbridge Rd
NUNW/HART CV10 81 H7
RIDG/WDGT B32 123 H4
Kingsbridge Wk
SMTHWK B66 87 M8 3
Kingsbrook Dr SOLH B91 147 M5
Kingsbury Cl RUSH/SHEL WS4 53 M1
WALM/CURD B76 74 B7
Kingsbury Rd COVN CV6 133 H7
ERDE/BCHGN B24 90 C3
TPTN/OCK DY4 67 L5 4
WALM/CURD B76 74 A8
WALM/CURD B76 75 L3

Kingsclere Wk
  ETTPK/GDPK/PENN WV4 ...... 49 G6 🔟
Kingscliff Rd SMHTH B10 ...... 108 E5
Kings Cl ALE/KHTH/YWD B14 .. 125 C7
Kingscote Cl REDE B98 .... 189 H6
Kingscote Gv COVS CV3............ 177 L1
Kingscote Rd DOR/KN B93 ...... 172 C3
  EDG B15 .... 106 B7
Kings Ct STRBR DY8 .... 101 L8
Kingscroft Cl CBROM B36 .... 92 D6 🔟
  LGN/SDN/BHAMAIR B26 ...... 109 L8 🔟
Kingscroft Cl FOAKS/STRLY B74 .. 55 L5
Kingscroft Rd FOAKS/STRLY B74 .. 55 L6
Kingsdene Av STRBR DY8 .... 101 C1
Kingsdown Av COVS CV3............ 153 K4
Kingsdown Rd BNTWD WS7 ...... 18 C4
  NFLD/LBR B31 .... 123 J4
Kingsfield Rd
  ALE/KHTH/YWD B14 .... 125 J5 🔟
Kingsford Cl CBROM B36 .... 92 B4 🔟
Kingsford Nouveau
  KGSWFD DY6 .... 83 M8 🔟
Kings Gdn BVILLE B50 .... 144 C1
Kings Gdns BDWTH CV12 .... 117 G3
Kings Green Av
  HWK/WKHTH B38 .... 144 D3
Kings Gv COVE CV2 .... 154 F2
Kingshayes Rd ALDR WS9 .... 40 F3
Kingshill Dr HWK/WKHTH B38 .. 144 D3
King's Hill Fld DARL/WED WS10 .. 52 C8
King's Hill La KNWTH CV8 ...... 177 K4
King's Hill Rd LICHS WS14 ...... 21 C7
Kingshurst RLSS CV31 .... 201 J7
Kingshurst Rd NFLD/LBR B31.... 143 L2
  SHLY B90 .... 146 D4
Kingshurst Wy
  CHWD/FDBR/MGN B37 .... 92 D8
Kingsland Av COVW CV5 .... 153 K3
Kingsland Dr DOR/KN B93 ...... 172 C2
Kingsland Rd KGSTG B44 .... 71 J1
  WOLV WV1 .... 2 C2
Kingslea Rd SOLH B91 .... 147 J3
Kingsleigh Dr CBROM B36 .... 91 M5 🔟
Kingsleigh Rd
  BFLD/HDSWWD B20 .... 88 F3
Kingsley Av
  DUNHL/THL/PER WV6............ 48 F1
  HEDN WS12 .... 13 C6 🔟
  REDE B98 .... 196 E2
Kingsley Cl CRTAM B79 .... 31 L7
Kingsley Crs BDWTH CV12 ...... 117 M2
Kingsley Gdns CDSL WV8 .... 34 C2
Kingsley Gv SEDG DY3 .... 65 L8
Kingsley Rd BHTH/HG B12 ...... 107 L8
  BVILLE B30 .... 144 B1
  KGSWFD DY6 .... 83 G8
Kingsley St DUDS DY2 .... 85 C8 🔟
  WSLW WS2 .... 52 F6
Kingsley Ter COVE CV2 .... 135 J5
Kingsley Wk COVE CV2 .... 135 K5 🔟
Kingslow Av
  ETTPK/GDPK/PENN WV4 ...... 49 H7
Kingsmead Ms COVS CV3 .... 155 H7 🔟
King's Meadow HAG/WOL DY9 .. 140 C3
Kingsmere Cl ERDW/BCHGN B24 .. 90 C3
Kings Mill Cl DARL/WED WS10 .. 52 C8
Kings Newnham La
  RRUGBY CV23...................... 157 L6
Kings Newnham Rd
  RRUGBY CV23...................... 157 M7
Kings Rd ALE/KHTH/YWD B14 .. 125 G7
  ERDW/GRVHL B23 .... 90 A1
  KGSTG B44 .... 71 M3
  KGSTG B44 .... 71 L3
  KGSTG B44 .... 71 J2
  KIDDW DY11 .... 137 G2
  RUSH/SHEL WS4 .... 40 A6
  SEDG DY3 .... 66 C5
  SPARK B11 .... 108 E8
  WOLVN WV10 .... 14 E7
Kings Street Prec
  DARL/WED WS10 .... 52 B7
Kingstanding Rd KGSTG B44 .... 71 K3 🔟
Kings Ter ALE/KHTH/YWD B14 .. 125 G7
Kingsthorpe Rd
  ALE/KHTH/YWD B14 .... 145 L1
Kingston Cl CRTAM B79 .... 32 A6
Kingston Ms RLSS CV31 .... 201 G7
Kingston Rd BORD B9 .... 107 M4
  COVW CV5 .... 153 K3
Kingston Rw CBHAMW B1 .... 6 C5 🔟
Kingston Wy KGSWFD DY6 ...... 83 G6
King St ALDR WS9 .... 40 D3
  BDWTH CV12 .... 117 G3
  BILS/COS WV14 .... 66 E5
  BILS/COS WV14 .... 67 J2
  BNTWD WS7 .... 18 D8
  BRLYHL DY5 .... 102 D5
  CDYHTH B64 .... 103 K4
  CRTAM B79 .... 45 M1
  DARL/WED WS10 .... 68 C3
  DUDS DY2 .... 85 G4
  HAG/WOL DY9 .... 120 D1
  HALE B63 .... 121 L1
  RLSN CV32 .... 200 E4
  RUGBYN/HIL CV21 .... 183 L1
  SMTHWK B66 .... 87 M6
  SPARK B11 .... 107 L6 🔟
  STRBR DY8 .... 101 J7
  WLNHL WV13 .... 51 M3
  WOLV WV1 .... 2 F5
  WSL WS1 .... 4 D8
King Street Pas BRLYHL DY5 .. 102 E5 🔟
  DUDS DY2 .... 85 H4
Kingsway CNCK/NC WS11 .... 16 E1 🔟
  LGN/QTN/QTN B68 .... 104 C1
  NUN CV11 .... 98 F1
  POL/KGSB/FAZ B78 .... 60 A7
  RLSS CV31 .... 200 D7
  RUGBYS/DCH CV22 .... 183 L4
  STRBR DY8 .... 101 H5
  STRPT DY13 .... 160 C6
  WNSFLD WV11 .... 37 L1
  WOLVN WV10 .... 36 E7
Kingsway Av TPTN/OCK DY4 .... 67 L5 🔟
Kingsway Dr HWK/WKHTH B38 .. 144 D3
Kingsway Rd WOLVN WV10 ...... 36 E7

Kingswear Av
  DUNHL/THL/PER WV6............ 48 D2
Kingswinford Rd BRLYHL DY5 .. 84 C6
  DUDN DY1............................ 84 C6
Kingswood Av CNCK/NC WS11 .. 16 A6 🔟
  RCOVN/BALC/EX CV7 .... 114 F5
Kingswood Cl COVN CV6 .... 134 B4
  HOCK/TIA B94...................... 173 J8
  SHLY B90 .... 147 H4
Kingswood Cft
  VAUX/NECH B7 .... 90 A6 🔟
Kingswood Dr CNCK/NC WS11 .. 17 K8
  FOAKS/STRLY B74 .... 71 K1
  GTWY WS6 .... 24 E1
Kingswood Gdns
  ETTPK/GDPK/PENN WV4 ...... 49 K7
Kingswood Rd MOS/BIL B13 .... 125 L1
  NFLD/LBR B31 .... 143 K7
  NUNW/HART CV10 .... 97 M2
  STRBR DY8 .... 101 G1
Kington Cl SHHTH WV12 .... 37 M5
Kington Gdns
  CHWD/FDBR/MGN B37 .... 110 D3
Kington Wy STETCH B33 .... 109 J4
King William St COV CV1 .... 9 J2
  STRBR DY8 .... 101 K5
Kiniths Crs HHTH/SAND B71 .... 87 J1
Kiniths Wy HHTH/SAND B71 .... 87 J1
  RMSLY B62 .... 104 C4
Kinlet Cl BDMR/CCFT WV3...... 48 E5
  REDE B98 .... 197 J2
Kinlet Gv NFLD/LBR B31 .... 144 A3
Kinloch Dr DUDN DY1 .... 84 D2
Kinnerley St WSL WS1 .... 5 J4
Kinnersley Cl REDE B98 .... 197 J2
Kinnersley Crs OLDBY B69 ...... 86 B8
Kinnerton Crs SLYOAK B29 ...... 123 K3
Kinross Av HEDN WS12 .... 12 C6
Kinross Cl NUNW/HART CV10 .. 98 D3
Kinross Crs GTB/HAM B43........ 70 F1
Kinross Rd RLSN CV32 .... 200 F1
Kinsall Gn TAM/AM/WIL B77 .... 47 C7
Kinsey Gv ALE/KHTH/YWD B14 .. 145 K1
Kinsham Dr SOLH B91 .... 147 M5
Kintore Cft RIDG/WDGT B32 .... 122 F6 🔟
Kintyre Cl RBRY B45 .... 142 C4 🔟
The Kintyre COVE CV2 .... 135 M6
Kinver Av KIDDW DY11 .... 160 E5
  SHHTH WV12 .... 37 M8
Kinver Cl COVE CV2 .... 135 J4 🔟
Kinver Crs ALDR WS9 .... 41 C4
Kinver Cft BHTH/HG B12 .... 107 J6 🔟
  WALM/CURD B76 .... 73 K5
Kinver Dr
  ETTPK/GDPK/PENN WV4 ...... 49 C8
Kinver Rd NFLD/LBR B31.......... 144 B3
Kinver St STRBR DY8 .... 101 H4
Kinwalsey La
  RCOVN/BALC/EX CV7 .... 113 J7
Kinwarton Cl
  LGN/SDN/BHAMAIR B26 ...... 109 H7
Kipling Av BILS/COS WV14........ 66 F4
Kipling Cl NUNW/HART CV10 .. 79 L8 🔟
  TPTN/OCK DY4 .... 67 L5
Kipling Ri CRTAM B79 .... 31 K5
Kipling Rd COVN CV6 .... 133 K5
  NFLD/LBR B31 .... 144 A1
  SEDG DY3 .... 65 J4
  SHHTH WV12 .... 38 C6
  WOLVN WV10 .... 36 B3
Kirby Av WWCK CV34 .... 199 K4
Kirby Cl BILS/COS WV14 .... 67 J2
  COV CV1 .... 134 B7
  KNWTH CV8 .... 156 D8
Kirby Corner Rd TLHL/CAN CV4 .. 152 F8
Kirby Rd COVW CV5 .... 153 K3
  WSNGN B18 .... 88 C7
Kirkby Gn SCFLD/BOLD B73 .... 72 E2
Kirkdale Av COVN CV6 .... 134 B2
Kirkham Gdns BRLYHL DY5 .... 84 A7
Kirkham Gv STETCH B33 .... 109 L1 🔟
Kirkham Wy TPTN/OCK DY4 .... 67 J3
Kirkland Wy POL/KGSB/FAZ B78 .. 44 F5
Kirkside Gv BRWNH WS8 .... 26 D6
Kirkstall Cl BLOX/PEL WS3 ...... 38 D3 🔟
Kirkstall Crs BLOX/PEL WS3 .... 38 D3
Kirkstone Cl BRLYHL DY5 .... 101 M5
Kirkstone Crs GTB/HAM B43.... 70 D7
  WMBN WV5 .... 64 D7
Kirkstone Rd BDWTH CV12 .... 116 E3
Kirkstone Wy BRLYHL DY5 ...... 101 M5
Kirkwall Rd RIDG/WDGT B32 .. 123 H4
Kirkwood Av ERDW/GRVHL B23.. 72 D6
Kirstead Gdns
  DUNHL/THL/PER WV6............ 48 F2
Kirtley TAM/AM/WIL B77 .... 46 C3
Kirton Cl COVN CV6 .... 133 K4 🔟
Kirton Gv DUNHL/THL/PER WV6 .. 49 L1
  SOLH B91 .... 147 L4
  STETCH B33 .... 109 L1 🔟
Kitchener Rd COVN CV6 .... 134 C4
  DUDS DY2 .... 85 K4
  SLYOAK B29 .... 124 F4
Kitchener St SMTHWK B66 ...... 88 B7
Kitchen La WNSFLD WV11 ...... 37 J5
Kitebrook Cl REDE B98 .... 197 J1
  SHLY B90 .... 147 L6 🔟
Kites Cl WWCK CV34 .... 199 J3
Kites Nest La
  RWWCK/WEL CV35 .... 190 B8
Kitsland Rd BKDE/SHDE B34 .... 92 C7
Kitswell Rd RIDG/WDGT B32.... 122 E5
Kittermaster Rd
  RCOVN/BALC/EX CV7 .... 130 F3
Kittiwake Dr BRLYHL DY5 .... 102 A6
  KIDD DY10.......................... 161 M2
Kittoe Rd FOAKS/STRLY B74.... 56 D2
Kitt's Green Rd STETCH B33 .... 109 M2
  STETCH B33 .... 110 A2
Kitwell La RIDG/WDGT B32 ...... 122 E5
Kitwood Av POL/KGSB/FAZ B78.. 47 K7
Kitwood Dr HIA/OLT B92 .... 128 B6
Kixley La DOR/KN B93.............. 149 C7
Klevedon Cl NUN CV11 .... 99 L4 🔟
Knaresdale Cl BRLYHL DY5 ...... 102 A6
Knaves Castle Av BRWNH WS8.. 26 D3
Knebley Crs NUNW/HART CV10 .. 99 G4
Knebworth Cl KGSTG B44 .... 71 J5 🔟

Knight Av COV CV1 .... 9 K7
Knightcote Dr SOLH B91 .... 147 M5
  RLSN CV32 .... 193 J8
Knightley Rd SOLH B91 .... 147 K3 🔟
Knightlow Av COVS CV3 .... 155 C8
Knightlow Cl KNWTH CV8 ...... 192 A2 🔟
Knighton Cl FOAKS/STRLY B74 .. 56 D2 🔟
Knighton Dr FOAKS/STRLY B74 .. 56 D8
Knighton Rd DUDS DY2 .... 103 H1 🔟
  FOAKS/STRLY B74 .... 42 B8
  HEDN WS12 .... 17 J2
  NFLD/LBR B31 .... 144 A1
Knights Av
  DUNHL/THL/PER WV6............ 35 J7
Knightsbridge Av BDWTH CV12 .. 98 F8
Knightsbridge Cl
  FOAKS/STRLY B74 .... 56 B1
Knightsbridge La SHHTH WV12 .. 37 M7
Knights Cl ERDW/GRVHL B23 .... 90 C3 🔟
  PENK ST19 .... 10 D6
Knights Ct CNCK/NC WS11 ...... 25 L1
Knights Crs
  DUNHL/THL/PER WV6............ 35 J6
Knightsford Cl REDW B97 .... 195 K3
Knights Hl FOAKS/STRLY B74 .. 54 F2
Knights Rd SPARK B11 .... 126 E1
Knights Templar Wy
  TLHL/CAN CV4 .... 152 E4 🔟
Knightstone Av WSNGN B18 .... 106 E1
Knightwick Crs
  ERDW/GRVHL B23 .... 72 A8
Knipersley Rd ERDW/GRVHL B23.. 72 E7
Knob Hl RRUGBY CV23............ 180 D7
Knoll Cl BNTWD WS7 .... 18 E8
Knoll Cft ALDR WS9 .... 41 C4
  COVS CV3 .... 154 A7
  SHLY B90 .... 171 H1
Knoll Dr COVS CV3 .... 154 A7
  WWCK CV34 .... 199 J3
The Knoll KGSWFD DY6 .... 83 J8
  RIDG/WDGT B32.................. 123 G4
Knottsall La LGLYGN/QTN B68 .. 104 F2
Knottsford Cl
  KGSWFD DY6 .... 101 L3 🔟
Knowesley Cl BRGRVE B60 ...... 185 M3 🔟
Knowlands Rd SOLH B91 .... 147 L6
Knowle Cl RBRY B45 .... 143 H6
  REDE B98 .... 189 G7
Knowle Hl ATHST CV9 .... 77 G1
  KNWTH CV8 .... 177 G7
Knowle Hill Rd DUDS DY2 .... 102 F1
Knowle La LICHS WS14 .... 28 F3
Knowle Rd BLKHTH/ROWR B65 .. 103 K1
  HIA/OLT B92 .... 149 J3
  SPARK B11 .... 126 E1
Knowles Av NUNW/HART CV10 .. 98 A1
Knowles Dr FOAKS/STRLY B74 .. 56 E6
Knowles Rd WOLV WV1 .... 3 L6
Knowles St DARL/WED WS10 .... 68 C2
Knowle Wood Rd DOR/KN B93 .. 172 F3
Knox Crs NUN CV11 .... 81 K6
Knox Rd BKHL/PFLD WV2 .... 50 A7
Knox's Grave La LICHS WS14 .. 29 M6
Knutsword Cl MOS/BIL B13 .... 126 B6 🔟
Kohima Dr STRBR DY8 .... 101 J8
Kossuth Rd BILS/COS WV14 .... 66 E4
Kurtus TAM/AM/WIL B77 .... 46 B7 🔟
Kyle Cl WOLVN WV10 .... 35 M4
Kyles Wy RIDG/WDGT B32 ...... 122 F6 🔟
Kynaston Crs CDSL WV8 .... 34 F3 🔟
Kynner Wy COVS CV3.............. 155 M5
Kyotts Lake Rd SPARK B11 ...... 107 L6
Kyrwicks La SPARK B11............ 107 L7
Kyter La CBROM B36 .... 91 L2 🔟

L

Laburnham Rd KGSWFD DY6 .... 83 J7
Laburnum Av
  CHWD/FDBR/MGN B37 .... 92 D7
  CNCK/NC WS11 .... 16 B6
  COVN CV6 .... 133 K8
  CRTAM B79 .... 31 M5
  KNWTH CV8 .... 191 L1
  SMTHWKW B67 .... 105 J1
Laburnum Cl BDWTH CV12 .... 116 C3
  BLOX/PEL WS3 .... 39 K3
  CHWD/FDBR/MGN B37 .... 92 D7 🔟
  CNCK/NC WS11.................... 16 C6
  HLYWD B47 .... 145 L8
  POL/KGSB/FAZ B78 .... 60 B7
  REDE B98 .... 196 C3 🔟
Laburnum Cft OLDBY B69 ...... 85 M3 🔟
Laburnum Dr WALM/CURD B76.. 73 L2
Laburnum Gv BNTWD WS7 ...... 18 D7
  BRGRVW B61 .... 185 L1
  KIDDW DY11 .... 136 E5
  NUNW/HART CV10 .... 80 B7
  RUGBYS/DCH CV22 .... 183 J5 🔟
  WSLW WS2 .... 52 D2
  WWCK CV34 .... 199 M4
Laburnum Rd ALDR WS9 .... 40 E2
  BVILLE B30 .... 124 D6
  DARL/WED WS10 .... 68 F2
  DSYBK/YTR WS5 .... 54 A8
  DUDN DY1.......................... 84 F1
  ETTPK/GDPK/PENN WV4 ...... 66 C2
  TPTN/OCK DY4 .... 67 K6
  WOLV WV1 .... 50 F5
Laburnum St BDMR/CCFT WV3.. 2 B7
Laburnum Wy NFLD/LBR B31 .. 143 L4 🔟
Lacell Cl WWCK CV34 .... 199 H4
Laches Cl WOLVN WV10 .... 14 B8
Laches La WOLVN WV10............ 22 C3
Ladbroke Dr WALM/CURD B76.... 73 K3
Ladbroke Gv ACGN B27 .... 127 G5
Ladbrook Cl REDE B98.............. 196 C6
Ladbrook Gv SEDG DY3 .... 83 L2

REDE B98 .... 196 E4
  WWCK CV34 .... 199 H5 🔟
Landor St WASH/WDE B8 .... 107 M2
Landport Rd WOLV WV1 .... 3 L8
Landrake Rd KGSWFD DY6 ...... 83 K8
Landsdown Pl WSNGN B18 ...... 88 E8 🔟
Landseer Gv KGSTG B44 .... 71 H1 🔟
Landsgate STRBR DY8 .... 119 L4
Landswood Cl KGSTG B44 .... 71 L4
Landswood Rd
  LGLYGN/QTN B68 .... 105 G1
Landywood Gn GTWY WS6 ...... 24 C3
Landywood La GTWY WS6 .... 24 B3
Lane Av WSLW WS2 .... 52 F2
Lane Cl WSLW WS2.................. 52 F2
Lane Cft WALM/CURD B76 ...... 73 L5
Lane Green Av CDSL WV8 .... 35 G4
Lane Green Rd CDSL WV8 .... 35 G3
Lane Rd
  ETTPK/GDPK/PENN WV4 ...... 66 C2
Lanes Cl WMBN WV5 .... 64 B8
Lanesfield Dr
  ETTPK/GDPK/PENN WV4 ...... 66 C1
Laneside COVS CV3.................. 155 J7
Laneside Av FOAKS/STRLY B74 .. 55 K6
Laneside Gdns WSLW WS2 ...... 52 E3
Lane St BILS/COS WV14 .... 67 H2
Langbank Av COVS CV3............ 155 G5
Langcliffe Av WWCK CV34 ...... 199 K4
Langcomb Rd SHLY B90 .... 146 E5
Langdale Av COVN CV6 .... 134 D2
Langdale Cl RLSN CV32 .... 201 H2
Langdale Ct TAM/AM/WIL B77 .. 32 J7 🔟
Langdale Cft HDSW B21 .... 88 C6 🔟
Langdale Dr BILS/COS WV14.... 51 H6
  CNCK/NC WS11.................... 15 M6
  NUN CV11 .... 81 L7
Langdale Rd GTB/HAM B43 .... 70 D6
Langdale Wy HAG/WOL DY9 .... 120 B1
Langdon St BORD B9 .... 107 M3 🔟
Langfield Rd DOR/KN B93 ...... 148 E6
Langford Av GTB/HAM B43 ...... 70 C5
Langford Cft SOLH B91 .... 148 A3 🔟
Langford Gv HRBN B17 .... 124 A2 🔟
Langham Cl
  LGN/SDN/BHAMAIR B26 ...... 109 L6
Langham Gn FOAKS/STRLY B74 .. 55 K4
Langholm Dr HEDN WS12 ...... 17 J3
  SCFLD/BOLD B73 .... 72 B4 🔟
Langland Dr SEDG DY3 .... 66 A5
Langley Av BILS/COS WV14 ...... 67 C5
Langley Cl REDE B98 .... 197 H4
Langley Crs LGLYGN/QTN B68.. 104 F1
Langley Dr CVALE B35 .... 91 L4
Langley Gdns BDMR/CCFT WV3.. 48 D6
  LGLYGN/QTN B68 .... 104 E1
Langley Green Rd OLDBY B69 .. 104 E1
Langley Hall Dr MGN/WHC B75.. 57 M7
Langley Hall Rd HIA/OLT B92 .. 127 G6
  MGN/WHC B75.................... 57 M8
Langley Heath Dr
  WALM/CURD B76 .... 73 K2
Langley High St OLDBY B69 .... 86 E8
Langley Ri HIA/OLT B92 .... 128 B2
Langley Rd
  ETTPK/GDPK/PENN WV4 ...... 48 D3
  LGLYGN/QTN B68 .... 104 E1
  SMTH B10............................ 108 B5
Langleys Rd SLYOAK B29 .... 124 C4
Langlodge Rd COVN CV6 .... 133 M3
Langmead Cl WSLW WS2 .... 52 B2
Langnor Rd COVE CV2 .... 135 C6
Langsett Rd WOLVN WV10 .... 3 J2
Langstone Rd
  ALE/KHTH/YWD B14 .... 145 M3
  DUDN DY1.......................... 84 C4
Langton Cl COVS CV3 .... 155 C5
Langton Pl BILS/COS WV14 ...... 51 L7
Langton Rd WASH/WDE B8 .... 108 C1 🔟
Langtree Av SOLH B91 .... 147 M4
Langtree Cl HEDN WS12 .... 17 H4
Langwood Ct TLHL/CAN CV4 .. 152 F6
Langwood Ct CBROM B36 .... 91 M5 🔟
Langworth Av ACGN B27 .... 109 C8 🔟
Lannacombe Rd NFLD/LBR B31.. 143 J7
Lansbury Av DARL/WED WS10 .. 68 A1
Lansbury Dr CNCK/NC WS11 .... 16 C1
Lansbury Gn CDYHTH B64 ...... 103 M5 🔟
Lansbury Rd CDYHTH B64 ...... 103 M5 🔟
Lansdale Av HIA/OLT B92 .... 128 D5
Lansdown Cl COVE CV2 .... 135 C3
Lansdowne Av WOLVN WV10 .... 14 C3
Lansdowne Circ RLSN CV32 .... 200 E4 🔟
Lansdowne Cl BDWTH CV12 .... 116 E2 🔟
  BILS/COS WV14 .... 66 E6
  DUDS DY2 .... 85 K7
Lansdowne Crs RLSN CV32 .... 200 E4 🔟
  TAM/AM/WIL B77 .... 46 B4
Lansdowne Rd BILS/COS WV14 .. 51 J6
  ERDE/BCHGN B24 .... 90 D2
  HALE B63 .... 121 H3
  HDSW B21 .... 88 E6
  RLSN CV32 .... 200 E4 🔟
  RMSLY B62 .... 104 D5
  WOLV WV1 .... 2 D3
Lansdowne St COVE CV2 .... 9 L4
  RLSN CV32 .... 200 E4
  WSNGN B18 .... 106 D1
Lansdown Gn KIDDW DY11 .... 136 F8
Lant Cl RCOVN/BALC/EX CV7.. 151 M6
Lantern Rd DUDS DY2 .... 103 G3 🔟
Lapal La RIDG/WDGT B32 ...... 122 E5
Lapal La North RMSLY B62 .... 122 C2
Lapal La South RMSLY B62 .... 122 C2
Lapley Cl WOLV WV1 .... 50 F3 🔟
Lapper Av
  ETTPK/GDPK/PENN WV4 ...... 66 D3
Lapping TAM/AM/WIL B77 ...... 46 E7 🔟
Lapwood Cl GTWY WS6 .... 24 A4
Lapwing Dr HIA/OLT B92 .... 129 M6
Lapwing Av KGSWFD DY6 .... 83 L8
  KIDD DY10.......................... 161 M4
Lapworth Cl REDE B98 .... 196 D6
Lapworth Dr SCFLD/BOLD B73 .. 72 A2
Lapworth Gv BHTH/HG B12 .... 107 K7 🔟
Lapworth Rd COVE CV2 .... 135 C4
Lara Cl HRBN B17 .... 105 M5
Lara Gv TPTN/OCK DY4 .... 85 L3 🔟
Larch Av HDSW B21 .... 88 B5

Larch Cl *KINVER* DY7......**118** A2
  LICHS WS14......**21** J6
  RUGBYS/DCH CV22......**182** F3
Larch Cft
  CHWD/FDBR/MGN B37......**110** F3
  OLDBY B69......**85** M3 🔲
Larches Cottage Gdns
  KIDDW DY11......**161** H2 🔲
Larches La *LICHS* WV3......**2** A5
Larches Rd *KIDDW* DY11......**161** H2
Larches St *SPARK* B11......**107** L7
The Larches
  POL/KGSB/FAZ B78......**60** B6 🔲
  RCOVN/BALC/EX CV7......**116** C5
Larchfield Cl
  BFLD/HDSWWD B20......**88** F2
Larchfields *KNWTH* CV8......**180** E1
Larch Gv *SEDG* DY3......**66** C6
  WWCK CV34......**199** L4 🔲
Larchmere Dr *BRGRVW* B61......**185** H2
  HLGN/YWD B28......**126** D5
  WNSFLD WV11......**37** L2
Larch Rd *KGSWFD* DY6......**83** J6
Larch Tree Av *TLHL/CAN* CV4......**152** E2
Larchwood Crs
  FOAKS/STRLY B74......**55** J5 🔲
Larchwood Dr *CNCK/NC* WS11......**16** E1 🔲
Larchwood Gn
  DSYBK/YTR WS5......**69** M1 🔲
Larchwood Rd *DSYBK/YTR* WS5......**69** L1
  RCOVN/BALC/EX CV7......**116** C5
Larcombe Dr
  ETTPK/GDPK/PENN WV4......**50** B8 🔲
Large Av *DARL/WED* WS10......**68** A1
Lark Cl *ALE/KHTH/YWD* B14......**145** L3
Larkfield Av *CBROM* B36......**91** M5
Larkfield Rd *REDE* B98......**196** E4
Larkfield Wy *COVW* CV5......**132** C2
Larkhill *KIDD* DY10......**137** J6
Larkhill Rd *STRBR* DY8......**119** C1
Larkhill Wk
  ALE/KHTH/YWD B14......**145** H4
  WOLVN WV10......**36** E4
Lark Meadow Dr
  CHWD/FDBR/MGN B37......**110** D2 🔲
Larkspur *TAM/AM/WIL* B77......**60** B1
Larkspur Av *BNTWD* WS7......**18** E8
Larkspur Cft *CBROM* B36......**91** H5
Larkspur Dr *WOLVN* WV10......**22** F6
Larkspur Rd *DUDS* DY2......**85** K5
Larkspur Wy *BRWNH* WS8......**26** B7
Larkswood Dr
  ETTPK/GDPK/PENN WV4......**65** C2
  SEDG DY3......**66** B6
Larne Rd
  LGN/SDN/BHAMAIR B26......**109** L6
Lassington Cl *REDE* B98......**197** J2
Latches Cl *DARL/WED* WS10......**52** C7 🔲
Latchford Cl *REDE* B98......**189** J7
Latelow Rd *STECH* B33......**109** L3
Latham Av *GTB/HAM* B43......**70** C6 🔲
Latham Crs *TPTN/OCK* DY4......**85** L2 🔲
Latham Rd *COVW* CV5......**8** A1
Latherford Cl *WOLVN* WV10......**14** C8
Latherford La *WOLVN* WV10......**14** F8
Lath La *SMTHWK* B66......**87** H5
Lathom Gv *STECH* B33......**91** K8
Latimer Cl *KNWTH* CV8......**191** K3
Latimer Gdns *EDG* B15......**107** H6 🔲
Latimer Pl *WSNGN* B18......**88** C7
Latimer Rd *ALVE* B48......**167** L8
Latymer Cl *WALM/CURD* B76......**73** L6 🔲
  WLNHL WV13......**51** H4
Lauder Cl *SEDG* DY3......**66** A4
Lauderdale Av *COVN* CV6......**134** B2
Lauderdale Cl
  RUGBYN/HIL CV21......**182** F1 🔲
Lauderdale Gdns
  WOLVN WV10......**36** C2 🔲
Launceston Cl *DSYBK/YTR* WS5......**54** B3 🔲
  TAM/AM/WIL B77......**46** B3 🔲
Launceston Dr *NUN* CV11......**99** K1
Launceston Rd *DSYBK/YTR* WS5......**54** B6
The Launde
  ALE/KHTH/YWD B14......**146** B2
Laundry Rd *SMTHWK* B66......**106** A2
Laural Dr *SMTHWK* B66......**87** J8
Laureates Wk *FOAKS/STRLY* B74......**56** E4
Laurel Av *BHTH/HG* B12......**107** L8 🔲
  POL/KGSB/FAZ B78......**47** L6
Laurel Bank *CRTAM* B79......**31** M7
Laurel Cl *COVE* CV2......**135** G3 🔲
  LICH WS13......**21** H5
  REDE B98......**196** C3
Laurel Dr *BNTWD* WS7......**19** C6
  FOAKS/STRLY B74......**55** J5
  HEDN WS12......**17** J1
  NUNW/HART CV10......**79** L6
  RUGBYS/DCH CV22......**182** F4 🔲
  SMTHWK B66......**87** L5
Laurel Gdns *ACGN* B27......**109** G8
  HDSW B21......**88** C4 🔲
  RUGBYS/DCH CV22......**183** K5
Laurel Gv *BDMR/CCFT* WV3......**49** J7
  BILS/COS WV14......**67** L1
  BRGRVW B61......**185** K1
  BVILLE B30......**124** C7
Laurel La *HALE* B63......**121** M2
Laurel Rd *BVILLE* B30......**144** E1
  DSYBK/YTR WS5......**53** M8
  DUDN DY1......**84** E1
  HDSW B21......**88** C3
  TPTN/OCK DY4......**67** K6
Laurels Crs
  RCOVN/BALC/EX CV7......**151** G7
The Laurels *BDWTH* CV12......**116** C3
  LGN/SDN/BHAMAIR B26......**110** A8 🔲
  POL/KGSB/FAZ B78......**60** B6 🔲
Laurence Gv
  DUNHL/THL/PER WV6......**35** J6 🔲
Lauriston Cl *DUDN* DY1......**84** D2 🔲
Lavender Av *COVN* CV6......**133** G4
Lavender Cl *COVEN* WV9......**35** K2
Lavender Gv *BILS/COS* WV14......**51** K7
Lavender Hall La
  RCOVN/BALC/EX CV7......**150** F4

Lavender La *STRBR* DY8......**119** H2
Lavender Rd *DUDN* DY1......**84** F2
  TAM/AM/WIL B77......**46** C1
Lavendon Rd *PBAR/PBCH* B42......**70** E8
Lavinia Rd *RMSLY* B62......**122** C2
Law Cliff Rd *PBAR/PBCH* B42......**70** F7
Law Cl *OLDBY* B69......**137** J2
Lawden Rd *SPARK* B11......**107** M5 🔲
Lawford Av *LICHS* WS14......**21** J6
Lawford Cl *COVS* CV3......**155** J4
  VAUX/NECH B7......**7** M3
Lawford Gv *DIG/EDG* B5......**107** J5 🔲
  SHLY B90......**146** B3
Lawford Heath La
  RRUGBY CV23......**181** M8
Lawford La *RUGBYS/DCH* CV22......**182** F4
  RLSS CV31......**200** F8
  RUGBYS/DCH CV22......**183** L2 🔲
Lawfred Av *WNSFLD* WV11......**37** H8
Lawley Cl *RUSH/SHEL* WS4......**39** M4
  TLHL/CAN CV4......**152** E3
Lawley Middleway
  ......**7** L2
Lawley Rd *BILS/COS* WV14......**50** F7
Lawley St *DUDN* DY1......**84** E4
  WBROM B70......**86** D2
The Lawley *HALE* B63......**121** C4
Lawn Av *STRBR* DY8......**119** J1
Lawnoaks Cl *BRWNH* WS8......**26** B3
Lawn Rd *BKHL/PFLD* WV2......**50** C7
Lawnsdale Cl
  CSHL/WTROR B46......**93** K6 🔲
Lawnsdown Rd *BRLYHL* DY5......**102** D6
Lawnsfield Gv
  ERDW/GRVHL B23......**72** B6 🔲
Lawnside Rd *BILS/COS* WV14......**51** H5
The Lawns *BDWTH* CV12......**116** B3
Lawn St *STRBR* DY8......**119** J1
Lawnswood *KINVER* DY7......**100** E1
  WALM/CURD B76......**73** L5
Lawnswood Av *BNTWD* WS7......**26** D1
  DUNHL/THL/PER WV6......**35** J5
  ETTPK/GDPK/PENN WV4......**66** C1
  SHLY B90......**147** H2
  STRBR DY8......**101** G1
Lawnswood Cl *HEDN* WS12......**17** H4 🔲
Lawnswood Dr *ALDR* WS9......**40** E2
  KINVER DY7......**100** E3
Lawnswood Gv *HDSW* B21......**88** A4
Lawnswood Ri
  DUNHL/THL/PER WV6......**35** K5
Lawnswood Rd *SEDG* DY3......**66** B8
  STRBR DY8......**101** G2
Lawnwood Rd *DUDS* DY2......**103** G3
Lawrence Av *WNSFLD* WV11......**37** K7
  WOLVN WV10......**50** E1
Lawrence Ct *CRTAM* B79......**31** L7 🔲
Lawrence Dr *WALM/CURD* B76......**74** B7
Lawrence Gdns *KNWTH* CV8......**176** D7
Lawrence La *CDYHTH* B64......**103** J4 🔲
Lawrence Saunders Rd
  COVN CV6......**133** M8
Lawrence Sheriff St
  RUGBYN/HIL CV21......**183** L3 🔲
Lawrence St *HAG/WOL* DY9......**102** A7 🔲
  WLNHL WV13......**51** L2
Lawrence Wk *GTB/HAM* B43......**71** H1 🔲
Lawson Cl *ALDR* WS9......**54** F1
Lawson St *CBHAMNE* B4......**7** H2
Law St *HHTH/SAND* B71......**69** G8
Lawton Cl *OLDBY* B69......**86** A7
Laxey Rd *LDYWD/EDGR* B16......**106** A2
Laxford Cl *BHTH/HG* B12......**107** J7
Laxton Cl *KGSWFD* DY6......**83** J5
Laxton Gv *YDLY* B25......**109** H4 🔲
Lay Gdns *RLSS* CV31......**201** J8
Lazy Hl *ALDR* WS9......**41** G3
  HWK/WKHTH B38......**144** F3
Lazy Hill Rd *ALDR* WS9......**41** G4
Lea Av *DARL/WED* WS10......**68** A4
Lea Bank Av *KIDDW* DY11......**136** E8
Lea Bank Rd *DUDS* DY2......**102** F2
Leabon Gv *HRBN* B17......**124** A1 🔲
Leabrook
  LGN/SDN/BHAMAIR B26......**109** K5
Leabrook Rd *DARL/WED* WS10......**68** B4
Leabrook Rd North
  DARL/WED WS10......**68** B4
Lea Castle Cl *KIDD* DY10......**137** J1
The Lea Cswy *KIDDW* DY11......**160** E1 🔲
Leach Green La *RBRY* B45......**142** E6
Leach Heath La *RBRY* B45......**142** D6
Leacliffe Wy *FOAKS/STRLY* B74......**55** K2
Leacote Dr
  DUNHL/THL/PER WV6......**49** G1
Lea Crs *RUGBYN/HIL* CV21......**159** H8
Leacrest Rd *COVN* CV6......**133** L3
Leacroft *SHHTH* WV12......**38** A6
Leacroft Av *WOLVN* WV10......**36** C5
Leacroft Cl *ALDR* WS9......**40** F4
Leacroft Gv *HHTH/SAND* B71......**68** F5
Leacroft La *CNCK/NC* WS11......**15** J7 🔲
Leacroft Rd *KGSWFD* DY6......**83** J7
  PENK ST19......**10** D3
Lea Croft Rd *REDW* B97......**196** B8
Leadbetter Dr *BRGRVW* B61......**185** H3
Lea Dr *LGN/SDN/BHAMAIR* B26......**109** L7
Lea End La *ALVE* B48......**168** A1
Leafdown Cl *HEDN* WS12......**17** H1
Leafenden Av *BNTWD* WS7......**18** B4
Leafield Cl *COVE* CV2......**135** K5 🔲
Leafield Crs *STECH* B33......**91** L8 🔲
Leafield Gdns *RMSLY* B62......**104** B5
Leafield Rd *HIA/OLT* B92......**127** M4
Leaf La *COVS* CV3......**154** D7
Leaford Wy *KGSWFD* DY6......**83** K6
Leafy Gld *FOAKS/STRLY* B74......**55** L2
Leafy Ri *SEDG* DY3......**84** A1
Leagh Cl *KNWTH* CV8......**176** F6
Lea Green Av *TPTN/OCK* DY4......**67** G8
Lea Green La *HLYWD* B47......**146** A7
Lea Hall Dr *BNTWD* WS7......**18** B4
Lea Hall Rd *STECH* B33......**109** K2
Leahill Cft
  CHWD/FDBR/MGN B37......**110** D3
Lea Hill Rd *BFLD/HDSWWD* B20......**89** G3
Leaholme Gdns *HAG/WOL* DY9......**119** M3

Leahouse Gdns
  LGLYGN/QTN B68......**104** E2
Lea House Rd *BVILLE* B30......**124** E6
Leahouse Rd *LGLYGN/QTN* B68......**104** E2
Leahurst Crs *HRBN* B17......**124** A1
Lea La *GTWY* WS6......**24** E3
Lea Manor Dr
  ETTPK/GDPK/PENN WV4......**65** J2
Leam Cl *NUN* CV11......**99** K4
Leam Crs *HIA/OLT* B92......**128** A4
Leam Dr *BNTWD* WS7......**19** H6
Leam Gn *TLHL/CAN* CV4......**153** H8
Leamington Cl *CNCK/NC* WS11......**16** A5
Leamington Rd *BHTH/HG* B12......**107** M8
  COVS CV3......**154** A6
  KNWTH CV8......**179** M5
Leamore Cl *WSLW* WS2......**38** E6
Leamore La *BLOX/PEL* WS3......**39** G6
  WSLW WS2......**38** E5
Leamount Dr *KGSTG* B44......**72** A3
Leam Rd *BDMR/CCFT* WV3......**49** L6
Leam St *RLSS* CV31......**200** A6
Leam Ter *RLSS* CV31......**200** F5
Leander Cl *BNTWD* WS7......**18** B4
  GTWY WS6......**24** D4 🔲
Leander Gdns
  ALE/KHTH/YWD B14......**125** K8
Leander Rd *HAG/WOL* DY9......**120** D1 🔲
Lea Park Ri *BRGRVW* B61......**165** K8
Leapgate La *STRPT* DY13......**161** J8
Lea Rd *BDMR/CCFT* WV3......**49** L6
  SPARK B11......**126** B1
Lear Rd *WMBN* WV5......**64** F6
Leas Cl *BDWTH* CV12......**116** E2
Leason La *WOLVN* WV10......**36** E5
Leasow Dr *EDG* B15......**124** B2
Leasowe Rd *RBRY* B45......**142** D5
  TPTN/OCK DY4......**85** J1
Leasowe's Av *COVS* CV3......**177** K1
Leasowes Ct *HALE* B63......**121** L3 🔲
Leasowes Dr
  DUNHL/THL/PER WV6......**48** B1
  ETTPK/GDPK/PENN WV4......**49** H7
Leasowes La *RMSLY* B62......**122** C1 🔲
Leasowes Rd
  ALE/KHTH/YWD B14......**125** K4 🔲
The Leasowe *LICH* WS13......**20** E4
The Leasow *ALDR* WS9......**40** C8
The Leas *WOLVN* WV10......**23** G6
Lea St *KIDD* DY10......**137** K8
The Lea *KIDDW* DY11......**136** E8
  STECH B33......**109** L2
Leatherhead Cl *AST/WIT* B6......**89** K7 🔲
Leathermill La
  NUNW/HART CV10......**80** B2
Lea Vale Rd *STRBR* DY8......**119** K3
Leavesden Gv
  LGN/SDN/BHAMAIR B26......**109** L8
Lea Vw *ALDR* WS9......**40** C8
  SHHTH WV12......**37** L8
Leaward Cl *NUNW/HART* CV10......**98** C3
Lea Wood Gv *KIDDW* DY11......**136** E8
Lea Wk *RBRY* B45......**142** D5
Lea Yield Cl *SLYOAK* B29......**124** E6
Lebanon Gv *BNTWD* WS7......**18** D5
Lechlade Cl *REDE* B98......**189** G6
Lechlade Rd *GTB/HAM* B43......**70** C5
Leckie Rd *WSLW* WS2......**53** J1
Ledbrook Rd *RLSN* CV32......**193** H8
Ledbury Cl *ALDR* WS9......**41** G4
  LDYWD/EDGR B16......**106** E3
  REDE B98......**197** K3
Ledbury Dr *WOLV* WV1......**50** F4 🔲
Ledbury Rd *RLSS* CV31......**200** F5
Ledbury Wy *WALM/CURD* B76......**73** L5
Ledsam Gv *RIDG/WDGT* B32......**105** K7
Ledsam St *LDYWD/EDGR* B16......**106** E3
Lee Bank Middleway *EDG* B15......**6** D9
Leebank Rd *HALE* B63......**121** J3
Leech St *TPTN/OCK* DY4......**68** A8
Lee Cl *WWCK* CV34......**199** J3
Lee Crs *EDG* B15......**107** C5
Leeder Cl *COVN* CV6......**134** A3
Leedham Av
  TAM/AM/WIL B77......**32** C8 🔲
Lee Gdns *SMTHWKW* B67......**87** J8
Leeming Cl *TLHL/CAN* CV4......**153** C7
Lee Mt *EDG* B15......**107** G5 🔲
Lee Rd *CDYHTH* B64......**103** K5
  HLYWD B47......**145** L6
  RLSS CV31......**200** C6
Lees Rd *BILS/COS* WV14......**67** K2 🔲
Lees St *WSNGN* B18......**88** D8
Lees Ter *WBROM* B70......**68** E5
The Lee *COVW* CV5......**153** G1
Legge La *BILS/COS* WV14......**67** H3
  CBHAMW B1......**6** B3
Legge St *AST/WIT* B6......**7** J1
  BKHL/PFLD WV2......**50** C7
  WBROM B70......**87** H2
Legion Cl *CNCK/NC* WS11......**17** L7
Legion Rd *RBRY* B45......**142** C6
Legs La *WOLVN* WV10......**36** D2
Le Hanche Cl
  RCOVN/BALC/EX CV7......**115** L6
Leicester Cswy *COV* CV1......**134** B8
Leicester Cl *SMTHWKW* B67......**105** J4
Leicester Crs *ATHST* CV9......**63** J4
Leicester La *RLSN* CV32......**193** C6
  RLSN CV32......**193** J4
Leicester Pl *HHTH/SAND* B71......**69** H6
Leicester Rd *BDWTH* CV12......**116** F1
  NUN CV11......**81** H8
  RUGBYN/HIL CV21......**159** L7
Leicester Rw *COV* CV1......**8** F2
Leicester Sq *BDWTH* CV12......**116** F2 🔲
  RLSN CV32......**200** E4
  WSL WS1......**4** F7
Leigham Dr *HRBN* B17......**105** K6
Leigh Av *BNTWD* WS7......**18** K6
  COVS CV3......**178** A2
Leigh Cl *RUSH/SHEL* WS4......**53** L1
Leigh Rd *MGN/WHC* B75......**57** M7
  RUGBYN/HIL CV21......**159** K5

  RUSH/SHEL WS4......**53** L1
  WASH/WDE B8......**90** C7
Leighs Cl *RUSH/SHEL* WS4......**40** A4
Leighs Rd *RUSH/SHEL* WS4......**39** M4
Leigh St *COV* CV1......**9** K2
Leighswood Av *ALDR* WS9......**40** C5
Leighswood Cl *CNCK/NC* WS11......**17** K8
Leighswood Gv *ALDR* WS9......**40** E6
Leighswood Rd *ALDR* WS9......**40** F7
Leighton Cl *DUDN* DY1......**84** C3 🔲
  GTB/HAM B43......**71** G2
  RLSN CV32......**201** G1
  TLHL/CAN CV4......**177** H3
Leighton Rd *BILS/COS* WV14......**67** L1
  ETTPK/GDPK/PENN WV4......**49** K7
  MOS/BIL B13......**125** K3
Leith Gv *HWK/WKHTH* B38......**144** C5
Lelant Gv *HRBN* B17......**105** L8
Lellow St *HHTH/SAND* B71......**69** G5
Le More *FOAKS/STRLY* B74......**56** E3
Lemox Rd *WBROM* B70......**68** E5
Lench Cl *RMSLY* B62......**104** A4 🔲
Lench's Cl *MOS/BIL* B13......**125** K3
Lench St *CBHAMNE* B4......**7** G2
Len Davies Rd *SHHTH* WV12......**37** L6
Lennox Cl *COVS* CV3......**155** H7
Lennox Gdns *BDMR/CCFT* WV3......**49** K6
Lennox Gv *SCFLD/BOLD* B73......**72** E6 🔲
Lennox St *LOZ/NWT* B19......**89** H7
Lenton Cft
  LGN/SDN/BHAMAIR B26......**127** J1
Lenton's La *COVE* CV2......**135** M1
Lenwade Rd *LGLYGN/QTN* B68......**105** H5
Leofric St *COVN* CV6......**133** L8
Leomansley Cl *LICH* WS13......**20** D6 🔲
Leomansley Rd *LICH* WS13......**20** D6 🔲
Leomansley Vw *LICH* WS13......**20** C6
Leominster Rd *SPARK* B11......**126** C2
Leonard Av *KIDD* DY10......**137** L4
  LOZ/NWT B19......**89** G5 🔲
Leonard Gv *LOZ/NWT* B19......**89** H5 🔲
Leonard Rd *LOZ/NWT* B19......**89** G5
  STRBR DY8......**101** G8
Leopold Av *BFLD/HDSWWD* B20......**70** L8 🔲
Leopold Rd *COV* CV1......**9** L3
Leopold St *BHTH/HG* B12......**107** K5
Lepid Gv *SLYOAK* B29......**124** B3
Lerryn Cl *KGSWFD* DY6......**83** K8
Lerwick Cl *KGSWFD* DY6......**83** K8
Lesingham Dr *TLHL/CAN* CV4......**152** C4
Lesley Dr *KGSWFD* DY6......**101** J1
Leslie Dr *TPTN/OCK* DY4......**67** L4
Leslie Ri *OLDBY* B69......**86** A5
Leslie Rd *BFLD/HDSWWD* B20......**89** H3
  FOAKS/STRLY B74......**55** M3
  LDYWD/EDGR B16......**106** D3
  WOLVN WV10......**50** D1
Lesscroft Cl *COVEN* WV9......**35** M3
Lester Gv *ALDR* WS9......**55** J3
Lester St *BILS/COS* WV14......**51** K8
Lestock Cl *RUGBYS/DCH* CV22......**183** G3
Leswell Gv *KIDD* DY10......**137** K7 🔲
Leswell La *KIDD* DY10......**137** K7 🔲
Leswell St *KIDD* DY10......**137** K7 🔲
Letchlade Cl *COVE* CV2......**135** M1
Levante Gdns *STECH* B33......**109** H3 🔲
Levedale Rd *PENK* ST19......**10** B4
  RSTAF ST18......**10** A2
Leve La *WLNHL* WV13......**51** M4
Level St *BRLYHL* DY5......**102** C2
Leven Cft *WALM/CURD* B76......**73** L6
Leven Dr *WNSFLD* WV11......**37** M4
Leven Wy *COVE* CV2......**135** L5
Levenwick Wy *KGSWFD* DY6......**83** L3 🔲
The Leveretts *HDSW* B21......**88** A2
Lever St *BKHL/PFLD* WV2......**3** C8
Leverton Ri *WOLVN* WV10......**36** A7
Leveson Av *GTWY* WS6......**24** C2
Leveson Cl *DUDS* DY2......**85** J5 🔲
Leveson Crs
  RCOVN/BALC/EX CV7......**150** F7
Leveson Dr *TPTN/OCK* DY4......**67** J7
Leveson Rd *WNSFLD* WV11......**37** K5
Leveson St *WLNHL* WV13......**51** L3
Levett Rd *LICHS* WS14......**30** A4
  TAM/AM/WIL B77......**32** F8 🔲
Levetts Flds *LICH* WS13......**21** C6
Levetts Hollow *HEDN* WS12......**17** H2
Levington Cl
  DUNHL/THL/PER WV6......**48** D1
Levy Cl *RUGBYN/HIL* CV21......**183** K2 🔲
Lewis Av *WOLV* WV1......**50** F2
Lewis Cl *LICHS* WS14......**21** J6
  SHHTH WV12......**38** B8
Lewis St *ATHST* CV9......**63** K7
Lewis Gv *WNSFLD* WV11......**37** H7
Lewisham Rd *SMTHWK* B66......**87** L6
  WOLVN WV10......**35** M3
Lewisham St *HHTH/SAND* B71......**87** H1
Lewis Rd *BVILLE* B30......**124** E8
  COV CV1......**134** B8
  HAG/WOL DY9......**102** B8
  LGLYGN/QTN B68......**104** F6
  RLSS CV31......**201** J8
Lewis St *BILS/COS* WV14......**51** J7
  TPTN/OCK DY4......**68** B8
  WSLW WS2......**53** H2
Lewthorn Ri
  ETTPK/GDPK/PENN WV4......**66** B1
Lexington Gn *BRLYHL* DY5......**102** A6 🔲
Leybourne Crs *COVEN* WV9......**35** K3
Leybourne Gv *YDLY* B25......**108** F7
Leybrook Rd *RBRY* B45......**142** F5
Leyburn Cl *COVN* CV6......**134** B2
  NUN CV11......**99** L3
  SHHTH WV12......**38** B1
  WNSFLD WV11......**199** K4 🔲
Leyburn Rd
  LDYWD/EDGR B16......**106** E4 🔲
Leycester Cl *NFLD/LBR* B31......**143** L6
Leycester Rd *KNWTH* CV8......**191** K5
Leycroft Av *STECH* B33......**110** B2
Leyes La *KNWTH* CV8......**177** G8
Leyfields *LICH* WS13......**20** F5
Ley Hill Farm Rd *NFLD/LBR* B31......**123** J8
Ley Hill Rd *MGN/WHC* B75......**57** C4
Leylan Cft *MOS/BIL* B13......**126** B6
Leyland Av *BDMR/CCFT* WV3......**49** K4

Leyland Cft *BLOX/PEL* WS3......**39** K1
Leyland Rd *BDWTH* CV12......**117** M3
  COVW CV5......**153** H1
  NUN CV11......**99** J4
  TAM/AM/WIL B77......**46** C3
Leyman Cl *ALE/KHTH/YWD* B14......**146** A1
Leymere Cl
  RCOVN/BALC/EX CV7......**131** G4
Ley Ri *SEDG* DY3......**66** A4 🔲
Leys Cl *HAG/WOL* DY9......**120** A3
Leys Crs *BRLYHL* DY5......**101** M2
Leysdown Gv *ACGN* B27......**127** G5 🔲
Leysdown Rd *ACGN* B27......**127** G5
Leyside *COVS* CV3......**155** J8
Leys La *RCOVN/BALC/EX* CV7......**131** G4
Leys Rd *BRLYHL* DY5......**101** M2
Leys Wood Cft
  LGN/SDN/BHAMAIR B26......**109** L7
Leyton Cl *BRLYHL* DY5......**102** B5
Leyton Gv *KGSTG* B44......**71** L4
Leyton Rd *HDSW* B21......**88** D5
Libbards Ga *SOLH* B91......**148** A5 🔲
Libbards Wy *SOLH* B91......**147** M5
Liberty Rd *TAM/AM/WIL* B77......**46** D8
Liberty St *NUN* CV11......**99** K2
Libra Cl *CRTAM* B79......**31** K6
Library Wy *RBRY* B45......**142** D6 🔲
Lich Av *WNSFLD* WV11......**37** J6
Lichen Cl *HEDN* WS12......**12** A8
Lichen Gn *TLHL/CAN* CV4......**153** H8
Lichfield Av *KIDDW* DY11......**136** D7
Lichfield Cl *NUN* CV11......**81** L6
  RCOVN/BALC/EX CV7......**96** E5
Lichfield Crs *POL/KGSB/FAZ* B78......**30** F6
Lichfield Rd *ALDR* WS9......**27** H6
  AST/WIT B6......**89** M5
  BLOX/PEL WS3......**25** M8
  BLOX/PEL WS3......**39** G3
  BNTWD WS7......**19** H7
  BRWNH WS8......**26** D5
  CNCK/NC WS11......**16** F5
  COVS CV3......**154** B5
  CSHL/WTROR B46......**93** G3 🔲
  FOAKS/STRLY B74......**42** D8 🔲
  MGN/WHC B75......**42** E8
  POL/KGSB/FAZ B78......**30** F6
  RUSH/SHEL WS4......**39** M6
  SHHTH WV12......**37** M6
  WALM/CURD B76......**75** H8
  WNSFLD WV11......**37** K6
Lichfield St *BILS/COS* WV14......**51** J7
  CRTAM B79......**31** L8
  POL/KGSB/FAZ B78......**45** K4
  RUSH/SHEL WS4......**53** K2
  TPTN/OCK DY4......**67** K5
  WOLV WV1......**2** F5
  WSL WS1......**5** G2
Lichwood Rd *WNSFLD* WV11......**37** K6
Lickey Coppice *RBRY* B45......**167** G1
Lickey Grange Dr *BRGRVE* B60......**166** E4
Lickey Gv *KIDDW* DY11......**160** F3
Lickey Rd *RBRY* B45......**142** F8
  STRBR DY8......**101** M7
Lickey Rock *BRGRVE* B60......**166** B4
Lickey Sq *RBRY* B45......**166** D3
Lickhill Rd North *STRPT* DY13......**160** B7
Liddon Gv *ACGN* B27......**127** G5 🔲
Liddon Rd *ACGN* B27......**127** G5
Lifford Cl *ALE/KHTH/YWD* B14......**144** F1
Lifford La *BVILLE* B30......**124** E5
Lifton Cft *KGSWFD* DY6......**83** K8
Light Ash *WOLVN* WV10......**22** K2
Lighthorne Av
  LDYWD/EDGR B16......**106** E2
Lighthorne Rd *SOLH* B91......**127** M7
Light La *COV* CV1......**8** E2
Lightning Wy *NFLD/LBR* B31......**143** M6
Lightoak Cl *REDW* B97......**196** A7
Lightwood Cl *DOR/KN* B93......**148** F5 🔲
Lightwood Rd *DUDN* DY1......**84** C2
Lightwoods Hl *SMTHWKW* B67......**105** J5
Lightwoods Rd *HAG/WOL* DY9......**120** A4
  SMTHWKW B67......**105** K4
Lilac Av *BHTH/HG* B12......**107** L8 🔲
  CNCK/NC WS11......**16** B6
  COVN CV6......**133** K8
  DSYBK/YTR WS5......**69** J6
  FOAKS/STRLY B74......**55** J6
  KGSTG B44......**71** J6
  TPTN/OCK DY4......**67** K5
Lilac Cl *REDE* B98......**196** C3 🔲
Lilac Dr *RUGBYS/DCH* CV22......**182** F3
  WMBN WV5......**64** D7
Lilac Gv *BNTWD* WS7......**18** D6
  DARL/WED WS10......**68** E3
  WSLW WS2......**52** C2
  WWCK CV34......**199** L4
Lilac La *GTWY* WS6......**24** D5
Lilac Rd *BDWTH* CV12......**99** H8
  CRTAM B79......**31** L5
  DUDN DY1......**84** F1
  SHHTH WV12......**38** C6
  WOLV WV1......**50** F5
Lilac Wy *RMSLY* B62......**104** D3
Lilian Gv *BILS/COS* WV14......**67** J4
Lilleshall Cl *REDE* B98......**197** J2
Lilleshall Crs *BKHL/PFLD* WV2......**50** B6 🔲
Lilleshall Rd
  LGN/SDN/BHAMAIR B26......**109** M6
Lilley Cl *COVN* CV6......**134** A3 🔲
Lilley Green Rd *ALVE* B48......**189** G2
Lilley La *NFLD/LBR* B31......**143** M5
Lillington Av *RLSN* CV32......**200** D3
Lillington Cl *LICH* WS13......**20** E2
  RLSN CV32......**200** C2
Lillington Gv *BKDE/SHDE* B34......**92** B8
Lillington Rd *COVE* CV2......**135** H4
  RLSN CV32......**200** E3
  SHLY B90......**146** F5
Lilycroft La *HWK/WKHTH* B38......**144** E6
Lily Rd *LGN/SDN/BHAMAIR* B26......**109** M7
Lily St *HHTH/SAND* B71......**69** G8
Limberlost Cl
  BFLD/HDSWWD B20......**88** E2
Limbrick Av *TLHL/CAN* CV4......**152** E4

Limbrick Cl *SHLY* B90 .... 146 D3
Limbury Gv *HIA/OLT* B92 .... 128 D5 🔢
Lime Av *RLSN* CV32................... 200 E1
   WSLW WS2 .... 52 C2
Lime Cl *HLYWD* B47 .... 145 L8
   TPTN/OCK DY4 .... 67 J8 🔢
   WBROM B70 .... 86 E1
   WSLW WS2 .... 52 C2
Lime Ct *SPARK* B11 .... 126 A1 🔢
Lime Gv *ATHST* CV9.................. 76 F1
   BHTH/HG B12 .... 107 K8
   BILS/COS WV14 .... 51 G5
   BNTWD WS7 .... 19 C7
   BRGRVW B61 .... 185 K1
   CHWD/FDBR/MGN B37 .... 110 F4
   KINVER DY7 .... 118 A2
   KNWTH CV8 .... 191 L1
   LICH WS13........................... 21 H5
   LOZ/NWT B19 .... 89 C5
   NUNW/HART CV10 .... 98 C1 🔢
   RUSH/SHEL WS4 .... 40 A7
   SCFLD/BOLD B73 .... 72 F6
   SMTHWK B66 .... 105 M1 🔢
   TLHL/CAN CV4 .... 152 F3
Limehurst Av *BDMR/CCFT* WV3 ... 49 G4
Limehurst Rd *RUSH/SHEL* WS4... 40 A8
Lime Kiln Cl *HWK/WKHTH* B38 ... 144 B6
Limekiln La
   ALE/KHTH/YWD B14 .... 145 L1
   HOCK/TIA B94..................... 171 C4
Lime Kilns *BLOX/PEL* WS3 .... 25 L4
Limepit La *DUDN* DY1 .... 84 E2 🔢
   HEDN WS12 .... 12 C7
Lime Rd *BILS/COS* WV14 .... 66 D4
   DARL/WED WS10 .... 68 D1
   HEDN WS12 .... 12 B5
   SEDG DY3 .... 66 D4
Limes Av *BLKHTH/ROWR* B65 .... 104 A3
   BRLYHL DY5 .... 84 A4
Limes Coppice
   NUNW/HART CV10 .... 79 J6
Limes Rd *DUDN* DY1 .... 84 F2
   DUNHL/THL/PER WV6 .... 35 H4
The Limes *BDWTH* CV12 .... 116 C3
   ERDE/BCHGN B24 .... 90 D2
   SPARK B11 .... 108 A7
Limestone Hall La
   RRUGBY CV23....................... 181 L1
Lime St *BDMR/CCFT* WV3 .... 2 B8
   BILS/COS WV14 .... 66 E5
   WSL WS1 .... 5 H3
Limes Vw *SEDG* DY3 .... 66 B4
Lime Tree Av
   DUNHL/THL/PER WV6 .... 48 E2 🔢
   RUGBYS/DCH CV22 .... 182 F6
   TLHL/CAN CV4 .... 152 E3
Lime Tree Crs *REDW* B97 .... 195 M1 🔢
Lime Tree Gdns *CDSL* WS8 .... 34 F2
Lime Tree Gv *NFLD/LBR* B31 ..... 144 A3 🔢
Lime Tree Rd *ACGN* B27 .... 109 C8 🔢
Limetree Rd *FOAKS/STRLY* B74... 55 H4
Lime Tree Wk *STRPT* DY13 .... 160 C8
Linaker Rd *COVS* CV3 .... 155 G8
Linchmere Rd *HDSW* B21 .... 88 A3
Lincoln Av *NUNW/HART* CV10....79 M6
   WLNHL WV13 .... 52 B3
Lincoln Cl *ACGN* B27 .... 127 J2
   LICH WS13.......................... 21 C2
   WWCK CV34 .... 199 J4 🔢
Lincoln Crs *KIDDW* DY11 .... 136 D7 🔢
Lincoln Cft *LICHS* WS14 .... 28 D7
Lincoln Dr *CNCK/NC* WS11 .... 16 D5
Lincoln Gn *WOLVN* WV10 .... 36 B3
Lincoln Gv
   CHWD/FDBR/MGN B37 .... 110 E5
Lincoln Rd *BRGRVW* B61 .... 185 J1
   DUDS DY2 .... 103 H2
   HHTH/SAND B71 .... 69 H4
   HIA/OLT B92 .... 127 H3
   SMTHWKW B67 .... 105 J3
   WSL WS1 .... 5 J2
Lincoln Rd North *HIA/OLT* B92... 127 J2
Lincoln St *BHTH/HG* B12 .... 107 J7
   COV CV1 .... 9 C1
   WOLVN WV10 .... 3 K3
Lincroft Crs *COVS* CV5 .... 153 H1
Lindale Av *CBROM* B36 .... 91 C7
Lindale Crs *BRLYHL* DY5 .... 101 M7
Lindale Dr *WMBN* WV5 .... 64 D7
Linden Av *BNTWD* WS7 .... 18 D5
   GTB/HAM B43 .... 70 B5 🔢
   KIDD DY10.......................... 137 L6
   OLDBY B69 .... 86 B5
   RMSLY B62 .... 104 C6
Linden Cl *TAM/AM/WIL* B77 ..... 46 D1 🔢
   WWCK CV34 .... 199 C3 🔢
Linden Dr *STRBR* DY8............... 119 C2
Linden Gdns *KIDD* DY10 .... 137 L6 🔢
Linden Gv *KIDD* DY10 .... 137 L6
Linden La *SHHTH* WV12 .... 38 C6
Linden Lea *BDMR/CCFT* WV3 .... 49 H4
   BDWTH CV12 .... 116 F2
Linden Rd *BVILLE* B30 .... 124 C6
   DUDN DY1 .... 84 F2
   SMTHWK B66 .... 105 L3
The Lindens
   DUNHL/THL/PER WV6 .... 49 J2
   RIDG/WDGT B32................. 105 J6
Linden Vw *HEDN* WS12 .... 16 F1
Lindenwood *SCFLD/BOLD* B73 ... 56 F7 🔢
Lindera *TAM/AM/WIL* B77 .... 46 E1 🔢
The Lindfield *COVS* CV3 .... 155 G5
Lindford Wy *HWK/WKHTH* B38 ...144 F4
Lindisfarne *TAM/AM/WIL* B77 ... 46 B3
Lindisfarne Dr *KNWTH* CV8 .... 192 A1
Lindley Av *TPTN/OCK* DY4 .... 85 K2
Lindley Rd *BDWTH* CV12 .... 116 B3 🔢
   COVS CV3 .... 154 F3
Lindon Cl *BRWNH* WS8 .... 26 E7
Lindon Dr *BRWNH* WS8 .... 26 E7
Lindon Rd *BRWNH* WS8 .... 26 E7
Lindon Vw *BRWNH* WS8 .... 26 E8

Lindrick Cl *BLOX/PEL* WS3 .... 38 D2 🔢
Lindridge Cl *REDE* B98 .... 197 L2 🔢
Lindridge Dr *WALM/CURD* B76 ... 74 A7
Lindridge Rd *ERDW/GRVHL* B23... 72 A8
   MGN/WHC B75...................... 57 K6
   SHLY B90............................ 146 D4
Lindrosa Rd *FOAKS/STRLY* B74 ... 55 L2
Lindsay Av *NFLD/LBR* B31 .... 144 A1 🔢
Lindsey Crs *KNWTH* CV8 .... 191 L4
Lindsey Pl *BRLYHL* DY5 .... 102 A2
Lindsey Rd *HHTH/SAND* B71 ..... 69 G6
Lindsworth Ap *BVILLE* B30 .... 145 G2
Lindsworth Rd *BVILLE* B30 .... 144 F2
Lineholt Cl *REDE* B98 .... 196 E7
Linehouse La *BRGRVE* B60 .... 166 B5
Linen St *WWCK* CV34 .... 199 H7
Linfield Gdns *SEDG* DY3 .... 66 A4
Linford Gv *YDLY* B25 .... 109 H4 🔢
Linford Wk *COVE* CV2 .... 135 K4
Lingard Cl *VAUX/NECH* B7 .... 89 M8
Lingard Rd *MGN/WHC* B75 .... 57 K8
Lingfield Av *REDE* B98 .... 197 J2
   WOLVN WV10 .... 22 B8
Lingfield Cl *GTWY* WS6 .... 24 D3
Lingfield Dr *GTWY* WS6 .... 24 D3
Lingfield Gdns
   BKDE/SHDE B34 .... 91 M7 🔢
Lingfield Gv
   DUNHL/THL/PER WV6 .... 48 D1
Lingfield Rd *BEWD* DY12 .... 136 B8
Lingfield Wy *KGSWFD* DY6 .... 83 L8
Lingham Cl *HIA/OLT* B92 .... 128 B6 🔢
Ling Rd *HEDN* WS12 .... 12 A8
Lingwood Dr *NUNW/HART* CV10...98 D2
Linhope Dr *KGSWFD* DY6 .... 83 L8 🔢
Link Rd *ALDR* WS9................... 40 F2
   LDYWD/EDGR B16 .... 106 C2
   WMBN WV5 .... 64 E6
Links Av
   DUNHL/THL/PER WV6 .... 35 H6
Links Dr *RBRY* B45 .... 142 E7
   SOLH B91 .... 127 M7
   STRBR DY8 .... 119 J3
Links Rd *COVN* CV6 .... 133 M5
   ETTPK/GDPK/PENN WV4 ..... 65 L2
   HLYWD B47........................ 145 L4
   LGLYGN/QTN B68 .... 104 F5
Links Side Wy *ALDR* WS9 .... 41 C5
Links Vw *FOAKS/STRLY* B74....... 55 L4
   RMSLY B62 .... 122 B1
Linkswood Cl *MOS/BIL* B13 ...... 125 M4
The Link *ACGN* B27 .... 126 D4
Linkway *RLSS* CV31 .... 200 C7
Linley Cl *ALDR* WS9 .... 40 C8
Linley Dr *WOLVN* WV10 .... 36 C4
Linley Gv *ALE/KHTH/YWD* B14 ... 125 G7
   SEDG DY3 .... 83 M3 🔢
Linley Rd *RUSH/SHEL* WS4 .... 40 B6
Linley Wood Rd *ALDR* WS9 .... 40 C8
Linnet Cl *COVS* CV3 .... 155 H8
   HEDN WS12 .... 12 B6
   RMSLY B62 .... 103 M7
   SLYOAK B29 .... 124 C5
Linnets Vw *SHHTH* WV12 .... 38 A5
Linnet Ri *KIDD* DY10 .... 161 K4
Linpole Wk
   ALE/KHTH/YWD B14 .... 145 G3
Linsey Rd *HIA/OLT* B92............. 128 A3
Linslade Cl
   ETTPK/GDPK/PENN WV4 ..... 66 B1
Linstock Wy *COVE* CV2 .... 134 F1 🔢
Linthouse La *WNSFLD* WV11 ..... 37 J5 🔢
Linthurst Newtown
   BRGRVE B60 .... 166 E8
Linthurst Rd *BRGRVE* B60 .... 166 E7
Lintly *TAM/AM/WIL* B77 .... 46 F4
Linton Av *SOLH* B91 .... 147 L4
Linton Cl *HALE* B63 .... 103 H8 🔢
   REDE B98 .... 197 K3
Linton Cft *BILS/COS* WV14 .... 67 H1
Linton Ms *REDE* B98 .... 197 K3
Linton Rd *CDYHTH* B64 .... 103 K2
   ETTPK/GDPK/PENN WV4 ..... 49 J8
   GTB/HAM B43 .... 71 G1
   SPARK B11 .... 126 E1
Linwood Dr *COVE* CV2 .... 135 K4
   HEDN WS12 .... 12 D6
Linwood Rd *DUDN* DY1 .... 66 F8
   HDSW B21.......................... 88 C5
   SOLH B91 .... 127 H8
Lionel St *CBHAMNW* B3 .... 6 E3
Lion Fields Av *COVW* CV5 .... 132 F7
Lion Pas *STRBR* DY8 .... 101 K8
Lion's Den *LICHS* WS14............. 27 J3
Lion Sq *KIDD* DY10 .... 137 J7 🔢
Lion St *KIDD* DY10 .... 137 J7
   STRBR DY8 .... 101 K8
Liskeard Cl *NUN* CV11 .... 81 L8
Liskeard Rd *DSYBK/YTR* WS5 .... 54 B6
Lisko Cl *STRBR* DY8 .... 101 L5
Lisle Av *KIDDW* DY11 .... 161 G2
Lismore Cl *RBRY* B45 .... 142 C4 🔢
Lismore Dr *HRBN* B17 .... 123 L2
Lisson Gv *KGSTG* B44 .... 71 K1
Listelow Cl *CBROM* B36 .... 91 M5 🔢
Lister Cl *TPTN/OCK* DY4 .... 85 L1 🔢
   WSLW WS2 .... 38 F8
Lister Rd *ATHST* CV9 .... 63 H4
   DUDS DY2 .... 85 G6
   KIDDW DY11 .... 160 F2
   WSLW WS2 .... 38 F8
Lister St *NUN* CV11 .... 99 H2
   VAUX/NECH B7 .... 7 J1
   WLNHL WV13 .... 51 M4
Listowel Rd
   ALE/KHTH/YWD B14 .... 125 H7
Lisures Dr *WALM/CURD* B76 ..... 73 H1
Little Acre *REDW* B97 .... 196 B8
Little Albert St *WSL* WS1.......... 4 F1 🔢
Little Ann St *DIG/EDG* B5.......... 7 K6
Little Aston Hall Dr
   FOAKS/STRLY B74 .... 41 L8
Little Aston La
   FOAKS/STRLY B74 .... 42 B7

Little Aston Park Rd
   FOAKS/STRLY B74 .... 55 L2
Little Aston Rd *ALDR* WS9 .... 41 G7
Little Barr St *BORD* B9.............. 7 M5
Little Birches
   BDMR/CCFT WV3 .... 49 K5 🔢
Little Brickiln St
   BKHL/PFLD WV1................... 2 E7 🔢
Little Bromwich Rd *BORD* B9 .... 108 F4
Little Brum *ATHST* CV9.............. 62 A3
Little Caldmore *WSL* WS1 .... 4 F5
Little Checkhill La *KINVER* DY7... 100 B1
Little Church La *CRTAM* B79 ..... 31 M8 🔢
Little Church St *COV* CV1 .... 9 G1 🔢
   RUGBYN/HIL CV21 .... 183 L2 🔢
Little Clothier St *WLNHL* WV13 ... 51 L2 🔢
Little Clover Cl *VAUX/NECH* B7... 90 A6 🔢
Little Cornbow *HALE* B63 .... 121 M2 🔢
Littlecote *CRTAM* B79 .... 31 H7 🔢
Littlecote Cft
   ALE/KHTH/YWD B14 .... 145 L2 🔢
Littlecote Dr *ERDW/GRVHL* B23... 72 B6
Little Cottage St *BRLYHL* DY5 ... 102 B2
Little Cft *GTB/HAM* B43 .... 70 A4
Little Cross St
   DARL/WED WS10 .... 52 B6 🔢
Little Cryfield *TLHL/CAN* CV4 ... 177 C3
Little Duke St *NUN* CV11 .... 98 F1
Little Edward St *BORD* B9......... 7 M6
Little Elborow St
   RUGBYN/HIL CV21 .... 183 L2 🔢
Little Fld *COVE* CV2 .... 134 E3
Little Fields Wy *OLDBY* B69 ...... 86 D6
Little Forge Rd *REDE* B98 .... 197 G6
Little Francis Gv
   VAUX/NECH B7 .... 89 M8 🔢
Little Gorway *WSL* WS1 .... 5 H7
Little Gra *LICH* WS13 .... 20 C4 🔢
Little Grebe Rd *KIDD* DY10 ...... 161 M2 🔢
Little Green La *BORD* B9 .... 108 B4 🔢
   SCFLD/BOLD B73 .... 72 F6
Little Hall Rd *VAUX/NECH* B7 .... 107 M1 🔢
Little Hardwick Rd *ALDR* WS9 ... 55 H3
Little Hayes *KIDDW* DY11 .... 137 C2
Little Hay La *LICHS* WS14......... 43 C3
Little Heath Cft
   BKDE/SHDE B34 .... 91 M6 🔢
Littleheath La *BRGRVE* B60 ...... 166 C7
Little Heath La *BRGRVE* B60 ..... 166 B7
Little Hl *DARL/WED* WS10 .... 68 D2 🔢
Little Hill Gv *HWK/WKHTH* B38 ... 144 E4
Little Hill Wy *RIDG/WDGT* B32... 123 H3
Little Johnson's La *ALDR* WS9 ... 54 F4
Little John St *BRLYHL* DY5 .... 102 B1
Little La *HHTH/SAND* B71 .... 69 H8
   SHHTH WV12 .... 38 B6
Little Lawford La
   RRUGBY CV23..................... 158 C6
Little Lawns Cl *BRWNH* WS8 ..... 26 D8
Little London *WSL* WS1 .... 4 F7
Little Marsh Gv *PENK* ST19 ...... 10 D4
Littlemead Av *NFLD/LBR* B31 ... 144 A4
Littlemead Rd *SHLY* B90 .... 146 C5
Little Moor Hl *SMTHWK* B67 .... 87 K8
Little Newport St *WSL* WS1 ...... 4 E5 🔢
Little Oaks Rd *AST/WIT* B6 .... 89 J5
Littleover Av *HLGN/YWD* B28 ... 126 D7
Little Pk *RIDG/WDGT* B32 .... 122 F1 🔢
Little Park St *COV* CV1 .... 9 H5 🔢
   WOLV WV1 .... 3 H5 🔢
Little Pennington St
   RUGBYN/HIL CV21 .... 183 K2 🔢
Little Pipe La *LICH* WS13 .... 19 L4
Little Pitts Cl *ERDE/BCHGN* B24 ... 73 H8
Little Potter St *BRLYHL* DY5 ...... 102 B3 🔢
Little Pountney St
   BKHL/PFLD WV2 .... 2 F8 🔢
Little Shadwell St
   CBHAMNE B4 .... 7 G2 🔢
Littleshaw Cft *HLYWD* B47 .... 170 A1
Littleshaw La *HLYWD* B47 .... 170 A1
Little's La *WOLV* WV1 .... 3 G3 🔢
Little South St *COV* CV1 .... 9 K4 🔢
Little Station St *WSL* WS1 .... 4 E4
Little St *DUDS* DY2 .... 85 H4 🔢
Little Sutton La *MGN/WHC* B75... 57 G4
Little Sutton Rd *MGN/WHC* B75... 57 C3
Littlethorpe *COVS* CV3 .... 155 H8
Littleton Cl *KNWTH* CV8 .... 176 E6
Littleton Crs *PENK* ST19 .... 10 D8
Littleton Cft *SOLH* B91 .... 148 A5 🔢
Littleton Dr *HEDN* WS12 .... 12 A6
Littleton Rd *SHHTH* WV12 .... 38 A6
Littleton St East *WSL* WS1 .... 4 F1
Littleton St West *WSLW* WS2 .... 4 E1
Littleton Wy *BNTWD* WS7 .... 18 B8
Littlewood *SOLH* B91 .... 147 M5 🔢
Littlewood La *GTWY* WS6 .... 24 C1
Littlewood Rd *GTWY* WS6 .... 24 C1
Little Woods *REDW* B97 .... 196 B8
Little Wood St *WLNHL* WV13 .... 51 L3
Littleworth Av *DUDN* DY1 .... 66 F7
Littleworth Gv *WALM/CURD* B76 ... 73 K1
Littleworth Hl *HEDN* WS12 .... 17 H1
Littleworth Rd *HEDN* WS12 ...... 17 H1
Litton *TAM/AM/WIL* B77 .... 47 G4
Liveridge Cl *DOR/KN* B93 .... 148 D7
Liverpool Cft
   CHWD/FDBR/MGN B37 .... 110 D4
Liverpool St *BORD* B9 .... 7 L6
Livery St *CBHAMNW* B3 .... 6 E2
   RLSN CV32........................ 200 D5
Livingstone Av
   DUNHL/THL/PER WV6 .... 34 C8
   RRUGBY CV23..................... 182 D1
Livingstone Rd
   ALE/KHTH/YWD B14 .... 125 J7
   BFLD/HDSWWD B20 .... 89 G4
   BILS/COS WV14 .... 50 F4
   BLOX/PEL WS3 .... 39 J3
   COVN CV6 .... 134 B6 🔢
   WBROM B70 .... 86 F4
Llangorse Cl *STRPT* DY13 .... 160 C6
Llewellyn Rd *RLSS* CV31 .... 200 E7
Lloyd Cl *NUN* CV11 .... 99 H3
Lloyd Crs *COVE* CV2 .... 155 J2

Lloyd Dr
   ETTPK/GDPK/PENN WV4 ..... 65 C3
Lloyd George Gv *CNCK/NC* WS11 ... 17 C3
Lloyd Rd *BFLD/HDSWWD* B20 .... 88 E1 🔢
   DUNHL/THL/PER WV6 .... 35 H8
Lloyds Rd *RMSLY* B62 .... 104 A6
Lloyd St *CNCK/NC* WS11 .... 16 B4
   DARL/WED WS10 .... 68 C2
   DUDS DY2 .... 85 H5 🔢
   DUNHL/THL/PER WV6 .... 49 K1
   HHTH/SAND B71 .... 87 J1
   SMTH B10........................... 108 B5
Loach Dr *COVE* CV2 .... 134 F1 🔢
Lobelia Cl *KIDDW* DY11 .... 137 C4
Locarno Rd *TPTN/OCK* DY4 ...... 67 K7
Lochalsh Gv *WNSFLD* WV11 ...... 37 M4
Lochmore Cl *HEDN* WS12 .... 11 K8
Lochsong Cl *TAM/AM/WIL* B77... 60 B1 🔢
Lock Cl *REDW* B97 .... 195 L1
Lock Dr *STETCH* B33................. 109 H2
Locke Cl *COVN* CV6 .... 133 L4
Locket Cl *WSLW* WS2 .... 52 C1
Lockfield Cl *STRBR* DY8 .... 101 K3 🔢
Lockhart Cl *KNWTH* CV8 .... 191 L1 🔢
Lockhart Dr *MGN/WHC* B75 ...... 57 C4
Lockheed Cl *RLSS* CV31 .... 200 D8
Lockhurst La *COVN* CV6 .... 134 B6
Locking Cft *CVALE* B35.............. 91 M2
Lockington Cft *RMSLY* B62 .... 104 D7
Lock Keepers Cl *CNCK/NC* WS11... 17 K8 🔢
Lock La *WWCK* CV34 .... 199 H4
Lockley Cl *WOLVN* WV10 .... 50 D1
Lock Rd *PENK* ST19 .... 10 D5
Lockside *ALDR* WS9 .... 40 C6
   WMBN WV5 .... 64 E6
Locksmith Cl *WLNHL* WV13 ...... 51 M3 🔢
Lock St *WOLV* WV1 .... 3 H3
Lockton Rd *BVILLE* B30 .... 124 C5
Lockwood Rd *NFLD/LBR* B31 .... 143 K1
Lode La *HIA/OLT* B92 .... 127 M4
   SOLH B91 .... 128 A6
Lodge Cl *ATHST* CV9................. 63 L7
   BEWD DY12 .... 160 B1 🔢
   DSYBK/YTR WS5 .... 54 B7 🔢
   RMSLY B62 .... 122 B2
Lodge Crs *DUDS* DY2 .... 102 E1
   HAG/WOL DY9 .... 119 M8
Lodge Cft *DOR/KN* B93 .... 148 F7
   NFLD/LBR B31 .... 123 J8
Lodge Dr
   LGN/SDN/BHAMAIR B26 ..... 109 J3
Lodge Farm Cl
   WALM/CURD B76 .... 73 K2 🔢
Lodgefield Rd *RMSLY* B62 .... 103 M6
Lodge Green La
   RCOVN/BALC/EX CV7 .... 131 C7
Lodge Green La North
   RCOVN/BALC/EX CV7 .... 131 C7
Lodge Gv *ALDR* WS9 .... 40 E8
Lodge Hill Rd *SLYOAK* B29 .... 124 B4
Lodge La *CNCK/NC* WS11 .... 23 M1
   KGSWFD DY6 .... 82 F7
   LICH WS13.......................... 19 H2
Lodgepool Cl *KGSTG* B44 .... 71 J1 🔢
Lodge Pool Dr *REDE* B98 .... 196 D4
Lodge Rd *AST/WIT* B6 .... 89 J5
   BILS/COS WV14 .... 67 K1
   BNTWD WS7 .... 18 C4 🔢
   COVS CV3 .... 154 F4
   DARL/WED WS10 .... 52 B8
   DOR/KN B93 .... 148 F7
   DSYBK/YTR WS5 .... 54 B8
   REDE B98 .... 196 C2
   RUGBYN/HIL CV21 .... 183 M1
   RUSH/SHEL WS4 .... 39 M4
   SMTHWK B66 .... 87 J6
   WBROM B70 .... 86 F2
   WOLVN WV10 .... 35 M5
   WSNGN B18 .... 88 C8
Lodge St *OLDBY* B69 .... 86 E6
   SHHTH WV12 .... 38 A8
Lodge Vw *GTWY* WS6 .... 24 A2
Loeless Rd *STETCH* B33 .... 109 L2
Lofthouse Crs *NFLD/LBR* B31 ... 143 K2
Lofthouse Gv *NFLD/LBR* B31 .... 143 K2 🔢
Lofthouse Rd
   BFLD/HDSWWD B20 .... 88 C3
Loftus Cl *NFLD/LBR* B31 .... 123 K5
Loftus Ct *BNTWD* WS7 .... 18 D8
Logan Cl *WOLVN* WV10 .... 36 A7 🔢
Logan Rd *COVE* CV2 .... 135 H6
Lole Cl *COVN* CV6 .... 134 E1
Lollard Cft *COVS* CV3 .... 154 B5
Lomaine Dr *BVILLE* B30 .... 144 C1
Lomas Dr *NFLD/LBR* B31 .... 143 J2
Lomas St *WOLV* WV1 .... 2 F1
Lomax Cl *LICH* WS13 .... 20 E4
Lomax Rd *HEDN* WS12 .... 12 F6
Lombard Av *DUDS* DY2 .... 103 H2
Lombard St *BHTH/HG* B12 .... 7 J9
   LICH WS13.......................... 20 F5
   WBROM B70 .... 87 G2
Lombard St West
   WBROM B70 .... 87 G2 🔢
Lombardy Cft *RMSLY* B62 .... 104 E7 🔢
Lombardy Gdns *SHHTH* WV12 ... 38 C6 🔢
Lombardy Gv *BNTWD* WS7 .... 18 D5
Lomita Crs *TAM/AM/WIL* B77 ... 46 B5 🔢
Lomond Cl *BKDE/SHDE* B34 ..... 92 C7
   CRTAM B79 .... 31 K5 🔢
Lomond Rd *SEDG* DY3 .... 66 C4
Lomond Wy *NUNW/HART* CV10 ... 80 A8
Lomsey Rd *TLHL/CAN* CV4 .... 152 E4
Londonderry Gv
   SMTHWKW B67 .... 87 K8 🔢
Londonderry La
   SMTHWKW B67 .... 105 H1
London Hts *DUDN* DY1 .... 84 C3 🔢
London La *BRGRVE* B60 .... 186 D7
London Rd *BFLD/HDSWWD* B20... 89 J3
   COV CV1 .... 9 J8
   COVS CV3 .... 154 D6
   COVS CV3 .... 179 G1 🔢
   KNWTH CV8 .... 179 H1
   LICHS WS14....................... 21 C8
   LICHS WS14....................... 43 J1

   MGN/WHC B75...................... 57 L1
   RRUGBY CV23..................... 181 M8
London St *SMTHWK* B66 .... 88 A3
Lones Rd *HHTH/SAND* B71 .... 87 M5
Long Acre *CDSL* WS8 .... 34 C3
   KIDD DY10.......................... 137 K6
   VAUX/NECH B7 .... 89 M7
Longacre *WLNHL* WV13 .... 51 L5
Longacres *HEDN* WS12 .... 13 K8
   WLNHL WV13 .... 51 L5
Long Acre St *WSLW* WS2 .... 53 H2 🔢
Longbank Rd *OLDBY* B69 .... 86 A5
Longboat La *STRBR* DY8 .... 101 J5
Longboat Quay *DUDS* DY2 .... 103 H1 🔢
Longborough Cl *REDW* B97 ...... 195 M7 🔢
Longbow Rd *SLYOAK* B29 .... 123 K6 🔢
Longbridge La *NFLD/LBR* B31 ... 143 M6
Long Bridge Rd *LICHS* WS14 ..... 21 C8
Long Brook La *KNWTH* CV8 .... 174 C1
Long Cl *HAG/WOL* DY9 .... 139 L1
Long Close Av *COVW* CV5 .... 132 F7
Long Compton Dr
   HAG/WOL DY9 .... 119 L7
Long Cft *HEDN* WS12 .... 16 A1
Longcroft Cl *CVALE* B35 .... 91 L2 🔢
The Longcroft *HALE* B63 .... 121 J1
   RUSH/SHEL WS4 .... 40 A6
Longdales Rd
   HWK/WKHTH B38 .... 144 C5 🔢
Longdon Av
   ETTPK/GDPK/PENN WV4 ..... 50 B8
Longdon Cl *REDE* B98 .... 196 F6
Longdon Dr *FOAKS/STRLY* B74 ... 56 C1
Longdon Rd *DOR/KN* B93 .... 148 E7
Longfellow Cl *REDW* B97 .... 195 M7
Longfellow Pl *CNCK/NC* WS11 ... 16 C1 🔢
Longfellow Rd *BNTWD* WS7 ...... 18 D4
   BVILLE B30 .... 144 B2
   COVE CV2 .... 155 G2
   SEDG DY3 .... 65 L8
Longfield Cl *HLGN/YWD* B28 .... 126 D7
   TAM/AM/WIL B77 .... 46 C1
Longfield Rd *HAG/WOL* DY9 ..... 102 B8
   NFLD/LBR B31 .... 123 J5 🔢
   RLSS CV31......................... 200 F7
Longford Cl *DOR/KN* B93 .... 172 F2
   RIDG/WDGT B32................. 122 E6 🔢
   WMBN WV5 .... 64 B8 🔢
Longford Gv *KGSTG* B44 .... 71 L2
Longford Rd *CNCK/NC* WS11 .... 16 B7
   COVN CV6 .... 134 E2
   KGSTG B44 .... 71 L3
   RCOVN/BALC/EX CV7 .... 116 E7
   WOLVN WV10 .... 50 D1
Longford Sq *COVN* CV6 .... 134 E1 🔢
   COVN CV6 .... 134 D1 🔢
Long Furlong
   RUGBYS/DCH CV22 .... 183 L6
Longham Cft *RIDG/WDGT* B32 ... 123 K1
Longhope Cl *REDE* B98 .... 197 L1
Longhurst Cft *NFLD/LBR* B31 ... 143 L4
Long Hyde Rd *SMTHWKW* B67... 105 K4
Long Innage *HALE* B63 .... 102 F7
Long Knowle La *WNSFLD* WV11 ... 36 F5
Longlake Av
   DUNHL/THL/PER WV6 .... 48 E2
Longlands Dr *TAM/AM/WIL* B77... 46 D1
Longlands Rd *RMSLY* B62 .... 122 C2
The Longlands *RBRY* B45 .... 167 H6 🔢
   WMBN WV5 .... 64 E7
Long La *BLKHTH/ROWR* B65 ..... 104 B4
   RCOVN/BALC/EX CV7 .... 133 H3
   RMSLY B62 .... 104 C5
   WNSFLD WV11 .... 24 B8
Longleat *CRTAM* B79 .... 31 H6
   GTB/HAM B43 .... 70 A4
   SHLY B90............................ 147 J8
Longleat Dr *DUDN* DY1 .... 84 C3 🔢
   SHLY B90............................ 147 J8
Longleat Gv *RLSS* CV31 .... 201 G7
Longleat Rd *ALDR* WS9 .... 40 E3
Long Ley *WOLVN* WV10 .... 3 M3
Longley Av *WALM/CURD* B76 .... 74 B8
Longley Crs
   LGN/SDN/BHAMAIR B26 ..... 127 J1
Long Leys Cft
   CSHL/WTROR B46 .... 92 F3 🔢
Longmeadow Cl
   MGN/WHC B75...................... 57 J8 🔢
Longmeadow Crs
   BKDE/SHDE B34.................. 92 C7
Long Meadow Dr *SEDG* DY3 ..... 65 M4
Longmeadow Gv
   NFLD/LBR B31 .... 143 L7
Long Meadow Rd *BRGRVE* B60 ... 166 A7
Longmeadow Rd
   DSYBK/YTR WS5 .... 54 C5
Long Mill Av *WNSFLD* WV11 ..... 36 F6
Long Ml North *WNSFLD* WV11 ... 36 F6
Long Ml South *WNSFLD* WV11 ... 36 F6
Longmoor Cl *REDW* B97 .... 187 M7
   WNSFLD WV11 .... 37 K8 🔢
Longmoor Rd *HALE* B63 .... 121 J2
   SCFLD/BOLD B73 .... 71 M2
Longmore Av *WSLW* WS2 .... 52 D4 🔢
Longmore St *BHTH/HG* B12 ..... 107 J6 🔢
   DARL/WED WS10 .... 68 D2
Long Mynd *HALE* B63 .... 121 H4
Long Mynd Cl *WNSFLD* WV11 ... 37 M4 🔢
Long Mynd Rd *NFLD/LBR* B31 ... 123 J3
Long Nuke Rd *NFLD/LBR* B31 ... 123 J6
Longrood Rd
   RUGBYS/DCH CV22 .... 183 H7
Longshaw Gv
   BKDE/SHDE B34.................. 92 B7 🔢
The Long Shoot *NUN* CV11 .... 81 M7
Longstaff Av *HEDN* WS12 .... 18 A1
Longstaff Cft *LICH* WS13 .... 20 D3
Longstone Rd *PBAR/PBCH* B42... 71 G6
Long St *ATHST* CV9 .... 63 C4 🔢
   POL/KGSB/FAZ B78 .... 47 L8
   SPARK B11 .... 107 L7
   WOLV WV1 .... 3 G4
Long Wd *BVILLE* B30 .... 124 C8
Longwood Cl *TLHL/CAN* CV4 .... 152 D7
Longwood La *RUSH/SHEL* WS4... 54 B3

Longwood Ri *SHHTH* WV12 38 B8
Longwood Rd *ALDR* WS9 54 F3
RBRY B45 142 E6
Lonicera Cl *DSYBK/YTR* WS5 69 M2 2
Lonscale Dr *COVS* CV3 153 M8
Lonsdale Cl *SHHTH* WV12 37 M8
Lonsdale Rd *BDMR/CCFT* WV3 2 C9
BILS/COS WV14 51 K7
DSYBK/YTR WS5 54 A7
HRBN B17 105 M7
RLSN CV32 200 F1
SMTHWK B66 87 H6
Lord Austin Dr *BRGRVE* B60 166 C4
Lord Lytton Av *COVE* CV2 155 H3
Lord's Dr *WSLW* WS2 53 J2
Lordsmore Cl *BILS/COS* WV14 67 H4
Lord St *BDMR/CCFT* WV3 2 C6
BILS/COS WV14 67 J2
COVW CV5 153 K3
VAUX/NECH B7 7 K1
WSL WS1 4 D8
Lord St West *BILS/COS* WV14 67 J2
Lordswood Cl *REDW* B97 195 K3
Lordswood Rd *HRBN* B17 105 L5
Lorenzo Cl *COVS* CV3 155 H7
Lorimer Wy *GTB/HAM* B43 55 H8
Lorne Gv *KIDD* DY10 137 L7
Lorne St *BNTWD* WS7 18 C5
KIDD DY10 137 L8
STRPT DY13 160 E8
TPTN/OCK DY4 67 K5
Lorrainer Av *STRBR* DY8 101 L5
Lorton *CRTAM* B79 31 H6
Lothersdale *TAM/AM/WIL* B77 46 F5
Lothians Rd *BLOX/PEL* WS3 25 L8
DUNHL/THL/PER WV6 35 H7 1
Lottie Rd *SLYOAK* B29 124 C4
Lotus *TAM/AM/WIL* B77 46 C2
Lotus Cft *SMTHWKW* B67 105 K1 2
Lotus Dr *CNCK/NC* WS11 12 C8 2
Lotus Wy *BLKHTH/ROWR* B65 103 L1 1
Loudon Av *COVN* CV6 133 L8
Loughshaw *TAM/AM/WIL* B77 47 G4
Loughton Gv *HALE* B63 121 K1
Louisa St *CBHAMW* B1 6 C4 3
Louise Cft *ALE/KHTH/YWD* B14 145 J3
Louise Lorne Rd *MOS/BIL* B13 125 K1
Louise Rd *HDSW* B21 88 D6
Louise St *SEDG* DY3 83 M2
Lovat St *WOLV* WV1 2 D5
Lovatt Cl *TPTN/OCK* DY4 68 A4 3
Lovatt Pl *CNCK/NC* WS11 12 C8
Lovatt St *CNCK/NC* WS11 12 C8
Loveday Cl *ATHST* CV9 63 H3 2
RLSN CV32 200 C3
Loveday St *CBHAMNE* B4 7 G2
Lovelace Av *SOLH* B91 148 B5
Love La *DUNHL/THL/PER* WV6 35 H7
GTWY WS6 24 F1
HAG/WOL DY9 102 C8
HLYWD B47 145 J6
STRBR DY8 119 L2
VAUX/NECH B7 7 J1
WSL WS1 4 F8
Lovell *CRTAM* B79 31 K7
Lovell Cl *RCOVN/BALC/EX* CV7 116 E5
SLYOAK B29 123 L7
Lovell Rd *BDWTH* CV12 116 E2 2
Love Lyne *REDW* B97 195 L8
Loveridge Cl *CDSL* WV8 34 C2
Lovett Av *OLDBY* B69 86 B8
Lowans Hill Vw *REDW* B97 196 A1
Low Av *GTB/HAM* B43 70 D3
Lowbridge Cl *SHHTH* WV12 38 A8
Lowbrook La *SHLY* B90 170 B1
Lowden Cft
LGN/SDN/BHAMAIR B26 127 J1
Lowdham *TAM/AM/WIL* B77 47 G4
Lowe Av *DARL/WED* WS10 51 M6
Lowe Dr *KGSWFD* DY6 101 J1
SCFLD/BOLD B73 72 B2
Lowe La *KIDDW* DY11 136 F2
Lower Av *RLSS* CV31 200 D6 4
Lower Beeches Rd
NFLD/LBR B31 143 G3
Lower Bentley La *BRGRVE* B60 194 C1
Lower Cape *WWCK* CV34 199 H5
Lower Chapel St *OLDBY* B69 86 A3
Lower Church La *TPTN/OCK* DY4 67 L7
Lower City Rd *OLDBY* B69 86 A4
Lower Common La *REDW* B97 195 M3
Lowercroft Wy
FOAKS/STRLY B74 42 C7
Lower Dartmouth St *BORD* B9 107 M3
Lower Darwin St *BHTH/HG* B12 7 J9
Lower Derry St *BRLYHL* DY5 102 B3
Lower Eastern Green La
COVW CV5 152 D1
Lower End *KNWTH* CV8 179 G7
Lower Essex St *DIG/EDG* B5 7 G8
Lower Ford St *COV* CV1 9 K5 1
Lower Forster St *WSL* WS1 5 G1
Lower Gambolds La
BRGRVE B60 185 M7
Lower Gn *TPTN/OCK* DY4 67 J8 2
Lower Grinsty La *REDW* B97 195 L6
Lower Ground Cl *AST/WIT* B6 89 K4 2
AST/WIT B6 89 K4 3
Lower Hall La *WSL* WS1 4 F4
Lower High St *CDYHTH* B64 103 G5
DARL/WED WS10 68 D3 2
STRBR DY8 101 K7
Lower Higley Cl
RIDG/WDGT B32 123 J1 2
Lower Holyhead Rd *COV* CV1 8 D4
Lower Horseley Flds *WOLV* WV1 3 L5
Lower House La *ATHST* CV9 61 K3
Lower Ladyes Hills *KNWTH* CV8 176 E7
Lower La *LICH* WS13 19 G3
Lower Leam St *RLSS* CV31 200 F5
Lower Lichfield St *WLNHL* WV13 51 M3
Lower Lickhill Rd *STRPT* DY13 160 B7
Lower Loveday St *LOZ/NWT* B19 6 F1
Lower Mill St *KIDD* DY10 137 H7 2
Lower Moor *SLYOAK* B29 124 C5 3
Lower North St *RUSH/SHEL* WS4 53 J2
Lowe Rd *COVN* CV6 133 L3

The Lower Pde
CSCFLD/WYGN B72 57 G8
Lowerpark *TAM/AM/WIL* B77 46 A4 2
Lower Parklands *KIDDW* DY11 137 H8
Lower Prestwood Rd
WNSFLD WV11 37 G6
Lower Queen St
CSCFLD/WYGN B72 73 G1
Lower Reddicroft
SCFLD/BOLD B73 57 G8 2
Lower Rd *HEDN* WS12 17 G2
RCOVN/BALC/EX CV7 117 M7
Lower Rushall St *WSL* WS1 5 G2
Lower Sandford St *LICH* WS13 20 E6
Lower Severn St *CBHAMW* B1 6 E6
Lower Shepley La *BRGRVE* B60 166 B7
Lowerstack Cft
CHWD/FDBR/MGN B37 110 D2 3
Lower St *DUNHL/THL/PER* WV6 35 J8
Lower Temple St *CBHAM* B2 6 F5 2
Lower Tower St *LOZ/NWT* B19 89 H8
Lower Trinity St *BORD* B9 7 L7
Lower Valley Rd *BRLYHL* DY5 101 L3
Lower Vauxhall *WOLV* WV1 2 A4
Lower Villiers St
BKHL/PFLD WV2 50 A6
RLSN CV32 200 E4
Lower Walsall St *WOLV* WV1 3 L6
Lower White Rd
RIDG/WDGT B32 105 H8
Lowes Av *WWCK* CV34 199 J4
Lowesmoor Rd
LGN/SDN/BHAMAIR B26 109 M6
Lowe St *BHTH/HG* B12 7 M9
DUNHL/THL/PER WV6 2 B1
Loweswater Cl *NUN* CV11 81 L7
Loweswater Rd *COVS* CV3 155 J4
STRPT DY13 160 C6
Lowfield Cl *RIDG/WDGT* B32 122 E2 1
Lowfield La *REDW* B97 187 M8
Lowforce *TAM/AM/WIL* B77 47 G4
Low Hill Crs *WOLVN* WV10 36 C5
Lowhill La *RBRY* B45 143 G7
Lowland Cl *CDYHTH* B64 103 K4 2
Lowland Rd *HEDN* WS12 12 A8
Lowlands Av
DUNHL/THL/PER WV6 35 J7
FOAKS/STRLY B74 55 J5
Lowlands La *REDE* B98 197 H2
Lowndes Rd *STRBR* DY8 101 J7
Lowry Cl *BDWTH* CV12 116 E1 3
DUNHL/THL/PER WV6 48 D1
SMTHWKW B67 87 K7
WLNHL WV13 51 H3
Low St *GTWY* WS6 24 A2
Low Thatch
HWK/WKHTH B38 144 C6 2
Lowther St *COVE* CV2 9 M2
Low Town *OLDBY* B69 86 E6 3
Low Wood Rd *ERDW/GRVHL* B23 72 C8
Loxdale Sidings *BILS/COS* WV14 67 K1
Loxdale St *BILS/COS* WV14 67 K1
DARL/WED WS10 68 D3 3
Loxley Av *ALE/KHTH/YWD* B14 146 A3
SHLY B90 146 D4
Loxley Cl *COVE* CV2 135 H3 3
NFLD/LBR B31 123 J5 3
REDE B98 189 H7
Loxley Rd *MGN/WHC* B75 57 H2
SMTHWKW B67 105 K4
Loxley Wy *RLSN* CV32 200 E2
Loxton Cl *FOAKS/STRLY* B74 42 B8
Loynells Rd *RBRY* B45 142 E6
Loyns Cl *CHWD/FDBR/MGN* B37 110 C2
Lozells Rd *LOZ/NWT* B19 88 F6
Lozells St *LOZ/NWT* B19 89 G6
Lozells Wood Cl *LOZ/NWT* B19 88 F6 3
Lucas Ct *RUGBYN/HIL* CV21 183 M1
Luce Cl *CVALE* B35 91 M1
Luce Rd *WOLVN* WV10 36 C7
Lucian Cl *COVE* CV2 135 L6
Lucknow Rd *SHHTH* WV12 38 A7 3
Luddington Rd *HIA/OLT* B92 128 C6
Ludford Cl *MGN/WHC* B75 57 J6 2
NUNW/HART CV10 96 F1 1
Ludford Rd *NUNW/HART* CV10 80 A7
RIDG/WDGT B32 122 E4
Ludgate *CRTAM* B79 31 L8
Ludgate Av *KIDDW* DY11 160 E1
Ludgate Cl *CSHL/WTROR* B46 92 E2 1
Ludgate Hl *CBHAMNW* B3 6 E3
Ludgate St *DUDN* DY1 84 F4 3
Lud La *CRTAM* B79 31 L8
Ludlow Cl
CHWD/FDBR/MGN B37 111 G3
HEDN WS12 17 G3 3
SHHTH WV12 37 M7
Ludlow La *WSLW* WS2 52 E1 3
Ludlow Rd *COVW* CV5 8 A6
KIDD DY10 161 J3
REDW B97 196 B2
WASH/WDE B8 108 D2
Ludlow Wy *DUDN* DY1 84 C3
Ludmer Wy
BFLD/HDSWWD B20 89 G3 1
Ludstone Av
ETTPK/GDPK/PENN WV4 49 H8
Ludstone Rd *SLYOAK* B29 123 K4
Luff Cl *COVS* CV3 154 F5
Lugtrout La *SOLH* B91 128 C7
Lulworth Cl *HALE* B63 103 G7
Lulworth Pk *KNWTH* CV8 177 G7
Lulworth Rd *BNTWD* WS7 18 E6
HLGN/YWD B28 126 E5
Lumley Gv
CHWD/FDBR/MGN B37 111 H3
Lumley Rd *WSL* WS1 5 K4
Lumsden Cl *COVE* CV2 135 K5
Lunar Cl *TLHL/CAN* CV4 153 H8
Lundy Vw *CBROM* B36 92 F7
Lunn Av *KNWTH* CV8 191 J2
Lunns Cft *LICH* WS13 21 G5
Lunt Gv *RIDG/WDGT* B32 105 H8
Lunt Pl *BILS/COS* WV14 51 L7
Lunt Rd *BILS/COS* WV14 51 K7
Lupin Gv *BORD* B9 108 D2
Lupin Rd *DUDS* DY2 85 K4
Lupton Av *COVS* CV3 154 A7

Lusbridge Cl *HALE* B63 120 F1
Luscombe Rd *COVE* CV2 135 J5
Luther Wy *COVW* CV5 152 D1
Lutley Av *HALE* B63 121 J1
Lutley Cl *BDMR/CCFT* WV3 49 J6
Lutley Dr *HAG/WOL* DY9 120 A2
Lutley Gv *RIDG/WDGT* B32 122 F4
Lutley La *HALE* B63 121 H1
Lutley Mill Rd *HALE* B63 121 J1
Luton Rd *SLYOAK* B29 124 D2
Lutterworth Rd *COVE* CV2 135 G8
NUN CV11 99 J3 3
Luttrell Rd *FOAKS/STRLY* B74 56 D5
Luxor La *COVW* CV5 131 M5
Lyall Gdns *RBRY* B45 142 C4
Lyall Gv *ACGN* B27 126 E3
Lychgate Av *HAG/WOL* DY9 120 A4
Lydate Rd *RMSLY* B62 122 D1
Lydbrook Covert
HWK/WKHTH B38 144 C5 3
Lydbury Gv *STETCH* B33 109 L1
Lyd Cl *WNSFLD* WV11 36 F8
Lydd Cft *CVALE* B35 91 M1
Lyddington Dr *RMSLY* B62 103 M6
Lyde Gn *HALE* B63 103 G6
Lydford Cl *COVE* CV2 135 G6
Lydford Gv *ERDE/BCHGN* B24 90 E3
Lydford Rd *BLOX/PEL* WS3 38 F3
Lydgate Rd *COVN* CV6 133 M8
KGSWFD DY6 83 K8
Lydget Gv *ERDW/GRVHL* B23 72 B6 3
Lydham Cl *BILS/COS* WV14 66 F1
ERDW/GRVHL B23 71 L7
REDE B98 188 C8
Lydia Cft *FOAKS/STRLY* B74 42 C7
Lydian Cl *DUNHL/THL/PER* WV6 2 D1
Lydiate Ash Rd *BRGRVW* B61 166 A2
Lydiate Av *NFLD/LBR* B31 143 H4
Lydiates Cl *SEDG* DY3 65 M6
Lydney Cl *REDE* B98 189 H7
SHHTH WV12 52 B1
Lydney Gv *NFLD/LBR* B31 143 K2
Lye Av *RIDG/WDGT* B32 122 E3
Lye Close La *RIDG/WDGT* B32 122 D3
Lyecroft Av
CHWD/FDBR/MGN B37 111 H3
Lye Cross Rd *OLDBY* B69 85 M6
Lygon Cl *REDE* B98 188 F8
Lygon Gv *RIDG/WDGT* B32 123 J1 3
Lymedene Rd *PBAR/PBCH* B42 70 F8
Lyme Green Rd *STETCH* B33 109 K1
Lymer Rd *WOLVN* WV10 36 A4
Lymesy St *COVS* CV3 154 B7
Lymington Cl *COVN* CV6 134 B5 1
Lymington Dr *COVN* CV6 116 F7
Lymington Rd *BNTWD* WS7 18 D4
WLNHL WV13 52 B3 3
Lymore Cft *COVE* CV2 135 L5
Lymsey Cft *STRBR* DY8 101 G2
Lyn Av *LICH* WS13 20 D4
Lynbrook Cl *DUDS* DY2 85 H7
HLYWD B47 145 L5
Lynbrook Rd *COVW* CV5 153 H5
Lynchgate Rd *TLHL/CAN* CV4 153 G7
The Lynch *NUN* CV11 99 H3
POL/KGSB/FAZ B78 47 K4
Lyncourt Gv *RIDG/WDGT* B32 104 F7
Lyncroft Rd *SPARK* B11 126 D3
Lyndale *TAM/AM/WIL* B77 46 D7
Lyndale Cl *COVW* CV5 153 G2
Lyndale Dr *WNSFLD* WV11 37 J7
Lyndale Rd *COVW* CV5 153 G2
DUDS DY2 85 J7
SEDG DY3 65 M3
Lynden Cl *BRGRVW* B61 185 J2
Lyndenwood *REDW* B97 195 L3
Lyndholm Rd *KIDD* DY10 137 L7
Lyndhurst Cl *COVN* CV6 116 F7 2
Lyndhurst Cft *COVW* CV5 152 A1 1
Lyndhurst Dr *KIDD* DY10 137 J5
STRBR DY8 101 K4
Lyndhurst Rd *BDMR/CCFT* WV3 49 L6
ERDE/BCHGN B24 90 D3
HEDN WS12 17 H4
HHTH/SAND B71 69 J6
Lyndon *HHTH/SAND* B71 69 H8
Lyndon Cl *BFLD/HDSWWD* B20 88 F3
CBROM B36 92 A5
HALE B63 103 J8
SEDG DY3 66 C4
Lyndon Cft
CHWD/FDBR/MGN B37 110 F6
Lyndon Gv *HHTH/SAND* B71 87 H1 2
KGSWFD DY6 82 F5
Lyndon Rd *HIA/OLT* B92 127 K3
RBRY B45 142 C6
SCFLD/BOLD B73 56 F8 3
STETCH B33 109 J2
Lyndworth Rd *BVILLE* B30 125 G6
Lyneham Cl *CRTAM* B79 31 M5
Lyneham Gdns *WALM/CURD* B76 73 L7
Lyneham Wy *CVALE* B35 91 K2 3
Lynehill La *PENK* ST19 10 B7
Lynfield Cl *HWK/WKHTH* B38 144 D6
Lynfield Rd *LICH* WS13 20 D4
Lyng Cl *COVW* CV5 152 E2
Lyng La *WBROM* B70 87 G3
Lynmouth Cl *ALDR* WS9 40 D8
NUN CV11 81 J8
Lynmouth Rd *COVE* CV2 135 J1
Lynn Gv *SLYOAK* B29 124 A2
Lynn La *ALDR* WS9 27 J7
Lynton Av *DUNHL/THL/PER* WV6 35 J6
HHTH/SAND B71 69 G6
SMTHWK B66 87 L7
Lynton Rd *AST/WIT* B6 89 L6
COVN CV6 134 D4
Lynval Rd *BRLYHL* DY5 102 D6
Lynwood Av *KGSWFD* DY6 82 F5
Lynwood Cl *SHHTH* WV12 38 C5 2
Lynwood Dr *KIDD* DY10 138 F3
Lyons Gv *SPARK* B11 126 A2
Lysander Rd *RBRY* B45 142 E3 3
Lysander St *COVS* CV3 155 H7 2
Lysander Wy *CNCK/NC* WS11 16 C2
Lyster Cl *WWCK* CV34 198 F5 1
Lysways St *WSL* WS1 5 G5
Lythall Cl *RLSS* CV31 201 K8

Lythalls La *COVN* CV6 134 B3
Lytham *TAM/AM/WIL* B77 33 G8
Lytham Cl *STRBR* DY8 119 L3
WALM/CURD B76 73 M7
Lytham Cft *EDG* B15 6 E9
Lytham Gv *BLOX/PEL* WS3 38 E1 3
Lytham Rd
DUNHL/THL/PER WV6 48 B1
RUGBYS/DCH CV22 183 H4
Lythwood Dr *BRLYHL* DY5 102 A5
Lyttelton Rd *LDYWD/EDGR* B16 106 B4
STETCH B33 109 H3
STRBR DY8 101 H8
WWCK CV34 199 J5
Lyttleton Av *BRGRVE* B60 185 J6
RMSLY B62 104 C6 1
Lyttleton Cl *COVS* CV3 155 L4
DUDS DY2 103 G1
Lyttleton St *WBROM* B70 87 G3
Lytton Av
ETTPK/GDPK/PENN WV4 65 H1
Lytton Gv *ACGN* B27 126 F4
Lytton La *RIDG/WDGT* B32 123 K2

M

Maas Rd *NFLD/LBR* B31 143 L1
Mabey Av *REDE* B98 188 D8 1
Macadam Cl *BNTWD* WS7 18 F5
Macarthur Rd *CDYHTH* B64 103 G5
Macaulay Rd *COVE* CV2 155 H1
RUGBYS/DCH CV22 183 J6
Macbeth Cl *RUGBYS/DCH* CV22 183 J7
Macdonald Cl *OLDBY* B69 86 B3
Macdonald Rd *COVE* CV2 155 H2
Macdonald St *DIG/EDG* B5 7 H9
Macefield Cl *COVE* CV2 135 H3
Mace St *CDYHTH* B64 103 J4
Mac Gregor Crs
TAM/AM/WIL B77 46 D1 3
Macgregor Tithe *CRTAM* B79 31 M8 4
Machin Rd *ERDW/GRVHL* B23 90 D1
Mackadown La *STETCH* B33 110 B3
Mackay Rd *BLOX/PEL* WS3 39 H3
Mackenzie Cl *COVW* CV5 132 E6
Mackenzie Rd *SPARK* B11 126 A3
Mackmillan Rd
BLKHTH/ROWR B65 104 A3
Macmillan Cl *OLDBY* B69 86 A3 3
Macrome Rd
DUNHL/THL/PER WV6 35 J5
Madam's Hill Rd *SHLY* B90 147 H6
Madden Pl *RUGBYS/DCH* CV22 183 G3
Maddocks Hl *CSCFLD/WYGN* B72 73 G3
Madehurst Rd
ERDW/GRVHL B23 72 C7 2
Madeira Av *CDSL* WV8 34 E3
Madeira Cft *COVW* CV5 153 J3
Madeley Rd *HAG/WOL* DY9 141 J6
KGSWFD DY6 101 L1
REDE B98 189 K7 1
SPARK B11 108 A8
Madin Rd *TPTN/OCK* DY4 85 J1
Madison Av *CBROM* B36 91 H7
WSLW WS2 52 F3 1
Madley Cl *RBRY* B45 142 C5
Madox Cl *CRTAM* B79 31 J5
Madresfield Dr *HALE* B63 121 M3 2
Maer Cl *BLKHTH/ROWR* B65 104 A2
Mafeking Rd *SMTHWK* B66 87 L6
Magdala St *WSNGN* B18 88 C8
Magdalen Cl *DUDN* DY1 84 E3 1
Magdalene Rd *WSL* WS1 5 K8
Magna Cl *GTWY* WS6 24 C2
Magness Crs *SHHTH* WV12 38 A8
Magnet La *RUGBYS/DCH* CV22 183 G5
Magnolia Cl *COVS* CV3 153 M8
SLYOAK B29 123 L6
Magnolia Gv *CDSL* WV8 34 E2 3
Magnolia Wy *STRBR* DY8 101 K5 2
Magnum Cl *FOAKS/STRLY* B74 55 K6 2
Magnus *TAM/AM/WIL* B77 46 C7
Magpie Cl *DUDS* DY2 103 J2 1
Magpie La
RCOVN/BALC/EX CV7 150 C7
Magpie Wy *KIDD* DY10 161 M3
Magyar Crs *NUN* CV11 99 K5
Maidavale Crs *COVS* CV3 154 A8
Maidendale Rd *KGSWFD* DY6 82 F6
Maidensbridge Gdns
KGSWFD DY6 82 F4 1
Maidensbridge Rd *KGSWFD* DY6 82 F4
Maidstone Dr *BNTWD* WS7 19 H7
STRBR DY8 101 J2
Maidstone Rd
BFLD/HDSWWD B20 89 J4
Maidwell Dr *SHLY* B90 147 J5
Main Av
LGN/SDN/BHAMAIR B26 129 G1
Main Rd *ATHST* CV9 61 L6
ATHST CV9 62 C7 2
ATHST CV9 63 J2
CRTAM B79 33 M3
LGN/SDN/BHAMAIR B26 128 D2
RCOVN/BALC/EX CV7 131 G4
Mainstone Cl *REDE* B98 197 J2 1
Mainstream Wy *VAUX/NECH* B7 108 A1
Main St *ALDR* WS9 41 J1
CRTAM B79 31 M4
KNWTH CV8 180 E1
LICHS WS14 28 D7
MKTBOS/BARL/STKG CV13 81 K2
RRUGBY CV23 158 F2
RRUGBY CV23 158 C1
RRUGBY CV23 182 E1
RUGBYN/HIL CV21 159 H6
RUGBYS/DCH CV22 183 G5
SPARK B11 107 L6
Mainwaring Dr
MGN/WHC B75 57 J3 2
Maisemore Cl *REDE* B98 189 H6
Maitland Rd *DUDN* DY1 84 B4
WASH/WDE B8 108 D1
Majestic Wy
BLKHTH/ROWR B65 104 A1
Major St *BKHL/PFLD* WV2 50 C6

Majuba Rd *LDYWD/EDGR* B16 106 A1
Makepeace Av *WWCK* CV34 199 K4
Malam Cl *TLHL/CAN* CV4 152 E4
Malcolm Av *BRGRVW* B61 185 J2
ERDE/BCHGN B24 73 G8
Malcolm Gv *RBRY* B45 142 E6
Malcolm Rd *SHLY* B90 146 F3
Malcolmson Cl *EDG* B15 106 D6
Maldale *TAM/AM/WIL* B77 47 G4
Malfield Dr *ACGN* B27 127 J2
REDW B97 195 K3
Malham Cl *NUN* CV11 99 L3
Malham Rd *STRPT* DY13 160 C6
TAM/AM/WIL B77 47 G4
WWCK CV34 199 K4 2
Malins Rd
ETTPK/GDPK/PENN WV4 50 B8
HRBN B17 106 B8
The Malins *WWCK* CV34 199 M7
Malkit Cl *WSLW* WS2 52 C1
Mallaby Cl *SHLY* B90 146 E5 1
Mallard Av *KIDD* DY10 161 M2
NUNW/HART CV10 80 A8
Mallard Cl *ACGN* B27 127 G2
BLOX/PEL WS3 25 L8 3
BRLYHL DY5 102 A6
REDE B98 188 D8 2
Mallard Dr *ERDW/GRVHL* B23 89 M2
OLDBY B69 104 D2
Mallender Dr *DOR/KN* B93 148 D6
Mallerin Cft *NUNW/HART* CV10 79 M8
Mallicot Cl *LICH* WS13 21 H4
Mallin St *SMTHWK* B66 87 H6
Mallory Crs *BLOX/PEL* WS3 39 H3
Mallory Dr *KIDDW* DY11 137 H4
WWCK CV34 199 H6
Mallory Ri *MOS/BIL* B13 126 A4
Mallory Rd
DUNHL/THL/PER WV6 48 C2
Mallory Wy
RCOVN/BALC/EX CV7 116 C8
Mallow Cl *DSYBK/YTR* WS5 69 L2 2
Malmesbury Rd *COVN* CV6 133 L3
SMHTH B10 108 C7
Malpas Dr *RIDG/WDGT* B32 123 G5
Malpass Gdns *CDSL* WV8 34 C1
Malpass Rd *BRLYHL* DY5 102 D6
Malt Cl *EDG* B15 106 B7
Malthouse Cl
NUNW/HART CV10 96 F1 2
Malthouse Cft *AST/WIT* B6 89 J5 2
Malthouse Gdns *LOZ/NWT* B19 89 H6
Malthouse Gv *YDLY* B25 109 J5 1
Malthouse La
DUNHL/THL/PER WV6 35 H7
HOCK/TIA B94 170 C7
KNWTH CV8 176 C7
PBAR/PBCH B42 71 H5
WASH/WDE B8 90 C7
Malt House La *WOLVN* WV10 14 F8
Malthouse Rd *TPTN/OCK* DY4 67 J8
Malthouse Rw
CHWD/FDBR/MGN B37 110 E5 1
The Maltings *RLSN* CV32 200 D3
WOLV WV1 3 G2
Malt Mill La *RMSLY* B62 104 A5
Malton Gv *MOS/BIL* B13 125 M6 1
Malvern Av *HAG/WOL* DY9 102 A8
NUNW/HART CV10 97 M2
Malvern Cl *HHTH/SAND* B71 69 H8 2
SHHTH WV12 51 M1
Malvern Ct *WOLVN* WV10 36 B5 1
Malvern Crs *DUDS* DY2 84 D7
Malvern Dr *ALDR* WS9 41 G5
KIDD DY10 161 J2
WALM/CURD B76 73 L5
WOLV WV1 50 F4 2
Malvern Hill Rd *VAUX/NECH* B7 90 A6
Malvern Park Av *SOLH* B91 148 B2
Malvern Rd *ACGN* B27 127 G1
BRGRVE B60 185 H6
COVW CV5 153 J1
LGLYGN/QTN B68 104 F5
RBRY B45 166 E3
RCOVN/BALC/EX CV7 151 G7
REDW B97 195 B5
Malvern St *BHTH/HG* B12 107 L8 3
Malvern Vw *KIDD* DY10 163 J4
KIDDW DY11 160 F4 1
Malvern View Rd *SEDG* DY3 84 B1 1
Mamble Rd *STRBR* DY8 101 J8
Manby Rd *CVALE* B35 91 L1
Manby St *TPTN/OCK* DY4 67 K5
Mancetter Rd *ATHST* CV9 63 K6
NUNW/HART CV10 80 B5
SHLY B90 147 G2 1
Manchester St *AST/WIT* B6 89 J8 3
OLDBY B69 86 F6
Mancroft Cl *KGSWFD* DY6 82 F6 3
Mancroft Gdns
DUNHL/THL/PER WV6 35 G8
Mancroft Rd
DUNHL/THL/PER WV6 35 G8
Mandale Rd *WOLVN* WV10 36 D7
Mandarin Av *KIDD* DY10 161 M2
Manderley Cl *COVW* CV5 132 A8
SEDG DY3 66 A3
Mander St *BDMR/CCFT* WV3 2 D8
Manderville Gdns *KGSWFD* DY6 83 G7
Mandeville Gdns *WSL* WS1 5 H5
Mandeville Wy *BRGRVW* B61 165 L8 3
Maney Cnr *CSCFLD/WYGN* B72 72 F1
Maney Hill Rd
CSCFLD/WYGN B72 73 G2
Manfield Av *COVE* CV2 135 L6
Manfield Rd *WLNHL* WV13 51 G2
Manifold Cl *BNTWD* WS7 19 H7 1
Manilla Rd *SLYOAK* B29 124 F4
Manitoba Cft
HWK/WKHTH B38 144 D5 3
Manley Cl *WBROM* B70 86 E2 3
Manley Rd *LICH* WS13 21 H4
Manlove St *BDMR/CCFT* WV3 2 B8
Manningford Rd
ALE/KHTH/YWD B14 145 K3 3
Mann's Cl *KNWTH* CV8 179 M5
Manor Abbey Dr *RMSLY* B62 122 C2
Manor Abbey Rd *RMSLY* B62 122 C1

Manor Av CNCK/NC WS11 .... 16 B4
 GTWY WS6 .... 24 E1
 KIDDW DY11 .... 136 E6
Manor Av South KIDDW DY11.. 136 H5
Manor Cl ATHST CV9 .... 61 M3
 CDSL WV8 .... 34 F2
 ETTPK/GDPK/PENN WV4 .... 65 K1
 KIDDW DY11 .... 136 E7
 STRPT DY13 .... 160 F8
 WLNHL WV13 .... 51 K2
Manor Court Av NUN CV11 .... 80 F8
Manor Court Rd BRGRVE B60.. 185 J5
 NUN CV11 .... 98 E1
Manor Dr SCFLD/BOLD B73 .... 72 F1
 SEDG DY3 .... 82 C3
 SEDG DY3 .... 83 M2
 WOLVN WV10 .... 23 H3
Manor Farm Dr SHHTH WV12.. 38 B8
Manor Farm Rd SPARK B11 .... 126 C1
Manorfield Cl PENK ST19 .... 10 C5
Manorford Av HHTH/SAND B71.. 69 L4
Manor Gdns STETCH B33 .... 109 H4
Manor Gv NFLD/LBR B31 .... 143 G4
Manor Hall Ms COVS CV3 .... 155 H7
Manor Hl SCFLD/BOLD B73 .... 72 F1
Manor House Cl
 RUGBYN/HIL CV21 .... 159 H6
 SLYOAK B29 .... 123 K4
Manor House Dr COV CV1 .... 8 E6
Manor House La
 CSHL/WTROR B46 .... 92 F1
 LGN/SDN/BHAMAIR B26 .... 109 J7
Manor House Pk CDSL WV8 .... 34 F1
Manor House Rd
 DARL/WED WS10 .... 68 D1
Manor La BGRVW B61 .... 142 A8
 CRTAM B79 .... 31 J2
 RMSLY B62 .... 122 C1
 STRBR DY8 .... 119 H2
Manor Pk KGSWFD DY6 .... 83 H7
 NFLD/LBR B31 .... 143 G4
Manor Park Rd CBROM B36 .... 92 B6
 NUN CV11 .... 80 E8
Manor Ri BNTWD WS7 .... 18 E4
 LICHS WS14 .... 21 C7
Manor Rd AST/WIT B6 .... 89 K4
 ATHST CV9 .... 63 J7
 COV CV1 .... 8 F7
 DARL/WED WS10 .... 69 H3
 DOR/KN B93 .... 172 D2
 ETTPK/GDPK/PENN WV4 .... 50 E8
 ETTPK/GDPK/PENN WV4 .... 65 K1
 FOAKS/STRLY B74 .... 55 L5
 HLYWD B47 .... 169 L2
 KNWTH CV8 .... 176 D7
 LDYWD/EDGR B16 .... 106 B4
 POL/KGSB/FAZ B78 .... 45 H4
 REDW B97 .... 194 E4
 RLSS CV32 .... 200 F2
 RUGBYN/HIL CV21 .... 183 M1
 SCFLD/BOLD B73 .... 56 F8
 SMTHWKW B67 .... 87 H8
 SOLH B91 .... 127 M8
 SOLH B91 .... 128 A8
 STETCH B33 .... 109 J2
 STRBR DY8 .... 101 H3
 STRPT DY13 .... 160 F8
 TAM/AM/WIL B77 .... 46 A1
 TPTN/OCK DY4 .... 85 K1
 WOLVN WV10 .... 36 A6
 WSLW WS2 .... 4 A2
Manor Rd North
 LDYWD/EDGR B16 .... 106 B4
 WSLW WS2 .... 4 A1
Manor Rd South DUNHL/THL/PER WV6.. 35 G8
Manor St DUNHL/THL/PER WV6.. 35 C8
Manor Wy HALE B63 .... 121 K4
 RMSLY B62 .... 122 A3
Mansard Cl BDMR/CCFT WV3.. 49 K5
 WNSFLD WV11 .... 36 F5
Manse Cl RCOVN/BALC/EX CV7.. 116 E4
Mansell Cl HALE B63 .... 102 F6
Mansell Rd REDW B97 .... 196 B6
 TPTN/OCK DY4 .... 67 L5
Mansel St COVN CV6 .... 134 C5
Mansfield Cl CRTAM B79 .... 31 J7
 YDLY B25 ....
Mansfield Rd AST/WIT B6 .... 89 H5
 YDLY B25 109
Mansion Cl DUDN DY1 .... 84 D2
Mansion Crs SMTHWKW B67 .... 105 J1
Mansion Dr BNTWD WS7 .... 27 H1
 TPTN/OCK DY4 .... 68 A8
Manston Dr
 DUNHL/THL/PER WV6.. 34 C8
Manston Hl PENK ST19 .... 10 C6
Manston Rd
 LGN/SDN/BHAMAIR B26 .... 109 M6
Manston Vw CRTAM B79 .... 32 A5
Manta Rd TAM/AM/WIL B77 .... 46 B7
Mantilla Dr COVS CV3.. 153 M8
Manton Cft DOR/KN B93 .... 172 C2
Manway Cl BFLD/HDSWWD B20.. 70 D8
Maple Av DARL/WED WS10 .... 69 G1
 RCOVN/BALC/EX CV7 .... 116 F4
Maplebeck Cl COVW CV5 .... 8 A4
Maple Cl BILS/COS WV14 .... 66 E6
 BNTWD WS7 .... 18 D6
 HDSW B21 .... 88 C4
 KIDDW DY11 .... 136 F5
 STRBR DY8 .... 119 H3
Maple Crs CNCK/NC WS11 .... 16 A5
Maple Cft ALE/KHTH/YWD B14.. 125 K7
Mapledene Rd
 LGN/SDN/BHAMAIR B26 .... 110 B7
Maple Dr DSYBK/YTR WS5.. 69 M1
 HDNS WS12 .... 12 B5
 KGSTG B44 .... 71 M5
 POL/KGSB/FAZ B78 .... 60 B6
 RUSH/SHEL WS4 .... 39 M5
 SEDG DY3 .... 83 M3
Maple Gn DUDN DY1 .... 66 E8
Maple Gv BDMR/CCFT WV3.. 49 G3
 BILS/COS WV14 .... 67 K1
 CHWD/FDBR/MGN B37 .... 92 D7
 KGSWFD DY6 .... 83 J7
 LICHS WS14 .... 21 J6
 LOZ/NWT B19 .... 89 H5

RUGBYN/HIL CV21 .... 183 L1
 WWCK CV34 .... 199 L4
Maple Leaf Dr
 CHWD/FDBR/MGN B37 .... 110 F5
Maple Leaf Rd
 DARL/WED WS10 .... 68 A4
Maple Ri LGLYGN/QTN B68 .... 105 G3
 TAM/AM/WIL B77 .... 46 F1
Maple Rd BDMR/CCFT WV3.. 49 G5
 BLOX/PEL WS3 .... 39 K3
 BVILLE B30 .... 124 C5
 CSCFLD/WYGN B72 .... 73 C2
 DUDN DY1 .... 85 G2
 NUNW/HART CV10 .... 80 C8
 RBRY B45 .... 142 D7
 RLSS CV31 .... 200 D7
 RMSLY B62 .... 104 B5
The Maples BDWTH CV12 .... 116 C3
Mapleton Av HLGN/YWD B28.. 126 F6
Mapleton Rd COVN CV6 .... 133 K5
 HLGN/YWD B28 .... 126 F7
Maple Tree La HALE B63 .... 103 G7
Maple Wy NFLD/LBR B31 .... 143 K5
Maplewood WALM/CURD B76.. 73 L5
Mapperley Cl COVE CV2 .... 135 L5
Mapperley Gdns MOS/BIL B13.. 125 C2
Mappleborough Rd SHLY B90.. 146 C4
Marans Cft HWK/WKHTH B38.. 144 B6
Marbury Cl NFLD/LBR B31 .... 143 L6
Marbury Ms BRLYHL DY5 .... 102 B4
Marchant Rd BDMR/CCFT WV3.. 49 K3
 BILS/COS WV14 .... 51 C6
March Cl GTWY WS6 .... 24 B3
March End Rd WNSFLD WV11.. 37 H8
Marchfont Cl NUN CV11 .... 99 K3
Marchmont Rd BORD B9 .... 108 E3
Marchmount Rd
 CSCFLD/WYGN B72 .... 73 C5
March Wy ALDR WS9 .... 41 C4
 COVS CV3 .... 155 H6
Marcliff Crs SHLY B90 .... 146 A3
Marconi Pl HEDN WS12 .... 13 C6
Marcos Dr CBROM B36 .... 92 D4
Marcot Rd HIA/OLT B92 .... 109 K8
Marcroft Pl RLSS CV31 .... 201 H7
Marden Cl WLNHL WV13 .... 51 K4
Marden Gv NFLD/LBR B31 .... 143 L6
Mardol Cl COVE CV2 .... 135 H6
Mardon Rd
 LGN/SDN/BHAMAIR B26 .... 109 M8
Maree Gv WNSFLD WV11 .... 37 M4
Marfield Cl WALM/CURD B76.. 73 L7
Margam Crs BLOX/PEL WS3.. 38 D3
Margam Ter BLOX/PEL WS3.. 38 D3
Margam Wy BLOX/PEL WS3.. 38 D3
Margaret Av BDWTH CV12.. 116 E2
 HALE B63 .... 121 K1
Margaret Dr CNCK/NC WS11.. 12 C7
 STRBR DY8 .... 119 M1
Margaret Gdns
 SMTHWKW B67 .... 87 J8
Margaret Gv HRBN B17 .... 106 A6
Margaret Rd ATHST CV9 .... 63 J6
 DARL/WED WS10 .... 68 A1
 HRBN B17 .... 106 A8
 SCFLD/BOLD B73 .... 72 B4
 WSLW WS2 .... 52 C2
Margaret St CBHAMNW B3 .... 6 E4
 WBROM B70 .... 86 F3
 WSLW WS2 .... 4 D1
Margaret V TPTN/OCK DY4.. 68 A4
Margeson Cl COVE CV2 .... 155 J3
Margesson Dr RBRY B45 .... 167 H4
Margetts Cl KNWTH CV8 .... 191 K1
Marholm Cl COVEN WV9 .... 35 K3
Marian Cft
 LGN/SDN/BHAMAIR B26 .... 110 B8
Maria St WBROM B70 .... 87 H5
Marie Brock Cl TLHL/CAN CV4.. 152 E3
Marie Cl ATHST CV9 .... 63 L6
Marie Dr ACGN B27 .... 126 F5
Marigold Cl HEDN WS12 .... 17 C2
Marigold Crs DUDN DY1 .... 84 E1
Marina Cl TLHL/CAN CV4.. 152 C6
Marina Crs HEDN WS12 .... 12 E8
Marine Crs STRBR DY8 .... 101 J4
Marine Dr KGSTG B44 .... 71 J7
Marine Gdns STRBR DY8 .... 101 J4
Mariner CRTAM B79 .... 31 J6
Mariner Av LDYWD/EDGR B16.. 106 C4
Marion Cl BRLYHL DY5 .... 102 D3
 SMTHWKW B67 .... 87 H7
Marion Wy HLGN/YWD B28.. 126 C6
Marion Rd COVN CV6 .... 134 B6
Marjorie Av BVILLE B30 .... 144 F2
Marjoram Cl HWK/WKHTH B38.. 144 D5
Markby Rd WSNGN B18 .... 88 C7
Mark Av DARL/WED WS10 .... 68 C2
Market End Cl BDWTH CV12.. 116 A3
Market Hall St CNCK/NC WS11.. 16 C4
Market La
 ETTPK/GDPK/PENN WV4.. 48 D7
 LICHS WS14 .... 28 C3
Market Pl BLOX/PEL WS3.. 38 F4
 CNCK/NC WS11 .... 16 B4
 DARL/WED WS10 .... 68 D5
 REDW B97 .... 196 C1
 TPTN/OCK DY4 .... 68 B8
 WLNHL WV13 .... 51 L3
Market St ATHST CV9 .... 63 H5
 BRGRVW B61 .... 185 L3
 CRTAM B79 .... 45 M1
 HEDN WS12 .... 12 F7
 KIDD DY10 .... 137 M8
 LICH WS13 .... 20 F5
 OLDBY B69 .... 86 E5
 PENK ST19 .... 10 C4
 POL/KGSB/FAZ B78 .... 47 L4
 RUGBYN/HIL CV21 .... 183 M1
 STRBR DY8 .... 101 L8
 WOLV WV1 .... 3 G5
 WWCK CV34 .... 199 H7
Market Wy HAG/WOL DY9 .... 120 A7
Markfield Rd
 LGN/SDN/BHAMAIR B26 .... 109 M5

Markford Wk LOZ/NWT B19 .... 89 H7
Markham Cresent
 HIA/OLT B92 .... 128 D4
Markham Cft COVEN WV9 .... 35 L3
Markham Dr KGSWFD DY6 .... 101 J1
Markholm Rd BRWNH WS8 .... 26 E8
Marklew Cl BRWNH WS8 .... 26 E8
Marklin Av WOLVN WV10 .... 36 B4
Mark Rd DARL/WED WS10 .... 68 C2
Marksbury Cl
 DUNHL/THL/PER WV6.. 35 L8
Marlbank Rd STRBR DY8 .... 101 L4
Marlborough Av BRGRVE B60.. 185 L5
Marlborough Cl
 FOAKS/STRLY B74 .... 42 C7
Marlborough Ct LICH WS13.. 20 F6
Marlborough Dr RLSS CV31.. 201 G7
 STRBR DY8 .... 119 L2
Marlborough Gdns
 DUNHL/THL/PER WV6.. 49 J1
 STRBR DY8 .... 101 H3
Marlborough Gv YDLY B25.. 109 H4
Marlborough Rd BORD B9.. 92 B5
 CBROM B36 .... 92 B5
 COVE CV2 .... 154 E3
 NUN CV11 .... 98 F1
 RUGBYS/DCH CV22 .... 183 J5
 SEDG DY3 .... 66 D7
 SMTHWK B66 .... 105 J2
Marlborough St BLOX/PEL WS3.. 38 F4
 KIDD DY10 .... 137 J8
Marlborough Wy
 TAM/AM/WIL B77 .... 46 C3
Marlbrook Cl HIA/OLT B92.. 128 A1
Marlbrook Dr
 ETTPK/GDPK/PENN WV4.. 49 M7
Marlbrook La BILS/COS WV14.. 166 B4
Marlburn Wy WMBN WV5.. 64 C7
Marlcliff Gv MOS/BIL B13.. 125 L7
Marlcroft COVS CV3 .... 155 J8
Marldon Rd
 ALE/KHTH/YWD B14.. 125 H7
Marlene Cft
 CHWD/FDBR/MGN B37 .... 111 H4
Marler Rd TLHL/CAN CV4.. 152 D6
Marley Rd KGSWFD DY6.. 101 L1
Marifield La REDE B98.. 188 F8
Marlin WALM/CURD B76.. 73 L6
Marling Cft HIA/OLT B92.. 128 C6
Marlissa Dr COVS CV3.. 134 C3
Marloes Wk RLSS CV31.. 201 G7
Marlow Cl COVW CV5.. 152 F1
 DUDS DY2 .... 103 J2
Marlowe Cl KIDD DY10.. 137 M7
 NUNW/HART CV10.. 79 K8
Marlowe Dr SHHTH WV12.. 37 L6
Marlow Rd ATHST CV9.. 61 G8
 ERDW/GRVHL B23.. 72 A8
 TAM/AM/WIL B77.. 32 B8
Marlow St
 BLKHTH/ROWR B65.. 104 A4
 WSLW WS2 .... 53 J1
Marlpit La MGN/WHC B75.. 57 H2
 REDW B97 .... 195 M4
Marlpool Cl KIDDW DY11.. 137 C4
Marlpool Dr BLOX/PEL WS3.. 39 K4
 REDW B97 .... 196 A2
Marlpool La KIDDW DY11.. 137 C4
Marlpool Pl KIDDW DY11.. 137 G5
Marl Rd DUDS DY2.. 102 F1
Marlston Wk COVW CV5.. 152 F1
Marl Top HWK/WKHTH B38.. 144 D3
Marlwood Cl COVN CV6.. 134 D1
Marmion Dr GTB/HAM B43.. 70 D3
Marmion Gv DUDN DY1.. 84 E5
Marmion St CRTAM B79.. 31 M8
Marmion Wy WBROM B70.. 68 D7
Marnel Dr BDMR/CCFT WV3.. 49 H5
Marner Crs COVN CV6.. 133 M8
Marner Rd BDWTH CV12.. 116 E2
 NUNW/HART CV10.. 98 F4
Marnhull Cl COVE CV2.. 155 K1
Marpool Ct KIDDW DY11.. 137 G5
Marquis Dr CDYHTH B64.. 103 L6
Marquis's Dr HEDN WS12.. 13 J2
Marrick TAM/AM/WIL B77.. 47 G5
Marriners La COVW CV5.. 132 F8
Marriott Rd BDWTH CV12.. 116 B3
 COVN CV6 .... 8 A1
 DUDS DY2 .... 103 G1
 SMTHWK B66 .... 87 H6
Marroway St
 LDYWD/EDGR B16.. 106 D2
Mars Cl BILS/COS WV14.. 66 E4
Marsdale Dr NUNW/HART CV10.. 98 C2
Marsden Rd HIA/OLT B92.. 127 J4
Marsden Rd REDE B98.. 196 C2
Marsett TAM/AM/WIL B77.. 47 C5
Marshall Cl ALDR WS9.. 54 F1
Marshall Gv KGSTG B44.. 71 K6
Marshall Lake Rd SHLY B90.. 147 H4
Marshall Rd LGLYGN/QTN B68.. 105 C4
 RCOVN/BALC/EX CV7.. 116 E5
 WLNHL WV13 .... 51 H4
Marshall St CBHAMW B1.. 6 E7
 SMTHWKW B67 .... 87 H6
 TAM/AM/WIL B77 .... 32 C8
Marsham Cl WWCK CV34.. 199 M5
Marsham Court Rd SOLH B91.. 127 K6
Marsham Rd
 ALE/KHTH/YWD B14.. 145 K2
Marshbrook Cl COVE CV2.. 135 J3
Marshbrook Rd
 ERDE/BCHGN B24.. 91 H1
Marsh Crs STRBR DY8.. 101 H2
Marshdale Av COVN CV6.. 134 C2
Marsh End HWK/WKHTH B38.. 144 E5
Marshfield Cl REDE B98.. 188 F6
Marshfield Dr TLHL/CAN CV4.. 177 H3
Marshfield Gdns
 ERDE/BCHGN B24.. 90 C3
Marsh Hl ERDW/GRVHL B23.. 90 A1
Marshland Wy WSLW WS2.. 52 C4
Marsh La CSHL/WTROR B46.. 92 F2
 ERDW/GRVHL B23.. 72 C8
 HHTH/SAND B71.. 69 H5
 HIA/OLT B92.. 130 B8
 LICHS WS14 .... 20 F8

LICHS WS14 .... 21 L8
 PENK ST19 .... 10 D3
 SOLH B91 .... 148 C2
 WALM/CURD B76.. 75 C8
 WOLVN WV10 .... 35 M3
 WSLW WS2 .... 4 D2
Marsh Lane Pde WOLVN WV10.. 36 A3
Marshmont Wy
 ERDW/GRVHL B23.. 72 E5
Marsh St WSLW WS2 .... 4 D2
Marsh Wy BRGRVW B61.. 165 K4
Marshwood Cft
 RIDG/WDGT B32.. 122 E2
Marsland Cl HRBN B17.. 106 A5
Marsland Rd HIA/OLT B92.. 127 J6
Marston Av DARL/WED WS10.. 52 A7
Marston Cl RLSN CV32.. 200 F3
 STRBR DY8 .... 119 H1
Marston Cft
 CHWD/FDBR/MGN B37.. 110 D6
Marston Dr
 CHWD/FDBR/MGN B37.. 92 E8
Marston Gv GTB/HAM B43.. 70 A3
Marston La BDWTH CV12.. 99 H8
 NUN CV11 .... 99 J5
 WALM/CURD B76.. 75 J4
Marston Rd BKHL/PFLD WV2.. 50 A6
 DUDN DY1 .... 84 B5
 HEDN WS12 .... 12 D7
 SCFLD/BOLD B73.. 72 E6
Marston St WLNHL WV13.. 52 A3
Marten Cl RWWCK/WEL CV35.. 198 E6
Martham Dr
 DUNHL/THL/PER WV6.. 48 F3
Martin Cl BILS/COS WV14.. 67 H6
 BRGRVW B61 .... 185 J4
 COVW CV5 .... 152 C1
 LGN/SDN/BHAMAIR B26.. 109 H7
Martin Cft LICH WS13.. 20 E4
Martindale CNCK/NC WS11.. 16 E3
Martindale Rd
 RCOVN/BALC/EX CV7.. 117 C5
Martindale Wk BRLYHL DY5.. 101 M4
Martin Dr SHHTH WV12.. 37 L4
Martingale Cl BRGRVE B60.. 185 J7
 DSYBK/YTR WS5.. 69 K1
Martin Hill St DUDS DY2.. 85 C5
Martin La RUGBYS/DCH CV22.. 183 H6
Martin Ri
 CHWD/FDBR/MGN B37.. 110 D5
Martin Rd BILS/COS WV14.. 67 K2
 DSYBK/YTR WS5.. 54 A5
 TPTN/OCK DY4.. 67 L8
Martins Dr ATHST CV9.. 63 H3
Martins Rd BDWTH CV12.. 116 C4
Martin St
 ETTPK/GDPK/PENN WV4.. 50 D7
Martlesham Sq CVALE B35.. 91 L1
Martley Cl REDE B98.. 196 F6
Martley Cft RIDG/WDGT B32.. 123 J7
 SOLH B91 .... 147 M5
Martley Dr HAG/WOL DY9.. 120 A1
Martley Rd OLDBY B69.. 86 B7
 RUSH/SHEL WS4.. 40 A4
Marton Av BNTWD WS7.. 18 E5
Marton Cl VAUX/NECH B7.. 89 M7
The Martyrs' Cl COVS CV3.. 9 C8
Marwood Cl NUN CV11.. 99 J6
Marwood Cft FOAKS/STRLY B74.. 55 L3
 WOLV WV1 .... 3 J6
Mary Herbert St COVS CV3.. 154 B6
Maryland Av BKDE/SHDE B34.. 91 J8
Maryland Dr NFLD/LBR B31.. 123 M8
Maryland Rd BRLYHL DY5.. 102 D6
Marylebone Cl STRBR DY8.. 101 L6
Mary Macarthur Dr
 CDYHTH B64.. 102 F4
Mary Rd HDSW B21.. 88 C6
 OLDBY B69 .... 86 A5
 STETCH B33 .... 109 H2
 WBROM B70 .... 87 H2
Mary Slessor St COVS CV3.. 155 H6
Marystow Cl COVW CV5.. 132 F5
Mary St BHTH/HG B12.. 107 J8
 CBHAMNW B3 .... 6 D2
 HEDN WS12 .... 12 F6
 WSLW WS2 .... 53 H2
Maryvale Ct LICHS WS14.. 21 H6
Mary Vale Rd BVILLE B30.. 124 C7
Marywell Cl RIDG/WDGT B32.. 122 F6
Masefield Av DUDN DY1.. 67 C6
Masefield Cl BILS/COS WV14.. 67 K3
 BNTWD WS7 .... 18 E4
 LICHS WS14 .... 21 H4
Masefield Dr CRTAM B79.. 31 L6
 CRTAM B79 .... 31 L7
Masefield Gv CNCK/NC WS11.. 16 C1
Masefield Ri RMSLY B62.. 122 B2
Masefield Rd BLOX/PEL WS3.. 39 J5
 SEDG DY3 .... 83 L1
 WOLVN WV10 .... 36 E4
Masefield Sq NFLD/LBR B31.. 144 A1
Masham Cl STETCH B33.. 109 H2
Mashie Gdns HWK/WKHTH B38.. 144 B4
Maslen Pl HALE B63.. 121 M2
Maslin Dr BILS/COS WV14.. 66 E4
Mason Av RLSN CV32.. 201 G2
Mason Cl REDW B97.. 196 B6
Mason Crs
 ETTPK/GDPK/PENN WV4.. 49 J8
Mason La HOCK/TIA B94.. 170 D4
Mason Rd COVN CV6.. 134 D4
 ERDE/BCHGN B24.. 90 E1
 KIDDW DY11 .... 137 G7
 REDW B97 .... 196 A5
 WSLW WS2 .... 38 F4
Masons Cl HALE B63.. 103 C7
Mason St BILS/COS WV14.. 66 F6
 BKHL/PFLD WV2.. 50 A6
 WBROM B70 .... 86 F1
Masons Wy HIA/OLT B92.. 127 J3
 HIA/OLT B92.. 127 J3
Massbrook Gv WOLVN WV10.. 36 D7
Massbrook Rd WOLVN WV10.. 36 D7

Masser Rd COVN CV6 .... 134 A1
Masshouse Circus Queensway
 CBHAMNE B4 .... 7 H4
Masshouse La DIG/EDG B5.. 7 J4
 HWK/WKHTH B38.. 144 D4
Masters La RMSLY B62.. 104 C4
Matchborough Wy REDE B98.. 197 G6
Matchlock Cl FOAKS/STRLY B74.. 55 J6
Matfen Av SCFLD/BOLD B73.. 72 C3
Mathe Cft RLSS CV31.. 201 L8
Math Meadow RIDG/WDGT B32.. 105 K8
Matlock Cl BLOX/PEL WS3.. 39 C2
 DUDS DY2 .... 103 H2
Matlock Dr CNCK/NC WS11.. 16 E1
Matlock Rd BLOX/PEL WS3.. 39 C2
 COV CV1 .... 134 B7
 SPARK B11 .... 126 D2
Matterson Rd COVN CV6.. 133 L8
Matthew La KIDDW DY11.. 161 K4
Matthews Cl
 BLKHTH/ROWR B65.. 103 M4
Mattox Rd WNSFLD WV11.. 37 H7
Matty Rd LGLYGN/QTN B68.. 105 C3
Maud Rd CSHL/WTROR B46.. 93 H2
 WBROM B70 .... 87 G4
Maudslay Rd COVW CV5.. 153 J3
Maughan St BRLYHL DY5.. 102 E5
 DUDN DY1 .... 84 E4
Maund Cl BRGRVE B60.. 185 J6
Maureen Cl TLHL/CAN CV4.. 152 A4
Maurice Gv WOLVN WV10.. 37 H1
Maurice Rd
 ALE/KHTH/YWD B14.. 125 J7
 SMTHWKW B67 .... 105 J3
Mavis Gdns LGLYGN/QTN B68.. 104 F5
Mavis Rd HEDN WS12.. 12 F6
 NFLD/LBR B31 .... 143 J4
Mavor Av BNTWD WS7.. 18 B4
Mavor Dr BDWTH CV12.. 116 B4
Mawgan Dr LICHS WS14.. 21 H7
Mawnan Cl
 RCOVN/BALC/EX CV7.. 116 F5
Maw St WSL WS1.. 5 G9
Maxholm Rd FOAKS/STRLY B74.. 55 K3
Max Rd COVN CV6.. 133 K8
 RIDG/WDGT B32.. 105 H8
Maxstoke Cl BLOX/PEL WS3.. 38 E2
 RCOVN/BALC/EX CV7.. 130 F4
 REDE B98 .... 197 H4
 TAM/AM/WIL B77 .... 60 A1
Maxstoke Cft SHLY B90.. 147 G5
Maxstoke La CSHL/WTROR B46.. 93 J7
 RCOVN/BALC/EX CV7.. 130 F7
Maxstoke Rd SCFLD/BOLD B73.. 72 E3
Maxstoke St BORD B9.. 107 M5
Maxted Rd ERDW/GRVHL B23.. 72 E3
Maxwell Av BFLD/HDSWWD B20.. 88 F4
Maxwell Cl LICH WS13.. 21 G6
Maxwell Rd BKHL/PFLD WV2.. 3 H8
Mayall Dr MGN/WHC B75.. 57 C1
Mayama Rd
 POL/KGSB/FAZ B78.. 45 K5
May Av BHTH/HG B12.. 107 L8
Maybank BORD B9.. 108 D2
Maybank Cl LICHS WS14.. 21 J5
Maybank Pl KGSTG B44.. 71 J7
Maybank Rd DUDS DY2.. 103 C2
Mayberry Cl
 ALE/KHTH/YWD B14.. 145 M3
Maybridge Dr SOLH B91.. 147 M5
Maybrook Rd BRWNH WS8.. 26 B8
 WALM/CURD B76.. 73 L8
Maybury Cl CDSL WV8.. 34 C1
Maybush Gdns WOLVN WV10.. 36 A4
May Cl BNTWD WS7.. 18 D4
Maycock Rd COVN CV6.. 133 L8
Maycroft Cl HEDN WS12.. 12 D6
Maydene Cft BHTH/HG B12.. 107 K7
Mayfair HAG/WOL DY9.. 120 B3
Mayfair Cl DUDN DY1.. 84 E4
 KGSTG B44 .... 71 M6
Mayfair Dr KGSWFD DY6.. 83 C6
 NUNW/HART CV10.. 97 K1
Mayfair Gdns BDMR/CCFT WV3.. 49 H1
 TPTN/OCK DY4.. 85 L1
May Farm Cl HLYWD B47.. 145 K7
Mayfield TAM/AM/WIL B77.. 47 C5
Mayfield Av PENK ST19.. 10 C5
Mayfield Cl BDWTH CV12.. 116 F2
 BRGRVW B61 .... 165 K4
 KIDDW DY11 .... 137 L3
 SOLH B91 .... 148 A4
Mayfield Crs
 BLKHTH/ROWR B65.. 103 L2
 KNWTH CV8 .... 192 A1
Mayfield Dr BRWNH WS8.. 25 M3
The Mayfields REDE B98.. 196 B3
Mayflower Cl LOZ/NWT B19.. 89 H7
Mayflower Dr BRLYHL DY5.. 83 L6
 COVE CV2 .... 155 H3
Mayford Gv MOS/BIL B13.. 125 M7
Maygrove Rd KGSWFD DY6.. 83 C6
Mayhurst Cl HLYWD B47.. 146 A7
 TPTN/OCK DY4.. 67 L5
Mayhurst Rd HLYWD B47.. 145 M6
Mayland Dr FOAKS/STRLY B74.. 55 K8
Mayland Rd LDYWD/EDGR B16.. 105 M2
May La ALE/KHTH/YWD B14.. 125 K8
 HLYWD B47 .... 145 K6
 RUGBYS/DCH CV22.. 183 H4
Maynard Av BDWTH CV12.. 116 B5
 STRBR DY8 .... 119 H2
 WWCK CV34 .... 199 L6
Mayne Cl RWWCK/WEL CV35.. 198 D7
Mayor's Cft TLHL/CAN CV4.. 152 F6
Maypole Cl BEWD DY12

CDYHTH B64 .... 102 F5 ◫
Maypole Ct *WMBN* WV5 .... 64 E7 ◫
Maypole Dr *STRBR* DY8 .... 101 J8
Maypole Flds *HALE* B63 .... 102 E6
Maypole Gv
 ALE/KHTH/YWD B14 ...... 145 M3
Maypole HI *HALE* B63 .... 102 E5
Maypole La
 ALE/KHTH/YWD B14 ...... 145 L3
 ATHST CV9 .... 62 A4 ◫
Maypole Rd *LGLYGN/QTN* B68 ... 104 F4
Maypole St *WMBN* WV5 .... 64 F6
May St *BLOX/PEL* WS3 .... 39 H7
 COVN CV6 .... 134 C5
Mayswood Dr
 DUNHL/THL/PER WV6 .... 48 D4
Mayswood Gv *RIDG/WDGT* B32 .. 123 H1
Mayswood Rd *HIA/OLT* B92 ..... 128 A3
Maythorn Av *WALM/CURD* B76 ... 73 L1
Maythorn Gdns
 DUNHL/THL/PER WV6 .... 49 G1
Maythorn Gv *SOLH* B91 .... 147 M5 ◫
Maytree Cl
 CHWD/FDBR/MGN B37 ...... 110 E3
May Tree Gv *GTWY* WS6 .... 24 E3
Maywell Dr *HIA/OLT* B92 .... 128 A3
Maywood Cl *KGSWFD* DY6 ...... 82 F7 ◫
Mcbean Rd
 DUNHL/THL/PER WV6 .... 49 K1
Mcconnell Cl *BRGRVE* B60 ..... 185 M6
Mcdonnell Dr
 RCOVN/BALC/EX CV7 .... 116 D7
Mcdougall Rd *DARL/WED* WS10 .. 69 G2
Mcghie St *HEDN* WS12 .... 12 F7
Mc Kean Rd *OLDBY* B69 .... 86 E5
Mclean Rd *WOLVN* WV10 .... 36 A3
Mcmahon Rd *BDWTH* CV12 ..... 116 C5
Meaburn Cl *SLYOAK* B29 .... 123 L6
Mead Cl *ALDR* WS9 .... 40 F7
Mead Crs *BORD* B9 .... 108 F2
Meadfoot Av
 ALE/KHTH/YWD B14 ...... 145 K2 ◫
Meadfoot Dr *KGSWFD* DY6 ..... 82 F6
Meadfoot Rd *COVS* CV3 .... 155 H7
The Meadlands *WMBN* WV5 ..... 64 C7
Meadow Av *HHTH/SAND* B71 .... 69 K4
Meadowbrook Rd *HALE* B63 .... 121 H2
 LICH WS13 .... 20 F7
Meadow Brook Rd
 NFLD/LBR B31 .... 123 K8
Meadow Cl *FOAKS/STRLY* B74 .. 55 K4
 HOCK/TIA B94 .... 172 A7
 HRBN B17 .... 105 M4
 POL/KGSB/FAZ B78 .... 60 B8 ◫
 RLSN CV32 .... 201 G1
 RRUGBY CV23 .... 180 E7
 RUSH/SHEL WS4 .... 40 A5 ◫
Meadow Ct *NUN* CV11 .... 98 F1
Meadow Cft
 DUNHL/THL/PER WV6 .... 48 B2 ◫
 HAG/WOL DY9 .... 139 K1
 HEDN WS12 .... 16 A1
 HLYWD B47 .... 169 L2 ◫
 LICH WS13 .... 21 L4 ◫
 RCOVN/BALC/EX CV7 .... 96 C4
Meadow Dr *HIA/OLT* B92 .... 129 L7
Meadowfield Rd *RBRY* B45 ..... 142 E6
Meadowfields Cl *STRBR* DY8 ... 101 J3
Meadow Gdns *ATHST* CV9 .... 62 A5
Meadow Grange Dr
 SHHTH WV12 .... 37 M6 ◫
Meadow Gv *GTWY* WS6 .... 24 E3
 HIA/OLT B92 .... 127 H4
Meadow Hill Cl *KIDDW* DY11 ... 136 E8
Meadow Hill Crs *REDE* B98 .... 188 D8
Meadow Hill Dr
 CNCK/NC WS11 .... 16 D3 ◫
Meadowhill Dr *STRBR* DY8 ..... 101 J3 ◫
Meadow Hill Rd
 HWK/WKHTH B38 .... 144 C3
Meadowhill Rd *REDE* B98 ...... 188 D8
Meadowlands Dr
 RUSH/SHEL WS4 .... 40 A5
Meadow La *ALVE* B48 .... 167 M7
 BILS/COS WV14 .... 66 E3 ◫
 SHHTH WV12 .... 37 L8
 WMBN WV5 .... 64 E5
 WOLVN WV10 .... 22 A7
Meadow Lark Cl *HEDN* WS12 .... 16 F1 ◫
Meadow Pk *CRTAM* B79 .... 31 K8
Meadowpark Rd *STRBR* DY8 .... 101 H5
Meadow Ri *BEWD* DY12 .... 136 B8
 BVILLE B30 .... 124 B6
Meadow Rd *ALDR* WS9 .... 54 E1
 ATHST CV9 .... 61 G8
 BDMR/CCFT WV3 .... 49 G5
 BRGRVW B61 .... 165 K5
 COVN CV6 .... 133 M1
 DUDN DY1 .... 84 E1
 HLYWD B47 .... 169 L2
 HRBN B17 .... 105 M4
 KNWTH CV8 .... 180 E1
 LGLYGN/QTN B68 .... 104 F3
 NUNW/HART CV10 .... 79 L5
 RIDG/WDGT B32 .... 104 A5
 RMSLY B62 .... 104 A7
 RUGBYN/HIL CV21 .... 159 H7
 SMTHWK B67 .... 105 L1
 WWCK CV34 .... 199 L6 ◫
Meadowside *NUN* CV11 .... 99 M5
Meadowside Cl *GTB/HAM* B43 ... 70 C4
Meadowside Rd
 FOAKS/STRLY B74 .... 56 D1
The Meadows *ALDR* WS9 .... 40 C8
 HAG/WOL DY9 .... 119 M6
 RWWCK/WEL CV35 .... 191 L6
Meadow St *ATHST* CV9 .... 63 H6
 CDYHTH B64 .... 103 K5 ◫
 COV CV1 .... 8 C5
 NUN CV11 .... 98 F1
 TAM/AM/WIL B77 .... 46 A2
 WOLV WV1 .... 2 C5
 WSL WS1 .... 4 D5
Meadowsweet Av
 HWK/WKHTH B38 .... 144 D6
Meadowsweet Wy
 KGSWFD DY6 .... 83 L7 ◫

Meadow V *CDSL* WV8 .... 34 F4
Meadowvale Rd *BRGRVW* B60 ... 166 A7
Meadow Vw *BNTWD* WS7 .... 19 H7
 MOS/BIL B13 .... 126 A5
 SEDG DY3 .... 66 A4 ◫
Meadow Wk
 ALE/KHTH/YWD B14 .... 145 J4
 CDYHTH B64 .... 103 H5
Meadow Wy *CDSL* WV8 .... 34 G3
 HEDN WS12 .... 17 G4
 RRUGBY CV23 .... 158 F2
 STRBR DY8 .... 101 G3
Mead Ri *EDG* B15 .... 106 D7
The Mead *SEDG* DY3 .... 65 M5 ◫
Meadthorpe Rd *KGSTG* B44 .... 71 H5
Meadvale Rd *RBRY* B45 .... 142 F7
Meadway *COVE* CV2 .... 134 F7
 STETCH B33 .... 109 M5
Meadway Cl *HEDN* WS12 .... 17 G2 ◫
 WS *BNTWD* WS7 .... 18 E8
The Meadway
 DUNHL/THL/PER WV6 ...... 34 E8
 REDW B97 .... 196 A4
Mears Cl *ERDW/GRVHL* B23 .... 72 B5 ◫
Mears Coppice *BRLYHL* DY5 .... 102 C7
Mears Dr *STETCH* B33 .... 109 H1
Mearse Cl *WNSFLD* WV11 ...... 88 E8
Mearse La *HAG/WOL* DY9 ...... 140 D7
 RBRY B45 .... 166 D4
Mease Av *BNTWD* WS7 .... 19 H7
Mease Cft *BORD* B9 .... 107 M3 ◫
Measham Gv
 LGN/SDN/BHAMAIR B26 ... 109 J8
Measham Wy *WNSFLD* WV11 .... 37 J6
Medcroft Av
 BFLD/HDSWWD B20 .... 88 C1
Medina Rd *COVN* CV6 .... 134 C4
 SPARK B11 .... 108 E4
Medina Wy *KGSWFD* DY6 ...... 83 G7 ◫
Medland Av *COVS* CV3 .... 153 K8
Medley Rd *SPARK* B11 .... 108 E3
Medlicott Rd *SPARK* B11 ...... 108 A8
Medway Cl *BRLYHL* DY5 .... 83 J7
Medway Cft *CBROM* B36 .... 92 D6 ◫
Medway Gv
 HWK/WKHTH B38 .... 144 C5
Medway Rd *BRWNH* WS8 .... 26 A3
Medwin Gv *ERDW/GRVHL* B23 ... 72 B6
Meerash La *BNTWD* WS7 .... 27 G2
Meer End Rd *KNWTH* CV8 ...... 175 C5
Meer End *KNWTH* CV8 .... 175 C5
Meerhill Av *SHLY* B90 .... 147 K7
Meeting House La
 NFLD/LBR B31 .... 143 L1
 RCOVN/BALC/EX CV7 ..... 151 G7
Meeting La *BRLYHL* DY5 ...... 101 M4
Meeting St *DARL/WED* WS10 ... 68 C2
 DUDS DY2 .... 103 G1
 TPTN/OCK DY4 .... 68 A7
Meg La *BNTWD* WS7 .... 18 F4
Melbourne Av *BRGRVW* B61 .... 185 J1
 LOZ/NWT B19 .... 89 H8
Melbourne Cl *BRGRVW* B61 .... 185 J2 ◫
 KGSWFD DY6 .... 101 J3
 NUN CV11 .... 99 J5 ◫
 WBROM B70 .... 68 C4
Melbourne Crs *HEDN* WS12 .... 17 K3 ◫
Melbourne Gdns
 DSYBK/YTR WS5 .... 5 M9 ◫
Melbourne Rd *BRGRVW* B61 .... 185 J1
 COVW CV5 .... 8 A6
 HALE B63 .... 103 M8
 HEDN WS12 .... 17 K3
 SMTHWK B66 .... 87 L6
Melbourne St *BKHL/PFLD* WV2 .. 3 G7 ◫
Melbury Cl *BDMR/CCFT* WV3 ... 2 C6
Melbury Gv
 ALE/KHTH/YWD B14 ...... 125 L3
Melbury Wy *CNCK/NC* WS11 .... 16 D3
Melchett Rd *BVILLE* B30 ...... 144 D2
Melcote Gv *KGSTG* B44 .... 71 J5
Meldon Dr *BILS/COS* WV14 .... 67 L3
Meldrum Rd *NUNW/HART* CV10 . 98 B2
Melen St *REDW* B97 .... 196 B1
Melford Cl *SEDG* DY3 .... 66 A3
Melford Hall Rd *SOLH* B91 .... 127 K6
Melford Ri *BNTWD* WS7 .... 18 C4
Melfort Cl *COVS* CV3 .... 155 K3 ◫
 NUNW/HART CV10 .... 79 M8
Melfort Gv *ALE/KHTH/YWD* B14 . 145 L2
Melksham Sq *CVALE* B35 ...... 91 L2 ◫
Mellis Gv *ERDW/GRVHL* B23 ... 71 L8
Mellish Ct *RUGBYS/DCH* CV22 . 183 J4 ◫
Mellish Dr *RUSH/SHEL* WS4 ... 53 M2
Mellish Rd *RUGBYS/DCH* CV22 . 183 J4
 RUSH/SHEL WS4 .... 53 L2
Mellor Dr *FOAKS/STRLY* B74 .. 56 C2
Mellors Cl *HRBN* B17 .... 123 M2
Mellowdew Rd *COVE* CV2 ...... 155 G1
 STRBR DY8 .... 101 G2
Mellowship Rd *COVW* CV5 ..... 132 A8
Mell Sq *SOLH* B91 .... 148 A1
Mellwaters Pk *TAM/AM/WIL* B77 . 47 G5 ◫
Melmerby *TAM/AM/WIL* B77 .... 47 G5
Melplash Av *SOLH* B91 .... 147 L1 ◫
Melrose Av *BDWTH* CV12 ...... 116 B6
 BHTH/HG B12 .... 107 L7 ◫
 HHTH/SAND B71 .... 69 H4
 SCFLD/BOLD B73 .... 72 C3
 SPARK B11 .... 108 A7 ◫
 STRBR DY8 .... 119 K3
Melrose Cl *HWK/WKHTH* B38 ... 144 D4 ◫
Melrose Dr
 DUNHL/THL/PER WV6 ...... 48 B1
 HEDN WS12 .... 17 G3
Melrose Gv *LOZ/NWT* B19 ..... 88 F6 ◫
Melrose Rd *BFLD/HDSWWD* B20 . 89 J4
Melstock Cl *TPTN/OCK* DY4 ... 67 H8
Melstock Rd
 ALE/KHTH/YWD B14 ...... 125 H6
Melton Av *HIA/OLT* B92 .... 127 M1
Melton Dr *EDG* B15 .... 107 G6
Melton Rd *ALE/KHTH/YWD* B14 . 125 K5
 RLSN CV32 .... 200 F1 ◫
Melverley Gv *KGSTG* B44 ..... 71 K6
Melverton Av *WOLVN* WV10 .... 36 B5
Melville Cl
 RCOVN/BALC/EX CV7 ..... 116 E5 ◫

Melville Rd *COV* CV1 .... 8 B4
 LDYWD/EDGR B16 .... 106 B4
Melvina Rd *VAUX/NECH* B7 .... 107 M1
Membury Rd *WASH/WDE* B8 .... 90 B7
Memorial Cl *WLNHL* WV13 ..... 51 L3
Memory La *DARL/WED* WS10 ... 52 B5
 WOLVN WV10 .... 36 F8
Menai Cl *SHHTH* WV12 .... 38 A7
Mendip Av *WASH/WDE* B8 ..... 90 C8 ◫
Mendip Cl *BKHL/PFLD* WV2 .... 50 D7
 BRGRVW B61 .... 165 L8 ◫
 SEDG DY3 .... 84 B2
Mendip Dr *NUNW/HART* CV10 .. 97 M2
Mendip Rd *HALE* B63 .... 121 H4
 HEDN WS12 .... 12 E4
 STRBR DY8 .... 101 M7
 WASH/WDE B8 .... 90 C8
Mendip Wy *TAM/AM/WIL* B77 .. 47 G4
Menin Crs *MOS/BIL* B13 ...... 125 M6 ◫
Menin Rd *MOS/BIL* B13 .... 125 M6
 TPTN/OCK DY4 .... 67 H8
Menteith St *STRPT* DY13 ...... 160 C6
Meon Gv *DUNHL/THL/PER* WV6 . 48 C1
 STETCH B33 .... 109 M5
Meon Ri *HAG/WOL* DY9 .... 120 A2
Meon Wy *WNSFLD* WV11 ...... 37 K6
Meranti Cl *SHHTH* WV12 ...... 38 A5
Mercer Av *COVE* CV2 .... 134 E8
 CSHL/WTROR B46 ...... 92 E2 ◫
Mercer Gv *WNSFLD* WV11 ..... 37 H6
Merchants Wy *ALDR* WS9 ..... 40 E6
 NUN CV11 .... 80 E8
Mercia Cl *BRGRVE* B60 .... 185 J6
 CRTAM B79 .... 31 J6
Mercia Dr *DUNHL/THL/PER* WV6 . 34 C8
Mercian Wy *TAM/AM/WIL* B77 .. 32 F8
 TAM/AM/WIL B77 .... 46 F2
Mercia Wy *WWCK* CV34 .... 199 L6
Mercot Cl *REDE* B98 .... 196 C7
Mercury Rd *CNCK/NC* WS11 ... 12 E8
Mere Av *CVALE* B35 .... 91 L2
Mere Cl *SHHTH* WV12 .... 37 L8
Merecote Rd *HIA/OLT* B92 .... 127 H6
Meredith Gn *KIDDW* DY11 .... 160 E4
Meredith Pool Cl *WSNGN* B18 . 88 D7 ◫
Meredith Rd *COVE* CV2 .... 155 H3
 SEDG DY3 .... 65 L8
 WNSFLD WV11 .... 37 C5
Mere Dr *MGN/WHC* B75 .... 56 F3
Mere Green Cl *MGN/WHC* B75 . 57 G3
Mere Green Rd *MGN/WHC* B75 . 57 G3
Mere La *PENK* ST19 .... 14 A1
Mere Oak Rd
 DUNHL/THL/PER WV6 ...... 34 C8
Mere Pool Rd *MGN/WHC* B75 .. 57 H3
Mere Rd *ERDW/GRVHL* B23 .... 90 B2
 STRBR DY8 .... 119 J1
Mereside Wy *HIA/OLT* B92 .... 127 J5
Meres Rd *HALE* B63 .... 103 G8
Merevale Av *NUN* CV11 .... 98 E1
Merevale Cl *REDE* B98 .... 197 H5
Merevale La *ATHST* CV9 .... 62 D6
Merevale Rd *ATHST* CV9 ...... 63 C4
 HIA/OLT B92 .... 127 M3
Merevale Vw *ATHST* CV9 ...... 63 G6
Mereworth Dr
 RUSH/SHEL WS4 .... 40 A5
Merganser *TAM/AM/WIL* B77 ... 46 E7
Merganser Wy *KIDD* DY10 .... 161 M2 ◫
Meriden Av *STRBR* DY8 .... 101 H7
Meriden Cl *CNCK/NC* WS11 .... 15 M5
 REDE B98 .... 197 J2 ◫
 STRBR DY8 .... 101 H6
Meriden Dr
 CHWD/FDBR/MGN B37 ..... 92 E7
Meriden Ri *HIA/OLT* B92 ...... 128 B2
Meriden Rd *HIA/OLT* B92 ...... 130 A6
 RCOVN/BALC/EX CV7 .... 113M6
 RCOVN/BALC/EX CV7 .... 131 G3
 WOLVN WV10 .... 35 L5
Meriden St *COV* CV1 .... 8 C3
 DIG/EDG B5 .... 7 J6
Merino Av *NFLD/LBR* B31 ..... 143 L5
Merlin Av *NUNW/HART* CV10 .. 79M7
Merlin Cl *CNCK/NC* WS11 ..... 16 A3
 DUDN DY1 .... 84 D5
 TAM/AM/WIL B77 ...... 46 E7
Merlin Dr *KIDD* DY10 .... 161 M2
Merlin Gv
 LGN/SDN/BHAMAIR B26 ... 109 M8
Merrick Cl *HALE* B63 .... 121 H5
Merrick Rd *WNSFLD* WV11 .... 37 L7
Merridale Av *BDMR/CCFT* WV3 . 49 K3
Merridale Crs *BDMR/CCFT* WV3 . 2 A5
Merridale Gdns *BDMR/CCFT* WV3 . 2 A6
Merridale Gv *BDMR/CCFT* WV3 . 49 J4
Merridale La *BDMR/CCFT* WV3 . 2 A5
Merridale Rd *BDMR/CCFT* WV3 . 49 K4
Merridale St West
 BDMR/CCFT WV3 .... 2 A8
Merridale St *BDMR/CCFT* WV3 . 2 B8
Merriemont Dr *RBRY* B45 ..... 166 E4
Merrill Cl *GTWY* WS6 .... 24 C3
Merrill Gdns *BRGRVE* B60 ..... 166 B4 ◫
Merrills Hall *WLNHL* WV11 .... 51 J1
Merrill's Hall La *WNSFLD* WV11 . 51 J1
Merrington Cl *SOLH* B91 ...... 148 A5 ◫
Merrion's Cl *GTB/HAM* B43 ... 70 C1
Merrishaw Rd *NFLD/LBR* B31 .. 143 L5
Merritts Brook Cl
 SLYOAK B29 .... 123 L8 ◫
Merritt's Brook La
 NFLD/LBR B31 .... 123 J8
Merritts Hl *NFLD/LBR* B31 .... 123 J7
Merrivale Rd *COVW* CV5 ...... 153 J2 ◫
 RMSLY B62 .... 104 F1
 SMTHWK B66 .... 105 L3
Merryfield Gv *HRBN* B17 ...... 124 A1
Merryfield Rd *DUDN* DY1 ..... 84 B4
Merryfields Wy *COVE* CV2 .... 135 L2
Merry Hl *BRLYHL* DY5 .... 102 A4
Merryhill Dr *WSNGN* B18 ..... 88 D7 ◫
Merse Rd *REDE* B98 .... 189 J7
Mersey Gv *HWK/WKHTH* B38 .. 144 C6
Mersey Rd *BDWTH* CV12 ..... 117 L3
 BLOX/PEL WS3 .... 39 J4

Merstal Dr *HIA/OLT* B92 ...... 128 D6
Merstone Cl *BILS/COS* WV14 .. 51 G7
Merstowe Cl *ACGN* B27 ...... 126 F2
Merton Cl *KIDD* DY10 .... 137 M6
 LGLYGN/QTN B68 .... 104 F3
Merton Rd *MOS/BIL* B13 ...... 125 M2
Merttens Dr
 RUGBYS/DCH CV22 .... 183 K3
Mervyn Pl *BILS/COS* WV14 .... 67 K2 ◫
Mervyn Rd *BILS/COS* WV14 ... 67 K2
 HDSW B21 .... 88 B4
Meryhurst Rd *DARL/WED* WS10 . 68 F1
Merynton Av *TLHL/CAN* CV4 .. 153 J7 ◫
Meschines St *COVS* CV3 ...... 154 B7
Mesnes Gn *LICHS* WS14 ...... 21 G6
Messenger La *WBROM* B70 ... 87 H2
Messenger Rd *SMTHWK* B66 .. 87 M7
Metcalf Cl *BNTWD* WS7 .... 19 G5
Metcalfe Cl *HEDN* WS12 ...... 13 C7 ◫
Metchley Ct *HRBN* B17 .... 124 B1 ◫
Metchley Cft *SHLY* B90 .... 147 K7 ◫
Metchley Dr *HRBN* B17 .... 106 A8
Metchley La *EDG* B15 .... 124 B1
 HRBN B17 .... 106 B7 ◫
Metchley Park Rd *EDG* B15 ... 106 C8
Metfield Cft *HRBN* B17 .... 124 B1
 KGSWFD DY6 .... 83 K7 ◫
Metlin Gv *STETCH* B33 .... 110 C2
Metro Wy *SMTHWK* B66 ...... 88 A6
Mews Rd *RLSN* CV32 .... 200 B5 ◫
The Mews *BDWTH* CV12 ..... 116 F3
 BLKHTH/ROWR B65 .... 104 A3 ◫
 KNWTH CV8 .... 191 J2
Meyrick Rd *WBROM* B70 ...... 68 E7
Meyrick Wk *LDYWD/EDGR* B16 . 106 D4
Miall Park Rd *SOLH* B91 ...... 127 J8 ◫
Miall Rd *HLGN/YWD* B28 ..... 126 E5
Mica Cl *TAM/AM/WIL* B77 ..... 46 F3
Michael Dr *EDG* B15 .... 107 G6
Michaelmas Rd *COVS* CV3 .... 8 B5
Michael Rd *DARL/WED* WS10 .. 51 M6
 SMTHWK B67 .... 87 J7
Michaelwood Cl *REDW* B97 ... 195 K3
Michell Cl *COVS* CV3 .... 154 F5
Michelle Cl *MOS/BIL* B13 ..... 125 L8 ◫
Michigan Cl *CNCK/NC* WS11 .. 16 F3 ◫
Micklehill Dr *SHLY* B90 ...... 146 F5
Mickle Meadow
 CSHL/WTROR B46 .... 92 F2
Mickleover Rd *WASH/WDE* B8 . 91 G8
Mickleton Rd *COVS* CV3 ...... 154 F5
Mickleton *TAM/AM/WIL* B77 ... 47 G5
Mickleton Av *STETCH* B33 .... 110 A5
Mickleton Cl *REDE* B98 ...... 196 C6
Mickleton Dr
 RWWCK/WEL CV35 .... 198 B3
Mickleton Rd *COVW* CV5 ..... 8 D8
 HIA/OLT B92 .... 127 H5
Micklewood Cl *PENK* ST19 ... 10 D6
Micklewood La *PENK* ST19 ... 14 F1
Mickley Av *WOLVN* WV10 ..... 36 C8
Midacre *WLNHL* WV13 .... 51 L4
Middleburg Cl *NUN* CV11 ..... 99 L5
Middle Acre Rd
 RIDG/WDGT B32 .... 123 J3
Middle Av *WLNHL* WV13 ...... 51 J5 ◫
Middle Bickenhill La
 HIA/OLT B92 .... 129 L1
Middleborough Rd *COV* CV1 .. 8 D2
Middlecotes *TLHL/CAN* CV4 .. 152 F4
Middle Crs *BLOX/PEL* WS3 ... 39 K6
Middle Cross *WOLV* WV1 .... 3 H6
Middle Dr *RBRY* B45 .... 167 H1
Middlefield *CDSL* WV8 .... 35 J3
Middlefield Av *DOR/KN* B93 .. 172 F1 ◫
 RMSLY B62 .... 104 D5
Middlefield Cl *RMSLY* B62 ... 104 D4 ◫
Middlefield Gdns *RMSLY* B62 . 104 D4
Middlefield La *HAG/WOL* DY9 . 119M7
Middlefield Rd *BRGRVE* B60 .. 185 M6
Middle Field Rd *NFLD/LBR* B31 . 143 M3
Middlefield Rd *OLDBY* B69 ... 85 L5
Middlefield Dr *COVS* CV3 .... 155 L4
Middle Gdns *WLNHL* WV13 ... 51 M3 ◫
Middlehill Ri
 RIDG/WDGT B32 .... 123 H2 ◫
Middle House Dr
 BRGRVE B60 .... 166 B4 ◫
Middlehouse La *REDE* B98 .... 188 C7 ◫
Middle La *CDSL* WV8 .... 34 A3
 CSHL/WTROR B46 ...... 76 C7
 HLYWD B47 .... 169 K2
 HWK/WKHTH B38 ...... 145 G6
Middle Leaford *STETCH* B33 .. 91 L8
Middle Leasowe
 RIDG/WDGT B32 .... 123 G1
Middle Lock La
 RWWCK/WEL CV35 .... 198 B3
Middlemarch Rd *COVN* CV6 ... 133M7
 NUNW/HART CV10 ...... 98 F4
Middle Meadow Av
 RIDG/WDGT B32 .... 105 G8 ◫
Middlemore La *ALDR* WS9 .... 40 C7
Middlemore La West *ALDR* WS9 . 40 C7
Middlemore Rd *NFLD/LBR* B31 . 143 M3
 SMTHWK B66 .... 87 M6
Middle Park Cl *SLYOAK* B29 .. 123 M5
Middle Park Rd *SLYOAK* B29 . 123 M5
Middle Piece Dr *REDW* B97 ... 195 L3
Middle Ride *COVS* CV3 ...... 155 J7 ◫
Middleton Rd *BRGRVE* B60 ... 194 E3
 BRGRVW B61 .... 165 K1
Middlesmoor *TAM/AM/WIL* B77 . 47 G5
Middleton Gdns *BVILLE* B30 .. 144 C1
Middleton Gra
 NFLD/LBR B31 .... 144 A1 ◫
Middleton Hall Rd *BVILLE* B30 . 144 C1
Middleton La *POL/KGSB/FAZ* B78.. 58 D7
Middleton Rd
 ALE/KHTH/YWD B14 ...... 125 K6 ◫
 BRGRVW B61 .... 185 K1
 BRWNH WS8 .... 26 C6
 FOAKS/STRLY B74 ...... 55 L4
 KIDDW DY11 .... 137 G4
 SHLY B90 .... 146 E3

Middletree Rd *HALE* B63 ...... 103 G6
Middle Vauxhall *WOLV* WV1 ... 2 B4 ◫
Middleway *HEDN* WS12 .... 13 L8
Middleway Av *STRBR* DY8 .... 101 G2
Middleway Gn *BILS/COS* WV14 . 51 G5
Middleway Rd *BILS/COS* WV14 . 51 G5
Middleway Vw *WSNGN* B18 ... 106 C2 ◫
Midford Gv *EDG* B15 .... 6 D9
Midgley Dr *FOAKS/STRLY* B74 . 56 F3
Midhill Dr *OLDBY* B69 .... 86 A7
Midhurst Dr *HEDN* WS12 ..... 13 G6
Midhurst Gv
 DUNHL/THL/PER WV6 ...... 35 G8
Midhurst Rd *BVILLE* B30 ..... 144 F2
Midland Cl *HDSW* B21 .... 88 E6 ◫
Midland Dr *CSCFLD/WYGN* B72. 57 G8
Midland Rd *BVILLE* B30 ...... 124 D8
 COVN CV6 .... 134 C8
 DARL/WED WS10 .... 52 A5
 FOAKS/STRLY B74 ...... 56 E6
 NUN CV11 .... 80 E8
 WSL WS1 .... 4 D4
Midland St *BORD* B9 .... 108 A2 ◫
Midvale Dr *ALE/KHTH/YWD* B14.. 145 H3
Milburn *TAM/AM/WIL* B77 ..... 47 G5
Milburn Hill Rd *TLHL/CAN* CV4 . 152 F8
Milburn Rd *KGSTG* B44 ...... 71 L2
Milby Dr *NUN* CV11 .... 81 K5
Milcote Cl *REDE* B98 .... 196 D6
Milcote Dr *SCFLD/BOLD* B73 .. 72 A2
 WLNHL WV13 .... 51 H4
Milcote Rd *SLYOAK* B29 ...... 123 L5
 SMTHKW B67 .... 105 K3
 SOLH B91 .... 147 M1
Milcote Wy *KGSWFD* DY6 ..... 82 F6
Mildenhall *CRTAM* B79 .... 32 A5
Mildenhall Rd *PBAR/PBCH* B42 . 70 E4
Mildred Rd *CDYHTH* B64 ..... 103 J3
Mildred Wy *OLDBY* B69 ...... 86 A7
Milebrook Gv
 RIDG/WDGT B32 .... 122 F5 ◫
Milebush Av *CBROM* B36 ..... 92 B4
Mile Flat *KGSWFD* DY6 .... 82 D6
Mile La *COVS* CV3 .... 9 H9
Miles Gv *DUDS* DY2 .... 85 K6
Miles Meadow *COVN* CV6 .... 134 F4
Miles Meadow Cl *SHHTH* WV12 . 38 A5
Milestone Dr *HAG/WOL* DY9 .. 139 K1
 RUGBYS/DCH CV22 ...... 183 K5
Milestone La *HDSW* B21 ..... 88 B5
Milestone Rd *SHHTH* WV12 ... 37 M5 ◫
Mile Tree La *COVE* CV2 ...... 117 J7
Milford Av *SHHTH* WV12 ..... 37 L8
 STRPT DY13 .... 160 C7 ◫
Milford Cl *COVW* CV5 .... 132 F7
 REDW B97 .... 195 M6
 STRBR DY8 .... 101 J2
Milford Ct *LOZ/NWT* B19 .... 89 H8
Milford Cft *BLKHTH/ROWR* B65 . 85 K7
Milford Gv *SHLY* B90 .... 148 A6
Milford Rd *BKHL/PFLD* WV2 .. 50 A6
 HRBN B17 .... 105 M8
Milford St *NUNW/HART* CV10 . 98 F3
Milhill Rd *REDE* B98 .... 197 J4
Milholme Gn *HIA/OLT* B92 ... 128 B6
Milking Bank *DUDN* DY1 ..... 84 C3
Milk St *DIG/EDG* B5.......... 7 K7
Millais Cl *BDWTH* CV12 ...... 116 E1
Millard Rd *BILS/COS* WV14 ... 66 F4
Mill Bank *CSHL/WTROR* B46 .. 95 H2
 SEDG DY3 .... 66 B5
Millbank *WWCK* CV34 .... 199 L3
Millbank Gv
 ERDW/GRVHL B23 .... 71 M7 ◫
Mill Bank Ms *KNWTH* CV8 .... 176 F7 ◫
Millbank St *WNSFLD* WV11 ... 37 K4
Millbrook Cl *CNCK/NC* WS11 .. 16 C7
Millbrook Dr *LICHS* WS14 .... 28 D7
 NFLD/LBR B31 .... 143 J5
Millbrook Rd
 ALE/KHTH/YWD B14 ...... 125 C7 ◫
Mill Burn Wy *BORD* B9 ...... 107 M3 ◫
Mill Cl *BRGRVE* B60 .... 185 K7 ◫
 COVN CV6 .... 134 F2
 HLYWD B47 .... 145 L6
 KIDD DY10 .... 138 F3
 NUN CV11 .... 99 K4
 SEDG DY3 .... 66 B7 ◫
Mill Crs *CNCK/NC* WS11 ..... 16 F3
 POL/KGSB/FAZ B78 .... 76 B1
Mill Cft *BILS/COS* WV14 ..... 51 J7 ◫
Millcroft Cl *RIDG/WDGT* B32 . 123 J3
Millcroft Rd *FOAKS/STRLY* B74 . 55 L5
Milldale Cl *KIDD* DY10 .... 137 J5
Milldale Crs *WOLVN* WV10 .... 36 B1
Milldale Rd *WOLVN* WV10 .... 36 B1
Mill Dr *SMTHWK* B66 .... 87 M8 ◫
Mill End *KNWTH* CV8 .... 176 F7 ◫
Millennium Cl *BLOX/PEL* WS3 . 39 L1
Millennium Wy *CDSL* WV8 .... 34 F1
 KNWTH CV8 .... 180 D2 ◫
Miller Cl *BRGRVE* B60 .... 185 J7
Miller Crs *BILS/COS* WV14 ... 66 E4
Millers Cl *WSLW* WS2 .... 52 D4
Millersdale Dr *HHTH/SAND* B71 . 69 K3
Millers Green *KGSWFD* DY6 .. 82 E5
Millers Rd *WWCK* CV34 ...... 199 H5
Miller St *AST/WIT* B6 .... 89 J8
Millers V *HEDN* WS12 .... 17 H4
 WMBN WV5 .... 64 B8
Millers Wk *BLOX/PEL* WS3 ... 39 J2
Mill Farm Rd *HRBN* B17 ..... 124 A2
Millfield Av *BLOX/PEL* WS3 ... 39 H3
 RUSH/SHEL WS4 ...... 39M4
Millfield Gdns *KIDDW* DY11 .. 137 H7 ◫
Millfield Rd *BFLD/HDSWWD* B20 . 70 D8
 BRGRVW B61 .... 185 H4
 BRWNH WS8 .... 26 C6
Millfields *STETCH* B33 .... 110 C3
Millfields Rd *BKHL/PFLD* WV2 . 50 E8
 HHTH/SAND B71 .... 68 F4
Millfields Wy *WMBN* WV5 .... 64 B8
Millfield Vw *HALE* B63 ...... 121 F7 ◫
Mill Gdns *HLGN/YWD* B28 ... 126 E8
Mill Gn *WOLVN* WV10 .... 36 B1
Mill Gv *CDSL* WV8 .... 35 G2
Millhaven Av *BVILLE* B30 .... 124 F7

Mill HI *COVS* CV3 .... 178 B2
  SMTHWKW B67 .... 105 K2
Millhouse Ct *COVN* CV6 .... 134 D6
Mill House Dr *RLSN* CV32 ...... 200 A5
  WWCK CV34 .... 200 A5
Millhouse Gdns *PENK* ST19 ..... 10 D4
Millhouse Rd *YDLY* B25 .... 108 F5
Millicent Cl *HEDN* WS12 .... 12 F7
Millichip Rd *WLNHL* WV13 ...... 51 J4
Milliners Ct *ATHST* CV9 .... 63 H5
Millington Rd *CBROM* B36 ...... 91 J5
  TPTN/OCK DY4 .... 67 K4
  WOLVN WV10 .... 36 C7
Millison Gv *SOLH* B91 .... 147 L6
Mill La *ALDR* WS9 .... 41 K1
  ALDR WS9 .... 41 L7
  ATHST CV9 .... 63 L7
  BDWTH CV12 .... 117 L2
  BNTWD WS7 .... 27 H1
  BRGRVW B61 .... 165 K2
  BRGRVW B61 .... 185 K3
  CNCK/NC WS11 .... 16 B8
  COVS CV3 .... 155 K3
  CRTAM B79 .... 32 A8
  DIG/EDG B5 .... 7 J7
  DOR/KN B93 .... 172 C1
  DUNHL/THL/PER WV6 .... 48 E3
  HOCK/TIA B94 .... 169 M4
  KIDD DY10 .... 138 F3
  KIDD DY10 .... 161 K3
  KIDDW DY11 .... 137 H3
  LICHS WS14 .... 28 E7
  NFLD/LBR B31 .... 143 K3
  OLDBY B69 .... 104 E1
  POL/KGSB/FAZ B78 .... 45 L5
  RCOVN/BALC/EX CV7 .... 96 A8
  RIDG/WDGT B32 .... 123 J3
  RLSN CV32 .... 193 K8
  RMSLY B62 .... 122 A1
  RUSH/SHEL WS4 .... 53 K1
  SHHTH WV12 .... 38 A8
  SOLH B91 .... 148 A1
  WMBN WV5 .... 64 F6
  WNSFLD WV11 .... 36 F6
Millmead Rd *SLYOAK* B29 .... 123 J3
Mill Pk *CNCK/NC* WS11 .... 16 F4
Mill Pl *BLOX/PEL* WS3 .... 53 J1
Mill Pool Cl *HAG/WOL* DY9 ..... 139 L1
  WMBN WV5 .... 64 B8
Millpool Gdns
  ALE/KHTH/YWD B14 .... 145 K2
Millpool Hill Alcester Road South
  ALE/KHTH/YWD B14 .... 145 K1
Mill Pool La *DOR/KN* B93 ...... 172 E5
Mill Pool Rd *HEDN* WS12 .... 12 F7
Millpool Wy *SMTHWKW* B67 ...... 105 L1
Mill Race La *COVN* CV6 .... 134 E2
  STRBR DY8 .... 101 L7
Millrace Rd *REDE* B98 .... 188 C7
Mill Race Vw *ATHST* CV9 .... 63 H3
Mill Rd *BRWNH* WS8 .... 26 E6
  CDYHTH B64 .... 103 J6
  RLSS CV31 .... 200 E5
  RUSH/SHEL WS4 .... 39 M4
Mills Av *WALM/CURD* B76 .... 73 J1
Millsboro Rd *REDE* B98 .... 196 C2
Millsbro Rd *REDE* B98 .... 196 D2
Mills Cl *WNSFLD* WV11 .... 36 F5
Mills Crs *BKHL/PFLD* WV2 ...... 3 J9
Millside *HLGN/YWD* B28 .... 146 C2
  WMBN WV5 .... 64 C8
Mills Rd *BKHL/PFLD* WV2 .... 3 J9
Mill St *AST/WIT* B6 .... 89 K8
  BDWTH CV12 .... 116 F2
  BILS/COS WV14 .... 51 G8
  BRLYHL DY5 .... 102 B3
  CDYHTH B64 .... 103 G6
  CNCK/NC WS11 .... 16 C4
  COV CV1 .... 8 D2
  CSCFLD/WYGN B72 .... 57 G8
  DARL/WED WS10 .... 52 A7
  KIDDW DY11 .... 137 G2
  NUN CV11 .... 99 G1
  PENK ST19 .... 10 C4
  REDW B97 .... 196 B1
  RLSS CV31 .... 200 E6
  STRBR DY8 .... 101 J3
  TPTN/OCK DY4 .... 68 B8
  WBROM B70 .... 87 G1
  WLNHL WV13 .... 52 A3
  WSLW WS2 .... 53 J2
  WWCK CV34 .... 199 K7
Mill Ter *BDWTH* CV12 .... 98 F8
Millthorpe Cl *WASH/WDE* B8 ... 90 D8
Mill Vw *STETCH* B33 .... 110 A1
Mill Wk *NUN* CV11 .... 99 G1
Millwalk Dr *COVEN* WV9 .... 35 L2
The Mill Wk *NFLD/LBR* B31 .... 145 K4
Millward St *BORD* B9 .... 108 A4
  WBROM B70 .... 86 E2
Millwright Cl *TPTN/OCK* DY4 .. 67 M8
Milner Crs *COVE* CV2 .... 135 J4
Milner Dr *CRTAM* B79 .... 33 J6
Milner Rd *SLYOAK* B29 .... 124 E4
Milner Wy *MOS/BIL* B13 .... 126 B5
Milo Crs *POL/KGSB/FAZ* B78 ... 45 L5
Milrose Wy *TLHL/CAN* CV4 ..... 152 D5
Milsom Gv *BKDE/SHDE* B34 ..... 92 B7
Milstead Rd
  LGN/SDN/BHAMAIR B26 ...... 109 L4
Milston Cl
  ALE/KHTH/YWD B14 .... 145 J3
Milton Av *CRTAM* B79 .... 31 L6
  WWCK CV34 .... 199 L4
Milton Cl *BDWTH* CV12 .... 117 H4
  DOR/KN B93 .... 172 D1
  KIDDW DY11 .... 136 E7
  REDW B97 .... 196 A5
  SHHTH WV12 .... 38 C6
  WSL WS1 .... 4 C9
Milton Crs *DUNHL/THL/PER* WV6 .. 48 C1
  YDLY B25 .... 109 H6
Milton Dr *HAG/WOL* DY9 .... 120 B6
Milton Pl *WSL* WS1 .... 4 D8
Milton Rd *BILS/COS* WV14 ..... 67 H6
  BRGRVW B61 .... 165 L5
  CNCK/NC WS11 .... 16 C1

Dor/Kn B93 .... 172 D1
  SMTHWKW B67 .... 87 H8
  WOLVN WV10 .... 36 E8
Milton St *BRLYHL* DY5 .... 84 B6
  COVE CV2 .... 154 E1
  HHTH/SAND B71 .... 68 F8
  LOZ/NWT B19 .... 89 J7
  WSL WS1 .... 4 D8
Milverton Cl *HALE* B63 .... 103 L7
  WALM/CURD B76 .... 73 K5
Milverton Crs West
  RLSN CV32 .... 200 C4
Milverton HI *RLSN* CV32 .... 200 C5
Milverton Lawn *RLSN* CV32 ..... 200 B5
Milverton Rd *COVE* CV2 .... 135 G2
  DOR/KN B93 .... 149 G8
  ERDW/GRVHL B23 .... 72 C8
Milverton Ter *RLSN* CV32 ...... 200 C5
Mimosa Cl *SLYOAK* B29 .... 123 M5
Mimosa Wk *KGSWFD* DY6 .... 83 J5
Mincing La *BLKHTH/ROWR* B65 ... 104 A2
Minden Gv *SLYOAK* B29 .... 123 M4
Minehead Rd *DUDN* DY1 .... 84 B5
  WOLVN WV10 .... 35 M3
Miner St *WSLW* WS2 .... 53 G2
Miners Wk *POL/KGSB/FAZ* B78 ... 47 K4
Minerva Cl *SMHTH* WV12 .... 52 C1
  TAM/AM/WIL B77 .... 32 B8
Minewood Cl *BLOX/PEL* WS3 ..... 38 D2
Minions Cl *ATHST* CV9 .... 63 H5
Minith Rd *BILS/COS* WV14 ...... 67 H5
Miniva Dr *WALM/CURD* B76 ...... 73 L3
Minivet Dr *BHTH/HG* B12 .... 107 J7
Minley Av *HRBN* B17 .... 105 K6
The Minories *DUDS* DY2 .... 85 G4
Minors HI *LICHS* WS14 .... 21 H7
Minstead Rd *ERDE/BCHGN* B24 ... 90 B4
Minster Cl *BLKHTH/ROWR* B65 ... 104 C2
  DOR/KN B93 .... 148 F5
  RWWCK/WEL CV35 .... 198 D7
Minster Dr *SMHTH* B10 .... 108 A6
Minsterley Cl
  BDMR/CCFT WV3 .... 49 J5
Minster Rd *COV* CV1 .... 8 C4
  STRPT DY13 .... 160 F6
The Minster *BDMR/CCFT* WV3 .... 49 K6
Mintern Rd *YDLY* B25 .... 109 G4
Minton Cl *WOLV* WV1 .... 50 E4
Minton Rd *COVE* CV2 .... 135 J4
  RIDG/WDGT B32 .... 123 K1
Minworth Rd *REDW* B97 .... 195 M3
Minworth Rd
  CSHL/WTROR B46 .... 92 F2
Mira Dr
  MKTBOS/BARL/STKG CV13 .... 81 G2
Miranda Cl *COVS* CV3 .... 155 H6
  RBRY B45 .... 142 E2
Mirfield Cl *COVEN* WV9 .... 35 L2
Mirfield Rd *SOLH* B91 .... 127 L7
  STETCH B33 .... 109 M3
Mission Cl *CDYHTH* B64 .... 103 L4
Mission Dr *TPTN/OCK* DY4 ..... 85 L1
Mistletoe Dr *DSYBK/YTR* WS5 .. 69 L2
Mitcham Cl *HEDN* WS12 .... 12 D6
Mitcham Gv *KGSTG* B44 .... 71 M4
Mitcheldean Covert
  ALE/KHTH/YWD B14 .... 145 H3
Mitcheldean Covert
Mitchell Av *BILS/COS* WV14 ... 66 F4
  TLHL/CAN CV4 .... 152 E7
Mitchell Rd *BDWTH* CV12 ...... 117 G3
Mitchell Rd *KGSWFD* DY6 ...... 101 K1
Mitford Dr *HIA/OLT* B92 ...... 128 B6
Mitre Cl *SHHTH* WV12 .... 38 B6
  WNSFLD WV11 .... 37 L2
Mitre Fold *WOLV* WV1 .... 2 F2
Mitre Rd *GTWY* WS6 .... 24 B3
  HAG/WOL DY9 .... 120 C8
Mitten Av *RBRY* B45 .... 142 D4
Mitton Rd *BFLD/HDSWWD* B20 ... 88 C3
Moat Av *COVS* CV3 .... 177 K1
Moat Brook Av *CDSL* WV8 ..... 34 C1
Moatbrook La *CDSL* WV8 ...... 34 B1
Moat Cl *KNWTH* CV8 .... 179 G7
Moat Coppice
  RIDG/WDGT B32 .... 122 E4
Moat Cft
  CHWD/FDBR/MGN B37 .... 110 E3
  WALM/CURD B76 .... 73 G7
Moat Dr *POL/KGSB/FAZ* B78 .... 45 J8
  RMSLY B62 .... 104 D4
Moat Farm Dr *BDWTH* CV12 ..... 116 A5
  RIDG/WDGT B32 .... 122 E4
Moat Farm Wy *BLOX/PEL* WS3 ... 25 L8
Moatfield Ter *DARL/WED* WS10 . 68 E2
Moat Green Av *WNSFLD* WV11 ... 37 J6
Moat House La
  CSHL/WTROR B46 .... 94 F4
  TLHL/CAN CV4 .... 153 G6
Moat House La East
  WNSFLD WV11 .... 37 H6
Moat House La West
  WNSFLD WV11 .... 37 H6
Moat House Rd *WASH/WDE* B8 ... 108 E1
Moat La *DIG/EDG* B5 .... 7 H7
  GTWY WS6 .... 24 E3
  LGN/SDN/BHAMAIR B26 ...... 109 J6
  SOLH B91 .... 128 A7
Moat Mdw *RIDG/WDGT* B32 ...... 123 J1
Moat Rd *LGLYGN/QTN* B68 ...... 104 F2
  TPTN/OCK DY4 .... 67 L6
  WSLW WS2 .... 52 E7
Moatside Cl *BLOX/PEL* WS3 .... 25 L8
Moat St *WLNHL* WV13 .... 51 L3
Mobberley Rd *BILS/COS* WV14 .. 66 E4
Mob La *RUSH/SHEL* WS4 .... 40 A3
Mockley Wood Rd *DOR/KN* B93 .. 148 F6
Modbury Av *RIDG/WDGT* B32 .... 123 H4
Modbury Cl *COVS* CV3 .... 154 B8
Moden Cl *SEDG* DY3 .... 66 B8
Moden HI *SEDG* DY3 .... 66 A7
Mogul La *HALE* B63 .... 102 E6
Moilliett Ct *SMTHWK* B66 .... 88 A7
Moilliett St *WSNGN* B18 ..... 106 B1
Moira Crs *ALE/KHTH/YWD* B14 .. 146 A1
Moises Hall Rd *WMBN* WV5 .... 64 F7
Moland St *AST/WIT* B6 .... 7 H1
Mole St *SPARK* B11 .... 107 M7

Molesworth Av *COVS* CV3 .... 154 E4
Molineux St *WOLV* WV1 .... 2 F3
Molineux Wy *WOLV* WV1 .... 2 F2
Mollington Crs *SHLY* B90 ...... 147 G2
Molyneux Rd *DUDS* DY2 .... 103 J3
Momus Bvd *COVE* CV2 .... 155 G3
Monarch Dr *TPTN/OCK* DY4 ...... 68 A7
Monarch's Wy
  BLKHTH/ROWR B65 .... 103 K1
  BRGRVE B60 .... 186 A5
  BRGRVW B61 .... 185 H3
  HAG/WOL DY9 .... 120 A2
  KGSWFD DY6 .... 82 C7
  KIDD DY10 .... 163 H8
  OLDBY B69 .... 86 A3
  REDW B97 .... 195 H3
  STRBR DY8 .... 101 L8
  WNSFLD WV11 .... 37 H2
  WSLW WS2 .... 52 E1
Monarch's Wy *DUDS* DY2 .... 102 F1
Mona Rd *ERDW/GRVHL* B23 ...... 72 D8
Monastery Dr *SOLH* B91 .... 127 J7
Monckton Rd *LGLYGN/QTN* B68 .. 104 E6
Moncrieff Cl *DUDS* DY2 .... 85 J5
Moncrieffe Cl *WSL* WS1 .... 5 J4
Money La *BRGRVW* B61 .... 141 J7
Monica Rd *SMHTH* B10 .... 108 D5
Monins Av *TPTN/OCK* DY4 ...... 85 L2
Monk Cl *TPTN/OCK* DY4 .... 85 M2
Monk Rd *WASH/WDE* B8 .... 90 F8
Monks Cl *WMBN* WV5 .... 64 C7
The Monk's Cft *COVS* CV3 ..... 154 A6
Monkseaton Rd
  CSCFLD/WYGN B72 .... 72 F3
Monksfield Av *DOR/KN* B93 .... 90 E1
Monkshood Ms
  ERDW/GRVHL B23 .... 71 M6
Monkshood Retreat
  HWK/WKHTH B38 .... 144 D5
Monks Kirby Rd
  WALM/CURD B76 .... 73 K2
Monks Pth *REDW* B97 .... 195 K1
Monkspath *SHLY* B90 .... 147 L2
  WALM/CURD B76 .... 73 K5
Monkspath Cl *SHLY* B90 .... 147 H6
Monkspath Hall La *SHLY* B90 .. 147 K6
  SOLH B91 .... 147 M5
Monks Rd *COV* CV1 .... 9 L5
  COVS CV3 .... 156 A6
Monksway *HWK/WKHTH* B38 ...... 144 F3
Monks Wy *TAM/AM/WIL* B77 ..... 32 B8
  WWCK CV34 .... 199 H7
Monkswell Cl *BRLYHL* DY5 ..... 102 B4
  SMHTH B10 .... 108 B6
Monkswood Crs *COVE* CV2 ...... 135 H5
Monkswood Rd *NFLD/LBR* B31 ... 144 A3
Monkton Rd *SLYOAK* B29 .... 123 L2
Monmer La *WLNHL* WV13 .... 51 M2
Monmore Cl *WOLV* WV1 .... 50 E5
Monmouth Cl *COVW* CV5 .... 152 F2
Monmouth Dr *HHTH/SAND* B71 ... 68 F6
  SCFLD/BOLD B73 .... 72 A1
Monmouth Gdns
  NUNW/HART CV10 .... 98 C1
Monmouth Rd *RIDG/WDGT* B32 ... 123 H5
  SMTHWKW B67 .... 105 J5
  WSLW WS2 .... 52 C2
Monsal Av *WOLVN* WV10 .... 3 J1
Monsaldale Cl *BRWNH* WS8 ..... 26 B6
Monsal Rd *PBAR/PBCH* B42 ..... 71 G6
Monsieurs Hall La *BRGRVW* B61 . 184 F2
Mons Rd *DUDS* DY2 .... 85 J4
Montague Rd *ERDE/BCHGN* B24 .. 90 E4
  HDSW B21 .... 88 D3
  LDYWD/EDGR B16 .... 106 C4
  RUGBYS/DCH CV22 .... 183 H8
  SMTHWK B66 .... 105 M2
  WWCK CV34 .... 199 J4
Montague St *AST/WIT* B6 ...... 89 M5
  DIG/EDG B5 .... 7 M5
Montalt Rd *COVS* CV3 .... 154 C6
Montana Av *PBAR/PBCH* B42 ... 70 E8
Montana Wk *NUNW/HART* CV10 .. 98 C2
Montcrieff Dr *RLSS* CV31 .... 201 G8
Monteagle Dr *KGSWFD* DY6 .... 83 H4
Montford Gv *SEDG* DY3 .... 66 B6
Montfort Rd *CSHL/WTROR* B46 . 93 K8
  WSLW WS2 .... 52 C2
Montgomery Av
  RWWCK/WEL CV35 .... 198 C7
Montgomery Cl *BRGRVW* B61 ... 165 G4
  COVS CV3 .... 179 G1
Montgomery Crs *BRLYHL* DY5 .. 102 D6
Montgomery Cft *SPARK* B11 ... 108 A6
Montgomery Dr
  RUGBYS/DCH CV22 .... 183 G4
Montgomery Rd *WSLW* WS2 ..... 52 C3
Montgomery St *SPARK* B11 .... 107 M6
Montgomery Wy
  WASH/WDE B8 .... 108 E1
Montjoy Cl *COVS* CV3 .... 155 H6
Montley *TAM/AM/WIL* B77 ..... 47 G5
Montpelier Rd
  ERDE/BCHGN B24 .... 90 E4
Montpellier Cl *COVS* CV3 .... 154 A7
Montpellier Gdns *DUDN* DY1 .. 84 C3
Montpellier St *BHTH/HG* B12 . 107 L7
Montrose Av *RLSN* CV32 ...... 200 D1
Montrose Cl *CNCK/NC* WS11 ... 12 D8
Montrose Dr *CVALE* B35 ...... 91 L2
  DUDN DY1 .... 84 E5
  NUNW/HART CV10 .... 98 D2
Montrose Rd
  RUGBYS/DCH CV22 .... 183 L4
Montsford Cl *DOR/KN* B93 .... 148 D7
Monument Av *HAG/WOL* DY9 .... 120 B6
Monument La *HAG/WOL* DY9 .... 120 B6
  RBRY B45 .... 166 D1
  SEDG DY3 .... 66 C4
Monument Rd
  LDYWD/EDGR B16 .... 106 D4
Monway Ter *DARL/WED* WS10 ... 68 C2
Monwode Lea La
  CSHL/WTROR B46 .... 95 H1
Monwood Gv *SOLH* B91 .... 147 K3
Monyhull Hall Rd *BVILLE* B30 . 144 F2

Moodyscroft Rd *STETCH* B33 ... 110 A2
Moon's La *GTWY* WS6 .... 24 B3
Moons Moat Dr *REDE* B98 ...... 189 H8
Moorbrooke *NUNW/HART* CV10 ... 79 L6
Moorcroft Dr *DARL/WED* WS10 .. 68 A3
Moorcroft Gdns *REDW* B97 ..... 195 M7
Moorcroft Rd *MOS/BIL* B13 .... 125 J3
Moordown Av *HIA/OLT* B92 ..... 127 L3
Moore Cl *DUNHL/THL/PER* WV6 .. 48 B2
  FOAKS/STRLY B74 .... 42 D7
  WWCK CV34 .... 199 J3
Moore Crs *LGLYGN/QTN* B68 .... 105 G2
Moorend Av
  CHWD/FDBR/MGN B37 .... 110 E5
Moor End La *ERDE/BCHGN* B24 .. 90 E1
Moore Rd *SHHTH* WV12 .... 38 B5
Moore's Rw *DIG/EDG* B5 .... 7 K7
Moore St *HEDN* WS12 .... 13 G6
  WOLV WV1 .... 3 L6
Moor Farm Cl *RRUGBY* CV23 .... 180 D7
Moorfield Av *DOR/KN* B93 ..... 148 D7
Moorfield Dr *BRGRVW* B61 ..... 185 K2
  HALE B63 .... 103 L8
  SCFLD/BOLD B73 .... 72 D5
Moorfield Rd *BKDE/SHDE* B34 .. 91 L7
  BKHL/PFLD WV2 .... 49 M6
The Moorfield *COVS* CV3 ...... 154 E5
Moorfoot Av *HALE* B63 .... 121 G4
Moorgate *CRTAM* B79 .... 31 L8
Moorgate Cl *REDE* B98 .... 189 J7
Moor Green La *MOS/BIL* B13 ... 125 G4
Moor Hall Dr *HAG/WOL* DY9 ... 140 E4
  MGN/WHC B75 .... 57 J4
Moor Hall La *PENK* ST19 ..... 10 E6
Moorhills Cft *SHLY* B90 ..... 146 F5
The Moorings *COVEN* WV9 ..... 35 K3
  OLDBY B69 .... 86 C5
Moorland Av *WOLVN* WV10 ..... 36 A7
Moorland Rd *BLOX/PEL* WS3 ... 38 E5
  CNCK/NC WS11 .... 12 C8
  LDYWD/EDGR B16 .... 106 B4
Moorlands Av *KNWTH* CV8 ..... 191 K2
Moorlands Dr *SHLY* B90 ...... 147 L2
Moorlands Rd *HHTH/SAND* B71 . 69 G4
The Moorlands
  FOAKS/STRLY B74 .... 56 D5
Moor La *AST/WIT* B6 .... 89 L2
  BLKHTH/ROWR B65 .... 103 L2
  CRTAM B79 .... 32 E7
  LICHS WS14 .... 42 C4
  TAM/AM/WIL B77 .... 32 B8
Moor Leasow *NFLD/LBR* B31 ... 144 A3
Moor Meadow Rd
  MGN/WHC B75 .... 57 H6
Moor Pk *BLOX/PEL* WS3 .... 38 F2
  DUNHL/THL/PER WV6 .... 34 B8
Moorpark Rd *NFLD/LBR* B31 ... 143 L4
Moor Pool Av *HRBN* B17 ...... 106 A7
Moor Rd *NUNW/HART* CV10 ..... 79 L8
Moors Cft *RIDG/WDGT* B32 .... 122 F4
Moorside Gdns *WSLW* WS2 ..... 52 F2
Moorside Rd
  ALE/KHTH/YWD B14 .... 146 A1
Moors La *NFLD/LBR* B31 ...... 123 J5
Moors Mill La *TPTN/OCK* DY4 . 68 A6
Moorsom St *AST/WIT* B6 ...... 89 J8
Moorsom Wy *BRGRVE* B60 ...... 185 M6
The Moors *CBROM* B36 .... 91 K5
Moor St *BRLYHL* DY5 .... 101 L2
  COVW CV5 .... 153 K4
  CRTAM B79 .... 31 L8
  DARL/WED WS10 .... 68 F3
  DIG/EDG B5 .... 7 H6
  WBROM B70 .... 87 G3
Moor Street Ringway
  CBHAMNE B4 .... 7 H6
Moor St South *BKHL/PFLD* WV2 . 50 A6
The Moor *WALM/CURD* B76 ...... 73 L5
Moorwood Crs
  NUNW/HART CV10 .... 79 L5
Moorwood La
  NUNW/HART CV10 .... 79 L5
Morar Cl *CVALE* B35 .... 91 M1
Moray Cl *RMSLY* B62 .... 104 C5
Morcom Rd *SPARK* B11 .... 108 C8
Morcrofts *BILS/COS* WV14 .... 67 L2
Mordaunt Dr *MGN/WHC* B75 .... 57 J3
Morden Rd *STETCH* B33 .... 109 H2
Moreall Mdw *TLHL/CAN* CV4 ... 177 H2
Moreland Cft
  WALM/CURD B76 .... 73 M7
The Morelands *NFLD/LBR* B31 . 143 M4
Morestead Av
  LGN/SDN/BHAMAIR B26 ...... 110 A8
Moreton Av
  ETTPK/GDPK/PENN WV4 ...... 66 C1
  GTB/HAM B43 .... 71 C3
Moreton Cl *RIDG/WDGT* B32 ... 105 K8
  TPTN/OCK DY4 .... 67 M3
Moreton Rd *SHLY* B90 .... 147 G3
  WOLVN WV10 .... 36 B4
Moreton St *CBHAMW* B1 .... 6 A2
  CNCK/NC WS11 .... 16 D1
Morford Rd *ALDR* WS9 .... 40 E6
Morgan Cl *RCOVN/BALC/EX* CV7 . 96 D5
  WLNHL WV13 .... 51 M1
Morgan Gv *CBROM* B36 .... 92 B2
Morgan Rd *POL/KGSB/FAZ* B78 . 45 L3
Morgans Rd *COVW* CV5 .... 152 A1
Morgrove Av *DOR/KN* B93 ..... 148 D7
Morillon Ct *KIDD* DY10 ...... 161 L4
Morjon Dr *GTB/HAM* B43 ...... 70 D3
Morland Rd *COVN* CV6 .... 134 A2
  GTB/HAM B43 .... 71 C1
Morley Gv *DUNHL/THL/PER* WV6 . 50 A1
Morley Rd *BNTWD* WS7 .... 18 F6
  WASH/WDE B8 .... 90 F7
Morlich Ri *BRLYHL* DY5 ...... 101 M5
Morlings Dr *BNTWD* WS7 ...... 18 E5
Morning Pines *STRBR* DY8 .... 119 J7
Morningside *COVW* CV5 .... 8 C9
  SCFLD/BOLD B73 .... 72 B5
Mornington Rd *SMTHWK* B66 ... 87 M6
Morpeth *TAM/AM/WIL* B77 ..... 46 A6
Morrell St *RLSN* CV32 .... 200 D4
Morris Av *COVE* CV2 .... 155 H1
  WSLW WS2 .... 52 C3

Morris Av *ACGN* B27 .... 127 H1
  RUGBYN/HIL CV21 .... 159 K7
Morris Cft *CBROM* B36 .... 92 C4
Morris Dr *NUN* CV11 .... 99 H4
Morris Field Cft
  HLGN/YWD B28 .... 146 C1
Morris HI *POL/KGSB/FAZ* B78 .. 47 K6
Morrison Av *WOLVN* WV10 ...... 36 B5
Morrison Rd *TPTN/OCK* DY4 .... 86 A1
Morris Rd *WASH/WDE* B8 .... 90 F7
Morris St *WBROM* B70 .... 87 G4
Morsefield La *REDE* B98 ...... 197 H4
Mortimer Rd *KNWTH* CV8 .... 191 K3
Mortimers Cl
  ALE/KHTH/YWD B14 .... 145 M4
Morton Cl *COVN* CV6 .... 133 L4
Morton Gdns
  RUGBYN/HIL CV21 .... 183 M3
Morton La *REDW* B97 .... 195 M7
Morton Rd *BRLYHL* DY5 .... 102 B6
  KIDD DY10 .... 162 F3
Morton St *RLSN* CV32 .... 200 D4
Morvale Gdns *HAG/WOL* DY9 .... 102 C8
Morvale Rd *HAG/WOL* DY9 ...... 102 C8
Morven Rd *SCFLD/BOLD* B73 .... 72 D3
Morville Cl *DOR/KN* B93 ...... 172 B2
Morville Cft
  ETTPK/GDPK/PENN WV4 ...... 66 F1
Morville Dr *DUDS* DY2 .... 103 H1
Morville St *LDYWD/EDGR* B16 .. 6 C6
Mosborough Crs *LOZ/NWT* B19 .. 89 G8
Mosedale Dr *WNSFLD* WV11 ..... 37 K8
Moseley Av *COVN* CV6 .... 8 A1
  COVN CV6 .... 133 L8
Moseley Ct *WNSFLD* WV11 ...... 37 K2
Moseley Dr
  CHWD/FDBR/MGN B37 .... 110 D5
Moseley Old Hall La
  WOLVN WV10 .... 22 E8
Moseley Rd *BHTH/HG* B12 ...... 7 L9
  KNWTH CV8 .... 191 M2
  WLNHL WV13 .... 51 H4
  WOLVN WV10 .... 22 E8
Moseley St *DIG/EDG* B5 .... 7 J8
  DUNHL/THL/PER WV6 .... 50 A2
  TPTN/OCK DY4 .... 68 A6
Mossbank Av *BNTWD* WS7 .... 18 E7
Moss Cl *ALDR* WS9 .... 40 E8
  HEDN WS12 .... 12 A3
  RUGBYS/DCH CV22 .... 183 J4
  RUSH/SHEL WS4 .... 53 L2
Mossdale *TAM/AM/WIL* B77 ..... 47 G5
Mossdale Cl *COVN* CV6 .... 133 L7
Mossdale Crs *NUNW/HART* CV10 . 98 D3
Mossdale Wy *SEDG* DY3 .... 66 C6
Moss Dr *CSCFLD/WYGN* B72 ..... 73 G2
Mossfield Rd
  ALE/KHTH/YWD B14 .... 125 J6
Moss Gdns *BILS/COS* WV14 .... 66 F2
Moss Gv *ALE/KHTH/YWD* B14 ... 125 J7
  KGSWFD DY6 .... 83 H6
Moss House Cl *EDG* B15 ...... 6 C6
Moss La *REDE* B98 .... 189 K5
Moss Lane Cl *REDE* B98 ..... 189 K5
Mossley Cl *BLOX/PEL* WS3 ... 38 D4
Mossley La *BLOX/PEL* WS3 ... 38 D3
Mosspaul Cl *RLSN* CV32 ..... 200 B3
Moss Rd *CNCK/NC* WS11 ...... 16 E2
  CNCK/NC WS11 .... 16 E2
  RLSS CV31 .... 200 E6
Mossvale Cl *CDYHTH* B64 .... 103 K4
Mossvale Gv *WASH/WDE* B8 ... 90 D8
Moss Wy *FOAKS/STRLY* B74 ... 55 K6
Mosswood Rd *SCFLD/BOLD* B73 . 72 D3
Mostyn Crs *HHTH/SAND* B71 .. 68 E6
Mostyn Rd *HDSW* B21 .... 88 D5
  LDYWD/EDGR B16 .... 106 C4
  STRPT DY13 .... 160 C7
Mostyn St *WOLV* WV1 .... 2 D1
Mott Cl *TPTN/OCK* DY4 ...... 68 A5
Mottistone Cl *COVS* CV3 .... 154 B7
Mottram Cl *WBROM* B70 ...... 86 E3
Mottrams Cl *CSCFLD/WYGN* B72 . 73 G3
Moule Cl *KIDDW* DY11 .... 136 F7
Moultrie Rd *RUGBYN/HIL* CV21 . 183 M3
Moundsley Gv
  ALE/KHTH/YWD B14 .... 145 L2
Mountain Ash Dr
  HAG/WOL DY9 .... 120 A3
Mountain Ash Rd *BRWNH* WS8 .. 26 C8
Mountain Pine Cl *HEDN* WS12 . 12 E5
Mount Av *BRLYHL* DY5 .... 102 B2
  HEDN WS12 .... 12 F6
Mountbatten Av *KNWTH* CV8 ... 192 A2
Mountbatten Cl *BNTWD* WS7 ... 18 D4
  WBROM B70 .... 87 K3
Mountbatten Rd *WSLW* WS2 .... 52 D3
Mount Cl *GTWY* WS6 .... 24 B3
  MOS/BIL B13 .... 125 K1
  SEDG DY3 .... 84 A3
  WMBN WV5 .... 64 E6
Mount Dr *BDWTH* CV12 .... 116 E2
  WMBN WV5 .... 64 E6
Mountfield Cl
  ALE/KHTH/YWD B14 .... 145 L3
Mountford Cl
  BLKHTH/ROWR B65 .... 104 A2
Mountford Crs *ALDR* WS9 .... 40 F5
Mountford Dr *MGN/WHC* B75 .. 57 G5
Mountford La *BILS/COS* WV14 . 51 H6
Mountford Rd *SHLY* B90 ..... 146 B4
Mountford St *SPARK* B11 .... 108 B8
Mount Gdns *CDSL* WV8 .... 34 D1
Mountjoy Crs *HIA/OLT* B92 .. 128 A2
Mount La *HAG/WOL* DY9 ...... 140 C1
  SEDG DY3 .... 84 A3
Mount Nod Wy *COVW* CV5 ..... 152 E2
Mount Pleasant
  ALE/KHTH/YWD B14 .... 125 K4
  BILS/COS WV14 .... 51 J7
  BRLYHL DY5 .... 102 C4
  GTWY WS6 .... 24 C2
  KGSWFD DY6 .... 100 F7
  REDE B98 .... 196 B3
  SMHTH B10 .... 107 M4

TAM/AM/WIL B77 46 A4
Mount Pleasant Av HDSW B21 88 C4
WMBN WV5 64 D6
Mount Pleasant Rd
BDWTH CV12 116 E2
Mount Pleasant St
BILS/COS WV14 66 F5
WBROM B70 87 G3
Mount Pleasant Ter
NUNW/HART CV10 80 D7
Mountrath St WSL WS1 4 E4
Mount Rd BLKHTH/ROWR B65 104 C2
BLOX/PEL WS3 39 L1
BNTWD WS7 18 F7
BRGRVW B61 165 H4
DUNHL/THL/PER WV6 48 E3
ETTPK/GDPK/PENN WV4 65 L1
ETTPK/GDPK/PENN WV4 66 D3
HDSW B21 88 B6 5
OLDBY B69 86 A5
STRBR DY8 101 H4
STRBR DY8 101 M8
WLNHL WV13 51 J5
WMBN WV5 64 E6
Mountside St HEDN WS12 12 F6
Mounts Rd DARL/WED WS10 68 D3
Mount St COVW CV5 153 K3
HALE B63 121 L3
HEDN WS12 12 F6
NUN CV11 98 F1
REDE B98 196 C2
STRBR DY8 101 L8
TPTN/OCK DY4 68 A7
VAUX/NECH B7 90 A7
WSL WS1 4 E5
Mounts Wy VAUX/NECH B7 90 A6 1
The Mount CDYHTH B64 103 L4
COVS CV3 154 B5
ERDW/GRVHL B23 90 B4
WALM/CURD B76 75 G8
Mount Vernon Dr
BRGRVW B61 165 L8 1
Mount Vw MGN/WHC B75 73 J1
Mountwood Covert
DUNHL/THL/PER WV6 48 F2
Mousehall Farm Rd
BRLYHL DY5 102 B6
Mouse Hl BLOX/PEL WS3 39 K2
Mouse La KIDDW DY11 136 F5
Mousesweet Cl DUDS DY2 103 J1
Mousesweet La DUDS DY2 103 J2 1
Mousesweet Wk
CDYHTH B64 102 F5 2
Mowbray Cl RBRY B45 142 E3 3
Mowbray Cft BNTWD WS7 18 C4
Mowbray St COVE CV2 9 M3
DIG/EDG B5 107 J5 3
Mowe Cft
CHWD/FDBR/MGN B37 110 E6
Moxhull Cl SHHTH WV12 38 A4
Moxhull Dr WALM/CURD B76 73 J5
Moxhull Gdns SHHTH WV12 38 A4 1
Moxhull Rd
CHWD/FDBR/MGN B37 92 E7
Moxley Rd DARL/WED WS10 67 M1
Moyle Crs COVW CV5 152 B1
Moyle Dr HALE B63 102 F6
Moyses Cft SMTHWK B66 87 L5 2
Mozart Ct CNCK/NC WS11 17 G3
Muchall Rd
ETTPK/GDPK/PENN WV4 49 L8
Much Park St COV CV1 9 G5
Mucklow Hl RMSLY B62 104 B8
Muirfield TAM/AM/WIL B77 32 F8 3
Muirfield Cl BLOX/PEL WS3 38 E2
Muirfield Crs OLDBY B69 85 L6 1
Muirfield Gdns
HWK/WKHTH B38 144 B4
Muirville Cl STRBR DY8 101 H2 3
Mulberry Cl RLSN CV32 200 E3
Mulberry Dr MOS/BIL B13 125 M4
Mulberry Gn DUDN DY1 66 D8 2
Mulberry Pl BLOX/PEL WS3 38 D4
Mulberry Rd BLOX/PEL WS3 38 D4
CNCK/NC WS11 16 C2
COVN CV6 134 E7
NFLD/LBR B31 124 A8
RUGBYS/DCH CV22 182 F3
Muldoon Cl CNCK/NC WS11 16 E1
Mull Cl RBRY B45 142 C4
Mull Cft CBROM B36 92 E6 1
Mullensgrove Rd
CHWD/FDBR/MGN B37 92 E8
Mullett Rd WNSFLD WV11 36 F6
Mullett St BRLYHL DY5 83 M8
Mulliners Cl
CHWD/FDBR/MGN B37 111 H3 2
Mulliner St COVN CV6 134 D8
Mullion Cft HWK/WKHTH B38 144 C4
Mulroy Rd FOAKS/STRLY B74 56 F7
Mulwych Rd STETCH B33 110 C2
Munches La HAG/WOL DY9 141 G5
Munro Cl KIDD DY10 138 A7
Munsley Cl REDE B98 197 K3
Munslow Gv NFLD/LBR B31 143 K5
Muntz Crs HOCK/TIA B94 172 A7
Muntz St SMHTH B10 108 B5
Murcroft Rd HAG/WOL DY9 120 B4
Murdoch Rd BILS/COS WV14 51 K7
Murdock Gv HDSW B21 88 C6 2
Murdock Rd HDSW B21 88 C5
SMTHWK B66 88 B7
Murdock Wy WSLW WS2 38 D8
Murray Ct SCFLD/BOLD B73 72 E2
Murrayian Cl
RUGBYN/HIL CV21 183 M2 2
Murray Rd COVN CV6 133 L6
Murrell Cl DIG/EDG B5 107 H6
Murton TAM/AM/WIL B77 47 G5 3
Musborough Cl CBROM B36 92 A4 2
Muscott Gv HRBN B17 105 L8
Muscovy Rd ERDW/GRVHL B23 90 A2
Musgrave Cl WALM/CURD B76 73 J2
Musgrave Rd WSNGN B18 88 D8
Mushroom Hall Rd
LGLYGN/QTN B68 86 F8 3
Musk La SEDG DY3 83 M2
Musk La West SEDG DY3 83 M2
Muswell Cl SOLH B91 128 B8
Muxloe Cl BLOX/PEL WS3 38 E2
Myatt Av ALDR WS9 40 D8
BKHL/PFLD WV2 50 C7
BNTWD WS7 18 E6
Myatt Cl BKHL/PFLD WV2 50 C7
Myddleton St WSNGN B18 106 E1
Myles Ct BRLYHL DY5 102 B1
Mylgrove COVS CV3 178 B1
Mynors Crs HLYWD B47 145 L8
Myring Dr MGN/WHC B75 57 K8
Myrtle Av ALE/KHTH/YWD B14 145 K3
BHTH/HG B12 107 L8 11
REDE B98 196 C3
Myrtle Cl SHHTH WV12 38 C6
Myrtle Gv BDMR/CCFT WV3 49 J7
COVW CV5 153 K4
Myrtle Rd DUDN DY1 84 E2
Myrtle St BKHL/PFLD WV2 50 D7
Myrtle Ter TPTN/OCK DY4 67 M3
Mythe La ATHST CV9 63 L5
Mythe Vw ATHST CV9 63 J4
Myton Crs WWCK CV34 200 A7
Myton Crofts RLSS CV31 200 B6
Myton Dr SHLY B90 146 B3
Myton Gdns WWCK CV34 199 L7
Myton La WWCK CV34 200 A7
Myton Rd WWCK CV34 199 L7
Mytton Cl DUDS DY2 85 J4
Mytton Gv TPTN/OCK DY4 67 J8
Mytton Rd BVILLE B30 124 A8
CSHL/WTROR B46 92 D2
Myvod Rd DARL/WED WS10 52 E8

N

Naden Rd LOZ/NWT B19 88 F7
Nadin Rd SCFLD/BOLD B73 72 E5
Naesby Rd
DUNHL/THL/PER WV6 48 D2 2
Nafford Gv
ALE/KHTH/YWD B14 145 K3
Nagersfield Rd BRLYHL DY5 101 L2
Nagington Dr PENK ST19 10 D6
Nailcote Av TLHL/CAN CV4 152 A4
Nailcote La
RCOVN/BALC/EX CV7 151 L6
Nailers Cl BRGRVE B60 185 J7 1
RIDG/WDGT B32 122 D3
Nailers Dr BNTWD WS7 19 G7
Nailors Fold BILS/COS WV14 67 G3 1
Nailstone Crs ACGN B27 127 G5
Nailsworth Rd DOR/KN B93 172 B3
REDE B98 196 D3
Nairn Cl HLGN/YWD B28 126 D8
NUNW/HART CV10 98 E3
REDE B98 197 J1 3
Nairn Rd BLOX/PEL WS3 38 E1
Nally Dr BILS/COS WV14 66 E3
Nanaimo Wy KGSWFD DY6 101 L1
Nansen Rd SPARK B11 126 A2
WASH/WDE B8 90 C8
Nantmel Gv RIDG/WDGT B32 123 G5
Naomi Wy ALDR WS9 40 F1
Napier TAM/AM/WIL B77 46 C2
Napier Dr TPTN/OCK DY4 68 A7
Napier Rd BKHL/PFLD WV2 50 B6
WSLW WS2 38 E8
Napier St COV CV1 9 K4
Napton Cl REDE B98 197 H4
Napton Dr RLSN CV32 200 E3
Napton Gn COVW CV5 152 E2
Napton Gv SLYOAK B29 123 L5
Narberth Wy COVE CV2 135 K6
Nares Cl RUGBYS/DCH CV22 183 J4 10
Narraway Gv TPTN/OCK DY4 68 B5 3
Narrowboat Wy DUDS DY2 84 E8
Narrow La BRWNH WS8 26 D5
RMSLY B62 104 C5
WSLW WS2 52 F6
Naseby Cl COVS CV3 155 K5
REDE B98 189 H7
Naseby Dr HALE B63 121 H3
Naseby Rd SOLH B91 127 M7
WASH/WDE B8 90 D8
Nash Av DUNHL/THL/PER WV6 48 C2
Nash Cl BLKHTH/ROWR B65 104 A4
Nashe Cl KIDD DY10 138 A8
Nash La HAG/WOL DY9 140 B6
Nash Sq PBAR/PBCH B42 89 H1
Nately Gv SLYOAK B29 123 M2
Nathan Cl MGN/WHC B75 57 G5
Naunton Cl SLYOAK B29 123 L5
Naunton Rd WSLW WS2 52 E2
Navenby Cl
ALE/KHTH/YWD B14 146 A2
Navigation La DARL/WED WS10 69 K3
Navigation St CBHAMW B1 6 E6
WOLV WV1 3 J7
WSLW WS2 4 D2
Navigation Wy COVN CV6 134 E5
WBROM B70 86 D3
Nayland Cft HLGN/YWD B28 126 E8
Naylor Cl KIDDW DY11 160 F2
Naylors Gv SEDG DY3 84 C1
Neachells Ct WLNHL WV13 51 J4
Neachells La WLNHL WV13 51 H1
WNSFLD WV11 37 H8
Neachless Av WMBN WV5 64 E8
Neachley Gv STETCH B33 109 K1
Neal Ct COVE CV2 135 L5 3
Neale Av COVW CV5 132 E7
Neale St WSLW WS2 4 B1
Neander CRTAM B79 31 K7
Nearhill Rd HWK/WKHTH B38 144 A5
Near Lands Cl RIDG/WDGT B32 122 F1
Nearmoor Rd BKDE/SHDE B34 92 B8
Neasden Gv KGSTG B44 71 M5
Neath Rd BLOX/PEL WS3 38 D3
Neath Wy BLOX/PEL WS3 38 D3
SEDG DY3 66 E7
Nebsworth Cl SHLY B90 127 H8
Nechells Park Rd VAUX/NECH B7 90 A6
Nechells Pkwy VAUX/NECH B7 7 M1
Nechells Pl VAUX/NECH B7 89 M7 2
Needham St VAUX/NECH B7 90 A6
Needhill Cl DOR/KN B93 148 D7
Needle Mill La REDE B98 188 C7
Needlers End La
RCOVN/BALC/EX CV7 150 D7
Needwood Cl BKHL/PFLD WV2 49 M7
Needwood Dr
ETTPK/GDPK/PENN WV4 66 D1 3
Needwood Gv HHTH/SAND B71 69 J4
Needwood Hl LICH WS13 20 E3 3
Neighbrook Cl REDW B97 195 K3
Neilston St RLSS CV31 200 E6
Nelson Av BILS/COS WV14 51 G6
WWCK CV34 199 L5 2
Nelson Dr HEDN WS12 17 J1
Nelson La WWCK CV34 199 L5
Nelson Rd AST/WIT B6 89 K4
DUDN DY1 84 F4
Nelson St CBHAMW B1 6 B4
COV CV1 9 K2
HHTH/SAND B71 69 G8
OLDBY B69 86 F7
WLNHL WV13 51 M2 1
Nelson Wy RUGBYS/DCH CV22 183 G4
Nene Cl COVS CV3 155 H6
STRBR DY8 119 L1
Nene Wy CBROM B36 92 D5
Neptune St TPTN/OCK DY4 67 H8
Nesbit Gv BORD B9 108 F2
Nesfield Cl HWK/WKHTH B38 144 A4
Nesfield Gv HIA/OLT B92 129 M6
Nesscliffe Gv ERDW/GRVHL B23 72 B6
Nest Common BLOX/PEL WS3 25 K8
Neston Gv STETCH B33 109 H3 3
Netheravon Cl
ALE/KHTH/YWD B14 145 H4 1
Nether Beacon LICH WS13 20 E4
Netherbridge Av LICHS WS14 21 J5
Netherby Rd SEDG DY3 66 A5
Nethercote Gdns SHLY B90 146 C2
Netherdale Cl
CSCFLD/WYGN B72 73 G6 2
Netherdale Rd
ALE/KHTH/YWD B14 145 L4 2
Netherend Cl HALE B63 102 E6
Netherend La HALE B63 102 F6
Netherend Sq HALE B63 102 E6 2
Netherfield REDE B98 196 E5
Netherfield Gdns ACGN B27 126 F2
Nethergate SEDG DY3 66 D8
Nether La BNTWD WS7 19 H5
Nethermill Rd COVN CV6 133 L8 2
Nethersole St
POL/KGSB/FAZ B78 47 L3
Netherstone Gv
FOAKS/STRLY B74 42 D8
Netherstowe LICH WS13 21 G3
Netherstowe La LICH WS13 21 G3
Netherton Gv STETCH B33 110 B2 3
Netherton La BEWD DY12 160 A3
Netherwood Cl SOLH B91 127 J7
Netherwood La DOR/KN B93 173 K7
Nethy Dr DUNHL/THL/PER WV6 34 F8
Netley Gv SPARK B11 126 D2
Netley Rd BLOX/PEL WS3 38 C3
Netley Wy BLOX/PEL WS3 38 C3
Nevada Wy
CHWD/FDBR/MGN B37 111 G4
Neve Av WOLVN WV10 36 D4
Nevill Cl RLSS CV31 200 D7
Neville Av
ETTPK/GDPK/PENN WV4 50 B7
KIDDW DY11 161 H2
Neville Cl REDE B98 188 D8
Neville Gv WWCK CV34 199 K4
Neville Rd CBROM B36 92 C4
ERDW/GRVHL B23 90 A2
SHLY B90 146 D4
Neville St TAM/AM/WIL B77 46 C2
Nevill St CRTAM B79 31 L8
Nevin Gv PBAR/PBCH B42 71 G8
Nevis Ct DUNHL/THL/PER WV6 49 J3
Nevis Gv SHHTH WV12 37 M4
Nevison Gv GTB/HAM B43 70 F1
Newark Cft
LGN/SDN/BHAMAIR B26 109 M7
Newark Rd DUDS DY2 103 H3
SHHTH WV12 38 A6 1
New Ash Dr COVW CV5 132 D8
Newbank Gv BORD B9 108 E2 2
New Barns La LICHS WS14 41 M1
New Bartholomew St
DIG/EDG B5 7 J5
New Birmingham Rd
OLDBY B69 85 L4
Newbold Cl COVS CV3 155 K4
DOR/KN B93 148 D8
Newbold Cft VAUX/NECH B7 89 M8 3
Newbold Pl RLSN CV32 200 E5 1
Newbold Rd RUGBYN/HIL CV21 159 J7
Newbolds Rd WOLVN WV10 36 E7
Newbold St RLSN CV32 200 E5
Newbold Ter RLSN CV32 200 E5
Newbold Ter East RLSN CV32 200 E5
Newbolt Rd BILS/COS WV14 51 J7
Newbolt St DSYBK/YTR WS5 53 J8
New Bond St BORD B9 107 M4
DUDS DY2 85 H5 3
Newborough Gv
HLGN/YWD B28 146 D1
Newborough Rd
HLGN/YWD B28 146 D1
Newbourne Hl ALVE B48 188 C1
Newbridge Av
DUNHL/THL/PER WV6 49 J2
Newbridge Crs
DUNHL/THL/PER WV6 49 J1
Newbridge Gdns
DUNHL/THL/PER WV6 49 J1 1
Newbridge Rd BORD B9 108 F5
KGSWFD DY6 83 G5
Newbridge St
DUNHL/THL/PER WV6 49 K1
New Brook St RLSN CV32 200 C5
New Buildings COV CV1 8 F4
Newburgh Crs WWCK CV34 199 J5
Newburn Cft
RIDG/WDGT B32 104 F8 1
Newbury Cl GTWY WS6 24 D2
RLSS CV31 201 G7 3
RMSLY B62 122 B2
Newbury La OLDBY B69 86 B7
Newbury Rd STRBR DY8 101 G3
WOLVN WV10 36 A3
Newby Cl COVS CV3 154 C7
Newby Gv
CHWD/FDBR/MGN B37 110 F1
New Canal St DIG/EDG B5 7 J5
Newcastle Cft CVALE B35 92 A2 1
New Church Rd
SCFLD/BOLD B73 72 E5
New Cl RWWCK/WEL CV35 198 D7 3
New College Cl WSL WS1 5 K8
Newcombe Rd COVW CV5 8 A8
HDSW B21 88 B3
Newcomen Cl BDWTH CV12 116 B5 1
BNTWD WS7 19 G5 1
Newcomen Dr TPTN/OCK DY4 85 K2
Newcomen Rd BDWTH CV12 116 B4
Newcott Cl COVEN WV9 35 K3
New Coventry Rd
LGN/SDN/BHAMAIR B26 109 K8
New Cft LOZ/NWT B19 89 J6
Newcroft Gv
LGN/SDN/BHAMAIR B26 109 J6
New Cross Av WOLVN WV10 50 F1
New Cross St
DARL/WED WS10 52 B8 2
TPTN/OCK DY4 67 J8
Newdegate Pl NUN CV11 99 G1 3
Newdegate Rd BDWTH CV12 116 E2
Newdegate St NUN CV11 99 G1
Newdigate RLSS CV31 201 G8
Newdigate Rd COVN CV6 134 D8
MGN/WHC B75 73 L1
New Dudley Rd KGSWFD DY6 83 G5
Newells Dr TPTN/OCK DY4 68 B6 2
Newells Rd
LGN/SDN/BHAMAIR B26 109 L5
New End Rd CSHL/WTROR B46 112 E2
New England RMSLY B62 104 C6
New England Cl OLDBY B69 86 C4 1
Newent Cl REDE B98 197 L2
SHHTH WV12 52 B1
Newent Rd NFLD/LBR B31 144 A1
Newey Av BDWTH CV12 116 B5
Newey Cl RBRY B45 142 E7 1
Newey Dr KNWTH CV8 191 L3
Newey Rd COVE CV2 155 H1
HLGN/YWD B28 126 D7
WNSFLD WV11 37 L5
Newey St DUDN DY1 84 E3
New Farm Rd HAG/WOL DY9 102 A8
Newfield Av KNWTH CV8 191 M2
Newfield Cl SOLH B91 128 B7
WSLW WS2 39 G8
Newfield Crs HALE B63 103 L8
Newfield Dr KGSWFD DY6 101 J1
Newfield Gdns HAG/WOL DY9 139 L1
Newfield La HALE B63 103 L8
Newfield Rd COV CV1 134 A8
HAG/WOL DY9 139 L1
OLDBY B69 86 D5
New Forest Rd BLOX/PEL WS3 39 J7
New Gas St WBROM B70 68 E8 2
Newgate St BNTWD WS7 18 E8
Newhall Crs HEDN WS12 16 F2
New Hall Dr WALM/CURD B76 73 J3
Newhall Farm Cl
WALM/CURD B76 73 H1 2
Newhall Hl CBHAMW B1 6 C3
New Hall Pl DARL/WED WS10 68 E2 3
Newhall Rd BLKHTH/ROWR B65 104 A2
COVE CV2 135 H6
New Hall St WLNHL WV13 51 L3
Newhall St CBHAMNW B3 6 D3
CNCK/NC WS11 16 B5
TPTN/OCK DY4 67 J5
WBROM B70 87 G3
WSL WS1 4 F5
Newham Gn
NUNW/HART CV10 80 A6 2
New Hampton Rd East
WOLV WV1 2 C2
Newhaven Cl COVN CV6 133 J7
VAUX/NECH B7 7 L1 2
New Hayes Rd HEDN WS12 18 A1
New Henry St LGLYGN/QTN B68 104 E1
Newhope Cl EDG B15 107 H5 2
New Hope Rd SMTHWK B66 106 A1
New Horse Rd GTWY WS6 24 C2
Newhouse Cft
RCOVN/BALC/EX CV7 150 F7 3
Newhouse Farm Cl
WALM/CURD B76 73 K2 7
Newhouse La BRGRVW B61 184 B5
Newick Av FOAKS/STRLY B74 55 M2
Newick Gv
ALE/KHTH/YWD B14 125 G8 1
Newick St DUDS DY2 103 G1
Newington Cl COVN CV6 133 H7
Newington Rd
CHWD/FDBR/MGN B37 110 F5 2
New Inn Rd LOZ/NWT B19 89 H4
New Inns Cl HDSW B21 88 B5
New Inns La RBRY B45 142 C4
New John St AST/WIT B6 89 J8
RMSLY B62 104 A4
New John St West
LOZ/NWT B19 88 F7
New King St DUDS DY2 85 G4 2
Newland Cl REDE B98 196 F6 2
RUSH/SHEL WS4 40 A3 1
Newland Gdns CDYHTH B64 103 J5
Newland Gv DUDS DY2 84 D6
Newland La
RCOVN/BALC/EX CV7 115 M6
Newland Rd COV CV1 134 B8
RLSN CV32 201 G2
SMHTH B10 108 D4
Newlands Cl KIDDW DY11 137 G6 3
PENK ST19 10 D6
WLNHL WV13 51 L4
Newlands Ct HEDN WS12 17 J5
Newlands Dr RMSLY B62 104 C6
Newlands La
CHWD/FDBR/MGN B37 110 E7
CNCK/NC WS11 17 G6
Newlands Rd ATHST CV9 62 A5
BVILLE B30 124 F6
DOR/KN B93 172 C1
Newland St RUGBYS/DCH CV22 183 J2
New Landywood La
WNSFLD WV11 24 C7
Newlyn Cl LICHS WS14 21 H6
NUN CV11 99 K1
Newlyn Rd CDYHTH B64 103 H5
NFLD/LBR B31 143 K2
Newman Av
ETTPK/GDPK/PENN WV4 66 D1
Newman Cl BDWTH CV12 116 F1 3
Newman College Cl
RIDG/WDGT B32 123 G5 1
Newman Pl BILS/COS WV14 51 K6
Newman Rd ERDE/BCHGN B24 90 D1
TPTN/OCK DY4 68 A4
WOLVN WV10 36 E4
Newmans Cl SMTHWK B66 106 A1 1
Newman Wy RBRY B45 142 E6
Newmarket Cl COVE CV2 135 F1
DUNHL/THL/PER WV6 35 L8 3
New Market St CBHAMNW B3 6 E4 1
Newmarket Wy CBROM B36 90 F6
Newmarsh Rd WALM/CURD B76 73 L7
New Meadow Cl NFLD/LBR B31 143 M3
New Meadow Rd REDE B98 196 F2
New Meeting St OLDBY B69 86 E5 3
New Mill La POL/KGSB/FAZ B78 45 L5
New Mills St WSL WS1 4 C8
New Mill St DUDS DY2 85 G4
Newmore Gdns DSYBK/YTR WS5 54 A7
Newnham Gv
ERDW/GRVHL B23 72 C7 3
Newnham Ri SHLY B90 147 H2
Newnham Rd COV CV1 134 D8 2
LDYWD/EDGR B16 106 A3 1
RLSN CV32 200 F2
New Penkridge Rd
CNCK/NC WS11 15 M3
New Pool Rd CDYHTH B64 102 F5
Newport TAM/AM/WIL B77 32 D8 1
Newport Cl REDW B97 195 M7
Newport Rd BHTH/HG B12 125 L1
CBROM B36 91 K5
COVN CV6 134 B4
Newport St WOLVN WV10 50 C1 1
WSL WS1 4 E3
Newquay Cl DSYBK/YTR WS5 54 C6
NUN CV11 81 K8
Newquay Rd DSYBK/YTR WS5 54 B6
New Rd ALDR WS9 40 E8
BDWTH CV12 115 K3
BEWD DY12 136 B8
BNTWD WS7 18 F7
BRGRVE B60 185 M6
BRGRVW B61 165 J3
BRGRVW B61 185 J2
BRWNH WS8 26 D6
COVN CV6 133 K4
CRTAM B79 33 J4
CSHL/WTROR B46 92 F2
DUDS DY2 85 G6
DUNHL/THL/PER WV6 49 J1
HALE B63 121 M1
HLYWD B47 145 K5
KIDD DY10 161 J1
LICHS WS14 28 D7
PENK ST19 10 C4
RBRY B45 142 C6
RCOVN/BALC/EX CV7 115 M7
SOLH B91 148 A2
STRBR DY8 101 L8
TAM/AM/WIL B77 46 D6
TPTN/OCK DY4 68 B7
WLNHL WV13 51 L4
WNSFLD WV11 36 F5
WOLVN WV10 22 B4
WOLVN WV10 23 G5
New Rowley Rd DUDS DY2 85 J6
Newsholme Cl WWCK CV34 199 J4 3
New Spring St WSNGN B18 106 E1
New Spring St North
WSNGN B18 88 E8
Newstead CRTAM B79 31 H7
Newstead Cl NUN CV11 99 K3 3
Newstead Rd KGSTG B44 71 L2
Newstead Wy COVS CV3 155 M4
New St ATHST CV9 62 A4
BDMR/CCFT WV3 49 H7
BDWTH CV12 117 G3
BKHL/PFLD WV2 50 E7 2
BLOX/PEL WS3 38 F4
BNTWD WS7 18 C6
BRLYHL DY5 102 E5
CBHAM B2 6 F5
CBROM B36 91 M5
CNCK/NC WS11 16 C4 1
DARL/WED WS10 52 B7
DARL/WED WS10 68 D4
DUDS DY2 85 H4 3
ERDW/GRVHL B23 72 D8
ETTPK/GDPK/PENN WV4 50 C8
GTWY WS6 24 E4
HEDN WS12 17 G1
KGSWFD DY6 83 G5
KGSWFD DY6 101 H1
KNWTH CV8 176 D7
POL/KGSB/FAZ B78 45 M5
POL/KGSB/FAZ B78 47 L8
POL/KGSB/FAZ B78 47 H5
RBRY B45 142 E3
RLSN CV32 193 J8
RLSS CV31 200 E6
RUGBYS/DCH CV22 183 J2
RUSH/SHEL WS4 40 B4
SEDG DY3 84 A2
SMTHWK B66 87 M7
STRBR DY8 101 H3
STRBR DY8 101 L8
TAM/AM/WIL B77 46 A5
TAM/AM/WIL B77 46 C2
TPTN/OCK DY4 67 J8
WBROM B70 68 E6
WBROM B70 87 H2
WLNHL WV13 51 J4

WNSFLD WV11 .... 37 L2
WSL WS1 .... 5 G4
WWCK CV34 .... 199 J7
New St North *HHTH/SAND* B71 ... 87 H2
New Summer St *LOZ/NWT* B19 ... 6 F1
New Swan La *WBROM* B70 .... 68 E8
Newton CI *COVE* CV2 .... 135 K6
GTB/HAM B43 .... 70 A5
NUNW/HART CV10 .... 79 M3
REDE B98 .... 196 D7
Newton Gdns *GTB/HAM* B43 ..... 69 M5
Newton La *CRTAM* B79 .... 33 L2
Newton Manor CI
GTB/HAM B43 .... 70 B5
New Town *BRLYHL* DY5 .... 101 M1
WSNGN B18 .... 88 D6
Newton PI *WSLW* WS2 .... 38 F7
WSNGN B18 .... 88 D6
Newton Rd *BRGRVE* B60 .... 185 L6
DOR/KN B93 .... 148 F6
GTB/HAM B43 .... 70 A5
HHTH/SAND B71 .... 69 K7
LICH WS13 .... 20 D3
SPARK B11 .... 107 M8
WSLW WS2 .... 38 F8
Newton Sq *GTB/HAM* B43 .... 70 C4
Newton St *CBHAMNE* B4 .... 7 H3
HHTH/SAND B71 .... 69 J6
New Town *BRLYHL* DY5 .... 101 M1
DUDS DY2 .... 103 H3
Newtown Dr *LOZ/NWT* B19 ..... 89 C7
Newtown La *CDYHTH* B64 .... 103 H4
HAG/WOL DY9 .... 141 H5
RBRY B45 .... 142 A4
Newtown Middleway
AST/WIT B6 .... 89 J8
Newtown Rd *BDWTH* CV12 ...... 116 D3
NUN CV11 .... 81 G8
Newtown Rw *CBHAMNE* B4 ...... 7 H1
LOZ/NWT B19 .... 89 J8
Newtown St *CDYHTH* B64 .... 103 H3
New Union St *COV* CV1 .... 8 F6
New Village *DUDS* DY2 .... 103 G4
New Wood CI *KINVER* DY7 ...... 107 C5
New Wood Gv *ALDR* WS9 .... 40 E2
New Wood La *KIDD* DY10 ...... 138 E5
Niall CI *EDG* B15 .... 106 D5
Niblett Hl *BRGRVE* B60 .... 164 F6
Nicholas Rd *FOAKS/STRLY* B74 ... 55 J5
Nicholas Wk *WALM/CURD* B76 ... 74 F7
Nicholds CI *BILS/COS* WV14 ..... 66 F4
Nicholls Rd *TPTN/OCK* DY4 ..... 67 J4
Nicholls St *COV* CV1 .... 9 L2
WBROM B70 .... 87 H3
Nicholls Wy *HEDN* WS12 .... 17 J4
Nichols CI *HIA/OLT* B92 .... 128 D6
Nicholson CI *WWCK* CV34 ..... 199 K4
Nigel Av *NFLD/LBR* B31 .... 123 L8
Nigel Rd *DUDN* DY1 .... 84 D3
WASH/WDE B8 .... 90 E7
Nightingale *TAM/AM/WIL* B77 ... 46 E7
Nightingale Av *CBROM* B36 ...... 92 E5
Nightingale CI *ATHST* CV9 .... 63 J4
HEDN WS12 .... 12 A6
Nightingale Crs *BRLYHL* DY5 .... 102 B6
SHHTH WV12 .... 37 M5
Nightingale Dr *KIDD* DY10 ..... 161 M3
TPTN/OCK DY4 .... 68 A3
Nightingale La *COVW* CV5 ...... 153 H5
Nightingale PI
BILS/COS WV14 .... 51 H6
Nightjar Gv *ERDW/GRVHL* B23 ... 72 A7
Nighwood Dr *FOAKS/STRLY* B74 ... 55 K6
Nijon CI *HDSW* B21 .... 88 A4
Nimbus *TAM/AM/WIL* B77 .... 60 B1
Nimmings CI *NFLD/LBR* B31 .... 143 J7
Nimmings Rd *RMSLY* B62 ...... 104 B4
Nineacres Dr
CHWD/FDBR/MGN B37 ...... 110 C3
Nine Days La *REDE* B98 .... 196 F7
Nine Elms La *WOLVN* WV10 .... 50 C1
Ninefoot La *TAM/AM/WIL* B77 ... 46 C5
Nine Leasowes *SMTHWK* B66 ... 87 J6
Nine Locks Rdg *BRLYHL* DY5 .... 102 B3
Nineveh Av *HDSW* B21 .... 88 D6
Nineveh Rd *HDSW* B21 .... 88 C6
Ninfield Rd *ACGN* B27 .... 126 E1
Ninian Wy *TAM/AM/WIL* B77 ... 46 C7
Nirvana CI *CNCK/NC* WS11 ..... 16 A3
Nith PI *DUDN* DY1 .... 84 F3
Niton Rd *NUNW/HART* CV10 ... 81 H7
Niven CI *COVW* CV5 .... 132 C7
Noble CI *WWCK* CV34 .... 199 H8
Nocke Rd *WNSFLD* WV11 .... 37 K4
Nock St *TPTN/OCK* DY4 .... 68 A2
Noddy Pk *ALDR* WS9 .... 40 F6
Noddy Park Rd *ALDR* WS9 ...... 40 F6
Nod Ri *COVW* CV5 .... 152 F2
Noel Av *BHTH/HG* B12 .... 107 L7
Noele Gordon Gdns *WSL* WS1 ... 4 E6
Noel Rd *LDYWD/EDGR* B16 .... 106 D4
Nolan CI *COVN* CV6 .... 116 B8
Nolton CI *GTB/HAM* B43 .... 70 B5
No Name Rd *BNTWD* WS7 ...... 18 C6
Nooklands Cft *STETCH* B33 .... 109 L3
The Nook *BRLYHL* DY5 .... 83 M8
GTWY WS6 .... 24 A4
NUN CV11 .... 99 J3
Noose Crs *WLNHL* WV13 .... 51 J3
Noose La *WLNHL* WV13 .... 51 J3
Nora Rd *SPARK* B11 .... 126 A2
Norbiton Rd *KGSTG* B44 .... 71 L5
Norbreck CI *GTB/HAM* B43 ..... 70 B5
Norbury Av *BLOX/PEL* WS3 ..... 39 K2
Norbury CI *REDE* B98 .... 188 F6
Norbury Crs
ETTPK/GDPK/PENN WV4 ..... 66 D1
Norbury Dr *BRLYHL* DY5 ...... 102 B4
Norbury Gv *HIA/OLT* B92 ...... 127 L2
Norbury Rd *BILS/COS* WV14 .... 51 K7
KGSTG B44 .... 71 K2
WBROM B70 .... 68 D6
WOLVN WV10 .... 36 D7
Norcombe Gv *SHLY* B90 .... 147 L8
Nordley Rd *WNSFLD* WV11 ..... 37 G3
Norfolk Av *HHTH/SAND* B71 ... 69 H6
Norfolk CI *BVILLE* B30 .... 124 F7
Norfolk Crs *ALDR* WS9 .... 40 F5

NUNW/HART CV10 .... 98 C2
Norfolk Dr *DARL/WED* WS10 .... 69 H1
POL/KGSB/FAZ B78 .... 45 K4
Norfolk Gdns *MGN/WHC* B75 .... 56 F5
Norfolk Gv *GTWY* WS6 .... 24 D4
Norfolk New Rd *WSLW* WS2 .... 52 E1
Norfolk PI *WSLW* WS2 .... 39 H8
Norfolk Rd *BDMR/CCFT* WV3 .... 2 A9
DUDS DY2 .... 84 E6
EDG B15 .... 106 B5
ERDW/GRVHL B23 .... 72 D8
LGLYGN/QTN B68 .... 104 F6
MGN/WHC B75 .... 57 G6
RBRY B45 .... 142 D4
STRBR DY8 .... 101 H5
Norfolk St *COV* CV1 .... 8 C4
RLSN CV32 .... 200 C4
Norfolk Ter *TLHL/CAN* CV4 .... 153 C6
Norgrave Rd *HIA/OLT* B92 ..... 128 A3
Norgrove La *REDE* B98 .... 195 H6
Norlan Dr *ALE/KHTH/YWD* B14 ... 145 K2
Norland Rd *ACGN* B27 .... 127 G4
Norley Gv *MOS/BIL* B13 .... 126 A6
Norman Ashman Coppice
COVS CV3 .... 156 A6
Norman Av *COVE* CV2 .... 135 K4
NUN CV11 .... 98 F1
RIDG/WDGT B32 .... 105 J6
Norman CI *CRTAM* B79 .... 31 J6
Normandy CI
RWWCK/WEL CV35 .... 198 E6
Normandy Rd
BFLD/HDSWWD B20 .... 89 H4
Norman Place Rd *COVN* CV6 ... 133 J2
Norman Rd *DSYBK/YTR* WS5 ... 54 A6
NFLD/LBR B31 .... 143 M2
PENK ST19 .... 10 D5
RUGBYN/HIL CV21 .... 159 K7
SMTHWK B67 .... 105 H4
Norman St *DUDS* DY2 .... 85 H5
WSNGN B18 .... 88 D3
Norman Ter
BLKHTH/ROWR B65 .... 104 A1
Normanton Av
LGN/SDN/BHAMAIR B26 ... 110 B8
Norrington Gv *NFLD/LBR* B31 ... 143 G2
Norrington Rd *NFLD/LBR* B31 ... 143 G2
Norris Dr *STETCH* B33 .... 109 J2
Norris Rd *BFLD/HDSWWD* B20 ... 89 K4
Norris Wy *MGN/WHC* B75 .... 57 H6
Northampton St *WSNGN* B18 .... 6 C1
North Av *BDWTH* CV12 .... 117 H3
BHAMNEC B40 .... 111 K8
COVE CV2 .... 154 E2
WNSFLD WV11 .... 37 G7
Northbourne Dr *NUN* CV11 ..... 99 J6
North Brook Rd *COVW* CV5 ... 133 H5
Northbrook Rd *SHLY* B90 ..... 127 G8
Northbrook St
LDYWD/EDGR B16 .... 106 D1
North CI *RLSN* CV32 .... 193 J8
Northcote Rd
RUGBYS/DCH CV22 .... 183 K3
STETCH B33 .... 109 H3
Northcote St *RLSS* CV31 ..... 200 F6
North Cl *WSL* WS2 .... 53 H1
Northcote Wk *ATHST* CV9 ...... 63 H3
Northcott Rd *BILS/COS* WV14 ... 67 J1
DUDS DY2 .... 103 H1
North Crs *WOLVN* WV10 .... 22 F6
Northdown Rd *SOLH* B91 ...... 147 K4
North Dr *BFLD/HDSWWD* B20 ... 88 F5
DIG/EDG B5 .... 107 G8
MGN/WHC B75 .... 57 G7
Northey Rd *COVN* CV6 .... 134 B5
Northfield CI *REDE* B98 .... 189 H7
Northfield Gv *BDMR/CCFT* WV3 ... 49 G6
Northfield Rd *BVILLE* B30 ..... 144 B1
COV CV1 .... 9 K6
DUDS DY2 .... 85 G8
HRBN B17 .... 123 L1
Northfields Wy *BRWNH* WS8 ... 26 B6
Northgate *ALDR* WS9 .... 40 E6
CDYHTH B64 .... 103 H5
North Ga *HRBN* B17 .... 106 A6
Northgate CI *KIDDW* DY11 ..... 160 E1
Northgate St *WWCK* CV34 .... 199 J6
Northgate Wy *ALDR* WS9 .... 40 E5
North Gn
ETTPK/GDPK/PENN WV4 ... 49 H7
North Holme *BORD* B9 .... 108 A3
Northland Rd *SHLY* B90 .... 147 M8
Northlands Rd *MOS/BIL* B13 ... 125 L4
Northleach Av *BVILLE* B30 ... 145 H3
Northleach CI *REDE* B98 ...... 188 F8
Northleigh Rd *WASH/WDE* B8 ... 90 E7
Northolt Dr *CVALE* B35 .... 91 L1
Northolt Gv *PBAR/PBCH* B42 ... 70 D4
North Ov *SEDG* DY3 .... 66 C8
Northover CI *COVEN* WV9 ...... 35 L3
North Park Rd
ERDW/GRVHL B23 .... 89 M2
North Pathway *HRBN* B17 .... 105 M6
North Rd *BFLD/HDSWWD* B20 ... 89 J3
BRGRVE B60 .... 185 L3
HRBN B17 .... 106 B7
SLYOAK B29 .... 124 C2
STRPT DY13 .... 160 E8
TPTN/OCK DY4 .... 67 M5
WOLV WV1 .... 2 F1
North Roundhay *STETCH* B33 ... 109 L1
Northside Dr *REDE* B98 .... 196 C6
Northside Dr *FOAKS/STRLY* B74 ... 55 K5
North Springfield *SEDG* DY3 .... 66 C4
North St *ATHST* CV9 .... 63 H3
BNTWD WS7 .... 18 D4
BRLYHL DY5 .... 85 L8
CNCK/NC WS11 .... 16 C7
COVE CV2 .... 134 E8
DARL/WED WS10 .... 52 C8
DUDS DY2 .... 85 H4
NUNW/HART CV10 .... 98 D2
RUGBYN/HIL CV21 .... 183 G1
SMTHWK B67 .... 87 K8
WOLV WV1 .... 2 F4
WSLW WS2 .... 53 J1

Northumberland Av
KIDDW DY11 .... 161 G2
NUNW/HART CV10 .... 98 C2
Northumberland CI
POL/KGSB/FAZ B78 .... 45 L4
Northumberland Rd *COV* CV1 .... 8 L4
RLSN CV32 .... 200 C3
Northumberland St
VAUX/NECH B7 .... 7 M3
Northvale CI *KNWTH* CV8 ..... 176 F7
North Vw *RCOVN/BALC/EX* CV7 ... 135 L4
North View Dr *BRLYHL* DY5 .... 84 C8
North Villiers St *RLSN* CV32 ... 200 E7
North Warwick St *BORD* B9 ... 108 B4
Northway *BHAMNEC* B40 ..... 111 K8
RLSS CV31 .... 200 F7
SEDG DY3 .... 66 A5
North Western CI *SMTHWK* B66 ... 87 K7
North Western Ter *WSNGN* B18 ... 88 D6
Northwick Crs *SOLH* B91 ..... 147 M4
Northwood Park CI
WOLVN WV10 .... 36 C2
Northwood Park Rd
WOLVN WV10 .... 36 C3
Northwood St *CBHAMW* B1 ...... 6 D3
North Worcestershire Pth
HAG/WOL DY9 .... 119 M7
HAG/WOL DY9 .... 141 G1
RBRY B45 .... 167 G2
Northycote La *WOLVN* WV10 ... 36 D1
Norton CI *CRTAM* B79 .... 32 A6
ETTPK/GDPK/PENN WV4 ... 65 G2
REDE B98 .... 197 K3
SMTHWK B66 .... 88 A8
Norton Crs *BILS/COS* WV14 .... 67 H4
BORD B9 .... 108 F2
DUDS DY2 .... 103 J2
Norton Dr *WWCK* CV34 .... 199 H3
Norton East Rd *CNCK/NC* WS11 ... 17 M8
Norton Gra *CNCK/NC* WS11 .... 25 K1
Norton Green La *CNCK/NC* WS11 ... 25 J1
DOR/KN B93 .... 172 F5
Norton Hall La *CNCK/NC* WS11 ... 25 J2
Norton Hill Dr *COVE* CV2 ..... 135 J7
Norton La *BNTWD* WS7 .... 19 H7
CNCK/NC WS11 .... 16 F6
GTWY WS6 .... 24 E1
SHLY B90 .... 170 B1
Norton Leys
RUGBYS/DCH CV22 .... 183 K7
Norton Rd *BLOX/PEL* WS3 ...... 25 L8
CSHL/WTROR B46 .... 93 K5
HEDN WS12 .... 17 K5
KIDD DY11 .... 137 M7
STRBR DY8 .... 119 H4
Norton Springs *CNCK/NC* WS11 ... 17 K8
Norton St *WSNGN* B18 .... 88 E7
Norton Ter *CNCK/NC* WS11 .... 17 K7
Norton Vw
ALE/KHTH/YWD B14 .... 125 H7
Nortune CI *HWK/WKHTH* B38 ... 144 B3
Norwich Av *KIDDW* DY11 ...... 136 D7
Norwich CI *LICH* WS13 .... 21 G2
NUN CV11 .... 81 L5
Norwich Cft
CHWD/FDBR/MGN B37 ...... 110 D4
Norwich Dr *COVS* CV3 .... 153 M8
HRBN B17 .... 105 K5
Norwich Rd *DUDS* DY2 .... 103 H3
WSLW WS2 .... 52 F4
Norwood Av *CDYHTH* B64 .... 103 J6
Norwood CI *COVE* CV2 .... 135 J3
LOZ/NWT B19 .... 88 F6
Norwood Rd *BORD* B9 .... 108 C3
BRLYHL DY5 .... 102 A2
Nottingham Dr *SHHTH* WV12 ... 38 A6
Nottingham Rd *LICHS* WS14 ... 30 A2
Nottingham Wy *BRLYHL* DY5 ... 102 D3
Nova Ct *PBAR/PBCH* B42 ...... 70 F4
Nova Scotia St *CBHAMNE* B4 .... 7 J4
Nowell St *DARL/WED* WS10 .... 52 C8
Nuffield Rd *COVN* CV6 .... 134 E6
Nugent CI *AST/WIT* B6 .... 89 J6
Nugent Gv *SHLY* B90 .... 171 H2
Nuneaton La
MKTBOS/BARL/STKG CV13 ... 81 K3
Nuneaton Rd *ATHST* CV9 .... 63 L8
BDWTH CV12 .... 99 M8
CSHL/WTROR B46 .... 95 J2
NUNW/HART CV10 .... 79 M3
RCOVN/BALC/EX CV7 .... 114 C2
Nunts La *COVN* CV6 .... 133 M2
Nunts Park Av *COVN* CV6 .... 133 M1
Nursery Av *ALDR* WS9 .... 40 F8
BHTH/HG B12 .... 107 K8
Nursery CI *BVILLE* B30 .... 124 D8
HAG/WOL DY9 .... 119 L8
KIDDW DY11 .... 136 F5
Nursery Cft *LICH* WS13 .... 20 D4
Nursery Dr *PENK* ST19 .... 10 C5
WMBN WV5 .... 82 D1
Nursery Gdns *CDSL* WV8 .... 34 D1
STRBR DY8 .... 101 K4
Nursery Gv *KIDDW* DY11 ...... 136 F4
Nursery La *POL/KGSB/FAZ* B78 ... 30 F2
RLSS CV31 .... 200 E8
Nursery Rd *ATHST* CV9 .... 63 K6
BLOX/PEL WS3 .... 38 F5
BVILLE B30 .... 124 C8
EDG B15 .... 106 B6
LOZ/NWT B19 .... 88 F6
NUNW/HART CV10 .... 79 J5
Nursery View CI *ALDR* WS9 .... 55 J3
Nursery Wk
DUNHL/THL/PER WV6 .... 35 H8
Nutbrook Av *TLHL/CAN* CV4 ... 152 C1
Nutbush Dr *NFLD/LBR* B31 ... 123 H7
Nutgrove CI
ALE/KHTH/YWD B14 .... 125 K6
Nuthatch Dr *BRLYHL* DY5 .... 102 A6
Nuthurst *MGN/WHC* B75 .... 73 L1
Nuthurst Crs *NUNW/HART* CV10 ... 97 G2
Nuthurst Dr *CNCK/NC* WS11 .... 24 D1
Nuthurst Gv
ALE/KHTH/YWD B14 .... 145 K3
DOR/KN B93 .... 172 E1
Nuthurst La *NUNW/HART* CV10 ... 97 G3

Nuthurst Rd *NFLD/LBR* B31 ... 143 K7
Nutley Dr *TPTN/OCK* DY4 ...... 68 B5
Nuttall Gv *HDSW* B21 .... 88 A6
Nymet *TAM/AM/WIL* B77 .... 46 C5

O

Oakalls Av *BRGRVE* B60 .... 185 M3
Oak Apple Rd *BRGRVW* B61 ... 165 M5
Oak Av *BHTH/HG* B12 .... 107 L8
GTWY WS6 .... 24 D4
HEDN WS12 .... 12 B5
RCOVN/BALC/EX CV7 .... 96 C3
WBROM B70 .... 86 F2
WSLW WS2 .... 52 C2
Oak Bank *WSNGN* B18 .... 88 E7
Oak Barn Rd *RMSLY* B62 ..... 104 B5
Oak CI *BDWTH* CV12 .... 117 G1
HRBN B17 .... 105 L7
KINVER DY7 .... 118 A2
KNWTH CV8 .... 178 D3
TPTN/OCK DY4 .... 67 L4
Oak Ct *HALE* B63 .... 121 K3
Oak Crs *BLOX/PEL* WS3 .... 39 H7
OLDBY B69 .... 85 M4
Oak Cft *CHWD/FDBR/MGN* B37 ... 110 C2
Oakcroft Rd *MOS/BIL* B13 .... 125 M6
Oakdale CI *BRLYHL* DY5 .... 83 M6
LGLYGN/QTN B68 .... 104 E3
Oakdale Rd *CBROM* B36 .... 91 J5
COVS CV3 .... 156 A6
LGLYGN/QTN B68 .... 104 D3
Oakdene Crs *NUNW/HART* CV10 ... 81 H6
Oakdene Dr *RBRY* B45 .... 167 G5
Oakdene Rd *BNTWD* WS7 ...... 18 E7
Oak Dr *ERDW/GRVHL* B23 ...... 72 A4
Oaken Covert *CDSL* WV8 .... 34 C2
Oaken Dr *CDSL* WV8 .... 34 C2
SHHTH WV12 .... 38 C6
SOLH B91 .... 127 K8
Oakenfield *LICH* WS13 .... 20 D3
Oaken Gdns *BNTWD* WS7 ...... 18 E5
Oaken Gv *CDSL* WV8 .... 34 C3
Oakenhayes Crs *BRWNH* WS8 ... 26 D4
WALM/CURD B76 .... 74 A8
Oakenhayes Dr *BRWNH* WS8 ... 26 D4
Oaken La *CDSL* WV8 .... 34 A2
CDSL WV8 .... 34 C2
Oaken Pk *CDSL* WV8 .... 34 E3
Oakenshaw Rd *REDE* B98 .... 196 D5
SHLY B90 .... 147 H4
Oakeswell St *DARL/WED* WS10 ... 68 E2
Oakey CI *COVN* CV6 .... 134 D1
Oakeywell St *DUDS* DY2 .... 85 H5
Oak Farm CI *WALM/CURD* B76 ... 73 L6
Oak Farm Rd *BVILLE* B30 .... 124 C8
Oakfield Av *BHTH/HG* B12 ... 107 L7
DUDN DY1 .... 66 F7
KGSWFD DY6 .... 83 J8
SPARK B11 .... 108 A7
Oakfield CI *SMTHWK* B66 ...... 88 A7
STRBR DY8 .... 101 K4
Oakfield Dr *BLOX/PEL* WS3 .... 25 L8
RBRY B45 .... 167 H1
Oakfield Gdns *ATHST* CV9 ...... 63 J6
Oakfield Rd *BHTH/HG* B12 ... 125 J1
CDSL WV8 .... 34 F3
COVN CV6 .... 133 K8
ERDE/BCHGN B24 .... 90 D2
HAG/WOL DY9 .... 120 D3
KIDDW DY11 .... 136 F8
RUGBYS/DCH CV22 .... 183 K3
SLYOAK B29 .... 124 E2
SMTHWK B66 .... 88 A8
STRBR DY8 .... 101 L4
Oakfields Wy *SOLH* B91 ...... 128 F8
Oakford Dr *COVW* CV5 .... 132 D3
Oak Gn *DUDN* DY1 .... 66 E8
Oak Gv *KIDD* DY10 .... 137 L8
NFLD/LBR B31 .... 143 J4
WNSFLD WV11 .... 37 M2
Oakhall Dr *DOR/KN* B93 ...... 172 D1
Oakham Av *DUDS* DY2 .... 85 J6
Oakham CI *REDE* B98 .... 196 E8
Oakham Crs *DUDS* DY2 .... 85 J6
Oakham Dr *DUDS* DY2 .... 85 K5
Oakham Rd *DUDS* DY2 .... 85 J5
HRBN B17 .... 105 M6
Oak HI *BDMR/CCFT* WV3 .... 49 G5
Oakhill Av *KIDD* DY10 .... 161 J1
Oakhill Crs *ACGN* B27 .... 126 F5
Oakhill Dr *BRLYHL* DY5 ...... 101 M6
Oak Hill Dr *EDG* B15 .... 106 C6
Oakhill Rd *CNCK/NC* WS11 .... 16 D3
Oakhurst *LICHS* WS14 .... 21 G4
Oakhurst Dr *BRGRVE* B60 .... 185 G2
Oakhurst Rd *ACGN* B27 ...... 126 F4
CSCFLD/WYGN B72 .... 72 F5
Oakland CI *SOLH* B91 .... 148 C1
Oakland Dr *SEDG* DY3 .... 83 M3
Oakland Gn *BRGRVW* B61 .... 185 L1
Oakland Rd *BLOX/PEL* WS3 .... 39 J6
HDSW B21 .... 88 B5
MOS/BIL B13 .... 125 L2
Oaklands *RMSLY* B62 .... 122 E1
WALM/CURD B76 .... 74 F8
Oaklands Av *HRBN* B17 ...... 105 L8
Oaklands CI *HEDN* WS12 ...... 12 A7
Oaklands Cft
WALM/CURD B76 .... 73 M6
Oaklands Dr
BFLD/HDSWWD B20 .... 88 D3
Oaklands Gn *BILS/COS* WV14 ... 51 G5
Oaklands Rd *BDMR/CCFT* WV3 ... 2 B5
FOAKS/STRLY B74 .... 56 F5
The Oaklands
CHWD/FDBR/MGN B37 ...... 110 C6
HEDN WS12 .... 11 J4
TLHL/CAN CV4 .... 152 E3
Oaklands Wy *BLOX/PEL* WS3 .... 39 M2
NFLD/LBR B31 .... 143 G4
Oak La *BNTWD* WS7 .... 18 D4
COVW CV5 .... 132 A4
HIA/OLT B92 .... 149 M4
KGSWFD DY6 .... 83 J4

Oakleaf CI *BRGRVE* B60 .... 185 M3
Oakleaf CI *RIDG/WDGT* B32 ... 123 G3
Oak Leaf Dr *MOS/BIL* B13 .... 125 L2
Oak Leasow *RIDG/WDGT* B32 ... 122 F1
Oakleigh *NFLD/LBR* B31 ...... 144 A3
Oakleigh Dr *CDSL* WV8 .... 34 E2
SEDG DY3 .... 66 A6
Oak Leigh Rd *STRBR* DY8 .... 119 L3
Oakleighs *STRBR* DY8 .... 101 G4
Oakley CI *KNWTH* CV8 .... 174 D4
Oakley Av *ALDR* WS9 .... 40 E8
TPTN/OCK DY4 .... 67 L7
Oakley CI *PENK* ST19 .... 10 E4
Oakley Gv
ETTPK/GDPK/PENN WV4 ... 49 H8
Oakley Rd *BVILLE* B30 .... 124 F8
ETTPK/GDPK/PENN WV4 ... 49 H8
SMHTH B10 .... 108 A6
Oak Leys *BDMR/CCFT* WV3 .... 49 G4
Oakley Wood Dr *SOLH* B91 ... 148 C1
Oakly Rd *REDE* B97 .... 196 B2
Oakmeadow CI
LGN/SDN/BHAMAIR B26 ... 109 H8
STETCH B33 .... 110 B3
Oakmeadow Wy
ERDE/BCHGN B24 .... 91 H2
Oakmoor Rd *COVN* CV6 ...... 134 C2
Oakmount CI *BLOX/PEL* WS3 .... 39 K2
Oakmount Rd *FOAKS/STRLY* B74 ... 55 L6
Oak Park Rd *STRBR* DY8 ..... 101 K4
Oakridge CI *REDE* B98 .... 189 G6
SHHTH WV12 .... 52 A1
Oakridge Dr *GTWY* WS6 .... 24 C3
SHHTH WV12 .... 52 A1
Oakridge Rd *RLSN* CV32 ..... 201 G1
Oak Ri *CSHL/WTROR* B46 ...... 93 K8
Oak Rd *ALDR* WS9 .... 40 E2
BLOX/PEL WS3 .... 25 K8
BRGRVW B61 .... 165 M5
DUDN DY1 .... 85 G2
LGLYGN/QTN B68 .... 105 G6
RUSH/SHEL WS4 .... 40 A5
TPTN/OCK DY4 .... 67 J7
WBROM B70 .... 86 F3
WLNHL WV13 .... 51 J3
Oakroyd Crs *NUNW/HART* CV10 ... 80 D6
Oaks Crs *BDMR/CCFT* WV3 ...... 2 B6
Oaks Dr *BDMR/CCFT* WV3 ...... 2 B5
CNCK/NC WS11 .... 16 A4
WMBN WV5 .... 64 E8
WOLVN WV10 .... 22 D5
Oaksdale Dr *HIA/OLT* B92 .... 128 C5
Oaks PI *COVN* CV6 .... 134 E2
Oaks Rd *KNWTH* CV8 .... 191 J3
The Oaks *BDWTH* CV12 ...... 116 D4
BKDE/SHDE B34 .... 91 M6
HWK/WKHTH B38 .... 144 D7
Oak St *BDMR/CCFT* WV3 .... 2 B6
BILS/COS WV14 .... 66 F6
BRLYHL DY5 .... 102 D4
DUDS DY2 .... 103 H4
DUDS DY2 .... 103 J1
KGSWFD DY6 .... 83 G8
RUGBYS/DCH CV22 .... 183 L3
Oakthorpe Dr
CHWD/FDBR/MGN B37 ...... 92 D8
Oakthorpe Gdns *OLDBY* B69 ... 85 L3
Oak Tree Av *COVS* CV3 .... 153 L8
REDW B97 .... 195 M1
Oak Tree CI *DOR/KN* B93 ..... 172 C1
RLSN CV32 .... 200 E3
Oaktree CI *ALVE* B48 .... 167 L6
POL/KGSB/FAZ B78 .... 60 B7
Oak Tree Crs *RMSLY* B62 ..... 104 D7
Oak Tree Gdns *STRBR* DY8 ... 101 L4
Oak Tree La *BVILLE* B30 ...... 124 C6
HLYWD B47 .... 145 M7
SLYOAK B29 .... 124 C4
Oak Tree Rd *COVS* CV3 .... 155 L4
The Oak Wk *NFLD/LBR* B31 ... 143 L4
Oak Wy *TLHL/CAN* CV4 .... 152 B3
Oakwood CI *ALDR* WS9 .... 40 C1
ATHST CV9 .... 62 A4
LICHS WS14 .... 28 E7
WNSFLD WV11 .... 37 M2
Oakwood Crs *DUDS* DY2 .... 84 D7
Oakwood Cft *SOLH* B91 ...... 148 A4
Oakwood Dr
ALE/KHTH/YWD B14 .... 145 H1
FOAKS/STRLY B74 .... 55 J5
Oakwood Gv *WWCK* CV34 .... 199 L4
Oakwood Rd *BLOX/PEL* WS3 .... 39 J6
HLYWD B47 .... 145 L7
SCFLD/BOLD B73 .... 72 C4
SMTHWK B67 .... 105 K1
SPARK B11 .... 126 A2
Oakwoods *CNCK/NC* WS11 .... 16 A5
Oakwood St *WBROM* B70 ...... 68 F8
Oakworth CI *COVE* CV2 .... 135 K5
Oasthouse CI *BRGRVE* B60 .... 185 H7
KGSWFD DY6 .... 82 E6
Oaston Rd *CBROM* B36 .... 92 B5
NUN CV11 .... 99 H1
Oatfield CI *BNTWD* WS7 .... 26 C1
Oatlands Wk
ALE/KHTH/YWD B14 .... 145 G3
Oatlands Wy
DUNHL/THL/PER WV6 .... 48 B2
Oatmill CI *DARL/WED* WS10 ... 52 C8
Oban Dr *NUNW/HART* CV10 ... 98 E3
Oban Rd *COVN* CV6 .... 116 D8
HIA/OLT B92 .... 127 K4
Oberon CI *NUN* CV11 .... 99 L4
RBRY B45 .... 142 E3
RUGBYS/DCH CV22 .... 183 H7
Oberon Dr *SHLY* B90 .... 146 E4
Occupation Rd *BRWNH* WS8 ... 40 E1
COVS CV3 .... 155 G2
Occupation St *DUDN* DY1 ...... 84 E3
Ocean Dr *DARL/WED* WS10 ... 68 B4
Ockam CI *NFLD/LBR* B31 ..... 144 A3
O'connor Dr *TPTN/OCK* DY4 ... 68 A4
Ocker Hill Rd *TPTN/OCK* DY4 ... 67 M4
Oddlcombe Cft *COVS* CV3 ... 154 D8
Oddingley Rd *NFLD/LBR* B31 ... 144 A3
Odell Crs *BLOX/PEL* WS3 .... 39 G5

Odell Pl *DIG/EDG* B5 .... 107 G8
Odell Rd *BLOX/PEL* WS3 .... 38 F6
Odensil Gn *HIA/OLT* B92 .... 127 M3
Odiham Cl *CRTAM* B79 .... 32 A5
Odin Cl *HEDN* WS12 .... 12 E8
Offadrive *CRTAM* B79 .... 31 M8
Offa Dr *KNWTH* CV8 .... 176 E8
Offa Rd *RLSS* CV31 .... 200 F7
Offa's Dr *DUNHL/THL/PER* WV6 ... 34 C8
Offa St *CRTAM* B79 .... 31 M8
Offchurch La *RLSS* CV31 .... 201 K7
Offchurch Rd *RLSN* CV32 .... 201 J1
Offenham Cl *REDE* B98 .... 188 F7
Offenham Covert
   HWK/WKHTH B38 .... 144 C5 ⊡
Offini Cl *SPARK* B11 .... 87 K3
Offmoor Rd *RIDG/WDGT* B32 .... 122 F5
Offmore Farm Cl *KIDD* DY10 ... 138 A7
Offmore La *KIDD* DY10 .... 137 L7
Offwell Rd *REDE* B98 .... 197 H4 ⊡
Ogbury Cl *ALE/KHTH/YWD* B14 .. 145 G3
Ogley Crs *BRWNH* WS8 .... 26 E6
Ogley Dr *MGN/WHC* B75 .... 57 L8
Ogley Hay Rd *BNTWD* WS7 ..... 18 E3
   BRWNH WS8 .... 26 E3
Ogley Rd *BRWNH* WS8 .... 26 E6
O'keeffe Cl *SPARK* B11 .... 107 M7 ⊡
Okehampton Rd *COVS* CV3 ..... 154 C8
Okement Dr *WNSFLD* WV11 ..... 36 F8
Okement Gv *RRUGBY* CV23 ..... 158 F8 ⊡
Oken Rd *WWCK* CV34 .... 199 H5 ⊡
Olaf Pl *COVE* CV2 .... 135 L6
Old Abbey Gdns *HRBN* B17 .... 124 B1 ⊡
Old Acre La *WALM/CURD* B76 .... 73 H7
Old Acre Dr *HDSW* B21 .... 88 C6
Oldacre Rd *LGLYGN/QTN* B68 .. 104 E6
Oldany Wy *NUNW/HART* CV10 ... 98 D3
Old Bank Rd *NFLD/LBR* B31 .... 143 M3
Old Barn Rd *BVILLE* B30 .... 124 A6
   STRBR DY8 .... 101 L4
Old Beeches *ERDW/GRVHL* B23 .. 72 A5
Old Bell Rd *ERDW/GRVHL* B23 .. 72 F7
Oldberrow Cl *SHLY* B90 .... 147 L7 ⊡
Old Birchills *WSLW* WS2 .... 53 G2
Old Birmingham Rd *ALVE* B48 .. 167 L5
   BRGRVE B60 .... 166 A6
Old Bridge St *LOZ/NWT* B19 .... 88 F7
Old Bridge Wk
   BLKHTH/ROWR B65 .... 85 K8
Old Bromford La *CBROM* B36 .... 90 F7
Old Brookside *STETCH* B33 .... 109 J3
Old Budbrooke Rd
   RWWCK/WEL CV35 .... 198 D7
Oldbury Cl *REDE* B98 .... 188 F7
Oldbury Ring Wy *OLDBY* B69 .. 86 D5
Oldbury Rd *BLKHTH/ROWR* B65 .. 104 B3
   NUNW/HART CV10 .... 79 G4
   OLDBY B69 .... 87 G6
   WBROM B70 .... 86 D2
Oldbury Road Industrial Est
   WBROM B70 .... 86 D3
Oldbury St *DARL/WED* WS10 .... 68 F2
Oldbury Vw *NUNW/HART* CV10 .. 79 M4
Old Bush St *BRLYHL* DY5 .... 102 C2 ⊡
Old Camp Hl *SPARK* B11 .... 7 M9
Old Cannock Rd *WOLVN* WV10 .. 23 K4
Old Castle Gv *BRWNH* WS8 .... 26 D3 ⊡
Old Chapel Rd *SMTHWKW* B67 .. 105 K2
Old Chester Rd South
   KIDD DY10 .... 161 K3 ⊡
Old Church Gn *STETCH* B33 .... 109 J3
Old Church Rd *COVN* CV6 ..... 134 D4
   CSHL/WTROR B46 .... 92 F2
   HRBN B17 .... 105 M8
Old Crest Av *REDE* B98 .... 196 C2
Old Croft La *CBROM* B36 .... 91 M6
Old Cross St *TPTN/OCK* DY4 .. 67 J8 ⊡
Old Crown Cl *RIDG/WDGT* B32 .. 122 F4
Old Crown Ms *COVE* CV2 .... 117 H8
Old Damson La *HIA/OLT* B92 .. 128 D3
Old Dickens Heath Rd
   SHLY B90 .... 146 E8
Olde Hall Rd *WOLVN* WV10 .... 23 G6
Old End La *BILS/COS* WV14 .... 67 G6
Old Fallings Crs *WOLVN* WV10 .. 36 D7
Old Fallings La *WOLVN* WV10 .. 36 D7
Old Fallow Av *CNCK/NC* WS11 .. 16 C2
Old Fallow Rd *CNCK/NC* WS11 .. 16 C2
Old Falls Cl *GTWY* WS6 .... 24 B2 ⊡
Old Farm Gv
   ALE/KHTH/YWD B14 .... 126 A8
Old Farm La *CSHL/WTROR* B46 .. 94 E1
Old Farm Meadow
   BDMR/CCFT WV3 .... 49 G5
Old Farm Rd *ATHST* CV9 .... 63 K7
   STETCH B33 .... 109 J1
Oldfield Dr *STRBR* DY8 .... 119 L2 ⊡
Oldfield Rd *BTHH/HG* B12 .... 107 L7
   BILS/COS WV14 .... 66 E5
   COVW CV5 .... 153 H2
Oldfields *CDYHTH* B64 .... 103 H5
   HAG/WOL DY9 .... 119 M7
Old Fordrove *WALM/CURD* B76 .. 73 H2
Old Forest Wy *BKDE/SHDE* B34 .. 91 M7
Old Forge Dr *REDE* B98 .... 196 F4
Old Grange Rd *SPARK* B11 .... 126 A1
Old Green La *DOR/KN* B93 .... 173 M3
Old Grove Gdns *HAG/WOL* DY9 .. 120 B2
Old Hall Cl *STRBR* DY8 .... 101 L6
Old Hall La *ALDR* WS9 .... 54 F8
   CNCK/NC WS11 .... 16 F6
Old Hall St *WOLV* WV1 .... 3 G7
Oldham Av *COVE* CV2 .... 155 H1
Old Ham La *HAG/WOL* DY9 .... 120 A3
Old Hampton La *WNSFLD* WV11 .. 37 G3
Old Hawne La *HALE* B63 .... 103 L8
Old Heath Crs *WOLV* WV1 .... 50 E4 ⊡
Old Heath Rd *WOLV* WV1 ..... 50 E3
Old Hedging La
   TAM/AM/WIL B77 .... 46 B8 ⊡
Old Hednesford Rd
   CNCK/NC WS11 .... 16 F2
   HEDN WS12 .... 16 F2
Old HI *DUNHL/THL/PER* WV6 .. 35 H8
Old Hinckley Rd *NUN* CV11 .... 81 H8
Old Hobicus La
   LGLYGN/QTN B68 .... 86 F8 ⊡

Old Holly La *ATHST* CV9 .... 63 G3
Old Horns Crs *PBAR/PBCH* B42 ... 71 J3 ⊡
Oldhouse Farm Cl
   HLGN/YWD B28 .... 126 D7 ⊡
Old House La
   RCOVN/BALC/EX CV7 .... 114 E6
   RMSLY B62 .... 141 M4
Oldington Gv *SOLH* B91 .... 147 L5
Oldington La *STRPT* DY13 .... 160 F5
Old Kingsbury Rd
   WALM/CURD B76 .... 74 A8
Oldknow Rd *SMHTH* B10 .... 108 C7
Old Landywood La
   WNSFLD WV11 .... 24 A7
Old La *ALVE* B48 .... 189 H1
   BLOX/PEL WS3 .... 39 G6
   DUNHL/THL/PER WV6 .... 48 D3
   WOLVN WV10 .... 23 G6
Old Leicester Rd
   RUGBYN/HIL CV21 .... 159 L6
Old Level Wy *DUDS* DY2 .... 103 H1 ⊡
Old Lime Gdns
   HWK/WKHTH B38 .... 144 C5 ⊡
Old Lindens Cl *FOAKS/STRLY* B74 .. 55 J6
Old Lode La *HIA/OLT* B92 ..... 127 M3
Old London Rd *LICHS* WS14..... 29 H4
Old Manor Cl *POL/KGSB/FAZ* B78 .. 45 J8
Old Meadow Rd
   NFLD/LBR B31 .... 144 A6 ⊡
Old Meeting Rd *BILS/COS* WV14.. 67 G5
Old Meeting St *MHTH/SAND* B71 .. 68 F8
Old Mill Av *TLHL/CAN* CV4 ..... 153 M8
Old Mill Br *WWCK* CV34 .... 199 K7
Old Mill Cl *SHLY* B90 .... 146 B3
Old Mill Gdns *RUSH/SHEL* WS4 .. 40 A3
Old Mill Gv
   BFLD/HDSWWD B20 .... 89 G3 ⊡
Old Mill Rd *CSHL/WTROR* B46 .. 93 K6
Old Milverton La *RLSN* CV32 .. 200 C1
Old Milverton Rd *RLSN* CV32 .. 200 A2
Old Moat Dr *NFLD/LBR* B31.... 143 M2
Old Moat Wy *WASH/WDE* B8 .. 90 F7
Oldnall Cl *HAG/WOL* DY9 ..... 120 D1
Oldnall Rd *HAG/WOL* DY9 ..... 120 E1
   KIDD DY10 .... 161 K1
Oak Cl *ALDR* WS9 .... 40 F5
Old Oak Rd *HWK/WKHTH* B38 .. 144 E3
Old Oscott HI *KGSTG* B44....... 71 J4
Old Oscott La *KGSTG* B44....... 71 J5
Old Pk *SLYOAK* B29 .... 123 L8
Old Park Farm La *OLDBY* B69 .. 86 E8
Old Park Rd *DARL/WED* WS10... 52 C7
   DUDN DY1 .... 84 D1
   HEDN WS12 .... 13 L8
Old Park Wk *LOZ/NWT* B19 .... 89 J6
Old Penkridge Rd
   CNCK/NC WS11 .... 16 A3
Old Pleck Rd *WSLW* WS2 ..... 4 A6
Old Port Cl *TPTN/OCK* DY4 .... 85 M3 ⊡
Old Portway *HWK/WKHTH* B38 .. 144 C6
Old Postway *LOZ/NWT* B19 .. 89 H6 ⊡
Old Quarry Cl *RBRY* B45 .... 142 D5 ⊡
Old Quarry Dr *SEDG* DY3 .... 66 B8
Old Rectory Gdns *ALDR* WS9 .. 41 G7
Old Rectory La *ALVE* B48 .... 167 M6
Old Rd *RCOVN/BALC/EX* CV7 .. 131 J4
Old School Cl *WLNHL* WV13 .. 51 L3 ⊡
Old School Dr
   BLKHTH/ROWR B65 .... 104 A2 ⊡
Old School Ms *RLSN* CV32 .... 200 F2 ⊡
Old Scott Cl *STETCH* B33 .... 110 A3
Old Smithy Pl *WSNGN* B18 .... 88 E8 ⊡
Old Snow HI *CBHAMNW* B3..... 6 F2
Old Stafford Rd *WOLVN* WV10 .. 22 A1
Old Station Rd *BRGRVE* B60 .. 185 L5
   HIA/OLT B92 .... 129 K3
   STETCH B33 .... 109 H1
Old Stone Cl *RBRY* B45 .... 142 D4
Old Stowheath La
   WLNHL WV13 .... 51 G4 ⊡
Old Town Cl
   HWK/WKHTH B38 .... 144 D3 ⊡
Old Town La *BLOX/PEL* WS3 .... 39 K2
Old Vicarage Cl *BLOX/PEL* WS3 .. 39 L3
Old Walsall Rd *GTB/HAM* B43 .... 70 D5
Old Warstone La *WNSFLD* WV11 .. 23 M5
Old Warwick Ct *HIA/OLT* B92 .. 127 J4 ⊡
Old Warwick Rd *HIA/OLT* B92 .. 127 J4 ⊡
   HOCK/TIA B94 .... 172 B8
   RLSS CV31 .... 200 C6
Oldway Dr *SOLH* B91 .... 148 C3
Old Well Cl *RUSH/SHEL* WS4 .. 39 M6
Old Wharf Rd *STRBR* DY8 .... 101 K7
Oldwich La East *KNWTH* CV8 .. 174 C4
Oldwich La West *DOR/KN* B93 .. 174 A5
Old Winnings Rd
   RCOVN/BALC/EX CV7 .... 115 K6
Olga Dr *TPTN/OCK* DY4 .... 67 M4
Olinthus Av *WNSFLD* WV11 .... 37 J4
Olive Av *COVE* CV2 .... 135 H8
   ETTPK/GDPK/PENN WV4 .... 50 C8 ⊡
Olive Dr *RMSLY* B62 .... 104 A5 ⊡
Olive Hill Rd *RMSLY* B62 .... 104 B5
Olive La *RMSLY* B62 .... 104 A5
Oliver Cl *DUDS* DY2 .... 85 J5 ⊡
Oliver Ct *BLKHTH/ROWR* B65 .. 103 M3 ⊡
Olivers Crs *BILS/COS* WV14 .... 67 J3
Oliver Rd *ERDW/GRVHL* B23 .... 72 D7
   LDYWD/EDGR B16 .... 106 D3
   SMTHWK B66 .... 106 A2
Oliver St *COVN* CV6 .... 134 D7
   RUGBYN/HIL CV21 .... 183 K2
   VAUX/NECH B7 .... 89 L8
Olivier Wy *RCOVN/BALC/EX* CV7.. 135 M5
Ollerton Rd
   LGN/SDN/BHAMAIR B26 .... 109 K6
Ollison Dr *FOAKS/STRLY* B74.... 55 K3
Olliver Cl *RIDG/WDGT* B32 .... 122 D3
Olorenshaw Rd
   LGN/SDN/BHAMAIR B26 .... 110 B8
Olton Bvd East *ACGN* B27 .... 127 C3
Olton Bvd West *SPARK* B11 .... 126 D2
Olton Cft *ACGN* B27 .... 127 H2
Olton Pl *NUNW/HART* CV10 .... 98 D1
Olton Pl *SHLY* B90 .... 126 F8
Olton Whf *HIA/OLT* B92 .... 127 J3
Olympus Av *RLSS* CV31 .... 200 B7

Olympus Cl *COVW* CV5 ..... 131 M5
Olympus Dr *TPTN/OCK* DY4 .. 68 B7
Omar Rd *COVE* CV2 .... 155 H3
Ombersley Cl *OLDBY* B69 .... 86 B8 ⊡
   REDE B98 .... 196 F6
Ombersley Rd *BTHH/HG* B12 .. 107 L7
   HALE B63 .... 121 K3 ⊡
Onibury Rd *HDSW* B21 .... 88 B4
Onley Ter *TLHL/CAN* CV4 .... 153 G6
Onslow Crs *HIA/OLT* B92 .... 127 L4
Onslow Cft *RLSN* CV32 .... 200 D3
Onslow Rd *SPARK* B11 .... 126 E1
Ontario Cl *HWK/WKHTH* B38 .. 144 E5
Oozells St *CBHAMW* B1 .... 6 C6
Open Field Cl *NFLD/LBR* B31.. 143 M3
Openfield Cft *CSHL/WTROR* B46 .. 93 G3
The Orangery *HAG/WOL* DY9 .. 120 B6
Oratory Dr *COVS* CV3 .... 155 G7 ⊡
Orchard Av *CNCK/NC* WS11 .... 16 A3
   SOLH B91 .... 128 B8
Orchard Cl *ATHST* CV9 .... 63 M5
   ATHST CV9 .... 77 G1
   BLKHTH/ROWR B65 .... 103 L2
   CSHL/WTROR B46 .... 93 K6 ⊡
   GTWY WS6 .... 24 C2 ⊡
   HAG/WOL DY9 .... 139 M1
   HALE B63 .... 103 G7 ⊡
   HDSW B21 .... 88 D4
   LICH WS13 .... 20 C4
   NUNW/HART CV10 .... 79 L6
   PENK ST19 .... 10 D4
   POL/KGSB/FAZ B78 .... 45 J7
   RUSH/SHEL WS4 .... 40 A7 ⊡
   TAM/AM/WIL B77 .... 46 A8
   WALM/CURD B76 .... 74 F7
   WLNHL WV13 .... 51 M4
Orchard Ct *ATHST* CV9 .... 63 H6
   BDMR/CCFT WV3 .... 48 F6
   COVS CV3 .... 155 K4
   KGSWFD DY6 .... 83 H7
Orchard Crs *COVS* CV3 .... 8 C9
   PENK ST19 .... 10 D4
Orchard Cft *RBRY* B45 .... 167 H5
Orchard Dr *COVW* CV5 .... 152 A1
   NFLD/LBR B31 .... 143 K6
Orchard Gv *ALDR* WS9 .... 54 F1
   ETTPK/GDPK/PENN WV4 .... 65 L1
   FOAKS/STRLY B74 .... 56 D2
   SEDG DY3 .... 83 M2
Orchard La *CDSL* WV8 .... 34 F2
   HAG/WOL DY9 .... 102 C7
   WOLVN WV10 .... 23 G2
Orchard Pl *STUD* B80 .... 197 K5
Orchard Ri *ATHST* CV9 .... 62 A3 ⊡
   LGN/SDN/BHAMAIR B26 .... 109 K6
Orchard Rd *BRGRVW* B61 .... 185 K1
   DSYBK/YTR WS5 .... 69 M2
   DUDS DY2 .... 103 G3
   ERDE/BCHGN B24 .... 72 E8
   HOCK/TIA B94 .... 172 A7
   WLNHL WV13 .... 51 M4
   WNSFLD WV11 .... 37 J4
The Orchards *FOAKS/STRLY* B74 .. 56 E4
   HLYWD B47 .... 145 L6
   KIDDW DY11 .... 136 F4
   SHLY B90 .... 171 H1 ⊡
Orchard St *BDWTH* CV12 .... 98 F8
   BRLYHL DY5 .... 102 B1
   CRTAM B79 .... 31 M8
   KIDD DY10 .... 137 J7
   NUN CV11 .... 99 H1 ⊡
   OLDBY B69 .... 85 K3 ⊡
   REDW B97 .... 196 C2
   TAM/AM/WIL B77 .... 46 A2
The Orchard *ATHST* CV9 .... 62 A6 ⊡
   BILS/COS WV14 .... 51 J8 ⊡
   BLOX/PEL WS3 .... 39 H3
   BRGRVW B61 .... 185 J1
   CHWD/FDBR/MGN B37 .... 110 D5
   DUNHL/THL/PER WV6 .... 35 J7
Orchard Wy *ACGN* B27 .... 126 F1
   GTB/HAM B43 .... 70 D4
   HLYWD B47 .... 145 L5
   KNWTH CV8 .... 179 G7
   NUNW/HART CV10 .... 80 A7
   RRUGBY CV23 .... 180 D7
   RUGBYS/DCH CV22 .... 183 H5
Orcheston Wk
   ALE/KHTH/YWD B14 .... 145 H4
Orchid Cl *SMTHWK* B66 .... 87 H6
Orchid Dr *LOZ/NWT* B19 .... 89 H7 ⊡
Ordnance Rd *COVN* CV6 .... 134 C8 ⊡
Oregon Cl *KGSWFD* DY6 .... 83 K7
Oregon Dr *SHHTH* WV12 ..... 38 C6 ⊡
Oregon Gdns *BNTWD* WS7 .... 18 D5
Orford Gv *HDSW* B21 .... 88 A6
Orford Ri *NUNW/HART* CV10 .. 97 J1
Oriel Cl *CNCK/NC* WS11 .... 16 C5
   DUDN DY1 .... 84 C1
Oriel Dr *WOLVN* WV10 .... 36 B2
Oriole Gv *KIDD* DY10 .... 161 M3
Orion Cl *GTWY* WS6 .... 24 D4
   WASH/WDE B8 .... 108 F1 ⊡
Orion Crs *COVE* CV2 .... 135 J3
Orion Wy *CNCK/NC* WS11 .... 12 D8
Orkney Av *BKDE/SHDE* B34 .. 91 K7
Orkney Cl *NUNW/HART* CV10 .. 98 E3
Orkney Cft *CBROM* B36 .... 92 F6
Orkney Dr *TAM/AM/WIL* B77 .. 46 D6
Orlando Cl
   RUGBYS/DCH CV22 .... 183 H7 ⊡
   WSL WS1 .... 4 F5
Orlescote Rd *TLHL/CAN* CV4 .. 153 H7
Ormande Cl *HALE* B63 .... 102 F6
Orme Cl *STRBR* DY8 .... 101 L5
Ormes La *DUNHL/THL/PER* WV6.. 49 G2
Ormond Pl *BILS/COS* WV14 .... 51 J7
Ormond Rd *RBRY* B45 .... 142 C4
Ormsby Gv *ACGN* B27 .... 126 F6 ⊡
Ormscliffe Rd *RBRY* B45 .... 142 F7
Orphanage Rd
   CSCFLD/WYGN B72 .... 73 G7
   ERDE/BCHGN B24 .... 72 E8 ⊡
Orpington Dr *COVN* CV6 .... 134 B1
Orpington Rd *KGSTG* B44 .... 71 J2 ⊡
Orpwood Rd *STETCH* B33 .... 109 L3

Orson Leys *RUGBYS/DCH* CV22 .. 183 K6
Orton Av *WALM/CURD* B76 .... 73 K7
Orton Cl *CSHL/WTROR* B46 .... 92 E2
Orton Gv
   ETTPK/GDPK/PENN WV4 .... 65 H1
Orton La
   ETTPK/GDPK/PENN WV4 .... 64 D2
Orton Rd *COVN* CV6 .... 134 A2
Orton Wy *CVALE* B35 .... 91 L3
Orwell Cl *NUNW/HART* CV10 .. 79 L8
   STRBR DY8 .... 119 H1
   WNSFLD WV11 .... 37 K8
Orwell Dr *HHTH/SAND* B71 .... 69 H7
   NFLD/LBR B31 .... 143 M5
Orwell Pas *DIG/EDG* B5 .... 7 H6
Orwell Rd *COV* CV1 .... 9 L7
   WSL WS1 .... 5 L5
Osbaston Cl *COVW* CV5 .... 152 C1
Osberton Dr *DUDN* DY1 .... 84 D3
Osborne Cl *ERDW/GRVHL* B23 .. 72 D8
   ETTPK/GDPK/PENN WV4 .... 49 K8
   HDSW B21 .... 88 D5
   WBROM B70 .... 87 G2 ⊡
Osborn Rd *SPARK* B11 .... 108 A7
Osbourne Cft *SHLY* B90 .... 147 H8 ⊡
Oscott Rd *PBAR/PBCH* B42 .... 89 J2
Oscott School La *KGSTG* B44 .. 71 J3
Osier Gv *ERDW/GRVHL* B23 .. 71 M7
Osier Pl *WOLV* WV1 .... 3 M4
Osier St *WOLV* WV1 .... 3 M4
Osler St *LDYWD/EDGR* B16 .. 106 D3
Oslo Gdns *COVE* CV2 .... 135 L6
Osmaston Rd *HRBN* B17 .... 123 L2
   STRBR DY8 .... 119 J3
Osmington Gv *HALE* B63 .... 103 H7 ⊡
Osprey *TAM/AM/WIL* B77 .... 46 E7
Osprey Cl *COVE* CV2 .... 135 M7
   NUN CV11 .... 99 M5 ⊡
Osprey Dr *DUDN* DY1 .... 84 D4
Osprey Gv *HEDN* WS12 .... 17 G4
Osprey Park Dr *KIDD* DY10 .. 161 M2
Osprey Rd *ERDW/GRVHL* B23 .. 72 A7
   HIA/OLT B92 .... 127 H3
Ostler Cl *KGSWFD* DY6 .... 82 F6
Oswald Rd *RLSN* CV32 .... 200 B4
Oswald St *REDW* B97 .... 196 C2
Oswald Wy
   RUGBYS/DCH CV22 .... 183 H2 ⊡
Oswestry Cl *REDW* B97 .... 196 A6
Oswin Gv *COVE* CV2 .... 155 G1
Oswin Pl *BLOX/PEL* WS3 .... 39 K8
Oswin Rd *BLOX/PEL* WS3 .... 39 K8
Othello Cl *RUGBYS/DCH* CV22 .. 183 H8
Other Rd *REDE* B98 .... 196 C1 ⊡
Otherton Cl *PENK* ST19 .... 10 C5
Otherton La *PENK* ST19 .... 10 D7
Otley Gv *BORD* B9 .... 109 G2
Otterburn Cl *HEDN* WS12 .... 17 K8
Otter Cft *BKDE/SHDE* B34 .... 92 B8
Otterstone Cl *SEDG* DY3 .... 66 F3
Ottery *TAM/AM/WIL* B77 .... 46 E8
Oughton Rd *BHTH/HG* B12 .. 107 L6 ⊡
Oulton Cl *KIDDW* DY11 .... 137 H5
Oundle Rd *KGSTG* B44 .... 71 K6
Ounsdale Crs *WMBN* WV5 .... 64 E6
Ounsdale Dr *DUDS* DY2 .... 103 G1
Ounsdale Rd *WMBN* WV5 .... 64 D6
Ounty John La *STRBR* DY8 .. 119 L5
Ousterne La
   RCOVN/BALC/EX CV7 .... 114 B2
Outermarch Rd *COVN* CV6 .. 134 A6
Outmore Rd *STETCH* B33 .... 109 M4
Outwood Cl *REDE* B98 .... 196 C6 ⊡
Outwoods Cl *ATHST* CV9 .... 63 G6
Oval Rd *ERDE/BCHGN* B24 .... 90 C4
   TPTN/OCK DY4 .... 67 K6
The Oval *DARL/WED* WS10 .... 68 D1
   DUDN DY1 .... 84 C5 ⊡
   SMTHWKW B67 .... 105 H3
Overberry Cl *COVE* CV2 .... 135 H3 ⊡
Overbrook Cl *SEDG* DY3 .... 84 A3 ⊡
Over Brunton Cl *NFLD/LBR* B31 .. 143 M3
Overbury Cl *NFLD/LBR* B31.... 144 A2
   RMSLY B62 .... 121 M3
Overbury Rd *NFLD/LBR* B31.... 144 A1
Overdale Av *WALM/CURD* B76 .. 73 K8
Overdale Cl *SHHTH* WV12 .... 52 A2
Overdale Dr *WSLW* WS2 .... 52 A2
Overdale Rd *COVW* CV5 .... 153 G2
   RIDG/WDGT B32 .... 105 J8
Overell Gv *RLSN* CV32 .... 200 A3
Overend Rd *HALE* B63 .... 103 H7
Overend St *WBROM* B70 .... 87 H2
Overfield Dr
   ETTPK/GDPK/PENN WV4 .... 66 E2
Overfield Rd *DUDN* DY1 .... 84 C5
   RIDG/WDGT B32 .... 123 J4
Over Green Dr
   CHWD/FDBR/MGN B37 .... 92 D8
Overhill Rd *BNTWD* WS7 .... 18 D3
Overlea Av *ACGN* B27 .... 126 F2
Over Mill Dr *SLYOAK* B29 .... 124 F3 ⊡
Overmoor Cl *LOZ/NWT* B19 .. 89 G6 ⊡
Over Pool Rd *WASH/WDE* B8 .. 90 E7
Overseal Rd *WNSFLD* WV11 .. 37 J3
Overslade Crs *COVN* CV6 .... 133 J6
Overslade La
   RUGBYS/DCH CV22 .... 183 H6
Overslade Manor Dr
   RUGBYS/DCH CV22 .... 183 K5 ⊡
Overslade Rd *SOLH* B91 .... 147 K3
Oversley Cl *WALM/CURD* B76 .. 73 L7
Over St *COVN* CV6 .... 134 C7
Overton Cl *HLGN/YWD* B28 .... 126 D7
Overton Dr *CSHL/WTROR* B46 .. 93 G3 ⊡
Overton Gv *ACGN* B27 .... 127 G5 ⊡
Overton La *BNTWD* WS7 .... 27 G1
Overton Pl *HHTH/SAND* B71 .. 69 H7 ⊡
   ACGN B27 .... 126 F5
Overtons Cl *RLSS* CV31 .... 201 K8 ⊡
Overwood Cft
   WASH/WDE B8 .... 108 C2 ⊡

Overwoods Rd
   TAM/AM/WIL B77 .... 46 D8
Owenford Rd *COVN* CV6 .... 134 A6
Owen Pl *BILS/COS* WV14 .... 51 H9
Owen Rd *BDMR/CCFT* WV3 .... 2 B8
   BILS/COS WV14 .... 51 H6
   WLNHL WV13 .... 51 M4
Owens Cft *HWK/WKHTH* B38 .. 144 E4
Owen St *ATHST* CV9 .... 63 H5
   DARL/WED WS10 .... 52 B6
   DUDS DY2 .... 85 J5
   TPTN/OCK DY4 .... 67 J8
Owens Wy *CDYHTH* B64 .... 103 L4
Ownall Rd *BKDE/SHDE* B34 .. 92 A7
Oxbarn Av *BDMR/CCFT* WV3 .. 49 J6
Oxbridge Wy *CRTAM* B79 .... 31 H7
Ox Cl *COVE* CV2 .... 134 E7
Oxendon Wy *COVS* CV3 .... 155 J5
Oxenton Cft *HALE* B63 .... 121 H3 ⊡
Oxford Canal Pth
   RUGBYN/HIL CV21 .... 159 M6
Oxford Canal Wk
   RRUGBY CV23 .... 157 L3
Oxford Cl *GTWY* WS6 .... 24 D3
   NUN CV11 .... 81 K5
   WASH/WDE B8 .... 90 F8
Oxford Dr *ACGN* B27 .... 127 H1
   STRBR DY8 .... 119 K1
Oxford Gn *CNCK/NC* WS11 .... 16 D5
Oxford Pl *RLSN* CV32 .... 200 E4 ⊡
Oxford Rd *ACGN* B27 .... 127 G2
   CNCK/NC WS11 .... 16 D5
   ERDW/GRVHL B23 .... 90 D1
   KNWTH CV8 .... 179 K4
   MOS/BIL B13 .... 125 J3
   RRUGBY CV23 .... 180 A8
   SMTHWK B66 .... 87 L5
   WBROM B70 .... 86 F2
Oxford Rw *RLSN* CV32 .... 200 D4
Oxford St *BILS/COS* WV14 .... 51 J8
   BVILLE B30 .... 124 E6
   COV CV1 .... 9 K4
   DARL/WED WS10 .... 68 F3
   DIG/EDG B5 .... 7 J7
   DUDN DY1 .... 84 F4 ⊡
   KIDD DY10 .... 137 J8
   RLSN CV32 .... 200 D4
   WOLV WV1 .... 3 H6
   WSLW WS2 .... 4 A7
Oxhayes Cl
   RCOVN/BALC/EX CV7 .... 151 G7
Oxhill Cl *REDE* B98 .... 197 J4 ⊡
Oxhill Rd *HDSW* B21 .... 88 A2
   SHLY B90 .... 146 A3
Ox Leasow *RIDG/WDGT* B32 .. 123 G3
Oxleasow Rd *REDE* B98 .... 189 J8
Oxley Av *WOLVN* WV10 .... 36 A7
Oxley Cl *DUDS* DY2 .... 102 F3
   GTWY WS6 .... 24 D4
Oxley Dr *COVS* CV3 .... 178 A2
Oxley Gv *SLYOAK* B29 .... 123 L5
Oxley La *WOLV* WV1 .... 2 F2
Oxley Links Rd *WOLVN* WV10 .. 35 M5
Oxley Moor Rd *COVEN* WV9 .. 35 L5
   WOLVN WV10 .... 35 L5
Ox Leys Rd *MGN/WHC* B75 .. 73 M1
Oxley St *WOLV* WV1 .... 2 F1
Oxlip Cl *DSYBK/YTR* WS5 .... 69 L2 ⊡
Oxpiece Dr *CBROM* B36 .... 91 H5 ⊡
Oxstall Cl *WALM/CURD* B76 .. 74 B8
Ox St *SEDG* DY3 .... 66 B8
Oxted Cl *WNSFLD* WV11 .... 37 K8 ⊡
Oxted Cft *ERDW/GRVHL* B23 .. 90 C2
Oxwood La *RMSLY* B62 .... 142 B1
Oxygen St *VAUX/NECH* B7 .... 7 J1

P

Pace Crs *BILS/COS* WV14 .... 67 K3
Pacific Av *DARL/WED* WS10 .... 68 B4
Packhorse La *HWK/WKHTH* B38.. 145 H7
   COVW CV5 .... 132 F7
Packington Av *BKDE/SHDE* B34.. 92 B4
Packington La
   CSHL/WTROR B46 .... 111 L1
   POL/KGSB/FAZ B78 .... 30 D8
   RCOVN/BALC/EX CV7 .... 112 F4
   RCOVN/BALC/EX CV7 .... 130 E2
Packington Pl *RLSS* CV31 .. 200 E6 ⊡
Packmore St *WWCK* CV34 .... 199 K5
Packwood Cl
   BFLD/HDSWWD B20 .... 88 E3 ⊡
   DOR/KN B93 .... 172 C1
   REDW B97 .... 195 K4
   RLSS CV31 .... 201 G8
   WLNHL WV13 .... 51 K5
Packwood Ct *SLYOAK* B29 .. 123 K4 ⊡
Packwood Dr *GTB/HAM* B43 .. 70 B4
Packwood Gn *COVW* CV5 .... 152 E2
Packwood La *HOCK/TIA* B94.... 172 E8
Packwood Rd *HOCK/TIA* B94 .. 172 E7
   LGN/SDN/BHAMAIR B26 .... 109 M5
   OLDBY B69 .... 85 L4
Padarn Cl *SEDG* DY3 .... 66 A4
Padbury *COVEN* WV9 .... 35 M2 ⊡
Padbury La *BNTWD* WS7 .... 19 H4
Paddeston Cl
   WASH/WDE B8 .... 108 B1 ⊡
Paddiford Pl
   NUNW/HART CV10 .... 98 B2 ⊡
Paddington Rd *HDSW* B21 .... 88 A4 ⊡
Paddock Dr *DOR/KN* B93 .... 172 E3
   LGN/SDN/BHAMAIR B26 .... 109 L6
Paddock La *ALDR* WS9 .... 40 E8
   GTWY WS6 .... 24 E2
   REDE B98 .... 196 C6
   WSL WS1 .... 5 H3
Paddocks Cl *KNWTH* CV8 .... 180 L2
   POL/KGSB/FAZ B78 .... 47 K4
Paddocks Gn *WSNGN* B18 .... 88 B3 ⊡
Paddock's Rd *HLYWD* B47 .... 145 K7
The Paddocks *BDWTH* CV12.... 117 M2
   RRUGBY CV23 .... 180 D8 ⊡
   WWCK CV34 .... 199 K6 ⊡
The Paddock *BILS/COS* WV14.. 67 H4
   BRGRVE B60 .... 185 H7

CDSL WV8 ... 34 E3
DUNHL/THL/PER WV6 ... 48 B1 5
HAG/WOL DY9 ... 119 M5
LICHS WS14 ... 21 G8
SEDG DY3 ... 66 C8 3
WMBN WV5 ... 64 C7 10
Paddock Vw
DUNHL/THL/PER WV6 ... 35 M8 2
Padgate Cl CVALE B35 ... 91 M2
Padgets La REDE B98 ... 197 H1
Padmore Ct RLSS CV31 ... 200 F7 1
Padstow TAM/AM/WIL B77 ... 32 D8 2
Padstow Cl NUN CV11 ... 81 K8
Padstow Rd TLHL/CAN CV4 ... 152 C5
Paganal Dr WBROM B70 ... 87 J4 2
Paganel Dr DUDN DY1 ... 85 G2
Paganel Rd SLYOAK B29 ... 123 L3
Page Rd TLHL/CAN CV4 ... 152 C6
Pages Cl MGN/WHC B75 ... 57 G8
Pages La GTB/HAM B43 ... 70 C3 3
Paget Cl BILS/COS WV14 ... 66 F5 3
BRGRVW B61 ... 185 J3
PENK ST19 ... 10 E6
Paget Ct COVN CV6 ... 134 F2
Paget Dr BNTWD WS7 ... 18 C4
Paget Rd DUNHL/THL/PER WV6 ... 49 K2
ERDE/BCHGN B24 ... 91 H2
Pagets Cha HEDN WS12 ... 18 A1
Paget's La KNWTH CV8 ... 179 H8
Paget St WOLV WV1 ... 2 D2 1
Pagham Cl COVEN WV9 ... 35 K3
Pagnell Gv MOS/BIL B13 ... 126 A7
Paignton Rd LDYWD/EDGR B16 ... 106 B2
Pailton Cl COVE CV2 ... 135 G3
Pailton Gv SLYOAK B29 ... 123 M4 1
Pailton Rd RRUGBY CV23 ... 158 F2
SHLY B90 ... 147 M4
Painswick Cl DSYBK/YTR WS5 ... 69 M2 4
REDE B98 ... 196 E7
Painswick Rd HLGN/YWD B28 ... 126 C6
Paint Cup Rw DUDS DY2 ... 103 G3
Painters Cft BILS/COS WV14 ... 67 J4
Pakefield Rd BVILLE B30 ... 144 F2
Pakenham Cl
WALM/CURD B76 ... 73 K5 4
Pakenham Rd EDG B15 ... 107 G6
Pake's Cft COVN CV6 ... 133 L8 3
Palace Cl BLKHTH/ROWR B65 ... 104 B1
Palace Dr SMTHWK B66 ... 87 G5
Palace Rd BORD B9 ... 108 C4
Palefield Rd SHLY B90 ... 147 K7
Pale La HRBN B17 ... 105 K5
Palermo Av COVS CV3 ... 154 C7
Pale St SEDG DY3 ... 66 C8
Palethorpe Rd TPTN/OCK DY4 ... 67 L5 3
Palfrey Rd STRBR DY8 ... 101 H6
Pallett Dr NUN CV11 ... 81 L6
Palmcourt Av HLGN/YWD B28 ... 126 C6
Palm Cft BRLYHL DY5 ... 102 A5
Palmer Cl WNSFLD WV11 ... 37 K4
Palmer La COV CV1 ... 8 F4
Palmers Cl CDSL WV8 ... 35 G3
SHLY B90 ... 126 F8
Palmers Gv CBROM B36 ... 91 J5 3
Palmers Rd REDE B98 ... 197 L1 1
Palmerston Dr OLDBY B69 ... 86 B3
Palmerston Rd COVW CV5 ... 153 K5
SPARK B11 ... 107 M7
Palmer St BORD B9 ... 7 M6
Palmers Wy CDSL WV8 ... 35 G4
Palm Tree Av COVE CV2 ... 135 G3
Palmvale Cft
LGN/SDN/BHAMAIR B26 ... 109 L7
Palomino Pl
LDYWD/EDGR B16 ... 106 D3 3
Pamela Rd NFLD/LBR B31 ... 143 L3
Pancras Cl COVE CV2 ... 135 J4
Pan Cft CBROM B36 ... 91 G6
Pandora Rd COVE CV2 ... 135 J6
Pangbourne Rd COVE CV2 ... 135 G5 3
Pangfield Pk COVW CV5 ... 153 G1
Pannel Cft LOZ/NWT B19 ... 89 H7
Panther Cft BKDE/SHDE B34 ... 92 B8
Pantolf Pl RUGBYN/HIL CV21 ... 159 J6
Papenham Gn TLHL/CAN CV4 ... 152 E5
Paper Mill Dr REDE B98 ... 188 F7
Paper Mill End PBAR/PBCH B42 ... 71 H7
Papworth Dr BRGRVW B61 ... 165 K8 3
Papyrus Wy CBROM B36 ... 91 K4
Parade CBHAMNW B3 ... 6 C4
RLSN CV32 ... 200 D4
The Parade BRWNH WS8 ... 26 C4
CDYHTH B64 ... 103 J5
DUDN DY1 ... 84 F3
KGSWFD DY6 ... 82 F6 4
NUN CV11 ... 99 G2
Paradise DUDS DY2 ... 85 H5
Paradise Circus Queensway
CBHAMNW B3 ... 6 D4
CBHAMW B1 ... 6 D5
Paradise La BLOX/PEL WS3 ... 39 K2
HLGN/YWD B28 ... 126 C7
WOLVN WV10 ... 22 B3 1
Paradise Rw BRGRVE B60 ... 185 K3 3
Paradise St CBHAM B2 ... 6 E5
COV CV1 ... 9 H7
WBROM B70 ... 87 H2
WWCK CV34 ... 199 K5
Paradise Wy
RCOVN/BALC/EX CV7 ... 135 L4
Paragon Wy
RCOVN/BALC/EX CV7 ... 116 F5
Parbrook Cl TLHL/CAN CV4 ... 152 C5
Parbury TAM/AM/WIL B77 ... 46 B8
The Parchments LICH WS13 ... 20 F4
Pardington Cl HIA/OLT B92 ... 128 C5 2
Pargeter Rd SMTHWKW B67 ... 105 K3
Pargeter St STRBR DY8 ... 119 K1
WSLW WS2 ... 4 A1
Par Gn NFLD/LBR B31 ... 144 A4
Parish Gdns HAG/WOL DY9 ... 119 M4 3
Parish Hl BRGRVW B61 ... 165 H4
Park Ap ERDW/GRVHL B23 ... 90 A3
Park Av BLKHTH/ROWR B65 ... 104 A2
BNTWD WS7 ... 18 F8
BVILLE B30 ... 124 E8
CNCK/NC WS11 ... 17 L8
COVN CV6 ... 134 A2
CSHL/WTROR B46 ... 93 K7 2
ETTPK/GDPK/PENN WV4 ... 50 A8
LGLYGN/QTN B68 ... 104 F2
NUN CV11 ... 99 J2
POL/KGSB/FAZ B78 ... 47 L5
SOLH B91 ... 148 B2
TPTN/OCK DY4 ... 67 J8 7
WLNHL WV13 ... 51 K3
WMBN WV5 ... 64 D8
WOLV WV1 ... 2 D4
WSNGN B18 ... 88 E6
Park Cl BRWNH WS8 ... 26 D5
DUDN DY1 ... 66 F6
ERDE/BCHGN B24 ... 73 H8
GTWY WS6 ... 24 C2
HIA/OLT B92 ... 128 B3 1
KNWTH CV8 ... 176 F8
OLDBY B69 ... 86 A6
Park Ct REDE B98 ... 196 E2
Park Crs HHTH/SAND B71 ... 87 H1
WOLV WV1 ... 2 D4
Park Cft HLYWD B47 ... 145 L8
Parkdale Av DARL/WED WS10 ... 68 E1
Parkdale Cl ERDE/BCHGN B24 ... 90 D3
Parkdale Dr NFLD/LBR B31 ... 143 L6
Park Dl East WOLV WV1 ... 2 A3
Parkdale Rd
LGN/SDN/BHAMAIR B26 ... 110 A7
Park Dl West WOLV WV1 ... 2 A3
Park Dr ETTPK/GDPK/PENN WV4 ... 50 A8
FOAKS/STRLY B74 ... 56 A1
FOAKS/STRLY B74 ... 56 D3 2
RLSS CV31 ... 200 C6
Park Edge HRBN B17 ... 106 A6
Park End LICHS WS14 ... 21 J6
Parkend RUGBYN/HIL CV21 ... 159 M6
Park End Dr RIDG/WDGT B32 ... 123 H4
Parker Pl STRPT DY13 ... 161 G6
Parker Rd WNSFLD WV11 ... 37 K4
Parkers Ct COVEN WV9 ... 22 A4
Parker St BLOX/PEL WS3 ... 38 E4
LDYWD/EDGR B16 ... 106 D4 3
Parkes Av CDSL WV8 ... 34 F3
Parkes Hall Rd DUDN DY1 ... 66 E8
Parkes La SEDG DY3 ... 66 E6
TPTN/OCK DY4 ... 67 K5
Parkes St BRLYHL DY5 ... 102 B2
SMTHWKW B67 ... 105 K1
WLNHL WV13 ... 51 M4
WWCK CV34 ... 199 H6
Parkeston Crs KGSTG B44 ... 71 M4
Park Farm Rd GTB/HAM B43 ... 70 F2
TAM/AM/WIL B77 ... 46 A4
Parkfield RIDG/WDGT B32 ... 122 D3
Parkfield Av TAM/AM/WIL B77 ... 46 A5
Parkfield Cl EDG B15 ... 107 G6 1
REDE B98 ... 188 F7
RMSLY B62 ... 104 E8
TAM/AM/WIL B77 ... 46 A5
Parkfield Colliery
ETTPK/GDPK/PENN WV4 ... 50 D8
Parkfield Crs BKHL/PFLD WV2 ... 50 C7
TAM/AM/WIL B77 ... 46 A4
Parkfield Dr CBROM B36 ... 92 A4
KNWTH CV8 ... 176 F8
Parkfield Gv BKHL/PFLD WV2 ... 50 C7
Parkfield Rd CSHL/WTROR B46 ... 93 K6
DUDS DY2 ... 85 H7
ETTPK/GDPK/PENN WV4 ... 50 B7 2
LGLYGN/QTN B68 ... 104 E2
RCOVN/BALC/EX CV7 ... 115 L7
RUGBYN/HIL CV21 ... 159 H7
STRBR DY8 ... 101 M8
WASH/WDE B8 ... 108 C2
Parkgate Rd COVN CV6 ... 133 M2
Park Gate Rd KIDD DY10 ... 137 M3
Park Gv CSHL/WTROR B46 ... 93 G2
Park Hall Cl DSYBK/YTR WS5 ... 54 A7
Park Hall Crs CBROM B36 ... 91 M5
Parkhall Cft CBROM B36 ... 92 A6
Park Hall Rd DSYBK/YTR WS5 ... 54 A7
ETTPK/GDPK/PENN WV4 ... 66 B1
Park Head Crs DUDS DY2 ... 84 F5 3
Park Head Rd DUDS DY2 ... 84 F5
Park Hl BLKHTH/ROWR B65 ... 103 M4
DARL/WED WS10 ... 69 G1
KNWTH CV8 ... 176 F8
MOS/BIL B13 ... 125 J1
Park Hill Dr BFLD/HDSWWD B20 ... 88 D1
Parkhill Dr COVW CV5 ... 132 D8
Park Hill La COVW CV5 ... 132 E7 2
Parkhill Rd BNTWD WS7 ... 18 E5
Park Hill Rd HRBN B17 ... 106 A7
SMTHWKW B67 ... 87 K8
Parkhill Rd WALM/CURD B76 ... 73 K7
Park Hill St DUDS DY2 ... 85 J5
Parkhouse Av WNSFLD WV11 ... 36 F7
Parkhouse Dr
ERDW/GRVHL B23 ... 71 L8 2
Parkhouse Gdns SEDG DY3 ... 84 A1 1
Parkinson Dr ATHST CV9 ... 63 J3
Parkland Av KIDDW DY11 ... 136 F8
Parkland Cl COVN CV6 ... 134 A2 1
Parklands Av RLSN CV32 ... 201 G1
Parklands Dr FOAKS/STRLY B74 ... 56 D5
Parklands Gdns WSL WS1 ... 5 K6
Parklands Rd BILS/COS WV14 ... 67 H2 2
DARL/WED WS10 ... 52 C8
WOLV WV1 ... 50 E4
The Parklands BDMR/CCFT WV3 ... 49 H3
ERDW/GRVHL B23 ... 72 B7
HAG/WOL DY9 ... 120 A2
Park La AST/WIT B6 ... 89 J6
CVALE B35 ... 73 M8
DARL/WED WS10 ... 52 D7
GTWY WS6 ... 24 D2
HALE B63 ... 102 E7
HDSW B21 ... 87 M3
KGSWFD DY6 ... 83 J6
KIDD DY10 ... 162 E3
KIDDW DY11 ... 137 H8
LGN/SDN/BHAMAIR B26 ... 129 G1
LICHS WS14 ... 28 E8
NUNW/HART CV10 ... 97 G8
NUNW/HART CV10 ... 97 K1
OLDBY B69 ... 86 E7
POL/KGSB/FAZ B78 ... 45 J3
RCOVN/BALC/EX CV7 ... 96 E8
RCOVN/BALC/EX CV7 ... 150 F3
WOLVN WV10 ... 36 C7
Park La East TPTN/OCK DY4 ... 85 M1
Park La West TPTN/OCK DY4 ... 85 J1
Park Lime Dr RUSH/SHEL WS4 ... 53 M1
Park Meadow Av
BILS/COS WV14 ... 51 G5
Park Ms SLYOAK B29 ... 123 M4 2
The Park Paling COVS CV3 ... 154 C6
Park Pl VAUX/NECH B7 ... 90 A6 5
Park Retreat SMTHWK B66 ... 105 M1
Park Rdg FOAKS/STRLY B74 ... 56 E6
Park Ridge Dr HALE B63 ... 102 F7
Park Ri BDMR/CCFT WV3 ... 49 J3
Park Rd AST/WIT B6 ... 89 L6
ATHST CV9 ... 61 M4
BDWTH CV12 ... 116 F3
BILS/COS WV14 ... 51 G8
BLOX/PEL WS3 ... 38 F4
BNTWD WS7 ... 18 C5
BNTWD WS7 ... 18 F8
BRLYHL DY5 ... 102 D5
CNCK/NC WS11 ... 16 B4
CNCK/NC WS11 ... 17 L8
COV CV1 ... 8 F7
CSHL/WTROR B46 ... 93 K7
DARL/WED WS10 ... 51 M7
DSYBK/YTR WS5 ... 54 B8
DUDN DY1 ... 66 F7
DUDS DY2 ... 85 G7
ERDW/GRVHL B23 ... 90 A3
HAG/WOL DY9 ... 120 A7
HALE B63 ... 102 F7
KNWTH CV8 ... 176 E7
MOS/BIL B13 ... 125 K1
OLDBY B69 ... 86 A5
POL/KGSB/FAZ B78 ... 47 M5
RLSN CV32 ... 200 D1
RUGBYN/HIL CV21 ... 183 L1
RUSH/SHEL WS4 ... 40 A8
SCFLD/BOLD B73 ... 56 F8
SEDG DY3 ... 83 M1
SMTHWKW B67 ... 105 K4
SPARK B11 ... 126 A2
STRBR DY8 ... 101 H8
TAM/AM/WIL B77 ... 46 A8
WLNHL WV13 ... 51 K2
WOLVN WV10 ... 23 H5
WSNGN B18 ... 88 D6
Park Rd East WOLV WV1 ... 2 C2
Park Rd South WSNGN B18 ... 88 F8
Park Rd West STRBR DY8 ... 101 G8
WOLV WV1 ... 2 B3
Parks Crs WNSFLD WV11 ... 37 L1
Parkside COV CV1 ... 9 G6
RIDG/WDGT B32 ... 123 G4
TAM/AM/WIL B77 ... 46 C4
Parkside Av WLNHL WV13 ... 51 J3
Parkside Cl DARL/WED WS10 ... 68 F2 2
Parkside La CNCK/NC WS11 ... 15 L5
Parkside Rd BFLD/HDSWWD B20 ... 70 C8
HALE B63 ... 103 H8
Parkside Wy
FOAKS/STRLY B74 ... 55 L5 2
NFLD/LBR B31 ... 143 G4
Park Sq CSHL/WTROR B46 ... 111 H5
Parkstone Av BRGRVW B61 ... 185 H5
Parkstone Cl RUSH/SHEL WS4 ... 40 A4
Parkstone Rd COVN CV6 ... 134 D3 2
Park St AST/WIT B6 ... 89 L6
BLKHTH/ROWR B65 ... 104 B4
CDYHTH B64 ... 103 H3
CNCK/NC WS11 ... 16 C7
COVN CV6 ... 134 C6 2
CRTAM B79 ... 31 L8
DARL/WED WS10 ... 52 A8
DIG/EDG B5 ... 7 H6 1
GTWY WS6 ... 24 C2
HAG/WOL DY9 ... 102 D8
KGSWFD DY6 ... 83 H7
KIDDW DY11 ... 137 H7
NUN CV11 ... 99 H2
OLDBY B69 ... 86 D7
RLSN CV32 ... 200 D5 4
STRBR DY8 ... 101 K5 3
STRBR DY8 ... 119 L1
TPTN/OCK DY4 ... 67 L8
WBROM B70 ... 87 H2 1
WSL WS1 ... 4 E2
Park St South BKHL/PFLD WV2 ... 50 A7
Park Ter DARL/WED WS10 ... 51 M7
HDSW B21 ... 88 C5
The Park REDW B97 ... 187 G6
Park Vw DARL/WED WS10 ... 52 A7
HOCK/TIA B94 ... 172 A7
SCFLD/BOLD B73 ... 56 E7
Park View Cl
RCOVN/BALC/EX CV7 ... 116 E6
Parkview Crs WSLW WS2 ... 52 E1
Parkview Dr WASH/WDE B8 ... 90 E7 2
Parkview Rd BILS/COS WV14 ... 51 G5
Park View Rd FOAKS/STRLY B74 ... 56 B2
HAG/WOL DY9 ... 120 D1
NFLD/LBR B31 ... 143 K2
Parkville Av HRBN B17 ... 123 M2
Parkville Cl COVN CV6 ... 134 A2
Parkville Hwy COVN CV6 ... 133 M2
Park Wk BRLYHL DY5 ... 102 D5
RUGBYN/HIL CV21 ... 183 L1
Park Wy RBRY B45 ... 142 F4
REDE B98 ... 188 E8
WNSFLD WV11 ... 37 L4
Parkway RCOVN/BALC/EX CV7 ... 135 M5
WASH/WDE B8 ... 90 E8
Parkway Rd DUDN DY1 ... 84 E3
The Parkway CDSL WV8 ... 34 B7
DUNHL/THL/PER WV6 ... 34 C8
RUSH/SHEL WS4 ... 40 A5
Parkwood Cl BRWNH WS8 ... 26 E8
Parkwood Cft
PBAR/PBCH B42 ... 70 F4 1
Parkwood Dr SCFLD/BOLD B73 ... 72 A3
Park Wood La TLHL/CAN CV4 ... 152 B6
Parkwood Rd BRGRVW B61 ... 185 J2
Parliament St AST/WIT B6 ... 89 K7
SMHTH B10 ... 108 A5
WBROM B70 ... 87 H4
Parlows End
HWK/WKHTH B38 ... 144 B6 3
Parmington Cl REDW B97 ... 195 M7
Parnell Cl RUGBYN/HIL CV21 ... 183 K2 3
Parr Cl RLSS CV31 ... 200 B7
Parrotts Gv COVE CV2 ... 117 H8
Parry Rd COVE CV2 ... 134 F6
KIDDW DY11 ... 160 F2
WNSFLD WV11 ... 37 L5
Parsonage Dr HALE B63 ... 102 E6 3
RBRY B45 ... 167 H1
Parsonage St
HHTH/SAND B71 ... 69 H7 2
OLDBY B69 ... 86 F7
Parson's Hl BVILLE B30 ... 144 F3
HWK/WKHTH B38 ... 144 F3
LGLYGN/QTN B68 ... 104 F4
Parson's Nook COVE CV2 ... 134 E8
Parsons Rd REDE B98 ... 196 C3
Parsons St DUDN DY1 ... 85 G4
Parson St TAM/AM/WIL B77 ... 46 C6
Partons Rd
ALE/KHTH/YWD B14 ... 125 H7
Partridge Av
DARL/WED WS10 ... 51 M7 1
Partridge Cl
CHWD/FDBR/MGN B37 ... 111 G2
HEDN WS12 ... 12 B6 1
Partridge Cft COVN CV6 ... 134 E4
LICH WS13 ... 21 G5
Partridge Gv KIDD DY10 ... 161 M3 2
Partridge La REDW B97 ... 195 L6
Partridge Ml BLOX/PEL WS3 ... 39 J2 1
Partridge Rd
LGN/SDN/BHAMAIR B26 ... 109 L4
STRBR DY8 ... 119 G1 2
Passey Rd MOS/BIL B13 ... 126 B3
Passfield Av HEDN WS12 ... 13 G6 3
Passfield Rd STETCH B33 ... 109 K2
Pasture Ga CNCK/NC WS11 ... 16 A3
The Pastures
DUNHL/THL/PER WV6 ... 48 B1 3
Pasture Vw BLOX/PEL WS3 ... 39 K4
Patch La REDE B98 ... 196 D7
Pat Davis Ct KIDD DY10 ... 137 J6 2
Patent Dr DARL/WED WS10 ... 68 B2
Paternoster Rw DIG/EDG B5 ... 7 H5 1
KIDDW DY11 ... 137 H7 4
WOLV WV1 ... 2 E4
Paterson Pl BRWNH WS8 ... 26 F8
Pathlow Crs SHLY B90 ... 146 E4
The Patios KIDDW DY11 ... 137 G6
Paton Gv MOS/BIL B13 ... 125 K3
Patricia Cl TLHL/CAN CV4 ... 152 A4
Patricia Av ALE/KHTH/YWD B14 ... 146 A1
ETTPK/GDPK/PENN WV4 ... 50 A8
Patricia Crs DUDN DY1 ... 66 F7
Patricia Dr TPTN/OCK DY4 ... 85 L3
Patrick Gregory Rd
WNSFLD WV11 ... 37 K6
Patrick Rd
LGN/SDN/BHAMAIR B26 ... 109 J6
Patriot Cl WSL WS1 ... 53 H8 1
Patshull Av WOLVN WV10 ... 35 M2
Patshull Cl GTB/HAM B43 ... 70 B4
Patshull Gv WOLVN WV10 ... 35 M2 2
Pattens Rd WWCK CV34 ... 199 M4
Patterdale Rd CNCK/NC WS11 ... 16 E1
ERDW/GRVHL B23 ... 90 B1
Patterdale Wy BRLYHL DY5 ... 101 M5
Patterton Dr WALM/CURD B76 ... 73 K5
Pattingham Rd
DUNHL/THL/PER WV6 ... 48 A3
Pattison Gdns
ERDW/GRVHL B23 ... 90 B3 1
Pattison St DSYBK/YTR WS5 ... 53 J8
Paul Byrne Ct
BFLD/HDSWWD B20 ... 88 F4
Pauline Av COVN CV6 ... 134 F3
Paul Pursehouse Rd
BILS/COS WV14 ... 67 H2 3
Pauls Coppice BRWNH WS8 ... 26 D8
Paul St BILS/COS WV14 ... 66 E4
BKHL/PFLD WV2 ... 2 E8
DARL/WED WS10 ... 68 E3
Paul V TPTN/OCK DY4 ... 67 M8
Pavenham Dr DIG/EDG B5 ... 125 G1
Pavilion Av SMTHWKW B67 ... 105 J2
Pavilion Gdns DUDS DY2 ... 103 G3
Pavilion Rd PBAR/PBCH B42 ... 89 K2
Pavilion Wy COVW CV5 ... 153 K2
Pavillion Cl ALDR WS9 ... 40 F5
Pavior's Rd BNTWD WS7 ... 26 C1
Paxford Cl REDE B98 ... 188 F7
Paxford Wy NFLD/LBR B31 ... 123 K7
Paxmead Cl COVN CV6 ... 133 L3
Paxton Av DUNHL/THL/PER WV6 ... 48 C2
Paxton Cl BRGRVE B60 ... 185 M4
Paxton Rd COVN CV6 ... 8 A1
HAG/WOL DY9 ... 120 E1
WSNGN B18 ... 88 E8
Payne Cl RLSN CV32 ... 200 E3
Paynell Cl COVN CV6 ... 133 M3 4
Payne's La COVE CV2 ... 9 L4
RUGBYN/HIL CV21 ... 183 H2
Payne St
BLKHTH/ROWR B65 ... 104 A4 12
Payton Cl OLDBY B69 ... 86 C4
Payton Rd HDSW B21 ... 88 B5
Peace Cl GTWY WS6 ... 24 C2 2
Peach Av DARL/WED WS10 ... 52 A7
Peachley Cl HALE B63 ... 121 M3 3
Peach Ley Rd SLYOAK B29 ... 123 K6
Peach Rd SHHTH WV12 ... 37 L7
Peacock Av COVE CV2 ... 135 K4
WNSFLD WV11 ... 37 L6
Peacock Cl TPTN/OCK DY4 ... 85 M1
Peacock Rd DARL/WED WS10 ... 51 M6
MOS/BIL B13 ... 125 K7
Peak Cft CBROM B36 ... 91 H5
Peak Dr SEDG DY3 ... 84 B2
Peake Av NUN CV11 ... 81 J5
Peake Crs BRWNH WS8 ... 26 D8
Peake Dr TPTN/OCK DY4 ... 85 M1
Peake Rd BRWNH WS8 ... 26 D8
Peak House Rd GTB/HAM B43 ... 70 C2
Peakman Cl RBRY B45 ... 142 E7 2
Peakman St REDW B97 ... 196 C1
Peak Rd STRBR DY8 ... 101 M7 3
Peal St WSL WS1 ... 5 G3
Pearce Cl DUDN DY1 ... 84 C5
Pearl Gv ACGN B27 ... 126 F2
Pearman Rd RBRY B45 ... 142 B4
SMTHWK B66 ... 105 L2
Pearmans Cft HLYWD B47 ... 145 L7
Pearsall Dr OLDBY B69 ... 86 C5
Pears Cl KNWTH CV8 ... 176 D8
Pearson Av COVN CV6 ... 134 F4
Pearson St BKHL/PFLD WV2 ... 2 F9
BRLYHL DY5 ... 102 B2
CDYHTH B64 ... 103 J4
HAG/WOL DY9 ... 120 D1
WBROM B70 ... 86 F1
Pear Tree Av NUNW/HART CV10 ... 80 C7
POL/KGSB/FAZ B78 ... 60 B8
TPTN/OCK DY4 ... 67 K8
Peartree Av WLNHL WV13 ... 51 M4 3
Pear Tree Cl CRTAM B79 ... 33 J6
GTB/HAM B43 ... 69 M4
HEDN WS12 ... 12 A6
KIDD DY10 ... 137 M6 1
SHLY B90 ... 146 B3
STETCH B33 ... 109 H3 4
Pear Tree Ct
BLKHTH/ROWR B65 ... 104 B2
Pear Tree Crs SHLY B90 ... 146 A2
Pear Tree Dr GTB/HAM B43 ... 70 A4
Peartree Dr STRBR DY8 ... 119 L3
Pear Tree Gv SHLY B90 ... 146 B3
Pear Tree La BILS/COS WV14 ... 67 H5
BRWNH WS8 ... 26 A3
Peartree La CDYHTH B64 ... 103 J4
DUDS DY2 ... 84 D8
Pear Tree La WNSFLD WV11 ... 36 F4
Pear Tree Rd BKDE/SHDE B34 ... 92 A7 3
GTB/HAM B43 ... 69 M4
SMTHWKW B67 ... 105 J1
Pear Tree Wy
RUGBYS/DCH CV22 ... 182 F4
Peascroft La BILS/COS WV14 ... 51 J7
Peasefield Cl HDSW B21 ... 88 A5 3
Peat Cl RUGBYS/DCH CV22 ... 183 J4
Pebble Cl STRBR DY8 ... 101 M8
TAM/AM/WIL B77 ... 46 F2
Pebble Mill Cl CNCK/NC WS11 ... 16 D3
Pebble Mill Dr CNCK/NC WS11 ... 16 D3
Pebble Mill Rd DIG/EDG B5 ... 124 F1
Pebworth Av SHLY B90 ... 147 M7
Pebworth Cl COVW CV5 ... 152 F2
REDE B98 ... 189 G6
SLYOAK B29 ... 124 F2 1
Pebworth Gv DUDN DY1 ... 84 E2
STETCH B33 ... 110 A5
Peckham Rd KGSTG B44 ... 71 L3
Peckover Cl
BLKHTH/ROWR B65 ... 103 M4
Peddimore La WALM/CURD B76 ... 74 B7
Pedmore Cl REDE B98 ... 196 F6
Pedmore Court Rd
STRBR DY8 ... 119 M4 5
Pedmore Gv KGSTG B44 ... 71 K3
Pedmore Hall La HAG/WOL DY9 ... 120 A5
Pedmore La HAG/WOL DY9 ... 120 A4
Pedmore Rd BRLYHL DY5 ... 102 D1
HAG/WOL DY9 ... 102 B8
Peel Cl COVN CV6 ... 134 C7
DARL/WED WS10 ... 52 B5
HIA/OLT B92 ... 129 M7
POL/KGSB/FAZ B78 ... 45 J8
WLNHL WV13 ... 51 L4
Peel Dr HEDN WS12 ... 12 E5
Peelers Wy TAM/AM/WIL B77 ... 45 M4
Peel La COVN CV6 ... 134 D8
Peel Rd WWCK CV34 ... 199 J5
Peel St BDMR/CCFT WV3 ... 2 E6
COVN CV6 ... 134 D7 1
DUDS DY2 ... 85 J5
HHTH/SAND B71 ... 69 G8
KIDDW DY11 ... 137 H8
TPTN/OCK DY4 ... 85 L1
WLNHL WV13 ... 51 L4 3
WSNGN B18 ... 88 C8
Peel Wy OLDBY B69 ... 86 A3
Pegasus Wk SLYOAK B29 ... 124 B4
Peglee Wk ALE/KHTH/YWD B14 ... 145 G3
Pegmill Cl COVS CV3 ... 154 D5
Pelham Dr DUDN DY1 ... 84 E3
Pelham Ldg KIDD DY10 ... 137 K8
Pelham Rd WASH/WDE B8 ... 108 F1
Pelham St BDMR/CCFT WV3 ... 2 B7
Pelsall La BLOX/PEL WS3 ... 39 H2
RUSH/SHEL WS4 ... 39 L5
Pelsall Rd BRWNH WS8 ... 26 B6
Pemberly Rd ACGN B27 ... 126 E4
Pemberton Cl SMTHWK B66 ... 105 M2 3
Pemberton Crs
DARL/WED WS10 ... 69 G1
Pemberton Rd BILS/COS WV14 ... 67 H4
WBROM B70 ... 68 E7
Pemberton St WSNGN B18 ... 6 B1
Pembridge Cl BRLYHL DY5 ... 102 D4 3
REDE B98 ... 197 H3
RIDG/WDGT B32 ... 122 E6
Pembridge Rd DOR/KN B93 ... 172 C2
Pembroke Av BKHL/PFLD WV2 ... 50 E6
Pembroke Cl BDWTH CV12 ... 116 A4 2
SHHTH WV12 ... 37 M7
WWCK CV34 ... 199 K5 3
Pembroke Cft HLGN/YWD B28 ... 126 E8
Pembroke Gdns STRBR DY8 ... 101 G3 2
Pembroke Rd BHTH/HG B12 ... 125 L1
HHTH/SAND B71 ... 68 F4
Pembroke Wy HHTH/SAND B71 ... 68 F6
HLGN/YWD B28 ... 126 E8
NUN CV11 ... 99 H2 2
STRPT DY13 ... 160 C7
Pembrook Rd COVN CV6 ... 134 A3
Pembury Av COVN CV6 ... 134 E2
Pembury Cl FOAKS/STRLY B74 ... 55 K7 1
Pembury Cft KGSTG B44 ... 71 L4
Penarth Gv COVS CV3 ... 155 K6
Pencombe Dr
ETTPK/GDPK/PENN WV4 ... 50 B8
Pencraig Cl KNWTH CV8 ... 176 F8
Pencroft Rd BKDE/SHDE B34 ... 91 M6
Penda Gv DUNHL/THL/PER WV6 ... 34 D8

Pendeen Rd
ALE/KHTH/YWD B14 .... **146** A1
Pendeford Av
DUNHL/THL/PER WV6 .... **35** J5
Pendeford Cl
DUNHL/THL/PER WV6 .... **35** J5
Pendeford La *CDSL* WV8 ...... **35** G2
Pendeford Mill La *CDSL* WV8 ... **35** G2
Pendennis Cl *BVILLE* B30 .... **124** B8
Pendennis Dr *OLDBY* B69 ..... **85** L5 ▣
Penderel Cl *WOLVN* WV10 ..... **22** E7
Penderel St *BLOX/PEL* WS3 .... **39** G4
Pendigo Wy *BHAMNEC* B40 ... **129** J1
Pendinas Dr *CDSL* WV8 .... **34** F2 ▣
Pendle HI *HEDN* WS12 .... **17** G1
Pendleton Gv *ACGN* B27 .... **126** F5
Penkridge Bank *HEDN* WS12 ... **12** D2
Penkridge Cl *WSLW* WS2 .... **53** H1
Penkridge Gv *STECH* B33 ...... **109** K1 ▣
Penkridge Rd *PENK* ST19 .... **11** C5
Penkridge St *WSLW* WS2 .... **53** H2
Penkridge Whf *PENK* ST19 ..... **10** D5
Penk Ri *DUNHL/THL/PER* WV6 .. **48** F1
Penleigh Gdns *WMBN* WV5 .... **64** D6
Penley Gv *WASH/WDE* B8 ..... **90** F7
Penmanor *BRGRVE* B60 .... **186** B5
Penmire Gv *ATHST* CV9 .... **62** A2
Pennant Gv *SLYOAK* B29 .... **123** L3
Pennant Rd
BLKHTH/ROWR B65 .... **103** M2
CDYHTH B64 .... **103** H4
Pennard Gv *RIDG/WDGT* B32 .. **123** K1
Penn Cl *BLOX/PEL* WS3 .... **39** G4
Penn Common Rd
ETTPK/GDPK/PENN WV4 .... **65** J4
Penncricket La
BLKHTH/ROWR B65 .... **104** C2
Penn Croft La
ETTPK/GDPK/PENN WV4 .... **65** L4
Pennhouse Av
ETTPK/GDPK/PENN WV4 .... **49** K8
Pennine Dr *CNCK/NC* WS11 ... **16** C3
SEDG DY3 .... **84** B2
Pennine Rd *BRGRVE* B61 .... **165** L8
Pennine Wy *NUNW/HART* CV10 . **97** M2
SHHTH WV12 .... **52** B1
STRBR DY8 .... **101** L7
TAM/AM/WIL B77 .... **46** F5
Pennington Cl *WBROM* B70 .... **86** E3
Pennington Ms
RUGBY/HIL CV21 .... **183** K2 ▣
Pennington St
RUGBY/HIL CV21 .... **183** K2 ▣
RUGBY/HIL CV21 .... **183** L2 ▣
Pennington Wy *COVN* CV6 ..... **134** C5
Penn Rd *BKHL/PFLD* WV2 .... **2** E8
BLKHTH/ROWR B65 .... **104** C2
ETTPK/GDPK/PENN WV4 .... **65** J1
SEDG DY3 .... **65** A1
Penn Road Island
BDMR/CCFT WV3 .... **2** E7
Penns Cl *RLSN* CV32 .... **193** J8
Penns Lake Rd *WALM/CURD* B76 . **73** J6
Penns La *CSCFLD/WYGN* B72 .. **73** H6
CSHL/WTROR B46 .... **93** K6 ▣
Penn St *BDMR/CCFT* WV3 ..... **2** D8
CBHAMNE B4 .... **3** H1
CDYHTH B64 .... **103** K5 ▣
Penns Wood Cl *SEDG* DY3 ..... **66** A3
Penns Wood Dr
WALM/CURD B76 .... **73** K6
Pennwood La
ETTPK/GDPK/PENN WV4 .... **65** K2
Pennyacre Rd
ALE/KHTH/YWD B14 .... **145** H3
Pennycress Gdns
WOLVN WV10 .... **22** F6 ▣
Penny Cress Gn *CNCK/NC* WS11 . **25** K1
Pennyfield Cft *STECH* B33 ...... **109** J2 ▣
Pennyhill La *HHTH/SAND* B71 .. **69** J6
Pennymoor Rd
TAM/AM/WIL B77 .... **46** F6 ▣
Penny Park La *COVN* CV6 .... **133** K2
Pennyroyal Cl *DSYBK/YTR* WS5 . **69** P3
Penny Royal Cl *SEDG* DY3 ...... **84** B3 ▣
Pennystone Cl *RLSS* CV31 ...... **201** H7
Penrice Dr *DUDS* DY2 .... **85** K4
Penrith Cl *BRLYHL* DY5 .... **101** M5 ▣
RLSN CV32 .... **200** A3
Penrith Cft *RIDG/WDGT* B32 ... **123** H5
Penrith Gv
CHWD/FDBR/MGN B37 .... **111** C3 ▣
Penrose Cl *TLHL/CAN* CV4 ...... **152** E6 ▣
Penrhyn Cl *KNWTH* CV8 .... **177** C8 ▣
Penryn Cl *DSYBK/YTR* WS5 ..... **54** B6
NUN CV11 .... **81** L8
Penryn Rd *DSYBK/YTR* WS5 .... **54** B6
Pensby Cl *MOS/BIL* B13 .... **126** A5
Pensford Rd *NFLD/LBR* B31 .... **144** A2
Pensham Cft *SHLY* B90 .... **147** L7
Penshaw Cl *COVN* WV10 .... **35** L2
Penshaw Gv *MOS/BIL* B13 ..... **126** B4 ▣
Penshurst Wy *NUN* CV11 ...... **99** K5
Pensilva Wy *COV* CV1 .... **9** K2
Pensnett Rd *BRLYHL* DY5 .... **102** A1
DUDN DY1 .... **84** C6
Penstone La
ETTPK/GDPK/PENN WV4 .... **64** C1
Pentire Rd *LICHS* WS14 .... **21** H7
Pentlands Gdns
DUNHL/THL/PER WV6 .... **49** J3 ▣
Pentos Dr *SPARK* B11 .... **126** B1
Pentridge Cl *WALM/CURD* B76 . **73** K8

Penzance Wy *NUN* CV11 .... **81** K8
Penzer Dr *RBRY* B45 .... **167** H5
Penzer St *KGSWFD* DY6 .... **83** H6
Peolsford Rd *BLOX/PEL* WS3 .... **39** L1
Peplins Wy *BVILLE* B30 .... **144** F2
Peplow Rd *STECH* B33 .... **109** L1
Pepperbox Dr *TPTN/OCK* DY4 .. **67** L8 ▣
Pepper HI *STRBR* DY8 .... **119** L1
Pepper La *COV* CV1 .... **8** F5
Pepperwood Cl *BRGRVW* B61 .. **165** H2
Pepys Cnr *TLHL/CAN* CV4 ...... **152** C2
Perch Av
CHWD/FDBR/MGN B37 .... **110** E2 ▣
Perch Rd *WSLW* WS2 .... **52** E1 ▣
Percival Rd
LDYWD/EDGR B16 .... **106** A4 ▣
Percy Crs *KNWTH* CV8 .... **191** J3
Percy Rd *KNWTH* CV8 .... **191** J3
SPARK B11 .... **126** B2
WWCK CV34 .... **199** J5
Percy St *COV* CV1 .... **8** C4 ▣
Peregrine Cl *DUDN* DY1 .... **84** D4
Peregrine Dr *COVW* CV5 .... **132** E8
Peregrine Gv *KIDD* DY10 .... **161** J3
Pereira Rd *HRBN* B17 .... **106** A6
Perimeter Rd *BHAMNEC* B40 ... **129** H1
Perivale Gv *BILS/COS* WV14 .... **67** H5 ▣
Perivale Wy *STRBR* DY8 .... **101** L5
Periwinkle Cl *BRWNH* WS8 ..... **26** B7
Perkins Cl *DUDN* DY1 .... **67** G7
Perott Dr *MGN/WHC* B75 .... **57** H3
Perrett Wk *KIDDW* DY11 .... **137** C2
Perrin Av *KIDDW* DY11 .... **160** F1
Perrins Gv *WASH/WDE* B8 ...... **90** F7
Perrins La *HAG/WOL* DY9 .... **120** D1
Perrins Ri *HAG/WOL* DY9 .... **120** D1
Perrott Gdns *STRBR* DY8 .... **101** L4 ▣
Perrott St *WSNGN* B18 .... **88** B7
Perry Av *PBAR/PBCH* B42 .... **89** C1
Perry Barr La *DUDS* DY2 .... **85** H5
Perry Common Rd
ERDW/GRVHL B23 .... **71** M7
Perry Cl *LGLYGN/QTN* B68 ...... **104** F6
Perrycrofts Crs *CRTAM* B79 .... **32** A6
Perryfields Cl *REDE* B98 .... **196** D7
Perryfields Crs *BRGRVW* B61 ... **165** K8
Perryfields Rd *BRGRVW* B61 ... **185** H2
Perryford Dr *SOLH* B91 .... **147** M5
Perry Hall Dr *SHHTH* WV12 ..... **37** M8
Perry Hall Rd *WNSFLD* WV11 ... **37** K7
Perry Hill Crs *LGLYGN/QTN* B68 . **104** F6
Perry Hill La
LGLYGN/QTN B68 .... **104** F6 ▣
Perry Hill Rd *LGLYGN/QTN* B68 . **105** G6
Perry La *BRGRVW* B61 .... **185** K3 ▣
KIDD DY10 .... **161** K5
Perryman Dr *POL/KGSB/FAZ* B78 . **60** D5
Perry Park Crs *PBAR/PBCH* B42 . **70** F7
Perry Park Rd *CDYHTH* B64 .... **103** M4
Perry St *BILS/COS* WV14 .... **67** J2
DARL/WED WS10 .... **52** B5
DARL/WED WS10 .... **68** D4
SMTHWK B66 .... **87** K6
TPTN/OCK DY4 .... **85** L1 ▣
Perry Villa Dr *PBAR/PBCH* B42 . **71** H8
Perrywell Rd *AST/WIT* B6 .... **89** L1
PBAR/PBCH B42 .... **89** K1
Perry Wood Rd *PBAR/PBCH* B42 . **70** F5
Persehouse St *WSL* WS1 .... **5** H2
Pershore Cl *BLOX/PEL* WS3 ..... **38** D3
BVILLE B30 .... **124** E7
DIG/EDG B5 .... **107** H7
HALE B63 .... **121** L3
KIDDW DY11 .... **136** E7
Pershore Rd South *BVILLE* B30 . **144** D2
Pershore Rd *BLOX/PEL* WS3 .... **38** D3
DIG/EDG B5 .... **7** G7
Pershore Wy *BLOX/PEL* WS3 ... **38** D3
Perth Ri *COVW* CV5 .... **152** E1
Perth Rd *SHHTH* WV12 .... **37** M7
Perton Brook V
DUNHL/THL/PER WV6 .... **48** B3
Perton Gv *DUNHL/THL/PER* WV6 . **48** D3
SLYOAK B29 .... **123** L4
Perton Rd *DUNHL/THL/PER* WV6 . **48** D3
Pestilence La *ALVE* B48 .... **168** B5
Peter Av *BILS/COS* WV14 .... **67** K3
Peterborough Dr
CNCK/NC WS11 .... **17** G4
Peterbrook Cl *REDE* B98 .... **196** D6
Peterbrook Ri *SHLY* B90 .... **146** B4
Peterbrook Rd *SHLY* B90 .... **146** B4
Peterdale Dr
ETTPK/GDPK/PENN WV4 .... **65** K2
Peterhead *TAM/AM/WIL* B77 ... **32** D8
Peters Av *NFLD/LBR* B31 .... **143** K3
Petersfield *CNCK/NC* WS11 ..... **16** D1
Petersfield Rd
BLKHTH/ROWR B65 .... **104** C2
Petersfield Rd *HLGN/YWD* B28 . **126** C6
Peter's Finger *BRGRVW* B61 .... **185** K4 ▣
Petersham Pl *EDG* B15 .... **106** C7
Petersham Rd *KGSTC* B44 ...... **72** A4
Peter's Hill Rd *BRLYHL* DY5 ..... **102** A6 ▣
Petershouse Dr
FOAKS/STRLY B74 .... **42** D8 ▣
Peter's La *BNTWD* WS7 .... **19** L8
Peters St *WBROM* B70 .... **68** E4
Peters Wk *COVN* CV6 .... **134** E1
Petford St *CDYHTH* B64 .... **103** J4
Petitor Crs *COVN* CV2 .... **135** G4
Pettitt Cl *ALE/KHTH/YWD* B14 . **145** J3
Petton Cl *REDE* B98 .... **197** K2
Pettyfield Cl
LGN/SDN/BHAMAIR B26 .... **109** L7 ▣
Pettyfields Cl *DOR/KN* B93 ..... **148** E8
Petworth Cl *WLNHL* WV13 ...... **51** K5
Petworth Gv
LGN/SDN/BHAMAIR B26 .... **109** J7
Pevensey Cl *DUDS* DY2 .... **85** K5
Peverell Dr *HLGN/YWD* B28 ... **126** D6
Peveril Dr *COVS* CV3 .... **153** M8
Peveril Gv *WALM/CURD* B76 .... **73** J1 ▣
Peverill Rd
DUNHL/THL/PER WV6 .... **48** D1

ETTPK/GDPK/PENN WV4 .... **66** C2
Pevril Wy *GTB/HAM* B43 .... **70** D3
Peyto Cl *COVN* CV6 .... **134** C3
Pheasant Cl *BDWTH* CV12 ..... **116** B4 ▣
Pheasant Cft *CBROM* B36 ...... **92** E5
KIDD DY10 .... **161** L3 ▣
Pheasant La *REDE* B98 .... **196** D6
Pheasant Rd *SMTHWKW* B67 .. **105** H3
Pheasant St *BRLYHL* DY5 .... **102** A2
Philip Cv *CNCK/NC* WS11 ...... **12** C7
Philip Rd *HALE* B63 .... **121** K2
TPTN/OCK DY4 .... **68** B8
Philip Sidney Rd *SPARK* B11 ... **125** M2
Philip St *BILS/COS* WV14 .... **67** H4
Philip Victor Rd
BFLD/HDSWWD B20 .... **88** D4
Phillimore Rd *WASH/WDE* B8 .. **90** B8
Phillippes Rd *WWCK* CV34 ..... **199** K4 ▣
Phillip Rd *WSLW* WS2 .... **53** C7
Phillips Av *WNSFLD* WV11 ...... **37** K4
Phillips St *AST/WIT* B6 .... **89** J7
Phillips Ter *REDE* B98 .... **196** D1
Phipson Rd *SPARK* B11 .... **125** M2
Phoenix Gn *EDG* B15 .... **106** C6
Phoenix Pk *BLKHTH/ROWR* B65 . **104** B4
Phoenix Ri *DARL/WED* WS10 ... **68** B3
ERDW/GRVHL B23 .... **71** M6
Phoenix Rd *CNCK/NC* WS11 ... **16** E3
TPTN/OCK DY4 .... **67** K7
WLNHL WV13 .... **51** H2
Phoenix St *BKHL/PFLD* WV2 ... **50** B7
WBROM B70 .... **68** D8
Phoenix Wy *COVN* CV6 .... **134** C3
Picasso Cl *CNCK/NC* WS11 ..... **17** H3 ▣
Piccadilly
CHWD/FDBR/MGN B37 .... **111** C4
Piccadilly Crs
POL/KGSB/FAZ B78 .... **60** D4 ▣
Pickard St *WWCK* CV34 .... **199** L6
Pickenham Rd
ALE/KHTH/YWD B14 .... **145** L4
Pickering Cft *RIDG/WDGT* B32 . **123** C4
Pickering Rd *WNSFLD* WV11 ... **37** H8
Pickersleigh Cl *HALE* B63 ...... **121** L2 ▣
Pickford Cl *NUN* CV11 .... **99** L4 ▣
Pickford Grange La *COVW* CV5 . **132** A2
Pickford Green La *COVW* CV5 .. **132** A7
Pickford St *DIG/EDG* B5 .... **7** K6
Pickford Wy *COVW* CV5 .... **132** F7
Pickrell Rd *BILS/COS* WV14 .... **66** F4
Pickwick Gv *MOS/BIL* B13 ..... **126** A3
Pickwick Pl *BILS/COS* WV14 .... **67** J1 ▣
Picton Cft
CHWD/FDBR/MGN B37 .... **111** H3 ▣
Picton Gv *MOS/BIL* B13 .... **125** M8
Picturedrome Wy
DARL/WED WS10 .... **52** B7 ▣
Piddock Rd *SMTHWK* B66 ...... **87** L8
Pierce Av *HIA/OLT* B92 .... **127** J2
Piercy St *WBROM* B70 .... **86** E2
Piers Cl *WWCK* CV34 .... **199** K5 ▣
Piers Rd *WSNGN* B18 .... **88** E6
Piggots Cft
CHWD/FDBR/MGN B37 .... **110** D2
Pike Cl *BFLD/HDSWWD* B20 .... **88** D4
Pike Dr *CHWD/FDBR/MGN* B37 . **111** C2
Pikehelve St *TPTN/OCK* DY4 .... **68** C6
WBROM B70 .... **68** C6
Pike HI *BRGRVE* B60 .... **166** E6
Pikehorne Cft *CBROM* B36 ..... **92** B3 ▣
Pike Rd *WSLW* WS2 .... **52** E1
Pikers La *COVW* CV5 .... **132** C2
Pikes Pool La *BRGRVE* B60 ..... **186** B4
The Pikes *RBRY* B45 .... **142** D5
Pilkington Av
CSCFLD/WYGN B72 .... **72** F2
Pilkington Rd *COVW* CV5 .... **153** H5
Pillaton Cl *PENK* ST19 .... **10** D6
Pillaton Dr *HEDN* WS12 .... **12** A7
Pilling Cl *COVE* CV2 .... **135** K5
Pilson Cl *CBROM* B36 .... **91** K5 ▣
Pimbury Rd *SHHTH* WV12 ...... **38** B6
Pimlico Ct *SEDG* DY3 .... **84** B2
Pimpernel Dr *DSYBK/YTR* WS5 . **69** L2
Pinbury Cft
CHWD/FDBR/MGN B37 .... **110** F5 ▣
Pinchers Cl *HAG/WOL* DY9 ..... **140** C5
Pinders La
RUGBY/HIL CV21 .... **183** M1 ▣
Pineapple Gv *BVILLE* B30 ...... **125** C5 ▣
Pineapple Rd *BVILLE* B30 ...... **125** C6
Pine Av *DARL/WED* WS10 ...... **52** D8
SMTHWK B66 .... **87** J6
Pine Cl *BDMR/CCFT* WV3 .... **2** A6 ▣
CRTAM B79 .... **31** M5
GTWY WS6 .... **24** D1
KGSWFD DY6 .... **83** H8
KINVER DY7 .... **118** A2 ▣
SOLH B91 .... **147** K3 ▣
Pine Gn *DUDN* DY1 .... **66** E8
Pine Gv *ALE/KHTH/YWD* B14 ... **125** L8
BNTWD WS7 .... **18** D8
RBRY B45 .... **166** D3
Pinehurst *RLSN* CV32 .... **193** J8
Pinehurst Dr *HWK/WKHTH* B38 . **144** D2
Pine Leigh *FOAKS/STRLY* B74 ... **56** F4
Pineneedle Cft *SHHTH* WV12 .. **52** C1
Pineridge Dr *KIDDW* DY11 ..... **136** F8
Pine Rd *DUDN* DY1 .... **67** C8
OLDBY B69 .... **85** L5
The Pines *BDMR/CCFT* WV3 .... **49** H4
LICHS WS14 .... **21** K6
RBRY B45 .... **142** E4
SHLY B90 .... **147** H8
WSL WS1 .... **5** C5
Pine St *BLOX/PEL* WS3 .... **39** G4
Pine Tree Av *TLHL/CAN* CV4 ... **152** E3
Pine Tree Cl *HEDN* WS12 .... **12** E4
REDW B97 .... **195** M3
Pinetree Dr *FOAKS/STRLY* B74 . **55** H4
Pine Tree Rd *BDWTH* CV12 ..... **117** C1
Pineview *NFLD/LBR* B31 .... **143** K3
Pine Wk *CDSL* WV8 .... **34** D3
HAG/WOL DY9 .... **120** D2
NFLD/LBR B31 .... **143** M2
Pinewall Av *HWK/WKHTH* B38 . **144** D4
Pineways *FOAKS/STRLY* B74 ... **56** A2 ▣

STRBR DY8 .... **101** G3
Pineways Dr
DUNHL/THL/PER WV6 .... **49** J2
The Pineways *OLDBY* B69 ...... **86** A3 ▣
Pineway *ATHST* CV9 .... **61** C4
CNCK/NC WS11 .... **16** B1
Pinewood Cl
BDMR/CCFT WV3 .... **48** E5
BRWNH WS8 .... **26** C3
DSYBK/YTR WS5 .... **69** M1 ▣
KGSTG B44 .... **71** J6
KIDDW DY11 .... **137** C4
RBRY B45 .... **142** B5
SHHTH WV12 .... **38** B6
WMBN WV5 .... **64** E7
Pinewood Dr *COVS* CV3 .... **156** A6 ▣
RIDG/WDGT B32 .... **122** C5
Pinewood Gv *COVW* CV5 ...... **153** M5
SOLH B91 .... **147** K3 ▣
Pinewoods *NFLD/LBR* B31 ..... **123** K5 ▣
RMSLY B62 .... **104** E6 ▣
Pinewoods Av *HAG/WOL* DY9 . **139** K1
Pinewoods Cl *HAG/WOL* DY9 .. **139** K1
Pinfield Dr *RBRY* B45 .... **166** F4
Pinfold *BLOX/PEL* WS3 .... **39** C5
Pinfold Ct *DARL/WED* WS10 ... **52** A8 ▣
Pinfold Crs
ETTPK/GDPK/PENN WV4 .... **49** H7
Pinfold Gdns *WNSFLD* WV11 ... **37** H8
Pinfold Gv
ETTPK/GDPK/PENN WV4 .... **49** J8
Pinfold HI *LICHS* WS14 .... **28** D7
Pinfold La *ALDR* WS9 .... **54** F6
CNCK/NC WS11 .... **25** J1
ETTPK/GDPK/PENN WV4 .... **49** J8
GTWY WS6 .... **24** A3
PENK ST19 .... **10** B5
Pinfold Rd *LICH* WS13 .... **20** C4 ▣
SOLH B91 .... **128** C8
Pingle Cl *HHTH/SAND* B71 ..... **69** K4
Pingle Ct *NUN* CV11 .... **99** H3
Pingle La *BNTWD* WS7 .... **27** H1
Pink Green La *REDE* B98 .... **189** M5
Pinkney Pl *LGLYGN/QTN* B68 ... **105** C2
Pinley Flds *COVS* CV3 .... **154** F5
Pinley Gv *GTB/HAM* B43 .... **70** F2
Pinley Wy *SOLH* B91 .... **147** L5
Pinner Gv *RIDG/WDGT* B32 .... **123** J1 ▣
Pinner's Cft *COVE* CV2 .... **134** E8
Pinnock Pl *TLHL/CAN* CV4 ..... **152** D4
Pinson Rd *WLNHL* WV13 .... **51** H4
Pintail Dr *ERDW/GRVHL* B23 ... **90** A3
Pintail Gv *KIDD* DY10 .... **161** M2
Pinto Cl *LDYWD/EDGR* B16 ..... **106** D3
Pinwall La *ATHST* CV9 .... **63** K1
Pinza Cft *CBROM* B36 .... **91** H5 ▣
Piper Cl *DUNHL/THL/PER* WV6 . **48** D1
Piper Pl *STRBR* DY8 .... **101** K5
Piper Rd *BDMR/CCFT* WV3 ..... **48** F5
Pipers Cl *BRGRVE* B60 .... **185** H6
Pipers Cft *LICH* WS13 .... **20** E3
Pipers Gn *HLGN/YWD* B28 ..... **126** D8
Piper's La *KNWTH* CV8 .... **191** L1
NUNW/HART CV10 .... **79** C5
Pipers Rd *REDE* B98 .... **197** H7
Piper's Rw *WOLV* WV1 .... **3** H5
Pipes Meadow
BILS/COS WV14 .... **51** J8 ▣
Pipewell Cl *RUGBYS/DCH* CV22 . **183** G4
Pipit Ct *KIDD* DY10 .... **161** L3
Pippin Av *HALE* B63 .... **102** F6
Pirbright Cl *BILS/COS* WV14 ... **67** J2 ▣
Pirrey Cl *BILS/COS* WV14 .... **67** H4
Pitcairn Cl *BVILLE* B30 .... **124** F7
Pitcairn Dr *RMSLY* B62 .... **103** M7
Pitcairn Rd *SMTHWKW* B67 .... **105** H4
Pitclose Rd *NFLD/LBR* B31 ..... **143** M4
Pitfield Rd *STECH* B33 .... **110** B4
Pitfield Rw *DUDN* DY1 .... **85** G4 ▣
Pitfields Cl *LGLYGN/QTN* B68 .. **104** E5
Pitfields Rd *LGLYGN/QTN* B68 . **104** E5
Pitfield St *DUDN* DY1 .... **85** G4 ▣
Pithall Rd *BKDE/SHDE* B34 ..... **92** B8
Pit HI *KNWTH* CV8 .... **179** C8
Pit Leasow Cl *BVILLE* B30 ...... **124** F5
Pitman Rd *RIDG/WDGT* B32 ... **104** E8
Pitmaston Rd *HLGN/YWD* B28 . **126** E7
Pitsford St *WSNGN* B18 .... **88** E8
Pitt La *HIA/OLT* B92 .... **129** H3
Pitts Farm Rd *ERDE/BCHGN* B24 . **73** C8
Pitts La *KIDD* DY10 .... **137** J7 ▣
Pitt St *CBHAMNE* B4 .... **7** L3 ▣
KIDD DY10 .... **137** L4
Pixall Dr *EDG* B15 .... **106** F6
Pixhall Wk *CVALE* B35 .... **91** M2 ▣
Plainview Cl *FOAKS/STRLY* B74 . **55** J3
Plaistow Av *CBROM* B36 .... **91** C6
Plane Gv
CHWD/FDBR/MGN B37 .... **110** F4
Planetary Rd *WLNHL* WV13 .... **51** C2
Planetree Cl *BRGRVE* B60 ...... **185** M3
Plane Tree Cl *KIDD* DY10 .... **137** K6
Plane Tree Rd *DSYBK/YTR* WS5 . **69** M1
Planetree Rd *FOAKS/STRLY* B74 . **55** H5
Plane La *BRLYHL* DY5 .... **102** B1
Plank La *CSHL/WTROR* B46 ..... **92** E3
Planks La *WMBN* WV5 .... **64** D7
Plantagenet Dr
RUGBYS/DCH CV22 .... **183** J7
Plantation La
POL/KGSB/FAZ B78 .... **30** F8
SEDG DY3 .... **82** F1
Plantation Rd
DSYBK/YTR WS5 .... **69** L1 ▣
HEDN WS12 .... **13** H8
The Plantation *BRLYHL* DY5 ... **83** M6
Plant La *BNTWD* WS7 .... **18** B6
Plants Brook Rd
WALM/CURD B76 .... **73** K7
Plants Cl *GTWY* WS6 .... **24** B4
SCFLD/BOLD B73 .... **72** B4
Plants Gv *ERDE/BCHGN* B24 ... **73** H8 ▣

Plants Hill Crs *TLHL/CAN* CV4 .. **152** C4
Plants Hollow *BRLYHL* DY5 ..... **102** B4
Plant St *CDYHTH* B64 .... **103** H4
STRBR DY8 .... **101** J3
Plant Wy *BLOX/PEL* WS3 .... **39** K1
Plascom Rd *WOLV* WV1 .... **50** E4
Platts Crs *STRBR* DY8 .... **101** J3
Platts Dr *STRBR* DY8 .... **101** K5
Platts Rd *STRBR* DY8 .... **101** K5
Platt St *CNCK/NC* WS11 .... **12** E8
DARL/WED WS10 .... **52** B8
Playdon Gv
ALE/KHTH/YWD B14 .... **145** L2 ▣
Pleasant Cl *KGSWFD* DY6 ...... **101** G1
Pleasant Md *ALDR* WS9 .... **40** C8
Pleasant St *KIDD* DY10 .... **137** J6
WBROM B70 .... **68** C5
WBROM B70 .... **87** G4
Pleasant Vw *SEDG* DY3 .... **84** B3
Pleasant Wy *RLSN* CV32 .... **200** E3
Pleck Rd *WSLW* WS2 .... **4** A5
Plestowes Cl *SHLY* B90 .... **126** F8
Plexfield Rd
RUGBYS/DCH CV22 .... **183** G4
Pleydell Cl *COVS* CV3 .... **155** G8
Plimsoll Gv *RIDG/WDGT* B32 ... **105** G8
Plimsoll St *KIDDW* DY11 .... **137** H8
Plomer Cl
RUGBYS/DCH CV22 .... **183** G5 ▣
Plott La *RRUGBY* CV23 .... **180** C7
Plough And Harrow Rd
LDYWD/EDGR B16 .... **106** C4
Plough Av *RIDG/WDGT* B32 .... **123** G3
Plough Hill Rd
NUNW/HART CV10 .... **79** K7
Ploughmans Wk *BRGRVE* B60 . **185** H7
KGSWFD DY6 .... **82** E6 ▣
LICH WS13 .... **21** C2 ▣
Plover Cl *WOLVN* WV10 .... **22** E6
Ploverdale Crs *KGSWFD* DY6 ... **83** L6
Plover Cl *KIDD* DY10 .... **161** M4
Plowden Rd *STECH* B33 .... **109** K1
Plowman St *RUGBYN/HIL* CV21 . **183** K2
Plume St *VAUX/NECH* B7 .... **89** M6
Plumstead Rd *KGSTG* B44 ...... **71** L5
Plym Cl *WNSFLD* WV11 .... **37** C8
Plymouth Cl *COVE* CV2 .... **135** C6
NFLD/LBR B31 .... **143** L6 ▣
REDW B97 .... **196** A3
Plymouth Ct *REDW* B97 .... **196** A4
Plymouth Dr *RBRY* B45 .... **166** E5 ▣
Plymouth Pl *RLSS* CV31 .... **200** E4
Plymouth Rd *BVILLE* B30 .... **124** F6
RBRY B45 .... **166** E4
REDW B97 .... **196** B3
Pochard Cl *KIDD* DY10 .... **161** K4
Pointon Cl *BILS/COS* WV14 .... **66** E3
Poitiers Rd *COVS* CV3 .... **154** D7
Polden Cl *HALE* B63 .... **121** C4
Polesworth Cl *REDE* B98 .... **197** H4 ▣
Polesworth Gv
BKDE/SHDE B34 .... **91** M7 ▣
Pollard Rd *ACGN* B27 .... **127** C4
The Pollards *ERDW/GRVHL* B23 . **72** C5
Polo Flds *HAG/WOL* DY9 .... **119** M4
Polperro Dr *COVW* CV5 .... **132** E8
Pomeroy Cl *TLHL/CAN* CV4 .... **152** B6
Pomeroy Rd *GTB/HAM* B43 ..... **71** H1
RIDG/WDGT B32 .... **123** C4
Pommel Cl *DSYBK/YTR* WS5 ... **69** K1
Pond Crs *BKHL/PFLD* WV2 ..... **50** C6
Pond Gv *BKHL/PFLD* WV2 ...... **50** C6
Pond La *BKHL/PFLD* WV2 .... **3** H9
BKHL/PFLD WV2 .... **50** C6 ▣
Pondthorpe *COVS* CV3 .... **155** J7
Ponesfield Rd *LICH* WS13 ...... **20** F3
Ponesgreen *LICH* WS13 .... **20** F3
Pontypool Av *COVS* CV3 .... **155** K7
Pool Av *CNCK/NC* WS11 .... **17** M8
Pool Bank *REDE* B98 .... **196** C3
Pool Bank St *NUN* CV11 .... **98** F1
Pool Cl *RUGBYS/DCH* CV22 .... **183** H5
WOLVN WV10 .... **23** H4
Poole Crs *BILS/COS* WV14 ..... **67** H3
BRWNH WS8 .... **26** A3
HRBN B17 .... **124** A2
Poolehouse Rd *GTB/HAM* B43 . **70** C2
Pool End Cl *DOR/KN* B93 .... **148** D7
Poole Rd *COVN* CV6 .... **133** L7
Pooles Cl *KIDD* DY10 .... **137** J6 ▣
Pooles La *SHHTH* WV12 .... **38** C6
Poole St *STRBR* DY8 .... **119** J1
Poole's Wy *BNTWD* WS7 .... **19** C6
Pooley La *POL/KGSB/FAZ* B78 .. **47** K3
Pool Farm Rd *ACGN* B27 .... **127** C4
Poolfield Dr *SOLH* B91 .... **147** K2 ▣
Pool Furlong *HAG/WOL* DY9 ... **140** C4
Pool Hall Crs *BDMR/CCFT* WV3 . **48** D5
Pool Hall Rd *BDMR/CCFT* WV3 . **48** D5
Pool Hayes La *SHHTH* WV12 ... **37** L8
Poolhead La *HOCK/TIA* B94 .... **169** M6
Pool House Rd *WMBN* WV5 .... **64** B7
Pool La *OLDBY* B69 .... **104** D1
Pool Meadow *GTWY* WS6 ..... **24** B4
WALM/CURD B76 .... **73** L5 ▣
Pool Meadow *MOS/BIL* B13 ... **126** A4
SOLH B91 .... **148** D4
Pool Rd *BRWNH* WS8 .... **26** C3
HALE B63 .... **121** M2
NUNW/HART CV10 .... **80** D8
SMTHWK B66 .... **87** M8
WNSFLD WV11 .... **37** L7
Poolside Gdns *COVS* CV3 ...... **153** L8
Pool St *AST/WIT* B6 .... **89** K7
BKHL/PFLD WV2 .... **3** J7
DUDN DY1 .... **66** E7
WSL WS1 .... **5** H1
Pool Vw *GTWY* WS6 .... **24** E1
RUSH/SHEL WS4 .... **40** B6
Pope Gv *HEDN* WS12 .... **12** D7
Pope Rd *WOLVN* WV10 .... **36** E5
Popes La *HWK/WKHTH* B38 .... **144** B2
OLDBY B69 .... **86** F7
Pope St *CBHAMW* B1 .... **6** A2
RUGBYS/DCH CV22 .... **183** J2
SMTHWK B66 .... **87** M6 ▣

Poplar Av *ALE/KHTH/YWD* B14.... 125 J5
  BDWTH CV12 .... 117 H3
  BHTH/HG B12 .... 125 L1 🔟
  BNTWD WS7 .... 18 D7
  BRWNH WS8 .... 26 E5
  CHWD/FDBR/MGN B37..... 111 G5
  CNCK/NC WS11................................ 16 D1
  DSYBK/YTR WS5............................ 69 L1
  HRBN B17 .... 105 M3
  MGN/WHC B75 .... 57 K6 🔟
  OLDBY B69 .... 85 M5
  OLDBY B69 .... 86 E8
  TPTN/OCK DY4 .... 67 H8
  WBROM B70 .... 87 J3
  WNSFLD WV11 .... 36 F6
  WSLW WS2 .... 52 B1
Poplar Cl *BRGRVW* B61 .... 165 K6
  OLDBY B69 .... 86 A4
  WMBN WV5 .... 64 F7
  WSLW WS2 .... 52 C1
Poplar Crs *DUDN* DY1 .... 84 F2
Poplar Dr *AST/WIT* B6 .... 71 K8
  RBRY B45 .... 167 H5
Poplar Gn *DUDN* DY1 .... 66 E7
Poplar Gv *RUGBYN/HIL* CV21 ... 183 G5
  RMSLY B62 .... 141 L2
Poplar La *CNCK/NC* WS11 .... 15 K5
  RMSLY B62 .... 141 L2
Poplar Ri *FOAKS/STRLY* B74 ...... 42 B8
  OLDBY B69 .... 86 A5
Poplar Rd *ALE/KHTH/YWD* B14.. 125 J5
  BDMR/CCFT WV3 .... 49 L7
  BILS/COS WV14 .... 51 K6
  BRWNH WS8 .... 26 E5
  COVW CV5.................................. 153 K4
  DARL/WED WS10 .... 52 E8
  DOR/KN B93 .... 172 D2
  GTWY WS6 .... 24 D4
  KGSWFD DY6 .... 83 J8
  KIDDW DY11 .... 161 G1
  OLDBY B69 .... 86 E5
  REDW B97 .... 195 L2
  SMTHWK B66 .... 105 L4
  SOLH B91 .... 148 A1
  SPARK B11 .... 107 M8
  STRBR DY8 .... 119 J2
Poplars Dr *CBROM* B36............. 91 M5
  CDSL WV8 .... 34 D3
The Poplars *CNCK/NC* WS11 .... 16 C1 🔟
  NUNW/HART CV10........................ 98 B2
  SPARK B11 .... 108 A7 🔟
  STRBR DY8 .... 101 K3
Poplar St *BKHL/PFLD* WV2 .... 50 B7
  CNCK/NC WS11............................. 17 L7
  SMTHWK B66 .... 88 A4 🔟
Poplarwoods *RIDG/WDGT* B32.. 122 F3
Poppy Dr *DSYBK/YTR* WS5 .... 69 K2
Poppyfield Ct *TLHL/CAN* CV4 .... 177 H2
Poppy Gv *WASH/WDE* B8 .... 108 D1
Poppy La *ERDE/BCHGN* B24 ...... 73 G8
Poppymead *ERDW/GRVHL* B23 .. 71 M5
Porchester Cl *ALDR* WS9 .... 40 E3
  COVS CV3 .... 155 L3
Porchester Dr *LOZ/NWT* B19 .... 89 H7
Porchester St *LOZ/NWT* B19...... 89 H7
Porlock Cl *COVS* CV3 .... 154 C8
Porlock Crs *NFLD/LBR* B31 .... 143 H2
Porlock Rd *STRBR* DY8 .... 101 L7
Portal Rd *WSLW* WS2 .... 52 D3
Portchester Dr
  WNSFLD WV11 .... 37 H8 🔟
Porter Cl *CSCFLD/WYGN* B72 .... 72 F6
  TLHL/CAN CV4 .... 152 C5
Porters Cft *HRBN* B17 .... 105 L5
Porters Fld *DUDS* DY2 .... 85 H4 🔟
Portershill Dr *SHLY* B90 .... 147 G5
Porter St *DUDS* DY2 .... 85 H4
Porters Wy *BORD* B9 .... 108 C3
Portfield Dr *TPTN/OCK* DY4 ...... 85 L2
Portfield Gv *ERDW/GRVHL* B23 .. 72 E7
Porthkerry Gv *SEDG* DY3 .... 65 M6
Port Hope Rd *SPARK* B11 .... 107 L6
Porthouse Gv *BILS/COS* WV14 .. 66 F2 🔟
Portia Av *SHLY* B90.................... 146 F3
Portia Cl *NUN* CV11 .... 99 L5
Portland Av *ALDR* WS9 .... 40 F8
  CRTAM B79 .... 31 K5 🔟
Portland Crs *HAG/WOL* DY9 ..... 119 M4
Portland Dr *HAG/WOL* DY9 ...... 119 M4
  NUNW/HART CV10........................ 98 A1
Portland House *RLSN* CV32 ..... 200 D5 🔟
Portland Ms *RLSN* CV32 .... 200 D5 🔟
Portland Pl *BILS/COS* WV14 ...... 66 F6
  CNCK/NC WS11............................. 16 A4
  RLSN CV32 .... 200 C5
Portland Pl West *RLSN* CV32 ... 200 C5
Portland Rd *ALDR* WS9 .... 40 F7
  LDYWD/EDGR B16 .... 106 A3
Portland St *AST/WIT* B6............. 89 L6
  RLSN CV32 .... 200 D5
  WSLW WS2 .... 53 J2
Portland Ter *WSNGN* B18 .... 88 E8 🔟
Portleys La *POL/KGSB/FAZ* B78 .. 59 H1
Portman Rd
  ALE/KHTH/YWD B14................... 125 K6
Portobello Cl *WLNHL* WV13 .... 51 H4 🔟
Portobello Rd *WBROM* B70 .... 68 D5
Portree Av *COVS* CV3 .... 155 K3
Portrush Av *NFLD/LBR* B31 ...... 144 A4
Portrush Rd
  DUNHL/THL/PER WV6.................. 48 B1
Portsdown Cl *WOLVN* WV10 ...... 36 D6 🔟
Portsdown Rd *HALE* B63........... 121 H4
Portsea Cl *COVS* CV3 .... 154 B7
Portsea St *BLOX/PEL* WS3 .... 39 G7
Portswood Dr *COVEN* WV9 .... 35 K4
Portway Cl *KGSWFD* DY6 .... 83 J8
  RLSS CV31 .... 201 H7
  SOLH B91 .... 147 A4
  TLHL/CAN CV4 .... 152 C5
Portway Hi *OLDBY* B69 .... 85 M7
Portway Rd *BILS/COS* WV14 ...... 51 K6
  BLKHTH/ROWR B65..................... 103 M1
  DARL/WED WS10 .... 68 C3
  OLDBY B69 .... 86 B6
The Portway *KGSWFD* DY6 .... 83 J8
Portwrinkle Av *COVN* CV6 .... 134 E7
Posey Cl *HDSW* B21 .... 88 A2
Postbridge Rd *COVS* CV3 .... 154 B8

Post Office La *ATHST* CV9 .... 63 M6
Post Office Rd *ATHST* CV9 .... 62 A4
Poston Cft
  ALE/KHTH/YWD B14................... 145 H1 🔟
Potter Cl *ERDW/GRVHL* B23 ...... 72 B5
Potters Cl *RRUGBY* CV23 .... 157 J2
Potters Green Rd *COVE* CV2 ..... 135 J4
Potters La *AST/WIT* B6 .... 89 J6 🔟
  DARL/WED WS10 .... 68 C3
  POL/KGSB/FAZ B78 .... 47 L5
Potters Rd *BDWTH* CV12 .... 116 B4
Potterton Wy *SMTHWK* B66 ...... 87 K5
Pottery Rd *LGLYGN/QTN* B68 ... 105 G4
  SMTHWK B66 .... 87 L6
Potton Cl *COVS* CV3 .... 155 J7
Potts Cl *KNWTH* CV8 .... 192 A1
Pouk Hill Cl *WSLW* WS2 .... 52 E2
Pouk La *LICHS* WS14 .... 27 J5
Poultney Rd *COVN* CV6 .... 133 J7
Poultney St *WBROM* B70 .... 68 D6
Poulton Cl *MOS/BIL* B13 .... 125 L3 🔟
Pound Cl *LGLYGN/QTN* B68 ..... 104 D2 🔟
  RCOVN/BALC/EX CV7 .... 151 H2
  CSHL/WTROR B46...................... 111 L1
  RIDG/WDGT B32......................... 142 D2
  RLSN CV32 .... 200 E2
Poundley Cl *CBROM* B36............. 92 A5
Pound Rd *ALE/KHTH/YWD* B14 .. 145 J3
  DARL/WED WS10 .... 68 E2
  LGLYGN/QTN B68 .... 104 D3
  OLDBY B69 .... 104 D2 🔟
Pountney St *BKHL/PFLD* WV2 .... 2 F8
Powell Av *RIDG/WDGT* B32 ...... 104 E7 🔟
Powell Pl *BILS/COS* WV14 .... 67 J2 🔟
  TPTN/OCK DY4 .... 68 A8
Powell Rd *COV* CV1 .... 154 E1
Powell St *CBHAMW* B1 .... 6 B3
  HALE B63 .... 121 M2 🔟
  WOLVN WV10 .... 50 D1
Powell Wy *NUN* CV11 .... 98 E1 🔟
Power Crs *LDYWD/EDGR* B16 ... 106 E4 🔟
Powers Ct *RLSN* CV32 .... 200 D4 🔟
Powick Rd *ERDW/GRVHL* B23.... 90 B4
Powis Av *TPTN/OCK* DY4 .... 67 M6
Powis Gv *KNWTH* CV8 .... 177 G3 🔟
Powke La *BLKHTH/ROWR* B65 ... 103 L3
  CDYHTH B64.............................. 103 K2
Powlers Cl *HAG/WOL* DY9 .... 120 C3 🔟
Powlett St *BKHL/PFLD* WV2 .... 3 G7
Poxon Rd *ALDR* WS9 .... 40 E2
The Poynings
  DUNHL/THL/PER WV6.................. 35 G8 🔟
Poyser Rd *NUNW/HART* CV10...... 99 G5
Pratts La *STUD* B80 .... 197 L5
Premier Ct *BVILLE* B30 .... 145 G2
Premier St *VAUX/NECH* B7 .... 90 B5
Premier Wy *SCFLD/BOLD* B73.... 72 B3
Prentice Cl *RRUGBY* CV23 .... 158 F8 🔟
Prescelly Cl *NUNW/HART* CV10 .. 97 M2
Prescot Rd *HAG/WOL* DY9 .... 120 A1
Prescott Dr *PENK* ST19 .... 10 E4
Prestbury Rd *REDE* B98 .... 197 L2 🔟
Prestbury Rd *AST/WIT* B6........... 89 J5
Presthope Rd *SLYOAK* B29 ...... 123 M6
Preston Av *WALM/CURD* B76 ..... 73 J2
Preston Cl *REDE* B98 .... 188 F7
  TLHL/CAN CV4 .... 152 D6
Preston Rd
  LGN/SDN/BHAMAIR B26 .... 109 H7
  WSNGN B18 .... 88 C7
Prestons Rw
  ETTPK/GDPK/PENN WV4 .... 66 E2 🔟
Prestwick Cl *MGN/WHC* B75...... 57 G5
Prestwick Rd *CVALE* B35 .... 91 M1
  KGSWFD DY6 .... 83 G7
Prestwood Av *WNSFLD* WV11 .... 37 H5
Prestwood Dr *KINVER* DY7 .... 100 D5
Prestwood Rd *KINVER* DY7 ...... 100 C7
  SLYOAK B29 .... 123 M5
  WNSFLD WV11 .... 36 E8
Prestwood Rd West
  WNSFLD WV11 .... 37 H7
Pretoria Rd *BORD* B9 .... 108 C2
Priam Gv *BLOX/PEL* WS3 .... 25 M8
Price Av *POL/KGSB/FAZ* B78...... 45 H4
Price Crs *BILS/COS* WV14 .... 51 H6
Price Rd *DARL/WED* WS10 .... 69 G2
  HAG/WOL DY9 .... 102 E7
  RLSN CV32 .... 193 J8
Prices Rd *SEDG* DY3 .... 84 A2 🔟
Price St *BILS/COS* WV14 .... 51 K8
  CBHAMNE B4 .... 7 G2
  CNCK/NC WS11............................. 16 C4
  DUDS DY2 .... 85 J5
  SMTHWK B66 .... 87 M8
  WBROM B70 .... 87 G2
Pridmore Rd *COVN* CV6 .... 134 B6
Priestfield Cl *KGSTG* B44 .... 71 H3 🔟
Priestfield Rd *REDW* B97 .... 196 B8
Priestland Rd *BKDE/SHDE* B34... 91 M6
Priestley Cl *BFLD/HDSWWD* B20 .. 88 E4
  HALE B63 .... 102 F7
Priestley Rd *SPARK* B11 .... 107 L6
  WSLW WS2 .... 38 E8
Priest St *CDYHTH* B64............... 103 K4
Primley Av *CBROM* B36............... 91 H6
  TAM/AM/WIL B77 .... 46 D8
  WSLW WS2 .... 52 F4
Primley Cl *WSLW* WS2 .... 52 F3
Primrose Av *SPARK* B11 .... 108 A7 🔟
  TPTN/OCK DY4 .... 68 A5
  WOLVN WV10 .... 36 D5
Primrose Bank
  LGLYGN/QTN B68 .... 104 F1 🔟
Primrose Cl *BLOX/PEL* WS3 .... 25 L8
  BRGRVE B60.............................. 166 A7 🔟
  CDYHTH B64.............................. 102 F5
Primrose Crs *DUDN* DY1 .... 85 G1 🔟
Primrose Gdns *CDSL* WV8 .... 34 E2
  HWK/WKHTH B38 .... 144 D5 🔟
  WOLVN WV10 .... 22 F6
Primrose Hi *HWK/WKHTH* B38 .. 144 F4
  SMTHWKW B67 .... 105 H1
  STRBR DY8 .... 101 J3
  WWCK CV34 .... 199 H3

Primrose Hill St *COV* CV1............. 9 H2
Primrose La *HLGN/YWD* B28 ..... 126 D8
  WOLVN WV10 .... 36 D5
Primrose Meadow
  CNCK/NC WS11............................. 17 G3
Primrose Pk *BRLYHL* DY5 .... 84 A6
Primrose Rd *DUDS* DY2 .... 103 G1 🔟
Primrose Woods
  RIDG/WDGT B32......................... 122 F3
Primsland Cl *SOLH* B91 .... 148 A6
Prince Albert St *BORD* B9 .... 108 B4
Prince Andrew Crs *RBRY* B45 ... 142 C3 🔟
Prince Charles Cl *RBRY* B45 ..... 142 C3 🔟
Prince Charles Rd
  BILS/COS WV14 .... 67 K2 🔟
Prince Edward Dr *RBRY* B45 ..... 142 C2 🔟
Prince George Rd
  DARL/WED WS10 .... 52 E8
Prince of Wales La *SHLY* B90 .... 146 A3
Prince of Wales Rd *COVW* CV5... 153 J2
Princep Cl *GTB/HAM* B43 .... 71 H1 🔟
Prince Philip Cl *RBRY* B45 .... 142 C3 🔟
Prince Rd *BVILLE* B30 .... 144 D2
Prince's Av *NUN* CV11 .... 98 F2
  WSL WS1 .... 5 K3
  WSL WS1 .... 5 K2
Princes Cl *COVS* CV3 .... 154 F5
Princes Dr *CDSL* WV8 .... 34 E2
  KNWTH CV8 .... 176 E5
  RLSN CV32 .... 200 B5
  RLSS CV31 .... 200 B6
Princes Gdns *CDSL* WV8 .... 34 D2
Princes Ga *SOLH* B91 .... 147 M1
Princes Rd *ATHST* CV9 .... 61 G8
  OLDBY B69 .... 85 L3
  POL/KGSB/FAZ B78 .... 47 M3 🔟
  STRBR DY8 .... 119 H3
Princess Alice Dr
  SCFLD/BOLD B73........................ 72 B3
Princess Aly *WOLV* WV1 .... 3 G5
Princess Anne Rd
  BILS/COS WV14 .... 67 K2
  WSLW WS2 .... 52 D2
Princess Crs *HALE* B63 .... 103 J7
Princess Gv *HHTH/SAND* B71 ... 69 H5
Princess Rd *ATHST* CV9 .... 63 J5
  DIG/EDG B5 .... 107 J7
  LGLYGN/QTN B68 .... 105 H3
Princess Sq *BILS/COS* WV14 ..... 67 K2 🔟
Princess St *BNTWD* WS7 .... 18 C5
  CNCK/NC WS11............................. 12 C8
  COVN CV6 .... 134 D6
  WOLV WV1 .... 3 G5
Prince's St *CBHAMNE* B4 .... 7 K3
  NUN CV11 .... 98 F2
  RLSN CV32 .... 200 E4
  RUGBYN/HIL CV21 .... 183 K1
Prince St *ALDR* WS9 .... 40 D3
  CDYHTH B64.............................. 103 H4
  CNCK/NC WS11............................. 12 C7
  DUDS DY2 .... 85 G7
  WSLW WS2 .... 4 A6
Prince's Wy *SOLH* B91 .... 147 M2
Princethorpe Cl
  BKDE/SHDE B34 .... 92 B6 🔟
  SHLY B90 .... 146 E3 🔟
Princethorpe Rd *SLYOAK* B29... 123 M4
Princethorpe Wy *COVS* CV3 ..... 155 H6
Princeton Gdns *COVN* CV6 .... 35 K3 🔟
Prince William Cl *COVN* CV6 ..... 133 J7
  ERDW/GRVHL B23 .... 90 B3 🔟
Princip Cl *CBHAMNE* B4 .... 7 G2
Printing House St *CBHAMNE* B4 .. 7 G3
Prior Cl *KIDD* DY10 .... 138 A8
Prior Deram Wk *TLHL/CAN* CV4 .. 152 F5
Priors Cl *RCOVN/BALC/EX* CV7 .. 150 F7
Priorsfield Rd *KNWTH* CV8 ...... 176 B6
Priorsfield Rd North *COVN* CV6 .. 8 B1 🔟
Priorsfield Rd South *COVN* CV6... 8 B1
Priors Harnall *COV* CV1 .... 9 J1
Priors Mi *SEDG* DY3 .... 66 C7
The Priors *BDWTH* CV12 .... 117 G3
Priors Wy *ERDW/GRVHL* B23 ..... 72 A5
Priory Av *SLYOAK* B29 .... 124 F3
Priory Cl *CSHL/WTROR* B46 .... 93 L8 🔟
  DUDN DY1 .... 84 F3
  HOCK/TIA B94............................ 173 H8
  WBROM B70 .... 87 K3
Priory Ct *KNWTH* CV8 .... 191 K1
Priory Dr *LGLYGN/QTN* B68 .... 87 G8
Priory Field Cl *BILS/COS* WV14 .. 66 B4
Priory La *SEDG* DY3 .... 66 B6
Priory Ms *WWCK* CV34 .... 199 J6 🔟
Priory Rd *ALE/KHTH/YWD* B14 ... 125 G6
  ALE/KHTH/YWD B14................... 146 B1
  AST/WIT B6.................................. 89 M5
  BRGRVW B61 .... 164 E7
  DUDN DY1 .... 85 G3
  EDG B15 .... 106 F7
  HEDN WS12 .... 17 H1
  KNWTH CV8 .... 176 D8
  KNWTH CV8 .... 180 F1
  RMSLY B62 .... 122 C1
  SHLY B90 .... 146 C2
  STRBR DY8 .... 119 M2
  WWCK CV34 .... 199 J6
Priory Rw *COV* CV1 .... 9 G4
Priory St *COV* CV1 .... 9 G4
  DUDN DY1 .... 85 G4 🔟
  NUNW/HART CV10........................ 98 A2
  RLSS CV31 .... 200 D7
Priory Ter *RLSS* CV31 .... 200 D6
The Priory *SEDG* DY3 .... 66 B5
  STRPT SY13 .... 160 D8
Priory Wk *ATHST* CV9 .... 63 K7
  CSCFLD/WYGN B72 .... 72 F6
Pritchard Av *WNSFLD* WV11 .... 37 J7
Pritchard Cl *SMTHWK* B66 .... 87 M8 🔟🔟
Pritchard St *BRLYHL* DY5 .... 101 M2
  DARL/WED WS10 .... 68 D2
Pritchatts Rd *EDG* B15 .... 106 D8
Pritchett Av
  ETTPK/GDPK/PENN WV4 .... 66 D3
Pritchett Rd *NFLD/LBR* B31 ..... 143 M6
Pritchett St *AST/WIT* B6 .... 89 J8
Private Wy *RBRY* B45 .... 167 G1

Privet Cl *KGSTG* B44 .... 71 J2
Privet Rd *COVE* CV2 .... 134 F3 🔟
Probert Rd *WOLVN* WV10 .... 35 M4
Proctors Barn La *REDE* B98 ..... 196 F1 🔟
Proctor St *VAUX/NECH* B7 .... 89 L8
Proffitt Av *COVN* CV6 .... 134 E4
Proffitt Cl *WSL* WS1 .... 53 J1
Proffitt St *WSLW* WS2 .... 53 J1
Progress Dr *CNCK/NC* WS11 ...... 16 C6
Progress Wy *COVS* CV3 .... 155 L5
Prole St *WOLVN* WV10 .... 50 B1
The Promenade *BRLYHL* DY5 ... 102 B3
Prophets Cl *REDW* B97 .... 196 B2
Prospect Dr *LICHS* WS14 .... 21 K5
Prospect Gdns *STRBR* DY8 ..... 119 L1 🔟
Prospect Hi *KIDD* DY10 .... 137 J7
  REDW B97 .... 188 C8
  STRBR DY8 .... 119 L1
Prospect La *KIDD* DY10 .... 137 J7 🔟
  SOLH B91 .... 147 H8
Prospect Rd *BNTWD* WS7 .... 18 F7
  MOS/BIL B13 .... 125 K4
  RLSS CV31 .... 200 F8
  RMSLY B62 .... 104 A8
  SEDG DY3 .... 83 M3
Prospect Rd North *REDE* B98 ... 196 E1 🔟
Prospect Rd South *REDE* B98 ... 196 E1
Prospect Rw *DUDS* DY2 .... 85 H6
  STRBR DY8 .... 119 L2 🔟
Prospect St *BILS/COS* WV14 ..... 51 J7
  CRTAM B79 .... 31 L8
  TPTN/OCK DY4 .... 68 A5
Prosper Meadow *KGSWFD* DY6 .. 83 J6
Prospero Cl *RBRY* B45 .... 142 E3
Prosser St *BILS/COS* WV14 .... 51 J7
  WOLVN WV10 .... 36 C8
Prossers Wk *CSHL/WTROR* B46 .. 93 K6
Proud Cross Ringway
  KIDDW DY10 .... 137 G6
Proud's La *BILS/COS* WV14 .... 51 H5
Provence Cl *WOLVN* WV10 .... 50 D1
Providence Cl *BLOX/PEL* WS3 .... 39 G6
Providence Dr
  HAG/WOL DY9 .... 102 C7 🔟
Providence La *BLOX/PEL* WS3 ... 39 G6
Providence Rd *BRGRVW* B61 .... 185 K2
Providence Rw *BILS/COS* WV14... 66 F5
Providence St *CDYHTH* B64 ..... 103 H4
  COVW CV5.................................. 153 K5
  HAG/WOL DY9 .... 102 C7
  TPTN/OCK DY4 .... 68 A8
Pruden Av
  ETTPK/GDPK/PENN WV4 .... 66 D2
Pryor Rd *LGLYGN/QTN* B68 ..... 105 G2
Puckering's La *WWCK* CV34 ..... 199 J7 🔟
Pudsey Dr *MGN/WHC* B75........... 57 G2
Pugh Crs *WSLW* WS2 .... 52 C3
Pugh Rd *AST/WIT* B6.................. 89 L6
  BILS/COS WV14 .... 66 D3
  BILS/COS WV14 .... 67 J2
Pugin Cl
  DUNHL/THL/PER WV6.................. 48 B2 🔟
Pugin Gdns *ERDW/GRVHL* B23 .. 72 B5
Pullman Cl *TAM/AM/WIL* B77...... 46 E3
Puma Rd *COV* CV1 .... 9 H8
Puma Wy *COV* CV1 .... 9 H7
Pumphouse La *BRGRVE* B60..... 166 D5
  REDW B97.................................. 194 F5
Pump La *RCOVN/BALC/EX* CV7 .. 114 A2
Pump St *BKHL/PFLD* WV2 .... 50 E6
  KIDD DY10 .... 161 J1 🔟
Puppy Gn *TPTN/OCK* DY4 .... 67 L8
Purbeck Cl *HALE* B63................. 121 H5
Purbeck Cft *RIDG/WDGT* B32 ... 105 K8 🔟
Purbrook Rd *WOLV* WV1 .... 3 M8
Purbrook Rd *WOLV* WV1 .... 50 E3
Purcell Av *LICH* WS13 .... 20 F3
  NUN CV11 .... 99 L6
Purcell Rd *COVN* CV6 .... 134 F5
  WOLVN WV10 .... 36 B5
Purdy Rd *BILS/COS* WV14 .... 67 J4
Purefoy Rd *COVS* CV3 .... 154 B5
  MOS/BIL B13 .... 126 A8
Purley Chase La *ATHST* CV9 .... 79 G2
Purley Gv *ERDW/GRVHL* B23 ..... 71 L8
Purley Vw *ATHST* CV9 .... 63 K7
Purlieu La *KNWTH* CV8............... 176 A8
Purnells Wy *DOR/KN* B93 .... 148 E8
Purshall Cl *REDW* B97 .... 196 A2
Purslow Gv *NFLD/LBR* B31 ...... 143 L4
Purton Ms *RLSS* CV31 .... 201 G7
Putney Av *BFLD/HDSWWD* B20 .. 89 G4
Putney La *RMSLY* B62 .... 141 M3
Putney Rd *BFLD/HDSWWD* B20 .. 89 G4
Puxton Dr *KIDDW* DY11 .... 137 H4
Puxton La *KIDDW* DY11 .... 137 H4
Pye Green Rd *CNCK/NC* WS11 ... 12 C8 🔟
  CNCK/NC WS11............................. 16 B3
  HEDN WS12 .... 12 D5
Pype Hayes Rd
  ERDE/BCHGN B24 .... 91 H1
Pytman Dr *WALM/CURD* B76 ..... 73 L6
Pyt Pk *COVW* CV5 .... 153 G1

Q

The Quadrant *SEDG* DY3 .... 66 B4
Quadrille Lawns *COVEN* WV9 ..... 35 K3 🔟
Quail Gn *DUNHL/THL/PER* WV6 .. 48 D3
Quail Park Dr *KIDD* DY10 .... 161 L3 🔟
Qualcast Rd *WOLVN* WV10 .... 3 L4
Quantock Cl *HALE* B63 .... 121 H5
  RBRY B45 .... 142 F3
Quantock Dr *KIDD* DY10 .... 137 L7
  NUNW/HART CV10........................ 97 M2
Quantock Rd *STRBR* DY8 .... 101 M7 🔟
Quantry La *HAG/WOL* DY9........ 141 J6
Quarrington Gv
  ALE/KHTH/YWD B14................... 145 L2 🔟
Quarry Brow *SEDG* DY3 .... 66 C2
Quarry Cl *GTWY* WS6 .... 24 C2
  RUGBYN/HIL CV21 .... 159 K7 🔟
  RWWCK/WEL CV35...................... 191 K6
Quarryfield La *COV* CV1.............. 9 J7
Quarry Flds *RWWCK/WEL* CV35... 191 K6

Quarry Hi *HALE* B63.................. 121 K3 🔟
Quarry Hills La *LICHS* WS14 ...... 21 L5
Quarry House Cl *RBRY* B45 ...... 142 D4
Quarry La *ATHST* CV9 .... 79 J1
  BRGRVW B61 .... 185 H5
  HALE B63 .... 121 K3
  NFLD/LBR B31 .... 143 K2
  NUN CV11 .... 99 K4
  RMSLY B62 .... 121 K3
Quarry Park Rd *STRBR* DY8 ..... 119 L5
Quarry Ri *OLDBY* B69 .... 85 M5
Quarry Rd *DUDS* DY2 .... 102 F3
  KNWTH CV8 .... 176 C7
  SLYOAK B29 .... 123 K4
Quarry St *RLSN* CV32 .... 200 A4
The Quarry *KIDD* DY10 .... 137 K5
Quarry Wk *RBRY* B45................. 142 E6
Quarrywood Gv *COVE* CV2 .... 154 E1
Quayle Gv *STRBR* DY8 .... 101 H2
Quayside
  OLDBY B69 .... 86 C5 🔟
Queen Eleanors Dr
  DOR/KN B93 .... 148 F5
Queen Elizabeth Av *WSLW* WS2 .. 52 D3
Queen Elizabeth Rd *KIDD* DY10 .. 137 M7
  NUNW/HART CV10........................ 80 A7
  RBRY B45 .... 142 C3
Queen Isabel's Av *COVS* CV3 ... 154 B5
Queen Margaret's Rd
  TLHL/CAN CV4 .... 152 F5
Queen Mary's Rd
  BDWTH CV12 .... 99 G8 🔟
  COVN CV6 .... 134 B5
Queen Mary St *WSL* WS1 .... 4 D9
Queen Philippa St *COVS* CV3 ... 154 B7 🔟
Queen's Av *OLDBY* B69 .... 85 M4
  SHLY B90 .... 146 F3
Queensbridge Rd *MOS/BIL* B13 . 125 H3
  KNWTH CV8 .... 191 K2
  SMTHWKW B67 .... 87 L8
Queens Cl *ERDE/BCHGN* B24 ..... 90 D3
  KNWTH CV8 .... 191 K2
  SMTHWKW B67 .... 87 L8
Queens Crs *BILS/COS* WV14 ..... 51 K7
  STRBR DY8 .... 101 L6 🔟
Queen's Cross *DUDS* DY2 .... 84 F5
Queens Dr *BLKHTH/ROWR* B65... 104 B1
  BNTWD WS7 .... 18 D8
  BVILLE B30 .... 144 L1
Queensferry Cl
  RUGBYS/DCH CV22 .... 183 G5 🔟
Queens Gdns *BILS/COS* WV14 .. 51 H6
  CDSL WV8 .... 34 D2
  DUDS DY2 .... 103 G1 🔟
Queens Head Rd *HDSW* B21 ...... 88 C6
Queens Hi *HAG/WOL* DY9 .... 140 B6
Queensland Av *COVW* CV5 .... 153 K3
Queen's Lea *SHHTH* WV12 .... 38 A8
Queen's Park Rd *HRBN* B17 ..... 105 K7
Queen Sq *WOLV* WV1 .... 2 F5
Queen's Ride *MOS/BIL* B13 ...... 125 G1
Queens Rd *AST/WIT* B6 .... 89 L5
  ATHST CV9 .... 63 J5
  COV CV1 .... 8 C6
  DSYBK/YTR WS5........................... 5 M9
  ERDW/GRVHL B23 .... 90 A2
  KNWTH CV8 .... 191 K2
  LGLYGN/QTN B68 .... 87 H8
  LGN/SDN/BHAMAIR B26 .... 109 K4
  NUN CV11 .... 98 F1 🔟
  RRUGBY CV23............................. 157 J6
  RUSH/SHEL WS4 .... 40 A6
  SEDG DY3 .... 66 C5
  SMTHWKW B67 .... 87 L8
  STRBR DY8 .... 101 K7 🔟
  TPTN/OCK DY4 .... 67 K8
  WOLVN WV10 .... 14 F7
Queen's Sq *WWCK* CV34 .... 199 H8 🔟
Queen St *ALDR* WS9 .... 40 D3
  BDWTH CV12 .... 117 G3
  BHTH/HG B12 .... 107 M8
  BILS/COS WV14 .... 51 J8
  BNTWD WS7 .... 18 D7
  BRLYHL DY5 .... 84 B6 🔟
  BRLYHL DY5 .... 84 B7 🔟
  BRLYHL DY5 .... 102 E5 🔟
  CDYHTH B64.............................. 103 H4 🔟
  CNCK/NC WS11............................. 12 E8
  CNCK/NC WS11............................. 16 B4
  COV CV1 .... 9 H2
  CSCFLD/WYGN B72 .... 72 F1
  DARL/WED WS10 .... 67 M1
  GTWY WS6 .... 24 B3
  HALE B63 .... 121 L2 🔟
  KGSWFD DY6 .... 83 H6
  KIDD DY10 .... 137 J6
  LICH WS13 .... 20 E6
  OLDBY B69 .... 86 E5
  REDE B98 .... 196 C1 🔟
  RLSN CV32 .... 193 H8
  RLSN CV32 .... 200 E4
  RUGBYN/HIL CV21 .... 183 L2
  STRBR DY8 .... 101 H2
  STRBR DY8 .... 119 L3 🔟
  TPTN/OCK DY4 .... 67 K5 🔟
  WBROM B70 .... 87 H2
  WOLV WV1 .... 3 G5
  WSLW WS2 .... 4 C4
Queens Wy *POL/KGSB/FAZ* B78 .. 47 K7
  ATHST CV9 .... 77 G1
  BEWD DY12 .... 136 A8 🔟
Queensway *CRTAM* B79 .... 31 J2
  FOAKS/STRLY B74 .... 55 L5 🔟
  HAG/WOL DY9 .... 120 C3
  HALE B63 .... 121 L2 🔟
  LGLYGN/QTN B68 .... 104 F4
  NUNW/HART CV10........................ 81 H7
  RLSS CV31 .... 200 C7
Queensway Cl
  LGLYGN/QTN B68 .... 104 F4 🔟
Queenswood Rd
  MGN/WHC B75 .... 56 F9
  MOS/BIL B13 .... 125 L1
Queen Victoria Rd *COV* CV1 .... 8 E6 🔟
  COV CV1 .... 8 E6 🔟
Quenby Dr *DUDN* DY1 .... 84 E2
Quendale *WMBN* WV5 .... 64 C7
Quentin Dr *DUDN* DY1 .... 84 D5
Queslade Cl *GTB/HAM* B43 .... 70 D4
Queslett Rd *GTB/HAM* B43 .... 70 F3
  KGSTG B44 .... 71 J2

PBAR/PBCH B42 70 F3
Queslett Rd East
FOAKS/STRLY B74 55 L7
Quibery Cl REDE B98 197 K2
Quicksand La ALDR WS9 54 D1
Quigley Av BORD B9 107 M3 7
Quillets Rd STRBR DY8 101 G2 2
Quilletts Cl COVN CV6 134 E4
Quilter Cl BILS/COS WV14 66 E5
WSLW WS2 52 D2
Quilter Rd ERDE/BCHGN B24 90 F3 2
Quincey Dr ERDE/BCHGN B24 91 G2
Quincy Ri BRLYHL DY5 102 A6 3
Quinneys La REDE B98 196 F7
Quinton Av GTWY WS6 24 D2
Quinton Cl HIA/OLT B92 128 B1
REDE B98 197 H4 3
Quinton Expy RIDG/WDGT B32 122 F1
Quinton La RIDG/WDGT B32 105 H7
Quinton Pk COVS CV3 154 B6
Quinton Rd COV CV1 9 G8
COVS CV3 9 G8
HRBN B17 123 M2
Quinton Rd West
RIDG/WDGT B32 104 F8
Quorn Crs STRBR DY8 101 G2 3
Quorn Gv ERDE/BCHGN B24 90 F3
Quorn Wy COVS CV3 155 J6

R

Rabbit La WOLVN WV10 22 E6
Rabone La SMTHWK B66 87 M7
Raby Cl OLDBY B69 85 K5
Raby St BKHL/PFLD WV2 3 H8
Racecourse La STRBR DY8 119 J4
Racecourse Rd
DUNHL/THL/PER WV6 35 L8
Racemeadow Rd ATHST CV9 63 K4
Rachael Gdns DARL/WED WS10 69 G1
Rachel Cl TPTN/OCK DY4 68 A4
Rachel Gdns SLYOAK B29 124 B3
Radbourn Dr FOAKS/STRLY B74 57 G7
Radbourne Dr HALE B63 102 E6
Radbourne Rd SHLY B90 147 H2
Radbrook Wy RLSS CV31 201 H7 3
Radcliffe Dr RMSLY B62 104 C7
Radcliffe Rd COVW CV5 153 K5
Raddens Rd RMSLY B62 122 D2
Raddington Dr HIA/OLT B92 127 H5
Raddlebarn Farm Dr
SLYOAK B29 124 D4
Raddlebarn Rd SLYOAK B29 124 D4
Radford Av KIDD DY10 137 J6
Radford Cir COVN CV6 8 B1
Radford Cl ATHST CV9 63 J3
DSYBK/YTR WS5 69 L2
Radford Dr RUSH/SHEL WS4 40 A3
Radford La
ETTPK/GDPK/PENN WV4 48 D6
Radford Ri SOLH B91 128 C8 1
Radford Rd ALVE B48 168 A7
COVN CV6 133 L6
RLSS CV31 200 F6
SLYOAK B29 123 L6
Radley Dr NUNW/HART CV10 98 E4
Radley Gv SLYOAK B29 123 L3
Radley Rd HAG/WOL DY9 120 D1
RUSH/SHEL WS4 40 A7
The Radleys STETCH B33 110 B6
Radmore Cl BNTWD WS7 18 B5
Radnor Cl RBRY B45 142 F3
Radnor Cft DSYBK/YTR WS5 70 A2 1
Radnor Dr NUNW/HART CV10 98 C3
Radnor Gn HHTH/SAND B71 69 G6
Radnor Ri HEDN WS12 16 F1
Radnor Rd BFLD/HDSWWD B20 88 F5
LGLYGN/QTN B68 104 F6 2
SEDG DY3 66 A5
Radnor St WSNGN B18 88 E7
Radnor Wk COVE CV2 135 K5
Radstock Av CBROM B36 91 G6
Radstock Rd SHHTH WV12 38 A4
Radway Cl REDE B98 188 F6 1
Radway Rd SHLY B90 147 J6
Raeburn Rd GTB/HAM B43 71 G1
Raford Rd ERDW/GRVHL B23 72 B7
Ragees Rd STRBR DY8 101 K2
Raglan Av DUNHL/THL/PER WV6 48 A2 1
SMTHWK B66 106 A1
Raglan Cl FOAKS/STRLY B74 55 K2
NUN CV11 99 H1
SEDG DY3 65 M6
Raglan Gv KNWTH CV8 176 F8
Raglan Rd DIG/EDG B5 107 H7
HDSW B21 88 A5
SMTHWK B66 106 A1
Raglan St BDMR/CCFT WV3 2 D5
BRLYHL DY5 102 A1 1
COV CV1 9 J4
Raglan Wy
CHWD/FDBR/MGN B37 111 H3
Ragley Cl BLOX/PEL WS3 38 E4
DOR/KN B93 148 F6
Ragley Crs BRGRVE B60 185 L5
Ragley Dr GTB/HAM B43 70 B3
LGN/SDN/BHAMAIR B26 110 A7
WLNHL WV13 51 K5 3
Ragley Wy NUN CV11 99 K3
Raglis Cl REDW B97 195 L3
Ragnall Av STETCH B33 110 B6 1
Raikes La LICHS WS14 27 M7
Railswood Dr BLOX/PEL WS3 39 L2
Railway Dr BILS/COS WV14 51 J8
WOLV WV1 3 H4
Railway La BNTWD WS7 18 C4
WLNHL WV13 51 L4
Railway Rd BFLD/HDSWWD B20 89 K3
SCFLD/BOLD B73 56 F8
Railwayside Cl SMTHWK B66 87 J6 3
Railway St BILS/COS WV14 51 J8 4
CNCK/NC WS11 16 C5
CNCK/NC WS11 17 L8
RRUGBY CV23 182 E1
TPTN/OCK DY4 68 A8
WBROM B70 86 F1
WOLV WV1 3 H4
Railway Ter DARL/WED WS10 68 E3 1
RUGBYN/HIL CV21 183 M1
VAUX/NECH B7 89 M6
Rainbow St BILS/COS WV14 67 H2
BKHL/PFLD WV2 3 G9 1
Rainham Cl TPTN/OCK DY4 67 H8
Rainsbrook Dr NUN CV11 99 L4
SHLY B90 147 K7
Rainscar TAM/AM/WIL B77 46 F6
Raison Av NUN CV11 81 K5
Rake Hl BNTWD WS7 18 F5
Rake Wy EDG B15 6 B7
Raleigh Cl HDSW B21 87 M4
Raleigh Cft GTB/HAM B43 70 C2
Raleigh Rd BILS/COS WV14 67 K2
BORD B9 108 B3
COVE CV2 154 F2
Raleigh St HHTH/SAND B71 87 G1
WSLW WS2 4 A1
Ralph Crs POL/KGSB/FAZ B78 60 A7
Ralph Rd COVN CV6 133 K8
SHLY B90 147 H1
WASH/WDE B8 108 B1
Ralphs Meadow
RIDG/WDGT B32 123 H3
Ralston Cl BLOX/PEL WS3 38 E1
Ramillies Crs GTWY WS6 24 D4
Ramp Rd
CHWD/FDBR/MGN B37 111 G8
Ramsay Cl HHTH/SAND B71 69 K5
Ramsay Crs COVW CV5 132 F6
Ramsay Rd LGLYGN/QTN B68 105 G4
TPTN/OCK DY4 67 J6
WSLW WS2 38 E8
Ramsden Av NUNW/HART CV10 80 A6
Ramsden Cl SLYOAK B29 123 M6
Ramsden Rd ATHST CV9 63 L6
Ramsey Cl RBRY B45 142 C4 1
Ramsey Rd RLSS CV31 200 F7
VAUX/NECH B7 90 A6 6
Ranby Rd COVE CV2 9 L2
Randall Av ALVE B48 167 L7
Randall Cl KGSWFD DY6 101 K1
Randall Rd KNWTH CV8 191 K2
Randle Dr MGN/WHC B75 57 G2
Randle Rd HAG/WOL DY9 120 A1
NUNW/HART CV10 98 B1
Randle St COVN CV6 133 M8
Randolph Cl RLSS CV31 201 G7 3
Randwick Gv KGSTG B44 71 H4
Ranelagh Rd BKHL/PFLD WV2 50 A7
Ranelagh St RLSS CV31 200 E7
Ranelagh Ter RLSS CV31 200 D7
Range Meadow Cl RLSN CV32 200 B4
Range Wy POL/KGSB/FAZ B78 60 B8
Rangeways Rd KGSWFD DY6 101 K2
KIDDW DY11 136 E5
Rangeworthy Cl REDW B97 196 A6
Rangifer Rd
POL/KGSB/FAZ B78 45 K4 1
Rangoon Rd HIA/OLT B92 128 C1
Rankine Cl RUGBYN/HIL CV21 159 H6
Ranleigh Av KGSWFD DY6 101 K1
Rann Cl LDYWD/EDGR B16 106 E4 2
Rannoch Cl BRLYHL DY5 101 M5
STRPT DY13 160 C6
Rannoch Dr NUNW/HART CV10 80 A8
Rannock Cl COVS CV3 155 K3 2
Ranscombe Dr SEDG DY3 84 B3 5
Ransome Rd
RCOVN/BALC/EX CV7 96 E5
Ransom Rd COVN CV6 134 C5
ERDW/GRVHL B23 90 A1
Ranulf Cft COVS CV3 154 A6
Ranworth Ri
ETTPK/GDPK/PENN WV4 66 B1
Raphael Cl COVW CV5 153 G2
Ratcliffe Br ATHST CV9 63 K3
Ratcliffe Cl SEDG DY3 66 D6
Ratcliffe Rd ATHST CV9 63 K4
SOLH B91 128 A6 4
WNSFLD WV11 37 L7 3
Ratcliffe St ATHST CV9 63 H5
Ratcliff Wk OLDBY B69 86 D6 1
Ratcliff Wy TPTN/OCK DY4 68 A7
Rathbone Cl BILS/COS WV14 51 H8 2
DIG/EDG B5 107 J6 3
RCOVN/BALC/EX CV7 115 L7 2
Rathbone Rd SMTHWKW B67 105 K3
Rathlin Cl COVEN WV9 35 L2
Rathlin Cft CBROM B36 92 F8
Rathmore Cl STRBR DY8 119 J3 1
Rathwell Cl COVEN WV9 35 L3
Ratliffe Rd RUGBYS/DCH CV22 183 K6
Rattle Cft STETCH B33 109 J2 3
Raveloe Dr NUN CV11 99 H4
Ravenall Cl BKDE/SHDE B34 91 M6 2
Raven Cl CTWY WS6 24 B3 4
HEDN WS12 12 A6 3
HEDN WS12 17 J1
Raven Cragg Rd COVW CV5 153 J5 1
Raven Crs WNSFLD WV11 37 K5 3
Ravenfield Cl WASH/WDE B8 90 E8 2
Ravenhayes La
RIDG/WDGT B32 122 E7
Raven Hays Rd NFLD/LBR B31 143 G3
Ravenhill Dr CDSL WV8 34 E2
Ravenhurst Dr GTB/HAM B43 70 C2
Ravenhurst Ms
ERDW/GRVHL B23 90 C2
Ravenhurst Rd HRBN B17 106 A6
Ravenhurst St BHTH/HG B12 7 L9
Raven Rd DSYBK/YTR WS5 5 M9
Ravens Bank Dr REDE B98 189 H6
Ravensbourne Gv WLNHL WV13 52 A3
Ravenscroft STRBR DY8 101 G7 5
Ravenscroft Rd HIA/OLT B92 127 L5
SHHTH WV12 37 M8
Ravensdale Av RLSN CV32 200 A3 1
Ravensdale Cl DSYBK/YTR WS5 5 L8
Ravensdale Gdns
DSYBK/YTR WS5 5 L9
Ravensdale Rd COVE CV2 155 G2
SMHTH B10 108 D6 1
Ravenshaw La SOLH B91 148 E1
Ravenshaw Rd
LDYWD/EDGR B16 106 A3
Ravenshaw Wy SOLH B91 148 E3
Ravenshill Rd
ALE/KHTH/YWD B14 146 A1
Ravensholme
DUNHL/THL/PER WV6 48 D3
Ravensitch Wk BRLYHL DY5 102 C4 2
Ravensmere Rd REDE B98 196 F4
Ravensthorpe Cl COVS CV3 155 J5 2
Ravenstone TAM/AM/WIL B77 46 F5 3
Ravenswood EDG B15 106 C5
Ravenswood Cl
FOAKS/STRLY B74 56 F5
Ravenswood Dr SOLH B91 147 J4
Ravenswood Hl
CSHL/WTROR B46 93 K6
Raven Wy NUN CV11 99 K3
Rawdon Gv KGSTG B44 71 M5 4
Rawlings Rd SMTHWKW B67 105 L3
Rawlins Cft CVALE B35 91 M2
Rawlinson Rd RLSN CV32 200 F3 1
Rawlins St LDYWD/EDGR B16 106 E4
Rawnsley Dr KNWTH CV8 177 G7
Rawnsley Rd HEDN WS12 13 J6
Rawn Vw ATHST CV9 63 K7
Raybolds Bridge St
WSLW WS2 53 G1 1
Raybon Cft RBRY B45 142 E7 3
Raybould's Fold DUDS DY2 85 G8
Rayford Dr HHTH/SAND B71 69 G5
Raygill TAM/AM/WIL B77 46 F5
Ray Hall La GTB/HAM B43 69 L4
Rayleigh Rd BDMR/CCFT WV3 2 A9
Raymond Av PBAR/PBCH B42 70 F7
Raymond Cl COVN CV6 116 D8
WSLW WS2 39 H8
Raymond Gdns WNSFLD WV11 37 J8
Raymond Rd WASH/WDE B8 108 C1
Raymont Gv GTB/HAM B43 70 F1 1
Rayners Cft
LGN/SDN/BHAMAIR B26 109 K3 1
Raynor Crs BDWTH CV12 116 B4
Raynor Rd WOLVN WV10 36 D7
The Raywoods
NUNW/HART CV10 98 D2
Rea Av RBRY B45 142 C5
Reabrook Rd NFLD/LBR B31 143 K5
Rea Cl NFLD/LBR B31 143 L6
Readers Wk GTB/HAM B43 70 D4
Reading Av NUN CV11 81 K5
Reading Cl COVN CV6 134 F2 1
Read St COV CV1 9 K4
Rea Fordway RBRY B45 142 D4 4
Reansway Sq
DUNHL/THL/PER WV6 49 L1
Reapers Cl SHHTH WV12 38 B8
Reardon Ct WWCK CV34 199 J4 10
Reaside Crs
ALE/KHTH/YWD B14 124 F8
Reaside Cft BHTH/HG B12 107 J7 7
Reaside Dr RBRY B45 142 F5
Rea St DIG/EDG B5 7 J8
Rea St South DIG/EDG B5 7 H9
Rea Ter DIG/EDG B5 7 K6
Rea Valley Dr NFLD/LBR B31 143 M3
Reaview Dr SLYOAK B29 124 F3
Reaymer Cl WSLW WS2 38 F6
Reay Nadin Dr SCFLD/BOLD B73 71 M1
Rebecca Dr SLYOAK B29 124 C3
Rebecca Gdns
ETTPK/GDPK/PENN WV4 65 K1
Recreation Rd BRGRVW B61 185 K2
COVN CV6 134 E2
Recreation St DUDS DY2 85 H8 2
Rectory Av DARL/WED WS10 52 B7 2
Rectory Cl COVW CV5 133 G7 2
POL/KGSB/FAZ B78 45 J8
RCOVN/BALC/EX CV7 116 E4
STRBR DY8 119 M2
Rectory Dr
RCOVN/BALC/EX CV7 116 E4
Rectory Gdns SOLH B91 148 B2
STRBR DY8 119 M2 4
Rectory Gv WSNGN B18 88 C7
Rectory La CBROM B36 91 L5
COVW CV5 133 G7
Rectory Park Av MGN/WHC B75 73 J1
Rectory Park Cl MGN/WHC B75 73 J1
Rectory Park Rd
LGN/SDN/BHAMAIR B26 110 A8
Rectory Rd MGN/WHC B75 57 G8
NFLD/LBR B31 143 M2
RCOVN/BALC/EX CV7 96 C4
REDW B97 196 A4
SOLH B91 148 A2
STRBR DY8 119 M2
Rectory St STRBR DY8 101 H2
Redacre Rd SCFLD/BOLD B73 72 D3
Redacres DUNHL/THL/PER WV6 35 J7
Redbank Av ERDW/GRVHL B23 90 A2
Redbourn Rd BLOX/PEL WS3 38 E1
Red Brick Cl CDYHTH B64 103 H6 1
Redbrook Cl HEDN WS12 17 H4
Redbrook Covert
HWK/WKHTH B38 144 C5 6
Red Brook Rd WSLW WS2 38 E8
Redbrooks Cl SOLH B91 147 L4 3
Redburn Dr
ALE/KHTH/YWD B14 145 H3
Redcap Cft COVN CV6 134 B1 2
Redcar Cl RLSN CV32 200 F1
Redcar Cft CBROM B36 91 G5
Redcar Rd WOLVN WV10 36 B1
Redcliff TAM/AM/WIL B77 32 D8 3
Redcliffe Dr WMBN WV5 64 F7
Redcotts Cl WOLVN WV10 36 E6
Redcroft Dr ERDE/BCHGN B24 73 G8
Redcroft Rd DUDS DY2 85 J7 1
Reddal Hill Rd CDYHTH B64 103 J4
Red Deeps NUN CV11 99 H5
Reddicap Heath Rd
WALM/CURD B76 73 K1
Reddicap Hl WALM/CURD B76 73 H1
Reddicroft SCFLD/BOLD B73 57 G8 3
Reddings La CSHL/WTROR B46 76 E8
HLGN/YWD B28 126 C3
SPARK B11 126 C2
Reddings Rd MOS/BIL B13 125 H3
The Reddings HLYWD B47 145 L8 3
Redditch Ringway REDW B97 196 B2
Redditch Rd ALVE B48 167 M2
ALVE B48 188 A3
BRGRVE B60 185 H7
HWK/WKHTH B38 144 B5
STUD B80 197 H7 1
Redesdale Av COVN CV6 133 K8
Redfern Av KNWTH CV8 176 E7
Redfern Cl HIA/OLT B92 127 M4
Redfern Dr BNTWD WS7 18 F8
Redfern Park Wy SPARK B11 108 E8
Redfern Rd SPARK B11 108 E8
Redfly La BRLYHL DY5 84 A7
Redford Cl MOS/BIL B13 125 M3 1
Redgate Cl HWK/WKHTH B38 144 B3
Redhall Rd RIDG/WDGT B32 105 J6 1
SEDG DY3 84 A3
Red Hl REDE B98 196 D3
STRBR DY8 119 M1
Redhill Av WMBN WV5 64 E7
Redhill Cl CRTAM B79 31 L6
STRBR DY8 119 M1
Red Hill Cl STUD B80 197 J7
Red Hill Gv HWK/WKHTH B38 144 D6
Redhill La BRGRVW B61 142 A8
Red Hill Pl RMSLY B62 121 L6
Redhill Rd CNCK/NC WS11 16 D1
HWK/WKHTH B38 144 B6
NFLD/LBR B31 143 M5
YDLY B25 108 E7 1
Red Hill St WOLV WV1 2 F2
Red House Av
DARL/WED WS10 68 F2 3
Redhouse Cl DOR/KN B93 148 C8
Red House La ALDR WS9 40 C8
Red House Park Rd
GTB/HAM B43 70 C3
Redhouse Rd
DUNHL/THL/PER WV6 34 F8
Red House Rd STETCH B33 109 J2
Redhouse St WSL WS1 4 F8
Redhurst Dr WOLVN WV10 35 M2
Redlake TAM/AM/WIL B77 46 C5
Redlake Dr HAG/WOL DY9 119 M5
Redlake Rd STRBR DY8 119 M4
Redland Cl BRGRVE B60 166 A4
COVE CV2 135 H3
Redland La KNWTH CV8 179 L2
Redland Rd RLSS CV31 200 F8
Redlands Cl SOLH B91 128 B8
Redlands Rd SOLH B91 128 A8
Redlands Wy FOAKS/STRLY B74 55 L4
Red La COVN CV6 134 C8
KNWTH CV8 175 M1
KNWTH CV8 176 B5
NUNW/HART CV10 97 J6
SEDG DY3 65 M5
WNSFLD WV11 38 A3
Red Leasowes Rd HALE B63 121 K2
Redliff Av CBROM B36 92 B4 3
Red Lion Av CNCK/NC WS11 25 L1
Red Lion Cl OLDBY B69 85 L4
Red Lion Crs CNCK/NC WS11 25 L1
Red Lion La CNCK/NC WS11 25 L1
Red Lion St ALVE B48 167 M7
REDE B98 196 C1 6
WOLV WV1 2 E4
Redlock Fld LICHS WS14 20 E8
Red Lodge Dr
RUGBYS/DCH CV22 183 J5
Redmead Cl NFLD/LBR B31 144 A1
Redmoor Gdns
ETTPK/GDPK/PENN WV4 49 L8 3
Redmoor Rd RUGE WS15 18 D2
Redmoor Wy WALM/CURD B76 74 B7
Rednal Hill La RBRY B45 142 E7
Rednall Dr MGN/WHC B75 57 G2
Rednal Mill Dr RBRY B45 143 G6
Rednal Rd HWK/WKHTH B38 144 A5
Redpine Crest SHHTH WV12 52 B1
Red River Rd WSLW WS2 38 E8 2
Red Rock Dr CDSL WV8 34 D3
Redruth Cl COVN CV6 134 E5
DSYBK/YTR WS5 54 B6 2
KGSWFD DY6 83 H5
NUN CV11 99 K1
Redruth Rd DSYBK/YTR WS5 54 B6
Red Sands Rd KIDDW DY11 137 J5
Redstart Av KIDD DY10 161 M3
Redstone Cl REDE B98 189 G7
Redstone Dr WNSFLD WV11 37 K8
Redstone Farm Rd
HLGN/YWD B28 126 F7
Redthorn Gv STETCH B33 109 H2
Redvers Rd BORD B9 108 C4 3
Redwell Cl TAM/AM/WIL B77 32 B8 3
Redwing TAM/AM/WIL B77 46 E7
Redwing Cl BNTWD WS7 19 H8
Redwing Ct KIDD DY10 161 L4 2
Redwing Dr HEDN WS12 12 A6
Redwing Gv
ERDW/GRVHL B23 71 M6 4
Redwood Av DUDN DY1 66 D8
Redwood Cl BVILLE B30 144 C1
FOAKS/STRLY B74 55 K3
Redwood Cft
ALE/KHTH/YWD B14 125 J6 1
NUNW/HART CV10 98 E3
Redwood Dr BNTWD WS7 18 D5
CNCK/NC WS11 16 D2
OLDBY B69 85 M3
POL/KGSB/FAZ B78 60 B6 3
Redwood Gdns ACGN B27 108 F8 5
Redwood Rd BILS/COS WV14 67 H3
BVILLE B30 144 C1
DSYBK/YTR WS5 69 M1
KINVER DY7 118 A2
Redwood Wy WNSFLD WV11 37 M5
Reedham Gdns
ETTPK/GDPK/PENN WV4 49 H7
Reedly Rd SHHTH WV12 38 A4
Reedmace TAM/AM/WIL B77 46 A3 3
Reedmace Cl
HWK/WKHTH B38 144 D5 6
Reedswood Cl WSLW WS2 53 G2
Reedswood Gdns WSLW WS2 53 G2 1
Reedswood La WSLW WS2 53 G2
Reedswood Wy WSLW WS2 53 G1 2
Rees Dr COVS CV3 178 A1
WMBN WV5 64 F6
Reeve Ct KIDD DY10 161 L4
Reeve Dr KNWTH CV8 191 L1
Reeve La LICH WS13 20 F5
Reeves Gdns CDSL WV8 34 E1
Reeves Rd ALE/KHTH/YWD B14 125 G7
Reeves St BLOX/PEL WS3 38 F5
Reform St HHTH/SAND B71 87 H2
WBROM B70 87 H2
Regal Cft CBROM B36 90 F5
Regal Dr WSLW WS2 4 B6
Regan Av SHLY B90 146 E4
Regan Crs ERDW/GRVHL B23 72 C7
Regency Cl NUNW/HART CV10 81 H7
Regency Ct COVW CV5 153 K5
Regency Dr COVS CV3 153 K8
HWK/WKHTH B38 144 C3
KNWTH CV8 191 K2
Regency Gdns
ALE/KHTH/YWD B14 146 A2
Regency Wk FOAKS/STRLY B74 42 B8
Regent Av OLDBY B69 85 L4
Regent Cl DIG/EDG B5 107 H7
HALE B63 121 L1
KGSWFD DY6 83 G7
OLDBY B69 85 L5
Regent Dr OLDBY B69 85 L4
Regent Gv RLSN CV32 200 D5
Regent Pde CBHAMW B1 6 C2
Regent Park Rd SMHTH B10 108 A5
Regent Pl CBHAMW B1 6 C2
OLDBY B69 85 M3
RLSS CV31 200 E6 11
RUGBYN/HIL CV21 183 L1
Regent Rd
ETTPK/GDPK/PENN WV4 49 J8
HDSW B21 88 B5
HRBN B17 106 A7
OLDBY B69 85 L4
Regents Park Rd BRGRVE B60 185 M3
Regent St BDWTH CV12 117 G1
BILS/COS WV14 51 H7
BVILLE B30 124 E6
CBHAMW B1 6 C2
CDYHTH B64 103 K3 3
COV CV1 8 C7
DUDN DY1 67 G7
NUN CV11 99 H1
RLSN CV32 200 D5
RUGBYN/HIL CV21 183 L2
SMTHWK B66 87 L7
TPTN/OCK DY4 67 J5
WLNHL WV13 51 L2 4
Regina Av KGSTG B44 71 H5
Regina Cl RBRY B45 142 C4
Regina Crs COVE CV2 135 L6
DUNHL/THL/PER WV6 48 F1
Regina Dr PBAR/PBCH B42 89 H2
RUSH/SHEL WS4 53 L1
Reginald Rd SMTHWKW B67 105 K3
WASH/WDE B8 108 B1
Regis Gdns BLKHTH/ROWR B65 104 A4
Regis Heath Rd
BLKHTH/ROWR B65 104 B3
Regis Rd BLKHTH/ROWR B65 104 A3
DUNHL/THL/PER WV6 34 F8
Regis Wk COVE CV2 135 K6
Reid Av SHHTH WV12 38 B7
Reid Rd LGLYGN/QTN B68 105 G4
Reindeer Rd POL/KGSB/FAZ B78 45 J4
Reigate Av WASH/WDE B8 109 G1
Relay Dr TAM/AM/WIL B77 47 G6
Relko Dr CBROM B36 91 G6
Rembrandt Cl COVW CV5 153 G2
HEDN WS12 17 H3 5
Remburn Gdns WWCK CV34 199 K5 5
Remembrance Rd COVS CV3 155 H7
DARL/WED WS10 69 G2
Remington Dr CNCK/NC WS11 16 D5
Remington Pl WSLW WS2 39 G8 1
Remington Rd WSLW WS2 38 F7
Rendermore Cl PENK ST19 10 C6 2
Rene Rd TAM/AM/WIL B77 32 C8
Renfrew Cl STRBR DY8 101 G2
Renfrew Gdns KIDDW DY11 137 G8 2
Renfrew Sq CVALE B35 91 M1 4
Renison Rd BDWTH CV12 116 C4
Rennie Gv RIDG/WDGT B32 105 H8
Rennison Dr WMBN WV5 64 E7
Renolds Cl TLHL/CAN CV4 153 G3
Renown Cl BRLYHL DY5 83 M6 1
Renton Gv WOLVN WV10 35 L4
Renton Rd WOLVN WV10 35 L4
Repington Av ATHST CV9 63 H3
Repington Rd North
TAM/AM/WIL B77 32 E8 3
Repington Rd South
TAM/AM/WIL B77 32 E8 4
Repington Wy
MGN/WHC B75 57 M8 3
MGN/WHC B75 57 M7 1
Repton Av
DUNHL/THL/PER WV6 48 B2
Repton Cl CNCK/NC WS11 15 M5
Repton Dr COVN CV6 134 F3
Repton Gv BORD B9 108 F2
Repton Rd BORD B9 108 F2
Reservoir Cl WSLW WS2 52 F5
Reservoir Dr
CSHL/WTROR B46 94 D3 1
Reservoir Pas
DARL/WED WS10 68 D2 6
Reservoir Pl WSLW WS2 52 F5
Reservoir Retreat
LDYWD/EDGR B16 106 D4
Reservoir Rd
BLKHTH/ROWR B65 104 B2
ERDW/GRVHL B23 90 B1
HEDN WS12 17 H1
HIA/OLT B92 127 K5
KIDDW DY11 161 G2 3
LDYWD/EDGR B16 106 D3
LGLYGN/QTN B68 105 G1
RBRY B45 167 G2
SLYOAK B29 124 A2
Reservoir St WSLW WS2 52 F5
Retallack Cl SMTHWK B66 87 M5 2

Retford Dr WALM/CURD B76 ...... 73 J1
Retford Cl YDLY B25 ...... 109 C7
Retreat Gdns SEDG DY3 ...... 66 C6
The Retreat CDYHTH B64 ...... 103 J6
Revival Cl BLOX/PEL WS3 ...... 38 F4
Rex Cl TLHL/CAN CV4 ...... 152 B0
Reyde Cl REDW B97 ...... 195 K3
Reynards Cl REDW B97 ...... 195 K2
  SEDG DY3 ...... 66 C6
Reynolds Cl LICH WS13 ...... 20 F3
  SEDG DY3 ...... 82 C3
Reynolds Gv
  DUNHL/THL/PER WV6 ...... 34 D8
Reynolds Rd BDWTH CV12 ...... 116 E1
  HDSW B21 ...... 88 C6
Reynoldstown Rd CBROM B36 ...... 91 C5
Rhayader Rd NFLD/LBR B31 ...... 123 J8
Rhodes Cl SEDG DY3 ...... 83 L1
Rhone Cl SPARK B11 ...... 126 A2
Rhoose Cft CVALE B35 ...... 91 M2
Rhuddlan Wy KIDDW DY11 ...... 161 J4
Rhys Thomas Cl SHHTH WV12 ...... 52 B1
Ribbesford Av WOLVN WV10 ...... 35 M5
Ribbesford Cl HALE B63 ...... 103 H8
Ribbesford Crs
  BILS/COS WV14 ...... 67 H4
Ribble Cl BDWTH CV12 ...... 117 M3
Ribble Rd COVS CV3 ...... 9 M6
Ribblesdale TAM/AM/WIL B77 ...... 46 F5
Ribblesdale Rd BVILLE B30 ...... 124 E6
Ribbonfields NUN CV11 ...... 99 H2
Richard Cooper Rd LICHS WS14 ... 28 D8
Richard Joy Cl COVN CV6 ...... 134 A3
Richard Pl DSYBK/YTR WS5 ...... 54 A5
Richard Rd DSYBK/YTR WS5 ...... 54 A5
Richards Cl KNWTH CV8 ...... 176 D8
  NFLD/LBR B31 ...... 143 K7
  OLDBY B69 ...... 104 C1
Richards Gv RLSS CV31 ...... 200 E8
Richardson Cl WWCK CV34 ... 199 K4
Richardson Dr STRBR DY8 ...... 101 J3
Richards Rd TPTN/OCK DY4 ...... 67 K4
Richard St VAUX/NECH B7 ...... 89 K8
  WBROM B70 ...... 86 F2
Richard St South WBROM B70 ... 87 G3
Richard St West WBROM B70 .. 86 F3
Richard Williams Rd
  DARL/WED WS10 ...... 68 F3
Richborough Dr DUDN DY1 ...... 84 C2
Rich Cl WWCK CV34 ...... 199 L6
Riches St DUNHL/THL/PER WV6 .... 49 K2
Richford Gv STECH B33 ...... 110 B3
Richmond Aston Dr
  TPTN/OCK DY4 ...... 67 L8
Richmond Av BDMR/CCFT WV3 .. 49 K4
Richmond Cl
  BFLD/HDSWWD B20 ...... 88 E3
  CNCK/NC WS11 ...... 12 E8
  CRTAM B79 ...... 31 L8
Richmond Cft PBAR/PBCH B42 .... 70 D7
Richmond Dr BDMR/CCFT WV3 .. 49 J4
  DUNHL/THL/PER WV6 ...... 48 D7
  LICHS WS14 ...... 21 H6
Richmond Gdns WMBN WV5 ...... 64 E8
Richmond Gv STRBR DY8 ...... 101 J5
Richmond Hl LGLYGN/QTN B68 ... 87 C8
Richmond Hill Gdns EDG B15 ... 106 C7
Richmond Hill Rd EDG B15 ...... 106 C7
Richmond Pk KGSWFD DY6 ...... 83 C5
Richmond Pl
  ALE/KHTH/YWD B14 ...... 125 K5
Richmond Rd ATHST CV9 ...... 63 H6
  BDMR/CCFT WV3 ...... 49 J4
  DUDS DY2 ...... 85 G5
  HIA/OLT B92 ...... 127 J3
  HLYWD B47 ...... 146 A6
  NUN CV11 ...... 98 E2
  RBRY B45 ...... 142 C6
  SCFLD/BOLD B73 ...... 56 F7
  SEDG DY3 ...... 66 C6
  SMTHWK B66 ...... 105 L3
  WSNGN B18 ...... 88 F7
  YDLY B25 ...... 109 H3
Richmond St COVE CV2 ...... 154 E2
  HALE B63 ...... 121 L1
  WBROM B70 ...... 68 C8
  WSL WS1 ...... 5 H4
Richmond St South
  WBROM B70 ...... 68 C8
Richmond Wy
  CHWD/FDBR/MGN B37 ...... 111 G2
Rickard Cl DOR/KN B93 ...... 148 C8
Ricketts Cl STRPT DY13 ...... 160 F6
Rickman Dr EDG B15 ...... 107 H5
Rickyard Cl POL/KGSB/FAZ B78 ... 47 L3
  SLYOAK B29 ...... 123 L7
  YDLY B25 ...... 109 H4
Rickyard La REDE B98 ...... 189 H8
Rickyard Piece
  RIDG/WDGT B32 ...... 123 J1
Riddfield Rd CBROM B36 ...... 91 J5
Ridding Gdns
  POL/KGSB/FAZ B78 ...... 47 L5
Ridding La DARL/WED WS10 ...... 68 C3
Riddings Cl BEWD DY12 ...... 136 A8
Riddings Crs BLOX/PEL WS3 ...... 39 K1
Riddings La ATHST CV9 ...... 62 A2
The Riddings ATHST CV9 ...... 62 A2
  COVW CV5 ...... 153 H6
  HAG/WOL DY9 ...... 120 B3
  STECH B33 ...... 109 J1
  TAM/AM/WIL B77 ...... 32 C8
  WALM/CURD B76 ...... 73 M5
  WOLVN WV10 ...... 36 E6
Ridgacre La RIDG/WDGT B32 ... 105 C8
Ridgacre Rd HHTH/SAND B71 .... 68 F7
  RIDG/WDGT B32 ...... 104 F7
Ridgacre Rd West
  RIDG/WDGT B32 ...... 104 E7
Ridge Cl MOS/BIL B13 ...... 126 A7
  WSLW WS2 ...... 52 B2
Ridge Ct COVW CV5 ...... 132 E7
Ridgefield Rd. RMSLY B62 ...... 104 A5
Ridge Gv HAG/WOL DY9 ...... 102 A8
Ridge La NUNW/HART CV10 ...... 78 E3
  WNSFLD WV11 ...... 37 H6

Ridgeley Cl WWCK CV34 ...... 199 H3
Ridgemount Dr
  HWK/WKHTH B38 ...... 144 B6
Ridge Rd KGSWFD DY6 ...... 83 G8
Ridge St STRBR DY8 ...... 101 G7
Ridgethorpe COVS CV3 ...... 155 L8
Ridgewater Cl RBRY B45 ...... 142 F7
Ridge Wy ALDR WS9 ...... 54 F1
Ridgeway HRBN B17 ...... 105 M3
  SEDG DY3 ...... 66 B0
Ridgeway Av COVS CV3 ...... 154 A7
  RMSLY B62 ...... 104 E7
Ridgeway Ct WSLW WS2 ...... 52 D4
Ridgeway Dr
  ETTPK/GDPK/PENN WV4 ...... 65 K2
Ridgeway Rd STRBR DY8 ...... 101 K3
  TPTN/OCK DY4 ...... 67 L3
The Ridgeway BNTWD WS7 ...... 18 E8
  ERDW/GRVHL B23 ...... 71 L7
  STRPT DY13 ...... 160 D8
  WWCK CV34 ...... 199 L4
Ridgewood BKDE/SHDE B34 .... 91 M7
Ridgewood Av STRBR DY8 ...... 101 G7
Ridgewood Cl RLSN CV32 ...... 200 D5
  WSL WS1 ...... 5 G5
Ridgewood Dr MGN/WHC B75 .. 56 F4
Ridgewood Gdns KGSTG B44 ... 71 K6
Ridgewood Ri TAM/AM/WIL B77 .. 32 E8
Ridgley Rd TLHL/CAN CV4 ...... 152 C5
Ridgmont Cft RIDG/WDGT B32 ... 105 J8
Riding Cl HHTH/SAND B71 ...... 69 K6
Ridings Brook Dr
  CNCK/NC WS11 ...... 16 E3
Ridings La REDE B98 ...... 188 F6
Riding Wy SHHTH WV12 ...... 38 B7
Ridley La CSHL/WTROR B46 ...... 76 E8
Ridley St CBHAMW B1 ...... 6 D8
Ridpool Rd STECH B33 ...... 109 M2
Rifle Range Rd KIDDW DY11 ... 160 F2
Rifle St BILS/COS WV14 ...... 66 E5
Rigby Dr CNCK/NC WS11 ...... 16 C1
Rigby La BRGRVE B60 ...... 185 M5
Rigby St DARL/WED WS10 ...... 68 D4
Rigdale Cl COVE CV2 ...... 155 J3
Riland Rd MGN/WHC B75 ...... 57 H8
Riley Cl KNWTH CV8 ...... 192 A1
Riley Crs BDMR/CCFT WV3 ...... 49 K7
Riley Dr CBROM B36 ...... 92 E4
Riley Rd ALE/KHTH/YWD B14 ... 146 B2
Riley St WLNHL WV13 ...... 51 M3
Rilstone Rd RIDG/WDGT B32 ... 105 K8
Rindleford Av
  ETTPK/GDPK/PENN WV4 ...... 49 G7
Ringhills Rd CDSL WV8 ...... 34 F5
Ringinglow Rd KGSTG B44 ...... 71 G3
Ringmere Av CBROM B36 ...... 91 M5
Ring Rd BNTWD WS7 ...... 18 B6
Ring Road St Andrews
  WOLV WV1 ...... 2 D5
Ring Road St Davids WOLV WV1 .. 3 H4
Ring Road St Georges
  BKHL/PFLD WV2 ...... 2 F7
Ring Road St Johns
  BKHL/PFLD WV2 ...... 2 E7
Ring Road St Marks
  BDMR/CCFT WV3 ...... 2 D6
Ring Road St Patricks WOLV WV1 .. 3 G7
Ring Road St Peters WOLV WV1 ... 2 E4
Ringswood Rd HIA/OLT B92 ...... 127 J1
The Ring YDLY B25 ...... 109 G5
Ringway CNCK/NC WS11 ...... 16 C4
Ringway Hill Cross COV CV1 ...... 8 D3
Ringway Queens COV CV1 ...... 8 D6
Ringway Rudge COV CV1 ...... 8 D5
Ringway St Johns COV CV1 ...... 9 G6
Ringway St Patricks COV CV1 ...... 8 E7
Ringway Swanswell COV CV1 ...... 9 G2
The Ringway KIDD DY10 ...... 137 J7
Ringway Whitefriars COV CV1 ...... 9 J5
Ringwood Av ALDR WS9 ...... 40 F9
Ringwood Dr RBRY B45 ...... 142 E4
Ringwood Hwy COVE CV2 ...... 135 J3
Ringwood Rd WOLVN WV10 ...... 36 B4
Ripley Cl DUDS DY2 ...... 85 K5
Ripley Gv ERDW/GRVHL B23 ... 71 M8
Ripon Cl COVW CV5 ...... 132 E5
Ripon Dr HHTH/SAND B71 ...... 69 H4
Ripon Rd ALE/KHTH/YWD B14 ... 146 A1
  WOLVN WV10 ...... 36 A6
  WSLW WS2 ...... 52 F3
Rippingille Rd GTB/HAM B43 ... 71 G1
Ripple Rd BVILLE B30 ...... 124 F6
Risborough Cl COVW CV5 ...... 153 G2
Rischale Wy RUSH/SHEL WS4 ... 40 A5
Risdale Cl RLSN CV32 ...... 200 A3
Rise Av RBRY B45 ...... 142 E6
Riseley Crs DIG/EDG B5 ...... 107 H7
The Rise ALVE B48 ...... 167 M1
  CHWD/FDBR/MGN B37 ...... 110 E6
  KGSWFD DY6 ...... 83 J8
  PBAR/PBCH B42 ...... 70 E5
Rising Brook
  DUNHL/THL/PER WV6 ...... 48 F1
Rising La HOCK/TIA B94 ...... 173 J8
Rissington Av SLYOAK B29 ...... 124 E5
Ritchie Cl MOS/BIL B13 ...... 125 L4
Rivendell Gdns
  DUNHL/THL/PER WV6 ...... 34 F8
Riverbank Rd WLNHL WV13 ...... 52 B3
River Brook Dr BVILLE B30 ...... 124 F6
River Cl RCOVN/BALC/EX CV7 ... 116 D4
  RLSN CV32 ...... 200 A5
River Dr ATHST CV9 ...... 63 H3
Riverdrive TAM/AM/WIL B77 ... 45 M2
Riverfield Gv TAM/AM/WIL B77 ... 32 B8
Riverford Cft TLHL/CAN CV4 ... 177 H2
River Lee Rd SPARK B11 ...... 108 C3
Rivermead NUN CV11 ...... 98 E1
Rivermead Pk BKDE/SHDE B34 .. 91 L8
Riversdale Rd
  ALE/KHTH/YWD B14 ...... 146 B2
  ATHST CV9 ...... 63 K5
Riverside ATHST CV9 ...... 63 L6
Riverside Cl BRGRVE B60 ...... 166 A7
  COVS CV3 ...... 154 D7
Riverside Ct
  HWK/WKHTH B38 ...... 144 B2

Riverside Crs HLGN/YWD B28 .. 146 B1
Riverside Dr SOLH B91 ...... 148 C3
Riversleigh Dr STRBR DY8 ...... 101 J5
Riversley Rd NUN CV11 ...... 99 G2
River St DIG/EDG B5 ...... 7 L6
Riverway DARL/WED WS10 ...... 68 F3
Rivington Cl STRBR DY8 ...... 119 J1
Rivington Crs KGSTG B44 ...... 72 A4
Roach TAM/AM/WIL B77 ...... 46 B7
Roach Cl BRLYHL DY5 ...... 84 B8
  CHWD/FDBR/MGN B37 ...... 111 C2
Roach Crs WNSFLD WV11 ...... 37 K5
Roach Pool Cft
  LDYWD/EDGR B16 ...... 106 A3
Road Eastwood DUDS DY2 ...... 85 J7
Road No 1 KIDDW DY11 ...... 161 J3
Road No 2 KIDDW DY11 ...... 161 J2
Road No 3 KIDDW DY11 ...... 161 J3
Roanne Ringway NUN CV11 ...... 98 F1
Robert Av ERDW/GRVHL B23 ... 72 C7
Robert Cl COVS CV3 ...... 179 C1
  CRTAM B79 ...... 31 K6
Robert Cramb Av
  TLHL/CAN CV4 ...... 152 D5
Robert Rd BFLD/HDSWWD B20 .. 88 F4
  RCOVN/BALC/EX CV7 ...... 116 D5
  TPTN/OCK DY4 ...... 67 K7
Roberts Cl ALDR WS9 ...... 40 D3
  RRUGBY CV23 ...... 180 D7
Roberts Green Rd SEDG DY3 .... 84 C1
Roberts La HAG/WOL DY9 ...... 119 M5
Robertson Knoll CBROM B36 ... 91 K6
Robertsons Gdns
  VAUX/NECH B7 ...... 90 A6
Roberts Rd ACGN B27 ...... 127 C2
  BLOX/PEL WS3 ...... 39 K8
  DARL/WED WS10 ...... 69 J2
Robert St SEDG DY3 ...... 84 C1
Robert Wynd BILS/COS WV14 ... 66 D4
Robeson Cl TPTN/OCK DY4 ...... 67 H8
Robey's La POL/KGSB/FAZ B78 ... 47 H3
Robin Cl CBROM B36 ...... 92 E5
  HEDN WS12 ...... 12 A6
  KGSWFD DY6 ...... 83 L7
Robin Ct DGD DY10 ...... 161 L3
Robin Gv WNSFLD WV11 ...... 37 G6
Robin Hood Crs
  HLGN/YWD B28 ...... 126 C6
Robin Hood Cft
  HLGN/YWD B28 ...... 126 D8
Robin Hood La HLGN/YWD B28 .. 126 C6
Robin Hood Rd BRLYHL DY5 .... 102 D3
  COVS CV3 ...... 155 G7
Robin Rd ERDW/GRVHL B23 ...... 90 C1
Robins Cl GTWY WS6 ...... 24 B3
  STRBR DY8 ...... 119 J1
Robinsfield Dr NFLD/LBR B31 ... 143 L6
Robins Hill Dr ALVE B48 ...... 167 L8
Robinson Cl CRTAM B79 ...... 31 J6
Robinson Rd BDWTH CV12 ...... 116 B5
  BNTWD WS7 ...... 18 D4
Robinson's Wy WALM/CURD B76.. 74 B8
Robins Rd BNTWD WS7 ...... 18 B7
Robins Wy NUNW/HART CV10 ... 97 J3
Robotham Cl
  RUGBYN/HIL CV21 ...... 159 K7
Robottom Cl WSLW WS2 ...... 38 F7
Rocester Av WNSFLD WV11 ...... 37 J6
Rocheberie Wy
  RUGBYS/DCH CV22 ...... 183 K5
Roche Rd BLOX/PEL WS3 ...... 38 D4
Rochester Cl NUNW/HART CV10 .. 98 F2
  REDW B97 ...... 196 A5
Rochester Cft WSLW WS2 ...... 52 E1
Rochester Rd COVW CV5 ...... 153 J7
  NFLD/LBR B31 ...... 143 L1
Rochester Wy HEDN WS12 ...... 17 C4
The Roche BNTWD WS7 ...... 19 L5
Roche Wy BLOX/PEL WS3 ...... 38 D4
Rochford Cl HALE B63 ...... 121 K3
  RBRY B45 ...... 142 C6
  WALM/CURD B76 ...... 73 L5
  WSLW WS2 ...... 4 A7
Rochford Ct SHLY B90 ...... 147 L7
Rochford Gv
  ETTPK/GDPK/PENN WV4 ...... 49 H8
Rock Av RBRY B45 ...... 143 C6
Rock Cl COVN CV6 ...... 134 F4
  NUNW/HART CV10 ...... 97 K1
Rocken End COVN CV6 ...... 134 B5
Rocket Pool Dr BILS/COS WV14 ... 67 K3
Rockford Cl REDE B98 ...... 196 D8
Rockford Rd PBAR/PBCH B42 ... 70 E6
Rock Gv HIA/OLT B92 ...... 127 J2
Rock Hl BRGRVE B61 ...... 185 H6
  POL/KGSB/FAZ B78 ...... 44 A1
Rockingham Cl
  BLOX/PEL WS3 ...... 38 F4
  DOR/KN B93 ...... 172 B3
  SEDG DY3 ...... 83 M2
Rockingham Dr
  DUNHL/THL/PER WV6 ...... 48 C2
Rockingham Gdns
  FOAKS/STRLY B74 ...... 56 F7
Rockingham Hall Gdns
  HAG/WOL DY9 ...... 120 B6
Rockingham Rd YDLY B25 ...... 109 H5
Rockland Dr STECH B33 ...... 109 J1
Rockland Gdns WLNHL WV13 ... 51 K5
Rocklands Crs LICH WS13 ...... 21 H5
Rocklands Dr MGN/WHC B75 ... 56 F5
Rockley Gv RBRY B45 ...... 142 F6
Rockley Rd BLKHTH/ROWR B65 .. 85 L7
Rockmead Av KGSTG B44 ...... 71 K3
Rock Mill La RLSN CV32 ...... 200 A4
Rockmoor Cl STECH B33 ...... 110 C2
Rockrose Gdns WOLVN WV10 .. 22 E6
Rock St SEDG DY3 ...... 66 C5
The Rock DUNHL/THL/PER WV6... 35 H8
Rockville Rd WASH/WDE B8 ... 108 E1
Rockwell La ALVE B48 ...... 188 C1
Rockwood Rd ACGN B27 ...... 126 F5
Rocky La AST/WIT B6 ...... 89 J5
  BRGRVW B61 ...... 165 J5

KNWTH CV8 ...... 192 B3
  PBAR/PBCH B42 ...... 70 D7
  VAUX/NECH B7 ...... 89 M7
Rodbaston Dr PENK ST19 ...... 10 C8
Rodborough Rd DOR/KN B93 ... 172 C3
Rodbourne Rd HRBN B17 ...... 124 A2
Roddis Cl ERDW/GRVHL B23 ... 72 B5
Roden Av KIDD DY10 ...... 137 K6
Roderick Dr WNSFLD WV11 ...... 37 H6
Roderick Rd SPARK B11 ...... 108 A8
Rodhouse Cl TLHL/CAN CV4 ... 152 B4
Rodlington Av KGSTG B44 ...... 71 K4
Rodman Cl EDG B15 ...... 106 B5
Rodney Cl HIA/OLT B92 ...... 127 M4
  LDYWD/EDGR B16 ...... 106 E3
  RUGBYS/DCH CV22 ...... 183 C4
Rodney Rd HIA/OLT B92 ...... 127 M4
Rodway Cl BRLYHL DY5 ...... 102 B6
  ETTPK/GDPK/PENN WV4 ...... 66 B2
  LOZ/NWT B19 ...... 89 H6
Rodway Dr COVW CV5 ...... 152 B1
Rodwell Cl KGSTG B44 ...... 71 L5
Roebuck Cl BKDE/SHDE B34 ... 110 C1
Roebuck Gld SHHTH WV12 ...... 52 C1
Roebuck La SMTHWK B66 ...... 87 K6
  WBROM B70 ...... 87 J4
Roebuck Pl BLOX/PEL WS3 ...... 39 J7
Roebuck Rd BLOX/PEL WS3 ...... 39 J7
Roebuck St WBROM B70 ...... 87 K4
Roe Cl WWCK CV34 ...... 199 K5
Roedean Cl KGSTG B44 ...... 71 M6
Roford Ct SEDG DY3 ...... 66 C3
Rogerfield Rd
  ERDW/GRVHL B23 ...... 72 E7
Rogers Cl WNSFLD WV11 ...... 37 L4
Rogers Rd WASH/WDE B8 ...... 90 F8
Rokeby Cl WALM/CURD B76 ...... 73 J1
Rokeby Rd GTB/HAM B43 ...... 70 D3
Rokewood Cl KGSWFD DY6 ...... 83 H4
Rokholt Crs CNCK/NC WS11 ...... 16 A4
Roland Av COVN CV6 ...... 133 M2
Roland Gdns LOZ/NWT B19 ...... 89 C5
Roland Gv LOZ/NWT B19 ...... 89 C5
Roland Mt COVN CV6 ...... 134 A2
Roland Rd LOZ/NWT B19 ...... 89 C5
Roland Ter LOZ/NWT B19 ...... 89 C5
Rolfe St SMTHWK B66 ...... 87 L7
Rollason Cl COVN CV6 ...... 134 A5
Rollason Rd COVN CV6 ...... 134 A2
  DUDS DY2 ...... 85 H7
  ERDE/BCHGN B24 ...... 90 E2
Rollesby Dr WLNHL WV13 ...... 51 K5
Rolling Mill Cl DIG/EDG B5 ... 107 J6
Rollingmill St WSLW WS2 ...... 4 A4
Rollswood Dr SOLH B91 ...... 147 K1
Roman Cl BRWNH WS8 ...... 26 C3
Roman La FOAKS/STRLY B74 .... 55 M1
Roman Pk FOAKS/STRLY B74 ... 55 M1
Roman Rd COVE CV2 ...... 154 E2
  FOAKS/STRLY B74 ...... 42 A8
Roman Rd (Sandy La)
  STRBR DY8 ...... 119 C2
Roman Vw CNCK/NC WS11 ...... 16 D8
Roman Wy BLKHTH/ROWR B65 ... 104 A2
  BRGRVE B60 ...... 185 M1
  COVS CV3 ...... 178 B2
  CRTAM B79 ...... 31 J6
  CSHL/WTROR B46 ...... 93 J3
  EDG B15 ...... 124 B2
  LICHS WS14 ...... 21 H6
  POL/KGSB/FAZ B78 ...... 47 L7
Romany Rd RBRY B45 ...... 142 B4
Romany Wy STRBR DY8 ...... 119 C2
Roma Rd SPARK B11 ...... 108 C8
Romford Cl
  LGN/SDN/BHAMAIR B26 ... 109 M7
Romford Rd COVN CV6 ...... 133 M3
Romilly Av BFLD/HDSWWD B20 .. 88 F3
Romilly Cl STRBR DY8 ...... 101 J7
  WALM/CURD B76 ...... 73 L1
Romney TAM/AM/WIL B77 ...... 46 C6
Romney Cl HLGN/YWD B28 ...... 126 D6
Romney Wy GTB/HAM B43 ...... 71 H1
Romsey Av NUNW/HART CV10 ... 81 H5
Romsey Gv WOLVN WV10 ...... 36 A2
Romsey Rd WOLVN WV10 ...... 36 A2
Romsey Wy BLOX/PEL WS3 ...... 38 D2
Romsley Cl HALE B63 ...... 121 M3
  RBRY B45 ...... 142 C5
  REDE B98 ...... 197 K2
  RUSH/SHEL WS4 ...... 40 A3
Romsley Rd HAG/WOL DY9 ...... 102 A8
  LGLYGN/QTN B68 ...... 104 F3
  RIDG/WDGT B32 ...... 122 F5
Romulus Cl BFLD/HDSWWD B20 .. 88 F2
Ronald Gv CBROM B36 ...... 92 B4
Ronald Pl BORD B9 ...... 108 C3
Ronald Rd BORD B9 ...... 108 B3
Ron Davis Cl SMTHWK B66 ...... 87 M8
Ro-oak Rd COVN CV6 ...... 133 K8
Rood End Rd LGLYGN/QTN B68 .. 87 G7
  OLDBY B69 ...... 87 C6
Rooker Av BKHL/PFLD WV2 ...... 50 C7
Rooker Crs BKHL/PFLD WV2 ... 50 D7
Rookery Av BRLYHL DY5 ...... 101 L3
  ETTPK/GDPK/PENN WV4 ...... 66 C2
Rookery Cl REDW B97 ...... 196 B4
Rookery La BKHL/PFLD WV2 ...... 49 L7
  COVN CV6 ...... 133 M2
  POL/KGSB/FAZ B78 ...... 44 A3
Rookery Pk BRLYHL DY5 ...... 83 M8
Rookery Ri WMBN WV5 ...... 64 F7
Rookery Rd
  ETTPK/GDPK/PENN WV4 ...... 66 E2
  HDSW B21 ...... 88 C3
  SLYOAK B29 ...... 124 D3
  WMBN WV5 ...... 64 F7
Rookery St WNSFLD WV11 ...... 37 H6
The Rookery NUNW/HART CV10 .. 78 D3
  NUNW/HART CV10 ...... 79 J8
  RIDG/WDGT B32 ...... 122 E3
Rooks Meadow HAG/WOL DY9 .. 119 M7
Rooks Nest RRUGBY CV23 ...... 157 J2
Rookwood Dr
  DUNHL/THL/PER WV6 ...... 48 D4

Roosevelt Dr TLHL/CAN CV4 ... 152 B3
Rooth St DARL/WED WS10 ...... 68 F1
Roper Wy SEDG DY3 ...... 66 D7
Rosafield Av RMSLY B62 ...... 104 D7
Rosalind Av DUDN DY1 ...... 66 F7
Rosalind Gv WNSFLD WV11 ...... 37 L8
Rosamond St WSL WS1 ...... 4 C7
Rosary Rd ERDW/GRVHL B23 ... 90 B3
Rosaville Crs COVW CV5 ...... 132 E7
Rose Av ALVE B48 ...... 167 L8
  COVN CV6 ...... 133 K8
  KGSWFD DY6 ...... 83 K8
  LGLYGN/QTN B68 ...... 105 G6
Rose Bank Dr BLOX/PEL WS3 ... 53 J1
Rosebay Av HWK/WKHTH B38 ... 144 D5
Rose Bay Meadow
  CNCK/NC WS11 ...... 17 G3
Roseberry Av COVE CV2 ...... 134 F4
Rosebery Rd SMTHWK B66 ...... 106 A1
  TAM/AM/WIL B77 ...... 60 A1
Rosebery St BDMR/CCFT WV3 .. 2 C7
  WSNGN B18 ...... 106 E1
Rosebury Gv WMBN WV5 ...... 64 C7
Rose Cl SMTHWK B66 ...... 88 A8
Rose Cft KNWTH CV8 ...... 176 C7
Rosecroft Rd
  LGN/SDN/BHAMAIR B26 ... 110 A7
Rosedale Av
  ERDW/GRVHL B23 ...... 90 C2
  SMTHWK B66 ...... 88 A8
Rosedale Gv YDLY B25 ...... 109 C5
Rosedale Pl WLNHL WV13 ...... 51 L5
Rosedene Dr
  BFLD/HDSWWD B20 ...... 88 D3
Rose Dr BRWNH WS8 ...... 26 C8
Rosefield Cft AST/WIT B6 ...... 89 K6
Rosefield Pl RLSN CV32 ...... 200 D5
Rosefield Rd SMTHWKW B67 ... 105 L4
Rosefield St RLSN CV32 ...... 200 E5
Rosegreen Cl COVS CV3 ...... 154 C7
Rosehall Cl REDE B98 ...... 196 C7
  SOLH B91 ...... 147 K4
Rose Hl ATHST CV9 ...... 63 J6
  BRLYHL DY5 ...... 102 E4
Rosehill WEDN WS12 ...... 12 D5
Rose Hl RBRY B45 ...... 166 E1
  WLNHL WV13 ...... 51 L4
Rose Hill Cl CBROM B36 ...... 91 M5
Rose Hill Gdns WLNHL WV13... 51 L4
Rose Hill Rd BFLD/HDSWWD B20 .. 88 E4
Roseship Cl DSYBK/YTR WS5 ... 69 L2
Roseship Dr COVE CV2 ...... 134 F7
Roseland Av DUDS DY2 ...... 85 K4
Roseland Rd KNWTH CV8 ...... 191 K3
Roselands Av COVE CV2 ...... 135 H5
Roseland Wy EDG B15 ...... 6 B8
Rose La BNTWD WS7 ...... 19 C6
  NUN CV11 ...... 99 C2
Roseleigh Rd RBRY B45 ...... 142 F2
Rosemary Av BILS/COS WV14 ... 51 K7
  ETTPK/GDPK/PENN WV4 ...... 50 A7
  GTWY WS6 ...... 24 B2
  TLHL/CAN CV4 ...... 152 C2
Rosemary Crs DUDN DY1 ...... 66 D7
  ETTPK/GDPK/PENN WV4 ...... 50 A8
Rosemary Crs West
  ETTPK/GDPK/PENN WV4 ...... 49 M8
Rosemary Dr FOAKS/STRLY B74 ... 56 A2
  HEDN WS12 ...... 12 B8
Rosemary Hl KNWTH CV8 ...... 176 D8
Rosemary Hill Rd
  FOAKS/STRLY B74 ...... 56 A3
Rosemary La STRBR DY8 ...... 119 H2
Rosemary Nook
  FOAKS/STRLY B74 ...... 42 B4
Rosemary Rd CNCK/NC WS11 ... 24 B1
  HALE B63 ...... 121 H3
  KIDD DY10 ...... 137 M6
  STETCH B33 ...... 109 K3
  TAM/AM/WIL B77 ...... 46 C1
  TPTN/OCK DY4 ...... 67 H7
Rosemoor Dr BRLYHL DY5 ...... 101 M6
Rosemount Cl COVE CV2 ...... 135 J5
Rose Rd CSHL/WTROR B46 ...... 93 K5
  HRBN B17 ...... 106 B7
Rose St BILS/COS WV14 ...... 67 K3
Rosetti Cl KIDD DY10 ...... 138 A7
Roseville Gdns CDSL WV8 ...... 34 C1
Rosewood NUN CV11 ...... 99 K4
Rosewood Av
  RUGBYS/DCH CV22 ...... 183 K5
Rosewood Cl TAM/AM/WIL B77 ... 46 B1
Rosewood Ct
  TAM/AM/WIL B77 ...... 46 B1
Rosewood Crs RLSN CV32 ...... 200 F3
Rosewood Dr ERDW/GRVHL B23 ... 90 B3
  SHHTH WV12 ...... 37 M5
Rosewood Gdns WNSFLD WV11... 37 M2
Rosewood Pk GTWY WS6 ...... 24 B3
Rosewood Rd DUDN DY1 ...... 66 B7
Roshven Rd BHTH/HG B12 ...... 125 L1
Roslin Cl BRGRVE B60 ...... 185 M4
Roslin Gv LOZ/NWT B19 ...... 89 C6
Roslyn Cl SMTHWK B66 ...... 87 L7
Ross BLKHTH/ROWR B65 ...... 103 M3
Ross Cl COVW CV5 ...... 132 E8
  DUNHL/THL/PER WV6 ...... 49 J3
Ross Dr KGSWFD DY6 ...... 83 C6
Rosse Ct HIA/OLT B92 ...... 128 D4
Rossendale Cl HALE B63 ...... 103 H7
Rossendale Wy
  NUNW/HART CV10 ...... 98 B3
Ross Hts BLKHTH/ROWR B65 ... 103 M2
Rosslyn Av COVN CV6 ...... 133 J7
Rosslyn Rd WALM/CURD B76 ... 73 K7
Ross Wy NUN CV11 ...... 99 M6
Rostrevor Rd BORD B9 ...... 108 D4
Rosy Cross CRTAM B79 ...... 31 M8
Rothay TAM/AM/WIL B77 ...... 46 D5
Rotherby Gv
  CHWD/FDBR/MGN B37 ...... 110 F6
Rotherfield Cl RLSS CV31 ...... 200 F6

Rotherfield Rd
LGN/SDN/BHAMAIR B26 .... 109 M5
Rotherham Rd COVN CV6 .... 133 M3
Rotherhams Oak La
HOCK/TIA B94 .... 171 K7
Rothesay Av TLHL/CAN CV4 .... 152 F3
Rothesay Cl
NUNW/HART CV10 .... 98 E3 🔲
Rothesay Cft
RIDG/WDGT B32 .... 122 F6 🔲
Rothesay Dr STRBR DY8 .... 101 C2
Rothesay Wy SHHTH WV12 .... 37 M7 🔲
Rothwell Dr SHLY B90 .... 127 H8 🔲
Rothwell Rd WWCK CV34 .... 199 C3
Rotten Rw LICH WS13 .... 21 C6
Rotton Park Rd
LDYWD/EDGR B16 .... 106 B3
Rotton Park St
LDYWD/EDGR B16 .... 106 D2
Rough Hay Rd DARL/WED WS10 .... 52 A6
Rough Hill Dr
BLKHTH/ROWR B65 .... 85 K7
REDE B98 .... 196 E7
Rough Hills Rd BKHL/PFLD WV2... 50 D7
Roughknowles Rd
TLHL/CAN CV4 .... 152 B7
Roughlea Av CBROM B36 .... 91 K6 🔲
Roughley Dr MGN/WHC B75 .... 57 G3
Rough Rd KGSTG B44 .... 71 L2
The Rough REDW B97 .... 196 B5 🔲
Rouncil Cl HIA/OLT B92 .... 128 B6
Rouncil La KNWTH CV8 .... 191 C5
KNWTH CV8 .... 191 K3
The Roundabout
NFLD/LBR B31 .... 143 H4
Round Av RRUGBY CV23 .... 158 E8
Round Cft WLNHL WV13 .... 51 L3 🔲
Round Hl SEDG DY3 .... 66 B3
Round Hill Av HAG/WOL DY9 .... 120 A4
Roundhills Rd RMSLY B62 .... 104 D5
Roundhill Ter RMSLY B62 .... 104 C4 🔲
Roundhill Wy BRWNH WS8 .... 26 E3
Round House Rd COVS CV3 .... 154 E5
SEDG DY3 .... 84 C1
Roundlea Cl SHHTH WV12 .... 37 M6 🔲
Roundlea Rd NFLD/LBR B31 .... 123 J6
Round Rd ERDE/BCHGN B24 .... 90 F3
Round Saw Cft RBRY B45 .... 142 D5 🔲
Rounds Gdns
RUGBYN/HIL CV21 .... 183 K2 🔲
Rounds Green Rd OLDBY B69 .... 86 C6
Rounds Hl KNWTH CV8 .... 191 J3
Rounds Hill Rd BILS/COS WV14 .... 67 H2
Rounds Rd BILS/COS WV14 .... 67 H2
Round St DUDS DY2 .... 85 C7
RUGBYN/HIL CV21 .... 183 K2 🔲
Roundway Down
DUNHL/THL/PER WV6 .... 48 C2
Rousay Cl RBRY B45 .... 142 D4 🔲
Rousdon Gv GTB/HAM B43 .... 70 B5 🔲
CBROM B36 .... 92 D4
Rover Av ACGN B27 .... 127 H1
Rover Rd COV CV1 .... 9 M7
Rowallan Rd MGN/WHC B75 .... 57 H3
Rowan Cl BRGRVW B61 .... 185 J3 🔲
COVS CV3 .... 156 B6
HLYWD B47 .... 145 M8
LICH WS13 .... 21 H5 🔲
POL/KGSB/FAZ B78 .... 60 B7
WALM/CURD B76 .... 73 K3
Rowan Ct BVILLE B30 .... 144 E3 🔲
Rowan Crs BDMR/CCFT WV3 .... 49 K8
BILS/COS WV14 .... 66 F4
REDW B97 .... 195 L1
Rowan Dr HLGN/YWD B28 .... 126 E8 🔲
RUGBYS/DCH CV22 .... 182 F3
WNSFLD WV11 .... 37 M2
WWCK CV34 .... 199 L3
Rowan Gdns POL/KGSB/FAZ B78.. 47 M5
Rowan Gv BNTWD WS7 .... 18 D7
COVE CV2 .... 135 J3
Rowan Ri KCSWFD DY6 .... 83 J7
Rowan Rd CNCK/NC WS11 .... 16 A3
CSCFLD/WYGN B72 .... 73 C3
DSYBK/YTR WS5 .... 69 K1
NUNW/HART CV10 .... 80 A7
REDW B97 .... 195 L1
SEDG DY3 .... 66 C4
The Rowans BDWTH CV12 .... 116 C3 🔲
Rowantrees RBRY B45 .... 142 F8
Rowan Wy
CHWD/FDBR/MGN B37 .... 111 C4
NFLD/LBR B31 .... 143 K5 🔲
Roway La OLDBY B69 .... 86 C4
Rowborough Cl
RWWCK/WEL CV35 .... 198 C3 🔲
Rowbrook Cl SHLY B90 .... 146 C5 🔲
Rowcroft Covert BVILLE B30 .... 145 C2 🔲
Rowcroft Rd COVE CV2 .... 135 L7
Rowdale Rd PBAR/PBCH B42 .... 71 C6
Rowden Dr ERDW/GRVHL B23 .... 72 E7
SOLH B91 .... 147 J3
Rowena Gdns SEDG DY3 .... 66 A3
Rowheath Rd BVILLE B30 .... 144 D1
Rowington Av
BLKHTH/ROWR B65 .... 104 B2
Rowington Cl COVN CV6 .... 133 H7
Rowington Rd BKDE/SHDE B34 .... 92 C7
Rowland Av POL/KGSB/FAZ B78 .. 47 L2
Rowland Ct
RCOVN/BALC/EX CV7 .... 96 C4
Rowland Gdns WSLW WS2 .... 53 C2 🔲
Rowland Hill Av KIDDW DY11 .... 136 F9
Rowland Hill Dr
TPTN/OCK DY4 .... 86 A1 🔲
WSLW WS2 .... 52 C2
Rowlands Av WOLV WV1 .... 50 F3
WSLW WS2 .... 52 C2
Rowlands Cl WSLW WS2 .... 52 C1
Rowlands Crs SOLH B91 .... 127 M5
Rowlands Rd
LGN/SDN/BHAMAIR B26 .... 109 J6
Rowland St RUGBYN/HIL CV21 .. 183 K2 🔲
WSLW WS2 .... 53 C2
Rowland Way (Road 1A)
KIDDW DY11 .... 161 J4 🔲
Rowley Cl HEDN WS12 .... 12 E5 🔲

Rowley Dr COVS CV3 .... 178 F1
Rowley Gv STECH B33 .... 110 B2
Rowley Hall Av
BLKHTH/ROWR B65 .... 104 A2
Rowley Hill Vw CDYHTH B64 .... 103 K5 🔲
Rowley La COVS CV3 .... 179 H2
Rowley Pl RUSH/SHEL WS4 .... 39 M6
Rowley Rd KNWTH CV8 .... 178 D2
Rowley St WSL WS1 .... 5 H2
Rowley Vw BILS/COS WV14 .... 67 L2 🔲
DARL/WED WS10 .... 68 A1
WBROM B70 .... 86 F2
Rowley Village
BLKHTH/ROWR B65 .... 104 A2
Rowney Cft HLGN/YWD B28 .... 146 C1
Rowney Green La ALVE B48 .... 188 B2
Rowood Dr HIA/OLT B92 .... 128 C5 🔲
Rowthorn Cl FOAKS/STRLY B74.. 55 L6
Rowthorn Dr SHLY B90 .... 147 L7
Rowton Av
DUNHL/THL/PER WV6 .... 48 C2 🔲
Rowton Dr FOAKS/STRLY B74... 55 K8
Roxall Cl KIDD DY10 .... 139 G3
Roxburgh Cft RLSN CV32 .... 192 F8
Roxburgh Gv GTB/HAM B43 .... 71 C1
Roxburgh Rd NUN CV11 .... 99 J4
SCFLD/BOLD B73 .... 72 E2
Roxby Gdns
DUNHL/THL/PER WV6 .... 35 L8
Royal Cl BLKHTH/ROWR B65 .... 86 A3
BRLYHL DY5 .... 102 A5
Royal Crs COVS CV3 .... 155 C8
Royal Mail St CBHAMW B1 .... 6 E6
Royal Oak La
RCOVN/BALC/EX CV7 .... 116 A6
Royal Oak Rd
BLKHTH/ROWR B65 .... 85 K8
RMSLY B62 .... 122 D1
Royal Rd CSCFLD/WYGN B72 .. 57 C8
Royal Scot Gv WSL WS1 .... 53 H8 🔲
Royal Star Cl STECH B33 .... 110 A3 🔲
Royal Wy TPTN/OCK DY4 .... 85 L3
Roydon Rd ACGN B27 .... 127 C5
Roylesden Crs SCFLD/BOLD B73 .. 72 A3
Royston Cl COVS CV3 .... 155 L2
Royston Cft BHTH/HG B12 .... 107 K7 🔲
Royston Wy SEDG DY3 .... 66 A5
Rozel Av KIDD DY10 .... 137 M4
Rubens Cl COVW CV5 .... 153 C2
SEDG DY3 .... 66 B8
Rubery Farm Gv RBRY B45 .... 142 D5
Rubery La RBRY B45 .... 142 D4
Rubery La South RBRY B45 .... 142 D5 🔲
Rubery St DARL/WED WS10 .... 52 B3
Ruckley Rd SLYOAK B29 .... 123 M5 🔲
Rudge Av WOLV WV1 .... 50 F2
Rudge Cl SHHTH WV12 .... 52 A1
Rudge Cft STECH B33 .... 109 L1
Rudge Rd COV CV1 .... 8 D5
Rudgewick Cft AST/WIT B6 .... 89 K7 🔲
Rudyard Cl WOLVN WV10 .... 36 C1
Rudyard Gv STECH B33 .... 109 M2 🔲
Rudyngfield Dr STECH B33 .... 109 K2 🔲
Rufford CRTAM B79 .... 31 J7
Rufford Cl ERDW/GRVHL B23 .. 72 B5 🔲
Rufford Rd HAG/WOL DY9 .... 120 A1
Rufford St HAG/WOL DY9 .... 102 D7
Rufford Wy ALDR WS9 .... 40 C6
Rugby La RRUGBY CV23 .... 180 E7
Rugby Rd BTACH/HAR CV33 .. 193 K7
COVS CV3 .... 156 A8
KNWTH CV8 .... 156 E8
RLSN CV32 .... 200 B5
RRUGBY CV23 .... 157 K2
STRBR DY8 .... 101 H6
Rugby St WOLV WV1 .... 2 C2
Rugeley Av SHHTH WV12 .... 38 B5
Rugeley Cl TPTN/OCK DY4 .... 67 J8 🔲
Rugeley Rd BNTWD WS7 .... 18 D5
HEDN WS12 .... 13 L6
Ruislip Cl CVALE B35 .... 91 L1
Ruiton St SEDG DY3 .... 84 B1
Rumbow HALE B63 .... 121 M1
Rumbow La RMSLY B62 .... 141 H1
Rumbush La HOCK/TIA B94... 170 B4
SHLY B90 .... 146 E8
Rumer Hill Rd CNCK/NC WS11 .. 16 C6
Runcorn Cl
CHWD/FDBR/MGN B37 .... 111 G1 🔲
REDE B98 .... 196 D5
Runcorn Rd BHTH/HG B12 .... 107 K8
Runnemede Gdns
NUNW/HART CV10 .... 98 D2 🔲
Runnymede Dr
RCOVN/BALC/EX CV7 .... 151 G8
Runnymede Rd SPARK B11 .... 126 C2
Rupert Brooke Rd
RUGBYS/DCH CV22 .... 183 J6
Rupert Rd COVN CV6 .... 133 M5
Rupert St BDMR/CCFT WV3 .... 2 A4
VAUX/NECH B7 .... 89 L8
Rushall Cl RUSH/SHEL WS4 .... 53 M1
STRBR DY8 .... 101 J5
Rushall Manor Cl
RUSH/SHEL WS4 .... 53 M1
Rushall Manor Rd
RUSH/SHEL WS4 .... 53 M1
Rushall Rd WOLVN WV10 .... 36 C3
Rushbrook Cl BRWNH WS8 .... 26 C7
HIA/OLT B92 .... 127 J3
Rushbrooke Cl MOS/BIL B13 .. 125 K1 🔲
Rushbrooke Dr
SCFLD/BOLD B73 .... 72 A1
Rushbrook Gv
ALE/KHTH/YWD B14 .... 145 G1 🔲
Rushbury Cl BILS/COS WV14 .. 50 F8 🔲
SHLY B90 .... 147 H1 🔲
Rushden Cft KGSTG B44 .... 71 K4
Rushes Ml BLOX/PEL WS3 .... 39 J2
Rushey La SPARK B11 .... 108 E8
Rushford Av WMBN WV5 .... 64 E7 🔲
Rushford Cl SHLY B90 .... 147 L6
Rush Gn RIDG/WDGT B32 .... 123 J3
Rush La REDE B98 .... 188 F7
TAM/AM/WIL B77 .... 60 B2

Rushleigh Rd SHLY B90 .... 146 C5
Rushmead Gv RBRY B45 .... 142 E6
Rushmere Rd TPTN/OCK DY4 .... 67 L5
Rushmoor Cl
FOAKS/STRLY B74 .... 56 F7 🔲
Rushmoor Dr COVW CV5 .... 8 A4
Rushmore St RLSS CV31 .... 200 D6
Rushock Cl REDE B98 .... 197 G7
Rushton Cl
RCOVN/BALC/EX CV7 .... 151 G6
Rushwater Cl WMBN WV5 .... 64 C7 🔲
Rushwick Gv SHLY B90 .... 147 L7
Rushwood Cl RUSH/SHEL WS4 .. 53 L2
Rushy Piece RIDG/WDGT B32 .. 123 H2
Ruskin Av BLKHTH/ROWR B65 .. 104 B3
ETTPK/GDPK/PENN WV4 .... 66 D3
KIDD DY10 .... 138 A7
Ruskin Cl AST/WIT B6 .... 89 K6 🔲
COVN CV6 .... 133 H7
NUNW/HART CV10 .... 79 L8
RUGBYS/DCH CV22 .... 183 K7
Ruskin Gv ACGN B27 .... 126 F3
Ruskin Rd WOLVN WV10 .... 36 D5
Ruskin St WBROM B71 .... 69 C8
Russel Cft BRGRVE B60 .... 185 L6
Russell Bank Rd
FOAKS/STRLY B74 .... 56 C1
Russell Cl OLDBY B69 .... 86 B3
TPTN/OCK DY4 .... 68 A4
WNSFLD WV11 .... 37 K4
Russell Crs BILS/COS WV14 .... 51 K6
HLGN/YWD B28 .... 126 C3
KIDD DY10 .... 161 K1
MOS/BIL B13 .... 125 H2
Russell's Hall Rd DUDN DY1 .... 84 C4
The Russells MOS/BIL B13 .... 125 H2
Russell St BDMR/CCFT WV3 .... 2 E1
COV CV1 .... 9 C2
DARL/WED WS10 .... 68 D3 🔲
DUDN DY1 .... 84 F4
RLSN CV32 .... 200 D4
WLNHL WV13 .... 51 M3
Russell St North COV CV1 .... 9 C1 🔲
Russell Ter RLSS CV31 .... 200 E6
Russelsheim Wy
RUGBYS/DCH CV22 .... 183 L3 🔲
Russett Cl BNTWD WS7 .... 18 E7
DSYBK/YTR WS5 .... 54 B5
Russett Wy BRLYHL DY5 .... 83 M6 🔲
Russet Wy NFLD/LBR B31 .... 123 J7
Ruston St LDYWD/EDGR B16 .. 106 E4
Ruthall Cl SLYOAK B29 .... 124 A6 🔲
Ruth Cl DARL/WED WS10 .... 68 A3
Rutherford Gln NUN CV11 .... 99 K4
Rutherford Rd BRGRVE B60 .... 185 M7
ERDW/GRVHL B23 .... 72 C6 🔲
WSLW WS2 .... 38 E7
Rutherglen Av COVS CV3 .... 154 C7
Rutland Av
ETTPK/GDPK/PENN WV4 .... 65 H1
NUNW/HART CV10 .... 98 D1
Rutland Crs ALDR WS9 .... 40 F4
BILS/COS WV14 .... 51 H6
Rutland Cft COVS CV3 .... 155 K5
Rutland Dr BRGRVE B60 .... 185 L5
LGN/SDN/BHAMAIR B26 .... 109 J6
POL/KGSB/FAZ B78 .... 45 L4
Rutland Pl STRBR DY8 .... 101 H5
Rutland Rd DARL/WED WS10 .. 69 C1
HEDN WS12 .... 17 J4
HHTH/SAND B71 .... 69 C6
SMTHWK B66 .... 105 L4
Rutland St BLOX/PEL WS3 .... 39 J8
Rutley Gv RIDG/WDGT B32 .. 123 K1
Rutters Meadow
RIDG/WDGT B32 .... 122 F1
Rutter St WSL WS1 .... 4 E7
Ryan Av WNSFLD WV11 .... 37 L6
Ryan Pl DUDS DY2 .... 85 J1
Rycroft Gv STECH B33 .... 110 A3 🔲
Rydal TAM/AM/WIL B77 .... 46 E6
Rydal Av NUN CV11 .... 81 L7
Rydal Cl COVW CV5 .... 132 F5
FOAKS/STRLY B74 .... 55 K3
HEDN WS12 .... 12 E5 🔲
STRPT DY13 .... 160 D7
WNSFLD WV11 .... 37 C6
Rydal Dr DUNHL/THL/PER WV6 .. 48 D1
Rydding La HHTH/SAND B71 .. 69 C5
Rydding Sq HHTH/SAND B71 .. 68 F5
Ryde Av NUNW/HART CV10.. 81 H7
Ryde Gv ACGN B27 .... 126 E4
Ryde Park Rd RBRY B45 .... 143 G7
Ryder Cl RWWCK/WEL CV35 .. 198 D7 🔲
Ryder Rw RCOVN/BALC/EX CV7 .. 96 E5
Ryders Green Rd WBROM B70 .. 86 D1
Ryders Hayes La BLOX/PEL WS3 .. 39 L1
Ryders Hill Crs
NUNW/HART CV10 .... 80 A6
Ryder St CBHAMNE B4 .... 7 H3 🔲
STRBR DY8 .... 101 H3
WBROM B70 .... 68 D8
Ryebank Cl BVILLE B30 .... 124 A8
Ryeclose Cft
CHWD/FDBR/MGN B37 .... 111 H2
Rye Cft ACGN B27 .... 109 C8 🔲
HAG/WOL DY9 .... 120 C3
HLYWD B47 .... 145 L8
Ryecroft Av
ETTPK/GDPK/PENN WV4 .... 49 M8
Ryecroft Cl SEDG DY3 .... 66 A5 🔲
Ryecroft Dr BNTWD WS7 .... 18 E5
Ryecroft Pk WSLW WS2 .... 53 J2 🔲
Ryecroft Pl BLOX/PEL WS3 .... 39 K7
Ryecroft St WSLW WS2 .... 53 J2 🔲
Ryefield CDSL WV8 .... 35 J4
Ryefield Cl HAG/WOL DY9 .... 139 L1
SOLH B91 .... 127 J8
Ryefield La WALM/CURD B76 .. 74 F3
Ryegrass La REDW B97 .... 196 A7
Rye Gv SPARK B11 .... 126 D1
Rye Hl COVW CV5 .... 132 E7
The Ryelands RRUGBY CV23 .. 182 A6
Rye Piece Ringway
BDWTH CV12 .... 117 G2 🔲
Ryhope Cl BDWTH CV12 .... 116 A4 🔲
Ryknild Cl FOAKS/STRLY B74.... 42 D7

Ryknild St LICHS WS14 .... 21 J7
Ryland Cl HALE B63 .... 121 J3 🔲
RLSS CV31 .... 200 F7
TPTN/OCK DY4 .... 67 M8 🔲
Ryland Rd EDG B15 .... 107 C6
ERDE/BCHGN B24 .... 90 D4
SPARK B11 .... 126 B1 🔲
Rylands Dr
ETTPK/GDPK/PENN WV4 .... 65 L1
Ryland St LDYWD/EDGR B16 .... 6 A7
Ryle St BLOX/PEL WS3 .... 39 H3
Rylston Av COVN CV6 .... 133 L4
Rymond Rd BKDE/SHDE B34 .... 91 J7
Ryton TAM/AM/WIL B77 .... 46 D5
Ryton Cl REDE B98 .... 197 H4
SCFLD/BOLD B73 .... 56 F8
TLHL/CAN CV4 .... 152 F5
WNSFLD WV11 .... 36 E8
Ryton Gv BKDE/SHDE B34 .... 92 B8

S

Sabell Rd SMTHWKW B67 .... 87 K7
Sabrina Rd
DUNHL/THL/PER WV6 .... 48 C4
Saddington Rd COVS CV3 .... 155 J5 🔲
Saddlers Ms SOLH B91 .... 148 A4
The Saddlestones
DUNHL/THL/PER WV6 .... 48 B1 🔲
Saddleworth Rd GTWY WS6 .... 38 E1
Sadler Rd BRWNH WS8 .... 26 E5
COVN CV6 .... 133 L6
MGN/WHC B75 .... 57 C6
Sadlers Ct WSLW WS2 .... 52 F6
Sadlers Wk
LDYWD/EDGR B16 .... 106 E3 🔲
Sadlerswell La HOCK/TIA B94 .. 171 M7
Saffron Gdns
ETTPK/GDPK/PENN WV4 .... 65 L1
Sage Cft NFLD/LBR B31 .... 123 K8
WASH/WDE B8 .... 90 F8
St Agatha's Rd COVE CV2 .... 154 E2 🔲
WASH/WDE B8 .... 90 F8
St Agnes Cl MOS/BIL B13 .... 125 M3 🔲
St Agnes La MOS/BIL B13 .... 125 M3
St Agnes Wy NUN CV11 .... 99 K1
St Aidan's Rd CNCK/NC WS11 .. 16 C1
St Alban's Av WOLVN WV10 .. 136 E6
St Albans Cl RLSN CV32 .... 200 A3 🔲
SMTHWKW B67 .... 87 J7 🔲
WNSFLD WV11 .... 37 L5
St Albans Rd MOS/BIL B13 .... 125 L1
SMTHWKW B67 .... 87 J7
St Andrew Cl HEDN WS12 .... 13 L8
St Andrews TAM/AM/WIL B77 .. 46 F1
St Andrews Av BLOX/PEL WS3 .. 25 L8
St Andrews Cl HRBN B17 .... 123 L2
SEDG DY3 .... 83 L2
STRBR DY8 .... 119 K3
St Andrews Crs
RUGBYS/DCH CV22 .... 183 L5
St Andrews Dr
DUNHL/THL/PER WV6 .... 34 D8
NUN CV11 .... 99 M4
OLDBY B69 .... 85 M6
St Andrew's Rd BORD B9 .... 107 M3
COVW CV5 .... 153 K5
MGN/WHC B75 .... 57 C6
RLSN CV32 .... 192 F8
St Andrew's St BORD B9 .... 107 M3
DUDS DY2 .... 85 C8
St Andrews Wy BRGRVW B61.. 185 H5
St Annes Cl BFLD/HDSWWD B20 .. 88 D1
BNTWD WS7 .... 26 C1
St Annes Ct MOS/BIL B13 .... 125 J1 🔲
St Annes Gv DOR/KN B93 .... 148 E7
St Anne's Rd CDYHTH B64 .... 103 C4
LICH WS13 .... 20 F2 🔲
RUGBYS/DCH CV22 .... 183 J4
WLNHL WV13 .... 51 M2
WOLVN WV10 .... 35 M4
St Annes Wy KGSTG B44 .... 71 L6
St Ann's Rd COVE CV2 .... 154 E2
St Anthonys Dr BLOX/PEL WS3 .. 25 M8
St Athan Cft CVALE B35 .... 91 M2
St Augustine's Rd
LDYWD/EDGR B16 .... 106 B4
St Augustine's Wk COVN CV6 .. 133 L6 🔲
St Augustus Cl
HHTH/SAND B71 .... 87 K3 🔲
St Austell Cl CRTAM B79 .... 31 L7
NUN CV11 .... 81 L8 🔲
St Austell Rd COVE CV2 .... 155 J2
DSYBK/YTR WS5 .... 54 B6
St Bartholemews Cl
COVS CV3 .... 155 L3 🔲
St Bartholomew Ter
DARL/WED WS10 .... 68 D2 🔲
St Benedicts Cl ATHST CV9 .... 63 H5
WBROM B70 .... 87 K3 🔲
St Benedict's Rd BNTWD WS7 .. 18 F7
SMHTH B10 .... 108 D5
St Benedicts Rd WMBN WV5 .. 64 D7 🔲
St Bernards Cl HEDN WS12 .... 18 A1
St Bernards Rd
CSCFLD/WYGN B72 .... 73 C3
HIA/OLT B92 .... 127 C4
SOLH B91 .... 127 H8
St Bernards Wk COVS CV3 .... 155 H7
St Blaise Av CSHL/WTROR B46 .. 92 F2
St Blaise Rd MGN/WHC B75 .. 57 H2
St Brades Cl OLDBY B69 .... 86 A6
St Brides Cl SEDG DY3 .... 66 A5 🔲
WMBN WV5 .... 64 D7
Saintbury Dr SOLH B91 .... 148 A5 🔲
St Caroline Cl WBROM B70 .... 87 K2
St Catharines Cl WSL WS1 .... 5 J8
St Catherine's Cl COVS CV3 .... 154 F5 🔲
DUDS DY2 .... 85 L4 🔲
MGN/WHC B75 .... 57 K6
St Catherine's Crs
ETTPK/GDPK/PENN WV4 .... 65 L1 🔲
St Catherine's Rd BRGRVE B60.. 186 D7
LICH WS13 .... 20 F7 🔲
St Cecilia Cl KIDD DY10 .... 161 J3

St Chad's Circus Queensway
CBHAMNW B3 .... 6 F3
St Chad's Cl CNCK/NC WS11 .. 16 E1 🔲
SEDG DY3 .... 83 M2
St Chads Queensway
CBHAMNW B4 .... 7 G2
St Chad's Rd BILS/COS WV14 .. 51 K6
LICH WS13 .... 20 F4
MGN/WHC B75 .... 57 J8
RBRY B45 .... 142 D6
WOLVN WV10 .... 36 D5
St Christian's Cft COVS CV3 .... 9 H9
St Christian's Rd COVS CV3 .... 154 C5
St Christopher Cl HEDN WS12 .. 13 L8 🔲
HHTH/SAND B71 .... 87 J3 🔲
St Christophers
BFLD/HDSWWD B20 .... 88 D1
St Christopher's Cl
WWCK CV34 .... 199 H5 🔲
St Christopher's Dr
TAM/AM/WIL B77 .... 46 A4 🔲
St Clement's La
HHTH/SAND B71 .... 87 H1
St Clement's La
HHTH/SAND B71 .... 87 H1
St Clements Rd VAUX/NECH B7 .. 90 A7
St Columba's Cl COV CV1 .... 8 C2
St Columbas Dr RBRY B45 .... 143 H6
St Cuthbert's Cl WBROM B70 .. 87 K3
St David Cl HEDN WS12 .... 13 L7
St Davids Cl BLOX/PEL WS3 .... 25 M8
STRPT DY13 .... 160 C7
WBROM B70 .... 87 K3
St Davids Dr RIDG/WDGT B32 .. 104 F8
St Davids Gv
BFLD/HDSWWD B20 .... 88 D1
St Davids Orch COVS CV3 .... 155 M6
St Davids Pl BLOX/PEL WS3 .... 39 H3
St Davids Wy NUNW/HART CV10 .. 98 D1
St Denis Rd SLYOAK B29 .... 123 L7
St Dominic's Rd
ERDE/BCHGN B24 .... 90 C4
St Edburghs Rd STETCH B33.... 109 J4
St Editha's Cl CRTAM B79 .... 31 M8 🔲
St Edith Rd POL/KGSB/FAZ B78 .. 47 L5
St Edmonds Rd ATHST CV9 .... 61 G8
St Edmund's Cl
DUNHL/THL/PER WV6 .... 49 K2 🔲
WBROM B70 .... 87 K3 🔲
St Edward's Rd SLYOAK B29 .... 124 D3
St Eleanor Cl WBROM B70.......... 87 K2
St Elizabeth's Rd COVN CV6 .... 134 C4
St Francis Av SOLH B91 .... 127 J7
St Francis Cl BLOX/PEL WS3 .... 25 M8
HEDN WS12 .... 13 L8 🔲
St George Dr HEDN WS12 .... 13 L8
SMTHWK B66 .... 87 L6 🔲
St Georges Av
ERDW/GRVHL B23 .... 72 E8 🔲
RUGBYS/DCH CV22 .... 183 K5
St Georges Ct EDG B15 .... 106 E6
MGN/WHC B75 .... 57 K7
St Georges Ct FOAKS/STRLY B74 .. 42 C8
St Georges Pl WBROM B70 .... 87 G1
St George's Rd ATHST CV9 .... 63 H3
COV CV1 .... 9 M7
DUDS DY2 .... 85 H7
REDE B98 .... 196 D1
RLSS CV31 .... 200 D7
SHLY B90 .... 147 H5 🔲
STRBR DY8 .... 119 H3
St George's St
DARL/WED WS10 .... 52 B6 🔲
LOZ/NWT B19 .... 6 E1
St George's Ter KIDD DY10 .... 137 K7 🔲
St Georges Wy
NUNW/HART CV10 .... 98 F5
TAM/AM/WIL B77 .... 46 C1
St Gerards Rd SOLH B91 .... 147 J3
St Giles Av BLKHTH/ROWR B65.. 103 M1
St Giles Cl BLKHTH/ROWR B65 .. 103 M1
St Giles Crs WOLV WV1 .... 50 E3
St Giles Rd BNTWD WS7 .... 18 F7
RCOVN/BALC/EX CV7 .... 116 B7
STETCH B33 .... 110 B3
WLNHL WV13 .... 51 M4
WOLV WV1 .... 50 E3
St Giles St DUDS DY2 .... 85 C8
St Godwald's Crs
BRGRVE B60 .... 185 M5 🔲
St Godwald's Rd BRGRVE B60 .. 185 M6
St Helens Av TPTN/OCK DY4 .... 68 A8
St Helens Pas CBHAMW B1 .... 6 C3
St Helens Rd LICH WS13 .... 20 F2 🔲
RLSS CV31 .... 200 D8
SOLH B91 .... 127 L7
St Helen's Wy COVW CV5 .... 132 F5
St Heliers Rd NFLD/LBR B31 .... 143 J1
St Ives Cl CRTAM B79 .... 31 M7
St Ives Rd COVE CV2 .... 155 H2
DSYBK/YTR WS5 .... 54 B6
St Ives Wy NUN CV11 .... 99 K1
St James Av
BLKHTH/ROWR B65 .... 103 L1
St James Cl BLOX/PEL WS3 .... 25 M8 🔲
WBROM B70 .... 87 K3
St James' La COVS CV3 .... 155 H7 🔲
St James Meadow Rd
RLSN CV32 .... 200 A4
VAUX/NECH B7 .... 7 M3
St James Pl SHLY B90 .... 146 F5
VAUX/NECH B7 .... 7 H3
St James Rd CNCK/NC WS11 .. 16 A5 🔲
CNCK/NC WS11... 17 M8
EDG B15 .... 6 A9
HDSW B21 .... 88 B5 🔲
MGN/WHC B75 .... 57 G3
OLDBY B69 .... 86 B5
St James Ter DUDN DY1 .... 84 E4
St James's St DARL/WED WS10 .. 68 F4
SEDG DY3 .... 84 B2
WOLV WV1 .... 3 G6
St John Cl MGN/WHC B75 .... 57 K6
St Johns WWCK CV34 .... 199 K6
St Johns Av BLKHTH/ROWR B65.. 103 M1
KIDDW DY11 .... 136 E7
KNWTH CV8 .... 191 L2 🔲
St John's Cl ALDR WS9 .... 40 D2

CNCK/NC WS11 .... 16 B5
DOR/KN B93 .... 148 F7
LICH WS13 .... 20 F7 🔲
NUNW/HART CV10 .... 79 J5
SEDG DY3 .... 82 B3
WBROM B70 .... 87 K3
St John's Ct HEDN WS12 .... 17 J4
St Johns Dr LICHS WS14 .... 28 D8
St Johns Gv
CHWD/FDBR/MGN B37 .... 110 D3
St John's Hl SLYOAK B29 .... 28 D8
St John's La RRUGBY CV23 .... 158 E8
St Johns Rd BLOX/PEL WS3.......... 25 M8
BRWNH WS8 .... 26 E8
CNCK/NC WS11 .... 16 B5
DARL/WED WS10 .... 52 A8 🔲
DUDS DY2 .... 85 J5 🔟
HALE B63 .... 121 J1
HRBN B17 .... 106 B7
LGLYGN/QTN B68 .... 87 G8
RLSS CV31 .... 200 F1 🔲
SPARK B11 .... 108 A8
STRBR DY8 .... 101 L7
STRPT DY13 .... 160 E8
TPTN/OCK DY4 .... 67 K6
WNSFLD WV11 .... 37 L2
WSLW WS2 .... 52 F5
St John's Sq BKHL/PFLD WV2 .... 2 F7
St Johns St COV CV1 .... 9 G6
DUDS DY2 .... 85 G8
KIDDW DY11 .... 137 G7 🔲
KNWTH CV8 .... 191 K2
St John St BRGRVW B61 .... 185 K3
CRTAM B79 .... 31 M8 🔲
RUGBYN/HIL CV21 .... 183 L1
St Johns Wk PBAR/PBCH B42 ...... 89 H1
St Johns Wd RBRY B45 .... 142 F8 🔲
St Josephs Av NFLD/LBR B31 ...... 123 M8
St Josephs Ci BLOX/PEL WS3 .... 39 L1 🔟
St Josephs Rd WASH/WDE B8 ...... 90 F3
St Joseph St DUDS DY2 .... 85 H4 🔲
St Judes Ci ALE/KHTH/YWD B14.. 145 K3
MGN/WHC B75 .... 57 K7 🔲
St Jude's Crs COVS CV3 .... 155 H6 🔲
St Jude's Pas DIG/EDG B5 .... 6 F7 🔲
St Jude's Rd
DUNHL/THL/PER WV6 .... 49 K2
St Jude's Rd West
DUNHL/THL/PER WV6 .... 49 K2
St Katherine's Rd
LGLYGN/QTN B68 .... 105 G3
St Kenelms Av HALE B63 .... 121 H4
St Kenelm's Ci WBROM B70 .... 87 K3 🔲
St Kenelm's Rd RMSLY B62 .... 121 H8
St Klida's Rd WASH/WDE B8 .... 90 C8 🔲
St Laurence Av WWCK CV34 .... 199 H8
St Laurence Ci ALVE B48 .... 167 M7 🔲
St Laurence Rd NFLD/LBR B31 ..... 123 L8
St Lawrence Ci DOR/KN B93 .... 148 F8
St Lawrence Dr CNCK/NC WS11 ... 16 F3
St Lawrence Rd
NUNW/HART CV10 .... 96 F1
St Lawrence's Rd COV CV6............ 134 D4
St Lawrence Wy
DARL/WED WS10 .... 52 B7
St Leonards Ci
CHWD/FDBR/MGN B37 .... 110 E6
St Leonards Vw
POL/KGSB/FAZ B78 .... 47 K5
St Leonard's Wk KNWTH CV8 ...... 179 L4 🔲
St Loye's Ci RMSLY B62 .... 104 B5 🔲
St Lukes Ci BLKHTH/ROWR B65 ... 103 M1
CNCK/NC WS11 .... 16 A5
St Luke's Rd BNTWD WS7 .... 19 G7
COVN CV6 .... 134 B3
Saint Luke's Rd
DARL/WED WS10 .... 68 E2
St Luke's Rd DIG/EDG B5 .... 107 J6
St Lukes St CDYHTH B64 .... 103 H4
St Margaret Rd COV CV1 .... 9 L6
St Margaret's FOAKS/STRLY B74 .. 56 A2
St Margarets Av WASH/WDE B8 ... 90 F7
St Margarets Dr HALE B63 .... 121 K3 🔲
St Margarets Rd BLOX/PEL WS3 ... 39 L1
CRTAM B79 .... 31 M7 🔲
GTB/HAM B43 .... 70 D3
HIA/OLT B92 .... 127 J4 🔲
LICH WS13 .... 20 F2
RLSS CV31 .... 200 E8
WASH/WDE B8 .... 90 E7
St Mark's Av
RUGBYS/DCH CV22 .... 183 G6
St Marks Crs CBHAMW B1 .... 106 E2
St Mark's Ms RLSN CV32 .... 200 C4 🔲
St Mark's St BDMR/CCFT WV3 .... 2 B6
BLOX/PEL WS3 .... 39 L1
BNTWD WS7 .... 19 G7
BRWNH WS8 .... 26 E8
DUDS DY2 .... 85 K3
HAG/WOL DY9 .... 102 B8
RLSN CV32 .... 200 B4
SMTHWKW B67 .... 105 H2
TPTN/OCK DY4 .... 67 L5
St Mark's St BDMR/CCFT WV3 .... 2 B6
CBHAMW B1 .... 6 A3
St Martin's Circus Queensway
CBHAM B2 .... 7 G6
DIG/EDG B5 .... 7 G6
St Martin's Ci BKHL/PFLD WV2 ..... 50 C7 🔲
WBROM B70 .... 87 K3 🔲
St Martin's Dr TPTN/OCK DY4 ...... 67 L8
St Martin's Rd COVS CV3 .... 177 M2
KNWTH CV8 .... 178 A4
MGN/WHC B75 .... 57 K8
St Martin's St EDG B15 .... 6 B4
St Martin's Ter BILS/COS WV14..... 67 J2
St Marys ACGN B27 .... 126 F2
BILS/COS WV14 .... 66 C3
ERDE/BCHGN B24 .... 91 H1 🔲
WOLVN WV10 .... 23 G3
WWCK CV34 .... 199 H5 🔲
St Mary's Crs RLSS CV31 .... 200 F6
St Mary's Ci STRBR DY8 .... 119 M2
St Marys Ringway KIDDW DY11.... 137 F7
St Mary's Rd ATHST CV9 .... 63 J5
DARL/WED WS10 .... 68 D2
HRBN B17 .... 106 A8
LICH WS13 .... 20 F2

NUN CV11 .... 80 F8
RCOVN/BALC/EX CV7 .... 114 C1
RLSS CV31 .... 200 F6
St Mary's Rw CBHAMNE B4............. 7 G3
MOS/BIL B13 .... 125 K2
St Mary St COV CV1 .... 9 G5 🔲
TAM/AM/WIL B77 .... 46 C1
St Matthew Ci HEDN WS12 .... 13 L8
St Matthew's Ci BNTWD WS7 ...... 19 K6
St Matthews Rd
LGLYGN/QTN B68 .... 104 E3
St Matthews Rd SMTHWK B66 ..... 88 A8
St Matthew St WOLV WV1............. 3 M6
St Mawes Rd
DUNHL/THL/PER WV6 .... 48 D2
St Mawgen Ci CVALE B35 .... 92 A1
St Michael Rd LICH WS13 .... 21 G5 🔲
St Michaels Ci ATHST CV9 .... 61 G4 🔲
ATHST CV9 .... 63 K4
BLOX/PEL WS3 .... 39 K3
PENK ST19 .... 10 C5
RCOVN/BALC/EX CV7 .... 96 D5
St Michael's Ct
DUNHL/THL/PER WV6 .... 35 J8
St Michael's Crs OLDBY B69 .... 104 D1 🔲
St Michaels Dr HEDN WS12 .... 13 L8
St Michael's Gv DUDS DY2........... 85 K4
St Michael's Rd COVE CV2 .... 154 C2
PENK ST19 .... 10 C5
SCFLD/BOLD B73 .... 72 D5
SEDG DY3 .... 65 K8
WSNGN B18 .... 88 E6
WWCK CV34 .... 199 H5
St Michael's Sq PENK ST19 .... 10 C4 🔲
St Michael St WBROM B70 .... 87 G2
WSL WS1 .... 4 F6
St Michael's Wy
NUNW/HART CV10 .... 98 A1
TPTN/OCK DY4 .... 85 L2 🔲
St Modwena Wy PENK ST19 .... 10 D6
St Nicholas Av KNWTH CV8 .... 191 K2
St Nicholas Church St
WWCK CV34 .... 199 K7
St Nicholas Ci BLOX/PEL WS3 ...... 39 L1 🔲
St Nicholas Ct COV CV1 .... 8 E1
St Nicolas Gdns
HWK/WKHTH B38 .... 144 D3
St Nicolas Park Dr NUN CV11 .... 81 J6
St Nicolas Rd NUN CV11 .... 81 H8
St Osburg's Rd COVE CV2 .... 154 E2
St Oswalds Ci KIDD DY10 .... 137 K5 🔲
St Oswalds Rd SMHTH B10 .... 108 C5
St Patrick Ci HEDN WS12 .... 13 L8
St Patricks Ci
ALE/KHTH/YWD B14 .... 125 J7
KIDDW DY11 .... 136 F7
St Paul's Av BHTH/HG B12 .... 107 L8
St Paul's Ci CNCK/NC WS11 .... 16 F4
COVEN WV9 .... 22 A3 🔲
WSL WS1 .... 4 F2
St Paul's Ct TAM/AM/WIL B77 ...... 60 A1 🔲
CSHL/WTROR B46 .... 93 L6
WBROM B70 .... 68 C6
St Pauls Dr RMSLY B62 .... 104 B4
TPTN/OCK DY4 .... 85 M1 🔲
St Paul's Rd BHTH/HG B12 .... 107 K7
BNTWD WS7 .... 19 G7
COVN CV6 .... 134 C7
DARL/WED WS10 .... 52 F8
DUDS DY2 .... 85 H8
HEDN WS12 .... 17 J4
NUNW/HART CV10 .... 98 A2
SMTHWK B66 .... 87 H6
St Paul's Sq CBHAMNW B3............. 6 D3
St Paul's St WSL WS1 .... 4 E2
St Peter's Av ATHST CV9 .... 63 M6 🔲
St Peter's Ci ALDR WS9 .... 41 J1
ATHST CV9 .... 63 M6
CSCFLD/WYGN B72 .... 72 F2 🔲
CSHL/WTROR B46 .... 92 F3
St Peters Cl HLGN/YWD B28 ...... 126 B7 🔲
St Peter's Ci REDW B97 .... 196 B8
TAM/AM/WIL B77 .... 46 A4
TPTN/OCK DY4 .... 86 B1
St Peters Ct BLOX/PEL WS3 .... 38 F4
COV CV1 .... 9 J2 🔲
St Peters Dr BLOX/PEL WS3 .... 39 L1
NUNW/HART CV10 .... 97 K1
St Peters La HIA/OLT B92 .... 129 H5
St Peters Rd ATHST CV9 .... 63 L6
BFLD/HDSWWD B20 .... 89 G5
BNTWD WS7 .... 19 G7
DUDS DY2 .... 85 H7
HAG/WOL DY9 .... 120 A4
HEDN WS12 .... 17 H1
HRBN B17 .... 105 M8
RLSN CV32 .... 200 D5 🔲
St Peters Ter WSLW WS2 .... 53 J1 🔲
St Philips Av BDMR/CCFT WV3 ... 49 K6
St Philip's Gv BDMR/CCFT WV3 ... 49 K6
St Quentin St WSLW WS2............... 4 A7
St Saviour's Ci
BKHL/PFLD WV2 .... 50 D7 🔲
St Saviour's Rd
WASH/WDE B8 .... 108 C2 🔲
St Silas' Sq LOZ/NWT B19 .... 88 F6
St Simons Ci RUSH/SHEL WS4 ...... 40 B7
St Stephen's Av WLNHL WV13 .... 51 K3 🔲
St Stephens Gdns REDE B98....... 188 D8
St Stephen's Rd BNTWD WS7 ...... 18 F7
HHTH/SAND B71 .... 87 M5 🔲
SLYOAK B29 .... 124 F5
St Stephens St AST/WIT B6 .... 89 J7
Saints Wy NUNW/HART CV10 ..... 81 H8
St Thomas' Ci ALDR WS9 .... 40 F4
BLOX/PEL WS3 .... 39 J7
MGN/WHC B75 .... 57 K8
St Thomas Dr HEDN WS12 .... 13 L8
St Thomas' Rd COVN CV6 .... 134 C2
ERDW/GRVHL B23 .... 90 B3
St Thomas's Ct COV CV1 .... 8 C6 🔲

St Thomas St DUDS DY2 .... 85 G8 🔲
St Valentines Ci WBROM B70 .... 87 K3 🔲
St Vincent Crs WBROM B70 .... 68 D7
St Vincent St LDYWD/EDGR B16 ... 6 A5
St Vincent St West
LDYWD/EDGR B16 .... 106 E3
Saladin Av OLDBY B69 .... 86 C8
Salcombe Av
LGN/SDN/BHAMAIR B26 .... 110 A8
Salcombe Ci CNCK/NC WS11 ...... 15 M5
COVS CV3 .... 155 H7
NUN CV11 .... 81 K8
Salcombe Dr BRLYHL DY5 .... 102 A5
Salcombe Gv BILS/COS WV14 ...... 67 H4
Salcombe Rd SMTHWK B66 .... 87 M8 🔲
Salem St TPTN/OCK DY4 .... 68 B8
REDE B98 .... 196 F7
Salford Ci COVE CV2 .... 134 E8
REDE B98 .... 196 F7
Salford St AST/WIT B6 .... 90 A5
Salisbury Av COVS CV3 .... 154 A7
Salisbury Ci DUDN DY1 .... 84 D2
KNWTH CV8 .... 180 D2
LICH WS13 .... 21 G2 🔲
MOS/BIL B13 .... 125 J2
Salisbury Dr CNCK/NC WS11 ...... 16 F5
CSHL/WTROR B46 .... 93 G2
KIDDW DY11 .... 136 D7
NUNW/HART CV10 .... 80 A7 🔲
Salisbury Gv CSCFLD/WYGN B72 .. 73 G6
Salisbury Rd LOZ/NWT B19 .... 89 H5
MOS/BIL B13 .... 125 J1
SMTHWK B66 .... 105 M1
WASH/WDE B8 .... 90 C8
WBROM B70 .... 87 J4
Salisbury St BDMR/CCFT WV3 ...... 2 C7
DARL/WED WS10 .... 52 C6
Sallow Gv BRWNH WS8 .... 26 D4
Sally Ward Dr ALDR WS9 .... 40 E1
Salop Ci HHTH/SAND B71 .... 68 F6
Salop Dr CNCK/NC WS11 .... 16 D5
LGLYGN/QTN B68 .... 105 G3
Salop Rd LGLYGN/QTN B68 .... 105 G2
REDW B97 .... 196 B3
Salop St BHTH/HG B12 .... 107 K5
BILS/COS WV14 .... 67 J1
BKHL/PFLD WV2 .... 2 E6
DUDN DY1 .... 84 E3
OLDBY B69 .... 86 C4
Salstar Ci AST/WIT B6 .... 89 J7 🔲
Saltash Gv YDLY B25 .... 109 G4
Saltbrook Rd HAG/WOL DY9 ...... 102 E6
Salter Rd TPTN/OCK DY4 .... 67 K6
Salter's La CRTAM B79 .... 31 M7 🔲
HHTH/SAND B71 .... 87 J1
REDW B97 .... 195 L1
Salter's Rd ALDR WS9 .... 40 E2
Salter St HOCK/TIA B94 .... 171 G3
Salters V WBROM B70 .... 87 J4 🔲
Saltisford WWCK CV34 .... 199 H6
Saltisford Gdns WWCK CV34 ..... 199 H5 🔲
Salt La COV CV1 .... 8 F5
Saltley Rd VAUX/NECH B7 .... 89 M8
Saltley Viad VAUX/NECH B7 .... 90 A8
Saltney Ci ERDE/BCHGN B24 ...... 73 H8
Salts La POL/KGSB/FAZ B78 .... 59 K1
Saltwells La DUDS DY2 .... 102 E3
Saltwells Rd DUDS DY2 .... 103 H2
Salwarpe Gv SLYOAK B29 .... 123 K3
Salwarpe Rd BRGRVE B60 .... 165 J1
Sam Barber Ct HEDN WS12 .... 17 J3 🔲
Sambar Rd POL/KGSB/FAZ B78 ... 45 K4
Sambourn Ci SOLH B91 .... 128 C2
Sambourne Dr BKDE/SHDE B34 ... 92 B6
Sambrook Rd WOLVN WV10 .... 36 E7
Sam Gault Ci COVS CV3 .... 155 J6
Sammons Wy TLHL/CAN CV4 ..... 152 B4 🔲
Sampson Ci COVE CV2 .... 135 G4
HDSW B21 .... 88 A4 🔲
OLDBY B69 .... 86 A6
Sampson Rd SPARK B11 .... 107 M6
Sampson St DARL/WED WS10 ..... 68 F2 🔲
Sams La WBROM B70 .... 87 G3
Sam Spencer Ct KIDD DY10 .... 162 E4 🔲
Samuel Ci LICH WS13 .... 21 G3
Samuels Rd RIDG/WDGT B32 .... 104 E3
Samuel St BLOX/PEL WS3 .... 38 F4
Sanby Ci BDWTH CV12 .... 116 C1
Sanda Cft CBROM B36 .... 92 F7
Sandalls Ci NFLD/LBR B31 .... 143 H4
Sandal Ri SOLH B91 .... 148 C2
Sandals Ri RMSLY B62 .... 122 B2 🔲
Sandalwood Ci SHHTH WV12 ...... 37 M5 🔲
Sand Bank BLOX/PEL WS3 .... 38 F4 🔲
BLOX/PEL WS3 .... 38 F4 🔲
Sandbarn Ci SHLY B90 .... 147 K7 🔲
Sandbeds Rd SHHTH WV12 .... 52 A1
Sandbourne Dr BEWD DY12 ...... 160 A2
Sandbourne Rd WASH/WDE B8 .. 108 E1
Sanderling Ci WOLVN WV10 ...... 22 F6
Sanderling Ct KIDD DY10 .... 161 L4
Sanderling Ri BNTWD WS7 .... 18 F5
BRLYHL DY5 .... 83 L7
Sanders Ci ATHST CV9 .... 63 J4 🔲
DUDS DY2 .... 85 J6
REDW B97 .... 195 L1
Sanders Rd BRGRVW B61 .... 185 J4
COVN CV6 .... 116 F7
Sandfield Ci SHLY B90 .... 146 E5
Sandfield Gv SEDG DY3 .... 83 M3
Sandfield Rd HHTH/SAND B71 ... 69 J4
STRBR DY8 .... 101 K3
Sandfields Av SMHTH B10 .... 107 M5 🔲
Sandfields Rd LGLYGN/QTN B68.. 105 G3
Sandford Av
BLKHTH/ROWR B65 .... 104 A2
Sandford Ci COVE CV2 .... 135 H2
Sandford Ri
DUNHL/THL/PER WV6 .... 35 J7
Sandford Rd DUDN DY1 .... 84 C4 🔲
MOS/BIL B13 .... 125 L2
Sandford St LICH WS13 .... 20 F6
Sandgate Crs COVE CV2 .... 155 K5
Sandgate Rd HLGN/YWD B28 ..... 146 D1
TPTN/OCK DY4 .... 67 L5
Sandhills Ci SOLH B91 .... 147 M5
Sandhills Gn RBRY B45 .... 167 H5
Sandhills La RBRY B45 .... 167 H6
Sandhills Rd RBRY B45 .... 167 H5

Sandhill St BLOX/PEL WS3 .... 38 E4 🔲
Sandhurst Av CBROM B36 .... 91 H7
HAG/WOL DY9 .... 120 B3
Sandhurst Ci REDE B98 .... 189 C7 🔲
Sandhurst Dr
ETTPK/GDPK/PENN WV4 .... 65 L1
Sandhurst Gv COVN CV6 .... 133 M8
STRBR DY8 .... 101 J2
Sandiacre Ci COVE CV2 .... 155 J1
Sandilands Ci COV CV2 .... 155 J1
Sandland Ci BILS/COS WV14 ...... 51 K7 🔲
Sandland Rd SHHTH WV12 .... 38 A5
Sandmartin Ci DUDS DY2 .... 103 G3 🔲
Sandmartin Wy KIDD DY10 .... 161 L3 🔲
Sandmere Gv
ALE/KHTH/YWD B14 .... 146 B2 🔲
Sandmere Ri WOLVN WV10 .... 36 C4 🔲
Sandmere Rd
ALE/KHTH/YWD B14 .... 146 B2
Sandon Ci REDE B98 .... 196 E2
Sandon Gv ERDE/BCHGN B24 ..... 90 E1
Sandon Rd HAG/WOL DY9 .... 120 D1
HRBN B17 .... 105 M4
NUN CV11 .... 80 F8
SMTHWK B66 .... 105 L3
WOLVN WV10 .... 35 M3
Sandown TAM/AM/WIL B77 .... 32 D8
Sandown Av COVN CV6 .... 134 C3
GTWY WS6 .... 24 B2
Sandown Ci BNTWD WS7 .... 13 L7 🔲
RLSN CV32 .... 201 G1
Sandown Dr
DUNHL/THL/PER WV6 .... 48 D1
Sandown Rd CBROM B36 .... 91 H5
Sandpiper TAM/AM/WIL B77 .... 46 B8
Sandpiper Ci HAG/WOL DY9 ..... 102 D8 🔲
HEDN WS12 .... 13 G6
KIDD DY10 .... 161 M3 🔲
Sandpiper Gdns
HWK/WKHTH B38 .... 144 D6 🔲
Sandpiper Rd COVN CV6 .... 134 F2
Sand Pits CBHAMW B1.................. 6 B4
Sandpits Ci WALM/CURD B76 ...... 74 F7
Sandpits La
RCOVN/BALC/EX CV7 .... 133 J5
Sandra Ci ALDR WS9 .... 40 F8
Sandringham Av SHHTH WV12 .... 37 M7
Sandringham Ci BNTWD WS7 ...... 18 C4 🔲
BLKHTH/ROWR B65 .... 104 C1 🔲
Sandringham Pl STRBR DY8 ...... 101 H4 🔲
Sandringham Rd
ETTPK/GDPK/PENN WV4 .... 49 M8 🔲
PBAR/PBCH B42 .... 70 F7
RMSLY B62 .... 103 M6 🔲
STRBR DY8 .... 101 G4
WMBN WV5 .... 64 D7
Sandringham Wy BRLYHL DY5 ... 102 A5
Sandstone Av RBRY B45 .... 142 E5
Sandstone Ci SEDG DY3 .... 84 B1
Sandstone Rd BEWD DY12 .... 160 A2
Sand St WBROM B70 .... 86 C1
Sandway Gdns WASH/WDE B8 .... 90 F1
Sandway Gv MOS/BIL B13 .... 126 A6 🔲
Sandwell Av DARL/WED WS10 .... 51 M8
Sandwell Rd HDSW B21 .... 88 B4
WBROM B70 .... 87 G1
WOLVN WV10 .... 35 M4
Sandwell Rd North
HHTH/SAND B71 .... 87 H1
Sandwick Ci COVS CV3 .... 155 K5
Sandwood Dr KGSTG B44 .... 71 K5
Sandyacre Wy STRBR DY8 .... 101 M8 🔲
Sandy Crs WNSFLD WV11 .... 37 L5
MOS/BIL B13 .... 126 A6
Sandyfields Rd SEDG DY3 .... 65 K8
Sandygate Ci REDW B97 .... 195 K3
Sandy Gv BRWNH WS8 .... 26 D4
Sandy Hill Ri SHLY B90 .... 146 E1 🔲
Sandy Hill Rd SHLY B90 .... 146 E1
Sandy Hollow
DUNHL/THL/PER WV6 .... 49 G3
Sandy La AST/WIT B6 .... 89 L6
BRGRVW B61 .... 141 K8
CDSL WV8 .... 34 D1
CNCK/NC WS11 .... 15 L4
COVN CV6 .... 134 A8
CSHL/WTROR B46 .... 95 J1
DARL/WED WS10 .... 69 K2
DUNHL/THL/PER WV6 .... 35 J7
KIDD DY10 .... 138 F5
LICHS WS14 .... 30 A1
PBAR/PBCH B42 .... 71 H5
RCOVN/BALC/EX CV7 .... 114 C2
RLSN CV32 .... 200 A2
RUGBYN/HIL CV21 .... 183 J2
WOLVN WV10 .... 36 C5
Sandy Mt WMBN WV5 .... 64 F6
Sandy Mount Rd WSL WS1 .... 5 H1
Sandy Rd STRBR DY8 .... 119 H4
Sandys Gv TPTN/OCK DY4 .... 67 J8 🔲
Sandy Wy EDG B15 .... 6 B7
TAM/AM/WIL B77 .... 46 E2
Sangwin Rd TPTN/OCK DY4 .... 67 G6
Sankey Rd CNCK/NC WS11 .... 16 D2
Sansome Ri SHLY B90 .... 146 D3 🔲
Sansome Rd SHLY B90 .... 146 D3
Sanstone Ci BLOX/PEL WS3 .... 39 G2
Sanstone Rd BLOX/PEL WS3 ...... 38 F2
Santolina Dr DSYBK/YTR WS5 .... 69 L2
Santos Ci COVS CV3 .... 155 K5
Santridge La BRGRVW B61 .... 185 L1
Sant Rd NFLD/LBR B31 .... 143 H6 🔲
Sapcote Gv COVE CV2 .... 134 F1 🔲
The Saplings PENK ST19 .... 10 D4
WALM/CURD B76 .... 73 L5 🔲
Sapphire Dr HEDN WS12 .... 17 G2
RLSS CV31 .... 200 D8 🔲
Sapphire Ga COVE CV2 .... 155 G3

Saracen Dr
RCOVN/BALC/EX CV7 .... 150 C7
Sara Ci FOAKS/STRLY B74 .... 56 E2
Sarah Ci BILS/COS WV14 .... 67 J4
Sarah St BORD B9 .... 107 M3
Sarah Seager Ci STRPT DY13 ..... 160 C7 🔲
Saredon Ci BLOX/PEL WS3 .... 39 L4
Saredon Rd CNCK/NC WS11 .... 23 M1
GTWY WS6 .... 24 A2 🔲
WOLVN WV10 .... 23 H3
Sarehole Rd HLGN/YWD B28 ..... 126 C5
Sargeant St RLSS CV31 .... 200 D6
Sargent Ci GTB/HAM B43 .... 71 H1
Sark Dr CBROM B36 .... 92 F7
Satchwell Ct RLSN CV32 .... 200 D5 🔲
Satchwell Pl RLSS CV31 .... 200 E6 🔲
Satchwell St RLSN CV32 .... 200 D4 🔲
Saturn Rd CNCK/NC WS11 .... 12 C5
Saumur Wy RLSS CV31 .... 200 A7
Saunders Av BDWTH CV12 .... 116 F3
Saunders Ci HEDN WS12 .... 13 L7 🔲
Saunton Ci COVW CV5 .... 132 F4
Saunton Rd RUGBYS/DCH CV22 .. 183 K4
Saunton Wy SLYOAK B29 .... 124 A4
Saveker Dr WALM/CURD B76 ...... 73 J1
Savernake Ci RBRY B45 .... 142 E3 🔲
Saville Ci RBRY B45 .... 142 F6
Saville Gv KNWTH CV8 .... 177 G7
Savoy Ci RIDG/WDGT B32 .... 105 K8
Saw Mill Ci RUSH/SHEL WS4 ...... 53 J2
Saxelby Ci ALE/KHTH/YWD B14 .. 145 J3
Saxon Ci COVS CV3 .... 156 B6
GTWY WS6 .... 24 E3
POL/KGSB/FAZ B78 .... 47 K4
STUD B80 .... 197 J8
TAM/AM/WIL B77 .... 46 D7
Saxoncourt
DUNHL/THL/PER WV6 .... 35 G8
Saxondale Av
LGN/SDN/BHAMAIR B26 .... 109 K7
Saxon Dr BLKHTH/ROWR B65 ... 104 A1
Saxondrive CRTAM B79 .... 46 A1
Saxonfields
DUNHL/THL/PER WV6 .... 35 G8 🔲
Saxon Mill La CRTAM B79 .... 46 A1
Saxon Rd COVE CV2 .... 154 F1
PENK ST19 .... 10 C5
Saxons Wy ALE/KHTH/YWD B14.. 145 L3
Saxon Wk LICH WS13 .... 20 C7
Saxon Wy
CHWD/FDBR/MGN B37 .... 110 D2
Saxon Wood Ci
NFLD/LBR B31 .... 143 L3 🔲
Saxon Wood Rd SHLY B90 .... 147 H8
Saxton Dr FOAKS/STRLY B74 ...... 42 D7
Scafell Ci COVW CV5 .... 152 E1
Scafell Dr BILS/COS WV14 .... 51 K6
ERDW/GRVHL B23 .... 72 A8
Scafell Rd STRBR DY8 .... 101 M7
Scaife Rd BRGRVE B60 .... 185 M6
Scammerton TAM/AM/WIL B77 ... 46 F6
Scampton Ci
DUNHL/THL/PER WV6 .... 34 C8 🔲
Scampton Wy CRTAM B79 .... 32 A5 🔲
Scar Bank WWCK CV34 .... 199 J4
Scarborough Ci WSLW WS2 .... 52 F5 🔲
Scarborough Rd WSLW WS2 .... 4 A5
Scarborough Wy
TLHL/CAN CV4 .... 152 D6
Scarfield Hl ALVE B48 .... 167 H8
Scarsdale Rd PBAR/PBCH B42 ... 71 H5
Schofield Av HHTH/SAND B71 ..... 68 F5
Schofield Rd
CHWD/FDBR/MGN B37 .... 92 D8
Scholars Ga BNTWD WS7 .... 19 H7
STETCH B33 .... 109 M3 🔲
Scholfield Rd
RCOVN/BALC/EX CV7 .... 115 L7
Schoolacre Ri FOAKS/STRLY B74 .. 55 J4
Schoolacre Rd
BKDE/SHDE B34 .... 91 M7 🔲
School Av BRWNH WS8 .... 26 D5
School Ci BDMR/CCFT WV3 .... 48 F6
BNTWD WS7 .... 18 B5
CDSL WV8 .... 20 F7
CHWD/FDBR/MGN B37 .... 92 E7
CNCK/NC WS11 .... 17 L7
COVS CV3 .... 9 M6 🔲
OLDBY B69 .... 86 A6
WMBN WV5 .... 65 H5
School Crs CNCK/NC WS11 .... 17 L7
School Dr BILS/COS WV14 .... 67 G4 🔲
BRGRVE B60 .... 185 L3
HLYWD B47 .... 169 L2
STRBR DY8 .... 101 K5
The School Dr DUDS DY2............. 85 J7
Schoolfield Gv
RUGBYN/HIL CV21 .... 183 K2 🔲
Schoolfields Rd LICHS WS14 ...... 28 E8
Schoolgate Ci RUSH/SHEL WS4 ... 40 B4
School Gn BILS/COS WV14........... 51 G5
School Hi BTACH/HART CV33 ..... 201 M5
NUNW/HART CV10 .... 79 L6
Schoolhouse Ci
HWK/WKHTH B38 .... 144 F3 🔲
School House La COVE CV2......... 135 L7
School La ALVE B48 .... 167 M8
BKDE/SHDE B34 .... 91 M6
BLOX/PEL WS3 .... 25 J3
BLOX/PEL WS3 .... 39 K1
BNTWD WS7 .... 18 B5
BRGRVE B60 .... 165 M7
BRLYHL DY5 .... 101 M1
CRTAM B79 .... 33 K6
HAG/WOL DY9 .... 119 M8
HALE B63 .... 121 K3 🔟
KNWTH CV8 .... 174 C8
KNWTH CV8 .... 176 D8
NUNW/HART CV10 .... 79 J8
POL/KGSB/FAZ B78 .... 30 F6
POL/KGSB/FAZ B78 .... 44 B2
RCOVN/BALC/EX CV7 .... 116 C6
RLSS CV31 .... 201 J8
RRUGBY CV23........................... 180 D7
SOLH B91 .... 148 B1
STETCH B33 .... 109 K4
TAM/AM/WIL B77 .... 46 D7

WALM/CURD B76 .... **75** L6
WOLVN WV10 .... **23** H3
WOLVN WV10 .... **36** B3
School Rd *ALE/KHTH/YWD* B14 .. **125** K4
ALE/KHTH/YWD B14 ...... **145** M1
BRLYHL DY5 .... **102** E3
CNCK/NC WS11 .... **17** L7
DARL/WED WS10 .... **69** H3
DUNHL/THL/PER WV6 .... **48** E2
HLGN/YWD B28 .... **126** E5
HOCK/TIA B94 .... **171** J4
RBRY B45 .... **142** C7
SEDG DY3 .... **82** F2
SHLY B90 .... **146** F3
WMBN WV5 .... **64** F6
WMBN WV5 .... **64** A4
WNSFLD WV11 .... **36** F7
School St *BKHL/PFLD* WV2 ...... **2** E7
BRLYHL DY5 .... **84** B6
CDYHTH B64 .... **103** H4
DARL/WED WS10 .... **52** A7
DUDN DY1 .... **84** F4
KNWTH CV8 .... **180** E1
RRUGBY CV23 .... **157** M8
RRUGBY CV23 .... **182** E1
RUSH/SHEL WS4 .... **40** B4
SEDG DY3 .... **66** C5
STRBR DY8 .... **101** K8 ⑧
TAM/AM/WIL B77 .... **46** C1
WLNHL WV13 .... **51** K3
WOLV WV1 .... **2** E6
School St West
BILS/COS WV14 .... **67** G5 ③
School Wk *BILS/COS* WV14 ...... **51** G5
BNTWD WS7 .... **18** B5
NUN CV11 .... **99** J3
Scimitar Cl *CRTAM* B79 .... **31** J6
Scorers Cl *HIA/OLT* B92 .... **126** F7
The Scotchill *COVN* CV6 .... **133** K4
The Scotchings *CBROM* B36 ... **91** J5 ⑨
Scotch Orch *LICH* WS13 .... **21** H4
Scotia Rd *CNCK/NC* WS11 ...... **16** B2
Scotland La *RIDG/WDGT* B32 .. **122** F5
Scots Cl *RUGBYS/DCH* CV22 .... **183** C6
Scots La *COVN* CV6 .... **133** K7
Scott Av *DARL/WED* WS10 ...... **68** F3
ETTPK/GDPK/PENN WV4 ... **65** J1
NUNW/HART CV10 .... **81** H5
Scott Cl *LICHS* WS14 .... **20** F7
Scott Gv *HIA/OLT* B92 .... **127** J2
Scott Rd *DSYBK/YTR* WS5 ..... **54** B7
GTB/HAM B43 .... **70** D3
HIA/OLT B92 .... **127** J3
KNWTH CV8 .... **191** J2
REDW B97 .... **196** A5
RLSS CV31 .... **200** F7
TAM/AM/WIL B77 .... **46** C1
Scott's Green Cl *DUDN* DY1.... **84** D5
Scott's Rd *STRBR* DY8 .... **101** K7
Scott St *HEDN* WS12 .... **17** K2
TPTN/OCK DY4 .... **68** A8
Scotwell Cl *BLKHTH/ROWR* B65 .. **103**M2
Scout Cl *STECH* B33 .... **110** A3
Scribban Cl *SMTHWK* B66 ...... **105** M1 ⑧
Scribers La *HLGN/YWD* B28 ... **146** B1
Sculthorpe Rd *KIDD* DY10 ..... **138** F3
Seabroke Av
RUGBYS/DCH CV22 .... **183** K2
Seacroft Av *STECH* B33 .... **109** J4
Seafield *TAM/AM/WIL* B77 .... **32** D8
Seafield Cl *KGSWFD* DY6 ...... **101** J1 ③
Seafield La *ALVE* B48 .... **169** J7
Seaford Cl *COVE* CV2 .... **134** F1 ③
Seaforth Gv *WNSFLD* WV11 ... **37** M4 ③
Seagar St *HHTH/SAND* B71 .... **87** H1
Seager's La *BRLYHL* DY5 ...... **102** B3
Seagrave Rd *COV* CV1 .... **9** J6
Seagull Bay Dr *BILS/COS* WV14 .. **67** H4
Sealand Dr *BDWTH* CV12 ...... **116** D2
Seal Cl *WALM/CURD* B76 .... **73** J2
Seals Gn *HWK/WKHTH* B38 .... **144** B6
Sear Hills Cl
RCOVN/BALC/EX CV7 ...... **150** F7
Seaton *TAM/AM/WIL* B77 ...... **46** C5
WNSFLD WV11 .... **37** K8
Seaton Gv *MOS/BIL* B13 .... **125** H4 ③
Seaton Pl *STRBR* DY8 .... **101** C3
Sebastian Cl *COVS* CV3 .... **154** F8
Sebright Gn *KIDD* DY11 .... **137** C2 ③
Sebright Rd *KIDD* DY11 .... **137** C2
Second Av *BORD* B9 .... **108** D4 ③
BRWNH WS8 .... **26** E5
COVS CV3 .... **155** C4
KGSWFD DY6 .... **83** L6
SLYOAK B29 .... **124** F2
WOLVN WV10 .... **36** C6
Second Exhibition Av
BHAMNEC B40 .... **129** H1 ③
Sedge Av *HWK/WKHTH* B38 ... **144** D2
Sedgeberrow Covert
HWK/WKHTH B38 .... **144** C5 ②
Sedgeberrow Rd *HALE* B63 .... **121** L3 ③
Sedgefield Cl *DUDN* DY1 ...... **84** C2 ③
Sedgefield Gv
DUNHL/THL/PER WV6 .... **48** D7 ③
Sedgeford Cl *BRLYHL* DY5 ..... **102** B5 ③
Sedgehill Av *HRBN* B17 .... **123**M1
Sedgemere Gv
RCOVN/BALC/EX CV7 ...... **151** C8 ⑪
RUSH/SHEL WS4 .... **40** A5
Sedgemere Rd
LGN/SDN/BHAMAIR B26 ... **109** K4
Sedgemoor Av *BNTWD* WS7 ... **18** F8
Sedgemoor Rd *COVS* CV3 ...... **154** F8
Sedgley Gv *BFLD/HDSWWD* B20 .. **88** C1
Sedgley Hall Av *SEDG* DY3 .... **66** A5
Sedgley Rd
ETTPK/GDPK/PENN WV4 ... **65** K3
Sedgley Rd East *TPTN/OCK* DY4 .. **85** L1
Sedgley Rd West *TPTN/OCK* DY4 .. **67** G7
Sedgley St *BKHL/PFLD* WV2 ... **50** A6
Sedlescombe Pk
RUGBYS/DCH CV22 .... **183** K5
Seed Field Cft *COVS* CV3 ...... **154** B6
Seedhouse Ct *CDYHTH* B64 ... **103** L5 ⑬

Seeds La *BRWNH* WS8 .... **26** D5
Seeleys Rd *SPARK* B11 .... **126** B1
Seeney La *WALM/CURD* B76 ... **59** K1
Seeswood Cl *NUNW/HART* CV10 .. **98** A3
Sefton Dr *BLKHTH/ROWR* B65 .. **85** K7
Sefton Gv *DARL/WED* WS10 ... **68** A3
TAM/AM/WIL B77 .... **60** B1
TLHL/CAN CV4 .... **153** J7
Segbourne Rd *RBRY* B45 .... **142** C5
Segundo Cl *DSYBK/YTR* WS5 ... **69** J1
Segundo Rd *DSYBK/YTR* WS5 .. **69** K1
Selba Dr *KIDDW* DY11 .... **136** D7
Selborne Cl *WSL* WS1 .... **5** J3
Selborne Rd
BFLD/HDSWWD B20 .... **88** E3
DUDS DY2 .... **85** H6
RUGBYS/DCH CV22 .... **183** H5
Selborne St *WSL* WS1 .... **5** J3
Selbourne Crs *WOLV* WV1 ..... **50** F4
Selby Cl
LGN/SDN/BHAMAIR B26 ... **109** K4
Selby Gv *MOS/BIL* B13 .... **126** A8
Selby Wy *BLOX/PEL* WS3 ...... **38** C3
NUNW/HART CV10 .... **79** M7
Selcombe Wy
HWK/WKHTH B38 .... **144** D6
Selcroft Av *RIDG/WDGT* B32 ... **105** K8
Selecta Av *KGSTG* B44 .... **71** H3
Selker Dr *TAM/AM/WIL* B77 ... **32** D8
Selkirk Cl *HHTH/SAND* B71 .... **69** G7
Selly Av *SLYOAK* B29 .... **124** E3
Selly Cl *SLYOAK* B29 .... **124** F3
Selly Hall Cft *BVILLE* B30 ...... **124** D7
Selly Hill Rd *SLYOAK* B29 ...... **124** D3
Selly Oak Rd *BVILLE* B30 ...... **124** C6
Selly Pk Rd *SLYOAK* B29 .... **124** E3
Selly Whf *SLYOAK* B29 .... **124** C4
Sellywick Dr *SLYOAK* B29 ...... **124** F3
Selly Wick Rd *SLYOAK* B29 .... **124** F3
Sellywood Rd *BVILLE* B30 ...... **124** C6
Selma Gv
ALE/KHTH/YWD B14 .... **126** B8 ②
Selmans HI *BLOX/PEL* WS3 ..... **39** C2
KIDDW DY11 .... **136** F8 ③
Selsdon Rd *BLOX/PEL* WS3 .... **38** D2
Selsey Cl *COVS* CV3 .... **179** G1
Selsey Rd *HRBN* B17 .... **105**M2
Selston Rd *AST/WIT* B6 .... **89** J6
Selvey Av *GTB/HAM* B43 .... **70** F2
Selworthy Rd *CBROM* B36 ..... **92** D6
COVN CV6 .... **134** B2
Selwyn Cl *BKHL/PFLD* WV2 .... **50** A6
Selwyn Rd *BILS/COS* WV14 .... **51** K7
LDYWD/EDGR B16 .... **106** B2
Selwyn Wk *FOAKS/STRLY* B74... **56** A1
Semele Cl *RLSS* CV31 .... **201** J8
Seneschal Cl *COVS* CV3 .... **154** C6
Senneleys Park Rd
NFLD/LBR B31 .... **123** K4
Sennen Cl *NUN* CV11 .... **99** H7
WLNHL WV13 .... **51** K4 ③
Sensall Rd *HAG/WOL* DY9 ..... **120** D2
Sephton Dr
RCOVN/BALC/EX CV7 ...... **117** G7 ①
Serin Cl *KIDD* DY10 .... **161** K4
Serpentine Rd *AST/WIT* B6 .... **89** C4
HRBN B17 .... **106** A8
SLYOAK B29 .... **124** E2
The Serpentine *KIDDW* DY11 .. **161** C1
Settle Av *BKDE/SHDE* B34 ..... **91** K7
Settle Cft
CHWD/FDBR/MGN B37 ..... **110** D4 ③
Setton Dr *SEDG* DY3 .... **66** C6
Seven Acres *ALDR* WS9 .... **40** F8
Seven Acres La *REDE* B98 ..... **189** G8
Seven Acres Rd *NFLD/LBR* B31 .. **144** A4
RMSLY B62 .... **104** E8
Sevens Rd *HEDN* WS12 .... **18** A2
Seven Star Rd *SOLH* B91 ...... **127** L8
Seven Stars Rd *OLDBY* B69 ... **86** E6
Severn Cl *BRGRVE* B61 .... **165** L5 ③
CBROM B36 .... **92** D6
RLSN CV32 .... **201** C2 ③
SHHTH WV12 .... **37** L6
TPTN/OCK DY4 .... **67** K8
Severn Dr *BNTWD* WS7 .... **19** H7
BRLYHL DY5 .... **83** M6
DUNHL/THL/PER WV6 .... **48** C1
Severne Gv *ACGN* B27 .... **127** C4
Severne Rd *ACGN* B27 .... **127** C5
Severn Gv *KIDDW* DY11 .... **160** F2
SPARK B11 .... **108** A7 ③
Severn Rd *BDWTH* CV12 ...... **117** L2
BLOX/PEL WS3 .... **39** H5
BRWNH WS8 .... **26** A3
COV CV1 .... **9** L7
HALE B63 .... **102** F8
STRBR DY8 .... **119** K2
Severn St *CBHAMW* B1 .... **6** E7
Severn Wy *HLYWD* B47 .... **169** J3
Sevington Cl *SOLH* B91 .... **148** A5 ③
Sewall Hwy *COVE* CV2 .... **135** C8
COVN CV6 .... **134** E5
Seward Cl *LICHS* WS14 .... **21** H7
Seymour Cl *COVS* CV3 .... **155** C8
GTWY WS6 .... **24** B4 ③
RWWCK/WEL CV35 .... **198** D7 ②
SLYOAK B29 .... **124** F3
Seymour Dr *REDE* B98 .... **188** E8 ③
Seymour Gdns
FOAKS/STRLY B74 .... **56** C3 ①
Seymour Gv *RLSS* CV31 .... **200** B7 ②
Seymour Rd *HAG/WOL* DY9 ... **102** D8
KIDDW DY11 .... **136** F5 ③
NUN CV11 .... **99** H2
OLDBY B69 .... **87** C6
TPTN/OCK DY4 .... **68** A4
Seymour St *DIG/EDG* B5 ...... **7** J2 ③
Shackleton Dr
DUNHL/THL/PER WV6 .... **34** B8
Shackleton Rd *BLOX/PEL* WS3 .. **39** H3
Shadowbrook La *HIA/OLT* B92 .. **129** H6
Shadowbrook Rd *COVN* CV6 .. **133** L8 ③
Shadwell Dr *SEDG* DY3 .... **84** B3
Shadwell St *CBHAMNE* B4...... **7** C2

Shady La *KGSTG* B44 .... **71** H3
Shadymoor Dr *BRLYHL* DY5 ... **102** A5
Shaftesbury Av *HAG/WOL* DY9 .. **120** A2
RCOVN/BALC/EX CV7 ...... **115** L6
Shaftesbury Cl *BRGRVE* B60 .. **185** M3 ③
Shaftesbury Dr *HEDN* WS12 ... **13** C6
Shaftesbury Rd *COVW* CV5 .... **153** K5
DARL/WED WS10 .... **68** F3
Shaftesbury Sq
HHTH/SAND B71 .... **69** G8 ③
Shaftesbury St *HHTH/SAND* B71 .. **87** C1
WBROM B70 .... **86** F1
Shaft La *RCOVN/BALC/EX* CV7 .. **131** L1
Shaftmoor La *HLGN/YWD* B28 .. **126** C3
Shaftsbury Av *HALE* B63 ...... **102** F6 ③
Shaftsbury Cl *BILS/COS* WV14 .. **51** K6 ③
Shaftsbury Rd
LGN/SDN/BHAMAIR B26 ... **110** A8
Shakespeare Av
BDWTH CV12 .... **117** H3 ③
LICHS WS14 .... **20** F7
REDE B98 .... **196** E5 ③
Shakespeare Cl
BILS/COS WV14 .... **67** H3 ③
CRTAM B79 .... **31** L7
Shakespeare Crs *BLOX/PEL* WS3 .. **39** J5
NUN CV11 .... **99** L4
SHLY B90 .... **146** E4
Shakespeare Dr *KIDD* DY10 ... **137**M7
Shakespeare Gdns
RUGBYS/DCH CV22 .... **183** J6
Shakespeare Gv
CNCK/NC WS11 .... **16** B1 ③
Shakespeare Pl *BLOX/PEL* WS3 .. **39** J6
Shakespeare Rd *AST/WIT* B6 .. **89**M2
BNTWD WS7 .... **18** D5
SEDG DY3 .... **83** L1
SHLY B90 .... **147** H4
SMTHWKW B67 .... **105** H1
TPTN/OCK DY4 .... **67** L5
Shakespeare St *COVE* CV2 .... **154** F1
SPARK B11 .... **108** A3 ③
WOLV WV1 .... **3** J6
Shakleton Rd *COVW* CV5 ...... **8** A5
The Shales *WMBN* WV5 .... **64** C8 ③
Shale St *BILS/COS* WV14 ...... **51** C8
Shalford Rd *HIA/OLT* B92 ..... **127** J1
Shallcross La *SEDG* DY3 ...... **84** B2
Shalnecote Gv
ALE/KHTH/YWD B14 .... **145** H2 ③
Shambles *DARL/WED* WS10 ... **68** D3 ⑩
Shandon Cl *RIDG/WDGT* B32 .. **123** K2 ③
Shanklin Cl *GTWY* WS6 .... **24** D2
Shanklin Dr *NUNW/HART* CV10 .. **81** H7
Shanklin Rd *COVS* CV3 .... **178** F1
Shannon *TAM/AM/WIL* B77 .... **46** D5
Shannon Dr *BRWNH* WS8 ...... **26** A3
Shannon Rd *HWK/WKHTH* B38 .. **144** C6
Shapinsay Dr *RBRY* B45 .... **142** D4 ③
Shard End Crs *BKDE/SHDE* B34 .. **92** A4
Shardlow Rd *WNSFLD* WV11 ... **37** J5
The Shardway *BKDE/SHDE* B34 .. **92** A8
Sharesacre St *WLNHL* WV13 ... **51**M2
Sharington Cl *DUDS* DY2 ...... **85** J5 ③
Sharman Rd *WOLVN* WV10 .... **36** C7
Sharmans Cross Rd
SOLH B91 .... **147** K1 ③
Sharon Cl
ETTPK/GDPK/PENN WV4 ... **50** C8
Sharon Wy *HEDN* WS12 .... **17** H2
Sharp Cl *COVN* CV6 .... **134** A3 ③
Sharpe Cl *WWCK* CV34 .... **199** J5 ③
Sharpe St *TAM/AM/WIL* B77 .. **32** E8 ③
Sharpley Ct *COVE* CV2 .... **135** C5 ③
Sharps Cl *RBRY* B45 .... **142** E6
Sharrat Fld *MGN/WHC* B75 .... **57** H3
Sharratt Rd *BDWTH* CV12 ..... **116** D3
Sharrocks St *WOLV* WV1 ...... **3** J7
Shaw Av *KIDD* DY10 .... **137**M7
Shawbank Rd *REDE* B98 .... **196** F2
Shawberry Av *CVALE* B35 ..... **91** L2 ③
Shawberry Rd
CHWD/FDBR/MGN B37 ..... **92** D8 ②
Shawbrook Gv
ALE/KHTH/YWD B14 .... **145** L2 ③
Shawbury Cl *REDE* B98 .... **197** J2
Shawbury Gv *BHTH/HG* B12 ... **107** K5
DUNHL/THL/PER WV6 .... **34** C7
Shawbury La *CSHL/WTROR* B46 .. **95** C5
CSHL/WTROR B46 .... **95** J7
Shawbury Rd *WOLVN* WV10 ... **36** D8
Shawbury Village
CSHL/WTROR B46 .... **95** M7
Shaw Dr *BNTWD* WS7 .... **18** E4 ③
STECH B33 .... **109** J3
Shawe Av *NUNW/HART* CV10 .. **81** C6
Shaw Hall La *COVEN* WV9 ..... **22** A6
Shaw Hedge Rd *BEWD* DY12 .. **160** A1 ③
Shawhellier Av *BRLYHL* DY5 ... **102** C3
Shaw Hill Rd *WASH/WDE* B8 ... **108** E1
Shawhurst Cft *HLYWD* B47 .... **145** L6 ③
Shawhurst La *HLYWD* B47 ..... **145** L7
Shaw La *DUNHL/THL/PER* WV6 .. **48** E7
LICH WS13 .... **20** E5
RUGE WS15 .... **18** E1
Shawley Cft *ACGN* B27 .... **127** J1
Shaw Rd *BILS/COS* WV14 ...... **66** F4
BKHL/PFLD WV2 .... **50** A7
DUDS DY2 .... **84** F6
TPTN/OCK DY4 .... **86** A1
WOLVN WV10 .... **36** A7 ③
Shaws Cl *REDW* B97 .... **195** K3
Shawsdale Rd *CBROM* B36 .... **91** K6
Shaw's La *GTWY* WS6 .... **24** E3
Shaw's Pas *DIG/EDG* B5 .... **7** J3 ③
Shaw St *WBROM* B70 .... **68** C5 ⑨
WSLW WS2 .... **4** D1
Shayler Gv *BKHL/PFLD* WV2 ... **50** B6
Sheaf La
LGN/SDN/BHAMAIR B26 ... **127**M1
Shearwater Cl *KIDD* DY10 ..... **161** M4 ③
RBRY B45 .... **142** D7
Shearwater Wk
ERDW/GRVHL B23 .... **71** M7 ③
Sheaves Cl
ETTPK/GDPK/PENN WV4 ... **66** A2 ③
Shedden St *DUDS* DY2 .... **85** H5 ③

Sheddington Rd
ERDW/GRVHL B23 .... **72** B6
Sheen Rd *KGSTG* B44 .... **71** J1
Sheepclose Dr
CHWD/FDBR/MGN B37 ..... **110** E2 ⑧
Sheepcote Cl *RLSN* CV32 ...... **200** E4 ③
Sheepcote Gra *BRGRVE* B61 ... **165** K8
Sheepcote La *TAM/AM/WIL* B77 .. **46** D2
Sheepcote St *CBHAMW* B1 .... **6** B7
LDYWD/EDGR B16 .... **6** A5
Sheepcroft Cl *REDW* B97 ...... **195** K5
Sheepfold Cl
BLKHTH/ROWR B65 .... **103** L1
Sheepmoor Cl *HRBN* B17 ...... **105** K5
Sheepwash La *TPTN/OCK* DY4 .. **68** B3
Sheepy Rd *ATHST* CV9 .... **63** H2
Sheerwater Dr *BRLYHL* DY5 ... **102** A6
Sheet St *DIG/EDG* B5 .... **50** A5 ③
STECH B33 .... **109** L3 ③
Sheffield Cl *COVW* CV5 .... **154** F2
HOCK/TIA B94 .... **172** A7 ③
Sheffield Rd
ALE/KHTH/YWD B14 .... **145** G2
TPTN/OCK DY4 .... **67** M5 ③
Shelley Av *KIDD* DY10 .... **137** J6
Shelley Cl *BDWTH* CV12 .... **117** H4
BRGRVE B61 .... **165** L5
REDW B97 .... **196** A4
SEDG DY3 .... **83** L1
STRBR DY8 .... **101** L5 ③
Shelley Dr *AST/WIT* B6 .... **89** M2 ③
FOAKS/STRLY B74 .... **42** D7
Shelley Rd *BNTWD* WS7 .... **18** E4
CNCK/NC WS11 .... **16** C8
COVE CV2 .... **155** C2
CRTAM B79 .... **31** K6
SHHTH WV12 .... **38** C6
WOLVN WV10 .... **35** L4
Shellon Cl *COVS* CV3 .... **155** K5
Shelly Cl
CHWD/FDBR/MGN B37 ..... **110** D3
Shelly Crs *SHLY* B90 .... **147**M7
Shelly Cft *STECH* B33 .... **109** L2
Shelly La *SHLY* B90 .... **147**M7
Shelsley Av *OLDBY* B69 .... **86** B8
Shelsley Dr *MOS/BIL* B13 ..... **125**M4
Shelsley Cl *PENK* ST19 .... **10** E4
Shelsley Wy *SOLH* B91 .... **147**M4
Shelton Cl *DARL/WED* WS10 ... **53** C8
Shelton La *HALE* B63 .... **103** J8
Shelton St *TAM/AM/WIL* B77 .. **46** D6 ③
Sheltwood Cl *REDW* B97 ...... **195** L3 ③
Sheltwood La *BRGRVE* B60 .... **194** D1
Shelwick Gv *DOR/KN* B93 ..... **172** D1 ③
Shenley Av *DUDN* DY1 .... **66** F7
Shenley Fields Dr
NFLD/LBR B31 .... **123** J6
Shenley Fields Rd *SLYOAK* B29 .. **123** K6
Shenley Gdns *SLYOAK* B29 .... **123** L6
Shenley HI *NFLD/LBR* B31 ..... **123** J7
Shenley La *SLYOAK* B29 .... **123** K6
Shenstone Av *RMSLY* B62 ..... **122** C1
STRBR DY8 .... **119** H3
Shenstone Cl *BRGRVE* B60 .... **185** L2
FOAKS/STRLY B74 .... **42** C7 ③
Shenstone Ct
BDMR/CCFT WV3 .... **49** L7 ③
Shenstone Dr *ALDR* WS9 ...... **40** E5
RCOVN/BALC/EX CV7 ...... **150** E7
Shenstone Rd
ALE/KHTH/YWD B14 .... **145** L4
GTB/HAM B43 .... **70** C5
LDYWD/EDGR B16 .... **106** A2
Shenstone Valley Rd
RMSLY B62 .... **104** D7
Shenton Wk
CHWD/FDBR/MGN B37 ..... **92** D8
Shepheard Rd
LGN/SDN/BHAMAIR B26 ... **110** B8
Shepherd Dr *LICH* WS13 ...... **21** G3
TLHL/CAN CV4 .... **152** D2
Shepherd Dr *SHHTH* WV12 ... **37** M8 ③
Shepherds Brook Rd
HAG/WOL DY9 .... **102** B8
Shepherds Fold
BLKHTH/ROWR B65 .... **103**M3
Shepherds Gdns *EDG* B15 .... **6** B8
Shepherds Green Rd
ERDE/BCHGN B24 .... **90** D3
Shepherds Pool Rd
MGN/WHC B75 .... **57** J3
Shepherds Standing
BKDE/SHDE B34 .... **91** M7 ③
Shepherds Wy
ERDW/GRVHL B23 .... **72** A5
RBRY B45 .... **142** F7
Shepperton St *NUN* CV11 ..... **99** C3 ③
Sheppey Dr *CBROM* B36 .... **92** F8 ③
Shepwell Gn *WLNHL* WV13 .... **52** A4
Sherard Cft *CBROM* B36 .... **92** F8 ③
Sheraton Cl *ALDR* WS9 .... **40** F7
ERDW/GRVHL B23 .... **72** D6 ③
Sheraton Dr *KIDD* DY10 .... **137** L7
Sheraton Gra *STRBR* DY8 ..... **119** K3 ③
Sherborne Cl *BLOX/PEL* WS3 .. **39** C6 ③

Sherborne Gdns *CDSL* WV8 ... **34** E2
Sherborne Gv *CBHAMW* B1 ... **106** C2
Sherborne Rd *WOLVN* WV10 .. **36** B4
Sherbourne Av *SHHTH* WV12 .. **17** J1
NUNW/HART CV10 .... **79** M8
Sherbourne Cl *REDE* B98 ...... **197** H3 ③
Sherbourne Crs *COVW* CV5 ... **153** J1
Sherbourne Dr *ACGN* B27 ..... **127** C1 ③
Sherbourne Rd *ACGN* B27 .... **126** F1
BHTH/HG B12 .... **107** K7
CDYHTH B64 .... **103** L5
STRBR DY8 .... **119** M1 ③
Sherbourne St *COV* CV1 ...... **8** B5
Sherbrooke Av
TAM/AM/WIL B77 .... **46** C7
Sherbrook Rd *CNCK/NC* WS11 .. **16** A4
Sherdmore Cft *SHLY* B90 ...... **147** K7 ③
WSLW WS2 .... **52** F6
Sheridan Cl *RUGBYS/DCH* CV22 .. **183** K6
Sheridan Dr *NUNW/HART* CV10 .. **79** K8
Sheridan Gdns *SEDG* DY3 ..... **65** K8 ③
Sheridan St *HHTH/SAND* B71 .. **87** H1
WSLW WS2 .... **52** F6
Sheriff Av *TLHL/CAN* CV4 ..... **152** F6
Sheriff Dr *BRLYHL* DY5 .... **102** D3 ③
Sheriffs Cl *LICHS* WS14 .... **21** J7
Sheriffs Orch *COV* CV1 .... **8** E6
Sherifoot La *MGN/WHC* B75 .. **56** F2 ③
Sheringham *EDG* B15 .... **106** C5
Sheringham La *NUN* CV11 ..... **99** K3
Sheringham Rd *BVILLE* B30 ... **144** F2
Sherington Av *COVW* CV5 ..... **153** C2
Sherington Dr
ETTPK/GDPK/PENN WV4 ... **50** B8 ③
Sherlock Cl *SHHTH* WV12 ..... **38** B8
Sherlock Rd *COVW* CV5 .... **153** H2
Sherlock St *DIG/EDG* B5 ...... **107** J5
Sherrans Dell
ETTPK/GDPK/PENN WV4 ... **66** B2 ③
Sherratt Cl *WALM/CURD* B76 .. **73** K5
Sherringham Dr *SHHTH* WV12 .. **38** A4
Sherron Gdns *BHTH/HG* B12 .. **107** K8 ③
Sherston Covert *BVILLE* B30 .. **145** G3 ③
Shervale Cl
ETTPK/GDPK/PENN WV4 ... **49** L7 ③
Sherwin Av *BILS/COS* WV14 ... **66** E3
Sherwood Cl *ATHST* CV9 ...... **60** F4
HIA/OLT B92 .... **127** K5
HLGN/YWD B28 .... **126** D6
Sherwood Dr *BRLYHL* DY5 ..... **102** D4
CNCK/NC WS11 .... **16** E2
Sherwood Jones Cl *COVN* CV6 .. **133**M7
Sherwood Ms *HLGN/YWD* B28 .. **126** C7
Sherwood Rd *BRGRVE* B60 .... **185** L7
HLGN/YWD B28 .... **126** C6
SMTHWKW B67 .... **105** L4
STRBR DY8 .... **101** J6
Sherwood St *WOLV* WV1 ...... **2** E2
Sherwood Wk *RLSN* CV32 .... **201** L1 ③
RUSH/SHEL WS4 .... **40** B6
Shetland Cl *COVW* CV5 .... **152** E1 ③
DUNHL/THL/PER WV6 .... **35** M8 ③
LDYWD/EDGR B16 .... **106** D3
Shetland Dr *NUNW/HART* CV10 .. **98** D3
SMTHWK B66 .... **87** H5 ③
Shevlock Wy *COVN* CV6 .... **134** E7
Shidas La *OLDBY* B69 .... **86** C6
Shillcock Gv *LOZ/NWT* B19 ... **89** J8 ③
Shillingstone Cl *COVE* CV2 .... **155** L1 ③
Shilton Cl *SHLY* B90 .... **147** K7
Shilton Gv *SLYOAK* B29 .... **123** K5 ③
Shilton La *COVE* CV2 .... **135** J3
Shinwell Crs *OLDBY* B69 ...... **86** B3
Shipbourne Cl *RIDG/WDGT* B32 .. **105** K8
Shipley Flds
ERDE/BCHGN B24 .... **90** E2 ③
Shipley Gv *SLYOAK* B29 .... **123** L5 ③
Shipston Rd *COVE* CV2 .... **155** H3 ③
NFLD/LBR B31 .... **143**M4
Shipton Cl *DUDN* DY1 .... **84** C2
Shipton Rd *CSCFLD/WYGN* B72 .. **73** C2
Shipway Rd *YDLY* B25 .... **108** E6
Shire Cl *COVN* CV6 .... **134** F3
LDYWD/EDGR B16 .... **106** D3 ③
LGLYGN/QTN B68 .... **104** F3
Shirehall Pl *CNCK/NC* WS11 .. **16** F3 ③
Shirehampton Cl *REDW* B97 .. **195** K3
Shireland Brook Gdns
WSNGN B18 .... **106** B1 ③
Shireland Cl *BFLD/HDSWWD* B20 .. **88** C2
Shireland Rd *SMTHWK* B66 ... **105**M1
Shirelea Cl *BNTWD* WS7 .... **18** F5
Shirestone Rd *STECH* B33 ..... **110** C3
Shireview Rd *BLOX/PEL* WS3 .. **39**M1
Shirlett Cl *COVE* CV2 .... **134** F1
Shirley Dr *CSCFLD/WYGN* B72 .. **73** C1 ③
Shirley La *RCOVN/BALC/EX* CV7 .. **131** L8
Shirley Park Rd *SHLY* B90 ..... **146** F3 ③
Shirley Rd *ACGN* B27 .... **126** F3
BVILLE B30 .... **124** E8
COVE CV2 .... **135** K6
DUDS DY2 .... **85** J5
HLGN/YWD B28 .... **126** E5
LGLYGN/QTN B68 .... **87** C7
Shirral Gv
CHWD/FDBR/MGN B37 ..... **92** D4
Shirrall Dr *POL/KGSB/FAZ* B78 .. **58** B1
Shoal Hill Cl *CNCK/NC* WS11 .. **15** M4
Sholing Cl *CDSL* WV8 .... **35** K4
Shooters Cl *DIG/EDG* B5 ...... **107** H7 ③
Shooters HI *CSCFLD/WYGN* B72 .. **73** H3
Shop La *CDSL* WV8 .... **34** B4
Shopton Rd *BKDE/SHDE* B34 .. **91** L6
Shoreham Cl *WLNHL* WV13 .... **51** H4 ③
Shorncliffe Rd *COVN* CV6 ..... **133** J7 ③
Short Acre St *WSLW* WS2 ..... **53** H2
Shortbutts La *LICHS* WS14 .... **20** F7
Shorters Av
ALE/KHTH/YWD B14 .... **145**M1
Shortfield Cl
RCOVN/BALC/EX CV7 ...... **150** F6 ③
Short Heath Rd
ERDW/GRVHL B23 .... **72** C7

Shortland Cl *DOR/KN* B93 .... 148 E7
Shortlands
RCOVN/BALC/EX CV7 .... 116 B7 🔢
Shortlands Cl *BVILLE* B30 .... 144 E3
Shortlands La *BLOX/PEL* WS3 ..... 39 K1
Short La *GTWY* WS6 .... 24 C2 🔢
Shortley Rd *COVS* CV3 .... 154 C5
Short Rd *SMTHWKW* B67 .... 105 H2
WOLVN WV10 .... 36 C4
Short St *BILS/COS* WV14 .... 51 H7 🔢
BLKHTH/ROWR B65 .... 104 A3 🔢
BRWNH WS8 .... 26 D6
CNCK/NC WS11 .... 16 D2
COV CV1 .... 9 H6
DARL/WED WS10 .... 52 D6
DARL/WED WS10 .... 68 C2
DUDN DY1 .... 84 E3 🔢
HALE B63 .... 121 K1
NUNW/HART CV10 .... 98 A1
SHHTH WV12 .... 38 A8
STRBR DY8 .... 101 K8 🔢
WOLV WV1 .... 3 G4 🔢
WSLW WS2 .... 52 F6
The Shortwoods
POL/KGSB/FAZ B78 .... 47 L1 🔢
The Shortyard *KIDDW* DY11 .... 137 H1
Shorwell Pl *BRLYHL* DY5 .... 102 A4
Shottery Cl *COVW* CV5 .... 152 F2
Shottery Gv *WALM/CURD* B76 ..... 73 K4
Shottery Rd *SHLY* B90 .... 146 F4 🔢
Shotteswell Rd *SHLY* B90 .... 146 F6
Showell Circ *WOLVN* WV10 .... 36 C6
Showell Green La *SPARK* B11 ..... 125 M2
Showell La
ETTPK/GDPK/PENN WV4 .... 64 L2
RCOVN/BALC/EX CV7 .... 131 K4
Showell Rd *WOLVN* WV10 .... 36 B6
Showells Gdns *VAUX/NECH* B7 .... 90 A6 🔢
Shrawley Av *KIDDW* DY11 .... 160 F2
Shrawley Cl *HALE* B63 .... 121 L3
RBRY B45 .... 142 D6 🔢
Shrawley Rd *NFLD/LBR* B31 .... 144 A3
Shrewley Crs *STECH* B33 .... 110 C4
Shrewsbury Cl *BLOX/PEL* WS3 .... 38 D4
Shrewsbury Rd *KIDDW* DY11 .... 136 E7 🔢
Shrewton Av
ALE/KHTH/YWD B14 .... 145 H3
The Shrubberies *NUNW/HART* CV4... 7 🔢
Shrubbery Av *TPTN/OCK* DY4 ...... 67 H8
Shrubbery Cl *WALM/CURD* B76 .... 73 K4
Shrubbery Rd *BRGRVW* B61 .... 185 J4
Shrubbery St *KIDD* DY10 .... 137 K6
Shrublands Av
LGLYGN/QTN B68 .... 104 F6
Shrubland St *RLSS* CV31 .... 200 E7 🔢
Shrub La *ERDE/BCHGN* B24 .... 90 E1
Shuckburgh Gv *RLSN* CV32 .... 200 E3 🔢
Shugborough Dr *DUDN* DY1 ..... 84 C3
Shugborough Wy
CNCK/NC WS11 .... 16 F4
Shulman's Wk *COVE* CV2 .... 135 H6
Shultern La *TLHL/CAN* CV4 .... 153 H7
Shuna Cft *COVE* CV2 .... 135 L6
Shustoke La *DSYBK/YTR* WS5 ..... 69 M1
Shustoke Rd *BKDE/SHDE* B34 ..... 92 F7
SOLH B91 .... 128 B8 🔢
Shutlock La *MOS/BIL* B13 .... 125 H4
Shut Mill La *RMSLY* B62 .... 141 H4
Shuttington Br *CRTAM* B79 .... 33 H6
Shuttington Rd *CRTAM* B79 .... 32 F7
Shutt La *HOCK/TIA* B94 .... 170 F4
Shuttle St *COVN* CV6 .... 134 F5
Shyltons Cft *LDYWD/EDGR* B16 .. 106 F7
Sibdon Gv *NFLD/LBR* B31 .... 143 L5
Sibree Rd *COVS* CV3 .... 178 F1
Sibton Cl *COVE* CV2 .... 135 G4 🔢
Sidaway Cl *OLDBY* B69 .... 86 A7
Sidaway St *CDYHTH* B64 .... 103 J4 🔢
Sidbury Gv *DOR/KN* B93 .... 172 C3
Sidcup Cl *BILS/COS* WV14 .... 66 F2
Sidcup Rd *KGSTG* B44 .... 71 L4
Siddeley Av *COVS* CV3 .... 154 E4
KNWTH CV8 .... 191 J2
Siddons Cl *LICH* WS13 .... 20 D3
Siddons Rd *BILS/COS* WV14 ...... 67 K3
Siddons Wy *HHTH/SAND* B71 ..... 68 E6
Sidenhill Cl *SHLY* B90 .... 146 F5
Sidlaw Cl *HALE* B63 .... 121 H3
WOLVN WV10 .... 35 M7
Sidmouth Cl *COVE* CV2 .... 135 G6
NUN CV11 .... 81 K8
Sidney St *BKHL/PFLD* WV2 .... 2 E8
Sidon Hill Wy *HEDN* WV12 .... 17 G2
Sidwick Crs *BKHL/PFLD* WV2 .... 50 F7
Sigmund Cl *WOLV* WV1 .... 50 F2 🔢
Signal Gv *BLOX/PEL* WS3 .... 38 C4
Signal Hayes Rd
WALM/CURD B76 .... 73 K3
Silesbourne Cl *CBROM* B36 ...... 92 A4 🔢
Silhill Hall Rd *SOLH* B91 .... 127 L8
Silica Rd *TAM/AM/WIL* B77 ...... 46 F5
Silksby St *COVS* CV3 .... 9 L6
Sillins Av *REDE* B98 .... 196 E2
Sillins La *REDW* B97 .... 195 J7
Silva Av *KGSWFD* DY6 .... 101 K1
Silver Birch Cl
NUNW/HART CV10 .... 79 L6 🔢
Silver Birch Coppice
FOAKS/STRLY B74 .... 42 B8
Silver Birch Dr *HLYWD* B47 ...... 145 M1
KIDD DY10 .... 138 A8
Silver Birch Gv *RLSS* CV31 ...... 200 D8 🔢
Silver Birch Rd *BKHL/PFLD* WV2 .. 50 B6
CHWD/FDBR/MGN B37 .... 92 D7
CNCK/NC WS11 .... 25 M1
ERDE/BCHGN B24 .... 72 F7
FOAKS/STRLY B74 .... 55 K4
HEDN WS12 .... 12 B5
Silverbirch Rd *SOLH* B91 .... 148 C2
Silvercroft Av
BFLD/HDSWWD B20 .... 88 A1

Silverfield Cl
ALE/KHTH/YWD B14 .... 125 J5 🔢
Silver Fir Cl *HEDN* WS12 .... 12 E5
Silver Innage *HALE* B63 .... 103 G6
Silverlands Av
LGLYGN/QTN B68 .... 104 F2 🔢
Silverlands Cl *HLGN/YWD* B28 ... 126 D4
Silver Link Rd *TAM/AM/WIL* B77 ... 46 D4
Silvermead Rd *SCFLD/BOLD* B73 .. 72 E4
Silvermere Rd
LGN/SDN/BHAMAIR B26 .... 110 B7
Silver's Cl *BLOX/PEL* WS3 ...... 25 K8
Silverstone Cl *WSLW* WS2 .... 52 B7
Silverstone Dr *FOAKS/STRLY* B74... 55 K7
RCOVN/BALC/EX CV7 .... 116 C8
Silver St *ALE/KHTH/YWD* B14 .... 125 J5
BRLYHL DY5 .... 101 M3
BRWNH WS8 .... 26 C6
COV CV1 .... 8 F3
HLYWD B47 .... 145 J8
HWK/WKHTH B38 .... 145 J8
KIDD DY10 .... 137 J7
REDW B97 .... 196 C2 🔢
Silverthorne Av *TPTN/OCK* DY4 .. 67 H8
Silverthorne La *CDYHTH* B64 .... 102 F4
Silverton Crs *MOS/BIL* B13 ..... 126 B4
Silverton Rd *COVN* CV6 .... 134 D6
SMTHWKW B67 .... 87 J7
Silverton Wy *WNSFLD* WV11 ..... 37 K8
Silver Wk *NUNW/HART* CV10 ..... 98 D2
Silvester Ct *BILS/COS* WV14 .... 51 J7
Silvester Wy *STRBR* DY8 .... 101 M5
Silvington Cl *NFLD/LBR* B31 .... 124 A6 🔢
Simcox Gdns *BLOX/PEL* WDGT B32... 123 L8
Simcox Rd *DARL/WED* WS10 ..... 52 D8
Simcox St *HEDN* WS12 .... 17 H1 🔢
Simeon Bissell Cl
TPTN/OCK DY4 .... 67 L8 🔢
Simeon's Wk *BRLYHL* DY5 .... 102 D6
Simmonds Cl *BLOX/PEL* WS3 .... 39 H2
Simmonds Pl
DARL/WED WS10 .... 52 D6 🔢
Simmonds Rd *BLOX/PEL* WS3 .... 39 H2
Simmonds Wy *ATHST* CV9 ...... 63 H3
BRWNH WS8 .... 26 C6
Simmons Leasow
RIDG/WDGT B32 .... 123 H3
Simmons Rd *WNSFLD* WV11 ..... 37 M4
Simms La *DUDS* DY2 .... 85 G8
HLYWD B47 .... 145 L8
Simon Cl *HHTH/SAND* B71 .... 69 J4 🔢
Simon Rd *HLYWD* B47 .... 145 L6
Simon Stone St *COVN* CV6 ...... 134 D5 🔢
Simpkins Cl *ALDR* WS9 .... 40 E2
Simpson Gv *WOLVN* WV10 ...... 36 C7
Simpson Rd *CSCFLD/WYGN* B72... 73 G4
LICH WS13 .... 20 F2
WOLVN WV10 .... 36 C7
WSLW WS2 .... 38 F8
Simpson St *OLDBY* B69 .... 86 E6
Singer Cl *COVN* CV6 .... 134 F5 🔢
Singer Cft *CBROM* B36 .... 92 D4
Sion Av *KIDD* DY10 .... 137 L4
Sion Hl *KIDD* DY10 .... 137 L4
Sir Alfreds Wy *WALM/CURD* B76 .. 73 J2
Sir Harrys Rd *DIG/EDG* B5 ...... 107 G7
EDG B15 .... 106 F7
Sir Henry Parkes Rd *COVW* CV5... 153 H6
Sir Hilton's Rd *NFLD/LBR* B31 .. 143 M6
Sir John's Rd *SLYOAK* B29 ..... 125 G2
Sir Richards Dr *HRBN* B17 ..... 105 K6
Sir Thomas White's Rd
COVW CV5 .... 153 K3
Sir William Lyons Rd
TLHL/CAN CV4 .... 153 G7
Sir Winston Churchill Pl
COVS CV3 .... 156 A6 🔢
Sisefield Rd *HWK/WKHTH* B38 ... 144 E4
Siskin Cl *BNTWD* WS7 .... 19 H8
Siskin Dr *BHTH/HG* B12 .... 107 J7 🔢
KNWTH CV8 .... 179 C3
Siskin Pkwy East *KNWTH* CV8 ... 178 F4
Siskin Pkwy West *KNWTH* CV8 ... 178 F4
Siskin Rd *HAG/WOL* DY9 .... 120 A2 🔢
Siskin Wy *KIDD* DY10 .... 161 M4
Sister Dora Gdns *WSL* WS1 ..... 4 E4
Siviter's Cl *BLKHTH/ROWR* B65 .. 103 M2
Siviter's La *BLKHTH/ROWR* B65 .. 103 M2
Siviter St *HALE* B63 .... 121 M1 🔢
Six Acres *RIDG/WDGT* B32 ..... 123 C1
Skelcher Rd *SHLY* B90 .... 146 E1
Skelwith Ri *NUN* CV11 .... 81 L7
Skemp Cl *BILS/COS* WV14 ..... 67 H8
Sketchley La *ATHST* CV9 ...... 63 M1
Skidmore Av *BDMR/CCFT* WV3... 49 K5
TAM/AM/WIL B77 .... 60 A1
Skidmore Dr *WBROM* B70 .... 86 E2
Skidmore Rd *BILS/COS* WV14 .. 67 H3 🔢
Skilts Av *REDE* B98 .... 196 D4
Skinner La *DIG/EDG* B5 .... 7 H8
Skinner St *WOLV* WV1 .... 2 E5
Skip La *DSYBK/YTR* WS5 .... 54 C8
Skipness *TAM/AM/WIL* B77 ..... 32 C8 🔢
Skipton Gdns *COVE* CV2 .... 134 F7 🔢
Skipton Rd
DUNHL/THL/PER WV6 .... 35 L8 🔢
Skipton Pl *CNCK/NC* WS11 ..... 15 M6
Skipton Rd *LDYWD/EDGR* B16 .. 106 D4
Skipwith Cl *RRUGBY* CV23 ..... 157 H2
Skipworth Rd *COVS* CV3 ...... 155 L3
Skomer Cl *RBRY* B45 .... 142 B4
Sky Blue Wy *COV* CV1 .... 9 K4
Skye Cl *CBROM* B36 .... 92 F7
Skye Wk *CDYHTH* B64 .... 103 J4 🔢
Skylark Cl *BRLYHL* DY5 .... 84 A4 🔢
HEDN WS12 .... 12 A6
Skylark Wy *KIDD* DY10 .... 161 L3
Slack La *HDSW* B21 .... 88 C3
Slacky La *BLOX/PEL* WS3 ...... 39 K4
Sladd La *KIDDW* DY11 .... 136 F1 🔢
Slade Av *BNTWD* WS7 .... 18 E5
Sladefield Rd *WASH/WDE* B8 .. 90 E8

STRBR DY8 .... 101 M7 🔢
WOLVN WV10 .... 35 M7
Slade Gdns *CDSL* WV8 .... 34 E1
Slade Gv *DOR/KN* B93 .... 148 D7
Slade La *RWWCK/WEL* CV35 ... 198 D6 🔢
Slade La *HLGN/YWD* B28 ..... 146 C2
MGN/WHC B75 .... 57 L2
TAM/AM/WIL B77 .... 60 A1
Slade Lanker *BKDE/SHDE* B34 .. 91 L8
Sladepool Farm Rd
ALE/KHTH/YWD B14 .... 145 K2
Slade Rd *ERDW/GRVHL* B23 .... 90 B3
HALE B63 .... 103 G7
MGN/WHC B75 .... 57 L2
WOLVN WV10 .... 36 A2
Slade View Ri *HEDN* WS12 .... 13 L7
The Slad *STRPT* DY13 .... 161 H7
Slaithwaite Rd *HHTH/SAND* B71... 87 H1
Slaney Rd *WSLW* WS2 .... 52 F7
Slatch House Rd
SMTHWKW B67 .... 105 J3
Slateley Crs *SHLY* B90 .... 147 L7 🔢
Slater Rd *DOR/KN* B93 .... 172 C1
Slaters La *WSLW* WS2 .... 52 F6
Slaters Pl *WSLW* WS2 .... 52 F6
Slater St *BILS/COS* WV14 .... 67 J2 🔢
DARL/WED WS10 .... 52 B7
TPTN/OCK DY4 .... 68 B8
TPTN/OCK DY4 .... 85 L1 🔢
WLNHL WV13 .... 52 A2
Sleaford Gv *HLGN/YWD* B28 ... 126 E6
Sleaford Rd *HLGN/YWD* B28 ... 126 E6
Sleath's Yd *BDWTH* CV12 .... 116 F2 🔢
Sledmere Cl *COVN* CV6 .... 134 F2
Sledmore Rd *DUDS* DY2 ...... 85 H6
Sleets Yd *BDWTH* CV12 ...... 116 E3
Slideslow Av *BRGRVE* B60 .... 185 M3
The Slieve *BFLD/HDSWWD* B20... 88 E2
Slim Av *BILS/COS* WV14 ...... 67 J2
Slimbridge Cl *REDW* B97 ..... 196 C8
SHLY B90 .... 147 L7 🔢
Slim Rd *WSLW* WS2 .... 52 C3
Slims Ga *HALE* B63 .... 121 L1
Slingfield Rd *NFLD/LBR* B31 .. 144 A4
Slingsby *TAM/AM/WIL* B77 .... 46 A6
Slingsby Cl *NUN* CV11 .... 99 J3
The Sling *DUDS* DY2 .... 85 G7
KIDD DY10 .... 137 J8
Sloane St *CBHAMW* B1 .... 6 C4
Slowley Hl *RCOVN/BALC/EX* CV7... 95 L4
Smallbrook La *WMBN* WV5 .... 64 F6
Smallbrook Queensway
DIG/EDG B5 .... 6 F7
Small Cl *SMTHWKW* B67 .... 87 H8
Smalldale Rd *PBAR/PBCH* B42... 71 H6
Smalley Cl *CNCK/NC* WS11 .... 12 E8
Small Heath Br *SPARK* B11 ... 107 M6
Small Heath Hwy *SMHTH* B10... 107 M5
YDLY B25 .... 108 D7
Small La *HOCK/TIA* B94 ...... 170 C7
Smallridge Cl *WOLVN* WV10 .. 36 D6
Smallshire Wy *STRBR* DY8 .... 100 F5
Small St *HHTH/SAND* B71 ..... 68 F8
WSL WS1 .... 4 E5
Smallwood Cl
ERDE/BCHGN B24 .... 91 H2 🔢
WALM/CURD B76 .... 73 J2
Smallwood Rd *CDSL* WV8 ..... 35 J3
Smarts Av *LICHS* WS14 ...... 42 E6
Smarts Rd *BDWTH* CV12 ..... 116 D4
Smeaton Gdns *WNSFLD* WV10... 106 C1 🔢
Smedley Crooke Pl *ALVE* B48... 168 A3
Smeed Gv *ERDE/BCHGN* B24 .. 90 F2
Smercote Cft *BDWTH* CV12 ... 116 B4
Smestow La *SEDG* DY3 .... 82 A1
Smestow St *WOLVN* WV10 .... 3 H1
Smillie Pl *CNCK/NC* WS11 .... 16 D2
Smirrells Rd *HLGN/YWD* B28 .. 126 C8
Smith Av *DARL/WED* WS10 ... 68 B1
Smith Cl *BILS/COS* WV14 .... 67 H4
SMTHWKW B67 .... 105 H2
Smithfield Pas *DIG/EDG* B5... 7 G7 🔢
Smithfield Ri *LICH* WS13 .... 21 G5
Smithfield Rd *BLOX/PEL* WS3 .. 39 H4
Smithmoor Crs *HHTH/SAND* B71... 69 K5
Smith Pl *TPTN/OCK* DY4 ...... 85 M1 🔢
Smith Rd *DARL/WED* WS10 .... 68 D4
WSLW WS2 .... 4 A9
Smith's Cl *BNTWD* WS7 .... 18 B6
RIDG/WDGT B32 .... 122 F3
Smiths La *DOR/KN* B93 ...... 148 C7
Smith St *ATHST* CV9 .... 61 G4
BDWTH CV12 .... 116 C4
BILS/COS WV14 .... 51 H8
COVN CV6 .... 134 D8
DUDS DY2 .... 85 H6
LOZ/NWT B19 .... 89 G8
RLSS CV31 .... 200 D6 🔢
WWCK CV34 .... 199 J7
Smiths Wy *CSHL/WTROR* B46 .. 92 E2
Smithy Dr *BLOX/PEL* WS3 .... 39 L1
Smithy La *ATHST* CV9 .... 62 A7
BRLYHL DY5 .... 83 M5
LICH WS13 .... 20 E4 🔢
RRUGBY CV23 .... 157 M8
TAM/AM/WIL B77 .... 46 D6
The Smithy
LGN/SDN/BHAMAIR B26 .... 110 A7 🔢
Smorrall La *BDWTH* CV12 .... 115 J4
Smout Crs *BILS/COS* WV14 ... 66 B7 🔢
Smythe Gv *WWCK* CV34 ..... 199 J4 🔢
Snake La *ALVE* B48 .... 167 L7
Snakes Lake La *BRGRVW* B61... 165 H7
Snapdragon Dr *DSYBK/YTR* WS5... 69 J2
Snape Rd *COVE* CV2 .... 135 K8 🔢
WNSFLD WV11 .... 37 K5
Sneyd Hall Cl *BLOX/PEL* WS3 .. 38 E5 🔢
Sneyd Hall Rd *BLOX/PEL* WS3 .. 38 E4
Sneyd La *BLOX/PEL* WS3 ..... 38 E4
WNSFLD WV11 .... 38 A4
Snipe Cl *WOLVN* WV10 ...... 22 F6 🔢
Snowberry Dr *BRLYHL* DY5 ... 84 A4
Snowberry Gdns *ACGN* B27... 109 G8 🔢
Snowdon Cl *KIDDW* DY11 .... 137 G4
Snowdon Gv *HALE* B63 ...... 121 H4
Snowdon Ri *SEDG* DY3 ...... 66 B7 🔢
Snowdon Rd *CNCK/NC* WS11 .. 12 C7

South Car Park Rd
BHAMNEC B40 .... 129 J2
South Cl *CNCK/NC* WS11 ..... 16 A5
Southcote Gv
HWK/WKHTH B38 .... 144 B4
Southcott Av *BRLYHL* DY5 .... 102 B5
Southcott Wy *COVE* CV2 ..... 135 K4
South Crs *WOLVN* WV10 ...... 23 G7
South Dr *CSHL/WTROR* B46 .. 93 H7
DIG/EDG B5 .... 125 G1
MGN/WHC B75 .... 57 G7
Southdown Av *WSNGN* B18 .. 88 E7
South Dr *CSHL/WTROR* B46 .. 93 H7
Southern Cl *KGSWFD* DY6 .... 101 K2
Southerndown Rd *SEDG* DY3... 65 M5
Southern Rd *WASH/WDE* B8 .. 91 G8
Southey Cl *SHHTH* WV12 .... 38 C5
SOLH B91 .... 147 M5 🔢
Southey Rd *RUGBYS/DCH* CV22... 183 J6
Southfield Av *CBROM* B36 ... 91 M5
LDYWD/EDGR B16 .... 106 B2
Southfield Cl *NUNW/HART* CV10... 81 H7
Southfield Dr *HLGN/YWD* B28 .. 126 E8
KNWTH CV8 .... 176 E7
Southfield Gv *BDMR/CCFT* WV3... 49 G6
Southfield Rd
LDYWD/EDGR B16 .... 106 A2
WNSFLD WV11 .... 37 K8
Southfields Cl *CSHL/WTROR* B46... 93 L8
Southfields Cl *SOLH* B91 .... 147 K4
Southfield Wy *GTWY* WS6 ... 24 D3
South Gdns *HAG/WOL* DY9 ... 139 L1
Southgate *CDYHTH* B64 ..... 103 H5 🔢
CNCK/NC WS11 .... 15 M6
WOLV WV1 .... 2 D4 🔢
Southgate Cl *KIDDW* DY11 ... 160 E1
Southgate End
CNCK/NC WS11 .... 15 M6 🔢
Southgate Rd *KGSTG* B44 ... 71 J3
South Gn
ETTPK/GDPK/PENN WV4 ..... 49 H8
South Gv *ERDW/GRVHL* B23 .. 72 D8
LOZ/NWT B19 .... 88 F5 🔢
South Holme Rd *BORD* B9 ... 108 A4
Southlands *ATHST* CV9 ...... 63 J6
RLSS CV31 .... 200 F6
Southlands Rd *MOS/BIL* B13... 125 L4
Southlea Av *RLSS* CV31 ..... 200 C7 🔢
Southlea Cl *RLSS* CV31 ..... 200 C7 🔢
Southleigh Av *COVW* CV5 .... 153 K7
Southmead Crs *REDE* B98 ... 196 F4
Southmead Dr *BRGRVE* B60 .. 165 M7 🔢
Southminster Dr
ALE/KHTH/YWD B14 .... 125 J7 🔢
South Ov *SEDG* DY3 .... 66 C8
South Pde *CSCFLD/WYGN* B72... 57 G8
South Park Ms *BRLYHL* DY5 .. 102 A3 🔢
Southport Cl *COVS* CV3 ..... 154 F8
South Range *SPARK* B11 .... 107 M7 🔢
South Rdg *COVW* CV5 ...... 152 F1
South Rd *ALE/KHTH/YWD* B14... 125 J5
BRGRVE B60 .... 185 M6
ERDW/GRVHL B23 .... 90 D1
HAG/WOL DY9 .... 139 L1
NFLD/LBR B31 .... 143 K3
SMTHWKW B67 .... 87 K8
SPARK B11 .... 107 M6
STRBR DY8 .... 119 K1 🔢
TPTN/OCK DY4 .... 67 M5
WSNGN B18 .... 88 E7
South Road Av *WSNGN* B18 .. 88 E7
South Roundhay *STECH* B33 .. 109 L2
South St *ATHST* CV9 .... 63 H5
BRLYHL DY5 .... 102 A3 🔢
COV CV1 .... 9 K4
HRBN B17 .... 106 C2
KIDD DY10 .... 137 K7 🔢
REDE B98 .... 196 C2
WLNHL WV13 .... 51 J4
WOLVN WV10 .... 36 A7
WSL WS1 .... 4 D6
South Street Gdns *WSL* WS1... 4 D6
South Vw *GTB/HAM* B43 .... 70 C6
POL/KGSB/FAZ B78 .... 76 B1
South View Cl *CDSL* WV8 ... 34 F3
WOLVN WV10 .... 22 F7
South View Rd *RLSN* CV32 .. 193 G8 🔢
SEDG DY3 .... 182 D1
SEDG DY3 .... 65 M5
Southwark Cl *LICH* WS13 .... 21 G2 🔢
South Wy *BHAMNEC* B40 .... 129 K2
Southway *RLSS* CV31 ...... 200 E8
Southway Cl *COVW* CV5 .... 101 K1
Southwick Pl *BILS/COS* WV14... 51 H6 🔢
Southwick Rd *RMSLY* B62 ... 104 B5
Southwold Av *BVILLE* B30 ... 145 G2
Southwood Av *BKDE/SHDE* B34... 91 L6
Southwood Cl *KGSWFD* DY6 .. 83 J8
Southwood Covert
ALE/KHTH/YWD B14 .... 145 G3
Sovereign Cl *KNWTH* CV8 ... 191 K4
Sovereign Dr *DUDN* DY1 .... 84 B3
Sovereign Hts *NFLD/LBR* B31... 143 G4
Sovereign Rd *BVILLE* B30 ... 144 D1
COVW CV5 .... 153 K3
Sovereign Rw *COV* CV1 ..... 8 A5
Sovereign Wy *MOS/BIL* B13... 125 K1
Sowerby March
ERDE/BCHGN B24 .... 91 H1 🔢
Sowers Cl *SHHTH* WV12 .... 38 B8
Sowers Gdns *SHHTH* WV12... 38 B8 🔢
Spadesbourne Rd *BRGRVE* B60... 166 A7
Spa Gv *BVILLE* B30 .... 125 G5
Sparkbrook St *COV* CV1 .... 9 K3
Spark St *SPARK* B11 .... 107 M7 🔢
Sparrey Dr *SLYOAK* B29 .... 124 E5
Sparrow Cl *DARL/WED* WS10... 53 G1
Sparrow Cock La *DOR/KN* B93... 174 A7
Spearhill *LICHS* WS14 ...... 21 J6
Speed Rd *TPTN/OCK* DY4 .... 67 J7
Speedway La *KNWTH* CV8 ... 156 D6
Speedwell Cl *ALDR* WS9 .... 40 D7
WNSFLD WV11 .... 37 J8 🔢
Speedwell Dr
RCOVN/BALC/EX CV7 .... 150 E7
Speedwell Gdns *BRLYHL* DY5... 101 M7

WOLVN WV10 .... 22 F5
Speedwell La ATHST CV9 .... 61 M5
Speedwell Rd DIG/EDG B5 ... 107 H7
  YDLY B25 .... 108 E7
Speedy Cl CNCK/NC WS11 ... 12 C8
Spencer Av BEWD DY12 ...... 160 A1
  BILS/COS WV14 ...... 67 C5
  COVW CV5 .... 135 C5
Spencer Cl HHTH/SAND B71 . 69 K5
  SEDG DY3 .... 83 L1
Spencer Dr BNTWD WS7 ..... 18 C5
Spencer Rd COVW CV5 .... 8 D8
  LICHS WS14 .... 20 F7
Spencer's La
  RCOVN/BALC/EX CV7 .. 151 H3
Spencer St KIDDW DY11 ..... 161 G1
  RLSS CV31 .... 200 D6
  WSNGN B18 .... 6 C1
Spencer Yd RLSS CV31 ...... 200 D6
Spennells Valley Rd KIDD DY10 161 L2
Spenser Av
  DUNHL/THL/PER WV6 .. 48 C1
Spenser Cl CRTAM B79 ...... 31 L7
Spernall Gv SLYOAK B29 .... 123 L4
Spetchley Cl REDW B97 ..... 196 A4
Spey Cl DIG/EDG B5 .... 107 H7
Sphinx Dr COVS CV3 .... 154 F4
Spiceland Rd NFLD/LBR B31 . 123 K7
Spicer Pl RUSH/SHEL CV22 .. 183 H4
Spiers Cl DOR/KN B93 ...... 148 E7
Spies Cl RMSLY B62 .... 104 D7
Spies La RMSLY B62 .... 104 D8
Spills Meadow SEDG DY3 .... 66 C8
Spilsbury Cl RLSN CV32 .... 200 C3
Spilsbury Cft SOLH B91 .... 147 L5
Spindle Cl DUDN DY1 .... 137 H4
Spindle La SHLY B90 .... 146 E7
Spindle St COV CV1 .... 9 L1
Spindlewood Cl HEDN WS12 .. 17 H4
Spinners End Dr
  CDYHTH B64 .... 103 H4
Spinney Cl BLOX/PEL WS3 ... 39 L3
  BNTWD WS7 .... 18 E4
  CNCK/NC WS11 ...... 17 K8
  COVS CV3 .... 156 C6
  KIDDW DY11 .... 136 E7
  NFLD/LBR B31 ...... 143 L3
  POL/KGSB/FAZ B78 .. 47 K5
  RCOVN/BALC/EX CV7 . 96 C5
  STRBR DY8 .... 100 F2
Spinney Dr SHLY B90 .... 171 H1
Spinney Farm Rd
  CNCK/NC WS11 ...... 15 M6
Spinney Hl WWCK CV34 ...... 199 L4
Spinney La BNTWD WS7 ...... 18 D4
  NUNW/HART CV10 .... 98 A1
The Spinney ATHST CV9 ..... 63 L6
  BDMR/CCFT WV3 ..... 49 H4
  BFLD/HDSWWD B20 ... 88 C1
  FOAKS/STRLY B74 ... 41 M7
  HLYWD B47 .... 169 M1
  RLSN CV32 .... 200 B4
  RRUGBY CV23 .... 158 E8
  SEDG DY3 .... 84 A3
  TLHL/CAN CV4 ...... 177 J2
Spinning School La CRTAM B79 31 M8
Spiral Cl RMSLY B62 .... 104 C5
Spiral Gn ERDE/BCHGN B24 . 91 C1
Spirehouse La BRGRVE B60 . 166 B8
Spires Cft WOLVN WV10 .... 23 H4
The Spires LICHS WS14 .... 21 J7
  NUNW/HART CV10 .... 98 A1
Spire Vw BRGRVW B61 ...... 185 K2
Spitfire Rd ERDE/BCHGN B24 91 G3
Spitfire Wy CVALE B35 .... 91 L3
Splash La HEDN WS12 ...... 17 G2
Spode Pl CNCK/NC WS11 .... 16 F3
Spondon Gv BKDE/SHDE B34 . 92 A8
Spondon Rd WNSFLD WV11 .. 37 J5
Spon End COVW CV5 .... 8 A4
Spon La WBROM B70 .... 87 H4
Spon La South SMTHWK B66 . 87 H5
Spon St COV CV1 .... 8 D4
Spoon Dr HWK/WKHTH B38 .. 144 B3
Spooner Cft DIG/EDG B5 ... 107 J7
Spooners HIA/OLT B92 ..... 128 D6
Spouthouse La GTB/HAM B43 70 C6
Spout La WSL WS1 .... 4 E7
Spreadbury Cl HRBN B17 ... 105 K5
Sprengers Cl PENK ST19 ... 10 E1
Sprig Cft CBROM B36 ...... 91 G5
Spring Av
  BLKHTH/ROWR B65 ... 104 A3
  BLKHTH/ROWR B65 ... 104 B3
Springavon Cft HRBN B17 .. 105 M7
Springbank BORD B9 .... 108 D2
Springbank Rd EDG B15 .... 107 C6
Springbrook Cl CBROM B36 . 92 B4
Springbrook La HOCK/TIA B94 170 D6
Spring Cl COV CV1 .... 9 K3
  HAG/WOL DY9 .... 139 K1
  RUSH/SHEL WS4 ..... 40 A3
  SOLH B91 .... 147 K2
Spring Coppice Dr
  DOR/KN B93 .... 172 E2
Spring Ct WSL WS1 .... 5 K6
Spring Crs CDYHTH B64 .... 103 K6
Springcroft Rd SPARK B11 . 126 D3
Springfield ERDW/GRVHL B23 90 B2
Springfield Av BHTH/HG B12 107 L7
  BRGRVE B60 .... 185 L6
  HAG/WOL DY9 .... 120 C1
  SEDG DY3 .... 66 C4
Springfield Cl
  BLKHTH/ROWR B65 ... 85 L8
Springfield Crs BDWTH CV12 116 F3
  DUDS DY2 .... 85 K5
  HIA/OLT B92 .... 128 A2
  WALM/CURD B76 ..... 73 L4
  WBROM B70 .... 87 J4
Springfield Gv SEDG DY3 .. 66 B4
Springfield La
  BLKHTH/ROWR B65 ... 85 K8
  KIDD DY10 .... 137 K5
  WOLVN WV10 .... 36 B1
Springfield Pl COV CV1 ... 9 G1
Springfield Ri HEDN WS12 . 13 G7

Springfield Rd
  ALE/KHTH/YWD B14 .. 125 K5
  BILS/COS WV14 ..... 51 J6
  CBROM B36 .... 92 B5
  COV CV1 .... 9 G1
  MOS/BIL B13 .... 126 B4
  NUN CV11 .... 99 J3
  RMSLY B62 .... 104 A7
  TAM/AM/WIL B77 .... 46 B5
  WALM/CURD B76 ..... 73 L2
  WOLVN WV10 .... 3 J1
Springfields CSHL/WTROR B46 93 K8
  RUSH/SHEL WS4 ..... 39 M6
Springfields Rd BRLYHL DY5 101 M3
  LGLYGN/QTN B68 .... 105 C1
Springfields Rd SWNGN B18 106 E2
Springfield Ter
  BLKHTH/ROWR B65 ... 85 K8
Spring Gdns DUDS DY2 ..... 85 H5
Spring Grove Crs KIDDW DY11 160 F2
Spring Grove Gdns WSNGN B18 88 D7
Spring Grove Rd KIDDW DY11 160 F2
Spring Head DARL/WED WS10 68 B3
Spring Hl ERDE/BCHGN B24 . 90 D2
  KNWTH CV8 .... 179 G8
Springhill NUNW/HART CV10 79 L5
Spring Hl RCOVN/BALC/EX CV7 96 D6
  WSNGN B18 .... 106 E1
Springhill Av
  ETTPK/GDPK/PENN WV4 65 G2
Springhill Cl RUSH/SHEL WS4 40 B4
  SHHTH WV12 .... 38 B6
Springhill Gv
  ETTPK/GDPK/PENN WV4 65 G1
Spring Hill La
  ETTPK/GDPK/PENN WV4 64 E1
Springhill Pk
  ETTPK/GDPK/PENN WV4 64 F2
Spring Hill Pas WSNGN B18 106 E2
Springhill Ri BNTWD WV12 160 A1
Springhill Rd BNTWD WS7 .. 18 E7
  BRWNH WS8 .... 26 E6
Spring Hill Rd NUNW/HART CV10 80 A7
Springhill Rd WNSFLD WV11 37 H5
  WSL WS1 .... 5 H4
Spring La ERDE/BCHGN B24 . 90 E2
  HOCK/TIA B94 ...... 171 L8
  KNWTH CV8 .... 176 E8
  RLSS CV31 .... 201 J8
  RMSLY B62 .... 141 H1
  RUSH/SHEL WS4 ..... 40 A3
  SHHTH WV12 .... 51 M1
Springle Styche La BNTWD WS7 19 G4
Spring Meadow CDYHTH B64 103 K4
  GTWY WS6 .... 24 B4
  HALE B63 .... 121 K3
  TPTN/OCK DY4 ...... 68 F5
Springmeadow Gv
  LOZ/NWT B19 .... 89 H7
Spring Meadow Rd DUDS DY2 103 G3
Spring Parklands DUDN DY1 84 E5
Spring Pool WWCK CV34 .... 199 J6
Spring Rd COVE CV6 .... 134 D5
  DUDS DY2 .... 85 H7
  EDG B15 .... 107 H6
  ETTPK/GDPK/PENN WV4 50 E8
  LICH WS13 .... 21 H5
  RCOVN/BALC/EX CV7 . 117 L7
  RUSH/SHEL WS4 ..... 40 B4
  SMHK B66 .... 87 H5
  SPARK B11 .... 126 D2
Springs Av BRGRVW B61 ... 165 K4
Springslade Dr
  ERDE/BCHGN B24 .... 91 H2
The Springs CDYHTH B64 ... 103 L4
Spring St CNCK/NC WS11 ... 16 C5
  EDG B15 .... 107 H5
  HAG/WOL DY9 .... 120 C1
  HALE B63 .... 103 G7
  RUGBYN/HIL CV21 ... 183 M2
  TPTN/OCK DY4 ...... 67 L8
  TPTN/OCK DY4 ...... 68 A5
Springthorpe Gn
  ERDE/BCHGN B24 .... 91 G1
Springthorpe Rd
  ERDE/BCHGN B24 .... 91 H1
Springvale Av DSYBK/YTR WS5 54 A6
Spring Vale Cl BILS/COS WV14 66 E4
Spring Vale Rd
  BLKHTH/ROWR B65 ... 85 L8
Springvale Rd REDW B97 ... 195 K3
Springvale St WLNHL WV13 51 M2
Springvale Wy BILS/COS WV14 67 G1
Spring Wk HALE B63 .... 121 H4
  OLDBY B69 .... 86 E8
  WSLW WS2 .... 5 G2
Springwell Rd RLSS CV31 . 201 H7
Sproat Av DARL/WED WS10 . 52 A8
Spruce Gv ERDE/BCHGN B24 90 F3
Spruce Rd DSYBK/YTR WS5 . 69 M2
  HEDN WS12 .... 12 D4
Spruce Wy BDMR/CCFT WV3 . 49 H4
Spur Tree Av
  BDMR/CCFT WV3 ..... 48 E4
Squadron Cl CVALE B35 .... 92 A1
Square Cl RIDG/WDGT B32 . 123 G2
Square La RCOVN/BALC/EX CV7 114 F4
The Square ALVE B48 ...... 167 M7
  BKHL/PFLD WV2 ..... 3 H9
  HRBN B17 .... 105 M7
  KNWTH CV8 .... 191 K1
  NUN CV11 .... 99 J3
  SOLH B91 .... 148 A2
  TPTN/OCK DY4 ...... 68 B6
Squires Ct BRLYHL DY5 .... 102 A4
Squires Cft COVE CV2 ..... 135 K4
  WALM/CURD B76 ..... 73 L4
Squires Ga BNTWD WS7 .... 19 G5
Squires Rd RRUGBY CV23 .. 180 D7
Squires Wy TLHL/CAN CV4 . 153 H6
Squirrel Cl HEDN WS12 .... 12 A7
  HEDN WS12 .... 17 H3
Squirrel Hollow
  WALM/CURD B76 ..... 73 L3
Squirrels Hollow BNTWD WS7 18 E4
  LGLYGN/QTN B68 .... 105 H6

Squirrel Wk
  ETTPK/GDPK/PENN WV4 65 L1
  FOAKS/STRLY B74 ... 42 A8
Stable Cl SEDG DY3 .... 66 C7
Stable Cft HHTH/SAND B71 . 69 K6
Stableford Cl REDW B97 ... 196 B6
  RIDG/WDGT B32 ..... 123 K2
Stable La WOLVN WV10 ..... 14 E6
Stable Wy BRGRVE B60 ..... 185 J7
Stacey Cl CDYHTH B64 ..... 103 J4
Stacey Grange Gdns
  RBRY B45 .... 142 C7
Stackhouse Cl ALDR WS9 ... 40 E1
Stackhouse Dr BLOX/PEL WS3 39 L1
Stadium Cl COVN CV6 ...... 134 B3
  KIDD DY10 .... 161 K1
  WLNHL WV13 .... 51 M2
Stafford Cl BLOX/PEL WS3 . 39 G3
Stafford Crs LICHS WS14 .. 30 B2
Stafford Dr HHTH/SAND B71 68 F6
Stafford La CDSL WV8 ..... 34 B4
  CNCK/NC WS11 ...... 12 F8
  HEDN WS12 .... 17 C1
Stafford Rd CNCK/NC WS11 . 16 B4
  COVEN WV9 .... 22 A5
  DARL/WED WS10 ..... 51 M7
  GTWY WS6 .... 24 E7
  HDSW B21 .... 88 D5
  HEDN WS12 .... 12 A6
  LICH WS13 .... 20 C4
  PENK ST19 .... 10 C1
  WOLVN WV10 .... 22 A4
  WOLVN WV10 .... 36 A5
Stafford Street Jct WOLV WV1 2 F3
Stafford Wy GTB/HAM B43 .. 70 C6
Stagborough Wy HEDN WS12 16 F1
Stag Crs BLOX/PEL WS3 .... 39 J7
Stag Dr HEDN WS12 .... 12 A7
Stag Hill Rd BLOX/PEL WS3 39 J6
Stag Wk WALM/CURD B76 .... 73 H6
Staines Cl NUN CV11 ...... 81 K6
Stainforth Cl NUN CV11 ... 99 K3
Stainsby Av LOZ/NWT B19 . 89 G8
Stainsby Cft SHLY B90 .... 147 M8
Staircase La COVW CV5 .... 133 G6
Stakenbridge La KIDD DY10 153 L4
Staley Cft HEDN WS12 ..... 16 A1
Stalling's La KGSWFD DY6 . 83 H5
  KGSWFD DY6 .... 83 K4
Stambermill Cl
  HAG/WOL DY9 .... 102 B8
Stamford Av COVS CV3 ..... 154 A7
Stamford Crs BNTWD WS7 .. 18 E5
Stamford Cft SOLH B91 .... 147 M3
Stamford Gv
  BFLD/HDSWWD B20 ... 89 G3
Stamford Rd
  BFLD/HDSWWD B20 ... 89 G4
  BRLYHL DY5 .... 102 A7
  STRBR DY8 .... 101 K6
Stamford St STRBR DY8 .... 101 M8
Stanbrook Rd SHLY B90 ... 147 L8
Stanbury Av DARL/WED WS10 51 M7
Stanbury Rd
  ALE/KHTH/YWD B14 .. 145 M1
Stancroft Gv
  LGN/SDN/BHAMAIR B26 109 L5
Standard Av TLHL/CAN CV4 152 E7
Standard Wy VAUX/NECH B7 90 D5
Standbridge Wy TPTN/OCK DY4 67 L7
Standedge TAM/AM/WIL B77 46 E6
Standhills Rd KGSWFD DY6 83 J7
Standish Cl COVE CV2 ..... 155 J3
Standlake Av CBROM B36 .. 91 H6
Standlake Ms RLSS CV31 ... 201 G7
Stand St WWCK CV34 .... 199 H7
Stanfield Rd GTB/HAM B43 . 55 H8
Stanford Av PBAR/PBCH B42 70 E6
Stanford Cl PENK ST19 .... 10 C4
  REDW B97 .... 195 M7
Stanford Rd BKHL/PFLD WV2 50 A6
  BLKHTH/ROWR B65 ... 103 M2
Stanhope Rd SMTHWKW B67 105 K2
Stanhope St BDMR/CCFT WV3 2 D6
  BHTH/HG B12 .... 107 K6
  DUDS DY2 .... 103 J1
Stanhope Wy GTB/HAM B43 . 71 H1
Stanhurst Wy HHTH/SAND B71 69 L3
Stanier Av COV CV1 .... 8 B3
Stanier Cl RUSH/SHEL WS4 . 39 M6
Stanier Gv BFLD/HDSWWD B20 88 F3
Staniforth St AST/WIT B6 . 7 H1
Stanklyn La KIDD DY10 .... 161 L5
Stanley Av RIDG/WDGT B32 105 J6
  SHLY B90 .... 146 F1
  WALM/CURD B76 ..... 73 K1
Stanley Cl HLGN/YWD B28 . 126 E8
  REDE B98 .... 188 E8
  WNSFLD WV11 .... 37 H7
Stanley Ct DUNHL/THL/PER WV6 48 C1
Stanley Dr SEDG DY3 ...... 82 C3
Stanley Pl BILS/COS WV14 50 F8
  RUSH/SHEL WS4 ..... 40 A4
Stanley Rd ALE/KHTH/YWD B14 125 H6
  ATHST CV9 .... 63 H6
  COVW CV5 .... 153 K5
  DARL/WED WS10 ..... 52 B8
  HEDN WS12 .... 13 G7
  HHTH/SAND B71 ..... 69 J6
  LGLYGN/QTN B68 .... 105 G6

  NUN CV11 .... 80 E8
  RUSH/SHEL WS4 ..... 39 M7
  STRBR DY8 .... 119 K2
  VAUX/NECH B7 ...... 90 A6
  WOLVN WV10 .... 36 B4
Stanley St BLOX/PEL WS3 .. 39 G5
Stanmore Gv RIDG/WDGT B32 122 E2
Stanmore Rd
  LDYWD/EDGR B16 .... 106 A4
Stansfield Gv KNWTH CV8 . 192 B1
Stanton Av DUDN DY1 ..... 66 D7
Stanton Gv
  LGN/SDN/BHAMAIR B26 109 K5
  SHLY B90 .... 146 E1
  TPTN/OCK DY4 ...... 67 L8
Stanton Rd GTB/HAM B43 .. 70 B5
  RLSS CV31 .... 201 G7
  SHLY B90 .... 146 E1
  WOLV WV1 .... 3 M5
Stanville Rd
  LGN/SDN/BHAMAIR B26 110 A7
Stanway Gdns HHTH/SAND B71 69 H7
Stanway Gv KGSTG B44 .... 71 K2
Stanway Rd COVW CV5 ..... 8 B9
  HHTH/SAND B71 ..... 69 H7
  SHLY B90 .... 147 H1
Stanwell Rd ERDW/GRVHL B23 72 C7
Stanwick Av STETCH B33 .. 110 C2
Stapenhall Rd SHLY B90 ... 147 L8
Staple Flat BRGRVE B60 ... 166 A5
Stapleford Cft
  ALE/KHTH/YWD B14 .. 145 G3
Stapleford Gdns BNTWD WS7 19 H7
Stapleford Gv STRBR DY8 . 101 J3
Staple Hall Rd NFLD/LBR B31 143 M3
Staplehurst Rd
  HLGN/YWD B28 ...... 126 D5
Staple Lodge Rd NFLD/LBR B31 143 M4
Stapleton Rd REDE B98 .... 197 H2
  WALM/CURD B76 ..... 73 M7
Stapleton Dr
  CHWD/FDBR/MGN B37 110 C2
Stapleton Rd ALDR WS9 ... 40 D8
Stapylton Av HRBN B17 ... 105 M8
Starbank Rd SMHTH B10 ... 108 E5
Starbold Crs DOR/KN B93 . 148 F8
Star Cl TPTN/OCK DY4 .... 68 A8
  WSLW WS2 .... 52 D1
Starcross Cl COVE CV2 .... 135 C6
Starcross Rd ACGN B27 ... 127 C3
Stare Gn TLHL/CAN CV4 .... 153 H8
Stareton Cl TLHL/CAN CV4 153 J2
Star Hl EDG B15 .... 106 F5
Starkey Cft
  CHWD/FDBR/MGN B37 111 G3
Starkie Dr LGLYGN/QTN B68 105 G5
Starley Rd COV CV1 .... 8 D5
Starley Wy
  CHWD/FDBR/MGN B37 111 G7
Star St BDMR/CCFT WV3 ... 49 J5
  HAG/WOL DY9 .... 102 D8
Startin Cl RCOVN/BALC/EX CV7 116 D6
Statham Dr LDYWD/EDGR B16 106 A3
Station Ap DOR/KN B93 .... 172 D3
  FOAKS/STRLY B74 ... 42 D7
  KIDD DY10 .... 137 K8
  RBRY B45 .... 167 H5
  RLSS CV31 .... 200 D6
  SCFLD/BOLD B73 .... 56 F7
  SOLH B91 .... 147 L1
Station Av LDYWD/EDGR B16 106 A4
  TLHL/CAN CV4 ...... 152 B5
  WWCK CV34 .... 199 K5
Station Cl BLOX/PEL WS3 .. 38 F5
  CDSL WV8 .... 34 C2
Station Dr BRLYHL DY5 ... 101 M4
  FOAKS/STRLY B74 ... 56 F5
  HAG/WOL DY9 .... 119 L8
  HIA/OLT B92 .... 127 J4
  HOCK/TIA B94 ...... 170 B4
  KIDD DY10 .... 137 K8
  TPTN/OCK DY4 ...... 85 M1
  WOLVN WV10 .... 14 A8
Station Pl BLOX/PEL WS3 .. 38 F5
Station Rd ACGN B27 ..... 127 G2
  ALDR WS9 .... 40 E8
  ALE/KHTH/YWD B14 .. 125 H5
  ALVE B48 .... 167 L8
  AST/WIT B6 .... 89 K4
  BEWD DY12 .... 160 A2
  BILS/COS WV14 ..... 51 J8
  BLKHTH/ROWR B65 ... 104 B3
  BLOX/PEL WS3 ...... 39 L2
  BNTWD WS7 .... 27 J2
  BRGRVE B60 .... 166 E8
  BRLYHL DY5 .... 102 A1
  BVILLE B30 .... 124 C8
  CDSL WV8 .... 34 C2
  CDYHTH B64 .... 103 K5
  CHWD/FDBR/MGN B37 110 E5
  CSHL/WTROR B46 .... 76 B7
  CSHL/WTROR B46 .... 93 K5
  CSHL/WTROR B46 .... 94 B2
  DOR/KN B93 .... 172 C2
  ERDW/GRVHL B23 .... 72 D8
  GTWY WS6 .... 24 D1
  HAG/WOL DY9 .... 102 C7
  HAG/WOL DY9 .... 119 L7
  HDSW B21 .... 88 A5
  HEDN WS12 .... 13 G7
  HIA/OLT B92 .... 129 L6
  HLYWD B47 .... 169 L2
  HRBN B17 .... 106 A7
  HWK/WKHTH B38 ..... 144 D1
  KNWTH CV8 .... 191 K1
  LICH WS13 .... 21 G6
  LICHS WS14 .... 28 D7
  MKTBOS/BARL/STKG CV13 81 K1
  NFLD/LBR B31 ...... 143 L3
  OLDBY B69 .... 86 E8
  PENK ST19 .... 10 C4
  POL/KGSB/FAZ B78 .. 47 M2
  RCOVN/BALC/EX CV7 . 96 B5
  RCOVN/BALC/EX CV7 . 151 G6
  RUSH/SHEL WS4 ..... 39 L7
  SCFLD/BOLD B73 .... 72 E4
  SOLH B91 .... 147 M1
  STETCH B33 .... 109 H2

  WMBN WV5 .... 64 E5
  WOLVN WV10 .... 3 M1
  WOLVN WV10 .... 14 B8
  WWCK CV34 .... 199 K6
Station Sq COV CV1 .... 8 E7
Station St ATHST CV9 ..... 63 H5
  BLOX/PEL WS3 ...... 38 F5
  BRGRVE B60 .... 185 K3
  CDYHTH B64 .... 103 G5
  DARL/WED WS10 ..... 52 C7
  DIG/EDG B5 .... 6 F7
  GTWY WS6 .... 24 C2
  SCFLD/BOLD B73 .... 56 F8
  TPTN/OCK DY4 ...... 67 M8
  WSL WS1 .... 4 E2
  WSLW WS2 .... 4 D3
Station St East COVN CV6 . 134 C4
Station St West COVN CV6 . 134 B5
Station Wy
  CHWD/FDBR/MGN B37 129 H1
  REDW B97 .... 196 B2
Staunton Rd BLOX/PEL WS3 38 E2
  RLSS CV31 .... 200 E8
Staveley Rd
  ALE/KHTH/YWD B14 .. 125 H7
  DUNHL/THL/PER WV6 . 2 D1
Staverton Cl COVW CV5 ... 152 D2
Staverton Leys
  RUGBYS/DCH CV22 ... 183 L6
Stead Cl TPTN/OCK DY4 ... 67 M4
  WSLW WS2 .... 5 J2
Steadman Cft TPTN/OCK DY4 68 B5
Steatite Wy STRPT DY13 .. 160 C8
Stechford La WASH/WDE B8 91 J8
Stechford Rd BKDE/SHDE B34 91 H8
Steel Bright Rd SMTHWK B66 88 A7
Steel Dr WOLVN WV10 ..... 36 B5
Steele St RUGBYS/DCH CV22 183 H2
Steel Gv YDLY B25 .... 109 G6
Steelhouse La BKHL/PFLD WV2 3 J8
  CBHAMNE B4 .... 7 H3
Steel Rd NFLD/LBR B31 ... 143 K3
Steene Gv NFLD/LBR B31 .. 143 G2
Steeping Rd RRUGBY CV23 . 158 F8
Steeplefield Rd COVN CV6 . 133 L8
The Steeples STRBR DY8 .. 119 M2
Steepwood Cft BVILLE B30 144 B1
Steere Av CRTAM B79 ..... 32 A6
Stella Cft
  CHWD/FDBR/MGN B37 111 G3
Stella Gv GTB/HAM B43 ... 70 A5
Stella Rd TPTN/OCK DY4 .. 67 K7
Stenbury Cl WOLVN WV10 .. 36 D1
Stencills Dr RUSH/SHEL WS4 53 M2
Stencills Rd RUSH/SHEL WS4 53 M1
Stennels Av RMSLY B62 ... 122 C1
Stennels Cl COVN CV6 .... 133 K5
Stephens Cl WNSFLD WV11 . 37 K5
Stephenson Av WSLW WS2 .. 38 E7
  WSLW WS2 .... 39 G8
Stephenson Cl TAM/AM/WIL B77 46 E3
Stephenson Dr
  CHWD/FDBR/MGN B37 110 F3
  DUNHL/THL/PER WV6 . 34 C8
Stephenson Pl BEWD DY12 160 A2
Stephenson Rd
  RCOVN/BALC/EX CV7 . 116 F6
Stephenson Sq WSLW WS2 . 38 F8
Stephenson St BDMR/CCFT WV3 2 D6
  CBHAM B2 .... 6 E5
Stephens Rd WALM/CURD B76 73 L1
Stephen St
  RUGBYN/HIL CV21 ... 183 K2
Stepney Rd COVE CV2 ..... 154 E1
Stepping Stone La WSLW WS2 52 D1
Stepping Stones STRBR DY8 101 M8
Stepping Stones Rd COVW CV5 153 K1
Steppingstone St DUDN DY1 84 F4
Sterling Wy NUN CV11 .... 99 J5
Sterndale Rd PBAR/PBCH B42 71 C7
Steven Dr BILS/COS WV14 . 67 J4
Stevens Av RIDG/WDGT B32 123 H3
Stevens Dr HEDN WS12 .... 13 H7
Stevens Ga BKHL/PFLD WV2 2 F9
Stevenson Av REDE B98 ... 196 D2
Stevenson Rd COVN CV6 ... 133 L5
  CRTAM B79 .... 31 L7
Stevenson Wk LICHS WS14 . 20 F7
Stevens Rd HAG/WOL DY9 .. 120 B3
Steward St WSNGN B18 .... 106 E2
Stewart Cl TLHL/CAN CV4 . 153 H3
Stewart Ct KIDD DY10 .... 161 K1
Stewart Rd ALDR WS9 ..... 40 E2
  KGSWFD DY6 .... 101 H1
Stewarts Rd RMSLY B62 ... 104 B6
Stewart St BKHL/PFLD WV2 2 F8
  NUN CV11 .... 98 F2
Stewkins STRBR DY8 ...... 101 J5
Steyning Rd
  LGN/SDN/BHAMAIR B26 109 J3
Stickley La SEDG DY3 .... 84 A1
Stidfall Gv RLSS CV31 ... 201 H7
Stilehouse Crs
  BLKHTH/ROWR B65 ... 104 A3
Stilthouse Gv RBRY B45 .. 142 E6
Stiper's Hl CRTAM B79 ... 47 M3
Stirling Av RLSN CV32 ... 192 F6
Stirling Cl COVS CV3 .... 155 K5
Stirling Crs SHHTH WV12 . 37 M8
Stirling Pl CNCK/NC WS11 15 M5
Stirling Rd BILS/COS WV14 67 K2
  DUDS DY2 .... 85 J7
  LDYWD/EDGR B16 .... 106 D4
  SCFLD/BOLD B73 .... 72 B3
  SHLY B90 .... 147 J5
Stirrup Cl DSYBK/YTR WS5 69 K1
Stivichall Cft COVS CV3 . 153 M7
Stockbridge Cl
  DUNHL/THL/PER WV6 . 48 C1
Stockdale Pl EDG B15 .... 106 D3
Stockfield Rd ACGN B27 .. 126 F1
Stockhay La BNTWD WS7 .. 19 H8
Stockhill Dr RBRY B45 ... 142 D7
Stocking St HAG/WOL DY9 . 102 D7
Stockland Rd ERDW/GRVHL B23 90 A1
Stockmans Cl
  HWK/WKHTH B38 ..... 144 C5
Stocks Ct RUGBYS/DCH CV22 183 H5

Stockton Cl DOR/KN B93 .... 172 F1
  WALM/CURD B76 .... 74 A8
  WSLW WS2 .... 53 H1
Stockton Gv RLSN CV32 .... 200 E3
  STETCH B33 .... 110 B4
Stockton Rd COV CV1 .... 9 J1
Stockwell Av BRLYHL DY5 .... 102 B5
Stockwell End
  DUNHL/THL/PER WV6 .... 35 H7
Stockwell Ri HIA/OLT B92 .... 128 B6
Stockwell Rd
  DUNHL/THL/PER WV6 .... 35 H8
  HDSW B21 .... 88 C3
Stoke Gn COVS CV3 .... 154 E3
Stoke La
  MKTBOS/BARL/STKG CV13 .... 81 M1
  REDE B98 .... 188 F6
Stoke Rd BRGRVE B60 .... 185 M6
Stoke Rw COVE CV2 .... 154 E1
Stokes Av TPTN/OCK DY4 .... 67 L5
  WLNHL WV13 .... 51 K5
Stokesay Av
  DUNHL/THL/PER WV6 .... 48 D2
Stokesay Cl KIDDW DY11 .... 161 J3
  NUNW/HART CV10 .... 98 E2
  OLDBY B69 .... 85 L5
Stokesay Gv NFLD/LBR B31 .... 143 K5
Stokesay Ri DUDN DY1 .... 84 C2
Stoke's La CNCK/NC WS11 .... 17 J6
Stokes St BLOX/PEL WS3 .... 38 F5
Stom Rd BILS/COS WV14 .... 50 F8
Stoneacre Cl
  BDMR/CCFT WV3 .... 48 E4
Stone Av MGN/WHC B75 .... 57 L8
Stonebow Av SOLH B91 .... 147 M5
Stonebridge Crs
  CHWD/FDBR/MGN B37 .... 110 D1
Stonebridge Hwy COVS CV3 .... 178 A1
Stonebridge Rd
  CSHL/WTROR B46 .... 93 K8
  CSHL/WTROR B46 .... 111 L5
Stonebrook Wy COVN CV6 .... 134 D2
  RIDG/WDGT B32 .... 123 K3
Stonebury Av COVW CV5 .... 132 C1
Stonechat Cl KIDD DY10 .... 161 M3
Stonechat Dr
  ERDW/GRVHL B23 .... 90 A3
Stone Cl HWK/WKHTH B38 .... 144 D3
Stonecroft Av RBRY B45 .... 142 E6
Stonecrop Cl BRWNH WS8 .... 26 B7
  HWK/WKHTH B38 .... 144 D5
Stone Cross PENK ST19 .... 10 C4
Stonedown Cl
  ETTPK/GDPK/PENN WV4 .... 66 E2
Stonefield Cl COVE CV2 .... 135 L5
Stonefield Dr BRLYHL DY5 .... 83 L6
Stonefield Rd BILS/COS WV14 .... 51 H8
Stoneford Rd SHLY B90 .... 146 E1
Stonehaven TAM/AM/WIL B77 .... 32 D8
Stonehaven Dr COVS CV3 .... 178 A2
Stonehaven Gv
  HLGN/YWD B28 .... 126 F5
Stonehenge Cft
  HWK/WKHTH B38 .... 145 H4
Stone HI KIDD DY10 .... 162 B2
Stonehill Cft SHLY B90 .... 147 K7
Stonehouse Av WLNHL WV13 .... 51 K2
Stonehouse Cl REDW B97 .... 196 A4
  RLSN CV32 .... 193 H8
Stonehouse Crs
  DARL/WED WS10 .... 68 F3
Stonehouse Dr
  FOAKS/STRLY B74 .... 55 M1
Stonehouse Hill SLYOAK B29 .... 123 L3
Stonehouse La ALVE B48 .... 168 C3
  COVS CV3 .... 179 G1
  RCOVN/BALC/EX CV7 .... 96 B6
  RIDG/WDGT B32 .... 123 H3
Stonehouse Rd BRGRVE B60 .... 185 L4
  SCFLD/BOLD B73 .... 72 D2
Stonehurst Rd GTB/HAM B43 .... 71 C2
Stonelea ALDR WS9 .... 40 F8
Stonelea Cl HHTH/SAND B71 .... 69 J5
Stoneleigh Av KNWTH CV8 .... 176 E7
Stoneleigh Cl FOAKS/STRLY B74 .... 56 D5
  KNWTH CV8 .... 177 M7
  REDE B98 .... 196 D8
Stoneleigh Gdns CDSL WV8 .... 34 C1
Stoneleigh Rd
  BFLD/HDSWWD B20 .... 89 J4
  KNWTH CV8 .... 176 E7
  RLSN CV32 .... 192 D7
  SOLH B91 .... 127 H7
  TLHL/CAN CV4 .... 177 H3
Stoneleigh Wy SEDG DY3 .... 66 B7
Stonepit Cl
  NUNW/HART CV10 .... 79 M3
Stone Pine Cl HEDN WS12 .... 12 D5
Stonepit TAM/AM/WIL B77 .... 46 A4
Stone Rd EDG B15 .... 107 H6
Stonerwood Av
  HLGN/YWD B28 .... 126 C5
Stones Gn ERDW/GRVHL B23 .... 72 D7
Stone St DUDN DY1 .... 85 G4
  OLDBY B69 .... 86 E6
Stoneton Crs
  RCOVN/BALC/EX CV7 .... 150 E7
Stoneton Gv SLYOAK B29 .... 123 L3
Stone Upper Cl
  WALM/CURD B76 .... 73 J1
Stonewell Crs NUN CV11 .... 99 M5
Stone Yd DIG/EDG B5 .... 7 K7
Stoney Brook Leys WMBN WV5 .... 64 C8
Stoney Cl HIA/OLT B92 .... 128 D6
Stoney Cft CNCK/NC WS11 .... 16 D4
Stoneyfields Cl
  CNCK/NC WS11 .... 16 D3
Stoneyford Gv
  ALE/KHTH/YWD B14 .... 145 M1
Stoneyhurst Rd ERDE/BCHGN B24 .... 90 D4
Stoney La BHTH/HG B12 .... 107 M8
  BLOX/PEL WS3 .... 39 H2
  BRGRVE B60 .... 187 C3
  DUDS DY2 .... 103 C2
  HAG/WOL DY9 .... 139 J2
  HHTH/SAND B71 .... 87 H1
  KIDD DY10 .... 137 J5
  RIDG/WDGT B32 .... 104 F7

STECH B33 .... 109 J4
Stoney Lea Rd CNCK/NC WS11 .... 16 D3
Stoneymoor Dr CBROM B36 .... 92 B4
Stoney Rd COV CV1 .... 8 F8
  NUNW/HART CV10 .... 80 F7
Stoney Stanton Rd COV CV1 .... 134 D6
  COVN CV6 .... 134 D6
Stoneythorpe Cl SOLH B91 .... 147 M4
Stoneywood Rd COVE CV2 .... 135 K4
Stonleigh Av COVW CV5 .... 153 K6
Stonnal Gv ERDW/GRVHL B23 .... 72 E7
Stonnall Gv ALDR WS9 .... 40 F5
Stonnall Rd ALDR WS9 .... 41 C5
Stonor Park Rd SOLH B91 .... 127 K7
Stonor Rd HLGN/YWD B28 .... 146 E1
Stonydelph La TAM/AM/WIL B77 .... 46 E6
Stony La SMTHWKW B67 .... 87 J8
Stony St SMTHWKW B67 .... 87 K7
Stornoway Rd CVALE B35 .... 91 M1
The Storrs Wy
  RIDG/WDGT B32 .... 122 F6
Stot Fold Rd
  ALE/KHTH/YWD B14 .... 145 K3
Stour Cl BNTWD WS7 .... 18 E8
  HALE B63 .... 103 J7
Stourdell Rd HALE B63 .... 103 J7
Stourmore Cl SHHTH WV12 .... 38 B7
Stourport Rd BEWD DY12 .... 160 A2
  KIDDW DY11 .... 160 A2
Stour St WBROM B70 .... 86 C2
Stourton Cl DOR/KN B93 .... 148 F6
  WALM/CURD B76 .... 73 K1
Stourton Crs KINVER DY7 .... 100 D7
Stourton Dr
  ETTPK/GDPK/PENN WV4 .... 49 C8
Stourton Rd RIDG/WDGT B32 .... 104 F8
Stour Vale Rd HAG/WOL DY9 .... 102 D7
Stour Valley Cl BRLYHL DY5 .... 102 B6
Stour Dr BRLYHL DY5 .... 101 M7
Stowcroft LICH WS13 .... 21 G4
Stowe Hill Gdns LICH WS13 .... 21 C4
Stowell Rd KGSTG B44 .... 71 K6
Stowe Pl TLHL/CAN CV4 .... 152 A4
Stowe Rd LICH WS13 .... 20 F5
Stowe St BLOX/PEL WS3 .... 39 C6
  LICH WS13 .... 21 C5
Stow Gv CBROM B36 .... 91 J6
Stow Heath La WOLV WV1 .... 50 F6
Stow Heath Pl WOLV WV1 .... 50 F6
Stowmans Cl BILS/COS WV14 .... 66 F2
Strachey Av RLSN CV32 .... 200 C3
Straight Mile WOLVN WV10 .... 14 D7
Straight Rd SHHTH WV12 .... 38 A7
Straits Gn SEDG DY3 .... 83 M1
Straits Rd SEDG DY3 .... 83 M2
The Straits SEDG DY3 .... 83 L1
Strathcona Rd COVW CV5 .... 132 E2
Stratford Av ATHST CV9 .... 63 G6
Stratford Cl DUDN DY1 .... 84 C3
Stratford Dr ALDR WS9 .... 41 C5
Stratford Pl BHTH/HG B12 .... 107 L5
Stratford Rd BRGRVE B60 .... 185 L3
  HLGN/YWD B28 .... 126 C3
  HOCK/TIA B94 .... 171 M2
  SHLY B90 .... 146 F1
  SHLY B90 .... 147 H6
  SPARK B11 .... 107 M7
Stratford St COVE CV2 .... 154 E1
  SPARK B11 .... 108 A8
Stratford St North SPARK B11 .... 107 L5
Stratford Wy CNCK/NC WS11 .... 12 D8
Strathdene Rd SLYOAK B29 .... 124 A3
Strathearn Rd RLSN CV32 .... 200 C4
Strathern Dr BILS/COS WV14 .... 66 E4
Strathmore Av COV CV1 .... 9 J6
Strathmore Crs WMBN WV5 .... 64 E4
Strathmore Pl CNCK/NC WS11 .... 16 D3
Strathmore Rd TPTN/OCK DY4 .... 67 L5
Stratton St WOLVN WV10 .... 50 C1
Strawberry Cl OLDBY B69 .... 86 A6
Strawberry Flds
  RCOVN/BALC/EX CV7 .... 130 F4
Strawberry La GTWY WS6 .... 24 C5
  WLNHL WV13 .... 51 G2
Strawberry Wk COVE CV2 .... 135 H3
Stream Meadow
  RUSH/SHEL WS4 .... 40 A4
Stream Pk KGSWFD DY6 .... 101 H1
Stream Rd KGSWFD DY6 .... 83 H8
Streamside Cl COVW CV5 .... 132 E5
  PENK ST19 .... 10 D5
Streamside Wy HIA/OLT B92 .... 128 B1
  RUSH/SHEL WS4 .... 40 B5
Streatham Gv KGSTG B44 .... 71 L3
Streather Rd MGN/WHC B75 .... 57 C4
Streetly Crs FOAKS/STRLY B74 .... 56 B2
Streetly Dr FOAKS/STRLY B74 .... 56 B2
Streetly La FOAKS/STRLY B74 .... 56 C3
Streetly Rd ERDW/GRVHL B23 .... 72 B7
Streetly Wd FOAKS/STRLY B74 .... 55 L3
Streetsbrook Rd SHLY B90 .... 127 H8
  SOLH B91 ....
Streets Corner Gdns ALDR WS9 .... 40 E1
Streets La GTWY WS6 .... 24 C5
Streetway Rd LICH WS14 .... 28 F6
Strensham HI MOS/BIL B13 .... 125 J1
Strensham Rd MOS/BIL B13 .... 125 J1
Stretton Av COVS CV3 .... 155 C8
Stretton Dr RBRY B45 .... 166 E3
Stretton Gdns CDSL WV8 .... 34 C1
Stretton Gv SPARK B11 .... 108 A7
  WASH/WDE B8 .... 90 F7

Stretton Pl BILS/COS WV14 .... 66 E4
  DUDS DY2 .... 103 H1
Stretton Rd KIDDW DY11 .... 160 F1
  KNWTH CV8 .... 180 E2
  NUNW/HART CV10 .... 98 E2
  RRUGBY CV23 .... 180 E5
  SHHTH WV12 .... 38 A5
  SHLY B90 .... 146 F5
Stringer Cl MGN/WHC B75 .... 56 E1
Stringers HI HEDN WS12 .... 13 H6
Stringes La WLNHL WV13 .... 51 M3
Strode Rd BKHL/PFLD WV2 .... 50 A7
Stroma Wy NUNW/HART CV10 .... 98 D3
Stronsay Cl RBRY B45 .... 142 D4
Stroud Av WLNHL WV12 .... 52 A1
Stroud Cl SHHTH WV12 .... 52 A1
Stroud Rd SHLY B90 .... 146 D3
Strutt Cl EDG B15 .... 106 B5
Stuart Crs DUDS DY2 .... 85 J4
Stuart Ct COVN CV6 .... 134 E5
  RLSN CV32 .... 200 C4
Stuart Rd
  BLKHTH/ROWR B65 .... 104 B1
  RMSLY B62 .... 104 B1
Stuart's Dr STETCH B33 .... 109 H4
Stuart Wy NUNW/HART CV10 .... 80 A8
Stuarts Rd STETCH B33 .... 109 H3
Stuart St BLOX/PEL WS3 .... 38 F5
  VAUX/NECH B7 .... 90 A6
Stuarts Wy RIDG/WDGT B32 .... 122 F6
Stubbers Green Rd ALDR WS9 .... 40 B5
Stubbington Cl WLNHL WV13 .... 51 H4
Stubbs Cl BDWTH CV12 .... 116 E1
Stubbs Gv COVE CV2 .... 134 F8
Stubbs Rd BDMR/CCFT WV3 .... 49 L6
Stubby La WNSFLD WV11 .... 37 K7
Stubley Dr WOLVN WV10 .... 36 F3
Studland Gn COVE CV2 .... 155 L1
Studland Rd HLGN/YWD B28 .... 126 E5
Stud La STETCH B33 .... 109 K2
Studley Cft HIA/OLT B92 .... 128 A2
Studley Dr BRLYHL DY5 .... 102 A5
Studley Ga STRBR DY8 .... 101 H8
Studley Rd BDMR/CCFT WV3 .... 49 C5
  REDE B98 .... 196 F5
Studley St BHTH/HG B12 .... 107 L7
Sturgeon's HI LICHS WS14 .... 21 G6
Sturley Cl KNWTH CV8 .... 176 F7
Sturman Dr
  BLKHTH/ROWR B65 .... 104 A4
Sturminster Cl COVS CV3 .... 155 L1
Stychbrook Gdns LICH WS13 .... 20 F3
Styles Cl RLSS CV31 .... 200 E6
Styvechale Av COVW CV5 .... 153 K5
Suckling Green La CDSL WV8 .... 34 D3
Sudbury Cl RLSN CV32 .... 201 C3
  WNSFLD WV11 .... 37 J5
Sudbury Gv KGSTG B44 .... 71 M3
Sudeley TAM/AM/WIL B77 .... 46 B1
Sudeley Cl CBROM B36 .... 91 M4
Sudeley Rd NUNW/HART CV10 .... 99 C5
Suffield Gv ERDW/GRVHL B23 .... 71 L8
Suffolk Cl BDWTH CV12 .... 116 D2
  COVW CV5 .... 152 F2
  LGLYGN/QTN B68 .... 104 F1
  NUNW/HART CV10 .... 98 C2
  WNSFLD WV11 .... 37 C7
Suffolk Dr BRLYHL DY5 .... 102 A6
Suffolk Gv ALDR WS9 .... 40 F5
Suffolk Pl CBHAMW B1 .... 6 F7
  DUDS DY2 .... 84 E6
  WSLW WS2 .... 39 H8
Suffolk Rd DARL/WED WS10 .... 69 C2
  DUDS DY2 .... 84 E6
Suffolk St RLSN CV32 .... 200 E4
Suffolk Street Queensway
  CBHAMW B1 .... 6 E6
Suffolk Wy POL/KGSB/FAZ B78 .... 45 L4
Suffrage St SMTHWK B66 .... 87 M8
Sugarbrook La BRGRVE B60 .... 185 K8
Sugarbrook Rd BRGRVE B60 .... 185 L7
Sugar Loaf La KINVER DY7 .... 118 F5
Sugden Gv DIG/EDG B5 .... 7 C7
Suigrave Cl DUDN DY1 .... 84 E2
Sullivan Rd COVN CV6 .... 134 F6
Sumburgh Cft CVALE B35 .... 91 L2
Summercourt Dr KGSWFD DY6 .... 83 C8
Summercourt Sq KGSWFD DY6 .... 83 C8
Summer Cft LGZ/NWT B19 .... 89 H7
Summer Dr SEDG DY3 .... 84 A2
Summerfield Av KGSWFD DY6 .... 83 C6
  WBROM B70 .... 87 C1
Summerfield Cl
  TAM/AM/WIL B77 .... 46 B1
Summerfield Crs
  LDYWD/EDGR B16 .... 106 C2
Summerfield Dr SLYOAK B29 .... 123 L6
Summerfield La KIDDW DY11 .... 161 K6
Summerfield Rd BNTWD WS7 .... 18 E8
  DUDS DY2 .... 85 H6
  HAG/WOL DY9 .... 140 C3
  HIA/OLT B92 .... 127 L4
  LDYWD/EDGR B16 .... 106 C2
  TAM/AM/WIL B77 .... 46 B1
  WOLV WV1 .... 2 C5
Summerfields Av RMSLY B62 .... 104 D5
Summergate SEDG DY3 .... 84 B2
Summer Gv LICH WS13 .... 21 H3
Summer HI HALE B63 .... 121 M2
  KGSWFD DY6 .... 83 C7
Summerhill Av KIDDW DY11 .... 136 E7
Summerhill Rd BILS/COS WV14 .... 67 K6
Summer Hill Rd CBHAMW B1 .... 6 A3
Summerhill Rd TPTN/OCK DY4 .... 67 K6
Summer Hill St CBHAMW B1 .... 6 B4
Summer Hill Ter CBHAMW B1 .... 6 B4
Summerhouse Rd
  BILS/COS WV14 .... 66 E4
Summer La LOZ/NWT B19 .... 6 F1
  RUSH/SHEL WS4 .... 39 M3
  SEDG DY3 .... 84 A2
  WALM/CURD B76 .... 74 D7
Summerlee Rd
  ERDE/BCHGN B24 .... 90 F3
Summer Rd ACGN B27 .... 126 D3

  BLKHTH/ROWR B65 .... 104 B2
  DUDN DY1 .... 84 E1
  EDG B15 .... 107 C6
  ERDW/GRVHL B23 .... 72 D8
  KIDDW DY11 .... 161 C2
Summer Rw BKHL/PFLD WV2 2
  CBHAMNW B3 .... 6 D4
Summerside Av HEDN WS12 .... 18 A1
Summerside Rd HAG/WOL DY9 .... 102 C8
  HHTH/SAND B71 .... 87 H1
  KGSWFD DY6 .... 83 H7
  REDE B98 .... 196 C2
  STRBR DY8 .... 101 K8
  WLNHL WV13 .... 51 K3
Summerton Rd OLDBY B69 .... 86 B5
Summervale Cl
  HAG/WOL DY9 .... 119 L8
Summervale Rd HAG/WOL DY9 .... 119 L8
Summit Crs SMTHWK B66 .... 87 J5
Summit Gdns HALE B63 .... 121 K2
Summit Pl SEDG DY3 .... 83 M3
The Summit HAG/WOL DY9 .... 120 B1
Sumner Cl
  RWWCK/WEL CV35 .... 198 D7
Sumner Rd CSHL/WTROR B46 .... 93 L7
Sunart Wy NUNW/HART CV10 .... 80 A8
Sunbeam TAM/AM/WIL B77 .... 46 C2
Sunbeam Cl CBROM B36 .... 92 D4
Sunbeam Dr GTWY WS6 .... 24 C2
Sunbeam St BKHL/PFLD WV2 .... 2 A6
Sunbeam Wy STETCH B33 .... 110 A3
Sunbury Cl BILS/COS WV14 .... 67 H4
Sunbury Rd COVS CV3 .... 179 C1
  HALE B63 .... 121 K1
  NFLD/LBR B31 .... 143 J5
Suncliffe Dr KNWTH CV8 .... 191 L3
Suncroft BDWTH CV12 .... 116 E1
Sundbury Ri NFLD/LBR B31 .... 123 M8
Sunderland Dr STRBR DY8 .... 101 L5
Sunderton Rd
  ALE/KHTH/YWD B14 .... 145 J1
Sundew Cft CBROM B36 .... 91 H5
Sundew St COVE CV2 .... 135 H3
Sundial La GTB/HAM B43 .... 70 D4
Sundorne Cl COVW CV5 .... 152 E1
Sundour Crs WNSFLD WV11 .... 36 F4
Sundridge Rd KGSTG B44 .... 71 J1
Sunfield Gv SPARK B11 .... 126 C1
Sunfield Rd CNCK/NC WS11 .... 15 L4
Sunfields Cl POL/KGSB/FAZ B78 .... 45 L5
Sunleigh Gv ACGN B27 .... 127 J1
Sunley Dr HEDN WS12 .... 13 H6
Sunningdale RMSLY B62 .... 122 C1
  TAM/AM/WIL B77 .... 33 C8
Sunningdale Av COVN CV6 .... 134 B3
  DUNHL/THL/PER WV6 .... 34 B8
  KNWTH CV8 .... 191 M1
Sunningdale Cl
  BFLD/HDSWWD B20 .... 88 C1
  NUN CV11 .... 99 L4
  SCFLD/BOLD B73 .... 72 E3
  STRBR DY8 .... 101 K8
Sunningdale Dr OLDBY B69 .... 85 L6
Sunningdale Rd BRGRVW B61 .... 185 H5
  SEDG DY3 .... 65 M4
  SPARK B11 .... 126 C2
Sunningdale Wy BLOX/PEL WS3 .... 38 C2
Sunny Av BHTH/HG B12 .... 107 L8
Sunnybank Av COVS CV3 .... 154 FB
  KGSTG B44 .... 71 M6
Sunnybank Cl FOAKS/STRLY B74 .... 55 J3
Sunny Bank Rd
  LGLYGN/QTN B68 .... 105 C6
Sunnydene WASH/WDE B8 .... 90 E8
Sunny Hill Cl WMBN WV5 .... 64 F7
Sunnymead BRGRVE B60 .... 185 L4
Sunnymead Rd
  LGN/SDN/BHAMAIR B26 .... 109 K7
Sunnymead Wy
  FOAKS/STRLY B74 .... 55 K6
Sunnymede Rd KGSWFD DY6 .... 101 L1
Sunnyside ALDR WS9 .... 40 D3
  OLDBY B69 .... 85 M6
Sunnyside Av
  ERDW/GRVHL B23 .... 90 C2
Sunnyside Cl COVW CV5 .... 153 K2
  RCOVN/BALC/EX CV7 .... 151 C6
Sunnyside Gdns KIDDW DY11 .... 136 F4
Sunnyside La
  RCOVN/BALC/EX CV7 .... 151 C6
Sunridge Av LOZ/NWT B19 .... 89 H7
  WMBN WV5 .... 64 E6
Sunrise HI HEDN WS12 .... 12 F7
Sunset Cl CRTAM B79 .... 45 L1
  GTWY WS6 .... 24 D2
  POL/KGSB/FAZ B78 .... 47 L5
Sunset Pl
  ETTPK/GDPK/PENN WV4 .... 66 D2
Sunshine Cl KNWTH CV8 .... 191 L3
Sun St BRLYHL DY5 .... 102 D4
  WOLVN WV10 .... 2 J3
  WSL WS1 .... 4 D7
Sunway Gv COVS CV3 .... 153 M7
Surfeit HI CDYHTH B64 .... 103 J5
Surfeit Hill Rd CDYHTH B64 .... 103 H5
Surrey Cl CNCK/NC WS11 .... 16 D5
  NUNW/HART CV10 .... 98 C2
Surrey Crs HHTH/SAND B71 .... 68 E5
Surrey Dr BDMR/CCFT WV3 .... 49 J4
  POL/KGSB/FAZ B78 .... 45 L4
  STRBR DY8 .... 101 J1
Surrey Rd DUDS DY2 .... 84 E6
  KGSTG B44 .... 71 J1
Surrey Wk ALDR WS9 .... 40 E5
Sussex Av ALDR WS9 .... 40 E5
  DARL/WED WS10 .... 69 G4
  HHTH/SAND B71 .... 69 G7
Sussex Cl NUNW/HART CV10 .... 98 C2
Sussex Dr BDMR/CCFT WV3 .... 49 J4
  HEDN WS12 .... 12 F8
Sussex Rd COVW CV5 .... 153 K1
Sutherland Av COVW CV5 .... 152 C1
  SHLY B90 .... 147 C2
Sutherland Cl GTB/HAM B43 .... 71 H1
  WWCK CV34 .... 199 J4

Sutherland Dr BDWTH CV12 .... 116 E3
  MOS/BIL B13 .... 125 K1
  WMBN WV5 .... 64 E5
Sutherland Gv
  DUNHL/THL/PER WV6 .... 48 D1
Sutherland Rd CDYHTH B64 .... 103 J5
  ETTPK/GDPK/PENN WV4 .... 49 M8
  GTWY WS6 .... 24 C3
Sutherland St AST/WIT B6 .... 89 M5
Sutton Ap WASH/WDE B8 .... 108 C1
Sutton Av COVW CV5 .... 152 B1
  POL/KGSB/FAZ B78 .... 45 L3
Sutton Cl REDE B98 .... 197 H3
Sutton Ct
  ETTPK/GDPK/PENN WV4 .... 66 C3
  MGN/WHC B75 .... 56 F6
Sutton Crs WBROM B70 .... 86 E2
Sutton New Rd
  ERDW/GRVHL B23 .... 90 D1
Sutton Oak Rd
  SCFLD/BOLD B73 .... 55 L8
Sutton Park Ct KIDDW DY11 .... 161 C2
Sutton Park Ri KIDDW DY11 .... 160 E2
Sutton Park Rd KIDDW DY11 .... 160 E2
Sutton Rd ALDR WS9 .... 54 D4
  DARL/WED WS10 .... 51 L8
  DSYBK/YTR WS5 .... 54 D4
  ERDE/BCHGN B24 .... 72 E8
  KIDDW DY11 .... 137 G8
  POL/KGSB/FAZ B78 .... 45 L4
  WSL WS1 .... 5 J5
Sutton Stop COVE CV2 .... 117 H3
Sutton St AST/WIT B6 .... 89 K7
  EDG B15 .... 6 E8
  STRBR DY8 .... 101 J4
Swadling St RLSS CV31 .... 200 D7
Swain Crofts RLSS CV31 .... 200 F7
Swains Gv KGSTG B44 .... 71 K1
Swaledale Cl BRGRVE B60 .... 185 J7
Swale Gv HWK/WKHTH B38 .... 144 D5
  WLNHL WV13 .... 52 B3
Swale Rd WALM/CURD B76 .... 73 L4
Swallow Av CBROM B36 .... 92 E5
Swallow Cl BHTH/HG B12 .... 107 M8
  DARL/WED WS10 .... 68 F1
  DUDS DY2 .... 103 H3
Swallow Ct WOLVN WV10 .... 36 B6
Swallow Cft LICH WS13 .... 20 E4
Swallowdale ALDR WS9 .... 40 E1
  DUNHL/THL/PER WV6 .... 48 D3
Swallowdean Rd COVN CV6 .... 133 J5
Swallow Dr KIDD DY10 .... 161 L3
Swallowfall Av STRBR DY8 .... 119 C1
Swallowfield CRTAM B79 .... 31 J2
Swallowfields Dr HEDN WS12 .... 16 F2
Swallowfields Rd SEDG DY3 .... 66 A2
Swallow Rd COVN CV6 .... 133 M4
Swallows Cl BLOX/PEL WS3 .... 25 L8
Swallows' Meadow SHLY B90 .... 147 H5
Swallow St CBHAM B2 .... 6 E6
Swanage Gn COVE CV2 .... 155 L1
Swanage Rd SMHTH B10 .... 108 B5
Swan Av SMTHWK B66 .... 87 J6
Swan Bank
  ETTPK/GDPK/PENN WV4 .... 65 K1
Swan Cl GTWY WS6 .... 24 A3
  KIDD DY10 .... 138 F4
Swan Copse YDLY B25 .... 109 G8
Swancote Dr
  ETTPK/GDPK/PENN WV4 .... 49 C8
Swancote Rd DUDN DY1 .... 84 E5
  STETCH B33 .... 91 K8
Swancroft Rd COVE CV2 .... 134 E8
  TPTN/OCK DY4 .... 67 K5
Swanfield Rd STRBR DY8 .... 101 L4
Swanfields BNTWD WS7 .... 19 C7
Swan Gdns ERDW/GRVHL B23 .... 90 D1
Swan La BRGRVW B61 .... 165 H2
  BRGRVW B61 .... 184 C8
  COVE CV2 .... 9 M2
  STRBR DY8 .... 101 L3
  WBROM B70 .... 68 E8
  WOLVN WV10 .... 23 C4
Swanley Cl RIDG/WDGT B32 .... 122 E2
Swan Ms LICH WS13 .... 20 E5
Swanmore Cl BDMR/CCFT WV3 .... 49 J6
Swann Rd BILS/COS WV14 .... 66 E3
Swan Pool Gv
  RUSH/SHEL WS4 .... 40 B4
Swan Rd LICH WS13 .... 20 E6
Swansbrook Gdns
  HWK/WKHTH B38 .... 145 C3
Swanshurst La MOS/BIL B13 .... 126 A5
Swans Length ALVE B48 .... 167 L6
Swan St ALVE B48 .... 167 M7
  BRLYHL DY5 .... 84 A6
  DUDS DY2 .... 85 C5
  RLSN CV32 .... 200 E4
  STRBR DY8 .... 101 J8
  WOLV WV1 .... 3 L5
  WWCK CV34 .... 199 J7
Swanswood Gv
  CHWD/FDBR/MGN B37 .... 111 C2
Swarthmore Rd SLYOAK B29 .... 123 M6
Sweetbriar La SHHTH WV12 .... 38 B8
Sweetbriar Rd BKHL/PFLD WV2 .... 50 E6
Sweetbrier Dr STRBR DY8 .... 101 J4
Sweetman Pl
  DUNHL/THL/PER WV6 .... 2 B2
Sweetmoor Cl CBROM B36 .... 92 A5
Sweetpool La HAG/WOL DY9 .... 119 K8
Swift TAM/AM/WIL B77 .... 46 C2
Swift Cl BRGRVW B61 .... 185 J5
  CBROM B36 .... 92 E5
  KNWTH CV8 .... 191 L3
Swift Park Gv KIDD DY10 .... 161 M3
Swift's Cnr COVS CV3 .... 154 C5
Swillington Rd COVN CV6 .... 133 M8
Swinbrook Gv KGSTG B44 .... 71 J4
Swinbrook Wy SHLY B90 .... 147 H1
Swinburn Cl NUNW/HART CV10 .... 79 L8
Swinburne Av COVE CV2 .... 155 H3

Swinburne Rd REDW B97 .... 196 A6
Swincross Rd STRBR DY8 .... 119 M1
Swindale TAM/AM/WIL B77 .... 46 F6
Swindale Cft COVS CV3 .... 155 K5
Swindell Rd HAG/WOL DY9 .... 120 A4
Swindon Rd HRBN B17 .... 105 M2
  KGSWFD DY6 .... 82 D5
Swinfen Broun Rd LICH WS13 ...... 20 E5
Swinford Gv DOR/KN B93 .... 172 C2
Swinford Leys WMBN WV5 .... 64 B8
Swinford Rd SLYOAK B29 .... 123 L2
  STRBR 119 L3
  WOLVN WV10 .... 36 C8
Swin Forge Wy SEDG DY3 .... 82 C3
Swiss Dr STRBR DY8 .... 101 K3
Swiss Lodge Dr
  POL/KGSB/FAZ B78 .... 45 K5
Swynnerton Dr WNSFLD WV11 .... 37 K1
Sycamore TAM/AM/WIL B77 .... 46 C6
Sycamore Av BHTH/HG B12 .... 107 L8
  POL/KGSB/FAZ B78 .... 47 L5
  REDE B98 .... 196 C5
Sycamore CI KIDD DY10 .... 137 K6
  RUSH/SHEL WS4 .... 39 M5
  STRBR DY8 .... 119 H3
Sycamore Crs
  CHWD/FDBR/MGN B37 .... 110 E5
  ERDE/BCHGN B24 .... 90 D2
  RCOVN/BALC/EX CV7 .... 96 F5
Sycamore Dr BDMR/CCFT WV3 ... 49 H4
  HLYWD B47 .... 145 M8
Sycamore Gn CNCK/NC WS11 ..... 12 C7
  DUDN DY1 .... 66 D8
Sycamore Gv
  RUGBYN/HIL CV21 .... 183 L1
  WWCK CV34 .... 199 L4
Sycamore Paddock
  STRBR DY8 .... 101 L4
Sycamore PI BILS/COS WV14 ..... 67 L2
Sycamore Rd AST/WIT B6 .... 89 L5
  BNTWD WS7 .... 18 D6
  BVILLE B30 .... 124 D6
  COVE CV2 .... 134 F3
  DARL/WED WS10 .... 68 E3
  DSYBK/YTR WS5 .... 53 K8
  ERDW/GRVHL B23 .... 72 D6
  GTB/HAM B43 .... 70 C2
  HDSW B21 .... 88 B5
  HEDN WS12 .... 17 K1
  KGSWFD DY6 .... 83 J7
  NUNW/HART CV10 .... 80 B7
  OLDBY B69 .... 104 E1
  POL/KGSB/FAZ B78 .... 39 M5
  RUSH/SHEL WS4 .... 105 M2
  SMTHWK B66 .... 105 M2
  TPTN/OCK DY4 .... 67 K6
The Sycamores BDWTH CV12 .... 116 C3
  WOLVN WV10 .... 36 D5
Sycamore Wy ACGN B27 .... 127 C1
  HEDN WS12 .... 12 B5
Sydenham Dr RLSS CV31 .... 200 F7
Sydenham Rd SMTHWK B66 ..... 87 L6
  SPARK B11 .... 108 A7
  WOLV WV1 .... 5 H3
Sydnall CI REDW B97 .... 195 K3
Sydnall Flds COVN CV6 .... 134 D1
Sydnall Rd COVN CV6 .... 116 D8
Sydney CI WBROM B70 .... 68 A6
Sydney Rd BORD B9 .... 108 A3
  BRGRVW B61 .... 185 J2
  CDYHTH B64 .... 102 F4
  SMTHWK B67 .... 105 J3
Syerscote La CRTAM B79 .... 32 B2
Sykesmoor TAM/AM/WIL B77 .... 46 F6
Sylvan Av NFLD/LBR B31 .... 143 K2
Sylvan Dr COVS CV3 .... 153 K7
Sylvan Gn RMSLY B62 .... 104 D8
Sylvia Av NFLD/LBR B31 .... 143 M5
Synkere CI
  RCOVN/BALC/EX CV7 .... 115 L7
Sytch La WMBN WV5 .... 64 B8
Sywell Leys RUGBYS/DCH CV22 .. 183 K7

T

Tabbs Gdns KIDD DY10 .... 137 L6
Tabeners La ATHST CV9 .... 63 H6
Table Oak La KNWTH CV8 .... 174 E3
Tachbrook CI COVE CV2 .... 135 G3
Tachbrook Park Dr RLSS CV31 .. 200 C7
Tachbrook Rd RLSS CV31 .... 200 D7
Tachbrook St RLSS CV31 .... 200 E7
Tack Farm Rd STRBR DY8 .... 101 H4
Tackford CI CBROM B36 .... 92 A4
Tackford Rd COVN CV6 .... 134 E6
Tackley CI SHLY B90 .... 146 F5
Tadmore Rd BILS/COS WV14 .... 51 L8
Tadworth CI WOLV WV1 .... 50 E3
Tainters HI KNWTH CV8 .... 176 D7
Tait Cft HIA/OLT B92 .... 128 D5
Talaton CI COVEN WV9 .... 35 L3
Talbot TAM/AM/WIL B77 .... 46 C2
Talbot Av FOAKS/STRLY B74 .... 55 L2
Talbot CI ERDW/GRVHL B23 ..... 72 B5
  WSLW WS2 .... 53 G7
Talbot PI BILS/COS WV14 .... 51 C7
Talbot Rd BKHL/PFLD WV2 ..... 50 A7
  BRGRVE B60 .... 185 J6
  DUDS DY2 .... 102 F1
  SMTHWK B66 .... 105 L1
Talbots La BDWTH CV12 .... 116 C4
Talbot St BRLYHL DY5 .... 102 C4
Talbot Wy SMTH B10 .... 108 D6
Talford St AST/WIT B6 .... 89 J7
Talfourd St BORD B9 .... 108 B4
Talgarth Covert
  HWK/WKHTH B38 .... 144 C6
Talisman CI KNWTH CV8 .... 191 K2
Talke Rd DSYBK/YTR WS5 ..... 53 K8
Talladale RIDG/WDGT B32 ..... 122 F6
Talland Av COVN CV6 .... 134 E7

  TAM/AM/WIL B77 .... 32 C8
Tallants CI COVN CV6 .... 134 E5
Tallants Rd COVN CV6 .... 134 D5
Tallington Rd
  LGN/SDN/BHAMAIR B26 .... 110 A6
Tall Trees CI BRGRVW B61 ...... 165 K5
  FOAKS/STRLY B74 .... 56 B1
  SHHTH WV12 .... 38 B7
Tall Trees Dr HAG/WOL DY9 .... 120 B3
Talton CI SHLY B90 .... 147 L8
Tamar CI BRWNH WS8 .... 26 A3
  RRUGBY CV23 .... 158 F8
Tamar Dr CBROM B36 .... 92 D5
  SEDG DY3 .... 66 D7
  WALM/CURD B76 .... 73 M6
Tamar Gv DUNHL/THL/PER WV6 . 48 C1
  WLNHL WV13 .... 52 A3
Tamarisk CI SLYOAK B29 ...... 123 M5
Tamar Ri STRBR DY8 .... 101 L5
Tamar Rd BDWTH CV12 .... 117 L3
  TAM/AM/WIL B77 .... 46 E8
Tame Av BNTWD WS7 .... 19 H7
  DARL/WED WS10 .... 69 G1
Tame Bank POL/KGSB/FAZ B78 . 60 A7
Tame Br DSYBK/YTR WS5 ...... 69 K1
Tame CI WSL WS1 .... 4 F9
Tame Crs HHTH/SAND B71 ..... 69 G7
Tame Dr BLOX/PEL WS3 .... 39 L4
Tamedrive POL/KGSB/FAZ B78 .. 45 L1
Tame Gdns CNCK/NC WS11 .... 16 B5
Tame Ri LGLYGN/QTN B68 ...... 104 F5
Tame Rd AST/WIT B6 .... 89 L3
  LGLYGN/QTN B68 .... 104 E5
  TPTN/OCK DY4 .... 68 A8
Tamerton Rd RIDG/WDGT B32 .. 123 H4
Tameside Dr CVALE B35 .... 91 L4
  PBAR/PBCH B42 .... 89 K1
Tame St BILS/COS WV14 .... 51 K8
  TAM/AM/WIL B77 .... 46 A2
  WBROM B70 .... 68 D5
  WSL WS1 .... 4 F9
Tame St East WSL WS1 .... 5 G9
Tamworth CI BRWNH WS8 ..... 26 A3
Tamworth Rd ATHST CV9 ...... 61 G4
  FOAKS/STRLY B74 .... 57 G6
  LICHS WS14 .... 21 G8
  LICHS WS14 .... 29 M2
  MGN/WHC B75 .... 57 H6
  POL/KGSB/FAZ B78 .... 47 J4
  POL/KGSB/FAZ B78 .... 60 B7
  RCOVN/BALC/EX CV7 .... 95 M5
  TAM/AM/WIL B77 .... 32 F7
Tamworth Rd (Amington)
  TAM/AM/WIL B77 .... 32 C8
Tamworth Rd (Dosthill)
  TAM/AM/WIL B77 .... 46 A7
Tamworth St LICH WS13 .... 20 F5
Tanacetum Dr DSYBK/YTR WS5 . 69 L2
Tandy Dr ALE/KHTH/YWD B14 .. 145 K2
Tandy's La KIDD DY10 .... 163 J1
Tanfield CI DUNHL/THL/PER WV6 . 48 F2
Tanfield Rd DUDS DY2 .... 84 F6
  STECH B33 .... 109 K2
Tanford Rd HIA/OLT B92 .... 128 A2
Tanglewood CI
  BKDE/SHDE B34 .... 92 A8
  BRGRVE B60 .... 166 E7
  RIDG/WDGT B32 .... 122 F1
Tanglewood Gv SEDG DY3 ..... 66 A3
Tangmere CI
  DUNHL/THL/PER WV6 .... 34 C8
Tangmere Dr CVALE B35 .... 91 L2
Tanhill TAM/AM/WIL B77 .... 46 F6
Tanhouse Av GTB/HAM B43 .... 70 A6
Tanhouse Farm Rd
  HIA/OLT B92 .... 128 A3
Tanhouse La HALE B63 .... 103 G8
  REDE B98 .... 189 G7
Tanners CI MGN/WHC B75 ..... 57 K6
Tanners Green La HLYWD B47 .. 169 L3
Tanners' La
  RCOVN/BALC/EX CV7 .... 151 M4
Tannery CI ATHST CV9 .... 63 J5
  WSLW WS2 .... 53 H2
Tansey Green Rd BRLYHL DY5 .. 83 M5
Tansley CI DOR/KN B93 .... 172 D1
Tansley Gv KGSTG B44 .... 71 K4
Tansley Hill Av DUDS DY2 ..... 85 K5
Tansley Hill Rd DUDS DY2 ..... 85 J5
Tansley Rd KGSTG B44 .... 71 K5
Tansley Vw BKHL/PFLD WV2 ... 50 B6
Tansy TAM/AM/WIL B77 .... 46 A2
Tantany La HHTH/SAND B71 ... 87 G1
Tantarra St WSL WS1 .... 5 H3
Tanwood CI REDW B97 .... 195 L7
  SOLH B91 .... 147 M5
Tanwood La KIDD DY10 .... 163 L3
Tanworth Gv BRMHL/HG B12 ... 107 K8
Tanworth La SHLY B90 .... 147 C5
Tanyard LICH WS13 .... 21 G5
Tanyard CI ALVE B48 .... 167 M7
  TLHL/CAN CV4 .... 152 A4
Tanyard La ALVE B48 .... 167 L7
Tanyards ACGN B27 .... 127 H2
Tapestries Av WBROM B70 .... 86 E1
Taplow PI CNCK/NC WS11 .... 16 D1
Tappinger Gv KNWTH CV8 .... 177 C8
Tapton CI BLOX/PEL WS3 ..... 39 G2
Tarlington Rd COVN CV6 ..... 133 H7
Tarmac Rd
  ETTPK/GDPK/PENN WV4 .... 50 D7
Tarn CI BDWTH CV12 .... 116 E3
Tarquin CI COVS CV3 .... 155 H6
Tarragon CI COVE CV2 .... 135 H4
Tarragon Gdns
  NFLD/LBR B31 .... 143 G3
Tarrant Gv RIDG/WDGT B32 ... 105 K8
Tarrant Wk COVE CV2 .... 135 L8
Tarrington Covert
  HWK/WKHTH B38 .... 144 C5
Tarry Hollow Rd BRLYHL DY5 .. 83 M5
Tarry Rd WASH/WDE B8 ...... 108 C1
Tarvin Rd BRLYHL DY5 .... 102 B4
Taryn Dr DARL/WED WS10 .... 52 B6
Tasker St WBROM B70 .... 86 C1
  WSL WS1 .... 4 D5
Tasman Gv
  DUNHL/THL/PER WV6 .... 34 C8

Tat Bank Rd OLDBY B69 ...... 86 F7
Tatnall Gv WWCK CV34 .... 199 J5
Taunton Av WOLVN WV10 ..... 36 B1
Taunton Rd BHTH/HG B12 .... 125 L1
Taunton Wy COVN CV6 .... 133 L3
Taverners CI SHHTH WV12 .... 38 A4
Taverner's Gn
  BFLD/HDSWWD B20 .... 88 D2
Tavistock Av CRTAM B79 ..... 32 A6
Tavistock Rd ACGN B27 ...... 127 C6
Tavistock St RLSN CV32 ...... 200 D4
Tavistock Wk COVE CV2 ...... 135 G6
Tavistock Wy NUN CV11 ...... 81 J8
Taw CI CBROM B36 .... 92 D6
Tay Cft CHWD/FDBR/MGN B37 . 111 G1
Tay Gv HWK/WKHTH B38 ..... 144 D5
  RMSLY B62 .... 104 C5
Taylor Av BLOX/PEL WS3 ..... 39 H5
  RLSN CV32 .... 200 F3
Taylor CI KNWTH CV8 .... 176 F7
Taylor Rd ALE/KHTH/YWD B14 . 125 K8
  DUDS DY2 .... 103 J5
  ETTPK/GDPK/PENN WV4 .... 50 D8
Taylor's La WBROM B71 ...... 87 H1
  OLDBY B69 .... 86 C6
  SMTHWK B67 .... 87 K8
Taylors Orch ERDW/GRVHL B23 . 89 M1
Taylor St WNSFLD WV11 ...... 37 M8
Tay Rd COVN CV6 .... 133 M7
  RBRY B45 .... 142 F4
Taysfield Rd NFLD/LBR B31 ... 123 J7
Taywood Dr SMTH B10 ...... 108 A6
Teachers CI COVN CV6 .... 133 L8
The Tea Gdn
  RCOVN/BALC/EX CV7 .... 116 C5
Tealby Gv SLYOAK B29 ...... 124 E4
Teal Crs KIDD DY10 .... 161 L2
Teal Dr ERDW/GRVHL B23 .... 89 M2
Teall Rd WASH/WDE B8 ...... 90 C8
Tean CI BNTWD WS7 .... 19 H7
  SPARK B11 .... 126 C2
Teasdale Wy HAG/WOL DY9 .. 120 B1
Teasel CI WOLVN WV10 ..... 22 F6
Teasel Rd WNSFLD WV11 .... 37 J8
Teazel Av BVILLE B30 .... 124 B7
Tebworth CI COVN CV9 ...... 35 K3
Tedbury Crs ERDW/GRVHL B23 . 72 C7
Tedder Rd WSLW WS2 .... 52 D3
Teddesley CI CNCK/NC WS11 . 16 C2
Teddesley Gv STECH B33 .... 110 A1
Teddesley Rd PENK ST19 .... 10 D4
Teddesley St RUSH/SHEL WS4 . 53 K2
Teddesley Wy HEDN WS12 ... 12 B8
Teddington Gv PBAR/PBCH B42 . 89 C2
Ted Pitts La COVW CV5 ...... 132 F3
Tedstone Rd RIDG/WDGT B32 . 105 J8
Teesdale Av BKDE/SHDE B34 . 91 K7
Teesdale CI WOLV WV1 ...... 50 E3
Tees Gv HWK/WKHTH B38 .... 144 D5
Teeswater CI BRGRVE B60 ... 185 J7
Teign TAM/AM/WIL B77 ...... 60 E1
Teignmouth Rd SLYOAK B29 . 124 D3
Telephone Rd COVS CV3 .... 155 G4
Telfer Rd COVN CV6 .... 133 M6
Telford Av GTWY WS6 ...... 24 C2
  RLSN CV32 .... 192 F8
Telford CI BNTWD WS7 ...... 18 F5
  HHTH/SAND B71 .... 68 C5
  SMTHWK B67 .... 105 H4
  WSLW WS2 .... 38 E8
Telford Gdns BDMR/CCFT WV3 . 49 H6
Telford Gv HEDN WS12 ...... 12 F6
Telford Rd CRTAM B79 ...... 31 K5
  RCOVN/BALC/EX CV7 .... 117 C5
  WSLW WS2 .... 38 E8
Telford Wy SMTHWK B66 .... 87 K6
Teme Av KIDDW DY11 .... 160 F2
Teme Gv WLNHL WV13 ...... 52 B3
Teme Rd HALE B63 .... 102 F8
  STRBR DY8 .... 119 K2
Tempest St BKHL/PFLD WV2 .. 5 G6
  CRTAM B79 .... 31 L8
Templar Av TLHL/CAN CV4 ... 152 E4
Templars' Flds TLHL/CAN CV4 . 152 F6
The Templars OLDBY B69 .... 86 C8
  WWCK CV34 .... 199 K8
Templars Wy PENK ST19 .... 10 D5
Temple Av HLGN/YWD B28 ... 126 E7
  RCOVN/BALC/EX CV7 .... 150 D7
Temple Bar WLNHL WV13 .... 51 L2
Temple CI REDE B98 .... 196 D1
Templefield Gdns BORD B9 .. 108 A4
Templefield St BORD B9 ..... 108 A4
Temple Gv WWCK CV34 ..... 199 H8
Temple La DOR/KN B93 ...... 173 L1
Temple Meadows Rd
  HHTH/SAND B71 .... 69 J7
Templemore Dr GTB/HAM B43 . 70 C6
Temple Pas CBHAM B2 ...... 6 F5
Temple Rd DOR/KN B93 ...... 172 E2
  WLNHL WV13 .... 51 L2
Temple Rw CBHAM B2 .... 7 C5
Temple Rw West CBHAMNW B3 . 6 F4
Temple Sq WLNHL WV13 .... 51 L2
Temple St BILS/COS WV14 ... 51 J8
  BKHL/PFLD WV2 .... 2 F8
  CBHAM B2 .... 6 F5
  SEDG DY3 .... 84 B2
  WBROM B70 .... 87 G1
Tenacre La SEDG DY3 ...... 66 C8
Ten Acres End BVILLE B30 .. 124 F5
Tenacres La REDE B98 ..... 197 K2
Ten Ashes La RBRY B45 .... 167 G1
Tenbury CI ALDR WS9 ...... 41 C5
  REDE B98 .... 189 C7
  WSLW WS2 .... 52 B2
Tenbury Ct
  ETTPK/GDPK/PENN WV4 ... 49 H8
Tenbury Gdns
  ETTPK/GDPK/PENN WV4 ... 65 H1
Tenbury Rd
  ALE/KHTH/YWD B14 .... 125 H7
Tenby CI BDWTH CV12 ...... 116 A4
Tenby Rd MOS/BIL B13 ..... 126 B3

Tenby St CBHAMW B1 .... 6 B2
Tenby St North CBHAMW B1 .. 6 B2
Tenby Wy STRPT DY13 ...... 160 C7
Teneriffe Rd COVN CV6 ..... 134 D4
Tenlands Rd HALE B63 ...... 121 K2
Tenlons Rd NUNW/HART CV10 . 98 D3
Tennal Dr RIDG/WDGT B32 ... 105 J7
Tennal Gv RIDG/WDGT B32 .. 105 K7
Tennal La RIDG/WDGT B32 ... 105 J7
Tennal Rd RIDG/WDGT B32 .. 105 J7
Tennant St EDG B15 .... 6 B8
  NUN CV11 .... 99 J2
Tennis Ct BVILLE B30 .... 144 B1
The Tennis Ct EDG B15 ..... 106 E8
Tennscore Av GTWY WS6 ... 24 C2
Tennyson Av BNTWD WS7 .. 18 E4
  CRTAM B79 .... 31 L7
  FOAKS/STRLY B74 .... 42 D7
  RUGBYS/DCH CV22 .... 183 J6
Tennyson CI KNWTH CV8 .... 192 A1
Tennyson Rd BLOX/PEL WS3 . 39 J5
  COVE CV2 .... 155 G2
  REDW B97 .... 196 A5
  SEDG DY3 .... 65 L8
  SHHTH WV12 .... 38 C5
  SMTH B10 .... 108 C6
  WOLVN WV10 .... 36 E4
Tennyson St BRLYHL DY5 .... 84 B7
Tennyson Wy KIDD DY10 .... 137 M7
Tenter Ct HALE B63 .... 121 M1
Tenter Dr HALE B63 .... 122 A2
Tenterfields HALE B63 ...... 121 M1
Tenter St ATHST CV9 .... 63 H5
Tern CI ETTPK/GDPK/PENN WV4 . 66 B2
Tern Gv HWK/WKHTH B38 .... 144 C5
Terrace Rd ATHST CV9 ...... 63 H5
  LOZ/NWT B19 .... 88 E6
Terrace St BLKHTH/ROWR B65 . 103 M4
  BRLYHL DY5 .... 84 B4
  DARL/WED WS10 .... 68 D2
The Terrace BDMR/CCFT WV3 . 49 G4
  CDYHTH B64 .... 103 J5
Terry Av LICH WS13 .... 20 D3
Terry Dr WALM/CURD B76 .... 73 K4
Terrys CI REDE B98 .... 188 D8
Terry St DUDS DY2 .... 85 H4
Tessall La NFLD/LBR B31 .... 143 H3
Tetbury Gv NFLD/LBR B31 ... 143 H2
Tetley Av RUSH/SHEL WS4 ... 53 L1
Tetley Rd SPARK B11 .... 126 C2
Tetnall St DUDS DY2 .... 85 H5
Tettenhall Rd
  DUNHL/THL/PER WV6 ..... 49 K2
Teveray Dr PENK ST19 ..... 10 D6
Teviot Gdns BRLYHL DY5 .... 83 L7
Teviot Gv HWK/WKHTH B38 . 144 D5
Tewkesbury Dr BDWTH CV12 . 117 L2
  DUDS DY2 .... 103 H2
Tewkesbury Rd
  BFLD/HDSWWD B20 ...... 89 J4
  BLOX/PEL WS3 .... 38 C3
Tew Park Rd HDSW B21 .... 88 C6
Thackeray CI NUNW/HART CV10 . 97 L1
  RUGBYS/DCH CV22 .... 183 K6
Thackeray Dr CRTAM B79 ... 31 L6
Thackeray Rd BVILLE B30 ... 124 B8
Thackhall St COVE CV2 ..... 9 L2
Thame Ct HLYWD B47 .... 169 J3
Thames CI BDWTH CV12 .... 117 L2
  BRLYHL DY5 .... 83 M6
Thames Rd BLOX/PEL WS3 . 39 H5
Thanet CI KGSWFD DY6 ..... 83 G7
Thanet Gv PBAR/PBCH B42 . 89 C1
Thatchway Gdns
  HWK/WKHTH B38 .... 144 C6
Thaxted Rd STECH B33 .... 110 C2
Theatre Ap DIG/EDG B5 .... 7 C7
Theatre St WWCK CV34 .... 199 H6
Thebes CI COVW CV5 ...... 131 M5
Theddingworth CI COVS CV3 . 155 J5
Theibridge Rd NFLD/LBR B31 . 143 J2
Thelma Rd TPTN/OCK DY4 ... 67 J7
Thelma St WSL WS1 .... 4 D7
Thelsford Wy HIA/OLT B92 . 128 B5
Thena Gdns COVN CV6 ..... 134 E4
Theodore CI HRBN B17 .... 124 B1
  OLDBY B69 .... 86 C4
Theresa Rd SPARK B11 .... 107 M6
Thetford CI TPTN/OCK DY4 . 67 H8
Thetford Gdns WNSFLD WV11 . 37 H7
Thetford Rd PBAR/PBCH B42 . 70 F6
Thetford Wy DSYBK/YTR WS5 . 70 A2
Thickett CI WSLW WS2 ..... 52 F5
Thicknall Dr HAG/WOL DY9 . 119 M3
Thicknall La HAG/WOL DY9 . 139 M2
Thicknall HI HAG/WOL DY9 . 139 L1
Thickthorn CI KNWTH CV8 . 191 M2
Thimble End Rd
  WALM/CURD B76 .... 73 L3
Thimble Mill La AST/WIT B6 . 89 M6
  VAUX/NECH B7 .... 89 M6
Thimblemill Rd SMTHWK B67 . 105 H1
Thimbier Rd TLHL/CAN CV4 . 153 C6
Third Av BORD B9 .... 108 D3
  BRWNH WS8 .... 26 E4
  SLYOAK B29 .... 125 G2
  WOLVN WV10 .... 36 C6
Third Exhibition Av
  BHAMNEC B40 .... 129 H1
Third Rd BRGRVW B61 ..... 165 K1
Thirlestane CI KNWTH CV8 . 177 C7
Thirlmere Av NUN CV11 .... 81 K7
Thirlmere CI CNCK/NC WS11 . 16 C4
  DUNHL/THL/PER WV6 .... 35 H5
  TLHL/CAN CV4 .... 152 C2
Thirlmere Dr MOS/BIL B13 . 126 A5
  WNSFLD WV11 .... 37 J3
Thirlmere Gv
  DUNHL/THL/PER WV6 .... 48 D1
Thirlmere Rd BDWTH CV12 . 116 E3
  STRPT DY13 .... 160 D7
Thirlmere Wk BRLYHL DY5 . 101 M6
Thirsk Cft CBROM B36 ..... 91 C5
Thirsk Rd COVS CV3 .... 154 A8
Thirston CI WNSFLD WV11 . 37 L8
Thistle CI SEDG DY3 .... 66 D7

Thistle Cft WNSFLD WV11 ... 37 H8
Thistledown Av BNTWD WS7 . 18 E7
Thistle Down CI
  FOAKS/STRLY B74 .... 55 L3
Thistledown Dr HEDN WS12 . 17 H4
  WOLVN WV10 .... 22 E6
Thistledown Rd BKDE/SHDE B34 . 92 A6
Thistle Gn HWK/WKHTH B38 . 144 C6
Thistlegreen CI
  BLKHTH/ROWR B65 .... 85 K8
Thistlegreen Rd DUDS DY2 . 103 J1
Thistle La RIDG/WDGT B32 . 122 F5
Thistlewood Gv
  DOR/KN B93 .... 173 M7
Thistley Fld East COVN CV6 . 133 K7
Thistley Fld North COVN CV6 . 133 L6
Thistley Fld South COVN CV6 . 133 K7
Thistley Fld West COVN CV6 . 133 K7
Thistley Nook LICH WS13 ... 20 E4
Thomas Crs SMTHWK B66 .. 88 A8
Thomas Guy Rd WBROM B70 . 9 C8
Thomas Landsdail St COVS CV3 . 9 G8
Thomas Lane St COVN CV6 . 134 E4
Thomas Mason CI
  WNSFLD WV11 .... 37 H6
Thomas Naul Cft
  TLHL/CAN CV4 .... 152 D2
Thomas Sharp St
  TLHL/CAN CV4 .... 152 E6
Thomas St AST/WIT B6 ..... 89 K7
  BDWTH CV12 .... 116 E3
  BKHL/PFLD WV2 .... 2 F8
  RLSN CV32 .... 200 E4
  SMTHWK B66 .... 87 M8
  TAM/AM/WIL B77 .... 46 B1
  WBROM B70 .... 87 H3
  WSLW WS2 .... 4 C1
Thomas Wy RRUGBY CV23 . 158 E8
Thompson CI DUDS DY2 .... 102 F3
  WLNHL WV13 .... 51 L2
Thompson Dr VAUX/NECH B7 . 90 D5
Thompson Gdns SMTHWK B67 . 105 H1
Thompson Rd
  LGLYGN/QTN B68 .... 104 F1
  SMTHWK B67 .... 105 K1
Thompson's Rd
  RCOVN/BALC/EX CV7 ..... 115 J7
Thompson St BILS/COS WV14 . 51 H8
  WLNHL WV13 .... 51 L2
Thomson Av NFLD/LBR B31 . 144 A4
Thomson CI RUGBYN/HIL CV21 . 159 M7
Thor CI CNCK/NC WS11 .... 12 E8
Thoresby CRTAM B79 ...... 31 J7
Thornberry Dr DUDN DY1 .. 84 B5
Thornbridge Av PBAR/PBCH B42 . 71 G6
Thornbury Ct
  DUNHL/THL/PER WV6 .... 48 E2
Thornbury La REDE B98 .... 189 G6
Thornbury Rd
  BFLD/HDSWWD B20 ...... 89 H3
Thornby Av KNWTH CV8 .... 191 L2
  SOLH B91 .... 127 M8
  TAM/AM/WIL B77 .... 46 C5
Thornby Rd ERDW/GRVHL B23 . 72 A5
Thorncliffe Rd KGSTG B44 . 71 J3
Thorncliffe Wy
  NUNW/HART CV10 .... 79 J5
Thorn CI DARL/WED WS10 . 68 D3
Thorncroft Wy DSYBK/YTR WS5 . 69 M1
Thorne Av WOLVN WV10 ... 36 C6
Thorne Rd WLNHL WV13 ... 51 L1
Thornes Cft ALDR WS9 .... 41 J1
Thorne St BKHL/PFLD WV2 . 50 E6
Thorneycroft La WOLVN WV10 . 36 E8
Thorneycroft Rd
  BILS/COS WV14 .... 67 L2
Thorney Rd COVE CV2 ..... 134 F7
  FOAKS/STRLY B74 .... 55 K4
Thornfield Crs BNTWD WS7 . 18 E5
Thornfield Cft SEDG DY3 ... 66 C6
Thornfield Rd ACGN B27 ... 127 G3
Thorngrove Av SOLH B91 .. 148 A5
Thornham Wy
  ALE/KHTH/YWD B14 ...... 145 H4
Thornhill Dr NUN CV11 ..... 99 M5
Thornhill Pk FOAKS/STRLY B74 . 55 L5
Thornhill Rd BRLYHL DY5 .. 102 C4
  COV CV1 .... 134 B8
  DUDN DY1 .... 85 G1
  FOAKS/STRLY B74 .... 55 L5
  HALE B63 .... 121 J2
  HDSW B21 .... 88 D5
  HEDN WS12 .... 12 D6
  REDE B98 .... 189 J6
  SOLH B91 .... 128 A6
  SPARK B11 .... 126 B2
Thornhurst Av RIDG/WDGT B32 . 105 J6
Thornleigh SEDG DY3 ..... 66 B8
Thornley CI MOS/BIL B13 .. 125 L4
  RLSS CV31 .... 201 L8
  WNSFLD WV11 .... 37 K4
Thornley Gv WALM/CURD B76 . 74 A7
Thornley Rd WNSFLD WV11 . 37 K4
Thornley St WOLV WV1 .... 3 G3
Thorn Rd BVILLE B30 ..... 124 C6
Thorns Av BRLYHL DY5 .... 102 C4
Thornsett Gv HIA/OLT B92 . 126 F7
Thorns Rd BRLYHL DY5 .... 102 C5
  HAG/WOL DY9 .... 102 C7
Thorn Side LICH RLSN CV32 . 193 J7
Thornthwaite CI RBRY B45 . 142 F3
Thornton CI COVW CV5 .... 152 A1
  OLDBY B69 .... 86 A3
  WWCK CV34 .... 199 K4
Thornton Dr BRLYHL DY5 . 102 C4
Thornton Rd SHLY B90 .... 147 K7
  WASH/WDE B8 .... 90 F8
  WOLV WV1 .... 50 F4
Thorntons Wy
  NUNW/HART CV10 .... 97 L2
Thornwood CI LGLYGN/QTN B68 . 87 G8
Thornyfield CI SHLY B90 .. 147 G2
Thornyfield Rd SHLY B90 . 147 G2
Thornyhurst La LICHS WS14 . 27 L8
Thorpe Av BNTWD WS7 .... 18 B5
Thorpe CI BNTWD WS7 .... 18 B5
  MGN/WHC B75 .... 57 G6

Thorpe Rd WSL WS1....4 F7
Thorpe St BNTWD WS7....18 B5
Thorp St DIG/EDG B5....6 F7
Threadneedle St COV CV1....134 A7
Three Corner Cl SHLY B90....146 C5
Three Cornered Rd RLSN CV32....193 J7
Three Oaks Rd HLYWD B47....169 M1
Three Shires Oak Rd
SMTHWKW B67....105 K3
Three Spires Av COVN CV6....133 L8
Three Tuns La WOLVN WV10....36 A3
Threshers Dr SHHTH WV12....38 B7
Throckmorton Rd REDE B98....196 E6
Throne Cl BLKHTH/ROWR B65....86 A8
Throne Crs BLKHTH/ROWR B65....104 D1
Throne Rd BLKHTH/ROWR B65....86 A8
Throstles Cl GTB/HAM B43....70 C6
Thrush Rd LGLYGN/QTN B68....104 D3
Thruxton Cl
ALE/KHTH/YWD B14....145 K2
REDE B98....197 J2
Thurcroft Cl WASH/WDE B8....108 D1
Thuree Rd SMTHWKW B67....105 H3
Thurleigh Cl HAG/WOL DY9....119 M3
Thurlestone Rd COVN CV6....133 K5
NFLD/LBR B31....143 J6
Thurloe Crs RBRY B45....142 C4
Thurlow Cl ATHST CV9....63 H3
Thurlston Av HIA/OLT B92....127 K1
Thurlstone Dr
ETTPK/GDPK/PENN WV4....65 K1
Thurlstone Rd BLOX/PEL WS3....38 F2
Thurnmill Rd
RUGBYN/HIL CV21....158 F8
Thursfield Rd HHTH/SAND B71....69 J6
RLSN CV32....200 F2
TPTN/OCK DY4....67 L7
Thurso TAM/AM/WIL B77....32 C8
Thurston Av OLDBY B69....86 D7
Thynne St WBROM B70....87 J3
Tibbats Cl RIDG/WDGT B32....123 G2
Tibberton Cl BDMR/CCFT WV3....49 H6
HALE B63....122 A2
SOLH B91....147 L5
Tibberton Ct BRGRVE B60....185 J6
Tibbets La HRBN B17....123 L1
Tibbington Rd TPTN/OCK DY4....67 J6
Tibbington Ter TPTN/OCK DY4....67 J6
Tiber Cl COVW CV5....152 D1
Tiberius Cl CSHL/WTROR B46....93 K4
Tiber Wy RUGBYN/HIL CV21....159 K6
Tibland Rd ACGN B27....127 H4
Tidbury Cl REDW B97....196 A7
Tideswell Cl COVS CV3....155 L4
Tideswell Rd PBAR/PBCH B42....71 C7
Tidmarsh Cl
RCOVN/BALC/EX CV7....150 E7
Tidmarsh Rd
RWWCK/WEL CV35....191 L6
Tidmington Cl
RWWCK/WEL CV35....198 C3
Tidworth Cft
ALE/KHTH/YWD B14....145 L2
Tierney Dr TPTN/OCK DY4....68 A7
Tiffany La COVEN WV9....35 K3
Tiffield Rd YDLY B25....109 C8
Tigley Av RIDG/WDGT B32....123 H4
Tilbury Gv MOS/BIL B13....125 C4
Tildasley St WBROM B70....68 F8
Tildesley Cl PENK ST19....10 C5
Tildesley Dr SHHTH WV12....37 M8
Tile Cross Rd STETCH B33....110 C4
Tiled House La BRLYHL DY5....83 M7
Tile Hill La COVW CV5....153 H4
TLHL/CAN CV4....152 F4
Tilehouse REDW B97....196 B3
Tilehouse Green La
DOR/KN B93....148 D6
Tilehouse La SHLY B90....146 C8
Tile Hurst Dr TLHL/CAN CV4....152 B3
Tilehurst Dr TLHL/CAN CV4....152 B3
Tilesford Cl SHLY B90....147 L8
Tilewood Av COVW CV5....152 C1
Tilia Rd TAM/AM/WIL B77....32 E8
Tilley St DARL/WED WS10....52 C7
Tillington Cl REDE B98....197 J3
Tillyard Cft SLYOAK B29....124 A4
Tilshead Cl ALE/KHTH/YWD B14....145 J2
Tilsley Gv ERDW/GRVHL B23....71 M8
Tilston Dr BRLYHL DY5....102 B4
Tilton Rd BORD B9....108 A4
Timberdine Cl HALE B63....103 H7
Timberhonger La BRGRVW B61....184 D4
Timberlake Cl SHLY B90....147 M7
Timber La STRPT DY13....160 F8
Timberley La BKDE/SHDE B34....92 A7
Timbers Wy ERDE/BCHGN B24....91 K1
SPARK B11....107 L7
Timbertree Crs CDYHTH B64....103 J6
Timbertree Rd CDYHTH B64....103 J6
Times Square Av BRLYHL DY5....102 D3
Timmins Cl SOLH B91....128 C2
Timmis Cl BILS/COS WV14....66 F2
Timmis Rd HAG/WOL DY9....102 A7
Timothy Gv TLHL/CAN CV4....152 F4
Timothy Rd OLDBY B69....86 A4
Tinacre Hl DUNHL/THL/PER WV6....48 C2
Tinchbourne St DUDN DY1....85 G4
Tindal St BHTH/HG B12....107 K8
Tink-a-tank WWCK CV34....199 J6
Tinkers Farm Gv
NFLD/LBR B31....143 J2
Tinkers Farm Rd NFLD/LBR B31....143 J1
Tinkers Green Rd
TAM/AM/WIL B77....46 E7
Tinkers La HOCK/TIA B94....171 H6
Tinmeadow Crs RBRY B45....143 G6
Tinsley St DARL/WED WS10....68 C8
Tintagel Cl
DUNHL/THL/PER WV6....48 D2
Tintagel Dr DUDN DY1....84 C3
Tintagel Gv KNWTH CV8....191 M1
Tintagel Wy NUN CV11....81 L8
Tintern Cl BRGRVW B61....185 J3
FOAKS/STRLY B74....55 L6

KIDDW DY11....136 D7
Tintern Ct
DUNHL/THL/PER WV6....48 C1
Tintern Crs BLOX/PEL WS3....38 D3
Tintern Rd BFLD/HDSWWD B20....89 J4
Tintern Wy BDWTH CV12....117 G2
BLOX/PEL WS3....38 D3
Tipperary Cl CBROM B36....91 J5
Tipper's Hill La
RCOVN/BALC/EX CV7....96 B7
Tippett Cl NUN CV11....99 L6
Tipping's Hl REDW B97....196 A8
Tipps Stone Cl TPTN/OCK DY4....85 J1
Tipton Rd DUDN DY1....85 J2
OLDBY B69....86 A3
SEDG DY3....66 C6
TPTN/OCK DY4....85 J1
Tirley Rd STECH B33....109 L1
Tisdale Ri KNWTH CV8....176 F7
Titania Cl RBRY B45....142 E2
Titan Wy LICHS WS14....21 K5
Titchfield Cl WOLVN WV10....36 C1
Titford Cl OLDBY B69....104 D1
Titford La OLDBY B69....104 C1
Titford Rd OLDBY B69....86 E8
Tithe Barn Cl
RWWCK/WEL CV35....198 D6
Tithe Barn La HOCK/TIA B94....170 F8
Tithe Cft WOLVN WV10....3 M2
Tithe Rd WNSFLD WV11....37 H7
Titterstone Rd NFLD/LBR B31....143 L5
Tiverton Cl KGSWFD DY6....101 L2
Tiverton Dr NUN CV11....81 J8
Tiverton Rd COVE CV2....135 H8
SLYOAK B29....124 D3
SMTHWK B66....87 M8
Tivycourt Rd COVN CV6....134 E2
Tividale Cl HALE B63....85 L3
Tividale St TPTN/OCK DY4....85 L2
Tixall Rd HLGN/YWD B28....126 C8
Tocil Cft TLHL/CAN CV4....177 H1
Toler Rd NUN CV11....80 F8
Tollard Cl COVE CV2....135 K8
Toll End Rd TPTN/OCK DY4....68 A5
Tolley Rd KIDDW DY11....160 F4
Tollgate Cl NFLD/LBR B31....143 K5
Tollgate Dr BFLD/HDSWWD B20....88 E6
Toll Gate La CRTAM B79....31 J2
Tollhouse Rd BRGRVE B60....185 J7
Toll House Rd RBRY B45....143 G6
Tollhouse Wy SMTHWK B66....87 K6
Tolman Dr TAM/AM/WIL B77....46 A2
Tolson Av POL/KGSB/FAZ B78....45 M5
Tolson Cl TAM/AM/WIL B77....46 A6
Tolworth Gdns
BKHL/PFLD WV2....50 C6
Tolworth Hall Rd
ERDE/BCHGN B24....90 F2
Tom Brown St
RUGBYN/HIL CV21....183 M1
Tomey Rd SPARK B11....108 B1
Tom Henderson Cl COVS CV3....155 K6
Tomkinson Dr KIDDW DY11....160 F1
Tomkinson Rd
NUNW/HART CV10....98 C1
Tomlan Rd NFLD/LBR B31....144 A6
Tomlinson Rd CBROM B36....92 B4
Tompstone Rd HHTH/SAND B71....69 K5
Tomson Av COVN CV6....8 C1
Tom Ward Cl COVS CV3....155 J6
Tonadine Cl WNSFLD WV11....37 L4
Tonbridge Rd COVS CV3....154 E7
ERDE/BCHGN B24....90 E4
Tong St WSL WS1....5 K3
Top Croft Rd ERDW/GRVHL B23....72 D6
Topfield Wk
ALE/KHTH/YWD B14....145 H3
Topland Gv NFLD/LBR B31....143 G3
Topp's Dr BDWTH CV12....116 C4
Topp's Heath BDWTH CV12....116 C4
Top Rd BRGRVW B61....165 L1
RCOVN/BALC/EX CV7....117 L6
Topsham Cft
ALE/KHTH/YWD B14....125 H8
Torbay TAM/AM/WIL B77....32 C8
Torbay Rd COVW CV5....153 G1
Torcastle Cl COVN CV6....134 D6
Torc Av TAM/AM/WIL B77....46 C1
Torcross Av COVE CV2....135 G8
Torfield CDSL WV8....35 J3
Toronto Gdns RIDG/WDGT B32....105 J7
Torpoint Cl COVE CV2....135 G6
Torquose Gv HEDN WS12....17 G2
Torrance Rd
RUGBYN/HIL CV21....183 K2
Torre Av NFLD/LBR B31....143 J3
Torrey Gv WASH/WDE B8....109 C1
Torridge TAM/AM/WIL B77....46 E8
Torridge Dr WNSFLD WV11....37 G8
Torridon Cl STRPT DY13....160 C6
Torridon Cft MOS/BIL B13....125 H2
Torridon Rd WNSFLD WV11....37 M4
Torrington Av TLHL/CAN CV4....152 D5
Torside TAM/AM/WIL B77....46 F6
Torton Cl KIDDW DY11....161 L8
Torvale Rd
DUNHL/THL/PER WV6....48 E3
Tor Wy BLOX/PEL WS3....39 K2
Torwood Cl TLHL/CAN CV4....152 D7
Totnes Cl COVE CV2....135 G6
Totnes Rd SMTHWK B66....87 K7
Tottenham Crs KGSTG B44....71 M3
Touchwood Hall Cl SOLH B91....148 A1
Tove Cl RRUGBY CV23....158 F8
Towbury Cl REDE B98....196 D8
Towcester Cft CBROM B36....91 H5
Tower Cft
CHWD/FDBR/MGN B37....110 F1
Tower Hl PBAR/PBCH B42....70 E7
Tower Ri NR OLDBY B69....86 A6
Tower Rd AST/WIT B6....89 K6
BDWTH CV12....116 E3
HEDN WS12....12 D4
MGN/WHC B75....56 F2
OLDBY B69....86 A6

Towers Cl KIDD DY10....137 M8
KNWTH CV8....191 K4
Tower St COV CV1....8 F3
DUDN DY1....85 G4
LOZ/NWT B19....89 H8
SEDG DY3....66 B4
WOLV WV1....3 G5
WSL WS1....4 F2
Tower View Crs
NUNW/HART CV10....97 M2
Tower View Rd GTWY WS6....24 D5
Townend St WSLW WS2....4 D4
Townesend Cl WWCK CV34....199 K4
Town Feilds Cl SHLY B90....132 F6
Townfields LICH WS13....20 E6
Townfold BLOX/PEL WS3....39 L1
Townley Gdns
BFLD/HDSWWD B20....89 J4
SEDG DY3....66 B5
Townsend Av BRGRVE B60....185 M1
Townsend Dr NUN CV11....99 K2
WALM/CURD B76....73 K6
Townsend La RRUGBY CV23....182 F1
Townsend Wy CBHAMW B1....6 B4
Townshend Gv
CHWD/FDBR/MGN B37....110 D1
Townson Rd WNSFLD WV11....37 K5
Townwell Fold WOLV WV1....2 E5
Towpath Cl BORD B9....107 M3
Towyn Rd MOS/BIL B13....126 B4
Tozer St TPTN/OCK DY4....67 K6
Traceys Meadow RBRY B45....142 E6
Trafalgar Cl HEDN WS12....17 J1
Trafalgar Ct OLDBY B69....85 M4
Trafalgar Gv ERDE/BCHGN B24....90 D2
HDSW B21....88 C5
MOS/BIL B13....125 K2
OLDBY B69....85 M4
SMTHWK B66....105 M1
Trafford Cl ATHST CV9....63 H3
Trafford Dr NUNW/HART CV10....80 A7
Trajan Cl CSHL/WTROR B46....93 K4
Tram St KIDD DY10....137 J8
Tram Wy SMTHWK B66....87 H8
Tramway Cl BILS/COS WV14....51 L6
DARL/WED WS10....52 C6
Tranter Crs HEDN WS12....16 F3
Tranter Rd WASH/WDE B8....90 E8
Tranwell Cl COVEN WV9....35 K3
Traquain Dr DUDN DY1....84 E2
Travellers Cl BNTWD WS7....18 E8
Treaford La WASH/WDE B8....108 F1
Treasure Cl TAM/AM/WIL B77....46 C1
Tredington Cl REDE B98....196 F6
Tredington Rd COVW CV5....152 D1
Tree Acre Gv HALE B63....121 G1
Treedale Cl TLHL/CAN CV4....152 B5
Treeford Cl SOLH B91....147 K4
Trees Rd WSL WS1....5 G9
Treeton Cft STETCH B33....109 L3
Treetops Dr SHHTH WV12....38 C8
Trefoil Cl SLYOAK B29....123 L6
Tregarron Rd HALE B63....103 G8
Tregea Ri GTB/HAM B43....70 A6
Tregony Ri LICHS WS14....21 H7
Tregorrick Rd
RCOVN/BALC/EX CV7....116 E6
Tregullan Rd
RCOVN/BALC/EX CV7....116 F5
Trehern Cl DOR/KN B93....148 E8
Treherne Rd COVN CV6....133 M5
Trehernes Dr HAG/WOL DY9....119 M4
Trejon Rd CDYHTH B64....103 J5
Trelawney Rd
RCOVN/BALC/EX CV7....96 D5
Tremaine Gdns WOLVN WV10....3 H1
Tremelling Wy
RCOVN/BALC/EX CV7....96 D5
Tremont St WOLVN WV10....3 K3
Trenance Cl LICHS WS14....21 H6
Trenance Rd
RCOVN/BALC/EX CV7....116 E6
Trenchard Cl MGN/WHC B75....57 K8
Treneere Rd
RCOVN/BALC/EX CV7....116 E5
Trensale Av COVN CV6....153 K1
Trent Cl BNTWD WS7....19 H7
DUNHL/THL/PER WV6....48 C1
STRBR DY8....119 L1
Trent Crs HLYWD B47....169 J3
Trent Dr CBROM B36....92 D5
Trentham Av SHHTH WV12....37 L8
Trentham Cl CNCK/NC WS11....16 F4
NUN CV11....99 K5
Trentham Gdns KNWTH CV8....177 G8
Trentham Gv
LGN/SDN/BHAMAIR B26....109 J8
Trentham Ri BKHL/PFLD WV2....50 D6
Trentham Rd NUNW/HART CV10....79 L3
Trent Pl BLOX/PEL WS3....39 H5
Trent Rd BDWTH CV12....117 L3
BLOX/PEL WS3....39 L4
CNCK/NC WS11....12 C8
NUN CV11....81 H8
Trent St DIG/EDG B5....7 K6
Trent Valley Rd LICH WS13....21 G5
Trenville Av SPARK B11....107 M3
Tresco Cl RBRY B45....142 C4
Trescott Rd NFLD/LBR B31....143 H2
REDE B98....196 D2
Tresham Rd KGSTG B44....71 J4
KGSWFD DY6....83 H5
Tresillian Rd
RCOVN/BALC/EX CV7....116 F5
Trevanie Av RIDG/WDGT B32....105 G7
Treville Cl REDE B98....197 J2
Treviscoe Cl
RCOVN/BALC/EX CV7....116 E6
Trevithick Cl BNTWD WS7....19 G5
STRPT DY13....160 E8
Trevor Av GTWY WS6....24 E2
Trevor Cl TLHL/CAN CV4....152 B5
Trevorne Cl BHTH/HG B12....107 K7
Trevor Rd BLOX/PEL WS3....39 K1

Trevor St VAUX/NECH B7....90 A7
Trevor St West VAUX/NECH B7....90 A6
Trevor White Dr
RUGBYS/DCH CV22....183 M4
Trevose Av
RCOVN/BALC/EX CV7....116 F6
Trevose Cl BLKHTH/ROWR WS3....38 D2
Trevose Retreat
BHTH/HG B12....107 K8
Trewman Cl WALM/CURD B76....73 K5
Treyamon Rd DSYBK/YTR WS5....54 B6
Treynham Cl WLNHL WV13....51 G4
The Triangle COVW CV5....152 F1
Trident Cl ERDW/GRVHL B23....72 E6
WALM/CURD B76....73 K6
Trident Dr DARL/WED WS10....68 B2
LGLYGN/QTN B68....86 F8
Trigo Cft CBROM B36....91 G5
Trimpley Cl DOR/KN B93....172 C2
Trimpley Dr KIDDW DY11....136 E6
Trimpley Gdns
ETTPK/GDPK/PENN WV4....65 J2
Trimpley La BEWD DY12....136 B8
Trimpley Rd RIDG/WDGT B32....122 F5
Trinder Rd SMTHWKW B67....105 H4
Trindle Rd DUDN DY1....85 H3
DUDS DY2....85 H4
Tring Ct DUNHL/THL/PER WV6....49 K1
Trinity Cl CNCK/NC WS11....16 C5
HIA/OLT B92....127 M4
STRBR DY8....119 L1
Trinity Ct KIDD DY10....137 L7
Trinity Flds KIDD DY10....137 K7
Trinity Gv DARL/WED WS10....68 C2
Trinity Hl CSCFLD/WYGN B72....57 G8
Trinity La COV CV1....8 F4
Trinity Rd AST/WIT B6....89 H4
BILS/COS WV14....51 K8
DUDN DY1....85 G4
MGN/WHC B75....56 F4
POL/KGSB/FAZ B78....46 F8
SHHTH WV12....38 B7
STRBR DY8....101 L5
Trinity Rd North WBROM B70....87 H3
Trinity Rd South WBROM B70....87 H4
Trinity St BRLYHL DY5....102 B2
CDYHTH B64....103 J4
COV CV1....9 G4
OLDBY B69....86 E8
RLSN CV32....200 D4
SMTHWKW B67....87 L7
WBROM B70....87 H4
Trinity Ter SPARK B11....7 M9
Trinity Wk NUN CV11....99 H3
Trinity Wy WBROM B70....87 H4
Trippleton Av
RIDG/WDGT B32....122 F5
RIDG/WDGT B32....122 F6
Tristram Av NFLD/LBR B31....143 M4
Triton Cl GTWY WS6....24 D4
Trittiford Rd MOS/BIL B13....126 A7
Triumph TAM/AM/WIL B77....46 C3
Triumph Cl COVE CV2....155 J2
Trojan TAM/AM/WIL B77....46 C2
Troon TAM/AM/WIL B77....47 G1
Troon Cl BLOX/PEL WS3....38 E2
MGN/WHC B75....57 H5
Troon Ct DUNHL/THL/PER WV6....34 B8
Troon Pl STRBR DY8....101 G2
Trossachs Rd COVW CV5....152 D2
Trotter's La HHTH/SAND B71....68 E6
Troughton Crs COVN CV6....133 L8
Trouse La DARL/WED WS10....68 C2
Troutbeck Av TAM/AM/WIL B77....46 A6
Troutbeck Dr BRLYHL DY5....101 M5
Troutbeck Rd COVW CV5....152 D1
Troyes Cl COVS CV3....154 B6
Troy Gv ALE/KHTH/YWD B14....145 H1
Truda St WSL WS1....4 D7
Trueman Cl WWCK CV34....199 J5
Truemans Heath La
HLYWD B47....145 M6
Truggist La
RCOVN/BALC/EX CV7....151 H5
Truro Cl BLKHTH/ROWR B65....104 C1
LICH WS13....20 F2
NUN CV11....81 K8
Truro Dr KIDDW DY11....136 E8
Truro Rd DSYBK/YTR WS5....54 B6
Trustin Crs HIA/OLT B92....128 C5
Tryan Rd NUNW/HART CV10....98 C1
Tryon Pl BILS/COS WV14....51 J7
Trysull Av
LGN/SDN/BHAMAIR B26....128 A3
Trysull Gdns BDMR/CCFT WV3....49 H6
Trysull Holloway WMBN WV5....64 A2
Trysull Rd BDMR/CCFT WV3....49 H6
WMBN WV5....64 C4
Trysull Wy DUDS DY2....103 G1
Tudbury Rd NFLD/LBR B31....143 H1
Tudman Cl WALM/CURD B76....73 L6
Tudor Av COVW CV5....152 D2
Tudor Cl BNTWD WS7....18 F7
GTWY WS6....24 C2
HLYWD B47....145 L4
LICHS WS14....21 K7
MOS/BIL B13....125 K7
RCOVN/BALC/EX CV7....150 E7
SCFLD/BOLD B73....72 B3
Tudor Ct TPTN/OCK DY4....85 L1
WNSFLD WV11....37 K2
WWCK CV34....199 H8
Tudor Crs ATHST CV9....63 H4
BKHL/PFLD WV2....49 M7
TAM/AM/WIL B77....46 D1
Tudor Cft
CHWD/FDBR/MGN B37....110 D4
Tudor Gdns ERDW/GRVHL B23....90 C2
STRBR DY8....101 J8
Tudor Gv FOAKS/STRLY B74....55 L5
Tudor Hl SCFLD/BOLD B73....56 F6
Tudor Pl SEDG DY3....66 C7
Tudor Rd BLKHTH/ROWR B65....86 A8
BNTWD WS7....19 G7
DARL/WED WS10....67 M1
HEDN WS12....12 D5
RCOVN/BALC/EX CV7....116 F7
SCFLD/BOLD B73....72 B3

NUNW/HART CV10....80 A7
SCFLD/BOLD B73....56 F8
SEDG DY3....66 C7
WOLVN WV10....50 E1
Tudor St TPTN/OCK DY4....85 L1
WSNGN B18....106 B1
Tudor Ter DUDS DY2....85 J4
Tudor V SEDG DY3....66 C7
Tudor Wy GTWY WS6....24 B4
Tufnell Gv WASH/WDE B8....90 E6
Tugford Rd NFLD/LBR B31....124 A6
SLYOAK B29....124 B3
Tuke Pl LICH WS13....20 D4
Tulip Tree Av KNWTH CV8....176 F8
Tulliver Cl BDWTH CV12....116 F1
Tulliver Rd NUNW/HART CV10....99 C5
Tulliver St COVN CV6....133 M8
Tulyar Cl CBROM B36....91 G5
Tunnel Dr REDE B98....196 C3
Tunnel La ALE/KHTH/YWD B14....144 F1
BVILLE B30....144 F1
Tunnel Rd NUNW/HART CV10....97 G2
WBROM B70....68 E5
Tunnel St BILS/COS WV14....67 G5
Tunstall Rd KGSWFD DY6....83 L8
Turchill Dr WALM/CURD B76....73 L5
Turfpits La ERDW/GRVHL B23....72 B7
Turf Pitts La MGN/WHC B75....43 G8
Turlands Cl COVE CV2....135 L6
Turley St DUDN DY1....66 E7
Turls Hill Rd SEDG DY3....66 C5
Turls St SEDG DY3....66 C6
Turnberry TAM/AM/WIL B77....32 F8
Turnberry Gv CDSL WV8....34 B8
Turnberry Rd BLOX/PEL WS3....38 E2
PBAR/PBCH B42....70 F5
Turner Av
ETTPK/GDPK/PENN WV4....66 D3
Turner Cl BDWTH CV12....116 E1
CNCK/NC WS11....17 H3
Turner Dr BRLYHL DY5....102 B6
Turner Gv DUNHL/THL/PER WV6....48 E1
Turner Rd COVW CV5....153 H2
Turners Cft HHTH/SAND B71....69 L5
Turner's Gv SEDG DY3....84 A1
Turner's Hl BLKHTH/ROWR B65....85 M7
Turner's Hill Rd SEDG DY3....84 A1
Turner St DUDN DY1....84 F5
SEDG DY3....66 A1
SPARK B11....107 L1
TPTN/OCK DY4....67 K6
WBROM B70....86 E1
Turney Rd STRBR DY8....101 K7
Turnham Gn
DUNHL/THL/PER WV6....48 C2
Turnhouse Rd CVALE B35....91 M1
Turnley Rd BKDE/SHDE B34....92 A7
Turnpike Cl SPARK B11....107 L7
Turnpike Dr CSHL/WTROR B46....93 C2
Turnstone Dr WOLVN WV10....22 F6
Turnstone Rd KIDD DY10....161 L4
Turpin Ct RLSS CV31....200 D7
Turton Cl BLOX/PEL WS3....38 E1
Turton Rd TPTN/OCK DY4....67 K4
WBROM B70....86 F3
Turtons Cft BILS/COS WV14....66 F2
Turton St KIDD DY10....137 L5
Turton Wy KNWTH CV8....192 A1
Turves Gn NFLD/LBR B31....143 K5
Turville Rd BFLD/HDSWWD B20....89 G4
Tustin Gv ACGN B27....127 G5
Tutbury TAM/AM/WIL B77....46 A6
Tutbury Av
DUNHL/THL/PER WV6....48 D2
TLHL/CAN CV4....153 J8
Tutbury Cl HEDN WS12....17 G2
Tutehill TAM/AM/WIL B77....46 F6
Tutnall Cl BRGRVE B60....186 D4
Tutnall La BRGRVE B60....186 D4
Tuttle Hl NUNW/HART CV10....80 C7
Tuxford Cl WOLVN WV10....3 J1
Twatling Rd BRGRVW B61....166 E3
Tweeds Well
RIDG/WDGT B32....122 F6
Twenty One Oaks ATHST CV9....62 C7
Twickenham Ct STRBR DY8....101 C6
Twickenham Rd KGSTG B44....71 M4
Twiners Rd REDE B98....196 D4
Two Gates HALE B63....102 F8
Two Gates La HALE B63....103 G8
Two Woods La BRLYHL DY5....102 C4
Twycross Gv CBROM B36....91 M4
Twydale Av OLDBY B69....85 M4
Twyford Cl ALDR WS9....30 F5
Twyford Gv WNSFLD WV11....37 K6
Twyford Rd WASH/WDE B8....91 G4
Twyning Rd BVILLE B30....124 F6
LDYWD/EDGR B16....106 B1
Tybalt Cl COVS CV3....155 G4
Tyber Dr BFLD/HDSWWD B20....88 F2
Tyberry Cl SHLY B90....146 E4
Tyburn Gv ERDE/BCHGN B24....91 H2
Tyburn Rd ERDE/BCHGN B24....90 F4
WOLV WV1....51 G4
Tyburn Sq ERDE/BCHGN B24....91 H2
Tyebeams BKDE/SHDE B34....92 A3
Tye Gdns HAG/WOL DY9....119 M4
Tyler Ct ERDE/BCHGN B24....90 D2
Tyler Gdns WLNHL WV13....51 M4
Tyler Gv PBAR/PBCH B42....70 E4
Tyler Rd WLNHL WV13....51 L3
Tylers Gn HWK/WKHTH B38....144 F4
Tylers Gv SHLY B90....147 K7
Tylney Cl COVS CV3....155 M3
DIG/EDG B5....107 H6
Tyndale Crs GTB/HAM B43....71 G2
Tyndall Wk RIDG/WDGT B32....122 E3
Tyne Cl BRWNH WS8....17 M8
CHWD/FDBR/MGN B37....110 F1
Tyne Gv YDLY B25....109 H5
Tynemouth Cl COVE CV2....117 H3
Tyne Pl BRLYHL DY5....102 D3
The Tynes BRGRVE B60....185 J6
Tyning Cl COVEN WV9....35 K3

256 Tyn - Wak

Tyninghame Av
DUNHL/THL/PER WV6 35 H7
Tynings Cl KIDDW DY11 136 F4
Tynings La ALDR WS9 40 E8
Tynsall Av REDW B97 195 K3
Tynward Cl COVS CV3 153 M8 5
Tyrley Cl DUNHL/THL/PER WV6 48 F3
Tyrol Cl STRBR DY8 101 H7
Tyseley Hill Rd SPARK B11 126 E1 1
Tyseley La SPARK B11 126 E1
Tysoe Cl HOCK/TIA B94 172 A7
REDE B98 197 H4
Tysoe Cft COVS CV3 155 K5
Tysoe Dr WALM/CURD B76 73 K1
Tysoe Rd KGSTG B44 71 K6
Tythe Barn Cl BRGRVE B60 185 H6
Tythebarn Dr KGSWFD DY6 82 E6
Tythebarn La SHLY B90 146 E7
Tyzack Cl BRLYHL DY5 102 A3 7

U

Udall Rd BILS/COS WV14 67 H2
Uffculme Rd BVILLE B30 125 H5
Uffmoor Est HALE B63 121 J3 5
Uffmoor La HALE B63 121 J4
RMSLY B62 121 H7
Ufton Cl SHLY B90 147 J2
Ufton Crs SHLY B90 147 H2
Ufton Cft COVW CV5 152 E2
Ullapool Cl REDW B97 196 B8 1
Ullenhall Rd DOR/KN B93 148 E7
WALM/CURD B76 73 K4 1
Ullenwood HDSW B21 88 B6 5
Ulleries Rd HIA/OLT B92 127 L3
Ullrik Gn ERDE/BCHGN B24 90 D3
Ullswater TAM/AM/WIL B77 46 F6 6
Ullswater Av NUN CV11 81 K7
RLSN CV32 200 A3
STRPT DY13 160 D7
Ullswater Cl RIDG/WDGT B32 123 K3
Ullswater Gdns KGSWFD DY6 83 H7 5
Ullswater Pl CNCK/NC WS11 16 C4 2
Ullswater Ri BRLYHL DY5 84 B8 1
Ullswater Rd BDWTH CV12 116 E3
COVS CV3 155 J4
WNSFLD WV11 37 M4
Ulster Cl CNCK/NC WS11 16 E2
Ulster Dr KGSWFD DY6 101 J1
Ulverley Crs HIA/OLT B92 127 K5
Ulverley Green Rd HIA/OLT B92 127 K5
Ulverscroft Rd COVS CV3 154 A6
Ulwine Dr NFLD/LBR B31 143 K1
Umberslade Rd HOCK/TIA B94 170 F5
SLYOAK B29 124 E5
Underhill Cl REDE B98 196 D7
Underhill La WOLVN WV10 36 E2
Underhill Rd TPTN/OCK DY4 68 A7
WASH/WDE B8 108 D2
Underhill St OLDBY B69 86 E8 4
Underley Cl KGSWFD DY6 82 F6 5
The Underpass BHAMNEC B40 129 H1
Underwood Cl EDG B15 124 B2
ERDW/GRVHL B23 90 A1
REDW B97 195 L6
Underwood Rd
BFLD/HDSWWD B20 70 C8
Unett St LOZ/NWT B19 89 G8 4
SMTHWK B66 106 A1
Unicorn Av COVW CV5 152 C1
Unicorn Hl REDW B97 196 B1 4
Unicorn La COVW CV5 152 D1
Union La WMBN WV5 64 B4
Union Mill St WOLV WV1 3 J5
Union Pl COVN CV6 116 D8
Union Rd AST/WIT B6 89 M5
OLDBY B69 86 C3
RLSN CV32 200 C4
SHLY B90 147 G3
SOLH B91 148 A1
WBROM B70 86 C3
Union Rw HDSW B21 88 D5
Union St BILS/COS WV14 51 G8
BLKHTH/ROWR B65 104 A4 14
BNTWD WS7 18 C8
CBHAM B2 7 G5
CNCK/NC WS11 16 C7
DARL/WED WS10 68 D3
DUDS DY2 85 G4 10
HAG/WOL DY9 102 C8
KIDD DY10 137 J6 4
REDE B98 196 D2
RUGBYS/DCH CV22 183 L3
STRBR DY8 119 L1
TPTN/OCK DY4 67 K8
WBROM B70 87 H5
WLNHL WV13 51 L3
WOLV WV1 3 H5
WSL WS1 5 H2
Unity Cl DARL/WED WS10 68 A1 2
Unity Pl OLDBY B69 86 E5 5
Unketts Rd SMTHWKW B67 105 J2
Unwin Crs STRBR DY8 101 J8
Upavon Cl CVALE B35 91 L1
Upland Gv BRGRVW B61 185 L1
Upland Rd BRGRVW B61 185 L1
SLYOAK B29 124 E3
Uplands COVE CV2 134 E8
HALE B63 121 H3
Uplands Av BDMR/CCFT WV3 49 H5
BLKHTH/ROWR B65 104 B2
WLNHL WV13 51 H4
Uplands Cl DUDS DY2 85 J6
PENK ST19 10 C3
Uplands Dr BDMR/CCFT WV3 49 J5
SEDG DY3 66 B5
Uplands Gv WLNHL WV13 51 G4
Uplands Rd DUDS DY2 85 J6
HDSW B21 88 B3
WLNHL WV13 51 G4
The Uplands SMTHWKW B67 105 K1
Upleadon Cl REDW B97 195 L7 2
Upper Abbey St NUN CV11 80 F8
Upper Ashley St RMSLY B62 104 A4 13
Upper Balsall Heath Rd
BHTH/HG B12 107 K7 5
Upper Brook St WSLW WS2 4 C3
Upper Chapel St OLDBY B69 85 M3
Upper Church La TPTN/OCK DY4 67 K6
Upper Clifton Rd
SCFLD/BOLD B73 56 F8
Upper Cl RIDG/WDGT B32 123 H2
Upper Coneybere St
BHTH/HG B12 107 K6 5
Upper Crossgate Rd REDE B98 197 G5
Upper Dean St DIG/EDG B5 7 G7
Upper Eastern Green La
COVW CV5 132 A8
Upper Ettingshall Rd
BILS/COS WV14 66 E5
Upper Field Cl REDE B98 189 G7
Upperfield Wy COVS CV3 155 L4 5
Upper Forster St
RUSH/SHEL WS4 53 K2
Upper Gambolds La
BRGRVE B60 186 A8
Upper Gough St CBHAMW B1 6 E8
Upper Gn DUNHL/THL/PER WV6 35 H8
Upper Green La WSLW WS2 53 G1
Upper Grosvenor Rd
BFLD/HDSWWD B20 88 F3
Upper Grove St RLSN CV32 200 C4
Upper Gungate CRTAM B79 31 M7
Upper Hall Cl REDE B98 197 H4
Upper Hall La WSL WS1 4 F4
Upper Highgate St
BHTH/HG B12 107 K6
Upper High St CDYHTH B64 103 H4
DARL/WED WS10 68 D2 5
Upper Holland Rd
CSCFLD/WYGN B72 73 G1
Upper Holly Wk RLSN CV32 200 F4
Upper Landywood La
GTWY WS6 24 C5
Upper Lichfield St WLNHL WV13 51 L3
Upper Marshall St CBHAMW B1 6 E7 5
Upper Meadow Rd
RIDG/WDGT B32 105 G8
Upper Navigation St WSLW WS2 4 D2
Upper Pk COVS CV3 155 H8
Upper Ride COVS CV3 155 H8
Upper Rosemary Hl
KNWTH CV8 176 D8
Upper Rushall St WSL WS1 5 G3
Upper Russell St
DARL/WED WS10 68 D3 11
Upper St John St LICHS WS14 20 F7
Upper St Mary's Rd
SMTHWKW B67 105 K4
Upper Short St WSLW WS2 4 C3
Upper Sneyd Rd WNSFLD WV11 37 M3
Upper Spon St COV CV1 8 B5
Upper Spring La KNWTH CV8 176 D6
Upper St DUNHL/THL/PER WV6 35 H8
Upper Sutton St AST/WIT B6 89 K6 5
Upper Thomas St AST/WIT B6 89 K5 1
Upper Trinity St BORD B9 7 L7
Upper Vauxhall WOLV WV1 2 B4
Upper Villiers St
ETTPK/GDPK/PENN WV4 49 M7
Upper Well St COV CV1 8 E3
Upper William St CBHAMW B1 6 C7
Upper York St COV CV1 8 C6
Upper Zoar St BDMR/CCFT WV3 2 C8
Upton Cl REDE B98 197 K2 2
Upton Gdns BILS/COS WV14 51 G8 4
Upton Gv YDLY B25 109 G4
Upton Rd KIDD DY10 137 K4
RUGBYS/DCH CV22 183 H2
STETCH B33 109 G3
Upton St DUDS DY2 85 G8
Upwey Av SOLH B91 147 L1
Usk Wy CBROM B36 92 D5
Usmere Rd KIDD DY10 137 K5
Utrillo Cl COVW CV5 153 G2
Uttoxeter Cl
DUNHL/THL/PER WV6 35 M8 4
Uxbridge Av COVS CV3 155 G3
Uxbridge Cl SEDG DY3 84 B3 5
Uxbridge St HEDN WS12 17 G1
LOZ/NWT B19 89 H8

V

Valbourne Rd
ALE/KHTH/YWD B14 145 G1
Vale Av ALDR WS9 55 H3
Vale Cl LICH WS13 20 F4 5
RIDG/WDGT B32 123 K2
Vale Gdns PENK ST19 10 C5
Valencia Cft CVALE B35 91 M1 5
Valentine Cl FOAKS/STRLY B74 55 K6
Valentine Rd
ALE/KHTH/YWD B14 125 J4
LGLYGN/QTN B68 105 G3
Valepits Rd STETCH B33 110 A4
Valerie Gv GTB/HAM B43 70 A5
Vale Ri PENK ST19 10 C5
Vale Rd DUDS DY2 103 J1
Vale Rw SEDG DY3 66 B8 2
Vales Cl WALM/CURD B76 73 J6
Vale St BKHL/PFLD WV2 50 E7
HHTH/SAND B71 69 J7
SEDG DY3 66 B8
STRBR DY8 101 K5
The Vale COVS CV3 154 F5
SPARK B11 125 M3
Vale Vw ALDR WS9 54 F2
NUNW/HART CV10 98 C1
Valley Cl KIDDW DY11 136 C5
REDW B97 195 L7
Valley Dr RRUGBY CV23 159 K4
Valley Farm Rd RBRY B45 142 D7
Valley Gn GTWY WS6 24 C3
Valley La HOCK/TIA B94 173 H6
LICH WS13 21 H5
TAM/AM/WIL B77 46 C6 2
Valley Rd BLOX/PEL WS3 39 H5
BRGRVW B61 165 J6
CDYHTH B64 103 J6
COVE CV2 134 E7
FOAKS/STRLY B74 55 K6
GTB/HAM B43 70 A6
HAG/WOL DY9 102 D8
HEDN WS12 13 L7
HIA/OLT B92 128 A1
HOCK/TIA B94 170 E4
NUNW/HART CV10 97 K1
RLSN CV32 200 F3
RMSLY B62 104 D5
SEDG DY3 66 C7
SMTHWKW B67 105 K2
WOLVN WV10 36 D8
Valley Side BLOX/PEL WS3 39 K3
The Valley BNTWD WS7 18 B5
Valley Vw BRWNH WS8 26 E6
Vallian Cft CBROM B36 91 K6
Vanborough Wk DUDN DY1 84 E3
Vanbrugh Ct
DUNHL/THL/PER WV6 48 C2
Van Diemans Rd WMBN WV5 64 C8
Van Dyke Cl COVW CV5 153 G2 1
Van Gogh Cl CNCK/NC WS11 17 H3
Vanguard TAM/AM/WIL B77 46 B7
Vanguard Cl CBROM B36 91 J4 1
Vann Cl SMTHH B10 108 A5 2
Varden Cft DIG/EDG B5 107 H7
Vardon Dr COVS CV3 178 B1
Vardon Wy HWK/WKHTH B38 144 B4
Varley Rd ERDE/BCHGN B24 91 H1
Varley V ERDE/BCHGN B24 91 H1
Varlins Wy HWK/WKHTH B38 144 B7
Varney Av WBROM B70 87 H3
Vaughan Cl FOAKS/STRLY B74 42 D7
Vaughan Gdns CDSL WV8 34 D1 5
Vaughan Rd WLNHL WV13 51 H4
Vaughton Dr MGN/WHC B75 57 J7
Vaughton St BHTH/HG B12 107 K5
Vaughton St South
DIG/EDG B5 107 J6
Vauxhall Av COVW CV5 153 G4
WOLV WV1 2 B4
Vauxhall Cl COV CV1 9 K3 5
Vauxhall Crs CBROM B36 92 D4
Vauxhall Gdns DUDS DY2 85 J6
Vauxhall Gv VAUX/NECH B7 107 M2
Vauxhall Rd STRBR DY8 101 L8
VAUX/NECH B7 7 M3
Vauxhall St COV CV1 9 K3
DUDN DY1 84 F5
Vaynor Dr REDW B97 196 B5
Veasey Cl NUN CV11 99 J2
Vecqueray St COV CV1 9 K5
Velsheda Rd SHLY B90 146 E3
Venetia Rd BORD B9 108 A3
Venning Gv GTB/HAM B43 70 B6
Ventnor Av CBROM B36 91 H6
LOZ/NWT B19 89 G6
Ventnor Cl COVE CV2 155 J2
LGLYGN/QTN B68 105 G6
Ventnor Rd HIA/OLT B92 128 A2
Ventnor St NUNW/HART CV10 81 G7
Ventura Park Rd
POL/KGSB/FAZ B78 45 K2
Venture Wy VAUX/NECH B7 7 K1
Vera Rd
LGN/SDN/BHAMAIR B26 109 J6
Vera Roberts Wy
KIDDW DY11 160 F2 2
Verbena Gdns VAUX/NECH B7 89 L8 1
Verbena Rd NFLD/LBR B31 123 K8
Vercourt FOAKS/STRLY B74 55 M2
Verdi Ct LICH WS13 21 G3
Verdon Cl PENK ST19 10 E6 2
Vere St DIG/EDG B5 107 H5
Verity Wk STRBR DY8 101 J4
Vermont Gn CNCK/NC WS11 16 E2 5
Vermont Gv RLSS CV31 201 H7
Verney Av STETCH B33 110 B6 2
Vernier Av KGSWFD DY6 83 L8
Vernon Av BFLD/HDSWWD B20 88 D1
BRWNH WS8 26 E6
TPTN/OCK DY4 85 J1
Vernon Cl COV CV1 9 K3 4
FOAKS/STRLY B74 42 C8
REDE B98 188 D8
RLSN CV32 200 C2
RMSLY B62 104 B5 2
WLNHL WV13 51 J4
WNSFLD WV11 37 K1 1
Vernon Rd BILS/COS WV14 51 K7
LDYWD/EDGR B16 106 B4
LGLYGN/QTN B68 87 G7
RMSLY B62 104 A5 2
Vernons La NUNW/HART CV10 98 D1
Vernons Pl WOLVN WV10 23 H4
Vernon St WBROM B70 86 C2
Vernon Wy BLOX/PEL WS3 38 C4
Verona Cl NUN CV11 99 L4
Veronica Av
ETTPK/GDPK/PENN WV4 50 C8
Veronica Cl SLYOAK B29 123 K7
Veronica Rd KGSWFD DY6 83 L7
Verstone Cft NFLD/LBR B31 143 L3
Verstone Rd SHLY B90 147 G1
Verwood Cl WLNHL WV13 51 H4 4
Vesey Cl CSHL/WTROR B46 92 F3
FOAKS/STRLY B74 56 D3
Vesey Rd SCFLD/BOLD B73 72 F4
Vesey St CBHAMNE B4 7 G2
Vestry Cl CDYHTH B64 103 K4
Vestry Ct STRBR DY8 101 J7 2
Viaduct Dr
DUNHL/THL/PER WV6 35 M7
Viaduct St VAUX/NECH B7 7 M4
Vibart Rd
LGN/SDN/BHAMAIR B26 109 K5
Vicarage Cl ATHST CV9 63 J6
BRGRVE B60 185 M5
BRLYHL DY5 102 A6 6
BRWNH WS8 26 E5
BVILLE B30 124 F6
PBAR/PBCH B42 71 H6
POL/KGSB/FAZ B78 47 K8
TPTN/OCK DY4 67 J8 10
Vicarage Crs KIDD DY10 137 K8
REDW B97 196 A2
Vicarage Fld WWCK CV34 199 M5
Vicarage Gdns RMSLY B62 104 B4 1
WALM/CURD B76 73 K6 5
Vicarage Hl POL/KGSB/FAZ B78 58 F4
Vicarage La BRLYHL DY5 84 B5
CSHL/WTROR B46 92 F3
RCOVN/BALC/EX CV7 116 B6
Vicarage Pl WSL WS1 4 E4
Vicarage Prospect DUDN DY1 84 F4 2
Vicarage Rd
ALE/KHTH/YWD B14 125 G6
AST/WIT B6 89 L6
BILS/COS WV14 67 G6
BKHL/PFLD WV2 3 H8
BLOX/PEL WS3 39 L3
BRWNH WS8 26 D6
DARL/WED WS10 68 D2
EDG B15 106 D5
ETTPK/GDPK/PENN WV4 65 J2
HAG/WOL DY9 102 D8
HHTH/SAND B71 69 H7 5
HOCK/TIA B94 171 G2
HOCK/TIA B94 172 C6
HRBN B17 105 M8
KIDD DY10 162 C3
KNWTH CV8 177 M7
LGLYGN/QTN B68 104 F1
RLSN CV32 200 E2
RMSLY B62 104 A5
RUGBYS/DCH CV22 183 K3
SEDG DY3 66 C8
SMTHWKW B67 87 K8
STETCH B33 109 J4
STRBR DY8 101 H6
WNSFLD WV11 36 F7
WOLVN WV10 14 C7
WSNGN B18 88 E6
Vicarage Rd West DUDN DY1 67 G7
Vicarage St LGLYGN/QTN B68 86 F8
NUN CV11 99 G1
OLDBY B69 86 F8
Vicarage Ter WSLW WS2 4 A5
Vicarage Vw REDW B97 196 B2
Vicarage Wk WSL WS1 4 E4
Vicar St DARL/WED WS10 68 E2
DUDS DY2 85 G5
KIDD DY10 137 J7
SEDG DY3 66 B5
Vicars Wk HAG/WOL DY9 120 C3 5
Viceroy Cl EDG B15 107 G7
KGSWFD DY6 83 L8 5
Victor Cl BKHL/PFLD WV2 50 F7 2
Victoria Av BLOX/PEL WS3 39 G4
RMSLY B62 104 D7
RUGBYN/HIL CV21 183 K2
Victoria Dr POL/KGSB/FAZ B78 45 L5 2
Victoria Gdns CDYHTH B64 103 K3 4
LICH WS13 20 D7
Victoria Gv WMBN WV5 64 E5
Victoria Ms OLDBY B69 104 D2 3
RUSH/SHEL WS4 53 L2 5
Victoria Park Rd SMTHWK B66 87 M8
Victoria Pas WOLV WV1 2 F5
Victoria Pl KIDDW DY11 160 F2
Victoria Rd ACGN B27 127 G3
AST/WIT B6 89 J6
ATHST CV9 63 K7
BDMR/CCFT WV3 49 J6
BLOX/PEL WS3 39 L2
BRGRVW B61 164 D6
BRGRVW B61 185 L2
BRLYHL DY5 102 E4
BVILLE B30 124 E6
CDYHTH B64 103 K3
CRTAM B79 32 A8
CSCFLD/WYGN B72 57 G8
DARL/WED WS10 52 B7
DUNHL/THL/PER WV6 35 J8
ERDW/GRVHL B23 90 B2
HDSW B21 88 C6
HRBN B17 105 M8
LGLYGN/QTN B68 87 G7
NUNW/HART CV10 79 M5
RLSS CV31 200 C5
RMSLY B62 104 B5 5
SEDG DY3 66 C5 1
STETCH B33 109 H2
TPTN/OCK DY4 67 K8
WNSFLD WV11 36 F7
WOLVN WV10 36 D8
Victoria Sq CBHAMNW B3 6 E5
Victoria St BORD B9 108 B3
BRLYHL DY5 84 A6
BRLYHL DY5 102 B2
CNCK/NC WS11 16 B5
CNCK/NC WS11 16 C1
COV CV1 9 H2
DARL/WED WS10 68 C3
HALE B63 121 L1 5
HEDN WS12 13 G7
KGSWFD DY6 82 F4
NUN CV11 98 F1
REDE B98 196 C1 2
RLSS CV31 200 C6
RUGBYN/HIL CV21 183 J2
STRBR DY8 101 L8 7
WBROM B70 68 D8
WBROM B70 87 G2 5
WLNHL WV13 51 L2
WOLV WV1 2 F6
WWCK CV34 199 H6
Victoria Ter RLSS CV31 200 D6
RUSH/SHEL WS4 53 K2
Victor Rd HIA/OLT B92 128 C2
WSNGN B18 88 C7
Victor St BLOX/PEL WS3 39 L4
WSL WS1 4 E7
Victory Av BNTWD WS7 18 D6
DARL/WED WS10 68 A1
Victory Cl HEDN WS12 17 J1
Victory La WSLW WS2 52 E1
Victory Ri HHTH/SAND B71 69 H8 5
Victory Rd COVN CV6 134 C5
View Dr DUDS DY2 85 J5
Viewfield Av HEDN WS12 12 D6
Viewfield Crs SEDG DY3 66 B6
Viewlands Dr
DUNHL/THL/PER WV6 48 E3
View St HEDN WS12 12 D7
Vigo Cl ALDR WS9 40 D3
Vigo Pl ALDR WS9 40 E6
Vigo Rd ALDR WS9 40 D3
Vigo Ter ALDR WS9 40 D2
Viking Ri BLKHTH/ROWR B65 104 A1 1
Villa Cl BDWTH CV12 117 M4
Villa Crs BDWTH CV12 117 M4
Village Rd AST/WIT B6 89 L4
The Village KGSWFD DY6 83 J6
Village Wy BILS/COS WV14 50 F8
Villa Rd COVN CV6 133 M7
LOZ/NWT B19 88 F6
Villa St LOZ/NWT B19 88 F6
STRBR DY8 101 L5
Villa Wk LOZ/NWT B19 89 G7
Villette Gv ALE/KHTH/YWD B14 146 A1
Villiers Av BILS/COS WV14 51 H7
Villiers Rd BRGRVE B60 185 H6
KNWTH CV8 176 F8
Villiers St COVE CV2 9 M3
KIDD DY10 137 L8
NUN CV11 98 F2
RLSN CV32 200 E4
WLNHL WV13 51 L3
WSL WS1 4 E7
Vimy Rd DARL/WED WS10 68 E1
MOS/BIL B13 125 M5
Vincent Cl BHTH/HG B12 107 K7 6
Vincent Dr EDG B15 124 B2
Vincent Pde BHTH/HG B12 107 K7
Vincent Rd MGN/WHC B75 57 J6
Vincent St BHTH/HG B12 107 K8
COV CV1 8 C5 1
RLSN CV32 200 E4
WSL WS1 5 G7
Vince St SMTHWK B66 105 L2
Vinculum Wy WLNHL WV13 51 M5
Vine Av BHTH/HG B12 107 L8 15
Vinecote Rd COVN CV6 134 D1
Vine Crs HHTH/SAND B71 69 H7 4
Vine La CNCK/NC WS11 16 B8
HAG/WOL DY9 140 D2
HALE B63 121 M2
WWCK CV34 199 J5
The Vineries ACGN B27 127 J1
Vine St AST/WIT B6 89 M6
BRLYHL DY5 84 C8
COV CV1 9 H2
KIDD DY10 137 L5
REDW B97 196 B1
STRBR DY8 101 J4
Vineyard Rd NFLD/LBR B31 123 K8
Vinnall Gv RIDG/WDGT B32 122 F5
Vintage Cl STETCH B33 91 L8 5
Vinyard Cl WSNGN B18 88 D6 1
Violet Cl COVE CV2 135 G3
Violet Cft TPTN/OCK DY4 67 M4
Violet La HAG/WOL DY9 140 C1
Virginia Dr
ETTPK/GDPK/PENN WV4 65 K1
Virginia Pl NUNW/HART CV10 98 C2
Virginia Rd COV CV1 9 J3
Viscount Cl CVALE B35 91 L3
RLSS CV31 200 D7
Viscount Rd BNTWD WS7 18 C4
Vista Gn HWK/WKHTH B38 144 E4
The Vista SEDG DY3 66 B4
Vittoria St CBHAMW B1 6 C2
SMTHWK B66 88 B7
Vivian Cl HRBN B17 106 A8
Vivian Rd HRBN B17 106 A8
Vixen Cl WALM/CURD B76 73 H6 2
Vogue Cl COV CV1 9 J3
Voyager Dr CNCK/NC WS11 16 D7
Vulcan Rd BILS/COS WV14 51 K8
LICH WS13 21 J4
SOLH B91 128 A7
Vyrnwy Gv HWK/WKHTH B38 144 C5
Vyse St AST/WIT B6 89 M5
WSNGN B18 6 C1

W

Wackrill Dr RLSN CV32 201 G2
Waddell Cl BILS/COS WV14 66 D4
Waddens Brook La
WNSFLD WV11 37 J8
Waddington Av GTB/HAM B43 70 C4
Wade Av COVS CV3 153 M8
Wadebridge Dr NUN CV11 99 K1
Wade Gv WWCK CV34 199 J3
Wadesmill Lawns
WOLVN WV10 36 C1 4
Wade St LICH WS13 20 F6
Wadham Cl OLDBY B69 86 A7
Wadhurst Rd HRBN B17 105 M3
Wadleys Rd SOLH B91 127 K7 1
Waen Cl TPTN/OCK DY4 67 M5
Waggoners Cl BRGRVE B60 185 J7 5
KNWTH CV8 179 G8
Waggoner's La
POL/KGSB/FAZ B78 44 C5
Waggon La KIDD DY10 138 C2
Waggon St CDYHTH B64 103 K3 5
Waggon Wk HWK/WKHTH B38 144 A5
Wagoners Cl WASH/WDE B8 90 D7
Wagon La HIA/OLT B92 127 K1
LGN/SDN/BHAMAIR B26 109 L8
Wagstaff Cl BILS/COS WV14 67 H5 5
Wainbody Av North COVS CV3 153 L8
Wainbody Av South COVS CV3 177 K1
Wainrigg TAM/AM/WIL B77 46 F6 7
Wainwright Cl KGSWFD DY6 82 E6 2
Wainwright St AST/WIT B6 89 L6
Waite Rd WLNHL WV13 51 J5
Wakefield Cl ATHST CV9 77 G1 1
COVS CV3 155 K6 6
SCFLD/BOLD B73 72 E3
Wakefield Gv
CSHL/WTROR B46 92 F2 5
Wakeford Cl NUNW/HART CV10 78 E2
Wakeford Rd NFLD/LBR B31 144 A4
Wake Green Pk MOS/BIL B13 125 M3
Wake Green Rd MOS/BIL B13 125 L3
TPTN/OCK DY4 67 L4
Wake Gv WWCK CV34 198 F8 1
Wakehurst Cl NUN CV11 99 K5 4
Wakelam Gdns GTB/HAM B43 70 B4

Wakeley HI
  ETTPK/GDPK/PENN WV4 ...... 65 K1
Wakelin Rd SHLY B90 ...... 146 F6
Wakeman Gv STETCH 110 B6
Wakes CI WLNHL WV13 ...... 51 M4
Wakes Rd DARL/WED WS10 ...... 68 E3
Walcot CI MGN/WHC B75 ...... 56 F2
Walcot Dr GTB/HAM B43 ...... 70 C7
Walcot Gdns BILS/COS WV14 ...... 50 F8
Walcot Gn DOR/KN B93 ...... 172 E3
Waldale CI SHHTH WV12 ...... 38 A4
Walden Gdns
  ETTPK/GDPK/PENN WV4 ...... 49 J7
Walden Rd SPARK B11 ...... 126 E2
Waldeve Gv HIA/OLT B92 ...... 128 C5
Waldley Gv ERDE/BCHGN B24 ...... 91 C2
Waldron Av BRLYHL DY5 ...... 101 M3
Waldron CI DARL/WED WS10 ...... 52 D7
Waldrons Moor
  ALE/KHTH/YWD B14 ...... 125 C8
Walford Dr HIA/OLT B92 ...... 128 C3
Walford Gv WWCK CV34 ...... 199 K4
Walford Rd SPARK B11 ...... 108 A7
Walford St OLDBY B69 ...... 85 K3
Walhouse CI WSL WS1 ...... 5 H2
Walhouse Dr PENK ST19 ...... 10 D6
Walhouse Rd WSL WS1 ...... 5 H2
Walhouse St CNCK/NC WS11 ...... 16 C5
Walker Av BRLYHL DY5 ...... 102 B6
  HAG/WOL DY9 ...... 120 B2
  OLDBY B69 ...... 86 A6
  WOLVN WV10 ...... 36 C5
Walker Dr KIDD DY10 ...... 137 L4
  VAUX/NECH B7 ...... 90 C5
Walker PI BLOX/PEL WS3 ...... 39 J7
Walker Rd BLOX/PEL WS3 ...... 39 H5
Walkers Cft LICH WS13 ...... 21 C3
Walkers Fold SHHTH WV12 ...... 38 B7
Walkers Heath Rd
  HWK/WKHTH B38 ...... 144 F4
Walkers Orch KNWTH CV8 ...... 177 M7
Walkers Ri HEDN WS12 ...... 13 H5
Walkers Rd REDW B98 ...... 189 J7
Walker St DUDS DY2 ...... 103 C1
  TPTN/OCK DY4 ...... 68 A6
Walkers Wy CSHL/WTROR B46 ...... 93 L7
  RCOVN/BALC/EX CV7 ...... 116 D4
Walk La WMBN WV5 ...... 64 E7
Walkmill La CNCK/NC WS11 ...... 16 B8
Walkmill Wy CNCK/NC WS11 ...... 16 B8
The Walk SEDG DY3 ...... 66 B4
Walkwood Crs REDW B97 ...... 196 A7
Walkwood Rd REDW B97 ...... 196 A7
Wallace CI CNCK/NC WS11 ...... 17 K8
  OLDBY B69 ...... 86 B7
Wallace Ct GTWY WS6 ...... 24 B4
Wallace Ri CDYHTH B64 ...... 103 J6
Wallace Rd BILS/COS WV14 ...... 67 L2
  BRWNH WS8 ...... 26 C5
  COVN CV6 ...... 133 L5
  OLDBY B69 ...... 86 B7
  SLYOAK B29 ...... 124 F3
Wall Av CSHL/WTROR B46 ...... 93 K8
Wallbank Rd WASH/WDE B8 ...... 90 E7
Wallbrook St BILS/COS WV14 ...... 67 H5
Wall Cft ALDR WS9 ...... 40 F6
Wall Dr FOAKS/STRLY B74 ...... 56 D1
Wall End CI WSLW WS2 ...... 38 E6
Waller CI RWWCK/WEL CV35 ...... 191 K6
Waller St RLSN CV32 ...... 200 E3
Wallface WMBN/HART B71 ...... 68 E6
Wallheath Crs ALDR WS9 ...... 27 J8
Wall Heath La ALDR WS9 ...... 41 K1
Wall Hill Rd
  RCOVN/BALC/EX CV7 ...... 114 A6
Wallhouse La BRGRVE B60 ...... 194 D8
  REDW B97 ...... 195 C8
Walling Cft BILS/COS WV14 ...... 66 F2
Wallingford Av CNCK/NC WS11 ...... 81 K6
Wallington CI BLOX/PEL WS3 ...... 38 F3
Wallington Heath
  BLOX/PEL WS3 ...... 38 F3
Wall La LICHS WS14 ...... 28 B1
Wallows La WSL WS1 ...... 4 B9
  WSLW WS2 ...... 4 A9
Wallows PI BRLYHL DY5 ...... 84 A8
Wallows Rd BRLYHL DY5 ...... 102 A4
Wallows Wd SEDG DY3 ...... 83 L1
Wallsgrove CI RLSN CV32 ...... 200 F2
Wall St WOLV WV1 ...... 50 E3
Wall Well HALE B63 ...... 121 K2
Wall Well La HALE B63 ...... 121 K2
Walmead Cft HRBN B17 ...... 105 K6
Walmer Gv ERDW/GRVHL B23 ...... 71 M8
Walmer Meadow ALDR WS9 ...... 40 F6
The Walmers ALDR WS9 ...... 40 F6
Walmer Wy
  CHWD/FDBR/MGN B37 ...... 111 G2
Walmley Ash Rd
  WALM/CURD B76 ...... 73 G4
Walmley CI HALE B63 ...... 102 F6
  WALM/CURD B76 ...... 73 K5
Walmley Rd WALM/CURD B76 ...... 73 K4
Walnut CI CDSL WV8 ...... 34 F2
Walnut CI
  CHWD/FDBR/MGN B37 ...... 110 F4
  CNCK/NC WS11 ...... 16 D2
  HAG/WOL DY9 ...... 119 M4
  NUNW/HART CV10 ...... 79 C7
  NUNW/HART CV10 ...... 80 C7
Walnut Cft ATHST CV9 ...... 62 A5
Walnut Dr BDMR/CCFT WV3 ...... 49 H4
  CNCK/NC WS11 ...... 16 D3
  RLSN CV32 ...... 200 F1
  SMTHWK B66 ...... 87 L8
Walnut Gv LICHS WS14 ...... 21 K6
Walnut La BRGRVE B60 ...... 186 B5
  DARL/WED WS10 ...... 68 C3
  DSYBK/YTR WS5 ...... 69 L2
Walnut St COVE CV2 ...... 134 C4
Walnut Tree CI KNWTH CV8 ...... 191 L2
Walnut Wy NFLD/LBR B31 ...... 143 K6
  RUGBYS/DCH CV22 ...... 182 F4
Walpole St DUNHL/THL/PER WV6 ...... 2 B2
Walpole Wk WBROM B70 ...... 87 H4
Walrand CI CRTAM B79 ...... 31 M4

Walsal End La HIA/OLT B92 ...... 149 K2
Walsall Rd ALDR WS9 ...... 40 C3
  BLOX/PEL WS3 ...... 39 L3
  CNCK/NC WS11 ...... 16 C7
  CNCK/NC WS11 ...... 25 K1
  DARL/WED WS10 ...... 52 C7
  DSYBK/YTR WS5 ...... 69 K1
  FOAKS/STRLY B74 ...... 42 A7
  GTWY WS6 ...... 24 E1
  HHTH/SAND B71 ...... 71 M8
  LICH WS13 ...... 20 E6
  LICHS WS14 ...... 27 J5
  PBAR/PBCH B42 ...... 70 E5
  WLNHL WV13 ...... 51 M3
Walsall St BILS/COS WV14 ...... 51 H8
  DARL/WED WS10 ...... 52 B7
  DARL/WED WS10 ...... 68 D2
  TLHL/CAN CV4 ...... 152 E6
  WBROM B70 ...... 87 H2
  WLNHL WV13 ...... 51 M4
  WOLV WV1 ...... 3 J6
Walsall Wood Rd ALDR WS9 ...... 40 E3
Walsgrave Dr HIA/OLT B92 ...... 128 B6
Walsgrave Gdns COVE CV2 ...... 135 L6
Walsgrave Rd COVE CV2 ...... 9 L4
Walsham Cft BKDE/SHDE B34 ...... 92 A8
Walsh Dr WALM/CURD B76 ...... 73 K1
Walsh Gv ERDW/GRVHL B23 ...... 72 B5
Walsh La RCOVN/BALC/EX CV7 ...... 131 J3
Walsingham Dr
  NUNW/HART CV10 ...... 98 E6
Walsingham St WSL WS1 ...... 5 J4
Walstead Rd DSYBK/YTR WS5 ...... 54 A8
Walstead Rd West
  DSYBK/YTR WS5 ...... 53 J8
Waltdene CI GTB/HAM B43 ...... 70 C3
Walter Cobb Dr
  SCFLD/BOLD B73 ...... 72 E4
Walter Nash Rd East
  KIDDW DY11 ...... 161 G4
Walter Nash Rd West
  KIDDW DY11 ...... 160 E4
Walter Rd BILS/COS WV14 ...... 67 J2
  SMTHWKW B67 ...... 87 J7
Walters CI NFLD/LBR B31 ...... 143 K7
Walter Scott Rd BDWTH CV12 ...... 117 L4
Walters Rd LGLYGN/QTN B68 ...... 104 E6
Walters Rw DUDN DY1 ...... 84 E2
Walter St BLOX/PEL WS3 ...... 39 L4
  VAUX/NECH B7 ...... 89 M7
  WBROM B70 ...... 87 H3
Waltham CI BRGRVW B61 ...... 185 J4
Waltham Crs NUNW/HART CV10 ...... 79 M8
Waltham Gv KGSTG B44 ...... 71 M3
Walthamstow Ct
  BRLYHL DY5 ...... 102 B4
Walton Av BLKHTH/ROWR B65 ...... 103 M5
Walton CI
  BLKHTH/ROWR B65 ...... 103 L1
  COVS CV3 ...... 155 J6
  HALE B63 ...... 121 K3
  KIDDW DY11 ...... 160 F3
  TPTN/OCK DY4 ...... 99 L6
Walton Crs
  ETTPK/GDPK/PENN WV4 ...... 50 C8
Walton Cft SOLH B91 ...... 147 M4
Walton Dr HAG/WOL DY9 ...... 102 A8
Walton Gdns CDSL WV8 ...... 34 D1
Walton Gv BVILLE B30 ...... 144 F3
Walton Heath BLOX/PEL WS3 ...... 38 D2
Walton Pool La HAG/WOL DY9 ...... 140 D3
Walton Ri HAG/WOL DY9 ...... 140 E2
Walton Rd ALDR WS9 ...... 40 E4
  BRGRVW B61 ...... 185 L1
  DARL/WED WS10 ...... 69 C3
  ETTPK/GDPK/PENN WV4 ...... 50 D8
  LGLYGN/QTN B68 ...... 105 C4
  STRBR DY8 ...... 101 L7
Walton St TPTN/OCK DY4 ...... 67 K8
Wanderers Av BKHL/PFLD WV2 ...... 50 A7
Wanderer Wk ERDE/BCHGN B24 ...... 91 J4
Wandle Gv SPARK B11 ...... 126 E2
Wandsworth Rd KGSTG B44 ...... 71 J2
Wanley Rd COVS CV3 ...... 154 B7
Wannerton Rd KIDD DY10 ...... 158 F4
Wansbeck Gv HWK/WKHTH B38 ...... 144 C5
Wansbeck Wk SEDG DY3 ...... 66 D7
Wansfell CI TLHL/CAN CV4 ...... 152 E6
Wanstead Gv KGSTG B44 ...... 71 L4
Wantage Rd
  CSHL/WTROR B46 ...... 93 J4
Wappenbury CI COVE CV2 ...... 135 C2
Wappenbury Rd COVE CV2 ...... 135 H4
Wapping La REDE B98 ...... 189 M6
Warbage La HAG/WOL DY9 ...... 164 D5
Warbank CI ALVE B48 ...... 167 L7
Warbler PI KIDD DY10 ...... 161 L3
Ward CI WASH/WDE B8 ...... 90 E8
Warden Av SCFLD/BOLD B73 ...... 72 D5
Ward End CI WASH/WDE B8 ...... 90 D7
Ward End Hall Gv
  WASH/WDE B8 ...... 90 E7
Ward End Park Rd
  WASH/WDE B8 ...... 90 D8
Wardend Rd WASH/WDE B8 ...... 90 E7
Warden Rd COVN CV6 ...... 133 M7
  SCFLD/BOLD B73 ...... 72 D5
The Wardens Av COVW CV5 ...... 132 F7
The Wardens KNWTH CV8 ...... 177 C8
Ward Gv
  ETTPK/GDPK/PENN WV4 ...... 66 D2
  WWCK CV34 ...... 199 M6
Wardle PI HEDN WS12 ...... 12 B8
Wardles La GTWY WS6 ...... 24 D3
Wardle St CRTAM B79 ...... 31 L8
Wardlow CI
  ETTPK/GDPK/PENN WV4 ...... 49 M7
Wardlow CI VAUX/NECH B7 ...... 89 L3
Wardour Dr
  CHWD/FDBR/MGN B37 ...... 111 G3
Wardour Gv KGSTG B44 ...... 72 A5
Ward Rd CDSL WV8 ...... 34 D2
  DUNHL/THL/PER WV6 ...... 48 D2
Ward St BILS/COS WV14 ...... 66 F5
  BKHL/PFLD WV2 ...... 50 F7
  HEDN WS12 ...... 12 D7
Warwick St BHTH/HG B12 ...... 7 L4
  BILS/COS WV14 ...... 51 J8
  COVW CV5 ...... 153 K5
  RLSN CV32 ...... 200 D4

LOZ/NWT B19 ...... 7 G1
  WLNHL WV13 ...... 51 M2
  WOLV WV1 ...... 3 J5
  WSL WS1 ...... 5 H1
Wareham CI COVE CV2 ...... 135 L8
Wareham Rd RBRY B45 ...... 142 F3
Wareing Dr ERDW/GRVHL B23 ...... 72 B5
Warewell St WSL WS1 ...... 5 J4
Waring CI TPTN/OCK DY4 ...... 67 J5
Waring Rd TPTN/OCK DY4 ...... 67 L5
Warings Green Rd
  HOCK/TIA B94 ...... 171 H5
War La HRBN B17 ...... 105 M8
Warley Cft LGLYGN/QTN B68 ...... 105 H5
Warley Hall Rd
  LGLYGN/QTN B68 ...... 105 H4
Warley Rd LGLYGN/QTN B68 ...... 87 G8
Warmington CI COVS CV3 ...... 155 J5
Warmington Dr
  SCFLD/BOLD B73 ...... 72 F1
Warmington Gv WWCK CV34 ...... 198 F5
Warmington Rd HLYWD B47 ...... 145 L7
  LGN/SDN/BHAMAIR B26 ...... 110 A8
Warmley CI
  DUNHL/THL/PER WV6 ...... 35 M8
  SOLH B91 ...... 128 B8
Warmwell CI COVE CV2 ...... 155 K1
Warner CI WWCK CV34 ...... 199 H4
Warner Dr BRLYHL DY5 ...... 102 B4
Warner PI BLOX/PEL WS3 ...... 39 K7
  CDSL WV8 ...... 34 D2
Warner Rd DARL/WED WS10 ...... 69 G3
Warner Rw COVN CV6 ...... 134 D6
Warple Rd BHTH/HG B12 ...... 7 L9
Warple Rd RIDG/WDGT B32 ...... 105 G8
Warren Av WOLVN WV10 ...... 36 D8
Warren CI HEDN WS12 ...... 13 L8
  LICHS WS14 ...... 21 J7
  RLSN CV32 ...... 200 D2
  TPTN/OCK DY4 ...... 67 K8
Warren Dr BLKHTH/ROWR B65 ...... 85 K8
  DOR/KN B93 ...... 172 E2
  SEDG DY3 ...... 66 A3
Warren Farm Rd KGSTG B44 ...... 71 K5
Warren Fld KNWTH CV8 ...... 179 L4
Warren Gdns KGSWFD DY6 ...... 83 G7
Warren Gn TLHL/CAN CV4 ...... 152 D5
Warren Hill Rd KGSTG B44 ...... 71 L6
Warren La RBRY B45 ...... 166 F2
Warren PI BRWNH WS8 ...... 26 E6
Warren Rd BNTWD WS7 ...... 18 E8
  BVILLE B30 ...... 124 E6
  KGSTG B44 ...... 71 L7
  WASH/WDE B8 ...... 90 C7
Warrens End HWK/WKHTH B38 ...... 144 D5
Warrens Hall Rd DUDS DY2 ...... 85 J6
Warrington CI WALM/CURD B76 ...... 73 L4
Warrington Dr
  ERDW/GRVHL B23 ...... 72 B6
Warsash CI WOLV WV1 ...... 50 F5
Warstock La
  ALE/KHTH/YWD B14 ...... 145 L1
Warstock Rd
  ALE/KHTH/YWD B14 ...... 145 K1
Warston Av RIDG/WDGT B32 ...... 123 H2
Warstone Dr HHTH/SAND B71 ...... 87 J1
Warstone La CBHAMW B1 ...... 6 C2
Warstone Pde East WSNGN B18 ...... 6 B1
Warstone Rd WOLVN WV10 ...... 23 M4
Warstones Crs
  ETTPK/GDPK/PENN WV4 ...... 49 H8
Warstones Dr
  ETTPK/GDPK/PENN WV4 ...... 49 G8
Warstones Gdns
  ETTPK/GDPK/PENN WV4 ...... 49 G7
Warstones Rd
  ETTPK/GDPK/PENN WV4 ...... 65 H1
Warstone Ter HDSW B21 ...... 88 C5
Wartell Bank KGSWFD DY6 ...... 83 H6
Warton CI KNWTH CV8 ...... 192 A1
Warwards La SLYOAK B29 ...... 124 E4
Warwell La
  LGN/SDN/BHAMAIR B26 ...... 109 H7
Warwick Av BRGRVE B60 ...... 185 L5
  COVW CV5 ...... 153 L6
  DARL/WED WS10 ...... 69 C2
  DUNHL/THL/PER WV6 ...... 48 D2
  WLNHL WV13 ...... 52 B3
Warwick CI CNCK/NC WS11 ...... 16 D5
  LGLYGN/QTN B68 ...... 104 F3
  WBROM B70 ...... 68 C6
Warwick Dr ATHST CV9 ...... 63 H3
  CDSL WV8 ...... 34 C2
Warwick Gdns
  NUNW/HART CV10 ...... 98 C2
  OLDBY B69 ...... 86 A3
Warwick Gra SOLH B91 ...... 127 K6
Warwick Gv HIA/OLT B92 ...... 127 H4
Warwick Hall Gdns
  BRGRVE B60 ...... 185 L5
Warwick Hwy REDE B98 ...... 196 E4
Warwick La COV CV1 ...... 8 F5
Warwick New Rd RLSN CV32 ...... 200 B5
Warwick Pas CBHAM B2 ...... 7 G5
Warwick PI RLSN CV32 ...... 200 B5
Warwick Rd ACGN B27 ...... 126 E1
  COV CV1 ...... 8 E6
  COVS CV3 ...... 8 D9
  DOR/KN B93 ...... 148 E4
  DOR/KN B93 ...... 173 G2
  DUDS DY2 ...... 103 J2
  KNWTH CV8 ...... 180 E2
  LGLYGN/QTN B68 ...... 105 H6
  RWWCK/WEL CV35 ...... 191 H5
  SCFLD/BOLD B73 ...... 72 A3
  SOLH B91 ...... 127 L8
  SOLH B91 ...... 148 A1
  SPARK B11 ...... 108 A8
  STRBR DY8 ...... 101 H4
  TAM/AM/WIL B77 ...... 46 C7

RUGBYS/DCH CV22 ...... 183 L3
  RUSH/SHEL WS4 ...... 53 K2
  STRPT DY13 ...... 160 E8
  WOLV WV1 ...... 3 J6
Warwick Ter RLSN CV32 ...... 200 C4
Warwick Wy ALDR WS9 ...... 40 E4
Wasdale CI RLSN CV32 ...... 200 A3
Wasdale Dr KGSWFD DY6 ...... 83 J7
Wasdale Rd BRWNH WS8 ...... 26 B7
  NFLD/LBR B31 ...... 143 K1
Waseley Rd RBRY B45 ...... 142 C5
Washbrook La CNCK/NC WS11 ...... 25 H1
  COVW CV5 ...... 132 E4
Washbrook Rd WASH/WDE B8 ...... 90 E7
Washford Dr REDE B98 ...... 197 G6
Washford Gv YDLY B25 ...... 108 F5
Washford La REDE B98 ...... 197 H5
Washington Dr
  BFLD/HDSWWD B20 ...... 88 F2
Washington St CBHAMW B1 ...... 6 D7
  DUDS DY2 ...... 103 H2
  KIDDW DY11 ...... 137 C8
Wash La YDLY B25 ...... 109 C4
Washwood Heath Rd
  WASH/WDE B8 ...... 90 C7
Wasperton CI CBROM B36 ...... 91 M5
  COVS CV3 ...... 155 K6
Wassell Ct HALE B63 ...... 121 J3
Wassell Dr BEWD DY12 ...... 160 A1
Wassell Grove Rd
  HAG/WOL DY9 ...... 120 C4
Wassell Rd BILS/COS WV14 ...... 51 H6
  HAG/WOL DY9 ...... 120 C3
  HALE B63 ...... 121 J3
Waste La ATHST CV9 ...... 62 C3
  COVN CV6 ...... 133 J4
  RCOVN/BALC/EX CV7 ...... 151 J7
Wast Hill Gv HWK/WKHTH B38 ...... 144 D6
Wasthill La HWK/WKHTH B38 ...... 144 B8
Wastwater Ct
  DUNHL/THL/PER WV6 ...... 48 D1
Watchbury CI CBROM B36 ...... 92 A4
Watch CI COV CV1 ...... 8 D4
Watchman Av BRLYHL DY5 ...... 102 D6
Watchtower Rd STRPT DY13 ...... 161 H7
Watcombe Rd COVE CV2 ...... 135 J5
Waterbrook CI PENK ST19 ...... 10 C6
Watercall Av COVS CV3 ...... 154 A8
Waterdale B90 ...... 147 H8
  WMBN WV5 ...... 64 C8
Waterfall CI
  RCOVN/BALC/EX CV7 ...... 131 C4
  SMTHWK B66 ...... 87 J6
Waterfall La CDYHTH B64 ...... 103 L4
Waterfall Rd BRLYHL DY5 ...... 102 A6
Waterfield CI TPTN/OCK DY4 ...... 67 C8
Waterford PI STETCH B33 ...... 110 B2
Waterford Rd KGSWFD DY6 ...... 83 H6
Waterfront East BRLYHL DY5 ...... 102 C1
Waterfront Wy BRLYHL DY5 ...... 102 C1
Waterfront West BRLYHL DY5 ...... 102 B1
Waterglade La WLNHL WV13 ...... 51 L4
Waterhaynes CI RBRY B45 ...... 142 F2
Waterhead CI WOLVN WV10 ...... 36 E3
Waterhead Dr WOLVN WV10 ...... 36 F3
Water La HHTH/SAND B71 ...... 69 K6
Waterlinks Bvd AST/WIT B6 ...... 89 L6
Waterloo Av
  CHWD/FDBR/MGN B37 ...... 110 F1
Waterloo Bvd HEDN WS12 ...... 17 J1
Waterloo Ct WWCK CV34 ...... 199 C5
Waterloo PI RLSN CV32 ...... 200 D4
Waterloo Rd
  ALE/KHTH/YWD B14 ...... 125 J5
  SMTHWK B66 ...... 105 J2
  WOLV WV1 ...... 2 E4
  YDLY B25 ...... 108 F7
Waterloo St CBHAM B2 ...... 6 F5
  COV CV1 ...... 9 K2
  DUDN DY1 ...... 84 E5
  KIDD DY10 ...... 137 J7
  RLSS CV31 ...... 200 F6
  TPTN/OCK DY4 ...... 67 K8
Waterloo St East
  TPTN/OCK DY4 ...... 67 K8
Waterman Rd COVN CV6 ...... 134 D4
Watermeadow Dr
  RUSH/SHEL WS4 ...... 40 A4
Watermere RUSH/SHEL WS4 ...... 40 B5
Water Mill CI SLYOAK B29 ...... 124 B2
Watermill CI WOLVN WV10 ...... 36 B2
Water Orton La
  WALM/CURD B76 ...... 74 B8
Water Orton Rd CBROM B36 ...... 92 A5
Water Rd SEDG DY3 ...... 84 A3
Watersbridge Gdns
  NUNW/HART CV10 ...... 99 C4
Waterside COVE CV2 ...... 117 C2
  POL/KGSB/FAZ B78 ...... 47 L4
Waterside CI ERDE/BCHGN B24 ...... 91 L1
  WOLVN WV10 ...... 22 C3
Waterside Vw BRLYHL DY5 ...... 101 M4
  WSNGN B18 ...... 88 B2
Waterside Wy BRWNH WS8 ...... 26 A3
Water Side Wy COVEN WV9 ...... 35 L3
Watersmead CI HEDN WS12 ...... 17 J1
Watersmeet Gv COVE CV2 ...... 134 F7
Watersmeet Rd COVE CV2 ...... 134 F7
Waterson Cft
  CHWD/FDBR/MGN B37 ...... 111 H2
Water St BNTWD WS7 ...... 18 C5
  CBHAMNW B3 ...... 6 E3
  KGSWFD DY6 ...... 83 H6
  WBROM B70 ...... 87 H5
  WOLVN WV10 ...... 2 H2
Waters Vw BLOX/PEL WS3 ...... 25 M3
Water Tower La KNWTH CV8 ...... 176 D7
Waterward CI HRBN B17 ...... 106 A8
Waterways Dr OLDBY B69 ...... 86 C4
Waterways Gdns STRBR DY8 ...... 101 J4
Waterworks Dr NFLD/LBR B31 ...... 123 H8
Waterworks Rd
  LDYWD/EDGR B16 ...... 106 D4
Waterworks St AST/WIT B6 ...... 89 M5
Watery La ALVE B48 ...... 168 C3
  ATHST CV9 ...... 61 M3

CSHL/WTROR B46 ...... 94 B3
  DOR/KN B93 ...... 173 J2
  HAG/WOL DY9 ...... 139 K6
  LICH WS13 ...... 18 F2
  LICH WS13 ...... 21 C2
  RCOVN/BALC/EX CV7 ...... 114 B8
  RCOVN/BALC/EX CV7 ...... 133 L1
  REDE B98 ...... 196 F3
  RIDG/WDGT B32 ...... 122 F2
  SHLY B90 ...... 171 G1
  SMTHWKW B67 ...... 87 L8
  STRBR DY8 ...... 101 J3
  TPTN/OCK DY4 ...... 67 K8
  WLNHL WV13 ...... 51 J2
  WSL WS1 ...... 4 D7
Watery Lane Middleway
  BORD 107 M3
Watford Gap Rd MGN/WHC B75 ...... 42 E6
Watford Rd BVILLE B30 ...... 124 D8
Wathan Av BILS/COS WV14 ...... 66 D3
Wathen Rd RLSN CV32 ...... 200 E3
  WWCK CV34 ...... 199 J5
Watkins Gdns NFLD/LBR B31 ...... 143 M2
Watkins Rd SHHTH WV12 ...... 38 A8
Watland Gn BKDE/SHDE B34 ...... 91 L8
Watling Rd KNWTH CV8 ...... 176 F7
Watling St BRWNH WS8 ...... 26 F4
  NUN CV11 ...... 81 M5
  POL/KGSB/FAZ B78 ...... 47 J8
  TAM/AM/WIL B77 ...... 46 A5
  TAM/AM/WIL B77 ...... 46 D6
Watney Gv KGSTG B44 ...... 72 A5
Watson CI CSCFLD/WYGN B72 ...... 72 F3
  WWCK CV34 ...... 199 J4
Watson Rd BILS/COS WV14 ...... 66 D3
  COVW CV5 ...... 153 H3
  DARL/WED WS10 ...... 51 L8
  WASH/WDE B8 ...... 90 D8
  WOLVN WV10 ...... 35 M3
Watsons CI DUDS DY2 ...... 85 J5
Watson's Green Flds
  DUDS DY2 ...... 85 K5
Watson's Green Rd DUDS DY2 ...... 85 J5
Watt Ct STRPT DY13 ...... 160 E2
Wattisham Sq CVALE B35 ...... 91 L1
Wattis Rd SMTHWKW B67 ...... 105 L3
Wattle Rd WBROM B70 ...... 86 E2
Watton CI BILS/COS WV14 ...... 66 E4
Watton Gn CVALE B35 ...... 91 L3
Watton La CSHL/WTROR B46 ...... 93 G3
Watt Rd ERDW/GRVHL B23 ...... 90 C1
  TPTN/OCK DY4 ...... 67 M5
Watts CI TPTN/OCK DY4 ...... 67 G8
Watt's Rd SMTHWK B10 ...... 108 B5
Watt St HDSW B21 ...... 88 B6
  SMTHWK B66 ...... 87 M7
Wattville Rd HDSW B21 ...... 88 A5
Watwood Rd SHLY B90 ...... 146 D2
Waugh CI
  CHWD/FDBR/MGN B37 ...... 110 F3
Waugh Dr HALE B63 ...... 121 H5
Wavebeck Ct RRUGBY CV23 ...... 158 F8
Waveley Rd COV CV1 ...... 8 B4
Wavell Rd BRLYHL DY5 ...... 102 D6
  WASH/WDE B8 ...... 90 C8
  WSLW WS2 ...... 52 C3
Wavendon CI COVE CV2 ...... 135 K4
Waveney Av
  DUNHL/THL/PER WV6 ...... 48 C1
Waveney Cft CBROM B36 ...... 92 D5
Waveney Gv CNCK/NC WS11 ...... 15 M4
Waverhill Rd HDSW B21 ...... 88 D6
Waverley Av GTB/HAM B43 ...... 70 F1
  NUN CV11 ...... 99 K5
Waverley CI KIDD DY10 ...... 137 K5
Waverley Crs
  ETTPK/GDPK/PENN WV4 ...... 49 L7
  ETTPK/GDPK/PENN WV4 ...... 66 D2
  RMSLY B62 ...... 141 K1
Waverley Gdns WMBN WV5 ...... 64 F6
Waverley Rd BLOX/PEL WS3 ...... 38 D3
  DARL/WED WS10 ...... 52 B7
  KNWTH CV8 ...... 191 L2
  RLSS CV31 ...... 200 F7
  SMTHWK B10 ...... 108 C7
Waverley Sq NUN CV11 ...... 99 K4
Waverley St DUDS DY2 ...... 84 E5
Waverton Ms RLSS CV31 ...... 201 C7
Wavytree CI WWCK CV34 ...... 199 H6
Waxland Rd HALE B63 ...... 121 M3
Way Cft KIDDW DY11 ...... 160 E5
Wayfield CI SHLY B90 ...... 147 G2
Wayfield Rd SHLY B90 ...... 147 G2
Wayford Dr CSCFLD/WYGN B72 ...... 73 H6
Wayford Gld WLNHL WV13 ...... 51 K3
Wayside
  CHWD/FDBR/MGN B37 ...... 110 E5
Wayside Acres CDSL WV8 ...... 34 C3
Wayside Dr FOAKS/STRLY B74 ...... 56 A2
Wayside Gdns SHHTH WV12 ...... 38 C8
Wayside Wk WSLW WS2 ...... 52 E2
Waystone La HAG/WOL DY9 ...... 164 B2
Wealden Hatch WOLVN WV10 ...... 36 C1
Wealdstone Dr SEDG DY3 ...... 84 B3
Weale Gv WWCK CV34 ...... 199 K3
Weaman St CBHAMNE B4 ...... 7 G3
Weatheroak CI REDW B97 ...... 195 L4
Weatheroak HI ALVE B48 ...... 168 F4
Weatheroak Rd SPARK B11 ...... 108 A8
Weatheroaks ALDR WS9 ...... 40 F1
Weather Oaks HRBN B17 ...... 105 M8
Weatheroaks RMSLY B62 ...... 104 E6
Weaver Av
  LGN/SDN/BHAMAIR B26 ...... 109 J3
  WALM/CURD B76 ...... 73 L4
Weaver CI BRLYHL DY5 ...... 83 M7
Weaver Dr RUGBYN/HIL CV21 ...... 183 G1
Weaver Gv WLNHL WV13 ...... 52 B3
Weaver Ri DUDS DY2 ...... 103 H2
Weavers Wk COVN CV6 ...... 134 F5
Webb Av DUNHL/THL/PER WV6 ...... 34 C8
Webbcroft Rd STETCH B33 ...... 109 J1
Webb Ellis Rd
  RUGBYS/DCH CV22 ...... 183 J3

Webb La *HLGN/YWD* B28............ 126 C7
Webb Rd *TPTN/OCK* DY4............. 68 A6
Webb St *BILS/COS* WV14............. 67 C3
   NUNW/HART CV10...................... 98 A2
   WLNHL WV13............................... 51 K3
Webley Ri *WOLVN* WV10............. 36 D1
Webster Av *KNWTH* CV8............ 176 F7
Webster Cl *CSCFLD/WYGN* B72..... 72 F6
   SPARK B11................................... 107 M7
Webster Rd *WLNHL* WV13........... 51 L2
   WSLW WS2................................... 39 H8
Webster Steet *COVN* CV6........... 134 C6
Weddell Wynd *BILS/COS* WV14.... 67 K4
Weddington La
   NUNW/HART CV10........................ 80 E2
Weddington Rd *NUN* CV11.......... 81 H8
Weddington Ter *NUN* CV11......... 81 G8
Wedge St *WSL* WS1......................... 5 H7
Wedgewood Av *WBROM* B70..... 68 D6 🔲
   COVE CV2.................................... 135 J5
Wedgewood Cl *BNTWD* WS7........ 19 C6
Wedgewood Dr
   BFLD/HDSWWD B20..................... 88 F3
Wedgewood Pl *WBROM* B70...... 68 D6 🔲
Wedgewood Rd
   RIDG/WDGT B32........................ 105 G8
Wedgnock Gn *WWCK* CV34........ 199 H5 🔲
Wedgnock La *WWCK* CV34.......... 199 G4
Wedgwood Cl *WMBN* WV5.......... 64 D6 🔲
   WOLV WV1..................................... 50 E4 🔲
Wednesbury Oak Rd
   TPTN/OCK DY4............................ 67 L4
Wednesfield Rd *WLNHL* WV13..... 51 L2
   WOLVN WV10.................................. 3 K3
Wednesfield Wy *WLNHL* WV13.... 51 H1
   WNSFLD WV11............................. 37 J8
Wedon Cl *TLHL/CAN* CV4.......... 152 C6
Weeford Dr *BFLD/HDSWWD* B20.. 88 D1
Weeford Rd *MGN/WHC* B75.......... 57 J4
Weights La *REDE* B98.................. 188 D6
   REDW B97.................................. 188 A6
Weirbrook Cl *SLYOAK* B29......... 124 A6 🔲
Welbeck Av *WOLVN* WV10........... 36 B6
Welbeck Dr *WALM/CURD* DY11.... 158 B8
   RUSH/SHEL WS4............................ 40 B6 🔲
Welbeck Gv
   ERDW/GRVHL B23......................... 71 M8 🔲
Welbury Gdns
   DUNHL/THL/PER WV6.................... 35 K8
Welby Rd *HLGN/YWD* B28.......... 126 D4
Welches Cl *NFLD/LBR* B31......... 123 M8
Welcombe Dr
   WALM/CURD B76......................... 73 J6 🔲
Welcombe Gv *SOLH* B91............ 147 K2
Welcome Dr *BRGRVW* B61......... 165 L4 🔲
Welcome St *ATHST* CV9.............. 63 J5 🔲
Welford Av
   LGN/SDN/BHAMAIR B26........... 109 K5
Welford Cl *REDE* B98................ 196 D8
Welford Gv *FOAKS/STRLY* B74.... 56 C2
   RWWCK/WEL CV35..................... 198 B2
Welford Pl *COVN* CV6................ 134 B6
Welford Rd *BFLD/HDSWWD* B20.. 88 E5
   SCFLD/BOLD B73......................... 72 C4
   SHLY B90.................................... 147 G1
   TAM/AM/WIL B77......................... 46 A8
Welgarth Av *COVN* CV6............. 133 J7
Welham Cft *SHLY* B90............... 147 L7
Welland Av *CSHL/WTROR* B46..... 92 F3
   RUGBYN/HIL CV21...................... 159 G8 🔲
Welland Dr *STRBR* DY8............ 101 L5
Welland Gv *ERDE/BCHGN* B24.... 91 C2
   WLNHL WV13............................... 52 A3
Welland Rd *COV* CV1................ 121 L3 🔲
   HALE B63.................................. 121 L3 🔲
Well Cl *CBROM* B36................... 91 J5 🔲
   REDW B97................................. 196 C8
Wellcroft Rd *BKDE/SHDE* B34..... 91 L6
Wellcroft St *DARL/WED* WS10.... 68 D2
Wellesbourne *CRTAM* B79.......... 32 A5 🔲
Wellesbourne Cl
   BDMR/CCFT WV3......................... 48 F5 🔲
   REDE B98.................................. 196 C1 🔲
Wellesbourne Dr *DUDN* DY1....... 66 F6
Wellesbourne Rd
   BFLD/HDSWWD B20..................... 88 F4
   COVW CV5................................. 152 E2
Wellesley Dr *TPTN/OCK* DY4...... 67 K8 🔲
Wellesley Gdns *MOS/BIL* B13.... 126 B4
Wellesley Rd *LGLYGN/QTN* B68... 86 F7
Wellfield Cl *CNCK/NC* WS11..... 15 M6 🔲
Wellfield Gdns *DUDS* DY2.......... 85 J7
Wellfield Rd *ALDR* WS9............... 40 F5
   HLGN/YWD B28.......................... 126 F7
Wellhead La *PBAR/PBCH* B42..... 89 J3
Wellington Av *BDMR/CCFT* WV3.. 49 K6
Wellington Cl *KGSWFD* DY6...... 101 J1
Wellington Crs *LICH* WS13........ 21 M1
Wellington Dr *CNCK/NC* WS11.... 15 M5
Wellington Gv *SOLH* B91.......... 127 K7
Wellington Pl *WLNHL* WV13........ 51 K2
Wellington Rd
   BFLD/HDSWWD B20..................... 88 F3
   BILS/COS WV14.......................... 51 C7
   BRGRVE B60............................. 185 M5
   DSYBK/YTR WS5......................... 54 A7 🔲
   DUDN DY1.................................. 84 F4
   EDG B15................................... 107 G7
   RLSN CV32................................ 200 F2
   SMTHWKW B67......................... 105 L2
   TPTN/OCK DY4............................ 67 L8
Wellington St *CDYHTH* B64....... 103 K3
   COV CV1....................................... 9 J2
   HHTH/SAND B71.......................... 86 F7 🔲
   OLDBY B69.................................. 86 F7 🔲
   REDE B98................................. 196 C1 🔲
   WSLW WS2.................................. 52 F6
   WSNGN B18................................ 88 B8
Wellington St South
   WBROM B70................................ 87 G1 🔲
Wellington Wy *CVALE* B35.......... 91 M3
Well La *BLOX/PEL* WS3............... 39 H6
   DIG/EDG DY9................................. 7 J1
   GTWY WS6................................. 24 E4
   WNSFLD WV11............................. 51 G1

Wellman Cft *SLYOAK* B29.......... 124 B4
Wellman's Rd *WLNHL* WV13....... 52 A4
Well Meadow *RBRY* B45............ 142 E7 🔲
Well Pl *BLOX/PEL* WS3................. 39 J5
Wells Av *DARL/WED* WS10.......... 51 M7
Wells Cl *CNCK/NC* WS11............ 12 C8
   DUNHL/THL/PER WV6.................... 48 B1 🔲
   HHTH/SAND B71......................... 69 H5
   KIDDW DY11............................. 136 E7 🔲
   TAM/AM/WIL B77......................... 79 K8
   TPTN/OCK DY4............................ 67 L4
Wellsford Av *HIA/OLT* B92......... 127 L1
Wells Green Rd *HIA/OLT* B92.... 127 L1 🔲
Well Spring Cl *ATHST* CV9.......... 63 K5
Wells Rd *BILS/COS* WV14............ 67 J2
   BLKHTH/ROWR B65.................... 104 C2 🔲
   BRLYHL DY5.............................. 101 M2
   ETTPK/GDPK/PENN WV4............... 49 K8
   LGN/SDN/BHAMAIR B26............ 128 A1
   RUGBYN/HIL CV21...................... 183 M2
Wells St *RUGBYN/HIL* CV21....... 183 M2 🔲
Welney Gdns *COVEN* WV9........... 35 L2
Welsby Av *GTB/HAM* B43............ 70 C6
Welsh Cl *WWCK* CV34............... 199 J3
Welsh House Farm Rd
   RIDG/WDGT B32........................ 123 K1
Welshmans HI *SCFLD/BOLD* B73 .. 71 M3
Welsh Rd *COVE* CV2.................. 154 F1
   RLSN CV32................................ 201 K2
Welton Cl *RMSLY* B62................ 122 B3 🔲
Welwyndale Rd
   CSCFLD/WYGN B72...................... 73 G7
Wembley Gv *YDLY* B25.............. 109 G5 🔲
Wembrook Cl *NUN* CV11............ 99 H3
Wembury *TAM/AM/WIL* B77........ 32 C8
Wem Gdns *WNSFLD* WV11.......... 37 H7
Wendell Crest *WOLVN* WV10....... 36 D2 🔲
Wendiburgh St *TLHL/CAN* CV4... 152 B6
Wendover Ri *COVW* CV5........... 153 G1
Wendover Rd
   BLKHTH/ROWR B65...................... 85 L7
   ERDW/GRVHL B23........................ 72 A6
   ETTPK/GDPK/PENN WV4................ 66 C3
Wendron Cl *BRGRVE* B60.......... 185 M3 🔲
Wendron Gv
   ALE/KHTH/YWD B14................... 145 H1
Wenlock *TAM/AM/WIL* B77.......... 46 B2 🔲
Wenlock Av *BDMR/CCFT* WV3..... 49 J5
Wenlock Cl *HALE* B63............... 121 H5 🔲
   SEDG DY3.................................. 66 A6 🔲
Wenlock Dr *BRGRVW* B61......... 165 L8 🔲
Wenlock Gdns *BLOX/PEL* WS3.... 39 J8
Wenlock Rd *BFLD/HDSWWD* B20.. 89 K4
   STRBR DY8................................ 101 M7 🔲
Wenlock Wy *NUNW/HART* CV10.... 97 M1
Wenman St *BHTH/HG* B12......... 107 K7
Wensley Cft *HIA/OLT* B92.......... 126 F7
Wensleydale Rd
   PBAR/PBCH B42.......................... 70 F7
Wensley Rd
   LGN/SDN/BHAMAIR B26........... 109 K7
Wentbridge Rd *WLNHL* WV13..... 51 G4
Wentworth Av *CBROM* B36.......... 91 M5 🔲
Wentworth Dr *BRGRVE* B60....... 166 E8 🔲
   LICHS WS14............................... 21 H8
   NUN CV11.................................. 99 L4
   RMSLY B62............................... 85 L6
Wentworth Ga *HRBN* B17......... 105 M7
Wentworth Gv *WNSFLD* WV11.... 37 H6 🔲
Wentworth Park Av *HRBN* B17 .. 105 M7
Wentworth Ri *RMSLY* B62......... 122 B2 🔲
Wentworth Rd
   BLOX/PEL WS3............................ 38 D2 🔲
   FOAKS/STRLY B74....................... 56 E5
   HIA/OLT B92............................. 127 K2
   HRBN B17................................ 105 M7
   RLSS CV31................................ 201 H7 🔲
   RUGBYS/DCH CV22................... 183 K4 🔲
   STRBR DY8............................... 101 H6
   WOLV WV10................................ 36 D3
Wentworth Wy
   RIDG/WDGT B32........................ 123 K2
Wenyon Cl *TPTN/OCK* DY4......... 85 M1 🔲
Weoley Av *SLYOAK* B29............ 124 A3
Weoley Castle Rd *SLYOAK* B29 .. 123 K4
Weoley HI *SLYOAK* B29............. 124 A5
Weoley Park Rd *SLYOAK* B29.... 123 M4
Wergs Dr *DUNHL/THL/PER* WV6.. 34 E6
Wergs Hall Rd *CDSL* WV8.......... 34 D4
Wergs Rd *DUNHL/THL/PER* WV6 .. 34 E7
Werneth Gv *BLOX/PEL* WS3........ 38 E1
Wesley Av *CDSL* WV8.................. 34 F3
   GTWY WS6................................. 24 B2
   HALE B63................................. 102 F6
Wesley Cl *BNTWD* WS7.............. 18 D4
Wesley Gv *DARL/WED* WS10....... 68 C2
Wesley Pl *HEDN* WS12................ 13 C6 🔲
   TPTN/OCK DY4............................ 68 A6
Wesley Rd *BRLYHL* DY5............. 83 M8 🔲
   CDSL WV8.................................. 34 F3
   ERDW/GRVHL B23........................ 72 D8
Wesley's Fold
   DARL/WED WS10......................... 52 B7 🔲
Wesley St *BILS/COS* WV14.......... 67 J3
   BKHL/PFLD WV2........................... 50 E7
   OLDBY B69................................. 86 E5 🔲
   WBROM B70................................ 86 F2 🔲
Wesley Wy *TAM/AM/WIL* B77...... 46 C1
Wessenden *TAM/AM/WIL* B77.... 46 F6 🔲
Wessex Cl *BDWTH* CV12............ 116 E1 🔲
   BRWNH WS8............................... 26 D6
Wessex Dr *CNCK/NC* WS11......... 16 D3
Wessex Rd *BKHL/PFLD* WV2........ 50 D7
Wesson Gdns *HALE* B63............ 102 C5 🔲
Wesson Rd *DARL/WED* WS10....... 52 A6
West Acre *WLNHL* WV13............ 51 K4
West Av *BDMR/CCFT* WV3......... 117 H3
   BFLD/HDSWWD B20..................... 88 D1
   CBROM B36................................ 92 B5
   COVE CV2................................. 154 E3
   OLDBY B69................................. 85 M5
   REDE B98................................. 196 C2

   WNSFLD WV11............................. 37 G7
Westbook Wy *WMBN* WV5.......... 64 D8
West Bvd *RIDG/WDGT* B32........ 105 J8
Westbourne Av *BKDE/SHDE* B34 .. 91 J7
   CNCK/NC WS11............................ 16 B3
   GTWY WS6................................. 24 C1
Westbourne Cl *BRGRVW* B61..... 185 J4 🔲
Westbourne Crs *EDG* B15......... 106 E5 🔲
Westbourne Cresent
   BNTWD WS7................................ 18 F6 🔲
Westbourne Gdns *EDG* B15....... 106 E6
Westbourne Gv
   RUGBYS/DCH CV22................... 183 K4 🔲
Westbourne Rd
   DARL/WED WS10......................... 52 D6 🔲
   EDG B15................................... 106 D6
   ETTPK/GDPK/PENN WV4............... 49 L8
   HDSW B21................................. 88 B4
   HIA/OLT B92............................. 127 K6
   RMSLY B62............................... 104 C7
   RUSH/SHEL WS4........................... 53 L1 🔲
   WBROM B70................................ 86 F4
West Bromwich Ringway
   WBROM B70................................ 87 G2 🔲
West Bromwich Rd
   DSYBK/YTR WS5........................... 53 J7 🔲
   WSL WS1...................................... 4 F9
West Bromwich St *OLDBY* B69.... 86 D4
   WSL WS1...................................... 4 F6
Westbrook Av *ALDR* WS9............ 40 D8
Westbury Av *DARL/WED* WS10.... 52 D7
Westbury Rd *COVW* CV5........... 133 H8
   DARL/WED WS10......................... 52 D7
   HRBN B17................................ 105 M2
   NUNW/HART CV10........................ 99 B1
Westbury St *WOLV* WV1.............. 3 G4
Westcliff Dr *WWCK* CV34.......... 199 J3
Westcliffe Dr *COVS* CV3........... 153 M8 🔲
Westcliff Pl *NFLD/LBR* B31....... 143 K1
Westcombe Gv
   RIDG/WDGT B32........................ 122 E4 🔲
West Coppice Rd *BRWNH* WS8..... 26 A5
Westcote Av *NFLD/LBR* B31...... 143 G3
Westcote Cl *HIA/OLT* B92......... 127 L3
Westcotes *TLHL/CAN* CV4......... 152 F4
Westcott Cl *STRBR* DY8............ 101 K2 🔲
Westcott Rd
   LGN/SDN/BHAMAIR B26........... 109 L5
Westcroft Av *WOLVN* WV10......... 36 E4
Westcroft Gv *NFLD/LBR* B31..... 144 A2
Westcroft Rd *CDSL* WV8............ 34 D7
   SEDG DY3................................. 65 M3
Westcroft Wy
   ALE/KHTH/YWD B14................... 145 M4
Westdean Cl *RMSLY* B62........... 122 A1
West Dr *BFLD/HDSWWD* B20...... 88 F5
   DIG/EDG B5.............................. 125 G1
   POL/KGSB/FAZ B78...................... 45 J3
West End Av *SMTHWK* B66........ 87 G6
Westerdale Cl *SEDG* DY3........... 66 C6
Westerham Cl *DOR/KN* B93...... 148 D7 🔲
Westeria Cl *CBROM* B36............. 92 A5
Westering Pkwy *WOLVN* WV10 ... 36 C1
Westerings
   BFLD/HDSWWD B20..................... 89 G3 🔲
Western Av *BRLYHL* DY5........... 101 M3
   RMSLY B62............................... 122 C1
   SEDG DY3................................. 65 M5
Western By-pass *LICH* WS13...... 20 D5
Western Rd *CDYHTH* B64.......... 103 H5
   ERDE/BCHGN B24....................... 90 E2
   HAG/WOL DY9.......................... 139 M1
   HEDN WS12................................ 13 J5
   OLDBY B69................................ 86 F8
   SCFLD/BOLD B73........................ 72 E4
   STRBR DY8............................... 119 K1
   WSNGN B18............................... 106 D1
Western Wy *DARL/WED* WS10.... 68 A2
   KIDDW DY11............................. 136 E8
Westfield Av
   ALE/KHTH/YWD B14................... 145 M3
Westfield Cl *DOR/KN* B93......... 172 C3
   NUNW/HART CV10........................ 81 H7
Westfield Dr *WMBN* WV5............ 64 D6
Westfield Gv *BDMR/CCFT* WV3.... 49 G5
Westfield Mnr *MGN/WHC* B75 ... 56 E1 🔲
Westfield Rd *ACGN* B27............ 126 F2
   ALE/KHTH/YWD B14................... 125 H5
   BILS/COS WV14.......................... 50 F6
   BRLYHL DY5.............................. 102 D5
   DUDS DY2.................................. 85 H6
   EDG B15................................... 106 B5
   RMSLY B62............................... 104 C4
   RUGBYS/DCH CV22................... 183 K3 🔲
   SEDG DY3................................. 66 B4
   SMTHWKW B67......................... 87 K8
Westfields *BRGRVW* B61........... 165 J5
Westford Gv *HLGN/YWD* B28 ... 146 C2 🔲
Westgate *ALDR* WS9.................. 40 C5
   HEDN WS12................................ 13 K7
West Ga *LDYWD/EDGR* B16....... 106 C2
Westgate Cl *SEDG* DY3.............. 66 C6 🔲
   WWCK CV34............................. 199 H7 🔲
West Gn
   ETTPK/GDPK/PENN WV4............... 49 G8
West Green Cl *EDG* B15............ 106 F5
Westgrove Av *SHLY* B90............ 147 K7
Westhaven Dr *NFLD/LBR* B31..... 123 J6
Westhaven Rd
   CSCFLD/WYGN B72...................... 57 G8 🔲
Westhay Rd *HLGN/YWD* B28...... 126 F6
Westhead Rd *KIDD* DY10......... 137 L1
Westhead Rd North *KIDD* DY10 .. 137 L1
West Heath Rd *NFLD/LBR* B31... 143 M4
   WSNGN B18............................. 106 D1 🔲
Westhill *BDMR/CCFT* WV3......... 49 G3
West Hill Av *HEDN* WS12............ 13 G3
Westhill Cl *HIA/OLT* B92........... 127 J5 🔲
Westhill Rd *COVN* CV6.............. 133 K7
   SEDG DY3................................. 65 M3
West Holme *BORD* B9............... 108 A3 🔲
Westholme Cft *BVILLE* B30....... 124 C6

Westhouse Gv
   ALE/KHTH/YWD B14................... 145 H1
Westland Av *BDMR/CCFT* WV3.... 49 K3
Westland Cl *ERDW/GRVHL* B23.... 72 D8
Westland Gdns
   BDMR/CCFT WV3......................... 49 K3
   STRBR DY8................................ 101 K6
Westland Rd *BDMR/CCFT* WV3.... 49 K3
Westlands Rd *MOS/BIL* B13...... 125 L6
   WALM/CURD B76......................... 73 K7
Westlea Rd *RLSS* CV31............. 200 F7 🔲
Westleigh Av *COVW* CV5........... 153 K6 🔲
Westleigh Rd *WMBN* WV5.......... 64 D8
Westley Cl *HLGN/YWD* B28....... 126 F7
West Leyes *RUGBYN/HIL* CV21... 183 K2 🔲
Westley Rd *ACGN* B27............... 126 F2
Westley St *BORD* B9....................... 7 M6
   DUDN DY1.................................. 84 F5
Westmead Crs
   ERDE/BCHGN B24....................... 91 G1 🔲
West Mead Dr
   ALE/KHTH/YWD B14................... 125 J7
Westmead Dr *LGLYGN/QTN* B68.. 104 T1 🔲
West Ms *KGSTG* B44.................. 71 H3
West Mill Cft *HWK/WKHTH* B38 .. 144 C6 🔲
Westminster Rd
   KIDDW DY11............................. 136 E7 🔲
Westminster Av
   ETTPK/GDPK/PENN WV4............... 49 M8
Westminster Cl
   BRGRVW B61............................. 185 H4 🔲
   DUDN DY1.................................. 84 E3
Westminster Dr
   ALE/KHTH/YWD B14................... 125 H7
   NUNW/HART CV10........................ 79 M7
Westminster Rd
   BFLD/HDSWWD B20..................... 89 G3
   CNCK/NC WS11............................ 12 C7
   COV CV1...................................... 8 D7
   HHTH/SAND B71.......................... 69 H4
   KIDDW DY11............................. 136 D7
   RUSH/SHEL WS4......................... 39 M6
   SLYOAK B29.............................. 124 E4
   STRBR DY8................................ 101 G3
Westmore Wy *DARL/WED* WS10 .. 53 H8
Westmorland Av
   NUNW/HART CV10........................ 98 C5
Westmorland Cl
   POL/KGSB/FAZ B78...................... 45 L4 🔲
Westmorland Rd *COVE* CV2...... 155 K1 🔲
   HHTH/SAND B71.......................... 69 G7
Weston Av *OLDBY* B69............... 85 M4
   SPARK B11............................... 108 A7 🔲
Westonbirt Cl *KNWTH* CV8........ 176 F7
Weston Cl *CNCK/NC* WS11......... 17 G4
   DOR/KN B93............................. 172 E3
   RLSS CV31................................ 201 C7 🔲
   WSL WS1...................................... 4 F9
   WWCK CV34............................. 199 K6 🔲
Weston Crs *ALDR* WS9............... 54 F1
Weston Dr *BILS/COS* WV14......... 67 G1
   DARL/WED WS10......................... 68 A3
   GTWY WS6................................. 24 C5
Weston La *BDWTH* CV12........... 117 M2 🔲
   SPARK B11............................... 126 C1
Weston Rd *LICH* WS13................ 20 C5
   LOZ/NWT B19............................. 88 F6
   SMTHWKW B67......................... 105 K3
Weston St *COV* CV1....................... 9 H2
   WSL WS1...................................... 4 F9
Westover Rd
   BFLD/HDSWWD B20..................... 88 C1
West Park Av *NFLD/LBR* B31..... 143 J3
West Park Rd *SMTHWKW* B67 ... 87 H4
West Pathway *HRBN* B17........... 106 A7 🔲
Westport Crs *WNSFLD* WV11....... 37 K8
Westray Cl *RBRY* B45............... 142 C4
West Rdg *COVW* CV5................ 132 E8
Westridge *SEDG* DY3................. 66 A5
Westridge Rd *MOS/BIL* B13...... 126 A7
West Ri *MGN/WHC* B75............. 57 G7
West Rd *BRGRVE* B60............... 185 L3
   GTB/HAM B43............................ 70 C6
   HALE B63................................. 102 F7
   TPTN/OCK DY4............................ 67 M5
West Rd South *HALE* B63......... 102 F7
Westside Dr *RIDG/WDGT* B32 .. 123 H4 🔲
West St *BLKHTH/ROWR* B65 ..... 104 A4 🔲
   BLOX/PEL WS3............................ 39 G6
   BRLYHL DY5.............................. 102 D5
   CNCK/NC WS11............................ 16 C7
   COV CV1...................................... 9 K4
   CRTAM B79................................ 32 A8 🔲
   DUDN DY1.................................. 84 F3
   DUNHL/THL/PER WV6.................... 36 A8
   REDW B97................................. 196 C2
   RRUGBY CV23............................ 182 E1
   STRBR DY8................................ 101 K8
   TAM/AM/WIL B77......................... 46 A2
   VAUX/NECH B7............................. 7 K2 🔲
   WWCK CV34............................. 199 H8
West Vw *NUNW/HART* CV10....... 79 J5
   WASH/WDE B8........................... 108 D1
   WOLVN WV10.............................. 22 F7 🔲
West View Dr *KGSWFD* DY6........ 83 J8
West View Rd *MGN/WHC* B75..... 57 J7
   RLSN CV32................................ 193 G8
   RUGBYS/DCH CV22................... 183 H3
Westville Av *KIDDW* DY11......... 136 E8
Westville Rd *WSLW* WS2............. 52 E2
Westward Cl *KGSTG* B44............. 71 K5
Westwood Av *STRBR* DY8......... 119 G2
Westwood Crs *ATHST* CV9.......... 63 H6
Westwood Gv *SOLH* B91........... 147 K2
Westwood Heath Rd
   TLHL/CAN CV4.......................... 152 A7
Westwood Rd *AST/WIT* B6.......... 89 L3
   ATHST CV9................................ 63 H6
   SCFLD/BOLD B73......................... 71 L1
Westwoods Hollow *BNTWD* WS7.. 18 F5
Westwood St *BRLYHL* DY5........ 101 L4
Westwood Vw
   ERDE/BCHGN B24....................... 91 G2
Westwood Wy *TLHL/CAN* CV4 ... 152 C7
Wetherby Cl *WOLVN* WV10......... 36 B1
Wetherby Rd *ACGN* B27............ 127 G3 🔲

   BLOX/PEL WS3............................ 38 E1
Wetherfield Rd *SPARK* B11....... 126 E2
Wexford Cl *DUDN* DY1............... 84 D3
Wexford Rd *COVE* CV2............. 135 H4
Weybourne Rd *KGSTG* B44......... 71 J3
Weycroft Rd *ERDW/GRVHL* B23... 71 M6
Weyhill Cl *COVEN* WV9............... 35 J3
Weymoor Rd *HRBN* B17........... 123 L2
Weymouth Dr *FOAKS/STRLY* B74.. 56 D1
Whaley's Cft *COVN* CV6............ 133 L5
Wharf Ap *ALDR* WS9.................. 40 D6
Wharf Cl *LICHS* WS14................ 21 C6 🔲
Wharfdale Rd *SPARK* B11......... 108 F8 🔲
   YDLY B25.................................. 108 F8
Wharfedale Cl *KGSWFD* DY6....... 82 F6
Wharfedale St *DARL/WED* WS10.. 68 D3
Wharf La *BNTWD* WS7................ 26 D2
   BRGRVE B60............................. 186 F4
   SOLH B91................................. 128 B7
   WSNGN B18................................ 88 E8
Wharf Rd *BVILLE* B30............... 144 E3 🔲
   COV CV1.................................. 134 D8
   DUDN DY1.................................. 85 C5
   TPTN/OCK DY4............................ 68 C8
Wharfside *OLDBY* B69................ 86 D6 🔲
Wharf St *AST/WIT* B6................. 89 L6
   WOLV WV1.................................... 3 J6
   WSLW WS2................................... 4 E2
   WSNGN B18................................ 88 E7
   WWCK CV34............................. 199 L5
Whar Hall Rd *HIA/OLT* B92....... 128 C5
Wharrington Cl *REDE* B98........ 196 E5 🔲
Wharrington HI *REDE* B98........ 196 E5
Wharton Av *HIA/OLT* B92.......... 128 C6
Wharton St *VAUX/NECH* B7........ 90 B5
Wharwell La *GTWY* WS6............. 24 E4
Whatcote Gn *HIA/OLT* B92........ 128 B5
Whateley Av *BLOX/PEL* WS3....... 39 K7
Whateley Crs *CBROM* B36.......... 92 B5
Whateley Gn *FOAKS/STRLY* B74... 56 E5
Whateley Hall Cl
   DOR/KN B93............................. 149 G6 🔲
Whateley Hall Rd *DOR/KN* B93 .. 148 F6
Whateley La *TAM/AM/WIL* B77.... 60 D1
Whateley Pl *BLOX/PEL* WS3....... 39 K7 🔲
Whateley Rd *BLOX/PEL* WS3....... 39 K7
   HDSW B21................................. 88 C5
Whateley's Dr *KNWTH* CV8........ 191 L1
Wheatcroft Av *BEWD* DY12....... 160 A1
Wheatcroft Cl *BNTWD* WS7......... 18 E8
   PENK ST19.................................. 10 C5
   RMSLY B62............................... 104 D5
Wheatcroft Dr
   CHWD/FDBR/MGN B37............... 111 H4 🔲
   CHWD/FDBR/MGN B37............... 111 G4 🔲
Wheatcroft Gv *DUDS* DY2.......... 85 K4
Wheatcroft Rd *STETCH* B33...... 109 K3
   *Wheate Cft *TLHL/CAN* CV4....... 152 D3 🔲
Wheaten Cl
   CHWD/FDBR/MGN B37............... 111 H2 🔲
Wheatfield Av
   RUGBYS/DCH CV22................... 183 G4
Wheatfield Cl *CBROM* B36.......... 92 E6 🔲
Wheatfield Vw *NFLD/LBR* B31.... 123 H8
Wheat Hl *DSYBK/YTR* WS5.......... 54 B7 🔲
Wheathill Cl
   ETTPK/GDPK/PENN WV4............... 65 J2 🔲
   RLSN CV32................................ 200 C3
Wheatlands *HEDN* WS12............ 17 G4 🔲
Wheatlands Cft *STETCH* B33 ... 110 C2 🔲
The Wheatlands
   DUNHL/THL/PER WV6.................... 48 B2
Wheatley Cl *HIA/OLT* B92......... 128 C5 🔲
   LGLYGN/QTN B68........................ 105 G5
   MGN/WHC B75............................ 57 G2 🔲
Wheatley Rd *BKHL/PFLD* WV2..... 50 C7
   WBROM B70................................ 86 E1
Wheatmill Cl *KIDD* DY10......... 138 F3 🔲
Wheatmoor Ri *MGN/WHC* B75.... 57 J7
Wheaton Cl *WOLVN* WV10.......... 36 A6
Wheaton V *BFLD/HDSWWD* B20 .. 88 C2
Wheatridge Cl *KGSWFD* DY6...... 82 E5 🔲
Wheatridge Rd *BRGRVE* B60 .... 185 H7
Wheats Av *HRBN* B17............... 123 M2
Wheatsheaf Rd *CDSL* WV8.......... 35 J4
   LDYWD/EDGR B16....................... 106 B3
   OLDBY B69................................ 85 K5
Wheatstone Cl *SEDG* DY3......... 66 C7 🔲
Wheatstone Gv *STETCH* B33...... 91 K8 🔲
Wheat St *NUN* CV11.................. 99 G1
Wheel Av *CDSL* WV8................... 34 D2
Wheeler Cl *CDSL* WV8................ 34 C1
   DOR/KN B93............................. 173 M6
Wheeler Rd *WNSFLD* WV11........ 37 G5
Wheeler's Fold *WOLV* WV1........... 3 C5
Wheelers La *MOS/BIL* B13........ 125 J7
   MOS/BIL B13............................. 125 L6
Wheeler St *LOZ/NWT* B19.......... 89 H6
   STRBR DY8............................... 101 K8
Wheeley Moor Rd
   CHWD/FDBR/MGN B37............... 92 E8
Wheeley Rd *ALVE* B48............... 167 H8
   HIA/OLT B92............................. 128 B6
Wheeleys La *EDG* B15................... 6 C9
Wheeleys Rd *EDG* B15............. 106 F6
Wheel La *LICH* WS13................... 6 C6
Wheelock Cl *FOAKS/STRLY* B74... 55 K6
Wheelwright Cl *BRGRVE* B60 ... 185 J7 🔲
Wheelwright La *COVN* CV6....... 134 A1
Wheelwright Rd
   ERDE/BCHGN B24....................... 90 C3
Wheldrake Av *BKDE/SHDE* B34... 92 A8
Wheler Rd *COVS* CV3............... 154 C5
Whernside Dr
   DUNHL/THL/PER WV6.................... 35 L8
Wherretts Well La *SOLH* B91..... 128 C8
Whetstone Gv *WOLVN* WV10...... 36 B5
Whetstone La *ALDR* WS9............ 40 F8
Whetstone Rd *WOLVN* WV10...... 36 B5
Whettybridge Rd *RBRY* B45...... 142 C7 🔲
Whetty La *RBRY* B45................ 142 B7
Whichcote Av
   RCOVN/BALC/EX CV7.................. 131 G4 🔲
Whichford Av
   WALM/CURD B76......................... 73 H7 🔲
Whichford Gv *BORD* B9............ 108 F3 🔲
While Rd *CSCFLD/WYGN* B72...... 72 F1
Whilmot Cl *WOLVN* WV10........... 22 F7

Whimbrel Gv KIDD DY10 .... 161 L4 [2]
Whinberry Ri BRLYHL DY5 .... 84 A4 [3]
Whinchat Gv KIDD DY10 .... 161 L3
Whinfield Rd BRGRVW B61 .... 164 F7
Whinyates Ri CNCK/NC WS11 .... 16 D5 [1]
Whiston Gv WNSFLD WV11 .... 37 L6
Whitacre La LICHS WS14 .... 27 J6
Whitacre Rd BORD B9 .... 108 C2
  DOR/KN B93 .... 148 F6
  NUN CV11 .... 81 J8
  RLSN CV32 .... 200 E3
Whitaker Rd COVW CV5 .... 153 G1
Whitbourne Cl
  BHTH/HG B12 .... 107 M8 [10]
Whitburn Av PBAR/PBCH B42 .... 70 E8
  KIDDW DY11 .... 136 F7
Whitburn Rd BDWTH CV12 .... 116 A4
Whitby Cl BLOX/PEL WS3 .... 38 D2
Whitby Rd BHTH/HG B12 .... 125 L1
Whitby Wy CNCK/NC WS11 .... 16 A5
Whitchurch Cl REDE B98 .... 196 D7 [2]
Whitchurch Wy TLHL/CAN CV4 .... 152 D6
Whitcot Gv NFLD/LBR B31 .... 143 K5 [2]
Whitebeam Cl BRWNH WS8 .... 26 C7
  TLHL/CAN CV4 .... 152 B4 [2]
Whitebeam Cft
  HWK/WKHTH B38 .... 144 C5 [1]
White Beam Rd
  CHWD/FDBR/MGN B37 .... 111 H4
Whitebeams Cl SEDG DY3 .... 84 A1 [5]
White City Rd BRLYHL DY5 .... 102 E4
White Cl HAG/WOL DY9 .... 120 A3 [3]
Whitecrest GTB/HAM B43 .... 70 E3
Whitecroft Rd
  LGN/SDN/BHAMAIR B26 .... 110 B8
White Falcon Ct SOLH B91 .... 147 K3 [2]
White Farm Rd
  FOAKS/STRLY B74 .... 56 C1
White Field Av HRBN B17 .... 105 L7 [1]
Whitefield Cl CDSL WV8 .... 34 F3 [1]
  TLHL/CAN CV4 .... 152 B7
Whitefields Crs SOLH B91 .... 147 M3
Whitefields Ga SOLH B91 .... 147 L4
Whitefields Rd SOLH B91 .... 147 L4
Whitefriars Dr HALE B63 .... 121 L1 [1]
White Friars La COV CV1 .... 9 H6
White Friars St COV CV1 .... 9 H5
Whitegate Dr KIDDW DY11 .... 160 E2
Whitegates Rd BILS/COS WV14 .... 67 H3
Whitehall Cl NUWHART CV10 .... 79 L3
  HALE B63 .... 121 M1
Whitehall Dr DUDN DY1 .... 84 E3
  HALE B63 .... 121 M1
Whitehall Rd BORD B9 .... 108 C4
  CDYHTH B64 .... 103 G4 [1]
  ETTPK/GDPK/PENN WV4 .... 65 M1
  HALE B63 .... 121 M1
  HDSW B21 .... 88 E6
  KGSWFD DY6 .... 83 G7
  RUGBYN/HIL CV21 .... 183 M2
  STRBR DY8 .... 119 M3
  TPTN/OCK DY4 .... 68 B8
  WBROM B70 .... 86 C1
  WSL WS1 .... 4 F7
Whitehead Dr KNWTH CV8 .... 177 G6 [2]
  WALM/CURD B76 .... 74 B7 [1]
Whitehead Gv
  RCOVN/BALC/EX CV7 .... 150 F6
Whitehead Rd AST/WIT B6 .... 89 J6
Whitehill La SLYOAK B29 .... 123 L8
Whitehill Rd KIDDW DY11 .... 160 E2
Whitehorn Dr RLSN CV32 .... 200 F3
Whitehorse Cl COVN CV6 .... 116 F7
White Horse Rd BRWNH WS8 .... 26 C3
Whitehouse Av
  BDMR/CCFT WV3 .... 49 C5
  DARL/WED WS10 .... 51 M6 [2]
  DARL/WED WS10 .... 68 D2
White House Av WNSFLD WV11 .... 37 K6
White House Cl RBRY B45 .... 166 E4
  SOLH B91 .... 147 K2
Whitehouse Common Rd
  MGN/WHC B75 .... 57 J6
  NUNW/HART CV10 .... 98 B2
  WNSFLD WV11 .... 37 K4 [1]
Whitehouse Cresent
  BNTWD WS7 .... 18 F6 [1]
White House Gn SOLH B91 .... 147 K2
Whitehouse La REDE B98 .... 197 J2
Whitehouse Pl RBRY B45 .... 142 D7 [1]
Whitehouse Rd KIDDW DY11 .... 161 H1
  POL/KGSB/FAZ B78 .... 47 K6
White Houses La WOLVN WV10 .... 22 E7
Whitehouse St AST/WIT B6 .... 89 K7
  BILS/COS WV14 .... 67 G5 [3]
  TPTN/OCK DY4 .... 85 L3
  WSLW WS2 .... 53 H2 [2]
Whitehouse Wy ALDR WS9 .... 54 D1
White House Wy SOLH B91 .... 147 L2
Whitelaw Crs COVW CV5 .... 132 F7
Whitemoor Dr SOLH B91 .... 147 L6
Whitemoor Rd KNWTH CV8 .... 191 L1
White Oak Dr BDMR/CCFT WV3 .... 49 G4
  KGSWFD DY6 .... 83 G7
Whitepits La ALVE B48 .... 189 K1
White Rd RIDG/WDGT B32 .... 105 H7
  SMTHWK B67 .... 87 K7
  SPARK B11 .... 108 A6
White Rw WMBN WV5 .... 64 A4
Whitesands Cl TAM/AM/WIL B77 .... 32 C8
White's Dr SEDG DY3 .... 66 C5
Whiteside Cl COVS CV3 .... 155 K5
Whiteslade Cl DOR/KN B93 .... 148 E6 [1]
Whitesmith Cl SEDG DY3 .... 66 B5 [5]
White's Rd HHTH/SAND B71 .... 69 G7
Whites Rw KNWTH CV8 .... 191 L3
Whitestitch La
  RCOVN/BALC/EX CV7 .... 130 F3
Whitestone Rd HALE B63 .... 103 L7
  NUN CV11 .... 99 L6
White St BHTH/HG B12 .... 107 L8
  COV CV1 .... 9 G3
  WSL WS1 .... 4 E5
Whites Wd WMBN WV5 .... 64 B8
Whitethorn Cl HEDN WS12 .... 12 E5 [1]

Whitethorn Crs
  FOAKS/STRLY B74 .... 55 H4
Whitethorn Rd STRBR DY8 .... 101 L4
Whitewood Gld SHHTH WV12 .... 52 C1 [1]
Whitfield Gv EDG B15 .... 107 H5 [5]
Whitfield Rd HEDN WS12 .... 13 G6
Whitford Dr BRGRVW B61 .... 185 H5
Whitford Dr SHLY B90 .... 147 M6
Whitford Gdns BRGRVW B61 .... 185 H3 [1]
Whitford Rd BRGRVW B61 .... 185 H3
Whitgreave Av WOLVN WV10 .... 22 F6 [4]
  WOLVN WV10 .... 36 C5
Whitgreave St WBROM B70 .... 86 C2
Whiting TAM/AM/WIL B77 .... 46 B6
Whitland Cl RBRY B45 .... 142 F7
Whitland Dr
  ALE/KHTH/YWD B14 .... 145 K2
Whitley Av TAM/AM/WIL B77 .... 32 C8
Whitley Cl DUNHL/THL/PER WV6 .... 48 F3
Whitley Court Rd
  RIDG/WDGT B32 .... 105 G7
Whitley Dr FOAKS/STRLY B74 .... 55 L5
Whitley St DARL/WED WS10 .... 68 C2
Whitley Village COVS CV3 .... 154 D6
Whitlock Gv
  ALE/KHTH/YWD B14 .... 145 L2
Whitminster Av
  ERDE/BCHGN B24 .... 90 F2
Whitminster Cl SHHTH WV12 .... 52 A1 [1]
Whitmore Hl WOLV WV1 .... 2 E4
Whitmore Park Rd COVN CV6 .... 134 A2
Whitmore Rd SMHTH B10 .... 108 A5
  STRBR DY8 .... 101 H8
Whitmore St WOLV WV1 .... 3 G4 [2]
  WSL WS1 .... 4 C8
  WSNGN B18 .... 88 F8
Whitnash Cl
  RCOVN/BALC/EX CV7 .... 150 E7
Whitnash Gv COVE CV2 .... 135 M8
Whitney Av STRBR DY8 .... 101 H7 [2]
Whittaker Av BKHL/PFLD WV2 .... 50 C6
Whittall Dr East KIDDW DY11 .... 160 F4
Whittall Dr West KIDDW DY11 .... 160 E4
Whittall St CBHAMNE B4 .... 7 G3
Whittimere St WSL WS1 .... 5 G2
Whittingham Gv WNSFLD WV11 .... 37 K7
Whittingham Rd HALE B63 .... 103 L8
Whittington Cl
  ALE/KHTH/YWD B14 .... 125 J8
  HHTH/SAND B71 .... 69 K5 [2]
  WWCK CV34 .... 199 M5 [8]
Whittington Common Rd
  LICHS WS14 .... 29 L1
Whittington Gv STETCH B33 .... 109 K3
Whittington Hall La
  KINVER DY7 .... 118 C3
Whittington La ATHST CV9 .... 62 E3
Whittington Ov STETCH B33 .... 109 L3
Whittington Rd STRBR DY8 .... 119 H2
Whittle Cl COVS CV3 .... 155 K5
  RUGBYS/DCH CV22 .... 183 H6
Whittle Cft CVALE B35 .... 91 K2 [2]
Whittleford Gv CBROM B36 .... 92 A4
Whittleford Rd
  NUNW/HART CV10 .... 98 A1
Whitton St DARL/WED WS10 .... 52 C7
Whitville Cl KIDDW DY11 .... 137 G6 [2]
Whitwell Dr SHLY B90 .... 147 L7 [1]
Whitworth Av COVS CV3 .... 154 F4
Whitworth Cl DARL/WED WS10 .... 52 C6
Whitworth Dr HHTH/SAND B71 .... 69 J4
Whoberley Av COVW CV5 .... 153 H2
Whyley St WBROM B70 .... 86 E1
Whyley Wk OLDBY B69 .... 86 E8 [3]
Whynot St HALE B63 .... 102 F8 [1]
Wibert Cl SLYOAK B29 .... 124 E4
Wichnor Rd HIA/OLT B92 .... 109 K8
Wickham Cl COVN CV6 .... 133 K3
Wickham Gdns WNSFLD WV11 .... 36 E7
Wicklow Cl HALE B63 .... 121 H4
Wiclif Wy NUNW/HART CV10 .... 97 M2
Widdecombe Cl COVE CV2 .... 135 H5
Widdrington Cl COV CV1 .... 134 A8
Wideacre Dr KGSTG B44 .... 71 J6
Wide Acres RBRY B45 .... 142 D4
Widney Av ALDR WS9 .... 40 F4
  SLYOAK B29 .... 124 A3
Widney Cl DOR/KN B93 .... 148 D8 [1]
Widney La SOLH B91 .... 147 M5
Widney Manor Rd SOLH B91 .... 148 A3
Widney Rd DOR/KN B93 .... 148 C8
Wigeon Gv WOLVN WV10 .... 36 C1
Wigford Rd TAM/AM/WIL B77 .... 46 A8
Wiggins Cft WALM/CURD B76 .... 73 K2
Wiggins Hill Rd
  WALM/CURD B76 .... 74 D5
Wigginsmill Rd DARL/WED WS10 .... 68 B4
Wiggin St LDYWD/EDGR B16 .... 106 D2
Wigginton Rd CRTAM B79 .... 31 M7
Wight Cft CBROM B36 .... 92 F4
Wightman Cl LICHS WS14 .... 21 J7
Wightwick Bank
  DUNHL/THL/PER WV6 .... 48 B5
Wightwick Cl BLOX/PEL WS3 .... 38 F4 [1]
Wightwick Gv
  DUNHL/THL/PER WV6 .... 48 E3
Wightwick Hall Rd
  DUNHL/THL/PER WV6 .... 48 C4
Wigmore Gv KGSTG B44 .... 71 M5 [1]
Wigmore La HHTH/SAND B71 .... 69 L5
Wigorn La HAG/WOL DY9 .... 119 M5
Wigorn Rd SMTHWK B67 .... 105 K4
Wigston Rd COVE CV2 .... 62 A8
  NUNW/HART CV10 .... 79 L6
Wilberforce Wy SOLH B91 .... 128 C6
Wilbraham Rd WSLW WS2 .... 4 A3
Wilcote Gv ACGN B27 .... 127 C5 [1]
Wilcox Av HEDN WS12 .... 12 F6
Wildacres STRBR DY8 .... 101 G7
Wildcroft Rd COVW CV5 .... 153 G3
Wilde Cl ALE/KHTH/YWD B14 .... 145 H1
Wilderness La GTB/HAM B43 .... 70 B2
Wildey Rd BDWTH CV12 .... 116 B3
Wildfell Rd ACGN B27 .... 127 H3
Wild Goose La REDE B98 .... 197 H5
Wildmoor Cl COVN CV6 .... 134 F1

Wildmoor La BRGRVW B61 .... 165 L4
Wildmoor Rd SHLY B90 .... 126 F8
Wildtree Av WOLVN WV10 .... 36 E1
Wiley Av DARL/WED WS10 .... 52 A7
Wiley Av South DARL/WED WS10 .... 52 A8
Wilford Gv SOLH B91 .... 147 M3
Wilford Rd HHTH/SAND B71 .... 69 H7
Wilkes Av WSLW WS2 .... 52 D2
Wilkes Cl BLOX/PEL WS3 .... 39 J2
Wilkes Cft SEDG DY3 .... 66 B6 [3]
Wilkes Rd CDSL WV8 .... 34 D2
Wilkin Rd BRWNH WS8 .... 26 A3
Wilkinson Av BILS/COS WV14 .... 67 J2
Wilkinson Cl BNTWD WS7 .... 18 F5
  SCFLD/BOLD B73 .... 72 F3
Wilkinson Rd DARL/WED WS10 .... 51 L8
Wilkinson Wy CSHL/WTROR B46 .... 94 E3
Wilkins Rd BILS/COS WV14 .... 51 H6
Willard Rd YDLY B25 .... 109 G7 [1]
Willaston Rd STETCH B33 .... 110 B6
Willclare Rd
  LGN/SDN/BHAMAIR B26 .... 109 L7
Willcock Rd BKHL/PFLD WV2 .... 50 C6
Willday Dr ATHST CV9 .... 63 H3
Willenhall La COVS CV3 .... 155 K5
  WSLW WS2 .... 38 D6
Willenhall Rd BILS/COS WV14 .... 51 K7
  DARL/WED WS10 .... 52 B5
  WLNHL WV13 .... 51 H4
  WOLV WV1 .... 50 F4
Willenhall St DARL/WED WS10 .... 52 A6 [2]
Willerby Fold WOLVN WV10 .... 36 D1 [2]
Willersey Rd MOS/BIL B13 .... 126 B5
Willes Rd RLSN CV32 .... 200 E5
  WSNGN B18 .... 88 C7
Willes Ter RLSS CV31 .... 200 F5
Willett Av BNTWD WS7 .... 18 C8
Willett Rd HHTH/SAND B71 .... 69 J5
Willetts Dr HALE B63 .... 120 F1
Willetts Rd NFLD/LBR B31 .... 144 C8
Willetts Wy CDYHTH B64 .... 103 K3 [3]
Willey Gv ERDE/BCHGN B24 .... 90 F3
William Arnold Cl COVE CV2 .... 154 E1 [1]
William Booth La CBHAMNE B4 .... 6 F2 [1]
William Bree Rd COVW CV5 .... 132 A8
William Bristow Rd COVS CV3 .... 154 C6
William Cook Rd
  WASH/WDE B8 .... 90 F8 [1]
William Cree Cl KNWTH CV8 .... 180 D2
William Green Rd
  DARL/WED WS10 .... 69 G2 [1]
William Groubb Cl COVS CV3 .... 155 J6
William Harper Rd WLNHL WV13 .... 51 M4
William Henry St
  VAUX/NECH B7 .... 89 L7 [1]
William Ker Rd TPTN/OCK DY4 .... 68 A8
William Mckee Cl COVS CV3 .... 155 J6
William Morris Gv
  CNCK/NC WS11 .... 16 C1 [3]
William Rd SMTHWKW B67 .... 105 H2
Williams Cl SHHTH WV12 .... 38 A8
Williamson Av HEDN WS12 .... 18 A1
Williamson St BDMR/CCFT WV3 .... 2 D8
William St BDWTH CV12 .... 117 H5
  BRLYHL DY5 .... 102 A2
  EDG B15 .... 6 C8
  NUN CV11 .... 99 J2
  REDW B97 .... 196 C1 [4]
  RLSN CV32 .... 200 E5
  RUGBYN/HIL CV21 .... 183 M2
  RUSH/SHEL WS4 .... 53 K2
  WBROM B70 .... 68 C8
William St North LOZ/NWT B19 .... 6 F1
William St West SMTHWK B66 .... 87 M6
William Tarver Cl WWCK CV34 .... 199 L6
William Wiggin Av
  BLOX/PEL WS3 .... 38 F3
Willingsworth Rd
  DARL/WED WS10 .... 68 A4
Willington Rd CRTAM B79 .... 31 M6
Willington St NUN CV11 .... 80 E8 [1]
Willingworth Cl
  ETTPK/GDPK/PENN WV4 .... 66 E2
Willis Gv BDWTH CV12 .... 117 G2
Willis Pearson Av
  BILS/COS WV14 .... 67 K3
Willis St KIDDW DY11 .... 137 G8
Willmore Gv HWK/WKHTH B38 .... 144 D5
Willmore Rd
  BFLD/HDSWWD B20 .... 89 H3
Willmott Cl MGN/WHC B75 .... 57 H2
Willmott Rd MGN/WHC B75 .... 57 H2
Willoughby Av KNWTH CV8 .... 191 J2
Willoughby Cl COVS CV3 .... 155 J5
  PENK ST19 .... 10 D6 [2]
Willoughby Dr SOLH B91 .... 147 M4
Willoughby Gv SLYOAK B29 .... 123 L4 [2]
Willoughby Rd CRTAM B79 .... 31 J6
Willow Av BNTWD WS7 .... 19 G7
  DARL/WED WS10 .... 68 D3
  HRBN B17 .... 105 L3
  WNSFLD WV11 .... 36 F5
Willow Bank BDMR/CCFT WV3 .... 49 G4
Willowbank POL/KGSB/FAZ B78 .... 45 M4
Willow Bank Rd DOR/KN B93 .... 148 D7
Willow Brook Rd ALVE B48 .... 167 L6
  KNWTH CV8 .... 180 E1 [1]
Willow Cl BDWTH CV12 .... 98 E8
  BRGRVW B61 .... 185 J3
  CDYHTH B64 .... 103 J4 [3]
  HAG/WOL DY9 .... 119 K8
  NUNW/HART CV10 .... 79 L6
  POL/KGSB/FAZ B78 .... 46 D6
Willow Coppice
  RIDG/WDGT B32 .... 123 G4 [3]
Willow Ct SMTHWK B66 .... 87 H5
Willow Ctyd COVE CV2 .... 135 H6
Willowdale Gra
  DUNHL/THL/PER WV6 .... 35 J8 [3]
Willow Dr CDSL WV8 .... 34 F2 [1]
  HDSW B21 .... 88 A4
  OLDBY B69 .... 86 A6
  SHLY B90 .... 171 H1
Willow End HAG/WOL DY9 .... 120 B2

Willowfield Dr KIDDW DY11 .... 137 G5
Willowfields Rd NUN CV11 .... 99 L4 [1]
Willow Gdns BRGRVW B61 .... 185 J2
  LDYWD/EDGR B16 .... 106 D1 [3]
Willow Gv TLHL/CAN CV4 .... 153 G3
  WNSFLD WV11 .... 37 M1
Willow Hts CDYHTH B64 .... 103 L5 [3]
Willowherb Cl
  CNCK/NC WS11 .... 17 G5 [1]
  COVS CV3 .... 155 K5 [3]
  DSYBK/YTR WS5 .... 69 L2 [10]
Willowherb Wy SHLY B90 .... 146 E8 [1]
Willow Meer KNWTH CV8 .... 176 F6 [1]
Willow Ms SLYOAK B29 .... 123 M4 [1]
Willow Park Dr STRBR DY8 .... 119 L3
Willow Ri BRLYHL DY5 .... 102 A4
Willow Rd BDMR/CCFT WV3 .... 49 H5
  BRGRVW B61 .... 185 J2 [2]
  BRGRVW B61 .... 185 J3 [5]
  BVILLE B30 .... 124 D5
  DUDN DY1 .... 84 E1
  GTB/HAM B43 .... 70 D4
  NUNW/HART CV10 .... 80 C8
  SOLH B91 .... 147 J3
Willows Brook Rd RMSLY B62 .... 104 D5
Willows Crs BHTH/HG B12 .... 107 H8
Willow Sheets Meadow
  RLSN CV32 .... 193 J7 [1]
Willowside RUSH/SHEL WS4 .... 40 A5
Willowsmere Dr LICHS WS14 .... 21 K6
Willows Rd BHTH/HG B12 .... 107 J8
  RUSH/SHEL WS4 .... 40 A5
  WSL WS1 .... 5 K3
The Willows ACGN B27 .... 126 F3
  ATHST CV9 .... 63 J3
  BDWTH CV12 .... 116 C3
  CNCK/NC WS11 .... 16 A4
  HLYWD B47 .... 145 J1
  WALM/CURD B76 .... 73 K3 [1]
  WMBN WV5 .... 64 D8 [1]
Willowtree Cl LICH WS13 .... 20 F3 [3]
Willow Tree Dr RBRY B45 .... 167 H5 [1]
Willow Wy
  CHWD/FDBR/MGN B37 .... 110 F3
  REDW B97 .... 195 M1
Wills Av HHTH/SAND B71 .... 68 F6
Willsbridge Covert
  BVILLE B30 .... 145 G3 [1]
Wills St LOZ/NWT B19 .... 88 F6
Wilmcote Cl BHTH/HG B12 .... 107 J7 [1]
Wilmcote Ct BRGRVW B61 .... 185 H5
Wilmcote Dr MGN/WHC B75 .... 56 F7
Wilmcote Gn COVW CV5 .... 152 E2 [2]
Wilmcote Rd SOLH B91 .... 127 K7 [1]
Wilmington Rd
  RIDG/WDGT B32 .... 104 F7
Wilmore La HLYWD B47 .... 169 J1
Wilmot Av CSHL/WTROR B46 .... 93 K7 [1]
Wilmot Dr ERDW/GRVHL B23 .... 72 E7
  TPTN/OCK DY4 .... 67 J7 [2]
Wilmot Gdns DUDN DY1 .... 84 E3 [2]
Wilmott Cl LICH WS13 .... 20 E6 [2]
Wilnecote Gv PBAR/PBCH B42 .... 89 C1
  RLSS CV31 .... 200 F8 [1]
Wilnecote La
  TAM/AM/WIL B77 .... 46 C5 [1]
Wilner's Vw BLOX/PEL WS3 .... 25 K8
Wilsford Cl ALE/KHTH/YWD B14 .... 145 H4
  RUSH/SHEL WS4 .... 40 A5
Wilson Cl RUGBYS/DCH CV22 .... 183 G3
Wilson Dr MGN/WHC B75 .... 57 M8 [2]
  MGN/WHC B75 .... 57 L8 [2]
Wilson Gn COVS CV3 .... 155 K4
Wilson Gv CNCK/NC WS11 .... 17 G3 [1]
  KNWTH CV8 .... 192 A1 [1]
Wilson Rd BILS/COS WV14 .... 67 G6
  BRLYHL DY5 .... 102 A1
  LGLYGN/QTN B68 .... 105 H5
  LOZ/NWT B19 .... 89 H5
  SMTHWK B66 .... 105 M1
Wilson's La COVN CV6 .... 116 D8
  RCOVN/BALC/EX CV7 .... 116 E7
Wilsons Rd DOR/KN B93 .... 149 G7
Wilson St TPTN/OCK DY4 .... 67 L8
Wilteil Rd LICHS WS14 .... 20 F7
Wilton Av KIDDW DY11 .... 136 E6
Wilton Cl SEDG DY3 .... 66 C5
Wilton Rd BFLD/HDSWWD B20 .... 88 F4
  ERDW/GRVHL B23 .... 72 D3
  RCOVN/BALC/EX CV7 .... 150 F7
  SPARK B11 .... 107 M1
Wilton St LOZ/NWT B19 .... 89 H6
Wiltshire Cl BDWTH CV12 .... 116 E2 [1]
  COVW CV5 .... 153 H2
  WSLW WS2 .... 53 H1 [1]
Wiltshire Dr HALE B63 .... 102 F6
Wiltshire Wy HHTH/SAND B71 .... 69 G6
Wimblebury Rd HEDN WS12 .... 17 K1
Wimbledon Dr STRBR DY8 .... 119 M3
Wimborne Dr COVE CV2 .... 155 K1
Wimborne Rd WOLVN WV10 .... 36 E7
Wimbourne Cl
  NUNW/HART CV10 .... 79 L8
Wimbourne Rd
  LDYWD/EDGR B16 .... 106 B2
  WALM/CURD B76 .... 73 L1
Wimperis Wy GTB/HAM B43 .... 71 G1
Wimpole Gv KGSTG B44 .... 71 M6 [3]
Wimshurst Meadow
  WOLVN WV10 .... 36 D1 [1]
Wincanton Cft CBROM B36 .... 91 G5
Winceby Pl TLHL/CAN CV4 .... 152 B4 [1]
Winceby Rd
  DUNHL/THL/PER WV6 .... 48 D2 [1]
Winchat Cl COVS CV3 .... 155 K4 [1]
Winchcombe Cl DUDN DY1 .... 84 C2 [1]
  HIA/OLT B92 .... 127 M3 [6]
Winchcombe Rd HIA/OLT B92 .... 136 E7 [1]
Winchester Av
  NUNW/HART CV10 .... 98 C7
Winchester Cl
  BLKHTH/ROWR B65 .... 104 C1 [3]
  HAG/WOL DY9 .... 119 J5
  LICH WS13 .... 21 G2 [2]
Winchester Dr
  CHWD/FDBR/MGN B37 .... 110 D3
  STRBR DY8 .... 119 L2 [2]

Winchester Gdns
  NFLD/LBR B31 .... 143 L2
Winchester Ri DUDN DY1 .... 84 E3 [1]
Winchester Rd
  BFLD/HDSWWD B20 .... 89 H4 [1]
  CNCK/NC WS11 .... 16 E2
  HHTH/SAND B71 .... 68 F5
  POL/KGSB/FAZ B78 .... 45 K2 [2]
  WOLVN WV10 .... 36 A3
Winchester St COV CV1 .... 9 J3
Winchfield Dr HRBN B17 .... 105 K5
Wincote Dr
  DUNHL/THL/PER WV6 .... 49 G1
Wincrest Wy BKDE/SHDE B34 .... 92 A8
Windermere
  TAM/AM/WIL B77 .... 46 E6 [2]
Windermere Av COVS CV3 .... 155 J4 [2]
  COVW CV5 .... 152 C1 [3]
  NUN CV11 .... 81 K6 [2]
Windermere Dr
  FOAKS/STRLY B74 .... 55 K2
  KGSWFD DY6 .... 83 H7
  RLSN CV32 .... 200 B3
Windermere Pl
  CNCK/NC WS11 .... 16 C4 [1]
Windermere Rd
  DUNHL/THL/PER WV6 .... 35 H5
  HDSW B21 .... 88 C3
  MOS/BIL B13 .... 125 M4
Windermere Wy STRPT DY13 .... 160 E8 [3]
Winderton Av
  RWWCK/WEL CV35 .... 198 B3 [2]
Winding Ml North
  BRLYHL DY5 .... 102 C6 [1]
Winding Ml South
  BRLYHL DY5 .... 102 C6 [2]
The Windings LICH WS13 .... 20 F4
Windlass Cft NFLD/LBR B31 .... 143 K1 [2]
Windleaves Rd CBROM B36 .... 92 C6
Windmill Av CSHL/WTROR B46 .... 93 K6 [2]
  RBRY B45 .... 142 C5
Windmill Bank WMBN WV5 .... 64 E6 [2]
Windmill Cl CRTAM B79 .... 31 L5
  KNWTH CV8 .... 176 E7 [2]
  LICH WS13 .... 20 D5
  NFLD/LBR B31 .... 124 A8 [2]
Windmill Crs BDMR/CCFT WV3 .... 48 E4
  SMTHWK B66 .... 88 A8
Windmill Dr REDW B97 .... 195 M5
Windmill End DUDS DY2 .... 85 J8
Windmill Gv KGSWFD DY6 .... 82 E5
Windmill Hl HALE B63 .... 103 H8 [3]
  NFLD/LBR B31 .... 123 M8
  RLSN CV32 .... 193 H8
The Windmill Hl COVW CV5 .... 132 E6
Windmill Hl ATHST CV9 .... 62 B7
  BDMR/CCFT WV3 .... 48 E4
  DOR/KN B93 .... 172 D4
  LICH WS13 .... 20 E3
  NUNW/HART CV10 .... 97 J7
  RCOVN/BALC/EX CV7 .... 114 D7
  RCOVN/BALC/EX CV7 .... 175 H1
  RUGE WS15 .... 18 E1
  SMTHWK B66 .... 105 M1
Windmill Prec SMTHWK B66 .... 88 A8 [2]
Windmill Rd ATHST CV9 .... 63 H4
  COVN CV6 .... 134 E2
  NUNW/HART CV10 .... 80 B6
  RCOVN/BALC/EX CV7 .... 116 E6
  RLSS CV31 .... 200 D8
  SHLY B90 .... 146 C3
Windmill St CBHAMW B1 .... 6 D4
  DARL/WED WS10 .... 68 D2
  DUDN DY1 .... 84 E3 [3]
  SEDG DY3 .... 66 B8
  WSL WS1 .... 4 F5
Windmill Vw DUDN DY1 .... 66 F6
Windridge Cl COVS CV3 .... 155 G7
Windridge Crs HIA/OLT B92 .... 128 D5 [2]
The Windrow
  DUNHL/THL/PER WV6 .... 48 B1 [2]
Windrush Cl REDW B97 .... 196 B7
Windrush Gv SLYOAK B29 .... 124 E5
Windrush Rd CNCK/NC WS11 .... 12 C7 [2]
  HLYWD B47 .... 145 M6
Windsor Av
  ETTPK/GDPK/PENN WV4 .... 49 J7
  LGLYGN/QTN B68 .... 86 C5
Windsor Cl BLKHTH/ROWR B65 .... 104 A1
  BNTWD WS7 .... 18 C4 [2]
  CRTAM B79 .... 32 A6
  HALE B63 .... 121 K2
  NFLD/LBR B31 .... 143 L7
  RBRY B45 .... 142 E3 [2]
Windsor Ct SEDG DY3 .... 83 M4
Windsor Crs DUDS DY2 .... 85 H7
Windsor Dr ERDE/BCHGN B24 .... 73 C8
  HIA/OLT B92 .... 127 M3
  KIDD DY10 .... 137 G5
Windsor Gdns BDMR/CCFT WV3 .... 48 E6
  BRGRVE B60 .... 185 L3 [2]
  CDSL WV8 .... 34 D2
Windsor Ga SHHTH WV12 .... 52 A1 [3]
Windsor Gv RUSH/SHEL WS4 .... 40 A3
  STRBR DY8 .... 101 J4
Windsor Holloway KINVER DY7 .... 118 A4
Windsor Pl ERDW/GRVHL B23 .... 90 C2 [2]
  RLSN CV32 .... 200 D4 [1]
Windsor Rd BLKHTH/ROWR B65 .... 86 A4
  BVILLE B30 .... 124 F8
  CBROM B36 .... 92 E6 [2]
  ETTPK/GDPK/PENN WV4 .... 50 D8
  GTWY WS6 .... 24 C1
  HALE B63 .... 121 K1
  HHTH/SAND B71 .... 68 F5
  LGLYGN/QTN B68 .... 104 E2
  POL/KGSB/FAZ B78 .... 47 L2
  REDW B97 .... 188 B8
  SCFLD/BOLD B73 .... 72 B4
  STRBR DY8 .... 119 H2
  TPTN/OCK DY4 .... 67 L5
  WMBN WV5 .... 64 D7
Windsor St BILS/COS WV14 .... 51 G7
  BRGRVE B60 .... 185 K3
  COV CV1 .... 8 C5
  NUN CV11 .... 98 F1
  REDW B97 .... 196 B1

RLSN CV32 .... 200 D4
WSL WS1 .... 4 F7
Windsor St South VAUX/NECH B7 .. 7 L2
Windsor Vw
  RIDG/WDGT B32 .... 122 F6
Windsor Wk DARL/WED WS10 .. 52 B5
Windsor Wy RUSH/SHEL WS4 .. 40 B6
Winds Point HAG/WOL DY9 ...... 119 L7
Windward Wy CBROM B36 ...... 92 D6
Windy Arbour KNWTH CV8 ...... 191 M1
Windyridge Rd
  WALM/CURD B76 .... 73 K7
Winfield Rd NUN CV11 .... 80 F8
Winford Av KGSWFD DY6 ...... 101 J1
Winforton Cl REDE B98 .... 197 J2
Wingate Cl BVILLE B30 .... 144 D1
Wingate Rd WSLW WS2 .... 52 C3
Wing Cl WSLW WS2 .... 52 D1
Wingfield Cl
  CHWD/FDBR/MGN B37 ...... 110 D2
Wingfield Rd CSHL/WTROR B46 .. 93 K6
  PBAR/PBCH B42 .... 71 G6
Wingfield Wy COVN CV6 .... 133 L3
Wingrave Cl WOLVN WV10 ...... 36 B5
Winifred Av COVW CV5 .... 8 B7
Winkle St WBROM B70 .... 86 F1
Winleigh Rd
  BFLD/HDSWWD B20 .... 88 D3
Winn Cl
Winnall Cl BILS/COS WV14 ...... 67 H3
Winnallthorpe COVS CV3 ...... 155 J7
Winnie Rd SLYOAK B29 .... 124 C4
Winnington Rd WASH/WDE B8 .. 90 E6
Winnipeg Rd HWK/WKHTH B38 .. 144 E5
Winsford Av COVW CV5 .... 152 F1
Winsford Cl HALE B63 .... 103 L7
  RCOVN/BALC/EX CV7 .... 150 E7
  WALM/CURD B76 .... 73 J2
Winsham Gv HDSW B21 .... 88 B5
Winsham Wk COVS CV3 .... 178 A2
Winslow Cl REDE B98 .... 197 K2
  RLSN CV32 .... 200 A4
Winslow Dr
  DUNHL/THL/PER WV6 ...... 49 J1
Winson Green Rd WSNGN B18 .. 88 C8
Winson St WSNGN B18 .... 106 B1
Winsor Av HEDN WS12 .... 12 F7
Winstanley Rd STETCH B33 ...... 109 H3
Winster Av DOR/KN B93 .... 172 C1
Winster Cl RCOVN/BALC/EX CV7 . 115 L6
Winster Gv KGSTG B44 .... 71 H3
Winster Rd GTB/HAM B43 ...... 70 B5
  WOLV WV1 .... 50 F4
Winston Av COVE CV2 .... 135 M4
Winston Cl COVE CV2 .... 135 K4
Winston Dr BFLD/HDSWWD B20 .. 88 F4
  RMSLY B62 .... 141 L1
Winstone Cl REDE B98 .... 196 E1
Winston Rd CDSL WV8 .... 82 C3
Winterbourne Cft
  ALE/KHTH/YWD B14 .... 145 L3
Winterbourne Rd SOLH B91 .... 147 K1
Winter Cl BRGRVW B61 .... 165 K7
  LICH WS13 .... 21 H3
Winterfold Cl KIDD DY10 ...... 137 M7
Winterley Gdns SEDG DY3 ...... 66 C7
Winterley La RUSH/SHEL WS4 .. 40 A6
Winterton Rd KGSTG B44 ...... 71 L2
Winthorpe Dr SOLH B91 .... 148 A5
Wintney Cl HRBN B17 .... 105 L6
Winton Gv WALM/CURD B76 .... 73 L7
Winward Rd REDE B98 .... 197 K4
Winwick Pl RUGBYS/DCH CV22 . 183 G5
Winwood Heath Rd RMSLY B62 .. 141 J3
Winwood Rd
  BLKHTH/ROWR B65 .... 104 C2
Winwoods Gv
  RIDG/WDGT B32 .... 122 E5
Winyate HI REDE B98 .... 196 E3
Winyates Wy REDE B98 .... 197 J1
Wirehill Dr REDE B98 .... 196 E4
Wiremill Cl KGSTG B44 .... 71 J7
Wirral Rd NFLD/LBR B31 ...... 123 K7
Wiscombe Av PENK ST19 .... 10 C4
Wiseacre Cft SHLY B90 .... 146 C3
Wise Gv WWCK CV34 .... 199 J3
Wiseman Gv ERDW/GRVHL B23 .. 72 B4
Wisemore WSL WS1 .... 4 E1
  WSLW WS2 .... 4 E1
  WSLW WS2 .... 53 J2
Wise St RLSS CV31 .... 200 D6
Wise Ter RLSS CV31 .... 200 D6
Wishaw Cl REDE B98 .... 196 E5
  SHLY B90 .... 146 C3
Wishaw Gv
  CHWD/FDBR/MGN B37 ...... 92 D8
Wishaw La POL/KGSB/FAZ B78 .. 58 F2
  WALM/CURD B76 .... 74 C6
Wisley Gv KNWTH CV8 .... 177 G8
Wisley Wy RIDG/WDGT B32 .. 105 K8
Wissage Ct LICH WS13 .... 21 J5
Wissage La LICH WS13 .... 21 H4
Wissage Rd LICH WS13 .... 21 H5
Wistaria Cl NFLD/LBR B31 .... 123 L1
Wisteria Gv KGSTG B44 .... 71 J3
Wistmans Cl DUDN DY1 .... 84 B4
Wistwood Hayes WOLVN WV10 .. 36 D1
Witham Cft SOLH B91 .... 148 A4
Withdean Cl SPARK B11 .... 108 B8
Witherford Cl SLYOAK B29 .... 124 A5
Witherford Cft SHLY B90 ...... 147 H3
Witherley Rd ATHST CV9 ...... 63 K6
Withern Wy SEDG DY3 .... 84 B2
Withers Rd CDSL WV8 .... 34 F2
Withers Wy HHTH/SAND B71 .. 87 H1
Withington Covert
  BVILLE B30 .... 145 H3
Withington Gv DOR/KN B93 .. 172 C1
Withybed Cl ALVE B48 .... 167 L7
Withybed La ALVE B48 .... 167 L7
Withybrook Cl COVE CV2 ...... 135 K3
Withybrook Rd SHLY B90 ...... 146 F4
Withy Gv CHWD/FDBR/MGN B37 . 92 C8
Withy Hill Rd WMBN WV5 .... 57 K6
Withymere La WMBN WV5 .... 65 C5
Withymoor Rd DUDS DY2 ...... 103 J1
  STRBR DY8 .... 101 L6

Withy Rd BILS/COS WV14 ...... 67 G2
Withywood Cl SHHTH WV12 .. 37 M4
Witley Av HALE B63 .... 121 J1
  SOLH B91 .... 148 A3
Witley Cl KIDDW DY11 .... 160 F3
Witley Crs OLDBY B69 .... 86 C8
Witley Farm Cl SOLH B91 ...... 148 A3
Witley Rd NFLD/LBR B31 ...... 144 B3
Witney Cl CRTAM B79 .... 31 K6
Witney Dr
  CHWD/FDBR/MGN B37 ...... 110 D3
Witney Gv WOLVN WV10 ...... 35 M2
Witton La AST/WIT B6 .... 89 K4
Witton Lodge Rd
  ERDW/GRVHL B23 .... 71 M6
Witton Rd AST/WIT B6 .... 89 J1
  ETTPK/GDPK/PENN WV4 .. 49 L7
Witton St BORD B9 .... 107 M3
  STRBR DY8 .... 119 J1
Wivelden Av STRPT DY13 ...... 161 H7
Wixford Gv SHLY B90 .... 147 H3
Wobaston Rd CDSL WV8 ...... 35 H2
  COVEN WV9 .... 35 J1
  WOLVN WV10 .... 35 M1
Woburn Av SHHTH WV12 ...... 37 M7
Woburn Av SHHTH WV12 ...... 37 M7
Woburn Cl BRGRVW B61 ...... 185 H4
  RLSS CV31 .... 201 G7
Woburn Crs GTB/HAM B43 .... 70 B4
Woburn Dr BRLYHL DY5 ...... 101 M5
  CDYHTH B64 .... 103 L6
  NUNW/HART CV10 .... 98 B7
Woburn Gv ACGN B27 .... 127 G4
Wodehouse Cl WMBN WV5 .... 64 C3
Wodehouse La SEDG DY3 ...... 65 J5
  WOLVN WV10 .... 3 L1
Woden Av WNSFLD WV11 .... 37 G7
Woden Cl WMBN WV5 .... 64 C3
Woden Crs WNSFLD WV11 .... 37 G7
Woden Rd East
  DARL/WED WS10 .... 52 F8
Woden Rd North
  DARL/WED WS10 .... 52 C8
Woden Rd South
  DARL/WED WS10 .... 68 D4
Woden Rd West
  DARL/WED WS10 .... 68 B1
Wold Wk MOS/BIL B13 .... 125 M7
Wolfe Rd CVW CAN CV4 ...... 152 D6
Wolfsbane Dr DSYBK/YTR WS5 .. 69 L2
Wolfson Dr EDG B15 .... 124 B1
Wolgarston Wy PENK ST19 .... 10 C6
Wollaston Ct STRBR DY8 ...... 101 G7
Wollaston Crs WNSFLD WV11 .. 37 H7
Wollaston Rd KINVER DY7 .... 101 G6
  STRBR DY8 .... 101 J6
Wollerton Gv MGN/WHC B75 .. 57 K7
Wollescote Dr SOLH B91 ...... 147 M3
Wollescote Rd
  HAG/WOL DY9 .... 120 A2
Wolmer Rd WNSFLD WV11 .... 37 K3
Wolseley TAM/AM/WIL B77 .... 46 D3
Wolseley Av ACGN B27 .... 127 H1
Wolseley Bank WOLVN WV10 .. 36 D6
Wolseley Cl CBROM B36 .... 92 E4
  WOLVN WV10 .... 36 D6
Wolseley Ga WOLVN WV10 .... 36 D6
Wolseley Rd BILS/COS WV14 .. 50 F6
  WBROM B70 .... 68 D7
Wolseley St BORD B9 .... 107 M3
Wolsey Rd LICH WS13 .... 20 D3
  RUGBYS/DCH CV22 .... 183 H8
Wolston Cl SHLY B90 .... 126 F8
Wolston La KNWTH CV8 ...... 180 D2
Wolverbury Rd
  CHWD/FDBR/MGN B37 ...... 110 F6
  COVW CV5 .... 8 C8
  DUDS DY2 .... 85 J4
  RBRY B45 .... 106 D5
Wolverton Rd
  CHWD/FDBR/MGN B37 ...... 110 F6
  COVW CV5 .... 8 C8
  DUDS DY2 .... 85 J4
  RBRY B45 .... 106 D5
Wombourne Cl SEDG DY3 .... 66 A5
Wombourne Pk WMBN WV5 .. 82 D1
Wombourne Rd SEDG DY3 .... 82 D2
Wombrook Dl WMBN WV5 .... 64 B7
Woodacre Rd ERDE/BCHGN B24 .. 91 G1
Woodall Rd BFLD/HDSWWD B20 .. 88 K4
Woodall St BLOX/PEL WS3 .... 39 G5
  CDYHTH B64 .... 103 G4
Woodard Rd TPTN/OCK DY4 .. 68 A6

Wood Av SEDG DY3 .... 84 A1
  WNSFLD WV11 .... 37 G7
Woodbank Rd SEDG DY3 ...... 66 A6
Woodbank Rd SEDG DY3 ...... 165 K5
Woodbine Av SPARK B11 ...... 108 C4
Woodberrow La REDW B97 .. 195 L6
Woodberry Dr WALM/CURD B76 .. 73 L3
Woodberry Wk ACGN B27 .... 127 H2
Wood Green Rd
  DARL/WED WS10 .... 68 D2
Woodbine Cft
  LGN/SDN/BHAMAIR B26 .. 109 L7
Woodbine St RLSN CV32 ...... 200 C5
Woodbourne EDG B15 .... 106 B5
Woodbourne Rd HRBN B17 .. 105 M5
  SMTHWKW B67 .... 105 J3
Woodbridge Cl BLOX/PEL WS3 . 38 E2
  RUSH/SHEL WS4 .... 40 B4
Woodbridge Rd MOS/BIL B13 .. 125 K2
Woodbrooke Rd BVILLE B30 .. 124 E6
Woodburn Cl COVW CV5 ...... 152 F1
  REDW B97 .... 195 L7
  RMSLY B62 .... 104 D5
Woodbury Cl BRLYHL DY5 .... 102 C4
  REDW B97 .... 195 L7
  RMSLY B62 .... 104 D5
  STRPT DY13 .... 160 D8
Woodbury Gv SOLH B91 ...... 147 M5
Woodbury Rd KIDDW DY11 .. 160 F3
  RMSLY B62 .... 104 E5
  STRPT DY13 .... 160 D8
Woodbury Rd North
  STRPT DY13 .... 160 C8
Woodbury Rd West
  STRPT DY13 .... 160 D8
Woodchester HAG/WOL DY9 .. 139 M1
Woodchester Rd DOR/KN B93 . 172 C3
Wood Cl CSHL/WTROR B46 .... 93 K6
Woodclose Av COVN CV6 ...... 133 K7
Woodclose Rd
  CHWD/FDBR/MGN B37 ...... 110 D2
Woodcock Cl NFLD/LBR B31 .. 142 F4
Woodcock Gdns WOLVN WV10 . 22 F6
Woodcock La ACGN B27 .... 127 H2
  NFLD/LBR B31 .... 123 J5
Woodcock La North ACGN B27 . 127 H1
  LGN/SDN/BHAMAIR B26 .. 127 J1
Woodcock St VAUX/NECH B7 .. 7 H2
Woodcombe Cl BRLYHL DY5 .. 101 M6
Wood Common Gra
  BLOX/PEL WS3 .... 39 J1
Woodcote Av KNWTH CV8 .... 176 B7
  NUN CV11 .... 81 K5
Woodcote Dr DOR/KN B93 .... 172 F3
  RWWCK/WEL CV35 .... 191 K6
  WASH/WDE B8 .... 90 D8
Woodcote La BRGRVW B61 .. 164 B7
  KNWTH CV8 .... 191 J6
Woodcote Rd
  DUNHL/THL/PER WV6 ...... 49 G1
  ERDE/BCHGN B24 .... 73 H8
  RLSN CV32 .... 200 D3
  WWCK CV34 .... 199 K5
Woodcote Wy FOAKS/STRLY B74.. 55 K7
  WSNGN B18 .... 106 B5
Wood Ct BFLD/HDSWWD B20 .. 88 E3
Woodcraft Cl TLHL/CAN CV4 .. 152 E3
Wood Cft HLYWD B47 .... 145 M7
Woodcroft Av
  BFLD/HDSWWD B20 .... 88 C2
  CRTAM B79 .... 31 M7
  TPTN/OCK DY4 .... 67 G8
Woodcroft Cl BRGRVE B60 .. 166 D8
  CDYHTH B64 .... 103 K5
Woodcross La BILS/COS WV14 .. 66 E3
Woodcross St BILS/COS WV14 . 66 E3
Woodend BFLD/HDSWWD B20 .. 70 C7
Woodend Cl REDW B97 .... 195 M3
Woodend Cft TLHL/CAN CV4 .. 152 C5
Wood End La ERDE/BCHGN B24 .. 90 D2
  HOCK/TIA B94 .... 170 C8
  RCOVN/BALC/EX CV7 ...... 114 E1
Woodend Pl
  DUNHL/THL/PER WV6 ...... 48 F1
Wood End Rd DSYBK/YTR WS5 .. 54 B5
  ERDE/BCHGN B24 .... 90 D2
  WNSFLD WV11 .... 37 G5
Woodfall Av BVILLE B30 ...... 124 D8
Woodfield Av BRLYHL DY5 .... 83 M6
  CDYHTH B64 .... 103 H5
  ETTPK/GDPK/PENN WV4 .. 49 K7
  HAG/WOL DY9 .... 120 D3
  OLDBY B69 .... 104 E1
Woodfield Cl CNCK/NC WS11 .. 17 K6
  DSYBK/YTR WS5 .... 54 C8
  MGN/WHC B75 .... 56 F5
  REDE B98 .... 188 E8
Woodfield Crs BHTH/HG B12 .. 107 L7
  KIDDW DY11 .... 137 G3
Woodfield Dr CNCK/NC WS11 . 17 K6
Woodfield Hts
  DUNHL/THL/PER WV6 ...... 49 H1
Woodfield La RMSLY B62 ...... 141 H5
Woodfield Rd
  ALE/KHTH/YWD B14 .... 125 K5
  BHTH/HG B12 .... 107 L7
  COVW CV5 .... 153 J5
  SEDG DY3 .... 84 A1
  SOLH B91 .... 127 M7
Woodfields Dr LICHS WS14 .. 21 J7
Woodfield Wy BHTH/HG B12 . 107 L7
  KIDDW DY11 .... 137 G3
Woodfold Cft ALDR WS9 ...... 40 F6
Woodford Av CBROM B36...... 91 L5
Woodford Cl COVEN WV9 .... 35 K3
  NUNW/HART CV10 .... 98 A1
  RCOVN/BALC/EX CV7 ...... 116 B8
Woodford Crs BNTWD WS7 .. 18 F6
Woodford End
  CNCK/NC WS11 .... 16 D1
Woodford Green Rd
  HLGN/YWD B28 .... 126 E5
Woodford La NUNW/HART CV10 . 79 M2
  WMBN WV5 .... 64 B8
Woodford Wy HEDN WS12 .... 17 G4
Woodfort Rd GTB/HAM B43 .. 70 C6
Woodgate Dr RIDG/WDGT B32 . 122 E4
Woodgate Gdns
  RIDG/WDGT B32 .... 122 E3

Woodgate La RIDG/WDGT B32 .. 122 E3
Woodgate Rd BRGRVE B60 .. 194 A4
Woodgate Wy HAG/WOL DY9 .. 140 C6
Woodglade Cft
  HWK/WKHTH B38 .... 144 C3
Woodgreen GTWY WS6 .... 14 C7
Woodgreen Rd REDW B97 .... 195 L6
Woodgreen Cft
  LGLYGN/QTN B68 .... 105 G6
Wood Green Rd
  DARL/WED WS10 .... 68 D2
Woodgreen Rd
  LGLYGN/QTN B68 .... 105 G6
Wood Green Rd WSNGN B18 .. 106 B1
Woodhall Cl NUN CV11 .... 99 K3
  TPTN/OCK DY4 .... 67 M4
Woodhall Cft HIA/OLT B92 .. 127 K2
Woodhall Rd
  ETTPK/GDPK/PENN WV4 .. 65 J1
Woodham Cl RBRY B45 .... 142 C4
Woodhams Rd KNWTH CV8 .. 179 G2
Woodhaven CNCK/NC WS11 . 15 M7
  RUSH/SHEL WS4 .... 40 B4
Wood Hayes Rd WOLVN WV10 . 36 F1
Woodhill Cl WMBN WV5 ...... 64 D7
Wood Hill Ri COVN CV6 ...... 134 A3
Woodhouse La COVS CV3 .... 155 J5
Woodhouse La
  TAM/AM/WIL B77 .... 32 E8
Woodhouse Orch
  HAG/WOL DY9 .... 140 C6
Woodhouse Rd
  DUNHL/THL/PER WV6 ...... 48 F2
  RIDG/WDGT B32 .... 105 J7
Woodhouse Rd North
  DUNHL/THL/PER WV6 ...... 48 F1
Woodhouses La BNTWD WS7 . 19 J7
Woodhouses Rd BNTWD WS7 . 19 L6
Woodhouse St WWCK CV34 .. 199 H7
Woodhouse Wy CDYHTH B64 . 103 G4
Woodhurst Cl
  TAM/AM/WIL B77 .... 32 D8
Woodhurst Rd MOS/BIL B13 . 125 L1
Wooding Crs TPTN/OCK DY4.. 67 M4
Woodington Rd MGN/WHC B75.. 57 L8
Woodland Av BRLYHL DY5 .... 102 E4
  COVW CV5 .... 153 K6
  DUDN DY1 .... 85 G2
  DUNHL/THL/PER WV6 ...... 48 F2
  KIDDW DY11 .... 136 F6
  STRBR DY8 .... 119 K8
Woodland Cl HAG/WOL DY9 .. 120 B4
  HEDN WS12 .... 12 F5
  SHHTH WV12 .... 38 B7
Woodland Ct HEDN WS12 .... 16 A1
  LICHS WS14 .... 42 E6
Woodland Crs BDMR/CCFT WV3 . 49 H6
Woodland Dr SMTHWK B66 .. 87 J6
Woodland Gv GTB/HAM B43.. 70 C2
  SEDG DY3 .... 83 M2
Woodland Ri CDYHTH B64 .. 103 K5
  SCFLD/BOLD B73 .... 72 F1
Woodland Rd BDMR/CCFT WV3 . 49 H6
  BRGRVW B61 .... 164 D6
  HDSW B21 .... 88 A5
  KNWTH CV8 .... 176 F6
  NFLD/LBR B31 .... 143 M2
  REDW B97 .... 195 M2
  RMSLY B62 .... 104 B5
  TAM/AM/WIL B77 .... 46 E1
Woodlands Av CSHL/WTROR B46.. 92 F7
  DSYBK/YTR WS5 .... 54 C8
Woodlands Cl
  POL/KGSB/FAZ B78 .... 47 L8
Woodlands Cottages
  ETTPK/GDPK/PENN WV4 .. 65 K1
Woodlands Crs BLOX/PEL WS3.. 25 K8
Woodlands Farm Rd
  ERDE/BCHGN B24 .... 91 K1
Woodlands La BDWTH CV12 . 116 C1
  SHLY B90 .... 146 F5
  WOLVN WV10 .... 36 D1
Woodlands Paddock
  ETTPK/GDPK/PENN WV4 .. 65 J1
Woodlands Park Rd BVILLE B30.. 124 A7
Woodlands Rd BDWTH CV12 . 116 C2
  COVS CV3 .... 156 B6
  KIDD DY10 .... 137 L1
  RBRY B45 .... 142 B6
  SPARK B11 .... 126 A2
  WASH/WDE B8 .... 108 D1
  WMBN WV5 .... 64 E8
Woodlands St SMTHWK B66 . 88 A8
Woodlands Wy
  CHWD/FDBR/MGN B37 ...... 111 H2
Woodland Wy BNTWD WS7 .. 18 E7
  POL/KGSB/FAZ B78 .... 47 K5
Wood La ALDR WS9 .... 41 L5
  BFLD/HDSWWD B20 .... 88 E3
  BLOX/PEL WS3 .... 25 K8
  BRGRVW B61 .... 165 G2
  CHWD/FDBR/MGN B37 .. 110 E5
  ERDE/BCHGN B24 .... 91 G3
  FOAKS/STRLY B74 .... 55 J4
  HEDN WS12 .... 17 G1
  HIA/OLT B92 .... 149 K4
  HOCK/TIA B94 .... 170 C4
  HRBN B17 .... 105 L7
  MKTBOS/BARL/STKG CV13 . 81 H2
  RCOVN/BALC/EX CV7 ...... 96 B3
  RIDG/WDGT B32 .... 122 E4
  RUGBYN/HIL CV21 .... 159 L8
  RLSN CV32 .... 200 E1
  STRBR DY8 .... 101 B4
  TPTN/OCK DY4 .... 67 G6
  WLNHL WV13 .... 51 L3
  WOLVN WV10 .... 15 K7
Woodlands Cl SHHTH WV12 . 38 C6
Woodlawn Gv KGSWFD DY6 .. 83 H1
Woodlea Dr ERDE/BCHGN B24.. 90 D3
  SOLH B91 .... 127 J8
Wood Leasow
  RIDG/WDGT B32 .... 123 H3
Woodleaves HLYWD B47 ...... 145 K5

Woodleigh Av HRBN B17 ...... 124 B1
Woodleigh Cl HALE B63 ...... 103 L7
The Woodleys
  CSCFLD/WYGN B72 .... 72 F4
  TLHL/CAN CV4 .... 152 D8
The Woodleys
  ALE/KHTH/YWD B14 .... 145 M1
Woodloes Av North
  WWCK CV34 .... 199 J3
Woodloes Av South
  WWCK CV34 .... 199 J4
Woodloes La
  RWWCK/WEL CV35 .... 199 J2
  WWCK CV34 .... 199 K3
Woodloes Rd SHLY B90 ...... 146 F6
Woodman Cl DARL/WED WS10 . 68 F1
  HALE B63 .... 122 A2
Woodman Gv GTWY WS6 .... 24 C1
  HAG/WOL DY9 .... 140 B1
Woodman Rd
  ALE/KHTH/YWD B14 .... 145 L4
  HALE B63 .... 122 A2
Woodmeadow Rd BVILLE B30 . 92 F6
Woodnorton Dr MOS/BIL B13 . 125 J3
Woodnorton Rd
  BLKHTH/ROWR B65 .... 104 D3
Woodpecker Gv CBROM B36 .. 92 E6
Woodpecker Wy HEDN WS12 . 17 G2
Woodperry Av SOLH B91 ...... 148 A4
Wood Piece La REDE B98 .... 189 H6
Woodridge Av COVW CV5 .... 132 D7
Woodridge Rd HALE B63 .... 103 L8
Wood Ridings LICH WS13 .... 20 E4
Wood Rd CDSL WV8 .... 34 B1
  DUNHL/THL/PER WV6 ...... 48 F2
  SEDG DY3 .... 84 A2
  WMBN WV5 .... 64 F6
Woodroffe Wk COVN CV6 .... 134 E1
Woodrough Dr MOS/BIL B13 . 125 K3
Woodrow Centre REDE B98 . 196 E5
Woodrow Cl BRGRVW B61 .. 165 K4
Woodrow Crs DOR/KN B93 .. 148 E3
Woodrow La BRGRVW B61 .. 165 L4
  KIDD DY10 .... 161 G1
Woodrow North REDE B98 .. 196 E6
Woodrow South REDE B98 .. 196 E6
Woodruff Wy DSYBK/YTR WS5.. 69 L2
Woodrush Dr HLYWD B47 .. 145 L8
Woods Bank Ter
  DARL/WED WS10 .... 52 A8
Woods Crs BRLYHL DY5 ...... 102 E4
Woods Cft LICH WS13 .... 20 E4
Woodsetton Cl DUDN DY1 .. 66 F7
Woodshill Av RBRY B45 ...... 166 E3
Woodshires Rd COVN CV6 .. 116 D8
  HIA/OLT B92 .... 127 J6
Woodside ATHST CV9 .... 62 A4
  CHWD/FDBR/MGN B37 .. 110 C1
  FOAKS/STRLY B74 .... 56 C3
  RCOVN/BALC/EX CV7 ...... 96 B4
Wood Side WNSFLD WV11 .... 37 L5
Woodside Av North COVS CV3 . 153 K7
Woodside Av South COVS CV3 . 153 K8
Woodside Cl ATHST CV9 ...... 61 G4
  DSYBK/YTR WS5 .... 54 B8
Woodside Crs DOR/KN B93 . 172 F1
Woodside Dr FOAKS/STRLY B74.. 42 A8
  RBRY B45 .... 166 F5
Woodside Gv CDSL WV8 ...... 34 F3
Woodside Pk
  RUGBYN/HIL CV21 .... 159 L8
Woodside Pl HEDN WS12 .... 12 B8
Woodside Wy ALDR WS9 .... 40 F8
  RIDG/WDGT B32 .... 122 E5
  SHHTH WV12 .... 38 C6
  SOLH B91 .... 127 J8
Woods La BRLYHL DY5 .... 102 B6
  CDYHTH B64 .... 103 G5
Woodsome Gv
  ERDW/GRVHL B23 .... 72 A6
Woodsorrel Rd DUDN DY1 .. 84 D1
The Woods MOS/BIL B13 .... 125 K3
Woodstile BKDE/SHDE B34 .. 91 M7
Woodstile Cl MGN/WHC B75 . 57 H2
Woodstock Cl
  DSYBK/YTR WS5 .... 69 L2
  DUDN DY1 .... 84 E5
  STRBR DY8 .... 101 G4
Woodstock Crs DOR/KN B93 . 172 D2
Woodstock Dr FOAKS/STRLY B74.. 56 B1
  HEDN WS12 .... 12 B8
  STRBR DY8 .... 101 G3
Woodstock Rd COVS CV3 .... 154 B6
  HDSW B21 .... 88 D5
  MOS/BIL B13 .... 125 L1
  NUN CV11 .... 99 J4
  WOLV WV1 .... 50 F4
Woodston Gv SOLH B91 .... 148 A5
Wood St ATHST CV9 .... 61 G5
  BDWTH CV12 .... 116 E1
  BILS/COS WV14 .... 51 H8
  DARL/WED WS10 .... 52 D7
  DUDS DY2 .... 84 D7
  ETTPK/GDPK/PENN WV4 .. 66 E2
  HAG/WOL DY9 .... 102 D8
  KIDDW DY11 .... 137 H7
  NUNW/HART CV10 .... 98 D1
  RLSN CV32 .... 200 E1
  RUGBYN/HIL CV21 .... 159 L8
  STRBR DY8 .... 101 B4
  TPTN/OCK DY4 .... 67 G6
  WLNHL WV13 .... 51 L3
  WOLVN WV10 .... 15 K7
Woodtherne Cl PENK ST19 .. 10 D6
Woodthorne Rd
  DUNHL/THL/PER WV6 ...... 34 E7
Woodthorne Rd South
  DUNHL/THL/PER WV6 ...... 34 E8

Woodthorpe Dr
 HAG/WOL DY9 .... 120 B2 🔲
Woodthorpe Gdns
 ALE/KHTH/YWD B14 .... 125 J8 🔲
Woodthorpe Rd
 ALE/KHTH/YWD B14 .... 125 H8
Woodvale Dr HLGN/YWD B28 .. 146 C4
Woodvale Rd HLGN/YWD B28 .. 146 C1
 RIDG/WDGT B32 .... 122 E4 🔲
Woodview Dr EDG B15 .... 107 C6
Woodview Rd ATHST CV9 .... 63 J6
Woodville Gdns SEDG DY3 ...... 66 D4 🔲
Woodville Rd
 ALE/KHTH/YWD B14 .... 125 K4
 HRBN B17 .... 105 L7
 WWCK CV34 .... 199 J5 🔲
Woodward Pl HAG/WOL DY9 .. 120 A1 🔲
Woodward Rd KIDDW DY11 ...... 161 C2
Woodwards Cl WSLW WS2 .... 52 F5
Woodwards Pl WSLW WS2 .... 52 F5 🔲
Woodwards Rd WSLW WS2 ...... 52 F5 🔲
Woodward St
 HHTH/SAND B71 .... 87 J1 🔲
Woodway ERDE/BCHGN B24 ...... 72 F8
 RWWCK/WEL CV35 .... 198 C6
Woodway Av
 RWWCK/WEL CV35 .... 198 D7
Woodway Cl COVE CV2 .... 135 J5
Woodway La COVE CV2 .... 135 K2
Woodway Wk COVE CV2 .... 135 J5
Woodwells Rd WASH/WDE B8 .... 90 E8
Woody Bank GTWY WS6 .... 24 C3
Woolacombe Lodge Rd
 SLYOAK B29 .... 124 A3
Woolaston Rd REDE B98 .... 197 C5
Woolgrove St COVN CV6 .... 134 E2 🔲
Woolhope Cl REDE B98 .... 197 J2
Woolmore Rd ERDW/GRVHL B23 .. 90 A1
Woolpack Cl
 BLKHTH/ROWR B65 .... 103 L1
Woolpack Wy ATHST CV9 .... 63 H5 🔲
Wooton Gv KGSTG B44 .... 72 A5 🔲
Wootton Av WNSFLD WV11 ...... 37 H6
Wootton Cl HEDN WS12 .... 16 F3 🔲
Wootton Rd RLSN CV32 .... 200 D3
Wootton Green La
 RCOVN/BALC/EX CV7 ...... 150 E4
Wootton La
 RCOVN/BALC/EX CV7 ...... 150 D4
Wootton Rd BDMR/CCFT WV3 .... 49 G6
 NFLD/LBR B31 .... 143 L6
Woottons Ct CNCK/NC WS11 .... 16 D4
Wootton St BDWTH CV12 .... 117 C2
Worcester Cl CNCK/NC WS11 .. 16 D5 🔲
 COVW CV5 .... 132 F6
 HAG/WOL DY9 .... 119 L8
 LICH WS13 .... 20 F2
 MGN/WHC B75 .... 57 H2
Worcester Ct
 BDMR/CCFT WV3 .... 49 L7 🔲
Worcester Gn HHTH/SAND B71 .. 69 G6
Worcester La
 DUNHL/THL/PER WV6 ...... 48 B1 🔲
Worcester La HAG/WOL DY9.....119 M5
 MGN/WHC B75 .... 57 H2
 STRBR DY8 .... 119 M3
Worcester Ri SLYOAK B29 .... 124 F4 🔲
Worcester Rd BRGRVW B61 ...... 185 K4 🔲
 DUDS DY2 .... 103 J2
 HAG/WOL DY9 .... 119 L8
 KIDD DY10 .... 137 J8 🔲
 KIDD DY10 .... 162 D4
 KIDDW DY11 .... 161 L5
 KNWTH CV8 .... 191 M2
 LGLYGN/QTN B68 .... 104 E5
 LICHS WS14 .... 30 A2
 WLNHL WV13 .... 52 B3
Worcester St BKHL/PFLD WV2 .. 2 E7
 KIDD DY10 .... 137 J7
 RUGBYN/HIL CV21 .... 183 L1
 STRBR DY8 .... 119 L1
Word Hi HRBN B17 .... 105 K6
Wordsley Cl REDE B98 .... 188 F6
Wordsworth Av CRTAM B79 ...... 31 L1
 ETTPK/GDPK/PENN WV4 ...... 66 C1
 REDW B97 .... 196 A5
 WWCK CV34 .... 199 G8
Wordsworth Cl
 CNCK/NC WS11 .... 16 B1 🔲
 LICHS WS14 .... 20 F8
 TPTN/OCK DY4 .... 67 K5
Wordsworth Ct
 DUNHL/THL/PER WV6 .... 48 C1 🔲

Wordsworth Crs KIDD DY10 .... 137 M7
Wordsworth Dr KNWTH CV8 .... 192 A1
Wordsworth Rd BDWTH CV12 .. 117 H4
 BLOX/PEL WS3 .... 39 J5
 BNTWD WS7 .... 18 E5
 COVE CV2 .... 155 C1
 RUGBYS/DCH CV22 .... 183 J7
 SEDG DY3 .... 65 M8
 SHHTH WV12 .... 38 C6
 SMHTH B10 .... 108 B6
 WOLVN WV10 .... 36 E5
Wordsworth St HHTH/SAND B71 .. 69 G8
Worfield Cl RUSH/SHEL WS4 .... 53 L1
Worfield Gdns BDMR/CCFT WV3 .. 49 K7
World's End Av
 RIDG/WDGT B32 .... 105 H7
World's End La
 RIDG/WDGT B32 .... 105 H8
Worlds End Rd
 BFLD/HDSWWD B20 .... 88 E2
Worleys Wharf Av
 DARL/WED WS10 .... 69 J3
Worsdell Cl COV CV1 .... 8 C2
Worsey Dr TPTN/OCK DY4 ...... 68 B7 🔲
Worsfold Cl COVW CV5 .... 132 E6
Worth Crs STRPT DY13 .... 160 B7
Worthen Gv NFLD/LBR B31 .... 143 L5 🔲
The Worthings BVILLE B30 .... 124 F7
Worthy Down WNSFLD WV11 .... 37 K8 🔲
Wortley Av WOLVN WV10 ...... 36 C7 🔲
Worton Rd HAG/WOL DY9 ...... 120 C3
Wragby Cl COVEN WV9 .... 35 M2
Wrekin Cl HALE B63 .... 121 G4
 KIDDW DY11 .... 160 F3
Wrekin Dr BDMR/CCFT WV3 .... 49 J5
 BRGRVW B61 .... 185 L8
 DUNHL/THL/PER WV6 .... 34 E8
 HAG/WOL DY9 .... 120 B1
Wrekin Gv SHHTH WV12 .... 37 M4 🔲
Wrekin La
 DUNHL/THL/PER WV6 .... 34 E8
Wrekin Rd KGSTG B44 .... 71 K7
 SCFLD/BOLD B73 .... 72 E4 🔲
Wrekin Vw BRWNH WS8 .... 26 E8
 HEDN WS12 .... 12 A5
Wrekin View Rd SEDG DY3 ...... 66 A5
Wren Av DUNHL/THL/PER WV6 .... 48 B2
Wrenbury Dr COVN CV6 .... 134 E1 🔲
Wrens Av KGSWFD DY6 .... 101 L1
 TPTN/OCK DY4 .... 67 G8
Wrens Hill Rd DUDN DY1 ...... 66 E8
Wren's Nest Rd DUDN DY1 ...... 66 E8
 DUDN DY1 .... 66 F7
Wrens Park Av WALM/CURD B76 .. 73 J6
Wren St COVE CV2 .... 9 L3
 DUDN DY1 .... 66 F7
 DUDS DY2 .... 84 F8
Wrentham St DIG/EDG B5........ 6 F9
Wretham Rd LOZ/NWT B19 ...... 88 F7
Wrexham Av WSLW WS2 .... 52 D4
Wright Av WNSFLD WV11 .... 37 H6
Wright Cl POL/KGSB/FAZ B78 .. 60 B8
Wrighton Cl SHHTH WV12 ...... 38 A5
Wrighton Dr SEDG DY3 .... 84 A4
Wright Rd WASH/WDE B8 .... 90 C8
Wright's Av CNCK/NC WS11 .... 16 D1
Wright's La CDYHTH B64 ...... 103 K3
Wright St BILS/COS WV14 ...... 67 J2 🔲
 COV CV1 .... 134 C8
 HALE B63 .... 121 M1 🔲
 SMHTH B10 .... 108 B5
 WOLVN WV10 .... 50 B1 🔲
Wrigsham St COVS CV3 .... 9 G8
Wrottesley Park Rd CDSL WV8 .. 34 B7
 DUNHL/THL/PER WV6 .... 34 B8
Wrottesley Rd
 DUNHL/THL/PER WV6 .... 34 F8
 GTB/HAM B43 .... 70 B4
Wrottesley Rd West
 DUNHL/THL/PER WV6 .... 34 D7
Wrottesley St DIG/EDG B5........ 7 G7 🔲
Wroxall Cl BRLYHL DY5 .... 101 M5
Wroxall Dr COVS CV3 .... 155 H8
Wroxall Gv MOS/BIL B13 ...... 125 L7
Wroxall Rd SOLH B91 .... 127 J7
Wroxham Gln WLNHL WV13 ...... 51 K5 🔲
Wroxton Rd YDLY B25 .... 109 J5
Wulfric Rd PENK ST19 .... 10 E5
Wulfruna Gdns
 BDMR/CCFT WV3 .... 49 K4
Wulfruna St WOLV WV1 .... 2 E4
Wyatt Cl DIG/EDG B5 .... 107 G8
Wyatt Ct BDWTH CV12 .... 116 F2 🔲

Wyatt Rd MGN/WHC B75 .... 57 M7
Wychall Dr WOLVN WV10 .... 36 C1
Wychall La HWK/WKHTH B38 .. 144 B3
 NFLD/LBR B31 .... 144 A3
Wychall Park Gv
 HWK/WKHTH B38 .... 144 B3
Wychall Rd NFLD/LBR B31 .... 143 M2
Wychbold Cl REDW B97 .... 195 L7 🔲
 SHHTH WV12 .... 38 B4
Wychbold Ct HAG/WOL DY9 .... 120 A5
Wychbold Crs STECH B33 ...... 110 A2
Wychbury WALM/CURD B76 ...... 73 L4 🔲
Wychbury Ct HALE B63 .... 121 L2 🔲
Wychbury Dr HAG/WOL DY9 .... 120 A6
Wychbury Rd BDMR/CCFT WV3 .. 49 G6
 BRLYHL DY5 .... 102 C5
 HAG/WOL DY9 .... 120 C4
 RIDG/WDGT B32 .... 122 E5
Wyche Av ALE/KHTH/YWD B14 .. 145 H1
Wych-elm Cl
 RUGBYS/DCH CV22 .... 182 F4 🔲
Wych Elm Dr RLSS CV31 ...... 200 D8 🔲
Wychelm Farm Rd
 ALE/KHTH/YWD B14 .... 145 L4
Wych Elm Rd BRWNH WS8 ...... 26 B8
Wychnor Gv HHTH/SAND B71 .... 69 J3 🔲
Wychwood Av COVS CV3 .... 178 A1
 DOR/KN B93 .... 148 F5
Wychwood Crs
 LGN/SDN/BHAMAIR B26 .... 109 L7
Wychwood Dr REDW B97 .... 196 B7
Wyckham Cl HRBN B17 .... 123 L1
Wyckham Rd CBROM B36 .... 92 D6
Wycliffe Gv COVE CV2 .... 154 F1
Wycliffe Rd West COVE CV2 .. 154 F8
Wycome Rd HLGN/YWD B28 .... 126 D7
Wye Cliff Rd
 BFLD/HDSWWD B20 .... 88 F5
Wye Cl BDWTH CV12 .... 117 M3
 DUNHL/THL/PER WV6 .... 48 D1 🔲
 RLSN CV32 .... 201 C2
 WALM/CURD B76 .... 73 L6
Wyemanton Cl GTB/HAM B43 .... 70 A4
Wye Rd BLOX/PEL WS3 .... 39 J4
Wykeham Gv
 DUNHL/THL/PER WV6.......... 48 B2
Wykeley Rd COVE CV2 .... 155 C1
Wyken Av COVE CV2 .... 135 H8
Wyken Cl DOR/KN B93 .... 172 C3
Wyken Cft COVE CV2 .... 135 H8
Wyken Grange Rd COVE CV2 .. 135 C8
Wyken Wy COVE CV2 .... 134 E8
Wyke Rd COVE CV2 .... 155 C1
Wyld Cl HHTH/SAND B71 ...... 68 E5
Wyld Ct COVW CV5 .... 132 F8
Wylde Crs BLKHTH/ROWR B65 .. 104 A1
Wylde Green Rd
 CSCFLD/WYGN B72 .... 73 G4
Wyley Rd COVN CV6 .... 133 M8
Wymering Av WNSFLD WV11 .... 37 K6
Wynall La HAG/WOL DY9 ...... 120 D1
Wynall La South HAG/WOL DY9 .. 120 E2
Wynbrook Gv SHLY B90 .... 147 L7 🔲
Wynchcombe Av
 ETTPK/GDPK/PENN WV4 ...... 65 H1
Wyncote Cl KNWTH CV8 .... 191 L1
Wyndcliff Rd BORD B9 .... 108 B4
Wyndham Gdns BVILLE B30 .... 144 B1
Wyndham Rd
 LDYWD/EDGR B16 .... 106 D4
Wyndhurst Rd STECH B33 ...... 109 J1
Wyndley Dr SCFLD/BOLD B73 .. 72 F1
Wyndley La SCFLD/BOLD B73 .. 72 E1
Wyndmill Crs HHTH/SAND B71 .. 69 K4
Wynds Covert BVILLE B30 .... 145 H3 🔲
Wyndshiels CSHL/WTROR B46 .. 93 L7 🔲
Wynds Point NFLD/LBR B31 .. 123 M8
The Wynd SEDG DY3 .... 66 B4
Wynfield Gdns
 ALE/KHTH/YWD B14 .... 125 J8
Wynford Rd ACGN B27 .... 109 C8
Wyn-griffith Dr TPTN/OCK DY4 .. 85 L2
Wynn Cl BEWD DY12 .... 136 B8
Wynne Crs
 ETTPK/GDPK/PENN WV4 ...... 65 G2
Wynn Rd
 ETTPK/GDPK/PENN WV4 ...... 49 K7
Wynn St EDG B15 .... 6 E9
Wynstead Covert
 BVILLE B30 .... 145 C3 🔲
Wynter Rd RUGBYS/DCH CV22 .. 183 H2
Wyntor La HHTH/SAND B71 .... 68 F5
Wynyates CRTAM B79 .... 31 J7 🔲

Wyre Cl ALDR WS9 .... 40 D1
Wyre Rd STRBR DY8 .... 101 J6
Wyrley Cl BRWNH WS8.......... 26 D2
 LICHS WS14 .... 20 E8 🔲
 SHHTH WV12 .... 38 A6
Wyrley La BLOX/PEL WS3 ...... 25 J4
Wyrley Rd AST/WIT B6.......... 89 L2
 MGN/WHC B75 .... 57 H4
 WNSFLD WV11 .... 37 L7
Wyrley St WOLV WV10.......... 3 L4
Wyrley Wy ERDW/GRVHL B23 .. 71 L7
Wythall Green Wy HLYWD B47 .. 169 J2
Wythall Rd HALE B63 .... 121 L3
Wythwood Gv HLYWD B47 .... 146 A7 🔲
 TPTN/OCK DY4 .... 67 L5 🔲
Wythwood Rd HLYWD B47 .... 145 M7
Wyver Crs COVE CV2 .... 155 J3
Wyvern Cl FOAKS/STRLY B74 .. 56 F6 🔲
 SHHTH WV12 .... 37 L6
Wyvern Gv HEDN WS12 .... 12 E8
 SLYOAK B29 .... 124 A3
Wyvern Rd FOAKS/STRLY B74.. 56 F6
Wyvis Cl DUNHL/THL/PER WV6 .. 49 J3

Y

Yale Dr WNSFLD WV11 .... 37 J8
Yardley Cl LGLYGN/QTN B68 .. 104 F4
 REDE B98 .... 197 J2 🔲
 WWCK CV34 .... 199 K3
Yardley Fields Rd STECH B33 .. 109 H3
Yardley Green Rd BORD B9 .... 108 D3
Yardley Rd ACGN B27 .... 127 C1
 YDLY B25 .... 109 H7
Yardley St BRLYHL DY5 ...... 102 A7
 COV CV1 .... 9 J2
 DARL/WED WS10 .... 52 A6
Yardley Wood Rd
 ALE/KHTH/YWD B14 .... 146 A2
 MOS/BIL B13 .... 125 M4
Yare Gv WLNHL WV13 .... 52 B4 🔲
Yarmouth Gn TLHL/CAN CV4 .. 152 C5
Yarnborough Hl STRBR DY8 .. 119 L3
Yarnbury Cl
 ALE/KHTH/YWD B14 .... 145 J4 🔲
Yarn Cl HLYWD B47 .... 145 L8
Yarner Cl DUDN DY1 .... 84 C4
Yarnfield Rd SPARK B11 ...... 126 E2
Yarningale Cl REDE B98 ...... 196 D7
Yarningale Rd
 ALE/KHTH/YWD B14 .... 125 C8
 COVS CV3 .... 155 G8 🔲
Yarnold La BRGRVW B61 ...... 165 C6
Yarrow Cl BLOX/PEL WS3 ...... 25 L8
 WNSFLD WV11 .... 37 K8 🔲
Yarrow Dr HWK/WKHTH B38 .. 144 D5 🔲
Yarwell Cl WOLVN WV10 .... 3 H1
Yateley Av PBAR/PBCH B42 .... 70 E6
Yateley Crs PBAR/PBCH B42.... 70 E6
Yateley Rd EDG B15 .... 106 C6
Yates Av RUGBYN/HIL CV21 .. 159 K7
Yatesbury Av CVALE B35 ...... 91 K2
Yates Cft FOAKS/STRLY B74 .. 42 D7
Yates La RMSLY B62 .... 104 C3
Yeadon Cl REDW B97 .... 195 L4
Yeadon Gdns BDMR/CCFT WV3 .. 49 H5
Yeames Cl GTB/HAM B43 ...... 55 C8
Yellowhammer Ct KIDD DY10 .. 161 L4
Yelverton Cl BLOX/PEL WS3 .. 38 F1 🔲
Yelverton Dr EDG B15 .... 106 C6
Yelverton Rd COVN CV6 ...... 134 A5
Yeman Rd LGLYGN/QTN B68 .. 105 H2
Yemscroft GTWY WS6 .... 24 E5 🔲
Yenton Cl POL/KGSB/FAZ B78.. 45 L4
Yenton Gv CSCFLD/WYGN B72 .. 73 C7
Yeoman Cl KIDD DY10 .... 161 J2 🔲
Yeomanry Cl WWCK CV34 .... 199 K6 🔲
Yeovilton CRTAM B79 .... 32 A5 🔲
Yerbury Gv ERDW/GRVHL B23 .. 71 L8
Yew Cl COVS CV3 .... 155 C5
Yew Croft Av HRBN B17 ...... 105 L7
Yewdale HRBN B17 .... 124 A1 🔲
Yewdale Crs COVE CV2 ...... 135 J4
Yewhurst Rd SOLH B91 ...... 147 H1
The Yews BDWTH CV12 ...... 116 C3
Yew St BDMR/CCFT WV3 .... 2 B6
Yew Tree Av HAG/WOL DY9.... 140 B5
 LICHS WS14 .... 21 J6
Yew Tree Cl CNCK/NC WS11 .. 17 L8

Yewtree Dr BRGRVE B60 ...... 185 M3
Yew Tree Gdns CDSL WV8 .... 34 E1 🔲
Yew Tree Hl RRUGBY CV23 .... 157 J2
Yew Tree Hills DUDS DY2.... 103 G2
Yewtree La BLKHTH/ROWR B65 .. 103 H1
Yew Tree La BILS/COS WV14.... 67 H4
 BRGRVW B61 .... 165 H3
 DARL/WED WS10 .... 68 A3
 DUNHL/THL/PER WV6 .... 34 D7
 LGN/SDN/BHAMAIR B26 .... 109 J6
 RMSLY B62 .... 142 C2
 SOLH B91 .... 128 C8
Yew Tree Pl RMSLY B62 ...... 121 K8
Yew Tree Ri WALM/CURD B76 .. 73 K2
Yewtree Rd FOAKS/STRLY B74 .. 55 H5
 SCFLD/BOLD B73 .... 72 E6
Yew Tree Rd AST/WIT B6...... 89 L4
 CBROM B36 .... 92 C5
 DSYBK/YTR WS5............ 53 L8
 DUDS DY2 .... 103 G1
 EDG B15 .... 6 C9
 HALE B63 .... 121 J2
 KIDD DY10 .... 137 K8
 MOS/BIL B13 .... 125 H3
 RUSH/SHEL WS4 .... 39 M4
 SMTHWKW B67 .... 105 J1
Yockleton Rd STECH B33 .... 110 A2
York Av ATHST CV9 .... 63 J4
 BDMR/CCFT WV3 .... 49 J4
 BDWTH CV12 .... 117 H3
 BRGRVW B61 .... 185 J1 🔲
 WLNHL WV13 .... 52 B3
 WSLW WS2 .... 52 F3
Yorkbrooke Dr
 LGN/SDN/BHAMAIR B26 .. 109 M8 🔲
York Cl BVILLE B30 .... 124 E7
 COVS CV3 .... 155 G8
 LICH WS13 .... 21 G2
 TPTN/OCK DY4 .... 85 H1
York Crs BDMR/CCFT WV3 .... 49 H4
 DARL/WED WS10 .... 52 B7
 STRBR DY8 .... 101 H6
 WBROM B70 .... 68 E7
Yorkdale Cl SEDG DY3 .... 84 B2 🔲
York Dr CBROM B36 .... 90 F5 🔲
Yorke Av BRLYHL DY5 .... 101 L4
York Gdns BDMR/CCFT WV3 .. 49 J4
Yorklea Cl
 CHWD/FDBR/MGN B37 .... 110 D3
Yorklea Cft
 CHWD/FDBR/MGN B37 .... 110 D3 🔲
Yorkminster Dr
 CHWD/FDBR/MGN B37 .... 111 G2
York Rd ALE/KHTH/YWD B14 .. 125 J5
 BDMR/CCFT WV3 .... 48 F5
 BLKHTH/ROWR B65 .... 104 C2
 BRGRVW B61 .... 185 K1 🔲
 CNCK/NC WS11 .... 16 D6
 DUDS DY2 .... 103 J2
 ERDW/GRVHL B23 .... 90 D1
 HDSW B21 .... 88 D5
 HLGN/YWD B28 .... 126 D4
 LDYWD/EDGR B16 .... 106 B4
 RLSS CV31 .... 200 D5
 RUSH/SHEL WS4 .... 39 M4
Yorksand Rd POL/KGSB/FAZ B78.. 45 K5
York St COV CV1 .... 8 C6
 HRBN B17 .... 106 B7
 KIDD DY10 .... 137 J6
 NUN CV11 .... 98 E1
 RUGBYN/HIL CV21 .... 183 K1
 WOLV WV1 .... 3 J6
Yorks Wood Dr
 CHWD/FDBR/MGN B37 ...... 92 C8
York Ter WSNGN B18 .... 89 G8 🔲
Young Cl WWCK CV34 .... 198 F8 🔲
Young St WBROM B70 .... 86 E2
Yoxall Gv STETCH B33 ...... 109 L2
Yoxall Rd SHLY B90 .... 147 H3
Yule Rd COVE CV2 .... 135 H8
Yvonne Rd REDW B97 .... 196 M1

Z

Zion Cl GTWY WS6 .... 24 B2
Zions Cl CDYHTH B64 .... 103 K4 🔲
Zoar St BDMR/CCFT WV3........ 2 C7
 SEDG DY3 .... 84 A2
Zorrina Cl NUNW/HART CV10 .. 79 M8
Zortech Av STRPT DY13 ...... 160 E5
Zouche Cl STRBR DY8 .... 101 J5 🔲

Index - featured places

A1 Trading Estate
 SMTHWK B66 .... 87 M6
A1 Trading Estate
 SMTHWKW B67 .... 105 L4
Abberley Industrial Centre
 SMTHWK B66 .... 88 B8
Abbey Clinic
 COVW CV5 .... 8 A8
Abbey C of E Junior &
 Infant School
 NUN CV11 .... 80 F8
Abbey College
 CBHAMNW B3 .... 6 F4
Abbey County Infant School
 SMTHWKW B67 .... 105 J3
Abbey CP School
 BLOX/PEL WS3 .... 38 C2
Abbey Fields Swimming Pool
 KNWTH CV8 .... 176 C8
Abbey Gallery
 NUN CV11 .... 99 G1
The Abbey High School
 REDE B98 .... 196 C1

Abbey Industrial Estate
 COVE CV2 .... 135 K7
Abbey Road Junior School
 SMTHWKW B67 .... 105 J4
Abbey Trading Centre
 REDE B98 .... 188 C8
Abbey Tutorial College
 CBHAMNW B3 .... 6 E3
Abbotsford
 Independent School
 KNWTH CV8 .... 176 D7
ABC Cinema
 NUNW/HART CV10 .... 98 E7
Abbey County Infant School
Albert Bradford School
 SMTHWK B66 .... 87 J6
Albert Pritchard Infant School
 DARL/WED WS10 .... 52 E8
Albion Business Park
 SMTHWK B66 .... 87 J5
Albion Industrial Estate
 COVN CV6 .... 134 B6
Albion Industrial Estate
 WBROM B70 .... 86 E3
Albion Junior School
 HHTH/SAND B71 .... 87 L5

Adderley Junior &
 Infant School
 WASH/WDE B8 .... 108 A2
Adderley Trading Estate
 WASH/WDE B8 .... 108 A1
Adrian Boult Hall
 CBHAMNW B3 .... 6 E5
Advance Business Park
 HEDN WS12 .... 16 F2
Alan Cotterell Practice
 BKHL/PFLD WV2 .... 3 G7
Albert Bradford School
 SMTHWK B66 .... 87 J6
Albert Pritchard Infant School
 DARL/WED WS10 .... 52 E8
Albion Business Park
 SMTHWK B66 .... 87 J5
Albion Industrial Estate
 COVN CV6 .... 134 B6
Albion Industrial Estate
 WBROM B70 .... 86 E3
Albion Junior School
 HHTH/SAND B71 .... 87 L5

Albion Road Junior School
 WLNHL WV13 .... 52 A3
Albright Home &
 Hospital PRU
 BLKHTH/ROWR B65 .... 104 B1
Alcott Hall Junior &
 Infant School
 CHWD/FDBR/MGN B37 .... 110 A4
Alderbrook School
 SOLH B91 .... 147 K3
Aldergate Medical Centre
 CRTAM B79 .... 31 M7
Alderman Callow School &
 Community College
 TLHL/CAN CV4 .... 152 E7
Alderman Harris Junior &
 Infant School
 TLHL/CAN CV4 .... 152 D6
Aldermans Green Primary
 School
 COVE CV2 .... 135 G2
Alderman Smith School
 NUNW/HART CV10 .... 98 B3

Aldermoor Farm Infant School
 COVS CV3 .... 154 F4
Aldermoor Farm Junior School
 COVS CV3 .... 154 F5
Aldermoor Lane Welfare Clinic
 COVS CV3 .... 154 E4
Aldersley High School
 CDSL WV8 .... 35 J4
Aldridge & Brownhills
 Magistrates Court
 ALDR WS9 .... 40 F7
Aldridge Road School Clinic
 KGSTG B44 .... 71 H4
Aldridge School
 ALDR WS9 .... 40 E8
Alexander Industrial Park
 BILS/COS WV14 .... 67 G1
Alexandra High School
 TPTN/OCK DY4............ 67 M7
The Alexandra Hospital
 REDE B98 .... 197 G1
Alexandra Industrial Estate
 TPTN/OCK DY4............ 67 K4

Alexandra Medical Centre
HALE B63 .... 103 K8
Alexandra Theatre
CBHAMW B1 .... 6 F6
Al Hijrah Mosque
SMHTH B10 .... 108 D4
Al Hijraj School
SMHTH B10 .... 108 E4
Alice Stevens School
COVS CV3 .... 154 E7
Allaware Gallery
ALE/KHTH/YWD B14 .... 145 K4
Allen Brown Gallery
LICHS WS14 .... 29 J5
Allens Rough
Community Primary School
SHHTH WV12 .... 38 A4
Allesley Hall Primary School
COVW CV5 .... 152 F1
Allesley Park Medical Centre
COVW CV5 .... 153 G1
Allesley Primary School
COVW CV5 .... 132 E6
Alliance Business Park
NUN CV11 .... 99 K2
All Saints C E Primary School
WMBN WV5 .... 64 A5
All Saints C of E First School
BDWTH CV12 .... 117 G3
All Saints C of E First School
NUNW/HART CV10 .... 99 G4
All Saints C of E Middle School
WWCK CV34 .... 199 L4
All Saints C of E Primary School
COV CV1 .... 9 K7
All Saints C of E Primary School
HHTH/SAND B71 .... 69 G7
All Saints C of E School
STRPT DY13 .... 161 G8
All Saints C of E
Community Primary School
RWWCK/WEL CV35 .... 191 L8
All Saints Hospital
WSNGN B18 .... 88 C8
All Saints Industrial Estate
WSNGN B18 .... 88 E8
All Saints School
BKHL/PFLD WV2 .... 3 J9
All Souls RC Infant School
COVW CV5 .... 153 J3
Alma Industrial Estate
DARL/WED WS10 .... 52 A7
Alpha Business Park
COVE CV2 .... 135 H4
Alston Junior School
BORD B9 .... 108 F2
Alumrock Medical Centre
WASH/WDE B8 .... 108 C1
The Alumwell School
WSLW WS2 .... 52 E4
Alvechurch C of E
Middle School
ALVE B48 .... 167 L7
Alvis Retail Park
COVW CV5 .... 8 B3
Amblecote Primary School
STRBR DY8 .... 101 K5
Amington Industrial Estate
TAM/AM/WIL B77 .... 46 E2
Amington Industrial Estate
TAM/AM/WIL B77 .... 47 G3
Ammond Business Centre
NUN CV11 .... 99 J2
Amptronik Trading Estate
SEDC DY3 .... 82 B1
Anderton Park Junior &
Infant School
BHTH/HG B12 .... 125 L1
Anglesey Business Park
HEDN WS12 .... 17 J1
Anglesey Junior &
Infant School
LOZ/NWT B19 .... 89 G6
Anglesey Junior School
LOZ/NWT B19 .... 89 G7
Anita Myatt Health Centre
ETTPK/CDPK/PENN WV4 .... 65 H1
Anjuman-e-naqeebul
Islam Mosque
WASH/WDE B8 .... 90 B8
Ankermoor County
Primary School
TAM/AM/WIL B77 .... 32 C8
Ankerside Shopping Centre
CRTAM B79 .... 45 M1
Annie Lennard Infant School
SMTHWK B67 .... 105 J2
Annie Osborn Primary School
COVE CV2 .... 135 H6
Apex Business Park
CNCK/NC WS11 .... 17 L8
Arbury Hall
NUNW/HART CV10 .... 98 A6
Arbury Medical Centre
NUNW/HART CV10 .... 98 C2
Arcadian Centre & Cinema
DIG/EDG B5 .... 7 G7
Archbishop Grimshaw
Comprehensive School
CHWD/FDBR/MGN B37 .... 110 D2
Archbishop Ilsley RC School
ACGN B27 .... 127 G3
Arches Industrial Estate
COVW CV5 .... 8 A4
Arden High School
DOR/KN B93 .... 148 F8
Arden Hill County
Infant School
ATHST CV9 .... 63 J6
Arden School
BORD B9 .... 108 B3
Arden School
SMTHWK B67 .... 87 K8
Arden Tree Surgery
HOCK/TIA B94 .... 173 G5
Argyle Street Clinic
TAM/AM/WIL B77 .... 46 C1

Arley & Gun Hill School
RCOVN/BALC/EX CV7 .... 96 E5
Arley Industrial Estate
RCOVN/BALC/EX CV7 .... 96 D5
Arley Sports Centre
RCOVN/BALC/EX CV7 .... 96 C3
Armoury Trading Estate
SPARK B11 .... 108 C7
Arnold Lodge School
RLSN CV32 .... 200 D3
Arran Medical Centre
CBROM B36 .... 92 E6
Arriva Business Park
KIDDW DY11 .... 161 G4
Arrow Business Park
REDE B98 .... 196 F2
Arrowcrest First School
REDE B98 .... 196 E3
Art Gallery
BRGRVW B61 .... 185 H3
The Art Gallery
WWCK CV34 .... 199 H8
Arthur Terry School
FOAKS/STRLY B74 .... 56 E2
Asda Shopping Centre
COVE CV2 .... 135 M6
Ashcroft County
Infants School
CRTAM B79 .... 32 A6
Ashford Industrial Estate
BKHL/PFLD WV2 .... 50 D6
Ashfurlong Health Centre
MGN/WHC B75 .... 57 J5
Ash Green School
RCOVN/BALC/EX CV7 .... 116 B7
Ashmore Industrial Estate
WSLW WS2 .... 53 H2
Ashmore Park Clinic
WNSFLD WV11 .... 37 L5
Ashtree Medical Centre
BVILLE B30 .... 124 E7
Ashwood Park CP School
STRBR DY8 .... 101 H4
Astley C of E School
NUNW/HART CV10 .... 97 J6
Aston Cross Business Park
AST/WIT B6 .... 89 L7
Aston Expressway
Industrial Estate
AST/WIT B6 .... 89 J8
Aston Fields Industrial Estate
BRGRVE B60 .... 185 L7
Aston Fields Middle School
BRGRVE B60 .... 186 A5
Aston Health Centre
BFLD/HDSWWD B20 .... 89 J4
Aston Industrial Estate
BDWTH CV12 .... 117 H3
Aston Manor Cricket &
Lucas Sports Club
PBAR/PBCH B42 .... 71 H8
Aston Manor School
AST/WIT B6 .... 89 K7
Aston Tower Junior &
Infant School
AST/WIT B6 .... 89 K6
Aston Villa Football Club
AST/WIT B6 .... 89 K4
Aston Villa Football Club
POL/KGSB/FAZ B78 .... 59 J7
At 7 Sports Centre
COVN CV6 .... 134 E6
Atherstone College
ATHST CV9 .... 63 H5
Atherstone Golf Club
ATHST CV9 .... 63 J7
Atherstone North
County Middle School
ATHST CV9 .... 63 J4
The Atherstone Surgery
ATHST CV9 .... 63 J5
Atherstone Town Cricket Club
ATHST CV9 .... 63 K4
Atherstone United
Football Club
ATHST CV9 .... 63 H3
Atlas Estate
SPARK B11 .... 108 B8
Atlas Estate
SPARK B11 .... 108 E8
Atlas Trading Estate
BILS/COS WV14 .... 67 K3
Attleborough Sports Club
NUN CV11 .... 99 J3
Attock Community
Sports & Cricket Club
MOS/BIL B13 .... 126 A4
Attwood Business Centre
HAG/WOL DY9 .... 102 D8
Audley JMI School
STECH B33 .... 109 K1
Autobase Industrial Estate
OLDBY B69 .... 85 M2
Avenue Clinic
NUN CV11 .... 80 E8
Avon Business Park
CNCK/NC WS11 .... 16 A6
Avoncroft College
BRGRVE B60 .... 185 J8
Avoncroft Museum of Historic
Buildings
BRGRVE B60 .... 185 J8
Aylesbury Hotel
HOCK/TIA B94 .... 172 B6
Baba Balak Nah Temple
WSL WS1 .... 4 E5
Bablake Junior School
COV CV1 .... 8 D2
Bablake School
COV CV1 .... 8 C2
Baddesley Ensor First School
ATHST CV9 .... 62 B4
Baddesley Ensor
Junior School
ATHST CV9 .... 62 A4
Baginton Fields School
COVS CV3 .... 178 F1

Balliol Business Park
COVEN WV9 .... 35 J2
Balsall Common Health Clinic
RCOVN/BALC/EX CV7 .... 150 F6
Balsall Common
Primary School
RCOVN/BALC/EX CV7 .... 150 F8
Banners Gate Infant &
Junior School
SCFLD/BOLD B73 .... 71 L1
Barber Institute of Fine Arts
EDG B15 .... 124 D1
Barford Junior & Infant School
LDYWD/EDGR B16 .... 106 C2
Barkers Butts Rugby
Football Club
COVW CV5 .... 132 C3
Barnfield Trading Estate
TPTN/OCK DY4 .... 67 J7
Barnt Green Cricket Club
RBRY B45 .... 167 G4
Barnt Green Surgery
RBRY B45 .... 167 H6
Barons Court Industrial Estate
ALDR WS9 .... 40 C3
The Barr Beacon School
ALDR WS9 .... 54 F8
Barrs Hill School &
Community College
COV CV1 .... 8 C1
Bartley Green Football Club
RIDG/WDGT B32 .... 123 C4
Bartley Green Health Centre
RIDG/WDGT B32 .... 122 F4
Bartley Green School
RIDG/WDGT B32 .... 123 G4
Barton Industrial Estate
BILS/COS WV14 .... 51 J6
The Baskerville School
HRBN B17 .... 105 L8
Batmans Hill County
Primary School
TPTN/OCK DY4 .... 67 J4
Bayer Hall Clinic
BILS/COS WV14 .... 67 G5
Bayton Road Industrial Estate
RCOVN/BALC/EX CV7 .... 116 F6
Beacon CP School
SHHTH WV12 .... 38 B5
Beaconside First &
Middle School
RBRY B45 .... 142 C7
Beacon Trading Estate
ALDR WS9 .... 40 E7
Bearwood Medical Centre
SMTHWKW B67 .... 105 K3
Bearwood Road
Junior & Infant School
SMTHWKW B67 .... 105 K3
Beauchamp Industrial Park
TAM/AM/WIL B77 .... 46 B5
Beau Desert Golf Club
HEDN WS12 .... 13 M5
Beaufort School
CBROM B36 .... 91 H8
Beauty Bank County
Primary Junior &
Infant School
STRBR DY8 .... 101 K7
Beckminster Special School
BDMR/CCFT WV3 .... 49 K6
Bedworth Health Centre
BDWTH CV12 .... 116 F3
Bedworth Leisure Centre
BDWTH CV12 .... 117 G3
Bedworth Rugby
Football Club
BDWTH CV12 .... 116 D4
Beechdale Centre Surgery
WSLW WS2 .... 38 E8
Beechdale CP School
WSLW WS2 .... 39 G8
Beeches First School
RBRY B45 .... 142 F3
Beeches Hospital
WOLV WV1 .... 2 A3
Beechwood Business Park
HEDN WS12 .... 16 F2
Beecroft Hill Special School
CNCK/NC WS11 .... 16 B3
Belbroughton C of E
First School
HAG/WOL DY9 .... 140 C7
Belfont Trading Estate
HALE B63 .... 122 A1
The Belfry Golf Centre
WALM/CURD B76 .... 75 G2
Belgrade Theatre
COV CV1 .... 8 E4
Belgrave County High School
TAM/AM/WIL B77 .... 46 D4
Belgrave Recreation Centre
TAM/AM/WIL B77 .... 46 C4
Bell Barn Shopping Centre
EDG B15 .... 6 D9
Belle Vue Medical Centre
EDG B15 .... 107 H6
Belle Vue Primary School
STRBR DY8 .... 101 G2
Bellfield Junior & Infant School
NFLD/LBR B31 .... 143 K1
Bell Green Health Centre
COVE CV2 .... 135 G4
Bells Farm Junior &
Infant School
ALE/KHTH/YWD B14 .... 145 G3
Bennetts Well Junior &
Infant School
CHWD/FDBR/MGN B37 .... 110 D2
Bennick Trading Estate
CNCK/NC WS11 .... 16 C1
Benson Industrial Estate
WSNGN B18 .... 88 D7
Benson Junior Mixed School
WSNGN B18 .... 88 D7
Bentley Bridge Business Park
WNSFLD WV11 .... 37 G8

Bentley Drive JMI School
WSLW WS2 .... 52 F2
Bentley Heath C of E
Primary School
DOR/KN B93 .... 148 D8
Bentley Lane Industrial Park
WSLW WS2 .... 52 F2
Bentley Mill Industrial Estate
WSLW WS2 .... 52 D4
Bentley West Primary School
WSLW WS2 .... 52 C2
Berkswell C of E
Primary School
RCOVN/BALC/EX CV7 .... 151 G2
Bescot Industrial Estate
DARL/WED WS10 .... 68 B2
Bewdley C of E Middle School
BEWD DY12 .... 160 A2
Bewdley High School
BEWD DY12 .... 160 A3
Bewdley Tennis Club
BEWD DY12 .... 160 A2
Bgw Business Park
BRGRVE B60 .... 185 K7
Bhylls Acre County
Primary School
BDMR/CCFT WV3 .... 48 F6
Bickford Road Industrial Estate
AST/WIT B6 .... 89 L4
Bilbrook C of E Middle School
CDSL WV8 .... 34 F2
Bilbrook Medical Centre
CDSL WV8 .... 34 F2
Billesley Infant and
Junior School
MOS/BIL B13 .... 126 A7
Bilston
College of Further Education
BILS/COS WV14 .... 50 F6
Bilston Community College
BILS/COS WV14 .... 51 G8
Bilston Community College
BKHL/PFLD WV2 .... 50 D6
Bilston Health Centre
BILS/COS WV14 .... 51 H7
Bilston Industrial Estate
BILS/COS WV14 .... 67 L1
Bilston Key Industrial Estate
BILS/COS WV14 .... 51 L8
Bilston Leisure Centre
BILS/COS WV14 .... 51 H7
Bilston Public
Library & Art Gallery
BILS/COS WV14 .... 51 J7
Bilston Town Football Club
BILS/COS WV14 .... 51 K7
Bilton C of E Middle School
RUGBYS/DCH CV22 .... 183 H7
Bilton County First School
RUGBYS/DCH CV22 .... 183 G5
Bilton Industrial Estate
COV CV1 .... 9 M7
Bilton Industrial Estate
HWK/WKHTH B38 .... 144 C5
Bingley Junior School
BDMR/CCFT WV3 .... 2 B9
Binley Business Park
COVS CV3 .... 155 L4
Binley Woods County
Middle School
COVS CV3 .... 156 C6
Birchbrook Industrial Park
LICHS WS14 .... 28 C7
Birch Business Park
CNCK/NC WS11 .... 16 D7
Birch Coppice Industrial Estate
POL/KGSB/FAZ B78 .... 47 J8
Birchen Coppice First &
Middle School
KIDDW DY11 .... 160 E3
Birchensale Middle School
REDW B97 .... 196 A1
Birches First School
CDSL WV8 .... 34 F4
Birches Green Junior &
Infant School
ERDE/BCHGN B24 .... 90 F2
Birchills C of E School
WSLW WS2 .... 4 C1
Birchills Health Centre
WSLW WS2 .... 53 G2
Birchley Industrial Estate
OLDBY B69 .... 86 C8
Birchley School
BLKHTH/ROWR B65 .... 104 B1
Birch Road East
Industrial Estate
AST/WIT B6 .... 89 M3
Birchwood Primary School
Polesworth
POL/KGSB/FAZ B78 .... 47 K6
Birds Bush County
Primary School
TAM/AM/WIL B77 .... 46 C5
Birmingham Alexander
Stadium
PBAR/PBCH B42 .... 71 H7
Birmingham Area Civil
Service Sports Club
HIA/OLT B92 .... 128 E3
Birmingham Business Centre
WBROM B70 .... 87 K3
Birmingham Cathedral
CBHAMNW B3 .... 6 F4
Birmingham Central Mosque
BHTH/HG B12 .... 107 J6
Birmingham Central
Synagogue
DIG/EDG B5 .... 107 H7
Birmingham Childrens
Hospital N H S Trust
CBHAMNE B4 .... 7 G3
Birmingham City Council
ALE/KHTH/YWD B14 .... 146 A1
Birmingham City Council
AST/WIT B6 .... 89 M6
Birmingham City Council
BFLD/HDSWWD B20 .... 88 E3

Birmingham City Council
BFLD/HDSWWD B20 .... 88 C2
Birmingham City Council
BHTH/HG B12 .... 107 K8
Birmingham City Council
BKDE/SHDE B34 .... 91 M6
Birmingham City Council
CBHAM B2 .... 7 G5
Birmingham City Council
CBHAMNE B4 .... 7 L4
Birmingham City Council
CBHAMNE B4 .... 7 H2
Birmingham City Council
CBHAMNB B3 .... 6 E4
Birmingham City Council
CBHAMW B1 .... 6 C4
Birmingham City Council
CBHAMW B1 .... 6 D6
Birmingham City Council
CBHAMW B1 .... 6 D5
Birmingham City Council
CSCFLD/WYGN B72 .... 73 G1
Birmingham City Council
DIG/EDG B5 .... 7 H7
Birmingham City Council
DIG/EDG B5 .... 7 J6
Birmingham City Council
DIG/EDG B5 .... 107 H6
Birmingham City Council
ERDE/BCHGN B24 .... 72 E8
Birmingham City Council
HDSW B21 .... 88 E6
Birmingham City Council
HRBN B17 .... 105 K7
Birmingham City Council
HRBN B17 .... 105 M3
Birmingham City Council
HRBN B17 .... 106 B7
Birmingham City Council
LDYWD/EDGR B16 .... 106 C4
Birmingham City Council
LGN/SDN/BHAMAIR B26 .... 110 B7
Birmingham City Council
LOZ/NWT B19 .... 89 J7
Birmingham City Council
NFLD/LBR B31 .... 123 J7
Birmingham City Council
NFLD/LBR B31 .... 143 G3
Birmingham City Council
NFLD/LBR B31 .... 143 H5
Birmingham City Council
SLYOAK B29 .... 124 E3
Birmingham City Council
SPARK B11 .... 107 M7
Birmingham City Council
SPARK B11 .... 108 E7
Birmingham City Council
VAUX/NECH B7 .... 7 L1
Birmingham City Council
WASH/WDE B8 .... 90 C8
Birmingham City Council
WASH/WDE B8 .... 90 D8
Birmingham City Council
YDLY B25 .... 109 G5
Birmingham City Football Club
BORD B9 .... 108 A4
Birmingham College
ACGN B27 .... 127 G2
Birmingham Conservatoire
CBHAMW B1 .... 6 D5
Birmingham Crown Court
CBHAMNE B4 .... 7 H4
Birmingham
Dental Hospital & School
CBHAMNE B4 .... 7 G2
Birmingham
International Airport
LGN/SDN/BHAMAIR B26 .... 111 G8
The Birmingham Mint
WSNGN B18 .... 6 A1
The Birmingham
Nuffield Hospital
EDG B15 .... 106 D8
Birmingham One Industrial
Estate
CBHAMW B1 .... 6 B4
Birmingham Railway Museum
SPARK B11 .... 108 D8
Birmingham Repertory Theatre
CBHAMW B1 .... 6 D5
Birmingham Womens
Hospital NHS Trust
EDG B15 .... 106 B8
Bishop Challoner RC School
ALE/KHTH/YWD B14 .... 125 J5
Bishopsgate Business Park
COV CV1 .... 134 B8
Bishop Milner RC
Secondary School
DUDN DY1 .... 84 E2
Bishop Ullathorne RC School
COVS CV3 .... 177 K1
Bishop Veseys Grammar School
FOAKS/STRLY B74 .... 57 G7
Bishop Walsh RC School
WALM/CURD B76 .... 73 H3
Bishop Wilson C of E
Junior & Infant School
CHWD/FDBR/MGN B37 .... 111 G3
Bishop Wulstan RC
High School
RUGBYS/DCH CV22 .... 183 L3
Blackbrook Valley
Industrial Estate
DUDS DY2 .... 84 E7
Black Country Family Practice
TPTN/OCK DY4 .... 67 J2
Black Country Museum
DUDN DY1 .... 85 H1
Blackheath Junior &
Infant School
BLKHTH/ROWR B65 .... 103 M4
Black Lake Industrial Estate
HHTH/SAND B71 .... 68 C7
Blackwell Golf Club
BRGRVE B60 .... 166 E8
Blackwood School
FOAKS/STRLY B74 .... 55 J4

Blakebrook School
KIDDW DY11 .... 137 C7

Blake County High School
HEDN WS12 .... 12 D7

Blakedown C of E
Primary School
KIDD DY10 .... 139 C3

Blakeley Heath CP School
WMBN WV5 .... 64 E8

Blakeley School
OLDBY B69 .... 86 C4

Blakenhale Infant School
STECH B33 .... 109 M4

Blakenhale Junior
Mixed School
STECH B33 .... 109 M4

Blakenhall Industrial Estate
BKHL/PFLD WV2 .... 49 M6

Blakesley Hall Junior
Mixed School
YDLY B25 .... 109 H4

Blakesley Surgery
YDLY B25 .... 109 J4

Blandford Mere
Primary School
KGSWFD DY6 .... 83 J6

Bleakhouse Clinic
LGLYGN/QTN B68 .... 105 G4

Bleakhouse Junior School
LGLYGN/QTN B68 .... 105 C3

Bloomsbury Health Centre
VAUX/NECH B7 .... 89 L8

Blossomfield Infant School
SHLY B90 .... 147 H2

Blowers Green Primary School
DUDS DY2 .... 84 F5

Bloxwich Business Park
WSLW WS2 .... 38 F6

Bloxwich C of E Primary School
BLOX/PEL WS3 .... 38 F4

Bloxwich Hospital
BLOX/PEL WS3 .... 38 F5

Bloxwich Lane Industrial Estate
WSLW WS2 .... 52 E2

Bloxwich Leisure Centre
BLOX/PEL WS3 .... 39 C5

Blue Coat C E School
COV CV1 .... 9 L8

Blue Coat C of E Infant School
WSL WS1 .... 5 G5

Blue Coat C of E Junior School
WSL WS1 .... 5 H4

Bluecoat C of E Comprehensive
School
WSL WS1 .... 5 G4

Blue Coat School
EDG B15 .... 106 C7

Blythe School
CSHL/WTROR B46 .... 111 L1

BMI Priory Hospital
EDG B15 .... 107 G8

Boddis Industrial Park
CDYHTH B64 .... 103 L3

Boldmere Clinic
SCFLD/BOLD B73 .... 72 D4

Boldmere Middle &
Infant School
SCFLD/BOLD B73 .... 72 D4

Boldmere St Michaels
Football Club
SCFLD/BOLD B73 .... 72 D5

Bond's Hosp & Bablake
Old School
COV CV1 .... 8 D4

Boney Hay Primary School
BNTWD WS7 .... 18 E4

Bordesley Green
Junior & Infant School
BORD B9 .... 108 E3

Bordesley Green
Trading Estate
BORD B9 .... 108 C3

Bordesley Trading Estate
WASH/WDE B8 .... 108 B2

Boscomoor Industrial Estate
PENK ST19 .... 10 C6

Bosworth Wood
Junior & Infant School
CBROM B36 .... 92 D4

Boughton Road Industrial
Estate
RUGBYN/HIL CV21 .... 159 M7

Boulton Industrial Centre
WSNGN B18 .... 88 F8

Boulton Junior & Infant School
HDSW B21 .... 88 C6

Boundary Industrial Estate
WOLVN WV10 .... 22 A8

Bournbrook & Varsity Medical
Practice
SLYOAK B29 .... 124 D2

Bourneville Surgery
BVILLE B30 .... 124 D6

Bournville College of Further
Education
BVILLE B30 .... 124 C6

Bournville College of Further
Education
NFLD/LBR B31 .... 124 A6

Bournville Junior &
Infant School
BVILLE B30 .... 124 C6

Bournville School
NFLD/LBR B31 .... 124 A7

Bournville School of Art
BVILLE B30 .... 124 C6

Boydell Galleries
ERDW/GRVHL B23 .... 72 E8

Brackendale Shopping Centre
SHHTH WV12 .... 52 B1

Bradford Street Clinic
WSL WS1 .... 4 E3

Braidwood Day Special School
ERDW/GRVHL B23 .... 71 M7

Bramford CP School
DUDN DY1 .... 66 E7

Brandhall Clinic
LGLYGN/QTN B68 .... 104 F5

Brandon Court Leofric
Business Park
COVS CV3 .... 155 L6

Brandon Way Industrial Estate
WBROM B70 .... 86 D2

Brasshouse Language Centre
LDYWD/EDGR B16 .... 6 B7

Brewery
WOLV WV1 .... 2 D5

Briars Country Club
KIDDW DY11 .... 136 E6

Brickhouse Junior &
Infant School
BLKHTH/ROWR B65 .... 103 L2

Brickkiln Primary School
BDMR/CCFT WV3 .... 2 C6

Bridge Field
WWCK CV34 .... 199 L7

Bridgeman Street
Trading Estate
WSLW WS2 .... 4 C2

Bridge School
ERDW/GRVHL B23 .... 90 C1

Bridgeside Industrial Estate
TAM/AM/WIL B77 .... 46 A2

Bridgeside Trading Estate
TAM/AM/WIL B77 .... 46 A3

Bridgetown Primary School
CNCK/NC WS11 .... 16 C7

The Bridge Trading Estate
SMTHWK B66 .... 87 M7

Bridgtown Business Centre
CNCK/NC WS11 .... 16 C7

Bridgtown Gallery
CNCK/NC WS11 .... 16 B7

Bridley Moor High School
REDW B97 .... 196 A1

The Brierley Hill Health Centre
BRLYHL DY5 .... 102 B2

Brierley Hill Leisure Centre
BRLYHL DY5 .... 102 C3

Brierley Hill Primary School
BRLYHL DY5 .... 102 C3

The Brier School
BRLYHL DY5 .... 102 C2

Brindley Business Park
HEDN WS12 .... 16 F2

Brinklow C of E First School
RRUGBY CV23 .... 157 K1

Bristnall Hall High School
LGLYGN/QTN B68 .... 105 H2

Britannia High School
BLKHTH/ROWR B65 .... 104 B3

The British School
HRBN B17 .... 106 A4

Broadcott Industrial Estate
CDYHTH B64 .... 103 L4

Broad Heath School
COVN CV6 .... 134 D6

Broadmeadow Health Centre
BVILLE B30 .... 144 F3

Broad Street Gallery
WOLV WV1 .... 3 G4

Broad Street Health Centre
COVN CV6 .... 134 D6

Broad Street Old Boys
Rugby Football Club
COVS CV3 .... 155 M4

Broad Street Rugby
Football Club
COVE CV2 .... 135 G5

Broadwalk Retail Park
WSL WS1 .... 53 H7

Broadway Medical Centre
DSYBK/YTR WS5 .... 53 K7

Broadway School
BFLD/HDSWWD B20 .... 89 J3

Broadway Surgery
DSYBK/YTR WS5 .... 53 K7

Broadwell Industrial Park
OLDBY B69 .... 86 D4

Broadwyn Trading Estate
CDYHTH B64 .... 103 L5

Brockmoor Industrial Estate
BRLYHL DY5 .... 101 L2

Brockmoor Primary School
BRLYHL DY5 .... 102 A2

Bromford Junior Mixed School
CBROM B36 .... 91 H5

Bromford Road
Industrial Estate
OLDBY B69 .... 86 E4

Bromley Hills Primary School
KGSWFD DY6 .... 83 K8

Bromley Primary School
BRLYHL DY5 .... 83 M8

Bromsgrove Business Centre
BRGRVW B61 .... 185 K3

Bromsgrove Clinic
BRGRVW B61 .... 185 K2

Bromsgrove District Council
BRGRVE B60 .... 185 M2

Bromsgrove Lower School
BRGRVE B60 .... 185 K4

Bromsgrove Museum & Tourist
Information Centre
BRGRVW B61 .... 185 L2

Bromsgrove Private Hospital
BRGRVE B60 .... 186 F4

Bromsgrove Rovers
Football Club
BRGRVW B61 .... 185 L2

Bromsgrove Rugby
Football Club
BRGRVE B60 .... 186 A5

Bromsgrove School
BRGRVE B60 .... 185 K4

Brookfields Junior &
Infant School
WSNGN B18 .... 6 A1

Brookhurst Primary School
RLSN CV32 .... 200 B4

Brooklands Industrial Estate
CHWD/FDBR/MGN B37 .... 110 F5

Brook Park Industrial Estate
HAG/WOL DY9 .... 102 D8

The Brook Primary School
STRBR DY8 .... 101 K4

Brook School
RUGBYS/DCH CV22 .... 183 K3

Brookside Surgery
RRUGBY CV23 .... 180 D7

Brook Street Business Centre
TPTN/OCK DY4 .... 67 J7

Brookvale Primary School
ERDW/GRVHL B23 .... 89 M1

Brookvale Trading Estate
AST/WIT B6 .... 89 L2

Brownhills Business Park
BRWNH WS8 .... 26 D8

Brownhills Clinic
BRWNH WS8 .... 26 D6

Brownhills
Comprehensive School
BRWNH WS8 .... 26 D4

Brownhills West
Primary School
BRWNH WS8 .... 26 A3

Browning Street
Industrial Estate
LDYWD/EDGR B16 .... 6 A6

Brownmead Junior &
Infant School
BKDE/SHDE B34 .... 92 A6

Brunswick Park Trading Estate
DARL/WED WS10 .... 68 F1

Brymill Industrial Estate
TPTN/OCK DY4 .... 67 J3

BSA Business Park
SMTHM B10 .... 108 B7

BT Tower
CBHAMNW B3 .... 6 E3

Buckpool
Comprehensive School
STRBR DY8 .... 101 K2

Budbrooke Combined School
RWWCK/WEL CV35 .... 198 D7

Budbrooke Industrial Estate
WWCK CV34 .... 199 G6

Budbrooke Medical Centre
RWWCK/WEL CV35 .... 198 D6

Budbrooke Road
Industrial Estate
RWWCK/WEL CV35 .... 198 F6

Buddhist Fat Yue Temple
BRLYHL DY5 .... 102 C2

Bull Ring Shopping Centre
DIG/EDG B5 .... 7 G6

Bull Ring Trading Estate
BORD B9 .... 7 K7

Bull Street Industrial Estate
BRLYHL DY5 .... 101 M4

The Bungalow Queensbury Day
Special School
ERDE/BCHGN B24 .... 90 D2

Buntsford Hill Business Park
BRGRVE B60 .... 185 K7

Burbidge Industrial Estate
BORD B9 .... 108 C2

Burlish Park First School
STRPT DY13 .... 160 D8

Burlish Park Middle School
STRPT DY13 .... 160 D7

Burman Infant School
SHLY B90 .... 146 E3

Burnsall Road Industrial
Estate
COVW CV5 .... 153 G5

Burnt Tree CP School
OLDBY B69 .... 85 L3

Burnt Tree Industrial Estate
TPTN/OCK DY4 .... 85 M3

Burntwood Baths
BNTWD WS7 .... 18 D7

Burntwood Health Centre
BNTWD WS7 .... 19 G7

Burntwood Town
Shopping Centre
BNTWD WS7 .... 18 C6

Burton Green Primary School
KNWTH CV8 .... 175 M2

Burton Industrial Estate
CDYHTH B64 .... 103 J5

Bushbury Baths
WOLVN WV10 .... 36 C4

Bushbury Health Centre
WOLVN WV10 .... 36 C3

Bushbury Infant School
WOLVN WV10 .... 36 C4

Busill Jones JMI School
BLOX/PEL WS3 .... 38 D5

The Business Centre
REDW B97 .... 196 B1

The Business Centre
YDLY B25 .... 108 D7

Butts Primary School
RUSH/SHEL WS4 .... 53 L2

Butts Stadium
COV CV1 .... 8 B5

Byng Kenrick Central School
STECH B33 .... 110 B2

CAB
CBHAMNE B4 .... 7 G4

Cadbury Sixth Form College
HWK/WKHTH B38 .... 144 D4

Cake Gallery
BVILLE B30 .... 144 E2

Calderfields Golf Club
RUSH/SHEL WS4 .... 54 A3

Caldmore JMI School
WSL WS1 .... 4 F5

Caldmore Medical Centre
WSL WS1 .... 4 F6

Callowbrook First School
RBRY B45 .... 142 C5

Calshot Junior & Infant School
PBAR/PBCH B42 .... 70 E5

Calthorpe Special School
BHTH/HG B12 .... 107 L5

Camp Hill Clinic
NUNW/HART CV10 .... 80 A7

Camp Hill County
Middle School
NUNW/HART CV10 .... 80 C7

Camp Hill Industrial Estate
BHTH/HG B12 .... 107 L5

Camp Hill Old
Edwardians Rugby
Football Club
SHLY B90 .... 146 F2

Campion School
RLSS CV31 .... 201 G8

Canalside Industrial Estate
BRLYHL DY5 .... 102 A4

Canning Wharf
CBHAMNW B3 .... 6 D4

Cannock Chase Council
CNCK/NC WS11 .... 16 B7

Cannock Chase Football Club
HEDN WS12 .... 12 E5

Cannock Chase High School
CNCK/NC WS11 .... 16 C3

Cannock Chase Hospital
CNCK/NC WS11 .... 16 C3

Cannock Chase
Technical College
CNCK/NC WS11 .... 16 C6

Cannock Chase
Technical College
CNCK/NC WS11 .... 16 B4

Cannock Industrial Centre
CNCK/NC WS11 .... 16 B8

Cannock & Rugeley Cricket Club
HEDN WS12 .... 13 L8

Cannon Business Park
BILS/COS WV14 .... 67 G4

Cannon Park Primary School
TLHL/CAN CV4 .... 153 H8

Canon Evans Infant School
BDWTH CV12 .... 116 E3

Canon Maggs C of E
Junior School
BDWTH CV12 .... 116 F3

Canterbury Cross
Primary School
BFLD/HDSWWD B20 .... 89 H3

Canwell C of E Primary School
MGN/WHC B75 .... 57 M1

Cape Hill Medical Centre
SMTHWK B66 .... 106 A1

Cape Industrial Estate
WWCK CV34 .... 199 J5

Cape Primary School
SMTHWK B66 .... 106 A1

Cardinal Griffin RC School
CNCK/NC WS11 .... 16 B2

Cardinal Newman RC School &
Community College
COVN CV6 .... 133 K3

Cardinal Newman
Secondary Modern
HRBN B17 .... 105 L3

Cardinal Wiseman RC School
COVE CV2 .... 135 J4

Cardinal Wiseman RC School
KGSTG B44 .... 71 K3

Caretaker Hill Farm School
COVN CV6 .... 133 L6

Caretaker Howes School
COVS CV3 .... 154 B7

Carlton Business Centre
VAUX/NECH B7 .... 90 A8

Carlyle Business Park
WBROM B70 .... 68 D8

Carlyon Road Industrial Estate
ATHST CV9 .... 63 K5

Carters Green Medical Centre
WBROM B70 .... 87 G1

Cascades Swimming Baths
STECH B33 .... 109 J2

Cashmore Middle School
RLSS CV31 .... 200 C7

Cashs Business Centre
COV CV1 .... 134 B8

Caslon Primary School
HALE B63 .... 120 F1

Castle Bromwich
Business Park
ERDE/BCHGN B24 .... 91 K4

Castle Bromwich
Cricket Club
CBROM B36 .... 92 A5

Castle Bromwich
Infant School
CBROM B36 .... 92 C5

Castle Bromwich
Junior School
CBROM B36 .... 92 B6

Castlecroft Primary School
BDMR/CCFT WV3 .... 48 F5

Castle Meadows Surgery
SEDG DY3 .... 84 B3

Castle School
BLOX/PEL WS3 .... 38 F6

Castle Vale Health Centre
CVALE B35 .... 91 L2

Castle Vale Housing
Action Trust
CVALE B35 .... 91 M1

Castle Vale Industrial Estate
WALM/CURD B76 .... 73 L8

Castle Vale School
CVALE B35 .... 91 M2

Castle Vale Shopping Centre
CVALE B35 .... 91 K2

Cathedral Gallery
LICH WS13 .... 20 C1

Cathedral Lanes
Shopping Centre
COV CV1 .... 8 F4

Catherine De Barnes
C of E Junior &
Infant School
SOLH B91 .... 128 F8

Catshill Clinic
BRGRVW B61 .... 165 L5

Catshill Middle School
BRGRVW B61 .... 165 K5

Catshill Primary School
BRGRVW B61 .... 165 L5

Catshill Village Surgery
BRGRVW B61 .... 165 L4

Causeway Green
Primary School
LGLYGN/QTN B68 .... 104 D2

Cavendish Surgery
WSNGN B18 .... 106 B1

Cedars Surgery
HIA/OLT B92 .... 127 J4

Centech Business Park
REDE B98 .... 189 K7

Centenary Business Centre
NUN CV11 .... 99 J2

Central City Industrial Estate
COVN CV6 .... 134 D8

Central Clinic
DUDS DY2 .... 85 H4

Central Jamia
Mosque Ghamkolvia
SMHTH B10 .... 108 B6

Central Six Retail Park
COV CV1 .... 8 D7

Central Surgery
RUGBYN/HIL CV21 .... 183 L2

Central Trading Estate
KGSWFD DY6 .... 83 K4

Centre Link Industrial Estate
VAUX/NECH B7 .... 89 M7

Centrovell Industrial Estate
NUN CV11 .... 99 G3

Century Industrial Estate
KGSTG B44 .... 71 J2

Chace Avenue Surgery
COVS CV3 .... 154 F8

Chace Primary School
COVS CV3 .... 155 G7

Chaddesley Corbett
Endowed School
KIDD DY10 .... 163 J5

Chadsgrove School
BRGRVW B61 .... 165 K5

Chadsmead County
Primary School
LICH WS13 .... 20 E4

Chadsmoor C E Junior School
CNCK/NC WS11 .... 16 E1

Chadsmoor County
Infants School
CNCK/NC WS11 .... 16 E1

Chadsmoor Medical Practice
CNCK/NC WS11 .... 12 C8

Chad Vale Primary School
HRBN B17 .... 106 B6

Challenge Business Park
COV CV1 .... 134 B8

Chamber of Commerce and
Industry
BDMR/CCFT WV3 .... 2 A4

Chancel Industrial Estate
DARL/WED WS10 .... 52 B8

Chancel Industrial Estate
KGSWFD DY6 .... 83 J5

Chancel Industrial Estate
WLNHL WV13 .... 51 M3

Chancel Way Industrial Estate
PBAR/PBCH B42 .... 71 K8

Chandos Junior & Infant School
DIG/EDG B5 .... 107 J6

Chapel Fields Primary School
HIA/OLT B92 .... 127 K2

Chapelhouse Surgery
HALE B63 .... 102 F7

Chapel Street Industrial Estate
DUDS DY2 .... 103 H1

Charford First School
BRGRVE B60 .... 185 K6

Charlemont Primary School
HHTH/SAND B71 .... 69 J5

Charles Street Industrial Estate
TPTN/OCK DY4 .... 68 C2

Charnwood Business Park
BILS/COS WV14 .... 51 G4

Charnwood County
Primary School
LICH WS13 .... 21 G2

Chase Park Industrial Estate
BNTWD WS7 .... 18 B6

Chaseside Industrial Estate
HEDN WS12 .... 16 F2

Chase Terrace County Primary
School
BNTWD WS7 .... 18 D5

Chasetown CP School
BNTWD WS7 .... 18 C8

Chasetown High School
BNTWD WS7 .... 26 C1

Chasewater Industrial Estate
BNTWD WS7 .... 18 C7

Chase Watersports Centre
BRWNH WS8 .... 26 A2

Chasewood Park
Business Centre
HEDN WS12 .... 17 J4

Cheapside Industrial Estate
BHTH/HG B12 .... 7 K8

Chelmsley Wood
Industrial Estate
CHWD/FDBR/MGN B37 .... 92 F8

Chelmsley Wood
Shopping Centre
CHWD/FDBR/MGN B37 .... 110 F3

Chelsea Trading Estate
AST/WIT B6 .... 89 L7

Cherry Oak School
SLYOAK B29 .... 124 C4

Cherry Orchard Primary School
BFLD/HDSWWD B20 .... 88 E2

Cherry Tree Sports Club
COVN CV6 .... 134 C3

Cherry Trees Special School
WMBN WV5 .... 64 D7

Cheslyn Hay CP School
GTWY WS6 .... 24 A2

Cheslyn Hay High School
GTWY WS6 .... 24 A2

Cheston Industrial Estate
AST/WIT B6 .... 89 M6

Cheswick Green Junior & Infant
School
SHLY B90 .... 147 J8

Chetwynd Middle School
NUN CV11 ...... 99 K6
Cheylesmore Welfare Clinic
COVS CV3 ...... 154 C7
Chilcote Junior School
HLGN/YWD B28 ...... 146 D1
Child Health Centre
SCFLD/BOLD B73 ...... 71 M1
Chillington Works
Industrial Estate
WOLV WV1 ...... 3 M7
Chinese Quarter
DIG/EDG B5 ...... 7 G7
Chiropodist Surgery
KGSTG B44 ...... 71 L6
The Chiropody Surgery
YDLY B25 ...... 109 H4
Chivenor Junior &
Infant School
CVALE B35 ...... 91 L3
Chivers Coton First School
NUN CV11 ...... 98 F2
Christ Church C of E
Primary School
LICH WS13 ...... 20 D6
Christ Church C of E
Infant School
DUNHL/THL/PER WV6 ...... 2 D1
Christ Church C of E
Infant School
DUNHL/THL/PER WV6 ...... 48 F2
Christ Church C of E
Primary School
BLOX/PEL WS3 ...... 39 H6
Christ Church C of E
Primary School
OLDBY B69 ...... 86 E5
Christ Church C of E School
SPARK B11 ...... 107 M6
Christ Church School
DUNHL/THL/PER WV6 ...... 49 G1
Christ Church School
PENK ST19 ...... 14 A3
Christ the King RC
Infant School
COVN CV6 ...... 133 K7
Christ the King RC
Junior School
COVN CV6 ...... 133 K6
Chuckery Primary School
WSL WS1 ...... 5 J3
Churchfields High School
HHTH/SAND B71 ...... 69 J8
Church Hill Middle School
REDE B98 ...... 189 H7
Church Lane Health Centre
STETCH B33 ...... 109 K2
Church of Christ the
King School
KGSTG B44 ...... 71 L5
Church of the Ascension C of E
Primary School
KGSWFD DY6 ...... 83 G5
Church Street Surgery
KIDD DY10 ...... 137 J7
Cinema
DIG/EDG B5 ...... 6 F6
City Estate
CDYHTH B64 ...... 103 H5
City Hospital NHS Trust
WSNGN B18 ...... 106 D1
City Plaza Shopping Centre
CBHAM B2 ...... 6 F5
City Technology College
CHWD/FDBR/MGN B37 ...... 110 E1
City Trading Estate
LDYWD/EDGR B16 ...... 106 E2
Clapham Terrace County
First School
RLSS CV31 ...... 200 E6
Claregate Primary School
DUNHL/THL/PER WV6 ...... 35 K6
Clarkes Industrial Estate
SCFLD/BOLD B73 ...... 72 E3
Claybrook Primary School
REDE B98 ...... 197 K4
Clent Parochial First School
HAG/WOL DY9 ...... 140 D3
Cleton Street Business Park
TPTN/OCK DY4 ...... 85 M2
Clifford Bridge Primary School
COVS CV3 ...... 155 L2
Clifton Infant School
BHTH/HG B12 ...... 107 L8
Clifton Junior School
BHTH/HG B12 ...... 107 L8
Clifton Mosque
BHTH/HG B12 ...... 107 K8
Clifton Road Industrial Estate
BHTH/HG B12 ...... 107 K8
Clinton Combined School
KNWTH CV8 ...... 191 J2
Closers Business Centre
NUN CV11 ...... 99 H3
Clothier Street Primary School
WLNHL WV13 ...... 51 L2
Club House
WOLVN WV10 ...... 35 M6
CMT Industrial Estate
OLDBY B69 ...... 86 E5
Coalpool Clinic
BLOX/PEL WS3 ...... 39 K7
Cobham Business Centre
BORD B9 ...... 108 B3
Cockshut Hill School
LGN/SDN/BHAMAIR B26 ...... 109 L5
Cocks Moors Woods
Leisure Centre
ALE/KHTH/YWD B14 ...... 145 K1
Codsall Clinic
CDSL WV8 ...... 34 E2
Codsall County High School
CDSL WV8 ...... 34 E2
Codsall County Middle School
CDSL WV8 ...... 34 E2
Cofton Medical Centre
NFLD/LBR B31 ...... 143 L6

Cofton Primary School
NFLD/LBR B31 ...... 143 L7
Coldland Colts Football Club
SOLH B91 ...... 128 D7
Colebourne Primary School
BKDE/SHDE B34 ...... 91 J8
Colemore School
ALE/KHTH/YWD B14 ...... 125 H6
Coleshill Clinic
CSHL/WTROR B46 ...... 93 L7
Coleshill C of E Primary School
CSHL/WTROR B46 ...... 93 L7
Coleshill Heath
Primary & Junior School
CHWD/FDBR/MGN B37 ...... 111 G4
Coleshill Industrial Estate
CSHL/WTROR B46 ...... 93 K3
Coleshill Leisure Centre
CSHL/WTROR B46 ...... 93 K7
Coleshill School
CSHL/WTROR B46 ...... 111 L2
Coleshill Town Council
CSHL/WTROR B46 ...... 93 L7
Coleshill Town Football Club
CSHL/WTROR B46 ...... 111 L2
College Annexe
COV CV1 ...... 8 C7
College High School
ERDW/GRVHL B23 ...... 71 L7
College of Adult Education
WOLV WV1 ...... 3 G6
College of Food
Tourism & Creative Studies
CBHAMNW B3 ...... 6 D4
Colley Lane Health Clinic
HALE B63 ...... 103 G7
Colley Lane Primary School
HALE B63 ...... 103 G7
Collingwood Junior School
WOLVN WV10 ...... 36 C3
Colmers Farm
Grant Maintained School
RBRY B45 ...... 142 F5
Colmers Farm Junior &
Infant School
RBRY B45 ...... 142 F5
Colmore Junior &
Infant School
ALE/KHTH/YWD B14 ...... 125 H6
Comberton Gallery
KIDD DY10 ...... 137 M8
Comberton Middle School
KIDD DY10 ...... 161 M1
Community Leisure Centre
TPTN/OCK DY4 ...... 67 H7
Conway Junior & Infant School
SPARK B11 ...... 107 M7
Coombswood & Hanne Surgery
CDYHTH B64 ...... 103 M6
Cooper & Jordan C of E
Junior & Infant School
ALDR WS9 ...... 41 G7
Coppice County Junior School
HIA/OLT B92 ...... 128 C6
Coppice High School
WNSFLD WV11 ...... 37 L6
Coppice Junior & Infant School
MGN/WHC B75 ...... 57 G4
Corbett Hospital
STRBR DY8 ...... 101 L6
Corbett Infant School
SMTHWK B66 ...... 87 M8
Corbetts Industrial Estate
DUDS DY2 ...... 85 G7
Corley Cricket Club
RCOVN/BALC/EX CV7 ...... 115 G7
Corley School
RCOVN/BALC/EX CV7 ...... 114 F7
Corngreaves Junior &
Infant School
CDYHTH B64 ...... 103 H4
Cornwall Industrial Estate
WASH/WDE B8 ...... 108 A1
Cornwall Road Industrial Estate
SMTHWK B66 ...... 88 A6
Corpus Christi Primary School
WNSFLD WV11 ...... 37 L5
Corpus Christi RC Junior & Infant
School
COVS CV3 ...... 155 H6
Corpus Christi RC School
STETCH B33 ...... 109 H3
Coseley Medical Centre
BILS/COS WV14 ...... 67 G5
Coseley Secondary School
BILS/COS WV14 ...... 66 F4
Coseley Swimming Pool
BILS/COS WV14 ...... 67 G5
Cotteridge Junior &
Infant School
BVILLE B30 ...... 124 E8
Cottesbrook Junior School
ACGN B27 ...... 127 G1
Cotton Green CP School
CRTAM B79 ...... 31 K6
Cotwell End County
Primary School
SEDG DY3 ...... 66 A6
Council Offices
COV CV1 ...... 9 G5
Coundon Court
School & Community College
COVN CV6 ...... 133 J6
Coundon Court
School & Community College
COVN CV6 ...... 134 C6
Coundon Primary School
COVN CV6 ...... 133 J4
County Bridge Primary School
WSLW WS2 ...... 52 C4
Court Farm Junior &
Infant Schools
ERDW/GRVHL B23 ...... 72 C7
Courthouse Infant School
COVN CV6 ...... 134 E5
Coventry Cathedral
COV CV1 ...... 9 G4

Coventry City Council
COV CV1 ...... 8 D6
Coventry City Council
COV CV1 ...... 9 G6
Coventry City Council
COVE CV2 ...... 135 G4
Coventry City Council
COVE CV2 ...... 155 J2
Coventry City Council
COVS CV3 ...... 154 D6
Coventry City Football Club
COV CV1 ...... 8 E4
Coventry City Football Club
COV CV1 ...... 9 L3
Coventry Health Authority
COV CV1 ...... 8 F6
Coventry Health Authority
COV CV1 ...... 134 A7
Coventry Health Authority
COVE CV2 ...... 135 L7
Coventry Muslim School
COV CV1 ...... 9 J1
Coventry Muslim School
COVN CV6 ...... 134 C5
Coventry &
North Warwickshire
County Council
COVS CV3 ...... 154 F3
Coventry Preparatory School
COVW CV5 ...... 153 M5
Coventry RFC
COVN CV6 ...... 8 B2
Coventry Rugby Club
COV CV1 ...... 8 B6
Coventry Technical College
COV CV1 ...... 8 B6
The Coventry Toy Museum
COV CV1 ...... 9 H6
Coventry Trading Estate
COVS CV3 ...... 179 G1
Coventry Trading Estate
KNWTH CV8 ...... 179 G3
Coventry University
COV CV1 ...... 9 J4
Coventry University
COV CV1 ...... 9 G5
Coventry
University Technocentre
COV CV1 ...... 9 G7
Coventry &
Warwickshire Hospital
COV CV1 ...... 9 G2
Coventry Welsh Rugby
Football Club
COVN CV6 ...... 116 B8
Crabbs Cross Medical Centre
REDW B97 ...... 196 C7
Crabbs Cross Surgery
REDW B97 ...... 196 B7
Crabtree Clinic
CHWD/FDBR/MGN B37 ...... 110 D3
Cradley C of E Primary School
HALE B63 ...... 103 C6
Cradley Heath
Community
Recreation Centre
DUDS DY2 ...... 103 J3
Cradley High School
HALE B63 ...... 102 F7
Cradley Town Football Club
HALE B63 ...... 121 G7
Craig Croft Child Health Clinic
CHWD/FDBR/MGN B37 ...... 111 G3
Craig Croft Medical Centre
CHWD/FDBR/MGN B37 ...... 111 G3
Cranmore County
Infant School
SOLH B91 ...... 147 J4
Cranmore Industrial Estate
SHLY B90 ...... 147 J5
Crescent Industrial Park
DUDS DY2 ...... 84 F6
Crescent School
RUGBYS/DCH CV22 ...... 183 H5
Crescent Theatre
LDYWD/EDGR B16 ...... 6 B6
Crescent Works Industrial Park
DARL/WED WS10 ...... 52 B4
Crestwood Park Primary School
KGSWFD DY6 ...... 83 J3
Crestwood School
KGSWFD DY6 ...... 83 K3
Cricket Club
GTB/HAM B43 ...... 70 B7
Cricket Club
WWCK CV34 ...... 199 J4
Criterion Theatre
COVW CV5 ...... 8 A9
Crocketts Lane Infant School
SMTHWK B66 ...... 87 M8
Croft Foundry Industrial Estate
WLNHL WV13 ...... 51 L3
Croft Infant School
WSLW WS2 ...... 53 H1
Croft Medical Centre
RLSS CV31 ...... 201 G8
Croft Middle School
NUNW/HART CV10 ...... 98 C2
Cromwell Junior &
Infant School
VAUX/NECH B7 ...... 89 M7
Cronehills Health Centre
WBROM B70 ...... 87 G2
Cronehills JMI School
WBROM B70 ...... 87 H1
Cronin Vet Surgery
GTB/HAM B43 ...... 70 A5
Crossfield Industrial Estate
LICH WS13 ...... 21 J5
Crossings Industrial Estate
BLOX/PEL WS3 ...... 38 E5
Cross Quays Business Park
OLDBY B69 ...... 86 A3
Cross Road Industrial Estate
COVN CV6 ...... 134 D6
Cross Street Health Centre
DUDN DY1 ...... 85 G4

Crown Court
COV CV1 ...... 9 G5
Crown Meadow
Primary School
ALVE B48 ...... 167 M7
Crown Medical Practice
TAM/AM/WIL B77 ...... 32 E8
Crystal Leisure Centre
STRBR DY8 ...... 101 L8
Cubbington C of E
Combined School
RLSN CV32 ...... 193 K8
Culwell Industrial Park
WOLVN WV10 ...... 3 J3
Culwell Trading Estate
WOLVN WV10 ...... 3 L1
Curdworth Primary School
WALM/CURD B76 ...... 75 G7
Curu Nanak Sikh Temple
WOLVN WV10 ...... 50 C1
Dadsford Bridge
Industrial Estate
STRBR DY8 ...... 101 J3
Dalehouse Lane
Industrial Estate
KNWTH CV8 ...... 177 G7
Dame Elizabeth
Cadbury School
BVILLE B30 ...... 124 C6
Dame Ellen Pinsent School
HRBN B17 ...... 106 A3
Dame Ellen Pinsent School
MOS/BIL B13 ...... 125 L6
Damson Wood County
Infant School
HIA/OLT B92 ...... 128 B6
Danesmore Park
Primary School
WNSFLD WV11 ...... 37 K4
Darlaston Clinic
DARL/WED WS10 ...... 52 A7
Darlaston Community School
DARL/WED WS10 ...... 51 M7
Darlaston Football Club
DARL/WED WS10 ...... 52 B7
Dartmouth
Comprehensive School
GTB/HAM B43 ...... 70 B2
Dartmouth School
COVE CV2 ...... 135 H8
Davenal House Surgery
BRGRVE B60 ...... 185 L2
Daw End School
RUSH/SHEL WS4 ...... 39 M7
Dawley Brook CP School
KGSWFD DY6 ...... 83 G6
Dawley Trading Estate
KGSWFD DY6 ...... 83 H5
Day School
CRTAM B79 ...... 31 M8
Daylesford Hall Infant School
HIA/OLT B92 ...... 127 L2
Deanery C of E Junior School
WALM/CURD B76 ...... 73 K5
Deansfield High School
WOLV WV1 ...... 51 G3
Deedmore School
COVE CV2 ...... 135 G5
Deeleys Industrial Estate
WSLW WS2 ...... 38 F7
Deepdale Industrial Estate
DUDN DY1 ...... 84 C2
Deer Park Business Centre
KNWTH CV8 ...... 193 H1
Delph Industrial Estate
BRLYHL DY5 ...... 102 A4
Delta Business Centre
CNCK/NC WS11 ...... 16 B7
Delves Junior & Infant School
DSYBK/YTR WS5 ...... 53 L8
Dental Health Centre
KGSTG B44 ...... 71 K3
The Dentists Surgery
WWCK CV34 ...... 199 J4
Devonshire Road Junior School
SMTHWKW B67 ...... 87 K7
Deykin Avenue Junior &
Infant School
AST/WIT B6 ...... 89 L3
Deyncourt CP School
WNSFLD WV11 ...... 36 F6
Dingle Primary School
KGSWFD DY6 ...... 101 L1
Dingleside Middle School
REDE B98 ...... 196 F5
Doctor Blacker &
Partners Surgery
BRGRVE B60 ...... 185 L4
Dodford Primary School
BRGRVW B61 ...... 164 E8
Doranda Way Industrial Estate
HHTH/SAND B71 ...... 87 K4
Dordon Community
Primary School
POL/KGSB/FAZ B78 ...... 47 L7
The Dormston School
SEDG DY3 ...... 66 C5
Dormston Trading Estate
DUDN DY1 ...... 84 D1
Dorothy Pattison Hospital
WSLW WS2 ...... 52 F4
Dorothy Purcell Junior School
BILS/COS WV14 ...... 67 M2
Dorridge Cricket Club
DOR/KN B93 ...... 172 C6
Dorridge Gallery
DOR/KN B93 ...... 172 D2
Dorridge Junior &
Infant School
DOR/KN B93 ...... 172 D2
Dorrington Junior &
Infant School
PBAR/PBCH B42 ...... 70 E7
Dosthill School
TAM/AM/WIL B77 ...... 46 A8
Doulton Trading Estate
BLKHTH/ROWR B65 ...... 103 K1

Dovecote Junior &
Infant School
CDSL WV8 ...... 35 J4
The Dovecote Surgery
LGLYGN/QTN B68 ...... 105 H6
Downing Close Health Clinic
DOR/KN B93 ...... 172 C1
Dows Surgery
REDW B97 ...... 196 C1
Dr Arora Surgery
PBAR/PBCH B42 ...... 71 H8
Dr Browns Surgery
BORD B9 ...... 108 E4
Dreamwell Industrial Estate
SPARK B11 ...... 108 E7
Dr Gonzales Surgery
KGSTG B44 ...... 71 K5
Driffold Gallery
SCFLD/BOLD B73 ...... 72 F2
Dr Lewiss Surgery
BORD B9 ...... 108 E4
Dr M Allbeson & Partners
PENK ST19 ...... 10 C4
Droicon Industrial Estate
BLKHTH/ROWR B65 ...... 103 M1
Drs Shirazi & Fitzgerald Surgery
NUN CV11 ...... 99 G2
Druids Heath Golf Club
ALDR WS9 ...... 41 G5
Dudley Central Trading Estate
DUDS DY2 ...... 85 G5
Dudley College
DUDN DY1 ...... 85 G3
Dudley College of Technology
BRLYHL DY5 ...... 102 B2
Dudley County Court
BRLYHL DY5 ...... 102 C1
Dudley Health Authority
DUDN DY1 ...... 84 E5
Dudley Kingswinford
Rugby Football Club
KGSWFD DY6 ...... 82 E6
Dudley Leisure Centre
DUDN DY1 ...... 84 F4
Dudley Metropolitan
Borough Council
BRLYHL DY5 ...... 101 L3
Dudley Metropolitan
Borough Council
BRLYHL DY5 ...... 102 B3
Dudley Metropolitan
Borough Council
DUDN DY1 ...... 66 D3
Dudley Metropolitan
Borough Council
DUDN DY1 ...... 84 D6
Dudley Metropolitan
Borough Council
DUDN DY1 ...... 85 G3
Dudley Metropolitan
Borough Council
DUDN DY1 ...... 85 G4
Dudley Metropolitan
Borough Council
DUDS DY2 ...... 84 F5
Dudley Metropolitan
Borough Council
DUDS DY2 ...... 85 H6
Dudley Metropolitan
Borough Council
DUDS DY2 ...... 103 H3
Dudley Metropolitan
Borough Council
HAG/WOL DY9 ...... 120 C1
Dudley Metropolitan
Borough Council
HALE B63 ...... 121 M2
Dudley Metropolitan
Borough Council
SEDG DY3 ...... 66 B4
Dudley Metropolitan
Borough Council
STRBR DY8 ...... 101 K8
Dudley Metropolitan
Borough Council
STRBR DY8 ...... 119 K1
Dudley Metropolitan
District Council
STRBR DY8 ...... 101 J3
Dudley Mosque &
Muslim Community Centre
DUDN DY1 ...... 85 H3
Dudley Priority Health
N H S Trust
DUDN DY1 ...... 84 C6
Dudley Priority Health
N H S Trust
KGSWFD DY6 ...... 83 J7
Dudley School
DUDN DY1 ...... 84 F3
Dudley Town Hall
DUDN DY1 ...... 85 G4
Dudley Water Sports Centre
DUDS DY2 ...... 102 F2
Dudley Wood Primary School
DUDS DY2 ...... 103 G3
Dudley Zoological Society Ltd
DUDN DY1 ...... 85 H3
Dumolos County
Primary School
TAM/AM/WIL B77 ...... 46 D8
Duncan Street Surgery
BKHL/PFLD WV2 ...... 50 B6
Dunlop Road
REDW B97 ...... 196 A8
Dunstall Hill Industrial Estate
DUNHL/THL/PER WV6 ...... 36 A8
Dunton Trading Estate
VAUX/NECH B7 ...... 90 B6
Durbar Avenue
Industrial Estate
COVN CV6 ...... 134 B5
Durberville Road
Industrial Estate
BKHL/PFLD WV2 ...... 50 D6
Eagle Industrial Estate
TPTN/OCK DY4 ...... 68 B6

Eagle Industrial Estate
WBROM B70................ 68 C5
Eagle Trading Estate
HALE B63.................. 121 L1
Earl Place Business Park
TLHL/CAN CV4.......... 153 G4
Earlsdon Primary School
COVW CV5.................. 8 A8
The Earls High School
HALE B63.................. 121 M1
Earlson Business Centre
COVW CV5................. 153 K5
Earlswood Trading Estate
HOCK/TIA B94............ 170 A7
East Birmingham College
STECH B33............... 109 M5
Eastbourne House School
ACGN B27................. 127 G1
East Cannock Industrial Estate
HEDN WS12................ 16 F2
Eastern Green Junior School
COVW CV5................ 132 B8
Eastfield Junior & Infant School
WOLV WV1.................. 3 M5
East Park Medical Practice
WOLV WV1................. 50 E3
East Park Primary School
WOLV WV1................. 50 F5
East Park Trading Estate
WOLV WV1.................. 3 M8
Eastwood Industrial Estate
WSNGN B18............... 106 D1
Eaton Wood Medical Centre
ERDE/BCHGN B24......... 91 H2
Eburne Primary School
COVE CV2................ 135 K2
Eclipse Trading Estate
TPTN/OCK DY4............ 67 J8
Edgar Stammers
Junior & Infant School
BLOX/PEL WS3............. 39 K6
Edgaston Shopping Centre
LDYWD/EDGR B16......... 106 E5
Edgbaston C of E
College for Girls
EDG B15................. 106 C5
Edgbaston College
EDG B15................. 106 F8
Edgbaston Health Clinic
EDG B15................. 106 D8
Edgbaston Health Clinic
SOLH B91................ 127 K7
Edgbaston High
School for Girls
EDG B15................. 106 D6
Edgwick Community
Primary School
COVN CV6................ 134 C5
Edgewood Road Clinic
RBRY B45................ 142 F7
Edgwick Park Industrial Estate
COVN CV6................ 134 C5
Edwards Street Day Hospital
WBROM B70................ 87 C2
Edward Street Hospital
WBROM B70................ 87 C2
Elgar House Surgery
REDW B97................ 196 B1
Elliot Court Coventry
Business Park
COVW CV5................ 153 G4
Elliots Field Retail Park
RUGBYN/HIL CV21......... 159 L7
The Ellowes Hall Gm School
SEDG DY3................. 66 A8
Elm Court Meriden
Green Business Park
COVW CV5................ 132 A5
Elmdon Trading Estate
CHWD/FDBR/MGN B37...... 111 C8
Elmfield School
STRBR DY8............... 119 L2
Elmore Green Primary School
BLOX/PEL WS3............. 38 E4
Elms Farm Junior &
Infant School
LGN/SDN/BHAMAIR B26.... 110 A6
Elms Health Centre
HALE B63................ 103 C7
Elm Street Infant School
WLNHL WV13............... 52 A2
Elm Terrace Clinic
OLDBY B69................ 85 M4
Elston Hall Primary School
WOLVN WV10............... 36 B3
Embassy Industrial Estate
HAG/WOL DY9............. 102 D8
Empire Industrial Park
ALDR WS9................ 40 D5
Emscote County First School
WWCK CV34............... 199 M5
Emscote Lawn
Preparatory School
WWCK CV34............... 199 L5
English Martyrs RC
Junior & Infant School
SPARK B11............... 126 A1
Ensign Business Centre
TLHL/CAN CV4............ 152 D7
Enterprise Trading Estate
BRLYHL DY5.............. 102 E2
Erdington Hall Primary School
ERDE/BCHGN B24.......... 90 D3
Erdington Industrial Park
ERDE/BCHGN B24.......... 91 K1
Erdington Medical Centre
ERDE/BCHGN B24.......... 90 C3
Ernesford Grange
Primary School
COVS CV3................ 155 J4
Ernesford Grange School &
Community College
COVS CV3................ 155 H5
Essington Light
Industrial Estate
WNSFLD WV11.............. 37 K1
Etone Community School
NUN CV11................. 81 H8

Etone Sports Centre
NUN CV11................. 81 H8
Ettingshall Lodge Surgery
BKHL/PFLD WV2............ 50 E6
Ettingshall Primary School
BILS/COS WV14........... 50 F7
European Business Park
OLDBY B69................ 86 C6
Eve Hill Medical Practice
DUDN DY1................. 84 F3
Eversfield Preparatory School
SOLH B91................ 147 M1
Exchange Industrial Estate
CNCK/NC WS11............. 16 C7
Exhall Business Park
RCOVN/BALC/EX CV7....... 116 F5
Exhall Cedars First School
RCOVN/BALC/EX CV7....... 116 F5
Exhall Grange School
RCOVN/BALC/EX CV7....... 116 B8
Express Way Industrial Estate
AST/WIT B6................ 89 J7
Eye Infirmary
BDMR/CCFT WV3............. 2 B5
Fairey Industrial Estate
TAM/AM/WIL B77........... 46 B5
Fairfax School
MGN/WHC B75.............. 57 K8
Fairfield First School
BRGRVW B61.............. 165 H2
Fairfield Villa Football Club
BRGRVW B61.............. 165 H2
Fairhaven Primary School
STRBR DY8............... 101 H2
Fair View Industrial Estate
WALM/CURD B76............ 74 F6
Fairway Primary School
HWK/WKHTH B38........... 144 B3
Falcon Lodge Clinic
MGN/WHC B75.............. 57 L8
Falcon Lodge Junior School
MGN/WHC B75.............. 57 K8
Fallings Park Industrial Estate
WOLVN WV10............... 36 D8
Farndale Junior School
DUNHL/THL/PER WV6........ 49 L1
Fazeley Health Centre
POL/KGSB/FAZ B78......... 45 L5
Fazeley Industrial Estate
DIG/EDG B5................ 7 K5
Featherstone Health Centre
WASH/WDE B8............. 108 E1
Featherstone Junior &
Infant School
ERDW/GRVHL B23........... 90 C1
Feldon Lane Clinic
RMSLY B62............... 104 C6
Fernbank Medical Centre
WASH/WDE B8............. 108 E1
Ferndale Primary School
GTB/HAM B43.............. 70 C5
Fillongley C of E School
RCOVN/BALC/EX CV7....... 114 B2
Finham Park School
COVS CV3................ 153 L8
Finham Primary School
KNWTH CV8............... 177 M2
Fircroft College
SLYOAK B29.............. 124 B5
Fire Station
CBHAMNE B4................ 7 H2
Firs Industrial Estate
STRPT DY13.............. 161 G6
Firs Junior & Infant School
CBROM B36................ 91 J5
First Community Health
GTWY WS6................. 24 D3
Fir Tree Junior & Infant School
DSYBK/YTR WS5............ 69 L1
Fitzwarren School
TPTN/OCK DY4............. 67 L7
Five Ways CP School
HEDN WS12................ 17 H3
Five Ways Shopping Centre
EDG B15................... 6 A8
Flax Hill Junior School
CRTAM B79................ 31 M6
Fletchamstead
Highway Industrial Estate
COVW CV5................ 153 H6
Fletchworth Gate
Industrial Estate
COVW CV5................ 153 H5
Florendine County
Primary School
TAM/AM/WIL B77........... 32 D8
Foleshill C of E Junior &
Infant School
COVN CV6................ 134 E3
Foleshill Leisure Centre
COVN CV6................ 134 B6
Foley Park Primary School
KIDDW DY11.............. 161 H2
The Foot Clinic (1996) Ltd
CBHAMNW B3................ 6 E4
Fordhouse Road
Industrial Estate
WOLVN WV10............... 36 A5
Fordhouses Cricket Club
WOLVN WV10............... 36 B1
Fords Hospital
COV CV1.................. 8 F5
Forge Trading Estate
RMSLY B62............... 104 A8
Formans Trading Estate
SPARK B11............... 126 B2
Fort Industrial Park
ERDE/BCHGN B24.......... 91 K4
Forum Health Centre
COVE CV2................ 155 H1
Foundry Road Junior &
Infant School
WSNGN B18................ 88 B7
Four Dwellings JMI School
RIDG/WDGT B32........... 104 F8
Four Oaks Junior &
Infant School
FOAKS/STRLY B74.......... 56 C1

Four Oaks Medical Centre
MGN/WHC B75.............. 56 F3
Four Oaks Saints Cricket Club
FOAKS/STRLY B74.......... 42 C8
Four Seasons Art Gallery
ERDE/BCHGN B24........... 72 E8
Foxford School
COVN CV6................ 116 F8
The Fox Hollies Leisure Centre
ACGN B27................ 126 E4
Fox Hollies Special School
ACGN B27................ 126 E4
Fox Hollies Surgery
HLGN/YWD B28............ 126 E4
Foxmill Estate Rear of 3
SPARK B11............... 126 B3
Foxyards County
Primary School
TPTN/OCK DY4............. 67 C8
Franche Clinic
KIDDW DY11.............. 136 F5
Franche CP School
KIDDW DY11.............. 136 F5
Frank F Harrison
Community School
WSLW WS2................. 38 D6
Frankley Health Centre
RBRY B45................ 142 D4
Frankley Industrial Park
RBRY B45................ 142 F4
Frankley Middle School
RBRY B45................ 142 F3
Frank Whittle Junior &
Infant School
COVE CV2................ 135 K5
Frederick Bird Primary School
COV CV1................. 134 D8
Friar Park Clinic
DARL/WED WS10............ 69 H2
The Friary County High School
LICH WS13................ 20 C3
Friary Grange Sports Centre
LICH WS13................ 20 D3
Fulfen County Primary School
BNTWD WS7................ 19 H6
Gallagher Retail Park
COVN CV6................ 134 D5
Galley Common First School
NUNW/HART CV10........... 79 K3
Galley Common Medical Centre
NUNW/HART CV10........... 97 K1
Gannow Middle School
RBRY B45................ 142 B6
Garratts Green Trading Estate
STECH B33............... 109 M4
Garretts Green Trading Estate
STECH B33............... 110 A4
Gas Street Basin
CBHAMW B1................. 6 C6
Gatehouse Trading Estate
BRWNH WS8................ 26 E4
Gate Lane Industrial Estate
SCFLD/BOLD B73........... 72 E3
Gate Medical Centre
WASH/WDE B8............. 90 B7
George Auden School
NFLD/LBR B31............ 123 K8
George Dixon GM School
HRBN B17................ 106 A3
George Dixon GM
School Annexe
HRBN B17................ 106 A4
The George Eliot Hospital
NHS Trust
NUNW/HART CV10........... 98 F3
George Eliot School
NUN CV11................. 99 H4
George Fentham
Junior & Infant School
HIA/OLT B92............. 129 J7
George Salter High School
WBROM B70................ 86 E1
Gibbons Industrial Park
KGSWFD DY6............... 83 L6
Gilberstone Primary School
HAG/WOL DY9............. 102 E7
G K Davies Industrial Estate
HAG/WOL DY9............. 102 E7
Glebefields Health Centre
TPTN/OCK DY4............. 67 L5
Glebefields Junior &
Infant School
TPTN/OCK DY4............. 67 L4
The Glebeland Surgery
HAG/WOL DY9............. 140 C7
Glendale First School
NUNW/HART CV10........... 98 D3
Glenmead Junior &
Infant School
PBAR/PBCH B42............ 71 H5
Glenthorne CP School
GTWY WS6................. 24 C2
Glynne Primary School
KGSWFD DY6.............. 101 C1
Golden Hillock
Community School
SPARK B11............... 108 B8
Goldtel Industrial Estate
ETTPK/GDPK/PENN WV4...... 50 E8
Goldthorne Medical Centre
ETTPK/GDPK/PENN WV4...... 50 A7
Goldthorn Park
Primary School
ETTPK/GDPK/PENN WV4...... 50 B8
Golf Club Bungalow
TAM/AM/WIL B77........... 47 C1
Golf Clubhouse
LICHS WS14............... 42 C7
Golf Club Leisure Centre
RLSN CV32............... 200 F4
Good Hope Hospital
MGN/WHC B75.............. 57 H7
Good Shepherd RC
Junior & Infant School
COVN CV6................ 134 D4

Goodyers End County
First School
RCOVN/BALC/EX CV7....... 116 C5
Gorsemoor CP School
HEDN WS12................ 17 H4
Goscote Hospital
BLOX/PEL WS3............. 39 K5
Goscote Industrial Estate
BLOX/PEL WS3............. 39 J4
Gosford Industrial Estate
COV CV1.................. 9 K5
Gosford Park Primary School
COV CV1.................. 9 K5
Gossey Lane Junior &
Infant School
STECH B33............... 110 A3
Grace Mary CP School
OLDBY B69................ 86 A6
Grafton Manor Hous
BRGRVW B61.............. 184 F6
Graiseley Primary School
BKHL/PFLD WV2............. 2 E9
Granby Business Park
STECH B33............... 110 B4
Grand Theatre
WOLV WV1.................. 3 C4
Grange Farm Primary School
COVS CV3................ 153 M8
Grangehurst Primary School
COVE CV2................ 134 F1
The Grange School
HAG/WOL DY9............. 120 F4
Gravel Hill Surgery
WMBN WV5................. 64 F7
Grazebrook Industrial Park
DUDS DY2................. 84 F7
Great Barr Gm School
KGSTG B44................ 71 H4
Great Barr Junior &
Infant School
PBAR/PBCH B42............ 71 G4
Great Bridge Industrial Estate
TPTN/OCK DY4............. 68 A6
Great Bridge Junior &
Infant School
TPTN/OCK DY4............. 68 A7
Great Western Industrial Estate
WSNGN B18................ 88 C7
Great Wyrley County
High School
GTWY WS6................. 24 D1
Greenacres County
Primary School
TAM/AM/WIL B77........... 32 F8
Greenacres Junior &
Infant School
BILS/COS WV14........... 51 K7
Greenbank Surgery
HLGN/YWD B28............ 126 C4
Greenfield Primary School
STRBR DY8............... 119 K1
Greenfield Surgery
STRBR DY8............... 101 K8
Greenhill Galleries
MOS/BIL B13............. 125 L4
Greenhill Health Centre
LICH WS13................ 21 C6
Greenholm Junior &
Infant School
KGSTG B44................ 71 J6
Green Industrial Estate
HEDN WS12................ 13 C6
Greenlands Business Centre
REDE B98................ 196 F4
Green Meadow Junior &
Infant School
SLYOAK B29.............. 123 K6
Green Rock Junior &
Infant School
BLOX/PEL WS3............. 39 J4
Greet Primary Infant &
Junior School
SPARK B11............... 126 B1
Greets Green Road
Industrial Estate
WBROM B70................ 86 D1
Gregston Industrial Estate
OLDBY B69................ 86 F5
Grendon Junior &
Infant School
ALE/KHTH/YWD B14........ 145 L2
Grestone Junior &
Infant School
BFLD/HDSWWD B20.......... 88 C1
Greswolde Gallery
DOR/KN B93.............. 148 F7
Greswold Junior &
Infant School
SOLH B91................ 127 M7
Greysbrooke CP School
LICHS WS14............... 28 E7
Griff Clara Industrial Estate
NUNW/HART CV10........... 98 D6
Griffin Industrial Estate
OLDBY B69............... 104 D2
Griffins Brook Medical Centre
SLYOAK B29.............. 124 A6
The Griff School
BDWTH CV12.............. 116 F2
Groundmans House
King Henry VIII School
COVS CV3................ 178 F1
Grovelands Industrial Estate
RCOVN/BALC/EX CV7....... 116 E7
Grove Lane Junior &
Infant School
HDSW B21................. 88 D5
Grove Medical Centre
BKHL/PFLD WV2............. 3 K9
Grove Park Industrial Estate
CNCK/NC WS11............. 16 C7
Grove Surgery
SOLH B91................ 128 A8
Grove Vale Primary School
GTB/HAM B43.............. 70 B4
Grypon Industrial Estate
BFLD/HDSWWD B20.......... 89 C3

Guardian Angels RC
Junior & Infant School
BKDE/SHDE B34............ 92 C7
Gulson Hospital
COV CV1.................. 9 J5
Gulson Road Clinic
COV CV1.................. 9 J5
Gun Barrel Industrial Centre
CDYHTH B64.............. 103 L7
Guns Village Infant School
WBROM B70................ 86 F1
Guns Village Junior School
WBROM B70................ 86 E2
Gunter Primary School
ERDE/BCHGN B24.......... 91 J1
Gupta Trading Estate
OLDBY B69................ 86 D4
Guru Nanak Sikh Temple
BDMR/CCFT WV3............. 2 C9
Guru Nanak Sikh Temple
BKHL/PFLD WV2............ 50 A6
Guru Nanak Sikh Temple
NUN CV11................. 99 J3
Guy Motors Industrial Park
WOLVN WV10............... 36 C8
GWS Trading Estate
TPTN/OCK DY4............. 68 B4
Haden Hill Leisure Centre
CDYHTH B64.............. 103 K5
Haden Vale Surgery
CDYHTH B64.............. 103 J6
Hagley County Primary
Junior & Infant School
HAG/WOL DY9............. 119 M8
Hagley RC High School
STRBR DY8............... 119 K8
Halas Industrial Estate
RMSLY B62............... 104 A8
Halcyon Gallery
CBHAM B2.................. 6 F6
Haldon House Business Centre
BRLYHL DY5.............. 101 M4
Halesbury School
RMSLY B62............... 104 C5
Hales Industrial Park
COVN CV6................ 134 C1
Halesowen C of E
Primary School
HALE B63................ 121 M1
Halesowen College
HALE B63................ 103 M8
Halesowen College
HALE B63................ 121 L1
Halesowen Cricket Club
HALE B63................ 121 M3
Halesowen Harriers
Football Club
HALE B63................ 102 F8
Halesowen Health Centre
HALE B63................ 121 M2
Halesowen Industrial Park
RMSLY B62............... 104 A7
Halesowen Leisure Centre
HALE B63................ 121 M2
Halesowen Magistrates Court
HALE B63................ 121 M2
Hale Trading Estate
TPTN/OCK DY4............. 67 M8
Hall Green Infant &
Junior Schools
HLGN/YWD B28............ 126 C5
Hall Green Little Theatre
ACGN B27................ 126 E3
Hall Green Primary &
Infant School
HHTH/SAND B71............ 69 G4
Hall Green School
HLGN/YWD B28............ 126 C5
Hallmoor School
STECH B33............... 109 M2
Hall of Memory
CBHAMW B1................. 6 D5
Hamd House School
BORD B9................. 108 E3
Hamilton School
HDSW B21................. 88 B5
Hammerwich Hospital
BNTWD WS7................ 18 F8
Hammond Business Centre
NUN CV11................. 99 J2
Hampstead Clinic
GTB/HAM B43.............. 70 B6
Hamstead Hall School
BFLD/HDSWWD B20.......... 70 C7
Hamstead Infant School
GTB/HAM B43.............. 70 B6
Hamstead Junior School
GTB/HAM B43.............. 70 B6
Hamstead Road Surgery
BFLD/HDSWWD B20.......... 88 E5
Hanburys Farm
Primary School
TAM/AM/WIL B77........... 46 B4
Handsworth College
HDSW B21................. 88 E6
Handsworth Grammar
School for Boys
HDSW B21................. 88 D5
Handsworth Leisure Centre
BFLD/HDSWWD B20.......... 88 D5
Handsworth Medical Practice
HDSW B21................. 88 C5
Handsworth Mosque &
Islamic Centre
HDSW B21................. 88 B5
Handsworth Rugby Club
DSYBK/YTR WS5............ 70 B1
Handsworth Wood Girls
School & Sixth Form Centre
BFLD/HDSWWD B20.......... 88 D3
Hanford Close Industrial Estate
COVN CV6................ 134 C7
Hangley Hall
HAG/WOL DY9............. 120 F7
Harborne Cycle Surgery
HRBN B17................ 105 J7
Harborne Hill School
EDG B15................. 106 L1

Harborne Junior School
HRBN B17 .... 106 A7
Harborne Medical Practice
HRBN B17 .... 106 B7
Harborne Swimming Pool
HRBN B17 .... 105 M8
Harden Primary School
BLOX/PEL WS3 .... 39 J6
Harden Surgery
BLOX/PEL WS3 .... 39 J6
Hargate Junior & Infant School
HHTH/SAND B71 .... 87 G1
Harnall Lane Industrial Estate
COV CV1 .... 9 H1
Harnall Lane Medical Centre
COV CV1 .... 9 H1
Harris C of E High School
RUGBYS/DCH CV22 .... 183 K4
Harrisons Institute & Sports Club
GTWY WS6 .... 24 E4
Harry Cheshire County Secondary School
KIDDW DY11 .... 136 F7
Harry Mitchell Leisure Centre
SMTHWKW B67 .... 87 K8
Harry Taylor First School
REDW B97 .... 196 B7
Hartshill School
NUNW/HART CV10 .... 79 M5
Harvey Road Health Centre
LGN/SDN/BHAMAIR B26 .... 109 J6
Harvey Works Industrial Estate
HALE B63 .... 103 K7
Harvills Hawthorn Primary School
WBROM B70 .... 68 D6
Hasbury C of E School
HALE B63 .... 121 K3
Hasbury Primary School
HALE B63 .... 121 K3
Hatchford Brook Junior & Infant School
HIA/OLT B92 .... 128 A2
Hatchford Gm Primary School
CHWD/FDBR/MGN B37 .... 110 D3
Hateley Heath Junior & Infant School
HHTH/SAND B71 .... 68 F6
Hatherton Lane Junior Mixed & Infant School
WSLW WS2 .... 38 D7
Havergal C of E Primary School
WOLVN WV10 .... 23 G3
Hawbush Primary School
BRLYHL DY5 .... 101 M3
Hawkesbury Fields School
COVE CV2 .... 135 G2
Hawkesbury Lock Industrial Centre
RCOVN/BALC/EX CV7 .... 116 F7
Hawkes Green Medical Centre
CNCK/NC WS11 .... 17 G3
Hawkesley C of E Methodist Junior School
HWK/WKHTH B38 .... 144 C6
Hawkesley Health Centre
HWK/WKHTH B38 .... 144 C6
Hawkins Colliery Sports Club
GTWY WS6 .... 24 B1
Hawkins Sports Club
GTWY WS6 .... 24 B1
Hawksmill Industrial Estate
BORD B9 .... 108 A4
Hawthorn Primary School
KGSTG B44 .... 71 L6
Hawthorns Business Centre
SMTHWK B66 .... 87 L5
Hawthorns Industrial Estate
HDSW B21 .... 87 M4
Hawthorns Surgery
CSCFLD/WYGN B72 .... 72 F5
Haybridge High School
STRBR DY8 .... 119 K7
The Hayes Trading Estate
HAG/WOL DY9 .... 102 E7
Hayley Green Hospital
HALE B63 .... 121 H5
Hayward Industrial Park
ALDR WS9 .... 40 E6
Hazelhead Industrial Estate
COV CV1 .... 9 L6
Hazell Way Industrial Estate
NUNW/HART CV10 .... 98 D4
Hazel Slade CP School
HEDN WS12 .... 13 L7
Health Authority Team Base
BRGRVE B60 .... 185 M2
Hearsall Community Primary School
COVW CV5 .... 153 K4
Hearsall Secondary School
COVW CV5 .... 153 K3
Heartlands High School
VAUX/NECH B7 .... 107 M1
Heart of England Secondary School
RCOVN/BALC/EX CV7 .... 150 F7
Heathfield Gm High School
CDYHTH B64 .... 103 K3
Heathfield Primary School
LOZ/NWT B19 .... 89 G5
Heathfields County Infants School
TAM/AM/WIL B77 .... 46 D7
Heath Hayes CP School
HEDN WS12 .... 17 K3
The Heathlands J I N C School
BKDE/SHDE B34 .... 91 K6
Heath Lane Hospital
HHTH/SAND B71 .... 69 H6
Heath Mount Primary School
BHTH/HG B12 .... 107 J7
Heath Park Comprehensive School
WOLVN WV10 .... 36 E8

Heath Street Industrial Estate
SMTHWK B66 .... 88 B8
Heath Town Leisure Centre
WOLV WV10 .... 50 D1
Hebrew Congregation
CBHAMW B1 .... 6 E7
Hemdale Business Park
NUN CV11 .... 99 K2
Henley College
COVN CV6 .... 135 G5
Henley Industrial Park
COVE CV2 .... 135 J6
Henry Bellairs C of E Middle & Primary School
BDWTH CV12 .... 117 H2
Henry Hinde First School
RUGBYS/DCH CV22 .... 183 K4
Henry Hinde Middle School
RUGBYS/DCH CV22 .... 182 F3
Henry Parkes Junior & Infant School
TLHL/CAN CV4 .... 153 G5
Herald Business Park
COVS CV3 .... 155 K6
Herbert Art Gallery & Museum
COV CV1 .... 9 G5
Herbert Fowler Middle School
RCOVN/BALC/EX CV7 .... 96 D3
Herefordshire College of Technology
KIDD DY10 .... 137 J8
Hereford & Worcester County Council
BRGRVW B61 .... 185 K3
Hereford & Worcester County Council
REDE B98 .... 188 C7
Hereward College of Further Education
TLHL/CAN CV4 .... 152 D4
H Hayes Clinic
HEDN WS12 .... 17 J4
Higham C of E Primary School
MKTBOS/BARL/STKG CV13 ..... 81 L1
Higham Lane School
NUNW/HART CV10 .... 81 J7
High Arcal School
SEDG DY3 .... 66 D7
Highclare School
CSCFLD/WYGN B72 .... 73 G4
Highclare School
ERDW/GRVHL B23 .... 72 E8
Highcroft Hospital
ERDW/GRVHL B23 .... 90 B2
Highcroft Hospital
ERDW/GRVHL B23 .... 90 C1
Highfield Junior & Infant School
WASH/WDE B8 .... 90 C8
Highfields Junior & Infant School
BLKHTH/ROWR B65 .... 104 A5
Highfields Primary School
BILS/COS WV14 .... 67 G3
Highfields Primary School
BNTWD WS7 .... 19 G6
Highfields School
ETTPK/GDPK/PENN WV4 .... 49 G8
Highgate Medical Centre
BHTH/HG B12 .... 107 K6
Highgate Primary School
DUDS DY2 .... 84 D7
Highgate Trading Estate
BHTH/HG B12 .... 107 L6
Highgate United Football Club
SHLY B90 .... 146 C7
High School
BNTWD WS7 .... 18 E6
High Street Surgery
ERDW/GRVHL B23 .... 72 E8
Highters Heath JMI School
ALE/KHTH/YWD B14 .... 145 M2
Hillary Infant School
WSLW WS2 .... 4 A8
Hill Avenue Primary School
ETTPK/GDPK/PENN WV4 .... 66 D2
Hillcrest Business Park
DUDS DY2 .... 85 G6
Hillcrest Industrial Estate
CDYHTH B64 .... 103 H5
Hillcrest School
RIDG/WDGT B32 .... 123 J2
The Hillcrest School & Community College
DUDS DY2 .... 85 G8
Hill Farm Primary School
COVN CV6 .... 133 M6
Hillfields Health Centre
COV CV1 .... 9 H2
Hillmeads Health Centre
HWK/WKHTH B38 .... 144 E4
Hillstone Junior & Infant School House
BKDE/SHDE B34 .... 92 B8
Hillstone Primary School
BKDE/SHDE B34 .... 92 B8
Hill Top Industrial Estate
WBROM B70 .... 68 D5
Hilltop Medical Centre
LGLYGN/QTN B68 .... 105 G3
Hill West Junior & Infant School
FOAKS/STRLY B74 .... 56 D1
Hilton Cross Business Park
WOLVN WV10 .... 22 F7
Hilton Main Industrial Estate
WNSFLD WV11 .... 23 G8
Hilton Trading Estate
ETTPK/GDPK/PENN WV4 .... 66 D1
Himley Hall
SEDG DY3 .... 83 H2
Hindu Temple
COV CV1 .... 9 G1
Hindu Temple
COVN CV6 .... 134 D4
Hindu Temple
DARL/WED WS10 .... 52 D6

Hippodrome Theatre
DIG/EDG B5 .... 6 F7
Hive Industrial Centre
WSNGN B18 .... 88 D7
Hm Prison
WOLVN WV10 .... 22 D6
Hob Green Primary School
HAG/WOL DY9 .... 120 C3
Hobmoor Junior & Infant School
YDLY B25 .... 109 H5
Hobs Moat Medical Centre
HIA/OLT B92 .... 127 L3
Hockley Brook Trading Estate
WSNGN B18 .... 88 E7
Hockley Heath Pavilion
HOCK/TIA B94 .... 172 A7
Hockley Heath Primary School
HOCK/TIA B94 .... 171 M7
Hockley Hill Industrial Estate
WSNGN B18 .... 88 F8
Hockley Medical Practice
HDSW B21 .... 88 E6
Hodge Hill Girls School
CBROM B36 .... 91 G6
Hodge Hill School
CBROM B36 .... 91 G6
Holbrook Park Industrial Estate
COVN CV6 .... 134 B5
Holbrooks Primary School
COVN CV6 .... 134 C4
Holiday Wharf
CBHAMW B1 .... 6 D7
Holland House Infant School
CSCFLD/WYGN B72 .... 73 G1
Hollies Business Park
CNCK/NC WS11 .... 16 D4
The Hollies Clinic
LGLYGN/QTN B68 .... 104 F1
Hollies Industrial Estate
BKHL/PFLD WV2 .... 2 E8
Holloway Bank Trading Estate
DARL/WED WS10 .... 68 E4
Hollow Gallery
HIA/OLT B92 .... 127 H3
Holly Bush Medical Centre
RIDG/WDGT B32 .... 105 H6
Hollyfast Primary School
COVN CV6 .... 133 J6
Hollyfield Infant School
MGN/WHC B75 .... 73 K1
Holly Grove County Primary School
BNTWD WS7 .... 18 C4
Holly Hall Clinic
DUDN DY1 .... 84 D6
Holly Hall Secondary School
DUDN DY1 .... 84 D5
Holly Hill Methodist C of E First School
RBRY B45 .... 142 D3
Holly Lodge High School
SMTHWKW B67 .... 87 J6
Holly Park Industrial Estate
ERDE/BCHGN B24 .... 91 H3
Hollywalk Clinic
RLSN CV32 .... 200 E4
Hollywood Junior & Infant School
ALE/KHTH/YWD B14 .... 145 L4
Hollywood Primary School
ALE/KHTH/YWD B14 .... 145 L4
Holte School
LOZ/NWT B19 .... 89 H6
Holt Farm Primary School
RMSLY B62 .... 104 C4
Holy Child School
EDG B15 .... 106 F7
Holy Cross RC School
WALM/CURD B76 .... 73 L2
Holy Family RC Junior & Infant School
COVN CV6 .... 133 M2
Holy Family RC School
SMHTH B10 .... 108 D6
Holyhead Primary School
DARL/WED WS10 .... 68 B2
Holyhead School
HDSW B21 .... 88 B5
Holy Name RC Primary School
GTB/HAM B43 .... 70 C4
Holyoakes Field First School
REDW B97 .... 196 A1
Holy Rosary RC School
WOLV WV1 .... 50 E1
Holy Souls RC Primary School
ACGN B27 .... 127 G2
Holy Trinity C of E Infant School
BRWNH WS8 .... 26 B7
Holy Trinity C of E Junior & Infant School
BFLD/HDSWWD B20 .... 89 G3
Holy Trinity Primary School
BILS/COS WV14 .... 51 J8
Holy Trinity Primary School
WBROM B70 .... 87 H4
Holy Trinity RC Comprehensive School
SMHTH B10 .... 108 C4
Holy Trinity School
KIDD DY10 .... 137 K7
Honeybourne School
HLGN/YWD B28 .... 126 D5
Honiley Farm Business Park
KNWTH CV8 .... 174 F6
Hoobrook Industrial Estate
KIDDW DY11 .... 161 J2
Hood Street Industrial Estate
COV CV1 .... 9 J4
Hoo Farm Industrial Estate
KIDDW DY11 .... 161 J4
Horeston Grange Shopping Centre
NUN CV11 .... 81 L8

Hornchurch Close Industrial Estate
COV CV1 .... 8 F8
Horrell Road Health Centre
LGN/SDN/BHAMAIR B26 .... 109 L6
Horse Shoe Associated Football Club
SHLY B90 .... 146 D7
Hospital
LDYWD/EDGR B16 .... 106 E4
Hospital of St Cross
RUGBYS/DCH CV22 .... 183 M4
Howes Primary School
COVS CV3 .... 154 C8
Howley Grange Primary School
RMSLY B62 .... 104 E8
Hrs Business Park
STETCH B33 .... 110 A4
Hrs Industrial Estate
STETCH B33 .... 110 A4
Hugh Meadow Infant School
CSHL/WTROR B46 .... 93 K5
Hulbert Industrial Estate
DUDS DY2 .... 84 F7
Hunters Hill School
BRGRVE B60 .... 166 D7
Huntington CP School
HEDN WS12 .... 12 B5
Huntingtree Primary School
HALE B63 .... 121 J1
Hurley Primary School
ATHST CV9 .... 77 H1
Hurst Green Primary School
RMSLY B62 .... 104 C5
Hurst Street Primary School
BILS/COS WV14 .... 66 E5
Hussani Mosque
DUNHL/THL/PER WV6 .... 49 K1
Icknield First School
REDE B98 .... 197 J4
Ikon Gallery
CBHAMW B1 .... 6 C6
Imex Business Estate
STETCH B33 .... 91 J8
Imex Business Park
BKHL/PFLD WV2 .... 49 M6
Imex Business Park
BORD B9 .... 108 B3
Imex Business Park
SPARK B11 .... 108 D7
Imex Business Park
TPTN/OCK DY4 .... 85 L2
Imex Industrial Estate
WSNGN B18 .... 106 E1
Indian High Commission
WSNGN B18 .... 6 C1
Indoor Market
DARL/WED WS10 .... 68 D3
Industrial Estate
BHAMNEC B40 .... 129 H1
Industrial Estate
BRGRVW B61 .... 185 J4
Industrial Estate
SMTHWK B66 .... 87 L6
Industrial Estate
SMTHWK B66 .... 88 A6
Industrial Estate
WASH/WDE B8 .... 108 B2
Infant Welfare Clinic
GTB/HAM B43 .... 70 B3
Inglenook School
SLYOAK B29 .... 124 F2
International Convention Centre
CBHAMW B1 .... 6 C5
Ipsley Primary School
REDE B98 .... 196 D5
Izons Industrial Estate
WBROM B70 .... 86 D3
Jack O Watton Industrial Estate
CSHL/WTROR B46 .... 93 H2
Jalalabad Mosque & Islamic Centre
SLYOAK B29 .... 124 D3
Jalalabad Mosque & Madrassa
AST/WIT B6 .... 89 K5
The James Gilbert Rugby Football Museum
RUGBYN/HIL CV21 .... 183 L2
James Watt Industrial Park
SMTHWK B66 .... 88 A7
James Watt Junior & Infant School
HDSW B21 .... 88 C6
Jamia Mosque
COV CV1 .... 134 B8
Jamia Mosque
DUNHL/THL/PER WV6 .... 2 A2
Jamia Mosque Mehr-ul-millat
SPARK B11 .... 108 A8
Jami Mosque & Islamic Centre
SMHTH B10 .... 108 B5
Jane Lane School
WSLW WS2 .... 52 D2
Janet Shaw Clinic
CHWD/FDBR/MGN B37 .... 110 F5
Jerome CP School
CNCK/NC WS11 .... 17 K8
Jerome Retail Park
WSL WS1 .... 4 D4
Jervoise Junior & Infant School
SLYOAK B29 .... 123 L4
Jockey Road Surgery
SCFLD/BOLD B73 .... 72 B4
John Black Day Hospital
CHWD/FDBR/MGN B37 .... 110 F5
John Gulson Primary School
COV CV1 .... 134 B8
John Shelton Primary School
COVN CV6 .... 134 B1
John Taylor Gallery
WWCK CV34 .... 199 J7
John Willmott School
WALM/CURD B76 .... 73 K1

John Wood C of E Infants School
CNCK/NC WS11 .... 16 B5
Joseph Cash Primary School
COVN CV6 .... 134 A6
Joseph Chamberlain College
BHTH/HG B12 .... 107 H7
Joseph Leckie School
DSYBK/YTR WS5 .... 53 J8
Joseph Turner Junior & Infant School
TPTN/OCK DY4 .... 67 M6
Josiah Mason College
ERDW/GRVHL B23 .... 90 A1
Jubilee Park Primary School
TPTN/OCK DY4 .... 67 M5
Jubilee Sports Centre
NUNW/HART CV10 .... 98 E2
Junction Industrial Estate
SMTHWK B66 .... 87 K5
Junction Two Industrial Estate
OLDBY B69 .... 86 D7
J W Green Swimming Pools
BDMR/CCFT WV3 .... 2 B7
Karis Medical Centre
LDYWD/EDGR B16 .... 106 D4
Kates Hill County Primary School
DUDS DY2 .... 85 J5
Keelinge House Surgery
DUDN DY1 .... 84 D6
Kenilworth Business Centre
KNWTH CV8 .... 191 L2
Kenilworth Castle
KNWTH CV8 .... 176 B8
Kenilworth Rugby Football Club
KNWTH CV8 .... 192 B1
Kenilworth School
KNWTH CV8 .... 177 G8
Kenilworth Town Council
KNWTH CV8 .... 191 K1
Kenilworth Wardens Cricket Club
KNWTH CV8 .... 192 A2
Kent Close CP School
HHTH/SAND B71 .... 69 G6
Keresley Grange Primary School
COVN CV6 .... 133 K4
Keresley Health Centre
RCOVN/BALC/EX CV7 .... 115 K5
Keresley Newland Primary School
RCOVN/BALC/EX CV7 .... 115 K5
Key Business Park
ERDE/BCHGN B24 .... 91 J2
Key Industrial Park
WLNHL WV13 .... 51 H2
Keyway Retail Park
WLNHL WV13 .... 51 M5
Khalsa Industrial Estate
SMTHWK B66 .... 106 B1
Kidderminster College
KIDD DY10 .... 161 J1
Kidderminster General Hospital
KIDDW DY11 .... 137 G8
Kidderminster Golf Club
KIDD DY10 .... 161 K1
Kidderminster Harriers Football Club
KIDD DY10 .... 161 K1
Kidderminster Health Centre
KIDD DY10 .... 137 J7
Kidderminster Industrial Estate
KIDD DY10 .... 161 K2
Kidderminster Railway Museum Trust
KIDD DY10 .... 137 H8
Kineton Green Infant School
HIA/OLT B92 .... 127 K4
King Charles High School
KIDD DY10 .... 137 L8
King Charles Primary School
WSLW WS2 .... 52 D3
King David Junior & Infant School
MOS/BIL B13 .... 125 K3
King Edward Business Park
NUN CV11 .... 99 H1
King Edwards School
EDG B15 .... 124 E1
King Edwards VI Aston School
AST/WIT B6 .... 89 K7
King Edwards VI Camp Hill School for Boys
ALE/KHTH/YWD B14 .... 125 H6
King Edward VI College
STRBR DY8 .... 101 L7
King Edward VI County School
LICHS WS14 .... 21 G7
King Edward VI Five Ways School
RIDG/WDGT B32 .... 123 G5
King Edward VI Form College
NUN CV11 .... 99 H1
King Edward VI Handsworth School
HDSW B21 .... 88 C6
King Edward VI High School for Girls
EDG B15 .... 124 E1
King Edward VI Leisure Centre
LICHS WS14 .... 21 G7
Kingfield Industrial Estate
COVN CV6 .... 134 C5
Kingfisher Business Park
REDE B98 .... 196 D5
Kingfisher Gallery
COV CV1 .... 8 C7
Kingfisher Industrial Estate
WBROM B70 .... 86 C3
King George V Primary School
HHTH/SAND B71 .... 87 J2
King Henry VIII School
COVW CV5 .... 8 D8

Kingsbury Business Park
WALM/CURD B76.................... 74 C8
Kingsbury Junior and
Infant School
POL/KGSB/FAZ B78.......... 60 B7
Kingsbury Road School
ERDE/BCHGN B24.................... 90 E3
Kingsbury School
POL/KGSB/FAZ B78.......... 60 A7
Kings Business Centre
NUN CV11.................... 99 H1
Kings Business Park
KGSTG B44.................... 71 H2
Kings Heath Infant School
ALE/KHTH/YWD B14.......... 125 J4
Kings Heath School
MOS/BIL B13.................... 125 L7
Kings High School for Girls
WWCK CV34.................... 199 J7
Kings Hill Business Park
DARL/WED WS10.......... 68 C1
Kings Hill Clinic
DARL/WED WS10.......... 52 C8
Kings Hill JMI School
DARL/WED WS10.......... 52 C8
Kingshurst Clinic
CHWD/FDBR/MGN B37.... 92 E8
Kingshurst Infant School
CHWD/FDBR/MGN B37.... 92 E7
Kingshurst Junior School
CHWD/FDBR/MGN B37.... 92 E7
Kingshurst Parish Council Playing
Fields Pavilion
CHWD/FDBR/MGN B37.... 92 F8
Kingsland JMI School
KCSTG B44.................... 71 K1
Kingsley Preparatory School
DOR/KN B93.................... 172 D3
Kingsley School
RLSN CV32.................... 200 D4
Kingsmead County
High School
HEDN WS12.................... 17 G1
Kings Norton Boys School
BVILLE B30.................... 144 C8
Kings Norton Girls School
BVILLE B30.................... 124 C8
Kings Norton High School
HWK/WKHTH B38.......... 144 D5
Kings Norton Primary School
BVILLE B30.................... 144 E2
Kingsrise Primary School
KCSTG B44.................... 71 M3
Kings Road Industrial Estate
YDLY B25.................... 108 C7
Kingstanding Leisure Centre
KCSTG B44.................... 71 M5
Kingstanding Special School
KCSTG B44.................... 71 J4
Kingsthorne Primary School
KCSTG B44.................... 71 L4
Kingston Industrial Estate
BORD B9.................... 7 M7
The Kingswinford GM School
KGSWFD DY6.................... 83 H6
Kitchen Gallery
DOR/KN B93.................... 172 D2
Kitwell Primary School
RIDG/WDGT B32.......... 122 E6
Klaxon Tysley Industrial Estate
SPARK B11.................... 126 D1
The Knibbs Shopping Centre
WWCK CV34.................... 199 K6
Knightlow C of E First & Middle
Schools
RRUGBY CV23.................... 180 D6
Knoll School
KIDDW DY11.................... 136 E6
Knowle C of E Junior &
Infant School
DOR/KN B93.................... 149 G7
Knowle & Dorridge Cricket Club
DOR/KN B93.................... 172 L4
Knowle Football Club
DOR/KN B93.................... 149 G6
Knowle Village Cricket Club
DOR/KN B93.................... 149 G6
Krishna Temple
BKHL/PFLD WV2.......... 49 M6
Ladbroke Racing
COVE CV2.................... 9 M3
Lady Katherine Leveson School
DOR/KN B93.................... 149 M8
Ladypool Junior &
Infant School
SPARK B11.................... 107 M7
Ladywood Arts &
Leisure Centre
LDYWD/EDGR B16.......... 106 E3
Ladywood Middleway
Health Centre
CBHAMW B1.................... 106 E2
Ladywood School
LDYWD/EDGR B16.......... 106 E3
Ladywood Surgery
LDYWD/EDGR B16.......... 6 A6
La Galleria
CBHAMW B3.................... 6 D5
Lakeside Industrial Estate
REDE B98.................... 196 F2
Lakeside Medical Centre
DUNHL/THL/PER WV6.... 48 C1
Lakeside Primary School
TAM/AM/WIL B77.......... 46 C3
Lakeside Trading Centre
REDE B98.................... 196 E1
Lakey Lane Primary School
HLGN/YWD B28.......... 126 F5
Landywood County
Primary School
GTWY WS6.................... 24 D5
Lane Green County First School
CDSL WV8.................... 34 F1
The Lane Medical Centre
BHTH/HG B12.................... 107 M8
Lanesfield Primary School
ETTPK/GDPK/PENN WV4.... 66 E2

The Lanes Shopping Centre
SCFLD/BOLD B73.......... 72 F6
Langley High School
LGLYGN/QTN B68.......... 104 F1
Langley Junior & Infant School
HIA/OLT B92.................... 127 H7
Langley Primary School
OLDBY B69.................... 86 E8
Langley Public Baths
LGLYGN/QTN B68.......... 105 G1
Langley School
MGN/WHC B75.................... 57 L7
Langley Secondary School
HIA/OLT B92.................... 127 H6
Langton Medical Group
LICH WS13.................... 20 E3
Lansdowne Health Centre
WSNGN B18.................... 106 D1
Lapal Primary School
RMSLY B62.................... 122 D1
Lark Hall County Infants School
CRTAM B79.................... 31 L5
Larkhill Industrial Estate
KIDD DY10.................... 137 J6
Laurel House Surgery
CRTAM B79.................... 31 M8
Laurie Pike Health Centre
AST/WIT B6.................... 89 H5
Lawford Heath
Industrial Estate
RRUGBY CV23.................... 182 A6
Lawrence Sheriff School
RUGBYN/HIL CV21.......... 183 M2
League of Friends
Walsall Hospitals
WSL WS1.................... 4 F3
Leamington Cricket Club
RLSN CV32.................... 200 D3
Leamington Museum &
Art Gallery
RLSS CV32.................... 200 D5
Leamore Industrial Estate
BLOX/PEL WS3.......... 38 E6
Leamore Industrial Estate
WSLW WS2.................... 38 E6
Leamore Primary School
BLOX/PEL WS3.......... 39 G6
Lea Road Medical Practice
BDMR/CCFT WV3.......... 2 C9
Leasowes High School &
Community College
RMSLY B62.................... 104 C7
Leasowes Primary School
SMTHWK B66.................... 87 H6
Lea Street CP School
KIDD DY10.................... 137 K7
Leaverstock Industrial Estate
STECH B33.................... 110 A4
Lee Bank Business Centre
CBHAMW B1.................... 6 E7
Lee Bank Group Practice
EDG B15.................... 6 D8
Lee Bank Junior &
Infant School
EDG B15.................... 107 G5
Leek Wootton C of E
First School
RWWCK/WEL CV35.......... 191 L6
Lee Marston Hotel &
Leisure Complex
WALM/CURD B76.......... 75 L4
Leigh C of E Primary School
TLHL/CAN CV4.................... 152 B5
Leigh Junior & Infant School
WASH/WDE B8.................... 90 C7
Leighswood Infant &
Junior School
ALDR WS9.................... 40 F5
Leighswood Junior School
ALDR WS9.................... 40 F6
Leisure Centre
PENK ST19.................... 10 F5
Lemar Industrial Estate
BVILLE B30.................... 125 G4
Lench Estate
BLKHTH/ROWR B65.......... 103 M3
Lennon Indoor Market
KCSTG B44.................... 71 L2
Leona Trading Estate
RMSLY B62.................... 104 B4
Lewisham Industrial Estate
SMTHWK B66.................... 87 L6
Leyhill Health Centre
NFLD/LBR B31.................... 123 J7
Ley Hill Junior & Infant School
NFLD/LBR B31.................... 123 H8
Ley Hill Primary School
MGN/WHC B75.................... 56 F3
Ley Hill Surgery
MGN/WHC B75.................... 56 F4
Leys High School
REDE B98.................... 197 G7
Lichfield College
LICH WS13.................... 20 E6
Lichfield County Court
LICH WS13.................... 20 F5
Lichfield Cricket Club
LICH WS13.................... 20 E7
Lichfield District Council
BNTWD WS7.................... 18 D6
Lichfield District Council
POL/KGSB/FAZ B78.......... 45 L4
Lichfield Road Industrial Estate
CRTAM B79.................... 31 J6
Lichfield Rugby Union
Football Club
LICHS WS14.................... 21 K8
Lichfield Trading Estate
CRTAM B79.................... 31 J7
Lickey End First School
BRGRVE B60.................... 166 A7
Lickey Primary &
Middle School
RBRY B45.................... 166 D3
Lifford Trading Estate
BVILLE B30.................... 144 E1
Light Hall School
SHLY B90.................... 146 F5

Lightwoods Junior &
Infant Primary School
LGLYGN/QTN B68.......... 105 H5
Lillington Middle School
RLSN CV32.................... 200 F2
Lillington Primary School
RLSN CV32.................... 200 F2
Limbrick Wood Junior &
Infant School
TLHL/CAN CV4.................... 152 D2
Lindens JMI School
FOAKS/STRLY B74.......... 55 K7
Link One Industrial Park
WBROM B70.................... 68 C7
Linkway Retail Park
CNCK/NC WS11.................... 15 M7
Linthurst First School
BRGRVE B60.................... 166 E7
Lion Industrial Park
WWCK CV34.................... 40 E4
Lisle Court Medical Centre
RLSS CV31.................... 200 E7
Lisle Court Surgery
RLSS CV31.................... 200 E8
Little Aston CP School
FOAKS/STRLY B74.......... 42 A7
Little Heath Industrial Estate
COVN CV6.................... 134 E3
Little Heath Junior School
COVN CV6.................... 134 E4
Little London JMI School
WLNHL WV13.................... 51 L3
Little Sutton Junior &
Infant School
MGN/WHC B75.................... 57 H2
Littleton Business Park
HEDN WS12.................... 12 A6
Locarno Junior & Infant School
TPTN/OCK DY4.................... 67 K7
Locketts Surgery
COVN CV6.................... 133 L8
The Lock Museum
WLNHL WV13.................... 51 K4
Lode Heath High School
SOLH B91.................... 128 A7
Lodgefarm Junior School
WSLW WS2.................... 52 C1
Lodge Farm Middle School
REDE B98.................... 196 E3
Lodge Forge Trading Estate
CDYHTH B64.................... 103 G6
Lodge Junior & Infant School
WBROM B70.................... 86 F2
The Loft Theatre
RLSS CV31.................... 200 D5
Long Acre Trading Estate
VAUX/NECH B7.................... 90 A6
Longford County
Primary School
CNCK/NC WS11.................... 16 A5
Longford Industrial Estate
CNCK/NC WS11.................... 16 B7
Longford Medical Centre
COVN CV6.................... 116 E8
Longford Park Junior &
Infant School
COVN CV6.................... 134 E2
Long Knowle Primary School
WNSFLD WV11.................... 37 G5
Long Lane Industrial Estate
RMSLY B62.................... 104 B4
Long Lane Medical Centre
RMSLY B62.................... 104 B4
Long Lawford Combined
School
RRUGBY CV23.................... 158 E3
Long Ley Primary School
WOLVN WV10.................... 3 M2
Longmoor Day Special School
SCFLD/BOLD B73.......... 71 L2
Longwill Special School
NFLD/LBR B31.................... 123 L8
Longwood Primary School
POL/KGSB/FAZ B78.......... 45 G4
Lord Leycester Hospital
WWCK CV34.................... 199 J7
Lordswood Boys School
HRBN B17.................... 105 L5
Lordswood Girls School
HRBN B17.................... 105 L5
Lordswood Medical Practice
HRBN B17.................... 105 M7
Lower Farm JMI School
BLOX/PEL WS3.......... 39 G1
Lower Gornal Health Centre
SEDG DY3.................... 83 M3
Low Hill Medical Centre
WOLVN WV10.................... 36 C6
Loxdale Industrial Estate
BILS/COS WV14.................... 67 J1
Loxdale Primary School
BILS/COS WV14.................... 67 K1
Lozells Junior & Infant School
LOZ/NWT B19.................... 89 H6
Lucy Baldwin Hospital
STRPT DY13.................... 160 D8
Lugman Medical Centre
WSL WS1.................... 4 C7
Lutley Primary School
HALE B63.................... 121 H4
Lye Business Centre
HAG/WOL DY9.................... 102 D6
Lye C C
HAG/WOL DY9.................... 102 B8
Lye Mosque
HAG/WOL DY9.................... 102 C8
Lye Town Football Club
HAG/WOL DY9.................... 102 B8
Lyndon Green Junior School
LGN/SDN/BHAMAIR B26.... 109 K7
Lyndon School
HIA/OLT B92.................... 127 L2
Lyne Hill Industrial Estate
PENK ST19.................... 10 C6
Lyng Hall School
COVE CV2.................... 135 G3
Lyng Primary School
WBROM B70.................... 87 G3

Lythalls Lane Industrial Estate
COVN CV6.................... 134 C4
Magreal Industrial Estate
LDYWD/EDGR B16.......... 106 D2
Maguire Industrial Estate
TLHL/CAN CV4.................... 152 D5
Maidensbridge Primary School
KGSWFD DY6.................... 82 K4
Mainstream Industrial Park
VAUX/NECH B7.................... 90 A8
Malt Mill Industrial Estate
RMSLY B62.................... 104 B3
Mander Shopping Centre
WOLV WV1.................... 2 E5
Maney Hill Primary School
CSCFLD/WYGN B72.......... 73 H3
Manor CP School
POL/KGSB/FAZ B78.......... 45 J8
Manor Farm
Comprehensive School
RUSH/SHEL WS4.......... 39 M7
The Manor General Hospital
WSLW WS2.................... 4 A3
Manor High School
DARL/WED WS10.......... 69 H1
Manor Industrial Estate
WSLW WS2.................... 4 B3
Manor Park Community School
NUN CV11.................... 80 E8
Manor Park Industrial Estate
COVS CV3.................... 154 F5
Manor Park Junior &
Infant School
AST/WIT B6.................... 89 L5
Manor Park Primary School
COVS CV3.................... 154 A6
Manor Practice
CSCFLD/WYGN B72.......... 73 J3
Manor Primary School
FOAKS/STRLY B74.......... 55 L4
Manor Way Primary School
HALE B63.................... 122 A2
Manse Business Centre
NUN CV11.................... 99 J3
Mansfield Medical Centre
COVS CV3.................... 154 E3
Maple Business Park
VAUX/NECH B7.................... 89 M7
Mapledene Junior &
Infant School
LGN/SDN/BHAMAIR B26.... 110 C2
Maple Hayes School
LICH WS13.................... 20 B5
Maple Leaf Industrial Estate
WSLW WS2.................... 52 F2
Mappleborough Green
C of E School
STUD B80.................... 197 M3
Marcus Galleries
ALE/KHTH/YWD B14.......... 125 J8
Market Hall
COV CV1.................... 8 E5
Market Street Surgery
KGSWFD DY6.................... 83 H8
Marlborough Junior &
Infant School
BORD B9.................... 108 C4
Marlfield Farm First School
REDE B98.................... 188 F7
Marlow Estate
BLKHTH/ROWR B65.......... 103 M4
Marlpool First School
KIDDW DY11.................... 137 C5
Marmion Junior School
CRTAM B79.................... 31 L7
Marshalls Industrial Estate
BKHL/PFLD WV2.......... 50 A6
Marshbrook First School
PENK ST19.................... 10 C4
Marsh Hill Junior &
Infant Schools
ERDW/GRVHL B23.......... 89 M1
Marston Green Clinic
CHWD/FDBR/MGN B37.... 110 E6
Marston Green Infant School
CHWD/FDBR/MGN B37.... 110 E6
Marston Green Junior School
CHWD/FDBR/MGN B37.... 110 E6
Marston Road Industrial Estate
BKHL/PFLD WV2.......... 50 A4
Martindale Trading Estate
CNCK/NC WS11.................... 16 E3
Mary Ann Evans Hospice
NUNW/HART CV10.......... 98 E3
Mary Elliot School
WSLW WS2.................... 53 J1
Maryvale RC Primary School
KCSTG B44.................... 71 J3
Masjid E Noor Mosque
AST/WIT B6.................... 89 K6
Maternity Welfare Clinic
ETTPK/GDPK/PENN WV4.... 49 H7
Matthew Boulton
Technical College
DIG/EDG B5.................... 6 F9
Matthew Boulton
Technical College
DIG/EDG B5.................... 107 H5
Maxstoke Castle
CSHL/WTROR B46.......... 94 C6
Maybrook Industrial Estate
BRWNH WS8.................... 26 D8
Mayfield Preparatory School
WSL WS1.................... 5 J5
Mayfield School
LOZ/NWT B19.................... 89 G5
Maypole Gallery
WMBN WV5.................... 64 G9
Maypole Health Centre
ALE/KPATH/YWD B14.......... 145 L2
Meadow Green
Primary School
HLYWD B47.................... 169 L2
Meadow Mill Industrial Estate
KIDD DY10.................... 137 J8
Meadows First School
BRGRVW B61.................... 185 L2

Meadowside Surgery
HIA/OLT B92.................... 127 M3
Meadows Junior &
Infant School
NFLD/LBR B31.................... 143 J5
Meadow View Junior &
Infant School
GTB/HAM B43.................... 55 H8
Meadwood Industrial Estate
BILS/COS WV14.................... 51 H8
Media Centre
WOLV WV1.................... 3 G4
Medina Mosque
WSNGN B18.................... 88 E6
Mega Bowl
BRLYHL DY5.................... 102 B2
Mega Bowl
DIG/EDG B5.................... 7 H7
Mega Bowl
RCOVN/BALC/EX CV7.......... 135 M5
Menzies High School
HHTH/SAND B71.................... 69 G5
Meriden C of E School
RCOVN/BALC/EX CV7.......... 131 G3
Merridale Primary School
BDMR/CCFT WV3.......... 2 A7
Merstone School
CHWD/FDBR/MGN B37.... 110 E4
Mesnes Green Industrial Estate
LICHS WS14.................... 21 G6
Mesty Croft Primary School
DARL/WED WS10.......... 68 E2
Michael Drayton Middle School
NUNW/HART CV10.......... 79 L5
Middlemarch County
Junior School
NUNW/HART CV10.......... 98 F4
Middlemore Business Park
ALDR WS9.................... 40 C7
Middleway Industrial Estate
BHTH/HG B12.................... 107 K6
Midland Air Museum
KNWTH CV8.................... 178 F2
The Midland Bus &
Transport Museum
HLYWD B47.................... 169 J2
Midland House Dawley
Trading Estate
KGSWFD DY6.................... 83 H5
Midland Institute
CBHAMNW B3.................... 6 E4
Midland Oak Industrial Estate
COVN CV6.................... 134 C2
Midland Oak Industrial Estate
COVN CV6.................... 134 C4
Midland Oak Trading Estate
COVN CV6.................... 134 C3
Midlands Sports Centre for the
Disabled
RCOVN/BALC/EX CV7.......... 152 A6
Midland Trading Estate
RUGBYN/HIL CV21.......... 159 L6
Milby First & Middle Schools
NUN CV11.................... 81 K5
Mile Oak Business Park
POL/KGSB/FAZ B78.......... 45 G3
Milking Bank Primary School
DUDN DY1.................... 84 C3
Millbrook Industrial Estate
WOLVN WV10.................... 36 B6
Millfield County Primary School
POL/KGSB/FAZ B78.......... 45 L5
Millfield CP School
BRWNH WS8.................... 26 E6
Millfield Day Special School
HHTH/SAND B71.................... 69 H5
Millfields First School
BRGRVW B61.................... 185 H5
Mill Lodge Primary School
SHLY B90.................... 146 C3
Millstream Surgery
REDW B97.................... 195 M1
Milverton Combined School
RLSN CV32.................... 200 C3
Milverton House
Preparatory School
NUN CV11.................... 99 H2
Minster House Clinic
KIDD DY10.................... 137 J7
Minworth Junior &
Infant School
WALM/CURD B76.......... 74 B8
Mirah Day Hospital
NUN CV11.................... 80 E8
Mirfield Surgery
STETCH B33.................... 110 A2
Moat Farm Junior &
Infant School
LGLYGN/QTN B68.......... 105 G2
Moat Hall County
Primary School
GTWY WS6.................... 24 D2
Moatfield Middle School
REDE B98.................... 197 J4
Mobarak Health Centre
BHTH/HG B12.................... 107 J3
Molineux Youth &
Sports Centre
WOLV WV1.................... 2 E3
Monarch Industrial Estate
SPARK B11.................... 108 E7
Monkspath Business Park
SHLY B90.................... 147 J4
Monkspath Business Park
SOLH B91.................... 147 K5
Monkspath Junior &
Infant School
SHLY B90.................... 147 J5
Monkton Recreation Centre
PENK ST19.................... 10 B4

Monmore Park
Industrial Estate
BKHL/PFLD WV2 .... 50 D6
Montgomery Junior &
Infant School
SPARK B11 .... 108 A6
Monway Industrial Estate
DARL/WED WS10 .... 68 B2
Moons Moat First School
REDE B98 .... 189 H8
The Moore Group
Business Centre
WSL WS1 .... 4 F6
Moorgate County
Primary School
CRTAM B79 .... 31 M8
Moor Green Football Club Ltd
HLGN/YWD B28 .... 126 C6
Moor Green JMI School
MOS/BIL B13 .... 125 G4
Moor Green Lane
Medical Centre
MOS/BIL B13 .... 125 G4
Moor Hall Golf Club
MGN/WHC B75 .... 57 H4
Moor Hall Junior &
Infant School
MGN/WHC B75 .... 57 H3
Moorhill County Primary School
CNCK/NC WS11 .... 12 C8
Moorhill Primary School
CNCK/NC WS11 .... 16 C1
Moorlands Junior & Infant School
HHTH/SAND B71 .... 68 F5
Moor Lane Trading Estate
PBAR/PBCH B42 .... 89 K1
Moor Street Industrial Estate
BRLYHL DY5 .... 102 A2
Moreton Community School
WOLVN WV10 .... 36 D4
Morley Road Shopping Centre
BNTWD WS7 .... 18 F6
Moseley C of E Junior &
Infant School
MOS/BIL B13 .... 125 K3
Moseley Cricket Club
ALE/KHTH/YWD B14 .... 125 J7
Moseley Junior & Infant School
COVN CV6 .... 8 A1
Moseley Rugby Football Club
MOS/BIL B13 .... 125 J3
Moseley School
MOS/BIL B13 .... 126 B3
Mosque
NUN CV11 .... 98 F2
Mosque
SPARK B11 .... 107 M8
Mosque & Community Centre
RMSLY B62 .... 104 B5
Mosque Gamkol Sharif
SPARK B11 .... 107 M8
Mosque Ghousia
AST/WIT B6 .... 89 K6
Mosque Noor-ul-uloom
SMHTH B10 .... 108 C5
Mosque Taiyyibah
BDMR/CCFT WV3 .... 2 B8
Mosque & Teaching Centre
VAUX/NECH B7 .... 90 A6
Mossely Junior School
BLOX/PEL WS3 .... 38 D3
Moss Grove Surgery
KGSWFD DY6 .... 83 H7
Mossley Clinic
BLOX/PEL WS3 .... 38 E4
Mossley Primary School
BLOX/PEL WS3 .... 38 D3
Mount Carmel RC
Primary School
REDW B97 .... 195 L3
Mount Nod Primary School
COVW CV5 .... 152 E2
Mount Pleasant
Primary School
BRLYHL DY5 .... 102 C4
Mount School
BRGRVW B61 .... 165 M8
Moxley Industrial Centre
DARL/WED WS10 .... 68 A1
Moxley Medical Centre
DARL/WED WS10 .... 52 A7
Moxley Primary School
DARL/WED WS10 .... 67 M1
Mucklow Hill Industrial Estate
RMSLY B62 .... 104 A8
Mucklow Hill Trading Estate
RMSLY B62 .... 104 A8
Municipal Art Gallery
WOLV WV1 .... 2 F4
Museum
LICHS WS13 .... 28 B3
Museum & Art Gallery
CBHAMW B3 .... 6 E5
Museum & Art Gallery
RUGBYN/HIL CV21 .... 183 L2
Museum of British Road
Transport
COV CV1 .... 8 E4
The Museum of
Cannock Chase
HEDN WS12 .... 13 H7
Museum of the
Jewellery Quarter
WSNGN B18 .... 88 F8
Muslim Foundation Mosque
BFLD/HDSWWD B20 .... 89 G4
Myton School
WWCK CV34 .... 199 M7
Nailcote Hall
RCOVN/BALC/EX CV7 .... 151 L6
Nanaksar Gurdwara
Gursikh Temple
COV CV1 .... 134 B8
Nanak Sar Sikh Temple
WSLW WS2 .... 52 F5
The Nancy Doyle Clinic
BRGRVE B60 .... 185 L3

Nathaniel Newton First School
NUNW/HART CV10 .... 79 M5
National Centre for
Cosmetic Surgery
OLDBY B69 .... 86 E6
National Indoor Arena
CBHAMW B1 .... 6 B5
National Motor Cycle Museum
HIA/OLT B92 .... 129 L3
National Sea Life Centre
CBHAMW B1 .... 6 B5
The Natural Health Centre
BVILLE B30 .... 144 D3
Neachells Lane
Industrial Estate
WLNHL WV13 .... 51 H1
Nechells Junior &
Infant School
VAUX/NECH B7 .... 90 A5
Neil Astill Gallery
WWCK CV34 .... 199 H7
Neilston Street
Business Centre
RLSS CV31 .... 200 E7
Nelson Junior & Infant School
CBHAMW B1 .... 6 A5
Nelson Mandela Junior & Infant
School
BHTH/HG B12 .... 107 M8
Neptune Industrial Estate
WLNHL WV13 .... 52 A5
Netherbrook Primary School
DUDS DY2 .... 103 H3
Nether Stowe County
High School
LICH WS13 .... 20 F4
Netherton Business Park
DUDS DY2 .... 103 H2
Netherton C of E Junior School
DUDS DY2 .... 103 G1
Netherton Cricket Club
DUDS DY2 .... 102 F1
New Big School
RUGBYS/DCH CV22 .... 183 L3
Newbold Football Club
RUGBYN/HIL CV21 .... 159 H7
Newbold Leisure Centre
RUGBYN/HIL CV21 .... 159 H6
Newbold Riverside Primary
RUGBYN/HIL CV21 .... 159 J7
Newbridge Doctors Surgery
DUNHL/THL/PER WV6 .... 49 K1
Newbridge Preparatory School
DUNHL/THL/PER WV6 .... 49 J1
New Cross Hospital
WOLVN WV10 .... 36 F8
New Cross Industrial Estate
WOLV WV1 .... 50 E2
Newdigate County
Junior & Infant School
BDWTH CV12 .... 116 A4
Newfield Park Middle School
HALE B63 .... 103 L8
New Hall Junior & Infant School
MGN/WHC B75 .... 57 L8
Newhall Junior & Infant School
MGN/WHC B75 .... 58 A8
Newhampton Open
Door Theatre
WOLV WV1 .... 2 D2
New Inn Industrial Estate
COVN CV6 .... 134 D3
New Invention CP School
SHHTH WV12 .... 38 A6
Newman College
RIDG/WDGT B32 .... 123 G5
New Oscott Junior &
Infant School
SCFLD/BOLD B73 .... 72 A2
New Oxford Medical Centre
COV CV1 .... 8 E3
New Palace Theatre
REDW B97 .... 196 C1
Newton Industrial Estate
BORD B9 .... 108 B3
Newtown Health Centre
LOZ/NWT B19 .... 89 H7
Newtown Junior &
Infant School
WBROM B70 .... 86 B2
Newtown Swimming Pool
LOZ/NWT B19 .... 89 J7
NHS Health Authority
BRGRVW B61 .... 185 L2
Nicholas Chamberlaine School
BDWTH CV12 .... 117 H2
Ninestiles School
ACGN B27 .... 126 F4
Nonsuch Primary School
RIDG/WDGT B32 .... 123 G3
Norfolk House School
EDG B15 .... 106 B5
North Birmingham College
PBAR/PBCH B42 .... 71 J6
North Birmingham
Health Authority
BORD B9 .... 108 E4
North Birmingham
Health Authority
ERDE/BCHGN B24 .... 90 E1
North Bromsgrove High School
BRGRVE B60 .... 185 L3
Northbrook Health Centre
SHLY B90 .... 127 G8
Northbrook Sports Club
COVW CV5 .... 133 G5
North East
Worcestershire College
BRGRVE B60 .... 185 M2
North East Worcestershire
Community Health Care
NHS Trust
REDW B97 .... 196 C1
Northern Birmingham
Community NHS Trust
BORD B9 .... 108 F3

Northern Birmingham
Community NHS Trust
KGSTG B44 .... 71 L5
Northern Birmingham
Community NHS Trust
WALM/CURD B76 .... 73 K5
Northern Birmingham
Community NHS Trust
WSNGN B18 .... 88 D8
Northfield Health Centre
NFLD/LBR B31 .... 143 K2
Northfield Manor
Primary School
SLYOAK B29 .... 123 M6
Northfield Road
Primary School
DUDS DY2 .... 85 H4
Northlands County First School
RUGBYN/HIL CV21 .... 183 M1
North Leamington School
RLSN CV32 .... 200 C3
North Leamington School
RLSN CV32 .... 200 D1
Northmoor Industrial Estate
BRLYHL DY5 .... 102 B2
Northside Business Park
WSNGN B18 .... 88 C8
North Solihull Sports Centre
CHWD/FDBR/MGN B37 .... 110 E1
North Solihull Sports Centre
CHWD/FDBR/MGN B37 .... 110 E2
Northumberland
House Surgery
KIDDW DY11 .... 161 G2
North Walsall Junior &
Infant School
WSLW WS2 .... 53 J1
North Warwickshire College of
Technology & Art
NUN CV11 .... 81 J7
North Warwickshire Golf Club
RCOVN/BALC/EX CV7 .... 130 D5
North Warwickshire &
Hinckley College
ATHST CV9 .... 63 H5
Northycote High School
WOLVN WV10 .... 36 C2
Norton Canes Business Park
CNCK/NC WS11 .... 25 L1
Norton Canes High School
CNCK/NC WS11 .... 17 L6
Norton Canes Infant School
CNCK/NC WS11 .... 17 L7
Norton Canes Primary School
CNCK/NC WS11 .... 17 L7
Norton Medical Practice
STRBR DY8 .... 119 J2
Nuneaton & Bedworth Borough
Council
NUN CV11 .... 99 K3
Nuneaton & Bedworth Borough
Council
NUN CV11 .... 99 G1
Nuneaton Borough AFC
NUNW/HART CV10 .... 98 D1
Nuneaton
Co-operative Sports Club
NUN CV11 .... 98 F1
Nuneaton Indoor Market
NUN CV11 .... 81 G8
Nuneaton Museum &
Art Gallery Riversley Park
NUN CV11 .... 99 G2
Nuneaton Old
Edwardians Rugby
Football Club
NUNW/HART CV10 .... 81 G7
Nuneaton Private Hospital
NUNW/HART CV10 .... 99 G4
Nuneaton Rugby Football Club
NUN CV11 .... 99 K1
Oak Cottage Primary School
SOLH B91 .... 127 K7
Oakdale Trading Estate
KGSWFD DY6 .... 83 H4
Oakeswell Health Centre
DARL/WED WS10 .... 68 C2
Oakfield Junior School
ATHST CV9 .... 63 J6
Oakham Junior & Infant School
OLDBY B69 .... 85 M6
Oakham Surgery
OLDBY B69 .... 85 L5
Oakland Industrial Estate
HEDN WS12 .... 16 F2
Oaklands Academy of
Theatre Dance
BLOX/PEL WS3 .... 39 L1
Oaklands Primary School
ACGN B27 .... 127 G3
Oakleigh Trading Estate
BILS/COS WV14 .... 66 F3
Oakmeadow Junior School
WNSFLD WV11 .... 37 L6
Oak Street Trading Estate
BRLYHL DY5 .... 102 D4
Oakwood School
ALDR B90 .... 40 E2
Ocker Hill Junior &
Infant School
TPTN/OCK DY4 .... 68 A5
Odeon Cinema
CBHAM B2 .... 7 G6
Odeon Cinema
COV CV1 .... 9 H5
Odeon Cinema
CSCFLD/WYGN B72 .... 72 F2
Offmore Primary School
KIDD DY10 .... 137 M7
Ogley Hay Infant School
BRWNH WS8 .... 26 D5
Oldbury Green Retail Park
OLDBY B69 .... 86 D6
Oldbury Health Centre
OLDBY B69 .... 86 E5
Oldbury Jamia Mosque
SMTHWK B66 .... 87 H6

Oldbury Leisure Centre
OLDBY B69 .... 86 C7
Oldbury United Football Club
BLKHTH/ROWR B65 .... 104 C2
Old Bush Trading Estate
BRLYHL DY5 .... 102 C2
Old Church C of E JMI School
DARL/WED WS10 .... 52 A7
Old Edwardians Sports Club
HIA/OLT B92 .... 127 G8
Old Fallings Junior School
WOLVN WV10 .... 36 D4
Oldfields
CDYHTH B64 .... 103 H5
Old Forge Business Centre
REDE B98 .... 197 G5
Old Forge Trading Estate
HAG/WOL DY9 .... 102 C7
Old Hall Industrial Estate
BLOX/PEL WS3 .... 39 G5
Old Hall School
WSLW WS2 .... 38 C8
Old Hill Cricket Club
CDYHTH B64 .... 103 K6
Old Hill Junior & Infant School
CDYHTH B64 .... 103 K4
Oldknow School
SMHTH B10 .... 108 C6
Old Leamingtonians
Rugby Football Club
RLSN CV32 .... 192 C6
Old Limberlost Sports Club
BFLD/HDSWWD B20 .... 88 E2
Old Mill Surgery
NUN CV11 .... 98 F2
Old Mill Surgery
NUN CV11 .... 99 K3
Old Park Industrial Estate
DARL/WED WS10 .... 68 C1
Old Park Junior & Infant School
DARL/WED WS10 .... 52 C8
Old Park School
DUDN DY1 .... 84 D5
Old Rep Theatre
DIG/EDG B5 .... 6 F7
Old School House Surgery
RCOVN/BALC/EX CV7 .... 131 H5
Oldswinford C of E
Primary School
STRBR DY8 .... 119 L2
Old Swinford Hospital School
STRBR DY8 .... 119 L1
Old Warwickian Sports Ground
RWWCK/WEL CV35 .... 198 E8
Olive Hill School
RMSLY B62 .... 104 B6
Olympia Sports Centre
CNCK/NC WS11 .... 16 C4
One Stop Medical Centre
COV CV1 .... 8 E3
One Stop Shopping Centre
PBAR/PBCH B42 .... 89 H2
Open market
BDMR/CCFT WV3 .... 2 E6
Open Market
CBHAMNE B4 .... 7 G4
Open Markets
DIG/EDG B5 .... 7 H7
The Open University
HRBN B17 .... 106 B7
Oratory RC Primary School
LDYWD/EDGR B16 .... 106 D3
Orchard Business Park
RUGBYN/HIL CV21 .... 159 L8
Orchard Lane Clinic
HAG/WOL DY9 .... 102 C7
Orchard Retail Park
COVS CV3 .... 179 H1
Orthodontists Surgery
ACGN B27 .... 126 C2
Orthodontists Surgery
COV CV1 .... 8 F7
Osborne Junior & Infant School
ERDW/GRVHL B23 .... 72 E8
Oscott College
SCFLD/BOLD B73 .... 72 B4
Ounsdale High School
WMBN WV5 .... 64 D6
Ounsdale Sports Centre
WMBN WV5 .... 64 D6
Our Lady of Compassion Primary
School
HIA/OLT B92 .... 127 H6
Our Lady of Fatima RC
Parish School
HRBN B17 .... 105 K6
Our Lady of Lourdes RC
School & Church
MOS/BIL B13 .... 126 B7
Our Lady of St Kenelm RC
Primary School
HALE B63 .... 121 K1
Our Lady of the Wayside RC
Junior & Infant School
SHLY B90 .... 147 G5
Our Lady St Chads RC School
WOLVN WV10 .... 36 D5
Our Lady & St Teresas R C
Combined School
RLSN CV32 .... 193 H8
Our Ladys RC Junior &
Infant School
STECH B33 .... 110 B3
Owen Road Trading Estate
WLNHL WV13 .... 52 A4
Oxbarn Social & Sports Club
BDMR/CCFT WV3 .... 49 K6
Oxford Street Industrial Park
BILS/COS WV14 .... 51 K8
Packwood House
HOCK/TIA B94 .... 172 E8
Paddys Wide Water
Industrial Estate
BRLYHL DY5 .... 84 A8

Paganel Junior & Infant School
SLYOAK B29 .... 123 L3
Paget Junior & Infant School
ERDE/BCHGN B24 .... 91 G1
Palfrey Infant School
WSL WS1 .... 4 E1
Palfrey Junior Mixed School
WSL WS1 .... 4 D8
Pallasades Shopping Centre
CBHAM B2 .... 6 F6
Palmers Cross Primary School
DUNHL/THL/PER WV6 .... 35 H5
Park Attwood Clinic
BEWD DY12 .... 136 B1
Park Clinic
ERDW/GRVHL B23 .... 72 E8
Park Farm Industrial Estate
REDE B98 .... 197 G5
Parkfield Clinic
BKHL/PFLD WV2 .... 50 B7
Parkfield High School
ETTPK/GDPK/PENN WV4 .... 50 C8
Parkfield Primary School
ETTPK/GDPK/PENN WV4 .... 50 C8
Parkfield Primary School
TAM/AM/WIL B77 .... 46 A4
Parkfield Surgery
ETTPK/GDPK/PENN WV4 .... 50 B7
Parkgate Primary School
COVN CV6 .... 133 M2
Park Hall Junior Gm School
DSYBK/YTR WS5 .... 54 A6
Park Hall Primary School
DSYBK/YTR WS5 .... 54 A6
Park Hall School
CBROM B36 .... 92 C4
Park Hill County Middle School
KNWTH CV8 .... 177 G7
Park Hill Primary School
COVW CV5 .... 152 E1
Park Hill Primary School
DARL/WED WS10 .... 69 G1
Parkhill Primary School
MOS/BIL B13 .... 125 K1
Park Lane Industrial Estate
KIDDW DY11 .... 161 H1
Park Lane Industrial Estate
OLDBY B69 .... 86 E6
Park Lane Primary School
NUNW/HART CV10 .... 97 K2
Park Lane Trading Estate
WOLVN WV10 .... 36 C8
Park Medical Centre
SMHTH B10 .... 108 C6
Parkrose Industrial Estate
SMTHWK B66 .... 87 M5
Park St Surgery
RLSN CV32 .... 200 D4
Parkside Industrial Estate
WOLV WV1 .... 3 M7
Parkside Junior School
SMTHWK B66 .... 87 M8
Parkside Middle School
BRGRVW B61 .... 185 L2
Park Special School
CRTAM B79 .... 31 L6
Park Street Industrial Estate
COVN CV6 .... 134 C6
Park Street Industrial Estate
COVN CV6 .... 134 B6
Park Trading Estate
WSNGN B18 .... 88 C7
Parkview Gallery
ALE/KHTH/YWD B14 .... 125 H6
Park View Lower School
WASH/WDE B8 .... 90 D8
Parkview Trading Estate
HWK/WKHTH B38 .... 144 D2
Parkway Industrial Estate
VAUX/NECH B7 .... 7 L2
Pavilions Shopping Centre
CBHAMNE B4 .... 7 H5
P D H Industrial Estate
DARL/WED WS10 .... 68 A1
P D H Industrial Estate
WLNHL WV13 .... 51 H2
Pearl Hyde Junior &
Infant School
COVE CV2 .... 135 L8
Pear Tree Surgery
POL/KGSB/FAZ B78 .... 60 B8
Pedmore C of E
Primary School
HAG/WOL DY9 .... 119 M4
Pedmore Road
Industrial Estate
BRLYHL DY5 .... 102 D1
The Peel Medical Centre
CRTAM B79 .... 31 L8
Pegasus Junior &
Infant School
CVALE B35 .... 91 M1
Pelsall Clinic
BLOX/PEL WS3 .... 39 L1
Pelsall
Comprehensive School
RUSH/SHEL WS4 .... 39 M4
Pelsall Village JMI School
BLOX/PEL WS3 .... 39 K1
Pendeford Business Park
COVEN WV9 .... 35 K2
Pendeford Health Centre
COVEN WV9 .... 35 K3
Pendene
Complimentary
Medical Centre
WOLV WV1 .... 2 C1
Penkridge County Middle School
PENK ST19 .... 10 E3
Penkridge Parish Council
PENK ST19 .... 10 D4
Pennfields Health Centre
BDMR/CCFT WV3 .... 2 C8
Penn Hall Special School
ETTPK/GDPK/PENN WV4 .... 65 J2
Penn Hospital
ETTPK/GDPK/PENN WV4 .... 65 J1

Penn Industrial Estate
DUDS DY2 .... 103 H4
Penn Manor Medical Centre
ETTPK/GDPK/PENN WV4 .... 65 K1
Penns Primary School
CSCFLD/WYGN B72 .... 73 H7
Penryn School
KIDD DY10 .... 162 E5
Pens Meadow School
STRBR DY8 .... 101 K2
Pensnett School of Technology
BRLYHL DY5 .... 83 M8
Percy Business Park
OLDBY B69 .... 86 D6
Percy Shurmer Infant School
DIG/EDG B5 .... 107 J6
Percy Shurmer Junior School
BHTH/PBCH B12 .... 107 J6
Perry Beeches School
PBAR/PBCH B42 .... 71 G5
Perryfields High School
LGLYGN/QTN B68 .... 104 E5
Perryfields Junior &
Infants School
LGLYGN/QTN B68 .... 104 E6
Perry Hall Primary School
WNSFLD WV11 .... 37 K7
Personal & Child Health Centre
BVILLE B30 .... 124 E7
Perton Clinic
DUNHL/THL/PER WV6 .... 48 C1
Perton County First School
DUNHL/THL/PER WV6 .... 34 C8
Perton County Middle School
DUNHL/THL/PER WV6 .... 48 E1
Perton Parish Council
DUNHL/THL/PER WV6 .... 48 C1
Peterbrook Junior &
Infant School
SHLY B90 .... 146 B3
Peters Hill Primary School
BRLYHL DY5 .... 102 A6
Peugeot Works
COVS CV3 .... 154 E4
Pheasey Clinic
GTB/HAM B43 .... 71 G2
Pheasey Park Farm
Primary School
GTB/HAM B43 .... 71 G1
Phillips Street Industrial Estate
AST/WIT B6 .... 89 K7
Phoenix Industrial Estate
BILS/COS WV14 .... 67 K1
Phoenix International
Industrial Estate
WBROM B70 .... 68 D8
Phoenix Road Industrial Estate
WLNHL WV13 .... 51 H2
Phoenix Works
Industrial Estate
DARL/WED WS10 .... 52 C5
Pickwick Picture Gallery
COVW CV5 .... 133 J8
The Picture Gallery
ERDW/GRVHL B23 .... 72 D7
The Picture House
STRBR DY8 .... 119 L1
The Picture House
WASH/WDE B8 .... 90 E8
The Picture House
WLNHL WV13 .... 51 H1
Pineapple Junior &
Infant School
ALE/KHTH/YWD B14 .... 124 F8
Pines Day Special School
CBROM B36 .... 91 K5
Pinfold Industrial Estate
BLOX/PEL WS3 .... 39 G5
Pinfold Street JMI School
DARL/WED WS10 .... 52 A8
Pingles Leisure Centre
NUN CV11 .... 99 H3
Pitcheroak Day Special School
REDW B97 .... 195 M1
Planetary Industrial Estate
WLNHL WV13 .... 51 G1
Plantsbrook School
CSCFLD/WYGN B72 .... 73 G1
Plastic Surgery
SOLH B91 .... 128 A6
Playbox Theatre
KNWTH CV8 .... 191 L1
Pleck Business Park
WSLW WS2 .... 4 B3
Pleck Industrial Estate
WSLW WS2 .... 4 A5
Polesworth High School
POL/KGSB/FAZ B78 .... 47 K5
Polesworth Nethersoles
Infant School
POL/KGSB/FAZ B78 .... 47 L3
Polesworth Nethersoles Middle
School
POL/KGSB/FAZ B78 .... 47 M3
Polesworth Parish Council
POL/KGSB/FAZ B78 .... 47 L4
Polesworth Surgery
POL/KGSB/FAZ B78 .... 47 L3
Police Headquarters
CBHAMNE B4 .... 7 G3
Pool Hayes
Comprehensive School
SHHTH WV12 .... 37 M8
Pool Hayes Primary School
SHHTH WV12 .... 37 M7
Pool Road Business Centre
NUNW/HART CV10 .... 80 D8
Pool Road Industrial Estate
NUNW/HART CV10 .... 80 D8
Poplar Industrial Estate
STUD B80 .... 197 H7
Poplar Road Clinic
ALE/KHTH/YWD B14 .... 125 K4

Portfolio Gallery
CRTAM B79 .... 31 M8
Portway Road Industrial Estate
OLDBY B69 .... 86 C7
Potters Green School
COVE CV2 .... 135 K3
Pound Close Surgery
LGLYGN/QTN B68 .... 104 E2
Powke Lane Industrial Estate
CDYHTH B64 .... 103 L3
Premier Business Centre
HAG/WOL DY9 .... 102 E8
Premier Business Park
WSLW WS2 .... 4 C4
Premier Partnership Estate
KGSWFD DY6 .... 101 M1
Premier Trading Estate
VAUX/NECH B7 .... 89 K8
President Kennedy School &
Community College
RCOVN/BALC/EX CV7 ...... 133 M1
Priestley Smith Special School
ERDW/GRVHL B23 .... 71 M7
Primary School
TAM/AM/WIL B77 .... 46 E2
Primrose Hill Junior &
Infant School
HWK/WKHTH B38 .... 144 D5
Primrose Lane Health Centre
WOLVN WV10 .... 36 E5
Primrose Trading Estate
DUDS DY2 .... 103 H1
Prince Albert Junior &
Infant School
AST/WIT B6 .... 89 J5
Princefield First School
PENK ST19 .... 10 D5
Princes Drive Industrial Estate
KNWTH CV8 .... 176 E5
Princes End Junior School
TPTN/OCK DY4 .... 67 J6
Princess of Wales Hospital
BRGRVW B61 .... 185 L1
Princethorpe Junior &
Infant School
SLYOAK B29 .... 123 L4
Priorsfield Combined School
KNWTH CV8 .... 176 B6
Priory Clinic
DUDN DY1 .... 84 F2
Priory Courts
CBHAMNW B3 .... 7 G4
Priory Green Junior &
Infants School
COVEN WV9 .... 35 L3
Priory House Industrial Estate
WSNGN B18 .... 88 E8
Priory Junior Mixed &
Infants School
BLOX/PEL WS3 .... 38 F6
Priory New Way
Industrial Centre
AST/WIT B6 .... 89 J8
The Priory Primary School
DARL/WED WS10 .... 69 H3
The Priory Primary School
DUDN DY1 .... 84 F2
Priory Theatre
KNWTH CV8 .... 176 D8
Private Medical Clinic
BRGRVW B61 .... 185 L2
Progress Business Centre
CNCK/NC WS11 .... 16 C6
Prospect Business Park
CNCK/NC WS11 .... 16 A6
Prospect Trading Estate
CBHAMW B1 .... 6 C4
Providence Industrial Estate
HAG/WOL DY9 .... 102 D7
Provost Williams C E
Primary School
KNWTH CV8 .... 179 G8
Pulse Business Centre
WSL WS1 .... 4 F4
Pye Green Valley CP School
HEDN WS12 .... 12 E6
Quarry Bank Infant School
BRLYHL DY5 .... 102 E4
Quarry Bank Primary School
BRLYHL DY5 .... 102 E4
Quarry Bank Surgery
BRLYHL DY5 .... 102 E5
Queen Elizabeth Gm School
ATHST CV9 .... 63 K6
Queen Elizabeth Hospital
EDG B15 .... 124 C1
Queen Elizabeth Law Courts
CBHAMNE B4 .... 7 H4
Queen Elizabeth
Mercian High School
CRTAM B79 .... 31 M7
Queen Elizabeth
Psychiatric Hospital
EDG B15 .... 124 C1
Queen Elizabeths School
ATHST CV9 .... 63 J3
Queen Marys Grammar School
WSL WS1 .... 5 K5
Queen Marys High School
RUSH/SHEL WS4 .... 53 K2
Queensbridge School
MOS/BIL B13 .... 125 J3
Queens College
EDG B15 .... 106 D8
Queens County Junior &
Infant School
NUN CV11 .... 98 C1
Queens Court Trading Estate
WBROM B70 .... 86 D2
Queens Croft Special School
LICH WS13 .... 20 C6
Queen Street Industrial Estate
BNTWD WS7 .... 18 D8
Queensway Trading Estate
RLSN CV31 .... 200 D4
Queen Victoria Primary School
SEDG DY3 .... 66 B5

Quince Tree Special School
TAM/AM/WIL B77 .... 46 E1
Quincey Rise Surgery
BRLYHL DY5 .... 102 A6
Quinton Junior & Infant School
RIDG/WDGT B32 .... 104 E7
Quinton Local Authority
RIDG/WDGT B32 .... 105 H8
Racecourse Road
Industrial Estate
DUNHL/THL/PER WV6 .... 35 L8
Race Leys Middle School
BDWTH CV12 .... 116 F1
Racemeadow County
Infant School
ATHST CV9 .... 63 J4
Racing Club Warwick F C
WWCK CV34 .... 199 G8
Raddlebarn Junior &
Infant School
SLYOAK B29 .... 124 E4
Radford Primary School
COVN CV6 .... 133 M8
Radford Semele C of E
Combined School
RLSS CV31 .... 201 J8
Radleys Primary School
RUSH/SHEL WS4 .... 40 A6
Radway Industrial Estate
SHLY B90 .... 147 J6
Rag Market
DIG/EDG B5 .... 7 H7
Rakegate Infant School
WOLVN WV10 .... 35 M4
Rakegate Junior School
WOLVN WV10 .... 35 M4
Raleigh Industrial Estate
HDSW B21 .... 87 M4
Ramgarhia Gurdwara Temple
SMHTH B10 .... 108 B6
Ramgarhia Sabha Sikh Temple
WOLV WV1 .... 2 D3
Ramgarhia Sikh Temple
CBHAMW B1 .... 6 C3
Ramgarhia Sikh Temple
COVN CV6 .... 134 D3
Ravenhalls First School
REDE B98 .... 189 H7
Ravensdale Primary School
COVE CV2 .... 155 G1
Rawlett High School
CRTAM B79 .... 31 L4
Read Street Industrial Estate
COV CV1 .... 9 J4
Reaside Clinic
RBRY B45 .... 142 F4
Reaside Middle School
RBRY B45 .... 142 C4
Red Deeps Special School
NUNW/HART CV10 .... 99 G5
Redditch Borough Council
REDE B98 .... 188 C7
Redditch College of Further
Education
REDW B97 .... 196 C1
Redditch County Court
REDW B97 .... 196 B1
Redditch District Council
REDW B97 .... 196 B3
Redditch Golf Club
REDW B97 .... 195 L5
Redditch Magistrates Court
REDE B98 .... 196 C1
Redditch Mosque
REDE B98 .... 196 C1
Redditch United Football Club
REDW B97 .... 196 A1
Redhall Junior & Infant School
SEDG DY3 .... 84 A2
Redhill Junior & Infant School
YDLY B25 .... 108 E7
Redhill Primary School
CNCK/NC WS11 .... 12 C8
Redhill School
STRBR DY8 .... 101 M8
Red Hill Street Clinic
WOLV WV1 .... 2 F1
Redhouse Industrial Estate
ALDR WS9 .... 40 C7
Redhouse Industrial Estate
ALDR WS9 .... 40 E7
Redhouse JMI School
ALDR WS9 .... 40 C8
Rednal Hill Junior &
Infant School
RBRY B45 .... 142 F6
Redroofs Surgery
NUN CV11 .... 99 G2
Red Rooster Industrial Estate
ALDR WS9 .... 40 C7
Redwood Business Park
SMTHWK B66 .... 87 G6
Reflex Industrial Park
WLNHL WV13 .... 51 K2
Regency Business Centre
RLSN CV32 .... 200 D4
Regent Health Centre
RUGBYN/HIL CV21 .... 183 L1
Regent School
OLDBY B69 .... 85 L4
Regents Park Junior &
Infant School
SMHTH B10 .... 108 A5
Regional Health Authority
BKHL/PFLD WV2 .... 50 B6
Regis Comprehensive School
DUNHL/THL/PER WV6 .... 34 F8
Regis Medical Centre
BLKHTH/ROWR B65 .... 104 A4
Register Office
CBHAMW B1 .... 6 D6
Reliance Trading Estate
BILS/COS WV14 .... 50 F8
Reynalds Cross School
HIA/OLT B92 .... 127 H6
Richard Lee Junior &
Infant School
COVE CV2 .... 155 H2

Ridgacre House Surgery
RIDG/WDGT B32 .... 105 H7
The Ridge Primary School
STRBR DY8 .... 101 G8
Ridgeway Middle School
BNTWD WS7 .... 18 E8
Ridgeway Special School
WWCK CV34 .... 199 K4
Ridgeway Surgery
SEDG DY3 .... 66 B6
Ridgewood High School
KINVER DY7 .... 101 G8
Ridpool Junior Mixed School
STECH B33 .... 109 M3
Rigby Hall School
BRGRVE B60 .... 186 A5
Ringway Industrial Estate
LICH WS13 .... 21 G2
River Brook Medical Centre
BVILLE B30 .... 124 C8
Riverside Industrial Estate
POL/KGSB/FAZ B78 .... 45 M4
Riverside Industrial Estate
REDE B98 .... 197 G5
Riversley Park Clinic
NUN CV11 .... 99 G2
R M W Business Centre
HAG/WOL DY9 .... 102 D8
Robbins Business Park
TPTN/OCK DY4 .... 68 C6
Robert Clinic
BVILLE B30 .... 124 C8
Roberts Infant School
SEDG DY3 .... 84 B2
Roberts Primary School
SEDG DY3 .... 84 C1
Robin Hood Junior &
Infant School
HLGN/YWD B28 .... 126 F7
Rocklands Special School
LICH WS13 .... 21 G5
Rocky Lane Trading Estate
VAUX/NECH B7 .... 89 L7
Rokeby County First School
RUGBYS/DCH CV22 .... 183 L5
Rokeby Middle School
RUGBYS/DCH CV22 .... 183 L5
Roman Way First School
REDE B98 .... 197 H2
Rood End Primary School
LGLYGN/QTN B68 .... 87 G7
Rookery Road JMI Schools
HDSW B21 .... 88 C4
Rosedale C of E School
SHHTH WV12 .... 38 B8
Rose Theatre
KIDD DY10 .... 137 K5
Rosslyn School
HLGN/YWD B28 .... 126 E8
Rotton Park Medical Centre
LDYWD/EDGR B16 .... 106 B2
Rough Hay JMI School
DARL/WED WS10 .... 52 A6
Rounds Green Junior &
Infant School
OLDBY B69 .... 86 C6
Rovex Business Park
SPARK B11 .... 108 D8
Rowley Hall Junior &
Infant School
BLKHTH/ROWR B65 .... 104 A1
Rowley Regis College
BLKHTH/ROWR B65 .... 103 M2
Rowley Regis Hospital
BLKHTH/ROWR B65 .... 103 M3
Rowleys Green
Industrial Estate
COVN CV6 .... 134 C1
Royal Brierley Trading Estate
BRLYHL DY5 .... 102 A3
Royal College of Nursing
EDG B15 .... 106 E5
Royal Orthopaedic Hospital
NFLD/LBR B31 .... 123 M8
Royal Society of Arts
CBHAM B2 .... 6 F5
Royal Theatre
CDYHTH B64 .... 103 H4
Royal Wolverhampton
Junior School
BDMR/CCFT WV3 .... 49 L6
The Royal Wolverhampton
School
BKHL/PFLD WV2 .... 49 M6
Rubery Clinic
RBRY B45 .... 142 C6
The Rubicon Business Centre
REDE B98 .... 196 F3
Ruckleigh School
SOLH B91 .... 148 A1
Rufford Primary School
HAG/WOL DY9 .... 102 A8
Rugby Football Club
RUGBYS/DCH CV22 .... 183 J3
Rugby High School
RUGBYS/DCH CV22 .... 183 H7
Rugby Mosque
RUGBYN/HIL CV21 .... 183 M2
Rugby School
RUGBYS/DCH CV22 .... 183 L3
Rugby School Museum
RUGBYN/HIL CV21 .... 183 L2
Rugby School Sports Centre
RUGBYS/DCH CV22 .... 183 M3
Rugby Theatre
RUGBYN/HIL CV21 .... 183 L2
Rugby Welsh Rugby
Football Club
RUGBYN/HIL CV21 .... 183 K2
Rushall Primary School
RUSH/SHEL WS4 .... 39 M6
Russell Medical Centre
DARL/WED WS10 .... 68 D3
Russells Hall Hospital
BRLYHL DY5 .... 84 B6
Russells Hall Junior &
Infant School
DUDN DY1 .... 84 C4

Ryders Hayes Junior
Mixed & Infants School
BLOX/PEL WS3 .... 25 L8
Ryton C of E First School
KNWTH CV8 .... 179 L4
Saab Surgery
SPARK B11 .... 126 D2
Sacred Heart Junior &
Infant School
TPTN/OCK DY4 .... 85 K1
Sacred Heart Junior
Mixed School
BFLD/HDSWWD B20 .... 89 H4
Sacred Heart RC Primary &
Infant School
COVE CV2 .... 154 E2
Saddam Hussain Mosque
BFLD/HDSWWD B20 .... 89 H4
The Safe Harbour
Industrial Estate
AST/WIT B6 .... 71 K8
Sai Medical Centre
WSLW WS2 .... 4 B2
St Albans C of E Primary School
WNSFLD WV11 .... 37 M5
St Albans C of E School
BHTH/HG B12 .... 107 K6
St Alpheges C of E
Infant School
SOLH B91 .... 148 A2
St Alpheges Junior School
SOLH B91 .... 148 A3
St Ambrose Barlow RC
Primary School
HLGN/YWD B28 .... 126 E7
St Ambroses RC Infant School
KIDD DY10 .... 137 K7
St Andrews C of E First School
RBRY B45 .... 167 H5
St Andrews C of E
Infant School
COVW CV5 .... 132 A8
St Andrews C of E
Infant School
DUNHL/THL/PER WV6 .... 49 K1
St Andrews Industrial Estate
BORD B9 .... 108 A3
St Andrews Junior &
Infant School
BORD B9 .... 107 M3
St Andrews RC Junior &
Infant School
HIA/OLT B92 .... 127 L3
St Annes Industrial Estate
WLNHL WS13 .... 51 L2
St Annes RC Junior &
Infant School
BHTH/HG B12 .... 7 M9
St Annes RC Junior &
Infant School
CHWD/FDBR/MGN B37 ...... 110 E3
St Annes RC Primary School
COVS CV3 .... 154 F7
St Annes RC Primary School
FOAKS/STRLY B74 .... 55 J5
St Annes RC School
NUNW/HART CV10 .... 80 B6
St Anthonys Junior &
Infant School
WOLVN WV10 .... 36 B2
St Anthonys RC Junior &
Infant School
CHWD/FDBR/MGN B37 ...... 92 E8
St Anthonys RC Primary School
RLSS CV31 .... 201 G6
St Augustines Catholic Gm
School
REDW B97 .... 196 B8
St Augustines RC
Combined School
KNWTH CV8 .... 176 C6
St Augustines RC
Primary School
COVN CV6 .... 133 L6
St Barnabas C of E First School
KIDDW DY11 .... 136 F4
St Barnabas C of E
Primary School
ERDE/BCHGN B24 .... 90 E2
St Bartholomews C of E
Junior & Infant School
COVS CV3 .... 155 J5
St Bartholomews
Primary School
ETTPK/GDPK/PENN WV4 ...... 65 J2
St Bedes Catholic School
REDE B98 .... 196 D2
St Benedict Biscop Primary
School
WMBN WV5 .... 64 F6
St Benedicts Infant School
SMHTH B10 .... 108 D6
St Benedicts RC Junior &
Infant School
COV CV1 .... 9 K2
St Benedicts RC School
ATHST CV9 .... 63 K6
St Bernadette RC Junior & Infant
School
YDLY B25 .... 108 F5
St Bernadettes RC JMI School
BRWNH WS8 .... 26 D5
St Bernadettes RC
Primary School
WMBN WV5 .... 64 D7
St Bernards RC Junior &
Infant School
MOS/BIL B13 .... 126 A4
St Brigids RC Junior &
Infant School
NFLD/LBR B31 .... 143 K2
St Catherines RC
Junior & Infant School
EDG B15 .... 6 E8
St Chads Cathedral School
LICH WS13 .... 20 F5

St Chads Catholic Primary
School
SEDG DY3 .... **66** B6
St Chads Junior &
Infants School
LOZ/NWT B19 .... **89** H8
St Chad's RC Cathedral
CBHAMNE B4 .... **6** F2
St Chads Stowe Primary School
LICH WS13 .... **21** G5
St Christopher Primary School
COVW CV5 .... **153** H1
St Christophers RC
Primary School
CDSL WV8 .... **34** E2
St Clares Primary School
BFLD/HDSWWD B20 .... **88** F4
St Clements C of E Junior &
Infant School
VAUX/NECH B7 .... **89** M6
St Columbas RC Junior &
Infant School
RBRY B45 .... **143** H6
St Cuthberts RC School
WASH/WDE B8 .... **109** G1
St Dunstans RC Junior &
Infant School
ALE/KHTH/YWD B14 .... **125** J5
St Edmund Campion RC
Lower School
ERDE/BCHGN B24 .... **73** G7
St Edmund Campion RC School
ERDE/BCHGN B24 .... **72** F7
St Edmund & St John
Primary School
DUDS DY2 .... **85** J4
St Edmunds RC Primary School
WSNGN B18 .... **106** E1
St Edmunds RC School
DUNHL/THL/PER WV6 .... **49** J2
St Edwards RC Primary School
CSHL/WTROR B46 .... **93** L8
St Edwards RC Primary School
CSHL/WTROR B46 .... **111** L2
St Edwards RC School
SLYOAK B29 .... **124** E4
St Elizabeths Primary School
CRTAM B79 .... **31** L5
St Elizabeths RC Junior & Infant
School
COVN CV6 .... **134** C6
St Francis C of E Primary School
BVILLE B30 .... **124** B7
St Francis Junior &
Infant School
RUSH/SHEL WS4 .... **40** A4
St Francis of Assisi RC
Comprehensive School
ALDR WS9 .... **41** G8
St Francis RC Junior &
Infant School
LOZ/NWT B19 .... **88** F6
St Francis RC School
BDWTH CV12 .... **116** F2
St Francis RC School
BDWTH CV12 .... **117** G2
St Gabriels RC Primary School
TAM/AM/WIL B77 .... **46** C4
St George & St Teresa RC
Junior & Infant School
DOR/KN B93 .... **172** E1
St Georges C of E First School
KIDD DY10 .... **137** K6
St Georges C of E
Infants School
LOZ/NWT B19 .... **89** H8
St Georges C of E
Primary School
LOZ/NWT B19 .... **89** H8
St Georges C of E
Primary School
REDE B98 .... **196** D2
St Georges Junior Mixed School
LDYWD/EDGR B16 .... **106** D4
St Gerards
Orthopaedic Hospital
CSHL/WTROR B46 .... **93** L8
St Giles C of E Junior School
WLNHL WV13 .... **51** M3
St Giles School
RCOVN/BALC/EX CV7 .... **116** D5
St Gregorys RC Primary School
SMTHWKW B67 .... **105** J3
St Gregorys RC School
COVE CV2 .... **155** J2
St Huberts Primary School
LGLYGN/QTN B68 .... **105** G4
St James C of E Junior School
OLDBY B69 .... **86** B8
St James C of E
Primary School
STRBR DY8 .... **101** H6
St James C of E School
HDSW B21 .... **88** A4
St James Medical Centre
COVS CV3 .... **155** G8
St James Medical Centre
HDSW B21 .... **88** B5
St James Primary School
BRWNH WS8 .... **26** D5
St James RC Junior &
Infant School
RBRY B45 .... **142** E6
St James Road Museum &
Art Gallery
DUDN DY1 .... **85** L4
St John Bosco RC
Primary School
HHTH/SAND B71 .... **68** F6
St John Fisher Primary School
COVE CV2 .... **135** H7
St John Fisher RC
Junior & Infant School
NFLD/LBR B31 .... **143** M6
St John & St Monica RC
Junior & Infant School
MOS/BIL B13 .... **125** J1

St Johns C E Primary School
WNSFLD WV11 .... **37** L1
St Johns Ce School
LDYWD/EDGR B16 .... **106** E4
St Johns C of E Junior &
Infant School
LDYWD/EDGR B16 .... **106** E3
St Johns C of E Middle School
KIDDW DY11 .... **136** F7
St Johns C of E Primary School
COVW CV5 .... **153** G1
St Johns C of E Primary School
DARL/WED WS10 .... **68** D3
St John's Hospital
COV CV1 .... **8** F3
St Johns Hospital
LICH WS13 .... **20** E5
St Johns Hospital
LICH WS13 .... **20** F6
St Johns Middle School
BRGRVW B61 .... **185** K4
St Johns Middle School
KNWTH CV8 .... **191** K3
St Johns Preparatory School
LICH WS13 .... **20** F6
St Johns Primary School
SEDG DY3 .... **82** C3
St Johns Surgery
BRGRVW B61 .... **185** K3
St John the Baptist RC
Junior & Infant School
CBROM B36 .... **92** F6
St John the Divine C of E
Primary School
COVS CV3 .... **155** G8
St John Vianney RC Junior &
Infant School
COVW CV5 .... **152** F2
St John Wall RC School
HDSW B21 .... **88** A3
St Joseph & St Theresa RC
Primary School
BNTWD WS7 .... **18** C7
St Josephs Convent Preparatory
School
DUNHL/THL/PER WV6 .... **35** J7
St Josephs Convent School
KNWTH CV8 .... **176** F6
St Josephs RC First School
NUN CV11 .... **99** G2
St Josephs RC Junior &
Infant School
VAUX/NECH B7 .... **89** M7
St Josephs RC Primary School
HEDN WS12 .... **17** G1
St Josephs RC Primary School
LICHS WS14 .... **21** G6
St Josephs RC Primary School
STRBR DY8 .... **119** K3
St Josephs RC School
DARL/WED WS10 .... **52** A6
St Josephs RC School
MGN/WHC B75 .... **57** G6
St Josephs School
DUDS DY2 .... **85** J4
St Judes Junior & Infant School
DUNHL/THL/PER WV6 .... **49** K1
St Judes RC C of E School
BDMR/CCFT WV3 .... **49** K3
St Judes RC Junior &
Infant School
ALE/KHTH/YWD B14 .... **145** J3
St Kenelms C of E School
RMSLY B62 .... **141** L1
St Leonards C E Primary School
CRTAM B79 .... **32** A3
St Leonards C of E School
BILS/COS WV14 .... **50** F7
St Lukes C of E Junior &
Infant School
DIG/EDG B5 .... **107** H5
St Lukes C of E Primary School
REDW B97 .... **196** B3
St Lukes Infant School
BKHL/PFLD WV2 .... **50** A6
St Lukes Junior School
BKHL/PFLD WV2 .... **49** M6
St Margaret Marys RC
Primary School
ERDW/GRVHL B23 .... **72** A7
St Margarets C of E
Junior & Infant School
HIA/OLT B92 .... **127** K3
St Margarets C of E School
GTB/HAM B43 .... **70** C1
St Margarets Hospital
DSYBK/YTR WS5 .... **54** C5
St Maries RC Infant School
RUGBYS/DCH CV22 .... **183** L3
St Maries RC Junior School
RUGBYS/DCH CV22 .... **183** K3
St Marks Primary School
BRLYHL DY5 .... **84** A6
St Marks RC Junior &
Infant School
PBAR/PBCH B42 .... **70** D6
St Martin De Porres RC
Junior & Infant School
MOS/BIL B13 .... **125** L2
St Martins C of E
Primary School
BILS/COS WV14 .... **67** L3
St Martins C of E
Primary School
TPTN/OCK DY4 .... **67** M8
St Martins Industrial Estate
OLDBY B69 .... **86** E7
St Mary & John RCJ & I School
ERDE/BCHGN B24 .... **90** C3
St Mary Magdalene C of E
Junior & Infant School
HHTH/SAND B71 .... **69** H7
St Mary of the Angels RC School
ALDR WS9 .... **40** F8
St Mary & St Margarets C of E
Junior & Infant School
CBROM B36 .... **91** M5

St Marys C of E First School
KIDD DY10 .... **137** J5
St Marys C of E Junior &
Infant School
SLYOAK B29 .... **124** B4
St Marys C of E Primary School
BFLD/HDSWWD B20 .... **88** E4
St Marys C of E Primary School
KGSWFD DY6 .... **83** H6
St Marys RC Combined School
WWCK CV34 .... **199** J5
St Marys RC Junior &
Infant School
COVE CV2 .... **9** L4
St Marys RC Primary School
CNCK/NC WS11 .... **16** C5
St Marys RC Primary School
DARL/WED WS10 .... **68** D1
St Marys RC Primary School
WSL WS1 .... **5** H6
St Marys RC Primary School
WWCK CV34 .... **199** J3
St Marys RC School
BRLYHL DY5 .... **102** C3
St Marys RC School
HRBN B17 .... **106** A8
St Marys RC School
WOLVN WV10 .... **36** E6
St Marys & St Johns RC School
BKHL/PFLD WV2 .... **3** H9
St Matthews Bloxam C of E
Primary School
RUGBYS/DCH CV22 .... **183** J3
St Matthews C of E Junior &
Infant School
VAUX/NECH B7 .... **7** M1
St Matthews C of E School
SMTHWK B66 .... **87** M8
St Michaels C of E First School
PENK ST19 .... **10** C4
St Michaels C of E Junior &
Infant School
RIDG/WDGT B32 .... **123** G5
St Michaels C of E Primary
School
LICH WS13 .... **21** G5
St Michaels C of E
Primary School
LICHS WS14 .... **21** G6
St Michaels C of E School
BLOX/PEL WS3 .... **39** K3
St Michaels C of E
Secondary School
OLDBY B69 .... **86** B8
St Michaels School
WSNGN B18 .... **88** E6
St Nicholas C of E
Combined School
KNWTH CV8 .... **176** E8
St Nicholas Park Leisure Centre
WWCK CV34 .... **199** L6
St Nicholas RC School
SCFLD/BOLD B73 .... **72** D3
St Nicholas's C E First School
CDSL WV8 .... **34** D1
St Nicolas C of E Junior School
NUN CV11 .... **81** K7
St Oswalds C of E First School
KIDD DY10 .... **137** L4
St Oswalds C of E Primary School
RUGBYS/DCH CV22 .... **183** H2
St Patricks C of E Junior &
Infant School
HOCK/TIA B94 .... **171** G3
St Patricks Junior Middle &
Infant RC School
WSLW WS2 .... **53** H2
St Patricks Primary School
WNSFLD WV11 .... **37** G8
St Patricks RC Combined School
RLSS CV31 .... **200** D8
St Patricks RC Junior &
Infant School
CHWD/FDBR/MGN B37 .... **111** G3
St Patricks RC Primary School
COVE CV2 .... **135** H4
St Patricks RC School
WSNGN B18 .... **106** D1
St Pauls C E First School
COVEN WV9 .... **22** A2
St Pauls C of E
Combined School
RLSN CV32 .... **200** F4
St Pauls C of E First School
NUNW/HART CV10 .... **98** A2
St Pauls C of E Primary School
TPTN/OCK DY4 .... **67** K7
St Pauls RC School
HWK/WKHTH B38 .... **144** E4
St Peter & Paul RC
Primary School
COVE CV2 .... **135** K6
St Peter & Paul RC
Primary School
ERDE/BCHGN B24 .... **91** G2
St Peters C E Primary School
ALDR WS9 .... **41** J1
St Peters C E Primary School
HEDN WS12 .... **17** H1
St Peters C of E Middle School
REDE B98 .... **197** J3
St Peters Collegiate School
DUNHL/THL/PER WV6 .... **49** J2
St Peters RC First School
RLSN CV32 .... **200** D5
St Peters RC Junior &
Infant School
RIDG/WDGT B32 .... **123** G4
St Peters RC School
BRGRVE B60 .... **185** J5
St Peters & St. Pauls RC
Primary School
LICH WS13 .... **20** F4
St Peters Surgery
WSLW WS2 .... **53** H1

St Philips RC School
SMTHWK B66 .... **87** M7
St Philips Sixth Form College
LDYWD/EDGR B16 .... **106** D4
St Saviours Junior &
Infant School
WASH/WDE B8 .... **90** B8
St Stephens C of E
First School
REDE B98 .... **188** D8
St Stephens C of E
Middle School
REDE B98 .... **188** D8
St Stephens C of E
Primary School
WOLVN WV10 .... **50** C1
St Teresas RC Primary School
ETTPK/GDPK/PENN WV4 .... **50** C8
St Teresas RC School
BFLD/HDSWWD B20 .... **88** E3
St Thomas C of E School
WNSFLD WV11 .... **37** H6
St Thomas Community
High School
EDG B15 .... **6** D9
St Thomas More
Comprehensive RC School
BILS/COS WV14 .... **51** L6
St Thomas More Comprehensive
School
WLNHL WV13 .... **51** M5
St Thomas More RC First School
REDE B98 .... **196** F6
St Thomas More RC Primary
School
CNCK/NC WS11 .... **24** E1
St Thomas More RC Primary
School
COVS CV3 .... **154** B8
St Thomas More RC Primary
School
LGN/SDN/BHAMAIR B26 .... **109** M8
St Thomas More Primary School
NUNW/HART CV10 .... **98** E2
St Thomas of
Canterbury School
BLOX/PEL WS3 .... **39** K7
St Thomas RC Grammar School
HWK/WKHTH B38 .... **144** B2
St Vincent De Paul RC School
VAUX/NECH B7 .... **107** M1
St Wilfrids RC Junior &
Infant School
CBROM B36 .... **91** K5
Salford Trading Estate
AST/WIT B6 .... **90** A5
Salim Mosque
WASH/WDE B8 .... **90** C7
Salisbury Place Industrial Estate
BDMR/CCFT WV3 .... **2** C7
Salisbury Primary School
DARL/WED WS10 .... **52** C6
Saltbrook Trading Estate
HALE B63 .... **102** E6
Salters Meadow Health Centre
BNTWD WS7 .... **18** D6
Saltley Business Park
VAUX/NECH B7 .... **90** B7
Saltley Health Centre
WASH/WDE B8 .... **90** C8
Saltley Industrial Centre
WASH/WDE B8 .... **108** A2
Saltley Leisure Centre
BORD B9 .... **108** E2
Saltley School
BORD B9 .... **108** E2
Salvation Army
CBHAMNE B4 .... **6** F2
Sandown County First School
DUNHL/THL/PER WV6 .... **48** D1
Sandwell Area Health Authority
SMTHWK B66 .... **87** J6
Sandwell Area Health Authority
SMTHWK B66 .... **87** L8
Sandwell Borough
Football Club
OLDBY B69 .... **86** C6
Sandwell College
DARL/WED WS10 .... **68** E4
Sandwell College
SMTHWK B66 .... **87** L8
Sandwell College
WBROM B70 .... **87** G2
Sandwell District
General Hospital
HHTH/SAND B71 .... **69** H8
Sandwell Health Authority
WBROM B70 .... **86** F1
Sandwell Health
Authority Clinic
CDYHTH B64 .... **103** J4
Sandwell
Metropolitan
Borough Council
BLKHTH/ROWR B65 .... **104** C1
Sandwell
Metropolitan
Borough Council
CDYHTH B64 .... **103** K5
Sandwell
Metropolitan
Borough Council
GTB/HAM B43 .... **70** D6
Sandwell
Metropolitan
Borough Council
HHTH/SAND B71 .... **69** J5
Sandwell
Metropolitan
Borough Council
LGLYGN/QTN B68 .... **87** G7
Sandwell
Metropolitan
Borough Council
OLDBY B69 .... **86** C6

Sandwell
Metropolitan
Borough Council
SMTHWK B66 .... **87** L8
Sandwell
Metropolitan
Borough Council
SMTHWK B66 .... **87** L7
Sandwell
Metropolitan
Borough Council
TPTN/OCK DY4 .... **85** K2
Sandwell Park Industrial Estate
HHTH/SAND B71 .... **87** K4
Sandyhill Industrial Estate
SHLY B90 .... **146** E1
Sandy Lane Business Park
COV CV1 .... **134** A8
Sapcote Trading Centre
AST/WIT B6 .... **89** L2
Sapcote Trading Centre
CDYHTH B64 .... **103** K2
Sapcote Trading Centre
SMHTH B10 .... **108** C7
Sarehole Mill Museum
MOS/BIL B13 .... **126** B5
Sarehole Surgery
HLGN/YWD B28 .... **126** C5
Sarephed Medical Centre
SMTHWKW B67 .... **87** L8
Sargeant Turner Trading Estate
HAG/WOL DY9 .... **102** D7
Satellite Industrial Park
WLNHL WV13 .... **51** G1
Saxon Hill Special School
LICHS WS14 .... **21** G7
School House
POL/KGSB/FAZ B78 .... **60** A7
School House C of E School
KNWTH CV8 .... **179** G8
School of Jewellery
CBHAMW B1 .... **6** B2
Scotch Orchard County Primary
School
LICH WS13 .... **21** H4
Scott Arms Shopping Centre
GTB/HAM B43 .... **70** C4
Sears Retail Park
SHLY B90 .... **147** H4
Seikh Temple
COVN CV6 .... **134** B6
Selly Oak Health Centre
SLYOAK B29 .... **124** C4
Selly Oak Hospital
SLYOAK B29 .... **124** D4
Selly Oak Industrial Estate
SLYOAK B29 .... **124** C4
Selly Oak School
SLYOAK B29 .... **124** C5
Selly Park Girls School
SLYOAK B29 .... **124** F4
Selly Park Surgery
COVS CV3 .... **124** F3
Seven Stars Industrial Estate
COVS CV3 .... **154** E6
Severne Junior & Infant School
ACGN B27 .... **127** G5
Shaftmoor Industrial Estate
HLGN/YWD B28 .... **126** D3
Shard End Surgery
BKDE/SHDE B34 .... **92** A7
Sharmans Cross Junior &
Infant School
SOLH B91 .... **147** J1
Shaw Hill Junior &
Infant School
WASH/WDE B8 .... **108** D1
Shawhurst Primary School
HLYWD B47 .... **145** L7
The Sheila Godfrey Clinic
DOR/KN B93 .... **172** D2
Sheldon Cricket Club
YDLY B25 .... **109** H5
Sheldon Heath School
STECH B33 .... **110** A5
Shelfield Clinic
RUSH/SHEL WS4 .... **40** A5
Shelfield Community School
RUSH/SHEL WS4 .... **40** A3
Shell Corner Industrial Estate
RMSLY B62 .... **104** B5
Shenley Lane
Community Association
Sports Centre
SLYOAK B29 .... **123** L7
Shenstone Lodge School
LICHS WS14 .... **42** E3
Shenstone Parish Council
FOAKS/STRLY B74 .... **42** B7
Shenstone Sports Club
LICHS WS14 .... **28** E7
Shenstone Trading Estate
RMSLY B62 .... **122** A1
Shepperton Business Park
NUN CV11 .... **99** G4
Sherbourne Fields School
COVN CV6 .... **133** H8
Sherbourne Medical Centre
RLSN CV32 .... **200** D4
Shireland Hall Primary School
SMTHWK B66 .... **105** M2
Shireland High School
SMTHWKW B67 .... **105** K1
Shire Oak School
BRWNH WS8 .... **26** E8
Shires Industrial Estate
LICH WS13 .... **20** E7
Shirestone Primary School
STECH B33 .... **110** B3
Shiri Krishna Temple
DUDS DY2 .... **85** G5
Shirley Clinic
SHLY B90 .... **146** F2
Shirley Park Sports Club
SHLY B90 .... **171** L1
Shirley Road Health Clinic
ACGN B27 .... **126** F4
Shirley Temple
HLGN/YWD B28 .... **126** E8

Shopping Centre
LOZ/NWT B19.................... 89 G7
Short Heath Clinic
SHHTH WV12.................... 38 B7
Short Heath Junior &
Infant School
ERDW/GRVHL B23............ 72 B7
Shorth Heath Junior School
SHHTH WV12.................... 38 B8
Showcase Cinemas
ERDE/BCHGN B24.............. 91 H3
Showcase Cinemas
RCOVN/BALC/EX CV7...... 135 M4
Showcase Cinemas
WSLW WS2...................... 52 D4
Showell Green Surgery
SPARK B11...................... 126 A1
Showell Road Industrial Estate
WOLVN WV10.................... 36 B7
Shree Krishna Temple
HHTH/SAND B71................ 68 F8
Shree Ram Mandir
Hindu Temple
SPARK B11...................... 107 M7
Shri Guru Ravidass Temple
BKHL/PFLD WV2................ 50 B6
Shri Guru Ravidass Temple
WLNHL WV13.................... 51 K4
Shrubland Street
Community School
RLSS CV31...................... 200 E7
Shustoke C of E
Primary School
CSHL/WTROR B46.............. 94 E3
Sidemoor Primary School
BRGRVW B61.................... 185 J2
Sidney Stringer Community
Technology College
COV CV1.......................... 9 H3
Sikh Temple
COV CV1.......................... 9 G1
Sikh Temple
RLSS CV31...................... 200 E5
Sikh Temple
WLNHL WV13.................... 52 A3
Sikh Temple
WNSFLD WV11.................. 37 H8
Sikh Temple
WOLV WV1........................ 3 G4
Sikh Temple
WSL WS1.......................... 5 G7
Silver Birches Business Park
BRGRVE B60.................... 185 L7
Silver End Industrial Estate
BRLYHL DY5.................... 101 M4
Singh Sabha
Gurudwara Temple
BFLD/HDSWWD B20.......... 88 D2
Sion Hill County
Secondary School
KIDD DY10...................... 137 L3
Sir Robert Peel Hospital
POL/KGSB/FAZ B78............ 45 H3
Sir Theodore Pritchett
Junior & Infant School
ALE/KHTH/YWD B14.......... 145 H3
Sir Wilfred Martineau School
STETCH B33...................... 110 B2
Sir Wilfred Martineau School
STETCH B33...................... 110 A2
Skydome Leisure Complex
COV CV1.......................... 8 D5
Sladefield Infants School
WASH/WDE B8.................. 90 E8
Slade Junior & Infant N C
School
ERDW/GRVHL B23............ 90 B3
Sladen School
KIDD DY10...................... 137 K6
Sledmere Primary School
DUDS DY2........................ 85 H7
Small Health Medical Centre
BORD B9.......................... 108 A4
Small Heath Business Park
SMTH B10........................ 108 D6
Small Heath Grant
Maintained School
SMTH B10........................ 108 B6
Small Heath School &
Community Centre
SMTH B10........................ 108 B5
Small Heath Trading Estate
SPARK B11...................... 108 C7
Smestow Bridge
Industrial Estate
WMBN WV5...................... 64 A7
Smethwick Medical Centre
SMTHWK B66.................... 87 L7
Smethwick Swimming Centre
SMTHKW B67.................... 105 K3
Smiths Picture Gallery
WBROM B70...................... 87 G1
Smiths Wood Parish Council
CBROM B36...................... 92 E6
Smiths Wood Secondary School
CBROM B36...................... 92 E7
Sneyd Community School
BLOX/PEL WV3.................. 38 C3
Snow Hill Clinic
BKHL/PFLD WV2................ 3 G6
Sofer Gallery
CNCK/NC WS11................ 16 C8
Soho Health Centre
HDSW B21........................ 88 D6
Solihull College
CHWD/FDBR/MGN B37...... 111 G1
Solihull College
SHLY B90........................ 147 H2
Solihull College
SOLH B91........................ 147 L2
Solihull Football Club
SOLH B91........................ 147 J1
Solihull Health Authority
SHLY B90........................ 146 F3
Solihull Health Authority
SOLH B91........................ 148 A1
Solihull Hospital
SOLH B91........................ 148 B1

Solihull Ice Rink
HIA/OLT B92.................... 127 M2
Solihull Magistrates Court
SOLH B91........................ 148 A2
Solihull Metropolitan
Borough Council
SOLH B91........................ 148 A2
Solihull Rugby Union
Football Club
SOLH B91........................ 147 K1
Solihull School
SOLH B91........................ 148 B1
Sommerville Primary School
SMHTH B10...................... 108 C5
South Birmingham College
BHTH/HG B12.................. 107 L8
South Birmingham College
HLGN/YWD B28................ 126 C5
South Birmingham
College Technical Centre
HLGN/YWD B28................ 126 D4
South Birmingham
Health Authority
EDG B15.......................... 106 E5
South Birmingham
Health Authority
SLYOAK B29.................... 124 C4
South Birmingham
Mental Health NHS Trust
BVILLE B30...................... 145 H2
South Bromsgrove
High School
BRGRVE B60.................... 185 K5
Southern Birmingham
Community Health
NHS Trust
BHTH/HG B12.................. 107 K8
Southern Birmingham
Community Health
NHS Trust
MOS/BIL B13.................... 125 J2
Southfields Junior &
Infant School
COV CV1.......................... 9 K4
Southside Business Centre
BHTH/HG B12.................. 107 L8
South Staffordshire Council
CDSL WV8........................ 34 E2
South Staffs Business Park
CNCK/NC WS11................ 24 A1
South Warwickshire
Health Authority
RLSS CV31...................... 200 D7
South Warwickshire
Health Authority
WWCK CV34...................... 199 J5
South Warwickshire Hospital
WWCK CV34...................... 199 K5
South Warwickshire
Mental Health Services
NHS Trust
WWCK CV34...................... 199 H5
Sovereign Trading Estate
STRBR DY8...................... 101 J8
Sowe Valley Primary School
COVS CV3........................ 155 H5
Sparkbrook Health Centre
SPARK B11...................... 107 M6
Sparkbrook Street
Industrial Estate
COV CV1.......................... 9 K3
Sparkhill Swimming
Pool & Fitness Centre
SPARK B11...................... 126 A1
Sparrowdale School
ATHST CV9...................... 62 B1
Spartan Industrial Centre
WBROM B70...................... 68 C7
Speedwell Trading Estate
YDLY B25........................ 108 E7
Spennells First School
KIDD DY10...................... 161 L3
Spines Clinic
WMBN WV5...................... 64 D7
Spon Gate Junior &
Infant School
COV CV1.......................... 8 B4
Spon Lane Trading Estate
WBROM B70...................... 87 G3
Sports Centre
COV CV1.......................... 9 H4
Sports Centre
MOS/BIL B13.................... 125 G3
Sports Ground
COVS CV3........................ 154 E4
Springdale College
SLYOAK B29.................... 124 A4
Springdale Primary School
ETTPK/GDPK/PENN WV4.... 49 G8
Springfield House School
DOR/KN B93.................... 149 L8
Springfield Industrial Estate
OLDBY B69...................... 86 F6
Springfield Infant School
BLKHTH/ROWR B65............ 103 L1
Springfield Junior
Mixed School
MOS/BIL B13.................... 126 B3
Springfield Junior School
BLKHTH/ROWR B65............ 103 L1
Springfield Medical Practice
SPARK B11...................... 126 B2
Springhill Business Park
WSNGN B18...................... 106 E1
Springhill CP School
BNTWD WS7...................... 18 F7
Spring Hill Industrial Estate
RCOVN/BALC/EX CV7........ 96 D5
Springhill Medical Centre
BNTWD WS7...................... 18 E6
Spring Hill Medical Centre
RCOVN/BALC/EX CV7........ 96 D6
Spring Lane Industrial Estate
SHHTH WV12.................... 52 A1
Spring Road Industrial Estate
ETTPK/GDPK/PENN WV4.... 66 E1
Springvale Primary School
CNCK/NC WS11................ 16 C5

Sprint Industrial Estate
WOLVN WV10.................... 14 B7
Sri Guru Ravidass Temple
DARL/WED WS10.............. 52 B8
Stafford Road Sports Club
BLOX/PEL WS3.................. 38 F3
Staffordshire College of
Agriculture
PENK ST19........................ 14 C1
Staffordshire County Council
CNCK/NC WS11................ 16 A5
Staffordshire County Council
CRTAM B79...................... 32 A8
Staffordshire County Council
LICH WS13...................... 20 F6
Staffordshire County Council
PENK ST19...................... 10 D4
Staffordshire County Council
PENK ST19...................... 14 A4
Staffordshire
Regiment Museum
LICHS WS14...................... 30 A3
Staffs Moor Industrial Estate
CRTAM B79...................... 31 K8
Staffs Moor Industrial Estate
CRTAM B79...................... 31 L7
Stag Industrial Estate
BILS/COS WV14................ 67 L1
Stag Industrial Estate
COVN CV6........................ 134 B5
Stambermill Industrial Estate
HAG/WOL DY9.................. 102 B7
Stanhope Road Clinic
SMTHWKW B67.................. 105 K2
Stanton Road
Primary School
COVN CV6........................ 134 D6
Stanville Junior &
Infant School
LGN/SDN/BHAMAIR B26.... 110 A7
Starbank Junior &
Infant School
SMTH B10........................ 108 T5
Start Point Trading Estate
SPARK B11...................... 126 B1
Station Road Industrial Estate
BLKHTH/ROWR B65............ 104 B3
Station Road Industrial Estate
CSHL/WTROR B46.............. 93 K3
Status Business Centre
COVW CV5........................ 8 B7
Stechford Health Centre
STETCH B33...................... 109 J3
Stechford Junior &
Infant School
STETCH B33...................... 109 H3
Stechford Trading Estate
STETCH B33...................... 109 J1
Stephens Industrial Estate
SPARK B11...................... 126 D1
Stepping Stones
Medical Practice
DUDN DY1........................ 84 F4
Steps to Health
WOLVN WV10.................... 36 C6
Stevens Dental Health Centre
STRBR DY8...................... 119 K1
Stirchley Junior & Infant School
BVILLE B30...................... 124 E7
Stirchley Trading Estate
BVILLE B30...................... 124 F7
Stivichall Primary School
COVS CV3........................ 153 L7
Stock Exchange
CBHAMNW B3.................... 6 E4
Stockingford Clinic
NUNW/HART CV10.............. 98 B2
Stockingford First School
NUNW/HART CV10.............. 98 B2
Stockingford Middle School
NUNW/HART CV10.............. 98 B2
Stockland Clinic
ERDW/GRVHL B23............ 90 B1
Stockland Green Health Centre
ERDW/GRVHL B23............ 90 B1
Stockland Green
Secondary School
ERDW/GRVHL B23............ 90 B1
Stoke Aldermoor
Medical Centre
COVS CV3........................ 154 F5
Stoke Heath Junior &
Infant School
COVE CV2........................ 134 E7
Stoke Old Boys Rugby
Football Club
COVS CV3........................ 155 H4
Stoke Park School &
Community College
COVE CV2........................ 154 F1
Stoke Primary School
COVE CV2........................ 154 E1
Stoke Row Industrial Estate
COVE CV2........................ 154 E1
Stonebridge Trading Estate
COVS CV3........................ 178 E1
Stonebridge Trading Estate
KNWTH CV8...................... 178 E1
Stone C of E School
KIDD DY10...................... 162 C3
Stone Cross Clinic
HHTH/SAND B71................ 69 J4
Stoneleigh Deer Park Golf Ltd
KNWTH CV8...................... 178 C8
Stoneydelph County
Junior School
TAM/AM/WIL B77.............. 46 E4
Stoneydelph Infants School
TAM/AM/WIL B77.............. 46 E4
Stoney Lane Industrial Estate
KIDDW DY11...................... 137 H5
Stoney Stanton
Medical Centre
COVN CV6........................ 134 C7
Stourbridge Clinic
STRBR DY8...................... 119 M1
Stourbridge College
STRBR DY8...................... 101 J8

Stourbridge College
STRBR DY8...................... 119 L1
Stourbridge Cricket Club
STRBR DY8...................... 101 K6
Stourbridge Football Club
STRBR DY8...................... 101 K7
Stourbridge Galleries
STRBR DY8...................... 119 K1
Stourbridge Industrial Estate
STRBR DY8...................... 101 L1
Stourbridge Rugby Club
KINVER DY7...................... 100 F7
Stourminster School
KIDD DY10...................... 161 M1
Stourport on Severn
High School
STRPT DY13...................... 160 E8
Stourside Industrial Estate
KIDD DY10...................... 137 J8
Stourvale Trading Estate
HALE B63........................ 103 H7
Stowe C of E School
LICH WS13...................... 21 G5
Stowheath Industrial Estate
WOLV WV1........................ 50 E5
Stowheath Junior School
WLNHL WV13.................... 51 H4
Stowlawn Primary School
BILS/COS WV14................ 51 G5
The Straits Primary School
SEDG DY3........................ 65 H4
Stratford Road School Clinic
SPARK B11...................... 126 B3
Strawberry Lane
Industrial Estate
WLNHL WV13.................... 51 G2
Streetly Clinic Infant
Welfare Centre
FOAKS/STRLY B74.............. 55 J5
Streetly Hockey &
Cricket Club
FOAKS/STRLY B74.............. 55 L4
Streetly Methodist
Recreation Centre
FOAKS/STRLY B74.............. 55 K3
Streetly Road Surgery
ERDW/GRVHL B23............ 72 C7
Streetly School
FOAKS/STRLY B74.............. 55 K7
Streetsbrook Infant School
SHLY B90........................ 147 G1
Studley Cricket Club
STUD B80........................ 197 J7
Summerfield Hospital
WSNGN B18...................... 106 D1
Summerfield Junior &
Infant School
WSNGN B18...................... 106 C1
Summerfield School
WSNGN B18...................... 106 C1
Summerhill Industrial Estate
CBHAMW B1...................... 6 A3
Summerhill School
KGSWFD DY6.................... 82 F7
Summit Crescent
Industrial Estate
SMTHWK B66.................... 87 J3
Sundridge CP School
KGSTG B44...................... 71 J4
Sunrise Business Park
STRBR DY8...................... 101 J6
Sunshine Infant School
BLOX/PEL WS3.................. 39 G5
Superbowl
COVS CV3........................ 178 B5
Superbowl
RLSS CV31...................... 200 B7
Superintendent Public Baths
BVILLE B30...................... 124 D6
Superintendent Public Baths
ERDW/GRVHL B23............ 90 E1
Superintendent Public Baths
SLYOAK B29.................... 124 D4
Superintendent Public Baths
SPARK B11...................... 126 A2
Superintendent Public Baths
VAUX/NECH B7.................. 90 A6
Sutton Arts Theatre
CSCFLD/WYGN B72............ 73 C2
Sutton Coldfield
College of
Further Education
ERDE/BCHGN B24.............. 72 E8
Sutton Coldfield Girls School
SCFLD/BOLD B73.............. 72 F7
Sutton Coldfield Hospital
SCFLD/BOLD B73.............. 72 F1
Sutton Coldfield
Magistrates Court
FOAKS/STRLY B74.............. 56 F7
Sutton Coldfield Rugby Club
WALM/CURD B76................ 73 K4
Sutton Coldfield Town
Football Club
CSCFLD/WYGN B72............ 73 G2
Sutton Coldfield Town Hall
SCFLD/BOLD B73.............. 56 F7
Sutton College
CSCFLD/WYGN B72............ 73 G1
Sutton College
FOAKS/STRLY B74.............. 57 G7
Sutton College
SCFLD/BOLD B73.............. 57 G8
Sutton College of
Further Education
FOAKS/STRLY B74.............. 57 G7
Sutton Park First School
KIDDW DY11...................... 160 F1
Sutton Park Surgery
SCFLD/BOLD B73.............. 55 L8
Sutton School
DUDN DY1........................ 84 D5
Sutton Town Sports Club
CSCFLD/WYGN B72............ 73 G1
Sutton United F C
MGN/WHC B75.................. 57 J8

The Swallows
Industrial Estate
SHLY B90........................ 147 H5
Swan Lane Industrial Estate
WBROM B70...................... 68 E8
Swan Medical Centre
YDLY B25........................ 109 H6
Swanpool Medical Centre
TPTN/OCK DY4.................. 67 L5
Swanshurst School
MOS/BIL B13.................... 125 L6
Swanswell Medical Centre
COV CV1.......................... 9 G2
Swimming Baths
WOLV WV1........................ 2 D4
Sycamore Green CP School
DUDN DY1........................ 66 D8
Sycamore House
Medical Centre
WSL WS1.......................... 5 K6
Sydenham County
Middle School
RLSS CV31...................... 201 G7
Sydenham Industrial Estate
RLSS CV31...................... 200 F7
Tachbrook Park
Industrial Estate
WWCK CV34...................... 200 B8
Talbots Lane Trading Estate
BRLYHL DY5.................... 102 C4
Talisman Theatre & Arts Centre
KNWTH CV8...................... 191 K2
Tamar Medical Centre
DUNHL/THL/PER WV6........ 48 C1
Tamebridge Industrial Estate
PBAR/PBCH B42................ 89 J1
Tameside Junior &
Infant School
DARL/WED WS10.............. 69 G3
Tame Valley Junior &
Infant School
CBROM B36...................... 91 H5
Tame Valley Small
Business Centre
TAM/AM/WIL B77.............. 46 C7
Tamworth Borough Council
CRTAM B79...................... 31 L8
Tamworth Borough Council
TAM/AM/WIL B77.............. 46 E1
Tamworth Borough Council
TAM/AM/WIL B77.............. 46 F2
Tamworth Borough Council
TAM/AM/WIL B77.............. 46 B4
Tamworth Business Centre
TAM/AM/WIL B77.............. 46 F2
Tamworth College of Further
Education
CRTAM B79...................... 31 M7
Tamworth District Council
CRTAM B79...................... 31 K6
Tandon Medical Centre
SEDG DY3........................ 66 C8
Tardebigge C of E School
BRGRVE B60.................... 186 F6
Telford County Middle School
RLSN CV32...................... 192 F8
Telford United Football Club
CNCK/NC WS11................ 25 L1
Telsen Industrial Centre
AST/WIT B6...................... 89 K7
Templars Primary School
TLHL/CAN CV4.................. 152 E4
Temple Gallery
CBHAMNW B3.................... 7 G4
Temple Meadow
Primary School
RBDC B64........................ 103 K4
The Temple
BHTH/HG B12.................. 107 L6
The Temple
COV CV1.......................... 9 J1
The Temple
CSHL/WTROR B46.............. 76 A5
Tenacres First School
REDE B98........................ 197 K2
Tenlons Road Industrial Estate
NUNW/HART CV10.............. 98 D3
Terrace Industrial Estate
RUGBYN/HIL CV21............ 183 M1
Terry Business Centre
REDE B98........................ 196 D2
Tettenhall College
DUNHL/THL/PER WV6........ 49 H1
Theatre One
COV CV1.......................... 9 H3
Thomas Barnes CP School
POL/KGSB/FAZ B78............ 30 F6
Thorns County First School
KNWTH CV8...................... 191 M1
Thorns Primary School
BRLYHL DY5.................... 102 C5
The Thorns School
BRLYHL DY5.................... 102 C5
Thornton Junior Mixed School
WASH/WDE B8.................. 90 F8
Three Crowns Special School
DSYBK/YTR WS5................ 54 D4
Three Spires Industrial Estate
COVN CV6........................ 116 E7
Three Spires School
COVW CV5........................ 133 H7
Ticket Shop
CBHAM B2........................ 7 G5
Ticket Shop
CBHAMNW B3.................... 6 F5
Tidbury Green Primary School
SHLY B90........................ 170 C1
Tile Cross Trading Estate
STETCH B33...................... 110 B4
Tile Hill College of
Further Education
TLHL/CAN CV4.................. 152 A4
Tile Hill Wood School
TLHL/CAN CV4.................. 152 B3
Timberley Primary School
BKDE/SHDE B34................ 92 D1

Tindal Street Junior &
Infant School
BHTH/HG B12 .... 107 K8
Tipton Green Junior School
TPTN/OCK DY4 .... 85 K1
Tipton Sports & Leisure Centre
TPTN/OCK DY4 .... 67 M4
Tiverton Junior & Infant School
SLYOAK B29 .... 124 D3
Tiverton School
COVN CV6 .... 133 H8
Tividale Business Park
TPTN/OCK DY4 .... 85 M2
Tividale Comprehensive School
OLDBY B69 .... 86 A4
Tividale FC
OLDBY B69 .... 85 M4
Tividale Hall Junior &
Infant School
OLDBY B69 .... 85 L4
Tividale Junior & Infant School
OLDBY B69 .... 85 M3
Tividale Medical Centre
OLDBY B69 .... 86 B5
Tolson Industrial Estate
POL/KGSB/FAZ B78 ...... 45 L5
Tolsons Mill Industrial Estate
POL/KGSB/FAZ B78 ...... 45 L5
Topcliffe Primary School
CVALE B35 .... 91 L2
Torc High School
TAM/AM/WIL B77 .... 46 E3
Tower Hill Health Centre
PBAR/PBCH B42 .... 70 E7
Tower Works Industrial Estate
BDMR/CCFT WV3 .... 2 B7
Town Junior School
CSCFLD/WYGN B72 .... 73 G1
TP Riley Comprehensive School
BLOX/PEL WS3 .... 39 G3
Tractor Spares Industrial Estate
WLNHL WV13 .... 51 H3
Trading Estate
KIDD DY10 .... 162 B7
Trading Estate
WBROM B70 .... 86 F4
The Trafford Park
Industrial Estate
REDE B98 .... 196 D2
The Trafford Park
Industrial Estate
REDE B98 .... 196 D2
Trent Valley Trading Estate
LICH WS13 .... 21 G2
Trescott JMI School
NFLD/LBR B31 .... 143 H2
Trevor Street Industrial Estate
VAUX/NECH B7 .... 90 A7
Trident Business Park
NUN CV11 .... 99 H2
Trinity C of E Junior School
WOLVN WV10 .... 50 D1
Trinity R C School
RLSN CV32 .... 200 B3
Trinity School
WWCK CV34 .... 200 A7
Tromans Industrial Estate
DUDS DY2 .... 103 H2
Tudor Grange School
SOLH B91 .... 147 L3
Tudor Industrial Estate
SPARK B11 .... 108 F8
Turves Green Boys School
NFLD/LBR B31 .... 143 L5
Turves Green Girls School
NFLD/LBR B31 .... 143 L4
Tuttle Hill Industrial Estate
NUNW/HART CV10 .... 80 C6
Twickenham Primary School
KGSTG B44 .... 72 A4
Two Gates County
Primary School
TAM/AM/WIL B77 .... 46 A5
Two Gates Ragged School
HALE B63 .... 103 G8
Two Gates Trading Estate
TAM/AM/WIL B77 .... 46 B6
Tyburn Industrial Estate
ERDE/BCHGN B24 .... 91 H3
Tyntesfield School
RUGBYS/DCH CV22 .... 183 J5
Tyseley Industrial Estate
SPARK B11 .... 108 C8
UCI Cinema
BRLYHL DY5 .... 102 C3
UCI 8 Screens
SHLY B90 .... 147 J6
Uffculme Clinic
MOS/BIL B13 .... 125 J3
Uffculme Special School
MOS/BIL B13 .... 125 J4
Ulverley Junior & Infant School
HIA/OLT B92 .... 127 M5
Underhill Junior &
Infant School
WOLVN WV10 .... 36 F4
Underhill Primary School
WOLVN WV10 .... 36 F4
Union Business Park
WSLW WS2 .... 4 D3
Unisant Trading Estate
CDYHTH B64 .... 103 K3
University
COV CV1 .... 9 H6
University
COV CV1 .... 9 H4
University
COV CV1 .... 9 J5
University Hospital N H S Trust
SLYOAK B29 .... 124 C4
University (North Site)
WOLV WV1 .... 2 F3
University of
Aston In Birmingham
CBHAMNE B4 .... 7 J2
University of
Aston In Birmingham
CBHAMNE B4 .... 7 J3

University of Birmingham
EDG B15 .... 106 E7
University of Birmingham
EDG B15 .... 106 D8
University of Birmingham
EDG B15 .... 106 C7
University of Birmingham
EDG B15 .... 106 C8
University of Birmingham
EDG B15 .... 106 E7
University of Birmingham
EDG B15 .... 106 E6
University of Birmingham
EDG B15 .... 124 E2
University of Birmingham
EDG B15 .... 124 D1
University of Birmingham
SLYOAK B29 .... 123 M6
University of Birmingham
SLYOAK B29 .... 123 M7
University of Central England
BFLD/HDSWWD B20 .... 88 C2
University of Central England
CBHAMNE B4 .... 7 J1
University of Central England
CBHAMNE B4 .... 7 J2
University of Central England
CBHAMNW B3 .... 6 E5
University of Central England
EDG B15 .... 106 D5
University of Central England
PBAR/PBCH B42 .... 89 H2
University of Warwick
TLHL/CAN CV4 .... 153 G7
University of Wolverhampton
DUDN DY1 .... 84 F3
University (South Site)
WOLV WV1 .... 2 F4
Uplands Junior & Infant School
BDMR/CCFT WV3 .... 49 H5
Uplands Junior & Infant School
SMTHWKW B67 .... 105 K2
USAM Trading Estate
WOLVN WV10 .... 36 B3
Valley Infant School
HIA/OLT B92 .... 128 B2
Vaughan Trading Estate
TPTN/OCK DY4 .... 85 M2
Vauxhall Trading Estate
VAUX/NECH B7 .... 107 M1
Vaynor First School
REDW B97 .... 196 A6
Venkat Medical Centre
STECH B33 .... 110 C2
Ventura Retail Park
POL/KGSB/FAZ B78 ...... 45 L2
Ventura Shopping Centre
POL/KGSB/FAZ B78 ...... 45 L2
Vernon Trading Estate
RMSLY B62 .... 104 A5
Vesey Gallery
SCFLD/BOLD B73 .... 72 B4
Vets Surgery
NFLD/LBR B31 .... 144 A1
Victor Business Centre
REDE B98 .... 196 F2
Victoria Business Centre
RLSS CV31 .... 200 E6
Victoria Health Centre
SMTHWK B66 .... 105 M1
Victoria Infant School
TPTN/OCK DY4 .... 67 J8
Village Surgery
SHLY B90 .... 171 H1
Villiers Primary School
BILS/COS WV14 .... 51 H6
Villiers Trading Estate
BKHL/PFLD WV2 .... 49 M6
Vulcan House Business Centre
SOLH B91 .... 128 A7
Wainbody Wood School
TLHL/CAN CV4 .... 177 J3
Wake Green Football Club
SHLY B90 .... 146 C5
Wake Green Surgery
MOS/BIL B13 .... 125 L2
Walkmill Business Park
CNCK/NC WS11 .... 16 A8
Walkwood C of E Middle School
REDW B97 .... 196 A5
The Wallows Industrial Estate
BRLYHL DY5 .... 84 B8
Walmley Ash First School
WALM/CURD B76 .... 73 L6
Walmley Ash Middle School
WALM/CURD B76 .... 73 L6
Walmley Cricket Club
WALM/CURD B76 .... 73 J6
Walsall College of Arts &
Technology
WSL WS1 .... 4 E3
Walsall College of Technology
WSLW WS2 .... 4 E1
Walsall Community
Health Trust
WSL WS1 .... 4 E5
Walsall Cricket Club
WSL WS1 .... 5 J7
Walsall & District
Doctors on Call
BLOX/PEL WS3 .... 39 K5
Walsall Football Club
WSL WS1 .... 53 H8
Walsall Health Authority
WLNHL WV13 .... 51 K3
Walsall Health Authority
WSL WS1 .... 5 G1
Walsall Health Authority
WSLW WS2 .... 4 B3
Walsall Metropolitan
Borough Council
ALDR WS9 .... 40 D2
Walsall Metropolitan
Borough Council
WSL WS1 .... 4 F3
Walsall Metropolitan
Borough Council
WSL WS1 .... 4 F1

Walsall Metropolitan
Borough Council
WSL WS1 .... 5 L4
Walsall Rugby Club
WSL WS1 .... 5 H9
Walsall Wood Junior &
Infant School
ALDR WS9 .... 40 E1
Walsgrave C of E
Junior & Infant School
COVE CV2 .... 135 K7
Walsgrave General Hospital
COVE CV2 .... 135 L8
Walsgrave Health Centre
COVE CV2 .... 135 K7
Walsgrave Triangle
Business Park
RCOVN/BALC/EX CV7 ..... 135 L4
Ward End Junior &
Infant School
WASH/WDE B8 .... 90 E7
Ward End Medical Centre
WASH/WDE B8 .... 90 F8
Warley High School
LGLYGN/QTN B68 .... 104 E3
Warley Magistrates Court
OLDBY B69 .... 86 E6
Warren Farm Primary School
KGSTG B44 .... 71 M5
Warstones Primary School
ETTPK/GDPK/PENN WV4 ... 49 J7
Wartell Bank Industrial Estate
KGSWFD DY6 .... 83 H6
Warwick Castle
WWCK CV34 .... 199 J7
Warwick County &
Crown Courts
WWCK CV34 .... 199 H4
Warwick County &
Crown Courts
WWCK CV34 .... 199 J7
Warwick District Council
RLSN CV32 .... 200 D5
Warwick District Council
RLSN CV32 .... 200 E5
Warwick District Council
RLSN CV32 .... 200 C5
Warwick District Council
WWCK CV34 .... 199 J7
Warwick Museum
WWCK CV34 .... 199 H7
Warwick Road Surgery
SPARK B11 .... 108 C3
Warwick Road Trading Estate
SPARK B11 .... 126 B1
Warwickshire College
RLSN CV32 .... 200 B5
Warwickshire Constabulary
CSHL/WTROR B46 .... 93 K7
Warwickshire County Council
BDWTH CV12 .... 116 E2
Warwickshire County Council
CHWD/FDBR/MGN B37 ..... 110 C1
Warwickshire County Council
CSHL/WTROR B46 .... 93 K7
Warwickshire County Council
KNWTH CV8 .... 191 K1
Warwickshire County Council
NUN CV11 .... 99 G1
Warwickshire County Council
NUN CV11 .... 99 G1
Warwickshire County Council
NUN CV11 .... 99 G2
Warwickshire County Council
RLSS CV31 .... 200 D6
Warwickshire County Council
RWWCK/WEL CV35 .... 198 C5
Warwickshire County Council
WWCK CV34 .... 199 J5
Warwickshire County Council
WWCK CV34 .... 199 J6
Warwickshire County
Cricket Club
DIG/EDG B5 .... 107 H8
Warwickshire Museum
WWCK CV34 .... 199 K6
Warwickshire Museum
WWCK CV34 .... 199 J7
Warwickshire Nuffield Hospital
RLSN CV32 .... 192 C8
Warwickshire Post
Graduate Medical Centre
COV CV1 .... 9 G2
Warwickshire Racquet &
Centre
COVS CV3 .... 154 D6
Warwick Sports Club
WWCK CV34 .... 199 H6
Waseley Hills High School
RBRY B45 .... 142 B6
Washwood Heath School
WASH/WDE B8 .... 91 G8
Waterfront Business Park
BRLYHL DY5 .... 102 B1
Waterfront Business Park
BRLYHL DY5 .... 102 C2
Waterloo Industrial Estate
CBROM B36 .... 92 F8
Waterloo Road Jamia Mosque
DUNHL/THL/PER WV6 ..... 50 A1
Water Mill Primary School
SLYOAK B29 .... 124 B2
Water Orton Cricket Club
CSHL/WTROR B46 .... 92 F2
Water Orton Primary School
CSHL/WTROR B46 .... 92 F3
Waterside Industrial Estate
BKHL/PFLD WV2 .... 50 E7
Waterside Industrial Estate
BLKHTH/ROWR B65 .... 103 K1
Watery Lane Industrial Estate
WLNHL WV13 .... 51 H2
Watling Junior & Infant School
BRWNH WS8 .... 26 A3
Wattville Infant School
HDSW B21 .... 88 A6
Wattville Junior Mixed School
HDSW B21 .... 87 M5
Wattville Road
Industrial Estate
SMTHWK B66 .... 87 M6

Waverley School
SMHTH B10 .... 108 E5
WCC Sports Ground
WWCK CV34 .... 199 M6
Webheath First School
REDW B97 .... 195 L3
Webnor Industrial Estate
BKHL/PFLD WV2 .... 50 E7
Weddington County
First School
NUNW/HART CV10 .... 81 H6
Weddington Middle School
NUNW/HART CV10 .... 81 H6
Wedgnock Industrial Estate
WWCK CV34 .... 199 G5
Wednesbury Art Gallery
DARL/WED WS10 .... 68 D3
Wednesbury Chiropody
Surgery
DARL/WED WS10 .... 68 D2
Wednesbury Cricket Club
DARL/WED WS10 .... 68 E1
Wednesbury Leisure Centre
DARL/WED WS10 .... 68 C2
Wednesbury Medical Centre
DARL/WED WS10 .... 68 C3
Wednesbury Oak
Junior & Infant School
TPTN/OCK DY4 .... 67 L4
Wednesbury Rugby Club
DARL/WED WS10 .... 68 D4
Wednesbury Town Hall
DARL/WED WS10 .... 68 D3
Wednesfield Football Club
WNSFLD WV11 .... 37 G7
Wednesfield High School
WNSFLD WV11 .... 37 J8
Wednesfield Village
Primary School
WNSFLD WV11 .... 37 H8
Welfare Clinic
KNWTH CV8 .... 191 K1
Welford School
BFLD/HDSWWD B20 .... 88 E5
Welsh House Farm
Junior & Infant School
RIDG/WDGT B32 .... 123 K1
Welsh Rugby Club
HIA/OLT B92 .... 129 G3
Wembrook Primary School
NUN CV11 .... 99 G3
Weoley Castle Health Centre
SLYOAK B29 .... 123 L4
Weoley Castle Ruins & Museum
SLYOAK B29 .... 123 L3
Weoley Park Surgery
SLYOAK B29 .... 124 A4
Westacre Infant School
BDMR/CCFT WV3 .... 49 H4
West Birmingham
Community Health Council
CBHAMNW B3 .... 6 E3
West Bromwich
Albion Football Club Ltd
HHTH/SAND B71 .... 87 M4
West Bromwich
Dartmouth Cricket Club
HHTH/SAND B71 .... 87 K4
West Bromwich
Magistrates Court
WBROM B70 .... 87 G2
West Chadsmoor Clinic
CNCK/NC WS11 .... 12 C8
Westcroft Special School
WOLVN WV10 .... 36 F3
West Cross Shopping Centre
SMTHWK B66 .... 87 H6
Western Business Park
RMSLY B62 .... 103 M6
Westfield County
Primary School
WMBN WV5 .... 64 E6
Westfield First School
RUGBYS/DCH CV22 .... 183 K3
Westfield Lodge College
RUGBYS/DCH CV22 .... 183 K4
Westgate County First School
WWCK CV34 .... 199 H7
Westgate Trading Estate
ALDR WS9 .... 40 C7
West Heath Hospital
HWK/WKHTH B38 .... 144 A5
West Heath Junior
Mixed School
NFLD/LBR B31 .... 144 A4
Westhill College of Education
SLYOAK B29 .... 124 B5
West Hill Primary School
HEDN WS12 .... 12 F7
West House School
EDG B15 .... 107 G5
West Midlands County Council
HALE B63 .... 121 M2
West Midlands
Health Authority
LDYWD/EDGR B16 .... 106 C4
West Midlands Hospital
HALE B63 .... 103 H8
Westminster Industrial Estate
DUDS DY2 .... 103 H3
Westminster Junior School
BFLD/HDSWWD B20 .... 89 G4
Westminster Surgery
BFLD/HDSWWD B20 .... 89 G4
Weston In Arden Junior &
Infant School
BDWTH CV12 .... 117 L2
Weston Lane Industrial Estate
SPARK B11 .... 126 C1
West Orchard Shopping Centre
COV CV1 .... 8 F4
West Orchards Shopping Centre
COV CV1 .... 8 E5
West Park Hospital
WOLV WV1 .... 2 C4
West Park Infant School
WOLV WV1 .... 2 D3

West Park Junior School
WOLV WV1 .... 2 D2
Westwood Business Park
AST/WIT B6 .... 89 L4
Wharton Street
Industrial Estate
VAUX/NECH B7 .... 90 B5
Wheatsheaf Studio Theatre
COVE CV2 .... 134 F8
Wheelers Lane Junior
Mixed School
ALE/KHTH/YWD B14 ...... 125 K6
Wheelers Lane
Secondary School
ALE/KHTH/YWD B14 ...... 125 K6
Whetstone Field
Primary School
ALDR WS9 .... 54 F1
Whitacre Road
Industrial Estate
NUN CV11 .... 99 J1
Whitecrest Primary School
GTB/HAM B43 .... 70 E3
Whitehall Industrial Park
TPTN/OCK DY4 .... 68 C8
Whitehall Infant School
WSL WS1 .... 5 G8
Whitehall Junior
Community School
WSL WS1 .... 5 H8
Whitehall Medical Practice
RUGBYN/HIL CV21 .... 183 M3
Whiteheath Clinic
OLDBY B69 .... 86 B8
Whitehouse Common
Junior & Infant School
MGN/WHC B75 .... 57 H6
Whitesmore Secondary School
CHWD/FDBR/MGN B37 ..... 110 D4
Whitestone Clinic
NUN CV11 .... 99 L5
Whitford Hall School
BRGRVW B61 .... 185 H3
Whitgreave Infant School
WOLVN WV10 .... 36 C5
Whitgreave Junior School
WOLVN WV10 .... 36 C5
Whitgreave Primary School
WOLVN WV10 .... 22 F6
Whitley Abbey Primary School
COVS CV3 .... 154 E7
Whitmore Medical Centre
WOLV WV1 .... 2 E2
Whitmore Park Junior &
Infant School
COVN CV6 .... 133 L4
Whitmore Reans Health Centre
DUNHL/THL/PER WV6 ..... 2 B1
Whittington Oval Primary
School
STECH B33 .... 109 K3
Whittington Primary School
LICHS WS14 .... 30 C1
Whittles Art Gallery
MOS/BIL B13 .... 125 K2
Whoberley Clinic
COVW CV5 .... 153 G1
Whoberley Hall Primary School
COVW CV5 .... 153 G2
Wholesale Markets
DIG/EDG B5 .... 7 H7
Widney Junior School
SOLH B91 .... 147 K4
Wightwick Hall Special School
DUNHL/THL/PER WV6 ..... 48 C3
Wilden Village Cricket Club
STRPT DY13 .... 161 H8
Wilkes Green Junior &
Infant School
HDSW B21 .... 88 C4
Wilkinson Primary School
BILS/COS WV14 .... 67 K2
Willenhall Lane
Industrial Estate
BLOX/PEL WS3 .... 38 E5
Willenhall Leisure Centre &
Public Baths
WLNHL WV13 .... 51 M4
Willenhall Town Football Club
WLNHL WV13 .... 51 K2
Willenhall Trading Estate
WLNHL WV13 .... 51 K4
Willenhall Wood Junior & Infant
School
COVS CV3 .... 155 H7
William Baxter Special School
HEDN WS12 .... 12 E7
William Cowper Primary School
LOZ/NWT B19 .... 89 J7
William Macgregor
Primary School
TAM/AM/WIL B77 .... 46 B1
Willingsworth High School
TPTN/OCK DY4 .... 67 M3
Willows County Primary School
LICH WS13 .... 20 F3
Wilnecote Health Centre
TAM/AM/WIL B77 .... 46 D6
Wilnecote High School
TAM/AM/WIL B77 .... 46 D7
Wilnecote Junior School
TAM/AM/WIL B77 .... 46 D6
Wilson Stuart School
ERDE/GRVHL B23 .... 72 A7
Wiltell Road Industrial Estate
LICH WS13 .... 20 F6
Windmill Industrial Estate
COVW CV5 .... 132 D6
Windsor Gm High School
HALE B63 .... 121 K1
Windsor Industrial Estate
VAUX/NECH B7 .... 89 L8
Windward Way Industrial Estate
CBROM B36 .... 92 D5
Windy Arbor Junior School
CHWD/FDBR/MGN B37 ..... 111 H3
Winster Grove Industrial Estate
KGSTG B44 .... 71 J3

Winyates Health Centre
REDE B98 .... 197 J2
Wishaw Cricket Club
WALM/CURD B76........................ 74 E3
Witherley C of E Primary School
ATHST CV9 .... 63 M6
Witherley United Football Club
ATHST CV9 .... 63 L5
Withymoor Primary School
BRLYHL DY5 .... 102 B4
Withy Road Industrial Estate
BILS/COS WV14 .... 67 G2
Witton Industrial Estate
AST/WIT B6 .... 89 L3
Witton Park Industrial Estate
AST/WIT B6 .... 89 L4
Woden Avenue Junior &
Infant School
WNSFLD WV11 .... 36 F7
Woden Junior School
WOLVN WV10 .... 3 J1
Wodensborough High School
DARL/WED WS10 .... 68 F3
Wolgarston High School
PENK ST19 .... 10 E5
Wollescote Business Park
HAG/WOL DY9 .... 102 D8
Wollescote Primary School
HAG/WOL DY9 .... 120 D1
Wolston Business Park
KNWTH CV8 .... 180 E1
Wolston St Margarets
C of E First School
KNWTH CV8 .... 180 D1
Wolston Surgery
KNWTH CV8 .... 180 E1
Wolverhampton &
Biltson Athletic Club
DUNHL/THL/PER WV6 .... 35 K7
Wolverhampton
Borough Council
WOLV WV1 .... 2 E5
Wolverhampton
Borough Council
WOLV WV1 .... 2 F3

Wolverhampton Cricket Club
DUNHL/THL/PER WV6 .... 35 G7
Wolverhampton
Grammar School
BDMR/CCFT WV3 .... 49 K3
Wolverhampton
Healthcare N H S Trust
WOLVN WV10 .... 50 F1
Wolverhampton Metropolitan
Borough Council
BDMR/CCFT WV3 .... 49 J4
Wolverhampton Metropolitan
Borough Council
WOLV WV1 .... 3 G3
Wolverhampton University
WOLVN WV10 .... 36 A7
Wolverhampton
Wanderers Football Club
WOLV WV1 .... 2 E2
Wolverley High School
KIDDW DY11 .... 137 H1
Wolverley Sebright
First School
KIDDW DY11 .... 137 H2
Wombourne Cricket
Tennis & Bowling Club
WMBN WV5 .... 64 E6
Wombrook Industrial Estate
WMBN WV5 .... 64 C7
Woodacre Surgery
ERDE/BCHGN B24 .... 91 G2
Woodbourne Priory Hospital
HRBN B17 .... 106 A4
Woodcock Hill Junior &
Infant School
NFLD/LBR B31 .... 123 J6
Woodcross Clinic
BILS/COS WV14 .... 66 E3
Wood End Health Centre
COVE CV2 .... 135 H4
Wood End Junior &
Infant School
COVE CV2 .... 135 H4
Wood End Primary School
POL/KGSB/FAZ B78 .... 60 F4

Wood End Primary School
WNSFLD WV11 .... 37 H6
Woodgate Business Park
RIDG/WDGT B32 .... 122 F3
Woodgate Junior and
Infant School
RIDG/WDGT B32 .... 122 F4
Woodgate Valley Health Centre
RIDG/WDGT B32 .... 123 G3
Wood Green High School
DARL/WED WS10 .... 52 F8
Wood Green Junior School
DARL/WED WS10 .... 68 D1
Woodlands Infant School
SHLY B90 .... 146 F5
Woodlands JMI School
SHHTH WV12 .... 38 B7
Woodlands Junior &
Infant School
CBROM B36 .... 92 F7
Woodlands Primary School
TAM/AM/WIL B77 .... 46 C1
Woodlands Road Mosque
SPARK B11 .... 126 A3
Woodloes First & Middle School
WWCK CV34 .... 199 J4
Woodrow Primary School
REDE B98 .... 196 F6
The Woodrush High School
HLYWD B47 .... 145 L7
Woodrush Rugby Club
HWK/WKHTH B38 .... 168 F1
Woodsbank Trading Estate
DARL/WED WS10 .... 68 B1
The Woodsbank Trading Estate
DARL/WED WS10 .... 68 B1
The Woodsetton School
SEDG DY3 .... 66 D6
Woodside Industrial Estate
BRLYHL DY5 .... 84 D8
Woodside Medical Centre
TLHL/CAN CV4 .... 152 D3
Woodthorne Primary School
DUNHL/THL/PER WV6 .... 48 F1

Woodthorpe Primary School
ALE/KHTH/YWD B14 .... 125 J8
Woodthorpe Surgery
ALE/KHTH/YWD B14 .... 125 J8
Woodway Park School &
Community College
COVE CV2 .... 135 K3
Worcester Street Surgery
STRBR DY8 .... 101 K8
Wordsley Green Health Centre
STRBR DY8 .... 101 H3
Wordsley Hospital
STRBR DY8 .... 101 J2
Wrens Nest Junior School
DUDN DY1 .... 84 E1
Wrens Nest Secondary School
DUDN DY1 .... 66 F8
Wribbenhall First School
BEWD DY12 .... 136 A8
Wulfrun College
BDMR/CCFT WV3 .... 49 K3
Wulfrun College
WOLV WV1 .... 2 E3
Wulfrun Shopping Centre
WOLV WV1 .... 2 F6
Wulfrun Trading Estate
DUNHL/THL/PER WV6 .... 36 A8
Wychall Farm Infant School
NFLD/LBR B31 .... 144 A3
Wyken Croft Primary School
COVE CV2 .... 135 G8
Wyken Medical Centre
COVE CV2 .... 134 F7
Wylde Green College
SCFLD/BOLD B73 .... 72 F4
Wylde Green Primary School
SCFLD/BOLD B73 .... 72 F6
Wyndcliffe Infant School
BORD B9 .... 108 A4
Wyndcliffe Junior School
BORD B9 .... 108 B4
Wyndley Leisure Centre
SCFLD/BOLD B73 .... 56 E8
Wyndley Swimming Baths
SCFLD/BOLD B73 .... 72 E1

Wynford Industrial
Trading Estate
YDLY B25 .... 109 G8
Wythall Health Centre
HLYWD B47 .... 145 L6
Wythall Parish Council
HLYWD B47 .... 145 K8
Yardley Green Health Centre
BORD B9 .... 108 D4
Yardley Green Medical Centre
SMHTH B10 .... 108 A5
Yardley Junior School
LGN/SDN/BHAMAIR B26 .... 109 H6
Yardley Medical Centre
YDLY B25 .... 108 F6
Yardleys Lower School
SPARK B11 .... 126 C2
Yardleys School
SPARK B11 .... 126 C2
Yardleys Upper School
SPARK B11 .... 126 C1
Yardley Wood Health Centre
ALE/KHTH/YWD B14 .... 126 A8
Yardley Wood Junior
Mixed School
ALE/KHTH/YWD B14 .... 146 B1
Yarnfield Junior & Infant School
HLGN/YWD B28 .... 126 E2
Yenton Infant School
ERDE/BCHGN B24 .... 72 F7
Yenton Junior Mixed School
ERDE/BCHGN B24 .... 73 G8
Yew Tree Hills Infant School
DUDS DY2 .... 84 F8
Yew Tree Primary School
DSYBK/YTR WS5 .... 69 M1
Yew Tree Primary School
.... 128 C8
Yorkmead Junior &
Infant School
HLGN/YWD B28 .... 126 D3
Yorkswood Junior &
Infant School
CHWD/FDBR/MGN B37 .... 92 D8
Zip Theatre
WOLV WV1 .... 2 E2

K7
1 Cherry Orchard Crs

K8
1 The Hawnelands

L1
1 Lotus Wy
2 Walton Cl

L4
1 Great Western Dr

L5
1 Seedhouse Av
2 Willow Heights

L6
1 High Clere
2 The Woodlands

L7
1 Milverton Cl
2 Woodleigh Cl

L8
1 Beach St

M3
1 Churchill Dr
2 Heartland Ms
3 Oliver Ct

M4
1 Higgs Field Crs
2 Matthews Cl

M5
1 Castle Heights
2 Chapel Cl
3 Granville Rd
4 Lansbury Gn
5 Lansbury Rd

M6
1 Badgers Cft
2 Sandringham Rd

M7
1 Haden Hill Rd

M8
1 Dudley Rd

Page 104

A1
1 Viking Ri

A2
1 Belle Vue Gdns
2 Old School Dr

A3
1 Birmingham Rd
2 The Mews
3 Short St
4 Spring Av
5 Stilehouse Crs

A4
1 Bassano Rd
2 Beet St
3 Ben Willetts Wk
4 Birmingham Rd
5 Cross St
6 Downing Cl
7 Frank Tommey Cl
8 The Heathlands
9 High St
10 Lench Cl
11 Marlow St
12 Payne St
13 Sturman Dr
14 Union St
15 Upper Ashley St
16 West St

A5
1 Olive Dr
2 Vernon Rd

B1
1 Stuart Rd

B2
1 Greenwood Av
2 Highbury Cl

B3
1 Spring Av

B4
1 Vicarage Gdns

B5
1 St Loye's Cl
2 Vernon Cl
3 Victoria Rd

B6
1 Greenhill Rd

C1
1 Canterbury Cl
2 Durham Rd
3 Ely Cl
4 Richards Cl
5 Truro Cl
6 Winchester Cl

C2
1 Bond St
2 Wells Rd

C4
1 Culmore Rd
2 Fairfield Gv
3 Fairhaven Cft
4 Roundhill Ter

C5
1 Moray Cl

C6
1 Lyttleton Av

D1
1 St Michael's Crs
2 Titford Cl

D2
1 Pound Cl
2 Pound Rd
3 Victoria Ms

D4
1 Middlefield Cl

D5
1 Middlefield Gdns
2 Woodbury Cl

D7
1 Clarendon Pl

E1
1 Bridgewater Av
2 Cross St
3 Harvest Gdns
4 Woodfield Av

E2
1 Barlow Cl

E3
1 Hollyoake
2 Hollyoake Cl

E6
1 Elmdale
2 Hollymount
3 Pinewoods
4 Weatheroaks

E7
1 B4043
2 Chantry Dr
3 The Green
4 Hickmans Cl
5 Hoosen Cl
6 Lombardy Cft
7 Powell Av
8 Ridgacre Rd West
9 Ridgeway Av

E8
1 Collins Cl
2 Frankley Av
3 Samuels Rd

F1
1 Archer Cl
2 Primrose Bank

F2
1 Silverlands Av

F3
1 The Constables
2 Conway Av

F4
1 Queensway Cl

F5
1 Chance Cft
2 Mavis Gdns

F6
1 Perry Hill La
2 Radnor Rd

F8
1 Newburn Cft

Page 105

G8
1 Hopedale Rd
2 Middle Meadow Av
3 Suncroft

Page 106

A1
1 Bishops Cl
2 Curtis Cl
3 Newmans Cl

A3
1 Newnham Rd

A4
1 Percival Rd

A7
1 West Pathway

A8
1 Clarenden Pl
2 Harborne Park Rd
3 Waterward Cl

B1
1 Shireland Brook Gdns
2 West Heath Rd
3 Wood Green Rd

B7
1 Metchley La

C1
1 Ashover Gv
2 Bellefield Av
3 Canning Gdns
4 Enderby Gv
5 Halifax Cv
6 Heath Green Gv
7 Ivy Cv
8 Smeaton Gdns

C4
1 Clipper Vw

D1
1 Barrow Dr

D2
1 Heath St South
2 Hooper St
3 Willow Gdns

D3
1 Ascot Cl
2 Coxwell Gdns
3 Daisy Rd
4 Palomino Pl
5 Shire Cl

D4
1 Eldon Rd
2 Hickman Gdns
3 Parker St

D5
1 Augustus Ct
2 Grenfell Dr

E1
1 Boar Hound Cl
2 Bond Sq

E2
1 Spring Hill Pas

E3
1 Ashton Cft
2 Darnley Rd
3 Graston Cl
4 Sadlers Wk

E4
1 Arden Gv
2 Holy Well Cl
3 Leyburn Rd
4 Power Crs
5 Rann Cl

E5
1 Westbourne Crs

E6
1 Kelton Ct

F1
1 Moreton St
2 Pemberton St
3 Warstone Pde East

F2
1 Clement St
2 Crosby Cl
3 King Edwards Rd
4 Nelson St
5 Sand Pits
6 Summer Hill St
7 Townsend Wy

F3
1 Bellcroft
2 Ladycroft
3 Morville St

F4
1 Essington St
2 Glebeland Cl
3 St Martin's St
4 Shepherds Gdns

F5
1 Embassy Dr
2 Enfield Rd
3 George Rd

F6
1 Crondal Pl

F7
1 Kesteven Cl

Page 107

G1
1 Augusta St
2 Northampton St
3 Regent Pde
4 Regent St

G2
1 Charlotte St
2 Fleet St
3 Helena St
4 Louisa St
5 St Helens Pas
6 Scotland La

G3
1 Adelaide St
2 Hanwood Cl
3 Jinnah Cl

G3
1 Brindley Dr
2 Civic Cl
3 Cumberland St
4 Gas St
5 Kingston Rw

G4
1 Berkley St
2 Bexhill Gv
3 Bridge St
4 Communication Rw
5 Ridley St
6 Upper William St

G5
1 Elvetham Rd
2 Gaywood Cft
3 Lee Mt

G6
1 Parkfield Cl

G7
1 Courtlands Cl

H1
1 Bond St
2 Livery St
3 St Paul's Sq
4 William Booth La
5 William St North

H2
1 Church St
2 Ludgate Hl
3 Margaret St
4 New Market St
5 Temple Rw West

H3
1 Beak St
2 Bennett's Hl
3 Ethel St
4 John Bright St
5 Lower Severn St
6 Paradise St
7 Royal Mail St
8 Station St
9 Stephenson St
10 Swallow St
11 Temple Pas
12 Waterloo St

H4
1 Brownsea Dr
2 Chapmans Pas
3 Ellis St
4 Exeter Pas
5 Florence St
6 Hinckley St
7 John Bright St
8 Marshall St
9 St Jude's Pas
10 Suffolk Pl
11 Upper Marshall St
12 Windmill St

H5
1 Colbrand Gv
2 Newhope Cl
3 Whitfield Gv

H6
1 Cambridge Crs
2 Columbia Cl
3 Latimer Gdns
4 Tylney Cl

H7
1 Dalloway Cl
2 Shooters Cl
3 Spey Cl

J1
1 Bath St
2 Lawson St
3 Lench St
4 Little Shadwell St
5 St Mary's Rw
6 Staniforth St

J2
1 Albert St
2 Carrs La
3 Dale End
4 Dudley St
5 Fore St
6 Freeman St
7 High St
8 Orwell Pas
9 Paternoster Rw
10 Union St
11 Warwick Pas

J4
1 Bath Pas
2 Clarbrook St
3 Dean St
4 Gloucester St
5 Hurst St
6 Ladywell Wk
7 Skinner La
8 Smithfield Pas
9 Theatre Ap
10 Well St
11 Wrottesley St

J5
1 Hodnet Gv
2 Lawford Gv
3 Mowbray St

J6
1 Barrow Wk
2 Berrington Wk
3 Cliscold Cl
4 Cumberland Wy
5 Horton Sq
6 Kinver Cft
7 Longmore St
8 Rathbone Cl
9 Rolling Mill Cl

J7
1 Cobden Gdns
2 Fitters Mill Cl
3 Four Stones Gv
4 Hampden Retreat
5 Hawkins Cl
6 Minivet Dr
7 Reaside Cft
8 Siskin Dr
9 Willmcote Cl

K1
1 Enterprise Wy
2 Heneage St West
3 Legge St
4 Oxygen St
5 West St

K2
1 Ab Rw
2 Bartholomew Rw
3 Chapel St
4 Masshouse La
5 Nova Scotia St
6 Seymour St

K3
1 Andover St
2 Banbury St
3 Meriden St
4 New Bartholomew St
5 Shaw's Pas

K4
1 Bradford St
2 Chapel House St
3 Moore's Rw
4 Stone Yd

K6
1 Canford Cl
2 Charles Cl
3 Highgate Cl
4 Ketley Cft
5 Pentland Cft
6 Upper Coneybere St

K7
1 Hollycroft Gdns
2 Lapworth St
3 Royston Cft
4 Trevorne Cl
5 Upper Balsall Heath Rd
6 Vincent Cl

K8
1 Fenter Cl
2 Margaret St
3 Sherron Gdns
4 Tanworth Gv
5 Trevose Retreat

L1
1 Adams St
2 Great Brook St
3 Newhaven Cl
4 Windsor St

L2
1 Forster St
2 Gopsal St
3 Margaret St
4 Northumberland St
5 Pitt St
6 St James' Pl

L3
1 Belmont Pas
2 Fawdry St
3 Little Edward St

L4
1 Bromley St
2 Clyde St
3 Hack St

L5
1 Little Broom St
2 Old Camp Hl
3 Stratford Pl
4 Trinity Ter
5 Warner St

L6
1 Arundel Pl
2 John Kempe Wy
3 King St
4 Oughton Rd

L7
1 Grosmont Av
2 Hereford Av
3 Melrose Av
4 Noel Av
5 Oakfield Av
6 Springfield Av

M1
1 Kelsey Cl

M2
1 Dollman St
2 Isbourne Wy

M3
1 Alport Cft
2 Farmacre
3 Hoff Beck Court Ct
4 Langdon St
5 Mease Cft
6 Mill Burn Wy
7 Quigley Av
8 Towpath Cl

M4
1 Bordesley Park Rd
2 Darnel Cft
3 Emmeline St
4 Mount Pleasant

M5
1 Bassett Cft
2 Bolton Rd
3 Cooksey Rd
4 Gisborn Cl
5 Lawden Rd
6 Sandfields Av

M6
1 Claremont Rd
2 Downey Cl
3 Jackson Cl

M7
1 Florence Av
2 Hampson Cl
3 O'keeffe Cl
4 South Range

M8
1 Ash Gv
2 Ash Wy
3 Beach Av
4 Beach Brook Cl
5 Chesterton Av
6 Colville Wk
7 Iv Av
8 Swallow Cl
9 Trenville Av
10 Whitbourne Cl

Page 108

A1
1 Dereham Cl

A2
1 Garland St
2 Garrison St
3 Midland St

A3
1 East Holme
2 North Holme
3 Sydney Rd
4 West Holme

A4
1 Bamford Cl
2 Bowling Green Rd
3 Broseley Brook Cl
4 Camp St
5 Templefield Gdns

A5
1 Danford Gdns
2 Vann Cl

A6
1 Montgomery Cft
2 Taywood Dr

A7
1 Bickley Av
2 Boscombe Av
3 Melrose Av
4 Oakfield Av
5 The Poplars
6 Primrose Av
7 Severn Gv
8 Stretton Gv
9 Weston Av

A8
1 Inglewood Rd
2 Johnson Cl
3 Shakespeare St
4 Stratford St

B1
1 Adderley Gdns
2 Charles Cl
3 Paddeston St

B3
1 Grove Cottage Rd

B4
1 Bertram Rd
2 Eversley Rd
3 Hafton Gv
4 Holmwood Rd
5 Little Green La
6 North Warwick St

B5
1 East Farm Cft
2 Watt's Rd

B6
1 Byron Cl
2 Monkswell Cl

B8
1 Blundell Rd
2 Holte Rd

C1
1 Adderley Park Cl
2 Heartlands Pl
3 Lancelot Cl
4 Langton Rd

C2
1 Overwood Cft
2 St Saviour's Rd

C4
1 First Av
2 Imperial Rd
3 Redvers Rd

C7
1 Armoury Rd

C8
1 River Lee Rd

D1
1 Kellington Cl
2 Thurcroft Cl

D2
1 Delphinium Cl
2 Springbank

D3
1 Azalea Gv

D4
1 Rostrevor Rd
2 Second Av

D6
1 Ravensdale Rd

D7
1 James Rd

E2
1 Bramble Dell
2 Newbank Gv

E4
1 Marchmont Rd

E7
1 Redhill Rd

F1
1 Orion Cl

F2
1 Kenwood Rd

F3
1 Alston Gv
2 Bedworth Gv
3 Frankton Gv
4 Whichford Gv

F5
1 Washford Gv

F8
1 Acorn Cl
2 Collycoft Pl
3 Eaves Green Gdns
4 Juniper Cl
5 Redwood Gdns
6 Wharfdale Rd

Page 109

G1
1 Cotterills Av
2 Everton Rd
3 Gumbleberrys Cl

G3
1 Foxwell Cl

G5
1 Brantford Rd
2 Rosedale Gv
3 Wembley Gv

G6
1 Elgin Gv
2 Henshaw Gv

G7
1 Broadyates Gv
2 Willard Rd

G8
1 Ash Ms
2 Blossomville Wy
3 Cypress Sq
4 Honeysuckle Gv
5 Langworth Av
6 Lime Tree Rd
7 Rye Cft
8 Shropshire Gdns
9 Swan Copse

H1
1 Northcote Rd

H2
1 Elizabeth Rd
2 Frederick Rd

H3
1 Denton Gv
2 Levante Gdns
3 Neston Gv
4 Pear Tree Cl

H4
1 Bonham Rd
2 Laxton Gv
3 Linford Gv
4 Marlborough Gv
5 Rickyard Cl
6 Stuart's Dr

H5
1 Charminster Av
2 Eastleigh Gv
3 Hythe Gv
4 Tyne Gv

H7
1 Gideon Cl
2 Gladstone Rd
3 Warwell La

H8
1 Avocet Cl
2 Pennyfield Cft
3 Rattle Cft

J1
1 Franks Wy

J4
1 Abbess Gv
2 Grevis Rd

J5
1 Malthouse Gv

J6
1 Hob Moor Rd

K1
1 Kirkham Gv
2 Penkridge Gv

K2
1 Glendale Dr
2 Tanfield Rd

K3
1 Rayners Cft

K6
1 Arden Dr

L1
1 Beswick Gv
2 Farmcote Rd
3 Kirton Gv

L2
1 Bembridge Rd
2 Coppenhall Gv
3 Felton Cft

L3
1 Nooklands Cft

L5
1 Fleetwood Gv
2 Fontley Cl
3 The Hays Kent's Moat
4 Somerland Rd

L7
1 Horrell Rd

L8
1 Broadway Gv
2 Pettyfield Cl
3 Woodbine Rd

L8
1 Kings Cft

M2
1 Dewhurst Rd
2 Rudyard Gv

M3
1 Edmonds Cl
2 Scholars Ga

M4
1 Carters Hurst
2 Hollyfaste Rd

M6
1 Abigails Cl

M8
1 Brook Cl
2 Yorkbrooke Dr

Page 110

A2
1 Foxdale Gv
2 Heynesfield Rd

A3
1 Royal Star Cl
2 Rycroft Gv
3 Sunbeam Wy

A7
1 Collingdon Gv
2 Rosecroft Rd
3 The Smithy
4 Stanville Rd

B1
1 Hawkesford Rd
2 Heritage Wy
3 Netherton Gv
4 Waterford Pl

B3
1 Birchtrees Dr
2 Blackmoor Cft
3 Oakmeadow Cl

B5
1 Stockton Gv

C1
1 Ragnall Av
2 Verney Av

C1
1 Marian Cft

C2
1 Chelmsley Gv
2 Rockmoor Cl
3 Wheatlands Cft

C4
1 Crosskey Cl
2 Lambourne Gv

C4
1 Cumberford Av

C5
1 Hazeldene Rd

D2
1 Colletts Gv
2 Hillside Gdns
3 Stonebridge Crs
4 Townshend Gv

D3
1 Hipsmoor Cl
2 Lark Meadow Dr
3 Lowerstack Cft

D3
1 Grandys Cft
2 Yorklea Cft

D4
1 Crassington Gv
2 Settle Cft

D7
1 Martin Ri

E2
1 Farlow Cft
2 Marston Cft

E4
1 Anstey Cft
2 Elmore Cl
3 Hadfield Wy

E4
1 Chester Cl

E4
1 Ardeme Dr

H5
1 Malthouse Gv
2 Wood La

H6
1 Aylesford Dr
2 Hemlingford Cft
3 Hidcote Gv
4 The Rise

F1
1 Tyne Cl

F2
1 Ceolmund Crs

F3
1 Beauchamp Cl
2 Cole Ct
3 Stephenson Dr

F6
1 Earls Ferry Gdns
2 Glengarry Cl
3 Kintore Cft
4 Kyles Wy
5 Lady Bank
6 Marywell Cl
7 Rothesay Gv
8 The Storrs Wy
9 Stuarts Wy
10 Trippleton Av
11 Tweeds Well
12 Windsor Vw

Page 116

A4
1 Hamilton Cl
2 Pembroke Cl

A6
1 Corley Vw
2 Elwy Cir
3 Willow Coppice

A7
1 Exton Cl

B3
1 Himley Rd
2 Lindley Rd

B4
1 Pheasant Cl

B5
1 Newcomen Cl

C5
1 Shortlands

C7
1 The Chestnuts
2 The Elms
3 The Firs
4 The Maples
5 The Rowans

C8
1 Topp's Heath

D1
1 The Tea Gdn

D3
1 Brooklea

D7
1 All Saints Rd
2 Beechcroft
3 Walkers Wy

D8
1 Bramwell Gdns
2 Glenridding Cl

E2
1 Cotman Cl
2 Gainsborough Dr
3 Lowry Cl
4 Wessex Cl

E3
1 Ashford Cl
2 Lansdowne Cl
3 Lovell Rd
4 Wiltshire Cl

E3
1 Didsbury Rd

E5
1 Melville Rd

E6
1 Treviscoe Cl

E8
1 Harrow Cl

F1
1 Ascot Cl
2 Cheltenham Cl
3 Epsom Cl
4 Ernest Richards Rd
5 John Knight Rd
6 Newman Cl

F2
1 George Street Ringway
2 Mayfield Cl
3 Sleath's Yd
4 Wyatt Ct

F5
1 High St
2 Springfield Crs

F5
1 Rosemullion Cl

F7
1 Brockenhurst Wy
2 Lyndhurst Cl

G7
1 Anderton Cl
2 Ashurst Cl

Page 121

K3
1 Abberley Cl
2 Alvechurch Rd
3 Chaddesley Rd
4 Cookley Cl
5 Hanbury Cl
6 Hartlebury Rd
7 Harvington Rd
8 Hindlip Cl
9 Inkberrow Rd
10 Ombersley Rd
11 Quarry Hl
12 Rochford Cl
13 St Margarets Dr
14 School La
15 Spring Meadow
16 Walton Cl
17 Wolverley Rd

K4
1 Bredon Cl
2 Broome Cl
3 Claremont Wy
4 Honeybourne Cl
5 Instone Rd
6 Pickersleigh Cl
7 Queensway
8 Weeson Gdns
9 Wychbury Cl

M1
1 Birmingham Rd
2 Church La
3 High St
4 Skitter St
5 Tenter Ct
6 Wright St

H1
1 Hunnington Crs
2 Macklesfield Dr
3 Peachley Cl

H4
1 Seaton Gv

H7
1 Emsworth Gv

H8
1 Appleby Cl
2 Brandwood Gv
3 Cranton Cl
4 Topsham Cft

J1
1 St Anne's Ct
2 Strensham Hl

J3
1 Hill Crest Rd

J6
1 Redwood Cl

J7
1 Southminster Dr

Page 122

B2
1 Carisbrooke Dr
2 County Park Av
3 Cricklewood Dr
4 Masefield Ri
5 Sandals Ri
6 Wentworth Ri

E2
1 Hunnington Cl
2 Moat Coppice
3 Moat Farm Dr
4 Westcombe Gv
5 Woodvale Rd

F6
1 Earls Ferry Gdns
2 Glengarry Cl
3 Kintore Cft
4 Kyles Wy
5 Lady Bank
6 Marywell Cl
7 Rothesay Gv
8 The Storrs Wy
9 Stuarts Wy
10 Trippleton Av
11 Tweeds Well
12 Windsor Vw

Page 123

G1
1 Highfield La

G2
1 Oakleaf Cl

K2
1 Corley Vw
2 Elwy Cir
3 Willow Coppice

A7
1 Exton Cl

B3
1 Himley Rd
2 Lindley Rd

B4
1 Pheasant Cl

B5
1 Newcomen Cl

C5
1 Shortlands

C7
1 The Chestnuts
2 The Elms
3 The Firs
4 The Maples
5 The Rowans

C8
1 Topp's Heath

D1
1 The Tea Gdn

D3
1 Brooklea

D7
1 All Saints Rd
2 Beechcroft
3 Walkers Wy

D8
1 Bramwell Gdns
2 Glenridding Cl

E2
1 Cotman Cl
2 Gainsborough Dr
3 Lowry Cl
4 Wessex Cl

E3
1 Ashford Cl
2 Lansdowne Cl
3 Lovell Rd
4 Wiltshire Cl

K1
1 Highfield La

G2
1 Oakleaf Cl

K2
1 Newman College Cl

K4
1 The Woods

K4
1 Birches Cl
2 Leasowes Rd
3 Mount Pleasant

K5
1 Florence Rd
2 Richmond Pl

K6
1 Middleton Rd
2 Nutgrove Cl

K6
1 Grazebrook Cft

K7
1 Hollyhedge Cl

J1
1 First Meadow Piece
2 Lower Higley Cl
3 Lygon Gv
4 Pinner Gv

J3
1 Davena Dr

J5
1 Guardians Wy
2 Longfield Rd
3 Loxley Cl

K1
1 Clavedon Cl
2 Draycott Dr
3 Dunchurch Dr

J7
1 Kewstoke Cft

K2
1 Blakemore Cl
2 Buttermere Dr
3 Shandon Cl
4 Stableford Cl

K3
1 Bilbrook Gv
2 Flyford Cft
3 Wiltshire Cl

K4
1 Colmore Crs

K6
1 Malton Gv
2 Menin Crs

M7
1 Mayford Gv

M8
1 Brigfield Crs
2 Chells Gv

Page 125

G3
1 Heather Dl

G4
1 Brockley Gv
2 Derwent Gv

G7
1 Pineapple Gv

G7
1 Cornhill Gv

G7
1 County Cl

G8
1 Newick Gv

H2
1 Torridon Cft

H4
1 Emsworth Gv

F2
1 Aspen Cl
2 Haven Dr

F3
1 Balaclava Rd
2 Kingsfield Rd
3 Silverfield Cl

J6
1 Redwood Cl

J7
1 Southminster Dr

Page 126

A1
1 Frederick Rd
2 Lime Ct

A2
1 Geoffrey Rd
2 Nora Rd
3 Rhone Cl

A3
1 Greethurst Dr

A4
1 Adrian Cft

A6
1 Norley Gv
2 Sandway Gv

A8
1 Selborne Gv

B1
1 Ryland Rd

B6
1 Burke Av
2 Keel Dr
3 Penshaw Gv

B7
1 Knutswood Cl

B7
1 Saint Peters Cr

B8
1 Highfield Cl
2 Selma Gv

C5
1 Cambrai Dr
2 Southam Cl
3 Stonerwood Av

C7
1 Brookmeadow Ct

D4
1 Brooklands Gv

D5
1 Finmere Rd
2 Hazelmere Rd
3 Staplehurst Rd

D7
1 Glover Cl
2 Oldhouse Farm Cl

E1
1 Tyseley Hill Rd

E2
1 Fieldhead Rd
2 Hattersley Gv
3 Helstone Gv
4 Walden Rd

E4
1 Ferris Gv

E5
1 Durlston Gv
2 Endsleigh Gv
3 Englewood Dr

E6
1 Halewood Gv

E7
1 Hazelville Gv

E8
1 Diddington Av
2 Rowan Dr

F2
1 Aspen Cl
2 Haven Dr

F3
1 Boyd Gv
2 Chaucer Gv
3 Coppice Dr
4 Dogge Lane Cft
5 Hazeltree Cft

F5
1 Stonehaven Gv

F6
1 Mapleton Gv
2 Ormsby Gv

F7
1 Thornsett Gv

Page 127

G1
1 Beeches Av
2 Bramley Mews Cft
3 Hazel Gdns
4 Sherbourne Dr

G4
1 Easton Gv
2 Woburn Gv

G5
1 Broom Hall Gv
2 Chisholm Gv
3 Leysdown Gv
4 Liddon Gv
5 Overton Gv
6 Wilcote Gv

G6
1 Hindon Gv

H1
1 Conyworth Cl
2 Cowley Dr

H2
1 Henbury Rd
2 Tanyards

H3
1 Bretton Rd
2 Culham Cl
3 Hillborough Rd

H8
1 Rothwell Dr

J1
1 Woodcock La North

J2
1 Hanbury Cft

J4
1 Old Warwick Ct
2 Old Warwick Rd
3 St Margaret's Rd

J5
1 Westhill Cl

J8
1 Chesterton Cl
2 Miall Park Rd

K2
1 Cloudsley Gv
2 Woodhall Cft

K4
1 Finbury Cl

K7
1 Wadleys Rd
2 Wellington Gv
3 Wilmcote Dr

K8
1 Oaken Dr

L1
1 Wells Green Rd

L2
1 Kempsey Cl
2 Norbury Gv

L4
1 Bablake Cft

M3
1 Hob's Moat Rd
2 Winchcombe Rd

M4
1 Rodney Cl

M5
1 Dursley Cl

Page 128

A3
1 Cophams Cl
2 Highcroft Cl

A4
1 Arlescote Rd

A6
1 Banmoor Cl
2 Boulton Rd
3 Brandon Rd
4 Ratcliffe Rd

B1
1 Manor Rd

B1
1 Coventry Rd
2 Gillman Cl

C5
1 Park Cl

B6
1 Lingham Cl
2 Merryfield Cl

C7
1 Heath Gdns

B8
1 Beechnut Cl
2 Broomfields Rd
3 Shustoke Rd

C5
1 Joiners Cft
2 Pardington Cl
3 Rowood Dr
4 Wheatley Cl

C6
1 Brailes Cl
2 Finchall Cft

C7
1 Bourne Cl
2 Framefield Dr
3 Timmins Cl

D4
1 Radford Ri

D7
1 Markham Cresent
2 Rosse Ct

E6
1 Limbury Gv
2 Windridge Crs

E7
1 Burgess Cft
2 Chetland Cft
3 Cloudbridge Dr
4 Elmdon Coppice
5 Nichols Cl
6 Spooners Cl
7 Stoney Cl

F8
1 Bransford Ri

Page 133

L8
1 Nethermill Rd
2 Pake's Cft
3 Shadowbrook Rd
4 Steeplefield Rd
5 Teachers Cl

Page 134

A1
1 Parkland Cl

B1
1 Alder Meadow Cl
2 Redcap Cft

G5
1 Crummock Cl

B3
1 Allied Cl
2 Stadium Cl

B4
1 Holbrook La

B5
1 Lymington Cl
2 Rocken End

B6
1 Heera Cl
2 Livingstone Rd

B7
1 Spindle St

C1
1 Eagle St

C2
1 Marshdale Av

C3
1 Blackwell Rd
2 Dunmoe Cl
3 Gosport Rd
4 Horndean Cl

C4
1 Broad Street Jetty
2 Park St

C6
1 Hanford Cl

C8
1 Edward St
2 Ordnance Rd

D1
1 Cope Arnolds Cl
2 Garrigill Cl
3 Marlwood Cl
4 Oakey Cl

D3
1 Barton Rd
2 Parkstone Rd

D4
1 Friswell Cl
2 Simon Stone St

D5
1 Millhouse Cl
2 Stoney Stanton Rd
3 Warner Rw

D7
1 Peel St

E1
1 Heath Crs
2 Newnham Rd

E1
1 Dodgson Cl
2 Elmhurst Rd
3 Horse Shoe Rd
4 Kegworth Cl
5 Kendrick Cl
6 Longford Sq
7 Wrenbury Dr

E3
1 Oaks Pl
2 Tiveycourt Rd
3 Woolgrove St

E5
1 Stuart Ct

E6
1 Adam Rd
2 Belmont Rd
3 Birchgrave Cl
4 Bridge St
5 Cheswick Cl
6 Edale Wy
7 Heywood Cl

F1
1 Alison Sq
2 Hurn Wy
3 Linstock Wy
4 Loach Dr
5 Sapcote Gv
6 Seaford Cl

F2
1 Reading Cl

F3
1 Copperas St
2 Privet Rd

F7
1 Singer Cl

F7
1 Elderberry Wy
2 Rosehip Dr
3 Watersmeet Gv

Page 135

H3
1 Ashorne Cl
2 Bilberry Rd
3 Celandine Rd
4 Loxley Cl
5 Overberry Cl
6 Shirebrook Cl
7 Strawberry Wk

L5
1 Ashcroft Cl
2 Caspian Wy
3 Downton Cl
4 Mapperley Cl
5 Neal Ct
6 Sharpley Cl

L7
1 Beamish Cl
2 Boswell Dr
3 Darwin Cl
4 Hexby Cl
5 Nordic Drift

Page 137

G7
1 Blakebrook Cl
2 Clare's Cl
3 Habberley St
4 King Charles Cl
5 St John's St
6 Woodfield St

H6
1 Bradley Thursfield Ct

H7
1 Black Horse La
2 Lower Mill St
3 Millfield Gdns
4 Paternoster Rw

J5
1 Edinburgh Cl

J7
1 Bromsgrove Gv
2 Bull Ring
3 Callows La
4 Lion Sq
5 Pitts La
6 Prospect La

K7
1 Leswell Gv
2 Leswell La
3 St George's Ter
4 South St

L6
1 Linden Gdns

M6
1 Pear Tree Cl

M7
1 Browning Cl
2 Marlowe Cl
3 Norton Rd

Page 142

C4
1 Bishop Cl
2 Kintyre Cl
3 Lismore Cl
4 Ramsey Cl

D5
1 Chaddersley Cl
2 Cock Hill La
3 Old Quarry Cl
4 Round Saw Cft
5 Rubery La South

E3
1 Blackdown Cl
2 Garden Cl
3 Glen Devon Cl
4 Lysander Rd
5 Mowbray Cl
6 Savernake Cl
7 Windsor Cl

Page 143

G3
1 Handley Gv
2 Tarragon Gdns

G4
1 Manor Gv
2 Manor Pk

G6
1 Bomers Fld

H2
1 Borrowdale Gv
2 Masonleys Rd

H6
1 Cofton Ct

J1
1 Honiton Cl

J2
1 Cheverton Rd
2 Tinkers Farm Gv

J4
1 Cypress Gv

J5
1 Daffodil Wy

J7
1 Hopwood Gv

K1
1 Windlass Cft

K2
1 Lofthouse Gv

K4
1 Cedar Wy
2 The Mill Wk

K5
1 Rowan Wy
2 Whitcot Gv

K6
1 Hewell Cl

K7
1 Ditton Gv
2 Heronfield Dr

L1
1 Rochester Rd
2 Saxon Wood Cl

L3
1 Greenslade Cft

L4
1 Centenary Cl
2 Laburnum Wy

L5
1 Worthen Gv

L6
1 Beeches Farm Dr
2 Plymouth Cl

M2
1 Conifer Dr
2 Eastville
3 Hollow Cft

M4
1 Chirbury Gv

Page 144

A3
1 Crabtree Cl
2 Furlong Meadow
3 Lime Tree Gv
4 Oakleigh
5 Ockam Cft

B6
1 Arrowfield Gn
2 Batheaston Cl
3 Buckridge Cl
4 Driftwood Cl
5 Parlows End

C5
1 Beech Hurst
2 Longdales Rd
3 Lydbrook Covert
4 Offenham Covert
5 Old Lime Gdns
6 Redbrook Covert
7 Sedgeberrow Covert
8 Tarrington Covert
9 Whitebeam Cft

D5
1 Beech Wk
2 Harebell Gdns
3 Manitoba Cft
4 Monkshood Retreat
5 Primrose Gdns
6 Reedmace Cl
7 Stonecrop Cl
8 Tees Gv
9 Yarrow Wk

D6
1 Sandpiper Gdns

E3
1 Rowan Ct

E5
1 Hawkmoor Gdns

F3
1 Farnbury Cft
2 Hayle Cl
3 Schoolhouse Cl

F4
1 Cavendish Cl
2 Greaves Sq

Page 145

G3
1 Barnpark Covert
2 Cherhill Covert
3 Dorstone Covert
4 Drews Meadow Cl
5 Elkstone Covert
6 Goodrich Covert
7 Sherston Covert
8 Southwood Covert
9 Stapleford Cft
10 Swansbrook Gdns
11 Willsbridge Covert
12 Winterbourne Cft
13 Wynstead Covert

H3
1 Bell Meadow Wy
2 Easmore Cl
3 Gullswood Cl
4 Kingham Covert
5 Mitcheldean Covert
6 Topfield Wk
7 Withington Covert
8 Wynds Covert

K3
1 Allwell Dr
2 Bramshaw Cl
3 Manningford Rd
4 Nuthurst Gv

L2
1 Dickens Cl
2 Fletton Gv
3 Littlecote Cft
4 Playdon Gv
5 Quarrington Gv
6 Shawbrook Gv

M2
1 Hawkswood Gv

Page 146

C2
1 Cheyne Gdns
2 Hebden Gv
3 Millside
4 Westford Gv

E8
1 Campion Wy
2 Dickens Heath Rd
3 Hirdemonsay
4 Willowherb Wy

Page 147

G2
1 Mancetter Rd
2 Sutherland Av
3 Thornyfield Cl
4 Thornyfield Rd

G5
1 Harwood Gv

H1
1 Brobury Cft
2 Cornbury Gv
3 Cropthorne Gv
4 Rushbury Cl

H3
1 Bardon Dr
2 Featherstone Cl

H4
1 Bellamy Cl
2 Chalford Wy

H5
1 Cranmore Bvd
2 St George's Rd

H6
1 Monkspath Cl
2 Stratford Rd

H8
1 Chatsworth Cl
2 The Dingle
3 Osbourne Cft
4 Waterdale

K1
1 Sharmans Cross Rd

K2
1 Poolfield Dr

K3
1 Knightley Rd
2 Monwood Gv
3 Pine Cl
4 Pinewood Gv
5 White Falcon Ct

K6
1 Devitts Cl

K7
1 Colehurst Cft
2 Dunley Cft
3 Metchley Cft
4 Sandbarn Cl
5 Sherdmore Cft
6 Stonehill Wk
7 Tylers Gv

K8
1 Bretshall Cl

L1
1 Melplash Av

L4
1 Four Stones Cl
2 Hollyoak Gv
3 Redbrooks Cl

L5
1 Claston Dr
2 Tibberton Cl

L6
1 Baywell Cl
2 Kitebrook Cl

L7
1 Bellington Cft
2 Highdown Rd
3 Himbleton Cft
4 Monkspath
5 Oldberrow Cl
6 Rochford Cl
7 Slatsley Crs
8 Slimbridge Cl
9 Whitwell Dr
10 Wynbrook Gv

L8
1 Barham Cl
2 Bowbrook Av
3 Norcombe Gv

M3
1 Bowercourt Cl
2 Stamford Cft

M4
1 Alderton Cl
2 Branthill Cft
3 Cherrington Wy
4 Habberly Cft
5 Hazelton Cl
6 Northwick Crs
7 Stoneythorpe Cl

M5
1 Bushley Cft
2 Chadbury Cft
3 Greyhurst Cft
4 Hillfield Ms
5 Hollings Gv
6 Hunningham Gv
7 Littlewood Cl
8 Martley Cft
9 Maythorn Gv
10 Southey Cl
11 Tanwood Cl

M7
1 Appleby Gv
2 Besford Gv
3 Buckbury Cft
4 Chivington Cl
5 Hawbridge Cl
6 Timberlake Cl

M8
1 Stainsby Cft

Page 148

A4
1 Cranford Gv
2 Mayfield Cl
3 Oakwood Cl
4 Woodberry Av

A5
1 Cherrywood Crs
2 Glenfield Cl
3 Libbards Ga
4 Littleton Cft
5 Merrington Cl
6 Saintbury Dr
7 Sevington Cl
8 Thorngrove Av
9 Woodston Gv

Page 152

A1
1 Lyndhurst Cft
2 Thornton Cl

A4
1 Devereux Cl

B1
1 Coniston Dr
2 Hanwood Cl
3 Rodway Dr

B4
1 Brockhurst Dr

B4
1 Aspen Cl
2 Rodhouse Cl
3 Sammons Wy
4 Whitebeam Cl
5 Winceby Pl

C1
1 Hove Av
2 Olton Av
3 Windermere Av

C3
1 Howlette Rd

C4
1 Copland Pl
2 Franklin Gv

C5
1 Sorrel Cl
2 Woodend Cft

D1
1 Howard Cl
2 Kimberley Cl
3 Tredington Rd

D2
1 Ferndown Cl
2 George Hodgkinson Cl

D3
1 Wheate Cft

D4
1 Bradnick Pl

D5
1 Milrose Wy

E1
1 Cartmel Cl
2 Shetland Cl
3 Sundorne Cl

E2
1 Greenleaf Cl
2 Wilmcote Gn

E3
1 Chestnut Gv
2 The Oaklands

E6
1 Knights Templar Wy

E6
1 Penrose Cl
2 Wansfell Cl

F1
1 Amersham Cl
2 Bowfell Cl
3 The Chilterns
4 Hazlemere Cl
5 Woodburn Cl

F2
1 Honeybourne Cl

F4
1 Tile Hill La

Page 153

K3
1 Abercorn Rd
2 Fife Rd

L1
1 Bateman's Acre South
2 Chiltern Leys
3 Thamley Rd

L3
1 Allesley Old Rd

M2
1 Barras La
2 Chester St
3 Collett Wk
4 Dover St
5 Hawksworth Dr
6 Lower Holyhead Rd
7 Percy St
8 Queen Victoria Rd
9 Watch Cl

M8
1 Ilmington Cl
2 Norwich Dr
3 Tynward Cl
4 Westcliffe Dr

Page 154

A2
1 Bishop St
2 Bond St
3 Chapel St
4 Corporation St
5 Cross Cheaping
6 Hill St
7 Ironmonger Rw
8 Lamb St
9 St Agnes La
10 Well St

A4
1 Hornchurch Cl

B1
1 Arthur St
2 Byron St
3 Harnall La West
4 Little Church St
5 Russell St North
6 Springfield Wlk
7 Springfield Rd
8 Swanswell St

B3
1 St Mary St

C1
1 Adelaide St
2 Arnside Cl
3 Brook Cl
4 Cawthorne Cl
5 Clarence St
6 Dysart Cl
7 Jade Cl
8 Nelson St
9 Pensilva Wy
10 Priors Harnall
11 St Peter's Ct
12 Waterloo St
13 Wellington St

D2
1 Far Gosford St

E2
1 St Agatha's Rd

E6
1 Fairfield Ct

F2
1 Ethelfield Rd

F5
1 St Catherine's Cl

Page 155

G5
1 Chatham Cl

G7
1 Canon Hudson Cl
2 Chapel Farm Cl
3 Epsom Dr
4 Goodwood Cl
5 Oratory Dr

G8
1 Dunsmore Av
2 Yarningale Rd

H3
1 Hipswell Highway

H5
1 Barford Cl

H6
1 Fabian Cl
2 Mary Slessor St
3 Montjoy Cl
4 St Jude's Crs
5 Tarquin Cl

H7
1 Kingsmead Ms
2 Lysander St
3 Manor Hall Ms
4 St James' La

J3
1 Arthingworth Cl
2 Windermere Av

J5
1 Horninghold Cl
2 Ravensthorpe Cl
3 Saddington Rd
4 Theddingworth Cl
5 Warmington Cl
6 Woodhouse Cl

J6
1 John Mcguire Crs
2 Joseph Creighton Cl
3 Tom Ward Cl

J7
1 Middle Ride
2 Winnallthorpe

K1
1 Frampton Wk
2 Westmorland Rd

K3
1 Melfort Cl
2 Rannock Cl

K5
1 Jim Forrest Cl
2 Willowherb Cl

K6
1 Binley Gv
2 Bredon Av
3 Bromwich Cl
4 Buttermere Cl
5 Tom Henderson Cl
6 Wakefield Cl
7 Wasperton Cl

L1
1 Bryanston Cl
2 Shillingstone Cl
3 Swanage Gn

L3
1 The Greensward
2 Grimston Cl
3 St Bartholemews Cl

L4
1 Caulby Wk
2 Hardwyn Cl
3 Soredale Cft
4 Tideswell Cl
5 Upperfield Wy

M4
1 Brunton Cl
2 Bulwick Cl

Page 161

G2
1 Brinton Cl
2 Godson Pl
3 Reservoir Rd
4 Sutton Park Gv

G3
1 Goldthorn Pl

H7
1 Abbotts Cl

J1
1 Durham Cl
2 King George Av
3 York Av

J2
1 Fallowfields Cl
2 Greenacres Rd
3 Melbourne Cl
4 Willow Rd

J3
1 Cotton Pool Rd
2 Kidderminster Rd
3 Rowan Cl
4 Willow Rd

J4
1 Westbourne Cl

J7
1 Barn Cl
2 Countinghouse Wy
3 Martingale Cl
4 Nailers Cl
5 Waggoners Cl
6 Wheelwright Cl

K1
1 Jasmine Gv
2 York Rd

K2
1 Churchfields Cl
2 Churchfields Gdns
3 Conifer Gv
4 Forge Dr
5 Spire Vw

K3
1 George St
2 Mill La
3 Paradise Rw
4 Perry La
5 Station St

K4
1 Hanover St
2 Peter's Finger
3 Worcester Rd

K7
1 Mill Cl

L1
1 Belvedere Dr

Page 172

C1
1 Barwell Cl
2 Bentley Farm Cl
3 Oak Tree Cl
4 Withington Gv

Page 183

G3
1 Cunningham Wy North
2 Freemantle Rd

G4
1 Cunningham Wy North
2 Grenville Cl
3 Rodney Cl

G5
1 Assheton Cl
2 Cawston Wy
3 Cheshire Cl
4 Holyoak Cl
5 Plomer Cl
6 Queensferry Cl

H2
1 Oswald Wy

H5
1 Bawnmore Ct

H6
1 Hobley Cl

H7
1 Hamlet Cl
2 Orlando Cl

J2
1 Dryden Pl
2 Dryden Wk

J4
1 Armstrong Cl
2 Baffin Cl
3 Broom Cl
4 Ferndown Ct
5 Ferndown Ter
6 Hawkins Cl
7 Heather Cl
8 Mellish Ct
9 Melville Cl
10 Nares Cl

J5
1 Bathurst Cl
2 Cherry Gv
3 Laburnum Gv

K2
1 Alfred St
2 Bennett St
3 Easy La
4 Levy Cl
5 Little Pennington St
6 Parnell Cl
7 Pennington Ms
8 Pennington St
9 Round St
10 Schoolfield Cl
11 Stephen St
12 Torrance Rd

K3
1 Westfield Rd

K4
1 Wentworth Rd
2 Westbourne Gv

K5
1 Overslade Manor Dr

K6
1 Goldsmith Av

L1
1 Avon St
2 Duke St

L2
1 Bank St
2 Bloxam Pl
3 Drury La
4 Eastfield Pl
5 Elborow St
6 Evreux Wy
7 Henry St
8 Lawford Rd
9 Little Church St
10 Little Elborow St
11 Pennington St

L3
1 Bilton Rd
2 John Thwaites Cl
3 Lawrence Sheriff St
4 Russelsheim Wy

L7
1 Brafield Leys

M1
1 Pinders La

M2
1 Castle Ms
2 Murrayian Cl

Page 185

H3
1 Whitford Gdns

H4
1 Westminster Cl

H5
1 Carnoustie Cl

H6
1 Berrow Vw
2 Harbours Cl

H7
1 The Paddock

L3
1 Ednall La
2 Market St
3 Windsor Gdns

L4
1 Bant Mill Rd
2 Cedar Ter
3 Stonehouse Rd
4 Sunnymead

L6
1 Springfield Av

M3
1 Broom Cl
2 Knowesley Cl
3 Shaftesbury Cl
4 Wendron Cl

M4
1 Ambleside Wy
2 Davenport Dr
3 Derwent Wy
4 Granville Cl
5 Hedges Wy

M5
1 St Godwald's Crs

Page 196

A2
1 Coppice Cl

A4
1 Goldthorne Cl

A5
1 Rochester Cl
2 Tennyson Rd

A7
1 Walkwood Crs

B1
1 Adelaide St
2 Bates Hl
3 Fir Tree Cl
4 Unicorn Hl

B5
1 Highfield Av
2 Highfield Rd
3 The Rough

B6
1 Blythe Cl
2 Stableford Cl

B7
1 Glenfield Cl

B8
1 Ullapool Cl

C1
1 Abbey Rd
2 Fish Hl
3 Herbert St
4 Other Rd
5 Queen St
6 Red Lion St
7 Victoria St
8 Wellesbourne Cl
9 Wellington St
10 William St

C2
1 Evesham St
2 Silver St
3 Smallwood St

C3
1 Laburnum Cl
2 Lilac Cl

C4
1 Eastnor Cl
2 Gilbertstone Cl

C6
1 Mitcheldean Cl
2 Northside Cl
3 Outwood Cl

C8
1 Eunal Ct

D1
1 Grange Rd
2 Lady Harriet's La
3 Temple Cl

D7
1 Whitchurch Cl

E1
1 Brook St

E2
1 Holloway Pk

E3
1 Shakespeare Av

E5
1 Wharrington Cl

F6
1 Hampton Cl
2 Newland Cl

Page 197

H4
1 Harbury Cl
2 Maxstoke Cl
3 Offwell Rd
4 Polesworth Cl
5 Quinton Cl

L2
1 Kendal Cl
2 Lindridge Cl
3 Meriden Cl
4 Prestbury Cl

Page 198

D7
1 Church Pth
2 Damson Rd
3 Friary Cl
4 Hayward Cl
5 Hunt Cl
6 Lloyd Cl
7 Minster Cl
8 New Cl
9 Ryder Cl
10 Seymour Cl
11 Sumner Cl

Page 199

H5
1 Landor Rd
2 Oken Rd
3 St Christopher's Cl
4 St Mary's Cl
5 Saltisford Gdns
6 Wedgnock Gn

H7
1 Bowling Green St
2 Charter Apppoach
3 Cockspar row St
4 The Holloway
5 Market St
6 Monks Wy
7 Stand St
8 Westgate St
9 Woodhouse St

H8
1 Charter Apppoach
2 Queen's Sq
3 Stuart Cl
4 Tudor St

J3
1 Berwick Cl
2 Drayton Ct
3 Hicks Cl
4 Linden Cl
5 Moore Cl

Page 200

C4
1 Clarendon Pl
2 Milverton Crs West
3 St Mark's Ms
4 Stuart Ct

D4
1 Beauchamp Rd
2 Clarence Ter
3 Guy Pl East
4 Guy Pl West
5 Powers Ct
6 Satchwell St
7 Waterloo Pl
8 Windsor Pl

D5
1 Bedford Pl
2 John St
3 Kenilworth St
4 Park St
5 Portland House
6 Portland Ms
7 Rosefield Pl
8 St Peter's Rd
9 Satchwell Ct

D7
1 Central Av
2 Frances Havergal Cl
3 Tachbrook Rd

D8
1 Bonniksen Cl
2 Emerald Wy
3 Sapphire Dr
4 Silver Birch Cl
5 Spruce Gv
6 Wych Elm Dr

E3
1 Campion Gn
2 Shuckburgh Gv
3 Stockton Cl

E6
1 Baxter Ct
2 Chapel St
3 Church Ter
4 Clinton St
5 Cumming St
6 Gloucester St
7 Gundry Cl
8 Mill St
9 Moss St
10 Packington Pl
11 Regent Pl
12 Satchwell Pl

E7
1 Charles Gardner Rd
2 Claremont Rd
3 St John's Rd
4 Shrubland St

E8
1 Hitchman Ms

F2
1 The Greenways
2 Old School Ms
3 Thursfield Rd

F3
1 Rawlinson Rd

F4
1 Comyn St

F6
1 Clapham Sq
2 Northcote St
3 Rotherfield Cl

F7
1 Blakelands Av
2 Clapham St
3 Cundall Cl
4 Padmore Ct

F8
1 Bourton Dr
2 Craig Cl
3 Wilnecote Gv

Notes

Notes

Notes

Notes

Notes